THE WORLD ALMANAC BOOK OF WHO

THE WORLD ALMANAC BOOK OF WHO

By the Staff of The World Almanac ®

Hana Umlauf Lane, Editor

WORLD ALMANAC PUBLICATIONS
NEW YORK

Library of Congress Catalog Card Number 79-67561
Library of Congress Catalog Card Number (hardcover) 80-81180
Newspaper Enterprise Association, Inc. ISBN 0-911818-11-1
Ballantine Books ISBN 0-345-29177-8
Prentice Hall, Inc. ISBN 0-13-967844-1

Paperback Edition distributed in the United States
by Ballantine Books, a Division of Random House, Inc.
and in Canada by Random House of Canada, Ltd.
First American hardcover edition printed by Prentice-
Hall, Inc., 1980

Printed in the United States of America

Newspaper Enterprise Association, Inc.
World Almanac Publications
Jane D. Flatt, Publisher
200 Park Avenue, New York, NY 10017

TABLE OF CONTENTS

EDITOR'S NOTE

The entries in *The World Almanac Book of Who* are designed to give the reader the necessary information in as few words as possible.

Individuals are listed according to the names by which they are best known, including any titles. Names enclosed in parentheses alone signify parts of the individual's given name, i.e. **ELIOT, T**(homas) **S**(tearns). Names enclosed in parentheses and quotes signify nicknames, i.e. **GOODMAN, BENNY** ("The King of Swing"). Pseudonyms are enclosed in parentheses and preceded by "pseud.", i.e. **HIGGINS, JACK** (pseud.: Harry Patterson). When a pseudonym is used for the individual listing, the real name is enclosed in parentheses following "pseud. of", i.e. **LE CARRE, JOHN** (pseud. of David John Moore Cornwell). When a woman is best known by her married name, her given name (surname only) is given following "nee", i.e. **BLOOMER, AMELIA**, née Jenks.

The individual's birth date, the exact date whenever possible, follows the name. The birthplace appears in parentheses following the birth date. The death date, if applicable, follows the place of birth.

In many cases, major works of the individual, e.g. books, compositions, films, etc., are listed following the main body of the entry. In no case are the works given intended to be a complete listing of that individual's accomplishments, but are merely a representative selection made at the discretion of the editor.

Names which appear in capital letters within an entry signify cross-references to other entries in the book.

Most of the abbreviations used in this book require no explanation. The following is a selected list of abbreviations and acronyms which may be unclear to the reader.

AA, Academy Award
ABA, American Basketball Association
ABT, American Ballet Theatre
ACLU, American Civil Liberties Union
AEC, Atomic Energy Commission
AFL-CIO, American Federation of Labor
   and Congress of Industrial Organizations
A.-H., Austria-Hungary
AL, American League
Alta., Alberta
AP, Associated Press
ASCAP, American Society of Composers,
   Authors, and Publishers
B.C., British Columbia
C., College
c., circa
CIA, Central Intelligence Agency
cm., committee
cmsr., commissioner
Co., County, Company

Ct., Court
D (in parentheses only), Democrat
Del., delegate
dep., deputy
D.R., Dominican Republic
ERA, Earned Run Average
FAA, Federal Aviation Agency
FBI, Federal Bureau of Investigation
Fed (in parentheses only), Federalist
FDA, Food and Drug Administration
fl., flourished
Fndn., Foundation
Ft., Fort
FTC, Federal Trade Commission
HEW, Department of Health, Education, and
   Welfare
HUD, Departing of Housing and Urban
   Development
I., Island
Ind (in parentheses only), Independent

leg., legislature
m, meter
MVP, Most Valuable Player
NAACP, National Association for the
   Advancement of Colored People
NASCAR, National Association of Stock Car
   Auto Racing
NATO, North Atlantic Treaty Organization
N.B., New Brunswick
NBA, National Basketball Association
NFL, National Football League
Nfld., Newfoundland
NHL, National Hockey Legue
NL, National League
N.S., Nova Scotia
NYCB, New York City Ballet
NYSE, New York Stock Exchange
OAS, Organization of American States

Par., Parish
PBA, Professional Bowlers Association
Pen., Peninsula
Phil., Philharmonic
P.R., Puerto Rico
Prog (in parentheses only), Progressive
R (in parentheses only), Republican
R., River
RBIs, Runs Batted In
RR, Railroad
S.A., South Africa
Ter., Territory
Twp., Township
UN, United Nations
USAC, United States Auto Club
USIA, United States Information Agency
V.I., Virgin Islands

Hana Umlauf Lane

Hana Umlauf Lane, editor

WRITERS

U.S. WRITERS

ADE, GEORGE, Feb. 9, 1866 (Kentland, Ind.)–May 16, 1944. U.S. humorist, playwright. Author of a humorous column for the Chicago Record. *Fables in Slang,* 1899; *People You Knew,* 1903; *College Widow* (play), 1904; *The Sultan of Sulu* (musical), 1903; *Stories of the Streets and of the Town,* 1941.

AIKEN, CONRAD POTTER, Aug. 5, 1889 (Savannah, Ga.)–Aug. 17, 1973. U.S. poet, novelist, critic. Volumes of poetry include *Earth Triumphant* (1914), *The Charnel Rose* (1918), *Selected Poems* (1929; Pulitzer Prize in poetry, 1930), *The Human Heart* (1952). *Blue Voyage* (novel), 1927; *Ushant* (autobiography), 1952.

AKINS, ZOË, Oct. 30, 1886 (Humansville, Mo.)–Oct. 29, 1958. U.S. dramatist, screenwriter. Wrote light, romantic stage plays. *A Royal Fandango,* 1923; *The Greeks Had a Word for It,* 1930; *The Old Maid* (1935 Pulitzer Prize in drama), 1935; also wrote the screenplay based on EDNA FERBER's *Showboat.*

ALBEE, EDWARD FRANKLIN, Mar. 12, 1928 (Washington, D.C.). U.S. dramatist. Initially wrote one-act plays, including *The Zoo Story and Other Plays* (1960); his first full-length play, *Who's Afraid of Virginia Woolf?* (1962) was his greatest critical and popular success. *Tiny Alice,* 1965; *A Delicate Balance* (1967 Pulitzer Prize in drama), 1967; *Seascape,* 1975.

ALCOTT, LOUISA MAY, Nov. 29, 1832 (Germantown, Pa.)–Mar. 6, 1888. U.S. novelist. Her most famous book, *Little Women* (1868), sold millions of copies. *Little Men,* 1871; *Eight Cousins,* 1875; *Jo's Boys,* 1886. (Daughter of AMOS BRONSON ALCOTT.)

ALGER, HORATIO, JR., Jan. 13, 1832 (Revere, Mass.)–July 18, 1899. U.S. writer. His 100 best-selling books for boys told the stories of poor bootblacks and newsboys whose honesty and industry gained them economic success. *Ragged Dick,* 1867; *Luck and Pluck,* 1869; *Tattered Tom,* 1871.

ALGREN, NELSON, Mar. 28, 1909 (Detroit, Mich.). U.S. novelist. Wrote realistic novels, most of which were set in slums of Chicago's West Side. *The Man with the Golden Arm,* 1949; *A Walk on the Wild Side,* 1956.

ANDERSON, MAXWELL, Dec. 15, 1888 (Atlantic, Pa.)–Feb. 28, 1959. U.S. dramatist. *What Price Glory?* (with LAURENCE STALLINGS), 1924; *Both Your Houses* (1933 Pulitzer Prize in drama), 1933; *Winterset,* 1935; *Knickerbocker Holiday,* 1938; *Anne of a Thousand Days,* 1948; *The Bad Seed,* 1955.

ANDERSON, ROBERT WOODRUFF, Apr. 28, 1917. U.S. playwright. *Tea and Sympathy,* 1953; *I Never Sang for My Father,* 1968.

ANDERSON, SHERWOOD, Sept. 13, 1876 (Camden, Ohio)–Mar. 8, 1941. U.S. short-story writer, novelist, journalist, poet. His major work, *Winesburg, Ohio* (1919), is a collection of short stories about American small-town life. *The Triumph of the Egg,* 1921; *Dark Laughter,* 1925; *Tar, A Midwest Childhood,* 1926.

ARMOUR, RICHARD WILLARD, July 15, 1906 (San Pedro, Calif.). U.S. humorist noted for his satires of historical and literary scholarship. *It All Started with Columbus,* 1953; *Twisted Tales from Shakespeare,* 1957.

ASCH, SHOLEM, Nov. 1, 1880 (Kutno, Pol.)–July 10, 1957. U.S. novelist. Wrote Biblical novels, chiefly in Yiddish. *The Nazarene,* 1939; *The Apostle,* 1949; *Mary,* 1949; *Moses,* 1951.

AUCHINCLOSS, LOUIS STANTON, Sept. 27, 1917 (Lawrence, N.Y.). U.S. novelist, short-story writer. Chronicler of upper-class American life. *The Great World of Timothy Colt,* 1956; *Pursuit of the Prodigal,* 1959; *The Rector of Justin,* 1964; *The Winthrop Covenant,* 1976; *The Dark Lady,* 1977.

BACH, RICHARD DAVID, June 23, 1936 (Oak Park, Ill.). U.S. author, aviator. Wrote the best-selling adult fairy tale, *Jonathan Livingston Seagull,* 1970. *Stranger to the Ground,* 1963; *Illusions,* 1978.

BALDWIN, FAITH CUTHRELL, Oct. 1, 1893 (New Rochelle, N.Y.)–Mar. 19, 1978. U.S. writer of popular romantic novels. *Wife Versus Secretary,* 1935; *American Family,* 1935; *Station Wagon Set,* 1939; *The Velvet Hammer,* 1969; *New Girl in Town,* 1975.

BALDWIN, JAMES, Aug. 2, 1924 (New York, N.Y.). U.S. novelist, essayist. Spokesman for American blacks in the late 1950s and early 1960s. *Go Tell It on the Mountain,* 1953; *Notes of a Native Son,* 1955; *Nobody Knows My Name,* 1961; *Another Country,* 1962.

BARAKA, IMANU AMIRI, born LeRoi Jones, Oct. 30, 1934 (Newark, N.J.). U.S. playwright, poet, essayist, novelist. Author of violently anti-white plays, poems, and polemics. *Dutchman,* 1964; *The Toilet,* 1964; *The Slave,* 1966.

BARRY, PHILIP, June 18, 1896 (Rochester, N.Y.)–Dec. 3, 1949. U.S. playwright. Wrote sophisticated comedies of manners. *Holiday,* 1928; *Here Come the Clowns,* 1938; *The Philadelphia Story,* 1939.

BARTH, JOHN, May 27, 1930 (Cambridge, Md.). U.S. novelist. Author of experimental, often comic novels and novellas. *The Sot-Weed Factor,* 1962; *Giles Goat-Boy,* 1966; *Chimera,* 1972; *Letters,* 1979.

BARTHELME, DONALD, Apr. 7, 1931 (Philadelphia, Pa.). U.S. novelist, short-story writer. Author of experimental fiction, using parody and black humor. *Unspeakable Practices, Unnatural Acts,* 1968; *Sadness,* 1972; *Great Acts,* 1979.

BAUM, L(yman) FRANK, May 15, 1856 (Chittenango, N.Y.)–May 6, 1919. U.S. writer of children's stories. *Father Goose: His Book,* 1899; *The Wonderful Wizard of Oz,* 1900.

BAUM, VICKI, Jan. 24, 1888 (Vienna, Austria)–Aug. 29, 1960. Austrian-U.S. novelist, dramatist. Successfully dramatized her romantic novel *Grand Hotel* (1931), which was later made into a classic film.

BELLAMY, EDWARD, Mar. 26, 1850 (Chicopee Falls, Mass.)–May 22, 1899. U.S. author. Achieved fame with his Utopian romance, *Looking Backward, 2000–1887* (1888), which depicted a socialist world in 2000 A.D. *Equality,* 1897.

BELLOW, SAUL, June 10, 1915 (Lachine, Quebec, Can.). U.S. novelist. Author of rich, complex, often comic novels; won Nobel Prize in literature, 1976. *The Adventures of Augie March,* 1955; *Henderson the Rain King,* 1959; *Herzog,* 1964; *Mr. Sammler's Planet,* 1970; *Humboldt's Gift,* 1975.

BENCHLEY, NATHANIEL GODDARD, Nov. 13, 1915 (Newton, Mass.). U.S. novelist, editor, journalist. The son of ROBERT BENCHLEY, he edited a selection of his father's works; his novel *The Off-Islanders* (1961) provided the basis for the film *The Russians Are Coming, The Russians Are Coming* (1966). (Father of PETER BENCHLEY.)

BENCHLEY, PETER BRADFORD, May 8, 1940 (New York, N.Y.). U.S. novelist. Adapted his bestseller *Jaws* (1974) into an equally successful film (1975). *The Deep,* 1976; *The Island,* 1979. (Grandson of ROBERT BENCHLEY; son of NATHANIEL BENCHLEY.)

BENCHLEY, ROBERT CHARLES, Sept. 15, 1889 (Worcester, Mass.)-Nov. 21, 1945. U.S. humorist. Noted for his understated comic essays; also noted for the short films he wrote, directed, and acted in. *From Bed to Worse,* 1934; *My Ten Years in a Quandry,* 1936; *Benchley Beside Himself,* 1943; *Chips off the Old Benchley,* 1949. (Father of NATHANIEL BENCHLEY; grandfather of PETER BENCHLEY.)

BENÉT, STEPHEN VINCENT, July 22, 1898 (Bethlehem, Pa.)-Mar. 13, 1943. U.S. poet, short-story writer, novelist. Awarded two Pulitzer Prizes in poetry, for *John Brown's Body* (1928) and *Western Star* (1943). *The Devil and Daniel Webster* (short stories), 1937. (Brother of WILLIAM ROSE BENÉT.)

BENÉT, WILLIAM ROSE, Feb. 2, 1886 (Brooklyn, N.Y.)-May 4, 1950. U.S. poet, editor. Edited several magazines, including the *Saturday Review of Literature* which he helped found (1924); edited *The Reader's Encyclopedia* and *The Oxford Anthology of American Literature;* awarded 1942 Pulitzer Prize in poetry for *The Dust Which Is God* (1941). (Brother of STEPHEN VINCENT BENÉT.)

BENSON, SALLY, born Sara Mahala Redway Smith, Sept. 3, 1900 (St. Louis, Mo.)-July 19, 1972. U.S. novelist, short-story writer. Her best-selling novel, *Junior Miss* (1939), was made into a successful play, film, and radio series; her autobiographical novel, *Meet Me in St. Louis* (1942), was made into a classic film (1944).

BERRYMAN, JOHN, born John Smith, Oct. 25, 1914 (McAlester, Okla.)-Jan. 7, 1972. U.S. poet. His famous poem "Homage to Mistress Bradstreet" (1956) addressed the spirit of the colonial poet ANNE BRADSTREET; awarded 1965 Pulitzer Prize in poetry for *77 Dream Songs* (1964); committed suicide, 1972.

BIERCE, AMBROSE GWINETT, July 24, 1842 (Horse Cave Creek, Ohio)-1914? U.S. journalist, short-story writer. Noted for his cynical, sardonic, grotesque stories and his Civil War stories, the most famous of which is "Occurrence at Owl Creek Bridge." *Cobwebs from an Empty Skull,* 1874; *In the Midst of Life,* 1891; *The Devil's Dictionary,* 1906.

BLUME, JUDY, born Judy Sussman, Feb. 12, 1938 (Elizabeth, N.J.). U.S. novelist. Author of realistic novels, especially for preteens and teenagers. *Then Again, Maybe I Won't,* 1971; *Forever,* 1976; *Wifey,* 1978.

BLY, ROBERT, Dec. 23, 1926 (Madison, Minn.). U.S. poet. Leading figure in the revolt against rhetoric in poetry; prominent among anti-Vietnam War intellectuals as organizer of the American Writers Against the Vietnam War, 1966. *Silence in the Snowy Fields,* 1962; *The Light around the Body,* 1967; *Point Reyes Poems,* 1974.

BRADSTREET, ANNE DUDLEY, c.1612 (Northampton, Eng.)-Sept. 16, 1672. U.S. poet. The first important woman writer in America. *The Tenth Muse Lately Sprung Up in America,* 1650.

BRAND, MAX (pseud. of Frederick Faust), Mar. 20, 1892 (Seattle, Wash.)-May 16, 1944. U.S. novelist, screenwriter. "King of the pulp writers"; wrote some 85 books about the West, including *Destry Rides Again* (1930); wrote a series of books and screenplays about Dr. Kildare.

BROMFIELD, LOUIS, Dec. 27, 1896 (Mansfield, Ohio)-Mar. 18, 1956. U.S. writer. His books *The Green Bay Tree* (1924), *Possession* (1925), *Early Autumn* (1926; awarded 1927 Pulitzer Prize in fiction), and *A Good Woman* (1927) comprise a tetralogy called *Escape.*

BROOKS, GWENDOLYN ELIZABETH, June 7, 1917 (Topeka, Kan.). U.S. poet. The first black woman poet to win a Pulitzer Prize (1950; for *Annie Allen* [1949]) and to be elected to the National Inst. of Arts (1960); poet laureate of Illinois, 1969. *The World of Gwendolyn Brooks,* 1970.

BRYANT, WILLIAM CULLEN, Nov. 3, 1794 (Cummington, Mass.)-June 12, 1878. U.S. poet, critic, newspaper editor. Editor of the New York *Evening Post,* 1829-78; first effective U.S. theorist of poetry. Elected to American Hall of Fame, 1910. *To A Waterfowl,* 1815; *Thanatopsis,* 1817.

BUCK, PEARL, née Sydenstricker, July 26, 1892 (Hillsboro, W.Va.)-Mar. 6, 1973. U.S. novelist raised in China, where her parents were missionaries. *The Good Earth,* (1932 Pulitzer Prize in fiction), 1932; awarded Nobel Prize in literature, 1938. *A House Divided,* 1935; *Dragon Seed,* 1942; *Pavilion of Women,* 1946. *Imperial Women,* 1956; *The Time Is Noon,* 1967.

BUNTLINE, NED (pseud. of Edward Zane Carroll Judson), Mar. 20, 1823 (Stamford, N.Y.)-July 16, 1886. U.S. novelist, adventurer. Founded sensationalist magazine, *Ned Buntline's Own,* 1845; dismissed from the army for drunkenness and lynched (but secretly cut down) for murder, 1846; wrote some 400 sensationalist books, originating the so-called dime novel in the U.S., e.g., *Magdalena, the Beautiful Mexican Maid* (1847), *The Black Avenger* (1847), *The Mysteries and Miseries of New York* (1848); led Astor Place riot in New York City, 1849; organized the Know-Nothing Party, 1850s.

BURDICK, EUGENE, Dec. 12, 1918 (Sheldon, Ia.)-July 26, 1965. U.S. novelist, political theorist. *The Ugly American* (with WILLIAM J. LEDERER), 1958; *Fail-Safe* (with Harvey Wheeler), 1962.

BURNETT, FRANCES ELIZA HODGSON, Nov. 24, 1849 (Manchester, Eng.)-Oct. 29, 1924. U.S. novelist. Noted for writing children's books, especially *Little Lord Fauntleroy* (1886), which she also dramatized (1886). *Sara Crewe,* 1888; *The Secret Garden,* 1911.

BURROUGHS, EDGAR RICE, Sept. 1, 1875 (Chicago, Ill.)-Mar. 19, 1950. U.S. novelist. Best known for the series of 23 Tarzan books, the first of which was *Tarzan of the Apes* (1914).

BURROWS, ABE, Dec. 18, 1910 (New York, N.Y.). U.S. playwright, writer for radio, TV, and nightclubs. Coauthored several plays, including *Guys and Dolls* (1950), *How To Succeed in Business without Really Trying* (1961; Pulitzer Prize in drama, 1961). Author, director, *Cactus Flower,* 1965.

CAIN, JAMES MALLAHAN, July 1, 1892 (Annapolis, Md.)–Oct. 27, 1977. U.S. novelist. Writer of "hard-boiled" fiction. *The Postman Always Rings Twice,* 1934; *Double Indemnity,* 1936; *Mildred Pierce,* 1941; *Past All Dishonor,* 1946.

CALDWELL, ERSKINE BRESTON, Dec. 17, 1903 (White Oak, Ga.). U.S. novelist. Author of realistic stories about the rural South. *Tobacco Road,* 1932 (dramatized, 1939); *God's Little Acre,* 1933; *Have You Seen Their Faces* (with MARGARET BOURKE-WHITE, his first wife), 1937.

CALDWELL, (Janet Miriam) **TAYLOR,** Sept. 7, 1900 (Preswick, Eng.). U.S. novelist. Author of numerous best-selling romances. *Dynasty of Death,* 1938; *The Eagles Gather,* 1940; *This Side of Innocence,* 1946; *Dear and Glorious Physician,* 1959; *Captains and Kings,* 1972.

CAPOTE, TRUMAN, Sept. 30, 1924 (New Orleans, La.). U.S. novelist, short-story writer. *Other Voices, Other Rooms,* 1948; *Breakfast at Tiffany's,* 1958; *In Cold Blood,* 1966.

CAREY, ERNESTINE MOLLER GILBRETH, Apr. 5, 1908 (New York, N.Y.). U.S. author who wrote *Cheaper by the Dozen* (with her brother Frank Gilbreth, 1949) and *Belles on Their Toes* (1951), humorous books about growing up as one of the 12 children of Frank Gilbreth, a motion-study expert who attempted to apply his theories to his family.

CARNEGIE, DALE, Nov. 24, 1888 (Maryville, Mo.)–Nov. 1, 1955. U.S. author, teacher of public speaking. Noted as the author of *How to Win Friends and Influence People* (1936), his guide to achieving success through poise, concentration, and self-confidence. *How to Stop Worrying and Start Living,* 1948.

CATHER, WILLA, Dec. 7, 1876 (Winchester, Va.)–Apr. 24, 1947. U.S. novelist, short-story writer. Awarded 1923 Pulitzer Prize in fiction for *One of Ours* (1922). *O Pioneers!,* 1913; *My Antonia,* 1918; *Death Comes for the Archbishop,* 1927.

CHASE, MARY COYLE, Feb. 25, 1907 (Denver, Col.). U.S. playwright. Best known for her play *Harvey,* about an invisible six-foot rabbit; the play enjoyed great success on Broadway and won the 1945 Pulitzer Prize in drama. *Mrs. McThing,* 1952; *Bernardine,* 1952.

CHAYEFSKY, PADDY, Jan. 29, 1923 (New York, N.Y.). U.S. playwright, TV and film screenwriter. Best known for his 1950s TV screenplays about urban working-class life, especially *Marty* (1953) and *The Bachelor Party* (1954); awarded 1976 Academy Award for best original screenplay for *Network.*

CHEEVER, JOHN, May 27, 1912 (Quincy, Mass.). U.S. novelist, short-story writer. Noted for his subtle, comic writing about suburbia; awarded 1979 Pulitzer Prize in fiction for *The Stories of John Cheever* (1978). *The Wapshot Chronicle,* 1957; *The Wapshot Scandal,* 1964; *The Brigadier and the Golf Widow,* 1964; *Bullet Park,* 1969; *Falconer,* 1978.

CHESTNUTT, CHARLES WADDELL, June 20, 1858 (Cleveland, Ohio)–Nov. 15, 1932. U.S. novelist. One of the first black writers to gain recognition in the U.S. *Conjure Woman,* 1899; *The Wife of His Youth and Other Stories of the Color Line,* 1899; *The House behind the Cedars,* 1901.

CHOPIN, KATE O'FLAHERTY, Feb. 8, 1851 (St. Louis, Mo.)–Aug. 22, 1904. U.S. novelist, short-story writer. Wrote stories of Creole and Cajun life in Louisiana, including *Bayou Folk* (1894) and *A Night in Acadie* (1897); her novel, *The Awakening* (1899), dealing with female sexuality, aroused great criticism and was ignored for 60 years before being rediscovered.

CIARDI, JOHN, June 24, 1916 (Boston, Mass.). U.S. poet, critic, editor. Poetry editor of *The Saturday Review,* 1956– ; author of highly esteemed verse translations of DANTE's *Inferno* (1954), *Purgatorio* (1961) and *Paradiso* (1970). *Homeward to America,* 1940; *As If,* 1955; *I Marry You,* 1958; *I Met a Man,* 1961; *The Wish Tree,* 1962.

CLARK, WALTER VAN TILBURG, Aug. 3, 1909 (E. Oreland, Me.)–Nov. 11, 1971. U.S. novelist, short-story writer. Wrote books about the West. *The Ox-Bow Incident,* 1940.

CLAVELL, JAMES DUMARESQ, Oct. 10, 1924 (England). U.S. novelist, screenwriter, director. *King Rat,* 1962; *Taipan,* 1966; *Shogun,* 1975.

COFFIN, (Robert Peter) **TRISTAM,** Mar. 18, 1892 (Brunswick, Me.)–Jan. 20, 1955. U.S. writer. *Strange Holiness* (1936 Pulitzer Prize in poetry), 1935; *Golden Falcon,* 1929; *Red Sky in the Morning,* 1935; *Maine Ballads,* 1935.

CONNELLY, MARC(us) COOK, Dec. 13, 1890 (McKeesport, Pa.). U.S. dramatist. Best known for his Pulitzer Prize-winning play, *The Green Pastures* (1930); with GEORGE S. KAUFMAN, wrote *Dulcy* (1921), *To the Ladies* (1923), *Beggar on Horseback* (1923), *Merton of the Movies* (1925).

COOPER, JAMES FENIMORE, Sept. 15, 1789 (Burlington, N.J.)–Sept. 14, 1851. U.S. novelist. The first important native American novelist; wrote about the conflict between frontier life and encroaching civilization; best known for the so-called Leatherstocking Tales: *The Pioneers* (1827), *The Last of the Mohicans* (1826), *The Prairie* (1827), *The Pathfinder* (1840), *The Deerslayer* (1841).

COSTAIN, THOMAS BERTRAM, May 8, 1885 (Brantford, Ont., Can.)–Oct. 8, 1965. U.S. novelist, editor. Fiction editor of the *Saturday Evening Post,* 1920–34; his historical novels include *The Black Rose* (1945) and *The Silver Chalice* (1953).

COZZENS, JAMES GOULD, Aug. 19, 1903 (Chicago, Ill.)–Aug. 9, 1978. U.S. novelist. *SS San Pedro,* 1931; *Guard of Honor* (1949 Pulitzer Prize in fiction), 1948; *By Love Possessed,* 1957.

CRANE, (Harold) **HART,** July 21, 1899 (Garrestville, Ohio)–Apr. 27, 1932. U.S. poet. In his best-known work, *The Bridge* (1930), used the Brooklyn Bridge as a symbol of America. *White Buildings,* 1926; *Collected Verse,* 1933.

CRANE, STEPHEN TOWNLEY, Nov. 1, 1871 (Newark, N.J.)–June 5, 1900. U.S. novelist, short-story writer, poet. Wrote vividly realistic novels and stories; died of tuberculosis at age 28. *Maggie: A Girl of the Streets,* 1893; *The Red Badge of Courage,* 1895; *The Open Boat and Other Tales,* 1898.

CRICHTON (John) **MICHAEL,** Oct. 23, 1942 (Chicago, Ill.). U.S. novelist, filmmaker. Trained in medicine (M.D., 1969); has written mystery stories and science fiction; received 1969 Edgar award; his novels *The Andromeda Strain* (1969) and *The Terminal Man* (1972) were made into films; wrote and directed the films *Westworld* (1973), *Coma* (1978), and *The Great Train Robbery* (1979)—the last-named adapted from his 1975 novel.

CRISTOFER, MICHAEL, born Michael Anthony Procaccino, Jan. 22, 1945 (Trenton, N.J.). U.S.

playwright, actor. Awarded 1977 Pulitzer Prize in drama for his play *The Shadow Box* (1972). *Ice*, 1974; *Black Angel*, 1976.

CROUSE, RUSSEL M., Feb. 20, 1893 (Findlay, Ohio)–Apr. 3, 1966. U.S. playwright. Collaborated with HOWARD LINDSAY to write several successful Broadway plays, including *Life with Father* (1939), *State of the Union* (1946; Pulitzer Prize in drama, 1946), *Call Me Madam* (1950), and (with RICHARD RODGERS and OSCAR HAMMERSTEIN II) *The Sound of Music*, 1959.

cummings, e(dward) e(stlin), Oct. 14, 1894 (Cambridge, Mass.)–Sept. 3, 1962. U.S. poet noted for his eccentric language and typography, and his erotic verse. *The Enormous Room* (autobiographical novel), 1922; *Tulips Are Chimneys*, 1923; *Is 5*, 1926; *50 Poems*, 1940; *95 Poems*, 1958.

DANA, RICHARD HENRY, JR., Aug. 1, 1815 (Cambridge, Mass.)–Jan. 6, 1882. U.S. novelist, lawyer. Based his classic sea novel, *Two Years before the Mast* (1840), on a diary he kept on a voyage around Cape Horn; as a lawyer, wrote a standard manual of maritime law, *The Seaman's Friend* (1841).

DAY, CLARENCE SHEPARD, JR., Nov. 18, 1874 (New York, N.Y.)–Dec. 28, 1935. U.S. essayist whose sketches about his parents were adapted for the stage as *Life with Father* and *Life with Mother*, by HOWARD LINDSAY and RUSSEL CROUSE. *God and My Father*, 1932; *Life with Father*, 1935; *Life with Mother*, 1937.

DENNIS, PATRICK, born Edward Everett Tanner III, May 18, 1921 (Chicago, Ill.)–Nov. 6, 1976. U.S. novelist. Created the eccentric, lovable *Auntie Mame* (1955); drama critic, *The New Republic*, 1957–71. *Guestward Ho!*, 1956; *Little Me*, 1961.

DICKEY, JAMES LAFAYETTE, Feb. 2, 1923 (Atlanta, Ga.). U.S. poet, novelist. *Into the Stone*, 1960; *Buckdancer's Choice*, 1965; *Deliverance*, 1969.

DICKINSON, EMILY, Dec. 10, 1830 (Amherst, Mass.)–May 15, 1886. U.S. poet. A unique stylist who used irregular rhymes and startling imagery; the daughter of a prominent Amherst attorney, she withdrew from society before the age of 30; published virtually nothing during her lifetime. *Collected Poems*, 1924.

DIDION, JOAN, Dec. 5, 1934 (Sacramento, Calif.). U.S. novelist, journalist. *Run River*, 1963; *Slouching Towards Bethlehem*, 1968; *Play It as It Lays*, 1970; *A Book of Common Prayer*, 1977; *The White Album*, 1979. (Wife of JOHN GREGORY DUNNE.)

DOCTOROW, E(dgar) L(awrence), Jan. 6, 1931 (New York, N.Y.). U.S. novelist. Editor in chief of Dial Press, 1964–69. *Welcome to Hard Times*, 1960; *The Book of Daniel*, 1971; *Ragtime*, 1975.

DODGE, MARY ELIZABETH, née Mapes, Jan. 26, 1831 (New York, N.Y.)–Aug. 21, 1905. U.S. editor, writer of children's books. Edited *St. Nicholas* (1873–1905), a leading children's magazine; a foremost writer of children's fiction, including *Hans Brinker; or, The Silver Skates* (1865).

DONLEAVY, J(ames) P(atrick), Apr. 23, 1926 (Brooklyn, N.Y.). U.S.-Irish novelist. Best known for his lusty, picaresque first novel, *The Ginger Man* (1955). *The Saddest Summer of Samuel S.*, 1967; *The Beastly Beatitudes of Balthazar B.*, 1969.

DOOLITTLE, HILDA ("H. D."), Sept. 10, 1886 (Bethlehem, Pa.)–Sept. 27, 1961. U.S. poet. A prominent member of the imagist movement. *Sea Garden*, 1916; *Hymen*, 1921; *Red Shoes for Bronze*, 1931.

DOS PASSOS, JOHN RODERIGO, Jan. 14, 1896 (Chicago, Ill.)–Sept. 18, 1970. U.S. novelist, journalist. In his novels, *Manhattan Transfer* (1925) and the trilogy *U.S.A.* (1937), created an impressionistic picture of the first three decades of the 20th cent.

DOUGLAS, LLOYD CASSEL, Aug. 27, 1877 (Columbia City, Ind.)–Feb. 13, 1951. U.S. novelist, clergyman. Many of his popular novels dramatizing Christian faith and morals—including *Magnificent Obsession* (1929), *Green Light* (1935), and *The Robe* (1942)—were made into films.

DREISER, THEODORE HERMAN ALBERT, Aug. 27, 1871 (Terre Haute, Ind.)–Dec. 28, 1945. U.S. novelist. Pioneer of naturalism in American literature. *Sister Carrie*, 1900; *The Financier*, 1912; *The Titan*, 1914; *An American Tragedy*, 1925; *Dreiser Looks at Russia*, 1928.

DRURY, ALLEN STUART, Sept. 2, 1918 (Houston, Tex.). U.S. novelist, journalist. A Washington correspondent who has written a series of novels about U.S. and world politics. *Advise and Consent* (1960 Pulitzer Prize in fiction), 1959; *Capable of Honor*, 1966; *Preserve and Protect*, 1968; *Anna Hastings*, 1977; *A Novel of Capitol Hill*, 1979.

DUNBAR, PAUL LAWRENCE, June 27, 1872 (Dayton, Ohio)–Feb. 9, 1906. U.S. poet, short-story writer, novelist. The son of escaped slaves; noted for sentimental poems and stories about poor black people. *Lyrics of Lowly Life*, 1896; *Folks from Dixie*, 1898; *The Sport of the Gods*, 1898.

DUNNE, JOHN GREGORY, May 25, 1932 (Hartford, Conn.). U.S. writer. *The Studio*, 1969; *Vegas*, 1974; *True Confessions*, 1977. (Husband of JOAN DIDION.)

EBERHART, RICHARD GHORMLEY, Apr. 5, 1904 (Austin, Minn.). U.S. poet. Awarded 1966 Pulitzer Prize in poetry for his *Selected Poems* (1966). *A Bravery of Earth*, 1930; *The Vastness and Indifference of the World*, 1965; *Shifts of Being*, 1968.

ELLISON, RALPH WALDO, Mar. 1, 1914 (Oklahoma City, Okla.). U.S. novelist. His highly-praised *The Invisible Man* (1952) tells of a young black man's search for his own identity and place in society. *Shadow and Act*, 1964.

EMERSON, RALPH WALDO, May 25, 1803 (Boston, Mass.)–Apr. 27, 1882. U.S. philosopher, poet, essayist. The main spokesman for American transcendentalism; his philosophy was marked by moral optimism and belief in the individual, intuition, mystical unity of nature; his poems include "Brahma," "The Problem," "The Concord Hymn." *Essays*, 1841 and 1844; *Representative Men*, 1850; *The Conduct of Life*, 1860.

ERDMAN, PAUL E., May 19, 1932 (Stratford, Ont., Can.). U.S. novelist. Author of popular novels about the world of high finance. *The Billion-Dollar Sure Thing*, 1973; *The Silver Bears*, 1974; *The Crash of '79*, 1976.

FARRELL, JAMES T., Feb. 27, 1904 (Chicago, Ill.)–Aug. 22, 1979. U.S. novelist. Best known for his Studs Lonigan trilogy: *Young Lonigan* (1932), *The Young Manhood of Studs Lonigan* (1934) and *Judgment Day* (1935). *A World I Never Made*, 1936.

FAST, HOWARD (pseud.: E. V. Cunningham), Nov. 11, 1914 (New York, N.Y.). U.S. novelist, screenwriter. Noted for historical novels set at the time of the American Revolution; under his pseudonym, writes suspense novels, screenplays, and science fiction. *Conceived in Liberty*, 1939; *The Unvanquished*, 1942; *Citizen Tom Paine*, 1943; *Spartacus*, 1951.

FAULKNER, WILLIAM HARRISON, Sept. 25, 1897 (New Albany, Miss.)-July 6, 1962. U.S. novelist. One of the great writers of the 20th cent., he created Yoknapatawpha County, Miss. as a microcosm of the post-Civil War deep South; won Nobel Prize in literature, 1949; awarded Pulitzer Prizes in fiction in 1955 (for *A Fable*, 1954) and 1963 (for *The Reivers*, 1962). *The Sound and the Fury*, 1929; *As I Lay Dying*, 1930; *Sanctuary*, 1931; *Light in August*, 1932; *Absalom, Absalom!*, 1936; *The Hamlet*, 1940; *Intruder in the Dust*, 1948; *Requiem for a Nun*, 1951.

FEARING, KENNETH FLEXNER, July 28, 1902 (Oak Park, Ill.)-June 26, 1961. U.S. poet, novelist. In his poetry, such as *The Afternoon of a Pawnbroker and Other Poems* (1943), satirized the U.S. as a mechanized society; also wrote crime novels, including *The Big Clock* (1946).

FERBER, EDNA, Aug. 15, 1885 (Kalamazoo, Mich.)-Apr. 16, 1968. U.S. novelist, short-story writer, playwright. *So Big* (1925 Pulitzer Prize in fiction), 1924; *Show Boat*, 1926; *The Royal Family* (with GEORGE S. KAUFMAN), 1927; *Cimarron*, 1930; *Dinner at Eight*, 1932; *Stage Door*, 1936; *Giant*, 1952.

FERLINGHETTI, LAWRENCE MONSANTO, born Lawrence Ferling, Mar. 24, 1919 (Yonkers, N.Y.). U.S. poet, publisher. Leader of the San Francisco Renaissance; owned City Lights bookshop in San Francisco, the first all-paperback store; published City Lights Books. *Pictures of the Gone World*, 1955; *A Coney Island of the Mind*, 1958.

FIELD, EUGENE, Sept. 2, 1850 (St. Louis, Mo.)-Nov. 4, 1895. U.S. poet, journalist; wrote column the "Sharps and Flats" for Chicago *Daily News* (and the Chicago *Record*); known for children's poems "Little Boy Blue" and "Wynken, Blynken, and Nod." *A Little Book of Western Verse*, 1889; *With Trumpets and Drums*, 1892.

FIELD, RACHEL LYMAN, Sept. 19, 1894 (New York, N.Y.)-Mar. 15, 1942. U.S. novelist. Wrote popular New England novels and children's books. *Hitty, Her First Hundred Years*, 1929; *Time Out of Mind*, 1935; *All This, and Heaven Too*, 1938; *And Now Tomorrow*, 1942.

FINLEY, MARTHA, née Farquharson, Apr. 26, 1828 (Chillicothe, Ohio)-Jan. 30, 1909. U.S. novelist. Wrote stories for little girls, including the 28 volumes of Elsie Dinsmore tales (1868-1905), the most popular such books of the day.

FINNEY, JACK, ? (Milwaukee, Wisc.). U.S. novelist. Best known as author of the cult classic *Time and Again* (1970). *The Invasion of the Body Snatchers*, 1954.

FITZGERALD, F(rancis) SCOTT KEY, Sept. 24, 1896 (St. Paul, Minn.)-Dec. 21, 1940. U.S. novelist, short-story writer. The success of his first novel, *This Side of Paradise* (1920), made him at age 24 the spokesman for the "lost generation" of the Jazz Age. *The Beautiful and the Damned*, 1921; *The Great Gatsby*, 1925; *Tender Is the Night*, 1934; *The Last Tycoon* (unfinished), 1940.

FORBES, KATHRYN, born Kathryn Anderson McLean, Mar. 20, 1909 (San Francisco, Cal.)-May 15, 1966. U.S. short-story writer. Her 1943 collection of short stories, *Mama's Bank Account*, was

dramatized by John Van Druten as *I Remember Mama* (1944), later made into a popular television series (1949-57), and in 1979 produced as a Broadway musical.

FRANK, GEROLD, Aug. 2, 1907 (Cleveland, Ohio). U.S. biographer. Coauthored biographies with celebrities. *I'll Cry Tomorrow* (with LILLIAN ROTH and Mike Connolly), 1954; *Too Much Too Soon* (with Diana Barrymore), 1957; *Beloved Infidel* (with SHEILAH GRAHAM), 1958. *Judy*, 1975.

FRIEDMAN, BRUCE J., Apr. 26, 1930 (New York, N.Y.). U.S. novelist, short-story writer, playwright. *Stern*, 1962; *A Mother's Kisses*, 1964; *Scuba Duba* (play), 1967; *Steambath* (play), 1970; *The Lonely Guy's Book of Life*, 1978.

FRINGS, KETTI, ? (Columbus, Ohio). U.S. playwright, screenwriter. Wrote the 1958 Pulitzer Prize-winning play *Look Homeward, Angel* (1957); wrote the screenplays for *Come Back, Little Sheba* (1952) and *The Shrike* (1955).

FROST, ROBERT, Mar. 26, 1874 (San Francisco, Calif.)-Jan. 29, 1963. U.S. poet. Wrote poetry about rural New England, traditional in form and colloquial in style; awarded Pulitzer Prizes in poetry in 1924 (for *New Hampshire*, 1923), 1931 (for *Collected Poems*, 1931), 1937 (for *A Further Range*, 1937), and 1943 (for *A Witness Tree*, 1943).

GALLICO, PAUL WILLIAM, July 26, 1897 (New York, N.Y.)-July 15, 1976. U.S. novelist, journalist. Staff member of the New York *Daily News*, 1922-36. *The Snow Goose*, 1941; *Mrs. 'Arris Goes to Paris*, 1958; *The Poseidon Adventure*, 1969.

GANN, ERNEST KELLOGG, Oct. 13, 1910 (Lincoln, Neb.). U.S. novelist. *The High and the Mighty*, 1952; *Fate Is the Hunter*, 1961; *In the Company of Eagles*, 1966.

GARLAND, (Hannibal) HAMLIN, Sept. 14, 1860 (W. Salem, Wisc.)-Mar. 4, 1940. U.S. short-story writer, novelist, essayist. Wrote about the difficult lives of Midwest farmers; awarded 1922 Pulitzer Prize for his autobiographical volume, *A Daughter of the Middle Border* (1921). *Main-Travelled Roads*, 1891; *A Little Norsk*, 1892.

GEISEL, THEODORE SEUSS ("Dr. Seuss"), Mar. 2, 1904 (Springfield, Mass.). U.S. author/illustrator of children's books. Launched the "beginner book" industry. *Horton Hears a Who*, 1954; *How the Grinch Stole Christmas*, 1957; *The Cat in the Hat*, 1957; *One Fish Two Fish Red Fish Blue Fish*, 1960; *Hop on Pop*, 1963.

GILLES, D(onald) B(ruce), Aug. 30, 1947 (Cleveland, Ohio). U.S. playwright. *The Girl Who Loved the Beatles*, 1974; *When I Lived in Baton Rouge*, 1975; *The Legendary Stardust Boys*, 1978.

GINSBURG, ALLEN, June 3, 1926 (Paterson, N.J.). U.S. poet. Prominent Beat Generation figure. "Howl," 1955; "Home," 1956; "Kaddish," 1960; *The Fall of America*, 1973.

GLASGOW, ELLEN, Apr. 22, 1874 (Richmond, Va.)-Nov. 21, 1945. U.S. novelist. Author of realistic novels about the South, as represented by her native Virginia. *The Descendant*, 1897; *Barren Ground*, 1925; *In This Our Life* (1942 Pulitzer Prize in fiction), 1941.

GOLDEN, HARRY LOUIS, May 6, 1902 (New York, N.Y.). U.S. nonfiction writer. Editor and publisher of *The Carolina Israelite*, Charlotte, N.C., 1942- . *Only in America*, 1958; *For 2 Cents Plain*, 1959; *Mr. Kennedy and the Negroes*, 1964; *The Greatest Jewish City in the World*, 1972.

THE BOOK OF WHO

GORDONE, CHARLES, Oct. 12, 1927 (Cleveland, Ohio). U.S. playwright. Wrote the 1970 Pulitzer Prize–winning play *No Place to Be Somebody* (1970).

GRAU, SHIRLEY ANN, July 8, 1929 (New Orleans, La.). U.S. short-story writer, novelist. *The Black Prince and Other Stories,* 1955; *The Hard Blue Sky,* 1958; *The Keepers of the House* (1965 Pulitzer Prize in fiction), 1964.

GREY, ZANE, Jan. 31, 1872 (Zanesville, Ohio)–Oct. 23, 1939. U.S. novelist. Author of best-selling Western romances, 54 in all. *The Last of the Plainsmen,* 1908; *Riders of the Purple Sage,* 1912.

GUEST, EDGAR A(lbert), Aug. 20, 1881 (Birmingham, Eng.)–Aug. 5, 1959. U.S. poet. Syndicated sentimental verses for the Detroit *Free Press* from the age of 20. *A Heap O' Livin',* 1916; *Just Folks,* 1917; *Life's Highway,* 1933.

HAILEY, ARTHUR, Apr. 5, 1920 (Luton, Eng.). U.S. novelist. *Hotel,* 1965; *Airport,* 1968; *Wheels,* 1971; *The Moneychangers,* 1975; *Overload,* 1975.

HALEY, ALEX PALMER, Aug. 11, 1921. U.S. author. His highly acclaimed fictionalized account of his black heritage, *Roots* (1976; a special citation Pulitzer Prize, 1977), was adapted into a highly successful TV series. *The Autobiography of Malcolm X,* 1965.

HALL, JAMES, Apr. 22, 1887 (Colfax, Ia.)–July 5, 1951. U.S. novelist, short-story writer. Collaborated with CHARLES BERNARD NORDHOFF on seafaring trilogy composed of *Mutiny on the Bounty* (1932), *Men against the Sea* (1933), and *Pitcairn Island* (1934).

HALLECK, FITZ-GREENE, July 8, 1790 (Guilford, Conn.)–Nov. 19, 1867. U.S. poet. *Satirical Croaker Papers* (with Joseph Rodman Drake), 1819; *Fanny,* 1819; *Marco Bozzares,* 1821.

HANSBERRY, LORRAINE, May 19, 1930 (Chicago, Ill.)–Jan. 12, 1965. U.S. playwright. Her play *Raisin in the Sun* (1959) was the first on Broadway to be written by a black woman. *The Sign in Sidney Brustein's Window,* 1964; *To Be Young, Gifted, and Black,* 1969.

HARRIS, JOEL CHANDLER, Dec. 8, 1848 (Eatonton, Ga.)–July 3, 1908. U.S. journalist, short-story writer, novelist. Author of the Uncle Remus stories, humorous tales, written in Southern black dialect, that featured animal characters. *Uncle Remus, His Songs and His Sayings,* 1881; *The Tar Baby,* 1904; *Uncle Remus and Br'er Rabbit,* 1906.

HART, MOSS, Oct. 24, 1904 (New York, N.Y.)–Dec. 20, 1961. U.S. playwright. In collaboration with GEORGE S. KAUFMAN, wrote *You Can't Take It With You* (1936; Pulitzer Prize in drama, 1937) and *The Man Who Came to Dinner* (1939); with KURT WEILL and IRA GERSHWIN, wrote *Lady in the Dark,* 1941. *Act One* (autobiography), 1959.

HARTE, (Francis) BRET(t), Aug. 25, 1836 (Albany, N.Y.)–May 5, 1902. U.S. short-story and verse writer. *The Luck of Roaring Camp,* 1868; *The Outcasts of Poker Flat,* 1869; *Plain Language from James,* 1870.

HAWTHORNE, NATHANIEL, July 4, 1804 (Salem, Mass.)–May 19, 1864. U.S. novelist, short-story writer. *Twice-Told Tales,* 1837 and 1842; *The Scarlet Letter,* 1850; *The House of the Seven Gables,* 1851; *The Blithedale Romance,* 1852; *The Marble Faun,* 1860.

HECHT, BEN, Feb. 28, 1893 (New York, N.Y.)–Apr. 18, 1964. U.S. journalist, playwright, novelist, short-story writer. Collaborated with CHARLES MACARTHUR to write *The Front Page* (1928) and *Twentieth Century* (1933). *A Child of the Century,* 1954.

HELLER, JOSEPH, May 1, 1923 (Brooklyn, N.Y.). U.S. novelist. Best known for his comic novel *Catch-22* (1961), about the absurdities of war. *We Bombed in New Haven* (play), 1968; *Something Happened,* 1974; *Good as Gold,* 1979.

HELLMAN, LILLIAN, June 20, 1905 (New Orleans, La.). U.S. dramatist. Wrote the plays *The Children's Hour* (1934), *Watch on the Rhine* (1941), *Another Part of the Forest* (1946), and *The Little Foxes* (1959); later turned to writing successful autobiographical books, including *An Unfinished Woman* (1969) and *Pentimento* (1973).

HEMINGWAY, ERNEST, July 21, 1899 (Oak Park, Ill.)–July 2, 1961. U.S. novelist, short-story writer. Noted for his terse, understated style; awarded Nobel Prize in literature, 1954. *In Our Time,* 1924; *The Sun Also Rises,* 1926; *A Farewell to Arms,* 1929; *For Whom the Bell Tolls,* 1940; *The Old Man and the Sea* (1953 Pulitzer Prize in fiction), 1952.

HENRY, O., born William Sidney Porter, Sept. 11, 1862 (Greensboro, N.C.)–June 5, 1910. U.S. short-story writer. Prolific writer of short stories with a surprising twist at the end, including "The Gift of the Magi" and "The Ransom of Red Chief"; convicted of embezzling, served three years in prison, where he wrote extensively. *Cabbages and Kings,* 1904; *The Four Million,* 1906.

HERLIHY, JAMES LEO, Feb. 27, 1927 (Detroit, Mich.). U.S. novelist, playwright. His novels *All Fall Down* (1960) and *Midnight Cowboy* (1965) were made into successful films; his plays include *Blue Denim* (with William Noble; 1957) and *Crazy October* (1958).

HERSEY, JOHN RICHARD, June 17, 1914 (Tientsin, China). U.S. novelist, journalist. War correspondent during WW II. *A Bell for Adano* (1945 Pulitzer Prize in fiction), 1944; *Hiroshima,* 1946; *The Wall,* 1950; *The War Lover,* 1959; *The Child Buyer,* 1960.

HIGGINS, GEORGE V., Nov. 13, 1939 (Brockton, Mass.). U.S. novelist. Author of realistic novels about small time Boston criminals and political novels about Washington, D.C.; asst. atty. gen. for Massachusetts, 1967–70; asst. U.S. atty. for Massachusetts, 1970–73. *The Friends of Eddie Coyle,* 1972; *The Digger's Game,* 1973; *City on the Hill,* 1975.

HOLMES, OLIVER WENDELL, Aug. 29, 1809 (Cambridge, Mass.)–Oct. 7, 1894. U.S. poet, essayist. New England Brahmin; first dean of the Harvard Medical School; named the *Atlantic Monthly* and contributed to it charming, witty sketches; his poems include "Old Ironsides" (1830), "The Moral Bully" (1836), "The Chambered Nautilus" (1858); named to Hall of Fame for Great Americans, 1910. (Father of jurist OLIVER WENDELL HOLMES.)

HOWE, JULIA WARD, May 27, 1819 (New York, N.Y.)–Oct. 17, 1910. U.S. poet, writer, social reformer. Wrote the words for "The Battle Hymn of the Republic," 1862; also wrote poetry, biographies, and books on social themes; the first woman elected to the National Institute of Arts and Letters (1907), and the American Academy of Arts and Letters (1908). *On Sex and Education,* 1874; *Modern Society,* 1881; *Reminiscences,* 1899.

14

WRITERS

HOWELLS, WILLIAM DEAN, Mar. 1, 1837 (Martin's Ferry, Ohio)–May 11, 1928. U.S. novelist, editor, critic. Worked as an editor at *Atlantic Monthly* (1872–81) and *Harper's* (1886–91); a champion of realism and mentor of MARK TWAIN, H. GARLAND, STEPHEN CRANE, and others. *A Modern Instance,* 1882; *The Rise of Silas Lapham,* 1885; *Criticism and Fiction,* 1891.

HUBBARD, ELBERT, June 19, 1856 (Bloomington, Ill.)–May 7, 1916. U.S. writer, editor. Best known as the author of "A Message to Garcia," 1899. *One Day: A Tale of the Prairies,* 1893; *The Man of Sorrows,* 1906.

HUGHES, (James) LANGSTON, Feb. 1, 1902 (Joplin, Mo.)–May 22, 1967. U.S. poet. An important figure in the Harlem Renaissance; wrote in dialect, using blues and jazz rhythms, about black Americans. *Weary Blues,* 1926; *Shakespeare in Harlem,* 1942; *One-way Ticket,* 1949; *Simple Speaks His Mind,* 1950.

HUNTER, EVAN (pseud.: Ed McBain), Oct. 15, 1926 (New York, N.Y.). U.S. novelist. His novels *Blackboard Jungle* (1954) and *Strangers When We Meet* (1958) were made into films; under his pseudonym, writes police precinct novels, including *Cop Hater* (1956), *Lady Killer* (1958), *See Them Die* (1960).

HURST, FANNIE, Oct. 18, 1889 (Hamilton, Ohio)–Feb. 23, 1968. U.S. novelist, short-story writer. Author of popular, sentimental novels and stories. *Humoresque,* 1919; *Back Street,* 1931; *Imitation of Life,* 1933.

INGE, WILLIAM MOTTER, May 3, 1913 (Independence, Kan.)–June 10, 1973. U.S. playwright. Wrote dramas about small-town Midwestern life. *Come Back, Little Sheba,* 1950; *Picnic* (1953 Pulitzer Prize in drama), 1953; *The Dark at the Top of the Stairs,* 1957.

IRVING, JOHN, Mar. 2, 1942 (Exeter, N.H.). U.S. novelist. *Setting Free the Bears,* 1969; *The 158-Pound Marriage,* 1974; *The World According to Garp,* 1978.

IRVING, WASHINGTON (pseud.: Diedrich Knickerbocker), Apr. 3, 1783 (New York, N.Y.)–Nov. 28, 1859. U.S. essayist. The first American man of letters to be admired abroad; best-known sketches include "Rip Van Winkle" and "The Legend of Sleepy Hollow" (both 1820). *Salmagundi* (with Wm. Irving and J. K. Paulding), 1807–8; *A History of New York* (as Knickerbocker), 1809; *The Sketchbook of Geoffrey Crayon, Gent.,* 1820.

JACKSON, HELEN HUNT, née Fiske, Oct. 15, 1830 (Amherst, Mass.)–Aug. 12, 1885. U.S. novelist, poet, essayist. Her novel *Ramona* (1884), a historical romance sympathetic to the American Indians, helped change white attitudes.

JACKSON, SHIRLEY, Dec. 14, 1919 (San Francisco, Calif.)–Aug. 8, 1965. U.S. short-story writer, novelist. Noted for her tales dealing with the supernatural. *The Lottery,* 1949; *We Have Always Lived in the Castle,* 1953; *Life among the Savages,* 1953.

JAMES, HENRY, Apr. 15, 1843 (New York, N.Y.)–Feb. 28, 1916. U.S. novelist (later a British citizen). One of the greatest American novelists, his principal motif was the innocent American versus experienced Europeans. *The American,* 1877; *Daisy Miller,* 1879; *The Portrait of a Lady,* 1881; *Washington Square,* 1881; *The Spoils of Poynton,* 1897; *The Ambassadors,* 1903; *The Golden Bowl,* 1904; *The Turn of the Screw,* 1898. (Son of HENRY JAMES; brother of WILLIAM JAMES.)

JARRELL, RANDALL, May 6, 1914 (Nashville, Tenn.)–Oct. 14, 1965. U.S. poet, critic, novelist. *Blood for a Stranger,* 1942; *Little Friend, Little Friend,* 1945; *Losses,* 1948; *Pictures from an Institution,* 1954; *The Lost World,* 1965.

JEFFERS, (John) ROBINSON, Jan. 10, 1887 (Pittsburgh, Pa.)–Jan. 20, 1962. U.S. poet. Much of his powerful poetry is based on Greek myths. "Tamar," 1925; "The Woman at Point Sur," 1927; "Medea," 1946; *Hungerfield and Other Poems,* 1954 (1954 Pulitzer Prize in poetry).

JEWETT, SARAH ORNE, Sept. 3, 1849 (So. Berwick, Me.)–June 24, 1909. U.S. novelist, short-story writer. Author of realistic regional fiction centered in New England. *The Country of the Painted Firs,* 1896; *A Country Doctor,* 1884.

JONES, JAMES, Nov. 6, 1921 (Robinson, Ill.)–May 9, 1977. U.S. novelist. *From Here to Eternity,* 1951; *Some Came Running,* 1957; *The Thin Red Line,* 1962; *Whistle* (completed by WILLIE MORRIS), 1978.

JONG, ERICA MANN, Mar. 26, 1942 (New York, N.Y.). U.S. novelist, poet. Noted for her best-selling bawdy, quasi-autobiographical novels. *Fruits and Vegetables* (poems), 1971; *Fear of Flying,* 1973; *Loveroot* (poems), 1975; *How to Save Your Own Life,* 1977.

KANTOR, MCKINLAY, Feb. 4, 1904 (Webster City, Ia.). U.S. novelist. *Long Remember,* 1934; *Arouse and Beware,* 1936; *Andersonville* (1956 Pulitzer Prize in fiction), 1955.

KAUFMAN, GEORGE S(imon), Nov. 16, 1889 (Pittsburgh, Pa.)–June 2, 1961. U.S. dramatist, drama critic, director. Among some 40 collaborations on comedies, best known for his plays with MOSS HART, including the Pulitzer Prize–winner *You Can't Take It With You* (1936) and *The Man Who Came to Dinner* (1939). *Merton of the Movies* (with MARC CONNELLY), 1922; *June Moon* (with RING LARDNER), 1929; *The Royal Family* (with EDNA FERBER), 1927; *Of Thee I Sing* (with Morrie Ryskind; 1932 Pulitzer Prize in drama), 1931.

KEROUAC, JACK, born Jean-Louis Kerouac, 1922 (Lowell, Mass.)–Oct. 21, 1969. U.S. novelist, poet. A leading representative of the Beat Generation of the 1950s, which was defined by his book *On the Road* (1957). *The Subterraneans,* 1958; *The Dharma Bums,* 1958.

KERR, JEAN, née Collins, July 1923 (Scranton, Pa.). U.S. humorist, playwright. *Please Don't Eat the Daisies,* 1957; *The Snake Has All the Lines,* 1960; *Mary, Mary* (play), 1961. (Wife of WALTER KERR.)

KESEY, KEN, Sept. 17, 1935 (La Hunta, Col.). U.S. novelist, editor. *One Flew Over the Cuckoo's Nest* (also a successful play and film), 1962; *Sometimes a Great Notion,* 1964; *Garage Sale,* 1973.

KEY, FRANCIS SCOTT, Aug. 1, 1779 (Carroll Co., Md.)–Jan. 11, 1843. U.S. poet, attorney. After watching the bombardment of Ft. McHenry during the War of 1812, wrote "The Star-spangled Banner," which became the official U.S. national anthem in 1931.

KEYES, FRANCIS PARKINSON, July 21, 1885 (Charlottesville, Va.)–July 3, 1970. U.S. novelist. *The Old Grey Homestead,* 1919; *Dinner at Antoine's,* 1948.

KILMER, (Alfred) JOYCE, Dec. 6, 1886 (New Brunswick, N.J.)–July 30, 1918. U.S. poet. Best known for his poem "Trees" (1914); wrote for the *Sunday Magazine* and the book-review section of *The New York Times.*

THE BOOK OF WHO

KNOWLES, JOHN, Sept. 16, 1926 (Fairmont, W. Va.). U.S. novelist. A Separate Peace, 1960; Phineas, 1968; Spreading Fires, 1974.

KUMIN, MAXINE WINOKUR, June 6, 1925 (Philadelphia, Pa.). U.S. poet, novelist, children's-book writer. Nightmare Factory, 1970; Up Country (1973 Pulitzer Prize in poetry), 1972; House, Bridge, Fountain, Gate, 1975.

KUNITZ, STANLEY JASSPON, July 29, 1905 (Worcester, Mass.). U.S. poet, editor, teacher. Metaphysical poet. Intellectual Things, 1930; Selected Poems, 1928-1958 (1959 Pulitzer Prize in poetry), 1958.

LA FARGE, OLIVER HAZARD PERRY, Dec. 19, 1901 (New York, N.Y.)-Aug. 2, 1963. U.S. novelist, anthropologist. Wrote fiction based on his anthropological field work in Arizona, Guatemala, and Mexico. Laughing Boy (1930 Pulitzer Prize in fiction), 1929; Sparks Fly Upward, 1931; All the Young Men, 1935.

LANIER, SIDNEY, Feb. 3, 1842 (Macon, Ga.)-Sept. 7, 1881. U.S. poet, musician, critic. First flutist of the Peabody Orchestra, Baltimore, Md. Corn, 1874; The Symphony, 1875; Song of a Chattahoochee, 1877; The Marshes of Glynn, 1878.

LARDNER, RING(old) WILMER, Mar. 6, 1885 (Niles, Mich.)-Sept. 25, 1933. U.S. humorist, short-story writer. Author of brilliant, bitter satires about ordinary people, including You Know Me, Al (1916) and Gullible's Travels (1917); coauthored (with GEORGE S. KAUFMAN) the plays Elmer the Great (1928) and June Moon (1929).

LAZARUS, EMMA, July 22, 1849 (New York, N.Y.)-Nov. 19, 1887. U.S. poet, essayist. Best known for her sonnet "The New Colossus," engraved on the pedestal of the Statue of Liberty; spokesperson for Judaism. Admetus and Other Poems, 1871; Songs of a Semite, 1882.

LEDERER, WILLIAM JULIUS, Mar. 31, 1912 (New York, N.Y.). U.S. novelist, nonfiction writer. The Ugly American (with EUGENE BURDICK), 1958; A Nation of Sheep, 1961; Sarkhan, 1965.

LEE, (Nelle) HARPER, Apr. 28, 1926 (Monroeville, Ala.). U.S. novelist. The only novel she wrote was a sensational success: To Kill a Mockingbird (1960).

LEVERTOV, DENISE, Oct. 24, 1923 (Ilford, Essex, Eng.). U.S. poet. The Double Image, 1946; Here and Now, 1957; The Jacob's Ladder, 1962; The Sorrow Dance, 1967; The Poet in the World, 1974.

LEVIN, IRA, Aug. 27, 1929. U.S. novelist, playwright. No Time for Sergeants (play), 1956; Rosemary's Baby, 1967; The Stepford Wives, 1972; The Boys From Brazil, 1976; Deathtrap (play), 1978.

LEVIN, MEYER, Oct. 8, 1905 (Chicago, Ill.). U.S. novelist. Compulsion (dramatized, 1959), 1956; Gore & Igor, 1968.

LEWIS, (Harry) SINCLAIR, Feb. 7, 1885 (Sauk Centre, Minn.)-Jan. 10, 1951. U.S. novelist. The first American to receive the Nobel Prize in literature, 1930; his major novels portrayed the provincialism of small-town middle-class America. Main Street, 1920; Babbitt, 1922; Arrowsmith, 1925; Elmer Gantry, 1927; Dodsworth, 1929.

LINDBERGH, ANN MORROW, 1906 (Englewood, N.J.). U.S. writer, poet. Gift From the Sea, 1955; The Unicorn and Other Poems, 1956; Bring Me a Unicorn, 1972. (Wife of CHARLES A. LINDBERGH.)

LINDSAY, HOWARD, Mar. 29, 1889 (Waterford, N.Y.). U.S. playwright. With RUSSEL CROUSE, adapted for the stage Life with Father (1939), and played the leading role for more than 3,000 performances; also with Crouse, wrote Anything Goes (1934), State of the Union (1945; Pulitzer Prize in drama, 1946), and Call Me Madam (1950).

LINDSAY, (Nicholas) VACHEL, Nov. 10, 1879 (Springfield, Ill.)-Dec. 5, 1931. U.S. poet. Chanted his rhythmic and onomatopoeic poems from lecture platforms. General William Booth Enters into Heaven and Other Poems, 1913; The Congo, 1914; The Chinese Nightingale, 1917.

LOFTING, HUGH, Jan. 14, 1886 (Maidenhead, Eng.)-Sept. 26, 1947. Eng.-U.S. writer of children's stories. The Story of Dr. Doolittle, 1920; The Voyages of Dr. Doolittle, 1922; Dr. Doolittle and the Secret Lake, 1948.

LONDON, JACK, born John Griffith London, Jan. 12, 1876 (San Francisco, Calif.)-Nov. 22, 1916. U.S. novelist, short-story writer, essayist. Highest paid and best known writer of his time. The Son of the Wolf, 1900; The Call of the Wild, 1903; The Sea-Wolf, 1904; Martin Eden, 1909; John Barleycorn; or, Alcoholic Memoirs, 1913.

LONGFELLOW, HENRY WADSWORTH, Feb. 27, 1807 (Portland, Me.)-Mar. 24, 1882. U.S. poet. Ballads and Other Poems (including "The Wreck of the Hesperus," "The Village Blacksmith," "Excelsior"), 1842; Evangeline, 1847; The Song of Hiawatha, 1855; The Courtship of Miles Standish, 1858; Paul Revere's Ride, 1860.

LOOS, ANITA, Apr. 26, 1893 (Sisson, Calif.). U.S. screenwriter, novelist. Her popular, humorous novel, Gentlemen Prefer Blondes (1925), was adapted into a play (1925), a musical comedy (1949), and a film (1953).

LOTHROP, HARRIET MULFORD, née Stone (pseud.: Margaret Sidney), June 22, 1844 (New Haven, Conn.)-Aug. 2, 1924. U.S. children's-book writer. Five Little Peppers and How They Grew, 1881.

LOWELL, AMY LAWRENCE, Feb. 9, 1874 (Brookline, Mass.)-May 12, 1925. U.S. poet, critic. Championed the imagist poets, publishing a three-volume anthology Some Imagist Poets (1915, 1916, 1917); an unusual and controversial woman of her times, famous for unconventional habits, including smoking cigars; awarded posthumous Pulitzer Prize in poetry for What's O'Clock, 1925. Dome of Many-Colored Glass, 1912; Six French Poets (criticism), 1915. (Sister of PERCIVAL LOWELL.)

LOWELL, JAMES RUSSELL, Feb. 22, 1819 (Cambridge, Mass.)-Aug. 12, 1891. U.S. poet, critic, editor. Editor of the Atlantic Monthly, (1857-61) and the North American Review (1864-72). A Fable for Critics, 1848; The Vision of Sir Launfal, 1848; Fireside Travels, 1864; Democracy and Other Addresses, 1887.

LOWELL, ROBERT TRAILL SPENCE, Mar. 1, 1917 (Boston, Mass.)-Sept. 12, 1977. U.S. poet. Leader of the Confessional school of poetry in the 1950s. Lord Weary's Castle (1947 Pulitzer Prize in poetry), 1946; The Mills of the Kavanaughs, 1951; Life Studies, 1959; For the Union Dead, 1964; The Dolphin (1974 Pulitzer Prize in poetry), 1973.

MACARTHUR, CHARLES GORDON, Nov. 5, 1895 (Scranton, Pa.)-Apr. 21, 1956. U.S. journalist, playwright. Collaborated with BEN HECHT on the plays *The Front Page* (1928) and *Twentieth Century* (1932). (Husband of HELEN HAYES.)

MACLEISH, ARCHIBALD, May 7, 1892 (Glencoe, Ill.). U.S. poet, playwright, teacher, public official. Poet laureate of the New Deal; librarian of Congress, 1939–44; asst. secy. of state, 1944–45; awarded 1959 Pulitzer Prize in drama for *J.B.* (1958), and two Pulitzer Prizes in poetry: 1933 (for *Conquistador,* 1932) and 1953 (for *Collected Poems: 1917-1952,* 1952). *New Found Land,* 1930; *Frescoes for Mr. Rockefeller's City,* 1933; *America Was Promises,* 1939.

MAILER, NORMAN, Jan. 31, 1923 (Long Branch, N.J.). U.S. novelist, journalist. Perhaps the most famous U.S. postwar writer, known for his iconoclastic writing on American life; ran for mayor of New York City on platform of statehood for the city, 1969. *The Naked and the Dead,* 1948; *The White Negro* (essay), 1957; *An American Dream,* 1966; *Armies of the Night* (Pulitzer Prize in general nonfiction, 1969), 1968; *Marilyn,* 1973; *The Executioner's Song,* 1979.

MALAMUD, BERNARD, Apr. 26, 1914 (Brooklyn, N.Y.). U.S. novelist, short-story writer. Noted for creating a fictional world related to Jewish folklore. *The Natural,* 1952; *The Assistant,* 1957; *The Magic Barrel,* 1958; *The Fixer* (1966 Pulitzer Prize in fiction), 1966; *The Tenants,* 1971; *Dubin's Lives,* 1979.

MANCHESTER, WILLIAM, Apr. 1, 1922 (Attleboro, Mass.). U.S. novelist, biographer. Best known for his *The Death of a President* (1967), commissioned by JACQUELINE KENNEDY, who later changed her mind and unsuccessfully filed suit against Manchester to prevent publication. *A Rockefeller Family Portrait,* 1959; *Portrait of a President,* 1962; *The Arms of Krupp,* 1968; *American Caesar,* 1978.

MARKHAM, EDWIN CHARLES, Apr. 23, 1852 (Oregon City, Ore.)–Mar. 7, 1940. U.S. poet, lecturer. Best known as the author of the poem "The Man with the Hoe" (1899). *Lincoln and Other Poems,* 1901; *Field Folk: Interpretations of Millet,* 1906.

MARQUAND, J(ohn) P(hillips), Nov. 10, 1893 (Wilmington, Del.)–July 16, 1960. U.S. novelist. Wrote satires about New England middle- and upper-class society. *The Late George Apley,* (1938 Pulitzer Prize in fiction), 1937; *Wickford Point,* 1939; *H. M. Pulham, Esquire,* 1941.

MARSHALL, (Sarah) CATHERINE, née Wood, Sept. 27, 1914 (Johnson City, Tenn.). U.S. nonfiction writer, editor. Noted for *A Man Called Peter,* a best-selling biography of her husband, PETER MARSHALL, chaplain of the U.S. Senate; edited collection of her husband's sermons and prayers, *Mr. Jones, Meet the Master,* 1949. *Christy,* 1967.

MASTERS, EDGAR LEE, Aug. 23, 1869 (Garnett, Kan.)–Mar. 5, 1950. U.S. poet, novelist. Best known for his *Spoon River Anthology* (1915), free-verse monologues spoken from the grave by the former inhabitants of a small town. *The New Spoon River,* 1924; *Across Spoon River* (autobiography), 1936.

MCBAIN, LAURIE, Oct. 15, 1949 (Carmel, Calif.). U.S. novelist. Author of best-selling historical romances. *Devil's Desire,* 1974; *Moonstruck Madness,* 1977; *Tears of Gold,* 1979.

MCCARTHY, MARY THERESE, June 21, 1912 (Seattle, Wash.). U.S. novelist, critic. In addition to witty, acerbic novels, writes about politics, art, and travel. *The Company She Keeps,* 1942; *Venice Observed,* 1956; *Memories of a Catholic Girlhood,* 1957; *The Group,* 1963; *Birds of America,* 1971; *Watergate Portraits,* 1974. (Once married to EDMUND WILSON; sister of actor KEVIN MCCARTHY.)

MCCULLERS, CARSON, Feb. 19, 1917 (Columbus, Ga.)–Sept. 29, 1967. U.S. novelist. Wrote about outcasts and misfits. *The Heart Is a Lonely Hunter,* 1940; *A Member of the Wedding* (later dramatized and made into a film), 1946; *The Ballad of the Sad Café* (later dramatized by EDWARD ALBEE), 1951.

MCGINLEY, PHYLLIS, Mar. 21, 1905 (Ontario, Ore.)–Feb. 22, 1978. U.S. poet. *Love Letters of Phyllis McGinley,* 1954; *Merry Christmas, Happy New Year,* 1958; *Times Three: Selected Verse From Three Decades* (1961 Pulitzer Prize in poetry), 1960; *Sixpence in Her Shoe,* 1964.

MCKUEN, ROD, April 29, 1938 (Oakland, Calif.). U.S. poet. *Stanyan Street and Other Sorrows,* 1966; *Listen to the Warm,* 1967; *Lonesome Cities,* 1968; *Come to Me in Silence,* 1973.

MELVILLE, HERMAN, Aug. 1, 1819 (New York, N.Y.)–Sept. 28, 1891. U.S. novelist. Initially wrote novels reflecting his experiences as a cabin boy and seaman; after early success, sank into obscurity as a writer, but rediscovered and celebrated in the 1920s. *Typee,* 1846; *Omoo,* 1847; *White-Jacket,* 1850; *Moby Dick,* 1851; *Pierre,* 1852; *Billy Budd,* 1924.

METALIOUS, GRACE, née de Repentigny, Sept. 8, 1924 (Manchester, N.H.)–Feb. 25, 1964. U.S. novelist. *Peyton Place,* 1956; *Return to Peyton Place,* 1959; *The Tight White Collar,* 1960.

MICHENER, JAMES ALBERT, Feb. 3, 1907 (New York, N.Y.). U.S. novelist. Noted for best-selling books about exotic locales. *Tales of the South Pacific* (1948 Pulitzer Prize in fiction, adapted by RICHARD RODGERS and OSCAR HAMMERSTEIN into the musical *South Pacific),* 1947; *The Bridges at Toko-Ri,* 1953; *Sayonara,* 1954; *Hawaii,* 1959; *The Source,* 1965; *Centennial,* 1974; *Chesapeake,* 1978.

MILLAY, EDNA ST. VINCENT, Feb. 22, 1892 (Rockland, Me.)–Oct. 19, 1950. U.S. poet, dramatist. Best known for her early poem "Renascence" (1917) and the sonnets in *A Few Figs from Thistles* (1920). *The Harp Weaver* (1923 Pulitzer Prize in poetry), 1923.

MILLER, ARTHUR, Oct. 17, 1915 (New York, N.Y.). U.S. dramatist. Deals with social and political problems, including anti-semitism, fascism, political persecution. *All My Sons,* 1947; *Death of a Salesman* (Pulitzer Prize in drama, 1950), 1949; *The Crucible,* 1953; *The Misfits* (screenplay), 1961; *After the Fall* (about his marriage to MARILYN MONROE), 1964; *The Price,* 1968; *The Creation of the World and Other Business,* 1972.

MILLER, HENRY, Dec. 26, 1891 (New York, N.Y.). U.S. novelist. His sexually candid novels were banned in the U.S. and Great Britain until the 1960s. *Tropic of Cancer,* 1934 (France) and 1961 (U.S.); *Tropic of Capricorn,* 1939 (France) and 1961 (U.S.); *Rosy Crucifixion* trilogy: *Sexus* (1949), *Plexus* (1953), *Nexus* (1959).

MILLER, JASON, Apr. 22, 1939 (New York, N.Y.). U.S. playwright, actor. Awarded 1973 Pulitzer Prize in drama for *That Championship Season* (1972); played Father Karras in film *The Exorcist,* 1974.

MILLER, JOAQUIN, born Cincinnatus Hiner Miller, Sept. 8, 1837 (nr. Liberty, Ind.)–Feb. 17, 1913.

U.S. poet, journalist. Best known for his romantic poems about the Old West. *Pacific Poems*, 1871; *Songs of the Sierras*, 1871; *Songs of the Sunlands*, 1873.

MITCHELL, MARGARET, 1900 (Atlanta, Ga.)–Aug. 16, 1949. U.S. novelist. Her novel *Gone with the Wind* (1936), about the Civil War and Reconstruction, was the biggest seller in the U.S. up to its time and won the 1937 Pulitzer Prize in fiction; the film based on the novel won an Academy Award for best picture (1940) and held the record for gross earnings for more than 20 years.

MOORE, CLEMENT CLARKE, July 15, 1779 (New York, N.Y.)–July 10, 1863. U.S. writer, poet, educator. Best known as the author of "A Visit from St. Nicholas." (1823); with family inheritance, established Gen. Theological Seminary (1819), where he was prof. of Oriental and Greek literature, 1823-50.

MOORE, MARIANNE CRAIG, Nov. 17, 1887 (St. Louis, Mo.)–Feb. 5, 1972. U.S. poet. Wrote concise, witty, intellectual poems, notably "The Pangolin," "To a Steam Roller," "When I Buy Pictures," and "Poetry." *Poems*, 1921; *Observations*, 1924; *What Are Years?*, 1941; *Collected Poems* (1952 Pulitzer Prize in poetry), 1951.

MOORE, ROBIN, born Robert Lowell Moore, Jr., Oct. 31, 1925 (Concord, Mass.). U.S. novelist. *The Green Berets*, 1965; *The French Connection* (film adaptation awarded Academy Award for best picture in 1971), 1969.

NASH, (Frederic) OGDEN, Aug. 19, 1902 (Rye, N.Y.)–May 19, 1971. U.S. poet. Wrote sophisticated, satirical humorous verse, much of it published originally in *The New Yorker*, whose tone it helped set; wrote lyrics for *One Touch of Venus* (with S. J. PERELMAN, 1943) and *Two's Company* (1952). *The Bad Parent's Garden*, 1936; *I'm a Stranger Here Myself*, 1938; *Everyone but Thee and Me*, 1938.

NEMEROV, HOWARD, Mar. 1, 1920 (New York, N.Y.). U.S. poet, critic, novelist, teacher. *The Image and the Law*, 1947; *The Salt Garden*, 1955; *Mirrors and Windows*, 1958; *Blue Swallows*, 1967.

NORDHOFF, CHARLES BERNARD, Feb. 1, 1887 (Santa Barbara, Calif.)–Apr. 11, 1947. U.S. novelist. Travel and adventure writer; with JAMES NORMAN HALL, wrote the trilogy composed of *Mutiny on the Bounty* (1932), *Men against the Sea* (1933), and *Pitcairn's Island* (1934).

NORRIS, (Benjamin) FRANK(lin), Mar. 5, 1870 (Chicago, Ill.)–Oct. 25, 1902. U.S. novelist. An influential muckraker best known for his unfinished trilogy *The Epic of the Wheat*, which included *The Octopus* (1901) and *The Pit* (1903). *McTeague*, 1899; *Vandover and the Brute*, 1914.

OATES, JOYCE CAROL, June 16, 1938 (Lockport, N.Y.). U.S. novelist, short-story writer, poet, critic, teacher. *A Garden of Earthly Delights*, 1967; *Them*, 1969; *Wonderland*, 1971; *Do with Me What You Will*, 1973; *Childwold*, 1976.

O'CONNOR, EDWIN GREENE, July 29, 1918 (Providence, R.I.)–Mar. 23, 1968. U.S. novelist. Wrote about the Irish-American middle class. *The Last Hurrah*, 1956; *The Edge of Sadness* (1962 Pulitzer Prize in fiction), 1961.

O'CONNOR, (Mary) FLANNERY, Mar. 25, 1925 (Savannah, Ga.)–Aug. 3, 1964. U.S. short-story writer, novelist. Wrote fierce and funny stories grounded in her Southern and Roman Catholic background; from age 26 to her death, was confined to her Milledgeville, Ga., home with an incurable blood disease. *A Good Man Is Hard to Find*

and Other Stories, 1955; *Wise Blood*, 1952; *The Violent Bear It Away*, 1960; *Everything That Rises Must Converge*, 1965.

ODETS, CLIFFORD, July 18, 1906 (Philadelphia, Pa.)–Aug. 14, 1963. U.S. dramatist. Leading dramatist of the Depression, wrote plays of social protest for the Group Theatre in New York City. *Waiting for Lefty*, 1935; *Awake and Sing*, 1935; *Paradise Lost*, 1935; *Golden Boy*, 1937; *The Big Knife*, 1949; *The Country Girl*, 1950.

O'HARA, JOHN HENRY, Jan. 31, 1905 (Pottsville, Pa.)–Apr. 11, 1970. U.S. short-story writer, novelist. His short-story collection *Pal Joey* (1940) was made into a successful Broadway musical and later a film. *Appointment in Samarra*, 1934; *Butterfield 8* (made into a film, 1960), 1935; *The Doctor's Son and Other Stories*, 1935.

O'HARA, MARY, née Alsop, July 10, 1885 (Cape May, N.J.). U.S. novelist. Best known for her classic tale of a boy and his colt, *My Friend Flicka* (1941).

O'NEILL, EUGENE GLADSTONE, Oct. 16, 1888 (New York, N.Y.)–Nov. 27, 1953. U.S. dramatist. Only U.S. playwright to be awarded Nobel Prize in literature, 1936; received Pulitzer Prizes in drama in 1920 for *Beyond the Horizon* (1920), in 1922 for *Anna Christie* (1922), in 1928 for *Strange Interlude* (1928), and in 1957 for *A Long Day's Journey into Night* (1956). *The Emperor Jones*, 1921; *Desire under the Elms*, 1921; *Mourning Becomes Electra*, 1931; *Ah, Wilderness!* 1933; *The Iceman Cometh*, 1946.

PARKER, DOROTHY, née Rothschild, Aug. 22, 1893 (West End, N.J.)–June 7, 1967. U.S. humorist. Celebrated wit of the 1920s; member of the Algonquin Round Table group; book reviewer at *The New Yorker*, 1925-27. *Enough Rope*, 1926; "The Big Blonde," 1929.

PATRICK, JOHN, born John Patrick Goggan, May 17, 1905 (Louisville, Ky.). U.S. playwright. *Teahouse of the August Moon* (1954 Pulitzer Prize in drama), 1953; *Everybody Loves Opal*, 1961.

PERCY, WALKER, May 28, 1916 (Birmingham, Ala.). U.S. novelist, essayist. *The Moviegoer*, 1961; *The Last Gentleman*, 1966; *Love in the Ruins: The Adventures of a Bad Catholic at a Time near the End of the World*, 1971.

PERELMAN S(idney) J(oseph), Feb. 1, 1904 (New York, N.Y.)–Oct. 17, 1979. U.S. humorist. Noted for the mock gentility and unpredictable flights of baroque imagination in his pieces for *The New Yorker*; coauthored MARX brothers movies, including *Monkey Business* (1931) and *Horsefeathers* (1932). *Dawn Ginsbergh's Revenge*, 1929; *One Touch of Venus* (with OGDEN NASH), 1943; *The Best of S. J. Perelman*, 1947; *Chicken Inspector No. 23*, 1967; *Baby, It's Cold Inside*, 1970.

PLATH, SYLVIA, Oct. 27, 1932 (Boston, Mass.)–Feb. 11, 1963. U.S. poet. Best known for her posthumously published volume of poetry, *Ariel* (1968), written shortly before her suicide, and her novel *The Bell Jar* (1962), a fictionalized account of her nervous breakdown. *The Colossus*, 1960; *Crossing the Water*, 1971; *Winter Trees*, 1972. (Wife of TED HUGHES.)

PORTER, GENE(ra) GRACE, née Stratton, Aug. 17, 1868 (Wabash Co., Ind.)–Dec. 6, 1924. U.S. novelist. Wrote popular stories for young people. *Freckles*, 1904; *A Girl of the Limberlost*, 1909; *The Harvester*, 1911; *Laddie*, 1913.

PORTER, KATHERINE ANNE, May 15, 1890 (Indian Creek, Tex.). U.S. short-story writer, novelist. Master of the short story, especially "Noon Wine"

(1919), "Old Morality" (1919), "Theft" (1935), and "Hacienda" (1935). *Flowering Judas*, 1930; *Pale Horse, Pale Rider*, 1939; *The Leaning Tower*, 1944; *Ship of Fools*, 1962.

POTOK, CHAIM, Feb. 17, 1929 (New York, N.Y.). U.S. novelist. Noted for his novels about Jewish life. *The Chosen*, 1967; *The Promise*, 1969; *My Name Is Asher Lev*, 1972; *In the Beginning*, 1975.

POUND, EZRA, Oct. 30, 1885 (Hailey, Ida.)–Nov. 1, 1972. U.S. poet, critic, translator. Exerted a profound influence on 20th-cent. lit.; during WW II, broadcast fascist propaganda to the U.S.; indicted for treason, confined to hospital as insane, 1946–58; his most famous work is *Cantos*, a cycle of poetry written from 1925 to 1960.

PUZO, MARIO, Oct. 15, 1920 (New York, N.Y.). U.S. novelist. *The Fortunate Pilgrim*, 1965; *The Godfather*, 1969; *Fools Die*, 1978.

PYNCHON, THOMAS, May 8, 1937 (Glen Cove, N.Y.). U.S. novelist. Noted for his experimental, black-humor fiction. *V*, 1963; *The Crying of Lot 49*, 1966; *Gravity's Rainbow*, 1973.

RAND, AYN, Feb. 2, 1905 (St. Petersburg [now Leningrad]), Rus.). U.S. novelist, nonfiction writer. In her novels, created superior, self-made individuals to illustrate her philosophy of rational self-interest, which she called objectivism. *The Fountainhead*, 1943; *Atlas Shrugged*, 1957; *For the New Intellectual*, 1961.

RANSOM, JOHN CROWE, Apr. 30, 1888 (Pulaski, Tenn.). U.S. poet, critic. The foremost theorist of the post-WW I Southern literary renaissance; taught at Vanderbilt U., 1914–35; taught at Kenyon C., 1937–58; founded and edited the *Kenyon Review*, 1939–59; his *The New Criticism* (1941) initiated an influential school of criticism that focused on the text itself. *Chills and Fever*, 1924; *Two Gentlemen in Bonds*, 1927.

RAWLINGS, MARGARET KINNAN, Aug. 8, 1896 (Washington, D.C.)–Dec. 14, 1953. U.S. novelist. Wrote books set in the Florida backwoods. *South Under Moon*, 1933; *The Yearling* (1939 Pulitzer Prize in fiction), 1938; *The Sojourner*, 1953.

RICE (originally Reizenstein), **ELMER LEOPOLD,** Sept. 28, 1892 (New York, N.Y.)–May 8, 1967. U.S. dramatist. Noted for plays that dramatized liberal social and political views. *The Adding Machine*, 1924; *Street Scene* (1929 Pulitzer Prize in drama; later made into opera by KURT WEILL), 1929; *Counsellor-at-Law*, 1931; *We, the People*, 1933; *Between Two Worlds*, 1934.

RICHARDS, LAURA ELIZABETH, née Howe, Feb. 27, 1850 (Boston, Mass.)–Jan. 14, 1943. U.S. novelist, short-story writer. Wrote children's books; with her sister Maud Howe Elliot, won the first Pulitzer Prize (1917) in biography for the *Life of Julia Ward Howe* (1916), her mother. (Daughter of SAMUEL G. HOWE.)

RILEY, JAMES WHITCOMB, Oct. 7, 1849 (Greenfield, Ind.)–July 22, 1916. U.S. poet. "The poet of the common people"; early poems in Hoosier dialect earned him name of Hoosier Poet. *The Old Swimmin' Hole and 'Leven More Poems*, 1883; *Pipes o' Pan at Zekesbury*, 1888; *Home Folks*, 1900.

ROBBINS, HAROLD, May 21, 1916 (New York, N.Y.). U.S. novelist. *Never Love a Stranger*, 1948; *The Dream Merchants*, 1949; *A Stone for Danny Fisher*, 1952; *The Carpetbaggers*, 1961; *The Adventurers*, 1966; *The Inheritors*, 1969; *The Betsy*, 1971; *The Lonely Lady*, 1976; *Dreams Die First*, 1977.

ROBERTS, KENNETH LEWIS, Dec. 8, 1885 (Kennebunk, Me.)–July 21, 1957. U.S. novelist. Awarded 1957 Pulitzer Special Citation for his historical novels. *Arundel*, 1930; *Rabble in Arms*, 1933; *Northwest Passage*, 1937.

ROBINSON, EDWARD ARLINGTON, Dec. 22, 1869 (Head Tide, Me.)–Apr. 6, 1935. U.S. poet. Introduced naturalism to American poetry; best-known poems include "Richard Cory" and "Miniver Cheevy." *The Children of the Night*, 1897; *The Man against the Sky*, 1916; *Collected Poems* (Pulitzer Prize in poetry, 1922), 1921; *The Man Who Died Twice* (Pulitzer Prize in poetry, 1925), 1924; *Tristram* (1928 Pulitzer Prize in poetry), 1927.

ROETHKE, THEODORE, May 25, 1908 (Saginaw, Mich.)–Aug. 1, 1963. U.S. poet noted for his evocations of childhood, old age, and images of horticulture. *Open House*, 1941; *The Lost Son and Other Poems*, 1948; *The Waking* (1954 Pulitzer Prize in poetry), 1953; *Words for the Wind*, 1957.

ROGERS, ROSEMARY, Dec. 7, 1933 (Ceylon). U.S. novelist. Author of best-selling historical and contemporary romances. *Sweet Savage Love*, 1974; *Wicked Loving Lies*, 1976; *The Crowd Pleasers*, 1978; *The Insiders*, 1979.

RÖLVAAG, O(le) E(dvart), Apr. 22, 1876 (Dönna I., Nor.)–Nov. 5, 1931. Norwegian-U.S. novelist, educator. Noted for his portrayal of the Norwegian immigrants on the Dakota prairie; prof. of Norwegian at St. Olaf C., 1906–31. *Giants in the Earth*, 1927; *Peder Victorious*, 1929; *Their Father's God*, 1931.

ROSSNER, JUDITH LOUISE, née Perelman, Mar. 31, 1935 (New York, N.Y.). U.S. novelist. Best known for her best-selling novel *Looking for Mr. Goodbar* (1975), based on the murder of a young New York City woman. *Attachments*, 1977.

ROTH, PHILIP, Mar. 19, 1933 (Newark, N.J.). U.S. novelist, short-story writer. Writes about middle-class Jewish life. *Goodbye Columbus*, 1959; *Letting Go*, 1962; *Portnoy's Complaint*, 1969; *Our Gang*, 1971; *The Breast*, 1972; *The Professor of Desire*, 1978; *The Ghost Writer*, 1979.

RUARK, ROBERT CHESTER, Dec. 29, 1915 (Wilmington, N.C.)–June 30, 1965. U.S. novelist, journalist. *Grenadine Etching*, 1947; *I Didn't Know It Was Loaded*, 1948; *Something of Value*, 1955; *Poor No More*, 1959; *Uhuru*, 1962; *The Honey Badger*, 1964.

RUKEYSER, MURIEL, Dec. 15, 1913 (New York, N.Y.)–Feb. 12, 1980. U.S. poet, translator. Writes on social and political themes, including feminism; translated poetry of OCTAVIO PAZ. *Theory of Flight*, 1935; *Beast in View*, 1944; *The Speed of Darkness*, 1968; *Breaking Open*, 1973.

RUNYON, (Alfred) **DAMON,** Oct. 4, 1884 (Manhattan, Kan.)–Dec. 10, 1946. U.S. short-story writer, journalist. Wrote humorous stories about colorful Broadway and underworld characters. *Guys and Dolls* (made into a highly successful musical comedy, 1950), 1931; *Blue Plate Special*, 1934; *Money from Home*, 1935; *Runyon à la Carte*, 1944.

SACKLER, HOWARD, 1929 (New York, N.Y.). U.S. playwright. Wrote the (1969) Pulitzer Prize-winning play *The Great White Hope* (1968) about world heavyweight boxing champion Jack Johnson.

SALINGER, J(erome) D(avid), Jan. 1, 1919 (New York, N.Y.). U.S. novelist, short-story writer. Best known for his critically acclaimed novel *The*

THE BOOK OF WHO

Catcher in the Rye (1951), about a precocious, sensitive adolescent's flight from the "phony" adult world; ceased publishing and became a recluse, 1963. Nine Stories, 1953; Franny and Zooey, 1961; Raise High the Roof Beam, Carpenters, 1963; Seymour: An Introduction, 1963.

SANDBURG, CARL, Jan. 6, 1878 (Galesburg, Ill.)-July 22, 1967. U.S. poet, biographer. Influential in the pre-WW I Chicago Renaissance movement; noted for his vigorous free verse celebrating America and its common people; received 1940 Pulitzer Prize in history for the second section of his biography of ABRAHAM LINCOLN, The War Years (4 vols.), 1939). Chicago Poems, 1916; Good Morning, America, 1928; The People, Yes, 1936.

SAROYAN, WILLIAM, Aug. 31, 1908 (Fresno, Calif.). U.S. short-story writer, playwright. Noted for his optimism, sentimentality, and mastery of the vernacular. The Daring Young Man on the Flying Trapeze, 1934; My Name Is Aram, 1940; The Human Comedy, 1943; The Time of Your Life (awarded, but refused, 1940 Pulitzer Prize in drama), 1939.

SCHWARTZ, DELMORE, Dec. 8, 1913 (Brooklyn, N.Y.)-July 11, 1966. U.S. poet, short-story writer, critic, teacher. Member, editorial board of the Partisan Review, 1943-55; poetry editor, The New Republic, 1955-57. In Dreams Begin Responsibilities, 1938; The World Is a Wedding, 1948; Summer Knowledge, 1959; Successful Love, and Other Stories, 1961.

SEGAL, ERICH, June 16, 1937 (New York, N.Y.). U.S. novelist, teacher. Prof. of classics, Yale U., 1965-73. Love Story, 1970; Oliver's Story, 1977.

SENDAK, MAURICE BERNARD, June 10, 1928 (New York, N.Y.). U.S. author, illustrator. Author and illustrator of children's books, many of which have become modern classics. The Nutshell Library, 1963; Where the Wild Things Are, 1963; In the Night Kitchen, 1970.

SERLING, ROD, Dec. 25, 1924 (Syracuse, N.Y.)-June 28, 1975. U.S. writer. Best known as the writer/creator/narrator of TV series Twilight Zone, 1959-64; Peabody Award, 1957. Screenplays: Requiem for a Heavyweight (TV), 1963; Seven Days in May, 1964; Planet of the Apes, 1967.

SETON, ANYA, 1916 (New York, N.Y.). U.S. novelist. My Theodosia, 1941; Dragonwyck, 1944; Foxfire, 1950; Katherine, 1954; The Mistletoe and the Sword, 1955.

SEXTON, ANNE, née Harvey, Nov. 9, 1928 (Newton, Mass.)-Oct. 4, 1974. U.S. poet. Noted for honest revelations about her personal life, including emotional illness and recovery; apparently committed suicide, 1974. To Bedlam and Part Way Back, 1960; All My Pretty Ones, 1962; Live or Die (1966 Pulitzer Prize in poetry), 1966; Love Poems, 1969; Transformations, 1971.

SHAPIRO, KARL JAY, Nov. 10, 1913 (Baltimore, Md.). U.S. poet, critic. Noted for his outspoken, controversial criticism. Poem, Place and Thing, 1942; V-Letter and Other Poems (1945 Pulitzer Prize in poetry), 1944; Beyond Criticism, 1953; Poems of a Jew, 1958; In Defense of Ignorance, 1960; White Haired Lover, 1968.

SHAW, IRWIN, Feb. 27, 1913 (New York, N.Y.). U.S. novelist, short-story writer. Noted for works that explore contemporary social issues. The Young Lions, 1948; Two Weeks in Another Town, 1959; Rich Man, Poor Man, 1970; Evening in Byzantium, 1973.

SHELDON, SIDNEY, Feb. 11, 1917 (Chicago, Ill.). U.S. novelist. The Other Side of Midnight, 1973; A Stranger in the Mirror, 1976; Bloodline, 1977.

SHERWOOD, ROBERT, Apr. 4, 1896 (New Rochelle, N.Y.)-Nov. 14, 1955. U.S. dramatist. Noted for his social and political dramas; won Pulitzer Prizes in 1936 for Idiot's Delight (1936), in 1939 for Abe Lincoln in Illinois (1938), in 1941 for There Shall Be No Night (1940), and in 1949 for the biography Roosevelt and Hopkins: An Intimate History (1948); notable among his other dramas is The Petrified Forest (1935).

SHULMAN, MAX, Mar. 14, 1919 (St. Paul, Minn.). U.S. humorist. Noted for writing the stories that were adapted into the TV series The Many Loves of Dobie Gillis. The Tender Trap, 1954; Rally Round the Flag, Boys, 1957.

SIMON, (Marvin) NEIL, July 4, 1927 (New York, N.Y.). U.S. playwright. Extremely successful writer of comedies for Broadway; had four shows running simultaneously during the 1966-67 season, three during the 1969-70 season. Come Blow Your Horn, 1961; Barefoot in the Park, 1963; The Odd Couple, 1965; Sweet Charity, 1966; Plaza Suite, 1968; Promises, Promises, 1969; The Sunshine Boys, 1972; California Suite, 1976; Chapter Two, 1978; They're Playing Our Song, 1979.

SIMPSON, LOUIS, Mar. 27, 1923 (Jamaica). U.S. poet, teacher. The Arrivistes: Poems 1940-48, 1949; A Dream of Governors, 1959; At the End of the Open Road (1964 Pulitzer Prize in poetry), 1963; North of Jamaica, 1972.

SINCLAIR, UPTON BEALL, Sept. 20, 1878 (Baltimore, Md.)-Nov. 25, 1968. U.S. novelist. Noted for his muckraking novels, including The Jungle (1906), which led to reform of federal food inspection laws. King Coal, 1917; Oil!, 1927; World's End, 1940; Dragon's Teeth (1943 Pulitzer Prize in fiction), 1942.

SINGER, ISAAC BASHEVIS, July 14, 1904 (Radzymin, Pol.) Polish-U.S. novelist, short-story writer. Yiddish writer noted for his imagination, irony, and wit; under the name Warshofsky, wrote for Jewish Daily Forward; awarded Nobel Prize in literature, 1978. Satan in Goray, 1935; The Family Moskat, 1950; Enemies, A Love Story, 1970; Shosha, 1978.

SMITH, BETTY, Dec. 15, 1906 (Brooklyn, N.Y.). U.S. novelist, playwright. A Tree Grows in Brooklyn, 1943; Tomorrow Will Be Better, 1948; Joy in the Morning, 1963.

SNODGRASS, WILLIAM DEWITT, Jan. 5, 1926 (Wilkinsburg, Pa.). U.S. poet. Heart's Needle (1960 Pulitzer Prize in poetry), 1959. After Experience, 1968.

SOUTHERN, TERRY, May 1, 1928 (Alvarado, Tex.). U.S. novelist, short-story writer, screenwriter. A writer of black humor best known for Candy (1955), a parody of pornography; his screenplays include Dr. Strangelove Or: How I Learned to Stop Worrying and Love the Bomb (with STANLEY KUBRICK; 1963), The Loved One (with Ring Lardner, Jr.; 1964), and Easy Rider (1968).

STAFFORD, JEAN, July 1, 1915 (Covina, Calif.)-Mar. 26, 1979. U.S. short-story writer, novelist. Boston Adventure, 1944; Children Are Bored on Sundays, 1953; A Mother in History (study of the mother of LEE HARVEY OSWALD), 1966; Collected Stories (1970 Pulitzer Prize in fiction), 1969.

STALLINGS, LAURENCE, Nov. 25, 1894 (Macon, Ga.). U.S. playwright. What Price Glory? (with MAXWELL ANDERSON), 1924; First Flight (with

Anderson), 1925; *The Buccaneer* (with Anderson), 1925; *The First World War* (book), 1933.

STEFFENS, (Joseph) LINCOLN, Apr. 6, 1866 (San Francisco, Calif.)-Aug. 9, 1936. U.S. journalist. A leading muckraker; held editorial positions at *McClure's*, *The American*, and *Everybody's* magazines. *The Shame of the Cities*, 1904; *The Struggle for Self-Government*, 1906.

STEIN, GERTRUDE, Feb. 3, 1874 (Allegheny, Pa.)-July 27, 1946. U.S. writer, patron of the arts; in the 1920s conducted a celebrated salon for writers in her Paris home; the friend, patron, and mentor of many post-WW I American expatriates, whom she collectively named the Lost Generation; with her brother Leo, was one of the first collectors of avant-garde paintings. *Three Lives*, 1933; *The Autobiography of Alice B. Toklas*, 1933; *Four Saints in Three Acts* (opera libretto), 1934.

STEINBECK, JOHN ERNST, Feb. 27, 1902 (Salinas, Calif.)-Dec. 20, 1968. U.S. novelist. Noted for his novels about the disinherited; awarded Nobel Prize in lit., 1962. *Tortilla Flat*, 1935; *In Dubious Battle*, 1936; *Of Mice and Men*, 1937; *The Grapes of Wrath* (1940 Pulitzer Prize in fiction), 1939; *The Moon is Down*, 1942; *Cannery Row*, 1945; *The Pearl*, 1947; *East of Eden*, 1952; *The Winter of Our Discontent*, 1961.

STEVENS, WALLACE, Oct. 2, 1879 (Reading, Pa.)-Aug. 2, 1955. U.S. poet. Noted for his subtle verse on the theme of the interaction of reality and imagination; best-known poems include "Sunday Morning," "Le Monocle de Mon Oncle," and "Peter Quince at the Clavier"; v.p. of a Hartford, Conn., insurance company. *Harmonium*, 1923; *Ideas of Order*, 1935; *The Man with the Blue Guitar*, 1937; *Collected Poems* (1955 Pulitzer Prize in poetry), 1954.

STONE, IRVING, July 14, 1903 (San Francisco, Cal.). U.S. author. Noted for writing popular fictional biographies. *Lust for Life*, 1934; *Sailor on Horseback*, 1938; *The President's Lady*, 1951; *The Agony and the Ectasy*, 1961; *I Michelangelo, Sculptor*, 1962; *Passions of the Mind*, 1971.

STOWE, HARRIET (Elizabeth) **BEECHER,** June 14, 1811 (Litchfield, Conn.)-July 1, 1896. U.S. novelist. A prolific writer best known as the author of *Uncle Tom's Cabin* (1852), which prior to the Civil War aroused considerable anti-slavery feeling; a regular contributor to the *Atlantic Monthly*. *The Key to Uncle Tom's Cabin*, 1853; *Dred*, 1856; *Old Town Folks*, 1869. (Daughter of LYMAN BEECHER; sister of HENRY WARD BEECHER and CATHERINE ESTHER BEECHER.)

STRATEMEYER, EDWARD (pseuds.: Carolyn Keene, Arthur M. Winfield, Ralph Bonehill, Franklin W. Dixon), Oct. 4, 1862 (Elizabeth, N.J.)-May 10, 1930. U.S. writer of juvenile fiction. Under Winfield pseudonym began "Bound to Win" series, from 1894; started "Rover Boy" series, 1899; established Stratemeyer Literary Syndicate (1906), which mass-produced such series as the "Tom Swift," "Nancy Drew," "Bobbsey Twins," "Hardy Boys," and "Dana Girls"; since 1942, his daughter Harriet Stratemeyer Adams has headed the syndicate.

STYRON, WILLIAM, June 11, 1925 (Newport News, Va.). U.S. novelist. Best known as author of the controversial (1968) Pulitzer Prize-winning novel, *The Confessions of Nat Turner* (1967), about the leader of the 1831 slave rebellion. *Lie Down in Darkness*, 1951; *Set This House on Fire*, 1960; *Sophie's Choice*, 1979.

SUSANN, JACQUELINE, Aug. 20, 1921 (Philadelphia, Pa.)-Sept. 21, 1974. U.S. novelist. *Valley of the Dolls*, 1966; *The Love Machine*, 1969; *Once Is Not Enough*, 1973; *Yargo* (published posthumously), 1979.

TARKINGTON, (Newton) BOOTH, July 29, 1869 (Indianapolis, Ind.)-May 19, 1946. U.S. novelist. Noted for his novels about Midwestern life. *Penrod*, 1914; *Seventeen*, 1917; *The Magnificent Ambersons* (1919 Pulitzer Prize in fiction, later filmed by ORSON WELLES), 1918; *Alice Adams* (1922 Pulitzer Prize in fiction), 1921.

TEASDALE, SARA, Aug. 8, 1884 (St. Louis, Mo.)-Jan. 29, 1933. U.S. poet. Member of the *Poetry* magazine circle. *Sonnets to Duse and Other Poems*, 1907; *Rivers to the Sea*, 1915; *Love Songs* (1918 Pulitzer Prize in poetry), 1917; *Flame and Shadow*, 1920; *Strange Victory*, 1933.

TERHUNE, ALBERT PAYSON, Dec. 12, 1872 (Newark, N.J.)-Feb. 18, 1942. U.S. novelist. Prolific author of popular novels about dogs. *Lad, A Dog*, 1919; *Bruce*, 1920; *The Heart of a Dog*, 1924; *A Book of Famous Dogs*, 1937.

TERKEL, STUDS LOUIS, May 16, 1912 (New York, N.Y.). U.S. writer. Noted for his books based on extensive tape-recorded interviews. *Giants of Jazz*, 1956; *Division Street America*, 1966; *Hard Times*, 1970; *Working*, 1974; *Talking to Myself*, 1977.

THEROUX, PAUL, Apr. 10, 1941 (Medford, Mass.). U.S. novelist. *Waldo*, 1967; *Jungle Lovers*, 1971; *Saint Jack*, 1973; *The Black House*, 1974; *The Great Railway Bazaar*, 1975; *The Family Arsenal*, 1976; *The Consul's File*, 1977; *The Old Patagonian Express*, 1979.

THOMPSON, KAY, ? (St. Louis, Mo.). U.S. author, entertainer. Wrote novels about Eloise, the over-privileged six-year-old who terrorized New York City's Plaza Hotel. *Eloise*, 1955; *Eloise in Paris*, 1977.

THURBER, JAMES GROVER, Dec. 8, 1894 (Columbus, Ohio)-Nov. 2, 1961. U.S. humorist, cartoonist. A leading contributor to *The New Yorker*, 1927-52; his drawings first appeared in *Is Sex Necessary?* (1929), written with E. B. WHITE. *My Life and Hard Times*, 1933; *Fables for Our Time*, 1940; *The Male Animal* (play; with Elliot Nugent), 1941; "The Secret Life of Walter Mitty," 1942; *The Thurber Album*, 1952; *The Years with Ross*, 1959.

TRYON, THOMAS, Jan. 14, 1926 (Hartford, Conn.). U.S. author, actor. After an early career as a motion-picture actor, turned to writing supernatural fiction. *The Other*, 1971; *Harvest Home*, 1973; *Lady*, 1974; *Crowned Heads*, 1976.

TWAIN, MARK (pseud. of Samuel Langhorne Clemens), Nov. 30, 1835 (Florida, Mo.)-Apr. 21, 1910. U.S. writer. Great American humorist; a self-made man, worked as a printer at age 12, an itinerant typesetter at 17, later a river pilot; married an heiress; became internationally famous as a "people's author." *The Innocents Abroad*, 1869; *The Gilded Age* (with Charles Dudley Warner), 1873; *Tom Sawyer*, 1876; *The Prince and the Pauper*, 1882; *Life on the Mississippi*, 1883; *Huckleberry Finn*, 1885; *A Connecticut Yankee in King Arthur's Court*, 1889; *Pudd'n head Wilson*, 1894.

UPDIKE, JOHN HOYER, Mar. 18, 1932 (Shillington, Pa.). U.S. novelist, short-story writer, poet. Writes about contemporary American small-town and suburban life. *Rabbit, Run*, 1960; *Pigeon*

THE BOOK OF WHO

Feathers, and Other Stories, 1962; *The Centaur,* 1963; *The Music School,* 1967; *Couples,* 1968; *Rabbit Redux,* 1971; *Museums and Women and Other Stories,* 1972; *The Coup,* 1978; *Too Far To Go,* 1979.

URIS, LEON MARCUS, Aug. 13, 1924 (Baltimore, Md.). U.S. novelist. *Battle Cry,* 1953; *Exodus,* 1958; *Mila 18,* 1961; *QB VII,* 1970; *Ireland: A Terrible Beauty* (with Jill Uris), 1975; *Trinity,* 1976.

VIDAL, GORE, Oct. 3, 1925 (West Point, N.Y.). U.S. novelist, playwright, critic. *Williwaw,* 1946; *The City and the Pillar,* 1948; *Julian,* 1964; *Washington, D.C.,* 1967; *Myra Breckinridge,* 1968; *Burr,* 1973; *1876,* 1976; *Matters of Fact and Fiction,* 1977.

VONNEGUT, KURT, JR., Nov. 11, 1922 (Indianapolis, Ind.). U.S. novelist. Popular in the 1960s, especially among students, for his black-humor novels about the horrors of the 20th cent. *Piano Player* 1951; *Cat's Cradle,* 1963; *Slaughterhouse Five,* 1969; *Happy Birthday, Wanda June,* 1970; *Breakfast of Champions,* 1973; *Slapstick,* 1976.

WALLACE, IRVING, Mar. 19, 1916 (Chicago, Ill.). U.S. novelist. *The Chapman Report,* 1960; *The Prize,* 1962; *The Man,* 1964; *Seven Minutes,* 1964; *The Ward,* 1972; *The Fan Club,* 1974. With his son, David Wallenchinsky, has created "entertainment reference books," including *The People's Almanac* (1975), *The Book of Lists* (1977), and *The People's Almanac II* (1978).

WALLACE, LEW(is), Apr. 10, 1827 (Brookville, Ind.)-Feb. 15, 1905. U.S. soldier, lawyer, diplomat, novelist. Best known as author of *Ben Hur* (1880), adapted both into a play and film; during Civil War, rose to major general of volunteers; headed Andersonville court of inquiry. *The Fair God,* 1873; *The Prince of India,* 1893.

WAMBAUGH, JOSEPH, Jan. 22, 1937 (East Pittsburgh, Pa.). U.S. novelist. Formerly a Los Angeles Police Department detective; writes realistic novels about police work. *The New Centurions,* 1971; *The Blue Knight,* 1972; *The Onion Field,* 1973; *The Choirboys,* 1975; *The Black Marble,* 1978.

WARREN, MERCY OTIS, Sept. 23, 1728 (Barnstable, Mass.)-Oct. 19, 1814. U.S. playwright, historian. Called the Mother of the American Revolution; held a political salon during pre-Revolutionary days; wrote a three-volume history of the American Revolution, *History of the Rise, Progress and Termination of the American Revolution* (1805); wrote two anti-Tory satirical plays, *The Adulateur* (1773) and *The Group* (1775).

WARREN, ROBERT PENN, Apr. 24, 1905 (Guthrie, Ky.). U.S. novelist, poet, critic. Noted for novels with Southern themes and characters; expanded the New Criticism; won 1947 Pulitzer Prize in fiction for his novel *All the King's Men* (1946); won Pulitzers in poetry in 1958 for *Promises* (1957) and in 1979 for *Now and Then* (1978).

WEIDMANN, JEROME, Aug. 4, 1913 (New York, N.Y.). U.S. novelist; short-story writer. *I Can Get It for You Wholesale,* 1937; *What's in It for Me?,* 1938.

WELTY, EUDORA, Apr. 13, 1909 (Jackson, Miss.). U.S. short-story writer, novelist. Noted for using rural Mississippi dialect and speech patterns, and comic, sometimes grotesque characters. *A Curtain of Green,* 1941; *The Golden Apples,* 1949; *The Optimist's Daughter* (1973 Pulitzer Prize in fiction), 1972.

WEST, NATHANAEL, born Nathan Wallenstein Weinstein, Oct. 17, 1903 (New York, N.Y.)-Dec. 22, 1940. U.S. novelist. Noted for his surrealistic satires that anticipated black humor. *The Dream Life of Balso Snell, Miss Lonelyhearts,* 1933; *A Cool Million,* 1934; *The Day of the Locust,* 1939.

WHARTON, EDITH NEWBOLD, née Jones, Jan. 24, 1862 (New York, N.Y.)-Aug. 11, 1937. U.S. novelist, short-story writer. Wrote about upperclass New York society. *The House of Mirth,* 1905; *Ethan Frome,* 1911; *The Age of Innocence* (1921 Pulitzer Prize in fiction), 1920; *Hudson River Bracketed,* 1929.

WHEATLEY, PHILLIS, 1753? (Africa)-Dec. 5, 1784. American colonial poet. First important black poet in America; in childhood, brought to Boston as a slave in the Wheatley household, where she was educated; began writing poetry at age 13, published at age 20. *Poems on Various Subjects, Religious and Moral, by Phillis Wheatley, Negro Servant to Mr. John Wheatley of Boston, in New England,* 1773; *Memoir and Poems of Phillis Wheatley,* 1834; *The Letters of Phillis Wheatley, the Negro Slave-Poet of Boston,* 1864.

WHITE E(lwyn) B(rooks), July 11, 1899 (Mt. Vernon, N.Y.). U.S. humorist, essayist, novelist. Staff member and contributor to *The New Yorker,* 1927– ; his children's books, *Stuart Little* (1945), *Charlotte's Web* (1952), and *The Trumpet of the Swan* (1970), have become classics. *Is Sex Necessary?* (with JAMES THURBER), 1929; *One Man's Meat,* 1942; *Here is New York,* 1949; *The Elements of Style* (with William Strunk, Jr.), 1959.

WHITMAN, WALT(er), May 31, 1819 (West Hills, N.Y.)-Mar. 26, 1892. U.S. poet. His *Leaves of Grass* (1855), revolutionary in its use of free verse, made him a major poetic figure. "Song of Myself," 1856; "Out of the Cradle, Endlessly Rocking," 1857; "When Lilacs Last in the Dooryard Bloom'd," 1866; "O Captain! My Captain," 1866.

WHITTIER, JOHN GREENLEAF, Dec. 17, 1807 (Haverhill, Mass.)-Sept. 7, 1892. U.S. poet, social reformer. Popular poet of rural New England; a crusading abolitionist; founder of the Liberal party. "Snow-Bound," (1866); "Barbara Frietchie"; "The Barefoot Boy."

WIESEL, ELIE, Sept. 30, 1928 (Sighet, Rum.). U.S. novelist, nonfiction writer. Writes about the plight of the Jew. *Night,* 1960; *Dawn,* 1961; *The Accident,* 1962; *The Town Beyond the Wall,* 1964; *The Jews of Silence: A Personal Report of Soviet Jewry,* 1966.

WIGGLESWORTH, MICHAEL, Oct. 18, 1631 (Yorkshire, Eng.)-June 10, 1705. American colonial poet, clergyman. His poem "The Day of Doom: or, a Poetical Description of the Great and Last Judgment" (1662), was the first American best-seller. *God's Controversy with New England,* written c.1662, pub. 1873.

WILBUR, RICHARD PURDY, Mar. 1, 1921 (New York, N.Y.). U.S. poet. *The Beautiful Changes,* 1947; *Things of This World* (1956 Pulitzer Prize in poetry), 1956; *The Poems of Richard Wilbur,* 1963; *Walking to Sleep,* 1969; *Seed Leaves,* 1974.

WILDER, LAURA, née INGALLS, Feb. 7, 1867 (Lake Pepin, Wisc.)-Jan. 10, 1957. U.S. juvenile novelist. Created the Little House series, classic books about frontier family life; her books have been adapted into a popular TV series. *Little House in the Big Woods,* 1932; *Farmer Boy,* 1933; *Little House on the Prairie,* 1935; *On the Banks of Plum Creek,* 1937.

WILDER, THORNTON NIVEN, Apr. 17, 1897

(Madison, Wis.). U.S. playwright, novelist. His play *The Merchant of Yonkers* (1938), revised into *The Matchmaker* (1954), was later made into the musical *Hello Dolly! The Bridge of San Luis Rey* (1928 Pulitzer Prize in fiction), 1927; *Our Town* (1938 Pulitzer Prize in drama), 1938; *The Skin of Our Teeth* (1943 Pulitzer Prize in drama), 1942.

WILLIAMS, TENNESSEE, born Thomas Lanier Williams, Mar. 26, 1911 (Columbus, Miss.). U.S. dramatist. Major playwright, often deals with controversial themes such as homosexuality, pederasty, cannibalism, and castration. *The Glass Menagerie,* 1944; *A Streetcar Named Desire* (1947 Pulitzer Prize in drama), 1947; *Camino Real,* 1953; *Cat on a Hot Tin Roof* (1955 Pulitzer Prize in drama), 1955; *The Night of the Iguana,* 1962; *Suddenly Last Summer,* 1958; *Sweet Bird of Youth,* 1959; *Small Craft Warnings,* 1972.

WILLIAMS, WILLIAM CARLOS, Sept. 17, 1883 (Rutherford, N.J.)–Mar. 4, 1963. U.S. poet. Noted for his use of idiomatic speech patterns and details of commonplace experience; best-known work is the epic poem *Paterson* (5 vols., 1946–58); practiced medicine for 40 years in Rutherford. *Al Que Quiere?,* 1917; *Sour Grapes,* 1921; *Journey to Love,* 1955; *Pictures from Brueghel, and Other Poems,* 1962.

WILSON, SLOAN, May 8, 1920 (Norwalk, Conn.). U.S. novelist. *The Man in the Gray Flannel Suit,* 1955; *A Summer Place,* 1958; *Ice Brothers,* 1980.

WISTER, OWEN, July 14, 1869 (Philadelphia, Pa.)–July 21, 1938. U.S. novelist. His prototypal Western novel, *The Virginian* (1902), helped establish the cowboy as a U.S. folk hero. *Roosevelt: The Story of a Friendship, 1880–1919,* 1930.

WOLFE, THOMAS CLAYTON, Oct. 3, 1900 (Asheville, N.C.)–Sept. 15, 1938. U.S. novelist. *Look Homeward, Angel,* 1929; *Of Time and the River,* 1935; *The Web and the Rock,* 1939; *You Can't Go Home Again,* 1940.

WOUK, HERMAN, May 27, 1915 (New York, N.Y.). U.S. novelist. *The Caine Mutiny* (1952 Pulitzer Prize in fiction), 1951; *Marjorie Morningstar,* 1955; *The Winds of War,* 1971; *War and Remembrance* 1978.

WRIGHT, RICHARD, Sept. 4, 1908 (nr. Natchez, Miss.)–Nov. 28, 1960. U.S. novelist, short-story writer. Author of the first influential protest novel by a black writer, *Native Son* (1940), later staged on Broadway by ORSON WELLES. *Black Boy,* 1945; *The Outsider,* 1953; *White Man, Listen,* 1957.

YERBY, FRANK GARVIN, Sept. 5, 1916 (Augusta, Ga.). U.S. novelist. *The Foxes of Harrow,* 1946; *The Vixens,* 1947; *A Woman Called Fancy,* 1951; *The Serpent and the Staff,* 1958; *The Girl from Storyville,* 1972.

ZINDEL, PAUL, May 15, 1936 (New York, N.Y.). U.S. playwright, novelist. *The Effect of Gamma Rays on Man-in-the-Moon Marigolds* (1971 Pulitzer Prize in drama), 1970; *The Pigman,* 1968; *My Darling, My Hamburger,* 1969; *Pardon Me, You're Stepping on My Eyeball,* 1976.

BRITISH WRITERS

ADDISON, JOSEPH, May 1, 1672 (Milston, Eng.)–June 17, 1719. English poet, essayist, critic, playwright. Contributor to *The Tatler* (1709–11) and *The Spectator* (1711–12, 1714); poetry includes *The Campaign* (1704) and *The Spacious Firmament on High* (1712); plays include *Rosamund* (1705) and *Cato* (1713).

ANTHONY, EVELYN (pseud. of Evelyn Bridget Patricia Stephens Ward-Thomas), July 3, 1928. English novelist. *The Assassin,* 1970; *The Tamarind Seed,* 1971; *Stranger at the Gates,* 1973.

ARNOLD, MATTHEW, Dec. 24, 1822 (Laleham, Eng.)–Apr. 15, 1888. English poet, critic. Crusaded for classicism, critical traditionalism, and the idea that literature should ennoble. *Empedocles on Etna and Other Poems,* 1852; *Poems* (inc. "The Scholar Gypsy"), 1853; *New Poems* (inc. "Dover Beach"), 1867; *Culture and Anarchy,* 1869; *Literature and Dogma,* 1873.

AUDEN, W(ystan) H(ugh), Feb. 21, 1907 (York, Eng.)–Sept. 28, 1973. English–U.S. poet, dramatist, editor. Captured the spirit of post–WW I England, which he termed the "age of anxiety." *Poems,* 1928; *The Dance of Death,* 1933; *The Dog beneath the Skin* (with CHRISTOPHER ISHERWOOD), 1935; *The Age of Anxiety* (1948 Pulitzer Prize in poetry), 1947; *Homage to Clio,* 1960; *Epistle to a Godson and Other Poems,* 1972.

AUSTEN, JANE, Dec. 16, 1775 (Hampshire, Eng.)–July 18, 1817. English novelist. The spinster daughter of a country parson, she wrote masterful and technically innovative novels centered on the domestic life of provincial men and women. *Sense and Sensibility,* 1811; *Pride and Prejudice,* 1813; *Mansfield Park,* 1814; *Emma,* 1816; *Northanger Abbey,* 1818; *Persuasion,* 1818.

AYCKBOURN, ALAN, Apr. 12, 1939 (London, Eng.) English dramatist. A prolific playwright, he had four plays running simultaneously in London's West End in 1975. *The Norman Conquests,* 1975; *Absurd Person Singular,* 1975.

BAGNOLD, ENID (Lady Roderick Jones), Oct. 27, 1889 (Rochester, Eng.). English novelist, playwright. *Serena Blandish,* 1925; *National Velvet,* 1935; *The Chalk Garden,* 1956; *The Chinese Prime Minister,* 1961.

BARRIE, SIR J(ames) M(atthew), May 9, 1860 (Kirriemuir, Scot.)–June 19, 1937. Scottish dramatist, novelist. Best known for *Peter Pan* (1904); made a baronet, 1913; appointed to the Order of Merit, 1922. *The Little Minister,* 1897; *Quality Street,* 1901; *The Admirable Crichton,* 1902; *What Every Woman Knows,* 1908.

BEAUMONT, FRANCIS, 1584 (Grace-Dieu, Eng.)–Mar. 6, 1616. English dramatist. Best known for his collaborations with JOHN FLETCHER on several tragicomedies, including *Philaster* (1609), *A King and No King* (1611), and *The Maid's Tragedy* (c.1611), that influenced Restoration drama. *The Woman Hater,* c.1606; *The Knight of the Burning Pestle,* c.1607.

BECKETT, SAMUEL, Apr. 13, 1906 (Dublin, Ire.). English-French playwright, novelist. A major writer in the literature of the absurd; awarded Nobel Prize in literature, 1969; author of a trilogy composed of *Malloy* (1951), *Malone Dies* (1951), *The Unnameable* (1953). *Waiting for Godot,* 1952; *Endgame,* 1957; *Krapp's Last Tape,* 1958; *The Last Ones,* 1972.

BEERBOHM, SIR MAX, Aug. 24, 1872 (London, Eng.)–May 20, 1956. English essayist, caricaturist, parodist. Noted for his polished, elegant essays and brilliant parodies; succeeded G. B. SHAW as drama critic of *Saturday Review,* 1878. *The Poet's Corner,* 1904; *Zuleika Dobson,* 1911; *A Christmas Garland,* 1912; *And Even Now,* 1920; *Rossetti and His Circle,* 1922.

BEHAN, BRENDAN FRANCIS, Feb. 9, 1923 (Dublin, Ire.)–Mar. 20, 1964. Irish playwright noted

THE BOOK OF WHO

for the "gallows humor" of his plays. An Irish Republican Army member twice imprisoned for his political offenses. *The Quare Fellow,* 1956; *The Hostage,* 1958; *Borstal Boy,* 1958.

BEHN, APHRA, July 1640 (Kent, Eng.)–Apr. 16, 1689. English novelist, dramatist. Often called the first English professional writer; her novel *Oroonoko* (c.1678) was the first English philosophical novel.

BENNETT, (Enoch) ARNOLD, May 27, 1867 (Staffordshire, Eng.)–Mar. 27, 1931. English novelist noted for his realistic works about "Five Towns," a fictional English manufacturing district. *The Old Wives' Tale,* 1908; *Clayhanger,* 1910.

BETJEMAN, SIR JOHN, Apr. 6, 1906 (London, Eng.). English poet. Author of witty light verse; knighted, 1969; named poet laureate of England 1972. *Mount Zion,* 1933; *A Few Late Chrysanthemums,* 1954; *High and Low,* 1966.

BLAKE, WILLIAM, Nov. 28, 1757 (London, Eng.)–Aug. 12, 1827. English poet, artist . A mystic who experienced visions from his boyhood on, he created his own elaborate mythology with poetry and art; illustrated, engraved, and published all but the first of his many books. *Songs of Innocence,* 1789; *Songs of Experience,* 1794; *The Marriage of Heaven and Hell,* c.1790; *Milton,* 1804–08; *Jerusalem,* 1804–20.

BOSWELL, JAMES, Oct. 29, 1740 (Edinburgh, Scot.)–May 19, 1795. Scottish biographer, diarist. Best known for his masterwork, *The Life of Samuel Johnson, LL.D.* (1791). *An Account of Corsica,* 1768; *The Journal of a Tour to the Hebrides with Samuel Johnson, LL.D.,* 1785.

BOWEN, ELIZABETH, born Dorothea Cole, June 7, 1899 (Dublin, Ire.)–Feb. 22, 1973. English-Irish novelist, short-story writer. Author of stories and novels that explored psychological relationships within the upper class. *The House in Paris,* 1935; *The Death of the Heart,* 1938; *Look at All Those Roses,* 1941; *The Demon Lover,* 1945.

BRONTE, ANNE, Jan. 17, 1820 (Thornton, Yorkshire, Eng.)–May 28, 1849. English novelist, poet. Her first and best-known novel, *Agnes Grey* (1847), was published as a set with her sister EMILY BRONTE's *Wuthering Heights. The Tenant of Wildfell Hall,* 1848.

BRONTE, CHARLOTTE, Apr. 21, 1816 (Thornton, Yorkshire, Eng.)–Mar. 31, 1855. English novelist, poet. Author of romantic, emotional novels. *Jane Eyre,* 1847; *Shirley,* 1849; *Villette,* 1853; *The Professor,* 1857; *Poems of Currer, Ellis and Acton Bell,* 1846.

BRONTE, EMILY JANE, July 30, 1818 (Thornton, Yorkshire, Eng.)–Dec. 19, 1848. English novelist, poet. Her reputation rests on a single great novel, *Wuthering Heights* (1847); noted poems include "The Prisoner," "Remembrance," "The Old Stoic," "The Visionary."

BROOKE, RUPERT, Aug. 3, 1887 (Rugby, Eng.)–Apr. 23, 1915. English poet. Wrote two volumes of romantic and patriotic poetry in the early years of WW I; died at age 28 of blood poisoning while serving in the Royal Navy. *Poems,* 1911; *1914 and Other Poems,* 1915.

BROWNING, ELIZABETH BARRETT, Mar. 6, 1806 (Durham, Eng.)–June 29, 1861. English poet. Best known for her *Sonnets From the Portuguese* (1850), love poems addressed to her husband, the poet ROBERT BROWNING. *The Seraphim and Other Poems,* 1838; *Poems,* 1844; *Aurora Leigh,* 1856.

BROWNING, ROBERT, May 7, 1812 (Camberwell, Eng.)–Dec. 12, 1889. English poet. Master of dramatic monologue. *Bells and Pomegranates,* 1846; *Dramatis Personae,* 1864; *The Ring and the Book,* 4 vols., 1868–69; *Dramatic Idyls,* 2 vols., 1879–80.

BUNYAN, JOHN, Nov. 1618 (Bedfordshire, Eng.)–Aug. 31, 1688. English author. Best known for *Pilgrim's Progress* (1678), an allegory that describes the journey of Christian and his wife, Christiana, from the City of Destruction to the Celestial City; while imprisoned for 12 years for unlicensed preaching, wrote nine books, including *Grace Abounding to the Chief of Sinners* (1666).

BURGESS, ANTHONY, Feb. 25, 1917 (Manchester, Eng.). English novelist, critic. Noted for his comic imagination and use of language; best known for *A Clockwork Orange* (1962), a thriller set in a classless futuristic society. *Inside Mr. Enderby,* 1961; *MF,* 1971; *Napoleon Symphony: A Novel in Four Movements,* 1974.

BURNEY, FANNY FRANCES, June 13, 1752 (King's Lynn, Norfolk, Eng.)–Jan. 6, 1840. English novelist, diarist. Author of novels of manners. *Diaries and Letters, 1778–1840,* 1842–48; *Evelina, or the History of a Young Lady's Entrance into the World,* 1778; *Cecilia,* 5 vols., 1782.

BURNS, ROBERT, Jan. 25, 1759 (Ayrshire, Scot.)–July 21, 1796. Scottish poet. Best known for his descriptive, humorous, playful poems in conversational rhythms about rural Scotland, including "Auld Lang Syne," "Comin' Thru the Rye," "Flow Gently, Sweet Afton." *Poems, Chiefly in the Scottish Dialect,* 1786.

BUTLER, SAMUEL, Dec. 4, 1835 (Langar, Eng.)–June 18, 1902. English novelist, satirist, scholar. Best known for his ironic, witty novel, *The Way of All Flesh* (1903). *Erewhon,* 1872; *Evolution Old and New,* 1879; *The Authoress of the Odyssey,* 1897; *Shakespeare's Sonnets Reconsidered,* 1899; *Erewhon Revisited,* 1901.

BYRON, GEORGE GORDON NOEL, 6th BARON BYRON, Jan. 22, 1788 (London, Eng.)–Apr. 19, 1824. English poet. Embodied in his poetry and his profligate life-style the essence of Romanticism. *Hours of Idleness,* 1807; *English Bards and Scotch Reviewers,* 1809; *Childe Harold's Pilgrimage,* 1812, 1816, 1818; *The Siege of Corinth,* 1816; *Beppo,* 1818; *Don Juan,* 1819–24.

CARROLL, LEWIS (pseud. of Charles Lutwidge Dodgson), Jan. 27, 1832 (Cheshire, Eng.)–Jan. 14, 1898. English children's-book author, mathematician. Best known for the classic fantasies *Alice in Wonderland* (1865) and *Through the Looking Glass* (1872); a lecturer in mathematics, Oxford U., 1855–81; wrote several books on mathematical subjects. *The Hunting of the Snark, An Agony in Eight Fits,* 1872.

CARTLAND, BARBARA, July 9, 1904 (England). English novelist. Author of some 250 books, including over 170 romantic novels; her books have sold over 100 million copies.

CARY, (Arthur) JOYCE TUNEL, Dec. 7, 1888 (Londonderry, Ire.)–Mar. 29, 1957. Anglo-Irish novelist. Wrote humorous English social history and created eccentric characters, especially Gully Jimson, a painter and likable scoundrel in *The Horse's Mouth* (1944). *Mister Johnson,* 1939; *Except the Lord,* 1953.

CHAUCER, GEOFFREY, c.1340 (London, Eng.)–Oct. 25, 1400. English poet. A master storyteller, best known for *The Canterbury Tales* (c.1387–1400), a 17,000-line unfinished poem; introduced the heroic couplet into English literature. *The Book of the Duchess*, 1369; *The House of Fame*, c.1380; *Troilus and Criseyde*, c.1385.

CLELAND, JOHN, 1709 (London, Eng.)–Jan. 23, 1789. English novelist. Author of *Fanny Hill; or, Memoirs of a Woman of Pleasure* (1748–49) while in debtors' prison; the book, which became a classic of erotic literature, was suppressed many times, finally being cleared by the U.S. Supreme Court in 1966.

COLERIDGE, SAMUEL TAYLOR, Oct. 21, 1772 (Devonshire, Eng.)–July 25, 1834. English poet, critic, essayist. An important spokesman for English Romanticism; his *Lyrical Ballads* (1798), written jointly with WILLIAM WORDSWORTH, was a landmark of the Romantic movement; the philosophy of criticism expressed in his *Biographia Literia* (1817) had a profound impact on modern critical theory.

CONGREVE, WILLIAM, Jan. 24, 1670 (Yorkshire, Eng.)–Jan. 19, 1729. English dramatist. A master of Restoration comedy. *The Old Bachelor*, 1693; *The Double Dealer*, 1693; *Love for Love*, 1695; *The Way of the World*, 1700.

CONRAD, JOSEPH, born Jozef Teodor Konrad Korzeniowski, Dec. 3, 1857 (Berdichev, Pol. now in Ukrainian SSR.)–Aug. 3, 1924. British novelist, short story writer. Recognized as a master of English prose. Served as seaman in French (1874–78) and British (1878–94) merchant marine. *The Nigger of the 'Narcissus'*, 1897; *Lord Jim*, 1900; *Nostromo*, 1904; *The Secret Agent*, 1907.

COWARD, SIR NOEL PIERCE, Dec. 16, 1899 (Teddington, Eng.)–Mar. 26, 1963. English playwright, actor, composer, director. Noted for his versatility, wit, and sophistication, principally in comedies about the spoiled, snobbish rich. *Fallen Angels*, 1925; *Hay Fever*, 1925; *Private Lives*, 1930; *Design for Living*, 1932; *Blithe Spirit*, 1941.

COWPER, WILLIAM, Nov. 26, 1731 (Hertfordshire, Eng.)–Apr. 25, 1800. English poet. Foreshadowed Romanticism; best known for the poems that begin "Oh for a closer walk with God" and "God moves in a mysterious way" in *Olney Hymns* (1779), and for *The Task*, a long poem in blank verse extolling rural living.

DAHL, ROALD, Sept. 13, 1916 (Llandaff, Wales). British short-story and children's-book writer. Noted for his macabre stories; his children's books include *James and the Giant Peach* (1961) and *Charlie and the Chocolate Factory* (1964). *The Gremlins*, 1943; *Over to You*, 1946.

DEFOE (or De Foe) DANIEL, born Daniel Foe, c.1660 (London, Eng.)–Apr. 26, 1731. English journalist, novelist, pamphleteer. The father of modern journalism and of the English novel; single-handedly wrote and published a journal of European affairs, 1704–13; at age 59 wrote his first novel, *Life and Strange Adventures of Robinson Crusoe* (1719). *Moll Flanders*, 1722; *A Journal of the Plague Year*, 1722.

DE LA MARE, WALTER, Apr. 25, 1873 (Kent, Eng.)–June 23, 1956. English poet. The "poet of childhood," often wrote about nature, dreams, the supernatural. *Songs of Childhood*, 1902; *Peacock Pie*, 1913; *Memoirs of a Midget*, 1921; *Poems for Children*, 1930.

DEQUINCY, THOMAS, Aug. 15, 1785 (Manchester, Eng.)–Dec. 8, 1859. English essayist, critic. Established his reputation with *Confessions of An English Opium-Eater* (1822), a vivid account of the progress of the drug habit he had acquired at

Oxford; his essays include "On Murder Considered as One of the Fine Arts" and "On the Knocking at the Gate in *Macbeth*."

DICKENS, CHARLES JOHN HUFFON (pseud.: Boz), Feb. 7, 1812 (Portsmouth, Eng.)–June 9, 1870. English novelist. Under his pseudonym, contributed sketches to periodicals, collected as *Sketches by Boz* (1836); wrote and published prodigiously, gaining immense success, many of his characters becoming household words; buried in Westminster Abbey. *The Posthumous Papers of the Pickwick Club*, 1836–37; *Oliver Twist*, 1838; *A Christmas Carol*, 1843; *David Copperfield*, 1850; *Bleak House*, 1853; *Little Dorrit*, 1857; *A Tale of Two Cities*, 1859; *Great Expectations*, 1861.

DONNE, JOHN, 1572 (London, Eng.)–Mar. 31, 1631. English metaphysical poet. Progressed from worldly and ironic poems to deeper, more religious works; neglected until the 20th cent, when his works influenced W. B. YEATS, T. S. ELIOT, W. H. AUDEN, and other modern poets; a convert to Anglicanism, became an eloquent, influential preacher; dean of St. Paul's Cathedral, 1621–31; best-known poems include "A Valediction," "Go and Catch a Falling Star," "Hymn to God the Father," and "Death Be Not Proud."

DOWSON, ERNEST CHRISTOPHER, Aug. 2, 1867 (Lee, Kent, Eng.)–Feb. 23, 1900. English poet. One of the English decadents; his best-known poem is "Non Sum Qualis Eram Bonae sub Regno Cynarae" (in *Verses*, 1896), which contains the famous refrain "I have been faithful to thee, Cynara! in my fashion." *The Pierrot of the Minute*, 1897.

DRABBLE, MARGARET, June 5, 1939 (Sheffield, Eng.). English novelist, critic. Noted for her novels about intelligent women. *The Garrick Year*, 1964; *The Millstone*, 1965; *The Needle's Eye*, 1972.

DRYDEN, JOHN, Aug. 9, 1613 (Northamptonshire, Eng.)–May 1, 1700. English poet, dramatist, critic. The complete man of letters, noted particularly for his satiric verse; poet laureate of England, 1668–1700; based his blank-verse masterpiece, *All for Love* (1677), on SHAKESPEARE's *Antony and Cleopatra*. *The Conquest of Granada* (2-part drama), 1670–71; *Marriage à la Mode* (comedy), 1672; *Absalom and Achitophel* (2-part verse satire), 1681–82; *MacFlecknoe* (verse satire), 1682.

DU MAURIER, DAPHNE, May 13, 1907 (London, Eng.). English novelist. *Rebecca*, 1933; *Jamaica Inn*, 1936; *The Birds*, 1963.

DURRELL, LAWRENCE GEORGE, Feb. 27, 1912 (Darjeeling, India). Anglo-Irish novelist, poet, playwright, travel writer. Best known for his *The Alexandria Quartet: Justine* (1957), *Balthazar* (1958), *Mountolive* (1958), *Clea* (1960).

ELIOT, GEORGE (pseud. of Mary Ann Evans), Nov. 22, 1819 (Warwickshire, Eng.)–Dec. 22, 1880. English novelist. Wrote with humor and compassion about life in rural towns, stressing concern for moral development. *Adam Bede*, 1859; *The Mill on the Floss*, 1860; *Silas Marner*, 1861; *Middlemarch*, 1871–72.

ELIOT, T(homas) S(tearns), Sept. 26, 1888 (St. Louis, Mo.)–Jan. 4, 1965. English-U.S. poet, critic, playwright. A major figure in 20th-cent. literature; dwelled on the theme of emptiness of modern life, especially in *Prufrock and Other Observations* (1917), *Gerontion* (1920), *The Waste-Land* (1922), and *Ash Wednesday* (1943); substituted idioms and conversational speech for the poetic diction and abstractions of 19th-cent. poetry;

awarded Nobel Prize in literature, 1948. *Murder in the Cathedral* (verse drama), 1935; *The Cocktail Party* (play), 1949.

FARQUHAR, GEORGE, 1678 (Londonderry, Ire.)-Apr. 29, 1707. English dramatist. His plays marked the transition between Restoration and 18th-cent. drama. *The Constant Couple*, 1699; *The Beaux Stratagem*, 1707.

FIELDING, HENRY, Apr. 22, 1707 (nr. Glastonbury, Eng.)-Oct. 8, 1754. English novelist, playwright. Best known for his brilliant picaresque novels *Tom Jones* (1749) and *Joseph Andrews* (1742); a leading playwright of his day; appointed a justice of the peace, organized the detective force that became Scotland Yard. *Amelia*, 1751.

FLETCHER, JOHN, Dec. 1579 (Sussex, Eng.)-Aug. 1625. English playwright who collaborated with FRANCIS BEAUMONT on a series of plays, including *Philaster, The Maid's Tragedy, A King and No King* (all 1607-13).

FORD, FORD MADOX, born Ford Madox Heuffer, Dec. 17, 1873 (Surrey, Eng.)-July 26, 1939. English novelist, editor, critic. Best known for *The Good Soldier* (1915) and a series of novels published as *Parade's End* (1950).

FORD, JOHN, Apr. 1586 (Devonshire, Eng.)-c.1640. English dramatist. Wrote intricately plotted tragedies full of gloom, blood, and sexual abnormality. *'Tis Pity She's a Whore*, c.1627; *The Broken Heart*, c.1629; *Perkin Warbeck*, c.1633.

FORESTER, C(ecil) **S**(cott), Aug. 27, 1899 (Cairo, Egypt)-Apr. 2, 1966. English novelist. Wrote the Horatio Hornblower series, including *The Happy Return* (1937), *Flying Colors* (1938), and *A Ship of the Line* (1939). *The African Queen*, 1935.

FORSTER, E(dward) **M**(organ), Jan. 1, 1879 (London, Eng.)-June 7, 1970. English novelist, critic. Best known for *A Passage to India* (1924), a novel about conflicts between British colonists and native Indians; also wrote novels of manners about the British middle class. *Where Angels Fear to Tread*, 1905; *A Room with a View*, 1908; *Maurice*, 1923.

FOWLES, JOHN, Mar. 31, 1926 (Essex, Eng.). English novelist. *The Collector*, 1963; *The Magus*, 1966 (revised edition, 1978); *The French Lieutenant's Woman*, 1969; *The Ebony Tower*, 1974; *Daniel Martin*, 1977.

FRY, CHRISTOPHER, born Christopher Harris, Dec. 18, 1907 (Bristol, Eng.). English dramatist. Author of witty verse plays and religious dramas. *The Lady's Not for Burning*, 1949; *Venus Observed*, 1950; *A Sleep of Prisoners*, 1951. Translated JEAN GIRAUDOUX's *Tiger at the Gates* (1955) and JEAN ANOUILH's *Ring Round the Moon* (1950).

GALSWORTHY, JOHN (pseud. of John Sinjohn), Aug. 14, 1867 (Surrey, Eng.)-Jan. 31, 1933. English novelist, dramatist. Best known for the three trilogies: *The Forsyte Saga* (1922), *A Modern Comedy* (1928), and *End of the Chapter* (1934); wrote several successful dramas about social problems; refused knighthood, 1918; awarded Order of Merit, 1929; awarded Nobel Prize in literature, 1932.

GASKELL, ELIZABETH CLEGHORN, née Stevenson, Sept. 29, 1810 (London, Eng.)-Nov. 12, 1865. English novelist. Wrote about English country life and the problems of the working class; a friend of CHARLES DICKENS, GEORGE ELIOT, and CHARLOTTE BRONTË. *Mary Barton*, 1848; *Cranford*, 1853; *Ruth*, 1853; *North and South*, 1855.

GAY, JOHN, c.Sept. 16, 1685 (Devon, Eng.)-Dec. 4, 1732. English playwright, poet. His play *The Beggar's Opera* (1728), a satire on SIR ROBERT WALPOLE and the court of George II, provided the basis for BERTOLT BRECHT and KURT WEILL's *Threepenny Opera*.

GILBERT, SIR WILLIAM SCHWENCK, Nov. 18, 1836 (London, Eng.)-May 19, 1911. English dramatist. Collaborated with composer SIR ARTHUR SULLIVAN on comic operas; wrote highly satirical lyrics that poked fun at English society; first opera produced by RICHARD D'OYLY CARTE at the Savoy Theatre, London, after 1881; knighted, 1907. *Trial by Jury*, 1875; *H.M.S. Pinafore*, 1878; *The Pirates of Penzance*, 1880; *The Mikado*, 1885; *Yeoman of the Guard*, 1888; *The Gondoliers*, 1889.

GOLDING, WILLIAM GERALD, Sept. 19, 1911 (Cornwall, Eng.). English novelist. Best known for his allegorical cult novel *Lord of the Flies* (1954). *Pincher Martin*, 1956; *The Spire*, 1964.

GOLDSMITH, OLIVER, Nov. 10, 1728 (Ireland)-Apr. 4, 1774. Anglo-Irish poet, novelist, dramatist. His realistic works are characterized by a lively, humorous style. *The Vicar of Wakefield*, 1766; *The Deserted Village*, 1770; *She Stoops to Conquer*, 1773.

GRAHAME, KENNETH, Mar. 8, 1859 (Edinburgh, Scot.)-July 6, 1932. English writer of children's books. Best known for the classic children's book *The Wind in the Willows* (1908), about the adventures of Toad, Ratty, and Mole.

GRAVES, ROBERT, July 26, 1895 (London, Eng.). English poet, novelist, critic. *Claudius the God*, 1934; *I, Claudius*, 1935; *The White Goddess*, 1947; *Collected Poems*, 1965.

GRAY, THOMAS, Dec. 26, 1716 (London, Eng.)-July 30, 1771. English poet. Best known poet of his time, noted for his charming neoclassical light verse and melancholy lyrics and odes; refused position of poet laureate in favor of a life of scholarship at Cambridge; "Elegy Written in a Country Churchyard" (1751) is his most famous poem.

GREENE, GRAHAM, Oct. 2, 1904 (Hertfordshire, Eng.). English novelist, short-story writer, playwright. Noted for his "entertainments" and serious novels, which often are set in exotic locations and usually hinge on profound moral crises. *A Gun for Sale*, 1936; *The Power and the Glory*, 1940; *The Heart of the Matter*, 1948; *The Third Man*, 1949; *The Quiet American*, 1955; *Our Man in Havana*, 1958; *The Comedians*, 1966; *The Human Factor*, 1978.

GREGORY, LADY ISABELLA AUGUSTA, née Persse, Mar. 15, 1852 (Roxborough, Ire.)-May 22, 1932. Irish playwright. A major figure in the Irish literary renaissance; dir. of the Irish National Theatre (later the Abbey Theatre), for which she wrote one-act plays; collected and translated Celtic folk tales. *Spreading the News*, 1904; *The Rising of the Moon*, 1907; *Our Irish Theatre*, 1914.

HARDY, THOMAS, June 2, 1840 (Dorset, Eng.)-Jan. 11, 1928. English novelist, poet. His lyrics exerted a major influence on modern English verse; his melancholy, powerful novels deal with solitary men struggling against environment and fate. *Far from the Madding Crowd*, 1874; *The Return of the Native*, 1878; *Tess of the D'Urbervilles*, 1891; *Jude the Obscure*, 1896; *Wessex Poems*, 1898; *Collected Poems*, 1931.

HARRIS, FRANK, born James Thomas Harris, Feb. 14, 1856 (Galway, Ire.)-Aug. 26, 1931.

WRITERS

British-U.S. editor, journalist, biographer, novelist; led a scandalous life and wrote an even more scandalous autobiography, *My Life and Loves* (3 vols., 1923–27), which was banned in England and in the U.S.; wrote a malicious biographical series, *Contemporary Portraits* (1915–27).

HERRICK, ROBERT, 1591 (London, Eng.)-Oct. 1674. English poet. Major Cavalier poet noted for his simple, sensuous, graceful poems, including "Gather ye rosebuds while ye may." *Hesperides,* 1648.

HERRIOT, JAMES, Mar. 10, 1916 (Glasgow, Scot.). Scottish veterinarian, author. Author of best-selling books about the life of a rural Scottish veterinarian. *All Creatures Great and Small,* 1972; *All Things Wise and Wonderful,* 1977.

HEYER, GEORGETTE, Aug. 16, 1902 (Wimbledon, Eng.)-July 4, 1974. English novelist. Wrote historical novels set in Regency London and well-plotted mystery novels with a light, humorous touch. *A Blunt Instrument,* 1938; *The Spanish Bride,* 1940.

HILTON, JAMES, Sept. 9, 1900 (Lancashire, Eng.)-Dec. 20, 1954. English novelist. *Lost Horizon,* 1933; *Goodbye, Mr. Chips,* 1934; *Random Harvest,* 1941.

HOPKINS, GERARD MANLEY, July 28, 1844 (Stratford, Eng.)-June 8, 1889. English Jesuit priest, poet. His highly original poetry is characterized by alliteration, puns, internal rhymes, "sprung rhythm"; first published 30 years after his death; noted poems include "The Windhover," "Pied Beauty," "Carrion Comfort," and "God's Grandeur."

HOUSMAN, A(lfred) E(dward), May 26, 1859 (Worcestershire, Eng.)-Apr. 30, 1936. English poet. His volume of poetry titled *A Shropshire Lad* (1896) was influential as a reaction against Victorianism; an outstanding classical scholar. *Last Poems,* 1922; *More Poems,* 1936; *Collected Poems,* 1939.

HUGHES, TED, Aug. 16, 1930 (W. Yorkshire, Eng.). English poet. His verse is characterized by violent images and controlled diction and style. *The Hawk in the Rain,* 1957; *Lupercal,* 1960; *Crow: From the Life and Songs of the Crow,* 1971. (Husband of SYLVIA PLATH.)

HUGHES, THOMAS, Oct. 20, 1822 (Berkshire, Eng.)-Mar. 22, 1896. English reformer, author. Best known as the author of *Tom Brown's School Days* (1857) and *Tom Brown at Oxford* (1861). A founder (1854) of the Working Men's C. and its principal, 1872–83; founded an unsuccessful model community in Rugby, Tenn., 1879.

HUXLEY, ALDOUS LEONARD, July 26, 1894 (Surrey, Eng.)-Nov. 22, 1963. English novelist, essayist. His early novels were witty satires on contemporary life; later novels reflected his interest in drugs, mysticism, and the occult. *Antic Hay,* 1923; *Point Counter Point,* 1928; *Brave New World,* 1932; *Eyeless in Gaza,* 1936; *The Doors of Perception,* 1954.

ISHERWOOD, CHRISTOPHER, Aug. 26, 1904 (Cheshire, Eng.). English novelist, playwright. In his early novels, wrote about the social disintegration in Berlin during the rise of Nazism; his *Goodbye to Berlin* (1935) was adapted for the stage by John Van Druten as *I Am a Camera* (1951) and as the musical *Cabaret* (1966); coauthored plays with his friend W. H. AUDEN. *The Memorial,* 1932; *A Meeting by the River,* 1967; *Kathleen and Frank,* 1971.

JOHNSON, SAMUEL, Sept. 18, 1709 (Staffordshire, Eng.)- Dec. 13, 1784. English poet, critic, essayist, lexicographer. An outstanding literary figure of his time, his compassion, humor, good sense, and masterful use of language reached a wide variety of readers; best-known works include his pioneering *Dictionary of the English Language* (1755), his edition of Shakespeare's works, and his 10-volume *Lives of the Poets* (1779–81). *The Rambler,* 1750–52; *The Adventurer,* 1753–54; *The Idler,* 1758–60; *Journey to the Western Islands of Scotland,* 1775.

JONSON, BEN, June 11, 1572? (London, Eng.)-Aug. 6, 1637. English dramatist, poet. Best known for his four masterpieces of dramatic satire: *Volpone* (1606), *Epicoene* (1609), *The Alchemist* (1610), and *Bartholomew Fair* (1614); his most famous poems include "Drink to me only with thine eyes" and "Come, my Celia, let us prove" (both in *The Forrest,* 1616).

JOYCE, JAMES, Feb. 2, 1882 (Dublin, Ire.)-Jan. 13, 1941. Irish novelist. One of the foremost writers of the 20th cent.; his novels are characterized by subtle but frank portraits of human nature and original and varied style; introduced the use of interior monologue and symbolic motif; his masterpiece, *Ulysses* (1922), notable for its complex design and combination of realism and stream of consciousness, was banned as obscene in the U.S. until 1933. *Dubliners,* 1914; *A Portrait of the Artist As a Young Man,* 1914; *Finnegan's Wake,* 1939.

KEATS, JOHN, Oct. 31, 1795 (London, Eng.)-Feb. 23, 1821. English poet. One of the foremost English Romantic poets; though he died of tuberculosis at age 25, left a large and mature body of work; most famous poems include "To Psyche," "On Melancholy," "To a Nightingale," "Ode On a Grecian Urn," and "To Autumn"—all published in *Lamia, Isabella, The Eve of St. Agnes, and Other Poems* (1820).

KIPLING, (Joseph) RUDYARD, Dec. 30, 1865 (Bombay, India)-Jan. 18, 1936. English poet, novelist, short-story writer. Wrote many works about India; later called an imperialist and racist; best-known poems include "The White Man's Burden," "Mandalay," "Gunga Din," and "If"; won England's first Nobel Prize in literature, 1907; refused laureateship and Order of Merit. *The Jungle Book,* 1894; *Captains Courageous,* 1897; *Kim,* 1901; *Just So Stories,* 1902.

KNIGHT, ERIC MOWBRAY, Apr. 10, 1897 (Yorkshire, Eng.)-Jan. 21, 1943. English-U.S. writer. Best-known for the juvenile classic *Lassie Come Home* (1940), later adapted into films and a television series.

KYD, THOMAS, Nov. 5, 1558 (London, Eng.)-Dec. 1594. English dramatist. His play *The Spanish Tragedy* (c.1592) influenced the development of English drama.

LAMB, CHARLES, Feb. 10, 1775 (London, Eng.)-Dec. 27, 1834. English essayist. Best known for *Essays of Elia* (1823), including "A Dissertation on Roast Pig," "A Chapter on Ears," and "The Praise of Chimney Sweepers"; his dramatic essays helped revive Elizabethan drama; with his sister Mary Ann Lamb, wrote a popular children's book, *Tales from Shakespeare* (1807).

LANGLAND, WILLIAM, c.1330 (West Midlands?, Eng.)-c.1400. English poet. According to conjecture, wrote at least two of the three versions of *The Vision of William concerning Piers Plowman,* one of the greatest pre-Chaucerian English poems.

LARKIN, PHILIP ARTHUR, Aug. 9, 1922 (Coventry, Eng.). English poet, novelist, editor. Led the post-WW II antiromantic movement; writes subtle, cynical, witty poems critical of contemporary life. *The Less Deceived,* 1955; *The Whitsun Weddings,* 1964; *High Window,* 1974.

LAWRENCE, D(avid) H(erbert), Sept. 11, 1883 (Nottinghamshire, Eng.)–Mar. 2, 1930. English novelist, short-story writer, poet. His works reflected rejection of Western culture and interest in the natural, the primitive, and the mystical; his controversial novel *Lady Chatterley's Lover* (1928) was banned in England and the U.S. *Sons and Lovers,* 1913; *The Rainbow,* 1915; *Women in Love,* 1921.

LESSING, DORIS, Oct. 22, 1919 (Kermanshah, Iran). British novelist, short-story writer. Raised in Southern Rhodesia [now Zimbabwe], about which she wrote her first novel; her works are marked by strong interest in social causes. *The Grass is Singing,* 1950; *The Golden Notebook,* 1962; *Briefing for a Descent into Hell,* 1971; *The Summer before the Dark,* 1973.

LEWIS, C(live) S(taples), Nov. 29, 1898 (Belfast, Ire.)–Nov. 22, 1963. English novelist, critic, scholar. Noted for his science-fiction novels and Christian apologetics—especially *The Screwtape Letters* (1942)—and for his literary criticism. *The Allegory of Love,* 1936; *Out of the Silent Planet,* 1938; *That Hideous Strength,* 1945; *Studies of Medieval and Renaissance Literature,* 1966.

LEWIS, (Percy) WYNDHAM, Nov. 18, 1884 (at sea in the Bay of Fundy, off Maine)–Mar. 7, 1957. English novelist, essayist, artist. Chiefly known for his angry, satiric novels and political and literary essays; a leader of the vorticist movement; edited *Beast* 1914-15, the vorticist magazine, with EZRA POUND. *Tarr,* 1918; *The Art of Being Ruled,* 1926; *Time and Western Man,* 1927; *The Apes of God,* 1930; *The Human Age* (trilogy), 1928-55.

LLEWELLYN (Lloyd), RICHARD (David Vivian), 1907 (Pembrokeshire, Wales). Welsh novelist. *How Green Was My Valley,* 1939; *None But the Lonely Heart,* 1943.

LOVELACE, RICHARD, 1618 (Kent, Eng.)–1658. English poet; a Cavalier poet noted chiefly for two poems, "To Althea, from Prison" (famous for the line "Stone walls do not a prison make . . . "; 1642) and "To Lucasta, Going to the Wars" (famous for the line "I could not love thee dear, so much/Loved I not honor more . . ."; 1649).

LOWRY, (Clarence) MALCOLM, July 28, 1909 (Cheshire, Eng.)–June 27, 1957. English novelist. Noted for one book, the autobiographical novel *Under the Volcano* (1947); his other works, published posthumously, include *Dark as the Grave Wherein My Friend Is Laid* (1968) and *Lunar Caustic* (1968).

MACDIARMID, HUGH (pseud. of Christopher Murray Grieve), Aug. 11, 1892 (Dumfriershire, Scot.). Scottish poet, critic. A leader of the Scottish literary renaissance; founded the Scottish Nationalist Party. *A Drunk Man Looks at the Thistle,* 1926; *To Circumjack Cencrastus,* 1930; *At the Sign of the Thistle,* 1934; *Stony Limits,* 1934; *A Kist of Whistles,* 1947.

MALORY, SIR THOMAS, fl.mid 15th cent. English writer. Identity uncertain, widely believed to be the Sir Thomas Malory of Newbold Revell, Warwickshire, who represented Warwickshire in Parliament (1445), then was jailed eight times for church plundering, extortion, rape, etc.; wrote *Le Morte d'Arthur* (1485), the first English prose collection of Arthurian fables.

MANSFIELD (Beauchamp), KATHERINE, Oct. 14, 1888 (Wellington, N.Z.)–Jan. 9, 1923. British short-story writer. A master of the short story; died of tuberculosis. *In a German Pension,* 1911; *Bliss and Other Stories,* 1920; *The Garden Party and Other Stories,* 1922; *The Dove's Nest and Other Stories,* 1923; *Something Childish and Other Stories,* 1924.

MARLOWE, CHRISTOPHER, Feb. 26, 1564 (Canterbury, Eng.)–May 30, 1593. English dramatist, poet. First great English dramatist; introduced into drama the probing of a hero's inner conflicts; established blank verse in drama. *Tamburlaine the Great,* 1590; *The Tragical History of Dr. Faustus,* 1604; *The Famous Tragedy of the Rich Jew of Malta,* 1633; *The Troublesome Raigne and Lamentable Death of Edward the Second, King of England,* 1594.

MARVELL, ANDREW, Mar. 31, 1621 (Yorkshire, Eng.)–Aug. 18, 1678. English poet, pamphleteer, politician. Metaphysical poet best known for his early lyric verse, notably "The Garden" (1681), "The Definition of Love" (1681), "To His Coy Mistress" (1650), and "An Horatian Ode upon Cromwell's Return from Ireland" (1650).

MASEFIELD, JOHN, June 1, 1878 (Herefordshire, Eng.)–May 12, 1967. English poet. Best known for his poems about the sea (e.g., *Salt Water Ballads,* 1902); poet laureate of England, 1930-67. *The Everlasting Mercy,* 1911; *Dauber,* 1913; *Reynard the Fox,* 1919.

MAUGHAM W(illiam) SOMERSET, Jan. 25, 1874 (Paris, Fr.)–Dec. 16, 1965. English novelist, short-story writer, playwright. An expert storyteller who set his short stories and many of his novels in exotic locales; wrote plays—chiefly Edwardian social comedies—popular in their time. *Of Human Bondage,* 1915; *The Moon and Sixpence,* 1919; *The Constant Wife,* 1927; *Cakes and Ale,* 1930; *The Razor's Edge,* 1944.

MEREDITH, GEORGE, Feb. 12, 1828 (Portsmouth, Eng.)–May 18, 1909. English novelist, poet. Wrote intellectual, satiric novels. *The Ordeal of Richard Feverel,* 1859; *The Egoist,* 1879; *Diana of the Crossways,* 1885.

MILNE, A(lan) A(lexander), Jan. 18, 1882 (London, Eng.)–Jan. 31, 1956. English humorist, children's-book author. Created Winnie-the-Pooh and his friends Piglet, Kanga, Roo, and Eeyore, whose adventures have become classics. *When We Were Very Young,* 1924; *Winnie-the-Pooh,* 1926; *Now We Are Six,* 1927; *The House at Pooh Corner,* 1928.

MILTON, JOHN, Dec. 9, 1608 (London, Eng.)–Nov. 8, 1674. English poet, essayist. One of English literature's foremost poets; his masterpiece, *Paradise Lost* (1667, 1674), is considered by some to be the greatest English-language epic poem; also wrote E glish and Italian sonnets, political pamphlets; on becoming totally blind, worked through secretaries, including ANDREW MARVELL. "On the Morning of Christ's Nativity," 1629; *Comus,* 1634; *Areopagitica,* 1644; *Paradise Regained,* 1671; *Samson Agonistes,* 1671.

MITFORD, NANCY, Nov. 28, 1904 (London, Eng.)–June 30, 1973. English novelist, biographer, editor. Noted for her witty novels about upper-class British life and biographies of VOLTAIRE, MME. DE POMPADOUR, and LOUIS XIV; coedited *Noblesse Oblige* (1956), a series of essays contrasting upper- and lower-class language and behavior. *Love in a Cold Climate,* 1949; *Madame de Pompadour,* 1954; *The Sun King,* 1966.

MOORE, BRIAN, Aug. 25, 1921 (Belfast, Ire.). Irish-U.S. novelist. Best known for *The Lonely Passion of Judith Hearne* (1955) and other novels about lonely, self-deluded people. *The Luck of Ginger Coffey* (1960); *The Emperor of Ice Cream* (1965).

MOORE, GEORGE AUGUSTUS, Feb. 24, 1852 (County Mayo, Ire.)-Jan. 21, 1933. Irish novelist. Introduced naturalism to the Victorian novel. *Esther Waters*, 1894; *Hail and Farewell* (3-vol. autobiography), 1911, 1912, 1914.

MUNRO, H(ector) H(ugh) (pseud. Saki), Dec. 18, 1870 (Akyab, Burma)-Nov. 14, 1916. British short-story writer, journalist. Noted for his fantastic, witty stories about the Edwardian social scene. *Not So Stories*, 1902; *Reginald*, 1904; *Reginald in Russia*, 1910; *The Chronicles of Clovis*, 1911; *Beasts and Super-Beasts*, 1914.

MURDOCH, (Jean) IRIS, July 15, 1919 (Dublin, Ire.). English novelist, university lecturer. Noted for her intelligent, witty novels; since 1948, fellow and tutor in philosophy at Oxford U. *Under the Net*, 1954; *The Flight from the Enchanter*, 1956; *A Severed Head*, 1961; *The Nice and the Good*, 1968; *An Accidental Man*, 1971; *The Black Prince*, 1973; *The Sacred and Profane Love Machine*, 1974.

O'BRIEN, EDNA, Dec. 15, 1930 (County Clare, Ire.). Irish novelist. Best known for a trilogy about the relationships of two Irish women: *The Country Girls* (1960), *The Lonely Girl* (1962), and *Girls in Their Married Bliss* (1964). *Casualties of Peace*, 1966; *A Pagan Place*, 1971; *Night*, 1972.

O'CASEY, SEAN, born John O'Casey, Mar. 30, 1880 (Dublin, Ire.)-Sept. 18, 1964. Irish dramatist. Best known for plays he wrote for Dublin's Abbey Theatre, including *Juno and the Paycock* (1924) and *The Plough and the Stars* (1926)—realistic, often humorous, ultimately tragic dramas.

O'FAOLAIN, SEAN, born Sean Whelan, Feb. 22, 1900 (County Cork, Ire.). Irish short-story writer, novelist, essayist, biographer. Noted for his portraits of Ireland's lower and middle classes. *Midsummer Night Madness and Other Stories*, 1932; *A Nest of Simple Folk*, 1933; *A Life of Daniel O'Connell*, 1938.

O'FLAHERTY, LIAM, 1896 (Aran Is., Ire.). Irish novelist, short-story writer. Best known for the novel *The Informer* (1925), adapted by JOHN FORD into an Academy Award-winning film (1935).

ORTON, JOE, born John Kingsley Orton, Jan. 1, 1933 (Leicester, Eng.)-Aug. 9, 1967. English playwright. Wrote black comedies, combining murder, sexual perversion, and blackmail with genteel, epigrammatic dialogue; murdered by his lover, who then committed suicide. *Entertaining Mr. Sloane*, 1964; *What the Butler Saw*, 1969.

ORWELL, GEORGE (pseud. of Eric Arthur Blair), June 25, 1903 (Motihari, India)-Jan. 21, 1950. English novelist, essayist, critic. Best known for his satirical novels *Animal Farm* (1945) and *Nineteen Eighty-Four* (1949), in which the heroes are victims. *Down and Out in Paris and London*, 1933; *The Road to Wigan Pier*, 1937; *Homage to Catalonia*, 1938.

OSBORNE, JOHN JAMES, Dec. 12, 1929 (London, Eng.). British playwright, screenwriter. Leader of the "Angry Young Men" of the British theater in the 1950s and 1960s. Plays: *Look Back in Anger*, 1956; *The Entertainer*, 1957; *Luther*, 1961 (Tony Award, 1963); *Inadmissable Evidence*, 1964; *Time Present*, 1968. Films: *Tom Jones* (Best Picture AA), 1964.

OWEN, WILFRED, Mar. 18, 1893 (Shropshire, Eng.)-Nov. 4, 1918. English poet. An antiwar poet, killed in action a week before the end of WW I; a single volume of his work, *Poems* (1920), was published posthumously by his friend SIEGFRIED SASSOON.

PEPYS, SAMUEL, Feb. 23, 1633 (London, Eng.)-May 26, 1703. English diarist. A secy. to the admiralty, he kept the most famous diary in the English language; first published in 1825, the diary gives a brilliant description of early Restoration life.

PINERO, SIR ARTHUR WING, May 24, 1855 (London, Eng.)-Nov. 23, 1934. English playwright. Noted for his literate farces and serious, realistic dramas. *The Second Mrs. Tanqueray*, 1889; *Trelawney of the "Wells"*, 1898.

PINTER, HAROLD, Oct. 30, 1930 (London, Eng.). English playwright, screenwriter. His "comedies of menace" feature ordinary characters in an atmosphere of mystery and horror, along with understated and ambiguous dialogue and long silences; wrote screenplays for the films *The Servant* (1962), *Accident* (1967), and *The Go-Between* (1971). *The Caretaker*, 1960; *The Homecoming*, 1965.

POPE, ALEXANDER, May 21, 1688 (London, Eng.)-May 30, 1744. English poet. English verse satirist; became the literary dictator of his age; afflicted with a disease that produced curvature of the spine, never grew more than 4 ft., 6 in. tall. *The Rape of the Lock*, 1714; *Eloise to Abelard*, 1717; *The Dunciad*, 1728-43; *An Essay on Man*, 1743.

POTTER, (Helen) BEATRIX, July 28, 1866 (Middlesex, Eng.)-Dec. 22, 1943. English children's book author/illustrator. *The Tale of Peter Rabbit*, 1902; *The Tailor of Gloucester*, 1903; *The Tale of Squirrel Nutkin*, 1903; *The Tale of Mrs. Tiggy-Winkle*, 1905.

PRIESTLEY, J(ohn) B(oynton), Sept. 13, 1894 (Yorkshire, Eng.). English novelist, dramatist, essayist. Noted for ingenious works in which he distorts normal sequence of past, present, and future, thereby evoking the phenomenon of *déjà vu*. *The Good Companions*, 1929; *Dangerous Corner*, 1932; *When We Are Married*, 1938.

RATTIGAN, SIR TERENCE MERVYN, June 10, 1911 (London, Eng.). English playwright. Knighted, 1971. *O Mistress Mine*, 1945; *The Winslow Boy*, 1947; *Separate Tables*, 1954; *Ross*, 1960; *A Bequest to the Nation*, 1970.

READE, CHARLES, June 8, 1814 (Oxfordshire, Eng.)-Apr. 11, 1884. English novelist. Noted for his historical romances, notably *The Cloister and the Hearth* (1861) and *Griffin Gaunt* (1866), as well as for novels that exposed social injustice and led to reforms. *It Is Never Too Late to Mend*, 1856; *Hard Cash*, 1863.

RENAULT, MARY (pseud. of Mary Challens), Sept. 4, 1905 (London, Eng.). English novelist. Author of historical novels about classical, preclassical, and Hellenistic Greece. *The Last of the Wine*, 1956; *The King Must Die*, 1958; *The Mask of Apollo*, 1966; *The Persian Boy*, 1972.

RHYS, JEAN, 1894 (Dominica, W. Indies)-May 15, 1979. English novelist. Her early works about bohemian life in Europe of the 1920s and 1930s were rediscovered by feminists in the 1970s. *After Leaving Mr. MacKenzie*, 1931; *Good Morning, Midnight*, 1939; *Tigers Are Better Looking*, 1965; *Wide Sargasso Sea*, 1966.

RICHARDSON, SAMUEL, baptized Aug. 19, 1689 (nr. Derby, Eng.)-July 4, 1761. English novelist. Author of *Pamela: or, Virtue Unrewarded* (1740-41), often called the first modern English novel. *Clarissa; or, The History of a Young Lady*, 1747–48; *The History of Sir Charles Grandison*, 1753–54.

ROLFE, FREDERICK WILLIAM ("Baron Corvo") born Serafino Austin Lewis Mary, July 22, 1860 (London, Eng.)–Oct. 25, 1913. English novelist. Versatile, learned, extremely eccentric; best known as author of *Hadrian the Seventh* (1904), a bizarre book about a man rejected for the priesthood who becomes pope; gained fame posthumously with publication of A. J. A. Symmon's *The Quest for Corvo* (1934). *The Desire and Pursuit of the Whole*, 1934.

ROSSETTI, DANTE GABRIEL, born Gabriel Charles Dante, May 12, 1828 (London, Eng.)–Apr. 9, 1882. English poet, painter. A master of the sonnet; founded the Pre-Raphaelite Brotherhood, which romanticized the Middle Ages. "The Blessed Damzel," 1850; "Sister Helen," 1870; "The House of Life," 1881.

RUSKIN, JOHN, Feb. 8, 1819 (London, Eng.)–Jan. 20, 1900. English writer. Noted for his writing on art and social problems. *Modern Painters*, 5 vols., 1843–60; *The Seven Lamps of Architecture*, 1849; *The Stones of Venice*, 3 vols., 1851–53; *Fors Clavigera: Letters to the Workmen and Laborers of Great Britain*, 1871–84.

RYAN, CORNELIUS JOHN, June 5, 1920 (Dublin, Ire.)–Nov. 23, 1974. Irish-U.S. novelist, journalist. *The Longest Day*,1959; *A Bridge Too Far*,1974.

SACKVILLE, THOMAS, 1ST EARL OF DORSET, BARON BUCKHURST, 1536 (Sussex, Eng.)–Apr. 19, 1608. English statesman, poet, dramatist. With Thomas Norton and others, wrote *Gorboduc* (1561), a blank-verse drama generally considered the first English tragedy. *Mirror for Magistrates*, 1563.

SASSOON, SIEGFRIED LORRAINE, Sept. 8, 1886 (Kent, Eng.)–Sept. 1, 1967. English poet, novelist. Wrote grim, realistic antiwar poetry and fictionalized autobiographies. *The Old Huntsman*, 1917; *Counterattack*, 1918; *The Memoirs of George Sherston*, 1937; *The Old Century and Seven More Years*, 1938.

SCOTT, SIR WALTER, Aug. 15, 1771 (Edinburgh, Scot.)–Sept. 21, 1832. Scottish novelist, poet. Father of the historical novel; wrote romances of Scottish life; in his narrative poems, introduced the popular form of the verse tale; made baronet, 1820. *Waverly*, 1814; *The Heart of Midlothian*, 1818; *The Bride of Lammermoor*, 1819; *Ivanhoe*, 1820; *The Fortunes of Nigel*,1822.

SHAFFER, (Levin) **PETER,** May 15, 1926 (London, Eng.). English playwright. Noted for moving easily from farce to plays portraying the agony of the human soul. *Five-Finger Exercise*, 1958; *The Private Ear and the Public Eye*, 1962; *The Royal Hunt of the Sun*, 1964; *Black Comedy*, 1965; *The Battle of Shrivings*, 1970; *Equus*, 1973.

SHAKESPEARE, WILLIAM, Apr. 26, 1564 (Stratford-on-Avon, Eng.)–Apr. 23, 1616. English dramatist, poet. Widely considered the greatest writer in the English language; his plays have been performed almost continuously to this day; wrote comedies, histories, tragedies, as well as 154 sonnets and two heroic narratives. Comedies include: *The Comedy of Errors*, 1592/93; *The Taming of the Shrew*, 1593/94; *The Two Gentlemen of Verona*, 1594/95; *Midsummer Night's Dream*, 1595/96; *The Merchant of Venice*, 1596/97; *Twelfth Night*, 1601/02; *The Tempest*, 1611/12. Tragedies include: *Romeo and Juliet*, 1594/95; *Julius Caesar*, 1599/1600; *Hamlet*, 1600/01;

Othello, 1604/05; *King Lear*, 1605/06; *Macbeth*, 1605/06; *Antony and Cleopatra*, 1606/07; *Coriolanus*, 1607/08. Histories include: 1 and 2 *Henry IV*, 1597–98; *Richard II*, 1595; *Richard III*, 1592–93; *Henry VI* 1590–92.

SHAW, GEORGE BERNARD, July 26, 1856 (Dublin, Ire.)–Nov. 2, 1950. British playwright, critic. Major British dramatist; wrote "dramas of ideas" that reflected his passion for social reform; his plays are noted for their memorable characters, brilliant language and wit; journalist; political pamphleteer; a leader in the socialist Fabian Soc.; a music and drama critic, awarded Nobel Prize in literature, 1925. *Caesar and Cleopatra*, 1899; *Man and Superman*, 1905; *Major Barbara*, 1905; *Androcles and the Lion*, 1912; *Pygmalion*, 1913; *Saint Joan*, 1923.

SHELLEY, PERCY BYSSHE, Aug. 4, 1792 (Sussex, Eng.)–July 8, 1822. English romantic poet. His verse is noted for its grandeur, beauty, mastery of language, and influence on social and political thought; led a tempestuous, highly unconventional life; left England for Italy, where he wrote his best poetry; killed at age 29 when his boat capsized. *Queen Mab*, 1813; *The Cenci*, 1819; *Prometheus Unbound*, 1820; *Epipsychidion*, 1821; *Adonais*, 1821; *Hellas*, 1822. (Husband of MARY WOLLSTONECRAFT SHELLEY.)

SHERIDAN, RICHARD BRINSLEY BUTLER, baptized Nov. 4, 1751 (Dublin, Ire.)–July 7, 1816. Irish playwright, politician. Noted for his comedies of manners; in *The Rivals* (1775) and *The School for Scandal* (1777) combined Restoration wit with 18th-cent. sensibility; *malapropism*, term meaning confusion of near-homonyms, derives from his character Mrs. Malaprop, in *The Rivals*. *The Critic*, 1779.

SHUTE, NEVIL, Jan. 17, 1899 (London, Eng.)–Jan. 12, 1960. English novelist. Noted for his fast-paced novels filled with technological details; an aeronautical engineer who settled in Australia, where he wrote 26 books in 30 years. *On the Beach*, 1957.

SIDNEY, SIR PHILIP, Nov. 30, 1554 (Kent, Eng.)–Oct. 17, 1586. English poet, courtier, scholar, soldier. A model of the Renaissance gentleman; an influential patron, critic and poet; his *Arcadia* (1590) is the earliest known pastoral in English; his *Astrophel and Stella* (1591) began vogue for the sonnet sequence; knighted, 1583. *The Defense of Poesie*, 1595; *An Apology for Poetry*, 1595.

SILLITOE, ALAN, Mar. 4, 1928 (Nottingham, Eng.). English novelist. Noted for his angry accounts of working-class life. *Saturday Night and Sunday Morning*, 1958; *The Loneliness of the Long Distance Runner*, 1959.

SITWELL, DAME EDITH, Sept. 7, 1887 (Yorkshire, Eng.)–Dec. 9, 1964. English poet, prose writer. With her brothers, OSBERT and Sacheverell, a member of a celebrated literary family; turned from early frivolous verse to religious poetry; known for her eccentricity and wit. *Clowns Houses*, 1918; *Facade*, 1923; *A Poet's Notebook*, 1943; *Gardeners and Astronomers*, 1953.

SITWELL, SIR (Francis) **OSBERT SACHEVERELL, 5TH BARONET SITWELL,** Dec. 6, 1892 (London, Eng.)–May 4, 1969. English poet, novelist, short-story writer, critic. Best known for his five-volume reminiscences about his family, a portrait of British society in the Edwardian era, beginning with *Left Hand! Right Hand!* (1944). (Brother of EDITH SITWELL.)

SMOLLETT, TOBIAS GEORGE, baptized Mar. 19, 1721 (Cardross, Scot.)–Sept. 17, 1771. Scottish novelist. Wrote satiric novels, rich in comic characters, which give a panoramic view of his times. *Roderick Random*, 1748; *Peregrine Pickle*, 1751; *Ferdinand Count Fathom*, 1753; *Sir Lancelot Greaves*, 1760–62; *Humphrey Clinker*, 1771.

SNOW, C(harles) **P**(ercy), **BARON,** Oct. 15, 1905 (Leicester, Eng.). English novelist, scientist, government administrator. Best known for his controversial *The Two Cultures and the Scientific Revolution* (1959), an analysis of the breach between the scientific and literary communities, and for his 11-volume novel series, *Strangers and Brothers* (1940–70); knighted, 1957; made a life peer,1964.

SPARK, MURIEL SARAH, née Camberg, 1918 (Edinburgh, Scot.). Scottish novelist, critic, poet. Best known for her novel *The Prime of Miss Jean Brodie* (1961), which was adapted into a play and later a movie. *Child of Light: A Reassessment of Mary Shelley*, 1951.

SPENDER, STEPHEN HAROLD, Feb. 28, 1909 (London, Eng.). English poet, critic. In 1930s, wrote poetry of social protest; his poetry became increasingly autobiographical; since 1940s, he has concentrated on criticism and editing influential reviews, including *Horizon* (1939–41) and *Encounter* (1953–67). *Twenty Poems*, 1930; *The Destructive Element*, 1935; *The Still Centre*, 1939; *The Creative Element;* 1953; *The Making of a Poem*, 1955.

SPENSER, EDMUND, 1552/53 (London, Eng.)–Jan. 13, 1599. English poet. Best known for his unfinished masterpiece, *The Faerie Queene* (6 books; 1596), an allegory for which he invented the Spenserian stanza, a form later revived by the Romantic poets.

STEAD, CHRISTINA ELLEN, July 17, 1902 (Sydney, Aust.). British novelist. Noted for her intelligent, sophisticated, unsentimental writings; best known for *The Man Who Loved Children* (1940; rev. 1960), a novel depicting marriage as savage warfare.

STEELE, SIR RICHARD, 1672 (Dublin, Ire.)–Sept. 1, 1729. English journalist, essayist, dramatist, politician. With JOSEPH ADDISON, coauthored several periodicals, including the famous *Tatler*, *Spectator*, and *Guardian;* wrote several sentimental comedies; became a Whig member of Parliament; knighted, 1715. *The Funeral*, 1701; *The Lying Lover*, 1703; *The Conscious Lovers*, 1722.

STERNE, LAURENCE, Nov. 24, 1713 (County Tipperary, Ire.)–Mar. 18, 1768. English novelist. His novel *Tristram Shandy* (9 vols., 1759–67) anticipated the interior-monologue device of 20th-cent. fiction.

STEVENSON, ROBERT LOUIS BALFOUR, Nov. 13, 1859 (Edinburgh, Scot.)–Dec. 3, 1894. Scottish novelist, essayist, critic, poet. Wrote romantic adventure and mystery stories, especially popular among the young; in ill health most of his life, traveled constantly to find a favorable climate; lived his last five years on Samoa as a planter, collaborating on novels with his stepson. *New Arabian Nights*, 1882; *Treasure Island*, 1883; *A Child's Garden of Verses*, 1885; *Kidnapped*, 1806; *The Strange Case of Dr. Jekyll and Mr. Hyde*, 1886.

STOPPARD, TOM, July 3, 1937 (Czech.). English playwright. Author of plays noted for their verbal brilliance. *Rosencrantz and Guildenstern Are Dead*, 1967; *The Real Inspector Hound*, 1968; *Jumpers*, 1972; *Travesties*, 1975.

SWIFT, JONATHAN, Nov. 30, 1667 (Dublin, Ire.)–Oct. 19, 1745. Anglo-Irish satirist, poet, political pamphleteer, clergyman. Leading Tory writer; Irish national hero for *Drapier Letters* (1724) and *A Modest Proposal* (1729); best known for his satirical masterpiece, *Gulliver's Travels* (4 parts, 1726). "The Battle of the Books," 1704; "A Tale of a Tub," 1704; *Argument against Abolishing Christianity*, 1708; *Journal to Stella*, 1710–13.

SWINBURNE, ALGERNON CHARLES, Apr. 5, 1837 (London, Eng.)–Apr. 10, 1909. English poet, critic. Wrote poetry noted for its vigor, music, and prosodic innovations; a symbol of the mid-Victorian poetic revolt; suffered from epilepsy, alcoholism, and masochism. *Atalanta in Calydon*, 1865; *Poems and Ballads*, 1866; *Songs before Sunrise*, 1871; *Essays and Studies*, 1871.

SYNGE, JOHN MILLINGTON, Apr. 16, 1871 (nr. Dublin, Ire.)–Mar. 24, 1909. Irish dramatist, poet. Major figure of the Irish literary renaissance; wrote poetic dramas about the lives of peasants and fishers of the Aran Is. and western Ireland. *The Shadow of the Glen*, 1903; *Riders to the Sea*, 1904; *The Playboy of the Western World*, 1907; *Deirdre of the Sorrows*, 1910.

TENNYSON, ALFRED, 1ST BARON (known popularly as Alfred, Lord Tennyson), Aug. 6, 1809 (Lincolnshire, Eng.)–Oct. 6, 1892. English poet. Spokesman for the Victorian age; poet laureate of England, 1850–92; best-known poems include "The Lotus-Eaters," "The Lady of Shalott," "Morte d'Arthur," and "The Charge of the Light Brigade"; created a peer, 1884. *Idylls of the King*, 1859; *Enoch Arden*, 1864; *Demeter and Other Poems*, 1889.

THACKERAY, WILLIAM MAKEPEACE, July 18, 1811 (Calcutta, India)–Dec. 24, 1863. English novelist. Noted for his satirical novels about upper- and middle-class life in 19th-cent. London; best known for *Vanity Fair* (1848), in which he created the unscrupulous yet appealing Becky Sharp. *Book of Snobs*, 1848; *Th History of Henry Esmond Esq.*, 1852.

THOMAS, DYLAN, Oct. 27, 1914 (Swansea, Wales)–Nov. 9, 1953. Welsh poet, prose writer. Created an individualistic poetic style, based on sound and rhythm; died of alcoholism. *Portrait of the Artist as a Young Dog*, 1940; *Deaths and Entrances*, 1946; *A Child's Christmas in Wales*, 1954; *Under Milk Wood*, 1954; *Adventures in the Skin Trade*, 1955.

TOLKIEN, J(ohn) **R**(onald) **R**(euel), Jan. 3, 1892 (Bloemfontein, S. A.)–Sept. 2, 1973. English author, scholar. Created adult fairy tales which gained great popularity during the 1960s; a prominent philologist, taught at Oxford U., 1925–59. *The Hobbit*, 1938; *The Lord of the Rings*, (trilogy), 1954–56; *The Silmarillion*, 1977.

TROLLOPE, ANTHONY, Apr. 24, 1815 (London, Eng.)–Dec. 6, 1882. English novelist. Best known for his Barchester novels, chronicles of Victorian life in a cathedral town; his series of Palliser novels was adapted into a popular television series. *The Warden*, 1855; *Barchester Towers*, 1857; *Doctor Thorne*, 1858; *Phineas Finn*, 1869.

WALPOLE, HORACE (or Horatio) **4TH EARL OF ORFORD,** Sept. 24, 1717 (London, Eng.)–Mar. 2, 1797. English novelist, letter-writer. Wrote over 3,000 witty, charming letters (1626–96), giving a picture of Georgian England; his medieval horror tale, *The Castle of Otranto* (1765), began the fashion for Gothic romances. (Son of Sir ROBERT WALPOLE.)

WALTON, IZAAK, Aug. 9, 1593 (Stafford, Eng.)-Dec. 15, 1683. English writer. Best known as the author of *The Compleat Angler* (1676), a discourse on the pleasures of fishing that was revised and reissued several times; also wrote intimate biographies of friends, including JOHN DONNE and George Herbert.

WAUGH, ALEC, born Alexander Raban Waugh, July 8, 1898 (London, Eng.). English novelist, travel writer. Author of popular novels, many about tropical countries. *Island in the Sun*, 1956; *The Mule on the Minaret*, 1965; *A Spy in the Family*, 1970. (Brother of EVELYN WAUGH.)

WAUGH, EVELYN ARTHUR ST. JOHN, Oct. 18, 1903 (London, Eng.)-Apr. 10, 1966. English novelist. Wrote sophisticated satires on 20th-cent. life. *Decline and Fall*, 1928; *Vile Bodies*, 1930; *Black Mischief*, 1932; *Brideshead Revisited*, 1945; *The Loved One*, 1948. (Brother of ALEC WAUGH.)

WEBSTER, JOHN, c.1575 (London, Eng.)-c.1634. English dramatist. Best known for two revenge tragedies, *The White Devil* (c.1612) and *The Duchess of Malfi* (c.1613), notable for their graphic language, portrayal of evil and human suffering, and strong satiric element.

WEST, DAME REBECCA, born Cicily Isabel Fairfield, Dec. 25, 1892 (County Kerry, Ire.). English novelist, critic, journalist. Noted for social and cultural criticism—especially her reports on the Nuremberg trials, collected in *A Train of Powder* (1955), and her examination of Balkan politics, culture, and history in *Black Lamb and Grey Falcon* (2 vols., 1942).

WHITE, T(erence) H(anbury), May 29, 1906 (Bombay, Ind.)-Jan. 17, 1964. English novelist, social historian. Best known for his adaptation of Sir THOMAS MALORY's *Morte D'Arthur* as *The Once and Future King* (4 vols., 1939-58), which in turn was adapted into the musical *Camelot* (1960). *The Goshawk*, 1951; *A Book of Beasts*, 1954.

WILDE, OSCAR FINGALL O'FLAHERTIE WILLS, Oct. 16, 1854 (Dublin, Ire.)-Nov. 30, 1900. Anglo-Irish playwright, novelist. Wrote witty, sophisticated plays, such as his masterpiece, *The Importance of Being Earnest* (1895); renowned for his wit and eccentricity; at the height of his career, sentenced to two years' hard labor for homosexuality, during which time he wrote the confessional "De Profundis" (1905). *Lady Windermere's Fan*, 1892; *A Woman of No Importance*, 1893; *An Ideal Husband*, 1895; "The Ballad of Reading Gaol," 1898.

WODEHOUSE, SIR P(elham G(renville), Oct. 15, 1881 (Surrey, Eng.)-Feb. 14, 1975. English novelist, short-story writer, playwright, screenwriter. Prolific author best known for his farces about the English gentry in late Edwardian era, especially those featuring Bertie Wooster and his "gentleman's personal gentleman," the impeccable Jeeves; knighted, 1975. *The Man with Two Left Feet*, 1917; *The Inimitable Jeeves*, 1924; *Bertie Wooster Sees It Through*, 1955.

WOOLF, (Adeline) VIRGINIA, née Stephen, Jan. 25, 1882 (London, Eng.)-Mar. 28, 1941. English novelist, short-story writer, playwright, screenwriter. Prolific author best known for his farces about a poetic, symbolic style and stream-of-consciousness technique; her criticism includes the classic feminist essay, "A Room of One's Own" (1929); with her husband, Leonard Woolf, stood at the center of the Bloomsbury group; plagued by instability all her life, committed suicide by drowning. *Jacob's Room*, 1922; *Mrs. Dalloway*, 1925; *To the Lighthouse*, 1927; *Orlando*, 1928; *The Waves*, 1931 (Daughter of Sir LESLIE STEPHEN.)

WORDSWORTH, WILLIAM, Apr. 7, 1770 (Cumberland, Eng.)-Apr. 23, 1850. English poet. A leader of the English Romantic movement; known for his worship of nature and humanitarianism; with his friend S. T. COLERIDGE, wrote *Lyrical Ballads* (1798); poet laureate of England, 1843-50. *Poems in Two Volumes*, 1807; *The Prelude*, 1850.

YEATS, WILLIAM BUTLER. June 13, 1865 (Dublin, Ire.)-Jan. 28, 1939. Irish poet, playwright. Leader of the Irish literary renaissance; in his early, lyrical poetry, was influenced by the Pre-Raphaelites and Irish mythology; later turned to more realistic and profound themes; a founder of the Abbey Theatre in Dublin, for which he wrote and produced plays; awarded Nobel Prize in literature, 1923. *The Wanderings of Oisin*, 1889; *The Countess Cathleen*, 1899; *The Wild Swans at Coole*, 1917; *The Tower*, 1928; *Last Poems*, 1940.

FRENCH WRITERS

ANOUILH, JEAN, June 23, 1910 (Bordeaux, Fr.). French dramatist, screenwriter. *Antigone*, 1942; *Ring Round the Moon*, 1947; *The Waltz of the Toreadors*, 1952; *The Lark*, 1953; *Becket*, 1959.

ARAGON, LOUIS, Oct. 3, 1897 (Paris, Fr.). French poet, novelist, critic. A leader of the Dadaists and later of the surrealists; spokesman for the French Resistance during WW II; intellectual leader of the French Communist Party. *The Peasant of Paris*, 1926; *A Poet of Resurgent France*, 1946; *Background for Death*, 1965.

BALZAC, HONORE DE, May 20, 1799 (Tours, Fr.)-Aug. 18, 1850. French novelist. A founder of the realistic school; his masterpiece, *Le Comédie Humaine* (inc. *Eugénie Grandet*, 1833; and *Le Pere Goriot*, 1835), took 20 years to complete and constitutes a social history of France. *Les Chouans*, 1829; *La Peau de Chagrin*, 1831.

BAUDELAIRE, CHARLES, Apr. 9, 1821 (Paris, Fr.)-Aug. 31, 1867. French poet, critic, translator. Author of powerful, expressionistic poetry, much of which was barred during his lifetime; credited with inventing symbolism; translated E. A. POE; led an eccentric, decadent, tragic life. *Les Fleurs du Mal*, 1857; *Curiosités esthetiques*, 1868; *Petits Poèmes en proses*, 1869.

BEAUMARCHAIS, PIERRE AUGUSTIN CARON DE, Jan. 24, 1732 (Paris, Fr.)-May 18, 1799. French dramatist. Two of his comic masterpieces satirizing upper-class behavior were adapted into famous operas: *The Barber of Seville* (1775) for G. A. ROSSINI's opera of the same name and *The Marriage of Figaro* (1784) for W. A. MOZART's opera of the same name.

BEAUVOIR, SIMONE LUCIE ERNESTINE MARIE DE, Jan. 9, 1908 (Paris, Fr.). French novelist, essayist. Part of the existentialist movement; an influential feminist. *The Blood of Others*, 1948; *The Second Sex*, 1949-50; *The Mandarins*, 1955; *Memoirs of a Dutiful Daughter*, 1958; *The Coming of Age*, 1970.

BOULLE, PIERRE FRANÇOIS MARIE-LOUIS, Feb. 20, 1912 (Avignon, Fr.). French novelist. *The Bridge over the River Kwai*, 1952; *Planet of the Apes*, 1963.

WRITERS

BRETON, ANDRÉ, Feb. 19, 1896 (France)–Sept. 28, 1966. French poet, novelist, essayist. Founded the surrealist movement, writing its manifestos in 1924, 1930, and 1934; experimented with automatic writing.

BRUNHOFF, JEAN DE, 1899–1937. French author/illustrator. Wrote and illustrated a popular series of children's books about Babar, the king of the elephants. *The Story of Babar the Little Elephant,* 1931; *Babar's Travels,* 1935; *Babar the King,* 1936.

CAMUS, ALBERT, Nov. 7, 1913 (Mondovi, Algeria)–Jan. 4, 1960. French philosopher, novelist, dramatist, journalist. Wrote chiefly about the absurd—the meaninglessness of existence; associated with J. P. SARTRE and the existentialists; awarded Nobel Prize in literature, 1957. *The Stranger,* 1942; *Caligula,* 1944; *The Plague,* 1948; *The Rebel,* 1951; *State of Siege,* 1958.

CHATEAUBRIAND, FRANÇOIS RENÉ, VICOMTE DE, Sept. 4, 1768 (St. Malo, Fr.)–July 4, 1848. French novelist. Wrote the first romantic fiction. *Atala,* 1801; *René,* 1805; *Les Natchez,* 1826.

CHRETIEN DE TROYES, fl.1160–1190. French poet. His early Arthurian legends, written in eight-syllable rhymed couplets, incorporated the ideals of the 12th-cent. court to which he was attached. *Erec et Enide; Cliges; Lancelot, or The Knight of the Cart; Percival, or The Story of the Grail.*

CLAUDEL, PAUL LOUIS MARIE, Aug. 6, 1868 (Villeneuve-sur-Fère, Fr.)–Feb. 23, 1955. French dramatist, poet. Used religious symbols, exotic backgrounds, pantomime, ballet, music and film techniques in his plays. *Tidings Brought to Mary,* 1912; *The Satin Slipper,* 1929.

COCTEAU, JEAN, July 5, 1889 (Maisons-Lafitte, Fr.)–Oct. 11, 1963. French poet, novelist, playwright, essayist, filmmaker, craftsman, artist. Stood in the forefront of 20th-cent. avant-garde movements. *Orphée,* 1926; *Les Enfants Terribles,* 1929; *The Blood of the Poet* (film), 1933; *Beauty and the Beast* (film), 1946.

COLETTE (pseud.: Willy), born Sidonie Gabrielle Colette, Jan. 28, 1873 (St. Sauveur-en-Puisaye, Fr.)–Aug. 3, 1954. French novelist. Her novels about relationships between men and women are noted for their intimate style and deep feeling for nature; with her husband, wrote the early Claudine series under her pseudonym; the first woman pres. of the Goncourt Acad.; the second woman to be made grand officer of the French Legion of Honor. *Claudine at School,* 1900; *The Innocent Wife,* 1903; *Cheri,* 1920; *La Maison de Claudine,* 1922; *Sido,* 1929; *Gigi,* 1945.

CORNEILLE, PIERRE, June 6, 1606 (Rouen, Fr.)–Sept. 30, 1684. French dramatist. The father of French tragedy; borrowed themes from history and classic mythology. *Melite,* 1629; *Médée,* 1635; *Le Cid,* 1637; *Horace,* 1640; *Cinna,* 1640; *Polyeucte,* 1643; *Le Menteur,* 1643.

CREVECOEUR, MICHEL GUILLAUME JEAN DE (pseud.: Hector Saint-John de Crèvecoeur, J. Hector St. John, Agricola). Jan. 31, 1735 (Lesches, Fr.)–Nov. 12, 1813. French-U.S. writer, naturalist. In his *Letters from an American Farmer* (1782), painted a vivid picture of 18th-cent. American rural life. *Sketches of Eighteenth Century America,* 1925 (published posthumously).

CYRANO DE BERGERAC, SAVINIEN, Mar. 6, 1619 (Paris, Fr.)–July 28, 1655. French novelist, playwright. Wrote fantasies about trips to the sun and moon; his fiery temper, dueling skill, and long nose are fairly accurately portrayed in EDMOND ROSTAND's 1897 play, *Cyrano de Bergerac. Comical History of the States and Empires of the Moon,* 1656; *Comical History of the States and Empires of the Sun,* 1661.

DAUDET, ALPHONSE, May 13, 1840 (Nimes, Fr.)–Dec. 16, 1897. French novelist, short-story writer. Author of humorous, sympathetic stories of provincial and Parisian life. *Letters from My Mill,* 1866; *Le Petit Chose,* 1868; *Tartarin de Tarascon,* 1872, 1885, 1890.

DUMAS, ALEXANDRE (Dumas père), born Davy de la Pailleterie, July 24, 1802 (Villers-Cotterêts, Fr.)–Dec. 5, 1870. French novelist. Published almost 300 books working with a "factory" of collaborators; accused of pilfering plots and rewriting history; best known for his popular novels, including *The Count of Monte Cristo* (1844) and *The Three Musketeers* (1844). (Father of ALEXANDRE DUMAS, fils)

DUMAS, ALEXANDRE (Dumas fils), July 27, 1824 (Paris, Fr.)–Nov. 27, 1895. French dramatist, novelist. The illegitimate son of ALEXANDRE DUMAS (père); noted for his realistic comedies of manners produced during the reign of Napoleon III; his *La Dame aux Camélias* (novel, 1848; play, 1852) was the basis for GUISEPPE VERDI's opera *La Traviata.*

DURAS, MARGUERITE, née Donnadieu, Apr. 4, 1914 (Giadinh, Indochina [now Vietnam]). French novelist, playwright, screenwriter. *The Sea Wall,* 1952; *Hiroshima, Mon Amour* (screenplay), 1959; *The Rapture of L. V. Stein,* 1967.

ELUARD, PAUL, born Eugene Grindel, Dec. 14, 1895 (Paris, Fr.)–Nov. 18, 1952. French poet. A founder of the surrealist movement; one of the leaders of the French Resistance in WW II. *To Die of Not Being,* 1924; *The Immaculate Conception* (with ANDRÉ BRETON), 1930; *Cours naturel,* 1938; *Poèmes politiques,* 1948.

FEYDEAU, GEORGES LEON JULES MARIE, Dec. 8, 1862 (Paris, Fr.)–June 5, 1921. French dramatist. His bedroom farces, comedies of manners, and comedies of character dominated Paris for 15 years. *L'Hôtel du Libre-Echange,* 1894; *The Lady from Maxim's,* 1907; *Occupe-toi d'Amelie,* 1908.

FLAUBERT, GUSTAVE, Dec. 12, 1821 (Rouen, Fr.)–May 8, 1880. French novelist. The objective, detailed realism of his *Madame Bovary* (1857) made it a literary landmark; his story "Un Coeur Simple" (1875–77) is also a classic.

FRANCE, ANATOLE (pseud. of Jacques Anatole Thibault), Apr. 16, 1844 (Paris, Fr.)–Oct. 13, 1924. French novelist, poet, critic. The most prominent and prolific French man of letters of his day; awarded Nobel Prize in literature, 1921. *The Crime of Sylvester Bonnard,* 1881; *The Red Lily,* 1894; *Penguin Island,* 1909.

GAUTIER, (Pierre Jules) THEOPHILE, Aug. 31, 1811 (Hautes-Pyrénées, Fr.)–Oct. 23, 1872. French poet, novelist, critic. Advocated "art for art's sake"; a forerunner of the Parnassian school. *Mademoiselle de Maupin,* 1835; *Emaux et Camées,* 1852.

GENET, JEAN, Dec. 19, 1910 (Paris, Fr.). French dramatist, essayist. An aesthete, existentialist, pioneer of the theater of the absurd; spent much of his youth in reformatories and prisons, pardoned from life imprisonment after the intervention of A. GIDE, J. P. SARTRE, J. COCTEAU and others; his powerful, stylized dramas include *The Maids* (1948), *The Balcony* (1957), and *The Blacks* (1959).

THE BOOK OF WHO

GIDE, ANDRE PAUL GUILLAUME, Nov. 22, 1869 (Paris, Fr.)–Feb. 19, 1951. French novelist, essayist. Prolific, unconventional author, influential as a moralist and philosopher as well as a writer; one of the founders of the *Nouvelle Revue Française*, the most important literary journal of its time; awarded Nobel Prize in literature, 1947. *The Immoralist*, 1902; *Strait Is the Gate*, 1924; *Travels in the Congo*, 1927; *Return from the USSR*, 1936.

GIRAUDOUX, (Hippolyte) **JEAN,** Oct. 29, 1882 (Haute-Vienne, Fr.)–Jan. 31, 1944. French dramatist, novelist, diplomat. A prolific writer best known for his early fanciful novels and whimsical plays that, under the direction of Louis Jouvet, were popular in the 1930s. *My Friend from Limousin*, 1922; *Tiger at the Gates*, 1935; *Ondine*, 1939; *The Madwoman of Chaillot*, 1945.

GONCOURT, EDMOND LOUIS ANTOINE HUOT DE, May 26, 1822 (Nancy, Fr.)–July 16, 1896; and his brother **GONCOURT, JULES ALFRED HUOT DE,** Dec. 17, 1830 (Paris, Fr.)–June 20, 1870. French novelists, art critics, historians, diarists. Inseparable personally and professionally, known as *les deux Goncourt;* collaborated on several popular novels, including *Renée Mauperin* (1864), that initiated the naturalistic movement; wrote the *Journal des Goncourt* (9 vols., 1887–96), featuring accounts of Parisian society; Edmond's will provided funds for the Goncourt Acad., which annually awards the Goncourt Prize in fiction.

HUGO, VICTOR, Feb. 26, 1802 (Besançon, Fr.)–May 22, 1885. French poet, novelist, dramatist. Stood in the forefront of the Romantic movement; a peer under Louis-Philippe, elected to the popular assembly, 1848; opposed Napoleon III, exiled to the Channel Is. for 18 years; on his return, served as a senator under the Third Republic. *Les Feuilles d'automne* (poetry), 1831; *Notre Dame de Paris*, 1831; *Les Châtiments* (poetry), 1853; *Les Misérables* (novel), 1862.

HUYSMANS, (Joris) **KARL,** born Charles Marie George Huysmans, Feb. 5, 1848 (Paris, Fr.)–May 12, 1907. French novelist. First pres. of Goncourt Acad. *Marthe*, 1876; *Against Nature*, 1884.

IONESCO, EUGENE, Nov. 26, 1912 (Slatina, Rum.). French playwright. Inaugurated the theater of the absurd with his one-act classic, *The Bald Soprano* (1950). *The Chairs*, 1952; *Rhinoceros*, 1959; *Exit the King*, 1963.

LA BRUYERE, JEAN DE, Aug. 16, 1645 (Paris, Fr.)–May 10, 1696. French satirist. Best known for *Characters of Theophrastus Translated from the Greek, with Characters or the Manners of this Century* (1688), a social satire including more than 1000 character sketches and aphorisms describing the arrogance and stupidity of the ruling classes.

LA FAYETTE, MARIE MADELEINE PIOCHE DE LA VERGNE, COMTESSE DE, Mar. 16, 1634 (Paris, Fr.)–May 25, 1693. French novelist. Best known for *The Princess of Cleves* (1678), the realistic story of a married woman's struggle to remain faithful to her husband.

LA FONTAINE, JEAN DE, July 8, 1621 (Chateau-Thierry, Fr.)–Apr. 13, 1695. French poet. Noted for his *Selected Fables Versified* (1668–94), 12 books of 230 tales, taken largely from AESOP.

LAMARTINE, ALPHONSE DE, Oct. 21, 1790 (Mâcon, Fr.)–Feb. 28, 1869. French poet, novelist, statesman. His *Meditations poetiques* (1820) in-

fluenced the French Romantic movement; with *Histoire des Girondins* (1847), helped bring about the Revolution of 1848; headed the short-lived provisional government, before losing out to Napoleon III.

LA ROCHEFOUCAULD, FRANÇOIS, DUC DE, Sept. 15, 1613 (Paris, Fr.)–Mar. 17, 1680. French writer. Noted for *Reflexions ou sentences et maximes morales* (5 ed., 1665–78), pessimistic epigrams based on the belief that behavior derives from self-love.

LESAGE, ALAIN RENE, May 8, 1668 (Brittany, Fr.)–Nov. 17, 1747. French novelist, dramatist. His masterpiece, *The Adventures of Gil Blas of Santillane* (1715–35), was influential in the development of the realistic novel; first known French writer to live by writing alone. *Turcaret*, 1709.

MALLARME, STEPHANE, Mar. 18, 1842 (Paris, Fr.)–Sept. 9, 1898. French poet. Leader of the symbolist movement. *Hérodiade* (begun 1864, never completed); *L'Après-midi d'un Faune*, 1876; *Poésies Complètes*, 1887.

MALRAUX, ANDRE, Nov. 3, 1901 (Paris, Fr.)–Nov. 23, 1977. French novelist, art historian, public official. Participated in revolutionary movements in China and Indochina, 1924–27; fought against F. FRANCO in the Spanish Civil War, 1936–39; hero and leader of the French Resistance during WW II; French min. of information, 1945, 1958; min. of cultural affairs, 1959–69. *Man's Fate*, 1933; *Man's Hope*, 1937; *The Voices of Silence*, 1951; *Antimémoirs*, 1967.

MARTIN DU GARD, ROGER, Mar. 23, 1881 (Neuilly-sur-Seine, Fr.)–Aug. 22, 1958. French novelist, dramatist. Best known for the eight-part cyclical novel, *The World of the Thibaults* (1922–40), a panoramic survey of French society in the early 20th cent.; awarded Nobel Prize in literature, 1937. *Jean Barois*, 1913; *Le Testament du Père Leleu*, 1913; *La Gonfle*, 1928; *Un Taciturne*, 1931.

MAUPASSANT, (Henry Rene Albert) **GUY DE,** Aug. 5, 1850 (nr. Dieppe, Fr.)–July 6, 1893. French short-story writer. Master of the short story; best-known stories include "Ball of Fat," (1880), "A Piece of String," "The House of Mme. Tellier," (1881), "Moonlight," (1884), "Mlle. Fifi," (1882); suffering from insanity caused by syphilis, died in a sanitarium.

MAURIAC, FRANÇOIS, Oct. 11, 1885 (Bordeaux, Fr.)–Sept. 1, 1970. French novelist, essayist, dramatist. A major writer in the French Catholic tradition; awarded Nobel Prize in literature, 1952. *The Kiss to the Leper*, 1923; *Desert of Love*, 1925; *Viper's Tangle*, 1932; *Mémoires*, 1959–67.

MAUROIS, ANDRE, born Emile Salomon Wilhelm Herzog, July 26, 1885 (Elbeuf, Fr.)–Oct. 9, 1967. French biographer, novelist, essayist, man of letters. Best known for his biographies, especially those of P. SHELLEY, BYRON, VICTOR HUGO, GEORGE SAND, H. BALZAC, and M. PROUST; elected to French Academy, 1938; knighted by the British Empire, 1938. *Ariel*, 1923; *Byron*, 1930; *Olympio*, 1954; *Lélia*, 1952; *Prometheus, the Life of Balzac*, 1965; *The Quest for Proust*, 1950.

MERIMEE, PROSPER, Sept. 28, 1803 (Paris, Fr.)–Sept. 23, 1870. French dramatist, short-story writer, historian. Best known for his restrained, ironic short stories and novellas; elected to French Academy, 1844; made a senator, 1853. *Mateo Falcone*, 1829; *Colomba*, 1840; *Carmen* (the basis for G. BIZET's opera), 1847.

34

MISTRAL, FRÉDÉRIC, Sept. 8, 1830 (Maillane, Fr.)–Mar. 25, 1914. French poet. Led the 19th-cent. revival of Provençal language and literature; awarded Nobel Prize in literature, 1904. *Mirèio,* 1859; *My Origins,* 1906.

MOLIÈRE (pseud. of Jean Baptiste Poquelin), baptized Jan. 15, 1622 (Paris, Fr.)–Feb. 17, 1673. French dramatist. A versatile comic dramatist whose works range from high comedy to broad farce; championed natural man, ridiculed the pretensions and hypocrisy of the bourgeoisie. *The School for Wives,* 1662; *Tartuffe,* 1664; *Le Misanthrope,* 1666; *The Miser,* 1668; *Le Bourgeois Gentilhomme,* 1670; *The Imaginary Invalid,* 1673.

MONTAIGNE, MICHEL EYQUEM DE, Feb. 28, 1533 (Château de Montaigne, nr. Bordeaux, Fr.)–Sept. 13, 1592. French essayist. With his informal, unpretentious essays, established a new literary form; wrote three volumes of essays (1580, 1588, 1595); advocated humanistic morality.

MUSSET, (Louis-Charles) ALFRED DE, Dec. 11, 1810 (Paris, Fr.)–May 2, 1857. French poet, playwright. An important French romantic, best known for his satiric and lyrical poetry. *La Confession d'un enfant du siècle,* 1836; *Lorenzaccio,* 1834; *Il ne faut jurer de rien,* 1836; "La Nuit d'Octobre," 1837.

2 NIN, ANAÏS, Feb. 21, 1903 (Paris, Fr.)–Jan. 14, 1977. French-U.S. diarist, novelist, short-story writer. Became a cult figure for her poetic novels; won wide readership with her diaries, which spanned 60 years in the U.S. and bohemian Paris. *House of Incest,* 1934; *Winter of Artifice,* 1939; *Diary of Anaïs Nin,* 1966; *Delta of Venus,* 1977.

PÉGUY, CHARLES, Jan. 7, 1873 (Orleans, Fr.)–Sept. 5, 1914. French poet, philosopher. Founded the influential journal *Cahiers de la Quinzaine,* 1900; a Christian, socialist, and strong supporter of A. DREYFUS; killed in action in WW I. *Mystère de la charité de Jeanne d'Arc,* 1910; *Eve,* 1913.

PERSE, ST.-JOHN (pseud. of Marie René Auguste Alexis Léger), Mar. 31, 1887 (Saint-Léger des Feuilles, Guadeloupe)–Sept. 20, 1975. French poet, diplomat. Noted for his obscure poetry and use of exotic words; awarded Nobel Prize in literature, 1960. *Anabase,* 1925; *Exil,* 1942; *Winds,* 1946; *Seamarks,* 1957; *Chronique,* 1960; *Birds,* 1962.

PRÉVOST, ABBÉ, born Antoine François Prévost d'Exiles, Apr. 1, 1697 (Hesdin, Fr.)–Nov. 25, 2763. French novelist. Noted for *Histoire du Chevalier des Grieux et de Manon Lescaut* (1731), a classic "novel of feeling" later adapted into the operas *Manon* (1884) by JULES MASSENET and *Manon Lescaut* (1893) by GIACOMO PUCCINI.

PROUST, MARCEL, July 10, 1871 (Anteuil, Fr.)–Nov. 18, 1922. French novelist. Best known for his seven-volume semiautobiographical opus, *Remembrance of Things Past* (1913–27), told as an allegorical search for truth and written in a highly stylized style; the sickly child of wealthy parents, he lived virtually as a recluse in his cork-lined room after their deaths.

RABELAIS, FRANÇOIS, c.1490 (Poitou, Fr.)–probably Apr. 9, 1533. French novelist. Best known as author of the comic masterpiece *Gargantua and Pantagruel* (4 books, 1532–52; another volume, published after his death, is of questionable authorship); noted for his broad, often ribald humor (adjective *Rabelaisian* means coarsely and boisterously satirical); a monk, later an eminent physician and humanist.

RACINE, JEAN, Dec. 22, 1639 (La Ferté-Milon, Fr.)–Apr. 21, 1699. French dramatist. The model of French classicism; supplanted P. CORNEILLE as the foremost French tragic dramatist; a rival of MOLIÈRE; elected to the French Academy, 1672. *Andromaque,* 1667; *Britannicus,* 1669; *Bérénice,* 1670; *Bajazet,* 1672; *Mithridate,* 1673; *Iphigenie en Aulide,* 1674; *Phèdre,* 1677.

RESTIF DE LA BRETONNE, NICHOLAS EDME, born Nicholas-Edme Restif, Oct. 23, 1734 (Sacy, Fr.)–Feb. 3, 1806. French novelist. Called the Rousseau of the Gutter and the Voltaire of Chambermaids; wrote some 250 rambling, coarse, erotic novels about lower-class life. *Le Pied de Fanchette,* 1769; *Le Paysan perverti,* 1775; *Les Parisiennes,* 1787; *Monsieur Nicolas,* 16 vols., 1794–97.

RIMBAUD, (Jean Nicolas) ARTHUR, Oct. 20, 1854 (Charleville, Fr.)–Nov. 10, 1891. French poet. Wrote original, imaginative, dreamlike verse; his prose-poems anticipated the surrealists. *Illuminations,* 1886; *The Drunken Boat,* 1871; *A Season in Hell,* 1873.

ROBBE-GRILLET, ALAIN, Aug. 18, 1922 (Brest, Fr.). French novelist. Originated the French *nouveau roman,* the "antinovel" of the 1950s, which described images without commentary and was often marked by violence. *The Erasers,* 1953; *The Voyeur,* 1955; *Jealousy,* 1957; *Towards a New Novel,* 1963; *Last Year at Marienbad* (screenplay), 1961.

ROLLAND, ROMAIN, Jan. 29, 1866 (Clamecy, Fr.)–Dec. 30, 1944. French novelist, dramatist, biographer, essayist. An apostle of heroic idealism; best known as author of the epic *Jean Christophe* (10 vols., 1904–12), which introduced the *roman fleuve,* or novel cycle, to France; a political activist, was involved in the DREYFUS affair; awarded Nobel Prize in literature, 1914. *Life of Beethoven,* 1903; *Life of Michelangelo,* 1905; *The Soul Enchanted,* 1922–23.

RONSARD, PIERRE DE, Sept. 11, 1524 (La Possonnière, Fr.)–Dec. 27, 1585. French poet. Leader of the Pléiade, seven writers who advocated adopting the language and literary forms of the classics to French literature. *Les Amours,* 1552; *Les Hymnes,* 1555–56; *Sonnets pour Hélène,* 1578; *La Franciade,* 1572.

ROSTAND, EDMOND, Apr. 1, 1868 (Marseilles, Fr.)–Dec. 2, 1918. French dramatist. Best known for his play *Cyrano de Bergerac* (1897), a colorful combination of comedy and pathos that starred the famous actor Constant Coquelin. *L'Aiglon,* 1900.

SADE, MARQUIS DE, born Donatien Alphonse François, Comte de Sade, June 2, 1740 (Paris, Fr.)–Dec. 2, 1814. French writer. Noted for his licentious prose narratives and plays; imprisoned for scandalous conduct, institutionalized for a total of 27 years for sexual offenses; during his last confinement, directed inmates in theatrical performances. *The Adversities of Virtue,* 1787; *Crimes of Love,* 1788.

SAGAN, FRANÇOISE (pseud. of Françoise Quoirez), June 21, 1935 (Carjac, Fr.). French novelist. Author of short works in the tradition of the French psychological novel. *Bonjour Tristesse,* 1945; *A Certain Smile,* 1953; *Do You Like Brahms?,* 1959.

SAINT-EXUPERY, ANTOINE MARIE ROGER DE, June 29, 1900 (Lyons, Fr.)–July 31, 1944. French writer, aviator. Wrote poetic narratives about aviation, but best known for the fable *The*

Little Prince (1943), read both by children and adults; lost in action in WW II. *Southern Mail,* 1929; *Night Freight,* 1932; *Wind, Sand, and Stars,* 1939.

SAND, GEORGE (pseud. of Amandine Aurore Lucile Dupin, Baronne Dudevant), July 1, 1804 (Paris, Fr.)–June 8, 1876. French novelist. Wrote rustic tales of love that transcends convention and class; led an unconventional life, including liaisons with PROSPER MÉRIMÉE, ALFRED DE MUSSET, FRÉDÉRIC CHOPIN, others. *Indiana,* 1832; *Valentine,* 1832; *Lélia,* 1833, *Tales of a Grandmother,* 1873.

SÉVIGNÉ, MARIE DE RABUTIN CHANTAL, MARQUISE DE, Feb. 5, 1626 (Paris, Fr.)–Apr. 17, 1696. French writer. Wrote more than 1,500 letters, models of the epistolary genre, in French and other languages; the letters, written in an elegant but unaffected style, provide a portrait of her age.

STAËL, GERMAINE DE, born Anne Louise Germaine Necker, after her marriage, Baronne de Staël-Holstein, Apr. 22, 1766 (Paris, Fr.)–July 14, 1817. French woman of letters. A theorist of Romanticism, she publicized the German Romantic movement, held salons for leading intellectuals in Paris and Geneva. *Delphine,* 1802; *Corinne,* 1807; *D'l'Allemagne,* 1818; *Considérations sur les principaux événements de la Révolution française,* 1818.

STENDHAL (pseud. of Marie Henri Beyle), Jan. 23, 1783 (Grenoble, Fr.)–Mar. 23, 1842. French novelist. Best known for two masterpieces of psychological and political insight, *The Red and the Black* (1830) and *The Charterhouse of Parma* (1839).

SULLY PRUDHOMME, born René François Armand Prudhomme, Mar. 16, 1839 (Paris, Fr.)–Sept. 7, 1907. French poet. Leading member of the anti-Romantic Parnassans; elected to the French Acad., 1881; awarded Nobel Prize in literature, 1901. *Stances et poèmes,* 1865; *Les Épreuves,* 1866; *La Justice,* 1878; *Le Bonheur,* 1888.

VALÉRY, PAUL AMBROISE TOUSSAINT JULES, Oct. 30, 1871 (Sete, Fr.)–July 20, 1945. French poet, critic. Associated with the symbolists; elected to the French Acad., 1925; pres. of the Committee for Intellectual Cooperation of the League of Nations, 1936; appointed to chair of poetry at the College de France 1937. *La Jeune Parque,* 1917; *Charmes,* 1922; *Variété,* 5 vols., 1922–44.

VERLAINE, PAUL, Mar. 30, 1844 (Metz. Fr.)–Jan. 8, 1896. French poet. One of the first symbolists, noted for his original, musical poetry; prominent in the bohemian literary life of Paris; his marriage ended because of his liaison with protégé A. RIMBAUD, whom he shot and wounded in a quarrel; sentenced to two years in prison. *Poèmes saturniens,* 1866; *Fêtes galantes,* 1869; *Romances sans paroles,* 1874; *Parallelement,* 1889.

VIGNY, ALFRED VICTOR, COMTE DE, Mar. 27, 1797 (Loche, Fr.)–Sept. 17, 1863. French poet, playwright, novelist. A leading French Romantic who wrote deeply pessimistic poetry and prose; translated *Othello* (1829) and *The Merchant of Venice* (1829) into French verse; elected to the French Acad., 1845. *Cinq-Mars,* 1826; *The Military Necessity,* 1835; *Chatterton,* 1835; *The Fates,* 1864.

VILLON, FRANÇOIS, born François de Montaubier or François de Loges, 1431 (Paris, Fr.)–after 1463. French poet. A brilliant student who took the name of his patron; led a life of crime,

narrowly escaping the gallows in 1463; banished from Paris for 10 years, he disappeared. "Ballade des dames du temps jadis"; "Ballade pur prier Notre Dame"; *Little Testament,* 1456; *Grand Testament,* 1461.

ZOLA, ÉMILE, born Edouard Charles Antoine, Apr. 2, 1840 (Paris, Fr.)–Sept. 29, 1902. French novelist. Leader of the naturalist school; best known for *Les Rougon-Macquart* (1871–93), a 20-novel series, including *The Dram-Shop* (1877), *Nana* (1880), and *Germinal* (1885), portraying a family's fortunes under the Second Empire; wrote "J'accuse" (1898), an open letter supporting A. DREYFUS; received a state funeral, buried in the Pantheon.

OTHER FOREIGN WRITERS

AESCHYLUS, 525 B.C. (Eleusis, Gr.)–456 B.C. Greek playwright often called the originator of tragedy. A military hero, he is said to have fought at Marathon; his plays are heroic, shocking, with epic sweep, broad characterizations, and lofty themes; he began the use of true dialogue and introduced elaborate costumes; won many firsts in the annual Athenian competition; of some 90 plays only 7 survive: *The Persians, Prometheus Bound, Seven against Thebes, The Oresteia* (inc. *Agamemnon, Choephori,* and *Eumenides*), and *Supplicants.*

AESOP, c.620 B.C.–c.560 B.C. Greek fabulist. Semilegendary figure credited with composing hundreds of fables in which talking animals illustrate human follies and foibles—*Aesop's Fables,* collected in the 2nd or 3rd century B.C.

AGNON, SHMUEL YOSEF HALEVI (pseud.: Mazel Tov, Ironi), born Shmuel Yosef Czaczkes, July 17, 1888 (E. Galicia, Pol.)–Feb. 17, 1970. Israeli novelist, short-story writer. Moved from traditional Hassidic tales to nightmarish stories about the disintegration of social and religious forms; awarded Nobel Prize in literature (shared with NELLY SACHS), 1966. *The Bridal Canopy,* 1937; *In the Heart of the Seas,* 1947; *Days of Awe,* 1948; *A Guest for the Night,* 1967.

AKHMATOVA, ANNA, born Anna Andreyevna Gorenko, June 23, 1888 (nr. Odessa, Rus.)–Mar. 5, 1966. Soviet poet. A leader of the Acmeist movement, along with her first husband, NIKOLAI GUMILYOV, and OSIP MANDELSTAM. *Evening,* 1912; *The Rosary,* 1914; *Anno Domini MCMXXI,* 1922; *The Willow Tree,* 1940.

ALEICHEM, SHOLOM, born Solomon Rabinovitch, Feb. 18, 1859 (Pereyaslav, Rus.)–May 13, 1916. Russian writer of Yiddish short stories and plays. His three main characters—Tevye, Menachem Mendel, and Mottel— have become Jewish archetypes. *The Old Country,* tr. 1946; *Tevye the Dairyman,* tr. 1949; *Adventures of Mottel, the Cantor's Son,* 1953.

ALEIXANDRE, VICENTE, Apr. 26, 1898 (Seville, Sp.). Spanish poet. Member of the so-called Generation of 1927, writers inspired by Spain's golden age of literature; awarded Nobel Prize in literature, 1977. *Swords as Lips,* 1932; *Shadow of Paradise,* 1944; *Story of the Heart,* 1954; *Dialogues of Insight,* 1974.

ANDERSEN, HANS CHRISTIAN, Apr. 2, 1805 (Odense, Den.)–Aug. 4, 1875. Danish fairy-tale writer, poet, novelist. Best known for his 168 fairy tales (1835–1872), including "The Princess and the Pea," "The Little Match Girl," and "The Ugly Duckling."

ANDRIC, IVO, Feb. 10, 1892 (Travnik, now Yugo.)–Mar. 13, 1975. Yugoslav novelist, short-story writer, poet; awarded Nobel Prize in literature, 1961. *The Bridge on the Drina*, 1945; *The Travnik Chronicle*, 1945; *The Devil's Yard*, 1954.

APULEIUS, LUCIUS, c.123 (nr. present-day Bône, Alg.)–? Roman novelist, orator. His *Metamorphoses, or The Golden Ass*, is the only Latin novel to survive intact.

ARISTOPHANES, c.450 B.C. (Athens, Greece)–c.385 B.C. Greek playwright, poet. His 11 extant plays, the only surviving examples of Greek comedy, combine music, dance, word play, political satire, lyric poetry, and fantasy. *The Clouds*, 423 B.C.; *The Wasps*, 422 B.C.; *The Birds*, 414 B.C.; *Lysistrata*, 411 B.C.; *The Frogs*, 405 B.C.

ASTURIAS, MIGUEL ANGEL, Oct. 19, 1899 (Guatemala City, Guat.)–June 9, 1974. Guatemalan novelist, short-story writer. Author of works combining European sociopolitical realism and surrealistic tales of the land and people of Guatemala; awarded Nobel Prize in literature, 1967. *Strong Wind*, 1950; *The Green Pope*, 1954; *Las Ojos de los Enterrados*, 1960; *Mulata de Fol*, 1963.

BABEL, ISAAC EMMANVILOVICH, July 13, 1894 (Odessa, Rus.)–Mar. 17, 1941. Soviet short-story writer. Wrote about the civil war following the October Revolution; disappeared in 1938, reputedly either executed or died in a concentration camp. *Odessa Tales*, 1923-24; *Red Cavalry*, 1926.

BALL, HUGO, Feb. 22, 1886 (Pirmasens, Ger.)–Sept. 14, 1927. German poet, theatrical producer, Catholic theologian. Cofounder of Dada. *Hermann Hesse, His Life and His Work*, 1927.

BEMELMANS, LUDWIG, Apr. 27, 1898 (Beran, Austria)–Oct. 1, 1962. Austrian-U.S. writer, illustrator. Wrote and illustrated children's books, notably *Hansi* (1934) and the *Madeline* series (beginning in 1939); worked in various restaurants and hotels, including the Ritz, which he described in *Hotel Splendide* (1941).

BENAVANTE Y MARTÍNEZ, JACINTO, Aug. 12, 1866 (Madrid, Sp.)–July 14, 1954. Spanish playwright. Author of satires of upper-class life, reminiscent of Italian commedia dell'arte; awarded Nobel Prize in literature, 1922. *Bonds of Interest*, 1907; *Señora Ama*, 1908; *Passion Flower*, 1913.

BENN, GOTTFRIED, May 2, 1886 (Mansfeld, Ger.)–July 7, 1956. German poet, critic. Influenced by F. NIETZSCHE, he is best known for early expressionistic poems and poetic dramas; considered by many to be the most influential writer in post-Hitlerian Germany. *Morgue*, 1912; *Rubble*, 1919; *The Surveyor*, 1919; *Double Life* (autobiography), 1950.

BJØRNSON, BJØRNSTJERNE, Dec. 8, 1832 (Kuikne, Nor.)–Apr. 26, 1910. Norwegian writer, political leader. The national poet of Norway; Nobel Prize in literature, 1903. *The Bastard*, 1862; *Fisher Girl*, 1868; *Poems and Songs*, 1870.

BLOK, ALEKSANDR ALEKSANDROVICH, Nov. 28, 1880 (St. Petersburg, Rus.)–Aug. 9, 1921. Russian poet. Foremost Russian symbolist. *Verses about the Lady Beautiful*, 1904; *The Unknown Woman*, 1906; *The Twelve*, 1918; *The Scythians*, 1920.

BOCCACCIO, GIOVANNI, 1313 (Paris, Fr.)–Dec. 21, 1375. Italian poet, storyteller. With PETRARCH, a principal precursor of the Italian Renaissance. *Diana's Hunt*, 1336; *Decameron*, 1348-53; *Filostrato*; *Teseida*.

BÖLL, HEINRICH, Dec. 21, 1917 (Cologne, Ger.). German novelist, short-story writer, poet. Left-wing Catholic, critic of modern society; awarded Nobel Prize in literature, 1972. *Traveler, If You Come to Spa... 1950; Billiards at Half Past Nine*, 1961; *Group Portrait with Lady*, 1971.

BORGES, JORGE LUIS, Aug. 24, 1899 (Buenos Aires, Arg.). Argentine poet, critic, short-story writer, noted for his highly-original fictional narratives. *Historia universal de la infamia*, 1935; *Ficciones*, 1944; *El Aleph*, 1949; *Extraordinary Tales*, 1955; *Labrynths*, 1962.

BRECHT, BERTOLT, Feb. 10, 1898 (Augsburg, Ger.)–Aug. 11, 1956. German dramatist, poet. Developed anti-Aristotelian epic theater, intended to shock the audience into a critical examination of characters; founded the Berliner Ensemble theater. *Mann ist Mann*, 1926; *The Three-penny Opera*, 1928; *Rise and Fall of the Town of Mahogonny*, 1929; *Mother Courage and Her Children*, 1939; *The Good Woman of Setzuan*, 1938-40; *The Caucasian Chalk Circle*, 1944-45.

BULGAKOV, MIKHAIL AFANASYEVICH, May 15, 1891 (Kiev, Rus.)–Mar. 10, 1940. Soviet novelist, short-story writer, playwright. His sympathetic treatment of Russians hostile to the revolution and his satires on Soviet bureaucracy brought him official criticism. *The Deviliad*, 1925; *The Days of the Turbines*, 1926; *The Master and Margarita*, 1940.

BUNIN, IVAN ALEKSEYEVICH, Oct 10, 1870 (Voronezh, Rus.)–Nov. 8, 1953. Soviet short-story writer, novelist, poet. The first Soviet citizen to win a Nobel Prize in literature, 1933. *The Village*, 1910; *The Gentleman from San Francisco*, 1916.

CALDERON DE LA BARCA, PEDRO, Jan 17, 1600 (Madrid, Sp.)–May 25, 1681. Spanish dramatist. After the death of LOPE DE VEGA (1635), the foremost Spanish dramatist and the last great figure in the golden age of Spanish literature. *La Vida es sueño*, 1635; *El Alcalde de Zalamea*, c.1640; *El Mágico prodigioso*, 1637; *El Gran Teatro del Mundo*, c.1635.

CAMOES (or Camoens), LUIS DE VAZ, 1524? (Lisbon?, Port.)–June 10, 1580. Portuguese poet. Most celebrated figure in Portuguese literature; led a romantic life, including banishment from court for his romance with the queen's lady-in-waiting; wrote sonnets and lyrics; modeled his epic, *The Lusiads* (1572), on VERGIL.

ČAPEK, KAREL, 1890 (Male Svantanovice, Bohemia)–Dec. 25, 1938. Czech novelist, dramatist. Wrote two plays, *R.U.R.* (1920) and *The Insect Play* (1921), with his brother Joseph Čapek. *Hordubal*, 1933; *Meteor*, 1935; *An Ordinary Life*, 1936.

CARDUCCI, GIOSUE, July 27, 1835 (Val di Castello, It.)–Feb. 16, 1907. Italian poet, critic. Considered to be the national poet of modern Italy; awarded Nobel Prize in literature, 1906. *Rime*, 1857; *Hymn to Satan*, 1865; *Nuove poesie*, 1873; *Barbaric odes*, 1877, 1882, 1889; *Rime¡ nuove*, 1889.

CASANOVA DE SEINGALT, GIOVANNI GIACOMO, Apr. 2, 1725 (Venice, It.)–June 4, 1798. Italian adventurer, author. A man of learning and taste, led an adventurous life all over Europe as a gambler, spy, seducer; his memoirs, *History of My Life* (12 vols., 1826-38), though an exaggerated account of his erotic exploits, is of historical interest.

CATULLUS, GAIUS VALERIUS, c.84 B.C. (Verona, It.)–c.54 B.C. Roman lyric poet. Wrote love lyrics, epigrams, nuptial poems, and elegies. "Hail and farewell"; "Let us live and love, My Lesbia"; "I hate and I love"; *Attis; Thetis, Peleus.*

CERVANTES SAAVEDRA, MIGUEL DE, Sept. 29?, 1547 (Alcala de Henares)–Apr. 23, 1616. Spanish novelist, dramatist, poet. Best known for his masterpiece *Don Quixote* (1605), a novel describing the adventures of a country gentleman and his squire. *Novelas Ejemplares* ("12 Tales"), 1613.

CHEKHOV, ANTON PAVLOVICH, Jan. 17, 1860 (Taganrog, Rus.)–July 2, 1904. Russian dramatist, short-story writer. Author of works characterized by realism, simplicity, compassion, humor, an emphasis on internal life, and the inability to communicate. *Motley Stories,* 1886; *Ivanov,* 1887; *Twilight,* 1887; *Uncle Vanya,* 1889; *The Island of Sakhalin,* 1890; *The Seagull,* 1896; *The Three Sisters,* 1901; *The Cherry Orchard,* 1904.

COHEN, LEONARD NORMAN, Sept. 21, 1934 (Montreal, Can.). Canadian poet, novelist, singer, composer. Rose from an obscure romantic poet to an internationally famous pop singer in the 1960s; his most popular songs include "Suzanne" (1968) and "Hey, That's No Way to Say Goodbye" (1968). *The Spice Box of the Earth,* 1961; *Beautiful Losers,* 1966.

D'ANNUNZIO, GABRIELE, Mar. 12, 1863 (Pescara, It.)–Mar. 1, 1938. Italian novelist, short-story writer, dramatist, poet. Prolific, eccentric writer; led 12,000 men in march on Fiume (Sept. 1919), which he ruled until Jan. 1921, when he declared war on Italy; an enthusiastic fascist, given a hereditary title and made resident of the Royal Academy by MUSSOLINI. *Episcopo and Company,* 1896; *The Triumph of Death,* 1896; *The Dead City,* 1902.

DANTE ALIGHIERE, May 1265 (Florence, It.)–Sept. 14, 1321. Italian poet. The most famous Italian poet; his masterpiece, *The Divine Comedy* (c.1307–21), tells the story of his imaginary journey through Hell, Purgatory, and Heaven, guided by VERGIL, then by Beatrice (probably Beatrice Portinari, whom he idolized.) *The New Life,* c.1292.

DELEDDA, GRAZIA, Sept. 27, 1875 (Sardinia)–Aug. 16, 1936. Italian novelist. Described the inner lives of Sardinian peasants with sympathy and humor; awarded Nobel Prize in literature, 1926. *After the Divorce,* 1902; *Cenere,* 1904; *Reeds in the Wind,* 1913; *The Mother,* 1922; *Flight into Egypt.* 1925.

DINESEN, ISAK (pseud. of Baroness Karen Blixen, née Christentze Dinesen), Oct. 17, 1885 (Rungsted, Den.)–Sept. 7, 1962. Danish short-story writer. Wrote mainly in English; noted for her accounts of life on an East African coffee plantation, collected in *Out of Africa* (1937) and *Shadows on the Grass* (1961). *Seven Gothic Tales,* 1934; *Winter's Tales,* 1942.

DOSTOYEVSKY, FYODOR MIKHAILOVICH, Nov. 11, 1821 (Moscow, Rus.)–Feb. 9, 1881. Russian novelist. Author of powerful, realistic novels combining psychology and philosophy; his tragic life included four years of hard labor in a Siberian prison camp for association with radical Utopians. *Notes from the Underground,* 1864; *Crime and Punishment,* 1866; *The Possessed,* 1871; *The Brothers Karamazov,* 1880.

DÜRRENMATT, FRIEDRICH, Jan. 5, 1921 (Konolfingen, Switz.). Swiss playwright, novelist. Nicknamed the Helvetian Aristophanes for his humorous treatment of serious subjects. *Romulus the Great,* 1949; *The Marriage of Mr.* Mississippi, 1952; *The Visit,* 1958; *The Physicists,* 1962.

ECHEGARAY Y EIZAGUIRRE, JOSÉ, 1832 (Madrid, Sp.)–1916. Spanish dramatist, mathematician, physicist, economist, politician. Author of technically masterful melodramas; awarded Nobel Prize in literature (with FRÉDÉRIC MISTRAL), 1904. *Folly or Saintliness,* 1876; *The Great Galeoto,* 1895.

EHRENBERG (or Erenburg), **ILYA,** Jan. 27, 1891 (Kiev, Rus.)–Sept. 1, 1967. Soviet novelist, journalist. His novel critical of the post-Stalin period, *The Thaw* (1954), gave that era its name. *The Storm,* 1941; *The Tempering of Russia,* 1944.

ESENIN, SERGEI ALEKSANDROVICH, Oct. 3, 1895 (Konstantinovo |now Esenino|, Rus.)–Dec. 27, 1925. Soviet poet. Cult figure in the early Soviet period, connected with the imagists; wrote simple lyrics about rural Russia; an alcoholic, denounced for "hooliganism" and committed suicide at age 30. *Confessions of a Hooligan: Fifty Poems,* 1924. (Second of his three wives was ISADORA DUNCAN.)

EURIPIDES, 480 or 485 B.C. (Attica)–406 B.C. Greek playwright. One of the great tragedians; of some 92 plays he wrote, only 17 tragedies and 1 satyr play are extant; called the first realist, he wrote works noted for their psychological insight, religious skepticism, and technical innovations, including expository prologue and the problem-resolving *deus ex machina* device. *Medea,* 431 B.C.; *Hecuba,* 425? B.C.; *The Trojan Women,* 415 B.C.; *Electra,* 413 B.C.; *Orestes,* 408 B.C.

FEDIN, KONSTANTIN ALEKSANDROVICH, Nov. 24, 1892 (Saratov, Rus.). Soviet novelist. His novels deal with small-town life before and after the October Revolution. *Early Joys,* 1945–46; *No Ordinary Summer,* 1948; *The Bonfire,* 1962.

FEUCHTWANGER, LION, July 7, 1884 (Munich, Ger.)–Dec. 21, 1958. German novelist, playwright. Noted for his historical romances. *The Ugly Duchess,* 1923; *Josephus,* 1932; *The Jew of Rome,* 1935; *Josephus and the Emperor,* 1942.

FUENTES, CARLOS, Nov. 11, 1928 (Mexico City, Mex.). Mexican novelist, playwright, critic. Noted Latin American fiction writer; headed Mexican Dept. of Cultural Relations, 1956–59; Mexican amb. to France, 1975. *Good Conscience,* 1959; *Where the Air Is Clear,* 1960; *Our Land,* 1974.

GARCIA LORCA, FEDERICO, June 5, 1898 (Fuente Vaqueros, Sp.)–Aug. 19, 1936. Spanish poet, dramatist. A major modern Spanish literary figure; his passionate and violent works are derived from the folklore of his native Andalusia; killed by F. FRANCO's forces during the Spanish Civil War. *House of Bernarda Alba,* 1936; *Death of a Bullfighter,* 1937; *Blood Wedding,* 1939; *Gypsy Ballads,* 1953; *The Poet in New York,* 1955.

GARCIA-MARQUEZ, GABRIEL, 1928 (Colombia). Colombian novelist, short-story writer. A highly imaginative writer, deals with the extraordinary as if it were commonplace. *The Funeral of Mama Grande,* 1962; *No One Writes to the Colonel and Other Stories,* 1968; *One Hundred Years of Solitude,* 1970; *Leaf Storm and Other Stories,* 1972.

GIBRAN, KAHLIL, 1883 (Bechari, Leb.)–Apr. 10, 1931. Syrian-U.S. writer. Best known as author of *The Prophet* (1923), an extremely popular mystical prose-poem.

GJELLERUP, KARL ADOLF, June 2, 1857 (Roholte, Den.)–Oct. 11, 1919. Danish poet, novelist. Criticized his times, caricaturing the

Danish bourgeoisie; awarded Nobel Prize in literature (with his compatriot HENRIK PONTOPPIDAN), 1917. *The Young Denmark*, 1879; *The Disciple of the Teutons*, 1882; *The Pilgrim Kamanita*, 1906.

GOETHE, JOHANN WOLFGANG VON, Aug. 28, 1749 (Frankfurt, Ger.)–Mar. 22, 1832. German poet, dramatist, novelist. Leading *Sturm und Drang* ("Storm and Stress") dramatist; originated Weimar classicism in drama; originated the German novel of character development. *Faust*, 1770, 1831; *The Sorrows of Young Werther*, 1774.

GOGOL, NIKOLAI VASILYEVICH, Mar. 31, 1809 (Sorochintsy, Rus.)–Feb. 21, 1852. Russian short-story writer, novelist, dramatist. The father of Russian realism, although in some of his best work he combined realism and fantasy; depression and religious fanaticism led him to burn the second part of his novel *Dead Souls* (1842) and starve himself to death. *The Nose*, 1836; *The Inspector-General*, 1836; *Diary of a Madman*, 1842.

GOLDONI, CARLO, Feb. 25, 1707 (Venice, It.)–Feb. 6, 1793. Italian dramatist. The creator of modern Italian comedy; superseded the commedia dell'arte by eliminating masks and depicting ordinary Venetians realistically, in the manner of J. MOLIÈRE. *La locandiera*, 1753 (trans. *The Mistress of the Inn*, 1856); *Il ventaglio*, 1763 (trans. *The Fan*, 1911); *Il burbero benifico*, 1771 (trans. *The Beneficient Bear*, 1849).

GONCHAROV, IVAN ALEXANDROVICH, June 18, 1812 (Simbirsk [now Ulyanovsk], Rus.)–Sept. 27, 1891. Russian novelist. Best known for his novel *Oblomov* (1858), about a Russian nobleman from whose name the Russian word *oblomovism* ("indolence") was derived. *A Common Story*, 1847; *The Precipice*, 1869.

GORKY, MAXIM (pseud. of Aleksei Maximovich Pyeshkov), Mar. 14, 1868 (Nizhny Novgorod [now Gorky], Rus.)–1936. Soviet novelist, short-story writer, dramatist. The first proletarian writer; the father of Soviet literature and a founder of Socialist Realism. *The Lower Depths*, 1902; *Mother*, 1907; *Childhood, In the World, My Universities* (autobiographical trilogy) 1915–23.

GRASS, GÜNTER, Oct. 16, 1927 (Danzig [now Gdansk], Pol.). German novelist, playwright. The literary spokesman for Germans who grew up during the Nazi era. *The Tin Drum*, 1959; *Cat and Mouse*, 1961; *Dog Years*, 1965; *Local Anesthetic*, 1970; *From the Diary of a Snail*, 1973.

GRILLPARZER, FRANZ, Jan. 15, 1791 (Vienna, Austria)–Jan. 21, 1872. Austrian dramatist. Although now considered the greatest Austrian dramatist, was not well received in his time and gave up publishing after 1838. *The Golden Fleece*, 1821; *Hero and Leander*, 1831; *A Dream Is Life*, 1834; *The Jewess of Toledo; Family Strife in Hapsburg*, published posthumously.

GRIMM, JACOB LUDWIG CARL, Jan 4, 1785 (Hanau, Ger.)–Sept. 20, 1863; and his brother WILHELM CARL GRIMM, Feb. 24, 1786 (Hanau, Ger.)–Dec. 16, 1859. German philologists, folklorists, lexicographers. Best known as the coauthors of *Grimm's Fairy-Tales* (1812–15), based on their interviews with peasants; also began to write the great *German Dictionary*, which was not completed until 1954.

GUMILIOV, NIKOLAI STEPANOVICH, 1886–1921. Russian poet. With his wife, ANNA AKHMATOVA, a founder of the Acmeist movement, 1912; his poetry reflected his travels in Europe and Africa; executed by the Bolsheviks for alleged conspiracy. *The Pillar of Fire*, 1921.

HAMSUN, KNUT, born Knut Pedersen, Aug. 4, 1859 (Lom, Norway)–Feb. 19, 1952. Norwegian novelist. Lived as a vagabond in Norway and the U.S. until age 30; gained fame with his first novel, *Hunger* (1899); awarded Nobel Prize in literature, 1920. *Pan*, 1899; *The Growth of the Soil*, 1917.

HAŠEK, JAROSLAV MATEJ FRANTIŠEK, Apr. 30, 1883 (Prague, Czech.)–Jan. 3, 1923. Czech novelist, short-story writer. Best known for *The Good Soldier Schweik* (4 vols., 1920–23), a hilarious satire on military bureaucracy and an indictment of war.

HAUPTMANN, GERHART, Nov. 15, 1862 (Silesia)–June 8, 1946. German dramatist, poet. Foremost German playwright of the pre-WW I period; his first play, *Before Sunrise* (1889), brought naturalism to the German theater; awarded Nobel Prize in literature, 1912. *The Weavers*, 1892; *The Sunken Bell*, 1897.

HEIDENSTAM, (Carol Gustaf) VERNER VON, July 6, 1859 (Närke, Swed.)–May 20, 1940. Swedish poet, novelist, essayist. A major Swedish lyric poet, led the reaction against the naturalist movement in Sweden; awarded Nobel Prize in literature, 1916. *Pilgrimage and Wanderyears*, 1888; *Poems*, 1895; *The Tree of the Folkungs*, 2 vols., 1905–07; *New Poems*, 1915.

HEINE, HEINRICH, born Chaim Harry Heine, Dec. 13, 1797 (Düsseldorf, Ger.)–Feb. 17, 1856. German lyric poet. His poetry has been used in over 3,000 musical works, including those of F. SCHUBERT, R. SCHUMANN, F. MENDELSSOHN, F. LISZT. *Buch der Lieder*, 1827; *Letzte Gedichten*, 1847; *Reisebilder*, 4 vols., 1826–31.

HEREDIA, JOSÉ MARIA, Dec. 31, 1803 (Santiago, Cuba)–May 2, 1839. Cuban poet. The national poet of Cuba, one of the New World's first Romantic poets. *On the Temple Pyramid of Cholula*, 1820; *Ode to Niagara Falls*, 1824.

HESSE, HERMANN, July 2, 1877 (Württemberg, Ger.)–Aug. 9, 1962. German-Swiss novelist. Wrote lyrical, symbolic, ironic novels; underwent a revival in the 1960s, especially among students; awarded Nobel Prize in literature, 1946. *Demian*, 1919; *Steppenwolf*, 1927; *Magister Ludi*, 1943.

HEYSE, PAUL JOHANN LUDWIG VON, Mar. 15, 1830 (Munich, Ger.)–Apr. 2, 1914. German novelist, playwright. A master of the novella who was extremely popular in his day; the first German to win the Nobel Prize in literature, 1910. *The Maiden of Treppi*, 1858; *Andrea Delfin*, 1859.

HOLBERG, LUDWIG, BARON, Dec. 3, 1684 (Bergen, Nor.)–Jan. 28, 1754. Danish dramatist, essayist, poet. The foremost Scandinavian writer of the Enlightenment, called the Molière of the North; claimed by both Norway and Denmark as the founder of their literatures; his *Pedar Paars* (1719–20), a mock-heroic epic, is the earliest extant Danish-language epic. *The Political Tinker*, 1722.

HOMER, fl. 8th cent. B.C. (Asia Minor, probably Chios or Smyrna). Greek poet. Although his existence has long been disputed by scholars, it is now generally believed that a single, unifying intelligence, created the *Iliad* and the *Odyssey*—the two epic poems from which all Western literature has developed—from history, folk tales, and legends; blind, according to legend.

HORACE, born Quintus Horatius Flaccus, Dec. 8, 65 B.C. (Venusia, Apulia)–Nov. 27, 8 B.C. Roman poet. Great lyric poet, noted especially for his *Odes*

THE BOOK OF WHO

(23 B.C.–c.13 B.C.); his poetry reveals much about the Augustan age; adapted Greek meters to Latin; wrote under the patronage of Maecenas and AUGUSTUS. *Epodes*, 30 B.C.; *Satires*, c.35 B.C.–30 B.C.; *Epistles*, 20 B.C.–c.13 B.C.; *Ars Poetica*, c.13 B.C.–8 B.C.

HUIDOBRO, VICENTE, Jan. 10, 1893 (Santiago, Chile)–Jan. 2, 1948. Chilean poet, novelist, literary theorist. Father of the avante-garde movements of "creationism" and "ultraism." *I Will Not Serve* (manifesto), 1914; *Tour Eiffel*, 1917; *Satire or the Power of Words*, 1939; *Ultimas poemas*, 1948.

IBSEN, HENRIK JOHAN, May 20, 1828 (Skien, Nor.)–May 23, 1906. Norwegian dramatist. The father of modern drama; his realistic plays emphasized social problems, characterizations, and psychological conflicts. *Peer Gynt*, 1867; *A Doll's House*, 1879; *Ghosts*, 1881; *An Enemy of the People*, 1882; *The Wild Duck*, 1884; *Hedda Gabler*, 1890; *The Master Builder*, 1892.

JENSEN, JOHANNES VILHELM, Jan. 20, 1873 (Farsø, Den.)–Nov. 25, 1950. Danish novelist, poet, essayist. Created his own literary form—myth-based short prose tales related to the essay; awarded Nobel Prize in literature, 1944. *The Long Journey* (epic fantasy), 6 vols., 1908–22; *The Waving Rye*, 1959.

JIMÉNEZ, JUAN RAMÓN, Dec. 24, 1881 (Andalusia, Sp.)–May 29, 1958. Spanish lyric poet. His early poems reflect French symbolist influence; later, he wrote simplified, concise free verse; awarded Nobel Prize in literature, 1956. *Sonorous Loneliness*, 1911; *Diary of a Recently Married Poet*, 1917.

JOHNSON, EYVIND, July 29, 1900 (Overlulea, Swe.). Swedish novelist, short-story writer. Best known for his four-volume autobiographical work, *The Novel about Olov* (1934–37); awarded Nobel Prize in literature (with Harry Martinson), 1974. *Babinack*, 1932; *Rain at Daybreak*, 1933.

JUVENAL, born Decimus Junius Juvenalis, c.60 (Aquinum?)–c.140. Roman poet. Noted for satires written in hexameters in which he denounced the degeneracy of the Empire. *Satires*, 5 books, c.100–127.

KAFKA, FRANZ, July 3, 1883 (Prague, A.-H. [now Czech.])–June 3, 1924. German novelist, short-story writer. Wrote visionary tales of guilt-ridden, isolated, anxious men in an aimless, unfathomable world. *The Metamorphosis*, 1915; *The Penal Colony*, 1919; *The Trial*, 1925; *The Castle*, 1926; *Amerika*, 1927.

KAISER, GEORG, Nov. 25, 1878 (Mägdeburg, Ger.)–June 4, 1945. German playwright. Leading German expressionist playwright. *The Burghers of Calais*, 1914; *From Morn to Midnight*, 1916; *Trilogy: The Corals* (1917), *Gas* (1918), and *Gas II* (1920).

KARLFELDT, ERIK AXEL, July 20, 1864 (Dalecarlia, Swe.)–Apr. 8, 1931. Swedish poet. His verse, virtually unknown outside of Sweden, deals with nature and native folklore; awarded Nobel Prize in literature, 1931. *Fridolins Visor*, 1898; *Fridolins Lustgard*, 1901; *Hösthorn*, 1927.

KAWABATA, YASUNARI, June 11, 1899 (Osaka, Jap.)–Apr. 17, 1972. Japanese novelist. Author of melancholy, impressionistic novels and short stories; the first Japanese to be awarded the Nobel Prize in literature, 1968. *The Izu Dancer*, 1925; *Snow Country*, 1935; *Thousand Cranes*, 1955; *The House of the Sleeping Beauties and Other Stories*, trans. 1969.

KAZANTZAKIS, NIKOS, 1883 (Crete)–1957. Greek poet, novelist. Best known in the U.S. for his novel *Zorba the Greek* (1946), which was made into a successful film. *The Greek Passion*, 1938; *The Odyssey, A Modern Sequel*, 1938.

KHLEBNIKOV, VELIMIR VLADIMIROVICH, born Viktor Vladimirovich Khlebnikov, Nov. 9, 1885 (Tundutov, Rus.)–June 28, 1922. Russian poet. Influential avante-garde poet and a founder of futurism in Russia. *Zangezi*, 1922.

KIELLAND, ALEXANDER, Feb. 18, 1849 (Stavanger, Nor.)–Apr. 6, 1906. Norwegian novelist, short-story writer, dramatist. With H. IBSEN, B. BJØRNSON, and J. LIE, one of the "big four" of 19th-cent. Norwegian literature. *Workers*, 1881; *St. John's Festival*, 1887.

KLEIST, (Bernd) HEINRICH (Wilhelm) VON, Oct. 18, 1777 (Frankfort on the Oder, Ger.)–Nov. 21, 1811. German dramatist, writer of novellas. Best known for the historical tragedy *The Prince of Homburg* (1821) and the novella *Michael Kolhaas* (1808); unrecognized in his time; committed suicide.

KOESTLER, ARTHUR, Sept. 1905 (Budapest, Hung.). Hungarian-English novelist, essayist. Spokesman for the ex-communist left; his *Darkness at Noon* (1941) is based on the Moscow trials of the 1930s.

KOSINSKI, JERZY NIKODEM, June 14, 1933 (Lódź, Pol.). Polish-U.S. novelist. Gained fame for *The Painted Bird* (1965), a horrifying, surrealistic account of a six-year-old boy in Eastern Europe during WW II; came to U.S. in 1957. *Steps*, 1968; *Being There*, 1971, *The Devil Tree*, 1973; *Blind Dates*, 1977.

LAGERKVIST, PÄR FABIAN, May 23, 1891 (Växjö, Swe.)–July 11, 1974. Swedish novelist, dramatist, poet. Best known for his humanistic novels, especially *Barabbas* (1950); awarded Nobel Prize in literature, 1951. *The Man without a Soul*, 1936; *The Dwarf*, 1945; *The Sibyl*, 1956.

LAGERLÖF, SELMA, Nov. 20, 1858 (Varmland, Swe.)–Mar. 16, 1940. Swedish novelist, short-story writer. Best known for her classic children's stories, such as *The Wonderful Adventures of Nils* (1906); the first woman to win the Nobel Prize in literature, 1909. *Gösta Berling*, 1891; *The Ring of the Lowenskolds* (trilogy), 1925–28, trans. 1931.

LAMPEDUSA, GIUSEPPE DI, DUKE OF PARMA, PRINCE OF LAMPEDUSA, Dec. 23, 1896 (Palermo, Sicily)–1957. Italian novelist. Born into a wealthy aristocratic family; noted for *The Leopard* (trans. 1960), a historical novel set in late 19th cent. Sicily.

LAXNESS, HALLDÓR KILJAN, Apr. 23, 1902 (Laxnes, Iceland). Icelandic novelist, poet, playwright. A major figure in modern Icelandic literature; noted for his lyrical novels set in an Icelandic fishing village; awarded Nobel Prize in literature, 1955. *Independent People* (2 vols., 1934–35); *The Light of the World* (4 vols., 1937–40).

LEOPARDI, GIACOMO, CONTE, June 29, 1798 (Recanati, It.)–June 14, 1837. Italian poet, scholar. Foremost 19th-cent. Italian poet; noted for his lyrical, melancholy, pessimistic poems, written in a classical style. *Canzoni*, 1824; *Versi*, 1826; *Canti*, 1831, 1835, 1845.

LERMONTOV, MIKHAIL YURIEVICH, Oct. 15, 1814 (Moscow, Rus.)–July 27, 1841. Russian poet, novelist. One of the foremost Russian poets of the 19th cent.; progressed from early Romantic poetry to simpler, realistic works; led a Byronic life, twice exiled to the Caucasus, where he was killed in a duel. "The Novice," 1840; *A Hero of Our Time*, 1840; *The Demon*, 1841.

LEVER, CHARLES, Jan. 22, 1729 (Saxony)–Feb.

15, 1781. German dramatist, critic. Influential German exponent of the Enlightenment; a major influence in development of modern German theater. *Miss Sara Sampson*, 1755; *Minna von Barnhelm*, 1763; *Emilia Galotti*, 1772; *Nathan the Wise*, 1779.

LIE, JONAS LAURITZ IDEMIL, Nov. 6, 1833 (Modum, Nor.)-July 5, 1908. Norwegian novelist. One of the "four great ones" of 19th-cent. Norwegian literature. *The Visionary, or Pictures from Nordland*, 1894; *One of Life's Slaves*, 1895; *The Family at Gilje*, 1920.

LOUW, N. P. VAN WYK, June 11, 1906 (Sutherland, Cape Colony)-June 18, 1970. Afrikaans poet, playwright, critic. Leader of the 1930s revival of Afrikaans poetry. *Raka*, 1941; *Germanicus*, 1956; *Tristia*, 1962.

LUCIAN (or Lucianus), 125 (Samosata, Syria | now Samsat, Turkey|)-200. Greek satirist. A major figure in the revival of Greek literature under the Roman Empire; best known for his dialogues. *Dialogues of the Gods; Dialogues of the Dead; The Sale of Lives; How History Should be Written; The True History.*

MAETERLINCK, MAURICE POLYDORE MARIE BERNARD, Aug. 29, 1862 (Ghent, Belg.)-May 6, 1949. Belgian poet, playwright, prose writer (in French). Best known for his symbolist masterpiece, *Pelléas et Mélisande* (music by C. DE-BUSSY, 1892); awarded Nobel Prize in literature, 1911. *Hot House Blooms*, 1899; *The Life of the Bee*, 1901; *The Intelligence of Flowers*, 1907; *The Blue Bird*, 1909.

MANDELSTAM, OSIP EMILYEVICH, Jan. 15, 1891 (Warsaw, Pol.)-c.Dec. 27, 1938. Russian poet. Member of the Acmeist group; died in exile in Siberia. *The Stone*, 1913; *Tristia*, 1922.

MANN, HEINRICH, Mar. 27, 1871 (Lübeck, Ger.)-Mar. 12, 1950. German novelist. Critic of authoritarian Germany under Wilhelm II; his novel *Small Town Tyrant* (1905) became the classic film *The Blue Angel. In the Land of Cockaigne*, 1900; *Henri Quatre*, 2 vols., 1935, 1938. (Brother of THOMAS MANN.)

MANN, THOMAS, June 6, 1875 (Lübeck, Ger.)-Aug. 12, 1955. German-U.S. novelist. One of the foremost German writers; wrote the relationship of art to reality; exiled from Nazi Germany, 1933; became a U.S. citizen, 1944; awarded Nobel Prize in literature, 1929. *Buddenbrooks*, 1900; *Tonio Kröger*, 1903; *Death in Venice*, 1912; *The Magic Mountain*, 1924; *Doctor Faustus*, 1947; *The Confessions of Felix Krull*, 1954.

MANZONI, ALESSANDRO FRANCESCO TOMASO ANTONIO, Mar. 7, 1785 (Milan, It.)-May 22, 1873. Italian novelist, poet. Best known for his novel *The Betrothed* (3 vols., 1825-27), considered a masterpiece; made a senator of Italy, 1860; G. VERDI wrote *Requiem* for him, and it was first performed on the anniversary of his death. *Sacred Hymns*, 1812-22; *Il Conte di Carmagnola*, 1820; *The Fifth of May*, 1822; *Adelchi*, 1822.

MARTIAL, born Marcus Valerius Martial, Mar. 1, 38-41 (Bilbilus, Sp.)-c.103. Roman poet. Wrote some 1,500 epigrams as social and satiric comment, presenting a vivid picture of Rome in the 1st cent. A.D. *Book on Spectacles*, 80; *Guest Gifts, and Gifts to Take Home*, 84-85; *Epigrams*, 86-102.

MATSUO BASHŌ (a.k.a. Basho), born Matsuo Munefusa, 1644 (Iga Prov., |now Mie Pref.|, Jap.)-Oct. 12, 1694. Japanese poet. Foremost Japanese practitioner of haiku, which he developed; influenced by Zen Buddhism. "The Narrow Road to the Deep North," 1694.

MAYAKOVSKY, VLADIMIR VLADIMIROVICH, July 19, 1893 (Bagdadi, now in Georgian SSR)-Apr. 14, 1930. Soviet poet. Foremost poet of the Russian Revolution and early Soviet period; a leading futurist; noted for his original, technically innovative, vigorous, declamatory poetry. "A Cloud in Trousers," 1914; "The Backbone Flute," 1915; "Ode to the Revolution," 1918; "Left March," 1919; "150,000,000," 1920; "Vladimir Ilich Lenin," 1924; "Very Good!" 1927.

MCCULLOUGH, COLLEEN, June 1, 1937 (Wellington, Austrl.). Australian novelist. Noted for her best-selling romantic saga set in Australia, *The Thorn Birds* (1977).

MENANDER, 342 B.C. (Athens, Gr.)-292 B.C. Athenian dramatist. Considered by the ancient Greeks to be the greatest poet of New Comedy; works were later adapted by PLAUTUS and TERENCE, and thereby influenced the development of European comedy. *Dyscolus; Perikeiromenē; Second Adelphoe; Epitrepontes.*

MICKIEWICZ, ADAM BERNARD, Dec. 24, 1798 (Zozie, Belorussia)-Nov. 26, 1855. Polish poet. Considered the apostle of Polish national freedom; a romantic, influenced by BYRON and W. SCOTT; best known for his poetic epic *Master Thaddeus* (1834). *Poetry I*, 1822; *Poetry II*, 1823; *Crimean Sonnets*, 1826; *Konrad Wallenrod*, 1828.

MILOSZ, CZESLAW, June 30, 1911 (Lithuania). Polish poet, novelist, essayist. Considered a major poet in Poland, but best known in the West for the anticommunist essay "The Captive Mind" (1952). *The Valley of Issa*, 1955-57; *The Usurpers*, 1955; *Selected Poems*, trans. 1973.

MISHIMA, YUKIO (pseud. of Kimitake Hiraoka), Jan. 14, 1925 (Tokyo, Jap.)-Nov. 25, 1970. Japanese novelist, short-story writer. Wrote about the conflict between contemporary westernized Japan and the militaristic tradition of the old Japan; created his own private army; committed hara-kiri. *Confessions of a Mask*, 1948; *The Temple of the Golden Pavilion*, 1959; *Sea of Fertility*, 1970.

MISTRAL, GABRIELA, born Lucila Godoy Alcayaga, Apr. 7, 1889 (Vicuna, Chile)-Jan. 10, 1957. Chilean poet. Founded the modernist movement in Chilean poetry; wrote of her love for children and the downtrodden; the first Latin American woman to win the Nobel Prize in literature, 1945. *Sonnets of Death*, 1914; *Desolation*, 1922; *Tenderness*, 1924, 1945; *Tala*, 1938.

MOBERG, (Carl Artur) VILHELM, Aug. 20, 1898 (Algutsboda, Swe.)-Aug. 8, 1973. Swedish novelist, dramatist. Best known for his multivolume epic about the Swedish emigration to America in the 1850s: *The Emigrants* (1949-59), *Unto a Good Land* (1952), *The Last Letter Home* (1961).

MOLNÁR, FERENC, Jan. 12, 1878 (Budapest, Hung.)-Apr. 1, 1952. Hungarian playwright, novelist, journalist. Wrote plays about salon life in Budapest and moving short stories about the underdog; his play *Liliom* (1909) was adapted by R. RODGERS and O. HAMMERSTEIN into the musical *Carousel. The Guardsman*, 1910; *The Swan*, 1920; *The Red Mill*, 1923.

MONTALE, EUGENIO, Oct. 12, 1896 (Genoa, It.). Italian poet, translator. A major modern Italian poet; translated SHAKESPEARE, T. S. ELIOT, G. M. HOPKINS, others. *Cuttlefish Bones*, 1925; *Notebook of Translations*, 1948; *The Offender*, 1963.

~S

...BERTO, born Alberto Pincherle, ...(Rome, It.). Italian novelist. A social ...tes about alienation and isolation. ...*Indifference*, 1932; *Two Adoles-* ...*Disobedience*, 1948; *The Conform-* ...*e Empty Canvas*, 1960.

MURAS..., SHIKIBU, 978?-1026. Japanese novelist. Author of *Tales of Genji*, generally considered to be the first Japanese novel and notable for its picture of a unique court society and sensitivity to emotions and nature; a lady in the court of Empress Akiko, she also wrote a diary of historical and literary value (1007-1010).

NABOKOV, VLADIMIR, Apr. 22, 1899 (St. Petersburg, Rus. [now Leningrad, USSR])-July 2, 1977. Russian-U.S. novelist, short-story writer. A brilliant stylist, he gained international renown for *Lolita* (1955), a satirical novel about a middle-aged man's obsession for a 12-year-old nymphet; a distinguished lepidopterist. *The Defense*, 1930; *The Real Life of Sebastien Knight*, 1941; *Bend Sinister*, 1947; *Pale Fire*, 1962; *Ada*, 1969.

NAIPAUL, V(idiadhar) S(urajprasad), Aug. 17, 1932 (Trinidad). West Indian novelist, journalist. Noted for his satirical portraits of the vanishing culture of the East Indian in Trinidad. *The Mystic Masseur*, 1957; *A House for Mr. Biswas*, 1961; *In a Free State*, 1971; *Guerrillas*, 1975; *A Bend in the River*, 1979.

NEKRASOV, NIKOLAI ALEKSEYEVICH, Dec 10, 1821 (Yuzvin, Ukraine)-Jan. 8, 1878. Russian poet, journalist. Noted for his original and powerful poems, including "Red-nosed Frost" (1863) and "Who Can Be Happy and Free in Russia?" (1879); edited *The Contemporary* and made it a major literary journal, 1846-66; edited and published *Fatherland Annals*, 1868-78.

NERUDA, PABLO, born Neftali Ricardo Reyes, July 12, 1904 (Parral, Chile)-Sept. 23, 1973. Chilean poet, diplomat. Considered to be one of the most original poets in Spanish-language literature; served as Chilean ambassador to Mexico, 1940-42; became a militant communist; awarded Nobel Prize in literature, 1971. *Crespus culario*, 1923; *Twenty Love Poems and a Song of Despair*, 1924.

NESTROY, JOHANN NEPOMUK EDWARD AMBROSIUS, Dec. 7, 1801 (Vienna, Austria)-May 25, 1862. Austrian dramatist, actor. A major comic dramatist and actor; wrote 50 plays in which he played the major role; his play *Einen Jux er sich machen* (1842) was adapted by THORNTON WILDER as *The Matchmaker* (1955), and later, as the musical play and movie *Hello, Dolly*. *A Man Full of Nothing*, 1844.

OEHLENSCHLÄGER, ADAM GOTTLOB, Nov. 14, 1779 (Vesterbo, Den.)-Jan. 20, 1850. Danish poet, dramatist. Danish national poet and a leader of the Romantic movement in Denmark; his poem *The Golden Horns* (1802) marked the beginning of romanticism in Denmark. *Midsummer Night's Play*, 1802; *Poetic Writings*, 1805; *Aladdin*, 1805; *Baldur the Good*, 1807; *The Gods of the North*, 1819.

OMAR KHAYYAM, born Gheyas Od-Din Abu al-Fath 'Umar Ebn Ebrahim Ol-Khayyami, May 1048? (Nishapur, Persia)-Dec. 1122. Persian poet, mathematician, astronomer. During his lifetime, noted for his accomplishments in astronomy, law, history, medicine, and mathematics—but for poetry; *The Rubaiyat*, attributed to him, was discovered by the English Victorian poet EDWARD FITZGERALD, who freely translated it and arranged the quatrains in a continuous elegy (1859).

ORCZY, BARONESS (Emmuska), 1865 (Tarna-Eörs, Hung.)-Nov. 12, 1947. Hungarian novelist. Best known for *The Scarlet Pimpernel* (1905), a novel about the swashbuckling adventures of Sir Percy Blakeney during the French Revolution. *The Elusive Pimpernel*, 1908; *The Way of the Scarlet Pimpernel*, 1933.

OVID, born Publius Ovidius Naso, Mar. 20, 43 B.C. (Sulmo [now Sulmona], It.)-A.D. 17. Roman poet. His witty and cosmopolitan works were influential and much-translated; best known for *Metamorphoses*, 15 books of legends about the history of the world; first gained fame for his *Amores* (erotic poems); also wrote *The Art of Love*, three books of instructions on lovemaking.

OZAKI, KOYO, born Ozaki Tokutaró, Dec. 16, 1867 (Tokyo, Jap.)-Oct. 30, 1903. Japanese novelist, essayist, poet. A pioneer of modern Japanese literature; one of the founders of the influential literary magazine *Kenyusha*, 1885. *The Perfumed Pillow*, 1890; *Tears and Regrets*, 1896; *The Heart*, 1903; *The Gold Demon*, trans. 1917.

PASTERNAK, BORIS LEONIDOVICH, Feb. 10, 1890 (Moscow, Rus.)-May 30, 1960. Soviet poet, novelist, translator. Best known for his novel *Doctor Zhivago* (1957), which was repressed in the Soviet Union as anti-Soviet but gained international fame when published abroad; declined Nobel Prize in literature, 1958. *Over the Barriers*, 1917; *Childhood*, 1918; *1905*, 1926.

PATON, ALAN STEWART, Jan. 11, 1903 (Pietermanritzburg, Natal [now S. A.]). South African novelist, political activist. Served as pres. of the Liberal Party of South Africa from its founding in 1953 to its enforced dissolution in 1968. *Cry, The Beloved Country*, 1948; *Too Late the Phalarope*, 1953.

PAVESE, CESARE, Sept. 9, 1908 (Santo Stefano Belbo, It.)-Aug. 27, 1950. Italian translator, critic, editor, novelist, short-story writer, poet. Fostered appreciation of U.S. literature in Italy through his translations and critical articles; founded and served as editor of the publishing house Einaudi; Pavese Prize in literature established in his honor, 1957. *The Moon and the Bonfires*, 1950; *American Literature, Essays and Opinions*, 1951.

PAZ, OCTAVIO, Mar. 31, 1914 (Mexico City, Mex.). Mexican poet, critic, social philosopher. Learned, eclectic, experimental writer, concerned with Mexican identity. *Labyrinth of Solitude*, 1950; *Salamandra*, 1962; *Ladera este*, 1969; *Sun-stone*, 1970; *The Bow and the Lyre*, 1974.

PERETZ, I(saac) L(eib), May 18, 1852 or May 20, 1851 (Zamose, Pol.)-Apr. 3, 1915. Polish poet, short-story writer, dramatist. Father of modern Yiddish literature; leader of the Yiddisheit movement; wrote about the poor Jews of Eastern Europe, introducing Hasidic lore; author of the *Silent Souls* series.

PETRARCH (in full, Francesco Petrarca), July 20, 1304 (Arezzo, It.)-July 18/19, 1374. Italian poet, scholar. His work served as a model for Italian literature for three centuries; especially known for his vernacular lyrics inspired by his idealized love for the young Laura; crowned "Laureate of the civilized world," 1341. *Triumphs; Song Book; Africa; Ecologues; Letters.*

PETRONIUS, ARBITER, born Gaius Petronius, died 66. Roman satirist. Reputed to be author of the *Satyricon*, a prose romance interspersed with verse that is generally considered the first Western European novel.

PINDAR, 518/522 B.C. (Cynoscephalae, Gr.)-c.

438 B.C. Greek poet. Choral lyricist, master of *epinicia*—odes celebrating athletic victory; his four books of *epinicia*, published 1513, greatly influenced Western poets.

PIRANDELLO, LUIGI, June 28, 1867 (Agrigento, Sicily)–Dec. 10, 1936. Italian playwright, novelist, short-story writer. Important innovator in modern drama; invented "theatre within the theatre" with his play, *Six Characters in Search of An Author* (1921); awarded Nobel Prize in literature, 1934. *Henry IV*, 1922.

PLAUTUS, born Titus Maccius Plautus, c.254 B.C. (Umbria)–184 B.C. Roman dramatist. Romanized Greek models and created Latin literary idiom; his comedies featured coarse humor, stock comic figures. *Amphitryon; Asinaria; Casina; Epidicus; Mostellaria; Persa, Truculentus; Vidularia.*

PONTOPPIDAN, HENRIK, July 24, 1857 (Fredericia, Den.)–Aug. 21, 1943. Danish novelist, short-story writer. Created a realistic, comprehensive picture of Denmark in epic style; awarded Nobel Prize in literature (with Karl Gjellerup), 1917. *The Promised Land,* 3 vols., 1891–95; *Lucky Peter,* 5 vols., 1898–1904., *Kingdom of the Dead,* 5 vols., 1912–16.

PUSHKIN, ALEXANDER SERGEYEVICH, June 6, 1799 (Moscow, Rus.)–Feb. 10, 1837. Russian poet, novelist, dramatist, short-story writer. A leading figure in Russian literature; introduced Romanticism with *The Prisoner in the Caucasus* (1822); his works inspired operas by M. P. MOUSSORGSKY, N. A. RIMSKY-KORSAKOV, and P. I. TCHAIKOVSKY. *Boris Godunov,* 1831; *Eugene Onegin,* 1825–31; *Tales of Belkin,* 1831.

QUASIMODO, SALVATORE, Aug. 20, 1901 (Syracuse, Sicily)–June 14, 1968. Italian poet, translator, critic. Translated works by VERGIL, HOMER, AESCHYLUS, SOPHOCLES, EZRA POUND, E. E. CUMMINGS, SHAKESPEARE; awarded Nobel Prize in literature, 1959. *Acque e terre,* 1930; *La vita non e' un sogno,* 1949; *La terra imparrigiable,* 1958.

QUEVEDO Y VILLEGAS, FRANCISCO GÓMEZ DE, Sept. 17, 1580 (Madrid, Sp.)–Sept. 8, 1645. Spanish satirist, novelist. One of the foremost writers of the golden age of Spanish literature; a virtuoso of language. *The Life of a Scoundrel,* 1626; *Visions,* 1627; *Epístola satírica y censoria,* 1639.

RADISCHEV, ALEKSANDR NIKOLAYEVICH, Aug. 31, 1749 (Moscow, Rus.)–Sept. 24, 1802. Russian writer. Founded the revolutionary tradition in Russian literature; in his fictional journal, *A Journey from St. Petersburg to Moscow* (1790), collected examples of social injustice; spent 10 years in Siberia, committed suicide one year later.

REMARQUE, ERICH MARIA, born Erich Paul Remark, June 22, 1898 (Osnabrück, Ger.)–Sept. 25, 1970. German-U.S. novelist. Best known for the WW I novel *All Quiet on the Western Front* (1929), in which he recorded the horrors of war. *The Way Back,* 1931; *Three Comrades,* 1937; *A Time to Love and a Time to Die,* 1954.

REYMONT, WLADYSLAW STANISLAW, 1867 (Kobiele Wielkie, Pol.)–1925. Polish writer. Best known for *The Peasants* (4 vols., 1902–09), a prose epic of Polish village life; awarded Nobel Prize in literature, 1924. *The Comedienne,* 1896; *The Promised Land,* 1899.

RICHLER, MORDECAI, Jan. 27, 1931 (Montreal, Que., Can.). Canadian novelist, short-story writer, journalist. "New Generation" Canadian novelist best known for *The Apprenticeship of Duddy Kravitz* (1959), which was adapted into a success-

ful film. *Son of a Smaller Hero,* 1953; *A Choice of Enemies,* 1957; *The Incomparable Atuk,* 1963.

RICHTER, JOHANN PAUL FRIEDRICH (pseud.: John Paul), Mar. 21, 1763 (Bavaria, Ger.)–Nov. 14, 1825. German novelist. Combined idealism with *sturm und drang* in his writing. *Hesperus,* 1795; *Quintus Fixlein,* 1796; *Siebenkäs,* 1796–97.

RILKE, RAINER MARIA, Dec. 4, 1875 (Prague, A.-H. [now Czech.])–Dec. 29, 1926. Austrian-German lyric poet. Noted for his highly individualized style; his poems often are mystical, with death a frequent theme. *Stories of God,* 1904; *Poems from the Book of Hours,* 1905; *New Poems,* 2 vols., 1907–08; *Duino Elegies,* 1923.

SACHS, NELLY LEONIE, Dec. 10, 1891 (Berlin, Ger.)–May 12, 1970. German poet, dramatist. Escaped to Sweden from Nazi Germany; described her experiences and the sufferings of European Jews; awarded Nobel Prize in literature, (with SHMUEL YOSEF AGNON), 1966. *A Mystery Play of the Sufferings of Israel,* 1951; *The Seeker and Other Poems,* 1966; *Israel's Suffering,* 1969.

SAPPHO, fl. early 6th cent. B.C. (Mytilene, Lesbos). Greek lyric poet. Wrote concise, picturesque poetry in the vernacular vocabulary of the local Lesbian-Aeolic dialect; invented Sapphic meter; wrote of the loves and hates in an informal association of upper-class women, of which she was the leading spirit.

SCHNITZLER, ARTHUR, May 15, 1862 (Vienna, Aust.)–Oct. 21, 1931. Austrian playwright, novelist. Wrote psychological dramas about Viennese bourgeois life; along with others opposed to German naturalist drama, started the Young Vienna Group. *Anatol,* 1893; *The Reckoning,* 1895; *Merry-Go-Round,* 1897; *None but the Brave,* 1926; *Flight into Darkness,* 1931.

SEFERIS, GIORGOS (pseud. of Giorgos Sefiriades,) Mar. 13, 1900 (Izmir, Turk.)–1971. Greek poet. His poetry is characterized by symbolic evocations of classical Greek themes; first Greek to win Nobel Prize in literature, 1963. *Strophe,* 1931; *Mithistorima,* 1935.

SENGHOR, LÉOPOLD SÉDAR, Oct. 9, 1906 (Joal, now in Senegal). Senegalese poet, statesman. In his poetry and essays, asserts black African cultural values, or negritude, a concept he formulated with other African thinkers; first pres. of Senegal, 1960–   ; first African member of the French Acad. of Moral and Political Sciences. *Chants d'Ombre,* 1945; *Hosties Noires,* 1948; *Ethiopiques,* 1956.

SERVICE, ROBERT WILLIAM, Jan. 16, 1874 (Lancashire, Eng.)–Sept.11, 1958. Canadian writer, poet. Called the "Canadian Kipling," best known for his verse, including "The Shooting of Dan McGrew." *Songs of a Sourdough,* 1907; *Ballads of Cheechako,* 1909; *Bar Room Ballads,* 1940.

SHOLOKHOV, MIKHAIL ALEKSANDROVICH, May 24, 1905 (Veshenskaya, Rus.). Soviet novelist. Best known for *The Silent Don* (4 vols., 1928–40), a widely read novel in the USSR, considered a model of socialist realism; awarded Nobel Prize in literature, 1965; first officially sanctioned Soviet laureate.

SIENKIEWICZ, HENRYK, May 5, 1846 (Wola Orkrzejska, Pol.)–Nov. 15, 1916. Polish novelist, short-story writer. Wrote colorful historical novels, including a trilogy about the Polish nationalist struggle: *With Fire and Sword* (1883), *The Deluge* (1886), *Pan Michael* (1887–88); awarded Nobel Prize in literature, 1905. *Quo Vadis?,* 1895.

THE BOOK OF WHO

SILLANPÄÄ, FRANS EEMIL, Sept. 16, 1888 (Hämeenkyrö, Fin.)–June 3, 1964. Finnish novelist, short-story writer. The first Finnish writer to win the Nobel Prize in literature, 1939. *Meek Heritage,* 1919, *The Maid Silja,* 1931.

SINYÁVSKY, ANDREI (pseud.: Abram Terts) 1925 (USSR). Soviet short-story writer, critic. Became symbol of the oppressed Soviet artist when he was sentenced (1966) to seven years of hard labor for writings published in the West under the pseudonym Abram Terts. *The Trial Begins,* 1961; *Fantastic Stories,* 1963; *The Makepeace Experiment,* 1965.

SOLZHENITSYN, ALEXANDER ISAYEVICH, Dec. 11, 1918 (Rostov, Rus.). Soviet novelist. Gained international fame for *One Day in the Life of Ivan Denisovich* (1962), about a forced labor camp during the Stalinist era, based on his own imprisonment for writing a letter critical of Stalin in 1945; officially censured from 1963; awarded 1970 Nobel Prize in literature, but forced to decline it; arrested, accused of treason, deported to the West, 1974; accepted Nobel after arriving in Switzerland. *The First Circle,* 1964; *Cancer Ward,* 1966; *August 1914,* 1972; *The Gulag Archipelago,* 1974.

SOPHOCLES, c.496 B.C. (Colonus, Gr.)–406 B.C. Greek playwright, poet. With AESCHYLUS and EURIPIDES, one of the great tragedians of classical Greece; an innovator, he added a third actor, enlarged the chorus, and replaced the trilogy format with a single tragedy; of some 123 dramas, seven complete tragedies, part of satyr play, and over 1,000 fragments survive; born to the leisure class, became treasurer of Athens, an army general, and elder statesman. *Antigone,* c.441 B.C.; *Oedipus Rex,* c.429 B.C.; *Electra; Trachinae; Philoctetes,* 409 B.C.; *Oedipus at Colonus,* 406 B.C.

SPITTELER, CARL FRIEDRICH GEORGE, Apr. 24, 1845 (Liestal, Switz.)–Dec. 29, 1924. Swiss poet, novelist. Noted for his imaginative works, notably the epics *Prometheus and Epimetheus* (1881), *Olympischer Frühling* (2 vols., 1900-06, rev. 1910), and *Prometheus der Dulder* (1924); his novel *Imago* (1906) influenced the development of psychoanalysis; awarded Nobel Prize in literature, 1919.

STRINDBERG, (Johan) **AUGUST,** Jan. 22, 1849 (Stockholm, Swe.)–May 14, 1912. Swedish playwright, novelist, short-story writer. Innovator who began writing dramas of social criticism in the tradition of HENRIK IBSEN; later, focused on the conflict between the sexes. *The Father,* 1887; *Miss Julie,* 1888; *Creditors,* 1888.

TAGORE, RABINDRANATH, May 7, 1861 (Calcutta, India)–Aug. 7, 1941. Bengali poet, playwright, essayist, novelist. A prodigious and versatile author, regarded as a guru; set hundreds of poems to music; a leading painter; awarded Nobel Prize in literature, 1913; knighted in 1915, but surrendered it to protest the Amritsar Massacre (1919). *The Golden Boat,* 1893; *Late Harvest,* 1896; *Gitanjali,* 1912; *Sadhana: The Realization of Life,* 1913; *Chitra,* 1917; *Red Oleanders,* 1924.

TASSO, TORQUATO, Mar. 11, 1544 (Sorrento, It.)–Apr. 25, 1595. Italian poet. A major poet of the later Renaissance; periodically confined for delusions of persecution. *Rinaldo,* 1562; *Jerusalem Liberated,* 1581; *Jerusalem Conquered,* 1593.

TERENCE, born Publius Terentius Afer, 186/185 B.C. (Carthage, modern Tunisia)–159? B.C. Roman dramatist. After PLAUTUS, the greatest Roman comic dramatist; wrote six influential verse comedies freely adapted from the works of MENANDER and others. *The Adrian Girl,* 166 B.C.; *The Mother-in-Law,* 165 B.C.; *The Self-Tormentor,* 163 B.C.; *The Eunuch,* 161 B.C. *Phormio,* 161 B.C.; *The Brothers,* 160 B.C.

THESPIS, fl.6th cent. B.C. (District of Icaria). Greek poet. The founder of tragic drama; introduced monologues and dialogues in the existing choruses of hymns to Bacchus and other deities.

TOLSTOY, LEO NIKOLAYEVICH, COUNT, Sept. 9, 1828 (Yasnaya Polyana, Rus.)–Nov. 20, 1910. Russian novelist, philosopher. Considered to be one of world's greatest writers; born of noble family, he led a profligate life and married, fathering 13 children; after a spiritual crisis (*A Confession,* 1878-79), became a Christian anarchist, abandoning worldly goods and devoting himself to social reform; became the center of an admiring cult. *War and Peace,* 1865-69; *Anna Karenina,* 1875-77; *The Kreutzer Sonata,* 1889; *Resurrection,* 1889; *Hadji Murad,* 1896-1904.

TU FU, 712 (Hsiang-yang |now Honan Prov.|, China)–770. Chinese poet. Generally considered the greatest Chinese poet of all time; a classicist whose verse decries the tragedy of wars and the cruelty of court life.

TURGENEV, IVAN SERGEYEVICH, Nov. 9, 1818 (Orel, Rus.)–Sept. 3, 1883. Russian novelist, short-story writer. Best known for his controversial masterpiece *Fathers and Sons* (1862); attacked serfdom in a simple but powerful style; a Westerner in his writing, from 1845 he lived abroad, chiefly in Germany and France. *Notes of A Hunter: A Sportsman's Sketches,* 1852; *Rudin,* 1856; *A Nest of Gentlefolk,* 1859; *Virgin Soil,* 1877.

UNDSET, SIGRID, May 20, 1882 (Kallundborg, Den.)–June 10, 1949. Norwegian novelist. Best known for her three-volume historical novel, *Kristin Lavransdatter* (1920-22), a medieval woman's life story; awarded Nobel Prize in literature, 1928; came to U.S. after the Nazi invasion of Norway, 1940. *Jenny,* 1911; *The Master of Hestviken,* 4 vols., 1928-30; *Return to the Future,* 1942.

VEGA (Carpio), **LOPE** (Felix) **DE,** Nov. 25, 1562 (Madrid, Sp.)–Aug. 27, 1635. Spanish dramatist. Foremost dramatist of the golden age of Spanish literature; called the Phoenix of Genius; wrote over 1,500 plays, including tragedies, comedies of manners, and cloak-and-dagger intrigues, of which nearly 500 survive. *The King the Greatest Mayor,* 1620-23; *The Knight of Olmedo,* 1620-25; *Punishment without Revenge,* 1631.

VERGA, GIOVANNI, Sept. 2, 1840 (Sicily)–Jan. 27, 1922. Italian novelist. Founder and leading exponent of the Italian realist school; wrote about Sicilian peasants and fishermen with intensity and lyricism; his play *Cavalleria Rusticana* (1884) was adapted into an opera by PIETRO MASCAGNI. *I Malavoglia,* 1881; *Mastrodon Gesualdo,* 1889.

VERGIL (or Virgil), born Publius Vergilius Maro, Oct. 15, 70 B.C. (nr. Mantua, It.)–Sept. 21, 19 B.C. Roman poet. Dominated Latin literature during its golden age; the well-educated son of a prosperous farmer, he joined the literary circle of Maecenas and AUGUSTUS; wrote eclogues or bucolics (37 B.C.), idealizing rural life, and georgics (30 B.C.), realistic rural poetry; devoted the remainder of his life to the *Aeneid* (12 books, unfinished), a national epic, sophisticated in style and noble in purpose, relating the adventures of the Trojan warrior Aeneas, whom myths linked to the founding of Rome.

VOZNESENSKY, ANDREI ANDREYEVICH, 1933 (Moscow, USSR). Soviet poet. A popular poet who gave many public readings in the 1960s; a close friend and protégé of BORIS PASTERNAK; writing stopped by anti-modernist campaign, 1963; placed under close surveillance, 1971. *Parabola,* 1960; *Mosaic,* 1960; *The Triangular Pear,* 1962.
WEISS, PETER, Nov. 8, 1916 (Nowawes |now Babelsberg|, Ger.). German-Swedish dramatist, novelist. Noted for *The Persecution and Assassination of Jean Paul Marat as Performed by the Inmates of the Asylum of Charenton under the Direction of the Marquis de Sade* (1964) and *The Investigation* (1965).
WEST, MORRIS LANGLO, Apr. 26, 1916 (Melbourne, Austrl.). Australian novelist. Best known for his best-selling *The Devil's Advocate* (1959) and *The Shoes of the Fisherman* (1963), which reflect his background as a Christian Brother. *The Summer of the Red Wolf,* 1971; *The Salamander,* 1973; *The Navigator,* 1976.
WHITE, PATRICK VICTOR MARTINDALE, May 28, 1912 (London, Eng.). Australian novelist, playwright, short-story writer. His main theme is the quest for meaning and value in 20th-cent. Australia; awarded Nobel Prize in literature, 1973. *Happy Valley,* 1939; *The Tree of Man,* 1955; *Riders in the Chariot,* 1961; *The Eye of the Storm,* 1973.
YEVTUSHENKO, YEVGENY ALEKSANDROVICH, July 18, 1933 (Zima, USSR). Soviet poet. Popular spokesman for the post-Stalin generation of Soviet poets; was heavily censored for his *A Precocious Autobiography* (1963; published in France), but allowed to make several trips abroad; best known for "Babi Yar," a protest against anti-semitism. *Selected Poems,* 1962; *Bratskyaya Station,* 1966; *Stolen Apples* 1971
ZAMYATIN, YEVGENY IVANOVICH. Feb. 1, 1884 (Lebedyan, Rus.)-Mar. 10, 1937. Soviet novelist, playwright. Best known for his anti-utopian novel *We* (1924), circulated but never published in the Soviet Union.

DETECTIVE, GOTHIC, SUSPENSE WRITERS

ALLINGHAM, MARGERY, May 20, 1904 (London, Eng.)-June 30, 1966. English novelist. A leading mystery writer; created the erudite detective Albert Campion. *The Crime at Black Dudley,* 1928; *Mystery Mile,* 1929; *Police at the Funeral,* 1931; *Sweet Danger,* 1933; *Death of a Ghost,* 1934; *Flowers for the Judge,* 1936; *The Fashion in Shrouds,* 1938; *Traitor's Purse,* 1941; *Tiger in the Smoke,* 1963; *The China Governess,* 1963; *The Mind Readers,* 1965.
AMBLER, ERIC, June 28, 1909 (London, Eng.). English novelist. Author of literate international-intrigue stories; created TV detective series *Checkmate,* 1960; Mystery Writers of America Grand Master Award, 1975. *A Coffin for Dimitrios,* 1939; *Journey into Fear,* 1940; *The Light of Day,* 1963; *Dirty Story,* 1967; *The Levanter,* 1972.
BALL, JOHN DUDLEY, July 8, 1911 (Schenectady, N.Y.). U.S. mystery-story writer. His mystery novel *In the Heat of the Night* (1965), featuring Virgil Tibbs, one of the first black detective heroes, was made into an Academy Award–winning film. *Five Pieces of Jade,* 1972.
BERKELEY, ANTHONY (pseud.: A. B. Cox, Francis Iles), born Anthony Berkeley Cox, 1893-1970. English journalist, critic, mystery writer; anonymously published *The Layton Court Mystery,*

featuring the outrageous Roger Sheringham, 1925; as A. B. Cox, founded London's famous Detective Club in 1928, wrote the classic story *The Avenging Chance* (1929), which he later expanded into a satirical novel, *The Poisoned Chocolates Case* (1929); as Francis Iles, wrote the highly praised *Malice Aforethought* (1931), *Before the Fact* (1932, adapted by ALFRED HITCHCOCK in *Suspicion*), and *Trial and Error* (1937).
BIGGERS, EARL DERR, Aug. 26, 1884 (Warren, Ohio)-Apr. 5, 1933. U.S. mystery-story writer, novelist. Author of the Charlie Chan stories, first serialized in the *Saturday Evening Post* and later made into a popular film series of the 1930s and 1940s.
CARR, JOHN DICKSON (pseud.: Carter Dickson, Carr Dickson), 1906 (Uniontown, Pa.)-Feb. 27, 1976. U.S. mystery-story writer. Master| of the locked-room mystery; created Dr. Gideon Fell. *Hag's Nook,* 1933; *The Bride of Newgate,* 1950; *The Dead Man's Knock,* 1958; *The Arabian Nights Murder,* 1965; *Case of the Constant Suicides,* 1962; *Crooked Hinge,* 1964.
CHANDLER, RAYMOND, July 23, 1888 (Chicago, Ill.)-Mar. 26, 1959. U.S. short-story writer, novelist. Master of the "hard-boiled" crime story; created the tough private detective Philip Marlowe. *The Big Sleep,* 1939; *Farewell, My Lovely,* 1940; *The Lady in the Lake,* 1943; *The Long Goodbye,* 1954; *Playback,* 1958.
CHESTERTON, G(ilbert) K(eith), May 29, 1874 (London, Eng.)-June 14, 1936. English essayist, novelist, journalist, poet. Created detective series with Father Brown as the sleuth; a convert to Catholicism; called the Prince of Paradox for the religious dogma underlying his light style. *Tremendous Trifles,* 1909; *The Innocence of Father Brown,* 1911; *Come To Think of It,* 1930.
CHRISTIE, DAME AGATHA MARY CLARISSA (pseud.: Mary Westmacott), Sept. 15, 1890 (Devon, Eng.)-Jan. 12, 1976. English novelist, playwright. Extremely popular mystery novelist whose books have sold over 100,000,000 copies; created the fastidious Belgian detective Hercule Poirot and eccentric spinster Jane Marple; her play *The Mousetrap* (1952) is still running on the London stage. *The Murder of Roger Ackroyd,* 1926; *Murder at the Vicarage,* 1930; *Death on the Nile,* 1937; *And Then There Were None,* 1940; *Witness for the Prosecution* (play), 1954.
COLES, MANNING (pseud. of Cyril Henry Coles, 1899 |London, Eng.|-Oct. 9, 1965, and Adelaide Manning, 1891 |London, Eng.|-1959). English mystery writers. Invented the character Tommy Hambleton, a high-ranking English intelligence agent. *Drink to Yesterday,* 1940; *No Entry,* 1958.
COLLINS, (William) WILKIE, Jan. 8, 1824 (London, Eng.)-Sept. 23, 1889. English novelist. Wrote what are generally considered to be the first detective novels in English. *The Woman in White,* 1860; *The Moonstone,* 1868.
CONDON, RICHARD, Mar. 18, 1915 (New York, N.Y.). U.S. novelist. *The Manchurian Candidate,* 1959; *A Talent for Loving,* 1961; *Arigato,* 1972; *The Star-Spangled Crunch,* 1974; *Winter Kills,* 1974; *Bandicoot,* 1978.
CREASEY, JOHN (pseud.: J. J. Marric, Gordon Ashe, Robert Caine, many others), Sept. 17, 1908 (Surrey, Eng.)-June 9, 1973. English mystery writer. Wrote over 600 books using 28 pseudonyms. *Department Z,* series, 1932-68; *The Toff,* series, 1938-68; *Inspector West,* series, 1942-68; *Dr. Palfrey,* series, 1942-68.

THE BOOK OF WHO

CRISPIN, EDMUND (pseud. of Robert Bruce Montgomery), Oct. 2, 1921 (Buckinghamshire, Eng.)–Sept. 15, 1978. English detective novelist, musician, composer. Noted for his short stories and novels about Gervase Fen, an Oxford prof. and crime solver; wrote scores for many British films. *Obsequies at Oxford*, 1945; *The Moving Toyshop*, 1946; *Buried for Pleasure*, 1949.

CROFTS, FREEMAN WILLIS, June 1879 (Dublin, Ire.)–Apr. 11, 1957. Irish detective-story writer. Creator of Inspector French; introduced police routine to detective fiction; his first book, *The Cask* (1920), is a classic that helped launch the golden age of the detective story. *The Box Office Murders*, 1929; *The Mystery of the Sleeping Car Express*, 1956.

DEIGHTON, LEN, Feb. 18, 1929 (London, Eng.). English mystery and nonfiction writer. Author of complex, wry espionage thrillers. *The Ipcress File*, 1962; *Funeral in Berlin*, 1964; *The Billion Dollar Brain*, 1966; *Spy Story*, 1974; *The Battle of Britain*, 1977; *SS-GB*, 1979.

DOYLE, SIR ARTHUR CONAN, May 22, 1859 (Edinburgh, Scot.)–July 7, 1930. British novelist. Created Sherlock Holmes, one of the best-known characters in English literature; a physician by profession, he abandoned medicine after the success of the first Holmes story, *A Study in Scarlet* (1887); knighted, 1902. *The Sign of the Four*, 1890; *The Memoirs of Sherlock Holmes*, 1894; *Hound of the Baskervilles*, 1902; *Return of Sherlock Holmes*, 1905.

EBERHART, MIGNON GOOD, July 6, 1899 (Lincoln, Nebraska). U.S. mystery novelist. Author of over 50 gothic/mystery novels. *While the Patient Slept*, 1930; *The Cases of Susan Dare*, 1934; *The Bayou Road*, 1979.

FLEMING, IAN LANCASTER, May 28, 1908 (London, Eng.)–Aug. 12, 1964. English writer of adventure novels. Created Secret Agent 007, James Bond. *Casino Royale*, 1953; *From Russia With Love*, 1957; *Dr. No*, 1958; *Goldfinger*, 1959; *Thunderball*, 1961; *Chitty-Chitty-Bang-Bang* (for children), 1964.

FORSYTH, FREDERICK, Aug. 1938 (Kent, Eng.). English novelist, journalist. *The Day of the Jackal*, 1971; *The Odessa File*, 1972; *The Dogs of War*, 1974.

FRANCIS, DICK, Oct. 31, 1920 (nr. Tenby, Wales). Welsh jockey, mystery writer. Raced under the Queen Mother's colors for four years; writes mystery novels about jockeys and pilots. *Dead Cert*, 1962; *Odds Against*, 1965; *For Kicks*, 1965; *Flying Finish*, 1966; *Forfeit*, 1969; *High Stakes*, 1975; *In the Frame*, 1977; *Risk*, 1978.

FREELING, NICOLAS, 1927 (London, Eng.). English mystery novelist. His mysteries, featuring Inspector van der Valk, are noted for their characterizations and authentic descriptions of Dutch locales. *Love in Amsterdam*, 1962; *The King of the Rainy Country*, 1966.

GARDNER, ERLE STANLEY (pseud.: A. A. Fair, Carleton Kendrake), July 17, 1889 (Malden, Mass.)–May 11, 1970. U.S. detective-story writer. A trial lawyer by profession, he wrote crime stories for magazines, as well as over 100 books; several films and a long-running television series were based on his hero, Perry Mason. *The Case of the Velvet Claws*, 1932.

GILBERT, MICHAEL FRANCIS, July 17, 1912 (Lincolnshire, Eng.). English lawyer, detective-story writer. Prolific author of short stories, as well as mystery dramas and novels; editor of *Classics of Adventure and Detection*. *The Claimant*, 1957; *A Clean Kill*, 1960; *Game without Rules*, 1967; *Amateur in Violence*, 1973.

GILMAN, DOROTHY (pseud.: Dorothy Gilman Butters), June 25, 1923 (New Brunswick, N.J.). U.S. mystery writer. Created Mrs. Pollifax, the geriatric sleuth; under her pseudonym, writes books for young people. *The Unexpected Mrs. Pollifax*, 1966; *The Amazing Mrs. Pollifax*, 1970; *The Elusive Mrs. Pollifax*, 1971; *Mrs. Pollifax on Safari*, 1976.

HAMMETT (Samuel) **DASHIELL**, Mar. 27, 1894 (St. Mary's Co., Md.)–Jan. 10, 1961. U.S. writer. Invented the hard-boiled "private eye" in the first Sam Spade novel, *The Maltese Falcon* (1930); his Spade, along with Nick and Nora Charles, were the heroes of many radio and TV shows and films. *The Dain Curse*, 1929; *The Glass Key*, 1931; *The Thin Man*, 1934.

HIGGINS, JACK (pseud.: Harry Patterson), July 27, 1929 (Newcastle, Eng.). English author of best-selling suspense novels. *The Eagle Has Landed*, 1975; *Storm Warning*, 1976; *Day of Judgement*, 1979.

HIGHSMITH, PATRICIA, 1921 (Fort Worth, Tex.). U.S. novelist, short-story writer. Author of mystery stories, especially popular in Europe; her *Strangers on a Train* (1950) inspired an ALFRED HITCHCOCK film.

HOLT, VICTORIA (pseud. of Eleanor Burford Hibbert), 1906 (London, Eng.). English novelist. Prolific author of gothic and romantic fiction. *Mistress of Mellyn*, 1960; *Shivering Sands*, 1969; *Pride of the Peacock*, 1976.

INNES, MICHAEL (pseud. of John Innes MacKintosh Stewart), 1906 (nr. Edinburgh, Scot.). Scottish novelist, scholar, mystery writer. Under his own name, author of novels, short stories, biographies, and *Eight Modern Writers* (1963), the final volume of the *Oxford History of English Literature*; as Michael Innes, writes mysteries noted for their erudition, complex plotting, and humor, including *Hamlet, Revenge!* (1937) and *Lament for a Maker* (1938).

JAMES, P(hyllis) D(orothy), Aug. 3, 1920 (Oxford, Eng.). English mystery writer. Created the intelligent, perceptive poet and inspector, Adam Dalgliesh. *Cover Her Face*, 1962; *Unnatural Causes*, 1967; *Shroud for a Nightingale*, 1971; *An Unsuitable Job for a Woman*, 1975.

KEMELMAN, HARRY, Nov. 2, 1908 (Boston, Mass.). U.S. mystery writer. Created a series featuring Rabbi David Small as a detective. *Friday the Rabbi Slept Late*, 1964; *Saturday the Rabbi Went Hungry*, 1966; *Wednesday the Rabbi Got Wet*, 1976.

LATHEN, EMMA (pseud. of Mary J. Latis and Martha Hennissart). U.S. mystery writers. Respectively an attorney and economic analyst, they met as graduate students at Harvard U.; created the fictional character John Putnam Thatcher, senior vice-pres. of Sloan Guaranty Trust Co. and amateur detective. *Death Shall Overcome*, 1966; *Murder to Go*, 1969; *Sweet and Low*, 1974; *By Hook or by Crook*, 1975.

LE CARRE, JOHN (pseud. of David John Moore Cornwell), Oct. 19, 1931 (Dorsetshire, Eng.). English novelist. Noted for his realistic spy stories about aging, weary spies. *The Spy Who Came in from the Cold*, 1963; *Tinker, Tailor, Soldier, Spy*, 1974; *The Honourable Schoolboy*, 1977.

LE FANU, JOSEPH SHERIDAN, Aug. 28, 1814 (Dublin, Ire.)–Feb. 7, 1873. Irish mystery writer.

Founded, owned, and edited the *Dublin Evening Mail*, 1839–58; after his wife's death, withdrew from society and wrote supernatural stories. *Uncle Silas: A Tale of Bartram Haugh*, 1864; *Wylder's Hand*, 1864; *Checkmate*, 1871.

LEROUX, GASTON, May 6, 1868 (Paris, Fr.)–Apr. 15, 1927. French journalist, dramatist, mystery writer. His classic thriller *The Phantom of the Opera* (1911) was made into several successful films. *The Mystery of the Yellow Room*, 1907; *The Perfume of the Lady in Black*, 1907.

LEWIS, CECIL DAY (pseud.: Nicholas Blake), born Cecil Day-Lewis, Apr. 27, 1904 (Ballintubber, Ire.)–May 22, 1972. English poet. Prof. of poetry, Oxford U., 1951–56; poet-laureate of England, 1967–72; wrote detective novels under his pseudonym. *Overtures to Death*, 1938; *Pegasus and Other Poems*, 1957; *The Whispering Roots and Other Poems*, 1970.

LOCKRIDGE, RICHARD, Sept. 26, 1898 (St. Joseph, Mo.). U.S. novelist, short-story writer. With his wife Frances Lockridge, wrote 27 civilized, humorous mysteries about a husband-and-wife detective team, the Norths; after his wife's death (1963), wrote several other mystery stories. *The Norths Meet Murder*, 1946; *Death on the Aisle*, 1942; *Murder within Murder*, 1946; *The Tenth Life*, 1977.

LUDLUM, ROBERT (pseud.: Jonathan Ryder), May 25, 1927 (New York, N.Y.). U.S. novelist. Author of novels of adventure and intrigue. *The Scarlatti Inheritance*, 1971; *The Osterman Weekend*, 1972; *The Rhinemann Exchange*, 1974; *The Gemini Contenders*, 1976; *The Holcroft Covenant*, 1978; *The Matarese Circle*, 1979.

MACDONALD, JOHN DANN, July 24, 1916 (Sharon, Pa.). U.S. mystery novelist, short-story writer. Most of his stories and books, including the Travis McGee series, are set in Florida; Mystery Writers of America Grand Master Award, 1972. *The Brass Cupcake*, 1950; *The Deep Blue Good-By*, 1964; *The Last One Left*, 1967; *The Dreadful Lemon Sky*, 1975; *Condominium*, 1977.

MACDONALD, ROSS (pseud. of Kenneth Millar; other pseud.: John MacDonald, John Ross MacDonald), Dec. 13, 1915 (Los Gatos, Cal.). U.S. novelist, mystery writer. Created private detective Lew Archer. *The Dark Tunnel*, 1944; *The Moving Target*, 1949; *The Chill*, 1964; *The Far Side of the Dollar*, 1965; *The Goodbye Look*, 1969; *The Underground Man*, 1972.

MACINNES, HELEN CLARK, Oct. 7, 1907 (Glasgow, Scot.). Scottish-U.S. novelist. Author of popular espionage novels. *Above Suspicion*, 1941; *While We Still Live*, 1944; *Decision at Delphi*, 1960; *The Snare of the Hunter*, 1974; *The Salzburg Connection*, 1968.

MACLEAN, ALISTAIR STUART, 1922 (Glasgow, Scot.). Scottish novelist. Author of adventure novels, many of which have been made into films. *The Guns of Navarone*, 1957; *Ice Station Zebra*, 1963; *Where Eagles Dare*, 1967.

MARSH, DAME (Edith) **NGAIO**, Apr. 23, 1899 (Christchurch, N.Z.). New Zealand–British novelist, actress, theatrical producer. Known for mysteries featuring Inspector Roderick Alleyn of Scotland Yard; made a dame of the Order of the British Empire, 1948. *A Man Lay Dead*, 1934; *Overture to Death*, 1939; *Death of a Fool*, 1956; *Dead Water*, 1963.

MCCLURE, JAMES HOWE, Oct. 9, 1939 (Johannesburg, S.A.). South African crime novelist. *The Steam Pig*, 1971; *The Caterpillar Cop*, 1972: *The Gooseberry Fool*, 1974; *Rogue Eagle*, 1976; *The Sunday Hangman*, 1977.

MCNEILE, HERMAN CYRIL (pseud.: Sapper), Sept. 28, 1888 (Cornwall, Eng.)–Aug. 14, 1937. English novelist. Wrote crime and adventure fiction; under his pseudonym, created series about ex-policeman Bulldog Drummond; after McNeile's death, the series was continued by his friend and biographer Gerard Fairlie, after whom Drummond was modeled in part. *Bulldog Drummond: The Adventures of a Demobilized Officer Who Found Peace Dull*, 1920; *Bulldog Drummond Strikes Back*, 1933.

POE, EDGAR ALLEN, Jan. 19, 1809 (Boston, Mass.)–Oct. 7, 1849. U.S. poet, short-story writer, critic. Best known for his mysterious, macabre stories and poems ("To Helen," 1931; "The Raven," 1845; "Annabel Lee," 1847); invented the modern detective story. "The Masque of the Red Death," 1842; "The Fall of the House of Usher," 1839; "The Pit and the Pendulum," 1842; "The Tell-Tale Heart," 1843; "The Murders in the Rue Morgue," 1841; "The Mystery of Marie Roget," 1842; "The Gold Bug," 1843; "The Purloined Letter," 1844.

PRICE, ANTHONY, Aug. 16, 1928 (Hertfordshire, Eng.). English novelist. Author of historical mysteries. *The Labyrinth Makers*, 1970; *Our Man in Camelot*, 1975; *War Game*, 1976.

QUEEN, ELLERY (pseud. of Manford B. Lee, born Manford Lepofsky, Jan. 11, 1905 [New York, N.Y.]–Apr. 2, 1971; and Frederic Dannay, born Daniel Nathan, Oct. 20, 1905 [New York, N.Y.]). U.S. mystery writers. Cousins, they collaborated on novels, novellas, and short stories, using their pseudonym for their detective-hero; edited *Ellery Queen's Mystery Magazine*, from 1941, and over 70 anthologies and critical works. *The Roman Hat Mystery*, 1929.

RADCLIFFE, ANN, née Ward, July 9, 1764 (London, Eng.)–Feb. 7, 1823. English novelist. Wrote popular, classic Gothic romances set in Italy. *The Romance of the Forest*, 1791; *The Mysteries of Udolpho*, 1794; *The Italian; or, The Confessional of the Black Penitents*, 1797.

RINEHART, MARY ROBERTS, Aug. 12, 1876 (Pittsburgh, Pa.)–Sept. 22, 1958. U.S. novelist. Originated the "Had I But Known" school of detective novels. *The Circular Staircase*, 1908; *The Amazing Adventures of Letitia Carberry*, 1911; *Tish*, 1916; *The Bat* (play), 1920.

ROHMER, SAX (pseud. of Arthur Sarsfield Ward [or Wade]), 1883?–June 1, 1959. English mystery writer. Best known as author of 13-book series about Fu Manchu, the sinister Chinese criminal genius. *Dr. Fu Manchu*, 1913; *Re-enter Fu Manchu*, 1957; *The Return of Fu*, 1959.

SANDERS, LAWRENCE, 1920 (New York, N.Y.). U.S. writer. Noted for his best-sellers in which the heroes possess a touch of perversity. *The Anderson Tapes*, 1970; *The First Deadly Sin*, 1973; *The Marlow Chronicles*, 1977; *The Sixth Commandment*, 1979.

SAYERS, DOROTHY L(eigh), June 13, 1893 (Oxford, Eng.)–Dec. 17, 1957. English mystery novelist. Wrote sophisticated detective novels; created Lord Peter Wimsey, the aristocratic amateur detective; one of the first women graduates of Oxford U. *Clouds of Witness*, 1926; *Strong Poison*, 1930; *Murder Must Advertise*, 1933; *The Nine Tailors*, 1934.

SHELLEY, MARY WOLLSTONECRAFT, Aug. 30, 1797 (London, Eng.)–Feb. 1, 1851. English novelist. Best known as the author of *Franken-stein; or, The Modern Prometheus* (1818), a novel of terror; daughter of author and political philosopher WILLIAM GODWIN and MARY WOLLSTONECRAFT GODWIN, the first radical feminist; at age 18, eloped with PERCY BYSSHE SHELLEY.

SIMENON, GEORGES JOSEPH CHRISTIAN (at least 17 pseudonyms), Feb. 13, 1903 (Liege, Belg.). Belgian-French novelist. Incredibly prolific writer of hundreds of short novels involving acts of violence; created Inspector Maigret of the Paris police. *The Strange Case of Peter the Lett*, 1933; *The Patience of Maigret*, 1939; *The Man Who Watched the Trains Go By*, 1942; *Maigret's Memoirs*, 1963; *The Girl with a Squint*, 1978.

SJÖWALL, MAJ, Sept. 25, 1935 (Stockholm, Swed.). Swedish novelist, poet. With her husband, PER WAHLÖÖ, wrote a series of realistic police procedural novels featuring Martin Beck. *Roseanna*, 1967; *The Laughing Policeman*, 1970; *Murder at the Savoy*, 1971; *The Locked Room*, 1973; *The Terrorists*, 1976.

SPILLANE, MICKEY, born Frank Morrison Spillane, Mar. 9, 1918 (Brooklyn, N.Y.). U.S. writer of detective novels. As a comic-book writer, one of the originators of Captain Marvel and Captain America; created the tough detective Mike Hammer, whom he played in the 1963 film version of his novel *The Girl Hunters* (1962). *I, the Jury*, 1947; *My Gun Is Quick*, 1950; *The Big Kill*, 1951.

STEWART, MARY FLORENCE ELINOR RAINBOW, Sept 17, 1916 (Durham, Eng.). English novelist. Author of best-selling romantic suspense novels. *Nine Coaches Waiting*, 1959; *My Brother Michael*, 1960; *The Ivy Tree*, 1961; *The Moon-Spinners*, 1962.

STOKER, BRAM, born Abraham Stoker, 1847 (Dublin, Ire.)–Apr. 20, 1912. Irish novelist. Best known as author of *Dracula* (1897), the classic horror story of a Transylvanian count who was a vampire; managed the actor Sir HENRY IRVING for 27 years.

STOUT, REX TODHUNTER, Dec. 1, 1886 (Noblesville, Ind.)–Oct. 27, 1975. U.S. novelist. Created the eccentric, elephantine detective Nero Wolfe; founder of the Vanguard Press, 1926. *Fer-de-Lance*, 1934; *Too Many Cooks*, 1938; *Some Buried Caesar*, 1939; *Black Orchids*, 1942; *The Black Mountain*, 1954; *The Doorbell Rang*, 1965.

SYMONS, JULIAN GUSTAVE, May 30, 1912 (London, Eng.). English novelist, poet, biographer, critic. Prolific crime novelist specializing in violence behind bland, respectable faces; also a critic of crime novels, a social historian, and a literary critic. *The Immaterial Murder Case*, 1945; *The Progress of a Crime*, 1960.

TEY, JOSEPHINE (pseud. of Elizabeth MacKintosh; pseud.: Gordon Daviot), 1896 (Inverness, Scot.)–Feb. 13, 1952. Scottish mystery novelist, playwright. Created the elegant Scotland Yard investigator Alan Grant. *The Man in the Queue*, 1929; *A Shilling for Candles*, 1936; *Miss Pym Disposes*, 1946; *The Daughter of Time*, 1951; *The Singing Sands*, 1952.

UHNAK, DOROTHY, Apr. 24, 1930 (New York, N.Y.). U.S. mystery novelist, policewoman. Best known for her best-sellers *The Investigation* (1977) and *Law and Order* (1973); a NYC policewoman for 14 years, received the depart-ment's highest award for heroism. *Policewoman*, 1964; *The Bait*, 1968.

VAN DINE, S. S. (pseud. of William Huntington Wright), Oct. 15, 1888 (Charlottesville, Va.)–Apr. 11, 1939. U.S. mystery writer, editor, critic. Created Philo Vance, a wealthy, sophisticated, pompous detective. *The Benson Murder Case*, 1926; *The Bishop Murder Case*, 1929; *The Gracie Allen Murder Case*, 1938.

WAHLÖÖ, PER, May 8, 1926 (Gothenburg, Swed.)–June 23, 1975. Swedish novelist. As Peter Wahlöö, wrote two crime novels, *The Thirty-first Floor* (1966) and *The Steel Spring* (1970), about Chief Inspector Jensen; with his wife, MAJ SJÖWALL, wrote a series of police procedure novels featuring Martin Beck.

WALLACE, EDGAR, Dec. 1875 (Greenwich, Eng.)–Feb. 10, 1932. English writer, dramatist, journalist. Noted as an author of thrillers. *The Clue of the Twisted Candle*, 1916 (U.S.); *The Green Archer*, 1924 (U.S.); *On the Spot*, 1931 (U.S.); *My Hollywood Diary*, 1932 (U.S.).

WESTLAKE, DONALD EDWIN (pseud.: Richard Stark, Tucker Cole), July 12, 1933 (New York, N.Y.). U.S. novelist. After early "hard-boiled" novels, turned to humorous crime fiction. *Killing Time*, 1961; *The Fugitive Pigeon*, 1965; *The Hot Rock*, 1970; *Bank Shot*, 1972; *Jimmy the Kid*, 1974; *Nobody's Perfect*, 1977.

WHITNEY, PHYLLIS AYAME, Sept. 9, 1903 (Yokohama, Jap.). U.S. juvenile-story and mystery writer. *Mystery of the Haunted Pool*, 1960; *Secret of the Emerald Star*, 1964; *Seven Tears for Apollo*, 1963; *The Winter People*, 1969; *Spindrift*, 1975.

SCIENCE FICTION WRITERS

ALDISS, BRIAN WILSON, Aug. 18, 1925 (England). British science-fiction writer. *Hot House*, 1962; *Greybeard*, 1964; *Frankenstein Unbound*, 1973; *Brotherhood of the Head*, 1978.

ANDERSON, POUL WILLIAM, 1926 (Pennsylvania). U.S. science-fiction writer noted for his humor ("Nicholas Van Rijn" series) and time-travel ideas. *Trader to the Stars*, 1964; *Guardians of Time*, 1960; *Tan Zero*, 1970.

ASIMOV, ISAAC, Jan. 2, 1920 (USSR). U.S. science and science-fiction writer. Prof. of biochemistry, Boston U., 1955– ; prolific (over 200 works) author of fiction and nonfiction; his *Foundation* trilogy (1951–53) and his story "Nightfall" (1940) are regarded as being among the best sci-fi works ever written. *I, Robot*, 1950; *Caves of Steel*, 1954; *The Intelligent Man's Guide to Science*, 2 vols., 1960; *The Gods Themselves*, 1973.

BLISH, JAMES BENJAMIN, 1921 (Orange, N.J.)–July 30, 1975. U.S. science-fiction writer. Noted especially for the "Cities in Flight" series and for his visions of the satanic; wrote for the *Star Trek* TV series.

BRADBURY, RAY DOUGLAS, Aug. 22, 1920 (Waukegan, Ill.). U.S. science-fiction writer. Known for well-written stories combining fantasy and social criticism; his *The Illustrated Man* (1951) and *Fahrenheit 451* (1953) were made into films. *The Martian Chronicles* (short stories), 1950; *Dandelion Wine* (short stories), 1957; *The Halloween Tree* (short stories), 1972.

BROWN, FREDERIC WILLIAM, Oct. 29, 1906 (Cincinnati, Ohio)–Mar. 11, 1972. U.S. science-fiction writer noted for comedy and satire. *What Mad Universe*, 1949; *Martians, Go Home*, 1955.

BRUNNER, JOHN KILIAN HOUSTON, 1934 (England). English science-fiction writer. Noted for novels about ecological disaster. *Stand on Zanzibar,* 1969; *The Sheep Look Up,* 1972.

CAMPBELL, JOHN WOOD, June 8, 1910 (Newark, N.J.)–July 11, 1971. U.S. science-fiction editor, writer. Editor of *Astounding Science Fiction* magazine (now *Analog*), 1937–71; "discovered" I. ASIMOV, R. HEINLEIN, A.E. VAN VOGT, L. DEL RAY, others; helped Asimov develop the "Robotic Laws"; his emphasis on "hard" science and technical knowledge made him the midwife of modern sci-fi.; his highly-acclaimed story "Who Goes There?" was made into the film *The Thing* (1951).

CLARKE, ARTHUR CHARLES, Dec. 16, 1917 (England). English science and science-fiction writer. Many of his stories are marked by a sense of cosmic unity, as in *Childhood's End* (1953); his *Sentinel* (1951) was the basis for STANLEY KUBRICK's 1968 film *2001—A Space Odyssey;* in many of his nonfiction books, strongly advocates space flight.

DE CAMP, L(yon) SPRAGUE, Nov. 27, 1907 (New York, N.Y.). U.S. science-fiction and history writer. Primarily a fantasist known for his *Viagens Interplanetarias* stories; his nonfiction includes *Lest Darkness Fall* (1941), *Divide and Rule* (1948), *The Ancient Engineers* (1963).

DELANY, SAMUEL RAY, 1942 (New York, N.Y.). U.S. science-fiction writer. Known for his highly individualistic style and symbolism. *Toromon* trilogy, 1963–65; *Nova,* 1968; *Dahlgren,* 1974.

DEL REY, LESTER, born Ramon Alvarez del Rey, June 2, 1915 (Saratoga, Minn.). U.S. science-fiction writer. Known for his vivid writing and sympathetic treatment of characters; his classic novel *Nerves* (1942) prophetically describes a nuclear power plant accident; with his wife, Judy-Lynn, edits science fiction and fantasy for Ballantine Books. *The Eleventh Commandment,* 1962.

DICK, PHILIP KENDRICK, 1928 (Chicago, Ill.). U.S. science-fiction writer. Prolific novelist on a variety of themes. *Time out of Joint,* 1959; *Do Androids Dream of Electric Sheep?,* 1968.

DICKSON, GORDON RUPERT, 1923 (Alberta, Can.). U.S.-Canadian science-fiction writer. Best known for his *Dorsai* trilogy, including *Soldier, Ask Not* (1967). *Delusion World,* 1961; *The Alien Way,* 1965.

ELLISON, HARLAN JAY, May 27, 1934 (Cleveland, Ohio). U.S. science-fiction writer. Author of innovative, award-winning science-fiction short stories; noted science-fiction anthologist (*Dark Visions,* collections of 1968, 1972, 1976); writer for *"Star Trek"* and other TV shows.

FARMER, PHILIP JOSÉ, 1918 (Indiana). U.S. science-fiction writer. Best known for being one of the first to introduce sex into science fiction. *Lovers,* 1961; *Maker of Universes,* 1965.

HEINLEIN, ROBERT ANSON, July 7, 1907 (Butler, Mo.). U.S. science-fiction writer. Noted for writing "future history" and for the conservative ideology of his writings. *Farmer in the Sky,* 1950; *Stranger in a Strange Land,* 1961; *Orphans of the Sky,* 1963.

HERBERT, FRANK PATRICK, Oct. 8, 1920 (Tacoma, Wash.). U.S. science-fiction writer. Best known for his *Dune* trilogy, detailing the ecology of a desert world. *Dune,* 1965; *Hellstrom's Hive,* 1973; *Dune Messiah,* 1976; *The Illustrated Dune,* 1978.

KORNBLUTH, C(yril) M. (pseud.: Cyril Judd), 1923 (New York, N.Y.)–Mar. 21, 1958. U.S. science-fiction writer. Best known for his collaborations with FREDERIK POHL. *The Syndic,* 1953.

LE GUIN, URSULA, née Kroeber, Oct. 21, 1929 (Berkeley, Calif.). U.S. science-fiction and fantasy writer. Best known for her *Left Hand of Darkness* (1969); Newberry Award, 1971; National Book Award, 1973. *The Lathe of Heaven,* 1971; *The Dispossessed,* 1974.

LEM, STANISLAW, Dec. 9, 1921 (Lvov, Pol.). Polish writer. Best known for the surrealism of his themes and plots. *Solaris,* 1961; *The Invincible,* 1973.

LOVECRAFT, H(oward) P(hilips), Aug. 20, 1890 (Providence, R.I.)–Mar. 15, 1937. U.S. writer. Best known for nightmarish horror stories of demonism; all but one of his books were published after his death. *Dunwich Horror,* 1945.

NIVEN, LAURENCE (Larry) VON COTT, Apr. 30, 1938 (Los Angeles, Calif.). U.S. science-fiction writer. Best known for *The Mote in God's Eye* (with J. Pournelle, 1974). *Ringworld,* 1970; *Lucifer's Hammer* (with J. Pournelle), 1977.

PADGETT, LEWIS (pseud. of Henry Kuttner), 1915 (Los Angeles, Calif.)–Feb. 4, 1958. U.S. science-fiction writer. Best known for his many short stories written in collaboration with his wife, C. L. Moore. *Well of the Worlds,* 1952; *Mutant,* 1953.

POHL, FREDERIK, Nov. 26, 1919 (New York, N.Y.). U.S. science-fiction writer. Editor of *Galaxy,* 1962–69; collaborated with C. M. KORNBLUTH on many novels and stories. *The Space Merchants* (with Kornbluth), 1953.

SILVERBERG, ROBERT, Jan. 1935 (New York, N.Y.). U.S. science-fiction and nonfiction writer. Prolific novelist and short-story writer. *Nightwings,* 1969; *A Time of Changes,* 1971.

SMITH, CORDWAINER (pseud. of Paul Myron Anthony Linebarger), 1913 (Milwaukee, Wisc.)–Aug. 6, 1966. U.S. science-fiction writer. Fantasist with a surreal, elusive style; expert in psychological warfare. *The Planet Buyer,* 1964.

SMITH, EDWARD ELMER ("Doc"), 1890 (Sheboygan, Wisc.)–Aug. 31, 1965. U.S. science-fiction writer. Specialized in "space opera"; best known for his Lensman and Skylark series.

STAPLETON, WILLIAM OLAF, May 10, 1886 (England)–Sept. 6, 1950. English science-fiction writer. Best known for his compendious future histories, such as *Star Maker* (1937), and for *Odd John* (1936), the story of a strange superman.

STURGEON, THEODORE HAMILTON (pseud. of Edward Hamilton Waldo), Feb. 26, 1918 (Staten Is., N.Y.). U.S. science-fiction writer. Best known for his group-mind stories, including *More Than Human* (1953) and *Cosmic Rape* (1958). A script writer for *Star Trek* TV series.

VAN VOGT, ALFRED ELTON, 1912 (Winnipeg, Man.). Canadian science-fiction writer. Best known for *Slan* (1946), *The World of Null-A* (1948), and *The Weapon Shops of Isher* (1951).

VERNE, JULES, Feb. 8, 1828 (Nantes, Fr.)–Mar. 24, 1905. French novelist. Wrote some 50 romantic-adventure and science-fiction stories, many of which were translated and made into plays and films; anticipated many scientific achievements of the 20th cent., including submarines, aqualungs, television, and space travel; made an officer of the Legion of Honor, 1892. *Five Weeks in a Balloon,* 1863; *A Journey to the*

Center of Earth, 1864; Twenty Thousand Leagues under the Sea, 1870; Around the World in Eighty Days, 1873.

WELLS, H(erbert) G(eorge), Sept. 21, 1866 (Kent, Eng.)–Aug. 13, 1946. English writer. Prolific and popular author of science fiction, realistic novels, and imaginative social philosophy. The Time Machine, 1895; The Invisible Man, 1897; The War of the Worlds, 1898; Kipps, 1905; Tono-Bungay, 1909; Outline of History, 1920.

WILLIAMSON, JOHN ("Jack") STEWART, 1908 (Arizona). U.S. science-fiction writer. Best known

for The Humanoids (1949) and its forerunner, "With Folded Hands"; collaborated with F. POHL on Reefs of Space trilogy, 1964–69.

WYNDHAM, JOHN (in full, John Wyndham Parkes Lucas Beynon Harris), 1903 (England). English science-fiction writer. His The Midwich Cuckoos (1957) was filmed as The Village of the Damned. Day of the Triffids, 1951.

ZELAZNY, ROGER, May 13, 1937 (Cleveland, Ohio). U.S. science-fiction writer. The Dream Master, 1966; And Call Me Conrad, 1965; Lord of Light, 1967.

PUBLISHERS, EDITORS, AND JOURNALISTS

ADLER, JULIUS OCHS, Dec. 3, 1892 (Chattanooga, Tenn.)–Oct. 3, 1955. U.S. newspaper executive. Vice-Pres. and gen. mgr. of The New York Times, 1935–55; credited with development of Times as most renowned daily in the world.

ALEXANDER, SHANA, née Ager, Oct. 6, 1925 (New York, N.Y.). U.S. journalist, author. Reporter (1951–61), staff writer (1961–64), and columnist of "The Feminine Eye" (1961–64) for Life; editor of McCall's, 1969–71; columnist and contributing editor to Newsweek, 1972–75; commentator on TV's 60 Minutes, 1975–79. Shana Alexander's State-by-State Guide to Women's Legal Rights, 1975; Anyone's Daughter, 1979.

ALSOP, JOSEPH WRIGHT, JR. Oct. 11, 1910 (Avon, Conn.). U.S. journalist. With his brother, STEWART ALSOP, wrote the syndicated column "Matter of Fact" for the New York Herald-Tribune, 1945–58; also with his brother, wrote We Accuse (1955), The Reporter's Trade (1958), and Nixon and Rockefeller (1960).

ALSOP, STEWART JOHONNOT OLIVER, May 17, 1914 (Avon, Conn.)–May 26, 1974. U.S. journalist. With his brother, JOSEPH ALSOP, wrote the syndicated column "Matter of Fact", for the New York Herald-Tribune, 1945–58; editor at Saturday Evening Post, 1958–68; also with his brother, wrote We Accuse (1955), The Reporter's Trade (1958), and Nixon and Rockefeller (1960). Stay of Execution, 1973.

ANDERSON, JACK, Oct. 19, 1922 (Long Beach, Calif.). U.S. journalist. Began as staff member for Drew Pearson's column, "Washington Merry-Go-Round"; took over column upon Pearson's death, 1969. The Case Against Congress (with Pearson), 1969.

ASCOLI, MAX, June 25, 1898 (Ferrara, It.). U.S. writer, publisher. Editor and publisher of The Reporter, 1949–1968; author of several books on political economy. Fascism for Whom, 1938; The Power of Freedom, 1948.

ATKINSON, (Justin) BROOKS, Nov. 18, 1894 (Melrose, Mass.). U.S. drama critic. Writing for The New York Times, exerted tremendous influence on American theater, 1925–42; won Pulitzer Prize in correspondence, 1947. New Voices in the American Theatre, 1955; Broadway, 1970.

BAKER, RUSSELL WAYNE, Aug. 14, 1925 (Loudoun Co., Va.). U.S. journalist. Writes a nationally-syndicated humor column for The New York Times; Pulitzer Prize in commentary, 1979.

BALLANTINE, IAN KEITH, Feb. 15, 1916 (New York, N.Y.). U.S. publishing executive. Instrumental in development of U.S. paperback-book industry as pres. of Bantam Books (1945–52) and as head of his own Ballantine Books (1952–75); head of

Peacock Press, a trade-paperback division of Bantam Books, 1975–

BEADLE, ERASTUS FLAVEL, Sept. 11, 1821 (Pierstown, N.Y.)–Dec. 21, 1894. U.S. publisher. Publication of his Dime Song Book started a new era that climaxed with his publication of the first "dime novel," 1861; his inexpensive books won great popularity (one sold 500,000 copies) and were forerunners of today's paperbacks.

BERNSTEIN, CARL, Feb. 14, 1944 (Washington, D.C.). U.S. journalist, author. As a reporter with the Washington Post, with ROBERT WOODWARD played a major role in uncovering and publicizing the Watergate scandal, 1972–74; also with Woodward, wrote All The President's Men (1974) and The Final Days (1976), accounts of Watergate and its aftermath.

BISHOP, JIM, Nov. 21, 1907 (Jersey City, N.J.). U.S. journalist, author. Writer of best-selling, hour-by-hour accounts of the days on which Jesus Christ, Abraham Lincoln and John F. Kennedy were killed. The Day Lincoln Was Shot, 1955; The Day Christ Died, 1957; The Day Kennedy Was Shot, 1968.

BLACKWELL, (Samuel) EARL, JR., May 3, 1913 (Atlanta, Ga.). U.S. publisher. As founder of Celebrity Service (1939) and Celebrity Register Ltd. (1957), keeps track of U.S. celebrities; publishes annual list of "best-dressed" and "worst-dressed" celebrities.

BOMBECK, ERMA, Feb. 21, 1927 (Dayton, Ohio). U.S. newspaper columnist, author. Her syndicated column, "At Wit's End," deals humorously with her life as a contemporary suburban housewife. At Wit's End, 1967; The Grass is Greener over the Septic Tank, 1976; If Life Is a Bowl of Cherries, What Am I Doing in the Pits?, 1978.

BOURKE-WHITE, MARGARET, June 14, 1906 (New York, N.Y.)–Aug. 27, 1971. U.S. photographer. Noted as an innovator in photo essays; on Life magazine staff, 1936–69. Eyes on Russia, 1931; You Have Seen Their Faces, 1937; North of the Danube, 1939.

BRESLIN, JIMMY, Oct. 17, 1930 (New York, N.Y.). U.S. journalist, novelist. Wrote DAMON RUNYON–type column for the New York Herald-Tribune (1963–65), New York World-Journal-Tribune (1965–67), and New York magazine (1968–71), which he helped launch; ran for president of New York City Council (with NORMAN MAILER as mayoral candidate), 1969. Can't Anybody Around Here Play This Game?, 1963; The Gang that Couldn't Shoot Straight, 1969; How the Good Guys Finally Won, 1975; with Dick Schaap, Forty-Four Caliber, 1978.

BRINKLEY, DAVID McCLURE, July 10, 1920 (Wilmington, N.C.). U.S. TV news correspondent.

Best known as the partner of Chet Huntley in the popular award-winning NBC-TV *The Huntley-Brinkley Report*, 1956–70; on NBC *Nightly News*, 1970–   . Noted for his dry wit and terse style of news analysis.

BROUN, HEYWOOD CAMPBELL, Dec. 7, 1888 (Brooklyn, N.Y.)–Dec. 18, 1939. U.S. journalist, novelist. Wrote a liberal-oriented column for several New York City newspapers; helped found the Newspaper Guild, which annually presents an award in his name for reporting. *It Seems to Me*, 1935; *A Collected Edition*, 1941.

BROWN, HELEN GURLEY, Feb. 18, 1922 (Green Forest, Ark.). U.S. author, editor. Gained fame as author of the best-selling *Sex and the Single Girl* (1962); editor-in-chief of *Cosmopolitan*, 1965–   .

BUCHWALD, ART, Oct. 20, 1925 (Mt. Vernon, N.Y.). U.S. journalist. Author of a syndicated humor column. *Art Buchwald's Paris*, 1954; *How Much Is That in Dollars?*, 1961; *I Am Not a Crook*, 1974; *Down the Seine and Up the Potomac*, 1977.

BUCKLEY, WILLIAM FRANK, JR., Nov. 24, 1925 (New York, N.Y.). U.S. editor, writer, TV personality. Well-known U.S. political conservative; founder and editor of the *National Review*, 1955–   ; host of TV show *Firing Line*, 1966–   ; ran unsuccessfully for mayor of New York City, 1965. *God and Man at Yale*, 1951; *Saving the Queen* (novel), 1976; *Stained Glass* (novel), 1978.

CANFIELD, CASS, Apr. 26, 1897 (New York, N.Y.). U.S. publishing executive. Chm. of the exec. com. and editorial board of Harper and Bros. (1927–61) and Harper & Row (1962–67); senior editor at Harper & Row, 1967–   . *The Publishing Experience*, 1969; *Up and Down and Around*, 1971.

CERF, BENNETT ALFRED, May 25, 1898 (New York, N.Y.)–Aug. 27, 1971. U.S. publisher, editor, columnist. Pres. of Modern Library, 1925–71; founder (1927), pres. (1927–65), and chm. (1965–70) of Random House; won landmark court battle ending U.S. censorship ban on J. JOYCE's *Ulysses*, 1933; published the works of F. KAFKA, M. PROUST, E. O'NEILL, and W. FAULKNER; compiled over 20 anthologies of humor; panelist on TV show *What's My Line*, 1952–66.

CHAMBERS, (Jay David) WHITTAKER, Apr. 1, 1901 (Philadelphia, Pa.)–July 9, 1961. U.S. journalist. Principal figure in the controversial Hiss-Chambers espionage case, 1948–50; an editor of *New Masses, Daily Worker,* and *Time* magazines.

CHANCELLOR, JOHN WILLIAM, July 14, 1927 (Chicago, Ill.). U.S. broadcast journalist. With NBC News from 1950; host of TV's *Today Show*, 1961–62; dir. of Voice of America, 1966–67; NBC natl. affairs correspondent, 1967–   ; anchorman of *NBC Nightly News*, 1970–   .

CHANDLER, HARRY, May 17, 1864 (Landaff, N.H.)–Sept. 23, 1944. U.S. newspaper publisher. Joined *Los Angeles Times* in 1885, and built circulation from 1,400 to a combined daily and Sunday circulation of over one million by the time of his retirement in 1942. (Grandfather of OTIS CHANDLER.)

CHANDLER, OTIS, Nov. 23, 1927 (Los Angeles, Calif.). U.S. newspaper publisher. Publisher of the *Los Angeles Times*, 1960–   ; dir. of Times Mirror Co., 1962–   ; leading California philanthropist. (Grandson of HARRY CHANDLER.)

CHILDS, MARQUIS WILLIAM, Mar. 17, 1903 (Clinton, Ia.). U.S. journalist. Author of a syndicated political column; awarded the first Pulitzer Prize in

commentary, 1969. *Sweden, the Middle Way*, 1936.

CONSIDINE, ROBERT BERNARD, Nov. 4, 1906 (Washington, D.C.)–Sept. 25, 1975. U.S. journalist. For nearly 40 years worked for Hearst Publications as war correspondent, sportswriter, syndicated columnist, and editor. *MacArthur the Magnificent*, 1942; *The Babe Ruth Story*, 1948; *Toots*, 1969.

COOKE, (Alfred) ALISTAIR, Nov. 20, 1908 (Manchester, Eng.). English-U.S. journalist. Best known as the urbane master of ceremonies for TV's *Masterpiece Theater*, 1971–   . Host of TV's *Omnibus*, 1952–60; writer and narrator of TV's *America: A Personal History of the United States*, 1972–73. *Six Men*, 1977; *The Americans*, 1979.

COPLEY, HELEN KINNEY, Nov. 28, 1922 (Cedar Rapids, Ia.). U.S. newspaper publisher. An exec. with Copley Press, Inc., Copley News Service, and San Diego *Union—Evening Tribune*, 1973–   .

COSELL, HOWARD, born Howard William Cohen, Mar. 25, 1920 (Winston-Salem, N.C.). U.S. sportscaster, for ABC-TV, 1956–   ; known for his abrasive manner and personality. *Like It Is*, 1974.

COUSINS, NORMAN, June 24, 1915 (Union City, N. J.). U.S. magazine editor. Joined *Saturday Review* (1940), and transformed the struggling literary magazine into the prestigious organ that became synonymous with his name; a spokesman for nuclear control and world govt. *Present Tense: An American Editor's Odyssey*, 1967.

CRONKITE, WALTER LELAND, JR., Nov. 4, 1916 (St. Joseph, Mo.). U.S. broadcast journalist. As anchorman of *CBS Evening News* (1962–   ), the preeminent broadcast journalist in the U.S. Worked as a newspaper reporter and wire service correspondent prior to joining CBS.

CROWTHER, BOSLEY, July 13, 1905 (Lutherville, Md.). U.S. film critic. As film critic (1940–67) and critic emeritus (1967–   ) of *The New York Times*, an early champion of foreign films. *The Lion's Share: The Story of an Entertainment Empire*, 1957; *The Great Films: Fifty Golden Years of Motion Pictures*, 1967; *Vintage Films*, 1977.

CURTIS, CHARLOTTE MURRAY, Dec. 19, 1928 (Chicago, Ill.). U.S. journalist. Noted for her tongue-in-cheek society reporting and for upgrading the family/style section of *The New York Times;* reporter (1961–   ), women's news editor (1965–72), family/style editor (1972–74), associate editor and editor of the Op-Ed page (1974–   ), *The New York Times. First Lady*, 1963; *The Rich and other Atrocities*, 1976.

CURTIS, CYRUS HERMANN KOTZSCHMAR, June 18, 1850 (Portland, Me.)–June 7, 1933. U.S. publisher, philanthropist. Founded Curtis Publishing Co., 1891; publisher of *Ladies' Home Journal, Saturday Evening Post,* and the Philadelphia *Ledger*.

DANIEL, (Elbert) CLIFTON, JR., Sept. 19, 1912 (Zebulon, N.C.). U.S. journalist. Foreign correspondent, editor, and managing editor of *The New York Times*, 1964–   .

DOUBLEDAY, NELSON, June 16, 1889 (Brooklyn, N.Y.)–Jan. 11, 1949. U.S. publisher. Founded the communications empire that bears his name as a subscription-book business, 1910; incorporated in 1917, the business included Doubleday Publishers, Literary Guild, and Doubleday One Dollar Book Club.

DYSTEL, OSCAR, Oct. 31, 1912 (New York, N.Y.).

U.S. publisher. Magazine circulation and promotion expert; editor, *Coronet*, 1940-42 and 1944-48; managing editor, *Collier's*, 1948-49; as pres. (1954-78) and chm. and chief operating officer (1978-80) of Bantam Books, credited with developing firm into paperback industry leader.

FADIMAN, CLIFTON, May 15, 1904 (New York, N.Y.). U.S. literary critic, author. Editor at Simon and Schuster, 1929-35; book editor of *The New Yorker*, 1933-43; master of ceremonies for the radio program *Information Please*, 1938-48. *Party of One*, 1955.

FIELD, MARSHALL, III, Sept. 28, 1893 (Chicago, Ill.)-Nov. 8, 1956. U.S. publisher, philanthropist. Founded the Chicago *Sun* (later the Chicago *Sun-Times*), 1941; major stockholder in New York City's ill-fated *PM* newspaper, 1940-48. (Grandson of MARSHALL FIELD.)

FLANNER, JANET, Mar. 13, 1892 (Indianapolis, Ind.)-Nov. 7, 1978. U.S. journalist. Correspondent for *The New Yorker* for almost 50 years; wrote the "Letter from Paris" under the byline "Genet"; one of the few women to be awarded the French Legion of Honor.

FLYNT, LARRY C., Nov. 1, 1942 (Salyersville, Ky.). U.S. publisher. Publisher of *Hustler* (1974-   ), the most explicit of the mass-market "skin" magazines, and of *Chic, Los Angeles Free Press, Atlanta Gazette;* convicted, as publisher and editor of *Hustler*, of pandering obscenity and engaging in organized crime in Cincinnati, Ohio, 1977; under tutelage of RUTH CARTER STAPLETON, became "born again" Christian, 1977; paralyzed from midthigh down as result of a gun attack, 1978.

FRENEAU, PHILIP MORIN, Jan. 2, 1752 (New York N.Y.)-Dec. 19, 1832. U.S. poet, journalist. Often called the first professional U.S. journalist; edited the *National Gazette* for THOMAS JEFFERSON, 1791-93. Poems: "The British Prison Ship", 1781; "The Wild Honeysuckle," 1786; "The Indian Burying Ground," 1788.

FRIENDLY, FRED W., Oct. 30, 1915 (New York, N.Y.). U.S. communications executive, educator. Collaborated with Edward R. Murrow on *See It Now* (CBS-TV); pres. of CBS News, 1964-66; prof. of broadcast journalism at Columbia U. *Due to Circumstances beyond Our Control,* 1967.

FURNESS, BETTY, Jan. 3, 1916 (New York, N.Y.). U.S. broadcast journalist, consumer adviser, actress. Movie actress, 1932-37; on CBS radio in *Dimension of a Woman's World, Ask Betty Furness,* 1961-67; chairperson of President's Com. on Consumer Interests, 1967-69; currently a consumer specialist with NBC News in New York City.

GILLIATT, PENELOPE ANN, née Douglass, 1933 (London, Eng.). English film critic, writer. Film critic with the *London Observer* (1961-67) and *The New Yorker* (1968-   ); author of short stories, novels, nonfiction and the screenplay of the film *Sunday, Bloody Sunday* (1971). *Nobody's Business,* 1972; *Splendid Lives,* 1977.

GILMER, ELIZABETH MERIWHETHER, Nov. 18, 1870 (Montgomery Co., Tenn.)-Dec. 16, 1951. U.S. journalist. Under the byline "Dorothy Dix," wrote for 55 years a popular syndicated column advising the lovelorn. *Fables of the Elite,* 1902; *Hearts à la Mode,* 1923; *Dorothy Dix, Her Book,* 1926.

GODEY, LOUIS ANTOINE, June 6, 1804 (New York, N.Y.)-Nov. 29, 1878. U.S. publisher. His *Lady's Book,* established in 1830, was the leading fashion magazine for 19th-cent. American women.

GRAHAM, KATHARINE, née Meyer, June 16, 1917 (New York, N.Y.). U.S. publisher. Consistently voted to be one of the most influential women in the U.S. Member of editorial staff of the *Washington Post;* pres. of Washington Post Co., 1963-67; publisher of the *Washington Post,* 1968-78; chm. and chief exec. officer of Washington Post Co., 1973-   . (Wife of PHILIP GRAHAM.)

GRAHAM, PHILIP LESLIE, July 18, 1915 (Terry, S. D.)-Aug. 3, 1963. U.S. newspaper executive. Publisher of the *Washington Post,* 1946-63; committed suicide. (Husband of KATHARINE GRAHAM.)

GRAHAM, SHEILAH, ? (England). U.S. journalist. Hollywood gossip columnist and author of several nonfiction books, notably a number of reminiscences about her relationship with F. SCOTT FITZGERALD in his last years. *Beloved Infidel* (with GEROLD FRANK), 1958; *College of One,* 1967; *The Real F. Scott Fitzgerald,* 1976.

GREELEY, HORACE, Feb. 3, 1811 (Amerst, N.H.)-Nov. 29, 1872. U.S. newspaper editor. Noted as a crusader against slavery. As founder and editor of the New York *Tribune* (1841-72), created a powerful voice; Liberal Republican party presidential candidate, 1872.

GUNTHER, JOHN, Aug. 30, 1901 (Chicago, Ill.)-May 29, 1970. U.S. journalist, author. Noted for his popular books on regions of the world, culled from his travels and interviews with political leaders. Overseas correspondent with the Chicago *Daily News,* 1924-36. *Inside Europe,* 1936; *Inside U.S.A.,* 1947.

HARPER, JAMES, Apr. 13, 1795 (Newtown, N.Y.)-Mar. 25, 1869. U.S. publisher. Founder of Harper & Bros. (later Harper & Row), 1825; first to use steam-run presses; first to introduce electrotyping on large scale.

HEARST, WILLIAM RANDOLPH, Apr. 29, 1863 (San Francisco, Calif.)-Aug. 14, 1951. U.S. editor, publisher. Creator of Hearst Newspapers, at its peak the largest newspaper chain in the U.S.; used "yellow journalism" (sensationalism, glaring headlines, and exaggerated news), to build sales; transformed the San Francisco *Examiner* into a success; in New York City, fought JOSEPH PULITZER with the New York *Journal-American;* spent money lavishly, fought for social reform; U.S. rep. (D, N.Y.), 1903-07.

HEFNER, HUGH, Apr. 9, 1926 (Chicago, Ill.). U.S. editor, publisher. Editor and publisher of *Playboy* (1953-   ), *VIP* (1963-75), and *Oui* (1972-   ) magazines; pres. of Playboy Clubs International, Inc., 1959-

HENDIN, DAVID, Dec. 16, 1945 (St. Louis, Mo.). U.S. editor, journalist, writer. Vice-pres. and editor of United Features Syndicate and Newspaper Enterprise Assn., 1977-   . *Save Your Child's Life,* 1973; *Death as a Fact of Life,* 1973; *The Life Givers,* 1976; *The Genetic Connection* (with Joan Marks), 1978.

HIGGINS, MARGUERITE, Sept. 3, 1920 (Hong Kong)-Jan. 3, 1966. U.S. journalist. Only woman correspondent at the Korean War front; reported from Vietnam in the 1960s; awarded Pulitzer Prize in international reporting. *War in Korea: The Report of a Woman Combat Correspondent,* 1951.

HOPPER, HEDDA, born Elda Furry, June 2, 1890 (Hollidaysburg, Pa.)-Feb. 1, 1966. U.S. journalist. Wrote a chatty, caustic syndicated column about Hollywood.

HOWARD, ROY WILSON, Jan. 1, 1883 (Gano,

Ohio)–Nov. 20, 1964. U.S. newspaperman. With United Press from 1906; board chairman of UP, Newspaper Enterprise Association and their parent concern, the Scripps-Rae Newspaper chain (now Scripps-Howard), 1921-36; pres., 1936-52; chairman of the executive committee, 1953-64.

KERR, WALTER FRANCIS, July 8, 1913 (Evanston, Ill.). U.S. journalist, playwright. Drama critic at the New York *Herald-Tribune* (1951-66) and *The New York Times* (1966-   ). *Murder in Reverse* (play with wife JEAN KERR), 1935; *How Not to Write a Play*, 1956; *Tragedy and Comedy*, 1967.

KIPLINGER, WILLARD MONROE, Jan. 8, 1891 (Bellefontaine, Ohio). U.S. journalist. Editor, *Kiplinger Washington Letters*, 1923-   . *Washington Is Like That*, 1942.

KNOPF, ALFRED A., Sept. 12, 1892 (New York, N.Y.). U.S. publisher. With wife BLANCHE W. KNOPF, founded Alfred A. Knopf, Inc., publishers, 1915.

KNOPF, BLANCHE, née Wolf, 1894 (New York, N.Y.)–June 4, 1966. U.S. publishing executive. Pres. of Alfred A. Knopf, Inc., 1957-66; originated the idea for Borzoi imprint on Knopf books. (Wife of ALFRED A. KNOPF.)

KROCK, ARTHUR, Nov. 16, 1887 (Glasgow, Ky.)–Apr. 12, 1974. U.S. journalist. Chief Washington correspondent, *The New York Times* 1932-53; won four Pulitzer Prizes, in 1935 and 1938 for correspondence, a special commendation, and a special citation. *Memoirs: Sixty Years on the Firing Line*, 1970.

LANDERS, ANN, (pseud. of Esther Pauline Friedman), July 4, 1918 (Sioux City, Ia.). U.S. journalist. Syndicated advice columnist, 1955-   ; *Since You Asked Me*, 1962; *Teenagers and Sex*, 1964; *Truth is Stranger . . .*, 1968. (Twin sister of ABIGAIL VAN BUREN.)

LERNER, MAX, Dec. 20, 1902 (nr. Minsk, Rus.). U.S. journalist. Internationally syndicated columnist for the *New York Post*, 1949-   . *It Is Later than You Think*, 1943; *America as Civilization*, 1957; *The Age of Overkill*, 1962.

LEWIS, ANTHONY, Mar. 27, 1927 (New York, N.Y.). U.S. journalist. Reporter, Washington bureau of *The New York Times*, 1955-64; awarded Pulitzer Prize in national reporting, 1955; editorial columnist, *The New York Times*, 1969-   . *Gideon's Trumpet*, 1964; *Portrait of a Decade: The Second American Revolution*, 1964.

LIPPMANN, WALTER, Sept. 23, 1889 (New York, N.Y.)–Dec. 14, 1974. U.S. journalist. Syndicated political columnist for the New York *Herald-Tribune* (1931-62), and the *Washington Post* (1962-67); awarded special Pulitzer Prize citations for news analysis (1958) and for international reporting (1962); Presidential Medal of Freedom, 1964. *A Preface to Politics*, 1931; *The Good Society*, 1937; *The Communist World and Ours*, 1952; *Unity and the Common Market*, 1962.

LORIMER, GEORGE HORACE, Oct. 6, 1867 (Louisville, Ky.)–Oct. 22, 1937. U.S. editor, writer. As editor of the *Saturday Evening Post*, raised its circulation from 1,800 to 3 million, 1899-1936. *Letters from a Self-made Merchant to His Son*, 1902; *Old Gorgon Graham*, 1904.

LUCE, HENRY ROBINSON, Apr. 1, 1898 (Tengchow [now Pénglai], China)–Feb. 28, 1967. U.S. editor, publisher. The founder of *Time* (1932) and *Life* (1936); one of the most influential publishers in the U.S., and one of the most controversial; believing objective reporting was impossible, en-

couraged editors to present their own views, even in unsigned articles. (Husband of CLARE BOOTHE LUCE.)

MARQUIS, DONALD ROBERT PERRY, July 19, 1878 (Walnut, Ill.)–Dec. 29, 1937. U.S. journalist, humorist. Wrote the popular columns "The Sun Dial," for the New York *Sun*, and "The Lantern," for the New York *Tribune*; created Archy the cockroach, who reported in first-person lowercase the adventures of Mehitabel, the cat. *the lives and times of archy and mehitabel*, 1940.

MCCLURE, SAMUEL SIDNEY, Feb. 17, 1857 (County Antrim, Ire.)–Mar. 21, 1949. U.S. publisher, editor. Founded McClure's Syndicate, first newspaper syndicate in the U.S., 1894; formed S. S. McClure Co., publishers of *McClure's* Magazine, a respected literary journal, 1893.

MCGRAW, JAMES HERBERT, Dec. 17, 1860 (Panama, N.Y.)–Feb. 21, 1948. U.S. publisher. Merged his industrial-journal publishing firm with the Hill Publishing Co. to form McGraw-Hill, the world's largest publisher of technical books and journals, 1916.

MCGRORY, MARY 1918 (Boston, Mass.). U.S. journalist. Syndicated liberal columnist for the Washington *Star;* awarded Pulitzer Prize in commentary, 1975.

MCWHIRTER, (Alan) ROSS, Aug. 12, 1925 (London, Eng.)–Nov. 27, 1975. English editor, author. With his twin brother, NORRIS, compiler and editor of *The Guinness Book of World Records* (1955-75) and *The Dunlop Illustrated Encyclopedia of Facts* (1964-66); killed in an IRA terrorist attack after he had offered an $100,000 reward for information leading to arrest of IRA bombers.

MCWHIRTER, NORRIS DEWAR, Aug. 12, 1925 (London, Eng.). English editor, author. With his twin brother, ROSS, compiler and editor of *The Guinness Book of World Records* (1955-75; on his own, 1975-   ) and *The Dunlop Illustrated Encyclopedia of Facts* (1964-66).

MENCKEN, H(enry) **L**(ouis), Sept. 12, 1880 (Baltimore, Md.)–Jan. 29, 1956. U.S. journalist, critic, editor. Controversial editor of *The Smart Set* (1914-23) and *American Mercury* (1924-33); columnist on the Baltimore *Sun* and *Evening Sun*, 1906-56; attacked business, organized religion, and middle-class America; known for his razor-sharp and fastidious use of the language. *American Language*, 1919; *Prejudice*, 6 vols., 1919-27; *Happy Days*, 1940; *Newspaper Days*, 1941; *Heathen Days*, 1943.

MERZ, CHARLES, Feb. 23, 1893 (Sandusky, Ohio)–Aug. 31, 1977. U.S. editor, author. Editor of The New York *Times*, 1938-61. *The Great American Bandwagon*, 1928; *The Dry Decade*, 1931; *Days of Decision* (ed.), 1941.

MORRIS, WILLIE, Nov. 29, 1934 (Jackson, Miss.). U.S. editor, novelist, nonfiction writer. Editor (1963-67) and editor in chief (1967-71) of *Harper's. North toward Home*, 1967; *Yazoo*, 1971; *The Last of the Southern Girls*, 1973.

MOYERS, BILL DON, June 5, 1934 (Hugo, Okla.). U.S. journalist. Personal asst. to LYNDON B. JOHNSON, 1960-67; White House press secy. (to LBJ), 1965-67; publisher of *Newsday* (L.I.), 1967-70; contributing editor to *Newsweek*, 1974-   ; editor-in-chief of IV's *Bill Moyers' Journal* (PBS), 1970-76; editor and chief correspondent of TV's *CBS Reports*, 1976-   .

MUDD, ROGER, Feb. 9, 1928 (Washington, D.C.). U.S. TV newsman. Reporter for WTOP TV and

THE BOOK OF WHO

Radio, Washington, D.C., 1956-61; news broadcaster, with CBS-TV, 1961- .

MUIR, MALCOLM, July 19, 1885 (Glen Ridge, N.J.)-Jan. 30, 1979. U.S. publisher. As pres. of McGraw-Hill, Inc. (1928-37), created *Business Week* magazine, 1929; pres., publisher, editor-in-chief and board chm. of Newsweek Inc., 1937-61.

MYERSON, BESS, July 16, 1924 (New York, N.Y.). U.S. public official, columnist. Miss America, 1945; panelist on CBS-TV's *I've Got a Secret*, 1958-68; New York City commissioner of consumer affairs, 1969-74; columnist for New York *Daily News*, 1974-

NAST, CONDÉ, Mar. 26, 1874 (New York, N.Y.)-Sept. 19, 1942. U.S. magazine publisher. Worked for *Collier's*, 1900-07; moved on to manage Home Pattern Co., which he had founded in 1904; bought *Vogue* (1909), and started publishing empire that would include *House and Garden* and *Vanity Fair*.

NEWHOUSE, SAMUEL IRVING, May 24, 1895 (New York, N.Y.)-Aug. 29, 1979. U.S. publisher. Founded Newhouse chain of newspapers, magazines, and broadcasting stations when he bought the *Staten Island Advance*, 1921; a major endower of Syracuse U.'s Newhouse Communications Center.

NEWMAN, EDWIN HAROLD, Jan. 25, 1919 (New York, N.Y.). U.S. news commentator, author. News commentator with NBC-TV, 1952- ; has narrated many TV specials; drama critic for WNBC-TV, 1965-71; a defender of the clear use of the English language. *Strictly Speaking*, 1974; *A Civil Tongue*, 1976.

NIELSEN, ARTHUR CHARLES, Sept. 5, 1897 (Chicago, Ill.). U.S. market researcher. Organized A. C. Nielsen Co. to do market research on industrial equipment, 1923; started a food-and-drug research service to record retail sales of products; began a rating service for radio programs using "Nielsen Audimeter," 1941; pioneered TV ratings, 1950.

PALEY, WILLIAM S., Sept. 28, 1901 (Chicago, Ill.). U.S. communications executive. Pioneer in U.S. broadcasting industry who parlayed fortune from family cigar business into CBS, Inc., the communications conglomerate he founded in 1928; CBS pres. (1928-46) and chm. of the board (1946-); chm. of the board of trustees of Museum of Modern Art, 1972- ; trustee emeritus of Columbia U., 1973-

PARSONS, LOUELLA O., Aug. 6, 1881 (Freeport, Ill.)-Dec. 9, 1972. U.S. journalist. Internationally-syndicated gossip columnist for Hearst Newspapers during Hollywood's golden age; great rival of HEDDA HOPPER. *Tell It to Louella*, 1961.

PERKINS, MAXWELL EVARTS, Sept. 20, 1884 (New York, N.Y.)-June 17, 1947. U.S. editor. Preeminent editor of his day as editor-in-chief at Charles Scribner's Sons (1927-47); edited THOMAS WOLFE's first novels, *Look Homeward Angel* (1929) and *Of Time and the River* (1935); also worked with F. SCOTT FITZGERALD, ERNEST HEMINGWAY, RING LARDNER, TAYLOR CALDWELL, others.

PHILLIPS, JOHN SANBURN, July 2, 1861 (Council Bluffs, Ia.)-Feb. 28, 1949. U.S. editor, publisher. Partner with S. S. MCCLURE in the McClure Syndicate, 1886; a founder of *McClure's* Magazine (1893) and McClure & Phillips (later S. S. McClure) book publishers (1900); founded his own publishing firm and *American* magazine, 1906.

PITKIN, WALTER BOUGHTON, Feb. 6, 1878 (Ypsilanti, Mich.)-Jan. 25, 1953. U.S. psychologist, journalist, editor. Best known for writings on pop psychology, especially *Life Begins at Forty* (1932).

PORTER, SYLVIA FIELD, June 18, 1913 (Patchogue, N.Y.). U.S. journalist. Leading financial columnist with the *New York Post* (1935-77; wrote as S. F. Porter until 1942) and the New York *Daily News* (1978-). *Sylvia Porter's Income Tax Guide*, published annually since 1960; *Sylvia Porter's Money Book*, 1975.

POST, EMILY, née Price, Oct. 27, 1872 (Baltimore, Md.)-Sept. 25, 1960. U.S. journalist. Wrote the definitive book on proper social behavior, *Etiquette*, 1921 (in its 10th ed. by the time of her death); wrote a daily column on etiquette that was syndicated in more than 200 newspapers.

PULITZER, JOSEPH, Apr. 10, 1847 (Mako, Hung.)-Oct. 29, 1911. U.S. newspaper publisher, often called the father of modern American journalism. After serving the Union in the Civil War, settled in St. Louis as a reporter for a German-language daily, 1868; bought St. Louis *Dispatch* and combined it with St. Louis *Post*, 1878; bought *New York World* in 1883 and made it a leading newspaper, trading heavily on working-class appeal and sensationalism; because of blindness, retired from active participation, 1887-90; established (1903) and endowed by his will School of Journalism at Columbia U. and Pulitzer Prizes for journalistic excellence.

PUTNAM, GEORGE PALMER, Feb. 7, 1814 (Brunswick, Me.)-Dec. 20, 1872. U.S. publisher. Started first bookseller's trade journal, the *Bookseller's Advertiser*; founded G. P. Putnam and Son (later G. P. Putnam's Sons) book publishers, 1848.

PYLE, ERNIE (Ernest) TAYLOR, Aug. 3, 1900 (Dana, Ind.)-Apr. 18, 1945. U.S. journalist. Noted WW II correspondent in Europe, North Africa, and the Pacific; wrote about the experiences of ordinary G.I. Joe; awarded Pulitzer Prize for distinguished correspondence, 1944; killed by Japanese machine-gun fire on Ie Shima, 1945. *Here is Your War*, 1943; *Brave Men*, 1944; *Last Chapter*, 1946.

RATHER, DANIEL, Oct. 31, 1931 (Wharton, Tex.). U.S. broadcast journalist. As CBS-TV White House correspondent (1964, 1966-74), accompanied the U.S. pres. on many trips; co-anchorman of TV's *60 Minutes* (1975-); The Palace Guard (with Gary Gates), 1974; *The Camera Never Blinks* (with Mickey Herskowitz), 1977.

REASONER, HARRY, Apr. 17, 1923 (Dakota City, Ia.). U.S. TV news correspondent. Correspondent and reporter with CBS-TV news, 1956-70; anchorman of *ABC-TV News*, 1970-79; again with CBS-TV News, on *60 Minutes* and *CBS Reports*, 1979-

REED, JOHN, Oct. 22, 1887 (Portland, Ore.)-Oct. 19, 1920. U.S. journalist, poet. Radical journalist from a wealthy Portland, Ore., family; was an eyewitness to the 1917 Russian Revolution and became a close associate of V. I. LENIN; his account of the revolution, *Ten Days That Shook the World* (1919), is considered the best eyewitness account of the events.

REED, REX, Oct. 2, 1938 (Ft. Worth, Tex.). U.S. film critic, author. Film critic and syndicated columnist with the New York *Daily News*, 1971- . *Do You Sleep in the Nude?*, 1968; *Big Screen, Little Screen*, 1971; *Valentines and Vitriol*, 1977.

RESTON, JAMES BARRETT, Nov. 3, 1909

(Clydebank, Scot.). U.S. author, journalist. Washington correspondent (1953-64) and columnist, consultant (1974–) with The New York Times; dir. New York Times Co.; awarded Pulitzer Prize in national correspondence (1945) and in national reporting (1957). The Artillery of the Press, 1967; Sketches in the Sand, 1967.

ROYKO, MIKE, Sept. 19, 1932 (Chicago, Ill.). U.S. journalist. Columnist with Chicago Daily News (1959-78) and the Chicago Sun-Times (1978–); awarded Pulitzer Prize in commentary, 1972. Up Against It, 1967; I May Be Wrong but I Doubt It, 1968; Boss—Richard J. Daley of Chicago, 1971; Slats Grobnik and Some Other Friends, 1973.

SAFER, MORLEY, Nov. 8, 1931 (Toronto, Ont., Can.). U.S. broadcast journalist. With CBS-TV since 1964; Vietnam correspondent, 1964-71; cohost of the TV show 60 Minutes, 1971– .

SAFIRE, WILLIAM, Dec. 17, 1929 (New York, N.Y.). U.S. journalist. Special asst. to Pres. RICHARD M. NIXON, 1969-73; columnist with The New York Times, 1973– . The New Language of Politics, 1968 (rev. 1972); Full Disclosure, 1977.

ST. JOHNS, ADELA ROGERS, May 20, 1894 (Los Angeles, Calif.). U.S. journalist. Started at age 18 as a reporter for The Los Angeles Herald; became star reporter for the Hearst papers, covering the Lindbergh baby kidnapping and BRUNO HAUPTMANN trial. A Free Soul, 1924; Final Verdict, 1962; Some Are Born Great, 1974.

SALANT, RICHARD S., Apr. 14, 1914 (New York, N.Y.)-U.S. communications executive. Pres. of CBS News, 1961-1979; vice-chm. of NBC Network, 1979–

SALINGER, PIERRE, June 14, 1925 (San Francisco, Calif.). U.S. politician, journalist. Reporter for the San Francisco Chronicle, 1946-55; press secy. to Pres. JOHN F. KENNEDY, 1961-63; U.S. sen. (D, Calif.), 1964-65.

SALISBURY, HARRISON EVANS, Nov. 14, 1908 (Minneapolis, Minn.). U.S. journalist. Editor and writer for The New York Times since 1954; served as Times Moscow correspondent, 1949-54; Pulitzer Prize in international correspondence, 1955. The Shook-up Generation, 1958; Moscow Journal, 1961; Russia, 1965; The 900 Days: The Siege of Leningrad, 1969; To Peking and Beyond, 1973; The Gates of Hell, 1975; Russia in Revolution, 1978.

SARNOFF, DAVID, Feb. 27, 1891 (Uzlian, Rus.) -Dec. 12, 1971. U.S. communications executive. As a wireless operator, relayed first news of the sinking of the Titanic, 1912; invented the radio set, 1915; joined RCA Corp. in 1919, later serving as pres. (1930-47), chief exec. (1947-66), and board chm. (1947-71); a founder of the NBC network, 1926; a pioneer in TV experimentation. (Father of R. W. SARNOFF.)

SARNOFF, ROBERT WILLIAM, July 2, 1918 (New York, N.Y.). U.S. communications executive. As pres. of NBC (1955–), presided over network's entry into color television (first all-color U.S. station opened in 1956); inaugurated Monitor on radio, 1955. (Son of DAVID SARNOFF.)

SCHIFF, DOROTHY, Mar. 11, 1903 (New York, N.Y.). U.S. newspaper publisher. As publisher and editor-in-chief of the New York Post, gained reputation for crusading liberalism for herself and her paper, 1939-77.

SCHOENBRUN, DAVID FRANZ, Mar. 15, 1915 (New York, N.Y.). U.S. journalist. Foreign correspondent in France (1946-62) and chief of

Washington bureau (1962-63) for CBS; chief correspondent, Metromedia, 1964-65. The Three Lives of Charles DeGaulle, 1964; Vietnam: How We Got In, How To Get Out, 1968.

SCHORR, DANIEL LOUIS, Aug. 31, 1916 (New York, N.Y.). U.S. radio and TV correspondent. A longtime CBS-TV news correspondent (1966-76), dismissed for leaking a secret House Intelligence Com. report on the CIA to the Village Voice, 1977.

SCRIBNER, CHARLES, Feb. 21, 1821 (New York, N.Y.)-Aug. 26, 1871. U.S. publisher. In partnership with Isaac D. Baker, founded Baker and Scribner Publishers (Charles Scribner's Sons, from 1878), 1846; at first published philosophical and theological books, then turned to reprints and translations of British and European literary works; founder and publisher of Scribner's magazine, 1870-71.

SCRIPPS, E(dward) W(yllis), June 18, 1854 (nr. Rushville, Ill.)-Mar. 12, 1926. U.S. newspaper publisher. Beginning with the Cleveland Penny Press (1878), organized the first major chain of newspapers in the U.S., the Scripps-McRae League (now Scripps-Howard), 1895; established Newspaper Enterprise Assn. to supply cartoons and features to his chain, 1902; established the UP, 1907.

SCRIPPS, ELLEN BROWNING, Oct. 18, 1836 (London, Eng.)-Aug. 3, 1932. U.S. newspaper publisher, philanthropist. A shareholder and active participant in the operations of family-owned newspaper chain (later Scripps-Howard), 1867-1930; with brother E. W. SCRIPPS, founded the Marine Biological Assn. of San Diego (later called Scripps Inst. of Oceanography), 1903; founded Scripps C. for Women, 1927.

SEVAREID, (Arnold) ERIC, Nov. 26, 1912 (Velva, N.D.). U.S. broadcast journalist. Correspondent with CBS News, 1939-77; commentator on TV's CBS Evening News, 1964-77; consultant with CBS News, 1977– . Not So Wild a Dream, 1946; This Is Eric Sevareid, 1964.

SHAKESPEARE, FRANK JOSEPH, JR., Apr. 9, 1925 (New York, N.Y.). U.S. govt. official, broadcast executive. Exec. vice-pres. of CBS-TV stations, 1965-67; headed RICHARD NIXON's TV campaign, 1968; dir. of USIA, 1969-73; pres. of RKO Gen., Inc., 1975–

SHEEHY, GAIL HENION, Nov. 27, 1937 (Mamaroneck, N.Y.). U.S. journalist, writer. Hustling: Prostitution in Our Wide Open Society, 1973; Passages: Predictable Crises of Adult Life, 1976.

SIMON, RICHARD LEO, Mar. 6, 1899 (New York, N.Y.)-July 29, 1960. U.S. publisher. With Max L. Schuster, founder of Simon and Schuster, Inc., 1924; introduced Pocket Books, Inc., one of the first enterprises devoted to inexpensive reprints, 1939.

SMITH, (Albert) MERRIMAN, Feb. 10, 1913 (Savannah, Ga.)-Apr. 13, 1970. U.S. journalist. Dean of the White House correspondents; UPI correspondent, 1936-70 (covered White House from 1941); awarded Pulitzer Prize in national reporting, 1964; Thank You, Mr. President, 1946; Good New Days, 1962.

SMITH, HEDRICK LAURENCE, July 9, 1933 (Kilmalcolm, Scot.). U.S. journalist. Washington bureau chief of The New York Times, 1976– ; served as foreign correspondent for the Times in Moscow, the Middle East, and Vietnam; awarded Pulitzer Prize in international reporting, 1974. The Russians, 1976.

SMITH, HOWARD K., May 12, 1914 (Ferriday, La.). U.S. news commentator. Chief European correspondent and European dir. of London Bureau of CBS, 1946-57; correspondent with Washington

Bureau of CBS, 1957–61; news analyst for ABC-TV, 1962– .

STANTON, FRANK NICHOLS, Mar. 20, 1908 (Muskegon, Mich.). U.S. communications executive. Pres. (1946–71) and vice-chm. (1971–73) of CBS, Inc.; for many years the number-two man behind WILLIAM S. PALEY at CBS; instrumental in the development of TV segment of CBS, Inc.

STONE, I(sidor) **F**(einstein), Dec. 24, 1907 (Philadelphia, Pa.). U.S. journalist. Editorial writer for the *New York Post*, 1933–39; assoc. editor (1938–40) and Washington editor (1940–46) of *The Nation;* editor and publisher of *I. F. Stone's Weekly,* 1953–71; Distinguished Scholar in Residence at American U., 1975– .

SWAYZE, JOHN CAMERON, SR., Apr. 4, 1906 (Wichita, Kan.). U.S. news correspondent. Anchorman of NBC-TV's *Camel News Caravan,* 1948–56; panelist on the radio show *Who Said That?,* 1948–51.

SWOPE, HERBERT BAYARD, Jan. 5, 1882 (St. Louis, Mo.)–June 20, 1958. U.S. journalist. War correspondent with the New York *World,* 1914–16 (awarded Pulitzer Prize in reporting, 1917); as exec. editor (1920–29) of the *World,* known for crusading and fine writing; originated Op-Ed page, with the bylines of HEYWOOD BROUN, ALEXANDER WOOLLCOTT, others.

TARBELL, IDA MINERVA, Nov. 5, 1857 (Erie Co., Pa.)–Jan. 6, 1944. U.S. journalist. A leading muckraker. *The Early Life of Abraham Lincoln,* 1896; *The Life of Abraham Lincoln,* 1900; *History of the Standard Oil Company,* 1904.

THOMAS, HELEN, Aug. 4, 1920 (Winchester, Ky.). U.S. journalist. A reporter for UPI in Washington, D.C., 1943–74; first woman chief of the UPI White House bureau, 1974– .

THOMAS, LOWELL JACKSON, Apr. 6, 1892 (Woodington, Ohio). U.S. author, radio news commentator. A news commentator on radio since 1930; from 1935, has filmed and narrated travelogues and written books about his travels; host of TV series *High Adventure,* 1957–59. *The Seven Wonders of the World,* 1956; *With Lawrence in Arabia* (with Lowell Thomas, Jr.), 1971; *Good Evening, Everybody: From Cripple Creek to Samarkand,* 1976.

THOMPSON, DOROTHY, July 9, 1894 (Lancaster, N.Y.)–Jan. 31, 1961. U.S. journalist. Syndicated columnist for the New York *Herald-Tribune. The New Russia,* 1928; *I Saw Hitler,* 1932; *Listen, Hans,* 1942; *The Courage to Be Happy,* 1957. (Wife of SINCLAIR LEWIS, 1928–42.)

VAN BUREN, ABIGAIL (pseud. of Pauline Esther Friedman), July 4, 1918 (Sioux City, Ia.). U.S. journalist. Since 1956, has written "Dear Abby," a syndicated advice column. *Dear Abby,* 1957; *Dear Teenager,* 1959; *Dear Abby on Marriage,* 1962. (Twin sister of ANN LANDERS.)

VANDERBILT, AMY, July 22, 1908 (Staten Is., N.Y.)–Dec. 27, 1974. U.S. journalist. Wrote daily syndicated column on etiquette. *Amy Vanderbilt's Complete Book of Etiquette,* 1952; *Amy Vanderbilt's Etiquette,* 1972.

VILLARD, OSWALD GARRISON, Mar. 13, 1872 (Wiesbaden, Ger.)–Oct. 1, 1949. U.S. editor, journalist. As editor of *The Nation* (1918–32), made it a leading liberal journal; inherited New York *Evening Post,* served as owner and editor, 1897–1918; champion of minority rights, pacifism. *John Brown: A Biography Fifty Years After,* 1910; *Newspapers and Newspaper Men,* 1932. (Grandson of WILLIAM LLOYD GARRISON.)

WALLACE, DEWITT, Nov. 12, 1889 (St. Paul, Minn.). U.S. publisher. With his wife, LILA ACHESON WALLACE, founded the Reader's Digest Assn. in a small Greenwich Village, N.Y., office, 1921; developed firm into a large communications enterprise that publishes books and produces films, as well as the magazine.

WALLACE, LILA BELL, née Acheson, Dec. 25, 1889 (Vinden, Man., Can.). U.S. publisher. With husband DEWITT WALLACE, founded *Reader's Digest,* 1921.

WALLACE, MIKE, May 9, 1918 (Brookline, Mass.). U.S. TV interviewer, commentator. With CBS-TV since 1951, news correspondent since 1963; on *Mike Wallace Interviews* (1957–58), used aggressive style with which he has become associated; costar and coeditor of *60 Minutes,* 1968– .

WALTERS, BARBARA, Sept. 25, 1931 (Boston, Mass.). U.S. newscaster. The first woman to anchor an evening TV news program, joining *ABC Evening News* in 1976. With NBC-TV's *Today Show* from 1961, was a panel member (1963–74) and cohost (1974–76).

WHITE, THEODORE HAROLD, May 6, 1915 (Boston, Mass.). U.S. journalist, author. Best known for his meticulously detailed chronicles of U.S. presidential campaigns. Chief of China bureau of *Time* magazine, 1939–45; as foreign correspondent, covered Europe, NATO, and American politics, 1955–78. *Thunder Out of China* (with Annalee Jacoby), 1946; *Making of the President 1960,* 1961 (awarded Pulitzer Prize in general nonfiction, 1962); *Making of the President 1964,* 1965; *Making of the President 1968,* 1969; *In Search of History: A Personal Adventure,* 1978.

WHITE, WILLIAM ALLEN ("The Sage of Emporia"), Feb. 10, 1868 (Emporia, Kan.)–Jan. 29, 1944. U.S. journalist. As owner and editor, made *The Emporia Gazette* internationally famous as a representative of grass-roots political opinion, 1895–1944; awarded 1923 Pulitzer Prize in editorial writing for "To an Anxious Friend"; awarded 1947 Pulitzer Prize in biography for *The Autobiography of William Allen White* (1946). *The Editor and His People* (collection), 1924.

WICKER, THOMAS GRAY (pseud.: Paul Connolly), June 18, 1926 (Hamlet, N.C.). U.S. journalist, novelist. Chief of the Washington bureau of *The New York Times,* 1964–68; *Times* assoc. editor, 1968– ; writes thrillers under his pseudonym. *Kennedy Without Tears,* 1964; *JFK and LBJ: The Influence of Personality upon Politics,* 1968; *Facing the Lions,* 1973; *A Time to Die,* 1975.

WILSON, EARL, May 3, 1907 (Rockford, Ohio). U.S. columnist. His gossip column, "It Happened Last Night," has been syndicated nationwide since 1942.

WINCHELL, WALTER, Apr. 7, 1897 (New York, N.Y.)–Feb. 20, 1972. U.S. journalist. Wrote an internationally famous, much-imitated syndicated gossip column; had a popular, long-running radio gossip program (1930–50).

WOLFE, TOM (born Thomas Kennerly Wolfe, Jr.), Mar. 2, 1931 (Richmond, Va.). U.S. journalist. Leading exponent of the so-called New Journalism, which combines fictional techniques with nonfiction reporting in studies of contemporary American culture. *The Kandy-Kolored Tangerine-Flake Streamline Baby,* 1965; *The Electric Kool-Aid Acid Test,* 1968; *Radical Chic and Mau-mauing the Flak Catchers,* 1970.

WOODWARD, ROBERT UPSHUR, Mar. 26, 1943 (Geneva, Ill.). U.S. journalist. With *Washington Post* colleague CARL BERNSTEIN, uncovered the Watergate scandal that led to the resignation of Pres. RICHARD NIXON; with Bernstein, wrote *All the President's Men* (1974) and *The Final Days* (1976).

WOOLLCOTT, ALEXANDER, Jan. 19, 1887 (Phalanx, N.J.)–Jan. 23, 1943. U.S. journalist, critic. Drama critic with *The New York Times* (1914–22) and the New York *World* (1925–28); starred in weekly radio show *The Town Crier,* 1929–49; the model for Sheridan Whiteside in the GEORGE S. KAUFMAN and MOSS HART play *The Man Who Came to Dinner. While Rome Burns,* 1934; *Long Long Ago,* 1943.

ZENGER, JOHN PETER, 1697 (Germany)–July 28, 1746. U.S. printer, journalist. As publisher of the *New York Weekly Journal* (founded 1733), the central figure in a famous libel suit (1734–35); his acquittal is regarded as fundamental to the establishment of freedom of the press in America.

ARTISTS

U.S. ARTISTS

ABBOTT, BERENICE, 1898 (Springfield, Ohio). U.S. photographer. Photographed literary and artistic social circles, 1920s; teacher at New School for Social Research, New York City. *Changing New York,* 1937.

ADAMS, ANSEL, Feb. 20, 1902 (San Francisco, Calif.). U.S. landscape photographer. Used technical and artistic innovations to depict Western wilderness areas and mountain panoramas, emphasizing lighting effects and sharp detail. *This Is the American Earth,* 1960; *This We Inherit,* 1962.

ADDAMS, CHARLES SAMUEL, Jan. 7, 1912 (Westfield, N.J.). U.S. cartoonist. His macabre cartoons have appeared in *The New Yorker* since 1935. *Drawn and Quartered,* 1942; *Home Bodies,* 1954.

ALLSTON, WASHINGTON, Nov. 5, 1779 (nr. Georgetown, S.C.)–July 9, 1843. U.S. painter, author. Considered a pioneer of U.S. Romantic landscape painting. Paintings: *The Deluge,* 1804; *Moonlit Landscape,* 1819; *Belshazzar's Feast,* begun 1817. Books: *The Sylphs of the Seasons, with Other Poems,* 1813.

ARBUS, DIANE, Mar. 14, 1923 (New York, N.Y.)–July 26, 1971. U.S. photographer. Photographed the traumatic experiences of people; won Guggenheim Fellowship, (1959 and 1966) for project entitled "The American Experience"; committed suicide.

ARNO, PETER, born Curtis Arnoux Peters, Jan. 8, 1904 (New York, N.Y.)–Feb. 22, 1968. U.S. cartoonist, writer. His cartoons in *The New Yorker* and other magazines satirized cafe society, from 1925.

AUDUBON, JOHN JAMES, born Jean Rabine, Apr. 26, 1785 (Les Cayes, Haiti)–Jan. 27, 1851. U.S. naturalist, painter. Devoted his mature professional years almost entirely to illustrations of U.S. wildlife. *The Birds of America,* 1827–38; *Ornithological Biography* (with William MacGillivray), 1831–39; *Viviparous Quadrupeds of North America* (with his son John), 1845–48.

BECK, C(harles) C(larence), June 8, 1910 (Zimbrota, Minn.). U.S. cartoonist. Humor illustrator with Fawcett's pulp magazines, 1933–   ; chief artist for *Captain Marvell,* cartoon strip, 1939–54; created Captain Tootsie for Tootsie Roll Candy Co.

BELLOWS, GEORGE WESLEY, Aug. 12, 1882 (Columbus, Ohio)–Jan. 8, 1925. U.S. painter. A popular exponent of the U.S. realistic school; painted urban scenes, sports events, and landscapes with forceful brushstrokes. Paintings: *Stag at Sharkey's,* 1909; *The Cliff Dwellers,* 1913.

BENTON, THOMAS HART, Apr. 15, 1889 (Neosho, Mo.)–Jan. 19, 1975. U.S. painter, muralist. A regionalist painter who specialized in flowing, colorful mythic portrayals of rural American life; opposed abstract art because it was divorced from American traditions. Paintings: *Cotton Pickers,* 1932; *July Hay,* 1943; murals at the Harry S. Truman Library, Independence, Mo., 1959.

BINGHAM, GEORGE CALEB, Mar. 20, 1811 (Augusta Co., Va.)–July 7, 1879. U.S. painter. Specialized in scenes of Midwestern river life and colorful political campaigns. Paintings: *Fur Traders Descending the Missouri,* 1844; *Stump Speaking,* 1854.

BLOCK, HERBERT LAWRENCE ("Herblock"), Oct. 13, 1909 (Chicago, Ill.). U.S. cartoonist. A political cartoonist since 1929; widely known for his liberal views and biting satire; awarded Pulitzer Prize for editorial cartooning, 1942, 1954, and 1979.

BORGLUM, GUTZON, born John Gutson de la Mothe Borglum, Mar. 25, 1871 (nr. Bear Lake, Idaho T.)–Mar. 6, 1941. U.S. sculptor. Moved from specializing in horse sculptures to large monumental portraits; sculpted the heads of presidents Washington, Jefferson, Lincoln, and T. Roosevelt on Mt. Rushmore, 1927–41.

BULFINCH, CHARLES, Aug. 8, 1763 (Boston, Mass.)–Apr. 4, 1844. U.S. architect. Reputedly the first professional U.S. architect; introduced the neoclassical Adam style to the U.S. as the so-called Federal style; designed the Massachusetts State House (1787–88) and the rotunda of the U.S. Capitol (1818–30).

BURNHAM, DANIEL HUDSON, Sept. 4, 1846 (Henderson, Mass.)–June 1, 1912. U.S. architect, city planner. Led the so-called City Beautiful movement; guided the redevelopment of Chicago and Washington, D.C., along grand, classical lines; designed the triangular Flatiron Bldg., New York City (1902) and Union Station, Washington, D.C. (1906).

CALDER, ALEXANDER, July 22, 1898 (Lawnton, Pa.)–Nov. 11, 1976. U.S. sculptor. One of the inventors of the mobile (suspended sculpture made of separate, moving parts) and the stabile (stationary sheet-metal sculptures); made toys, jewelry, and furniture. Works: *Lobster Trap and Fish Tail,* 1939; *Spiral,* 1958; *Ticket Window,* 1965.

CANIFF, MILTON, Feb. 28, 1907 (Hillsboro, Ohio). U.S. cartoonist. Created the comic strips *Terry and the Pirates* and *Steve Canyon,* which pitted American heroes against sinister Orientals.

CAPP, AL, born Alfred Gerald Caplin, Sept. 28, 1909 (New Haven, Conn.)–Nov. 5, 1979. U.S. cartoonist. Created the *"Li'l Abner"* comic strip noted for broad satire of U.S. mores and politics and for voluptuously-drawn female hillbilly citizens of Dogpatch, U.S.A.

CASSATT, MARY, May 22, 1844 (Allegheny City,

THE BOOK OF WHO

Pa.)–June 14, 1926. U.S. painter, printmaker. Impressionist in France specializing in domestic scenes. Paintings: *Cup of Tea,* 1879; *Reading "Le Figaro,"* 1882; *Woman Bathing,* 1890; *The Coiffure,* 1890; *The Bath,* 1891–92.

CATLIN, GEORGE, July 16, 1796 (Wilkes-Barre, Pa.)–Dec. 23, 1872. U.S. painter, engraver, writer. Traveled among the American Indians; painted hundreds of Indian scenes; published travel books, including *My Life among the Indians* (1841).

CHURCH, FREDERICK EDWIN, May 4, 1826 (Hartford, Conn.)–Apr. 7, 1900. U.S. painter. Achieved dramatic light, water, and sunset effects in his grand, often exotic landscapes such as *Niagara Falls* (1857) and *Heart of the Andes* (1855).

COLE, THOMAS, Feb. 1, 1801 (Bolton-le-Moors, Eng.)–Feb. 8, 1848. U.S. painter. Founded the Hudson R. school; painted awesome Romantic landscapes; also painted large allegorical canvases. Paintings: *Voyage of Life* series, 1839–40; *Schroon Mountain,* 1838.

COPLEY, JOHN SINGLETON, July 3, 1738 (probably Boston, Mass.)–Sept. 9, 1815. U.S. painter. Painted realistic, strong portraits of New Englanders with their tools of trade; went to England (1775), where he painted realistic historical scenes. Paintings: *Boy with a Squirrel,* 1765; *Watson and the Shark,* 1778; *Death of Major Peirson,* 1782–84.

CUNNINGHAM, IMOGEN, Apr. 12, 1883 (Portland, Ore.)–June 24, 1976. U.S. photographer. Known for portraits and photographs of plants. Works: *Marsh at Dawn,* 1901; *Words beyond the World,* 1912; *Two Callas,* 1929.

CURRIER, NATHANIEL, Mar. 27, 1813 (Roxbury, Mass.)–Nov. 20, 1888. U.S. lithographer. Partner in Currier and Ives with JAMES MERRITT IVES, 1857–1888; produced more than 7,000 prints and titles between 1840 and 1890.

DAVIES, ARTHUR BOWEN, Sept. 26, 1862 (Utica, N.Y.)–Oct. 24, 1928. U.S. painter, printmaker, tapestry designer. Organized the Ashcan School exhibit, 1908; major figure in organizing the groundbreaking 1913 Armory Show of modern art. Works: *Along the Erie Canal,* 1890; *Crescendo,* 1910; *Dancers,* 1913.

DAVIS, STUART, Dec. 7, 1894 (Philadelphia, Pa.)–June 24, 1964. U.S. abstract artist. Sought inspiration in urban environment—taxis, chain-store fronts, neon sights, etc. Paintings: *Lucky Strike,* 1921; *Egg Beater* series, 1927–30; *Little Giant Still-Life,* 1950.

DUNCAN, DAVID DOUGLAS, Jan. 23, 1916 (Kansas City, Mo.). U.S. photojournalist. Photographer for *Life* magazine, 1946–56; freelance photographer, 1956–   ; photo correspondent in Vietnam for *Life* magazine and ABC-TV, 1967–68. *I Protest,* 1968; *Self-Portrait, U.S.A.,* 1969; *War without Heroes,* 1970; *Goodbye Picasso,* 1974; *Magic Worlds of Fantasy,* 1978.

DURAND, ASHER BROWN, Aug. 21, 1796 (Jefferson Village, N.J.)–Sept. 17, 1886. U.S. painter, engraver, illustrator. A founder (1826) and pres. (1845–61) of the National Acad. of Design. Works: *Declaration of Independence,* 1823; *Kindred Spirits,* 1849.

EAKINS, THOMAS, July 25, 1844 (Philadelphia, Pa.)–Jun. 25, 1916. U.S. artist. Prime exponent of native tradition of realism in American art; known for strong draftsmanship and dramatic compositions. Paintings: *The Surgical Clinic of Professor Gross,* 1875; *The Chess Players,* 1876; *The Concert Singer,* 1892; *The Thinker,* 1900.

EAMES, CHARLES, June 17, 1907 (St. Louis, Mo.)–Aug. 21, 1978. U.S. designer. Best known for series of chairs he designed, 1940s; molded plywood furniture, mass-produced by the Herman Miller Furniture Co., 1946; design consultant for IBM, in the 1960s.

FEIFFER, JULES, Jan. 26, 1929 (New York, N.Y.). U.S. cartoonist, writer. Cartoonist with the *Village Voice* (1956–   ), *Playboy* magazine (1959–   ), and the *London Observer* (1958–66 and 1972–   ). *Sick, Sick, Sick,* 1959; *The Great Comic Book Heroes,* 1965; *Feiffer on Nixon: The Cartoon Presidency,* 1974; *Knock, Knock,* 1976.

FRANKENTHALER, HELEN, Dec. 12, 1928 (New York, N.Y.). U.S. painter. Paintings: *Mountains and Sea,* 1952; *Open Wall,* 1953; *The Human Edge,* 1967.

FRENCH, DANIEL CHESTER, Apr. 20, 1850 (Exeter, N.H.)–Oct. 7, 1931. U.S. sculptor. Works: *The Minute Man,* 1875; the statue of Lincoln in the Lincoln Memorial, Washington, D.C., dedicated in 1922; *John Harvard,* 1884.

GIBSON, CHARLES DANA, Sept. 14, 1867 (Roxbury, Mass.)–Dec. 23, 1944. U.S. artist, illustrator. Best known for his "Gibson Girl" drawings; contributed illustrations to *Life* magazine and *Collier's Weekly;* illustrated *London As Seen by C. D. Gibson* (1895–97), *People of Dickens* (1897) and *The Education of Mr. Pipp* (1899).

GILBERT, CASS, Nov. 24, 1859 (Zanesville, Ohio)–May 17, 1934. U.S. architect. Designed the Woolworth Bldg., New York City, 1908–13; U.S. Sup. Ct. Bldg., Washington, D.C., completed 1935; Minnesota State Capitol, St. Paul, 1896–1903.

GORKY, ASHILE, born Vosdanig Adoian, 1905 (Khorkom Vari, Turkish Armenia)–July 21, 1948. Armenian-U.S. painter. Combined European expressionist and U.S. abstract expressionist styles. Paintings: *How My Mother's Embroidered Apron Unfolds in My Life,* 1944; *The Diary of a Seducer,* 1945; *The Bethrothal II,* 1947.

HARRISON, WALLACE KIRKMAN, Sept. 28, 1895 (Worcester, Mass.). U.S. architect. With the firm Harrison and Abramovitz, 1941–78; co-designer of Rockefeller Center, New York City, 1930; dir. of planning for UN Plaza, New York City, 1947; designed Met. Opera House, Lincoln Center, New York City, 1955; pres. of Architectural League of New York, 1946–47.

HASSAM, CHILDE, Oct. 17, 1859 (Boston, Mass.)–Aug. 27, 1935. U.S. impressionist painter, printmaker. Known for his scenes of New York life. Paintings: *Washington Arch, Spring,* 1890; *Southwest Wind,* 1905; *Church at Old Lyme,* 1906.

HENRI, ROBERT, June 25, 1865 (Cincinnati, Ohio)–July 12, 1929. U.S. painter. A leader of the modernist Ashcan school of artists; instructor at the Women's School of Design of Philadelphia, 1891–98; teacher at the Art Students' League of New York, 1915–28. Paintings: *Willie Gee,* 1904; *Himself* and *Herself,* 1913.

HICKS, EDWARD, Apr. 4, 1780 (Bucks County, Pa.)–Aug. 23, 1849. U.S. folk painter. Known for landscape paintings of Pennsylvania and New York farm country. Paintings: *The Peaceable Kingdom; The Cornell Farm,* 1836.

HOBAN, JAMES, 1762 (Callan, Ire.)–Dec. 8, 1831. U.S. architect. Designed the White House, Washington, D.C., 1793–1801; other works in-

ARTISTS

clude Grand Hotel (1793–95) and the State and War Offices (1818), both in Washington, D.C.

HOMER, WINSLOW, Feb. 24, 1836 (Boston, Mass.)–Sept. 29, 1910. U.S. painter. A Romantic painter in the tradition of native American realism; began as a painter of convivial social scenes, then turned to powerful, dramatic depictions of man-versus-the-sea; in his last years, painted atmospheric, impressionistic coastal views. Paintings: *Eight Bells,* 1866; *Snap the Whip,* 1872; *The Gulf Stream,* 1899.

HOOD, RAYMOND MATHEWSON, Mar. 28, 1881 (Pawtucket, R.I.)–Aug. 14, 1934. U.S. architect. Designer of Beaux Arts skyscrapers in Chicago and New York, including the McGraw-Hill Bldg., New York, 1930–31.

HOPPER, EDWARD, July 22, 1882 (Nyack, N.Y.)–May 15, 1967. U.S. painter. Chiefly depicted city scenes, with photographic realism. Paintings: *Model Reading,* 1925; *House by the Road,* 1925; *Nighthawks,* 1942; *Second-Story Sunlight,* 1960.

HUNT, RICHARD MORRIS, Oct. 31, 1827 (Brattleboro, Vt.)–July 31, 1895. U.S. architect. Established the French Beaux Arts style in U.S.; a founder of American Inst. of Architects; designed the Tribune Bldg. (1873) and the façade of the Met. Museum of Art (completed 1900–02), both in New York City.

INNESS, GEORGE, May 1, 1825 (Newburgh, N.Y.)–Aug. 3, 1894. U.S. painter. A landscapist of the Hudson R. school. Paintings: *The Lackawanna Valley,* 1855; *The Delaware Water Gap,* 1861; *Peace and Plenty,* 1865; *Autumn Oaks,* 1875.

IVES, JAMES MERRITT, Mar. 5, 1824 (New York, N.Y.)–Jan. 3, 1895. U.S. painter, lithographer, publisher. Partner with NATHANIEL CURRIER in Currier & Ives lithograph publishers, 1857–95.

JENNEY, WILLIAM LE BARON, Sept. 25, 1832 (Fairhaven, Mass.)–June 15, 1907. U.S. civil engineer, architect. An innovator in the development of the skyscraper; best known for designing and solving the structural problems in erecting the Insurance Bldg., Chicago (1884–85), often considered the first true skyscraper.

JOHNS, JASPER, May 15, 1930 (Augusta, Ga.). U.S. artist. A major pop artist known for using numbers, alphabetical letters, flags, targets in his work. Paintings: *Construction with a Piano,* 1954; *Book,* 1957; *Map,* 1961; *Field Painting,* 1964.

JOHNSON, PHILIP CORTELYOU, July 8, 1906 (Cleveland, Ohio). U.S. architect, theorist. One of the principal exponents of the so-called International style of architecture; best-known for functionalist glass-and-steel buildings such as the Seagram Bldg. (with M. VAN DER ROHE), New York City, 1958; Dir. of dept. of architecture at the Museum of Modern Art, New York City, 1932–40 and 1946–54. Coauthor (with H. R. Hitchcock) of *The International Style: Architecture Since 1922,* 1932.

KAHN, ALBERT, Mar. 21, 1869 (Westphalia, Ger.)–Dec. 8, 1942. U.S. architect. His Detroit firm designed over 2,000 industrial buildings, from 1904.

KENT, ROCKWELL, June 21, 1882 (Tarrytown Heights, N.Y.)–Mar. 13, 1971. U.S. painter, illustrator. Known for his stark, dramatic lithographs and exotic landscapes. Works: *The Road Roller,* 1909; *North Wind,* 1919; *Wilderness,* 1920.

LA FARGE, JOHN, Mar. 31, 1835 (New York, N.Y.)–Nov. 14, 1910. U.S. landscape and figure painter. National Academician at Soc. of American Artists, 1869; painted the altarpiece at St. Peter's Church, New York City, 1863; decorated New York City's Trinity Church. *Lectures on Art,* 1895, *Higher Life in Art,* 1908.

LANE, JOHN RICHARD, Aug. 12, 1932 (Jefferson City, Mo.). U.S. artist. Creative dir. (1969–75), editorial cartoonist (1975–78) for Newspaper Enterprise Assn. and art dir. (1978–   ) for NEA-United Features Syndicate; has illustrated numerous books, including *Rockin' Steady* (1974), *Giant Animals* (1977), and *How to Make Play Places and Secret Hidy Holes* (1979).

LATROBE, BENJAMIN HENRY, May 1, 1764 (Yorkshire, Eng.)–Sept. 3, 1820. U.S. architect. An exponent of the Classical Revival style; appointed architect of the Capitol, Washington, D.C., 1803; rebuilt the Capitol after it was destroyed in the War of 1812.

LICHTENSTEIN, ROY, Oct. 27, 1923 (New York, N.Y.). U.S. painter. A leader of the pop art movement. Paintings: *Flatten . . . sandfleas,* 1962; *Preparedness,* 1968.

MCKIM, CHARLES FOOLEN, Aug. 24, 1847 (Chester Co., Pa.)–Sept. 14, 1909. U.S. architect. A founder (1879) of McKim, Mead and White, the most prestigious U.S. architectural firm of the late 19th cent. and the designers of Boston Public Library (1895), the Washington Memorial Arch (New York, 1889), and Symphony Hall (Boston, 1901).

MILLS, ROBERT, Aug. 12, 1781 (Charleston, S.C.)–Mar. 3, 1855. U.S. neoclassical architect. Considered the first American-born professional architect; designed the original U.S. Post Office, the Treasury Office, and the Patent Office, all in Washington, D.C., 1836–51; also designed the Washington Monument, 1836.

MOSES, GRANDMA, born Anna Mary Robertson, Sept. 7, 1860 (Greenwich, N.Y.)–Dec. 13, 1961. U.S. folk painter. Best known for documentary paintings of U.S. rural life, including *Black Horses,* (1941) and *From My Window* (1946). Autobiography: *My Life's History,* 1952.

MOTHERWELL, ROBERT, Jan. 24, 1915 (Aberdeen, Wash.). U.S. painter. A founder of abstract expressionism; later adopted surrealist technique of automatism. Paintings: *Poncho Villa, Dead and Alive,* 1943; *Africa,* 1964–65; *Open* series, 1967–69.

MUYBRIDGE, EADWEARD JAMES, Apr. 9, 1830 (Kingston-on-Thames, Eng.)–May 8, 1904. U.S. photographer. Pioneer in photographic studies of motion and in moving-picture projection; invented zooproxiscope and motion photography; 1877; did motion studies of humans at the U. of Pennsylvania, 1884–87.

NAST, THOMAS, Sept. 27, 1840 (Landau, Ger.)–Dec. 7, 1902. U.S. cartoonist. With *Harper's Weekly,* 1858–86; known for the creation of the Democratic Party Donkey and the Republican Party Elephant, and for his brilliant cartoons savaging the corrupt Tammany Hall political machine.

NEVELSON, LOUISE, 1899 (Kiev, Rus.). U.S. sculptor, painter. Known for her large-scale wooden pieces. First exhibition, New York City, 1941. Sculptures: *Sky Cathedral,* 1958.

NEWMAN, BARNETT, Jan. 29, 1905 (New York, N.Y.)–July 3, 1970. U.S. abstract expressionist painter. Cofounder (with W. Baziotes, R. MOTHERWELL, and MARK ROTHKO) of the Subject of the Artist school, 1948; best known for his series of 14 paintings titled *Stations of the Cross,* 1966.

59

NOGUCHI, ISAMU, Nov. 17, 1904 (Los Angeles, Calif.). U.S. sculptor, designer. Designed fountain for Ford Pavillion at the New York World's Fair, 1939. Other works: *Kouros*, 1945; garden for UNESCO, Paris, 1958; *Euripides*, 1966.

O'KEEFFE, GEORGIA, Nov. 15, 1887 (Sun Prairie, Wisc.). U.S. painter. Best known for her semiabstract depictions of natural subjects. Paintings: *Black Iris*, 1926; *Cow's Skull: Red, White and Blue*, 1931; *Sky above Clouds IV*, 1965. (Wife of ALFRED STIEGLITZ.)

OLMSTED (or Olmstead), **FREDERICK LAW,** Apr. 26, 1822 (Hartford, Conn.)-Aug. 28, 1903. U.S. landscape architect. Pioneer in urban landscaping; best known for his designs for New York's Central Park (1857) and for the grounds of the 1893 Chicago World's Fair (now Jackson Park); chm. of the first Yosemite commission, 1864-90.

PARRISH, MAXFIELD FREDERICK, July 25, 1870 (Philadelphia, Pa.)-Mar. 30, 1966. U.S. painter, illustrator. Known for his highly original posters and book illustrations; member of the Natl. Acad. of Design, from 1906. Books illustrated: *Mother Goose in Prose, Knickerbocker's History of New York*.

PEALE, CHARLES WILSON, Apr. 15, 1741 (Queen Annes Co., Md.)-Feb. 22, 1827. U.S. painter. Best known for his portraits of American Revolutionary figures, including G. WASHINGTON, B. FRANKLIN, and T. JEFFERSON; founder of the first U.S. museum, the Peale Museum, 1786.

PEI, I(eoh) M(ing), Apr. 26, 1917 (Canton, China). U.S. architect. With Webb and Knapp, New York City, 1948-55; formed I. M. Pei and Partners, 1955-   ; known for innovative modernist structures. Buildings: National Airlines Terminal, Kennedy Airport, New York, N.Y., 1970; Herbert F. Johnson Museum of Art, Cornell U., 1973; Natl. Gallery of Art, East Bldg., Washington, D.C., 1978.

PHYFE, DUNCAN, 1768 (Loch Fannich, Scotland)-Aug. 16, 1854. U.S. cabinetmaker. Established Duncan Phyfe and Sons, 1837; known for his chairs, settees, tables.

POLLOCK, (Paul) **JACKSON,** Jan. 28, 1912 (Cody, Wyo.)-Aug. 11, 1956. U.S. painter. A leader of the abstract expressionist movement in America and an initiator of the op art movement of the 1950s and 1960s. Paintings: *Mural*, 1944; *Full Fathom Five*, 1947; *Autumn Rhythm*, 1955; *Portrait and a Dream*, 1953.

PORTMAN, JOHN CALVIN, Dec. 4, 1924 (Walhalla. S.C.). U.S. architect. Head of John Portman and Assoc., 1968-   ; known for distinctly designed hotels, many built for the Hyatt chain. Buildings: Hyatt Regency Hotel, Atlanta; Hyatt Regency, O'Hare Chicago; Bonaventure Hotel, Los Angeles; Peachtree Center Plaza Hotel, Atlanta.

RAY, MAN, born Emmanuel Radinski, Aug. 27, 1890 (Philadelphia, Pa.)-Nov. 18, 1976. U.S. painter, sculptor, photographer. Cofounder (with MARCEL DUCHAMP and Frances Picabia) of the Dada group, 1917; member of dada and surrealist groups, Paris, 1924-39; developed the rayograph technique in photography, 1921. Films: *Le Retour de la Raison*, 1923; *L'Etoile de Mer*, 1928. Paintings: *Observatory Time—The Lovers*, 1932-34.

REMINGTON, FREDERIC, Oct. 4, 1861 (Canton, N.Y.)-Dec. 26, 1909. U.S. painter, sculptor, illustrator. Best known for his colorful, exuberant paintings depicting scenes from the Old West. Paintings: *A Dash for the Timber, Past All Surgery*. Sculpture: *A Bronco Buster*.

RENWICK, JAMES, Nov. 3, 1818 (Bloomingdale, [now in New York City], N.Y.)-June 23, 1895. U.S. architect. Best known for his Gothic revival designs; buildings include Grace Church (1843-46) and St. Patrick's Cathedral in New York City (dedicated in 1879) and the Smithsonian Inst. and Corcoran Art Gallery (c. 1897) in Washington, D.C.

RICHARDSON, HENRY HOBSON, Sept. 29, 1838 (St. James Par., La.)-Apr. 27, 1886. U.S. architect. Worked in neo-Romanesque style; influenced the work of Louis Sullivan and FRANK LLOYD WRIGHT. Buildings: Trinity Church, Boston, 1872-77; Marshal Field Warehouse, Chicago, 1885-87.

RIPLEY, ROBERT LEROY, Dec. 25, 1893 (Santa Rosa, Calif.)-May 27, 1949. U.S. cartoonist. Best known for his "Believe it or Not" cartoons, first published in 1918 and syndicated in over 300 newspapers all over the world.

RIVERS, LARRY, born Yitzroch Loiza Grossberg Aug. 17, 1923 (New York, N.Y.). U.S. artist. A forerunner of the pop art movement; among the first to use popular images in his paintings. Paintings: *Double Portrait of Birdie*, 1954.

ROCKWELL, NORMAN, Feb. 3, 1894 (New York, N.Y.)-Nov. 8, 1978. U.S. illustrator, painter. Best known for his nostalgic, highly detailed covers for the *Saturday Evening Post*. Recipient of Presidential Freedom Medal, 1977. *Norman Rockwell's America*, 1975.

ROOT, JOHN WELLBORN, Jan. 10, 1850 (Lumpkin, Ga.)-Jan. 15, 1892. U.S. architect. In partnership with DANIEL H. BURNHAM, 1872-92; consulting architect for the corp. for the World's Columbian Exposition, 1890. Buildings: Chicago Acad. of Fine Arts, 1882; Chicago Daily News Bldg., 1890.

ROSENQUIST, JAMES ALBERT, Nov. 29, 1933 (Grand Forks, N. Dak.). U.S. painter. In the pop art movement; incorporates everyday images in huge canvases. Paintings: *F-111* (51 panels), 1965.

ROTHKO, MARK, Sept. 25, 1903 (Dvinska, Rus.)-Feb. 25, 1970. U.S. painter. A cofounder of the abstract expressionist group called The Ten, 1935. Works: *Subway* series, late 1930s; *Baptismal Scene*, 1945; *No. 2, 1948*, 1948; *Light, Earth and Blue*, 1954; *Black on Grey*, 1970.

RYDER, ALBERT PINKHAM, Mar. 19, 1847 (New Bedford, Mass.)-Mar. 28, 1917. U.S. painter. Best known for his seascapes and allegorical scenes. Paintings: *Toilers of the Sea*, c. 1884; *Jonah, Death on a Pale Horse*.

SAARINEN, EERO, Aug. 20, 1910 (Kirkkonummi, Fin.)-Sept. 1, 1961. U.S. architect. In partnership with his father, Eliel Saarinen, 1938-50. Buildings: Gen. Motors Technical Center, Warren, Mich., 1948-56; U.S. Embassy, London, 1955-60.

SAINT-GAUDENS, AUGUSTUS, Mar. 1, 1848 (Dublin, Ire.)-Aug. 3, 1907. U.S. sculptor. Executed both relief and in-the-round works in a Beaux Arts mode; the most famous American sculptor of his day. Works: monument to Admiral Farragut, 1880; *Amor Caritas*, 1887; designs for the U.S. $20 gold piece (1907) and the $10 gold piece.

SARGENT, JOHN SINGER, Jan. 12, 1856 (Florence, It.)-Apr. 15, 1925. U.S. portrait and genre painter. The most sought-after portraitist of the late-19th and early-20th centuries, in both Europe and the U.S.; a master of composition and surface effects. Paintings: *The Daughters of Edward Darly Boit*, 1882; *El Jaleo*, 1882; decorative murals for Boston Public Library, 1890-1916.

ARTISTS

SCHULZ, CHARLES MONROE ("Sparky"), Nov. 26, 1922 (Minneapolis, Minn.). U.S. cartoonist. Created syndicated comic strip *Peanuts*, 1950; numerous collections of cartoons published in books, 1952–   ; won Outstanding Cartoonist award, Natl. Cartoonist Soc., 1956; won Emmy award for *A Charlie Brown Christmas*, 1966.

SHAHN, BEN(jamin), Sept. 12, 1898 (Kaunas, Lith. [now USSR])–Mar. 14, 1969. U.S. painter, graphic artist. Worked with DIEGO RIVERA to execute *Man at the Crossroads* at New York City's Rockefeller Center, 1933; did a series of paintings of the trials of Sacco and Vanzetti (1931–32) and of Tom Mooney (1932–33). Other paintings: *Seurat's Lunch*, 1939; *Handball*, 1939.

SKIDMORE, LOUIS, Apr. 8, 1897 (Lawrenceburg, Mo.)–Sept. 27, 1962. U.S. architect. A partner in Skidmore, Owings and Merrill (1949–   ), an architectural firm that pioneered in commercial and institutional design and structure. Buildings: Connecticut Gen. Life Insurance Co., Hartford, Conn., 1954–57; U.S. Air Force Acad., 1954–62.

SLOAN, JOHN FRENCH, Aug. 2, 1871 (Lock Haven, Pa.)–Sept. 7, 1951. U.S. painter, etcher, lithographer, illustrator. Best known for his depictions of everyday life in New York City; a founder of the Ashcan school, 1908. Works: *Wake of the Ferry*, 1907; *Sunday, Women Drying Their Hair*, 1912; *Backyards, Greenwich Village*, 1914.

STEICHEN, EDWARD, Mar. 27, 1879 (Luxembourg)–Mar. 25, 1973. U.S. photographer. With ALFRED STIEGLITZ, founded the Photo-Secession Gallery, 1905; head of WW I U.S. Army Air Corps photography; celebrity photographer, 1923–38; created *The Family of Man* exhibition, 1955.

STIEGLITZ, ALFRED, Jan. 1, 1864 (Hoboken, N.J.)–July 13, 1946. U.S. photographer. Known as the father of modern photography; founded Photo-Secession Group, 1902; with EDWARD STEICHEN, opened Photo-Secession Gallery, 1905; best known for his 400-print series of his wife, GEORGIA O'KEEFFE.

STONE, EDWARD DURELL, Mar. 9, 1902 (Fayetteville, Ark.)–Aug. 6, 1978. U.S. architect. Organized his own firm, 1936; one of the designers for the Mus. of Modern Art, 1937. Buildings: U.S. Embassy, New Delhi, 1954; American Pavillion, Brussels World's Fair, 1958; John F. Kennedy Center for the Performing Arts (Washington, D.C.), 1964.

STUART, GILBERT CHARLES, Dec. 3, 1755 (N. Kingstown, Kings, R.I.)–July 9, 1828. U.S. painter. Best known for his portraits of early Americans. Painted three portraits of GEORGE WASHINGTON from life, 1795, 1796, and c. 1796. Paintings: *The Skater*.

SULLY, THOMAS, June 19, 1783 (Horncastle, Eng.)–Nov. 5, 1872. U.S. portrait painter. Executed some 2,000 portraits and 500 subject and historical pictures, including *Lady with a Harp* (1818), *The Passage of the Delaware* (1819), and *Col. Thomas Handasyd Perkins* (1831–32).

TIFFANY, LOUIS COMFORT, Feb. 18, 1848 (New York, N.Y.)–Jan. 17, 1933. U.S. painter, decorator, designer. Son of the jeweler, CHARLES LEWIS TIFFANY; organized the Soc. of American Artists, 1877; established an interior-decorating studio in New York (1878) that specialized in *Faverile* glass, which was executed in irridescent art nouveau style.

TRUMBULL, JOHN, June 6, 1756 (Lebanon, Conn.)–Nov. 10, 1843. U.S. painter, architect, writer. Best known for his paintings of the American Revolutionary era. Pres of American Acad. of Fine Arts, 1816.

UPJOHN, RICHARD, Jan. 22, 1802 (Shaftesbury, Eng.)–Aug. 17, 1878. U.S. architect. Best known for his Gothic revival churches; helped to found American Inst. of Architects, 1857. Buildings: St. John's Church, Maine, 1837; Trinity Church, New York City, 1839–46. Books: *Upjohn's Rural Architecture*, 1852.

WARHOL, ANDY, Aug. 6, 1928 (Pittsburgh or McKeesport, Pa.). U.S. artist. Leader of the pop art movement of the 1960s; known for his paintings of soup cans, sculptures of Brillo Soap Pad boxes; publisher of *Interview* magazine, 1969–   . Films: *My Hustler*, 1965; *The Chelsea Girls*, 1966. Books: *Andy Warhol's Index*, 1967; *The Philosophy of Andy Warhol from A–B and Back Again*, 1975; *Exposures*, 1979.

WARREN, WHITNEY, Jan. 29, 1864 (New York, N.Y.)–Jan. 24, 1943. U.S. architect. With McKim, Mead and White, 1894–98; formed Warren and Wetmore, 1898–1931; a founder of Soc. of Beaux Arts Architects of New York; designed many New York City landmarks, including the N.Y. Yacht Club, Grand Central Station (1913), and the Belmont, Vanderbilt, and Biltmore hotels.

WESTON, EDWARD, Mar. 24, 1886 (Highland Park, Ill.)–Jan. 1, 1958. U.S. photographer. Used only natural light; rarely cropped, enlarged, or retouched his negatives. *California and the West*, 1940; *The Cats of Wildcat Hill*, 1947; *Fifty Photographs*, 1947; *My Camera on Point Lobos*, 1950.

WHISTLER, JAMES ABBOTT MCNEILL, July 10, 1834 (Lowell, Mass.)–July 17, 1903. U.S. etcher, painter, lithographer. Expatriate American painter known for his studies in color tones. Pres. of Royal Soc. of British Artists, 1886–88; taught at Académie Carmen, Paris, 1898–1901. Works: *Thames* series of etchings, 1860; *At the Piano*, 1859; *Blue Wave*, 1860; *The Little Girl in White*, 1863; *Arrangement in Gray and Black No. 1: The Artist's Mother*, 1872.

WHITE, STANFORD, Nov. 9, 1853 (New York, N.Y.)–June 25, 1906. U.S. architect. With McKim, Mead, and White, 1880–1906; known for his design of the original Madison Square Garden, New York City, 1889; shot to death by H. K. THAW over his alleged affair with EVELYN NESBIT, Thaw's wife.

WHITNEY, GERTRUDE VANDERBILT, Apr. 19, 1877 (New York, N.Y.)–Apr. 18, 1942. U.S. sculptor. Conceived and financed the Whitney Museum of American Art, 1931.

WOOD, GRANT, Feb. 13, 1892 (nr. Anamosa, Ia.)–Feb. 12, 1942. U.S. painter. Depicted Midwestern rural life of the 1930s; best known for his *American Gothic* (1930).

WRIGHT, FRANK LLOYD, June 8, 1867 (Richland Center, Wisc.)–Apr. 9, 1959. U.S. architect, writer. One of the most influential U.S. architects in history; created so-called organic architecture. Buildings: Larkin Bldg., Buffalo, N.Y., 1904; Guggenheim Museum, New York City, 1943. Books: *An Organic Architecture*, 1939; *An American Architecture*, 1955.

FOREIGN ARTISTS

AALTO, HUGO ALVAR HENRICK, Feb. 3, 1898 (Kuortane, Fin.)–May 11, 1976. Finnish architect, city planner, furniture designer. One of the pioneers of 20th-cent. Scandinavian design; used

THE BOOK OF WHO

natural materials and irregular forms blended with natural surroundings. Structures: Viipuri Municipal Library, 1930–35; Säynatsälo town hall, 1950–52.

ADAM, ROBERT, July 3, 1728 (Kirkcaldy, Eng.)–Mar. 3, 1792. English architect, furniture designer, decorator. Initiated the elegant, airy, neoclassical "Adam style"; designed rooms at Osterly Park, Middlesex (1761–80), and at Syon House, Middlesex (1762–69).

ALBERTI, LEON BATTISTA, Feb. 14, 1401 (Genoa, It.)–Apr. 25, 1472. Italian architect, scholar. A typical Ren. man—poet, art theorist, moral philosopher, and mathematician; worked out scientific system of linear perspective used by most Italian Ren. artists; used classical motifs in his church and secular architectural designs; designed churches of San Sebastiano (1460) and Sant' Andrea (1472), both in Mantua; author of *Della pittura* (On Painting), 1435.

ALTDORFER, ALBRECHT, 1480 (Regensburg, Ger.)–1538. German painter, engraver, architect. One of the earliest European landscape artists; member of the Danube school. Paintings: *The Battle of Issus,* 1529; *The Fall and Redemption of Man* (a series of 40 engravings).

ANDREA DEL SARTO, born Andrea Domenico d'Agnolo di Francesco, July 16, 1486 (Florence, It.)–Sept. 28, 1530. Italian painter. Known for his draftsmanship and feeling for color and atmosphere; one of the leading fresco painters of the High Ren.; painted frescoes in Florence at the Church of Annunziata (1509 and 1525) and the Chiostro dello Scalzo (John the Baptist series, 1511–26).

ANGELICO, FRA, a.k.a. Giovanni da Fiesole, born Guido di Petro, 1387 (Vicchi, It.)–Feb. 18, 1455. Italian painter. Known for his altarpieces; his use of perspective and sense of form reflected Early Ren. influence, while his use of exclusively religious subjects, unmixed colors, and traditional composition linked him to his medieval predecessors.

ARP, HANS (or Jean), Sept. 16, 1887 (Strasbourg, Ger. |now Fr.|)–June 7, 1966. French painter, sculptor, poet. Pioneer abstract painter; one of the founders of Dadaism; became a surrealist, from 1925; wrote experimental poetry.

BACON, FRANCIS, Oct. 28, 1909 (Dublin, Ire.). English painter. Painted expressionist portraits distorted by terror, the subjects often shown screaming. Paintings: *Studies after Velazquez' Portrait of Pope Innocent X,* 1951–53.

BARTOLOMMEO, FRA, called Baccio della Porta, born Bartolommeo di Pagolo del Fattorino, Mar. 28, 1475 (Florence, It.)–Oct. 31, 1517. Italian painter. Painted religious subjects in the classical, monumental style of the High Ren.; introduced use of generalized, rather than contemporary, settings and costumes. Paintings: *Marriage of St. Catherine,* 1512; *St. Peter* and *St. Paul,* 1515.

BEARDSLEY, AUBREY VINCENT, Aug. 21, 1872 (Brighton, Eng.)–Mar. 16, 1898. English illustrator. Influential exponent of art nouveau; earned a reputation for decadence with his sinuous, sensual, and often macabre black-and-white drawings; art editor of *Yellow Book* (1894) and *Savory* (1895); illustrated *Morte d'Arthur* (1893–94) and *Salome* (1894).

BEATON, CECIL WALTER HARDY, Jan. 14, 1904 (London, Eng.)–Jan. 18, 1980. English photographer, theatrical designer. His stylish photographic portraits for *Vanity Fair, Vogue,* and other magazines stressed decorative, often artificial backgrounds; designed sets and costumes for the play *My Fair Lady,* 1956.

BECKMANN, MAX, Feb. 12, 1884 (Leipzig, Ger.)–Dec. 27, 1970. German expressionist painter. Used angular, contorted forms and bright, flat colors in his depictions of 20th-cent. savagery. Paintings: *Departure,* 1932–33; *Blindman's Bluff,* 1945.

BELLINI, GENTILE, c.1429 (Venice, It.)–buried Feb. 23, 1507. Italian painter. Painted portraits and narrative panoramas, especially of Venetian life. Paintings: *Portrait of Mohammed II,* c.1480; *Procession in the Piazza of San Marco,* 1496.

BELLINI, GIOVANNI, c.1430 (Venice, It.)–Nov. 1516. Italian painter. His adoption of oils enabled him to develop a style of rich coloring and warm lighting that defined subsequent Venetian art; his detailed settings marked him as a great landscape painter. Paintings: *St. Francis in Ecstasy,* 1480; *Allegory of Purgatory,* 1480s.

BERNINI, GIOVANNI LORENZO, Dec. 7, 1598 (Naples, It.)–Nov. 28, 1680. Italian sculptor, architect, painter, designer. Considered the founder of the Italian baroque style; stressed movement and theatr al effects in his religious and secular works. Sculpture: *Apollo and Daphne,* 1622–24; *Ecstasy of St. Theresa,* 1644–52; tomb of Urban VIII, 1628–47.

BONNARD, PIERRE, Oct. 3, 1867 (Fontenay-aux-Roses, Fr.)–Jan. 23, 1947. French painter, printmaker. A postimpressionist who used brilliant colors, warm lighting effects, and decorative patterns in his still-lifes, domestic interiors, and landscapes. Paintings: *The Open Window,* 1921; *The Breakfast Room,* 1930.

BORROMINI, FRANCESCO, born Francesco Castelli, Sept. 25, 1599 (Bissone, It.)–Aug. 3, 1667. Italian baroque architect. Used unusual solid geometric shapes for church floor-plans and spiral finials and concave façades as ornamentation; considered idiosyncratic, but strongly influenced late baroque architecture. Buildings: Church of San Carlo alle Quattro Fontane, Rome, 1638–1646; St. Agnese, Rome; Sant'Ivo alla Sapienz, Rome, 1642–60.

BOSCH, HIERONYMUS, born Jeroen Anthoiszoon or Jeroen von Aeken, c.1450 (Hertogenbosch, Neth.)–c.1516. Flemish painter. His fantastic, subtly colored landscapes and carefully detailed allegorical groups expressed a mystical obsession with sin and punishment. Paintings: *Garden of Earthly Delights,* 1505–10; *Crowning with Thorns.*

BOTTICELLI, SANDRO, born Alessandro di Mariano Filipepi, 1445 (Florence, It.)–May 17, 1510. Italian painter. One of the greatest artists of Early Ren. Florence; his use of relatively flat surfaces, flowing lines, soft lighting, quiet facial expressions, and allegorical details reflect a melancholy spirituality; career divided sharply between early works with classical subjects and later religious paintings. Paintings: *Primavera,* 1474–78; *Birth of Venus,* 1485–88.

BOUCHER, FRANÇOIS, Sept. 29, 1703 (Paris, Fr.)–May 30, 1770. French painter, tapestry and porcelain designer, engraver. His pastel colors, delicate composition, and sensuous treatment of pastoral and mythological subjects epitomized the sophisticated elegance of French rococo. Tapestries: *Pastorales.* Painting: *Triumph of Venus,* 1740.

BOUTS, DIERIK (or Dirk, Thierry, Dirck), c.1400–1415 (Haarlem, Neth.)–May 6, 1475. Dutch painter. His austere religious paintings were characterized by controlled, intense facial expressions. Paintings: *Last Supper,* 1464; *Last Judgement,* 1468.

BRAMANTE, DONATO (or Donino), born Donato d'Agnolo (or d'Angelo) 1444 (Monte Asdruvaldo, It.)-Apr. 11, 1514. Italian architect, town planner, writer. Through his many commissions in Milan and Rome, developed the classical High Ren. style in architecture; designed the Church of Sta. Maria delle Grazie (Milan) and the early 16th-cent. plan for rebuilding Rome, including the original design for St. Peter's.

BRANCUSI, CONSTANTIN, Feb. 21, 1876 (Hobita, Rum.)-Mar. 16, 1957. Rumanian-French sculptor. A pioneer in sculpture of abstract figures; stressed form over detail and the peculiar qualities of his various materials, including wood, marble, and polished bronze. Sculpture: *The Kiss,* 1908; *Bird in Space* (variations), 1924-40.

BRAQUE, GEORGES, May 13, 1882 (Argenteuil, Fr.)-Aug. 31, 1963. French painter, sculptor, and stage, book, and glass designer. Acknowledged as a principal founder of modern art; with PABLO PICASSO, developed cubism; known for his collage technique, still-lifes, and interiors. Paintings: *Houses at L'Estaque,* 1908; *Man with Guitar,* 1911; *The Yellow Tablecloth,* 1937.

BREUER, MARCEL LAJOS, May 21, 1902 (Pécs, Hung.). Hungarian-U.S. architect, furniture designer. Helped develop and popularize the sleek, streamlined International Style in architecture, furniture, and industrial design; invented the tubular metal chair; designed UNESCO headquarters in Paris (1953-58), St. John's Abbey in Collegeville, Minn. (1953-61), and the Whitney Museum in New York City (1966).

BRONZINO, IL, (also Agnolo or Angiolo di Cosimo) born Nov. 17, 1503 (Monticelli, It.)-Nov. 23, 1572. Italian painter, poet. Best known for his courtly portraits, whose elongated figures, smooth surfaces, and artificial colors typified Mannerism. Paintings: *Portrait of a Young Man; Venus, Cupid, Folly and Time,* c.1546.

BROWN, LANCELOT ("Capability Brown"), 1715 (Kirkharle, Eng.)-Feb. 6, 1783. English landscape gardener. Led the development of the informal, naturally contoured "English garden" style; responsible for the estates at Kew and Blenheim.

BRUEGEL (or Brueghel) **THE ELDER, PIETER,** 1525? (nr. Breda, Neth.)-Sept. 5/9, 1569. Flemish painter. Painted vigorous, almost primitive scenes of peasant life and Biblical allegories; his innovative landscapes and detailed crowd scenes are unified by rhythm of movement and warm color. Paintings: Months of the Year series, c.1565; *Tower of Babel,* 1563; *Peasant Dance,* 1565.

BRUNELLESCHI, FILIPPO, 1377 (Florence,♥.)-Apr. 15, 1446. Italian architect, engineer, inventor, sculptor. One of the founders of Ren. architecture, both esthetically and technologically; the chief developer of the rules of linear perspective in painting; designed the dome of Florence Cathedral (1418), as well as the Ospedale degli Innocenti (1421-55) and the Church of Santa Maria degli Angeli (begun 1434) in Florence.

BURNE-JONES, SIR EDWARD COLEY, born Edward Jones, Aug. 28, 1833 (Birmingham, Eng.)-June 17, 1898. English painter, designer. A Pre-Raphaelite painter of carefully drawn, artificially posed medieval and classical narrative scenes; a leader of the "artist-craftsman" movement. Paintings: *The Beguiling of Merlin,* 1872-77; *The Golden Stairs,* 1880. Book illustrations: *Chaucer,* 1896.

CALLICRATES (or Kallikrates), fl.5th cent. B.C. Athenian architect. One of the two builders of the Parthenon in Athens, c.440 B.C.; designed the temple of Athena Nike on the Acropolis.

CAMPIN, ROBERT, c.1378 (Tournai, Flanders)-Apr. 26, 1444. Flemish painter. One of the founders of the naturalistic Flemish painting tradition; often identified with the Master of Flémalle; the *Mérode Altarpiece* (1428) is attributed to him.

CANALETTO, born Giovanni Antonio Canal, Oct. 18, 1697 (Venice, It.)-Apr. 19, 1768. Italian painter, etcher. A pioneer of colorful, architecturally accurate *vedute* (cityscapes); did animated views of Venice and London.

CARAVAGGIO, MICHELANGELO MERISI (or Amerisi) **DA,** Sept. 28, 1573 (Caravaggio, It.)-July 18, 1610. Italian painter. A founder of the Italian baroque; used chiaroscuro (modeling via light and shade) for emotional impact in intensely realistic works. Paintings: *Young Bacchus,* c.1590; *Calling of St. Matthew,* c.1597; *Conversion of St. Paul,* 1600-01.

CARRACCI (or Caracci) family: **LUDOVICO,** Apr. 21, 1555 (Bologna, It.)-Nov. 13, 1619; **ANNIBALE,** Nov. 3, 1560 (Bologna, It.)-July 15, 1609; **AGOSTINO,** Aug. 16, 1557 (Bologna, It.)-Feb. 23, 1602. Italian family of painters. Among the founders of the Italian baroque; formed the influential Bologna Acad., 1582; joint works include frescoes in Palazzo Farnese (c.1595-1604) in Rome and Palazzo Fava in Bologna (1584).

CARTIER-BRESSON, HENRI, Aug. 22, 1908 (Chanteloup, Fr.). French photographer. Best known for his spontaneous, sympathetic portraits and documentary photographs.

CASTAGNO, ANDREA DEL, born Andrea di Bartolo di Simone, c.1421 (San Martino a Corella, It.)-Aug. 19, 1457. Italian painter. Early Florentine Ren. master; introduced naturalism and perspective into religious scenes. Paintings: *Last Supper,* 1445; *Trinity.*

CELLINI, BENVENUTO, Nov. 3, 1500 (Florence, It.)-Feb. 13, 1571. Italian goldsmith, sculptor, writer. Designed and executed lavishly intricate Mannerist metalworks, ranging from coins to helmets; known for his innovative, picaresque autobiography, which influenced subsequent views of the Ren.; created a gold and enamel saltcellar for Francis I and a bust of *Bindo Altoviti* (1550).

CEZANNE, PAUL, Jan. 19, 1839 (Aix-en-Provence, Fr.)-Oct. 22, 1906. French painter. Perhaps the most influential Western painter since GIOTTO; his works span the innovative era from impressionism to cubism; evolved a style that dynamically assembled simple masses of color and shape in contrasting planes of still-lifes, landscapes, and figure studies; laid the pictorial and imaginative groundwork for abstract art. Paintings: *Card Players,* 1890-92; *Mont Sainte-Victoire with Large Pine Trees,* 1885-87; *Grandes Baigneuses,* 1888-1905.

CHAGALL, MARC, July 7, 1887 (Liozno, Rus.). Russian-French painter, graphic artist, theatrical designer. Painted colorful fantasy narratives, usually expressing the mores, religion, and folklore of Eastern European Jews. Paintings: *I and My Village,* 1911; *Over Vitebsk,* 1923; *12 Tribes* (windows at the Hadassah Center in Jerusalem), 1962.

CHARDIN, JEAN BAPTISTE SIMEON, Nov. 2, 1699 (Paris, Fr.)-Dec. 6, 1779. French painter. Master of still-life and genre subjects who painted in a serene, sympathetic tone; turned to pastels late in life. Paintings: *Le Benedicte,* 1740; *Attributes of the Arts* and *Attributes of Music,* 1765.

CIMABUE, GIOVANNI, born Benvenuto di Giuseppi (or di Pepo), c.1240 (Florence, It.)-1302.

Italian painter, mosaicist. The first great Florentine master; developed the medieval Byzantine style with strong compositional control and classically dignified poses and faces; known as the teacher of GIOTTO. Paintings: *Madonna and Child Enthroned with Angels and Prophets,* early 1280s.

CLAUDE LORRAIN, born Claude Gellée, 1600 (Chamagne, Fr.)–Nov. 21, 1682. French painter. His idealized landscapes of ancient Roman countrysides and harbor views were inspired by classical antiquity. Paintings: *Embarkation of Ulysses,* 1646; *Pastoral Landscape,* 1647; *Rest on the Flight into Egypt,* 1661.

CONSTABLE, JOHN, June 11, 1776 (East Bergholt, Eng.)–Mar. 31, 1837. English painter. Noted for his Romantic views of English countryside in which man's works blend with serene nature; his early naturalistic precision gave way to more impressionistic handling. Paintings: *Salisbury Cathedral,* 1823; *Waterloo Bridge,* 1832.

CORBUSIER, LE, born Charles-Edouard Jenneret, Oct. 6, 1887 (La Chaux-de-Fonds, Switz.)–Aug. 27, 1965. Swiss architect, city planner. One of the founders of modern functionalist architecture; coined the phrase, "The house is a machine for living." Buildings: Palace of the League of Nations, Geneva, 1927–28; Convent of Sainte-Marie-de-la-Tourette, near Lyons, Fr., 1957–61; National Museum of Western Art, Tokyo, Jap., 1960; Carpenter Visual Art Center, Harvard U., 1964.

COROT, JEAN BAPTISTE CAMILLE, July 16, 1796 (Paris, Fr.)–Feb. 22, 1875. French painter. His freely-painted landscapes, with subtle atmospheric effects, influenced the impressionists; extremely popular in his day. Paintings: *Bridge of Narni,* 1820s; *Souvenir de Mortefontaine,* 1864.

CORREGGIO, born Antonio Allegri da Correggio, 1489 or 1494 (Correggio, It.)–Mar. 5, 1534. Italian painter. Founded Ren. Parma school; painted huge, dramatic fresco murals with foreshortened figures and (later) poetic, sensuous works. Paintings: *Mystic Marriage of St. Catherine,* c.1526; dome paintings at the Cathedral of Parma, 1526–30; *Leda,* 1530s.

COURBET, GUSTAVE, June 10, 1819 (Ornans, Fr.)–Dec. 31, 1877. French painter. Leader of realist movement in France, rebelling against romantic painting of the day; imprisoned for activities with Socialist party, 1871. Paintings: *The Stone Breakers,* 1849; *The Artist's Studio,* 1855.

CRANACH THE ELDER, LUCAS, born Lucas Müller, 1472 (Kronach, Ger.)–Oct. 16, 1553. German painter. Court painter at Wittenberg, 1505–50; propagandist for Protestant Ref., 1517; works include altarpieces, court portraits, portraits of Protestant Reformers, women.

CUYP, ALBERT JACOBSZ, baptized Oct. 20, 1620 (Dordrecht, Neth.)–Nov. 1691. Dutch painter. Best known for landscapes of Dutch countryside. Paintings: *Hilly Landscape with Cows and Shepherds,* 1665; *Castle by a River Bank,* 1645.

DALI, SALVADOR, May 11, 1904 (Figueras, Sp.). Spanish painter. Important Surrealist known for his outrageous attire and outlandish mustache; built Dali's Dream House, N.Y. World's Fair, 1937–39; costume and scenery designer for operas and ballets, 1939–42; elected to French Acad. of Fine Arts, 1979.

DAUMIER, HONORÉ, Feb. 20/26, 1808 (Marseilles, Fr.)–Feb. 11, 1879. French caricaturist, painter, sculptor. Best known for satiric cartoons and lithographs of 19th-cent. French politics and society.

DAVID, JACQUES-LOUIS, Aug. 30, 1748 (Paris, Fr.)–Dec. 29, 1825. French artist. Official painter to NAPOLEON I; painted portraits and historical subjects in the neoclassical style. Paintings: *The Oath of the Horatii,* 1784; *Marat,* 1793; *Coronation,* 1808.

DEGAS, (Hilaire Germaine) EDGAR, July 19, 1834 (Paris, Fr.)–Sept. 27, 1917. French artist. One of the greatest draftsmen of all time; with C. MONET, A. RENOIR, and others, organized the first impressionist exhibition, 1874; closely associated with the impressionist movement, although he rejected that classification; failing eyesight in his later years led him to abandon his precise, compositionally-innovative oil paintings for softer and more colorful pastels. Paintings: *Absinthe,* 1876; *Prima Ballerina,* c.1876.

DELACROIX, EUGENE, Apr. 26, 1798 (Charenton-Saint-Maurice, Fr.)–Aug. 13, 1863. French Romantic painter. Known for exotic subject-matter and vivid colors. Paintings: *Massacre at Chios,* 1824; murals in the Palais Bourbon, 1833; murals in Museum of History at Versailles, 1837.

DELLA ROBBIA, LUCA, born Luca di Simone di Marco, 1399/1400 (Florence, It.)–Feb. 1482. Italian Ren. sculptor. Founder of family studio; worked in enamelled terra-cotta and marble. Sculpture: *Singing Gallery,* 1431; tabernacle at Peretola, 1441; tomb of Benozzo Federighi, bishop of Fiesole, 1454–57.

DOMENICHINO, born Domenico Zampieri, Oct. 1581 (Bologna, It.)–Apr. 6, 1641. Italian baroque painter. Best known for such landscapes as *The Hunt of Diana* (1617–18) and *The Martyrdom of St. Sebastian* (1628–30).

DONATELLO, born Donato di Niccolò di Betto Bardi, 1386 (Florence, It.)–Dec. 13, 1466. Italian sculptor. First postclassical sculptor to render the human body as self-activating and functional; the principal creative genius of the Italian Early Ren. and the acknowledged mentor of MICHELANGELO. Sculpture: *St. George and the Dragon,* 1416–17; *David,* 1430–35; *Gattamelata,* 1447–53.

DUCCIO DI BUONINSEGNA, c.1255 (Siena, It.)–c.1318. Italian painter. Founder of the Sienese school of painting; with GIOTTO, one the key figures in the transition from Gothic to Ren. art; best-known work is the *Maestà* high altar for the Siena Cathedral, 1308–11.

DUCHAMP, MARCEL, July 28, 1887 (Blainville, Fr.)–Oct. 2, 1968. French-U.S. painter. Known as an "antiartist" because he eliminated the boundaries between works of art and everyday objects; an important cubist and a founder of Dadaism. Paintings: *Nude Descending a Staircase, No. 2,* 1912. Assemblages: *The Bride stripped bare by her Bachelors,* 1915–23.

DUFY, RAOUL, June 3, 1877 (Le Havre, Fr.)–Mar. 23, 1953. French painter, designer. Helped to popularize modern art, especially Fauvism. Paintings: *Bois de Boulogne,* 1929; *Deauville,* 1930.

DÜRER, ALBRECHT, May 21, 1471 (Nuremberg, Ger.)–Apr. 6, 1528. German painter, graphic artist. The great genius of the Northern Ren.; combined Italian Ren. elements with German expressionism in brilliantly executed altarpieces, religious paintings, self-portraits, and engravings. Paintings: *Self-Portrait,* 1498; *Four Apostles,* 1526. Woodcuts: *Apocalypse* series, 1498. Engravings: *Knight, Death, and the Devil,* 1513; *Melancholia I,* 1514.

EIFFEL, ALEXANDRE-GUSTAVE, Dec. 15, 1832

ARTISTS

(Dijon, Fr.)–Dec. 28, 1923. French engineer. Known for his design of the Eiffel Tower, 1887–89; built the first aerodynamic laboratory, at Auteuil, 1912.

ELSHEIMER, ADAM, Mar. 18, 1578 (Frankfurt-am-Main, Ger.)–Dec. 1610. German painter, etcher. A founder of modern landscape painting; known for small paintings on copper of Biblical and mythological subjects. Paintings: *Flight into Egypt,* 1609; *Philemon and Baucus; The Good Samaritan.*

ENSOR, JAMES SYDNEY, Apr. 13, 1860 (Ostend, Belg.)–Nov. 19, 1949. Flemish painter, printmaker. Created expressionist works noted for fantasy and social commentary; member of the progressive Les Vingt group of artists, 1883–88. Paintings: *Woman Eating Oysters,* 1882; *Scandalized Masks,* 1883; *Entry of Christ into Brussels,* 1888; *Masks,* 1890.

ERNST, MAX, Apr. 2, 1891 (Brühl, Ger.). German painter, sculptor. Worked in the expressionistic mode of surrealism, later converted to Dadaism. Paintings: *The Elephant of the Célebes,* 1921; *Here Everything Is Still Floating,* 1920; *The Great Forest,* 1927; *The Temptation of St. Anthony,* 1945; *The King Playing with the Queen,* 1944.

EYCK, JAN VAN, c.1395 (Maaseik, Flanders)–July 9, 1441. Flemish painter. His strongly realistic oil paintings, principally portraits and religious subjects, had a profound influence on later North ern European painters. Paintings: *Ghent Altarpiece,* completed 1432; *Giovanni Arnolfini and His Bride,* 1434.

FABERGÉ, PETER CARL, born Karl Gustavovich Fabergé, May 30, 1846 (St. Petersburg, Rus. [now Leningrad, USSR])–Sept. 24, 1920. Russian goldsmith, jeweler, decorator. Inherited family jewelry business, 1870; commissioned by Czar Alexander III to design the ceremonial eggs for his czarina, 1884.

FANTIN-LATOUR, (Ignace) HENRI JOSEPH THEODORE, Jan. 14, 1836 (Grenoble, Fr.)–Aug. 25, 1904. French painter, printmaker, illustrator. Best known for his realistic still-lifes and portraits. Paintings: *Hommage à Delacroix,* 1864; *Hommage à Monet,* 1870. Books illustrated: Jullien's *Wagner* (1886), and *Berlioz* (1888).

FRAGONARD, JEAN-HONORÉ, Apr. 5, 1732 (Grasse, Fr.)–Aug. 22, 1806. French painter. Painted landscapes, portraits, and fêtes-galantes in rococo style; decorated Madame du Barry's Pavillon de Louveciennes with four paintings depicting the *Progress of Love,* 1770.

FUSELI, HENRY, born Johann Heinrich Füssli, Feb. 7, 1741 (Zurich, Switz.)–Apr. 16, 1825. Anglo-Swiss painter. Romantic painter who used eerie, often grotesque imagery. Prof. of paining at the Royal Acad., London, 1799–1805. Paintings: *The Death of Cardinal Beaufort,* 1774; *The Oath of the Rütli,* 1778; *The Nightmare,* 1781.

GAINSBOROUGH, THOMAS, baptized May 14, 1727 (Sudbury, Eng.)–Aug. 2, 1788. English painter. Known for his portraits and landscapes of idyllic scenes, including his famous *The Blue Boy* (1770).

GAUGUIN, (Eugène Henri) PAUL, June 7, 1848 (Paris, Fr.)–May 8, 1903. French painter. Postimpressionist artist known for his use of color and "primitive" subject-matter and formats. Paintings: *Self-Portrait,* 1889; *Bonjour, Monsieur Gauguin,* 1889; *Whence Come We? What Are We? Whither Go We?,* 1897–98.

GERICAULT, (Jean Louis André) THÉODORE, Sept. 26, 1791 (Rouen, Fr.)–Jan. 26, 1824. French Romantic painter whose realistic and freely rendered paintings of historical and animal subjects caused a furor in official French art circles. Paintings: *Mounted Officer of the Imperial Guard,* 1812; *The Wounded Cuirassier,* 1814; *The Raft of the Medusa,* 1819.

GHIBERTI, LORENZO, orig. Lorenzo di Cione di Ser Buonaccorso, 1378 (Pelago, It.)–Dec. 1, 1455. Italian sculptor. A transitional figure between the elegant International Gothic style and the naturalistic Ren. era; his bronze-relief doors for the Baptistery in Florence, (first set, 1403–24; second set, the *Gates of Paradise,* 1425–52) broke new ground in perspective systems and in modeling of the human form.

GHIRLANDAJO, DOMENICO, born Domenico di Tommasio Bigardi, 1449 (Florence, It.)–Jan. 11, 1494. Italian painter. One of the principal painters of the Italian Early Ren.; MICHELANGELO studied in his studio. Paintings: fresco series in Sistine Chapel, Rome, 1481–82; two series of frescoes in Sta. Trinetà and Sta. Maria Novella, Florence, 1482–94.

GIACOMETTI, ALBERTO, Oct. 10, 1901 (Borgonovo, Switz.)–Jan. 11, 1966. Swiss sculptor, painter. Created a skeletal style; known for sculptures of solitary figures. Sculptures: *Observing Head,* 1927/28; *City Square,* 1948; *Chariot,* 1950.

GIORGIONE, born Giorgio da Castelfranco, 1477 (Castelfranco, It.)–1511. Italian painter. Venetian High Ren. painter whose luminous colors and deft brushwork had a profound influence on 16th-century Venetian painting. Paintings: *The Tempest,* 1505; *Fête Champetre,* c.1510.

GIOTTO, born Giotto di Bondone, 1276 (Vespignano, It.)–Jan. 8, 1337. Italian painter, architect. Often called the single most-influential artist in European history; his frescoes introduced the attitudes and concerns that would dominate European painting until the late 19th cent., including narrative drama, the dignity and beauty of the human form, and the construction of "realistic" pictorial space; inaugurated the great line of Florentine painters that stretched well into the 16th cent. Paintings: Arena Chapel fresco-cycle, Padua, 1305–06; *Enthroned Madonna,* 1310; Bardi Chapel fresco cycle, Florence, 1320s.

GIRARDON, FRANÇOIS, baptized Mar. 17, 1628 (Troyes, Fr.)–Sept. 1, 1715. French baroque sculptor. Employed at Versailles under LOUIS XIV; member of Royal Acad. of Painting and Sculpture, from 1657. Sculpture: *Apollo Tended by the Nymphs,* 1666; equestrian statue of Louis XIV, 1683–92; tomb of CARDINAL RICHELIEU, 1675.

GOGH, VINCENT VAN, Mar. 30, 1853 (Zindert, Neth.)–July 29, 1890. Dutch postimpressionist painter. Noted for powerfully expressive works rendered with thick brushwork and in brilliant colors; committed suicide. Paintings: *The Potato Eaters,* 1885; *Outdoor Cafe at Night, Arles,* 1888; *Sunflowers,* 1888; *Starry Night,* 1889.

GOYA (y Lucientes), FRANCISCO JOSÉ DE, Mar. 30, 1746 (Fuendetodos, Sp.)–Apr. 16, 1828. Spanish painter, etcher. First gained fame for his portraits and genre works, later executed powerful, Romantic depictions of the heroes of war; his last paintings are macabre renderings of nightmare subjects. Paintings: *Los Caprichos,* 1796; *May 3, 1808,* 1814–15; *The Witches' Sabbath.* Etchings: *The Disasters of War* series, 1810–13.

GRECO, EL, born Domenikos Theotokopoulos, 1541 (Candia, Crete)–Apr. 8, 1614. Greek painter, sculptor, architect. Known for his unorthodox, elongated treatment of devotional subjects and portraits; became a citizen of Spain, 1577; introduced Ren. and Mannerist elements into Spanish painting. Paintings: *The Burial of Count Orgaz,* 1586.

GROPIUS, WALTER ADOLPH, May 18, 1883 (Berlin, Ger.)–July 5, 1969. German architect, educator. Leader in the development of modern architecture; dir. of the Bauhaus, 1919–28; chm. of the architecture dept. at Harvard U., 1938–52.

GRÜNEWALD, MATHIAS, real name Mathis Gothart Nithart, c.1470 (Aschaffenburg, Ger.)–1528. German painter. Best known for his highly expressionistic and mystical treatment of religious subjects, especially in his *Isenheim Altarpiece,* begun 1517.

HALS, FRANS, 1581/85 (Antwerp, Belgium)–Sept. 1, 1666. Flemish painter. A baroque painter known for his brilliant portraits, particularly of the Dutch bourgeoisie of Haarlem. Paintings: *The Laughing Cavalier,* 1624; *The Governors of the Almshouse,* 1664; *Lady Regents of the Almshouse,* 1664.

HEPWORTH, DAME BARBARA, Jan. 10, 1903 (Wakefield, Eng.)–May 20, 1975. English abstract sculptor. Named Dame of the British Empire, 1965. Sculptures: *Reclining Figure,* 1932; *Wave,* 1943–44; *Winged Figure,* 1962; *Single Form,* 1962–63; *Four-Square,* 1966.

HILDEBRANDT, JOHANN LUCAS VON, Nov. 14, 1668 (Genoa, It.)–Nov. 16, 1745. Austrian baroque architect, military engineer. Appointed court engineer and architect to Prince Eugene and other Austrian aristocrats, 1700. Buildings: the Belvedere Palace, 1700–23; Austrian Chancellory, 1717–19.

HOBBEMA, MEINDERT, baptized Oct. 31, 1638 (Amsterdam, Neth.)–Dec. 7, 1709. Dutch baroque landscape painter. Paintings: *Water Mill,* 1665; *The Ruins of Brederode Castle,* 1671; *The Avenue, Middelharnis,* 1689.

HOGARTH, WILLIAM, Nov. 10, 1697 (London, Eng.)–Oct. 26, 1764. English painter, engraver. Best known for his morality pictures featuring brilliant characterizations and a wealth of detail. Paintings: *The Harlot's Progress* (series), 1732; *The Rake's Progress* (series), 1735; *Marriage à la Mode* (series), 1745.

HOLBEIN THE YOUNGER, HANS, 1497/98 (Augsburg, Ger.)–1543. German painter. Court painter of the Northern Ren. period, best known for his well executed and psychologically penetrating portraits. Paintings: *Sir Thomas More,* 1526; *Henry VIII,* 1540.

HOUDON, JEAN ANTOINE, Mar. 20, 1741 (Versailles, Fr.)–July 15, 1828. French neoclassical sculptor. Sculptures: *Voltaire,* 1781; *George Washington,* 1785; also did busts of THOMAS JEFFERSON, JOHN PAUL JONES, J. B. MOLIÈRE, J. J. ROUSSEAU, NAPOLEON I.

HUNT, (William) **HOLMAN,** Apr. 2, 1827 (London, Eng.)–Sept. 7, 1910. English painter. Cofounder (with JOHN MILLAIS and DANTE ROSSETTI) of the Pre-Raphaelite Brotherhood, 1848; known for his religious works, including *Rienzi* (1849) and *The Light of the World* (1854); author of *Pre-Raphaelitism and the Pre-Raphaelite Brotherhood,* 2 vols., 1905.

INGRES, JEAN-AUGUSTE-DOMINIQUE, Aug. 29, 1780 (Montauban, Fr.)–Jan. 14, 1867. French painter. One of the greatest draftsmen in European art history; known for his highly finished and sensual works; dir. of French Acad. of Rome,

1835–41. Paintings: *Jupiter and Thetis,* 1811; *The Apotheosis of Homer,* 1827.

JONES, INIGO, baptized July 19, 1573 (London, Eng.)–June 21, 1652. English architect, painter, designer. Highly influential architect in the Palladian manner; King's surveyor of works, 1615–42. Buildings: Banqueting House, Whitehall, 1619–22; Queen's Chapel at St. James Palace, 1623–27; restoration of St. Paul's Cathedral, London, 1634–42.

KANDINSKY, VASILY, Dec. 4, 1866 (Moscow, Rus.)–Dec. 13, 1944. Russian painter. Best known for his abstract paintings; founded the Munich group called The Blue Rider, 1911–14; teacher at the Bauhaus School of Design, 1921–33.

KLEE, PAUL, Dec. 18, 1879 (Munchenbuchsee, Switz.)–June 29, 1940. Swiss painter, etcher. Surrealist painter influenced by primitive African sculpture; prof. at the Düsseldorf Acad. of Art, 1930–33. Paintings: *Twittering Machine,* 1922; *The Mocker Mocked,* 1930; *Death and Fire,* 1930.

LA TOUR, GEORGE DE, Mar. 19, 1593 (nr. Luneville, Fr.)–Jan. 30, 1652. French painter. A baroque painter famed for portraying subjects in candlelight. Paintings: *The Mocking of Job, St. Joseph the Carpenter, The Fortune Teller.*

LEGER, FERNAND, Feb. 4, 1881 (Argentan, Fr.)–Aug. 17, 1955. French Cubist painter. Influenced by modern industrial technology. Paintings: *The Cyclist, Adam and Eve.*

LEIDEN, LUCAS VAN, born Lucas Hugensz, 1489–94 (Leiden, Neth.)–1533. Dutch painter, engraver. Paintings: *Muhammad and the Monk Sergius,* 1508; *Susanna and the Elders,* 1508; *The Poet Vergil Suspended in a Basket,* 1521.

LE NAIN, brothers. **ANTOINE,** 1588–May 25, 1648; **LOUIS,** 1593 (Laon, Fr.)–May 23, 1648; **MATHIEU,** 1607 (Laon, Fr.)–Apr. 20, 1677. French painters of peasant life; all received into the French Acad., 1648.

L'ENFANT, PIERRE CHARLES, Aug. 2, 1754 (Paris, Fr.)–June 14, 1825. French engineer, architect, urban designer. Designed basic plan for Washington, D.C., 1791–92; renovated old City Hall for U.S. Congress as Federal Hall, New York City, 1787.

LEONARDO DA VINCI, 1452 (Vinci, It.)–May 2, 1519. Italian painter, sculptor, architect, engineer. The archetypal Ren. man; brilliant draftsman and colorist who invented *sfumato* (smoky) style of painting; his *Notebooks* are a treasury of art criticism, scientific investigation, and prototype inventions centuries ahead of their time (e.g., the helicopter). Paintings: *The Last Supper,* 1495–97; *Mona Lisa,* 1503–06; *St. John the Baptist,* c.1514.

LIEBERMANN, MAX, July 20, 1847 (Berlin, Ger.)–Feb. 8, 1935. German postimpressionist painter. Known for his study of light and depiction of life of humble people. Paintings: *Women Plucking Geese,* 1872; *Old Folks' Home in Amsterdam,* 1880; *The Flax Spinners,* 1887.

LIPPI, FRA FILIPPO, 1402 (Florence, It.)–Oct. 9, 1469. Italian Ren. painter. Known for his sensual, elegant Madonnas. Paintings: *Madonna and Child,* 1437.

MAGRITTE, RENÉ FRANÇOIS-GHISLAIN, Nov. 21, 1898 (Lessines, Belg.)–Aug. 15, 1967. Belgian surrealist painter. Best known for his jolting juxtapositions of unrelated elements in realistic-looking pictures. Paintings: *The Rape,* 1934; *Golconda,* 1953.

MANET, EDOUARD, Jan. 23, 1832 (Paris, Fr.)-Apr. 30, 1883. French painter, printmaker. A forerunner of the impressionists. Paintings: *Le Dejeuner sur L'Herbe,* 1863; *Olympia,* 1863; *Bar at the Folies-Bergere,* 1882.

MANTEGNA, ANDREA, 1431 (Mantua, It.)-Sept. 13, 1506. Italian Ren. painter, engraver. Court painter in Mantua, 1459. Paintings: *Camera degli Sposi,* 1474; Ovetari Chapel frescoes, 1448–55; *Triumph of Caesar,* 1486.

MASACCIO, born Tommaso Guidi, Dec. 21, 1401 (Castello San Giovanni di Valdarno, It.)-1428. Italian painter. The most important and influential painter of the Early Ren. in Italy; introduced humanism into art. Paintings: *Madonna and Child with St. Anne,* 1424.

MASSYS (or Matsys, Messys, Metsys), **QUENTIN,** c.1466 (Louvain, Flanders)-1530. Flemish painter. Member of painters' guild of Antwerp, 1491–1530. Paintings: *St. Anne Altarpiece,* 1509; *The Money Changer and His Wife,* 1514.

MATISSE, HENRI-EMILE-BENOÎT, Dec. 31, 1869 (Le Cateau, Fr.)-Nov. 3, 1954. French painter. A leading fauvist. Paintings: *Woman with the Hat,* 1905; *The Red Studio,* 1911.

MEMLING (or Memlinc), **HANS,** c.1430 (Seligenstadt, Ger.)-Aug. 11, 1494. Flemish painter. Member of the painters' guild, Brussels, from 1467; known for use of color and emotive detail. Paintings: *Last Judgement,* 1472–73; *Virgin and Child,* 1487; *Madonna with Angels,* 1490.

MICHELANGELO, born Michelangelo di Lodovico Buonarroti Simoni, Mar. 6, 1475 (Caprese, It.)-Feb. 18, 1564. Italian painter, sculptor, architect. Giant of the High Ren.; known for monumental style, noble renderings of the human form; epitomized the High Ren. style, presaged baroque art and Mannerism; also wrote sonnets. Sculpture: *Pietà,* 1498; *David,* 1504. Paintings: ceiling of Sistine Chapel, 1508–12; *Last Judgement,* 1534–41. Architecture: Medici Chapel, 1520–34.

MIES VAN DER ROHE, LUDWIG, Mar. 27, 1886 (Aachen, Ger.)-Aug. 17, 1969. German architect. A leading practitioner of 20th-cent. functionalist architecture; head of School of Architecture at Chicago's Armour Inst., 1937–58. Buildings: Seagram Bldg., New York City, 1958.

MILLAIS, SIR JOHN EVERETT, June 8, 1829 (Southhampton, Eng.)-Aug. 13, 1896. English painter, illustrator. A founder of the Pre-Raphaelite Brotherhood; pres. of Royal Acad., 1896. Paintings: *The Return of the Dove to the Ark,* 1851; *The Order of Release,* 1852; *The Blind Girl,* 1856.

MILLET, JEAN-FRANÇOIS, Oct. 4, 1814 (Gruchy, Fr.)-Jan. 20, 1875. French painter. Known for his romanticized depictions of rural scenes. Paintings: *The Milkmaid,* 1844; *A Peasant Grafting a Tree,* 1855; *The Man with the Hoe,* 1863.

MODIGLIANI, AMEDEO, July 12, 1884 (Leghorn, It.)-Jan. 24, 1920. Italian painter, sculptor. Known for his unique, elongated portraits. Paintings: *Peasant Boy; Portrait of Mme. Modigliani; Woman Seated; Girl with Rose.*

MONDRIAN, PIET, born Pieter Cornelis Mondiaan, Mar. 7, 1872 (Amersfoort, Neth.)-Feb. 1, 1944. Dutch artist. A leader of the Dutch abstract art movement called De Stijl; Cubist phase, 1912–17; neoplastic phase, 1917–20; thereafter American phase. Paintings: *New York City,* 1943; *Broadway Boogie Woogie,* 1943.

MONET, CLAUDE, Nov. 14, 1840 (Paris, Fr.)-Dec. 5, 1926. French artist. One of the founders and a principal leader of the impressionist movement. Paintings: *Haystacks,* 1891; *Rouen Cathedral,* 1894.

MOORE, HENRY, July 30, 1898 (Castleford, Eng.). English abstract sculptor. Teacher of sculpture at Royal C. of Art (1925-32) and Chelsea School of Art (1932–39).

MORISOT, BERTHE, Jan. 14, 1841 (Bourges, Fr.)-Mar. 2, 1895. French impressionist painter, printmaker. Paintings: *Repose,* 1870; *The Artist's Sister, Mme. Portillon, Seated on the Grass,* 1873.

MORRIS, WILLIAM, Mar. 24, 1834 (Walthamstow, Eng.)-Oct. 1, 1896. English craftsman, poet. With his friends E. BURNE-JONES and D. G. ROSSETTI, formed Morris & Co., a firm of decorators that designed wallpaper, furniture, and tapestries that revolutionized Victorian taste; established Kelmscott Press (1890), where he designed type, page borders, and book bindings; his most notable poetic works include *The Defense of Guenevere and Other Poems* (1858), *The Life and Death of Jason* (1862), and *Earthly Paradises* (3 vols., 1868–70).

MUNCH, EDVARD, Dec. 12, 1863 (Löten, Norway)-Jan. 23, 1944. Norwegian expressionist painter, printmaker. Influenced the development of German expressionism; known for his shocking, agonized images of psychic traumas. Paintings: *The Shriek,* 1893; *The Kiss,* 1895.

MURILLO, BARTOLOMÉ ESTEBAN, baptized Jan. 1, 1618 (Seville, Sp.)-Apr. 13, 1682. Spanish baroque religious painter. Founder and first pres. of Acad. of Painting, Seville, 1660. Paintings: *Virgin of the Rosary,* 1642; *Immaculate Conception,* 1652; *Vision of St. Anthony,* 1656; *Self-Portrait,* 1675.

NERVI, PIER LUIGI, June 21, 1891 (Sorvino, It.)-Jan. 9, 1979. Italian architect, engineer. Prof. at U. of Rome, from 1947; invented *ferrocemento* (reinforced concrete); designed two sports palaces for Rome Olympic games, 1957–60; designed George Washington Bridge Bus Terminal, 1961-62.

PALLADIO, ANDREA, born Andrea di Pietro della Gondola, Nov. 30, 1508 (Padua, It.)-Aug. 1580. Italian architect. His neoclassical style had a tremendous influence on European domestic architecture; published *Le Antichita di Roma* (1554) and *I Quattro Libri dell'Architettura* (1570).

PHIDIAS, 500 B.C. (Athens, Gr.)-430 B.C. Greek sculptor. Works: Temple of Theseus; Athena Areia at Plataea; Olympian Zeus.

PICASSO, PABLO, Oct. 25, 1881 (Malaga, Sp.)-Apr. 8, 1973. Spanish painter, sculptor. Seminal modern artist; with GEORGES BRAQUE, founded Cubist movement, 1907-08. Paintings: *Demoiselles d'Avignon,* 1907; *Three Musicians; Guernica,* 1937; *Woman in White.*

PIERO DELLA FRANCESCA, 1410/20 (Borgo San Sepolcro, It.)-1492. Italian Ren. painter. Member of the Umbrian school; known for his monumental, architectonic frescos. Paintings: *The Story of the True Cross,* 1452-66.

PISSARRO, CAMILLE, July 10, 1830 (St. Thomas, V.I.)-Nov. 13, 1903. French impressionist painter. Best known for his paintings of the boulevards of Paris, streets of Rouen, landscapes of Normandy.

PONTORMO, JACOPO DA, born Jacopo Carrucci, May 24, 1494 (Pontormo, It.)-Jan. 2, 1557. Italian painter. An initiator of the Florentine Mannerist style. Paintings: piece for Church of Saint Michele, Florence, 1518; *Joseph in Egypt,* 1515.

THE BOOK OF WHO

POUSSIN, NICHOLAS, 1594 (Villers, Fr.)–Nov. 19, 1665. French painter. A leader of pictorial classicism in the baroque period.

PRAXITELES, fl. end of 5th century B.C. (Athens, Gr.). Greek sculptor. Best known for his statues of Hermes, Dionysus, Aphrodite of Canidus.

RAPHAEL, born Raffaello Sanzio or Santi, Mar. 28, 1483 (Urbino, It.)–Apr. 6, 1520. Italian painter. Exemplar of serene, classical High Ren. style. Paintings: *Coronation of the Virgin,* 1503; Vatican stanza, decorated for Pope Julius II, 1508.

REMBRANDT, born Rembrandt Harmensz van Rijn, July 15, 1606 (Leiden, Neth.)–Oct. 4, 1669. Dutch painter. Greatest practitioner of Northern baroque painting; known for brilliant use of light, revealing portraits. Paintings: *Clemency of Titus,* 1626; *The Anatomy Lesson of Dr. Tulp,* 1632; *Self-Portrait with Saskia,* 1635; *The Deposition,* 1653; *Three Trees,* 1643.

RENOIR, PIERRE-AUGUSTE, Feb. 25, 1840 (Limoges, Fr.)–Dec. 3, 1919. French impressionist painter. A leader and founder of the French impressionist movement. Paintings: *The Moulin de la Galette,* 1876; *Portrait of Mme. Charpentier and Her Children,* 1879.

REYNOLDS, SIR JOSHUA, July 16, 1723 (Plympton, Eng.)–Feb. 23, 1792. English painter. Known for his portraits; pres. of Royal Acad., from 1768; knighted, 1768. Paintings: *Captain John Hamilton,* 1746; *Commodore Augustus Keppel,* 1753; *Duchess of Devonshire and Her Daughter,* 1786.

RIVERA, DIEGO, Dec. 8, 1886 (Guanajuato, Mex.)–Nov. 25, 1957. Mexican painter. Helped to begin govt.-sponsored project for the decoration of public buildings with frescos, 1921; with BEN SHAHN, painted *Man at the Crossroads,* mural for RCA Bldg., New York City.

RODIN, AUGUSTE, Nov. 12, 1840 (Paris, Fr.)–Nov. 17, 1917. French sculptor. Best known for his *The Thinker* (1880), *Le Baiser* (1886), and *The Burghers of Calais* (1884–86).

ROUSSEAU, HENRI, May 21, 1844 (Laval, Fr.)–Sept. 2, 1910. French painter. Leader of the primitivist school of postimpressionism; a major influence on Cubism. Paintings: *Landscape with Tree Trunks,* 1887; *Myself: Portrait Landscape,* 1890; *The Child among the Rocks,* 1895; *The Repast of the Lion,* 1907; *Tropical Forest with Monkeys,* 1910.

RUBENS, PETER-PAUL, June 28, 1577 (Siegen, Ger.)–May 30, 1640. Flemish baroque painter. Known for his dynamic colors and well-rounded figures. Paintings: *The Rape of the Sabines,* 1635; *Venus and Adonis,* 1635; Self-Portrait, 1639; *Christ on the Cross,* 1635–40.

RUISDAEL, JACOB VAN, 1628/29 (Haarlem, Neth.)–Mar. 1682. Dutch baroque painter. Known for his landscapes. Paintings: *Dunes,* 1647; *Bentheim Castle,* 1653; *Jewish Cemetery,* 1660; *Wheatfields,* 1670.

SEURAT, GEORGES, Dec. 2, 1859 (Paris, Fr.)–Mar. 29, 1891. French painter. Founder of the 19th-cent. school of neoimpressionism; invented pointillist style. Paintings: *Sunday Afternoon on The Island of La Grande Jatte; Une Baignade, Asnieres.*

SISLEY, ALFRED, Oct. 30, 1839 (Paris, Fr.)–Jan. 29, 1899. French painter. Known for his impressionist landscapes. Paintings: *Flood at Port-Marly,* 1876.

STUBBS, GEORGE, Aug. 24, 1724 (Liverpool, Eng.)–July 10, 1806. English animal painter, anatomical draftsman. Executed 18 etched plates for Dr. John Burton's *Essay Towards a Complete New System of Midwifery,* 1751. Paintings: *Mares and Foals in a Landscape,* 1760–70.

TERBORCH, GERARD, 1617 (Zwolle, Neth.)–Dec. 8, 1681. Dutch baroque painter. Paintings: *The Swearing of the Oath of Ratification of the Treaty of Münster,* 1648; *Self-Portrait,* 1670.

TIEPOLO, GIOVANNI BATTISTA, Mar. 5, 1696 (Venice, It.)–Mar. 27, 1770. Italian artist. Known for his large-scale frescos; executed frescos for the Residenz, Würzburg, including *Olympus;* painted three ceilings at the Royal Palace, Madrid, for King Carlos III, 1762.

TINTORETTO, born Jacopo Robusti, 1518 (Venice, It.)–May 31, 1594. Italian Mannerist painter of the Venetian school. Paintings: *Vulcan Surprising Venus and Mars,* 1545; *The Last Supper,* 1547.

TITIAN, born Tiziano Vecellio, c.1487/90 (Pieve di Cadore, It.)–Aug. 27, 1576. Italian Ren. painter. Venetian painter known for his monumental compositions and sensual use of color. Paintings: *The Assumption,* 1516–18; *The Venus of Urbino,* 1538; *Equestrian Portrait of Charles V,* 1548; *The Death of Actaeon,* 1565.

TOULOUSE-LAUTREC, HENRI DE, Nov. 24, 1864 (Albi, Fr.)–Sept. 9, 1901. French artist. Known for his postimpressionist depictions of Parisian night life, such as *La Goulue at the Moulin Rouge* (1891).

TURNER, J(oseph) M(allard) W(illiam), Apr. 23, 1775 (London, Eng.)–Dec. 19, 1851. English Romantic painter. Best known for his impressionistic landscapes and seascapes. Paintings: *Snow Storm, The Burning of the Houses of Parliament.*

UCCELLO, PAOLO, born Paolo di Dono, 1397 (Pratovecchio, It.)–Dec. 12, 1475. Italian Ren. painter. Paintings: *Battle of San Romano,* 1542.

VAN DYCK, SIR ANTHONY, Mar. 22, 1599 (Antwerp, Belg.)–Dec. 9, 1641. Flemish artist. Appointed by King Charles I as Painter-in-Ordinary to the English court; his portraits set the style in English portraiture for almost 100 years.

VASARI, GIORGIO, July 30, 1511 (Arezzo, It.)–June 27, 1574. Italian Mannerist painter, architect, writer. Designed the Uffizi Palace, Florence, for COSIMO I DE MEDICI, 1560; author of *The Lives of the Most Eminent Italian Architects, Painters and Sculptors,* 1550.

VELAZQUEZ, DIEGO RODRIGUEZ DE SILVA Y, June 6, 1599 (Seville, Sp.)–Aug. 6, 1660. Spanish painter. Greatest Spanish Baroque painter; known for his technical excellence and highly effective sense of composition. Paintings: *Los Borrachos Bacchus,* 1629; *Surrender at Breda,* 1634; *Juan de Perera,* 1649; *Las Meninas,* 1656.

VERMEER, JAN, Oct. 30, 1632 (Delft, Neth.)–Dec. 15, 1675. Dutch painter. Dean of painters' guild at Delft, 1662–63 and 1670–71; known for his beautifully composed landscapes and interiors. Paintings: *View of Delft,* 1660; *Young Woman with a Water Jug,* 1663; *Artist and Model,* 1663; *Girl with a Red Hat,* 1667.

VERONESE, PAOLO, born Paolo Caliari, 1528 (Verona, It.)–Apr. 19, 1588. Italian painter of the 16th-cent. Venetian school; known for his devotional themes. Paintings: *Bevilicqua-Lazise Altarpiece,*1548; *The Temptation of St. Anthony,* 1552.

VUILLARD, (Jean) EDOUARD, Nov. 11, 1868 (Ciuseaux, Fr.)–June 21, 1940. French painter, graphic artist. With PIERRE BONNARD, developed the intimist style of painting; known for his domestic scenes. Paintings: *Self-Portrait*, 1892; *Woman Sweeping*, 1892; *Interior*, 1898.

WATTEAU, (Jean) ANTOINE, Oct. 10, 1684 (Valenciennes, Fr.)–July 18, 1721. French rococo painter. Known for paintings of "fêtes galantes"; elected to French Acad., 1712. Paintings: *The Embarkation for Cythera*.

WEYDEN, ROGER VAN DER, 1400 (Tournai, Flanders)–June 16, 1464. Flemish painter. City planner of Brussels, 1435–64; highly influential in the development of Flemish naturalism. Paintings: *Descent from the Cross*, 1435; Braque tryptych, 1450–52.

WREN, SIR CHRISTOPHER, Oct. 20, 1632 (E. Kroyle, Eng.)–Feb. 25, 1723. English architect, astronomer. Prof. of astronomy at Gresham C., 1657; rebuilt over 50 churches, including St. Martin's (Ludgate), St. Magnus (London Bridge); designed St. Paul's Cathedral and Chelsea Hospital, 1682–85.

ZURBARÁN, FRANCISCO DE, baptized Nov. 7, 1598 (Fuente de Cantos, Sp.)–Aug. 27, 1664. Spanish baroque painter. Known for his religious works. Paintings: *Immaculate Conception*, 1616; *Labours of Hercules*, 1634; *A Franciscan Monk*, 1630–32.

COMPOSERS, CONCERT, BALLET AND OPERA PERSONALITIES

U.S. COMPOSERS, CONCERT, BALLET, AND OPERA PERSONALITIES

AILEY, ALVIN, Jan. 5, 1931 (Rogers, Tex.). U.S. dancer, choreographer. Incorporates modern, jazz, and academic dance forms in his choreography; his ballets to traditional music include *Blues Suite* (1958) and *Revelations* (1960); formed the Alvin Ailey American Dance Theatre, 1958– .

ALBANESE, LICIA, July 22, 1913 (Bari, It.). U.S. operatic soprano. Debuted in Parma, It., 1934; debuted at Met. Opera, 1940; sang at the Met. for 25 years, in over 40 roles.

ANDERSON, MARIAN, Feb. 17, 1902 (Philadelphia, Pa.). U.S. contralto, concert artist. Has made many internatl. concert tours; the first black to perform in a major role at the Met. Opera (Ulrica in *Un ballo in maschera*), 1955; U.S. del. to the UN, 1955.

ARRAU, CLAUDIO, Feb. 6, 1903 (Chillan, Chile). Chilean-U.S. concert pianist. Child prodigy; began to make internatl. tours in 1912; came to the U.S. permanently, 1941; has won many internatl. awards.

ARROYO, MARTINA, Feb. 2, 1940 (New York, N.Y.). U.S. operatic soprano. Won Met. Opera "Auditions of the Air," 1958; famed as replacement for BIRGIT NILSSON in *Aida* at Met., 1965; with Zurich Opera, 1963–68; specializes in major dramatic roles in G. VERDI and G. ROSSINI operas.

BALANCHINE, GEORGE, born Georgy Melitonovich Balanchivadze, Jan. 9, 1904 (St. Petersburg, Rus. |now Leningrad, USSR|). Russian-U.S. choreographer. Most influential choreographer of classical ballet in the U.S. Chief choreographer of Ballets Russes, 1925; founded School of American Ballet, 1934; cofounder of Ballet Soc., 1946 (NYCB, from 1948); artistic dir., NYCB, 1948– . Major works: *The Prodigal Son*, 1929; *Agon; The Four Temperaments; Jewels; Vienna Waltzes; Tricolore*.

BARBER, SAMUEL, Mar. 9, 1910 (West Chester, Pa.). U.S. composer. Prolific modern composer known for his operas, songs, and string music. Opera: *Vanessa*, 1958 (awarded 1958 Pulitzer Prize). Other works: *Essays for Orchestra*, 1938 and 1942; *First Symphony*, 1936; *Piano Concerto*, 1962 (awarded 1963 Pulitzer Prize).

BARYSHNIKOV, MIKHAIL, Jan. 28, 1948 (Riga, USSR). Soviet-U.S. dancer. Leading premiere danseur. Member of Kirov Ballet from 1969 until defection to U.S. in 1974; guest artist with ballet

companies worldwide, 1974– ; soloist with ABT, 1974–78; soloist with NYCB, 1978–79; artistic dir. of ABT, 1980– ; choreographed *Nutcracker* for ABT, 1976.

BERNSTEIN, LEONARD, Aug. 25, 1918 (Lawrence, Mass.). U.S. composer, conductor. Immensely popular conductor of the New York Phil., 1958–69; his compositions, of both serious and show music, frequently reflect American themes. Works: *Jeremiah Symphony*, 1942; *Mass*, 1971; *An American Songbook*, 1978. Show music. *On the Town*, 1944; *Candide*, 1956; *West Side Story*, 1957.

BIGGS, E(dward George) POWER, Mar. 29, 1906 (Westcliff, Eng.)–Mar. 10, 1977. British-U.S. organist. Concert virtuoso who popularized the organ and, especially, Baroque music, through recitals, records and broadcasts; authority on music of J. S. BACH.

BRICO, ANTONIA, June 26, 1902 (Denver, Col.). U.S. conductor, teacher. Teacher and conductor of note as first woman to conduct Berlin Phil., 1930; founder of New York Women's Symphony, 1935; founder of Brico Symphony.

BUMBRY, GRACE MELZIA, Jan. 4, 1937 (St. Louis, Mo.). U.S. singer. Operatic mezzo-soprano; joint winner, Met. Auditions, 1958; debuts in Paris (1960), Bayreuth (1961), Covent Garden (1963), Met. Opera (1965).

CAGE, JOHN MILTON, JR., Sept. 5, 1912 (Los Angeles, Calif.). U.S. composer. Advocate of indeterminism in music; pieces composed for "prepared piano"; music dir. of MERCE CUNNINGHAM and Dance Co., 1944–66.

CALDWELL, SARAH, 1929 (Maryville, Mo.). U.S. conductor and opera producer. Established opera workshop, Boston U., 1948; after reorganization, 1st chairman of music theater dept., 1954; founder, artistic dir., and conductor of Opera Co. of Boston, 1957.

CALLAS, MARIA, born Cecilia Sophia Anna Maria Kalogeropoulos, Dec. 3, 1923 (New York, N.Y.)–Sept. 16, 1977. U.S. prima donna operatic soprano. Professional debut with Athens Royal Opera, 1939; vocal and dramatic versatility allowed her to sing both dramatic and lyric roles; sang 43 roles in over 500 performances in all major internatl. opera houses.

CLIBURN, VAN, born Harvey Levan, Jr., July 12, 1934 (Shreveport. La.). U.S. concert pianist. Concert debut, 1940; internatl. concert tours; gained internatl. fame by winning first prize at the Internatl. Tchaikovsky Piano Competition, Moscow, 1958.

COPLAND, AARON, Nov. 14, 1900 (Brooklyn,

THE BOOK OF WHO

N.Y.). U.S. composer. Founder (with ROGER SESSIONS) of Copland-Sessions Concerts, 1929-31. Works: *Billy the Kid* (ballet), 1938; *Rodeo* (ballet), 1942; *A Lincoln Portrait,* 1942; *Appalachian Spring,* 1944 (awarded Pulitzer Prizein music, 1945); film score for *The Heiress,* (AA, 1950).

CUNNINGHAM, MERCE, Apr. 16, 1919 (Centralia, Wash.). U.S. dancer, choreographer. Developed new forms of abstract dance movement called "choreography by chance"; with MARTHA GRAHAM Co., 1939-45; formed own co., 1952. Works: *Summerspace,* 1958; *Winterbranch,* 1965.

DAMROSCH, WALTER JOHANNES, Jan. 30, 1862 (Breslau, Ger. |now Wroclaw, Pol.|)- Dec. 22, 1950. U.S. conductor, composer. Specialized in Wagnerian opera; with Met. Opera Co., 1885-91 and 1900-02; founded Damrosch Opera Co., 1894-1900; pioneer of symphonic broadcasting; musical counsel, NBC, 1928-47; composed operas and other works.

DE MILLE, AGNES GEORGE, 1909 (New York, N.Y.). U.S. dancer, choreographer. Toured with humorous mime-dancers, 1929-40; choreographed *Rodeo* (1942), first ballet to include tap dancing; choreographed the musicals *Oklahoma* (1943), *Carousel* (1945), *Gentlemen Prefer Blondes* (1949), and *Paint Your Wagon* (1951); won Tony awards in 1947 and 1962; received Capezio Dance Award, 1966.

DORATI, ANTAL, Apr. 9, 1906 (Budapest, Hung.). U.S. composer, conductor. Conductor and musical dir. throughout Europe, 1924-40; Ballet Theatre, 1940-44; Dallas Symphony Orch., 1945-49; Minneapolis Symphony Orch., 1949-60; BBC Symphony Orch., 1962-66; Stockholm Phil., 1966-   ; musical dir. of Washington Natl. Symphony, 1969-77; Detroit Symphony Orch., 1977-   .

DUKE, VERNON, born Vladimir Dukelsky, Oct. 10, 1903 (Pskov, Rus.)-Jan. 17, 1969. U.S. composer. Composed ballets for S. DIAGHILEV; Broadway musical scores include *Cabin in the Sky,* 1940; songs include "April in Paris," "Autumn in New York."

DUNCAN, ISADORA, May 27, 1878 (San Francisco, Calif.)-Sept. 14, 1927. U.S. dancer. Rejected the formality of ballet; one of the first to interpret dance as a free form of art; popularized barefoot dance; found great success in Europe, especially England and Russia.

DUNHAM, KATHERINE, June 22, 1910 (Chicago, Ill.). U.S. dancer, choreographer. First to organize a black dance troupe of professional caliber; dance dir. of New York Labor Stage, 1939; established Dunham School of Dance (1945) and Katherine Dunham Dance Co. (1945); received *Dance Magazine* Award, 1968.

EGLEVSKY, ANDRE, Dec. 21, 1917 (Moscow, Rus.)-Dec. 4, 1977. Russian-U.S. ballet dancer. One of the greatest male classical dancers; with Ballet Russe (1933-35), Ballet de Monte Carlo (1935-37, 1938-42), American Ballet (1935), New York City Ballet (1951-58); repertoire included *Giselle* and *Swan Lake;* created roles in *Caracole* and *Scotch Symphony.*

FARRAR, GERALDINE, Feb. 28, 1882 (Melrose, Mass.)-Mar. 11, 1967. U.S. operatic soprano. With Met. Opera Co., 1906-22; lead roles included Madame Butterfly, Manon, Carmen.

FARRELL, EILEEN, Feb. 13, 1920 (Willimantic, Conn.). U.S. operatic soprano. Best known for her

roles in Wagnerian operas; sang with San Francisco and Chicago opera cos. before making Met. Opera debut, 1960.

FARRELL, SUZANNE, Aug. 16, 1945 (Cincinnati, Ohio). U.S. ballerina. With NYCB, 1961-69 and 1975-   ; created many roles in G. BALANCHINE ballets; received *Dance Magazine* Award, 1976.

FIEDLER, ARTHUR, Dec. 17, 1894 (Boston, Mass.)-July 10, 1979. U.S. conductor. Organized and conducted Esplanade concerts, Boston, 1929-79; conducted the Boston Symphony Pops Concerts, 1930-79.

FIRKUSNY, RUDOLF, Feb. 11, 1912 (Napajedla, Czech.). Czech-U.S. pianist. Child prodigy who first appeared with Czech Philharmonic Orch. in 1922; European concert tours, 1930-39; a U.S. resident since 1950; best known for his interpretations of L. BEETHOVEN and Czech composers.

GERSHWIN, GEORGE, Sept. 26, 1898 (Brooklyn, N.Y.)-July 11, 1937. U.S. composer. Composed Broadway musicals, concert music, songs with elements of jazz. Works: "Swanee," 1918; *Rhapsody in Blue,* 1924; *Porgy and Bess* (opera), 1925; *Lady Be Good,* 1924; *Funny Face,* 1927; *An American in Paris,* 1928; *Of Thee I Sing,* (first musical to win a Pulitzer Prize), 1931.

GRAHAM, MARTHA, May 11, 1893 (Pittsburgh, Pa.). U.S. dancer, teacher, choreographer of modern dance. Studied and worked with Denishawn Dancers, 1916-23; founder and artistic dir. of Martha Graham School of Contemporary Dance, 1927; over 150 choreographed works, including *Appalachian Spring* (1944); received 1956 *Dance Magazine* Award and 1960 Capezio Dance Award.

GREGORY, CYNTHIA KATHLEEN, July 8, 1946 (Los Angeles, Calif.). U.S. ballerina. Soloist with San Francisco Ballet, 1962-65; soloist with American Ballet Theatre, NYC, 1965-   .

HANDY, W(illiam) C(hristopher), Nov. 16, 1873 (Florence, Ala.)-Mar. 28, 1958. U.S. composer. First to write down and publish "blues" music; established popularity of the blues in band music; ignoring his blindness, conducted own orchestra, 1903-21. Works: "St. Louis Blues," 1914.

HANSON, HOWARD HAROLD, Oct. 28, 1896 (Wahoo, Neb.). U.S. composer, conductor. Dir. of Eastman School of Music at U. of Rochester, 1924-64; works include five symphonies, an opera (commissioned by the Met.); won Prix de Rome, 1921; awarded 1944 Pulitzer Prize in music, for his Fourth Symphony.

HEIFETZ, JASCHA, Feb. 2, 1901 (Vilna, Lith. |now USSR|). U.S. violin virtuoso. Child prodigy who played F. MENDELSSOHN Concerto at age seven; New York debut at Carnegie Hall, 1917; many internatl. tours; has transcribed works of J. S. BACH and A. VIVALDI for violin; named Chevalier, Legion of Honor, 1926.

HERBERT, VICTOR, Feb. 1, 1859 (Dublin, Ire.)-May 26, 1924. Irish-U.S. virtuoso cellist, conductor, composer. Best known for his operettas *Babes in Toyland* (1903) and *Naughty Marietta* (1910); conductor of Pittsburgh Symphony Orch., 1898-1904; cofounder of ASCAP, 1914; wrote music scores for plays, motion pictures (*The Fall of a Nation,* 1916).

HINDEMITH, PAUL, Nov. 16, 1895 (Hanau, Ger.)-Dec. 23, 1963; German-U.S. composer, musical theorist. Member of Frankfurt Opera Orch., 1915-23; his opera *Mathis der Maler* (1934) was banned by Nazis; has taught in Europe

COMPOSERS, CONCERT, BALLET AND OPERA

and the U.S.; works include chamber music, operas, instrumental music.

HINES, JEROME, born Jerome Heinz, Nov. 8, 1921 (Hollywood, Calif.). U.S. operatic bass. Made debut, 1941; with Met. Opera, from 1946; at Bayreuth, 1958-63; repertoire includes Mephistopheles, Boris Godunov, Grand Inquisitor (*Don Carlos*), and Swallow (*Peter Grimes*).

HORNE, MARILYN B., Jan 16, 1934 (Bradford, Pa.). U.S. operatic mezzo-soprano. Has appeared in most major internatl. opera houses; with Met. Opera, 1970-   ; best known for performances in coloratura roles such as *Carmen*; sang leading role on the sound track for the film *Carmen Jones*, 1954.

HOROWITZ, VLADIMIR, Oct. 1, 1904 (Kiev, Rus.). U.S. virtuoso pianist. Has done internatl. concert tours since 1924; best known for his interpretations of S. RACHMANINOV, F. CHOPIN, F. LISZT, S. PROKOFIEV, A. SCRIABIN, R. SCHUMANN; has won 12 Grammy awards (1966-76) for classical recordings.

HUMPHREY, DORIS, Oct. 17, 1895 (Oak Park, Ill.)-Dec. 29, 1958. U.S. dancer, choreographer, teacher. With Denishawn Co. (1917-28); and Humphrey-Weidman School & Co. (1928-44); artistic dir. of JOSE LIMON Co., 1942-58; influenced the U.S. modern-dance movement.

IVES, CHARLES EDWARD, Oct. 20, 1874 (Danbury, Conn.)-May 19, 1954. U.S. composer. Known for tonal, rhythmic, and harmonic experimentation; themes drawn from New England; awarded 1947 Pulitzer Prize in music for his *Third Symphony (The Camp Meeting)*.

JOFFREY, ROBERT, born Abdulla Jaffa Anver Bey Khan, Dec. 24, 1930 (Seattle, Wash.). U.S. dancer, choreographer, ballet dir. First choreographed ballet was *Persephone*, 1952; founder and dir. of ballet faculty of American Ballet Center, 1953-65; founder of R. Joffrey Ballet, 1956 (became City Center Joffrey Ballet, 1966).

JOPLIN, SCOTT, Nov. 24, 1868 (Texarkana, Tex.)-Apr. 1, 1917. U.S. ragtime pianist, composer. Entertained in vaudeville; ragtime instrumental music includes "Maple Leaf Rag."

KIRCHNER, LEON, Jan. 24, 1919 (Brooklyn, N.Y.). U.S. composer, pianist. Wrote mainly keyboard and string compositions; won 1967 Pulitzer Prize, for *String Quartet No. 3* (1966).

KOSTELANETZ, ANDRE, Dec. 22, 1901 (St. Petersburg, Rus. |now Leningrad, USSR|). Jan. 14, 1980. U.S. conductor. Gained fame with CBS radio broadcasts, from 1928; many concert tours and guest appearances with major internatl. orchs.

KOUSSEVITZKY, SERGE ALEXANDROVITCH, July 26, 1874 (Vyshni Volochek, Rus.)-June 4, 1951. Russian-U.S. conductor. With Boston Symphony Orch., 1924-49; founder and dir. of Berkshire Music Festival, 1937; organized Koussevitzky Fndn. (1942) to commission and perform new works; known for his interpretations of works by modern composers.

LAWRENCE, MARJORIE, Feb. 17, 1907 (Melbourne, Austrl.)-Jan. 13, 1979. Australian operatic soprano. Known for her roles in Wagnerian operas; only singer to ride a horse on stage in the finale of *Die Gotterdammerung* (as R. WAGNER intended); with Paris Opera, from 1933; Polio curtailed her career, 1941; The 1955 film *Interrupted Melody* told the story of her life.

LEINSDORF, ERICH, Feb. 4, 1912 (Vienna, Austria). U.S. conductor. With Met. Orch., 1937-43; music dir. of Phil. Orch. of Rochester (N.Y.)

1947-56; dir. of Met. Opera, 1957-62; music dir. of Boston Symphony Orch., 1962-69.

LEVINE, JAMES, June 23, 1943 (Cincinnati, Ohio). U.S. conductor, pianist. Asst. conductor of Cleveland Orch., 1964-70; music director of Met. Opera, 1975-   .

LIMON, JOSE ARCADIO, Jan. 12, 1908 (Cuiliacán, Mex.)-Dec. 2, 1972. Mexican-U.S. modern dancer, choreographer, teacher. Dancer with Humphrey & Weidman Co., 1930-40; founder of José Limón American Dance Co., 1947; artistic dir. of American Dance Theatre, 1964.

MAAZEL, LORIN, Mar. 6, 1930 (Paris, Fr.). U.S. conductor, violinist. Conductor at the Edinburgh, Bayreuth and Salzburg festivals, 1960-70; musical dir., Cleveland Orchestra, 1972-   .

MAKAROVA, NATALIA ROMANOVNA, Nov. 21, 1940 (Leningrad, USSR). Soviet-U.S. ballerina. Known for her performances in Romantic roles; after defection (1970) to U.S., with ABT, 1970-72.

MCBRIDE, PATRICIA, Aug. 23, 1942 (Teaneck, N.J.). U.S. ballerina. With NYCB, from 1959, now principal dancer; repertoire includes *Swan Lake, Harlequinade, Nutcracker, Jewels, Coppelia*.

MCCORMACK, JOHN, June 13, 1884 (Athlone, Ire.)-Sept. 16, 1945. U.S. operatic tenor. Made Covent Garden debut, 1907; known for effortless singing, diction, phrasing; sang mostly Italian opera, German lieder, Irish folk songs.

MCCRACKEN, JAMES EUGENE, Dec. 16, 1926 (Gary, Ind.). U.S. operatic tenor. Many roles in major international houses; known for his performances as Otello.

MELCHIOR, LAURITZ LEBRECHT HOMMEL, Mar. 20, 1890 (Copenhagen, Denmark)-Mar. 18, 1973. U.S. operatic tenor. Debuted as baritone (1913) and as a tenor (1918); specialized in Wagnerian roles, especially Tristan and Siegfried; sang with Metropolitan Opera, 1926-50.

MENUHIN, YEHUDI, Apr. 22, 1916 (New York, N.Y.). U.S. violin virtuoso. A child prodigy, he performed Mendelssohn *Violin Concerto* at age seven; has made many international concert tours, often with sister, Hephzibah Menuhin, pianist; dir., Bath Festival (now Menuhin Festival), 1958-68.

MERRILL, ROBERT, June 4, 1919 (Brooklyn, N.Y.). U.S. operatic baritone. Made debut, 1944; with Met. Opera, 1945-1975; roles include Escamillo (*Carmen*), Germont (*La Traviata*), Marcello (*La Boheme*), Iago (*Otello*); first American to sing 500 performances at Met. Opera.

MILNES, SHERRILL EUSTACE, Jan. 10, 1935 (Downers Grove, Ill). U.S. operatic baritone. With Met. Opera, 1965-   ; best known for his performances in G. VERDI operas.

MOFFO, ANNA, June 27, 1934 (Wayne, Pa.). U.S. operatic soprano. Made U.S. debut, 1957; with Met. Opera, from 1959-1969; repertoire includes *La Boheme, Rigoletto, Madama Butterfly, The Barber of Seville, Tosca.*

ORMANDY, EUGENE, Nov. 18, 1899 (Budapest, Hung.). U.S. conductor, music dir.; at age 5½, the youngest pupil at the Royal State Acad. of Music; toured Europe as child violinist; conductor of Minneapolis Symphony Orch., 1931-36; conductor and music dir. of Philadelphia Orch., from 1936.

PEERCE, JAN, born Jacob Pincus Perelmuth, June, 1904 (New York, N.Y.). U.S. operatic tenor. Made his Metropolitan Opera debut (1941) and his Broadway debut in *Fiddler on the Roof* (1971); first American singer to appear at the Bolshoi Opera, USSR.

PETERS, ROBERTA, May 4, 1930 (New York,

N.Y.). U.S. operatic soprano. Made Met. Opera debut as Zerlina in *Don Giovanni*, 1950; repertoire includes *Rigoletto* and *Magic Flute*.

PIATIGORSKY, GREGOR, Apr. 20, 1903 (Ekaterinoslav, Russia)–Aug. 6, 1976. U.S. cello virtuoso. Solo cellist, Imperial Opera, Moscow (1916–19) and Berlin Philharmonic (1923–28); U.S. debut, 1929.

PISTON, WALTER, Jan. 20, 1894 (Rockland, Maine)–Nov. 12, 1976. U.S. composer, teacher. Prof. of music, Harvard U., 1944–60; noted for his compositions in neoclassical style with romantic overtones; awarded Pulitzer prizes for third (1947) and seventh (1960) symphonies.

PONS, LILY, born Alice Josephine Pons, Apr. 16, 1904 (Draguignan, Fr.)–Feb. 13, 1976. U.S. coloratura soprano. With Met. Opera, 1931–56; repertoire included *Lakme* and *Lucia di Lammermoor;* in the films *I Dream Too Much* (1935) and *That Girl from Paris* (1936).

PONSELLE, ROSA MELBA, Jan. 22, 1897 (Meriden, Conn.). U.S. operatic soprano. Sang with Metropolitan Opera, 1918–37; repertoire included *La Forza del Destina, Carmen, Aida, La Traviata;* coach and artistic dir., Baltimore Civic Opera Co., 1954-

PREVIN, ANDRÉ, Apr. 6, 1929 (Berlin, Ger.). U.S. composer, conductor. With Houston Symphony (1967–69) and London Symphony Orch. (1968-   ); music dir. of Pittsburgh Symphony, 1976-   ; winner of four AAs.

PRICE, LEONTYNE, Feb. 10, 1927 (Laurel, Miss.). U.S. operatic soprano. Made debut with San Francisco Opera, 1957; with Met. Opera, 1961-   ; created role of Cleopatra (*Antony and Cleopatra*); also known for her role as Aida; has won 20 Grammy awards for classical vocal recordings; received Presidential Medal of Freedom, 1964.

REINER, FRITZ, Dec. 19, 1888 (Budapest, Hung.)–Nov. 15, 1963. Hungarian-U.S. conductor. With Cincinnati Symphony, 1922–31; at Curtis Inst. of Music (Philadelphia), 1931–41; with Pittsburgh Symphony, 1938–48; with Met. Opera, 1948–53; with Chicago Symphony, 1953–62; best known for interpretations of R. WAGNER and R. STRAUSS.

ROBBINS, JEROME, Oct. 11, 1918 (New York, N.Y.) U.S. ballet dancer, choreographer. Many Broadway musical appearances; with ABT, 1940–44; assoc. music dir. of NYCB, 1959-   .

ROBESON, PAUL BUSTILL, Apr. 9, 1898 (Princeton, N.J.)–Jan. 23, 1976. U.S. dramatic bass-baritone. Performed on stage, in films. Plays: *All God's Chillun Got Wings,* 1924; *The Emperor Jones,* 1924; *Show Boat,* 1928.

ROMBERG, SIGMUND, July 29, 1887 (Szeged, Hungary)–Nov. 9, 1951. U.S. composer. Wrote 40 scores for musicals; best known for his operettas, including *Maytime* (1917), *The Student Prince* (1924), and *The Desert Song* (1926).

ROSTROPOVICH, MSTISLAV, Mar. 27, 1927 (Baku, USSR). Soviet-U.S. cello virtuoso, conductor. Made cello debut, 1935; Soviet citizenship revoked, 1978; music dir. of Natl. Symphony Orch., 1977-   .

RUBINSTEIN, ARTHUR (or Artur), Jan. 28, 1887 (Lodz, Pol.). U.S. concert pianist. A child prodigy who made U.S. debut in 1906; famed for international concert performances and especially for his interpretations of F. CHOPIN.

SCHIPPERS, THOMAS, Mar. 9, 1930 (Kalamazoo, Mich.)–Dec. 16, 1977. U.S. conductor. With

New York City Opera, 1951–54; with Met. Opera, 1955–77; founder (with G. C. MENOTTI) of Festival of Two Worlds (Spoleto, It.), 1958.

SCHNABEL, KARL ULRICH, Aug. 6, 1909 (Berlin, Ger.). U.S. concert pianist. Internatl. career, including recitals, broadcasts, concert tours, and solos with major orchs. *Modern Technique of the Pedal,* 1954.

SCHOENBERG, ARNOLD, Sept. 13, 1874 (Vienna, Austria)–July 13, 1961. Austrian-U.S. composer, teacher. Invented the 12-tone row, 1921; at Prussian Acad. of Arts, 1925–33; prof. at UCLA, 1936–44. Works: *Verklärte Nacht,* 1889; *Gurrelieder,* 1913; *Pierrot Lunaire,* 1912.

SERKIN, RUDOLF, Mar. 28, 1903 (Eger, Bohemia). Austrian-U.S. pianist. A child prodigy who made European debut in 1915; U.S. debut, 1933; dir. of Curtis Inst. of Music, 1968–76; received Presidential Medal of Freedom, 1963.

SESSIONS, ROGER HUNTINGTON, Dec. 28, 1896 (Brooklyn, N.Y.). U.S. composer, teacher. With AARON COPLAND, organized Copland-Sessions Concerts for contemporary music, 1928; works include four symphonies, two operas, string and keyboard pieces, orchestral suites.

SILLS, BEVERLY, born Belle Silverman, May 25, 1929 (Brooklyn, N.Y.). U.S. operatic coloratura soprano. With radio's *Major Bowes Capital Family Hour,* 1934–41; with New York City Opera Co. since 1955-   , as Dir. since 1979; repertoire includes *Manon, La Traviata, Lucia di Lammermoor.* Autobiography: *Bubbles.*

STADE, FREDERICA VON, June 1, 1945 (Sommerville, N.J.). U.S. operatic mezzo-soprano. With Metropolitan Opera, 1970-   ; has made international opera house appearances; repertoire includes *Marriage of Figaro, Faust,* and *Don Giovanni.*

STERN, ISAAC, July 21, 1920 (Kreminiecz, Rus.). U.S. violinist. Made U.S. debut, 1931; many internatl. tours and solo and chamber-music recordings; won Grammy awards in 1971 and 1973.

STEVENS, RISË, born Risë Steenberg, June 11, 1913 (New York, N.Y.). U.S. operatic mezzosoprano. Made Metropolitan Opera debut, 1938; repertoire includes *Mignon, Carmen, Samson et Dalila,* and *Cosi Fan Tutte;* pres., Mannes College of Music, N.Y., 1975–78.

STOKOWSKI, LEOPOLD, Apr. 18, 1882 (London, Eng.)–Sept. 13, 1977. U.S. conductor. With Cincinnati Symphony, 1909–12; music dir. of Philadelphia Orch., 1912–36; organized All-American Youth Orch., 1940–41; formed American Symphony Orch., 1962.

SZELL, GEORGE, June 7, 1897 (Budapest, Hung.)–July 30, 1970. U.S. conductor. Made piano debut with Vienna Symphony at age 10; conductor of Berlin State Opera, 1924–29; with German Opera, Prague, 1930–33; with Met. Opera, 1942–45; principal conductor of Cleveland Orch., 1946–70.

TAYLOR, PAUL BELVILLE, July 29, 1930 (Allegheny County, Pa.). U.S. modern dancer, choreographer. Dancer, Martha Graham Dance Co., 1955–61; dir., choreographer, Paul Taylor Dance Co., 1955-   .

THARP, TWYLA, July 1, 1941 (Portland, Ind.). U.S. dancer, choreographer. With Paul Taylor Dance Co., 1963–65; freelance choreographer with own modern-dance troupe, 1965-   ; major choreography includes *Eight Jelly Rolls* (1971) and *Push Comes to Shove* (1976).

THOMAS, MICHAEL TILSON, 1944 (Hollywood, Calif.). U.S. conductor. Music dir. and conductor of

COMPOSERS, CONCERT, BALLET AND OPERA

Buffalo Phil. Orch., 1971–   ; dir. and conductor of New York Phil. Young People's Concerts (CBS-TV), 1971–77; won Grammy award, 1976.

THOMSON, VIRGIL, Nov. 25, 1896 (Kansas City, Mo.). U.S. composer, music critic. Works include chamber music, ballet, symphonies, choral works, operas (Four Saints in Three Acts, 1934; The Mother of Us All, 1947); music critic with the New York Herald-Tribune, 1940–54; won Pulitzer Prize in music, 1949.

TRAUBEL, HELEN, June 20, 1899 (St. Louis, Mo.)–July 28, 1972. U.S. operatic and concert soprano. Made Met. Opera debut, 1939; principal Wagnerian soprano at Met., 1939–53.

TUCKER, RICHARD, born Reuben Ticker, Aug. 28, 1914 (Brooklyn, N.Y.)–Jan. 8, 1975. U.S. operatic tenor. With Met. Opera, 1945–75; well-known cantor; repertoire included Aida, Pagliacci, La Juive, La Bohème.

VILLELLA, EDWARD, Oct. 1, 1936 (Long I., N.Y.). U.S. ballet dancer. With NYCB, 1957–   ; roles include Prodigal Son, Harlequinade; has starred in musicals (Brigadoon, 1962); won 1957 Emmy for Harlequinade (CBS Festival of Lively Arts).

WALLENSTEIN, ALFRED FRANZ, Oct. 7, 1898 (Chicago, Ill.). U.S. conductor, cellist. First cellist with Chicago Symphony Orch. (1922–29) and New York Phil. (1929–36); radio orchestra conductor with his Sinfonietta, from 1933; music dir. of Los Angeles Phil., 1943–56.

WARREN, LEONARD, born Leonard Vaarenov, Apr. 21, 1911 (New York, N.Y.)–Mar. 4, 1960. U.S. operatic baritone. With Met. Opera, 1939–60; popular radio and TV singer; known for roles in G. VERDI operas; died on stage at Met. during La Forza del Destino.

WATTS, ANDRÉ, June 20, 1946 (Nuremberg, Ger.). U.S. concert pianist. Made debut in Philadelphia Orch. Children's Concerts, 1955; made European debut with London Symphony Orch., 1966; won Grammy award, 1963.

ZIMBALIST, EFREM, May 7, 1889 (Rostov-on-Don, Rus.). Russian-U.S. violinist. Made debut in Berlin at age 17; extensive international tours; dir. of Curtis Inst. of Music. 1941–68. (Father of actor EFREM ZIMBALIST, JR.)

FOREIGN COMPOSERS, CONCERT, BALLET, AND OPERA PERSONALITIES

ALONSO, ALICIA, born Alicia Ernestina de la Caridad del Cobre Martinez Hoyo, Dec. 21, 1921 (Havana, Cuba). Cuban prima ballerina. Danced with the Ballet Theatre (now ABT), 1941, 1943–48, and 1951; formed Alicia Alonso ballet co. in Havana, 1948; prima ballerina and dir. of Ballet Nac. de Cuba, 1959–   ; bouts of blindness have caused temporary interruptions in her career; a pure, classical ballerina whose most famous role is Giselle.

ANSERMET, ERNEST ALEXANDRE, Nov. 11, 1883 (Vevey, Switz.)–Feb. 20, 1969. Swiss conductor. Noted for conducting I. STRAVINSKY and other modern composers; conductor for S. DIAGHILEV's Ballets Russes; founded Orchestre de la Swisse Romande, 1918; composed symphonic poem "Feuilles au Printemps."

ASHKENAZY, VLADIMIR, July 6, 1937 (Gorky, USSR). Russian pianist. Internatl. concert star; won second prize in Chopin Competition, 1955; winner of Tchaikovsky Piano Competition, 1962; London debut, 1963; performs frequently on records, TV.

ASHTON, SIR FREDERIC (WILLIAM MALLANDINE), Sept. 17, 1904 (Guayaquil, Ecuador). English choreographer. Founder, principal choreographer, and dir. of England's Royal Ballet, 1952–70; has choreographed for many ballet cos. worldwide.

BACH, CARL PHILIPP EMANUEL, Mar. 8, 1714 (Weimar, Ger.)–Dec. 14, 1788. German composer. Third son of J. S. BACH; court musician to FREDERICK THE GREAT, 1740–67; prolific composer; a pioneer in sonatas, symphonic orchestrations, and chamber music; wrote "Essay on Keyboard Instruments" (1753), a valuable source on 18th-cent. music technique.

BACH, JOHANN CHRISTIAN ("The English Bach"), Sept. 5, 1735 (Leipzig, Ger.)–Jan. 1, 1782. German composer, organist. Resident of Milan (and cathedral organist), (1754–59) and London, where he taught music to the royal family (1759–82); composed operas, sonatas, symphonies.

BACH, JOHANN SEBASTIAN, Mar. 21, 1685 (Eisenach, Ger.)–July 28, 1750. German composer. Founding father of a music dynasty, pioneer in the playing of and composition for keyboard instruments; musician for royalty and church in native Germany; became totally blind, 1749; wrote keyboard music, cantatas, concertos, masses, hymns. Mass in B Minor, 1724–46; Brandenburg Concertos, 1721; The Goldberg Variations, 1722; Well-Tempered Clavier, 1742.

BARBIROLLI, SIR JOHN, born Giovanni Battista Barbirolli, Dec. 2, 1899 (London, Eng.)–June 29, 1970. British conductor. Musical dir. of British Natl. Opera (1926–27), New York Phil. (1937–43).

BARTÓK, BÉLA, Mar. 25, 1881 (Nagyszentmiklos, A.-H. [now Hung.])–Sept. 26, 1945. Hungarian composer, pianist. Utilized Hungarian folk themes and a chromatic system of 12 tones to produce a variety of string, piano, and choral music. Operas: Bluebeard's Castle, 1911. Ballets: The Wooden Prince, 1916; The Wonderful Mandarin, 1919. Piano collection: Mikrokosmos, 1926–39.

BEECHAM, SIR THOMAS, Apr. 29, 1879 (St. Helen's, Eng.)–Mar. 8, 1961. British conductor. Introduced Britain to R. STRAUSS (1915), the Ballets Russes (1911) and Chaliapin (1913); founder of British Natl. Opera Co., London Phil. (1932) and Royal Phil. (1946); artistic dir. of Covent Garden, from 1933.

BEETHOVEN, LUDWIG VAN, baptized Dec. 17, 1770 (Bonn, Ger.)–Mar. 26, 1827. German composer. The prototypical Romantic composer of symphonies, sonatas, choral works, chamber music, etc. A child prodigy taught by W. A. MOZART (1787) and J. HAYDN (1792–94); spent most of his career in Vienna; composed many of finest works while almost totally deaf; first composer to make a living without church subsidy. First period (1794–1800): First Symphony. Second period (1801–14): Second–Eighth Symphonies, Moonlight Sonata, Appassionata, Fourth and Fifth Concerti, Battle Symphony, Fidelio. Third period (1815–27): Ninth Symphony, string quartets.

BÉJART, MAURICE, born Maurice-Jean de Berger, Jan. 1, 1927 (Marseilles, Fr.). French choreographer. Founded Ballet of the XXth Century Company, 1954; known for his radical contemporary interpretations of ballet classics, produced in a lavish manner.

BELLINI, VINCENZO, Nov. 3, 1801 (Catania, Sicily)–Sept. 23, 1835. Italian composer. Prime mover in the composition of bel canto opera.

73

THE BOOK OF WHO

Operas: *La Sonnambula,* 1831; *Norma,* 1831; *I Puritani,* 1835.

BERG, ALBAN, Feb. 9, 1885 (Vienna, Austria)-Dec. 24, 1935. Austrian composer. Composer of atonal music, influenced by A. SCHONBERG; wrote orchestral, chamber music and songs; best known for two operas, *Wozzeck* (1925) and *Lulu* (1937).

BERIOSOVA, SVETLANA, Sept. 24, 1932 (Kaunas, Lith [now USSR]). Russian-English ballerina. Prima with many ballet cos. (1948–75) chiefly with Sadler's Wells (now Royal) Ballet in England (1952–75); her Giselle most famous role.

BERLIOZ, (Louis) **HECTOR,** Dec. 11, 1803 (La Côte-Saint Andre, Fr.)-Mar. 8, 1869. French composer. Most important of the French Romantics; noted for symphonies and operas. Works: *Symphonie Fantastique,* 1830; *Romeo and Juliet,* 1839; *La Damnation de Faust,* 1846; *Les Troyens,* 1858–60; "Te Deum," 1849.

BING, SIR RUDOLPH, Jan. 9, 1902 (Vienna, Austria). Anglo-Austrian impresario. Held various managerial posts; most notably, gen. mgr. of Met. Opera, 1950–72; cofounder of Edinburgh Festival, 1947.

BIZET, GEORGES, born Alexandre Cesar Leopold Bizet, Oct. 25, 1838 (Paris, Fr.)-June 3, 1875. French composer. Known for his dramatic music and the opera *Carmen* (1875). Works: *L'Arlesienne,* 1872; *Jeux d'enfants,* 1871; Symphony in C Major, 1855.

BJÖRLING, JUSSI, born Johan Jonaton Björling, Feb. 2, 1911 (Stora Tuna, Swe.)-Sept. 9, 1960. Swedish singer. Operatic tenor; made debut, 1929; debut in U.S., 1937; known for elegant robustness of voice, particularly in G. VERDI and G. PUCCINI dramatic roles.

BLAIR, DAVID, born David Butterfield, July 27, 1932 (Halifax, Eng.)-Apr. 1, 1976. English dancer. With Royal Ballet, 1948–76; premier danseur, 1955–76; frequent partner of MARGOT FONTEYN; choreographer for ABT.

BÖHM, KARL, Aug. 28, 1894 (Graz, Austria). Austrian conductor. Still conducts symphonies and opera-co. orchs. worldwide; gen. music dir. at Darmstadt, 1927–31; dir. of Hamburg Opera, 1931–34; dir. of Dresden Opera, 1934–42; dir. of Vienna Opera, 1943–45; known for R. WAGNER and W. A. MOZART conducting.

BOITO, ARRIGO, born Enrico Giuseppi Giovanni Boito, Feb. 24, 1842 (Padua, It.)-June 10, 1918. Italian librettist, composer, critic. Wrote libretti for several famous operas of G. VERDI; as a critic, favored reform of Italian opera, 1860s. *Mefistofele,* 1875. Libretti: *La Gioconda,* 1876; *Simon Boccanegra,* 1881; *Otello,* 1887; *Falstaff,* 1893.

BORODIN, ALEKSANDR PROFIRYEVICH, Nov. 12, 1833 (St. Petersburg. Rus. [now Leningrad, USSR])-Feb. 27, 1887. Russian composer. A professional scientist and part-time musician, he became one of five influential figures in Russian nationalistic music for his three symphonies and the opera, *Prince Igor.*

BOULANGER, NADIA JULIETTE, Sept. 16, 1887 (Paris, Fr.)-Oct. 22, 1979. French music teacher/conductor. As a teacher of composition, influenced a whole generation of musicians and composers, including W. PISTON, A. COPELAND and V. THOMPSON. First woman to conduct Boston Symphony (1938) and N.Y. Philharmonic (1939).

BOULEZ, PIERRE, Mar. 26, 1925 (Montbrison, Fr.). French conductor, composer. Conductor of major orchs. worldwide; musical dir. of New York

Phil., 1971–77; head of Centre Georges Pompidou, Paris, 1978– . Works: *Sonatine,* 1946; *Structures, Book I,* 1952.

BOULT, SIR ADRIAN CEDRIC, Apr. 8, 1889 (Chester, Eng.). English conductor. Musical dir. and conductor of many orchestras, including Birmingham City Orch. (1924-30), the BBC Orch. (1930-42 and 1959-60), London Phil. (1950-57), and the Bach Choir (1928-33).

BRAHMS, JOHANNES, May 7, 1833 (Hamburg, Ger.)-Apr. 3, 1897. German composer. Prime exponent of the Romantic school of composition, in symphonies, chamber music, piano works, concerti, choral works, songs, lieder; protégé of R. SCHUMANN. Works: *A German Requiem,* 1868; Hungarian Dances, 1878–93; Violin Concerto in D Major, 1878; "Lullaby," 1868.

BREAM, JULIAN, July 15, 1933 (London, Eng.). British musician. Leading authority on music of 16th-18th cents. for guitar and lute; has own Julian Bream Consort, a performing group; protégé of A. SEGOVIA.

BRITTEN, (Edward) **BENJAMIN,** Nov. 22, 1913 (Lowestoft, Eng.)-Dec. 4, 1976. English composer. Leading figure in mid-20th-cent. chromatic composition, especially opera and religious works. Operas: *Peter Grimes,* 1945; *Rape of Lucretia,* 1946; *Billy Budd,* 1951; *Turn of the Screw,* 1954; *Death in Venice,* 1973. Other works: *The Young Person's Guide to the Orchestra,* 1945; *Curlew River,* 1964; *The Prodigal Son,* 1968.

BRUCKNER, (Josef) **ANTON,** Sept. 4, 1824 (Ansfelden, Austria)-Oct. 11, 1896. Austrian Romantic composer. Noted for nine monumental symphonies and for sacred music; organist at Linz (1856) and Vienna (1868); disciple of R. WAGNER.

BRUHN, ERIK, born Belton Evers, Oct. 3, 1928 (Copenhagen, Den.). Danish dancer. Ballet dancer with Royal Danish Ballet (1947-55), ABT (1955-58, 1960-61, 1968-69, and 1972–   ); noted for 19th-cent.-style roles; in recent years, has turned to character roles and modern dance (with JOSÉ LIMON Co.).

BÜLOW, BARON HANS GUIDO VON, Jan. 8 1830 (Dresden, Ger.)-Feb. 12, 1894. German conductor. First modern virtuoso conductor; a champion of R. WAGNER, he conducted the first performances of *Meistersinger* (1868) and *Tristan und Isolde* (1862); first to conduct from memory.

CABALLÉ, MONTSERRAT, Apr. 12, 1933 (Barcelona, Sp.). Spanish operatic soprano. Leading bel canto soprano; repertoire also includes W. A. MOZART and R. STRAUSS; Met. Opera debut, 1965.

CARUSO, ENRICO, Feb. 25, 1873 (Naples, It.)-Aug. 2, 1921. Italian operatic lyric tenor. Sang entire French and Italian repertoires; achieved fame singing Rodolfo in *La Bohème,* in Milan; Covent Garden, 1903-07; Met. Opera Co., 1908-21; first operatic singer to appreciate the potential of phonograph recordings.

CASADESUS, ROBERT, Apr. 7, 1899 (Paris, Fr.)-Sept. 19, 1972. French concert pianist and composer. Popular concert artist, 1917-72; gave many concerts with wife Gaby and son Jean; chm. of piano dept. (1935) and dir.-gen. (from 1955) at American Conservatory, Paris; composed piano pieces, symphonies, orchestral suites.

CASALS, PABLO, Dec. 30, 1876 (Vendrell, Sp.)-Oct. 22, 1973. Spanish cellist, conductor. Noted for his virtuoso interpretations of J. S.

COMPOSERS, CONCERT, BALLET AND OPERA

BACH; formed trio with Alfred Corot and Jacques Thibaud, 1905; founded (1919) and conducted (1920) Orquesta Pau Casals, Barcelona; inaugurated annual festivals.

CHALIAPIN, FYODOR IVANOVICH, Feb. 13, 1873 (Kazan, Russia)–Apr. 12, 1938. Russian operatic bass. With his powerful voice, gusto, and natural acting ability, considered one of opera's greatest performers. Dramatic roles: Boris in *Boris Godunov;* Philip II in *Don Carlos;* Mefistofele in *Faust.* Comic roles: Don Basilio in *Barber of Seville;* Leporello in *Don Giovanni.*

CHOPIN, FREDERIC FRANÇOIS, Feb. 22, 1810 (Zelazowa Wola, Pol.)–Oct. 17, 1849. Polish-French composer and pianist. Child prodigy; Vienna debut, 1829; Paris debut, 1832; London debut, 1837; piano compositions include concertos, sonatas, nocturnes, études, mazurkas, polonaises, waltzes.

CORELLI, FRANCO, born Dario Franco Corelli, Apr. 8, 1921 (Ancona, Italy). Italian operatic tenor. Specializes in heroic tenor roles, especially of R. WAGNER; debut, Spoleto, 1951; N.Y. Metropolitan Opera debut, 1961.

DEBUSSY, CLAUDE ACHILLE, Aug. 22, 1862 (St. Germain-en-Laye, Fr.)–Mar. 25, 1918. French Romantic composer. Works: "Prélude à L'Après-midi d'un Faune," 1894; "Clair de lune," 1890-1905; "La Mer," 1905; *Pelléas et Mélisande* (opera), 1902; "Jeux," 1912.

DE LARROCHA, ALICIA, May 23, 1923 (Barcelona, Sp.). Spanish concert pianist. Child prodigy who debuted in 1927; known for her interpretation of F. CHOPIN.

DELIBES, C. P. LÉO, born Clement-Philbert Delibes, Feb. 21, 1836 (St.-Germain-du-Val, Fr.)–Jan. 16, 1891. French composer. Known for his operettas, operas, and ballets, including *Coppelia* (1870) and *Lakme* (1883); accompanist at the Theatre Lyrique (1853) and the Paris Opera (1863); prof. of composition at the Conservatoire, 1881.

DELIUS, FREDERICK, Jan. 29, 1863 (Bradford, Eng.)–June 10, 1934. English composer. Involved in late-19th-cent. revival of English music. Works: *Koanga* (opera), 1904; *Village Romeo and Juliet* (opera), 1907; "Over the Hills and Far Away" (tone poem), 1895.

DE LUCA, GIUSEPPE, Dec. 25, 1876 (Rome. It.)–Aug. 26, 1950. Italian operatic baritone. Best known for his performances in W. A. MOZART and G. VERDI operas; La Scala debut, 1903; sang with Metropolitan Opera, 1915-41.

DE VALOIS, NINETTE, born Edris Stannus, June 6, 1898 (Baltiboys, Ire.). British dancer, choreographer, ballet director. Dancer with Ballets Russes, 1923-25; dir. of ballet at Abbey Theatre, Dublin, 1928-31; dir. of Vic-Wells Ballet, 1931-63 (later Sadler's Wells and Royal Ballet); founder and dir. of Sadler's Wells Ballet School (now Royal Ballet School), 1931.

DIAGHILEV, SERGEI PAVLOVICH, Mar. 31, 1872 (Novgorod Prov., Russia)–Aug. 19, 1929. Russian ballet, art, music impresario. Artistic dir. of Maryinsky Theatre, 1899-1901; formed Ballets Russes, 1911-29; in producing such innovative ballets as I. STRAVINSKY's *The Firebird* (1910) and *The Rite of Spring* (1913), revitalized ballet in Western Europe.

DOMINGO, PLACIDO, Jan. 21, 1941 (Madrid, Sp.). Spanish operatic tenor. Made his U.S. debut, 1961; internationally renowned for his interpretations of G. VERDI and G. PUCCINI roles and French and Italian verisimo operas.

DONIZETTI, GAETANO, Nov. 29, 1797 (Bergamo, It.)–Apr. 8, 1848. Italian composer. Composed over 65 operas; gained internatl. fame with *Anna Bolena,* 1830; romantic operas include *L' Elisir d'Amore* (1832), *Lucrezia Borgia* (1833), *Lucia di Lammermoor* (1835); comic operas include *La Fille du Regiment* (1840) and *Don Pasquale* (1843).

DUKAS, PAUL ABRAHAM, Oct. 1, 1865 (Paris, Fr.)–May 17, 1935. French composer. Known for his dramatic and program music, as well as his piano compositions; most popular work: *The Sorcerer's Apprentice,* 1897.

DVORÁK, ANTONIN, Sept. 18, 1841 (Nelahozeves, Bohemia)–May 1, 1904. Czech composer. His 19th-cent. Romantic music was influenced by Czech folk songs; wrote chamber music, symphonies, and concertos; dir. of Natl. Conservatory of Music, New York City, 1892-95. Works: *Slavonic Dances,* 1878; *Symphony from the New World,* 1893.

ELGAR, SIR EDWARD WILLIAM, June 2, 1857 (Broadheath, Eng.)–Feb. 23, 1934. English composer. Known for his orchestral works. Works: *Enigma Variations,* 1896; *Dream of Gerontius,* 1900; *Pomp and Circumstance* marches, 1901-30.

FALLA, MANUEL DE, Nov. 23, 1876 (Cadiz, Sp.)–Nov. 14, 1946. Spanish composer. Incorporated Spanish folk themes in his music; organized festival of traditional folk songs of southern Spain, 1922; Works: *La Vida Breve* (opera), 1905; *The Three-Cornered Hat* (ballet), 1919.

FAURÉ, GABRIEL URBAIN, May 13, 1845 (Pamiers, Fr.)–Nov. 4, 1924. French composer. Prof. of composition (1896) and dir. (1905-20) at Paris Conservatory; best known for his *Masse de Requiem,* 1887; wrote over 100 songs, plus piano works, incidental music, and chamber music.

FISCHER-DIESKAU, DIETRICH, May 28, 1925 (Berlin, Ger.). German operatic baritone. Made his debut, 1948; has sung in all major international opera houses; repertoire includes *Don Giovanni, Macbeth, Wozzeck, Almaviva;* noted as a singer of German lieder.

FLAGSTAD, KIRSTEN, July 12, 1895 (Hamar, Nor.)–Dec. 7, 1962. Norwegian operatic soprano. Best known for her roles in Wagnerian operas, especially as Brünnhilde; debut, 1913; Met. Opera debut, 1935; Covent Garden debut, 1936; first dir. of Royal Norwegian Opera, 1958-60.

FOKINE, MICHEL, born Mikhail Mikhaylovich Fokine, Apr. 26, 1880 (St. Petersburg, Rus. [now Leningrad, USSR])–Aug. 22, 1942. Russian-U.S. dancer, choreographer. Influenced the development of modern dance by incorporating mime, music, scenery, and costume into dance; choreographed *The Dying Swan* for PAVLOVA, 1905; chief choreographer for Ballets Russes, creating *The Firebird* (1910), and *Petrushka* (1911).

FONTEYN, MARGOT, born Margaret Hookham, May 18, 1919 (Reigate, Eng.). English prima ballerina. Has danced all standard classical roles; made debut in *Nutcracker* at Vic-Wells Ballet, 1934; pres. of Royal Acad. of Dancing, from 1954; received *Dance Magazine* Award, 1962. Autobiography: *Margot Fonteyn: An Autobiography,* 1975.

FRACCI, CARLA, Aug. 20, 1936 (Milan, It.). Italian prima ballerina. Best known for her interpretations of romantic roles; with La Scala Ballet, from 1954; principal dancer with ABT, 1967- .

FRANCA, CELIA, June 25, 1921 (London, Eng.).

THE BOOK OF WHO

English ballet dancer, director, choreographer. Debut, 1936; danced with numerous ccs., 1936–59; founder and artistic dir. of Natl. Ballet of Canada, 1951–74; cofounder of Natl. Ballet School, Toronto, 1959.

FRANCK, CÉSAR AUGUSTE, Dec. 10, 1822 (Liège, Belg.)–Nov. 8, 1890. French Romantic composer, organist. Organist at St. Clotilde's Church, Paris, from 1858; teacher at Paris Conservatoire, from 1872; known for his Symphony in D Minor, (1886–88).

GALWAY, JAMES, Dec. 8, 1939 (Belfast, Ire.). Irish virtuoso flutist. Internationally acclaimed flutist; a member of orchs. all over Europe; principal flutist with Berlin Phil., 1969–75.

GEDDA, NIKOLAI, born Nikolai Ustinov, July 11, 1925 (Stockholm, Swe.). Swedish operatic tenor. With Paris Opera, Covent Garden (1954), Salzburg, Met. Opera (1957); fluent in six languages; performs works by G. VERDI, G. PUCCINI, J. HAYDN, R. WAGNER, and others.

GLAZUNOV, ALEKSANDR KONSTANTINO-VICH, Aug. 10, 1865 (St. Petersburg, Rus. [now Leningrad, USSR])–Mar. 21, 1936. Russian composer. Wrote eight symphonies, the symphonic poem "Stenka Razin," the ballets *Raymonda* and *Les Saisons,* as well as concerti; dir. of St. Petersburg Conservatory, 1905–28.

GLINKA, MIKHAIL IVANOVICH, June 1, 1804 (Novospasskoye, Russia)–Feb. 15, 1857. Russian composer. Founder, Russian National School. Operas: *Life for the Tsar,* 1836; *Ruslan and Ludmila,* 1842.

GLUCK, CHRISTOPH WILLIBALD RITTERS VON, July 2, 1714 (Erasbach, Ger.)–Nov. 15, 1787. German composer. Best known for his operas based on simplicity, including *Orfeo ed Eurydice* (1762), *Alceste* (1767), and *Paride ed Elena* (1770).

GOBBI, TITO, Oct. 24, 1915 (Bassano del Grappa, It.). Italian operatic baritone. Made debut, 1937; has appeared throughout the world in all major opera houses; known for his roles in G. VERDI and G. PUCCINI operas, especially as Scarpia in *Tosca.*

GOULD, GLENN HERBERT, Sept. 25, 1932 (Toronto, Can.). Canadian concert pianist. Debuted with Toronto Symphony at age 15; known for his interpretations of J. S. BACH and Romantic composers.

GOUNOD, CHARLES FRANÇOIS, June 17, 1818 (Paris, Fr.)–Oct. 17, 1893. French composer. Best known for his operas, including *Faust* (1859) and *Romeo et Juliette* (1867); composed a large amount of sacred music; awarded Prix de Rome, 1839.

GRIEG, EDVARD HAGERUP, June 15, 1843 (Bergen, Nor.)–Sept. 4, 1907. Norwegian composer. Founder of Norwegian natl. school; music rooted in Norwegian folk tradition; composed songs, piano, choral and orchestral works; best known for his *Peer Gynt* Suites, inspired by the play by H. IBSEN.

HANDEL, GEORGE FREDERICK, Feb. 23, 1685 (Halle, Ger.)–Apr. 14, 1759. British composer. Known for operas, oratorios, instrumental music; music dir. to the Elector of Hanover (later King George I of England), 1710. Works: "Acis and Galatea," 1731; "Coronation Anthems," 1727; *Messiah,* 1741; "Water Music," 1740; "Royal Fireworks Music," 1749.

HAYDEN, MELISSA, born Mildred Herman, Apr. 25, 1923 (Toronto, Can.). Canadian ballerina. Danced with Ballet Theatre (1946–55) and N.Y.C. Ballet (1949–53; as principal dancer, 1953–73).

HAYDN, (Franz) JOSEPH, Mar. 31, 1732 (Rohrau, Austria)–May 31, 1809. Austrian composer. Worked under the patronage of the Esterhazy family, 1761–90; composed masses, chamber music, symphonies, operas, keyboard music; famous oratorios include *The Creation* (1789) and *The Seasons* (1801).

HESS, DAME MYRA, Feb. 25, 1890 (London, Eng.)–Nov. 25, 1965. British concert pianist. Best known for her work in chamber music; interpreted J. S. BACH, W. A. MOZART, L. BEETHOVEN, and R. SCHUMANN; named Dame Commander of the British Empire, 1941.

HOLST, GUSTAV THEODORE, born Gustavus Theodore von Holst, Sept. 21, 1874 (Cheltenham, Eng.)–May 25, 1934. English composer, music teacher. Known for Oriental and mystical themes; most popular work is "The Planets" (orchestral suite), 1914–16.

HONEGGER, ARTHUR OSCAR, Mar. 10, 1892 (Le Havre, Fr.)–Nov. 27, 1955. French composer. Advocate of polytonality; one of "Les Six" Parisian composers; operas include *Le Roi David* (1921), *Judith* (1926), and *Antigone* (1927); orchestral works include *Pacific 231,* 1924.

HUMPERDINCK, ENGELBERT, Sept. 1, 1854 (Sieberg, Ger.)–Sept. 27, 1921. German composer best known for his opera *Hansel und Gretel* (1893).

ITURBI, JOSÉ, Nov. 28, 1895 (Valencia, Sp.). Spanish-U.S. conductor, pianist. Conductor of musicals and films; many internatl. piano tours; artistic dir. of Valencia (Spain) Symphony Orch., 1956–

JANAČEK, LEOŠ, July 3, 1854 (Hukvaldy, Moravia [now Czech.])–Aug. 12, 1928. Czech composer. His music was influenced by Czech folk music; best known for his opera *Jenufa,* 1904.

JOOSS, KURT, Jan. 12, 1901 (Wasseralfingen, Ger.)–May 22, 1979. German-British dancer, teacher, choreographer, ballet director. First interl. choreographer to combine classical and modern dance; founder and dir. of Ballets Jooss, 1933–67.

KARAJAN, HERBERT VON, Apr. 5, 1908 (Salzburg, Austria). Austrian orchestral and operatic conductor. With Berlin State Opera, 1938–45; dir. and conductor of Vienna State Opera, 1945–64; musical dir. of Berlin Phil., 1954–

KHACHATURIAN, ARAM, June 6, 1903 (Tiflis, Rus. [now USSR])–May 1, 1978. Soviet composer. Uses themes based on Armenian folk music; named Artist of the Soviet Union, 1954; known for the "Saber Dance" from the ballet *Gayne.* Other works: "Masquerade Suite," 1944; *Spartacus* (ballet), 1953.

KLEMPERER, OTTO, May 14, 1885 (Breslau, Ger. [now Wroclaw, Pol.])–July 3, 1973. German conductor with German Natl. Theatre, Prague, 1907; with Los Angeles Phil., 1933–39; with Budapest Opera, 1947–50; known for his interpretations of L. BEETHOVEN and G. MAHLER.

KODÁLY, ZOLTÁN, Dec. 16, 1882 (Kecskemet, Hung.)–Mar. 6, 1967. Hungarian composer. Theory and composition teacher at Budapest U., 1907–41; published a collection of Magyar folk music with BELA BARTOK, 1907; style derived from Hungarian folk music. Works: *Psalmus Hungaricus,* 1923; *Hary Janos* (comic opera), 1926.

KREISLER, FRITZ, Feb. 2, 1875 (Vienna, Austria)–Jan. 29, 1962. Austrian-U.S. violin virtuoso. His technique capitalized on intensive vibrato and bow economy.

KUBELIK, RAFAEL JERONÝM, June 29, 1914 (Bychory, Czech.). Czech-Swiss conductor, composer. With Czech. Phil., 1936–39 and 1941–48; music dir. of Chicago Symphony, 1950–53; music dir. of Covent Garden Opera Co., 1955–58; first permanent music dir. of Met. Opera, 1971.

LALO, EDOUARD VICTOR ANTOINE, Jan. 27,

COMPOSERS, CONCERT, BALLET AND OPERA

1823 (Lille, Fr.)-Apr. 22, 1892. French composer. Composed impressionist-style music. Works: *Symphonie espagnole*, 1875; Cello Concerto, 1876; *Namouna* (ballet), 1882; Symphony in G Minor, 1887; *Le Roi d'Ys* (opera), 1888.

LANDOWSKA, WANDA LOUIS, July 5, 1879 (Warsaw, Pol.)-Aug. 16, 1959. French harpsichordist. Researched old music and keyboard instruments; founded a school of early-music interpretation, 1925; influenced the modern revival of interest in the harpsichord; known for her recording of J. S. BACH's "Well-Tempered Clavier."

LEHÁR, FRANZ, Apr. 30, 1870 (Kemárom, Hung.)-Oct. 24, 1948. Hungarian composer. Best known for his operetta *The Merry Widow* (1905).

LEHMANN, LILLI, Nov. 24, 1848 (Wurzburg, Ger.)-May 17, 1929. German operatic soprano, lieder singer. Known for her performances in *Tristan und Isolde* and *Fidelio*; coached by R. WAGNER for debut of *Der Ring des Nibelungen;* repertoire included 170 operatic roles and 600 lieder, mostly by Wagner and W. A. MOZART.

LEONCAVALLO, RUGGIERO, Mar. 8, 1858 (Naples, It.)-Aug. 9, 1919. Italian opera composer, librettist. Reacted against Wagnerian and Romantic Italian opera; best known for *Pagliacci* (1892).

LIND, JENNY, born Johanna Maria Lind, Oct. 6, 1820 (Stockholm, Swed.)-Nov. 2, 1887. Anglo-Swedish operatic and oratorio soprano. Known for her vocal purity and control; made debut in Stockholm, 1838; many internatl. concert and stage tours.

LISZT, FRANZ, Oct. 22, 1811 (Raiding, Hung.)-July 31, 1886. Hungarian piano virtuoso, composer. Advanced playing techniques and methods of composition for the piano; dir. of music at the Weimar Court, Germany, 1843-61; over 700 compositions, including Préludes (1856) and 20 Hungarian Rhapsodies (1851-86).

LUDWIG, CHRISTA, Mar. 16, 1928 (Berlin, Ger.). Austrian operatic mezzo-soprano. Known for her lieder singing; sang with N.Y. Met., 1966-71 and 1973-74; resident member, Staatsoper, Vienna, 1958-   ; repertoire includes *Norma, Lohengrin, Fidelio,* and *Cosi fan Tutti.*

LULLY, JEAN-BAPTISTE, Nov. 28, 1632 (Florence, It.)-Mar. 22, 1687. French composer. Court composer to LOUIS XIV; founder of French Natl. Opera; introduced minuet form to ballet; founder of Paris Opera, 1672. Works: *Au Clair de la Lune; Alceste* (opera), 1674.

MACKENZIE, SIR ALEXANDER CAMPBELL, Aug. 22, 1847 (Edinburgh, Scot.)-Apr. 28, 1935. Scottish composer. Helped to revive British music in late 19th cent.; works include *Scottish Rhapsodies* (1881), cantatas ("The Bride," 1881), and operas (*Colomba,* 1883). Knighted, 1894.

MAHLER, GUSTAV, July 7, 1860 (Kalištĕ, A.-H.)-May 18, 1911. Austrian composer, conductor. Dir. of Imperial Opera, Vienna, 1897-1907; dir. of Met. Opera, 1907; conductor of N.Y. Phil. Orch., 1911; major works include 10 symphonies, 44 lieder, various song cycles; known for complex Romantic symphonies employing enormous numbers of musicians and singers.

MANTOVANI, ANNUNZIO PAOLO, Nov. 15, 1905 (Venice, It.). Anglo-Italian conductor. Famous for the "Mantovani sound," harmonious orchestral arrangements of classics, light classics, and pop music that make good background music, from 1923.

MARKOVA, ALICIA, born Lilian Alicia Marks, Dec. 1, 1910 (London, Eng.). English ballerina. Made debut in DIAGHILEV Ballet at age 14; with Vic-Wells Ballet, 1931-35; dir. (with Anton Dolin) of Markova-Dolin Ballet, 1935-38; dir. of London's Festival Ballet, 1949-52; dir. of Met. Ballet, 1963-69; known for her outstanding performances as Giselle.

MASCAGNI, PIETRO, Dec. 7, 1863 (Levorno, It.)-Aug. 2, 1945. Italian composer. In the "Verismo" school; best known for his one-act opera *Cavalleria Rusticana* (1890).

MASSENET, JULES EMILE FRÉDÉRIC, May 12, 1842 (Montaud, Fr.)-Aug. 13, 1912. French composer. Prof. of music at Paris Conservatoire, 1878-94; composed orchestral and piano music; operas include *Manon* (1884) and *Thais* (1894); won 1863 Prix de Rome for his cantata "David Rizzio."

MASSINE, LEONIDE FEDOROVICH, Aug. 8, 1896 (Moscow, Russia)-Mar. 16, 1979. Russian-U.S. dancer, choreographer. Principal dancer, choreographer, Ballet Russe de Monte Carlo, 1932-38; choreographed "Le Sacre du Printemps," "Le Roi David"; danced in and choreographed the films *The Red Shoes* (1948) and *Tales of Hoffmann* (1952).

MEHTA, ZUBIN, Apr. 29, 1936 (Bombay, India). Indian conductor. Musical dir. of Montreal Symphony, 1961-67; music dir. of Los Angeles Phil., 1962-78; music dir. of New York Phil., 1978-   .

MELBA, NELLIE, born Helen Porter Mitchell, May 19, 1861 (Richmond, Austl.)-Feb. 23, 1931. Australian operatic soprano. Made debut, 1887; repertoire included 25 roles; best known for her roles in *Lakmé, Faust,* and *La Traviata;* famous for her pure tone and effortlessness in singing.

MENDELSSOHN(-Bartholdy), (Jakob Ludwig) **FELIX,** Feb. 3, 1809 (Hamburg, Ger.)-Nov. 4, 1847. German composer, pianist. Founder of Leipzig Conservatory of Music, 1843; Works: Overture to *A Midsummer Night's Dream,* 1826; five symphonies; String Octet, 1826; eight books of "Songs without Words."

MENOTTI, GIAN CARLO, July 7, 1911 (Cadegliano, It.). Italian composer, librettist, producer. Work includes chamber music, songs, operas (*The Consul, The Saint of Bleecker Street, Amahl and the Night Visitors);* established Festival of Two Worlds (Spoleto, It.), 1958; won 1950 and 1954 Pulitzer Prize in music and 1954 New York Drama Critics Circle award.

MEYERBEER, GIACOMO, born Jakob Liebmann Meyer Beer, Sept. 5, 1791 (Tasdorf, Ger.)-May 2, 1864. German operatic composer. Known for spectacular "grand opera" dramatic style. Works: *Robert le Diable,* 1831; *Les Huguenots,* 1836; *L'Africaine,* 1864.

MOISEYEV, IGOR ALEXANDROVICH, Jan. 21, 1906 (Kiev, Ukraine). Soviet ballet dancer, choreographer, director. Dancer, Bolshoi Ballet, 1924-39; dir. of choreography, Moscow Theater for Folk Art, 1936; created Moiseyev Folk Dance Ensemble, the first Soviet folk dance ensemble, 1937.

MONTEUX, PIERRE, Apr. 4, 1875 (Paris, Fr.)-July 1, 1964. French conductor. As conductor of S. DIAGHILEV's Ballets Russes, led world premieres of I. STRAVINSKY's *The Rite of Spring* (1913) and M. RAVEL's *Daphnis et Chloé* (1912); founder and dir. of Paris Symphony, 1929-38.

MONTEVERDI, CLAUDIO GIOVANNI ANTONIO, baptized May 15, 1567 (Cremona, It.)-Nov. 29, 1643. Italian composer. Founder of Italian opera; developed orchestration; music dir. at

THE BOOK OF WHO

St. Mark's Cathedral, Venice from 1613; works include madrigals, sacred music, and operas (*Favola d'Orfeo*, 1607; *L'incoronazione di Poppea*, 1642).

MOUSSORGSKY, MODEST PETROVICH, Mar. 21, 1839 (Karevo, Rus.)–Mar. 28, 1881. Russian composer. A founder of realistic natl. music in Russia; best known works include *Boris Godunov* (opera, 1874), *Pictures from an Exhibition* (piano suite, 1874), and *Night on Bald Mountain* (1860–66).

MOZART, WOLFGANG AMADEUS, Jan. 27, 1756 (Salzburg, Austria)–Dec. 5, 1791. Austrian composer. A child prodigy (violin), patronized by archbishop of Salzburg, 1775–81; chamber music composer to Emperor Joseph II, 1787; composed over 600 works, including chamber music, piano concerti, symphonies, operas (*The Marriage of Figaro* [1786], *Don Giovanni* [1787], *The Magic Flute* [1791]); one of the great musical geniuses of all time.

MUNCH, CHARLES, Sept. 26, 1891 (Strasbourg, Fr.)–Nov. 6, 1968. French conductor. Best known for his interpretations of BRAHMS, DEBUSSY, RAVEL; cofounder and conductor, Paris Philharmonic Orchestra, 1935–38; conductor, Boston Symphony Orch. (1949–62) and Tanglewood Berkshire Music Center (1951–62).

NIJINSKY, VASLAV, Mar. 12, 1890 (Kiev, Rus.)–Apr. 8, 1950. Russian ballet dancer. Leading dancer with Maryinsky Theatre, 1907–11; with Ballets Russes, 1909–12; created roles in *Les Sylphides, Le Spectre de la Rose, Scheherazade*; choreographed *L'Après-midi d'un Faune* and *The Rite of Spring.*

NILSSON, BIRGIT, May 17, 1918 (Karup, Swe.). Swedish operatic soprano. Made Met. Opera debut, 1959; named Swedish Royal Ct. singer; known for roles in R. WAGNER and G. VERDI operas; repertoire includes Brunnhilde, Isolde, Salomé, Elektra, Turandot, Tosca, Lady Macbeth.

NUREYEV, RUDOLF HAMETOVICH, Mar. 17, 1938 (Irkutsk, Rus.). Soviet-British ballet dancer. Soloist with Leningrad Kirov Ballet, 1958; following his defection from USSR, made Paris and U.S. debut, 1962; permanent guest artist at Royal Ballet, London; known for suspended leaps and fast turns; roles include *Swan Lake, Giselle, Don Quixote,* and *Romeo and Juliet.*

OFFENBACH, JACQUES, born Jakob Eberst, June 20, 1819 (Cologne, Ger.)–Oct. 5, 1880. French composer. Created the French operetta; organized and directed the Bouffes-Parisiens, 1855–66; operettas include *Orpheus in the Underworld* (1859) and *La Perichole* (1868); only grand opera is *The Tales of Hoffmann,* unfinished at his death.

OZAWA, SEIJI, Sept. 1, 1935 (Hoten, Jap.). Japanese conductor. Asst. conductor of New York Phil., 1961–62; music dir. of Ravinia Festival, 1964–69; conductor of Toronto Symphony Orch., 1965–69; music dir. of San Francisco Symphony Orch., 1968–   ; music dir. of Boston Symphony Orch., 1973–   .

PAGANINI, NICCOLO, Oct. 27, 1782 (Genoa, It.)–May 27, 1840. Italian composer, violin virtuoso. Composed 24 Capricci for unaccompanied violin, 1801–07; European tours, 1828–32; known for brilliant violin technique, pizzicato, fingering, improvisation.

PALESTRINA, GIOVANNI PIERLUIGI DA, c. 1525 (Palestrina, It.)–Feb. 2, 1594. Italian composer. Chapelmaster at St. John Latern (1550–60) and St. Maria Maggiore (1561–71), Rome; composed three masses (1565), setting the standard for ecclesiastical music; works include over 90 masses and 60 motets, plus lamentations and litanies.

PASTA, GIUDITTA, Apr. 9, 1798 (Saronno, It.)–Apr. 1, 1865. Italian operatic soprano. Known for her large vocal range; BELLINI's *Norma* (1831) and DONIZETTI's *Anna Bolena* (1830) were written for her.

PAVAROTTI, LUCIANO, Oct. 12, 1935 (Modena, It.). Italian lyric tenor. Made debut as Rodolfo *(La Bohème),* 1961; Met. Opera debut, 1968; roles include Edgardo *(Lucia di Lammermoor)* and the Duke *(Rigoletto).*

PAVLOVA, ANNA, Jan. 31, 1882 (St. Petersburg, Rus. [now Leningrad, USSR)–Jan. 23, 1931. Russian ballerina. With Maryinsky Theatre from 1899, as prima ballerina, 1906–13; with Ballets Russes tour, 1909; debut with Met. Opera, 1909; remembered for dancing in *Swan Lake.*

PETIPA, MARIUS, Mar. 11, 1818 (Marseilles, Fr.)–July 14, 1910. French dancer, choreographer. Greatly influenced modern classical Russian ballet; choreographed over 60 ballets; collaborated with P. I. TCHAIKOVSKY on *The Nutcracker* (1892) and *Sleeping Beauty* (1889).

PINZA, EZIO, May 18, 1892 (Rome, It.)–May 9, 1957. Italian operatic bass. Made debut in Rome, 1921; with Met. Opera, 1926–48; many Broadway musicals *(South Pacific,* 1949), and films.

PLISETSKAYA, MAYA MICHAILOVNA, Nov. 20, 1925 (Moscow, USSR). Soviet prima ballerina. Soloist with Bolshoi Ballet, from 1945; known for her fine technique; created the role of Carmen in *Carmen Suite,* 1967.

POULENC, FRANCIS, Jan. 7, 1899 (Paris, Fr.)–Jan. 30, 1963. French composer. Known for his sophisticated, comic style; sacred music includes *Mass in G Major,* 1937. Operas: *Les Mamelles de Tiresias,* 1947; *Dialogues of the Carmelites,* 1953–56.

PROKOFIEV, SERGE, Apr. 23, 1891 (Sontsovka, Rus.)–Mar. 5, 1953. Soviet composer. Influenced the development of Soviet and modern music; works include collaborations on the film *Aleksandr Nevsky* (1938) and the ballets *Romeo and Juliet* (1935–36) and *Peter and the Wolf* (1936); numerous symphonies, piano concerti.

PUCCINI, GIACOMO, Dec. 22, 1858 (Lucca, It.)–Nov. 29, 1924. Italian opera composer. Works include *La Bohème,* (1896), *Tosca,* (1900), *Madama Butterfly* (1904), and *Turandot* (left unfinished at death).

PURCELL, HENRY, c.1658 (London, Eng.)–Nov. 21, 1695. English composer. Composer to King Charles II from 1677; Chapel Royal organist, from 1682; known for his works *Dido and Aeneas* (opera, 1689) and *The Fairy Queen,* and for his incidental music to *A Midsummer Night's Dream.*

RACHMANINOFF, SERGEI VASILYEVICH, Apr. 1, 1873 (Oneg, Rus.)–Mar. 28, 1943. Russian-U.S. piano virtuoso, composer. Composed in the Romantic style; works include three symphonies and four piano concerti, as well as chamber music and other piano works.

RAMPAL, JEAN-PIERRE LOUIS, Jan. 7, 1922 (Marseilles, Fr.). French flutist. Has appeared internationally since 1945.

RAVEL, MAURICE JOSEPH, Mar. 7, 1875 (Ciboure, Fr.)–Dec. 28, 1937. French composer. Known for impressionist style and form. Works: *Pavanne for a Dead Infanta,* 1899; *Daphnis et Chloé* (ballet), 1912; *Boléro,* 1928.

RIMSKY-KORSAKOV, NIKOLAI ANDREYEVICH, Mar. 18, 1844 (Tikhvin, Rus.)–June 21, 1908. Russian composer, teacher, editor. Composed Romantic music. Operas: *The Snow Maiden,* 1882; *Sadko,* 1898; *Le Coq d'or,* 1909. Other works: *Scheherazade,* 1888; *Capriccio espagnol,* 1887; Russian Easter Festival Overture, 1888.

ROSSINI, GIOACCHINO ANTONIO, Feb. 29, 1792 (Pesaro, It.)–Nov. 13, 1868. Italian opera composer. Wrote 39 operas, including *The Barber of Seville* (1816), *The Siege of Corinth* (1826), and *William Tell* (1829).

RUBINSTEIN, ANTON GRIGORIEVICH, Nov. 28, 1829 (Russia)–Nov. 20, 1894. Russian composer, pianist. Founder and dir. of St. Petersburg Conservatory of Music, 1862–67; instituted the Rubinstein Prizes for piano playing and composition; works include symphonies, oratorios, piano pieces.

SAINT-SAËNS, (Charles) CAMILLE, Oct. 9, 1835 (Paris, Fr.)–Dec. 16, 1921. French composer, pianist. Organist at Church of the Madelaine, Paris, 1857–77; helped to found Société Nationale de Musique, 1871. Works: five symphonies; *Samson et Dalila* (opera), 1877; *Carnival of the Animals* (concerti).

SATIE, ERIK ALFRED-LESLIE, May 17, 1866 (Honfleur, Fr.)–July 1, 1925. French composer. Composed unconventional, witty music; influenced Les Six; composed chiefly piano works. Works: *Sarabandes,* 1887; *Gymnopédies,* 1888; *Socrate,* 1918; *Les Mariés de la tour Eiffel* (ballet), 1921.

SCARLATTI, ALESSANDRO, May 2, 1660 (Palermo, It.)–Oct. 24, 1725. Italian composer. Influenced the development of classical harmony; works include operas, sacred music, chamber music; wrote over 600 cantatas, 100 operas, 200 masses.

SCARLATTI, (Giuseppe) DOMENICO, Oct. 26, 1685 (Naples, It.)–July 23, 1757. Italian composer, harpsichordist. Noted for his keyboard sonatas and, especially, his music which aided the technical and musical development of the harpsichord.

SCHUBERT, FRANZ PETER, Jan. 31, 1797 (Himmelpfortyrund, Austria)–Nov. 19, 1828. Austrian composer. Combined classical and Romantic styles; created German lieder in 1814, when he set J. W. GOETHE's poem "Gretchen am Spinnrade" to music; works include lieder, song cycles, chamber music, symphonies, and piano music.

SCHUMANN, ROBERT, June 8, 1810 (Zwickau, Ger.)–July 29, 1856. German composer. Founder and editor of *Die Neue Zeitschrift für Musik;* dir. of music at Düsseldorf, 1850–53; known for piano music and song cycles *(Carnaval, Myrthen, Liederkreise* [1840]).

SCHWARZKOPF, ELISABETH, Dec. 9, 1915 (Jarotschin, Posen). German operatic soprano. Has sung at Vienna Staats Opera (1946–48), Covent Garden (1948–50), La Scala (1949–63) and N.Y. Metropolitan Opera (1964–66); roles include Manon, Violetta, Cio-Cio-San, Mimi, Donna Elvira; has made concert tours singing German lieder.

SCOTTO, RENATA, Feb. 24, 1934 (Savona, It.). Italian operatic soprano. At La Scala, from 1954; at Covent Garden, 1957; with Met. Opera, from 1965; repertoire includes *La Bohème, Manon, Don Giovanni,* and *Madama Butterfly.*

SCRIABIN, ALEKSANDR NIKOLAYEVICH, Jan. 6, 1872 (Moscow, Rus.)–Apr. 27, 1915. Russian composer, pianist, teacher. Moscow Conservatory, 1898–1903; European concert tours, from 1892; works include piano and orchestral music; experimented with harmony.

SEGOVIA, ANDRÉS, Feb. 18, 1894 (Linares, Sp.). Spanish classical-guitar virtuoso. Made debut in Granada, Sp., 1909; extensive international tours; has adapted for guitar the works of J. S. BACH, J. HAYDN, W. A. MOZART; awarded Spain's Gold Medal for meritorious work, 1967.

SHEARER, MOIRA, Jan. 17, 1926 (Dunfermline, Scot.). Scottish ballerina. With Sadler's-Wells Ballet, 1942; danced in films *The Red Shoes* (1948) and *Tales of Hoffmann* (1951); retired 1954.

SHOSTAKOVICH, DIMITRI, Sept. 25, 1906 (St. Petersburg, Rus. [now Leningrad, USSR])–Aug. 9, 1975. Soviet composer. Prof. at Leningrad Conservatory, 1937–75; compositions include 15 symphonies, chamber music, concerti, film scores; awarded 1958 Lenin Prize, 11th Symphony.

SIBELIUS, JEAN, Dec. 8, 1865 (Hameenlinna, Fin.)–Sept. 20, 1957. Finnish composer. Principal creator of Finnish natl. music; known for seven symphonies, tone poems ("Tapiola" [1925] and "Finlandia" [1900]), orchestral suites ("The Swan of Tuonela" [1893], violin music.

SLEZAK, LEO, Aug. 18, 1873 (Krasna Hora, Bohemia [now Czech.])–June 1, 1946. Austrian operatic tenor. Sang with Vienna Staatopera, 1901–26; made Covent Garden debut (1909) and Metropolitan Opera debut (1913); known for his Wagnerian roles. (Father of actor WALTER SLEZAK.)

SMETANA, BEDŘICH, Mar. 2, 1824 (Leitomischl, Bohemia)–May 12, 1884. Czech composer. Conductor with Natl. Theater, Prague, 1866–74; best known for his cycle of six symphonic poems *(My Country)* and his opera *The Bartered Bride,* (1886).

SOLTI, SIR GEORG, Oct. 21, 1912 (Budapest, Hung.). Anglo-Hung. conductor. With Budapest Opera House, 1930–39; with Munich Opera, 1952–60; music dir. of Covent Garden, 1961–71; with Chicago Symphony Orch., 1969–   ; artistic dir. and conductor of London Phil., 1979–   ; has won twelve Grammy awards and 5 Grand Prix du Disque Mondiale.

SOMES, MICHAEL, Sept. 28, 1917 (Horsley, Eng.). English ballet dancer. Principal dancer at Sadler's Wells Ballet, from 1938; frequent partner of M. FONTEYN; dir. of Royal Ballet, 1963–70.

STRAUSS (The Younger), JOHANN ("The Waltz King"), Oct. 25, 1825 (Vienna, Austria)–June 3, 1899. Austrian composer. Combined father's band with his (1849) and toured Europe, Russia and England, to 1874; wrote 400–500 pieces, mostly dance music and several operas. Works: *The Blue Danube,* 1867; *Artist's Life,* 1867; *Tales from the Vienna Woods,* 1868; *Wine, Women and Song,* 1869; *Wiener Blut,* 1871; *Die Fledermaus,* 1874.

STRAUSS, RICHARD, June 11, 1864 (Munich, Ger.)–Sept. 8, 1949. German composer. Known chiefly for operas *(Der Rosenkavalier,* 1911; *Salomé,* 1905; *Elektra,* 1909; *Ariadne auf Naxos,* 1912) and tone poems ("Don Juan," 1889; "Also

THE BOOK OF WHO

Sprach Zarathustra," 1896); pres. of Reichsmusik-kamer (Nazi govt. music agency), 1933–35.
STRAVINSKY, IGOR FYODOROVICH, June 17, 1882 (Oranienbaum, Rus.)–Apr. 6, 1971. U.S. composer. Best known for his ballets, including *The Firebird* (1910), *Petrouchka* (1911), and *The Rite of Spring* (1913); works also include chamber music, concerti, orchestral music.
SULLIVAN, SIR ARTHUR S(eymour). May 13, 1842 (London, Eng.)–Nov. 22, 1900. English composer, conductor. Most noted for collaboration with W. S. GILBERT (1871–1900), which produced enduringly popular satiric operas. Works: *Trial by Jury*, 1875; *H.M.S. Pinafore*, 1878; *The Pirates of Penzance*, 1880; *The Mikado*, 1885.
SUTHERLAND, DAME JOAN, Nov. 7, 1926 (Sydney, Austl.). Australian coloratura soprano. Best known for heroine roles in V. BELLINI and G. DONIZETTI operas; repertoire includes *Lucia di Lammermoor*, *La Traviata*, *Julius Caesar*, *Norma*, *Tales of Hoffmann;* named Dame of the British Empire, 1979.
TAGLIONI, MARIE, Apr. 23, 1804 (Stockholm, Swe.)–Apr. 24, 1884. Swedish-Italian ballet dancer. Popularized dancing on pointe; bell-like skirt worn in *La Sylphide* (1832) became accepted uniform for classical dancers; initiated system of ballet examination at Paris Opéra.
TCHAIKOVSKY, PETER ILYICH, May 7, 1840 (Votkinsk, Rus.)–Nov. 6, 1893. Russian composer. Advocate of Western style of music composition with Slavic character; known for classical ballet scores, including *Sleeping Beauty* (1890), *Swan Lake* (1877), and *The Nutcracker* (1892); composed six symphonies, eleven operas (*Eugene Onegin*, 1879), and many orchestral works (*Marche Slav* [1876], *1812 Overture* [1880], *Capriccio Italien* [1880]).
TEBALDI, RENATA, Jan. 2, 1922 (Pesaro, It.). Italian operatic lyric soprano. Made debut, 1944; at La Scala, 1946; made U.S. debut (San Francisco), 1950; with Met. Opera, 1955; repertoire includes *La Bohème*, *Madama Butterfly*, *Tosca*.
TELEMANN, GEORG PHILIPP, Mar. 14, 1681 (Magdeburg, Ger.)–June 25, 1767. German baroque composer. Music dir. at Frankfurt (1712–21) and Hamburg (1721–67); works include 40 operas and 600 overtures, as well as sacred music, vocal and instrumental music, and chamber music.
TETRAZZINI, LUISA, June 29, 1871 (Florence, It.)–Apr. 28, 1940. Italian operatic coloratura soprano. Made debut, 1895; at Covent Garden, 1907; at Met. Opera, 1908; after WW I, gave recitals and taught; the dish Chicken Tetrazzini is named after her.
TOSCANINI, ARTURO, Mar. 25, 1867 (Parma, It.)–Jan. 16, 1957. Italian conductor. Music dir. of La Scala, from 1898; conductor of New York Phil., 1928–36; dir. of NBC Symphony Orch., 1937–54; known for energetic interpretations of G. VERDI operas, L. BEETHOVEN symphonies, R. WAGNER's music; conducted from memory.
TUDOR, ANTONY, born William Cook, Apr. 4, 1908 (London, Eng.). English dancer, choreographer, teacher. Dir. and choreographer with Ballet Rambert, 1930–38; a founder of London Ballet, 1938; with ABT, 1939–   ; ballet dir. of Met. Opera, 1957–63; known for the development of the psychological ballet.
ULANOVA, GALINA SERGEYEVNA, Jan. 8, 1910 (St. Petersburg, Rus. [now Leningrad, USSR])

Russian prima ballerina. With Kirov Ballet, from 1934; with Bolshoi Ballet, 1944–62; presently ballet mistress and coach of Bolshoi Ballet; known for personality and warmth of dance in *Giselle, The Dying Swan, The Red Poppy;* author of *The Bolshoi Ballet Story* (1959).
VAUGHN WILLIAMS, RALPH, Oct. 13, 1872 (Down Ampney, Eng.)–Aug. 26, 1958. English composer. Founder of nationalist movement in English music; musical themes draw upon English folk songs of Tudor period. Works: *A London Symphony*, 1914; *A Pastoral Symphony*, 1921; Sixth Symphony, 1947.
VERDI, GIUSEPPE, Oct. 10, 1813 (Le Reneole, It.)–Jan. 27, 1901. Italian opera composer. Composed 27 operas, including *Nabucco* (1842), *Rigoletto* (1851), *Il Trovatore* (1853), *La Traviata* (1853), *Aida* (1872), *Otello* (1887), and *Falstaff* (1892); also known for his Requiem Mass (1874) and other sacred music.
VICKERS, JON, Oct. 29, 1926 (Prince Albert, Sask., Can.). Canadian operatic tenor. Made Covent Garden debut, 1957; Met. Opera debut, 1960; repertoire includes both lyrical and dramatic roles.
VILLA-LOBOS, HEITOR, Mar. 5, 1887 (Rio de Janeiro, Braz.)–Nov. 17, 1959. Brazilian composer, music educator. Proponent of Brazilian nationalism in music. Works: *Chôros*, 1920–29; twelve symphonies, 1920–58.
VIVALDI, ANTONIO, Mar. 4, 1678 (Venice, It.)–July 28, 1741. Italian composer, violin virtuoso. Composed instrumental music of late baroque period; composed over 450 concerti for solo instruments accompanied by string orchestra; most famous work is *The Four Seasons*.
WAGNER, RICHARD, May 22, 1813 (Leipzig, Ger.)–Feb. 13, 1883. German opera composer. Opera themes derived from medieval legends; involved in German revolution of 1848; forced into exile in 1849. Operas: *The Flying Dutchman*, 1843; *Tannhäuser*, 1845; *Lohengrin*, 1848; *Der Ring des Nibelungen*, 1876; *Tristan und Isolde*, 1857; *Parsifal*, 1882.
WALTER, BRUNO, born B. W. Schlesinger, Sept. 15, 1876 (Berlin Ger.)–Feb. 17, 1962. German conductor. With Vienna Opera, 1901–12; conducted premier of G. MAHLER's Ninth Symphony, 1912; with Met. Opera, from 1941; with New York Phil., 1947–49.
WEBER, CARL MARIA VON, Nov. 18, 1786 (Eutin, Ger.)–June 5, 1826. German composer. Founder of German natl. opera; works include piano compositions, chamber music, operas (*Euryanthe*, 1823; *Oberon*, 1826); dir. of Dresden Opera, 1817.
WEBERN, ANTON VON, Dec. 3, 1883 (Vienna, Austria)–Sept. 15, 1945. Austrian composer. Influenced 20th-cent. music by adopting the 12-tone system of composition of his teacher, A. SCHOENBERG; his music was banned by Nazi regime.
WEILL, KURT, Mar. 2, 1900 (Dessau, Ger.)–Apr. 3, 1950. German composer. Wrote several of the most popular operas of the 20th-cent. and was a major force in the musical theater. Husband of LOTTE LENYA, the legendary cabaret singer, he wrote much of his greatest music for her; a frequent collaborator with BERTOLT BRECHT. Works: *The Rise and Fall of the City of Mahagonny*, 1927; *Threepenny Opera*, 1928; *Knickerbocker Holiday*, 1938; *Lady in the Dark*, 1941; *One Touch of Venus*, 1943; *Street Scene*, 1947; *Lost in the Stars*, 1949.

PHILOSOPHERS AND RELIGIOUS LEADERS

U.S. PHILOSOPHERS AND RELIGIOUS LEADERS

ADLER, FELIX, Aug. 13, 1851 (Alzey, Ger.)–Apr. 24, 1933. U.S. educator, ethical reformer. Founded and lectured at the New York Society for Ethical Culture, 1876; professor of political and social ethics, Columbia U. 1902–33. *Creed and Deed,* 1877; *Life and Destiny,* 1905; *Religion of Duty,* 1905; *An Ethical Philosophy of Life,* 1918.

ALCOTT, AMOS BRONSON, Nov. 29, 1799 (Wolcott, Conn.)–Mar. 4, 1888. U.S. philosopher, teacher, reformer. A leader of the New England Transcendentalist group; started several innovative schools; founded Fruitlands, a cooperative vegetarian community, 1843; directed the Concord School of Philosophy, 1879–88; a nonresident member of Brook Farm. *Record of a School,* 1835. (Father of LOUISA MAY ALCOTT.)

ASBURY, FRANCIS, Aug. 20, 1745 (Handsworth, Eng.)–Mar. 31, 1816. U.S. bishop. His efforts did much to assure the continuance of the Methodist Episcopal Church in the new world; supt. of the church, 1784; bishop, 1785; church membership grew from 300 to over 200,000 at the time of his death.

BLAKE, EUGENE CARSON, Nov. 7, 1906 (St. Louis, Mo.). U.S. Presbyterian churchman, ecumenical leader. Pres., National Council of the Churches of Christ in the U.S.A., 1954–57; general secy., World Council of Churches, 1966–72; pres., Bread for the World, 1974– .

BOYD, MALCOLM, June 8, 1923 (Buffalo, N.Y.). U.S. Episcopal priest, author. Priest-activist involved in civil and gay rights; experimented with new ways of communicating the gospel through music and theater. *Are You Running with Me Jesus?,* 1965; *Free to Live, Free to Die,* 1967.

BREWSTER, WILLIAM, 1566 (Nottinghamshire, Eng.)–Apr. 10, 1644. English lay elder. Sailed to America on the *Mayflower* (1609) and became the spiritual leader of the Plymouth Colony; heavily influenced the formulation of the colony's doctrines, worship, and practices.

CABRINI, MARIA FRANCESCA, SAINT FRANCIS XAVIER, ("Mother Cabrini"), July 15, 1850 (Lodigiano, It.)–Dec. 22, 1917. Italian-U.S. religious worker who founded the Missionary Sisters of the Sacred Heart; first U.S. citizen to be canonized, 1946.

CARROLL, JOHN, Jan. 8, 1735 (Upper Marlboro, Md.)–Dec. 3, 1815. U.S. clergyman. The first R.C. bishop in the U.S.; founded Georgetown U., 1789; accompanied BENJAMIN FRANKLIN on a fruitless mission to persuade Canada to join the revolutionary cause.

COFFIN, WILLIAM SLOANE, JR., June 1, 1924 (New York, N.Y.). U.S. clergyman. A leader in the Vietnam War peace movement; chaplain, Yale U., 1958–75; pastor, Riverside Church (New York City), 1977– .

COHEN, MORRIS RAPHAEL, July 25, 1880 (Minsk, Rus.)–Jan. 28, 1947. U.S. philosopher, author. Prof. of philosophy, C. of the City of New York, 1912–38; first U.S. philosopher to work extensively on legal philosophy; a major contributor to logic and the philosophy of science and history. *Reason and Nature,* 1931; *Law and the Social Order,* 1933; *Preface to Logic,* 1944; *The Faith of a Liberal,* 1946.

COOKE, TERENCE JAMES, Mar. 21, 1921 (New York, N.Y.). U.S. R.C. cardinal (from 1969–). Archbishop of New York, 1968– ; has distinguished himself in areas of finance, fundraising, and supervision of building programs.

COTTON, JOHN, Dec. 4, 1585 (Derbyshire, Eng.)–Dec. 23, 1652. English Puritan leader of the Massachusetts Bay Colony in America. Influenced the Congregational Church immensely and pushed it in a theocratic direction; responsible for the expulsion of ANNE HUTCHINSON (1637) and ROGER WILLIAMS (1635) from the colony.

COUGHLIN, CHARLES EDWARD, Oct. 25, 1891 (Hamilton, Ont., Can.)–Oct. 27, 1979. U.S. R.C. priest. Gained prominence in 1930s through his radio addresses bitterly opposing administration of Pres. FRANKLIN D. ROOSEVELT, 1936; his magazine, *Social Justice* (1936–42), was banned from U.S. mails for violation of the Espionage Act.

CUSHING, RICHARD JAMES, Aug. 24, 1895 (Boston, Mass.)–Nov. 2, 1970. U.S. R.C. cardinal. Archbishop of Boston, 1944–70; highly successful director of the Boston office of the Society for the Propagation of the Faith; was called "the most pervasive social force" in Boston in the late 1940s and early 1950s.

DAVENPORT, JOHN, baptized Apr. 9, 1597 (Coventry, Eng.)–Mar. 11, 1670. American colonial clergyman. Led the settlers of the colony of New Haven, 1638; laid the foundation for the establishment of Yale C. in 1700 by founding Hopkins C.

DEWEY, JOHN, Oct. 20, 1859 (Burlington, Vt.)–June 1, 1952. U.S. philosopher, educator. Adherent of pragmatism as formulated by WILLIAM JAMES; helped inaugurate the theories and practice of progressive education. *The School and Society,* 1899; *Democracy and Education,* 1916.

DOUGLASS, TRUMAN B., July 15, 1901 (Grinnell, Ia.)–May 27, 1969. U.S. clergyman. A moving spirit in the unification of the Congregational, Evangelical, and Reformed denominations into the United Church of Christ, 1957; his early concern for blacks, problems of urban living, and ethics in mass communication profoundly affected modern Protestantism.

DURANT, WILLIAM JAMES, Nov. 5, 1885 (North Adams, Mass.). U.S. philosopher. Critic of popular philosophy and history; attempted to humanize knowledge by grounding the story of speculative thinking in the lives of great philosophers. *The Story of Philosophy,* 1926; *The Story of Civilization,* 10 vols., 1935–67.

EDDY, MARY MORSE, née Baker, July 16, 1821 (Bow, N.H.)–Dec. 3, 1910. U.S. religious leader, founder of the Christian Science movement. Attempting to relieve a chronic spinal malady, became interested in health; after a fall (1866) was healed by reading the New Testament (Matt. 9:1-8); developed a system of thought based on her experience and the Bible; organized first Christian Science Church, 1879; founded the *Christian Science Monitor,* 1883; substituted a "lesson-sermon" for a sermon preached from the pulpit. *Science and Health,* 1875; *Rudimental Divine Science,* 1908.

EDWARDS, JONATHAN, Oct. 5, 1703 (East

THE BOOK OF WHO

Windsor, Conn.)–Mar. 22, 1758. American colonial theologian, philosopher. The greatest theologian of American Puritanism; a leader of the Great Awakening of the 1740s; fought against the current theological stream of thought by emphasizing man's dependence on God, the role of love in religion, and the need for genuine faith in obtaining church membership. *History of the Work of Redemption*, 1737; *Freedom of the Will*, 1754; *Treatise on Religious Affections*, 1796.

ELIOT, JOHN, ("Apostle to the Indians"), Aug. 1604 (Widford, Eng.)–May 21, 1690. English Puritan missionary in colonial America. His translation of the Bible into the Algonquin language (1661–63) was the first Bible printed in North America; his work set a pattern for Indian missions for the next two centuries.

FOSDICK, HARRY EMERSON, May 24, 1878 (Buffalo, N.Y.)–Oct. 5, 1969. U.S. clergyman. Liberal Prot. minister who stood at the center of the Prot. liberal-fundamentalist controversies; pastor, Riverside Church (New York City) 1926–46; preached on the *National Vespers* nationwide radio program, 1926–46.

GRAHAM, WILLIAM FRANKLIN ("Billy"), Nov. 17, 1918 (Charlotte, N.C.). U.S. clergyman. Southern Baptist evangelist who first came to national attention with his Los Angeles campaign, 1949; his continued success has created a large organization that he leads on preaching tours worldwide. *Revival in Our Times*, 1950; *The Seven Deadly Sins*, 1955.

HARRIS, WILLIAM TORREY, Sept. 10, 1835 (Killingly, Conn.)–Nov. 5, 1909. U.S. philosopher. Leading U.S. Hegelian; interpreter of German philosophical thought to America; editor of the *Journal of Speculative Philosophy*, 1867–93; U.S. commissioner of education, 1889–1906; editor-in-chief of *Webster's New Internatl. Dictionary*, first edition, 1909. *Introduction to the Study of Philosophy*, 1889.

HECK, BARBARA, née Ruckle. 1734 (County Limerick, Ire.)–Aug. 17, 1804. Irish-American religious leader. Organized first Methodist church in America, in New York City, 1765; called the Mother of Methodism in the U.S.

HESBURGH, THEODORE MARTIN, May 25, 1917 (Syracuse, N.Y.). U.S. educator, religious leader. Ordained as R.C. priest, 1943; pres., Notre Dame U., 1952–   ; under his chairmanship (1969–72), U.S. Commission on Civil Rights issued a report (1970) critical of the government's failure to enforce civil rights legislation. Awarded Presidential Medal of Freedom, 1964.

HOCKING, WILLIAM E., Aug. 10, 1873 (Cleveland, Ohio)–June 12, 1966. U.S. philosopher. Prof. of philosophy, Harvard U., 1914–43; an idealist philosopher who attempted to discern speculative issues in the practical problems of living. *The Meaning of God in Human Experience*, 1912; *The Spirit of World Politics*, 1932.

HOFFER, ERIC, July 25, 1902 (New York, N.Y.). U.S. author, migrant worker, longshoreman, social philosopher. *The True Believer*, 1951; *The Passionate State of Mind*, 1955; *Reflections on the Human Condition*, 1972.

HOOKER, THOMAS, July 7, 1586 (Marfield, Eng.)–July 19, 1647. English clergyman. Founded Hartford, Conn., 1636; one of the drafters of the Connecticut Constitution, perhaps the first major document of American democracy, 1639.

HUBBARD, LAFAYETTE RONALD, Mar. 13, 1911 (Tilden, Neb.). U.S. religious leader, founder of Scientology. A science-fiction writer until 1950; formulated dianetics, a method of achieving mental and physical health, 1938; in the early 1950s, founded Scientology, a religious movement based on dianetics; withdrew from the director of the Church of Scientology, 1966. *Dianetics: The Modern Science of Mental Health*, 1977.

HUTCHINSON, ANNE, née Marbury, baptized July 20, 1591 (Lincolnshire, Eng.)–Aug. or Sept. 1643. American colonial religious liberal. Banished from the Massachusetts Bay Colony for her religious views, which opposed those of the New England Puritans and Calvinists, 1637; emigrated with her family to Rhode Island; killed in an Indian massacre.

JAMES, HENRY, June 2, 1811 (Albany, N.Y.)–Dec. 18, 1882. U.S. theologian. Rebelled against Calvinism; influenced by EMANUEL SWEDENBORG and in social philosophy, by CHARLES FOURIER. (Father of WILLIAM JAMES and novelist HENRY JAMES.)

JAMES, WILLIAM, Jan. 11, 1842 (New York, N.Y.)–Aug. 26, 1910. U.S. philosopher, psychologist. The first distinguished American psychologist and a leading philosopher of pragmatism; his functional psychology, experimental religious philosophy, and pragmatism function as an interrelated whole; his lively writing style spurred the influence and popularity of his ideas. *Principles of Psychology*, 1890; *The Varieties of Religious Experience*, 1902; *Pragmatism*, 1907. (Son of theologian HENRY JAMES; brother of novelist HENRY JAMES.)

JUNGREIS, ESTHER, 1938 (Hungary). U.S. revivalist. Founded Hineni ("Here I Am"), a Jewish revivalist organization, 1973; has lectured widely to bring assimilated Jews back into the fold.

KOHLER, KAUFMANN, May 10, 1843 (Fürth, Ger.)–Jan. 28, 1926. U.S. rabbi, leader of Reformed Judaism. Pres., Hebrew Union C., 1903–22; scholar and rabbi of Temple Beth-El (New York City), 1903–22; an editor of *The Jewish Encyclopedia. Backwards or Forwards: Lectures on Reform Judaism*, 1885; *The Origins of the Synagogue and the Church*, 1929.

KUHLMAN, KATHRYN, 1907 (Concordia, Mo.)–Feb. 20, 1976. U.S. religious leader, faith healer. Preached the Holy Spirit's power to cure; set up an organization devoted to missionary churches, drug rehabilitation, and the education of blind children.

LAMY, JOHN BAPTIST, born Jean Baptiste l'Amy, Oct. 11, 1814 (Lempdes, Fr.)–Feb. 13, 1888. U.S. R.C. priest. Archbishop of southwestern U.S., 1875–85; established the first school to teach English in Santa Fe, N.M.; successfully extended the R.C. faith to the Indians and whites of the Southwest. (The model for WILLA CATHER's protagonist in *Death Comes for the Archbishop*.)

LANGDON, WILLIAM CHAUNCEY, Aug. 19, 1831 (Burlington, Vt.)–Oct. 28, 1895. U.S. Episcopal clergyman. One of the early organizers of the Young Men's Christian Association in the U.S.; active in the ecumenical movement.

MARCUSE, HERBERT, July 19, 1898 (Berlin, Ger.)–July 29, 1979. German-U.S. political philosopher. Fled Nazi Germany, 1933; his ideas, notably that modern American society was repressive, became popular with American student radicals in the 1960s; taught at Columbia, Harvard, and Brandeis, and, since 1965, at the U. of California. *Eros and Civilization*, 1958; *One-Dimensional Man*, 1964.

MARSHALL, PETER, May 27, 1902 (Coatbridge, Scot.)–Jan. 25, 1949. U.S. Presbyterian clergyman. Chaplain to the U.S. Senate, 1947–48; known for his deft phraseology; subject of the book *A Man Called Peter* (by his wife, CATHERINE MARSHALL), as well as a film of the same name.

MATHER, COTTON, Feb. 12, 1663 (Boston, Mass.)-Feb. 13, 1728. American colonial clergyman. Pastor, Second Church of Boston; a prolific writer, helped establish New England as a cultural center; his interest in science led him to advocate inoculation for smallpox and the use of scientific evidence in witchcraft trials. *Magnalia Christi Americana,* 1702. (Son of INCREASE MATHER.)

MATHER, INCREASE, June 21, 1639 (Dorchester, Mass.)-Aug. 23, 1723. American colonial clergyman. Pastor of the Second Church of Boston, 1664-1723; pres. of Harvard C., 1685-1701; after Massachusetts' loss of its charter, obtained a new charter from King William, 1688; wrote the most outspoken and earliest public utterance in New England against the practices of the witchcraft—*Cases of Conscience Concerning Evil Spirits* (1693). (Father of COTTON MATHER.)

MCPHERSON, AIMEE SEMPLE, born A. Elizabeth Kennedy, Oct. 9, 1890 (Ingersoll, Ont., Can.)-Sept. 27, 1944. U.S. religious leader. Best-known woman evangelist of her day. Itinerant revivalist, 1916-23; founded the International Church of the Foursquare Gospel and built the Angelus Temple in Los Angeles, serving as its minister, 1923-44.

MOODY, DWIGHT LYMAN, Feb. 5, 1837 (Northfield, Mass.)-Dec. 22, 1899. U.S. evangelist, popular urban revivalist. Worked for YMCA; led a highly successful evangelist campaign in Great Britain, 1873-75; founded in Chicago two secondary schools and the Bible Inst. for Home and Foreign Missions (1889).

MOTT, JOHN RALEIGH, May 25, 1865 (Livingston Manor, N.Y.)-Jan. 31, 1955. U.S. evangelist, Methodist layman. Student secy., International Committee of the YMCA, 1888-1915; organized World Missionary Conference, 1910; pres., World's Alliance of YMCAs, 1926-37; shared Nobel Peace Prize with EMILY G. BALCH, for his work in international church and missionary movements, 1946.

MUHAMMAD, ELIJAH, born Elijah Poole, Oct. 7, 1897 (nr. Sandersville, Ga.)-Feb. 25, 1975. U.S. black nationalist leader. An automobile assembly-line worker, became follower of Wali Farad, who had founded Temple of Islam in Detroit; upon Farad's disappearance (1934), took over leadership of movement, which became known as the Nation of Islam or the Black Muslims; calling himself the "Messenger of Allah," preached that only salvation for U.S. black people was withdrawal into an autonomous state.

MUHLENBERG, HEINRICH MELCHIOR, Sept. 6, 1711 (Einbeck, Ger.)-Oct. 7, 1787. U.S. Lutheran clergyman, often called the patriarch of Lutheranism. Led all Lutheran groups in the colonies; organized first Lutheran synod in America, 1748; helped prepare a uniform liturgy, a hymnal, and an ecclesiastical constitution.

NEUMANN, JOHN NEPOMUCENE, SAINT, March 28, 1811 (Prahatice, Bohemia)-Jan. 5, 1860. U.S. R.C. bishop. As fourth bishop of Philadelphia see, oversaw much building and an expansion of membership, 1851-60; helped establish the Sisters of Notre Dame (1877) and the Sisters of the Third Order of St. Francis (1855); beatified, 1963; canonized, 1977.

NIEBUHR, REINHOLD, June 21, 1892 (Wright City, Mo.)-June 1, 1971. U.S. theologian, one of the most influential of the 20th cent. Prof., Union Theological Seminary (New York City), 1928-60; a critic of theological liberalism; proposed a Christian Realism that recognized the persistence of evil and the egotism and pride of nations and other social groups; political activist. *The Nature and Destiny of Man,* 1941, 1943; *Moral Man and Immoral Society,* 1932.

O'HAIR, MADALYN, née Mays, Apr. 13, 1919 (Pittsburgh, Pa.). U.S. lawyer. Well-known atheist, the principal in the U.S. Supreme Court case (1963) that removed Bible reading and prayer recitation from public schools. Originated *American Atheist Magazine,* 1965; dir. of the American Atheist Center, 1965-77; founder of the United World Atheists, 1970. *Why I Am an Atheist,* 1965.

OLCOTT, HENRY STEEL, Aug. 2, 1832 (Orange, N.J.)-Feb. 17, 1907. U.S. farmer, lawyer. A founder of the Theosophical Society, which he served as pres., 1875-1907. *A Buddhist Catechism,* 1881; *Theosophy, Religion and Occult Science,* 1885.

PAINE, THOMAS, Jan. 29, 1737 (Norfolk, Eng.)-June 8, 1809. American colonial political philosopher, pamphleteer. His *Common Sense* (1776), advocating immediate independence from England, was widely considered the best argument for the cause; published *Crisis* (12 issues), upholding the colonial cause, 1776-83; in *Rights of Man* (1791), inspired by the French Revolution, proposed to end poverty, illiteracy, unemployment, and war; published *Age of Reason* (2 vols., 1794 and 1796), a philosophical discussion of his deist beliefs.

PEALE, NORMAN VINCENT, May 31, 1898 (Bowersville, Ohio). U.S. clergyman. Prominent religious author and radio preacher on the national program *The Art of Living;* minister, Marble Collegiate Reformed Church (New York City), 1932- . *You Can Win,* 1938; *The Power of Positive Thinking,* 1952.

PEIRCE, CHARLES SANTIAGO SANDERS, Sept. 10, 1839 (Cambridge, Mass.)-Apr. 19, 1914. U.S. philosopher, logician. A founder of pragmatism; did valuable work in mathematics, pendulum work, and logic; considered the effects of an object to be part of its conception as a principle of method. *Collected Papers of Charles Sanders Peirce,* 8 vols., 1931-58.

PIKE, JAMES ALBERT, Feb. 14, 1913 (Oklahoma, City, Okla.)-Sept. 7, 1969. U.S. Episcopalian priest, lawyer. As dean of Cathedral of St. John the Divine in New York City (1952-58), spoke out against McCarthyism, advocated civil rights and planned parenthood; bishop of California, 1958-66; joined Center for Democratic Institutions, 1966; renounced church to form Fndn. for Religious Transition, 1968; died on an expedition to the Judean desert.

PRIESAND, SALLY, June 27, 1946 (Cleveland, Ohio). U.S. rabbi. The first U.S. woman to be ordained as a rabbi, 1972; asst. rabbi (1972-77) and associate rabbi (1977-79) of New York City's Stephen Wise Free Synagogue.

RAPP, GEORGE, Nov. 1, 1757 (Württemberg, Ger.)-Aug. 7, 1847. German-U.S. religious leader, founder of the Harmonists. Emigrated to Pennsylvania with a group of followers who literally interpreted the Bible, 1803; established a settlement called Harmony, where they lived communally and in celibacy; formed other settlements and continued as spiritual head of Harmonists until his death.

THE BOOK OF WHO

ROBERTS, (Granville) ORAL, Jan. 24, 1918 (Ada, Okla.). U.S. evangelist. Evangelist, 1936–41; began worldwide evangelistic ministry through crusades, radio, TV, and print media, 1947; founder and pres. of Oral Roberts U., Tulsa, Okla., 1963– . *If You Need Healing, Do These Things,* 1947; *God's Formula for Success and Prosperity,* 1956; *The Miracle Book,* 1972.

ROYCE, JOSIAH, Nov. 20, 1855 (Grass Valley, Calif.)–Sept. 14, 1916. U.S. idealist philosopher who stressed individuality, will and loyalty. *The Religious Aspect of Philosophy,* 1885; *The World and the Individual,* 1900–01; *The Philosophy of Loyalty,* 1908.

RUSSELL, CHARLES T., Feb. 16, 1852 (Pittsburgh, Pa.)–Oct. 31, 1916. U.S. religious leader. Founded the Russellites, a sect of millennialists; founded the journal *The Watchtower;* his sect formed the nucleus for the Jehovah's Witnesses.

RUTHERFORD, JOSEPH FRANKLIN ("Judge"), Nov. 8, 1869 (Booneville, Mo.)–Jan. 8, 1942. U.S. religious leader, author. Pres., Jehovah's Witnesses (called Russellites before 1925), 1916–42; indicted for obstructing the war effort by counseling people to be conscientious objectors, 1917.

SANTAYANA, GEORGE, Dec. 16, 1863 (Madrid, Sp.)–Sept. 26, 1952. U.S. philosopher, poet. Taught philosophy at Harvard U. (1889–1912), then resided chiefly in Europe; in early work, applied the psychological approach to life of the mind, later turned to a more classical philosophical approach. *The Sense of Beauty,* 1896; *The Life of Reason,* 1905–06; *Skepticism and Animal Faith,* 1923; *The Realms of Being,* 4 vols., 1927, 1930, 1937, and 1940.

SHEEN, FULTON JOHN, born Peter John Sheen, May 8, 1895 (El Paso, Ill.)–Dec. 9, 1979. U.S. R.C. bishop. Outstanding orator, well-known as a radio broadcaster from 1930; known for his attacks on communism and Freudianism. *The Cross and the Crisis,* 1938; *Communism and the Conscience of the West,* 1948.

SMITH, JOSEPH, Dec. 23, 1805 (Sharon, Vt.)–June 27, 1844. U.S. religious leader. Founder of the Church of Jesus Christ of Latter-day Saints, usually called the Mormon Church. At age 14 had a revelation; later visions told him of buried plates, which he allegedly received later from an angel (1827) and translated into *The Book of Mormon* (1830); founded church at Fayette, N.Y., 1830; moved colony to Ohio, Missouri, then Illinois; ruled despotically; arrested by non-Mormons, taken from jail in Carthage, Ill., by mob and assassinated.

SPELLMAN, FRANCIS JOSEPH, May 4, 1889 (Whitman, Mass.)–Dec. 2 1967. U.S. R.C. cardinal. Archbishop of New York, 1939–67; interests lay in education and charities; an advocate of state aid to parochial schools.

STAPLETON, RUTH, née Carter, c.1930 (Plains, Ga.). U.S. evangelist. A nondenominational Christian evangelist; spiritual adviser to LARRY FLYNT, the publisher of *Hustler;* based at "Holovita" (whole life), a retreat near Dallas, Tex. *The Gift of Inner Healing,* 1976; *The Experience of Inner Healing,* 1977. (Sister of JIMMY CARTER.)

SUNDAY, WILLIAM ASHLEY ("Billy"), Nov. 19, 1862 (Ames, Ia.)–Nov. 6, 1935. U.S. revivalist, professional baseball player. As an urban revivalist, possessed a theatrical mastery of idiomatic language; supported Prohibition; accepted the support of the Ku Klux Klan; conducted more than 300 revivals with an estimated attendance of 100 million.

THOREAU, HENRY DAVID, July 12, 1817 (Concord, Mass.)–May 6, 1862. U.S. essayist, poet, naturalist. Best known for his book *Walden* (1854), in which he described his solitary life in a cabin near Walden Pond; a member of the Transcendentalist group of the mid-19th cent. and a friend of RALPH WALDO EMERSON; came to the defense of JOHN BROWN's raid on Harper's Ferry, 1859. *Civil Disobedience,* 1845.

TILLICH, PAUL, Aug. 20, 1886 (Starzeddel, Prussia)–Oct. 22, 1965. German-U.S. philosopher, theologian. A Protestant thinker who attempted to bring Christianity and contemporary culture together; an opponent of the Nazi movement, he was barred from German universities and came to Union Theological Seminary (New York City), 1933; used a method of "correlation between the human questions of the times and the divine answers of Christian revelation." *The Courage to Be,* 1952; *Dynamics of Faith,* 1957; *Systematic Theology,* 1951, 1963.

TURNER, HENRY MCNEAL, Feb. 1, 1831 (Newberry Court House, S.C.)–May 8, 1915. U.S. Methodist Episcopal bishop, government worker. One of the principal advocates of the return of black people to Africa; the first black chaplain commissioned in the U.S., 1863; bishop of the African Methodist Episcopal Church, 1880.

VINCENT, JOHN HEYL, Feb. 23, 1832 (Tuscaloosa, Ala.)–May 9, 1920. U.S. Methodist bishop. Attempted to improve teaching methods used in Sunday schools; organized a Sunday-school teachers' institute at Chautauqua, N.Y., which grew into the Chautauqua movement, 1874; became a bishop in the American Methodist Church, 1888.

WATTS, ALAN WILSON, Jan. 6, 1915 (Chislehurst, Eng.)–Nov. 16, 1973. U.S. writer, lecturer on philosophy. For almost 40 years, interpreted Eastern thought to the West; gained considerable popularity in the late 1950s and 1960s as interest in the East grew in the U.S. *The Spirit of Zen,* 1936; *This Is It,* 1960.

WHITE, ELLEN GOULD, née Harmon, Nov. 26, 1827 (Gorham, Me.)–July 16, 1915. U.S. religious leader. As leader of the Seventh-Day Adventists, probably influenced the movement more than any other individual; her interpretation of Scripture did much to shape orthodoxy.

WILLIAMS, ROGER, c.1603 (London, Eng.)–March? 1683. English clergyman, founder of Rhode Island Colony in America. Became embroiled in dispute with the Massachusetts Colony over his claim that civil magistrates should have no authority over the consciences of men; banished in 1635; founded Providence, R.I., 1636; received charter from England for Rhode Island Colony, 1644. *The Bloody Tenent of Persecution for Cause of Conscience,* 1644.

WISE, ISAAC MAYER, Mar. 29, 1819 (Steingrub, Bohemia)–Mar. 26, 1900. German-U.S. rabbi, founder of Reform Judaism in the U.S. Tried to unify U.S. synagogues and give them common standards; founded Hebrew Union C., 1875; pres., 1875–1900; edited *The American Israelite* and *Die Deborah.*

YOUNG, BRIGHAM, June 1, 1801 (Whitingham, Vt.)–Aug. 29, 1877. U.S. Mormon leader, carpenter, glazier. One of the most influential Mormon leaders, he led the great migration west to the settlement at Salt Lake City, Utah, 1846–47; built the settlement into a prosperous, solid one; defied the U.S. government against attacks on the Mormons; accused of polygamy.

PHILOSOPHERS AND RELIGIOUS LEADE.

FOREIGN PHILOSOPHERS AND RELIGIOUS LEADERS

ABELARD, PIERRE, c.1079 (Nantes, Fr.)–Apr. 21, 1142. French philosopher, theologian. Affair with a student, HELOISE, led to his castration by ruffians hired by her uncle; espousal of nominalist doctrines led to his persecution.

ABRAHAM, fl. 1800? B.C. (Mesopotamia). First patriarch of the Jews. A central ancestral figure in Judaism, Islam, and Christianity; the model of a man of faith, tested by God; his journey to Canaan from Haran, his treatment of his nephew Lot, and his willingness to sacrifice his son Isaac expressed his devotion to God; received the promise of Canaan as the land of his people; began the tradition of circumcision.

ANAXAGORAS, c.500 B.C. (Clazomenae)–428 B.C. Greek philosopher. The first to introduce a dualistic explanation of the universe; gave first known explanation of moon phases and moon and sun eclipses; taught Pericles, EURIPIDES, and possibly SOCRATES.

ANAXIMANDER, 611 B.C.–547 B.C. Greek astronomer and philosopher. Generally credited with the discovery of obliquity of the ecliptic, the introduction of the sun dial, and the invention of geographic maps; formulated the doctrine of a single-world principle, the starting point and origin of the cosmic process that he called "the infinite."

ANGELA MERICI, SAINT, Mar. 21, 1474 (Desenzano, Rep. of Venice)–Jan. 27, 1540. Italian nun. Founded the Ursulines, the first religious order for the teaching of young girls, 1531; worked to increase the Christian influence on the family.

ANTISTHENES, 444? B.C. (Athens, Gr.)–371 B.C. Greek philosopher. Founder of the Cynics; in the quest for virtue, taught the importance of disregarding external goods, such as social convention and pleasure, and of looking to internal values, such as truth and knowledge of the soul.

ARISTOTLE, 384 B.C. (Stagira)–322 B.C. Greek philosopher. Studied under PLATO at the Athens Academy; tutor of ALEXANDER THE GREAT; taught in Athens as head of the Peripatetic school; the first proponent of the scientific method, and the first Western thinker to set forth coherent theories of logic and causality. *Prior Analytics; Posterior Analytics; Metaphysics; Physics; On the Soul; Generation; Nicomachean Ethics; Politics; Poetics; Rhetoric; On the Heavens; On Beginning and Perishing.*

AUGUSTINE, SAINT, Nov. 13, 354 (Tagaste, Numidia [now Algeria])–Aug. 28, 430. Early Christian church Father, philosopher. Through sermons, books, and pastoral letters, he exerted a tremendous influence in the Christian world; stood forth as a champion of orthodoxy against the Manicheans, Donatists, and Pelagians; fused the religion of the New Testament with the Platonic tradition of Greek philosophy. *The City of God; Confessions.*

AVERROES, 1126 (Cordoba, Sp.)–Dec. 10, 1198. Islamic philosopher. Integrated Islamic traditions and Greek thought; defended the philosophical study of religion against the philosophers; wrote commentaries on most of ARISTOTLE's works.

AVICENNA, 980 (Bukhara, Persia)–1037. Islamic physician, philosopher, scientist. The most famous philosopher and scientist of medieval Islam; his medical writings enjoyed immense prestige for hundreds of years; interpreted ARISTOTLE's writings in a Neoplatonic fashion. *Canon of Medicine.*

BAAL-SHEM-TOV, born Israel ben Eliezer, c.1700 (Tluste, Ukraine)–1760. Jewish teach tavern keeper, founder of modern Hasidism. F emphasis on the joy of religious devotion and re pudiation of the prevailing asceticism gained him a considerable following; taught that learning was not necessary for salvation; spent his time with simple people, dressing like them—a highly controversial practice.

BACON, SIR FRANCIS, BARON VERULAM, VISCOUNT ST. ALBANS, Jan. 22, 1561 (Eng.)–Apr. 9, 1626. English philosopher, essayist, statesman. An early advocate of inductive reasoning from intensive observation; his prestige made empirical science respectable and fashionable; knighted, 1603; made baron, 1618; made viscount, 1621; chan. of England, 1618–21. *Novum Organum,* 1620; *New Atlantis,* 1627; *Essayes,* 1597–1625.

BACON, ROGER, c.1214 (Eng.)–1294. English philosopher, friar. Considered natural science complementary to faith, not opposed to it, and battled for placing the sciences in the curriculum of university studies; knew how to make gunpowder. *Opus majus; Opus minor; Opus tertium.*

BARTH, KARL, May 10, 1886 (Basel, Switz.)–Dec. 9, 1968. Swiss theologian. Reasserted the principles of the Reformation in modern theology; developed a "theology of the word of God" in opposition to the anthropocentric theological writings of the 19th cent.; led church opposition against Hitler's Third Reich. *Der Römerbrief,* 1919; *Das Wort Gottes und die Theologie,* 1924; *Kirchliche Dogmatik,* 1932.

BENEDICT, SAINT, 480 (Nursia, It.)–547. Italian monk, the father of Western monasticism. Founded the monastery at Monte Cassino; his monastic rule, which included a year of probation and a vow of obedience, became the norm for monastic living throughout Europe.

BENTHAM, JEREMY, Feb. 15, 1748 (London, Eng.)–June 6, 1831. English philosopher, economist. Founded utilitarianism, the first systematic effort to describe and evaluate all human acts, institutions, and laws in terms of immediate sensible pleasures and pains; a pioneer in prison reform; proposed a scientific discipline for achieving solutions to social problems. *Introduction to the Principles of Morals and Legislation,* 1789.

BERDYAEV, NIKOLAI ALEKSANDROVICH, Mar. 6, 1874 (Kiev, Rus.)–Mar. 23, 1948. Russian philosopher, religious thinker. A former Marxist, he was leading thinker of Russian Orthodox Christianity; exiled in 1922, he lived in Berlin and Paris, where he wrote extensively, criticizing Russian communism and developing a Christian existentialist philosophy. *Freedom and the Spirit,* 1935; *The Destiny of Man,* 1937.

BERGSON, HENRI, Oct. 18, 1859 (Paris, Fr.)–Jan. 4, 1941. French philosopher. One of the first "process" philosophers, he proposed a theory of evolutionary vitalism and fought against a spacialized conception of time by stressing its quality of duration. *Time and Free Will,* 1910; *Matter and Memory,* 1911; *Creative Evolution,* 1911.

BERKELEY, GEORGE, Mar. 12, 1685 (Kilkenny, Ire.)–Jan. 14, 1753. Anglo-Irish philosopher, churchman. A subjective idealist, he argued that all qualities of the world are in the mind; Anglican bishop of Cloyne, 1734–53. *An Essay Towards a New Theory of Vision,* 1709; *A Treatise Concerning the Principles of Human Knowledge,* 1710.

BERNADETTE, SAINT, born Marie-Bernarde

THE BOOK OF WHO

Soubirous, Jan. 7, 1844 (Lourdes, Fr.)-Apr. 16, 1879. French visionary. A peasant girl who at age 14 claimed to see the Virgin Mary in a grotto near Lourdes on several occasions; became a Sister of Charity; canonized, 1933.

BESANT, ANNIE, Oct. 1, 1847 (London, Eng.)-Sept. 20, 1933. British social reformer, theosophist, Indian independence leader. A former Christian, she went through an atheist stage in the 1880s, when she advocated birth control and became a prominent Fabian socialist; converted to theosophy, 1889; pres., Theosophical Society, 1907-1933; went to India in 1916, establishing the Indian Home Rule League and promoting Jiddu Krishnamurti as the new messiah.

BIDDLE, JOHN, 1615 (Wotton-under-Edge, Eng.)-Sept. 22, 1662. British lay theologian. The father of English unitarianism, often imprisoned for his anti-Trinity views. *Twelve Arguments Against the Deity of the Holy Ghost,* 1644.

BLAVATSKY, HELENA PETROVNA, née Hahn, 1831 (Dnepropetrovsk, Rus.)-1891. Russian spiritualist, author. A cofounder of the Theosophical Society; fused Vedantic thought and Egyptian serpent worship into an occult system based on the belief in a pantheistic evolutionary process. *Isis Unveiled,* 1877; *The Secret Doctrine,* 1888; *Key to Theosophy,* 1889.

BOEHME, JAKOB, 1575 (Altseidenberg, Ger.)-Nov. 21, 1624. German Christian mystic, metaphysician. Out of a religious experience, developed a mystical strain of thought that employed a dialectical method; merged Renaissance nature-mysticism with Biblical religion. *The Aurora,* 1612; *The Way to Christ,* 1622; *The Great Mystery,* 1623.

BRUNNER, EMIL, Dec. 23, 1889 (Winterthur, Switz.)-Apr. 6, 1966. Swiss theologian. As professor of theology, U. of Zurich (1924-53), became the leading theologian in the Reformed tradition; opposed rational and liberal Christianity with a theology of revelation and divine encounter; in leaving some room for natural theology in his system, distinguished himself from KARL BARTH. *The Divine Imperative,* 1932; *Justice and the Social Order,* 1945; *Natural Theology,* 1946.

BUBER, MARTIN, Feb. 8, 1878 (Vienna, Aust.)-June 13, 1965. Jewish philosopher of encounter. Distinguished two fundamental relationships, "I-it" and "I-thou"; his relational thought led him to new insights into the Bible; edited the magazine *Der Jude* (1916-24). *I and Thou,* 1937; *The Eclipse of God,* 1952.

BUDDHA, GAUTAMA, born Siddhartha, c.563 B.C. (Kapilavastu, India)-486? B.C. Indian philosopher, religious leader, founder of Buddhism. Renounced wealthy heritage to lead an ascetic life; taught for 45 years and founded monastic orders; his teaching offered a prescription to cure suffering; considered everything impermanent; preached rigorous disciplines for overcoming dependency; his Buddhist movement played a central role in the entire Eastern world.

CALVIN, JOHN, July 10, 1509 (Noyon, Fr.)-May 27, 1564. French theologian, ecclesiastical statesman. Founder of Calvinism. Promulgated the doctrine of divine election and gave a preeminent place to the Holy Spirit; wrote his views with a clarity and force that did much to propel the Prot. movement; originated the form of church government called a presbytery. *Institutes of the Christian Religion,* 1536.

COMTE, AUGUSTE, Jan. 19, 1798 (Montpellier, Fr.)-Sept. 5, 1857. French philosopher, social reformer. Founded positivism and modern sociology; devised a scheme of social evolution, relating it to the stages of science. *The Course of Positive Philosophy,* 1830-42; *System of Positive Polity,* 1851-54.

CONDORCET, MARIE JEAN, MARQUIS DE, Sept. 17, 1743 (Ribemont, Fr.)-Mar. 29, 1794. French mathematician, philosopher. A leading thinker of the Enlightenment, he contributed to the theory of probability; took part in the French Revolution; devised a system of state education. *Sketch for a Historical Picture of the Human Mind.*

CONFUCIUS, born K'ung Ch'iu, c.551 B.C. (state of Lu [now Shantung Prov.], China)-478 B.C. Chinese philosopher. Most influential philosopher in Chinese history; spent his life teaching and seeking a government post through which to implement his ideas; his teachings emphasized moral character as the source of social order; wanted to reform men and thereby government; considered the founder of a new class in China, the literati; valued filial piety, loyalty, reciprocity, and sincerity; although his teachings were ignored by the rulers of his time, they survived and were used by generations of subsequent rulers.

CRANMER, THOMAS, July 2, 1489 (Aslacton, Eng.)-Mar. 21, 1556. English churchman. The first Prot. archbishop of Canterbury, 1533-56; one of the principal authors of the *Book of Common Prayer,* 1549; as legal adviser to Henry VIII, found legal rationales for the king's divorces; after the accession of QUEEN MARY I, convicted of heresy and burned.

CROCE, BENEDETTO, Feb. 25, 1866 (Pescasseroli, It.)-Nov. 20, 1952. Italian idealist philosopher who constructed a so-called Philosophy of the Spirit; a committed opponent of BENITO MUSSOLINI's fascism in Italy. *Philosophy of the Spirit,* 1902; *History as the Story of Liberty,* 1938.

DAMIEN, FATHER, born Joseph de Veuster, Jan. 3, 1840 (Tremeloo, Belg.)-Apr. 15, 1889. Belgian priest. As R.C. missionary to the leper colony in Molokai, Hawaii, cared for the physical and spiritual needs of 600 persons; when his character came under attack, ROBERT LOUIS STEVENSON wrote *Father Damien: An Open Letter to the Reverend Dr. Hyde,* 1890.

DEMOCRITUS, ("The Laughing Philosopher"). 460? B.C. (Abdera, Gr.)-370? B.C. Greek philosopher. The first developer of the atomic theory of the universe, holding that reality consists ultimately of atoms and the space between them; anticipated the distinction between primary and secondary qualities of matter later made by JOHN LOCKE.

DESCARTES, RENÉ, Mar. 31, 1596 (La Haye, Fr.)-Feb. 1, 1650. French philosopher, mathematician, scientist. Founder of modern philosophical rationalism; inventor of analytic geometry; made many advances in optics; crusaded to apply mathematical methods to all fields of knowledge; beginning with radical skepticism, attempted to prove through deductive steps the existence of the world and of God. *Discourse on Method,* 1637; *Meditations Concerning Primary Philosophy,* 1641; *Principles of Philosophy,* 1644.

DIDEROT, DENIS, Oct. 5, 1713 (Langres, Fr.)-July 30, 1784. French philosopher, writer. Chief editor (1745-72) of the *Encyclopédie,* a comprehensive compendium of knowledge and a symbol and stimulant of the Enlightenment; in his battle against censorship of the *Encyclopédie*, figured in the movement toward tolerance and freedom of expression. *La père de famille*, 1758; *Elements of Physiology*, 1774-80; *Jacques le fataliste*, 1796.

DIOGENES, c.412 B.C. (Sinope, Gr.)-323 B.C. Greek philosopher. Leader of the Cynics, a group that believed in self-sufficiency and disregard of luxuries; his high moral standards resulted in his famous search, with a lantern in daylight, for an honest man.

ECKHARD (or Eckart, Eckardt, Eccard, or Eckehart), **JOHANNES,** known as Meister Eckhard, 1260? (Hochheim, Ger.)-1327? German Dominican theologian, mystic, preacher. Founded German mysticism; the father of German philosophical language.

EMPEDOCLES, c.495 B.C. (Acragas, Sicily)-c.435 B.C. Greek pre-Socratic philosopher who postulated that the world is composed of four elements (air, water, earth, fire) and two forces (love and strife); considered physical motion the only kind of change possible.

EPICTETUS, c.50 (Hierapolis, Asia Minor)-c.138. Greek Stoic philosopher. Valued self-control and selflessness; believed that the will was the sole source of value; influenced Christian thinkers.

EPICURUS, 341 B.C. (Samos)-270 B. C. Greek philosopher. Considered pleasure to be the only good and the end of all morality, but it must be honorable, prudent, and just.

ERASMUS, DESIDERIUS, born Gerhard Gerhards, Oct. 26/27, 1466 (Rotterdam, Neth.)-July 12, 1536. Dutch humanist. Represented the northern Renaissance. The first editor of the Greek version of the New Testament; edited Greek and Latin classics; defended reason, tolerance, and faith; attacked MARTIN LUTHER's position on predestination. *Praise of Folly*, 1509; *The Education of a Christian Prince*, 1515.

EUCKEN, RUDOLPH CHRISTOPH, Jan. 5, 1846 (Aurich, Ger.)-Sept. 14, 1926. German philosopher. Developed a philosophy of ethical activism, a metaphysical-idealistic philosophy of life; an interpreter of ARISTOTLE; awarded Nobel Prize in literature, 1908. *The Truth of Religion*, 1901; *The Life of the Spirit*, 1909; *Knowledge and Life*, 1913.

FÉNELON, FRANÇOIS DE SALIGNAC de la Mothe, Aug. 6, 1651 (Périgord, Fr.)-Jan. 7, 1715. French theologian. The archbishop of Cambrai (from 1695), his liberal views on politics and education faced a concerted opposition from church and state. *Explications des maximes des saints*, 1697; *Télemaque*, 1699; *Lettre à l'Académie*, 1716.

FEUERBACH, LUDWIG ANDREAS, July 28, 1804 (Landshut, Ger.)-Sept. 13, 1872. German philosopher. Abandoned Hegelian idealism for naturalistic materialism; attacked orthodox religion and immortality; concluded that God is the outward projection of man's inner nature; influenced KARL MARX. *The Essence of Christianity*, 1841.

FICHTE, JOHANN, May 19, 1762 (Rammenau, Ger.)-Jan. 29, 1814. German philosopher. The successor to IMMANUEL KANT, he developed the first idealist system (ethical idealism) out of Kant's work; influential as a patriot and liberal. *Science of Knowledge*, 1794; *The Vocation of Man*, 1800.

FOX, GEORGE, July 1624 (Fenny Drayton, Eng.)-Jan. 13, 1691. English religious leader. Founded the Society of Friends, also known as the Quakers, 1668; on the basis of a personal religious

experience, emphasized a God-given "light within" as the source of authority and revelation; fought against slavery and war. *Journal*, 1694.

FRANCIS OF ASSISI, SAINT, c.1181 (Assisi, It.)-Oct. 3, 1226. Italian religious leader. After his conversion to holy life, he attempted to live literally by the Gospel, renouncing material goods and family ties; wandering as a street preacher, he gathered a large following, leading to the establishment of the Franciscan order of priests (formally chartered 1223).

GHAZALI, AL- (or Al-Gazel), c.1058 (Khurasan, now in Iran)-1111. Islamic philosopher. A mystical ascetic, he opposed the use of rational methods in pursuing religious truth; influential in suppressing Moslem rationalism. *Destruction of the Philosophers*.

GODWIN, WILLIAM, Mar. 3, 1756 (Isle of Ely, Eng.)-Apr. 7, 1836. English philosopher. Champion of atheism, anarchism, and personal freedom; defended the power of reason in making choices. *An Enquiry Concerning Political Justice...*, 1793; *Things as They Are, or, The Adventures of Caleb Williams*, 1794. (Husband of MARY WOLLSTONECRAFT.)

GREGORY XIII, born Ugo Buoncompagni, June 7, 1502 (Bologna, It.)-Apr. 10, 1585. Italian pope (1572-85). Reformed the Julian calendar, creating the Gregorian calendar, 1582; founded several colleges and universities, including Gregorian U., 1572; attempted to implement the decrees of the Council of Trent.

HÄRING, BERNARD, Nov. 10, 1912 (Böttingen, Ger.). German theologian. R.C. moral theologian influential in the reforms of Vatican II. *The Law of Christ*, 1956.

HEGEL, GEORG WILHELM FREDERICK, Aug. 27, 1770 (Stuttgart, Ger.)-Nov. 14, 1831. German idealist philosopher. Constructed a grand system that deeply influenced the modern movements of existentialism, Marxism, positivism, and analytical philosophy; believing that the limits IMMANUEL KANT placed on reason were wrong, he saw reason operating in history as a World Spirit infusing order in various areas of culture and society. *The Phenomenology of the Spirit*, 1807; *The Science of Logic*, 1812-16; *Philosophy of Right and Law*, 1820.

HEIDEGGER, MARTIN, Sept. 26, 1889 (Messkirch, Ger.)-May 26, 1976. German philosopher. The major German philosopher of existentialism; greatly influenced European culture between the World Wars; placed being or ontology at the center of his philosophy; coined his own terms in an attempt to revitalize philosophical terminology; brought the awareness of death into philosophical focus. *Being and Time*, 1927; *What is Metaphysics?*, 1929.

HERACLITUS, c.540B.C. (Ephesus, Asia Minor)-c.480 B.C. Greek philosopher. A cosmologist who taught that everything is in a state of flux; believed that everything carries within itself its opposite (life carries the potential of death, etc.); taught that fire is the underlying reality transformed into various manifestations.

HERDER, JOHANN GOTTFRIED VON, Aug. 25, 1744 (Mohrungen, East Prussia [now Morag, Pol.])-Dec. 18, 1803. German philosopher. Founder of German Romanticism; a leader of the *Sturm und Drang* literary movement; considered language and poetry to be natural human expressions; developed a profound philosophy of history emphasizing the unique contributions of each era

THE BOOK OF WHO

and an integrated view of culture. *Folk Songs,* 1778–79; *Outlines of a Philosophy of the History of Man,* 1784–91; *On the Origin of Language,* 1772.

HOBBES, THOMAS, Apr. 5, 1588 (Malmesbury, Eng.)–Dec. 4, 1679. English philosopher. An influential political philosopher who applied the mechanistic and scientific world view to society; had a pessimistic view of human nature; argued for absolutist government. *Leviathan,* 1651.

HUME, DAVID, Apr. 26, 1711 (Edinburgh, Scot.)–Aug. 25, 1776. Scottish philosopher. A philosophical skeptic, he questioned the existence of causality and substance; his writings jarred IMMANUEL KANT from his "dogmatic slumber" and challenged many others to deepen their thinking. *A Treatise of Human Nature,* 1739–40; *An Enquiry Concerning Human Understanding,* 1748; *Dialogues Concerning Natural Religion,* 1779.

HUSS, JOHN (Czech, Jan Hus), 1372 (Husinec, Bohemia)–July 6, 1415. Czech religious reformer. A forerunner of the Prot. Reformation, he was influenced by the writings of JOHN WYCLIFFE; denied the infallibility of the pope, proclaimed the ultimate authority of the Scriptures over the church, and proposed that the state had the right to rule the church; burned at the stake.

HUXLEY, THOMAS HENRY, May 4, 1825 (Middlesex, Eng.)–June 29, 1895. English philosopher, biologist. A leading advocate of Darwinism, vital to its tremendous influence in the late 19th cent; a marine zoologist and a tireless educator and popularizer of science. *Evolution and Ethics,* 1893. (Grandfather of ALDOUS HUXLEY.)

IGNATIUS OF LOYOLA, SAINT, born Iñigo de Onez y Loyola, Dec. 24, 1491 (Azpeitia, Sp.)–July 31, 1556. Spanish priest who founded the Jesuit order. After being wounded in battle, reoriented his life in a spiritual direction, attempting to imitate the life of Christ; underwent a 12-year education; in 1540, founded an order, the Society Of Jesus (Jesuits), that renounced some of the traditional forms of religious life, such as penitential garb, and stressed mobility, flexibility, and learning. *Spiritual Exercises; Constitutions.*

INGE, WILLIAM RALPH, June 6, 1860 (Yorkshire, Eng.)–Feb. 26, 1954. English theologian. Explored the mystical aspects of Christianity; known for his originality and pessimism; dean of St. Paul's Cathedral, 1911–34. *The Church in the World,* 1927; *Mysticism in Religion,* 1948.

ISAIAH, fl. 8th century B.C. (Jerusalem). Hebrew prophet. Called to prophecy c.742 B.C.; saw the advancement of Assyria as a divine warning; reputed to have suffered a martyr's death; Book of Isaiah in the Old Testament is named after him.

JASPERS, KARL THEODOR, Feb. 23, 1883 (Oldenburg, Ger.)–Feb. 26, 1969. German philosopher. Considered a prominent existentialist thinker, though he himself rejected the classification because it placed him within a restricted school of thought. *Man in the Modern Age,* 1933.

JEREMIAH, c.650B.C. (Anathoth, Judah)–585 B.C. Hebrew prophet whose life and teaching are recorded in the book of Jeremiah in the Old Testament. Denounced social injustice and false worship in Judah; saw Babylonian invasion and capture of Jerusalem as a punishment from God; urged people to make peace and believe in God, teaching that they could preserve their worship even in disaster and in exile.

JEROME, SAINT, born Eusebius Hieronymus, c.347 (Stridon, [now in Yugo.])–420. Christian Biblical scholar. A Father of the Roman Catholic Church. His preparation of a standard text of the Gospels for Latin-speaking Christians and new translation of the Psalms and Old Testament was the basis for the Vulgate, or authorized Latin text of the Bible.

JESUS CHRIST, c.6 B.C. (Bethlehem, Judea)–c.30 AD. The founder of Christianity. Son of Joseph the carpenter, but believed, by his followers, to have been miraculously conceived by his mother, the VIRGIN MARY; a wandering rabbi, gathered a large following drawn by his healing powers, teaching in parables, and authority; gathered 12 disciples; his attacks on hypocrisy offended privileged classes; betrayed by one of his disciples, Judas Iscariot, and seized by Roman soldiers and convicted of blasphemy; crucified; believed by his followers to have risen from the dead.

JOAN OF ARC (in French, Jeanne D'Arc), c.1412 (Domremy, Fr.)–May 30, 1431. French saint, national heroine. Called the "Maid of Orleans"; heard voices exhorting her to aid the dauphin (later King Charles VII), who furnished her with troops; defeated English at Patay, 1429; captured by Burgundians at Compiègne and sold to English, who turned her over to Ecclesiastical Court at Rouen; tried for heresy and witchcraft by French clerics supporting the English; turned over to secular court; burned at the stake; trial annulled, 1456; beatified, 1909; canonized, 1920.

JOHN OF THE CROSS, SAINT (Sp. San Juan de la Cauz), born Juan de Yepes y Alvarez, June 24, 1542 (Fontiveros, Sp.)–Dec. 14, 1591. Spanish monk, Doctor of the Church. A great lyric poet and profound mystic; founded the Discalced Carmelites, 1579; a close friend of ST. THERESA OF AVILA; his reforms of the order led to his imprisonment (1577–78) during which time he wrote his greatest poetry. *The Dark Night of the Soul; The Ascent of Mount Carmel.*

JOHN PAUL I, born Luciani Albino, Oct. 17, 1912 (Forno di Canale, Italy)–Sept. 29, 1978. Italian pope, for 34 days in 1978. A long-time pastor, taught the rural poor; vice rector, Bellumo Seminary, 1937–47; patriarch of Venice, 1969–78; cardinal of Venice, 1973–78.

JOHN PAUL II, born Karol Wojtyla, May 18, 1920 (Wadowice, Pol.). Polish pope (elected Oct. 16, 1978), the first non-Italian to be elevated to the papacy in 456 years. Prof. of Moral Theology, U. of Cracow and Lublin, 1953–58; archbishop of Cracow, 1963–78; cardinal, 1967–78. *Love and Responsibility,* 1960; *Person and Work,* 1969; *At the Bases of Renovation,* 1972.

KANT, IMMANUEL, Apr. 22, 1724 (Königsberg, E. Prussia [now Kalingrad, USSR])–Feb. 12, 1804. German philosopher. One of the foremost thinkers of the Enlightenment, he attempted to reconcile two previously divergent trends in philosophy—rationalism and empiricism; using a new method he called "transcendental," showed that "concepts without percepts are empty, percepts without concepts are blind." *Critique of Pure Reason,* 1781; *Prolegomena to Any Future Metaphysics,* 1783; *Critique of Practical Reason,* 1788; *Critique of Judgement,* 1790; *Metaphysics of Morals,* 1797.

KIERKEGAARD, SØREN, May 5, 1813 (Copenhagen, Den.)–Nov. 11, 1855. Danish philosopher, the father of existentialism. Developed a body of thought that stressed the primacy of personal experience and choice; a critic of official Christianity, laid out a tortuous version of an authentic religious life. *Either/Or,* 1843; *Fear and Trembling,* 1843;

The Concept of Dread, 1844; *Concluding Unscientific Postscript,* 1846.

KNOX, JOHN, c.1514 (Haddington, Scot.)–Nov. 24, 1572. Scottish religious leader, the founder of Scottish Presbyterianism. Zealously led the Prot. battle to win Scotland from the R.C. Church; a stirring preacher, he disseminated Prot. ideas and then fought the political establishment that resisted them. *Book of Common Order,* 1564; *History of the Reformation in Scotland,* 1684.

LAO-TZU, c.600 B.C. (Honan, China). Chinese philosopher. His life is shrouded in obscurity, but he was probably a recluse who shunned worldly life; a scholar at the Chou court; traditionally considered to be the author of the *Tao-te Ching,* a text of tremendous importance to Chinese cultural life.

LATIMER, HUGH, c.1485 (Thurcaston, Eng.)–Oct. 16, 1555. English priest, Prot. leader. His popular preaching and his martyrdom (1555) did much to further Prot. cause in England; attacked the superstitions of the clergy and the wealth of the R.C. Church.

LEE, ANN, Feb. 29, 1736 (Manchester, Eng.)–Sept 8, 1784. English religious leader, founder of American sect of Shakers. Joined the "Shaking Quakers" in England, becoming Ann the Word, 1758; founded a Shaker settlement at Watervliet, N.Y., 1776.

LEIBNIZ, GOTTFRIED VON, July 1, 1646 (Leipzig, Ger.)–Nov. 14, 1716. German philosopher and mathematician who made major contributions to mathematics, logic, and metaphysics. Invented, independently of ISAAC NEWTON, differential and integral calculus, 1684; based his metaphysics on the theory of monads (distinct simple substances); also contributed to symbolic logic. *Theodicy,* 1710; *Monadology,* 1714.

LOCKE, JOHN, Aug. 29, 1632 (Wrington, Eng.)–Oct. 28, 1704. English philosopher, founder of British empiricism; leading proponent of liberalism. His theory of knowledge, in an attempt to account for the rise of modern science, stressed the role of sensations on the blank mind *(tabula rasa);* his political philosophy argued for social contract, consent, the protection of property, and the separation of legislative and executive powers; greatly influenced the framers of the U.S. Constitution. *Essay Concerning Human Understanding,* 1690; *Two Treatises on Civil Government,* 1690.

LOMBARD, PETER, c.1100 (Novara, It.)–Aug. 21/22, 1160. Italian theologian. Best known for a series of four books, *Sentences,* which were the source of Catholic theology until replaced by T. AQUINAS's *Summa theologica.*

LUTHER, MARTIN, Nov. 10, 1483 (Eisleben, Ger.)–Feb. 18, 1546. German religious reformer, leader of the Prot. Reformation. As an Augustinian friar, he grappled with his own religious anxieties, developing his own reading of the Scriptures; feeling disgust at the prevailing ecclesiastical laxity, protested the sale of indulgences by posting his 95 theses at Wittenberg, Ger., 1517; as his breach with Rome widened, he attacked the authority of the priesthood to mediate between man and God and rejected the sacraments except as visible signs of an unseen grace; advocated salvation by faith alone; Lutheran religion named after him.

MAHAVIRA ("The Great One"), born Vardhamana, c.599 B.C. (Ksatriyakundagrama, India)–527 B.C. Indian ascetic, a founder of Jainism. Organized earlier Jaina doctrines and established the rules for the Jaina religious order, or *sangha;* practiced extreme asceticism and developed the doctrine of *ahimsa* (nonviolence); the five great vows of renunciation have been attributed to him.

MAIMONIDES, Mar. 30, 1135 (Cordoba, Sp.)–Dec. 13, 1204. Jewish philosopher, jurist, physician. Organized and clarified the Torah, the Jewish oral law; attempted to develop a more rational philosophy of Judaism by reconciling Aristotle, the Bible, and Jewish tradition. *Guide for the Perplexed; Mishneh Torah.*

MANI (also Manes or Manichaeus), Apr. 24, 216 (south Babylonia)–274? Persian religious leader, founder of the Manichaean religion. After a religious experience, traveled to northwest India, where he preached a dualistic doctrine of good and evil; advocated ascetic practices to liberate oneself from matter; died as a captive of Persian Zoroastrian priests.

MARCUS AURELIUS (surnamed Antoninus), born Marcus Annius Verus, Apr. 20, 121 (Rome, It.)–Mar. 17, 180. Roman emperor (161–180), Stoic philosopher. His *Meditations* are a classic and beautiful expression of Stoic philosophy; as emperor, repressed countless rebellions, implemented many reforms, and persecuted Christians.

MARITAIN, JACQUES, Nov. 18, 1882 (Paris, Fr.)–Apr. 28, 1973. French philosopher. An influential Catholic neo-Thomist thinker who defended the scholastic use of reason and fought against modern subjectivism. *Art and Scholasticism,* 1920; *True Humanism,* 1938; *Men and the State,* 1951.

MARY, also **SAINT MARY** or **VIRGIN MARY.** The Mother of Jesus. A figure of tremendous religious and cultural importance to Roman Catholic, Orthodox, and Anglican Christianity; considered a religious figure in her own right, as a mediator of grace.

MENCIUS (or Menz-tzu), born Meng K'o, c.371 B.C. (Tsou [modern Shantung Prov.], China)–c.289 B.C. Chinese philosopher, one of the greatest early Confucians. Stressed the innate goodness of human nature and the obligation of rulers to provide for the common people; known as the Second Sage.

MINDSZENTY, JÓZSEF, Mar. 29, 1892 (Szombathely, Hung.)–May 6, 1975. Hungarian Roman Catholic cardinal. Became a stirring symbol of resistance in his fight against fascism and communism in Hungary; arrested by fascist Hungarian government, 1944; arrested by communist government, 1948; granted protection in U.S. embassy from 1956 to 1971, when he was ordered to leave Hungary by the Vatican.

MOHAMMED, 570 (Mecca)–June 8, 632. Arabian prophet and founder of Islam. Called the Prophet of Allah; a wealthy merchant, he received a call from God (610); began to preach, but received with hostility in Mecca; learning of a plot to murder him, fled to Medina, an event called the *hegira,* 622; established a theocracy at Medina, from which his empire grew; victory over the Meccans at Badr increased his prestige; conquered Mecca (630) making all Arabia Islamic; each of his military victories was seen as confirming evidence of divine sanction for his message and mission.

MONTESQUIEU, CHARLES-LOUIS DE SE-CONDAT, BARON DE LA BRÈDE ET DE, Jan. 18, 1689 (Château de la Brède, Fr.)–Feb. 10, 1755. French liberal political philosopher whose writings inspired the Declaration of the Rights of Man and the U.S. Constitution. Reclassified governments according to their manner of conducting policy;

THE BOOK OF WHO

developed theory of the separation of powers; a social figure and satirist. *Persian Letters,* 1721; *Considerations on the Causes of Greatness of the Romans and Their Decline,* 1734; *The Spirit of the Laws,* 1748.

MOSES, c.1350? B.C. (Egypt)-c.1250? B.C. Hebrew prophet, Jewish religious leader, founder of the Hebrew nation. Called by God, who revealed himself as a burning bush; directed by God to lead his people, the Hebrews, out of bondage in Egypt, took them across the desert to the edge of Canaan; received the Ten Commandments from God on top of Mt. Sinai; died after seeing Canaan from Mt. Nebo.

NEWMAN, JOHN HENRY, Feb. 21, 1801 (London, Eng.)-Aug. 11, 1890. English churchman, cardinal (from 1879). A leader of the Oxford movement in the Church of England, and after his conversion, in the R.C. church. *Loss and Gain,* 1848; *The Idea of a University,* 1852; *Apologia pro vita sua,* 1864; *Grammar of Assent,* 1870.

NIETZSCHE, FRIEDRICH, Oct. 15, 1844 (Röcken, Ger.)-Aug. 25, 1900. German philosopher. A highly influential critic of his culture, he disparaged Christianity, conformism, and nationalism, displaying a remarkable psychological understanding for his time; saw the will-to-power as underlying many phenomena. *The Birth of Tragedy,* 1872; *Thus Spoke Zarathrustra,* 1883-91; *Beyond Good and Evil,* 1886.

OCKHAM, (or Occam), **WILLIAM OF,** 1285 (Ockham, Eng.)-1349. English philosopher. Made two fundamental contributions to the philosophy of science by denying the reality of PLATO's ideal forms in favor of immediately perceived phenomena and by devising "Ockham's razor," a rule of thought that forbids unnecessary complexity.

ORTEGA Y GASSET, JOSÉ, May 9, 1883 (Madrid, Sp.)-Oct. 18, 1955. Spanish philosopher. Perhaps the foremost Spanish thinker of the 20th cent., he sought to bring Spain out of its intellectual isolation; his main concern was to fashion a philosophy that brought reason and life together. *Revolt of the Masses,* 1932; *Concord and Liberty,* 1946.

PARMENIDES, fl. 450 B.C. (born at Elea, now in Italy). Greek pre-Socratic philosopher. The first Western thinker to use a rigorous logical method; postulated that reality is one, eternal, perfect being knowable only through the intellect.

PASCAL, BLAISE, June 19, 1623 (Clermont, Fr.)-Aug. 19, 1662. French philosopher, mathematician, physicist. Formulated the modern theory of probability; invented the first digital calculator (1642-44), the syringe, and the hydraulic press; discovered a law of atmospheric pressure; midway through his life, after a brush with death, turned to religion; his delineation of the "reasons of the heart" for having faith influenced modern existentialism. *Provincial Letters,* 1656; *Pensées,* 1670.

PATRICK, SAINT, c. 385 (nr. Severn, Britain)-461. Christian missionary. The patron saint of Ireland, also called the Apostle of Ireland; known for his successful conversion of Ireland to Christianity, after a vision called him to preach there; consecrated missionary bishop to Ireland, 432; introduced the Roman alphabet to Ireland. *Confessio; Epistola.*

PAUL, SAINT, born Saul, ? (Tarsus, Asia Minor)-c. 67. Christian missionary, theologian. Converted on the road to Damascus from a life of persecuting Christians; his preaching was influential in launching the Christian movement; his letters to outposts of Christians indelibly stamped Christian thinking; wrote the following New Testament books: Romans, 1 and 2 Corinthians, Galatians, Philippians, Colossians, and 1 Thessalonians.

PICO DELLA MIRANDOLA, COUNT GIOVANNI, Feb. 24, 1463 (Mirandola, It.)-Nov. 17, 1494. Italian humanist, philosopher. An eminent Renaissance thinker who championed human dignity and free will; developed a syncretic philosophy; used Kabbalistic doctrine to defend Christian theology. *Oration,* 1486.

PLATO, 427? B.C. (Athens, Gr.)-347? B.C. Greek philosopher who attempted to show the rational relationship between the soul, the state, and the cosmos. A student of SOCRATES; founded a school, the Academy, where he taught; traveled to Syracuse, Sicily, twice in a vain attempt to implement his political ideals; poetically presented the rational pursuit for truth and then demonstrated it with brilliance in all fields of knowledge; wrote in dialogue form, the dialectic method he considered the royal road to truth. *Republic; Phaedo; Symposium; Phaedrus; Timaeus; Apology; Meno.*

PLOTINUS, 205 (Egypt?)-270. Roman Neoplatonist philosopher. Transformed a revival of Platonism in the Roman Empire into what is now called Neoplatonism; although opposed to Christianity, his teaching affected Christian thought.

PRABHUPADA, SWAMI, born A. C. Bhaktivedanta Swami Prabhupada, c.1895 (Calcutta, Ind.)-Nov. 14, 1977. Indian spiritual leader. Founder of the Hare Krishna movement in the U.S., 1965; set up 108 temples in major cities around the world; wrote 52 books on ancient Vedic culture.

PROTAGORAS, c.485 B.C. (Abdera, Gr.)-c.410 B.C. Greek philosopher. Known as the first of the Sophists; his philosophy is summed up in the familiar dictum, "Man is the measure of all things"; generally credited with being the first to systemize the study of grammar.

PYTHAGORAS, c.582 B.C. (Samos)-c.497 B.C. Greek philosopher, mathematician, astronomer. Discovered the basic principles of musical pitch; his emphasis on the importance of numbers in the universe sparked much early mathematics, including the Pythagorean theorem on the length of the hypotenuse of a right triangle; the first to note that the morning and evening star were one planet; founded a mystical cult that lasted to about 350 B.C.

ROUSSEAU, JEAN JACQUES, June 28, 1712 (Geneva, Switz.)-July 2, 1778. French philosopher. A highly influential 18th-cent. thinker; in his political thought, went beyond the economic liberalism of social-contract theorists such as JOHN LOCKE to recognize the role of the general will of the people; his philosophy of education with its freely accepted "contract" between teacher and pupils inspired modern educational theory; the father of romantic sensibility in his longing for closeness with nature. *Discours sur l'origine de l'inégalité des hommes,* 1754; *La nouvelle Héloise,* 1761; *Contrat social,* 1762; *Émile,* 1762.

RUSSELL, BERTRAND ARTHUR WILLIAM, 3rd EARL, May 18, 1872 (Trelleck, Wales)-Feb. 2, 1970. British philosopher, mathematician, essayist. Beyond his eminent philosophical contributions, wrote popular books for the laymen and took controversial stands on public issues; made major contributions to symbolic logic; began as an idealist, but became a realist and logical atomist; arrested for resisting conscription in WW I and

90

later for his activity against the arms race; Nobel Prize in Literature, 1950. *Principia Mathematica*, with ALFRED N. WHITEHEAD, 3 vols, 1910–13; *Mysticism and Logic*, 1918; *History of Western Philosophy*, 1945.

SARTRE, JEAN-PAUL, June 21, 1905 (Paris, Fr.). French writer, philosopher. Leading thinker in the existentialist movement; active in the Resistance movement in WW II; one of the major playwrights and novelists of the 20th-cent. *Nausea*, 1938; *Being and Nothingness*, 1943; *No Exit*, 1944.

SCHELLING, FRIEDRICH VON, Jan. 27, 1775 (Leonberg, Ger.)–Aug. 20, 1854. German idealist philosopher. Laid the foundation for much of GEORG HEGEL's philosophy; identified reality with the necessary movement of thought; his philosophy of nature was very influential. *System of Transcendental Idealism*, 1800.

SCHLEGEL, FRIEDRICH VON, Mar. 10, 1772 (Hanover, Ger.)–Jan. 12, 1829. German writer, critic. Conceived many of the ideas of the early Romantic movement in Germany; founded Oriental studies in Germany with his work on India. *Thoughts on Poetry*, 1800; *Über die Sprache und Weischeit der Inder*, 1808.

SCHLEIERMACHER, FRIEDRICH, Nov. 21, 1768 (Breslau, Ger. [now Wroclaw, Pol.])–Feb. 12, 1834. German Prot. theologian, philosopher. Stressed the integrity of religion and located its distinctiveness in the awareness of absolute dependence. *On Religion: Speeches to its Cultured Despisers*, 1799; *The Christian Faith*, 1822.

SCHOPENHAUER, ARTHUR, Feb. 22, 1788 (Danzig, Ger. [now Gdansk, Pol.])–Sept. 21, 1860. German philosopher. Stressed the irrational impulses of life arising from the will over the predominantly rational emphasis of thought in vogue at the time; a pessimist, his world was characterized by conflict and unsatisfied desires; concluded that the renunciation of desire was the only possible escape from madness. *The World as Will and Representation*, 1819.

SENECA THE YOUNGER, c.3 B.C. (Corduba [now Cordoba, Sp.])–65. Roman philosopher, dramatist, statesman. The tutor of Nero, was very powerful at the beginning of Nero's reign; wrote brilliantly on Stoic doctrines; wrote nine tragedies; out of favor, took his own life on the orders of Nero.

SERRA, JUNÍPERO, born Miguel José Serra, Nov. 24, 1713 (Majorca)–Aug. 28, 1784. Spanish Franciscan missionary in Mexico and California. Founded the first mission in upper California, at San Diego, 1769; the guiding spirit behind the establishment of many other missions in the West; known for his asceticism and preaching.

SOCRATES, c.470 B.C. (Athens, Gr.)–399 B.C. Greek philosopher who introduced the Socratic method (eliciting truth through question-and-answer dialogue) to philosophy. Left no writings, known chiefly through the works of his pupil, PLATO; pursued his method in the marketplace, constantly challenging people to back up their ideas; emphasized moral conduct and ethics; believed in the unity of knowledge and virtue; conceived of the soul as the seat of moral character; brought to trial for corrupting youth, condemned, and forced to drink hemlock.

SPENCER, HERBERT, Apr. 27, 1820 (Derby, Eng.)–Dec. 8, 1903. English naturalist philosopher. Primary formulator of the doctrines of Social Darwinism and popularizer of the idea of "survival of the fittest"; helped establish sociology as a discipline; developed an individualistic doctrine of utilitarianism. *Social Statics*, 1851; *First Principles*, 1862; *The Study of Sociology*, 1872.

SPINOZA, BARUCH, Nov. 24, 1632 (Amsterdam, Neth.)–Feb. 21, 1677. Dutch philosopher. Influenced by RENÉ DESCARTES and the geometrical method; deduced the rationally-necessary character of reality; deep religious feeling animated his system; one of the first to raise questions of higher criticism of the Bible. *Theological-Political Treatise*, 1670; *Ethics*, 1677.

SWEDENBORG, EMANUEL, Jan. 29, 1688 (Stockholm, Swe.)–Mar. 29, 1772. Swedish scientist, mystic, philosopher, theologian. Wrote scientific treatises on the brain, psychology, and the animal kingdom; a 1745 revelation led him to spiritual matters; rejected many traditional doctrines, such as the Trinity, original sin, and eternal punishment; taught that gradual redemption occurs through stages, that heaven and hell are not places but states. *Arcana coelestia*, 1749–56; *Heaven and Hell*, 1758.

TAINE, HIPPOLYTE ADOLPHE, Apr. 21, 1828 (Vouziers, Fr.)–Mar. 5, 1893. French critic, philosopher. An influential French positivist who attempted to apply the scientific method to the humanities; prof. of aesthetics at École des Beaux-Arts, 1864–84. *The Origins of Contemporary France*, 6 vols., 1876–94; *On Intelligence*, 1871.

TEILHARD DE CHARDIN, PIERRE, May 1, 1881 (Sarcenat, Fr.)–Apr. 10, 1955. French R.C. priest, paleontologist, philosopher. Forged a synthesis between Christianity and contemporary theories of evolution; while working as a paleontologist in China, became involved in discovery of Peking Man's skull, 1923–46. *The Phenomenon of Man*, 1938–40; *The Divine Milieu*, 1960.

TERESA OF AVILA, born Teresa de Cepeda y Ahumda, Mar. 28, 1515 (Avila, Sp.)–Oct. 4, 1582. Spanish reformer, author. Reformed the Carmelite order, returning it to its original austerity of total withdrawal; established 16 other convents; wrote beautiful mystical literature. *The Way of Perfection*, 1583; *The Interior Castle*, 1588; *Life of the Mother Teresa of Jesus*, 1611.

THALES, c.634 B.C. (Miletus, Asia Minor)–c.546 B.C. Greek philosopher. The first recorded Western philosopher to give a rational rather than a mythological answer to the nature of the universe; considered water to be the basic constituent of the universe; according to belief, introduced geometry into Greece and predicted an eclipse of the sun.

THOMAS À BECKET (Saint Thomas Becket), c.1118 (London, Eng.)–Dec. 29, 1170. English ecclesiastic, confidant and right-hand man to King Henry II. Became archbishop of Canterbury, 1162; fought Henry over the church's right to use ecclesiastical courts in trying clergy for secular offenses and other issues; killed in Canterbury Cathedral by four of the king's barons for refusing to reinstate bishop suspended for crowning the king's son as prince.

THOMAS À KEMPIS, c.1379 (Kempen, Ger.)–Aug. 8, 1471. German monk, theologian. Reputed to be author of the *Imitation of Christ*, a great devotional work; copied and wrote at the Mt. St. Agnes convent; a representative of the *Devotio Moderna* movement of the late Middle Ages.

THOMAS AQUINAS, SAINT, c.1224 (Roccasecca, It.)–Mar. 7, 1274. Italian theologian, philosopher, Doctor of the Church. Devised one of the most powerful and comprehensive Roman Catholic systems of thought; the greatest figure of

THE BOOK OF WHO

Scholasticism; building on ARISTOTLE, defended the place of reason as a harmonious adjunct to faith; his synthesis was made the official R.C. philosophy in 1879. *Summa theologica,* 1267-73.
TORQUEMADA, TOMÁS DE, 1420 (Valladolid, Sp.)-Sept. 16, 1498. Spanish Dominican friar. First Grand Inquisitor in Spain; confessor to King FERDINAND V and Queen ISABELLA I, whom he convinced to expel all Jews refusing to be baptized, leading to expulsion of about 170,000 Jews, 1492; centralized the Inquisition and pronounced its guidelines.
UNAMUNO Y JUGO, MIGUEL DE, Sept. 2, 1864 (Bilbao, Sp.)-Dec. 31, 1936. Spanish philosopher, writer, educator. Concerned with immortality and the problems of modern Spain; father of the modern Spanish essay; lost many university posts because of his political involvement. *The Tragic Sense of Life in Men and in Peoples,* 1921.
URBAN II, born Odo of Lagery, c.1035 (Lagery, Fr.)-July 29, 1099. French pope (1088-99). Launched the Crusade movement, 1095; strengthened the papacy and reformed the church, building on the reforms started by Pope Gregory VII; attempted to clarify the church-state relationship; excommunicated King Philip I of France for repudiating his wife.
VOLTAIRE, FRANÇOIS MARIE AROUET DE, Nov. 21, 1694 (Paris, Fr.)-May 30, 1778. French philosopher, writer. Attacked tyranny, bigotry, and cruelty; fought against religious fanaticism and worked for political reform; imprisoned several times for his remarks, crusaded against persecution; wrote poetry, plays, novels, and letters; wrote first modern historical treatises using a critical method. *Le Siècle de Louis XIV,* 1751; *Essai sur les moeurs,* 1753, 1756; *Candide,* 1759.
WEIL, SIMONE, Feb. 3, 1909 (Paris, Fr.)-Aug. 24, 1943. French mystic, social philosopher, and activist in French Resistance during WW II. *Waiting for God,* 1951; *Gravity and Grace,* 1952; *The Need for Roots,* 1952; *Oppression and Liberty,* 1958.
WESLEY, JOHN, June 17, 1703 (Epworth, Eng.)-Mar. 2, 1791. English evangelist, theologian, a founder of the Methodist movement. Ordained an Anglican priest, 1728; led study group at Oxford called methodists, 1729; journeyed on mission to Georgia in America, 1735; upon return to England experienced a spiritual conversion; set up Methodist societies and became an influential revivalist, developing a theology suitable to revivals; rejected Calvinist doctrine of election.
WHITEHEAD, ALFRED NORTH, Feb. 15, 1861

(Ramsgate, Eng.)-Dec. 30, 1947. English mathematician, philosopher. Made important contributions to mathematics, logic, the philosophy of science, and metaphysics; late in life, developed a philosophy of organism that stressed the linkage of matter, space, and time. *Principia Mathematica,* with BERTRAND RUSSELL, 1910-13; *Science and the Modern World,* 1925; *Process and Reality,* 1929.
WILLEBRANDS, JOHANNES, Sept. 4, 1909 (Bovenkarspel, Neth.). Dutch cardinal (since 1969). Founded the Catholic Conference for Ecumenical Questions, 1952; pres., Secretariat for the Union of Christians, 1969; archbishop of Utrecht, 1975- .
WITTGENSTEIN, LUDWIG JOSEF JOHANN, Apr. 26, 1889 (Vienna, Austria)-Apr. 19, 1951. Austrian-English philosopher, teacher. Prof., Oxford U., 1930-47; molded the modern discipline of philosophy with his logical theories and philosophy of language; pioneered in the philosophical study of ordinary language. *Tractatus Logico-philosophicus,* 1921; *Philosophical Investigations,* 1953.
WYCLIFFE, JOHN, c.1320 (North Riding of Yorkshire, Eng.)-Dec. 31, 1384. English theologian, church reformer. A forerunner of the Reformation; challenged Church authority by claiming supreme authority for the Scriptures and holding that the Church did not have the only access to grace; promoted a notable translation of the Bible.
ZENO, c.490 B.C. (Elea, now in Italy)-c.430 B.C. Greek philosopher. Defended PARMENIDES by demonstrating, with his famous paradoxes, that motion and multiplicity are logically impossible; attempts to resolve his paradoxes sparked major mathematical and physical-science developments for the next 2,000 years.
ZOROASTER, c. 660 B.C. (Rhages, Medea)-c.583 B.C. Persian religious reformer, prophet, founder of Zoroastrianism, or Parsiism. After a revelation from Ahura Mazda, the Wise Lord, he preached his belief and converted King Vishtaspa; his teachings were monotheistic, although polytheism and a pronounced dualism were present; emphasized the vanquishing of the spirit of evil.
ZWINGLI, HULDRYCH, Jan. 1, 1484 (Wildhaus, Switz.)-Oct. 11, 1531. Swiss Prot. reformer, a leader of the Prot. Reformation. Preached his new views by means of scriptural study; his lectures on the New Testament sparked the Reformation in Switzerland, 1519. *Commentary on True and False Religion,* 1525; *67 Proofs,* 1522.

HISTORIANS, ECONOMISTS AND OTHER SCHOLARS

ACTON, JOHN EMERICH EDWARD, LORD ACTON, Jan. 10, 1834 (Naples, It.)-June 19, 1902. English historian. A Christian liberal who edited *The Rambler,* a Roman Catholic monthly; as prof. of modern history at Cambridge U. (1895-1902), planned the great *Cambridge Modern History.*
ADAMS, HENRY BROOKS, Feb. 16, 1838 (Boston, Mass.)-Mar. 27, 1918. U.S. historian, novelist. Edited the *North American Review,* 1870-76; prof. of history, Harvard U., 1870-77. *History of the United States,* 9 vols., 1898-91; *Mont-Saint-Michel and Chartres,* 1904; *The Education of Henry Adams,* pub. 1918.
ADLER, ALFRED F., Feb. 7, 1870 (Vienna, Aus-

tria)-May 28, 1937. Austrian psychiatrist. Founded the school of individual psychology. Postulated that a feeling of inferiority was the source of all personality difficulties and was compensated for with a need for power or self-assertion.
ANGELL, SIR NORMAN THOMAS, born Ralph Norman Angell Lane, Dec. 26, 1872 (Lincolnshire, Eng.)-Oct. 7, 1967. English economist, author. Rancher, prospector, and journalist in western U.S., to 1898; editor of *Foreign Affairs,* 1928-31; in his antiwar book, *The Great Illusion* (1910), argued that common economic interests of nations made war futile; awarded Nobel Peace Prize, 1933.
ARENDT, HANNAH, Oct. 14, 1906 (Hanover,

HISTORIANS, ECONOMISTS AND OTHER SCHOLARS

Ger.)–Dec. 4, 1975. German-U.S. political scientist, philosopher. Political theorist known for her study of totalitarianism and writings on Jewish affairs; a refugee from Nazi Germany. *The Origins of Totalitarianism*, 1951; *Eichmann in Jerusalem*, 1963.

BABBITT, IRVING. Aug. 2, 1865 (Dayton, Ohio)–July 15, 1933. U.S. scholar, educator, literary critic. With Paul Elmer Moore, founded modern humanistic movement; a foe of Romanticism and its offshoots, realism and naturalism, he championed the classical values of restraint and moderation. *Rousseau and Romanticism*, 1919; *Democracy and Leadership*, 1924.

BAGEHOT, WALTER, Feb. 3, 1826 (Somerset, Eng.)–Mar. 24, 1877. English economist, editor, literary critic, political analyst. As editor of *The Economist*, helped build its reputation, 1860–77; applied the concept of evolution to political societies. *The English Constitution*, 1867; *Physics and Politics*, 1872; *Lombard Street*, 1873; *Literary Studies*, 1879.

BANCROFT, GEORGE, Oct. 3, 1800 (Worcester, Mass.)–Jan. 17, 1891. U.S. diplomat, historian. Called the "Father of American History" for his 10-volume *A History of the United States* (1834–74). U.S. secy. of the navy, 1845–46; U.S. min. to England, 1846–49.

BARTLETT, JOHN, June 14, 1820 (Plymouth, Mass.)–Dec. 3, 1905. U.S. editor, bookseller. Compiled the famous *Familiar Quotations* (1855) that has become the standard reference work in its field.

BEARD, CHARLES AUSTIN, Nov. 27, 1874 (nr. Knightstown, Ind.)–Sept. 1, 1948. U.S. historian. Noted for his economic interpretation of U.S. institutional development; analyzed motivational factors in the founding of institutions; criticized scientific certitude in historical research. *An Economic Interpretation of the Constitution*, 1913.

BEDE, THE VENERABLE, 672–73 (Northumbria, Eng.)–May 25, 735. English historian, monk. His *Ecclesiastical History of the English People* (731) remains an indispensable source for the conversion of the Anglo-Saxon tribes to Christianity; set the example in England for dating events from the birth of Christ (A.D. and B.C.)

BENEDICT, RUTH, June 5, 1887 (New York, N.Y.)–Sept. 17, 1948. U.S. anthropologist. Demonstrated the role of culture in individual personality formation; a student and colleague of FRANZ BOAS at Columbia U. *Patterns of Culture*, 1934; *The Chrysanthemum and the Sword: Patterns of Japanese Culture*, 1946.

BETTLEHEIM, BRUNO, Aug. 28, 1903 (Vienna, Austria). Austrian-U.S. psychologist, educator. Authority on children, especially emotionally disturbed children. Taught educational psychology and headed Sonia Shankman Orthogenic School, at U. of Chicago, 1943–73. *Love Is Not Enough*, 1950; *The Informed Heart*, 1960; *The Children of the Dream*, 1969; *The Uses of Enchantment*, 1976.

BLACKSTONE, SIR WILLIAM, July 10, 1723 (London, Eng.)–Feb. 14, 1780. English jurist, writer. Best known for his *Commentaries on the Laws of England* (4 vols., 1765–69); appointed to the Court of King's Bench and knighted, 1770; an advocate of prison reform.

BOAS, FRANZ, July 9, 1858 (Minden, Ger.)–Dec. 22, 1942. German-U.S. anthropologist. As the first professor of anthropology, at Columbia U. (from 1899), exerted a great influence on the field;

trained many important U.S. anthropologists, including MARGARET MEAD; founded relativistic, culture-centered anthropology; specialist in the cultures and languages of American Indians. *The Mind of Primitive Man*, 1911 (rev. 1938); *Primitive Art*, 1927; *Race, Language and Culture*, 1940.

BOORSTIN, DANIEL J., Oct. 1, 1914 (Atlanta, Ga.). U.S. historian. A prolific writer on American history. Dir. of Smithsonian Inst.'s Museum of History and Technology, 1969–73; librarian of Congress, 1975–   . *The Americans*, 3 vols., 1958–73.

BOYD ORR, JOHN, FIRST BARON BOYD ORR OF BRECHIN MEARNS, Sept. 23, 1880 (Ayrshire, Scot.)–June 25, 1971. British nutritionist, agricultural scientist. A major contributor to the solution of world food problems and an advocate of world govt. Dir.-gen. of UN Food and Agric. Org., 1946–47; awarded Nobel Peace Prize, 1949. *Food and the People*, 1943; *The White Man's Dilemma*, 1953.

BRINTON, (Clarence) CRANE, Feb. 2, 1898 (Winsted, Conn.)–Sept. 7, 1968. U.S. historian. An authority on the history of ideas and an expert on the theory of revolution. Prof. at Harvard U., 1923–68. *The Anatomy of Revolution*, 1938.

BRONOWSKI, JACOB, Jan. 18, 1908 (Poland)–Aug. 22, 1974. U.S. historian, mathematician. A writer on science and human value; his *The Ascent of Man* (1973) was made into a popular TV series detailing the breakthroughs in human civilization. Senior fellow at Salk Inst. of Biological Studies, 1964–74.

BROOKS, VAN WYCK, Feb. 16, 1886 (Plainfield, N.J.)–May 2, 1963. U.S. literary critic, cultural historian. Viewed literature as an outgrowth of a natl. culture. *The Wine of the Puritans*, 1909; *America's Coming of Age*, 1915; *The Flowering of New England, 1815–65*, 1936 (Pulitzer Prize in history, 1937).

BURCKHARDT, JACOB, May 25, 1818 (Basel, Switz.)–Aug. 8, 1897. Swiss cultural historian. Famous for his pioneering study of Ren. Italy; saw individualistic modern man as originating at the Ren. and being threatened by industrialization. *The Civilization of the Renaissance in Italy*, 1860.

BURKE, EDMUND, Jan. 12, 1729 (Dublin, Ire.)–July 9, 1797. British political writer, statesman. A prominent conservative political theorist and a reformer in Parliament; worked for a more conciliatory policy with the American colonies; considered unrestricted rationalism to be destructive in human affairs. *Reflections on the Revolution in France*, 1790.

CARLYLE, THOMAS, Dec. 4, 1795 (Dumfriesshire, Scot.)–Feb. 5, 1881. Scottish essayist, historian. Noted for his spiritual autobiography, *Reminisences* (written 1866, pub. 1881) and *The French Revolution* (1837). Stressed the need for a strong, paternalistic govt.; believed that certain "heroes" molded history.

CASTAÑEDA, CARLOS, Dec. 25, 1931 (São Paulo, Braz.) U.S. anthropologist. Author of popular books about his experiences as the apprentice to a Yaqui Indian sorcerer. *The Teachings of Don Juan*, 1968; *Tales of Power*, 1969.

CATTON, BRUCE, Oct. 8, 1899 (Petoskey, Mich.)–Aug. 28, 1978. U.S. historian, editor, journalist. Noted for his works on the military history of the Civil War. Editor (1954–59) and senior editor (1959–78), *American Heritage*. *A Stillness at Appomattox*, 1953 (Pulitzer Prize in history, 1954).

THE BOOK OF WHO

CHAMPOLLION, JEAN FRANÇOIS, Dec. 23, 1790 (Figeac, Fr.)–Mar. 4, 1832. French archeologist. Founded the science of Egyptology. Using the Rosetta Stone, established the principles for deciphering Egyptian hieroglyphics.

CHOMSKY, NOAM, Dec. 7, 1928 (Philadelphia, Pa.). U.S. linguist, writer, political activist. Founded transformational or generative grammar, which revolutionized the scientific study of language; a prolific propagandist for radical causes. *Cartesian Linguistics,* 1966.

COMFORT, ALEX, Feb. 10, 1920 (London, Eng.). English fiction and nonfiction writer. A Ph.D. in biochemistry and dir. of research in gerontology at University C., London. Best known for *The Joy of Sex: A Gourmet's Guide to Love Making* (1973) and *More Joy* (1974).

COMMAGER, HENRY STEELE, Oct. 25, 1902 (Pittsburgh, Pa.). U.S. historian. Prolific writer on a wide range of topics; a Jeffersonian liberal. *The American Mind,* 1950.

DEUTSCH, HELENE, née Rosenbach, Oct. 9, 1884 (Przemysl, A.-H.). U.S. psychoanalyst. Grande dame of Boston psychoanalysis; a pioneer in the Freudian movement and last of the original Freudians. *The Psychology of Women,* 2 vols., 1944 (U.S.).

DE VOTO, BERNARD A., Jan. 11, 1897 (Ogden, Ut.)–Nov. 13, 1955. U.S. editor, critic, historian, novelist. Noted for his works on U.S. literature and the American frontier; wrote the "Easy Chair" column for *Harper's,* 1935–52. *Across the Wide Missouri,* 1947 (awarded Pulitzer Prize in history, 1948).

DEWEY, MELVIL, Dec. 10, 1851 (Adams Center, N.Y.)–Dec. 26, 1931. U.S. librarian. Devised the Dewey Decimal System of classification for library cataloging; founded the first training school for librarians; a founder of the *Library Journal* and American Library Assn.

DU PONT DE NEMOURS, PIERRE SAMUEL, Dec. 14, 1739 (Paris, Fr.)–Aug. 6, 1817. French economist. The main writer of the Physiocratic school of economics; an important figure in the Constituent Assembly during the French Revolution; emigrated to U.S., 1800; his two sons VICTOR MARIE and ÉLEUTHÈRE IRÉNÉE, founded the two U.S. branches of the family.

DURKHEIM, EMILE, Apr. 15, 1858 (Epinal, Fr.)–Nov. 15, 1917. French sociologist. One of the founders and leaders of modern sociology; formulated a rigorous methodology for sociology; founded *L'Année Sociologique,* 1896; conducted studies on suicide, moral education, population density, the division of labor, and primitive religion.

EISLEY, LOREN COREY, Sept. 3, 1907 (Lincoln, Neb.)–July 9, 1977. U.S. anthropologist, naturalist. A major interpreter of CHARLES DARWIN and poetic popularizer of biological science. *The Immense Journey,* 1957; *Darwin's Century,* 1958.

ELLIS, (Henry) HAVELOCK, Feb. 2, 1859 (Surrey, Eng.)–July 8, 1939. English scientist, man of letters. Pioneer writer on the psychology of sex; conducted the first study of homosexuality; wrote extensively about masturbation; an advocate of sex education. *Studies in the Psychology of Sex,* 1897–1928.

EVANS, BERGEN, Sept. 19, 1904 (Franklin, Ohio)–Feb. 4, 1978. U.S. grammarian, critic. Prof. of English at Northwestern U.; wrote the column "Skeptic's Corner" in *The American Mercury,* 1946–50; author of "The Last Word," a daily syndicated newspaper feature; host of several language-oriented TV shows. *Natural History of Nonsense,* 1946; *Dictionary of Contemporary American Usage,* 1957; *Dictionary of Quotations,* 1968.

FIEDLER, LESLIE, Mar 8, 1917 (Newark, N.J.). U.S. literary critic. Controversial critic who has applied Freudian and Jungian concepts to American literature and social thought. Prof. of English at State Univ. of New York at Buffalo, 1965–   . *Love and Death in the American Novel,* 1960.

FRASER, ANTONIA, née Pakenham, Aug. 27, 1932 (London, Eng.). English biographer. *Mary, Queen of Scots,* 1969; *Cromwell: The Lord Protector,* 1973; *Royal Charles,* 1979.

FRAZER, SIR JAMES GEORGE, Jan. 1, 1854 (Glasgow, Scot.)–May 7, 1941. Scottish anthropologist, classicist. Author of *The Golden Bough: A Study in Magic and Religion* (1890), a masterpiece on primitive culture; devised a theory of divine kingship and a theory of psychic development.

FRIEDMAN, MILTON, July 31, 1912 (Brooklyn, N.Y.) U.S. economist. Known for his work in monetary economics; supports laissez-faire economic policies, floating exchange rates, and a stable Federal Reserve policy; prof. at U. of Chicago, 1946–   ; awarded Nobel Prize in economics, 1976. *Capitalism and Freedom,* 1962.

FROMM, ERICH, March. 23, 1900 (Frankfurt, Ger.). U.S. psychoanalyst. Emphasized the role of social and cultural pressures on individuals. *Escape from Freedom,* 1941; *Man for Himself,* 1947; *The Art of Loving,* 1956.

GALBRAITH, JOHN KENNETH, Oct. 15, 1908 (Ontario, Can.). U.S. economist. Author of popular books on the U.S. economy; involved in several Democratic presidential campaigns, including those of A. STEVENSON, J. KENNEDY, and G. MCGOVERN; U.S. amb. to India, 1961–63; chm. of Americans for Democratic Action, 1967–69. *The Affluent Society,* 1958; *The New Industrial State,* 1967.

GIBBON, EDWARD, Apr. 27, 1737 (Surrey, Eng.)–Jan. 16, 1794. British historian. Best known as the author of *The History of the Decline and Fall of the Roman Empire* (1776–88); considered the greatest English historian of his century.

HALL, GRANVILLE STANLEY, Feb. 1, 1844 (Ashfield, Mass.)–Apr. 24, 1924. U.S. psychologist. Founded American experimental psychology; pioneer in child and educational psychology; a major exponent of SIGMUND FREUD's work.

HANDLIN, OSCAR, Sept. 19, 1915 (Brooklyn, N.Y.). U.S. historian. Influential in the field of U.S. social history; noted for his work on immigration to the U.S., *The Uprooted,* 1951 (Pulitzer Prize in history, 1952).

HARRINGTON, MICHAEL, Feb. 24, 1928 (St. Louis, Mo.). U.S. writer. Noted leftist author of *The Other America* (1963), which played a major role in awakening the U.S. to the problem of American poverty. *Twilight of Capitalism,* 1976.

HAYEK, FRIEDRICH AUGUST VON, May 8, 1899 (Vienna, Austria). Anglo-Austrian economist. Leading speaker for the Austrian school of economics, which favors a free-market economy and opposes govt. management; awarded Nobel Prize in economics (with GUNNAR MYRDAL), 1974. *Prices and Production,* 1931; *The Pure Theory of Capital,* 1941; *The Road to Serfdom,* 1944.

HERODOTUS, c. 485 B.C. (Halicarnassus [now Bodrum, Turk.])–430 B.C. Greek historian. As author of the first history of Western civilization, called the "Father of History." Wrote primarily about the Persian wars; though his history lacks accuracy, it is comprehensive and has a charming, anecdotal style.

HITE, SHERE D., Nov. 2, 1942 (St. Joseph, Mo.). U.S. author, cultural historian. Dir. of Natl. Org. of Women's Female Sexuality Project, 1972- . *Sexual Honesty: By Women for Women*, 1974; *The Hite Report: A Nationwide Study of Female Sexuality*, 1976.

HOFSTADTER, RICHARD, Aug. 6, 1916 (Buffalo, N.Y.)-Oct. 24, 1970. U.S. historian. Author of popular and controversial books on American social and intellectual history. *The American Political Tradition*, 1948; *Anti-Intellectualism in American Life* (Pulitzer Prize in general nonfiction, 1964), 1964.

HORNEY, KAREN, Sept. 16, 1885 (Hamburg, Ger.)-Dec. 4, 1952. Norwegian-Dutch psychoanalyst, writer, teacher. A co-founder of the American Institute for Psychoanalysis; stressed social and environmental factors in determining personality; studied the behavior of children. *The Neurotic Personality of Our Time*, 1937; *Neurosis and Human Growth*, 1950.

HOWE, IRVING, June 11, 1920 (New York, N.Y.). U.S. literary and social critic. A vocal radical; editor of *Dissent*; prof. of English at Hunter C., 1963- . *Sherwood Anderson*, 1951; *World of Our Fathers*, 1976 (National Book Award, 1977).

HULME, T(homas) **E**(rnest), Sept. 16, 1883 (Staffordshire, Eng.)-Sept. 28, 1917. English critic, philosopher, poet. Theorist of the Imagist movement, whose ideas were popularized by T. S. ELIOT and E. POUND. *Speculations*, 1924; *Notes on Language and Style*, 1929; *Further Speculations*, 1955.

JANEWAY, ELIOT, Jan. 1, 1913 (New York, N.Y.). U.S. economist, author. Economic advisor to many firms; author of syndicated newspaper column on the nation's business. *The Economics of Crisis*, 1968; *What Shall I Do with My Money?*, 1970.

JUNG, CARL GUSTAV, July 26, 1875 (Kessevil, Switz.)-June 6, 1961. Swiss psychologist, psychiatrist. Founder of analytic psychology. Differentiated people according to attitude types, extroverted and introverted; conducted studies in mental association; an associate of S. FREUD, split with him over the question of libido. *The Psychology of Dementia Praecox*, 1909; *The Psychology of the Unconscious*, 1916.

KAZIN, ALFRED, June 5, 1915 (Brooklyn, N.Y.). U.S. critic, writer. *On Native Grounds*, 1941; *Walker in the City*, 1951; *Starting Out in the Thirties*, 1965; *Bright Book of Life*, 1973.

KEYNES, JOHN MAYNARD, June 5, 1883 (Cambridge, Eng.)-Apr. 21, 1946. British economist. The most influential modern economist, whose ideas on the causes of prolonged unemployment demanded a greater role for govt. in the economy; argued that private and public expenditure determines the levels of income and employment. *Economic Consequences of the Peace*, 1919; *The General Theory of Employment, Interest and Money*, 1935.

KINSEY, ALFRED CHARLES, June 23, 1894 (Hoboken, N.J.)-Aug. 25, 1956. U.S. zoologist. Author of studies of the sexual life of human beings based on 18,500 personal interviews. *Sexual Behavior in the Human Male*, 1948; *Sexual Behavior in the Human Female*, 1953.

KRAFFT-EBBING, BARON RICHARD, Aug. 14,

1840 (Germany)-Dec. 22, 1902. German neurologist, psychiatrist. Initiated study of sexual deviation; coined the words *paranoia, sadism, masochism. Psychopathia Sexualis*, 1886.

LAROUSSE, PIERRE ATHANASE, Oct. 23, 1817 (Toucy, Fr.)-Jan. 3, 1875. French lexicographer, encyclopedist. Publisher of many of best education and reference books of 19th-cent. France, including the *Grand dictionnaire universel du XIX*[e] *siècle* (15 vols., 1866-76).

LASKI, HAROLD JOSEPH, June 30, 1893 (Manchester, Eng.)-Mar. 24, 1950. English political scientist, educator. Beginning as a pluralist, became a Marxist during the troubled 1930s. Prof. at London School of Economics, 1926-50; member of Executive Com. of the Labour Party, 1936-49.

LEAKEY, LOUIS SEYMOUR BAZETT, Aug. 7, 1903 (Kabete, Kenya)-Oct. 1, 1972. British archeologist, anthropologist. Made fossil discoveries in E. Africa that proved that humans existed much earlier than previously thought and that human evolution was centered in Africa, not Asia. *Stone-Age Africa*, 1936; *White African*, 1937; *Olduvai Gorge*, 1952. (Husband of MARY LEAKEY; father of RICHARD LEAKEY.)

LEAKEY, MARY, 1904 (London, Eng.). English anthropologist. Her discovery of fossils in Laetolil, Tanzania (1975), helped push back the dates of the first true man to almost four million years ago. (Wife of LOUIS B. LEAKEY; mother of RICHARD LEAKEY.)

LEAKEY, RICHARD ERSKINE, Dec. 19, 1944 (Nairobi, Kenya.). English anthropologist. Based on his discoveries in Koobi Fora in Kenya, he argued that three humanlike forms existed of which two died out and the third, Homo habilis, evolved into Homo erectus, the direct ancestor of Homo sapiens; dir. of Natl. Museum of Kenya, 1968- . *Origins* (with Roger Lewin), 1977; *People of the Lake* (with Roger Lewin), 1978. (Son of LOUIS and MARY LEAKEY.)

LEONTIEF, WASSILY, Aug. 5, 1906 (St. Petersburg, Rus. [now Leningrad, USSR]). U.S. economist. Originated the input-output analysis used in economic planning and in forecasting output and growth requirements. Prof. at Harvard U., 1931-75; prof. at N.Y.U., 1975- ; awarded Nobel Prize in economics, 1973.

LEVI-STRAUSS, CLAUDE, Nov. 28, 1908 (Brussels, Belg.). French anthropologist. Founder of structural anthropology; prof. at Institut d'Ethnologie, U. of Paris, 1948-59; prof. at College de France, 1959- ; elected to French Acad., 1973. *The Elementary Structures of Kinship*, 1949; *Structural Anthropology*, 1958; *From Honey to Ashes*, 1967.

LEWIS, OSCAR, Dec. 25, 1914 (New York, N.Y.)-Dec. 16, 1971. U.S. anthropologist. Noted for his theory that poverty creates an identifiable culture that transcends national differences. *Five Families*, 1959; *The Children of Sanchez*, 1961; *La Vida*, 1966; *Anthropological Essays*, 1970.

LIDDELL HART, B(asil) **H**(enry), Oct. 31, 1895 (Paris, Fr.)-Jan. 29, 1970. English military historian and strategist. Developed the "expanding torrent" method of attack; advocate of mechanized warfare, surprise, mobility, and airpower; military correspondent for the *Daily Telegraph* (1925-35) and *The Times* (1935-39).

LIVY, born Titus Livius, 59 B.C. (Patavium [now Padua, It.])-A.D. 17. Roman historian. The most famous of the ancient Roman historians. His *The Annals of the Roman People* consisted of 142

THE BOOK OF WHO

books covering the period 753 B.C. to 9 B.C.; only 35 survive.

MACAULAY, THOMAS BABINGTON, BARON MACAULAY OF ROTHLEY, Oct. 25, 1800 (Leicestershire, Eng.)-Dec. 28, 1859. English historian. His *History of England from the Accession of James the Second* (5 vols., 1849-61) is considered one of the great works of the 19th century; published poetry and essays, especially in *Edinburgh Review;* member of Parliament, 1830, 1839-47, and 1852-56; secy. of war, 1839-41; buried in Westminster Abbey.

MALTHUS, THOMAS ROBERT, Feb. 14, 1766 (Surrey, Eng.)-Dec. 29, 1834. English political economist. Pioneer in modern population-theory who warned that poverty was inevitable since population increases by geometrical ratio, while means of subsistence increase only arithmetically. *Essay on the Principles of Population,* 1798.

MEAD, MARGARET, Dec. 16, 1901 (Philadelphia, Pa.)-Nov. 15, 1978. U.S. anthropologist. Noted for her work on childhood and adolescence, the cultural conditioning of sexual behavior, national character, and culture change. Outspoken on contemporary social issues. Asst. curator (1926-42), assoc. curator (1942-64), and curator (1964-69) of ethnology at American Museum of Natural History. *Coming of Age in Samoa,* 1928; *Culture and Commitment,* 1970.

MENNINGER, KARL AUGUSTUS, July 22, 1893 (Topeka, Kan.). U.S. psychiatrist. A cofounder of the Menninger Fndn., a major center for the study and treatment of mental-health problems, 1941; a pioneer in the modern reform of mental hospitals.

MICHELET, JULES, Aug. 21, 1798 (Paris, Fr.)-Feb. 9, 1874. French historian. Great historian of the Romantic school, evoked the Middle Ages with brilliance. Work marred by his bias against the clergy, the nobility, and the monarchic institutions. *Histoire de France,* 1833-67.

MILL, JOHN STUART, May 20, 1806 (London, Eng.)-May 8, 1873. English economist, philosopher. Influential utilitarian who examined the rule of induction and who urged reform and expanded democracy; applied the principles of utility to political theory. *The Principles of Political Economy,* 1848; *On Liberty,* 1854; *Subjection of Women,* 1869; *Autobiography,* 1873.

MILLER, PERRY GILBERT, Feb. 25, 1905 (Chicago, Ill.)-Dec. 9, 1963. U.S. historian. A leader in American intellectual history who wrote extensively on the colonial period; argued that religion rather than economics was the primary motive behind the settling of New England. *The New England Mind,* 1939; *Errand into the Wilderness,* 1956.

MILLS, C. WRIGHT, Aug. 28, 1916 (Waco, Tex.)-Mar. 20, 1962. U.S. sociologist. Argued that social scientists should be activists rather than disinterested observers. *White Collar,* 1951; *The Power Elite,* 1956; *The Sociological Imagination,* 1959.

MONNET, JEAN OMER MARIE GABRIEL, Nov. 9, 1888 (Cognac, Fr.)-Mar. 16, 1979. French economist, govt. official. The architect of the European Common Market; played a leading role in the financial reconstruction of Poland, Austria, and Rumania following WW I; recapitalized the Diamond Match Co., after the scandal involving IVAR KREUGER; sent as the League of Nations representative to China, 1933; set up and obtained loans for the China Development Corp.; through his posts with the French govt., developed the

European Coal and Steel Community, which later became the Common Market, 1950.

MONTAGU, (Montague Francis) ASHLEY, June 28, 1905 (London, Eng.). British-U.S. anthropologist, author. Writes prolifically for the layman. *Man's Most Dangerous Myth: The Fallacy of Race,* 1942; *The Natural Superiority of Women,* 1953, 1958; *The Prevalence of Nonsense,* 1967.

MORISON, SAMUEL ELIOT, July 9, 1887 (Boston, Mass.)-May 15, 1976. U.S. historian. Prof. at Harvard U., 1925-55; official historian of Harvard U. and official U.S. naval historian for WW II. *The Growth of the American Republic* (with H.S. COMMAGER), 1930; *Admiral of the Ocean Sea,* 1942 (Pulitzer Prize in biography, 1943); *John Paul Jones,* 1958 (Pulitzer Prize in biography, 1959).

MUMFORD, LEWIS, Oct. 19, 1895 (Flushing, N.Y.). U.S. social critic. Wrote on architecture and the city. *Sticks and Stone,* 1924; *The Culture of Cities,* 1938; *The City in History,* 1961.

MYRDAL, GUNNAR, Dec. 6, 1898 (Gustafs, Swe.). Swedish economist, sociologist, public official. Involved in the development of Swedish welfare state and the United Nations; awarded Nobel Prize in economics (with F. VON HAJEK), 1974. *Asian Drama,* 3 vols., 1968.

NEARING, SCOTT, Aug. 6, 1883 (Morris Run, Pa.). U.S. sociologist. Well-known radical who fought against child labor, war, and big business; retired to become a homesteader in Maine. *Poverty and Riches,* 1916; *War,* 1931; *Living the Good Life,* 1954; *The Making of a Radical,* 1972.

NEVINS, ALLAN, May 20, 1890 (Camp Point, Ill.)-Mar. 3, 1971. U.S. historian. Prolific writer, noted for his masterful political biographies. As prof. of history at Columbia U. (1931-58), established Columbia's oral-history program. *Grover Cleveland—A Study in Courage,* 1932 (Pulitzer Prize in biography, 1933); *Hamilton Fish,* 1936 (Pulitzer Prize in biography, 1937).

OGDEN, ROBERT MORRIS, July 6, 1877 (Binghampton, N.Y.)-Mar. 2, 1959. U.S. psychologist, educator. As prof. of education at Cornell U. (1917-45), introduced Gestalt psychology to the U.S. *Psychology and Education,* 1926.

PACKARD, VANCE OAKLEY, May 22, 1914 (Granville Summit, Pa.). U.S. nonfiction writer. Author of popular sociological tracts. *The Hidden Persuaders,* 1957; *The Status Seekers,* 1959; *The Waste Makers,* 1960; *The Naked Society,* 1964; *The People Shapers,* 1977.

PARETO, VILFREDO, July 15, 1848 (Paris, Fr.)-Aug. 20, 1923. Italian sociologist, economist. Attempted to establish a theory applying mathematical analyses to economic and social phenomena; devised the "circulation of elites" concept; his ideas were largely incorporated into Italian fascism. *The Mind and Society,* 4 vols., trans. 1935.

PARSONS, TALCOTT, Dec. 13, 1902 (Colorado Springs, Col.)-May 8, 1979. U.S. sociologist. Attempted to construct a theoretical framework for classifying societies and their parts. Prof. at Harvard U., 1927-74. *The Social System,* 1951.

PARTRIDGE, ERIC HONEYWOOD, Feb. 6, 1894 (Gisborne, N.Z.)-June 1, 1979. British lexicographer, author. Expert on the English language and prolific author of popular books on slang, catch phrases, punctuation, clichés, correct usage, and other miscellany. *Usage and Abusage,* 1947; *A Dictionary of Underworld,* 1950; *A Dictionary of Slang and Unconventional English,* 1970.

HISTORIANS, ECONOMISTS AND OTHER SCHOLARS

PASSY, FREDERIC, May 20, 1822 (Paris, Fr.)–June 12, 1912. French economist. A pacifist, founded the International League for Permanent Peace (1867) and served as its gen. secy. until 1889. Awarded, with J. DUNANT, first Nobel Peace Prize, 1901. *Leçons d'économie politique,* 1860–61; *La question de la paix,* 1891.

PETER, LAWRENCE JOHNSTON, Sept. 16, 1919 (Vancouver, B.C., Can.). Canadian-U.S. educator, author. Formulated the "Peter Principle" on the level of competence in organizations. *The Peter Principle: Why Things Always Go Wrong,* 1969.

PIAGET, JEAN, Aug. 9, 1896 (Neuchâtel, Switz.). Swiss psychologist. Known for his theory on child cognition and intellectual development, which showed that a child thinks differently from an adult and that its cognitive development proceeds in genetically determined stages. Prof. at U. of Lausanne, 1937–54. *The Language and Thought of the Child,* 1926; *Biology and Knowledge,* 1971.

PLINY THE ELDER, born Gaius Plinius Secundus c.23 (Cisalpine, Gaul)–79. Roman naturalist. Noted for one surviving work, *Historia naturalis,* an encyclopedia of natural science, much of which is now known to be incorrect.

PLUTARCH, 46?–(Boetia)–c.120. Greek essayist, biographer. Deeply influenced early modern letters; attempted to portray character in his biographies of Roman soldiers, legislators, orators, and statesmen. *The Parallel Lives; Moralia.*

REUBEN, DAVID ROBERT, Nov. 29, 1933 (Chicago, Ill.). U.S. psychiatrist, author. *Everything You Always Wanted to Know about Sex,* 1969; *Any Woman Can!,* 1971; *How to Get More out of Sex,* 1974; *The Save-Your-Life Diet,* (with Barbara Reuben), 1975; *Everything You Always Wanted to Know about Nutrition,* 1978.

RHINE, JOSEPH BANKS, Sept. 19, 1895 (Waterloo, Pa.). U.S. parapsychologist. A pioneer in advocating scientific practices, particularly the use of statistics, in the study of telepathy, clairvoyance and other psychic phenomena of questionable reality.

RICARDO, DAVID, Apr. 19, 1772 (London, Eng.)–Sept. 11, 1823. English political economist. One of the first systematic economists; proposed an "iron law of wages," stating that wages tend to stabilize around the subsistence level; developed a theory of value and of comparative advantage in internatl. trade. *On the Principles of Political Economy and Taxation,* 1817.

RORSCHACH, HERMANN, Nov. 8, 1884 (Zurich, Switz.)–Apr. 2, 1922. Swiss psychiatrist. Developed the Rorschach ink-blot test (1921), as an aid in psychiatric diagnosis.

SAMUELSON, PAUL ANTHONY, May 15, 1915 (Gary, Ind.). U.S. economist. Noted for his widely-used introductory textbook, *Economics: An Introductory Analysis* (1948) and for important contributions to the mathematical structure of economic theory. Prof. at M.I.T., 1941–   ; awarded Nobel Prize in economics, 1970.

SCHLESINGER, ARTHUR MEIER, JR., Oct. 15, 1917 (Columbus, Ohio). U.S. historian, public official. Prof. at Harvard U. (1946–61) and City U. of N.Y. (1966–   ); cofounder of Americans for Democratic Action, 1947. *The Age of Jackson,* 1945 (Pulitzer Prize in history, 1946); *A Thousand Days,* 1965 (Pulitzer Prize in biography, 1966).

SCHLIEMANN, HEINRICH, Jan. 6, 1822 (Neubukow, Ger.)–Dec. 26, 1890. German archeologist. Noted as the discoverer of the ruins of Troy. A successful businessman who retired to devote himself to archeology out of his love for HOMER; discovered four superimposed towns, including Troy, at Hissarlik, Turkey, 1871; excavated at Mycenae (1876), Ithaca (1878), Bocotia (1881–82) and Tiryus (1884–85).

SCHUMPETER, JOSEPH, Feb. 8, 1883 (Triesch, A.-H. [now Czech.])–Jan. 8, 1950. Austrian-U.S. economist. Developed theories of capitalist development and business cycles; predicted that capitalism would perish from its success. *Capitalism, Socialism, and Democracy,* 3d ed., 1950.

SHIRER, WILLIAM LAWRENCE, Feb. 23, 1904 (Chicago, Ill.). U.S. nonfiction writer. *The Rise and Fall of the Third Reich: a History of Nazi Germany,* 1960; *The Rise and Fall of Adolf Hitler,* 1961; *The Collapse of the Third Republic, an Inquiry into the Fall of France in 1940,* 1969.

SKINNER, B(urrhus) F(rederic), Mar. 20, 1904 (Susquehanna, Pa.). U.S. behavioral psychologist who made major contributions to understanding of "instrumental learning" and the role of "reinforcement." *Walden Two,* 1960; *Beyond Freedom and Dignity,* 1971.

SMITH, ADAM, June 5, 1723 (Kircaldy, Scot.)–July 17, 1790. Scottish economist, philosopher. Noted as the author of *An Inquiry into the Nature and Causes of the Wealth of Nations* (1776), in which he postulated that wealth resides in labor; argued for the beneficent effect of the division of labor and a self-regulating free market in which an "invisible hand" turns private gain into public welfare. *Theory of Moral Sentiments,* 1759.

SONTAG, SUSAN 1933 (New York, N.Y.). U.S. critic, essayist, novelist. Best known for her critical essays on 1960s avant-garde culture, especially "Camp"; also has written experimental fiction. *Against Interpretation,* 1966; *The Benefactor* (novel), 1963; *Styles of Radical Will,* 1969; *On Photography,* 1977; *Illness as a Metaphor,* 1978.

SPENGLER, OSWALD, May 29, 1880 (Blankenburg-am-Harz, Ger.)–May 8, 1936. German writer on philosophy of history. Proposed in *The Decline of the West* (1926–28) that world history follows definite laws of growth and that Western culture had passed through a life cycle and was in a period of decline.

SPINGARN, JOEL ELIAS, May 17, 1875 (New York, N.Y.)–July 26, 1939. U.S. educator, literary critic. An exponent of the aesthetic school of criticism. Prof. of comparative literature at Columbia U., 1899–1911; a founder of Harcourt, Brace and Co., 1919; pres. of the NAACP, 1930–39; established the NAACP Springarn Medal for the black person of greatest service to his people. *The New Criticism,* 1911.

STEPHEN, SIR LESLIE, Nov. 28, 1832 (London, Eng.)–Feb. 22, 1904. English author, critic. The first serious critic of the novel. Editor of *The Dictionary of Natl. Biography,* 1882–91; as editor of *Cornhill* magazine (1871–82), encouraged writers. *History of English Thought in the Eighteenth Century,* 1876; *The English Utilitarians,* 3 vols., 1900 (Father of VIRGINIA WOOLF.)

STRABO, c.63 B.C. (Pontus [near northern coast of modern Turk.])–c.23. Greek geographer. His 17-volume *Geography,* provided a detailed description of the ancient world and a record of previous geographers' work (since lost).

THE BOOK OF WHO

STRACHEY, (Giles) LYTTON, Mar. 1, 1880 (London, Eng.)-Jan. 21, 1932. English biographer. Transformed the art of writing biography by writing brief, critical biographies; member of the Bloomsbury group. *Eminent Victorians,* 1918; *Queen Victoria,* 1921; *Portraits in Miniature,* 1931.

SUETONIUS, c.69-c.140. Roman biographer. Wrote lively biographies that deeply influenced history's view of Rome until the modern discovery of nonliterary evidence. *The Twelve Caesars* (trans. by ROBERT GRAVES, 1957); *Concerning Illustrious Men.*

TACITUS, CORNELIUS, c.56-c.120. Roman historian, orator, public official. Probably the greatest Roman historian. *Historiae; Dialogue on Orators; Life of Agricola; Germania; Annales.*

TATE, (John Orley) ALLEN, Nov. 19, 1899 (Winchester, Ky.). U.S. critic, poet, novelist. Major critic of the so-called "New Criticism"; regionalist advocate of the agrarian, conservative South. *Robert E. Lee,* 1932; *The Pope and Other Poems,* 1928; *The Fathers,* 1938.

THUCYDIDES, c.455 B.C. (Athens, Gr.)-c.400 B.C. Greek historian. In writing the *History of the Peloponnesian War,* became the earliest critical historian in antiquity; placed speeches in mouths of people in order to show their motives.

TOCQUEVILLE, ALEXIS DE, July 29, 1805 (Verneuil, Fr.)-Apr. 16, 1859. French writer, politician. Noted as the author of a perceptive study of the young U.S., *Democracy in America* (2 vols., 1835), in which he noted the distinctiveness of American institutions and the results of unprecedented equality. *L'Ancien Régime et la Révolution,* 1856.

TOYNBEE, ARNOLD, Apr. 14, 1889 (London, Eng.)-Oct. 22, 1975. English historian. Noted as author of the monumental *A Study of History* (12 vols., 1934-61), in which he analyzed the cyclical development and decline of civilizations. Prof. at London School of Economics, 1925-56.

TREITSCHKE, HEINRICH VON, Sept. 15, 1834 (Dresden, Ger.)-Apr. 28, 1896. German historian. Advocated German unification under Prussian leadership; an anti-Semitic and nationalist writer; editor of *Preussische Jahrbucher,* 1866-89. *History of Germany in the Nineteenth Century,* 7 vols., 1915-19.

TREVELYAN, GEORGE MACAULEY, Feb. 16, 1876 (Welcombe, Eng.)-July 21, 1962. English historian. Noted for his three-volume study of G. GARIBALDI (1907-11), for *British History in the Nineteenth Century, 1782-1901* (1922), and for *England Under Queen Anne* (3 vols., 1930-34). Prof. at Cambridge U., 1927-51.

TRILLING, LIONEL, July 4, 1905 (New York, N.Y.)-Nov. 5, 1975. U.S. critic author. Noted for his essays combining social, psychological, and political insights with literary criticism. *The Liberal Imagination,* 1950; *The Opposing Self,* 1955; *A Gathering of Fugitives,* 1956.

TUCHMAN, BARBARA, née Wertheim, Jan. 30, 1912 (New York, N.Y.). U.S. historian. Noted for her best-selling historical books. *The Guns of August* (Pulitzer Prize in history, 1963), 1962; *Stilwell and the American Experience in China, 1911-45* (Pulitzer in history, 1972), 1971; *A Distant Mirror,* 1978.

UNTERMEYER, LOUIS, Oct. 1, 1885 (New York, N.Y.)-Dec. 18, 1977. U.S. poet, editor, anthologist. Best known for his anthologies, especially *Modern American Poetry* (1919), *Modern British Poetry* (1920), and *A Treasury of the World's Great Poems* (1942).

VAN DOREN, CARL, Sept. 10, 1885 (Hope, Ill.)-July 18, 1950. U.S. author, editor. Member of group that established American literature and history as a central part of university curriculums. Prof. of English at Columbia U., 1911-30; literary editor of *The Nation* (1919-22), *Century* (1922-25), and *Literary Guild* (1926-34). *Benjamin Franklin,* 1938 (Pulitzer Prize in biography, 1939). (Brother of MARK VAN DOREN.)

VAN DOREN, MARK, June 13, 1894 (Hope, Ill.)-Dec. 10, 1972. U.S. critic, poet, educator. Prof. at Columbia U., 1920-59; literary editor (1924-28) and film critic (1935-38) for *The Nation. Collected Poems* (Pulitzer Prize in poetry, 1940), 1939. (Brother of CARL VAN DOREN.)

VAN-LAWICK-GOODALL, JANE, BARONESS, born Jane Goodall, Apr. 3, 1934 (London, Eng.). British ethologist. An authority on chimpanzees, discovered that they are not strict vegetarians and are crude toolmakers; has studied great apes at the Gombe Stream Game Reserve, Tanzania, from 1960. *My Friends the Wild Chimpanzees,* 1967; *In the Shadow of Man,* 1971.

VEBLEN, THORSTEIN BUNDE, July 30, 1857 (Cato Twp., Wisc.)-Aug. 3, 1919. U.S. economist, social critic. Coined the phrases "conspicuous consumption" and "pecuniary emulation" in his attempt to understand the emergence of big business in the U.S. *The Theory of the Leisure Class,* 1899; *The Theory of Business Enterprise,* 1904.

VELIKOVSKY, IMMANUEL, June 10, 1895 (Vitebsk, Rus.)-Nov. 17, 1979. Russian-U.S. writer. Proponent of the catastrophe theory of cosmology in a series of books that achieved worldwide popular success but were met with skepticism or hostility by the scientific community. *Worlds in Collision,* 1950; *Earth in Upheaval,* 1955; *Ages in Chaos,* 1952; *Oedipus and Akhnaton,* 1960.

WARD, BARBARA MARY, BARONESS JACKSON OF LODSWORTH, May 23, 1914 (York, Eng.). English economist. Noted for writings on political and economic affairs; counseled European economic unity and a liberal approach to the underdeveloped world; created baroness, 1976. *The Rich Nations and the Poor Nations,* 1962; *Nationalism and Ideology,* 1966; *Spaceship Earth,* 1966.

WEBER, MAX, Apr. 21, 1864 (Erfurt, Ger.)-June 14, 1920. German sociologist. A founder of modern sociology, credited with first noting the importance of bureaucracy in modern life; developed the famous thesis that the Protestant Ethic decisively influenced the rise of Western capitalism. *Protestant Ethic and the Spirit of Capitalism,* 1920.

WEBSTER, NOAH, Oct. 16, 1758 (West Hartford, Conn.)-May 28, 1843. U.S. lexicographer, writer. Known for his *American Spelling Book* (1783), which helped to standardize American spelling; agitated for U.S. copyright law. *American Dictionary of the English Language,* 1828.

WILSON, EDMUND, May 8, 1895 (Red Bank, N.J.)-June 12, 1972. U.S. literary and social critic. Noted for his influential critical writings on E. HEMINGWAY, J. DOS PASSOS, F. S. FITZGERALD, W. FAULKNER, and the symbolists, as well as his social studies of European revolutionary tradition and the American Depression. *Axel's Castle,* 1931; *American Jitters,* 1932; *To the Finland Station,* 1940; *The Boys in the Back Room,* 1941; *The Bit between My Teeth,* 1965.

WITTE, EDWIN EMIL, Jan. 4, 1887 (Jefferson Co., Wisc.)-May 20, 1960. U.S. economist. Leading prof. of economics at U. of Wisconsin, 1920-57; while serving on President's Com. on Economic Security (1934-35), authored Social Security Act of 1935, first govt.-sponsored old-age pension in U.S. history.

WOODSON, CARTER GODWIN, Dec. 19, 1875 (nr. New Canton, Va.)-Apr. 3, 1950. U.S. educator, historian. Devoted his life to research and publication in the field of black history. Organized Chicago Assn. for the Study of Negro Life and History, 1915; founded and edited the *Journal of Negro History,* 1916-50; founder (1922) and pres. (1922-50) of Associated Publishers, Inc., devoted to publishing books on blacks. *The Education of the Negro Prior to 1861,* 1915; *Negro Makers of History,* 1928.

XENOPHON, c.431 B.C. (Attica)-c.350 B.C. Greek historian. A disciple of SOCRATES; led a long retreat from the battle of Cunaxa (401 B.C.), which he described in *Anabasis. Memorabilia* (Recollections of Socrates); *Hellenica.*

YERKES, ROBERT MERANS, May 26, 1876 (Breadysville, Pa.)-Feb. 3, 1956. U.S. psychologist. One of the first comparative psychologists to work with animals in a laboratory setting; while at Yale U.'s Inst. of Psychology, founded experimental station near Orange Park, Fla. (1929), later named Yerkes Laboratories of Primate Biology and the nucleus of the present Yerkes Regional Primate Research Center. *The Great Apes: A Study of Anthropoid Life* (with A. W. Yerkes), 1929.

ZAMENHOF, LUDWIK LAZANZ ("Dr. Esperanto"), Dec. 15, 1859 (Bialystok, Pol.)-Apr. 14, 1917. Polish linguist. Creator of Esperanto, an internatl. language based on Indo-European languages, especially those of Western Europe. *Lingvo Internacia,* 1887; *Fundamento de Esperanto,* 1905.

EDUCATORS

ADLER, CYRUS, Sept. 13, 1863 (Van Buren, Ark.)-Apr. 7, 1940. U.S. educator, editor, Conservative Jewish leader. First pres., Dropsie C. for Hebrew and Cognate Learning, 1908-40; pres., Jewish Theological Seminary, 1924-40; founded American Jewish Historical Soc., 1892; planned and edited the *American Jewish Yearbook,* 1899-1905.

ANGELL, JAMES BURRILL, Jan. 7, 1829 (Scituate, R.I.)-Apr. 1, 1916. U.S. educator. Pres., U. of Vermont, 1866-71; as pres., U. of Michigan (1871-1909), elevated that school to academic prominence.

ARNOLD, THOMAS ("Arnold of Rugby"), June 13, 1795 (West Cowes, Isle of Wight)-June 12, 1842. English educator. As headmaster at Rugby (1828-42), set the pattern for the English public-school system. *History of Rome,* 3 vols., 1838-43; *Lectures on Modern History,* 1842. (Father of MATTHEW ARNOLD.)

BAKER, GEORGE PIERCE, Apr. 4, 1866 (Providence, R.I.)-Jan. 6, 1935. U.S. teacher. Started Harvard U. class for playwrights called "47 Workshop," 1905; students included EUGENE O'NEILL, PHILIP BARRY, THOMAS WOLFE, and JOHN DOS PASSOS; founded Yale Drama School, 1925.

BARNARD, FREDERICK AUGUSTUS PORTER, May 5, 1809 (Sheffield, Mass.)-Apr. 27, 1889. U.S. educator. Pres., U. of Mississippi, 1856-61; as pres., Columbia U., established Barnard C. for women, 1864-89.

BEECHER, CATHARINE ESTHER, Sept. 6, 1800 (East Hampton, N.Y.)-May 12, 1878. U.S. educator who promoted higher education for women. (Daughter of LYMAN BEECHER; sister of HARRIET BEECHER STOWE.)

BELL, ANDREW, Mar. 27, 1753 (St. Andrews, Scot.)-Jan. 27, 1832. Scottish educator, clergyman. Originated a system of education (Bell or Madras) in which the older students instruct the younger.

BETHUNE, MARY McLEOD, July 10, 1875 (Mayesville, S.C.)-May 18, 1955. U.S. educator. Founded Daytona Normal and Industrial Inst. for Negro Girls, 1904; merged school with Cookman Inst. (1923), to form Bethune-Cookman C., of which she was pres., 1923-42 and 1946-47; founded National Council of Negro Women, 1937; awarded Spingarn Medal (NAACP), 1935.

BLAIR, JAMES, 1655 (Scot.)-Apr. 18, 1743. Colonial clergyman, educator. Established the C. of William and Mary, the second-oldest institution of higher learning in the U.S.

BOK, DEREK CURTIS, May 22, 1930 (Ardmore, Pa.). U.S. educator. Dean, Harvard Law School, 1968-71; pres., Harvard U., 1971-   .

BREWSTER, KINGMAN, June 17, 1919 (Longmeadow, Mass.). U.S. educator, diplomat. Prof. of law at Harvard U. (1950-60) and Yale U. (1961-63); pres. of Yale U., 1963-77; chm. of Natl. Policy Panel of the UN, 1968; U.S. amb. to Great Britain, 1977-

BUTLER, NICHOLAS MURRAY, Apr. 2, 1862 (Elizabeth, N.J.)-Dec. 7, 1947. U.S. educator. Pres., Columbia U., 1901-45; helped establish Carnegie Endowment for International Peace and served as pres., 1925-45; won Nobel Peace Prize, 1931.

COMENIUS, JOHN AMOS, born Jan Amos Komensky, Mar. 28, 1592 (Nivnice, Moravia)-Nov. 15, 1670. Czech churchman, educator. Attempted to reform educational methods and advocated universal education; wanted knowledge organized systematically and in vernacular language; called the "grandfather" of modern education. *The Great Didactic,* 1628-32.

COMPTON, KARL TAYLOR, Sept. 14, 1887 (Wooster, Ohio)-June 22, 1954. U.S. educator, physicist. Pres., M.I.T., 1930-46; chm. of the atomic-bomb evaluation board, 1946.

CONANT, JAMES BRYANT, Mar. 26, 1893 (Dorchester, Mass.). U.S. educator, diplomat. Pres. of Harvard U., 1933-53; U.S. amb. to W. Germany, 1955-57. *The Chemistry of Organic Compounds,* 1923.

DOBIE, JAMES FRANK, Sept. 26, 1888 (Live Oak Co., Tex.)-Sept. 18, 1964. U.S. teacher, folklorist. Prof. of English, U. of Texas, 1933-47; wrote some 30 books chronicling the legends and stories of Texas and the Southwest.

DORIOT, GEORGES FREDERIC, Sept. 24, 1899 (Paris, Fr.). U.S. business executive, educator. Asst. dean (1926-31) and prof. of industrial management (1926-66) at Harvard Business School; through his course on manufacturing, credited with creating the professional management corps of U.S. business; pres. of American Research and Development Co., 1947-72.

DUNSTER, HENRY, 1609 (Lancashire, Eng.)-

THE BOOK OF WHO

Feb. 16, 1659. U.S. educator. First pres. of Harvard C., 1640-54.

EISENHOWER, MILTON STOVER, Sept. 15, 1899 (Abilene, Kan.). U.S. educator. Pres., Kansas St. U., 1943-50; pres., Pennsylvania St. U., 1950-56; pres., Johns Hopkins U., 1956-67 and 1971-72. (Brother of DWIGHT D. EISENHOWER.)

ELIOT, CHARLES WILLIAM, Mar. 20, 1834 (Boston, Mass.)-Aug. 22, 1926. U.S. educator. Pres., Harvard U. 1869-1909; helped establish Radcliffe C., 1894.

FRANCKE, AUGUST HERMANN, Mar. 22, 1663 (Lübeck, Ger.)-June 8, 1727. German preacher, educator. Founder of Pietism; founded a charity school in Halle (1698) that later became the Francke Inst.

FROEBEL (or Fröbel), FRIEDRICH WILHELM AUGUST, Apr. 21, 1782 (Oberweissbach, Ger.)-June 21, 1852. German educator. Founded the kindergarten system, 1837.

GALLAUDET, THOMAS HOPKINS, Dec. 10, 1787 (Philadelphia, Pa.)-Sept. 10, 1851. U.S. educator. Established the first free school for the deaf in the U.S., 1817; Gallaudet C. is named for him.

GIAMATTI, ANGELO BARTLETT, Apr. 4, 1938 (Boston, Mass.). U.S. educator. Pres., Yale U., 1978- .

GOHEEN, ROBERT FRANCIS, Aug. 15, 1919 (Vengurla, India). U.S. educator, diplomat. Pres., Princeton U., 1972-77; U.S. amb. to India, 1977- .

GRAY, HANNA HOLBORN, Oct. 25, 1930 (Heidelberg, Ger.). U.S. educator. Provost and prof. of history (1974-78) and acting pres. (1977-78) of Yale U.; pres., U. of Chicago, 1978- .

HARPER, WILLIAM RAINEY, July 26, 1856 (New Concord, Ohio)-Jan. 10, 1906. U.S. educator. First pres., U. of Chicago, 1891-1906.

HARVARD, JOHN, baptized Nov. 29, 1607 (London, Eng.)-Sept. 14, 1638. American colonial clergyman. Left his library and half of his estate to a newly founded college that was renamed in his honor, 1639.

HERBART, JOHANN FRIEDRICH, May 4, 1776 (Oldenburg, Ger.)-Aug. 14, 1841. German philosopher, educator. Noted for coordinating psychology and ethics in devising educational systems and methods.

HOPKINS, MARK, Feb. 4, 1802 (Stockbridge, Mass.)-June 17, 1887. U.S. educator, theologian. Noted for his ability to arouse students to express their own thoughts and natures; Pres. JAMES A. GARFIELD, a former student, reputedly said of him, "The ideal college is Mark Hopkins on one end of a log and a student on the other." Pres. of Williams C., 1836-72.

HUNTER, THOMAS, Oct. 18, 1831 (Ardglass, Ire.)-Oct. 14, 1915. U.S. educator. Organized and headed Normal C. of the City of New York, 1870-1906; college renamed after him, 1914.

KALLEN, HORACE MEYER, Aug. 11, 1882 (Silesia, Ger.)-Feb. 16, 1974. U.S. educator, philosopher. Prof. of philosophy, New School for Social Research, 1919-52. *William James and Henri Bergson,* 1914.

LANCASTER, JOSEPH, Nov. 25, 1778 (London, Eng.)-Oct. 24, 1838. English educator. Developed "Lancasterian schools," a system of mass education in which brighter children taught other children under the direction of an adult; emigrated to the U.S. (1818), where he established over 60 such schools.

LA SALLE, JEAN BAPTISTE DE, Apr. 30, 1651

(Reims, Fr.)-Apr. 7, 1719. French educator, Roman Catholic saint. Founded the Christian Bros., 1680-84; canonized, 1900.

LINCOLN, MARY JOHNSON, née Bailey, July 8, 1844 (S. Attleboro, Mass.)-Dec. 2, 1921. U.S. educator, author. Dir., Boston Cooking School, 1879-85; wrote several cookbooks, including *Mrs. Lincoln's Boston Cook Book,* (1884) and *Boston School Kitchen Textbook* (1887).

LYON, MARY, Feb. 28, 1797 (Buckland, Mass.)-Mar. 5, 1849. U.S. educator. Founded Mt. Holyoke C., the first women's college in the U.S., 1837.

MACKENZIE, JAMES CAMERON, Aug. 15, 1852 (Aberdeen, Scot.)-May 10, 1931. U.S. educator. Noted for raising scholarship standards in U.S. secondary schools. Founded Wilkes-Barre (Pa.) Academy (1878), Lawrenceville (N.J.) School (1882), and MacKenzie (N.Y.) school (1901); at Lawrenceville, introduced English house system, honor system, athletic fields, and golf links.

MACY, ANNE SULLIVAN, Apr. 14, 1866 (Feeding Hills, Mass.)-Oct. 20, 1936. U.S. teacher. Best known as the teacher and companion of HELEN KELLER. Blinded by a childhood illness; studied at the Perkins Inst. for the Blind; accompanied Keller through her education at Perkins, Cambridge School for Young Ladies, and Radcliffe C., 1889-1904.

MANN, HORACE, May 4, 1796 (Franklin, Mass.)-Aug. 2, 1859. U.S. educator, public official. As the first secy. of the Massachusetts Board of Education, 1837-48, established public-school system that became model for the nation; U.S. rep. (Whig, Mass.), 1849-53; pres., Antioch C., 1853-59.

MASON, LOWELL, Jan. 8, 1792 (Medfield, Mass.)-Aug. 11, 1872. U.S. educator, hymn writer. Organized Boston Academy of Music, 1833; devised system of musical instruction for children; wrote "Nearer, My God to Thee," 1859.

MATTFIELD, JACQUELYN PHILLIPS ANDERSON, Oct. 5, 1925 (Baltimore, Md.). U.S. educator. As pres. of Barnard C. (1976-), has attempted to keep it autonomous within Columbia U.

MCGUFFEY, WILLIAM HOLMES, Sept. 23, 1800 (Claysville, Pa.)-May 4, 1873. U.S. educator. Author of "eclectic readers," six volumes published between 1836 and 1857 that served as standard texts in 19th-cent. U.S. public schools; sold over 122 million copies, shaping the minds of three generations of school children.

MCLUHAN, HERBERT MARSHALL. July 21, 1911 (Edmonton, Alta., Can.). Canadian educator, author, expert on mass communications. *Understanding Media,* 1964; *The Medium Is the Message,* 1967.

MONTESSORI, MARIA, Aug. 31, 1870 (Chiaravalle, It.)-May 6, 1952. Italian educator. Originated the Montessori method of education which stresses development of initiative, and sense and muscle training, as well as the freedom of the child; opened her first school, in Rome, 1907.

NEILSON, WILLIAM ALLEN, Mar. 28, 1869 (Doune, Scot.)-Feb. 13, 1946. U.S. educator, editor, author. Pres., Smith C., 1917-39; editor in chief, *Webster's New International Dictionary,* 2nd edition, 1934; editor, Cambridge edition of *Shakespeare's Works,* 1906 and 1942. *Essentials of Poetry,* 1912.

PATTERSON, FREDERICK DOUGLAS, Oct. 10, 1901 (Washington, D.C.). U.S. educator. Pres. of Tuskegee Normal and Industrial Inst., 1935-53; organized United Negro C. Fund, 1943.

PEABODY, ELIZABETH PALMER, May 16, 1804 (Billerica, Mass.)–Jan. 3, 1894. U.S. educator. Founded first kindergarten in the U.S., 1860; published elementary-school textbooks in grammar and history.

PESTALOZZI, JOHANN HEINRICH, Jan. 12, 1746 (Zurich, Switz.)–Feb. 17, 1827. Swiss educational reformer. Stressed the importance of accurate observation of actual objects for clear, accurate thinking; influenced methods of instruction in elementary schools in Europe and the U.S.

PHILLIPS, JOHN, Dec. 6, 1719 (Andover, Mass.)–Apr. 21, 1795. U.S. merchant, educational benefactor. Founded Phillips Exeter Academy, at Exeter, N.H., 1781; helped found Phillips Academy, at Andover, Mass., 1778.

PORTER, SARAH, Aug. 16, 1813 (Farmington, Conn.)–Feb. 17, 1900. U.S. educator. Founded Miss Porter's School for Girls, at Farmington, Conn., 1843.

RAIKES, ROBERT, Sept. 4, 1736 (Gloucester, Eng.)–Apr. 5, 1811. British philanthropist. Pioneer of the Sunday-school movement.

SCOPES, JOHN THOMAS, 1900 (Salem, Ill.)–Oct. 21, 1970. U.S. schoolteacher. Taught the theory of evolution in defiance of a Tennessee state law, precipitating the "Scopes Trial," July 1925; convicted and fined, but rulings were later reversed.

SETON, ELIZABETH ANN, née Bayley ("Mother Seton"), Aug. 28, 1774 (New York, N.Y.)–Jan. 4, 1821. U.S. educator, religious leader. Founded the Sisters of St. Joseph, a teaching order instrumental in the establishment of the parochial school system in the U.S., 1809; canonized as the first U.S.-born saint, 1975.

STURM, JOHANNES VON, Oct. 1, 1507 (Schlesden, Ger.)–Mar. 3, 1589. German educator. Founded a school in Strasbourg that emphasized maintenance of strict discipline and mastery of the classics, 1537.

SUMNER, WILLIAM GRAHAM, Oct. 30, 1840 (Paterson, N.J.)–Apr. 12, 1910. U.S. educator, sociologist, economist. As prof. of political science, Yale U. (1872-1910), advocated free trade and sound currency and opposed socialism.

Folkways, 1907; *Science and Society* (4 vols.), 1927.

THOMAS, MARTHA CAREY, Jan. 2, 1857 (Baltimore, Md.)–Dec. 2, 1935. U.S. educator, prominent suffragist. Pres., Bryn Mawr C., 1894-1922. *The Higher Education of Women,* 1900.

VITTORINO DA FELTRE, born Vittorino Ramboldini (or de Ramboldoni), 1378 (Feltre, It.)–Feb. 2, 1446. Italian educator, humanist. Founded a school that admitted both noble and poor boys and girls, in Mantua, 1423; set the pattern for Renaissance schools.

WASHINGTON, BOOKER TALIAFERRO, Apr. 5, 1856 (Franklin Co., Va.)–Nov. 14, 1915. U.S. educator, social reformer. Established Tuskegee Inst., 1881, and headed it until his death; an educational leader and principal spokesman of black people. Elected to the American Hall of Fame, 1945. *Up From Slavery,* 1901.

WHEELOCK, ELEAZAR, Apr. 22, 1711 (Windham, Conn.)–Apr. 24, 1779. U.S. educator. Tutored American Indians, from 1743; founded Dartmouth C. and served as its first pres., 1770-79.

WHITE, ANDREW DICKSON, Nov. 7, 1832 (Homer, N.Y.)–Nov. 4, 1918. U.S. educator, diplomat. A founder (with EZRA CORNELL) of Cornell U. (1865), which he served as pres., 1868-85; U.S. min. to Germany (1879-81) and Russia (1892-94); U.S. amb. to Germany, 1897-1902.

WIGGIN, KATE DOUGLAS, née Smith, Sept. 28, 1856 (Philadelphia, Pa.)–Aug. 24, 1923. U.S. educator, writer. Founded, with her sister Nora, the California Kindergarten Training School, 1880; *Rebecca of Sunnybrook Farm,* 1903.

WILLARD, EMMA, née Hart, Feb. 23, 1787 (Berlin, Conn.)–Apr. 15, 1870. U.S. educator. Pioneer in the field of higher education for women. Established the Emma Willard School, 1821; elected to the American Hall of Fame, 1905.

WYTHE, GEORGE, 1726 (Elizabeth Co., Va.)–June 8, 1806. U.S. lawyer, educator. First prof. of law in the U.S., at William and Mary, 1779-89; taught THOMAS JEFFERSON, JOHN MARSHALL, and HENRY CLAY.

SCIENTISTS, PHYSICIANS, AND INVENTORS

U.S. SCIENTISTS, PHYSICIANS, AND INVENTORS

ABBE, CLEVELAND, Dec. 3, 1838 (New York, N.Y.)–Oct. 28, 1916. U.S. astronomer, meteorologist. Initiated daily weather bulletins, 1869; the first meteorologist of U.S. Weather Bureau; instrumental in initiating use of standard time zones.

ADAMS, WALTER SIDNEY, Dec. 20, 1876 (Syria)–May 11, 1956. U.S. astronomer. Developed a method of spectroscopic parallax that enabled calculation of distances of far-away stars, 1914; first discoverer of a white dwarf star, 1915.

AGASSIZ, JEAN LOUIS RODOLPHE, May 28, 1807 (Switzerland)–Dec. 12, 1873. U.S. zoologist, geologist. By examining modern glaciers and their effects on the land, discovered (c.1840) that glaciers and ice had once covered large parts of northern Europe and America (the Ice Age); the Agassiz Museum of Comparative History at Harvard University is named after him; named to Hall of Fame for Great Americans, 1915.

AIKEN, HOWARD HATHAWAY, Mar. 9, 1900

(Hoboken, N.J.)–Mar. 14, 1973. U.S. mathematician. Invented Mark I, first modern digital computer (completed 1944), which weighed 35 tons, was 51 ft. long, had a memory, and did only arithmetic.

ALEXANDERSON, ERNST FREDERICK WERNER, Jan. 25, 1878 (Sweden)–May 14, 1975. U.S. electrical engineer. Developed a high-frequency alternator able to produce continuous radio waves, thus revolutionizing radio communications, 1906; invented modern radio-tuning device, 1916; developed an early automatic-control system for sensitive manufacturing processes (the amplidyne); early TV pioneer, demonstrating it privately in 1927.

ALVAREZ, LUIS WALTER, June 13, 1911 (San Francisco, Calif.). U.S. physicist. His discovery of "resonance particles" led to major modern theories of subatomic particles (after 1945); made major contributions to aviation radar, including ground-control approach (GCA) landing systems, 1940-44; devised method of X-raying ancient buildings, including the Great Pyramid, to deter-

THE BOOK OF WHO

mine whether any chambers remained undiscovered; awarded Nobel Prize in physics, 1968.

ANDERSON, CARL DAVID, Sept. 3, 1905 (New York, N.Y.). U.S. physicist. Discovered and named the positron, 1932; discovered and named the first mesotron (now shortened to meson), the mu-meson, 1935; awarded Nobel Prize for physics, 1936.

ANDERSON, PHILIP WARREN, Dec. 13, 1923 (Indianapolis, Ind.). U.S. physicist. Noted for his basic studies of the electrical and magnetic properties of noncrystalline solids; awarded Nobel Prize in physics (with J. H. VAN VLECK and N. F. MOTT), 1977.

ANFINSEN, CHRISTIAN BOEHMER, Mar. 26, 1916 (Monessen, Pa.). U.S. biochemist. Studied how the structure of enzymes and other proteins relate to their physiological function; awarded Nobel Prize in chemistry (with STANFORD MOORE and W. H. STEIN), 1972. *The Molecular Basis of Evolution,* 1959.

ANGLE, EDWARD HARTLEY, June 1, 1855 (Herrick, Pa.)–Aug. 11, 1930. U.S. orthodontist. Founded modern orthodontia as the first specialist in field, c.1886; founded first School of Orthodontia, in St. Louis, 1895; initiated idea of normal occlusion (bite) of the teeth.

ARMSTRONG, EDWIN HOWARD, Dec. 18, 1890 (New York, N.Y.)–Feb. 1, 1954. U.S. inventor. Invented regenerative circuit, the first amplifying receiver and reliable transmitter, 1912; invented superheterodyne circuit, the basis for most modern radio, TV, and radar reception, 1918; invented FM broadcasting system, 1933; in long fight to defend his primary role in these inventions, lost to L. DE FOREST on the regenerative circuit and committed suicide in midst of suit over FM.

AXELROD, JULIUS, May 30, 1912 (New York, N.Y.). U.S. biochemist. Discovered two ways in which noradrenaline activity in the nervous system is stopped; awarded Nobel Prize in physiology or medicine (with B. KATZ and U. S. VON EULER), 1970.

BAEKELAND, LEO HENDRIK, Nov. 14, 1863 (Belgium)–Feb. 23, 1944. U.S. chemist. Invented Bakelite, one of the first plastics with widespread applications, 1909; founded Bakelite Corp., now part of Union Carbide, 1910.

BAILEY, LIBERTY HYDE, Mar. 15, 1858 (South Haven, Mich.)–Dec. 25, 1954. U.S. chemist. Founded modern science of horticulture, c.1885; leader in establishment of agricultural-extension courses in rural areas.

BALTIMORE, DAVID, Mar. 7, 1938 (New York, N.Y.). U.S. microbiologist. Conducted research into the process by which a virus can change the genetic makeup of a cell; demonstrated the existence of "reverse transcriptase," a viral enzyme that reverses the normal DNA-to-RNA process, 1970; awarded Nobel Prize in physiology or medicine (with RENATO DULBECCO and HOWARD TEMIN), 1975.

BANNEKER, BENJAMIN, Nov. 9, 1731 (Ellicott's Mills, Md.)–Oct. 1806. U.S. astronomer. A self-taught black scientist who published an annual almanac and astronomical ephemeris for years 1792–1802 for mid-Atlantic states, one of the most accurate and sophisticated in the world at that time; assisted in 1789 survey of District of Columbia; wrote essays and pamphlets against slavery and war.

BARDEEN, JOHN, May 23, 1908 (Madison, Wisc.). U.S. physicist. Only person to win two Nobel Prizes in one field; a discoverer (with W. B.

S. SHOCKLEY and W. H. BRATTAIN) of the transistor, c.1948; with L. N. COOPER and J. R. SCHRIEFFER, developed the BCS theory, which explains superconductivity according to fundamental physics, 1957; awarded 1956 Nobel Prize in physics (with Brattain and Shockley) and 1972 Nobel Prize in physics (with Cooper and Schrieffer).

BEADLE, GEORGE WELLS, Oct. 22, 1903 (Wahoo, Neb.). U.S. geneticist. Pioneer in the study of the chemical functions of genes in the production of enzymes, 1940s; awarded Nobel Prize in physiology or medicine (with E. L. TATUM and J. LEDERBERG), 1958.

BEAUMONT, WILLIAM, Nov. 21, 1785 (Lebanon, Conn.)–Apr. 25, 1853. U.S. surgeon. First to use an artificial opening (fistula) in a living body to study body processes; observed and made experiments in the process of digestion of a man whose stomach had been opened by a shotgun blast, 1822–33.

BEEBE, CHARLES WILLIAM, July 29, 1877 (Brooklyn, N.Y.)–June 4, 1962. U.S. naturalist, inventor. Invented the bathysphere; was the first man to descend in the ocean beyond a few hundred ft.—3,038 ft., 1934.

BELL, ALEXANDER GRAHAM, Mar. 3, 1847 (Edinburgh, Scot.)–Aug. 2, 1922. U.S.-Can. inventor. First to patent and commercially exploit the telephone, 1876; in addition to other inventions and improvements, supported other researchers; founded the journal *Science,* 1883; named to Hall of Fame for Great Americans, 1950; his famous first words on the telephone: "Watson, please come here. I want you."

BERLINER, EMILE, May 20, 1851 (Germany)–Aug. 3, 1929. U.S. inventor. Invented the flat, "platter," phonograph record; worked on improvements in the telephone and airplane motors; a leading advocate of compulsory pasteurization of milk.

BJERKNES, JACOB AALL BONNEVIE, Nov. 2, 1879 (Sweden)–July 7, 1975. Norwegian-U.S. meteorologist. With father, Vilhelm, worked out the theory of polar and tropical air masses and weather fronts, the basic ideas of modern meteorology.

BLACKWELL, ELIZABETH, Feb. 3, 1821 (England)–May 31, 1910. English-U.S. physician. First woman in U.S. to gain an M.D. degree, 1849; founded New York Infirmary (1857) and London School of Medicine for Women (1875).

BLOCH, FELIX, Oct. 23, 1905 (Zurich, Switz.). U.S. physicist. Devised methods for the study of magnetism in atomic nuclei (c.1945–46) that opened the way to more precise knowledge of nuclear structure, to very sensitive magnetometers, and to new techniques in analytic chemistry; first dir.-genl. of CERN, a multinational nuclear lab in Geneva, Switz.; awarded Nobel Prize in physics (with E. M. PURCELL), 1952.

BLOCH, KONRAD EMIL, Jan. 21, 1912 (Silesia, Ger.). U.S. biochemist. Traced the construction of cholesterol out of the simple two-carbon compound acetic acid, 1946–58; awarded Nobel Prize in physiology or medicine (with F. Lynen), 1964.

BORDEN, GAIL, Nov. 9, 1801 (Norwich, N.Y.)–Jan. 11, 1874. U.S. inventor. Invented evaporated milk (1853) and a variety of juice concentrates; father of the "instant food" industry.

BRATTAIN, WALTER HOUSER, Feb. 10, 1902 (Amoy, China). U.S. physicist. One of the discoverers of the transistor, 1948; awarded Nobel Prize in

SCIENTISTS, PHYSICIANS, AND INVENTORS

physics (with W. SHOCKLEY and J. BARDEEN), 1956.

BRAUN, WERNHER MAGNUS MAXIMILIAN VON, Mar. 23, 1912 (Germany)–June 16, 1977. U.S. engineer. Early pioneer of rocketry; led development of Germany's V-2 missiles in WW II (1938–45) and of U.S. rocket-engine program that culminated in manned flight to the moon (1950s–60s).

BRIDGMAN, PERCY WILLIAMS, Apr. 21, 1882 (Cambridge, Mass.)–Aug. 20, 1961. U.S. physicist. Pioneer in development of high-pressure chambers for study of matter at extreme pressures; a philosopher of science; awarded Nobel Prize in physics, 1946.

BRONK, DETLEV WULF, Aug. 13, 1897 (New York, N.Y.)–Nov. 17, 1975. U.S. biophysicist. Founded biophysics, the application of physics to biological processes; headed Rockefeller Inst., 1953–68.

BRUSH, CHARLES FRANCIS, Mar. 17, 1849 (Euclid, Ohio)–June 15, 1928. U.S. inventor, manufacturer. Invented a long-lasting arc light; installed first electric arc street-lighting, in Cleveland, Ohio (1879), and first electric store-lighting in Wanamaker's of Philadelphia (1878).

BRYCE, JAMES WARES, Sept. 5, 1880 (New York, N.Y.)–Mar. 27, 1949. U.S. inventor. Working at IBM from 1917 on, a major pioneer in the application of electronics to business machines, acquiring more than 500 patents; led in the development of visual display tubes.

BURBANK, LUTHER, Mar. 7, 1849 (Lancaster, Mass.)–Apr. 11, 1926. U.S. botanist. Pioneer in improving food plants through grafting, hybridization, etc.; developed a new potato and new varieties of plums and berries; also developed new flowers, including the Burbank rose and the Shasta daisy.

BUSH, VANNEVAR, Mar. 11, 1890 (Everett, Mass.)–June 28, 1974. U.S. electrical engineer. Built the first analog computer, 1925; as chm. of the U.S. Office of Scientific Research and Development in early 1940s, headed U.S. scientific war effort and early uranium research for the atomic bomb; instrumental in founding Manhattan Project (1942), which developed the fission bomb, and the National Science Fndn.

BUSHNELL, DAVID, 1742? (Saybrook, Conn.)–1824. U.S. inventor. Invented the first submarine, a one-man craft designed to attach a mine to an enemy hull, 1776.

CALVIN, MELVIN, Apr. 7, 1911 (St. Paul, Minn.). U.S. biochemist. Worked out the steps of the photosynthesis process, the process by which plants use carbon dioxide and water to form starch and oxygen, 1949–57; awarded Nobel Prize in chemistry, 1961.

CANNON, ANNIE JUMP, Dec. 11, 1863 (Dover, Del.)–Apr. 13, 1941. U.S. astronomer. Called the "Census Taker of the Sky," she catalogued and classified some 400,000 astronomical objects, 1897–1930; first woman to receive an honorary doctorate from Oxford U., 1925.

CAROTHERS, WALLACE HUME, Apr. 27, 1896 (Burlington, Ia.)–Apr. 29, 1937. U.S. chemist. Invented the first form of nylon (1931) and neoprene (a synthetic rubber).

CARVER, GEORGE WASHINGTON, 1864 (nr. Diamond Grove, Mo.)–Jan. 5, 1943. U.S. chemist. Born a slave, he revolutionized Southern agriculture by advocating planting peanuts and sweet potatoes, which enrich the soil, to replace cotton and tobacco, which impoverish it; developed over 400 byproducts of peanuts and sweet potatoes; refused offers of work from T. A. EDISON, HENRY FORD, and the USSR; took no personal profit from his discoveries; awarded Roosevelt Medal, 1939; his birthplace is a national monument.

CHAMBERLAIN, OWEN, July 10, 1920 (San Francisco, Calif.). U.S. physicist. With EMILIO SEGRÈ, discovered the antiproton, 1955; awarded Nobel Prize in physics (with Segrè), 1959.

COBLENTZ, WILLIAM WEBER, Nov. 20, 1873 (North Lima, Ohio)–Sept. 15, 1962. U.S. physicist. An early pioneer in infrared spectrophotometry, which enables detection of atomic groupings within molecules; founded radiometry section of Natl. Bureau of Standards; major figure in establishment of internatl. radiation standards.

COLT, SAMUEL, July 19, 1814 (Hartford, Conn.)–Jan. 10, 1862. U.S. inventor. Invented Colt revolver, 1835 (introduced, 1852); founded Colt's Armory in Hartford, Conn. (1842), which made extensive use of assembly-line techniques and interchangeable parts.

COMMONER, BARRY, May 28, 1917 (Brooklyn, N.Y.). U.S. biologist, environmentalist. A major advocate of environmental protection and the use of solar energy. *Science and Survival,* 1966; *The Politics of Energy,* 1979.

COMPTON, ARTHUR HOLLY, Sept. 10, 1892 (Wooster, Ohio)–Mar. 15, 1962. U.S. physicist. Discovered and named the photon, the particle unit of light, thus giving confirmation to MAX PLANCK's quantum theory, 1923; first to prove that cosmic rays were particles, not electromagnetic forces; awarded Nobel Prize in physics (with C. T. R. WILSON), 1927.

COOLIDGE, WILLIAM DAVID, Oct. 23, 1873 (Hudson, Mass.)–Feb. 3, 1975. U.S. physicist. Developed a method of making fine wire from tungsten (1908), making possible the mass production of long-lived light bulbs, radio tubes, etc.; also developed a tungsten-using X-ray tube ("Coolidge tube") that made mass production possible, 1913.

COOPER, LEON N., Feb. 28, 1930 (New York, N.Y.). U.S. physicist. With J. BARDEEN and J. R. S. SCHRIEFFER, developed an effective theory of superconductivity, 1957; awarded Nobel Prize in physics (with Bardeen and Schrieffer), 1972.

CORI, CARL FERDINAND, Dec. 5, 1896 (Prague, Czech.) and **GERTY THERESA CORI,** née Radnitz, Aug. 15, 1896 (Prague, Czech.)–Oct. 26, 1957. U.S. biochemists. Worked out details of glycogen breakdown and resynthesis through use of phosphates; discoverers of "Cori ester," the basic phosphate of this process, which is essential to the understanding of muscular energy; awarded Nobel Prize in physiology or medicine (with B. A. HOUSSAY), 1947.

CURTISS, GLENN HAMMOND, May 21, 1878 (Hammondsport, N.Y.)–July 23, 1930. U.S. inventor. Pioneer in aviation who built his first successful plane in 1908; his major contribution was the development of powerful, lightweight engines; held a variety of air records, 1908–10; invented the hydroplane, 1911.

DAVISSON, CLINTON JOSEPH, Oct. 22, 1881 (Bloomington, Ill.)–Feb. 1, 1958. U.S. physicist. By diffracting an electron beam with a nickel crystal, demonstrated that an electron has a wave motion, 1927; awarded Nobel Prize in physics (with G. P. THOMSON), 1937.

DEBAKEY, MICHAEL ELLIS, Sept. 7, 1908 (Lake Charles, La.). U.S. surgeon. Has made major advances in heart surgery and heart transplants.

THE BOOK OF WHO

DEBYE, PETER JOSEPH WILHELM, Mar. 24, 1884 (Netherlands)–Nov. 2, 1966. Dutch-U.S. physical chemist. Developed basic theory of dipole movements, fundamental to the understanding of chemical bonds (the unit of dipole moment is called a debye) and contributed to the Debye-Hückel theory of ion behavior in solutions; awarded Nobel Prize in chemistry, 1936.

DE FOREST, LEE, Aug. 26, 1873 (Council Bluffs, Ia.)–June 30, 1961. U.S. inventor. Invented the triode, the basis of the first electronic-sound amplification before transistors, 1906; invented first sound-on-film system, 1923; owned over 300 patents.

DELBRÜCK, MAX, Sept. 4, 1906 (Berlin, Ger.). U.S. biologist, physicist. A founder of molecular biology through his basic discoveries in bacterium and virus reproduction and mutation, 1940; awarded Nobel Prize in physiology or medicine (with A. D. HERSHEY and S. E. LURIA), 1969.

DICK, ALBERT BLAKE, Apr. 16, 1856 (Bureau Co., Ill.)–Aug. 15, 1934. U.S. inventor. Invented the mimeograph process and machines, c.1887; founded A. B. Dick Co., a duplicator manufacturer, 1887.

DREW, CHARLES RICHARD, June 3, 1904 (Washington, D.C.)–Apr. 1, 1950. U.S. surgeon. An expert on blood plasma who organized and operated the first blood bank (1940, in New York City); the segregation rules of that time forbade Dr. Drew, a black, to donate his own blood to the bank; awarded Spingarn Medal, 1943.

DULBECCO, RENATO, Feb. 2, 1914 (Italy). U.S. molecular biologist. Developed laboratory techniques for the study of animal viruses; awarded Nobel Prize in physiology or medicine (with DAVID BALTIMORE and HOWARD TEMIN), 1975.

DUNNING, JOHN RAY, Sept. 24, 1907 (Shelby, Neb.)–Aug. 25, 1975. U.S. physicist. First to demonstrate fission of uranium-235, 1940; developed gas-diffusion method of concentrating U-235.

DU PONT, FRANCIS IRÉNÉE, Dec. 3, 1873 (Wilmington, Del.)–Mar. 16, 1942. U.S. chemist, financier. Made basic discoveries in the field of smokeless powder and minerals-separation processes; founded F. I. du Pont & Co., investment bankers, 1931.

DU VIGNEAUD, VINCENT, May 18, 1901 (Chicago, Ill.)–Dec. 11, 1978. U.S. chemist. Synthesized penicillin (1946) and two hormones; awarded Nobel Prize in chemistry, 1955.

EASTMAN, GEORGE, July 12, 1854 (Waterville, N.Y.)–Mar. 14, 1932. U.S. inventor. Invented photographic emulsion gel (1878) and its application to paper (1884) to make film; patented celluloid film, 1889; developed the Kodak, the first low-price, popularly available camera; pioneer in such business practices as sickness benefits, employee life insurance, and pensions.

EDELMAN, GERALD MAURICE, July 1, 1929 (New York, N.Y.). U.S. biochemist. First to work out the structure of an antibody molecule (1969), independently of R. R. PORTER; awarded Nobel Prize in physiology or medicine (with Porter), 1972.

EDISON, THOMAS ALVA, Feb. 11, 1847 (Milan, Ohio)–Oct. 18, 1931. U.S. inventor. Called the "Wizard of Menlo Park"; invented stock ticker (1869), the first electric light bulb (1879), and nearly 1,300 other items; made major contributions to the development of motion pictures, telephones, electrical generating systems; discovered the "Edison effect," the basis of modern electronics, 1883; the total value of his inventions was estimated at $25 billion before his death; named to Hall of Fame for Great Americans, 1960.

EINSTEIN, ALBERT, Mar. 14, 1879 (Ulm, Ger.)–Apr. 18, 1955. U.S.-Swiss-German physicist. Revolutionized cosmology and physics with his special (1905) and general (1915) theories of relativity, the former containing the equation $E = mc^2$, the basis of atomic power, and the latter revealing that gravity bends light; showed that ISAAC NEWTON's physics did not apply on the subatomic and cosmic level; awarded 1921 Nobel Prize in physics for his explanation of the photoelectric effect (1905), which verified MAX PLANCK's quantum theory.

ENDERS, JOHN FRANKLIN, Feb. 10, 1897 (West Hartford, Conn.). U.S. microbiologist. Discovered a method to culture viruses outside of living bodies, the first step in the development of the polio vaccine, 1948–49; awarded Nobel Prize in physiology or medicine (with T. H. WELLER and F. C. ROBBINS), 1954.

ERLANGER, JOSEPH, Jan. 5, 1874 (San Francisco, Calif.)–Dec. 5, 1965. U.S. physiologist. Using an oscillograph to study nerve impulses, showed that velocity of impulse varied directly with the thickness of nerve fiber (1920s); awarded Nobel Prize in physiology or medicine (with H. S. GASSER), 1944.

EWING, WILLIAM MAURICE, May 12, 1906 (Lockney, Tex.). U.S. geologist. Pioneer in studies of the ocean floor; discovered that the mid-Atlantic ridge continues into the Pacific and Indian oceans and that there is a chasm running along the center of the ridge; proposed theory of polar warming and the melting of Arctic ice with consequent increase in temperate-zone snow, to explain the Ice Age.

FEYNMAN, RICHARD PHILIPS, May 11, 1918 (New York, N.Y.). U.S. physicist. Worked out the behavior of electrons with greater mathematical precision than ever before (quantum electrodynamics); awarded Nobel Prize in physics (with J. S. SCHWINGER and S. I. TOMONAGA), 1965.

FITCH, JOHN, Jan. 21, 1743 (Windsor, Conn.)–July 2, 1798. U.S. inventor. Built the first steamboat to carry passengers (between Trenton, N.J. and Philadelphia), 1790.

FRANCK, JAMES, Aug. 26, 1882 (Hamburg, Ger.)–May 21, 1964. U.S. physicist. With G. HERTZ, demonstrated an aspect of MAX PLANCK's quantum theory by bombarding gases with electrons to induce light emission; awarded Nobel Prize in physics (with G. Hertz), 1925.

FULLER, R(ichard) BUCKMINSTER, July 12, 1895 (Milton, Mass.) U.S. engineer, architect, author. Developer of the geodesic dome (c. 1940), which utilizes his *Dymaxion* principle of maximum output for minimum input. *Operating Manual for Spaceship Earth,* 1969; *Utopia or Oblivion,* 1969; *Synogetics,* 1975.

FULTON, ROBERT, Nov. 14, 1765 (Little Britain [now Fulton], Pa.)–Feb. 24, 1815. U.S. inventor. First to develop a profitable, practical steamship, 1807.

GAMOW, GEORGE, Mar. 4, 1904 (Odessa, Rus.)–Aug. 19, 1968. U.S.-Russian physicist. Made fundamental contributions to early nuclear theory, from 1928 on; a major formulator of "Big Bang" theory of the origin of the universe; with EDWARD TELLER, worked out theory of the nature of red giant stars, an early step in understanding stellar evolution, 1942; worked out process by which

SCIENTISTS, PHYSICIANS, AND INVENTORS

elements were created in the "Big Bang," 1948; suggested idea of "genetic code" in arrangement of components of DNA, 1954.

GARAND, JOHN C., Jan. 1, 1888 (St. Remi, Que., Can.)-Feb. 16, 1974. U.S. gun designer. Developed the Garand semiautomatic rifle (M-1) for the U.S. Army, 1930.

GASSER, HERBERT SPENCER, July 5, 1888 (Platteville, Wisc.)-May 11, 1963. U.S. physiologist. With JOSEPH ERLANGER, showed that different nerve fibers carry specific impulses, such as those for pain or heat; awarded Nobel Prize in physiology or medicine (with Erlanger), 1944.

GATLING, RICHARD JORDAN, Sept. 12, 1818 (Winton, N.C.)-Feb. 26, 1903. U.S. inventor. Invented the first machine-gun, 1862; improved planting machines; his name is the origin of the slang word *gat,* meaning a gun.

GELL-MANN, MURRAY, Sept. 15, 1929 (New York, N.Y.). U.S. physicist. Received his Ph.D. at age 22; introduced concept of "strangeness" to nuclear-particle theory, 1953; proposed the "Eight-fold Way," a system of grouping nuclear particles, one of which was found in 1964; introduced idea of "quarks," particles with fractonal electric charges, as basic building blocks of matter; awarded Nobel Prize in physics, 1969.

GESELL, ARNOLD LUCIUS, June 21, 1880 (Alma, Wisc.)-May 29, 1961. U.S. psychologist. Made a major contribution to the description and understanding of the normal mental development of infants and children, from 1911. *Atlas of Infant Behavior* (with collaborators), 1934; *The Child from 5 to 10* (with collaborators), 1946; *Youth: The Years from 10 to 16,* 1956.

GIAEVER, IVAR, Apr. 5, 1929 (Bergen, Nor.). U.S. physicist. Made basic discoveries in the phenomenon of electron "tunneling" and superconductivity, 1960; awarded Nobel Prize in physics (with L. ESAKI and B. D. JOSEPHSON), 1973.

GIAUQUE, WILLIAM FRANCIS, May 12, 1895 (Niagara Falls, Ont., Can.). U.S. chemist. Discovered the isotopes of oxygen, 1929; devised a new method for achieving temperatures very near to absolute zero, 1926 (first successful use, 1935); awarded Nobel Prize in chemistry, 1949.

GIBBS, JOSIAH WILLARD, Feb. 11, 1839 (New Haven, Conn.)-Apr. 28, 1903. U.S. physicist. Possibly the greatest U.S. scientist; worked out most of the details of chemical thermodynamics and statistical mechanics, in the 1870s; his work was virtually ignored for over a decade; named to Hall of Fame for Great Americans, 1950.

GLASER, DONALD ARTHUR, Sept. 21, 1926 (Cleveland, Ohio). U.S. physicist. Invented the bubble chamber, vital to recent study of high-energy particles, 1952; awarded Nobel Prize in physics, 1960.

GODDARD, ROBERT HUTCHINGS, Oct. 5, 1882 (Worcester, Mass.)-Aug. 10, 1945. U.S. physicist. Father of modern rocketry; tested first liquid-fueled rocket engine, 1923; devised prototypes of many modern rocket systems, including combustion chambers, steering mechanisms, and multistages; his work, ignored by the U.S. govt., was financed by Daniel Guggenheim at CHARLES LINDBERGH's urging; the U.S. finally "discovered" his work when German rocket experts acknowledged Goddard as the master, 1945.

GOEPPERT-MAYER, MARIE, June 28, 1906 (Germany)-Feb. 20, 1972. German-U.S. physicist. Proposed idea of nuclear shells, independently of

H. D. JENSEN, 1949; awarded Nobel Prize in physics (with Jensen and E. P. WIGNER), 1963.

GOETHALS, GEORGE WASHINGTON, June 29, 1858 (Brooklyn, N.Y.)-Jan. 21, 1928. U.S. engineer. Chief engineer for and administrator of the Panama Canal project, 1907-14.

GOLDMARK, PETER CARL, Dec. 2, 1906 (Budapest, Hung.)-Dec. 7, 1977. U.S. inventor. Developed color television (1940) and the first commercially successful long-playing record (1948).

GOODYEAR, CHARLES, Dec. 29, 1800 (New Haven, Conn.)-July 1, 1860. U.S. inventor. Invented the vulcanized-rubber process, patented in 1844; died a pauper.

GORGAS, WILLIAM CRAWFORD, Oct. 3, 1854 (Mobile, Ala.)-July 3, 1920. U.S. surgeon. Organized anti-mosquito controls in the Panama Canal Zone, ending malaria and yellow-fever epidemic and thus making the construction of the canal possible without massive loss of life from disease, 1904; named to Hall of Fame for Great Americans, 1950.

GRAY, ASA, Nov. 18, 1810 (Paris, N.Y.)-Jan. 30, 1888. U.S. botanist. The major contributor to knowledge of North American plants; a major early supporter of CHARLES DARWIN in the U.S.; named to Hall of Fame for Great Americans, 1900.

GREENWOOD, CHESTER, Dec. 4, 1858 (Farmington, Mass.)-July 5, 1937. U.S. inventor. Invented modern ear muffs, 1874.

GRINNEL, GEORGE BIRD, Sept. 20, 1849 (Brooklyn, N.Y.)-Apr. 11, 1938. U.S. naturalist. Founder of the Audubon Soc., 1886; originated the idea of Glacier Natl. Park, 1885; a pioneer conservation advocate and expert in Plains Indian folklore.

GUILLEMIN, ROGER, Jan. 11, 1924 (Dijon, Fr.). U.S. physiologist. Isolated the hormone stomatostatin (1973) and (with A. SCHALLY) the hormone TRH (1968-69), important in the treatment of some pituitary deficiencies; awarded Nobel Prize in physiology or medicine (with Schally and R. S. YALOW), 1977.

GUTTMACHER, ALAN FRANK, May 19, 1898 (Baltimore, Md.)-Mar. 18, 1974. U.S. physician. Called the "Father of birth control in the U.S."; as pres. of Planned Parenthood Federation of America (1962-74), advocated unlimited access to contraceptive information and liberal abortion regulations; chief of obstetrics and gynecology at Mt. Sinai Hospital in New York City, 1952-62.

HALE, GEORGE ELLERY, June 29, 1868 (Chicago, Ill.)-Feb. 21, 1938. U.S. astronomer. Prime mover behind the Yerkes Observatory and Yerkes telescope (largest refracting telescope in the world), the Mount Wilson observatory (1908), and the Mount Palomar observatory (1948); invented the spectroheliograph, 1889.

HALL, CHARLES MARTIN, Dec. 6, 1863 (Thompson, Ohio)-Dec. 27, 1914. U.S. chemist. Independently of P. L. T. Heroult, discovered an inexpensive way of refining aluminum by electrolysis, thus making the metal available for widespread use, 1886.

HALSTED, WILLIAM STEWART, Sept. 23, 1852 (New York, N.Y.)-Sept. 7, 1922. U.S. surgeon. Developed local anesthesia, 1885; the first to use rubber gloves in surgery, 1890; founded first surgical school in the U.S., at Johns Hopkins, c.1890; his techniques and demands for careful work laid the basis for modern surgery.

HARKINS, WILLIAM DRAPER, Dec. 28, 1873

THE BOOK OF WHO

(Titusville, Pa.)–Mar. 7, 1951. U.S. chemist. Predicted the existence of the neutron and deuterium; introduced idea of "packing fraction" and from that idea, hypothesized the process of nuclear fusion as the source of solar energy.

HARTLINE, HALDAN KEFFER, Dec. 22, 1903 (Bloomsburg, Pa.). U.S. physiologist. Made major advances in the study of individual retinal cells; awarded Nobel Prize in physiology or medicine (with G. WALD and R. A. Granit), 1967.

HENCH, PHILIP SHOWALTER, Feb. 28, 1896 (Pittsburgh, Pa.)–Mar. 31, 1965. U.S. physician. Discovered that cortisone, a hormone, alleviated arthritis, 1948; awarded Nobel Prize in physiology or medicine (with E. C. KENDALL and T. REICHSTEIN), 1950.

HENRY, JOSEPH, Dec. 17, 1797 (Albany, N.Y.)–May 13, 1878. U.S. physicist. Made major contributions to the development of electromagnets, 1829–31; the major contributor to the invention of the telegraph, 1831–37; the first to describe (but not to make) an electric motor, 1831; discovered self-induction, 1832; invented the electric relay, 1835; first secy. of the Smithsonian Inst., 1846; originated the gathering of weather reports that grew into the U.S. Weather Bureau; unit of inductance, the "henry," named for him.

HERSHEY, ALFRED DAY, Dec. 4, 1908 (Owosso, Mich.). U.S. biologist. Confirmed earlier indications that nucleic acid in cells was the material basis of the genetic code; awarded Nobel Prize in physiology or medicine (with M. DELBRUCK and S. E. LURIA), 1969.

HILLIER, JAMES, Aug. 22, 1915 (Brantford, Ont., Can.). Canadian-U.S. physicist. Designed and constructed the first practical electron microscope, 1937.

HOFSTADTER, ROBERT, Feb. 5, 1915 (New York, N.Y.). U.S. physicist. Did basic studies in the structure of neutrons and protons, 1961; predicted the existence of massive mesons; awarded Nobel Prize in physics (with R. L. MÖSSBAUER), 1961.

HOLLEY, ROBERT WILLIAM, Jan. 28, 1922 (Urbana, Ill.). U.S. chemist. Isolated three varieties of transfer-RNA (1962) and worked out the structure of one (1965); awarded Nobel Prize in physiology or medicine (with H. G. KHORANA and M. W. NIRENBERG), 1968.

HOWE, ELIAS, July 9, 1819 (Spencer, Mass.)–Oct. 3, 1867. U.S. inventor. Invented the first practical sewing machine, the first modern invention to lighten the load of women's household chores, by placing the eye near the needle's point and using two threads, 1846; sold the English rights for $1,250; U.S. patent, confirmed in 1854, finally brought him license fees from competitors; named to Hall of Fame for Great Americans, 1915.

HUBBLE, EDWIN POWELL, Nov. 20, 1889 (Marshfield, Mo.)–Sept. 28, 1953. U.S. astronomer. Discovered that nebulae (other galaxies) were far removed from the sun's galaxy, 1924; showed that these nebulae were receding at a speed directly proportioned to their distance (Hubble's constant, 1929), thus establishing the idea of the expanding universe.

HUGGINS, CHARLES BRENTON, Sept. 22, 1901 (Halifax, N.S., Can.). Canadian-U.S. surgeon. First to show that some cancers could be controlled by chemicals, in this case the female sex hormone for male prostate cancer, 1943; awarded Nobel Prize in physiology or medicine (with F. P. ROUS), 1966.

HYATT, JOHN WESLEY, Nov. 28, 1837 (Starkey, N.Y.)–May 10, 1920. U.S. inventor. Invented and named celluloid, the first synthetic plastic, 1869.

IPATIEFF, VLADIMIR NIKOLAEVICH, Nov. 21, 1867 (Moscow, Rus.)–Nov. 29, 1952. Russian-U.S. chemist. Determined the structure of isoprene, the basic molecule of rubber, 1897; discovered high-temperature catalytic reactions in hydrocarbons, 1900; developed the process for making low-grade gasoline into "high octane," 1930s.

JANKSY, KARL GUTHE, Oct. 22, 1905 (Norman, Okla.)–Feb. 14, 1950. U.S. radio engineer. First to detect and determine the source of radio waves from outside the solar system, the beginning of radio astronomy, 1932.

KAMEN, MARTIN DAVID, Aug. 27, 1913 (Toronto, Ont., Can.). Canadian-U.S. biochemist. Discovered carbon-14 isotope, a basic tool of biochemical and archeological research, 1940; the first to show that in photosynthesis, the liberated oxygen comes from water, not carbon dioxide.

KENDALL, EDWARD CALVIN, Mar. 8, 1886 (S. Norwalk, Conn.)–May 4, 1972. U.S. biochemist. Isolated thyroxine, the basic substance of the thyroid hormone, 1916; isolated most of the hormones produced by the adrenal cortex, 1930s; awarded Nobel Prize in physiology or medicine (with P. S. HENCH and T. REICHSTEIN), 1950.

KENNELLY, ARTHUR EDWIN, Dec. 17, 1861 (Bombay, India)–June 18, 1939. English-U.S. electrical engineer. Independently of O. HEAVISIDE, hypothesized the existence of the Kennelly-Heaviside layer of charged particles in the upper atmosphere that makes long-distance radio transmission possible, 1902.

KHORANA, HAR GOBIND, Jan. 9, 1922 (Raipur, India). U.S. chemist. Worked out most of the genetic code, independently of M. W. NIRENBERG; awarded Nobel Prize in physiology or medicine (with Nirenberg and R. W. HOLLEY), 1968.

KRAFT, CHRISTOPHER COLUMBUS, Feb. 28, 1924 (Phoebus, Va.). U.S. aeronautical engineer. Flight dir. of U.S. manned space-flight program, 1959–70.

KÜBLER-ROSS, ELISABETH, c.1926 (Zurich, Switz.). Swiss-U.S. physician. International consultant in the care of the dying and medical pioneer in the study of how people die; board chm. of Shanti-Nilaya, a healing and growth center in Escondido, Calif. *On Death and Dying,* 1969; *Death—The Final Stage of Growth,* 1975.

KUIPER, GERARD PETER, Dec. 7, 1905 (Harenkarspel, Neth.)–Dec. 23, 1973. U.S. astronomer. Detected the atmosphere of Saturn's moon Titan; discovered and named Miranada (1948), a moon of Uranus, and Nereid (1949), a moon of Neptune; proposed the theory that planets and moons are formed by independent condensations, 1951.

LAND, EDWIN HERBERT, May 7, 1909 (Bridgeport, Conn.). U.S. inventor. Invented the Polaroid lens, 1932; discovered a method of producing the full spectrum by using only two colors; invented the instant (Land) camera, 1947.

LANDSTEINER, KARL, June 14, 1868 (Vienna, Austria)–June 26, 1943. U.S. physician. Discovered human blood groups, thus making transfusions safe, 1900; the first to isolate the polio virus, 1908; awarded Nobel Prize in physiology or medicine, 1930.

LANGLEY, SAMUEL PIERPONT, Aug. 22, 1834 (Roxbury, Mass.)–Feb. 27, 1906. U.S. astronomer, inventor. Invented a bolometer capable of measuring minute quantities of heat, 1881; a pioneer in development of the airplane, he worked out basic aerodynamic principles and built several unsuccessful planes, until one equipped with a powerful engine flew in 1914.

LANGMUIR, IRVING, Jan. 31, 1881 (Brooklyn, N.Y.)–Aug. 16, 1957. U.S. chemist. Made a basic improvement in light bulbs by filling them with nitrogen; invented a hydrogen blowtorch capable of temperatures close to 6,000 C (10,700 F); the first to study mononuclear films, for which he received the 1932 Nobel Prize in chemistry, 1932.

LARSON, JOHN AUGUSTUS, Dec. 11, 1892 (Nova Scotia, Can.)–U.S. psychiatrist. Invented the "lie detector" or polygraph, 1921.

LAWRENCE, ERNEST ORLANDO, Aug. 8, 1901 (Canton, S. D.)–Aug. 27, 1958. U.S. physicist. Invented the cyclotron to increase vastly the energy of charged particles bombarding atomic nuclei, thus making possible most major advances in recent nuclear physics, 1930; awarded Nobel Prize in physics, 1939.

LEDERBERG, JOSHUA, May 23, 1925 (Montclair, N.J.). U.S. geneticist. With E. L. TATUM, discovered sexual reproduction in bacteria, thus expanding the value of bacteria in genetic research, c. 1947; showed that some viruses could transfer genetic material from one bacterium to another, 1952; awarded Nobel Prize in physiology or medicine (with Tatum and G. W. BEADLE), 1958.

LEE, TSUNG-DAO, Nov. 24, 1926 (Shanghai, China). U.S. physicist. With C. N. YANG, showed that the principle of conservation of parity (mirror equivalence of right- and left-handedness) did not apply in "weak" nuclear interactions; awarded Nobel Prize in physics (with Yang), 1957.

LEY, WILLY, Oct. 2, 1906 (Berlin, Ger.)–June 24, 1969. U.S. engineer. Founded the German Rocket Soc. (1972) and introduced WERNHER VON BRAUN to rocketry; his strong advocacy of rocketry prepared the U.S. for space exploration in the 1960s.

LIBBY, WILLARD FRANK, Dec. 17, 1908 (Grand Valley, Col.). U.S. chemist. Discovered and developed the carbon-14 dating technique, 1947; awarded Nobel Prize in chemistry, 1960.

LIPMANN, FRITZ ALBERT, June 12, 1899 (Königsberg, Ger. |now Kaliningrad, USSR|). U.S. biochemist. Made fundamental discoveries about the function of phosphates in animal metabolism; discovered coenzyme A, a basic catalyst in animal metabolism; awarded Nobel Prize in physiology or medicine (with H. A. KREBS), 1953.

LOEWI, OTTO, June 3, 1873 (Frankfurt-am-Main, Ger.)–Dec. 25, 1961. U.S. physiologist. Discovered acetylcholine, a chemical transmitter of nerve impulses, 1921; awarded 1936 Nobel Prize in physiology or medicine (with H. H. Dale), but was forced to turn over his prize money to the Nazis in 1938 as the price for emigration.

LOWELL, PERCIVAL, Mar. 13, 1855 (Boston, Mass.)–Nov. 12, 1916. U.S. astronomer. Established Lowell observatory in Arizona, 1894; predicted the existence of the planet Pluto prior to its 1930 discovery. (Brother of the poet AMY LOWELL.)

LURIA, SALVADOR EDWARD, Aug. 13, 1912 (Turin, It.). U.S. biologist. Made basic discoveries in mutation of bacteria and viruses, 1940s; awarded Nobel Prize in physiology or medicine (with M. DELBRUCK and A. D. HERSHEY), 1969.

MARSH, OTHNIEL CHARLES, Oct. 29, 1831 (Lockport, N.Y.)–Mar. 18, 1899. U.S. paleontologist. The first prof. of paleontology in the U.S., at Yale C., 1866; discovered the pterodactyl, 1871; discovered some 1,000 fossil vertebrates; through fossils of extinct horses, traced a complete evolutionary line, thus giving powerful support to CHARLES DARWIN's evolutionary theory.

MASTERS, WILLIAM HOWELL, Dec. 27, 1915 (Cleveland, Ohio). U.S. physician, educator. Noted for his important research in the field of sex therapy, with wife Virginia E. Johnson; with Johnson, wrote *Human Sexual Response* (1966), *Human Sexual Inadequacy* (1970), *The Pleasure Bond* (1975), and *Homosexuality in Perspective,* 1979.

MAYO, WILLIAM JAMES, June 29, 1861 (Le Sueur, Minn.)–July 28, 1939 and his brother **MAYO, CHARLES HORACE,** July 19, 1865 (Rochester, Minn.)–May 26, 1939. U.S. surgeons. Cofounders of the Mayo (Clinic) Fndn. for Medical Education and Research (1915) with a contribution to the U. of Minnesota of $2,800,000.

MCCORMICK, CYRUS HALL, Feb. 15, 1809 (Rockbridge Co., Va.)–May 13. 1884. U.S. inventor. Invented the first reaper to combine effectively all the basic elements of the modern reaper. 1831; established a farm-machine business (1848) that later (1902) became the Internatl. Harvester Co.

MCMILLAN, EDWIN MATTISON, Sept. 18, 1907 (Redondo Beach, Calif.). U.S. physicist. Discovered the first transuranium element, neptunium, 1940; devised improvements in the cyclotron to create the synchrotron, vastly increasing the energy to which particles could be accelerated; awarded Nobel Prize in chemistry (with G. T. SEABORG), 1951.

MERGENTHALER, OTTMAR, May 11, 1854 (Württemburg, Ger.)–Oct. 28, 1899. U.S. inventor. Invented the Linotype machine (1885), which mechanized typesetting.

MICHELSON, ALBERT ABRAHAM, Dec. 19, 1852 (Prussia)–May 9, 1931. U.S. physicist. Progressively refined the measure of the speed of light to within 5.5 km per second of the presently accepted value, 1882–1927; with E. W. MORLEY, failed to show that light moved more rapidly if projected in the direction of earth's motion, thus throwing great doubt on the then-prevailing theory of light waves (1887) and initiating the revolution in physics by K. LORENZ, M. PLANCK, and A. EINSTEIN; the first to measure the width of a star by interferometry, 1920; awarded Nobel Prize in physics, (the first U.S. winner), 1907.

MILLIKAN, ROBERT ANDREWS, Mar. 22, 1868 (Morrison, Ill.)–Dec. 19, 1953. U.S. physicist. In subtle experiments with ionized oil droplets, determined the value of the charge on a single electron, proving beyond doubt that electricity consists of particles, 1910; verified A. EINSTEIN's photoelectric explanation experimentally and derived a value for Planck's constant, 1916; invented the term *cosmic rays,* 1925; awarded Nobel Prize in physics, 1923.

MOORE, STANFORD, Sept. 4, 1913 (Chicago, Ill.). U.S. biochemist. Made a basic contribution to the development of chromatographic techniques in the study of protein structures; with W. H. STEIN, determined the constituents of ribonuclease; awarded Nobel Prize in chemistry (with C. B. ANFINSEN and Stein), 1972.

MORGAN, THOMAS HUNT, Sept. 25, 1866 (Lexington, Ky.)–Dec. 4, 1945. U.S. geneticist. Established and completed the work of G. MENDEL by mapping gene positions on the chromosomes of fruit flies and discovering the "crossing-over" phenomenon by which gene-linkage on a specific chromosome is occasionally broken, 1907–26; awarded Nobel Prize in physiology or medicine, 1933. *Theory of the Gene,* 1926.

MORLEY, EDWARD WILLIAMS, Jan. 29, 1838 (Newark, N.J.)–Feb. 24, 1923. U.S. chemist. Collaborated with A. A. MICHELSON in the famous experiments with light that began the modern revolution in physics.

MORSE, SAMUEL FINLEY BREESE, Apr. 27, 1791 (Charlestown, Mass.)–Apr. 2, 1872. U.S. inventor. With great assistance from J. HENRY, invented the first practical telegraph (1840), which was first built in 1844; devised "Morse code" for use with the telegraph; named to Hall of Fame for Great Americans, 1900.

MORTON, WILLIAM THOMAS GREEN, Aug. 9, 1819 (Charlton City, Mass.)–July 15, 1868. U.S. dentist. First to patent and publicize the use of ether as an anesthetic; named to Hall of Fame for Great Americans, 1920.

MUIR, JOHN, Apr. 21, 1838 (Dunbar, Scot.)–Dec. 24, 1914. U.S. naturalist. The primary force behind the first U.S. land-conservation laws and establishment of Yosemite and Sequoia natl. parks; explored most of the Sierra (1868–74) and a large portion of Alaska and the Yukon.

MULLER, HERMAN JOSEPH, Dec. 21, 1890 (New York, N.Y.)–Apr. 5, 1967. U.S. biologist. Discovered the mutagenic effects of X rays, thus speeding up the process of mutation for genetic studies, 1926; when study of mutations revealed that most are lethal, became an early advocate of limiting exposure to X rays and the use of sperm banks to conserve healthy genes; awarded Nobel Prize in physiology or medicine, 1946.

NATHANS, DANIEL, Oct. 30, 1928 (Wilmington, Del.). U.S. biologist. Found that the restriction enzyme discovered by H. O. SMITH could break up the DNA of a cancer virus, leading to a complete mapping of the genetics of the virus, 1971; awarded Nobel Prize in physiology or medicine (with Smith and W. ARBER), 1978.

NEUMANN, JOHN VON, Dec. 28, 1903 (Budapest, Hung.)–Feb. 8, 1957. U.S. mathematician. Developed "game theory," 1926–44; directed construction of computers that helped solve problems in engineering the H-bomb; did major advanced work in mathematical physics; received Fermi Award, 1956.

NIRENBERG, MARSHALL WARREN, Apr. 10, 1923 (New York, N.Y.). U.S. biochemist. First to discover an element of the genetic code, relating a particular group of three DNA nucleotides to the building of a particular amino acid, 1961; awarded Nobel Prize in physiology or medicine (with H. G. KHORANA and R. W. HOLLEY), 1968.

NORTHROP, JOHN HOWARD, July 5, 1891 (Yonkers, N.Y.). U.S. biochemist. His work, from 1930, in enzyme crystallization and analysis proved conclusively that enzymes are proteins; awarded Nobel Prize in chemistry (with J. B. SUMNER and W. M. STANLEY), 1946.

OCHOA, SEVERO, Sept. 24, 1905 (Luarca, Spain). U.S. biochemist. First to synthesize RNA, 1955; awarded Nobel Prize in physiology or medicine (with Arthur Kornberg), 1959.

OPPENHEIMER, J. ROBERT, Apr. 22, 1904 (New York, N.Y.)–Feb. 18, 1967. U.S. physicist. His basic theoretical work led to the discovery of the positron and to advances in neutron bombardment; headed Los Alamos, N.M., laboratories during the development of the first A-bombs, 1943–45; chm. of the gen. advisory com. of the AEC, 1947–53; proclaimed a security risk for his reluctance to proceed with H-bomb development, 1954; received Fermi Award, 1963.

OTIS, ELISHA GRAVES, Aug. 3, 1811 (Halifax, Vt.)–Apr. 8, 1861. U.S. inventor. Invented the first elevator with a reliable safety device to prevent its falling if the cable were to break, 1852.

PALADE, GEORGE EMIL, Nov. 19, 1912 (Jassy, Rumania). U.S. physiologist. Discovered the function of ribosomes as the sites of protein manufacture, 1956; awarded Nobel Prize in physiology or medicine (with A. CLAUDE and C. R. De Duve), 1974.

PAPANICOLAOU, GEORGE NICHOLAS, May 13, 1883 (Greece)–Feb. 19, 1962. U.S. physiologist. Devised a simple test (Pap smear) for early discovery of cervical cancer, 1928; work was ignored until 1940.

PAULI, WOLFGANG, Apr. 25, 1900 (Vienna, Austria)–Dec. 15, 1958. U.S.-Austrian physicist. Pronounced the "Pauli exclusion principle," a fundamental explanation of the behavior of a class of atomic particles, 1925; the first to postulate the existence of the neutrino, 1931; awarded Nobel Prize in physics, 1945.

PAULING, LINUS CARL, Feb. 28, 1901 (Portland, Ore.). U.S. chemist. Made basic theoretical contributions to understanding the structure of molecules and the nature of chemical bonds, 1939; first to suggest a helical structure for protein molecules, early 1950s; a major advocate of nuclear disarmament and an end to nuclear testing; a major advocate of large doses of vitamin C to prevent the common cold; awarded Nobel Prize in chemistry, 1954; awarded Nobel Peace Prize, 1962.

PENZIAS, ARNO ALLAN, Apr. 26, 1933 (Munich, Ger.). U.S. physicist. With R. W. WILSON, discovered the cosmic background-radiation theoretically left over from the "Big Bang" that began the universe, 1964; awarded Nobel Prize in physics (with R. W. Wilson and P. L. KAPITSA), 1978.

PINCUS, GREGORY, Apr. 9, 1903 (Woodbine, N.J.)–Aug. 22, 1967. U.S. biologist. Invented the birth-control pill, 1955.

PURCELL, EDWARD MILLS, Aug. 30, 1912 (Taylorville, Ill.). U.S. physicist. Discovered, independently of F. BLOCH, nuclear magnetic resonance and used it to devise methods for the study of magnetism in atomic nuclei and new techniques in analytic chemistry; in radio astronomy, discovered the radio emission of neutral hydrogen in interstellar space, 1951; awarded Nobel Prize in physics (with Bloch), 1952.

RABI, ISIDOR ISAAC, July 29, 1898 (Austria-Hungary). U.S. physicist. Developed technique of using molecular beams (see O. STERN) as a means to measure magnetic properties of atoms and molecules, from 1933; worked on the development of radar and the A-bomb; chairman of the scientific advisory com. of the AEC, 1952–56; awarded Nobel Prize in physics, 1944.

RAINWATER, L. JAMES, Dec. 9, 1917 (Council, Ida.). U.S. physicist. Proposed that some atomic nuclei can be very asymmetrical, not spherical, and suggested why, 1949; awarded Nobel Prize in physics (with BEN MOTTELSON and AAGE BOHR), 1975.

REBER, GROTE, Dec. 22, 1911 (Wheaton, Ill.). U.S. radio astronomer. Built the first radio telescope (1937) and was the only radio astronomer in the world from 1937 to 1945; mapped high-frequency sources (1938–42) and low-frequency sources (from 1951).

REED, WALTER, Sept. 13, 1851 (Belroi, Va.)–Nov. 23, 1902. U.S. bacteriologist. Led the commission that tracked the carrier of yellow fever to a particular mosquito, 1900; proved the cause was a filterable virus, 1901; his discoveries contributed greatly to the successful construction of the Panama Canal; named to Hall of Fame for Great Americans, 1945.

REMSEN, IRA, Feb. 10, 1846 (New York, N.Y.)–Mar. 4, 1927. U.S. chemist. Discovered the chemical sweetener later named saccharin, 1879.

RICHARDS, THEODORE WILLIAM, Jan. 31, 1868 (Germantown, Pa.)–Apr. 2, 1928. U.S. chemist. Determined the atomic weight of most elements as accurately as possible with purely chemical means; confirmed by chemical means F. SODDY's prediction of the existence of isotopes, c.1915; awarded Nobel Prize in chemistry, 1914.

RICHTER, BURTON, Mar. 22, 1931 (Brooklyn, N.Y.). U.S. physicist. Independently of SAMUEL C. C. TING, discovered the J-(psi) particle, 1974; his discovery helped confirm the theory of charmed quarks; awarded Nobel Prize in physics (with Ting), 1976.

RICHTER, CHARLES FRANCIS, Apr. 26, 1900 (Butler Co., Ohio). U.S. seismologist. Developed a method for calculating the severity of earthquakes and a scale to measure earthquake intensity (Richter scale).

ROBBINS, FREDERICK CHAPMAN, Aug. 25, 1916 (Auburn, Ala.). U.S. microbiologist. With J. ENDERS and T. WELLER, discovered (1952) how to cultivate viruses in tissue culture, which contributed directly to the development of a polio vaccine; awarded Nobel Prize in physiology or medicine (with Enders and Weller), 1954.

ROEBLING, JOHN AUGUSTUS, June 12, 1806 (Prussia)–July 22, 1869. U.S. engineer. First to recognize the strength and resilience of steel wire and to weave wire into cable, about 1845; pioneered in the design and construction of suspension bridges, including the Brooklyn Bridge.

ROUS, FRANCIS PEYTON, Oct. 5, 1879 (Baltimore, Md.)–Feb. 16, 1970. U.S. physician. The first to isolate a cancer-causing virus, 1910; awarded Nobel Prize in physiology or medicine (with C. B. HUGGINS), 1966.

RUSSELL, HENRY MORRIS, Oct. 25, 1877 (Oyster Bay, N.Y.)–Feb. 18, 1957. U.S. astronomer. Independently of E. HERZSPRUNG, devised a scale of stellar types on which the life-cycle of stars could be plotted, 1913; did pioneering work in determining the sun's composition, 1929.

SABIN, ALBERT BRUCE, Aug. 26, 1906 (Bialystok, Rus.). U.S. microbiologist. Developed the oral vaccine for polio, using "attenuated" live viruses, 1959.

SAGAN, CARL, Nov. 9, 1934 (New York, N.Y.). U.S. astronomer. Specializes in planetary surfaces and atmospheres; advocates the search for extraterrestrial intelligence; a science popularizer. *The Dragons of Eden,* 1977 (Pulitzer prize in nonfiction, 1978); *Broca's Brain,* 1979.

SALK, JONAS EDWARD, Oct. 28, 1914 (New York, N.Y.). U.S. microbiologist. Developed the first polio vaccine, using dead viruses, 1952-55.

SCHALLY, ANDREW, Nov. 30, 1926 (Wilno, Pol.). U.S. biochemist. Isolated the hormone LHRH (1971), vital to human ovulation, and with R. GUILLEMIN, the vital pituitary hormone TRH (1968-69); awarded Nobel Prize in physiology or medicine (with Guillemin and R. S. YALOW), 1977.

SCHRIEFFER, JOHN ROBERT, May 31, 1931 (Oak Park, Ill.). U.S. physicist. With J. BARDEEN

and L. N. COOPER, developed an effective theory of superconductivity, 1957; awarded Nobel Prize in physics (with Bardeen and Cooper), 1972.

SCHWINGER, JULIAN SEYMOUR, Feb. 12, 1918 (New York, N.Y.). U.S. physicist. Made a basic theoretical contribution to the development of quantum electrodynamics; awarded Nobel Prize in physics (with R. P. FEYNMAN and S. I. TOMONAGA), 1965.

SEABORG, GLENN THEODORE, Apr. 19, 1912 (Ishpeming, Mich.). U.S. physicist. Made basic discoveries in the physics and chemistry of transuranian elements, 1940-70; chm. of the AEC, 1961-71; awarded Nobel Prize in chemistry (with E. M. MCMILLAN), 1951.

SEGRÈ, EMILIO, Feb. 1, 1905 (Tivoli, Italy). U.S. physicist. Discovered element 43, technetium, the first artificially produced element, 1937; with O. CHAMBERLAIN, demonstrated the existence of the antiproton, 1955; awarded Nobel Prize in physics (with Chamberlain), 1959.

SHANNON, CLAUDE ELWOOD, Apr. 30, 1916 (Gaylord, Mich.). U.S. mathematician. The founder of information theory, which has had a major impact on computer development, communications technology, biology, and other fields. *Mathematical Theory of Communications,* 1949.

SHOCKLEY, WILLIAM BRADFORD, Feb. 13, 1910 (London, Eng.). U.S. physicist. A major contributor to the invention of the transistor and development of semiconductor technology; awarded Nobel Prize in physics (with J. BARDEEN and W. H. BRATTAIN), 1956.

SIKORSKY, IGOR IVANOVICH, May 25, 1889 (Kiev, Rus.)–Oct. 26, 1972. U.S. aviation engineer. Built and flew the first multimotored plane, 1913; developed the early transoceanic amphibian plane; developed the first successful helicopter, 1939.

SMITH, HAMILTON O., 1931 (New York, N.Y.). U.S. biochemist. Discovered a restriction enzyme that always breaks certain DNA molecules at the same place, 1970; developed new techniques to isolate and purify restriction enzymes; awarded Nobel Prize in physiology or medicine (with D. NATHANS and W. ARBER), 1978.

SPERRY, ELMER AMBROSE, Oct. 12, 1860 (Cortland, N.Y.)–June 16, 1930. U.S. inventor. Developed the gyroscopic compass, 1896-1910; obtained over 400 patents for a wide variety of electrical devices and industrial processes; a founder of the Sperry-Rand Corp.

SPITZER, LYMAN, June 26, 1914 (Toledo, Ohio). U.S. astronomer. His research on the formation of stars out of interstellar gas in magnetic fields led to work on hydrogen fusion and one of the first suggestions that fusion reactions could be contained in magnetic "bottles."

SPOCK, BENJAMIN MCLANE, May 2, 1903 (New Haven, Conn.). U.S. pediatrician. A major influence on modern U.S. child-rearing practices and health care; ran for U.S. pres. on the Peace and Freedom party ticket, 1972; his *Common Sense Book of Baby and Child Care* (1946) has sold over 24 million copies.

STANLEY, FRANCIS EDGAR, June 1, 1849 (Kingfield, Me.)–July 31, 1918. U.S. inventor. Invented the Stanley Steamer, a steam-powered automobile, 1897.

STANLEY, WENDELL MEREDITH, Aug. 16, 1904 (Ridgeville, Ind.)–June 15, 1971. U.S. biochemist. First to crystallize viruses, thus opening the way to understanding their molecular structure; awarded

THE BOOK OF WHO

Nobel Prize in chemistry (with J. NORTHROP and J. SUMNER), 1946.

STEIN, WILLIAM HOWARD, June 25, 1911 (New York, N.Y.). U.S. biochemist. With S. MOORE, determined the constituents of ribonuclease and developed automated techniques for analysis of amino acids in enzymes; awarded Nobel Prize in chemistry (with C. B. ANFINSEN and Moore), 1972.

STEINMETZ, CHARLES PROTEUS, born Karl August Rudolf Steinmetz, Apr. 9, 1865 (Breslau, Ger. [now Wroclaw, Pol.])–Oct. 26, 1923. U.S. electrical engineer. Established the mathematical methods of electrical engineering; worked out the necessary mathematics to predict the efficiency of electrical motors (1892) and alternating-current circuits (1893); designed a generator able to produce an electrical discharge of immense power in order to study effects of lightning.

SUMNER, JAMES BATCHELLER, Nov. 19, 1887 (Canton, Mass.)–Aug. 12, 1955. U.S. biochemist. First to crystallize an enzyme and to prove that enzymes were proteins, 1926; awarded Nobel Prize in chemistry (with J. H. NORTHROP and W. M. STANLEY), 1946.

SUTHERLAND, EARL WILBUR, Nov. 19, 1915 (Burlington, Kan.). U.S. biochemist. Conducted basic studies in roles of enzymes and hormones in carbohydrate metabolism; awarded Nobel Prize in physiology or medicine, 1971.

SZILARD, LEO, Feb. 11, 1898 (Budapest, Hung.)–May 30, 1964. U.S. physicist. Developed the first method of separating isotopes of radioactive elements, 1934; ghosted the famous letter from A. EINSTEIN to Pres. F. D. ROOSEVELT advocating development of an atomic bomb, 1939; worked with E. FERMI in building the first nuclear reactor, 1942; did basic research in biophysics, after 1946; received Atoms for Peace award, 1959.

TATUM, EDWARD LAWRIE, Dec. 14, 1909 (Boulder, Col.)–Nov. 5, 1975. U.S. biochemist. With G. W. BEADLE, did basic research in the study of the chemical function of genes in the production of enzymes; awarded Nobel Prize in physiology or medicine (with Beadle and J. LEDERBERG), 1958.

TAYLOR, FREDERICK WINSLOW, Mar. 20, 1856 (Philadelphia, Pa.)–Mar. 21, 1915. U.S. engineer. Father of scientific management; conducted the first time-and-motion studies to improve efficiency, 1881.

TELLER, EDWARD, Jan. 15, 1908 (Budapest, Hung.). U.S. physicist. Called the "Father of the H-bomb" for devising a secret element that made the device practical and leading the H-bomb project as administrator (1949–52); received Fermi Award, 1962.

TEMIN, HOWARD MARTIN, Dec. 10, 1934 (Philadelphia, Pa.). U.S. molecular biologist. Conducted research into the process by which a virus can change the genetic makeup of a cell; awarded Nobel Prize in physiology or medicine (with DAVID BALTIMORE and RENATO DULBECCO), 1975.

TESLA, NIKOLA, July 9, 1856 (Croatia)–Jan. 7, 1943. U.S. electrical engineer. Regarded by many as one of the most brilliant men in history; developed (by 1885) the principles and devices that made alternating current practical and dominant in the U.S.; his wide-ranging experiments in electricity contributed to most developments in electronics.

TING, SAMUEL CHAO CHUNG, Jan. 26, 1936 (Ann Arbor, Mich.). U.S. physicist. Discovered the J(-psi) particle, independently of BURTON RICHTER, 1974; his discovery helped confirm the theory of charmed quarks; awarded Nobel Prize in physics (with Richter), 1976.

TOWNES, CHARLES HURD, July 28, 1915 (Greenville, S.C.). U.S. physicist. An inventor of the maser, 1953; contributed to the theory of the laser, 1958; awarded Nobel Prize in physics (with A. M. PROKHOROV and N. G. BASOV), 1964.

UREY, HAROLD CLAYTON, Apr. 29, 1893 (Walkerton, Ind.). U.S. chemist. Proved the existence of deuterium, or heavy hydrogen, 1931; did basic research in isotope separation essential to the development of the A-bomb, 1930s; developed the basic theories of evolution of the elements in stellar activity, c.1950; major advocate of the condensation theory of planet formation; awarded Nobel Prize in chemistry, 1934.

VAN ALLEN, JAMES ALFRED, Sept. 7, 1914 (Mount Pleasant, Ia.). U.S. physicist. Helped develop the proximity fuse, c.1942; a major advocate of the space program, 1945–58; pioneered in the use of rockets and satellites for scientific purposes; discovered the magnetosphere (or Van Allen radiation belts) around the earth, 1958.

VAN VLECK, JOHN HASBROUCK, Mar. 13, 1899 (Middletown, Conn.). U.S. physicist. Made basic contributions to the understanding of magnetic forces within and between atoms; awarded Nobel Prize in physics (with N. F. MOTT and P. W. ANDERSON), 1977.

WAKSMAN, SELMAN ABRAHAM, July 22, 1888 (Russia)–Aug. 16, 1973. U.S. microbiologist. Discovered streptomycin, a breakthrough in the search for antibiotics, 1943; coined the word *antibiotics*; awarded Nobel Prize in physiology or medicine, 1952.

WALD, GEORGE, Nov. 18, 1906 (New York, N.Y.). U.S. chemist. Did basic research in the chemistry of vision, in the 1940s and 1950s; in the late 1960s became a spokesman for the anti-Vietnam War movement and later, anti-nuclear power groups; awarded Nobel Prize in physiology or medicine (with H. K. HARTLINE and R. A. Granit) 1967.

WALKER, MARY, Nov. 26, 1832 (Oswego, N.Y.)–Feb. 21, 1919. U.S. physician. Graduated from Syracuse Medical C. (1855), six years after E. BLACKWELL became first U.S. female physician; asst. surgeon in Union Army; only woman ever to receive Medal of Honor, 1865; arrested several times for wearing a frock coat and trousers on the street, a custom she had picked up during the Civil War, in the late 1860s; active in The Mutual Dress Reform and Equal Rights Assn.

WATSON, JAMES DEWEY, Apr. 6, 1928 (Chicago, Ill.). U.S. biochemist. With F. H. C. CRICK, worked out the structure of DNA; awarded Nobel Prize in physiology or medicine (with Crick and M. H. F. WILKINS), 1962.

WATSON, JOHN BROADUS, Jan. 9, 1878 (Greenville, S.C.)–Sept. 25, 1958. U.S. psychologist. Founded behaviorist psychology, the study of human behavior as almost entirely the product of conditioned response and learning.

WELLER, THOMAS HUCKLE, June 15, 1915 (Ann Arbor, Mich.). U.S. microbiologist. With J. F. ENDERS and F. C. ROBBINS, devised methods to cultivate viruses in the laboratory, 1948–49; awarded Nobel Prize in physiology or medicine (with Enders and Robbins), 1954.

WESTINGHOUSE, GEORGE, Oct. 6, 1846 (Central Bridge, N.Y.)–Mar. 12, 1914. U.S. engineer. Invented the air brake, 1868; developed many important railroading devices and systems for piping gas; founded Westinghouse Electric Co., 1886; bought N. TESLA's patents in alternating current and made it the standard form of electrical transmissions in the U.S.

WHITNEY, ELI, Dec. 8, 1765 (Westboro, Mass.)-Jan. 8, 1825. U.S. inventor. Invented the cotton gin, which made cotton-growing highly profitable, 1793; devised precision-machining methods that made musket parts interchangeable, 1801; the first to use assembly-line methods in industry; named to Hall of Fame for Great Americans, 1900.

WIENER, NORBERT, Nov. 26, 1894 (Columbia, Mo.)-Mar. 18, 1964. U.S. mathematician. Made fundamental contributions to mathematics, 1930s; founder of cybernetics, the science of communication and control within and between machines, animals, and organizations, on which much modern automation is based. *Cybernetics,* 1948.

WIGNER, EUGENE PAUL, Nov. 17, 1902 (Budapest, Hung.). U.S. physicist. Worked out the theory of neutron absorption, essential to reactor operation, 1936; worked out the theory of parity conservation; helped in construction of the first atomic reactor, 1942; awarded Nobel Prize in physics (with M. GOEPPERT-MAYER and J. D. H. JENSEN), 1963.

WILSON, ROBERT W., Jan. 10, 1936 (Houston, Tex.). U.S. physicist. With A. A. PENZIAS, discovered the cosmic radiation background that tends to support the Big Bang theory of the origin of the universe; awarded Nobel Prize in physics (with Penzias and P. L. KAPITSA), 1978.

WOODWARD, ROBERT BURNS, Apr. 10, 1917 (Boston, Mass.)-July 8, 1979. U.S. chemist. Made fundamental contributions to the processes of molecular-structure determination, leading to his synthesis of quinine (1944), cholesterol (1951), strychnine (1954), reserpine (1956), and others; worked out the structures of many substances, including penicillin (1945).

WRIGHT, WILBUR, Apr. 16, 1867 (Millville, Ind.)-May 30, 1912; and his brother **ORVILLE WRIGHT,** Aug. 19, 1871 (Dayton, Ohio)-Jan. 30, 1948. U.S. inventors. Made the first powered, controlled, and sustained airplane flight, Dec. 17, 1903; invented ailerons; designed internal-combustion engines with lower weight-to-horsepower ratios; developed the first practical airplane, 1905; both elected to Hall of Fame for Great Americans, Wilbur in 1955 and Orville in 1965.

YALOW, ROSALYN, née Sussman, July 19, 1921 (New York, N.Y.). U.S. medical physicist. Made a major contribution to the development of radioimmunoassay techniques for measuring concentrations of biological substances in the body, 1950s-60s; awarded Nobel Prize in physiology or medicine (with R. GUILLEMIN and A. SCHALLY), 1977.

YANG, CHEN NING, Sept. 22, 1922 (China). U.S. physicist. With T.-D. LEE, proved that the law of parity conservation did not hold true in "weak" nuclear interactions, 1956; awarded Nobel Prize in physics (with Lee), 1957.

ZINN, WALTER H., Dec. 10, 1906 (Kitchener, Ont., Can.). U.S. physicist. Developed the first so-called breeder reactor, 1951.

ZWORYKIN, VLADIMIR KOSMA, July 30, 1889 (Russia). U.S. physicist. The father of electronic TV; invented the iconoscope (1923), or TV transmitter, and the kinescope (1924), or TV receiver; developed the first practical TV system, 1938; his innovations made practical the electron microscope, 1939.

BRITISH SCIENTISTS, PHYSICIANS, AND INVENTORS

ABEL, SIR FREDERICK AUGUSTUS, July 17, 1827 (England)-Sept. 6, 1902. English chemist. Pioneered in smokeless powders; with SIR JAMES DEWAR, invented cordite, c.1889; knighted, 1891.

ADRIAN, EDGAR DOUGLAS, BARON OF CAMBRIDGE, Nov. 30, 1889 (London, Eng.)-Aug. 4, 1977. English physiologist. Conducted research on the electrical activity of sensory and muscular nerve cells and in the brain; awarded Nobel Prize in physiology or medicine, (with C. S. SHERRINGTON), 1932.

APPLETON, SIR EDWARD VICTOR, Sept. 6, 1892 (England)-Apr. 21, 1965. English physicist. Discovered the Appleton, or F, layer of the ionosphere, a reliable reflector of the shorter shortwave radio waves, thus making possible more dependable long-distance radio communication and aiding development of radio, 1926; knighted, 1941; awarded Nobel Prize in physics, 1947.

ASTON, FRANCIS WILLIAM, Sept. 1, 1877 (England)-Nov. 20, 1945. English chemist, physicist. Developed the mass spectrograph, which accurately distinguishes atoms of the same element with minutely different masses (isotopes), 1920; discovered many isotopes; awarded Nobel Prize in chemistry, 1922.

BABBAGE, CHARLES, Dec. 26, 1792 (England)-Oct. 18, 1871. English mathematician, inventor. Created the first reliable actuarial tables; showed that a flat fee for postage made more money than fees based on distance, c.1835; developed the first speedometer; invented skeleton keys and the cow-catcher; one of first to conceive of and try to build a computer, after 1822.

BAIRD, JOHN LOGIE, Aug. 13, 1888 (Scotland)-June 14, 1946. Scottish engineer. First man to demonstrate television of objects in motion, 1926; first demonstrated television, 1924; went on to work on color and stereoscopic television; his early system used mechanical scanners, not the electronic scanners of modern television.

BARTON, DEREK HAROLD RICHARD, Sept. 18, 1918 (Gravesend, Eng.). English organic chemist. Father of conformational analysis in organic chemistry, the study of molecular structure in three dimensions, 1949; developed theory of phenol and alkaloid structure (1956) that simplified understanding of the biosynthesis of these complex substances; awarded Nobel Prize in chemistry (with O. Hassel), 1969.

BAYLISS, SIR WILLIAM MADDOCK, May 2, 1860 (England)-Aug. 27, 1924. English physiologist. With E. H. STARLING, discovered hormones, 1902.

BESSEMER, SIR HENRY, Jan. 19, 1813 (England)-Mar. 15, 1898. English metallurgist, inventor. Discovered "blast furnace" method of making steel directly from cast iron by blowing air directly on molten iron to burn off carbon impurities; reduced the cost of high-grade steel by ten times, making modern steel construction possible, 1856-1860.

BLACKETT, LORD PATRICK MAYNARD STUART, Nov. 18, 1897 (London, Eng.)-July 13, 1974. English physicist. Improved upon and made extensive use of the Wilson cloud chamber to get the first photographs and precise knowledge of subatomic particle reaction (1925) and cosmic rays (1932); did basic work in tracing changes in earth's magnetic field; dir. of British Naval Operations Research in WW II; awarded Nobel Prize in physics, 1948; made a life peer, 1969.

BOOLE, GEORGE, Nov. 2, 1815 (England)–Dec. 8, 1864. English mathematician. Originated Boolean algebra, the basis of symbolic logic and the beginning of the attempt to place mathematics on a firm logical basis, 1854. *An Investigation of the Laws of Thought,* 1854.

BOYLE, ROBERT, Jan. 25, 1627 (Ireland)–Dec. 30, 1691. Anglo-Irish physicist, chemist. A major founder of modern science in his firm advocacy of careful experimentation, thorough description, and publication of findings; major advocate of the idea that elements were irreducible material substances, not mystical properties; did major experimental work in the study of vacuums and gases; discovered Boyle's law (volume of gas changes in simple inverse proportion to pressure), 1661; first to distinguish between acids, bases, and neutral substances. *The Sceptical Chemist,* 1661.

BRADLEY, JAMES, Mar. 1693 (England)–July 13, 1762. English astronomer. Discovered "aberration of light," the first observational proof of the heliocentric theory; first to calculate with relative accuracy the speed of light; discovered "nutation," the shift in the earth's axis caused by lunar gravity.

BRAGG, SIR WILLIAM HENRY, July 2, 1862 (England)–Mar. 12, 1942. English physicist. With his son, W. L. BRAGG, pioneered in the study of molecular structures by x-ray diffraction in crystals, which made possible the analysis of the structure of such substances as DNA; awarded Nobel Prize in physics (with W. L. BRAGG), 1915; knighted, 1920.

BRAGG, SIR WILLIAM LAWRENCE, Mar. 31, 1890 (Adelaide, Austrl.)–July 1, 1971. Australian-English physicist. With his father, W. H. BRAGG, pioneered in x-ray crystallography; became dir. of Cavendish Lab. at Cambridge (replacing ERNEST RUTHERFORD), 1938; awarded Nobel Prize in physics (with W. H. BRAGG), 1915 (the youngest man ever to win a Nobel); knighted, 1941.

BRAID, JAMES, 1795 (Scotland)–Mar. 25, 1860. Scottish surgeon. Established the reality of and named hypnotism, c.1842.

BRIGGS, HENRY, Feb. 1561 (England)–Jan. 26, 1630. English mathematician. Invented common logarithmic notation; worked out logarithmic tables for numbers from 1 to 20,000, 1624; invented modern method of long division.

CAVENDISH, HENRY, Oct. 10, 1731 (France)–Feb. 24, 1810. English chemist, physicist. Discovered hydrogen, c.1766; first to measure weights of gases to determine density; first to show that hydrogen, when burned, produces water; discovered argon, 1785; first to work out the constant of gravitational force and to compute accurately the mass and density of the Earth, 1798; an eccentric, he published few of his findings and much of his work remained unknown for many years.

CAYLEY, SIR GEORGE, Dec. 27, 1773 (England)–Dec. 15, 1857. English engineer. Built the first successful glider, 1853; founded science of aerodynamics, developing the basic elements (fixed wings, tail with elevators and rudder, etc.) of modern airplanes; invented the caterpillar tractor.

CHADWICK, SIR JAMES, Oct. 20, 1891 (England)–July 24, 1974. English physicist. Discovered the neutron, a major step in the develop-

ment of atomic fission; awarded Nobel Prize in physics, 1935; knighted, 1945.

CHAIN, ERNST BORIS, June 19, 1906 (Berlin, Ger.). English biochemist. With H. W. FLOREY, the first to isolate penicillin, during 1940s; awarded Nobel Prize in physiology or medicine (with H. W. FLOREY and A. FLEMING), 1945.

COCKCROFT, SIR JOHN DOUGLAS, May 27, 1897 (England)–Sept. 18, 1967. English physicist. Pioneered in development of particle accelerators, with E. T. S. WALTON; first to cause a nuclear reaction without using natural radioactivity, 1932; knighted, 1948; awarded Nobel Prize in physics (with Walton), 1951.

CRAPPER, THOMAS, 1837 (England)–1910. English sanitary engineer, inventor. Invented the valve-and-siphon arrangement that made the modern flush toilet possible.

CRICK, FRANCIS HARRY COMPTON, June 8, 1916 (England). English biochemist, physicist. With J. D. WATSON, discovered the double-helix structure of DNA, the basic substance of the chromosome and thus of heredity, 1953; awarded Nobel Prize in physiology or medicine (with Watson and M. H. F. WILKINS), 1962.

CROOKES, SIR WILLIAM, June 17, 1832 (London, Eng.)–Apr. 4, 1919. English physicist. Discovered thallium, 1861; invented radiometer, 1875; was a major pioneer in development and study of the vacuum electron tube, which led to x-ray tubes, cathode-ray tubes, and display tubes used in television and radar, 1875; knighted, 1897; invented spinthariscope, a device for monitoring alpha particles, 1903.

DALTON, JOHN, Sept. 6?, 1766 (England)–July 27, 1844. English chemist. First to propound the modern view of the theory that elements are composed of atoms, 1803; the first to devise a table of atomic weights; a pioneer in meteorology, keeping detailed weather records from 1787 to his death; the first to describe color-blindness, 1794. *New System of Chemical Philosophy,* 1808.

DARWIN, CHARLES ROBERT, Feb. 12, 1809 (England)–Apr. 19, 1882. English naturalist. Developed the theory of organic evolution through natural selection (1844–58), sparking the revolution in biological sciences, after a five-year voyage (1831–36) on the H.M.S. *Beagle* to South America and the Galapagos Is.; his study of finch species (Darwin's finches) on the islands and his reading (1838) of THOMAS MALTHUS's *Essay on the Principle of Population* provided the bases of the evolutionary theory, which was firmly established before his death. *Origin of Species,* 1859; *The Descent of Man,* 1871.

DARWIN, SIR GEORGE HOWARD, July 9, 1845 (England)–Dec. 7, 1912. English astronomer. Discovered that the rate of the earth's rotation and angular momentum were decreasing because of tidal friction and that the moon's distance from Earth was increasing, 1879; knighted, 1905. (Son of CHARLES DARWIN.)

DAVY, SIR HUMPHREY, Dec. 17, 1778 (Cornwall, Eng.)–May 29, 1829. English chemist. Discovered potassium, sodium (1807), barium, magnesium, strontium, calcium (1808); correctly identified chlorine as an element, named it, and discovered that it supported combustion; discovered nitrous oxide (1800), the first chemical anesthetic (laughing gas); invented the Davy lamp, which decreased danger of gas explosions in mines, 1815; knighted 1812; baronet, 1815.

DEWAR, SIR JAMES, Sept. 20, 1842 (Scot-

SCIENTISTS, PHYSICIANS, AND INVENTORS

land)–Mar. 27, 1923. British-Scottish physicist. First to liquefy (1898) and then solidify (1899) hydrogen, reaching a temperature of only 14 degrees above absolute zero; his research in low-temperature preservation led to the Thermos bottle; invented cordite, the first practical smokeless powder; knighted, 1901.

DIRAC, PAUL ADRIEN MAURICE, Aug. 8, 1902 (England). English physicist, mathematician. His development of the hypothesis of wave mechanics of electrons led to the hypothesis of antiparticles, 1930; awarded Nobel Prize in physics (with EDWIN SCHRÖDINGER), 1933.

DUNLOP, JOHN BOYD, Feb. 5, 1840 (Scotland)–Oct. 23, 1921. Scottish veterinary surgeon. Invented the pneumatic tire, c.1887.

FARADAY, MICHAEL, Sept. 22, 1791 (England)–Aug. 25, 1867. English physicist, chemist. Discovered benzene, 1825; first to define the laws of electrolysis, 1832; first to convert electromagnetic forces into continuous mechanical motion, 1821; invented the transformer and electric generator, 1831; discovered electrical induction; the first to hypothesize electromagnetic "lines of force," a beginning of field theory; the key pioneer in the development of modern electricity; refused knighthood.

FLAMSTEED, JOHN, Aug, 19, 1646 (England)–Dec. 31, 1719. English astronomer. Created first great star maps using telescopic observations, 1675–1719; first Astronomer Royal; established observatory at Greenwich that later marked the prime meridian.

FLEMING, SIR ALEXANDER, Aug. 6, 1881 (Scotland)–Mar. 11, 1955. Scottish bacteriologist. Discovered penicillin by accident (1928) and demonstrated that it killed some bacteria and did no harm to human cells; knighted, 1944; awarded Nobel Prize in physiology or medicine (with E. B. CHAIN and H. W. FLOREY), 1945.

FLOREY, HOWARD WALTER, BARON FLOREY OF ADELAIDE, Sept. 24, 1898 (Adelaide, Austrl.)–Feb. 22, 1968. Australian-English pathologist. With E. B. CHAIN, isolated penicillin from the mold in which it was discovered by ALEXANDER FLEMING; awarded Nobel Prize in physiology or medicine (with Chain and Fleming), 1945; awarded life peerage, 1965.

GABOR, DENNIS, June 5, 1900 (Budapest, Hung.)–Feb. 8, 1979. British physicist. Invented holography, a technique of three-dimensional photography based on creating an interference pattern of two light beams on film, 1947; awarded Nobel Prize in physics, 1971.

GALTON, SIR FRANCIS, Feb. 16, 1822 (Birmingham, Eng.)–Jan. 17, 1911. English anthropologist. Founded modern technique of weather mapping, 1863; began a system of fingerprint identification; studied the hereditary basis of intelligence and coined the term *eugenics*; knighted, 1909.

GILBERT, WILLIAM, May 24, 1544 (England)–Dec. 10, 1603. English physician, physicist. Pioneer in research into magnetism and electric phenomena; coined the terms *electric* and *magnetic poles;* the first to suggest that the earth was like a magnet and that heavenly bodies were kept in place by magnetism; court physician to ELIZABETH I and JAMES I. *De Magnete...,* 1600.

GRAHAM, THOMAS, Dec. 20, 1805 (Glasgow, Scot.)–Sept. 16, 1869. Scottish chemist. Discovered "Graham's law" of gas diffusion, 1831; discovered and named the processes of dialysis and osmosis, 1861; founded colloid chemistry.

HALDANE, JOHN BURDON SANDERSON, Nov. 5, 1892 (England)–Dec. 1, 1964. English-Indian geneticist. Conducted basic studies of sex-linkage in chromosomes and of mutation rate; contributed to development of the heart-lung machine; used himself as subject in experiments on the human body under stress. *Science and Ethics,* 1928; *Biochemistry of Genetics,* 1953.

HALLEY, EDMUND, Nov. 8, 1656 (England)–Jan. 14, 1742. English astronomer. First to predict the appearance of a comet (now named for him) in 1758, on the basis of his study of records of comet sightings, 1705; first professional astronomer to catalogue southern hemisphere stars; first to prepare mortality tables, 1693; first to produce a meteorological chart, 1686; a close friend of ISAAC NEWTON.

HAMILTON, SIR WILLIAM ROWAN, Aug. 4,1805 (Dublin, Ire.)–Sept. 2, 1865. Irish mathematician. Discovered quaternions, an essential element of the mathematics of three-dimensional space, 1843; his work in optics and dynamics presaged the appearance of quantum mechanics, 1835; knighted, 1835.

HARDEN, SIR ARTHUR, Oct. 12, 1865 (England)–June 17, 1940. English biochemist. Discovered the coenzyme, a nonprotein necessary to the function of enzymes, c.1904; his discovery of enzymes' use of phosphates began the study of intermediate metabolism; awarded Nobel Prize in chemistry (with HANS VON EULER-CHELPIN), 1929.

HARVEY, WILLIAM, Apr. 1, 1578 (England)–June 3, 1657. English physician. The father of modern physiology, through his discovery of the circulation of the blood, 1616; adapted GALILEO's experimental approach to physiology and ended the influence of GALEN on medical studies.

HAWORTH, SIR WALTER NORMAN, Mar. 19, 1883 (England)–Mar. 19, 1950. English chemist. Conducted basic studies of sugars; devised modern ring form of representing sugar molecules; one of the first to synthesize vitamin C, and coined the name *ascorbic acid,* 1934; awarded Nobel Prize in chemistry (with Paul Karrer), 1937.

HEAVISIDE, OLIVER, May 13, 1850 (London, Eng.)–Feb. 3, 1925. English physicist. Did basic work in the application of mathematics to electrical engineering and electromagnetic theory; shortly after A. E. KENNELLY in 1902, predicted the existence of an electrically charged layer in the upper atmosphere now called the KENNELLY-HEAVISIDE layer.

HERSCHEL, SIR JOHN FREDERICK, Mar. 7, 1792 (England)–May 11, 1871. English astronomer. Continued the work of his father, WILLIAM HERSCHEL, with double stars and nebulae; completed EDMUND HALLEY's catalogue of the stars of the southern hemisphere, 1847; the first to identify the Magellanic Clouds as star clusters; the first to measure accurately the brightness of stars; coined terms *positive* and *negative* in photography; knighted, 1831; made a baronet, 1837.

HERSCHEL, SIR WILLIAM, born Friedrich Wilhelm Herschel, Nov. 15, 1738 (Hanover, Ger.)–Aug. 25, 1822. German-English astronomer. With his sister Caroline, built the best telescope of his time, 1774; discovered Uranus, the first new planet found since ancient times, 1781; the first to determine that many double stars were not simply line-of-sight pairs, but revolved about each other, 1793; the first to hypothesize that the sun was in motion, 1805; the first to hypothesize other galaxies; discovered infrared radiation, 1800; knighted, 1816.

HEWISH, ANTONY, May 11, 1924 (England). English radio astronomer. Discovered pulsars, 1967; awarded Nobel Prize in physics (with M. Ryle), 1974.

HINSHELWOOD, SIR CYRIL NORMAN, June 19, 1897 (London, Eng.)-Oct. 9, 1967. English physical chemist. Conducted basic studies in kinetics (rate at which chemical reactions occur at various temperatures); awarded Nobel Prize in chemistry (with N. N. SEMENOV), 1956; knighted, 1948.

HINTON, SIR CHRISTOPHER, LORD HINTON OF BANKSIDE, BARON OF DULWICH, May 12, 1901 (England). English nuclear engineer. Built the first large-scale nuclear power plant (Calder Hall, Eng., 1956); knighted, 1957; made a baron, 1965.

HODGKIN, ALAN LLOYD, Feb. 5, 1914 (England). English physiologist. With A. F. HUXLEY, discovered the "sodium pump" action of nerve-cell impulse transmission, 1952; awarded Nobel Prize in physiology or medicine (with A. F. HUXLEY and J. C. ECCLES), 1963.

HOOKE, ROBERT, July 18, 1635 (Isle of Wight, Eng.)-Mar. 3, 1703. English physicist. Discovered Hooke's law of elasticity (1678), and worked from this to devise the hairspring of modern watches; coined the word *cell*, 1665.

HOPKINS, SIR FREDERICK GOWLAND, June 30, 1861 (England)-May 16, 1947. English biochemist. Discovered the first "essential amino acid," tryptophan, 1900; suggested the necessity of trace substances in the diet, 1906; awarded Nobel Prize in physiology or medicine (with C. Eijkman), 1929.

HUGGINS, SIR WILLIAM, Feb. 7, 1824 (London, Eng.)-May 12, 1910. English astronomer. The first to discover a "red shift" in the spectrum of a receding star, 1868; the first to devise a method of photographic spectroscopy in astronomy, 1875; the first to consistently use spectroscopy in astronomy; knighted, 1897.

HUTTON, JAMES, June 3, 1726 (Edinburgh, Scot.)-Mar. 26, 1797. Scottish geologist. Founded the science of geology; formulated principle of "uniformitarianism," that the forces now slowly changing the earth's surface had always operated in the same way at the same rate (as opposed to "catastrophism"), 1785; anticipated Darwin in idea of organic evolution by natural selection, 1797.

HUXLEY, ANDREW FIELDING, Nov. 2, 1917 (London, Eng.). English physiologist. With A. L. HODGKIN, discovered the "sodium pump" action of nerve-cell impulse transmission, 1952; Nobel Prize in physiology or medicine (with A. L. Hodgkin and J. C. ECCLES), 1963.

HUXLEY, THOMAS HENRY, May 4, 1825 (England)-June 29, 1895. English biologist. Primary advocate of CHARLES DARWIN's natural selection theory (from 1858 on), and a major science popularizer; coined the word *agnostic*. (Grandfather of ALDOUS and ANDREW FIELDING HUXLEY.)

JEANS, SIR JAMES HOPWOOD, Sept. 11, 1877 (London, Eng.)-Sept. 17, 1946. English mathematician, astronomer. First to suggest the "continuous creation" theory of the origin of the universe, 1928; popularizer of astronomy; knighted, 1928. *Universe around Us,* 1929; *Through Space and Time,* 1934.

JENNER, EDWARD, May 17, 1749 (England)-Jan. 24, 1823. English physician. Discovered and named the process of vaccination for prevention of smallpox, the first disease to be conquered by modern medicine, 1796.

JOSEPHSON, BRIAN DAVID, Jan. 4, 1940 (Cardiff, Wales). British physicist. Noted for his basic research in electron "tunneling" and superconductivity, 1962; awarded Nobel Prize in physics (with I. GIAEVER and L. ESAKI), 1973.

JOULE, JAMES PRESCOTT, Dec. 24, 1818 (England)-Oct. 11, 1889. English physicist. Credited with the accurate determination of the mechanical equivalent of heat, a fundamental contribution to understanding the law of conservation of energy, 1847; with William Thomson (BARON KELVIN), discovered the Joule-Thomson effect (the cooling of expanding gas in a vacuum), essential to low-temperature studies, 1852; the electrical unit of work is named after him.

KATZ, SIR BERNARD, Mar. 26, 1911 (Leipzig, Ger.). British physiologist. Conducted basic research on nerve function and transmission of nerve impulses to muscular fiber; awarded Nobel Prize in physiology or medicine (with J. AXELROD and U. S. VON EULER), 1970.

KELVIN, WILLIAM THOMSON, 1ST BARON, June 26, 1824 (Belfast, Ire.)-Dec. 17, 1907. British physicist, mathematician. Devised the Kelvin scale of temperature, based on absolute zero; argued correctly that gas has no energy or motion at absolute zero, 1848; coined term *kinetic energy,* 1856; made major contributions to thermodynamics, mathematics of electricity and magnetism, and law of energy conservation; made many practical inventions, including a receiver that made the transatlantic cable useful; knighted, 1866; raised to permanent peerage, 1892.

KREBS, SIR HANS ADOLF, Aug. 25, 1900 (Germany). English biochemist. In basic studies of carbohydrate metabolism, discovered and outlined the Krebs cycle, which creates the body's energy through complex processes of carbon dioxide breakdown and oxygen-hydrogen combination; awarded Nobel Prize in physiology or medicine (with F. A. LIPMANN), 1953; knighted, 1958.

LISTER, JOSEPH, BARON LISTER OF LYME REGIS, Apr. 5, 1827 (England)-Feb. 10, 1912. English surgeon. Introduced the use of antiseptic practices in surgery and in hospitals, 1867.

LOCKYER, SIR JOSEPH NORMAN, May 17, 1836 (England)-Aug. 16, 1920. English astronomer. A pioneer in solar spectroscopy, 1860s; with P. Janssen, discovered helium by studying solar spectra, 1868; knighted after helium was discovered on earth, 1897.

LOVELL, SIR ALFRED CHARLES BERNARD, Aug. 31, 1913 (Gloucestershire, Eng.) English astronomer. A leader in the development of radio astronomy and a major force behind the construction of the Jodrell Bank radio telescope (completed 1957), the first major radio telescope in the world; knighted, 1961.

LYELL, SIR CHARLES, Nov. 14, 1797 (Scotland)-Feb. 22, 1875. Scottish geologist. Verified and popularized the geological views of J. HUTTON, establishing uniformitarianism as the basis of modern geology. *The Principle of Geology,* 1830-33.

MACLEOD, JOHN JAMES RICKARD, Sept. 6, 1876 (Scotland)-Mar. 16, 1935. Scottish physiologist. With F. G. BANTING, credited for first isolation of insulin; he had merely lent his lab to Banting and C. H. Best, but as the senior and most prestigious, took credit for the work; awarded Nobel Prize in physiology or medicine, 1923.

MARTIN, ARCHER JOHN PORTER, Mar. 1, 1910 (London, Eng.). English biochemist. With R. L. M. SYNGE, developed paper chromatography, a method of separating and identifying the parts of such complex substances as protein, which has led to major advances in research in chemistry, biology, and medicine; awarded Nobel Prize in chemistry (with Synge), 1952.

MAXIM, SIR HIRAM STEVENS, Feb. 5, 1840 (Brockway's Mills, Me.)-Nov. 24, 1916. English inventor. Invented the first fully automatic machine gun (1883), which was adopted by the British army in 1889.

MAXWELL, JAMES CLERK, Nov. 13, 1831 (Edinburgh, Scot.)-Nov. 5, 1879. Scottish mathematician, physicist. Worked out the mathematics that expressed and united electricity and magnetism, discovering that an electromagnetic field moved outward at the speed of light and postulating that light itself was an electromagnetic radiation far beyond the light spectrum; developed the Maxwell-Boltzmann kinetic theory of gases, which proved heat to be a form of motion, 1860.

MEDAWAR, PETER BRIAN, Feb. 28, 1915 (Rio de Janeiro, Braz.). British biologist. Discovered that immunity is acquired in the embryo stage or in very early infancy, c.1950; awarded Nobel Prize in physiology or medicine (with F. M. BURNET), 1960.

MICHELL, JOHN, 1724 (England)-Apr. 21, 1793. English geologist. Considered to be the father of seismology for suggesting the existence of earthquake waves and that timing the waves could reveal the center of the quake.

MOSELEY, HENRY GWYN-JEFFREYS, Nov. 23, 1887 (Weymouth, Eng.)-Aug. 10, 1915. English physicist. Developed the concept of the atomic number, based on his postulation of a positive nuclear charge characteristic of each element that could be determined by finding the X-ray radiation wavelength characteristic of each element, 1914; his X-ray analysis technique was a major advance in chemical analysis; killed in the Gallipoli campaign in WW I.

MOTT, SIR NEVILL FRANCIS, Sept. 30, 1905 (Leeds, Eng.). English physicist. Conducted basic studies of electrical conduction in noncrystalline solids; awarded Nobel Prize in physics (with P. W. ANDERSON and J. H. VAN VLECK), 1977.

NAPIER, JOHN, LAIRD OF MERCHISTON, 1550 (Scotland)-Apr. 4, 1617. Scottish mathematician. Discovered the usefulness of exponential notation; worked out the first tables of logarithms (a word he coined), thus vastly simplifying routine calculations, 1614; introduced the use of the decimal point.

NEWTON, SIR ISAAC, Dec. 25, 1642 (England)-Mar. 20, 1727. English scientist, mathematician. One of the greatest scientific minds in history, from whose work stems all modern science and technology; first to demonstrate that white light was a combination of all colors, 1666; developed the calculus independently of G. LEIBNIZ, 1670-85; devised the reflecting telescope, 1668; first enunciated the three laws of motion and the law of universal gravitation, 1687. *Philosophiae naturalis principia mathematica,* 1687.

NICHOLSON, WILLIAM, 1753 (London, Eng.)-May 21, 1815. English chemist. Discovered elec-

trolysis, the making of a chemical reaction by applying an electric current, 1790.

NIGHTINGALE, FLORENCE ("The Lady with the Lamp"), May 12, 1820 (Florence, It.)-Aug. 13, 1910. English nurse. Founded trained nursing as a profession; a pioneer in the development of civil and military nursing and hospital care, 1856-60.

NORRISH, RONALD GEORGE WREYFORD, Nov. 9, 1897 (Cambridge, Eng.). English chemist. With G. PORTER, made studies of chemical reactions that take place in as little as one-billionth of a second, 1949-55; awarded Nobel Prize in chemistry (with Porter and M. EIGEN), 1967.

OUGHTRED, WILLIAM, Mar. 5, 1575 (England)-June 30, 1660. English mathematician, minister. Invented the slide rule, 1622; introduced the multiplication sign and the trigonometry abbreviations sin, cos, and tan.

OWEN, SIR ROBERT, July 20, 1804 (Lancaster, Eng.)-Dec. 18, 1892. English zoologist. Made primary contributions to comparative anatomy; coined the term *dinosaur* (1842) and made major advances in understanding the extinct reptiles; discovered the parathyroid glands, 1852; the most virulent opponent of CHARLES DARWIN's theory of evolution.

PARSONS, SIR CHARLES ALGERNON, June 13, 1854 (London, Eng.)-Feb. 11, 1931. English engineer. Made the first practical steam turbine (1884) and adapted it for use in steamships (1890s).

PERKIN, SIR WILLIAM HENRY, Mar. 12, 1838 (London, Eng.)-July 14, 1907. English chemist. Discovered aniline purple or mauve, the first synthetic dye, 1856; discovered the first synthetic aromatic for use in perfume, 1868; first to synthesize an amino acid (glycine), 1858; discovered the important chemical reaction named for him, 1867.

PERUTZ, MAX FERDINAND, May 19, 1914 (Vienna, Austria). British biochemist. Worked out the structure of hemoglobin, 1960; made a basic contribution to the technique of X-ray diffraction analysis, 1953; awarded Nobel Prize in chemistry (with J. C. Kendrew), 1962.

PORTER, GEORGE, Dec. 6, 1920 (England). English chemist. With R. G. W. NORRISH, worked on ultrafast chemical reactions; awarded Nobel Prize in chemistry (with Norrish and M. EIGEN), 1967.

PORTER, RODNEY ROBERT, Oct. 8, 1917 (England). English biochemist. First to work out the structure of an antibody molecule (1969), independently of G. M. EDELMAN; awarded Nobel Prize in physiology or medicine (with Edelman), 1972.

POWELL, CECIL FRANK, Dec. 5, 1903 (England)-Aug. 9, 1969. English physicist. Developed the process for registering the tracks and interactions of atomic particles directly on a photographic emulsion, 1930s; discovered the pi-meson, or pion, 1947; awarded Nobel Prize in physics, 1950.

PRIESTLEY, JOSEPH, Mar. 13, 1733 (England)-Feb. 6, 1804. English chemist, clergyman. His basic studies in gases resulted in the discovery of ammonia, sulphur dioxide, hydrogen chloride, and most notably, oxygen (1774); invented carbonated water, 1773; a radical in politics, his outspoken sympathy with the French Revolution forced him to flee to the U.S., 1794; also made major contributions to education (de-emphasizing the classics) and to liberal theology and political theory.

THE BOOK OF WHO

RAMSAY, SIR WILLIAM, Oct. 2, 1852 (Glasgow, Scot.)-July 23, 1916. Scottish chemist. Discovered argon (1894, with J. W. S. RAYLEIGH), helium on earth (1895), and neon, krypton, xenon (1898), and radon (1910); awarded Nobel Prize in chemistry, 1904.

RANKINE, WILLIAM JOHN MACQUORN, July 5, 1820 (Edinburgh, Scot.)-Dec. 24, 1872. Scottish physicist, engineer. A fundamental contributor to modern engineering who consistently related scientific theory to practical engineering issues; basic work in metal fatigue (1843), applied mechanics (1858), systematic theory of steam engines (1859), and soil mechanics.

RAYLEIGH, JOHN WILLIAM STRUTT, 3RD BARON, Nov. 12, 1842 (England)-June 30, 1919. English physicist. His basic research in waves led to advances in measurements of electricity and magnetism; with W. RAMSAY, discovered the first inert gas (argon), 1894; awarded Nobel Prize in physics, 1904.

RICHARDSON, SIR OWEN WILLANS, Apr. 26, 1879 (England)-Feb. 15, 1959. English physicist. Worked out the mathematics of ion emission from heated substances, thus contributing directly to the development of electronic-tube technology; awarded Nobel Prize in physics, 1928.

ROSS, SIR RONALD, May 13, 1857 (India)-Sept. 16, 1932. English bacteriologist. Discovered the cause and carrier of malaria, 1898; awarded Nobel Prize in physiology or medicine, 1902.

RUMFORD, BENJAMIN THOMPSON, COUNT, Mar. 26, 1753 (Woburn, Mass.)-Aug. 21, 1814. English-U.S. physicist. First to conclude that heat was a form of motion, not a fluid, and to attempt to derive a value for the mechanical equivalent of heat, 1798; introduced JAMES WATT's steam engine to Europe; founded the Royal Inst., for the dissemination of scientific information, 1799; endowed a chair of applied science at Harvard and the Rumford Medals; made a count of the Holy Roman Empire by the elector of Bavaria, for whom he worked, 1791.

RUTHERFORD, ERNEST, 1ST BARON RUTHERFORD OF NELSON, Aug. 30, 1871 (New Zealand)-Oct. 19, 1937. British physicist. Discovered and named alpha, beta (1897), and gamma (1900) radiation; discovered and named the "half-life" phenomenon of radioactivity, c. 1902; the first to achieve a manmade nuclear reaction, turning nitrogen atoms into oxygen by bombarding them with alpha particles, 1917; awarded Nobel Prize in chemistry, 1908; instrumental in rescuing many Jewish scientists from Nazi Germany; buried in Westminster Abbey.

SHERRINGTON, SIR CHARLES SCOTT, Nov. 27, 1857 (London, Eng.)-Mar. 4, 1952. English neurologist. Pioneer in neurophysiology; did basic studies in reflexes (c.1906), the kinetic sense (c.1894), and the motor areas of the brain; awarded Nobel Prize in physiology or medicine (with E. D. ADRIAN), 1932.

SIEMENS, SIR WILLIAM, Apr. 4, 1823 (Germany)-Nov. 18, 1883. English inventor of the open-hearth steel-making process, 1861.

SIMPSON, SIR JAMES YOUNG, June 7, 1811 (Scotland)-May 6, 1870. Scottish obstetrician. A founder of modern gynecology; the first to use anesthesia in childbirth, 1847; appointed official physician to Queen VICTORIA, 1847.

SMITHSON, JAMES, 1765 (France)-June 26, 1829. English chemist, mineralogist. Published 27 scientific papers; elected to Royal Acad. at age 22;

provided funds for the founding of the Smithsonian Inst., Washington, D.C.; the mineral smithsonite (carbonate of zinc) is named after him.

SODDY, FREDERICK, Sept. 2, 1877 (England)-Sept. 22, 1956. English chemist. With E. RUTHERFORD, worked out an explanation of radioactive breakdown, c.1902; worked out the theory of isotopes and coined that term, 1912; awarded Nobel Prize in chemistry, 1921.

STARLING, ERNEST HENRY, Apr. 17, 1866 (London, Eng.)-May 2, 1927. English physiologist. With W. M. BAYLISS, discovered and named hormones, 1902.

STEPHENSON, GEORGE, June 9, 1781 (England)-Aug. 12, 1848. English inventor of the first practical and commercially-successful steam locomotive, 1825.

SWAN, SIR JOSEPH WILSON, Oct. 31, 1828 (England)-May 27, 1914. English chemist, inventor. Invented "dry plate" photography (1871) and bromide paper for photographic prints (1879); invented one of the first light bulbs (1860) and developed a practical one (1880) independently of T. A. EDISON.

SYNGE, RICHARD LAURENCE MILLINGTON, Oct. 28, 1914 (Liverpool, Eng.). English biochemist. With A. J. P. MARTIN, developed paper chromatography techniques, 1944; awarded Nobel Prize in chemistry (with Martin), 1952.

THOMSON, SIR GEORGE PAGET, May 3, 1892 (Cambridge, Eng.)-Sept. 10, 1975. English physicist. Discovered electron diffraction, independently of C. J. DAVISSON; awarded Nobel Prize in physics (with Davisson), 1933; (Son of J. J. THOMSON.)

THOMSON, SIR JOSEPH JOHN, Dec. 18, 1856 (England)-Aug. 30, 1940. English physicist. Discovered the electron, 1897; opened the field of subatomic physics; awarded Nobel Prize in physics, 1906; seven of his students, including his son, G. P. THOMSON, won Nobel Prizes.

TINBERGEN, NIKOLAAS, Apr. 15, 1907 (The Hague, Neth.). English ethologist. Conducted fundamental studies of the social behavior of animals; awarded Nobel Prize in physiology or medicine (with K. Z. LORENZ and K. VON FRISCH), 1973.

TODD, ALEXANDER ROBERTUS, BARON TODD OF TRUMPINGTON, Oct. 2, 1907 (Glasgow, Scot.). Scottish biochemist. His basic research in and synthesis of nucleic acid components (1940s) prepared the way for fine-structure analysis of DNA; awarded Nobel Prize in chemistry, 1957.

TREVITHICK, RICHARD, Apr. 13, 1771 (England)-Apr. 22, 1833. English engineer. Made a major contribution to the development of high-pressure steam engines; built the first locomotive, 1803.

TYNDALL, JOHN, Aug. 2, 1820 (Ireland)-Dec. 4, 1893. Irish physicist. His investigations of light-scattering by colloidal particles provided the explanation for why the sky is blue, c. 1870; popularized the idea of heat as motion and the law of conservation of energy.

WALLACE, ALFRED RUSSEL, Jan. 8, 1823 (England)-Nov. 7, 1913. English naturalist. Simultaneously with, but independently of C. R. DARWIN, proposed the theory of evolution by natural selection, 1858.

WALTON, ERNEST THOMAS SINTON, Oct. 6, 1903 (Ireland). Irish physicist. With J. D. COCKROFT, devised the voltage-multiplier particle ac-

SCIENTISTS, PHYSICIANS, AND INVENTORS

celerator (1929) and obtained the first nuclear reaction with artificially accelerated particles, 1932; awarded Nobel Prize in physics (with Cockroft), 1951.

WATSON-WATT, SIR ROBERT, Apr. 13, 1892 (Scotland)–Dec. 5, 1973. Scottish physician. Invented the first practical radar, c.1935; knighted, 1942.

WATT, JAMES, Jan. 19, 1736 (Scotland)–Aug. 19, 1819. Scottish engineer. Father of the Industrial Revolution; invented the first efficient steam engines (1769) and the first reciprocal steam engine (c.1771), and was the first to use a steam engine to turn a wheel (1781); invented the first automatic governor, to regulate the flow of steam; invented and defined the idea of horsepower.

WHEATSTONE, SIR CHARLES, Feb. 6, 1802 (Gloucester, Eng.)–Oct. 19, 1875. English physicist. Anticipated S. F. B. MORSE in the invention of the telegraph, 1837; the first to use and popularize the Wheatstone bridge, a device for precision measurement of electrical resistance, 1843; invented the stereoscope.

WILKINS, MAURICE HUGH FREDERICK, Dec. 15, 1916 (New Zealand). English physicist. His X-ray diffraction studies of DNA provided J. WATSON and F. CRICK with essential data for determining DNA's structure, 1953; awarded Nobel Prize in physiology or medicine (with Crick and Watson), 1963.

WILKINSON, SIR GEOFFREY, July 14, 1921 (England). English chemist. Conducted basic research in organometallic compounds; awarded Nobel Prize in chemistry (with E. O. FISCHER), 1973.

WILLIAMSON, ALEXANDER WILLIAM, May 1, 1824 (London, Eng.)–May 6, 1904. English chemist. First to provide an understanding of reversible chemical reactions, to describe clearly dynamic equilibrium, and to explain the function of a catalyst, 1854; his studies of ethers and alcohols laid important groundwork for later understanding of chemical structure.

WILSON, CHARLES THOMSON REES, Feb. 14, 1869 (Scotland)–Nov. 15, 1959. Scottish meteorologist, physicist. His basic research in cloud formation led to his invention of the Wilson cloud chamber (1911), an essential device in the study of nuclear radiation until 1952; awarded Nobel Prize in physics (with A. H. COMPTON), 1927.

YOUNG, THOMAS, June 13, 1773 (England)–May 10, 1829. English physicist. Discovered how the lens of the eye changes shape to focus at different distances; discovered the cause of astigmatism, 1801; provided conclusive evidence of the wave nature of light, 1803; first to state the three-color theory; one of the first to decipher Egyptian hieroglyphics, c.1815.

GERMAN SCIENTISTS, PHYSICIANS, AND INVENTORS

AGRICOLA, GEORGIUS, born Georg Bauer, Mar. 24, 1494 (Saxony)–Nov. 21, 1555. German mineralogist, physician. Called the father of mineralogy because of his written descriptions of Saxon mining knowledge and machinery (published 1556).

ALBERTUS MAGNUS (Albert the Great), born Albert, Count von Bollstädt, 1193 (Germany)–Nov. 15, 1280. German botanist, chemist, alchemist, philosopher. Introduced Aristotelian natural philosophy to northern Europe, 1245–54; a teacher of THOMAS AQUINAS in Paris; an early advocate of personal observation and skepticism in the sciences.

ALDER, KURT, July 10, 1902 (Germany)–June 20, 1958. German organic chemist. With OTTO DIELS, worked out (1928) the Diels-Alder reaction that became the basis of many modern synthetic products, ranging from rubber to many plastics and insecticides; awarded Nobel Prize in chemistry (with Diels), 1950.

BAEYER, JOHANN FRIEDRICH WILHELM ADOLF VON, Oct. 31, 1835 (Berlin, Ger.)–Aug. 20, 1917. German chemist. Discovered barbituric acid (basis of barbiturates), 1864; synthesized indigo, 1880; developed "strain" theory to explain why small carbon rings commonly hold only five or six carbon atoms, 1886; awarded Nobel Prize in chemistry, 1905.

BEHRING, EMIL ADOLF VON, Mar. 3, 1854 (Germany)–Mar. 31, 1917. German bacteriologist. Discovered antitoxin serums against tetanus and diphtheria; awarded Nobel Prize in physiology or medicine, 1901.

BENZ, KARL FRIEDRICH, Nov. 25, 1844 (Germany)–Apr. 4, 1929. German engineer. Designed and built first feasible automobile with internal combustion engine, 1885.

BERGIUS, FRIEDRICH KARL RUDOLF, Oct. 11, 1884 (Germany)–Mar. 30, 1949. German chemist. Using high-pressure processes, developed methods of making gasoline from coal and heavy oil; discovered ways to break down wood molecules to produce alcohol and sugar; his processes played vital role in German economy during WW II; awarded Nobel Prize in chemistry (with Carl Bosch), 1931.

BESSEL, FRIEDRICH WILHELM, July 22, 1784 (Prussia)–Mar. 17, 1846. Prussian astronomer. Brought modern precision to processes of measurement in astronomy and geodetics; established exact positions of some 50,000 stars; first to accurately measure the distance of a star from the earth, thus multiplying by many times the idea of the size of the universe; first to hypothesize the existence of binary stars and of Neptune.

BETHE, HANS ALBRECHT, July 2, 1906 (Strasbourg, Ger. [now France]). German-U.S. physicist. Developed modern view of stellar energy as the result of combining hydrogen atoms to form helium, with resulting conversion of some hydrogen mass into energy, 1938; contributed to development of atomic weapons and energy; awarded Fermi Prize, 1961; awarded Nobel Prize in physics, 1967.

BOTHE, WALTHER WILHELM GEORG FRANZ, Jan. 8, 1891 (nr. Berlin, Ger.)–Feb. 8, 1957. German physicist. Devised a method of studying cosmic rays ("coincidence counting") that permitted measurement of extremely brief time-intervals (less than a billionth of a second) and demonstration of the law of conservation of energy and momentum at the atomic level; awarded Nobel Prize in physics (with Max Born), 1954.

BRAUN, KARL FERDINAND, June 6, 1850 (Germany)–Apr. 20, 1918. German physicist. Invented the oscillograph, 1897; helped develop use of crystals in radios, c. 1875; awarded Nobel Prize in physics (with G. MARCONI), 1909.

BUCHNER, EDUARD, May 20, 1860 (Munich, Ger.)–Aug. 24, 1917. German chemist. While attempting to demonstrate that dead yeast could not turn sugar into alcohol, proved the opposite, end-

THE BOOK OF WHO

ing serious debate over whether life must be present to cause certain chemical reactions, 1896; awarded Nobel Prize in chemistry, 1907; killed in action in WW I.

BUNSEN, ROBERT WILHELM, March 31, 1811 (Germany)–Aug. 16, 1899. German chemist, inventor. Pioneer in study of arsenic, gas analysis methods, heat measurement; first to demonstrate that burning magnesium could make a very bright light; did not invent Bunsen burner, but popularized it; invented spectroscopy (with G. R. KIRCHHOFF), 1859.

BUTENANDT, ADOLF FRIEDRICH JOHANN, Mar. 24, 1903 (Germany). German chemist. Pioneer in isolation and analysis of sex hormones; isolated estrone, androsterone, and progesterone; awarded Nobel Prize in chemistry (with L. Ruzicka), 1939, but was forced by Nazi government to refuse the prize (finally accepted it in 1949).

CHLADNI, ERNST FLORENS FRIEDRICH, Nov. 30, 1756 (Germany)–Apr. 3, 1827. German physicist. Founded the science of acoustics, by working out the quantitative rules of the transmission of sound, c.1809; determined the speed of sound in many gases.

CLAUSIUS, RUDOLF JULIUS EMMANUEL, Jan. 2, 1822 (Germany)–Aug. 24, 1888. German physicist. Discovered second law of thermodynamics, 1850; coined the word *entropy*.

DAIMLER, GOTTLIEB WILHELM, Mar. 17, 1834 (Germany)–Mar. 6, 1900. German inventor. Invented the high-speed, gasoline-burning internal-combustion engine that made the automobile practical, 1883; by installing such an engine on a bicycle, made the first motorcycle, 1885; founded Daimler motor company (1890), and developed the Mercedes automobile.

DIELS, OTTO PAUL HERMANN, Jan. 23, 1876 (Berlin, Ger.)–Mar. 7, 1954. German chemist. With KURT ALDER, discovered Diels-Alder reaction, essential to the synthesis of many complex compounds, 1928; awarded Nobel Prize in chemistry (with Alder), 1950.

DIESEL, RUDOLF, Mar. 18, 1858 (Paris, Fr.)–Sept. 30, 1913. German inventor of the diesel engine (1897).

EHRLICH, PAUL, Mar. 14, 1854 (Germany)– Aug. 20, 1915. German bacteriologist. Discovered "silver bullets," chemicals that act primarily on disease-causing organisms without affecting healthy cells, for sleeping sickness and syphilis (1909), thus founding modern chemotherapy; made major contributions to studies of immunization and serum therapy; awarded Nobel Prize in physiology or medicine (with I. I. MECHNIKOFF), 1908.

EIGEN, MANFRED, May 9, 1927 (Germany). German physicist. Made major contributions to the study of chemical reactions that take place in as little as a billionth of a second; awarded Nobel Prize in chemistry (with R. G. NORRISH and G. PORTER), 1967.

FAHRENHEIT, GABRIEL DANIEL, May 14, 1686 (Danzig, Ger. [now Gdansk, Pol.])–Sept. 16, 1736. German-Dutch physicist. Invented mercury thermometer, 1714; devised Fahrenheit scale.

FISCHER, EMIL HERMANN, Oct. 9, 1852 (Germany)–July 15, 1919. German chemist. Pioneer in stereochemistry, the study of the three-dimensional structure of complex compounds (during 1880s), conducted nucleic acid research and protein-structure and synthesis studies (1907); awarded Nobel Prize in chemistry, 1902.

FISCHER, ERNST OTTO, Nov. 10, 1918 (Munich, Ger.). German chemist. Noted for his fundamental research in organo-metallic chemistry, in the 1950s and 1960s; awarded Nobel Prize in chemistry (with G. WILKINSON), 1973.

FISCHER, HANS, July 27, 1881 (Germany)–Mar. 31, 1945. German chemist. Worked out the composition and structure of the heme molecule, a vital part of the blood, 1929; did the same for chlorophyll, in the late 1930s; awarded Nobel Prize in chemistry, 1930.

FLEMMING, WALTHER, April 21, 1843 (Germany)–Aug. 5, 1905. German anatomist. Discovered chromosomes and the details of mitosis (process of cell division), c. 1881.

FORSSMANN, WERNER, Aug. 19, 1904 (Germany)–June 1, 1979. German surgeon. Demonstrated (on himself) that a catheter introduced at a vein in the elbow could safely be pushed through to the heart (1929), making possible new techniques in diagnosis and therapy; awarded Nobel Prize in physiology or medicine (with A. Courand and D. W. Richards), 1956.

GAUSS, KARL FRIEDRICH, born Johann Friedrich Karl Gauss, Apr. 30, 1777 (Germany)–Feb. 23, 1855. German mathematician. One of the world's greatest mathematicians; discovered method of least-squares, c.1795; developed concept of complex numbers and proved the fundamental theorems of algebra (1799) and arithmetic (1801); made major contributions to calculations of asteroid orbits; calculated location of the earth's magnetic poles; devised units of measurement for magnetic phenomena, 1832; the unit of magnetic flux was named for him.

GEIGER, (Johannes) HANS WILHELM, Sept. 30, 1882 (Germany)– Sept. 24, 1945. German physicist. Introduced the Geiger counter, the first successful device for detecting and measuring radioactivity, 1913; redesigned it with the help of A. Müller, 1928.

GEISSLER, HEINRICH, May 26, 1814 (Germany)–Jan. 24, 1879. German inventor. Invented a pump that could produce the most thorough vacuum possible in tubes (now called Geissler tubes), which made possible basic advances in atomic physics, 1855.

GUERICKE, OTTO VON, Nov. 20, 1602 (Germany)–May 11, 1686. German physicist. Invented first air pump, 1650; the first to create a vacuum.

GUTENBERG, JOHANNES, c.1398 (Mainz, Ger.)–1468. German inventor. Invented movable type and the printing press, enabling a revolution in the spread of learning and ideas, c.1454.

HAECKEL, ERNST, Feb. 16, 1834 (Germany)–Aug. 8, 1919. German biologist. Popularized the phrase "ontogeny recapitulates phylogeny"; coined the term *ecology*.

HAHN, OTTO, Mar. 8, 1879 (Germany)–July 28, 1968. German physical chemist. Discovered uranium fission, 1938; with LISE MEITNER, discovered protactinium (1918) and nuclear isomers (1921); awarded Nobel Prize in chemistry, 1944.

HEISENBERG, WERNER KARL, Dec. 5, 1901 (Germany)–Feb. 1, 1976. German physicist. Discovered the "uncertainty principle," which stated that the position and momentum of a particle could not be known simultaneously at one instant of time, thus introducing the element of chance into modern physics and weakening the deterministic cause-and-effect view, 1927; awarded Nobel Prize in physics, 1932.

HELMHOLTZ, HERMANN LUDWIG FERDINAND VON, Aug. 31, 1821 (Prussia)–Sept. 8, 1894. German physiologist, physicist. Did basic studies in the function of the eye and ear; made a basic contribution to the law of conservation of energy, 1847.

HERTZ, GUSTAV LUDWIG, July 22, 1887 (Hamburg, Ger.)–Oct. 30, 1975. German physicist. With J. FRANCK, demonstrated an aspect of MAX PLANCK's quantum theory by bombarding gases with electrons to stimulate light emissions; awarded Nobel Prize in physics (with J. Franck), 1925.

HERTZ, HEINRICH RUDOLF, Feb. 22, 1857 (Hamburg, Ger.)–Jan. 1, 1894. German physicist. The first to observe the photoelectric effect, 1888; demonstrated the existence of electromagnetic waves (1888), confirming J. C. MAXWELL's hypothesis, and demonstrated that they obeyed the same laws as light; discovered "long waves," the basis of radio; unit of electromagnetic frequency is named after him.

HEVELIUS, JOHANNES, Jan. 28, 1611 (Danzig [now Gdansk], Pol.)–Jan. 28, 1687. German astronomer. An early mapper of the moon's surface; his names for the moon's mountains and "seas" are still in use.

HOPPE-SEYLER, ERNST FELIX, Dec. 26, 1825 (Freiburg, Ger.)–Aug. 10, 1895. German biochemist. Established biochemistry as a distinct discipline, 1872–1877; discovered the enzyme invertase (1871) and lecithin; constructed the present system of classifying proteins.

HUMBOLDT, FRIEDRICH WILHELM HEINRICH ALEXANDER, FREIHERR VON, Sept. 14, 1769 (Berlin, Ger.)–May 6, 1859. German naturalist, explorer. Traveled throughout Europe, the Americas, and Russian Asia, collecting plants, studying rivers, ocean currents, volcanoes, and temperature changes, and measuring geomagnetism; suggested building the Panama Canal; made the first isothermic and isobaric maps; wrote *Kosmos,* a five-volume review of astronomy and earth sciences, 1835–60; during his life, contributed his entire fortune to the advancement of science.

JENSEN, J. HANS DANIEL, June 25, 1907 (Hamburg, Ger.)–Feb. 11, 1973. German physicist. Proposed the idea of nuclear shells, independently of M. GOEPPERT-MAYER, 1949; awarded Nobel Prize in physics (with Goeppert-Mayer and E. P. WIGNER), 1963.

KEKULÉ VON STRADONITZ, FRIEDRICH AUGUST, Sept. 7, 1829 (Darmstadt, Ger.)–July 13, 1896. German chemist. Suggested ideas of Kekulé structures (the representation of molecules as specific patterns of atoms) and tetravalent carbon, 1858; proposed "ring" theory for benzene structure, 1865; his ideas provided the foundation of modern advances in organic chemistry.

KEPLER, JOHANNES, Dec. 27, 1571 (Germany)–Nov. 15, 1630. German astronomer. Discovered that the orbits of the planets are ellipses with the sun at one focus, 1609; did fundamental work in optics; developed tables of planetary motion based on data collected by TYCHO BRAHE. *Astronomia Nova,* 1609.

KIRCHHOFF, GUSTAV ROBERT, Mar. 12, 1824 (Königsberg, Prussia [now Kalingrad, USSR])–Oct. 17, 1887. German physicist. With R. W. BUNSEN, invented spectroscopy, 1859; discovered cesium (1860) and rubidium (1861); developed techniques of solar spectroscopy; first to propose the idea of "black body" radiation.

KOCH, ROBERT, Dec. 11, 1843 (Germany)–May 27, 1910. German bacteriologist. Developed basic modern techniques and rules of bacteriol-

ogy; pioneered in the use of gels as culture mediums; discovered the causative agents of anthrax (1876), tuberculosis (1882), and cholera; discovered the louse and tsetse fly vectors of bubonic plague and sleeping sickness, 1897–1906; awarded Nobel Prize in physiology or medicine, 1905.

KOLBE, ADOLPH WILHELM HERMANN, Sept. 27, 1818 (Germany)–Nov. 25, 1884. German chemist. A pioneer in the synthesis of organic compounds from inorganic substances; developed new methods of synthesis, one of which made possible the mass production of acetylsalicylic acid (aspirin), 1859.

KOSSEL, ALBRECHT, Sept. 16, 1853 (Germany)–July 5, 1927. German biochemist. First to isolate and begin analysis of nucleic acid (DNA and related substances), discovering it contained adenins, guanine, cytosine and thymine—now known to be the elements of the genetic code; also made extensive studies of proteins; awarded Nobel Prize in physiology or medicine, 1910.

LAMBERT, JOHANN HEINRICH, Aug. 26, 1728 (Mulhouse, Alsace [now France])–Sept. 25, 1777. German mathematician, physicist. Proved pi to be an irrational number; did basic studies of light reflection and coined the term *albedo,* 1760; the first to measure light intensities accurately.

LAUE, MAX THEODORE FELIX VON, Oct. 9, 1879 (Germany)–Apr. 23, 1960. German physicist. Discovered X-ray diffraction by crystals, making it possible to determine the wavelengths of X rays and the atomic structures of crystals; awarded Nobel Prize in physics, 1914.

LINDE, KARL PAUL GOTTFRIED VON, June 11, 1842 (Bavaria, Ger.)–Nov. 16, 1934. German engineer, chemist. Developed the first efficient refrigerator; devised new method of liquefying gases in quantity, 1895; discovered how to separate large quantities of pure liquid oxygen from liquid air, thus sparking advances in high-temperature industrial processes, 1901.

MAYER, JULIUS ROBERT, Nov. 25, 1814 (Germany)–Mar. 20, 1878. German physicist. In advance of J. P. JOULE and H. HELMHOLTZ, respectively, worked out the mechanical equivalent of heat and the law of conservation of energy, 1842; the first to argue that all energy on earth ultimately derived from the sun; his contributions went unrecognized until the 1860s.

MESMER, FRANZ (or Friedrich) **ANTON,** May 23, 1734 (Germany)–Mar. 5, 1815. German physician. The modern discoverer of cure by suggestion in certain cases, which he attributed to "magnetic" force; his work, though discredited (1784), prepared the way for the discovery of hypnotism and the investigation of hysterical symptoms.

MESSERSCHMITT, WILHELM, June 26, 1898 (Frankfurt-am-Main, Ger.)–Sept. 15, 1978. German aviation engineer. Designed the Me 262, the first jet to fly in combat, 1944; also designed the Me-109, the major German fighter in WW II.

MÖBIUS, AUGUST FERDINAND, Nov. 17, 1790 (Germany)–Sept. 26, 1868. German mathematician, astronomer. Made basic contributions to mathematics, especially geometry; a founder of topology; best known for discovering and analyzing the Möbius strip, a three-dimensional band with one edge and one surface that remains whole even when split down the middle.

MOHS, FRIEDRICH, Jan. 29, 1773 (Germany)–Sept. 29, 1839. German mineralogist. Devised the Mohs scale of comparative mineral hardness, ranging from talc at 1 to diamond at 10.

THE BOOK OF WHO

MÖSSBAUER, RUDOLF LUDWIG, Jan. 31, 1919 (Munich, Ger.). German physicist. Discovered the so-called Mössbauer effect, describing the behavior of gamma waves emitted and absorbed by crystals under particular conditions, 1958; this effect permitted the first laboratory test of ALBERT EINSTEIN's general theory of relativity; awarded Nobel Prize in physics (with R. HOFSTADTER), 1961.

NERNST, WALTHER HERMANN, June 25, 1864 (Prussia)–Nov. 18, 1941. German physical chemist. Discovered the third law of thermodynamics, that entropy nears zero at a temperature of absolute zero, 1906; explained why a chlorine-and-hydrogen mixture will explode on exposure to light, thus making clear the existence of chemical "chain reactions," 1918; awarded Nobel Prize in chemistry, 1920.

NICHOLAS OF CUSA (or Nichola Cusanus), born Nicholas Krebs, 1401 (Germany)–Aug. 11, 1464. German philosopher. On intuition alone, hypothesized that the earth turned on its axis and revolved around the sun, that space was infinite, and that the stars were other suns and had planets, 1440; invented concave-lens spectacles for the near-sighted; became a cardinal, 1448.

OHM, GEORG SIMON, Mar. 16, 1787 (Germany)–July 7, 1854. German physicist. Defined the relationships between the difference in potential, the resistance of the conductor, and the amount of electric current that would flow through a wire, 1827; both the ohm (the unit of resistance) and the mho (the unit of conductance), are named for him.

OSTWALD, FRIEDRICH WILHELM, Sept. 2, 1853 (Riga, Lat. [now USSR])–Apr. 4, 1932. German physical chemist. A major founder of modern physical chemistry; made basic contributions to the understanding of how catalysts work; awarded Nobel Prize in chemistry, 1909.

OTTO, NIKOLAUS AUGUST, June 10, 1832 (Germany)–Jan. 26, 1891. German inventor. First to build a four-stroke internal combustion engine, the type used almost universally today, 1876.

PLANCK, MAX KARL ERNST LUDWIG, Apr. 23, 1858 (Kiel, Ger.)–Oct. 3, 1947. German physicist. Began modern physics with his proposal of the quantum theory, which states that electromagnetic radiation consists of quanta (particles of energy) directly proportional in size to the frequency of the radiation; awarded Nobel Prize in physics, 1918.

PRANDTL, LUDWIG, Feb. 4, 1875 (Germany)–Aug. 15, 1953. German physicist. Often considered the father of aerodynamics; his discovery of the "boundary layer" led to understanding of streamlining, 1904; made fundamental contributions to wing theory and turbulence study.

REGIOMONTANUS, born Johann Müller, June 6, 1436 (Germany)–July 6, 1476. German astronomer. His updated tables of planetary motion were widely used by explorer-navigators, including C. COLUMBUS; the first to observe and study the comet later called Halley's; the primary exponent in his day of a stationary, nonspinning earth.

RIEMANN, GEORG FRIEDRICH BERNHARD, Sept. 17, 1826 (Germany)–July 20, 1866. German mathematician. A major creative source of mathematics in modern theoretical physics through his development of a non-Euclidean geometry of curved space, 1854.

RITTER, JOHANN WILHELM, Dec. 16, 1776 (Silesia, Ger. [now Pol.]). German physicist. Discovered the ultraviolet end of the light spectrum, 1801; discovered the electroplating process, 1800.

ROENTGEN, WILHELM KONRAD, Mar. 27, 1845 (Germany)–Feb. 10, 1923. German physicist. Discovered X rays while experimenting with cathode rays (1895)—a discovery that revolutionized medicine, led directly to the discovery of radioactivity, and is often considered the beginning of modern physics; awarded the first Nobel Prize in physics, 1901; the unit of X-radiation is named after him.

SCHWABE, HEINRICH SAMUEL, Oct. 25, 1789 (Germany)–Apr. 11, 1875. German pharmacist, astronomer. Discovered the sun-spot cycle, after 18 years of observation and recordkeeping, 1843.

SCHWANN, THEODOR, Dec. 7, 1810 (Germany)–Jan. 11, 1882. German physiologist. The primary developer of the cell theory of life, 1839; the first to isolate an animal enzyme (pepsin), 1836.

SPEMANN, HANS, June 27, 1869 (Stuttgart, Ger.)–Sept. 12, 1941. German zoologist. His basic research in embryology revealed the role of hormones in organizing the development of embryo cells, 1920s; awarded Nobel Prize in physiology or medicine, 1935.

STAHL, GEORG ERNST, Oct. 21, 1660 (Germany)–May 14, 1734. German chemist. Father of "phlogiston theory" of combustion (1700), which held that some materials contained "phlogiston" that was used up in the combustion process; his theory dominated chemical thought until A. LAVOISIER.

STERN, OTTO, Feb. 17, 1888 (Germany)–Aug. 17, 1969. German-U.S. physicist. Developed molecular beams as a tool for studying the structure of molecules; measured the magnetic moment of the proton, 1933; awarded Nobel Prize in physics, 1943.

STRUVE, FRIEDRICH GEORG WILHELM VON, Apr. 15, 1793 (Altona, Ger.)–Nov. 23, 1864. German-Russian astronomer. Established binary-star studies with a catalogue of over 3,000 binaries, 1837.

VIRCHOW, RUDOLPH, Oct. 13, 1821 (Prussia)–Sept. 5, 1902. German pathologist. Founder of cellular pathology, 1858; first to describe leukemia, 1845; entered politics to fight for social reforms as a first step in preventing disease, 1862.

WALDEYER, HEINRICH WILHELM GOTTFRIED VON, Oct. 6, 1836 (Germany)–Jan. 23, 1921. German anatomist. Proposed the theory that the nervous system is made up of discrete cells, c. 1870; coined the words *neuron* and *chromosome*.

WALLACH, OTTO, Mar. 27, 1847 (Königsberg, Prussia [now Kaliningrad, USSR])–Feb. 26, 1931. German organic chemist. His basic research on the molecular structure of terpenes (such as menthol and camphor) contributed to the development of the perfume industry and understanding of steroids; awarded Nobel Prize in chemistry, 1910.

WARBURG, OTTO HEINRICH, Oct. 8, 1883 (Freiburg, Ger.)–Aug. 1, 1970. German biochemist. His basic research in the details of cell respiration helped to clarify the functions of several vitamins and enzymes, 1920s and 1930s; awarded Nobel Prize in physiology or medicine, 1931.

WASSERMAN, AUGUST VON, Feb. 21, 1866 (Bamberg, Ger.)–Mar. 15, 1925. German bacteriologist. Developed the prevalent diagnostic test for syphilis, 1906.

SCIENTISTS, PHYSICIANS, AND INVENTORS

WEBER, ERNST HEINRICH, June 24, 1795 (Wittenberg, Ger.)-Jan. 26, 1878. German physiologist. Developed the theory of the "just noticeable difference," a way of measuring the acuity of the senses and the foundation of experimental psychology, 1830s; his ideas were popularized by G. T. Fechner.

WEIZSÄCKER, CARL FRIEDRICH, June 28,1912 (Kiel, Ger.). German astronomer. Originated the modern nebular hypothesis for the origin of the solar system, 1944.

WIELAND, HEINRICH OTTO, June 4, 1877 (Germany)-Aug. 5, 1957. German chemist. Did basic research in the structure of steroids, 1912-20; conducted basic research in how food is converted to energy, 1920s; awarded Nobel Prize in chemistry, 1927.

WIEN, WILHELM, Jan. 13, 1864 (E. Prussia)-Aug. 31, 1928. German physicist. His basic research in black-body radiation proved that the wavelength of radiation shortens as the temperature of the emitting body increases, 1839; awarded Nobel Prize in physics, 1911.

WINDAUS, ADOLF, Dec. 25, 1876 (Berlin, Ger.)-June 9, 1959. German chemist. Worked out the structure of cholesterol, 1901-31; synthesized histamine, 1907; did basic research in steroids; awarded Nobel Prize in chemistry, 1928.

WUNDT, WILHELM, Aug. 16, 1832 (Germany)-Aug. 31, 1920. German physiologist. Founded the science of experimental psychology, 1862; established the first psychology laboratory, in Leipzig, 1879.

ZEPPELIN, FERDINAND, GRAF VON, July 8, 1838 (Germany)-Mar. 8, 1917. German inventor, military officer. Invented the dirigible, which made the first directed flight by man, July 2, 1900.

ZSIGMONDY, RICHARD ADOLF, Apr. 1, 1865 (Vienna, Austria)-Sept. 23, 1929. German chemist. Pioneer in colloid studies with the ultramicroscope (which he helped develop, 1903); awarded Nobel Prize in chemistry, 1925.

FRENCH SCIENTISTS, PHYSICIANS, AND INVENTORS

AMPÈRE, ANDRÉ-MARIE, Jan. 22, 1775 (France)-June 10, 1836. French mathematician, physicist. Founded the study of electromagnetics (then called electrodynamics), 1820; stated the basic concept of the solenoid (which he named); stated Ampère's law, which describes mathematically the magnetic force between two electric currents; the unit of rate of motion of electric current was named an *ampere* by W. T. KELVIN, 1883.

BECQUEREL, ANTOINE HENRI, Dec. 15, 1852 (Paris, Fr.)-Aug. 25, 1908. French physicist. Discovered radioactivity, showing that atoms were composed of still smaller charged particles; awarded Nobel Prize in physics (with MARIE and PIERRE CURIE), 1903.

BERTHELOT, PIERRE EUGÈNE MARCELIN, Oct. 27, 1827 (France)-Mar. 18, 1907. French chemist. Synthesized methyl alcohol, ethyl alcohol, methane, benzene, acetylene; first to synthesize organic compounds that do not occur in nature; did extensive studies of the heat of chemical reaction; French senator, 1881-1907; foreign minister, 1895; secy. of French Acad., 1889-1907.

BINET, ALFRED, July 8, 1857 (France)-Oct. 18, 1911. French physiologist. Inventor of standardized tests for general intelligence.

BLÉRIOT, LOUIS, July 1, 1872 (France)-Aug. 2, 1936. French aviator, inventor. First to fly an airplane across the English Channel, July 25, 1909; invented auto lights.

BUFFON, GEORGE-LOUIS LECLERC, COMTE DE, Sept. 7, 1707 (France)-Apr. 16, 1788. French naturalist. Wrote first 36 volumes of *Natural History* (1749-88), an attempt at a complete description of nature (eight more volumes appeared after his death); first to develop theory of geological eras, 1778; first to theorize the earth might be older than the biblically determined 6,000 years; first to propose idea of organic evolution.

CAILLETET, LOUIS PAUL, Sept. 21, 1832 (France)-Jan. 5, 1913. French physicist. Independently of R. P. Pictet, was first to liquify oxygen, nitrogen, and carbon monoxide by compressing and cooling them, then allowing them to expand to further decrease their temperatures to the critical point.

CARNOT, NICOLAS LEONARD SADI, June 1, 1796 (Paris, Fr.)-Aug. 24, 1832. French physicist. First to compute mathematically the relation between heat and work, thus founding study of thermodynamics.

CARREL, ALEXIS, June 28, 1873 (Lyons, Fr.)-Nov. 5, 1944. French-U.S. surgeon. Developed method for suturing blood vessels end-to-end, 1902; pioneer in the preservation of body organs by perfusion and in design of early "artificial heart" machines; awarded Nobel Prize in physiology or medicine, 1912.

CHARCOT, JEAN-MARTIN, Nov. 29, 1825 (Paris, Fr.)-Aug. 16, 1893. French neurologist. A pioneer in the study of neurological disease and in determining areas of the nervous system responsible for specific functions; a pioneer in the study of hysteria and in the use of hypnosis for such studies.

CHARDONNET, LOUIS MARIE, May 1, 1839 (France)-Mar. 12, 1924. French chemist. Invented rayon ("Chardonnet silk"), the first common artificial fiber, 1884.

CHARLES, JACQUES ALEXANDRE CÉSAR, Nov. 12, 1746 (France)-Apr. 7. 1823. French physicist. First to express the law that the volume of a gas is proportional to its absolute temperature where pressure is held constant (called Charles's law or Gay-Lussac's law); constructed first hydrogen balloon, 1783.

CORIOLIS, GASPARD DE, May 21, 1792 (Paris, Fr.)-Sept. 19, 1843. French physicist. Worked out the mathematics of motion on a spinning surface (Coriolis forces), essential to meteorology, ballistics, rocket launches, etc., c.1840; first to give the exact modern definitions of kinetic energy and work.

COULOMB, CHARLES AUGUSTIN DE, June 14, 1736 (France)-Aug. 23, 1806. French physicist. Discovered Coulomb's law (of the force of electrical attraction and repulsion), 1785.

CURIE, MARIE, née Sklodowska, Nov. 7, 1867 (Warsaw, Pol.)-July 4, 1934. Polish-French chemist. Using piezoelectric phenomenon to measure intensity of radiation, determined that uranium was the source of radioactivity in uranium compounds; discovered polonium and radium (1898) as further sources of radioactivity in compounds; coined word *radioactive;* awarded Nobel Prize in physics (with husband PIERRE CURIE and A. H. BECQUEREL), 1903; was excluded from French Acad. by one vote, because of her sex; died of leukemia.

CURIE, PIERRE, May 15, 1859 (Paris, Fr.)-Apr. 19, 1906. French chemist. With his brother, dis-

THE BOOK OF WHO

covered and named piezoelectric phenomenon, the basis of microphones and record players, 1880; was first to measure heat and radioactivity; made other discoveries under the guidance of his wife, MARIE CURIE; awarded Nobel Prize in physics, with Marie Curie and A. H. BECQUEREL.

CUVIER, BARON GEORGES LÉOPOLD CHRÉTIEN FRÉDÉRIC DAGOBERT, Aug. 23, 1769 (France)–May 13, 1832. French anatomist. Founded comparative anatomy and paleontology; developed principles of classification still in use, with emphasis on internal structure rather than outward appearance.

DAGUERRE, LOUIS JACQUES MANDÉ, Nov. 18, 1789 (France)–July 12, 1851. French inventor, artist. One of the inventors of photography; used copper plates and silver salts to achieve photographic image, 1837.

FERMAT, PIERRE DE, Aug. 17, 1601 (France)–Jan. 12, 1665. French mathematician. Founded modern number theory and, with BLAISE PASCAL, the probability theory.

FOUCAULT, JEAN BERNARD LÉON, Sept. 18, 1819 (Paris, Fr.)–Feb. 11, 1868. French physicist. The first to arrive at an almost precise measure of the speed of light and to demonstrate that light-speed slowed down in water, 1853; the first to demonstrate the rotation of the earth, using the Foucault pendulum, 1851; invented the gyroscope, 1852.

FOURIER, JEAN BAPTISTE JOSEPH BARON, Mar. 21, 1768 (Fr.)–May 16, 1830. French mathematician. Discovered Fourier's theorem of periodic oscillation, fundamental to the study of any wave phenomenon and the basis of dimensional harmonic analysis, 1807; made a baron by NAPOLEON I.

GASSENDI, PIERRE, Jan. 22, 1592 (France)–Oct. 24, 1655. French physicist, philosopher. Described and named the aurora borealis, 1621; the first to observe a transit of Mercury, 1631; studied velocity of sound; an early advocate of atomism and mechanistic view of nature; opponent of RENÉ DESCARTES.

GAY-LUSSAC, JOSEPH LOUIS, Dec. 6, 1778 (France)–May 9, 1850. French chemist. Showed that all gases expand equally with rise in temperature, 1802; propounded law of combining volumes, or Gay-Lussac's law, 1808; discovered boron, 1808; showed iodine to be an element, 1813; made two balloon ascensions for scientific purposes, reaching a then-record altitude of 23,018 ft., 1804; his careful techniques made a major contribution to analytic chemistry.

GRIGNARD, FRANÇOIS AUGUSTE, May 6, 1871 (France)–Dec. 13, 1935. French chemist. Discovered Grignard reagents, magnesium compounds vital to the development of many synthetics, 1900; awarded Nobel Prize in chemistry (with PAUL SABATIER), 1912.

JACOB, FRANÇOIS, June 17, 1920 (France). French biologist. With J. MONOD, demonstrated that the function of some genes is to regulate the action of others; also with Monod, proposed the existence of messenger RNA, which regulates the building of enzymes, 1961; awarded Nobel Prize in physiology or medicine (with Monod and A. M. LWOFF), 1965.

JOLIOT-CURIE, JEAN FRÉDERIC, Mar. 19, 1900 (Paris, Fr.)–Aug. 14, 1958; and his wife, **IRÈNE JOLIOT-CURIE,** Sept. 12, 1897 (Paris, Fr.)–Mar. 17, 1956. French physicists. Discovered "artificial radioactivity," the creation of radioactive isotopes

of common elements by atomic-particle bombardment, 1934; the major contributors to France's independent development of nuclear power; awarded Nobel Prize in chemistry, 1935.

JOUFFROY D'ABBANS, CLAUDE FRANÇOIS, MARQUIS DE, 1751 (France)–1832. French engineer who built first practical steamboat, 1783.

LAENNEC, RENÉ THÉOPHILE, Feb. 17, 1781 (France)–Aug. 13, 1826. French physician. Invented and named the stethoscope, 1819.

LAGRANGE, JOSEPH LOUIS, COMTE DE, Jan. 25, 1736 (Piedmonte, It.)–Apr. 10, 1813. French mathematician, astronomer. The basic contributor to mathematical analysis and number theory and to analytic and celestial mechanics; his work on the gravitational relations among three bodies resulted in the discovery of "Lagrange points" at which a very small body maintains a stable orbit while under the influence of two much larger bodies; instrumental in the establishment of the metric system; his *Analytic Mechanics* (1788) laid the basis of this field of mathematics.

LAMARCK, JEAN BAPTISTE PIERRE ANTOINE DE MONET, CHEVALIER DE, Aug. 1, 1744 (France)–Dec. 18, 1829. French naturalist. Did the basic work of classifying invertebrates, 1801–22; first to fully develop a theory of evolution which, though based on false ideas of inheritance of acquired characteristics, pushed the problem of evolution into the forefront of biological science.

LAPLACE, PIERRE SIMON, MARQUIS DE, Mar. 28, 1749 (Beaumont-en-Auge, Fr.)–Mar. 5, 1827. French mathematician, astronomer. Did basic work in celestial mechanics; with JOSEPH LAGRANGE, showed that planetary orbits are extraordinarily stable; his work in probability theory modernized that subject, 1812–20; proposed nebular hypothesis of solar system formation; pres. of French Acad., 1817.

LAVOISIER, ANTOINE LAURENT, Aug. 26, 1743 (Paris, Fr.)–May 8, 1794. French chemist. The father of modern chemistry through his emphasis on precise measurements; disproved G. E. STAHL's phlogiston theory of combustion (1774) and defined the role of oxygen, which he named (1779); based on similar work with hydrogen, concluded that human energy derived from oxidation of hydrogen and carbon; instrumental in establishing chemical nomenclature, 1787; wrote *Elementary Treatise on Chemistry*, first modern textbook on the subject, 1789; entered French Acad. at age 24, 1768.

LWOFF, ANDRÉ MICHAEL, May 8, 1902 (France). French microbiologist. Discovered lysogeny, in which viral DNA incorporates itself into chromosomes of bacteria and is thereafter passed on to future generations of bacteria; awarded Nobel Prize in physiology or medicine (with J. MONOD and F. JACOB), 1965.

MAGENDIE, FRANÇOIS, Oct. 15, 1783 (Bordeaux, Fr.)–Oct. 7, 1855. French physiologist. Laid the groundwork for modern nutritional studies in experiments showing the dietary necessity of a variety of foods containing nitrogen (protein); experimented with the effects of drugs on the human system; his spinal-cord studies of the 1820s showed the functions of sensory and motor nerve-roots; established the first medical school laboratory, early 1830s.

MESSIER, CHARLES, June 26, 1730 (France)–Apr. 11, 1817. French astronomer. In a fanatical search for comets, compiled a list of over 100 blurry objects that he determined were not comets; these objects much later were found to be nebulas, galaxies, and star clusters, now often referred to by their so-called Messier number.

MONOD, JACQUES LUCIEN, Feb. 9, 1910 (Paris, Fr.)–May 31, 1976. French biochemist. With F. JACOB, proposed the existence of messenger RNA, which regulates the building of enzymes, 1961; also with Jacob, found that some genes serve only to regulate the function of other genes; wrote the best-seller *Chance and Necessity*, (1971), in which he argued that human life was no more than a chance collection of atoms; awarded Nobel Prize in physiology or medicine (with Jacob and A. M. LWOFF), 1965.

MONTGOLFIER, JOSEPH MICHEL, Aug. 26, 1740 (France)–June 26, 1810; and his brother **JACQUES ÉTIENNE MONTGOLFIER,** Jan. 7, 1745 (France)–Aug. 2, 1799. French inventors. Invented the hot-air hydrogen balloon, 1783; the first men literally to travel through the air.

NÉEL, LOUIS EUGÈNE FÉLIX, Nov. 22, 1904 (Lyon, Fr.). French physicist. Made fundamental contributions to the understanding of the varieties and properties of magnetism, in the 1930s and 1940s; awarded Nobel Prize in physics (with H. O. G. Alfven), 1970.

PARÉ, AMBROISE, 1510 (France)–Dec. 20, 1590. French surgeon. Often considered the father of modern surgery; made several advances in the treatment of wounds and in improving cleanliness.

PASTEUR, LOUIS, Dec. 27, 1822 (France)–Sept. 28, 1845. French chemist. Proposed the "germ" theory of disease, perhaps the greatest single advance in the history of medicine, late 1860s; discovered "pasteurization," gentle heating to kill harmful bacteria in wine and milk, 1860s; proved that total sterility was possible in the laboratory, 1864; discovered the process of using "attenuated" germs in inoculations against some diseases (1881), leading to the prevention of rabies (1885); made basic discoveries in polarimetry, 1848–58; elected to French Acad., 1873; the first head of the Pasteur Inst., founded for him by the French govt. in 1888.

PEREGRINUS DE MARICOURT, PETRUS, c. 1220–? French scholar. The first to describe the modern compass, suggesting it be mounted on a pivot and encircled by a scale denoting directions, 1269; author of the first significant work describing magnetism, *Epistola de Magnete.*

PINEL, PHILIPPE, Apr. 20, 1745 (France)–Oct. 26, 1826. French physician. A primary founder of psychiatry; the first to identify insanity with disease (rather than demons) and to propose that extreme stress, physiological damage, or heredity might be the cause, 1790 on; described many psychotic systems and invented the term *alienation* for mental disorder. *Treatise on Mental Alienation,* 1801.

POINCARÉ, JULES HENRI, Apr. 29, 1854 (Nancy, Fr.)–July 17, 1912. French mathematician. Made important contributions in most areas of mathematics, especially the three-body problem and tidal forces. (Cousin of RAYMOND POINCARÉ.)

POISSON, SIMÉON-DENIS, June 21, 1781 (France)–Apr. 25, 1840. French mathematician. Made major contributions to the application of mathematics to electromagnetics and mechanics and to the development of the mathematics of probability.

RÉAUMUR, RENÉ ANTOINE FERCHAULT DE,

Feb. 28, 1683 (La Rochelle, Fr.)–Oct. 17, 1757. French physicist. Proved that digestion was a process of chemical dissolving and not mechanical grinding, 1752; devised the Réaumur thermometer and temperature scale, 1731; the first to demonstrate the importance of carbon in steel-making.

SABATIER, PAUL, Nov. 5, 1854 (France)–Aug. 14, 1941. French chemist. Discovered nickel catalysis, which made possible the mass production from inedible vegetable oils of margarine, shortening, and other edible fats; awarded Nobel Prize in chemistry (with F. A. GRIGNARD), 1912.

SCALIGER, JOSEPH JUSTUS, Aug. 5, 1540 (France)–Jan. 21, 1609. French scholar. Father of modern chronology; founder of the Julian Day system, 1583.

VIETA, FRANCISCUS, 1540 (France)–Dec. 13, 1603. French mathematician. Considered the father of modern algebra; introduced the use of letters for unknowns and constants, 1591.

OTHER FOREIGN SCIENTISTS, PHYSICIANS, AND INVENTORS

ÅNGSTROM, ANDERS JONAS, Aug. 13, 1814 (Sweden)–June 21, 1874. Swedish physicist, astronomer. A pioneer in astronomical spectroscopy, he discovered the sun was made of hydrogen and other elements, 1862; first to use 10^{-10} meter as a unit to measure wavelengths of light (this unit was named after him in 1905).

ARBER, WERNER, 1929 (Switzerland). Swiss microbiologist. Noted for his basic contributions to the study and isolation of a restriction enzyme that breaks up certain DNAs at random points, 1968; awarded Nobel Prize in physiology or medicine (with D. NATHANS and H. O. SMITH), 1978.

ARCHIMEDES, c.287 B.C. (Syracuse, Sicily)–c.212 B.C. Greek mathematician, engineer. Discovered principle of buoyancy while in a bathtub (and shouted "Eureka!"); developed the mathematical principles of the lever; derived more accurate values for "pi."

ARRHENIUS, SVANTE AUGUST, Feb. 19, 1859 (Sweden)–Oct. 2, 1927. Swedish chemist. Founded modern physical chemistry through his theory that some atoms (ions) carry electric charges, c.1884; awarded Nobel Prize in chemistry, 1903.

AVOGADRO, AMADEO, CONTE DI QUAREGNA, June 9, 1776 (Piedmont, It.)–July 9, 1856. Italian physicist. Coined the word *molecules* and was the first to draw the distinction between molecules and atoms, 1811; his ideas were not accepted until about 1858.

BANTING, SIR FREDERICK GRANT, Nov. 14, 1891 (Ont., Can.)–Feb. 21, 1941. Canadian physiologist. First to isolate insulin (1922), thus providing an effective treatment for diabetes; awarded Nobel Prize in physiology or medicine, 1923.

BARNARD, CHRISTIAAN NEETHLING, Nov. 8, 1922 (South Africa). South African surgeon. Performed first successful heart transplant, Dec. 3, 1967; patient lived $1^1/_2$ years after the operation.

BASOV, NIKOLAI GENNADIEVICH, Dec. 14, 1922 (Voronezh, USSR). Soviet physicist. With ALEKSANDR PROKHOROV, worked out theoretical principles of the maser (microwave amplification by stimulated emission of radiation); awarded Nobel Prize in physics, (with Prokhorov and CHARLES H. TOWNES), 1964.

BERNOULLI, DANIEL, Jan. 29, 1700 (Nether-

THE BOOK OF WHO

lands)–Mar. 17, 1782. Swiss mathematician. Discovered Bernoulli's principle, that fluid pressure decreases as velocity of flow increases, c.1733; also made major contributions to study of behavior of gases and to differential calculus.

BERZELIUS, BARON JÖNS JAKOB, Aug. 20, 1779 (Sweden)–Aug. 7, 1848. Swedish chemist. Devised first relatively accurate list of atomic weights, 1828; devised atomic symbols, 1813; discovered selenium (1818), silicon (1824), and thorium (1829); dominated world of chemistry from 1830 to his death.

BOHR, AAGE NIELS, June 19, 1922 (Denmark). Danish physicist. Discovered the connection between collective motion and particle motion in atomic nuclei by work on problem of asymmetrical nuclei, 1950–53; awarded Nobel Prize in physics (with JAMES RAINWATER and BEN MOTTELSON), 1975. (Son of NIELS BOHR.)

BOHR, NIELS HENRIK DAVID, Oct. 7, 1885 (Copenhagen, Den.)–Nov. 18, 1962. Danish physicist. A major theoretician and administrative force in modern physics; revolutionized physics by combining elements of MAX PLANCK's quantum theory with classic mechanics to explain electromagnetic radiation, 1913; framed "principle of complimentarity," allowing subatomic phenomena to be viewed in two contradictory ways, with each valid in its own terms, 1927; brought to U.S. the news that uranium would apparently undergo fission when bombarded by neutrons, and predicted that the fissionable isotope was U-235, 1939; played major role in rescue of many Danish Jews from Hitler, 1940–43; worked on U.S. atom bomb project, 1943–45; organized first Atoms for Peace conference, 1955; awarded Nobel Prize in physics, 1922.

BORDET, JULES JEAN BAPTISTE VINCENT, June 13, 1870 (Belgium)–Apr. 6, 1961. Belgian bacteriologist. His discoveries in immunology (1895 and later) laid the basis for most modern work in the field, including the Wasserman test for syphilis; discovered and developed a vaccine against the whooping cough bacillus, 1906; awarded Nobel Prize in physiology or medicine, 1919.

BOVET, DANIELE, Mar. 23, 1907 (Neuchâtel, Switz.). Swiss-Italian pharmacologist. With others, discovered sulphanilamide, 1936; discovered the first antihistamines (1937), and the use of curare as a muscle relaxant in surgery; awarded Nobel Prize in physiology or medicine, 1957.

BRAHE, TYCHO, born Tyge, Dec. 14, 1546 (Sweden)–Oct. 24, 1601. Danish astronomer. The last naked-eye astronomer; observed first recorded exploding star seen in Europe and named the phenomenon a "nova," 1572; built first major astronomical observatory, 1580; made first scientific observations of a comet; his research made Gregorian calendar reform possible; his data became basis for the laws of planetary motion devised by JOHANNES KEPLER.

BURNET, SIR FRANK MACFARLANE, Sept. 3, 1899 (Austrl.). Australian physician. First to perceive that immunological resistance to foreign proteins might not be inborn, but might be developed very early in life; awarded Nobel Prize in physiology or medicine (with P. B. MEDAWAR), 1960.

CANDOLLE, AUGUSTINE PYRAME, Feb. 4, 1778 (Geneva, Switz.)–Sept. 9, 1841. Swiss botanist. Began a 21-volume encyclopedia of plants; coined *taxonomy* for science of classification; taxonomic system for plants still commonly used.

CASSINI, GIOVANNI (Jean) **DOMENICO DOMINIQUE**, June 8, 1625 (nr. Nice, Fr.)–Sept. 11, 1712. French-Italian astronomer. Determined rotation periods of Mars and Jupiter, 1665-66; discovered four of Saturn's satellites, 1671-84; discovered Cassini's diversion, the gap in Saturn's rings, 1675; first to arrive at a close approximation of the sun's true distance from earth, 1672.

CELSIUS, ANDERS, Nov. 27, 1701 (Sweden)–Apr. 25, 1744. Swedish astronomer. Devised the Celsius (centigrade scale of temperature with 100° between the freezing and boiling points of water).

CHERENKOV, PAVEL ALEKSEYEVICH, Aug. 10, 1904 (Russia). Soviet physicist. First to observe Cherenkov radiation, a glow caused by the movement of elementary particles through a medium, such as water, at a rate faster than the speed of light in that medium, 1934; awarded Nobel Prize in physics (with I. M. FRANK and I. J. TAMM), 1958.

CLAUDE, ALBERT, Aug. 24, 1898 (Luxembourg). Belgian-U.S. microbiologist. Made fundamental discoveries in the anatomy of cells (including mitochondria) and developed centrifuge techniques for separating the parts of cells; awarded Nobel Prize in physiology or medicine (with G. E. PALAD and C. De Duve), 1974.

COPERNICUS, NICOLAS, Feb. 19, 1473 (Poland)–May 24, 1543. Polish astronomer. Worked out the mathematics of a heliocentric solar system, beginning in 1512; first to explain precession of equinoxes as caused by earth's wobbling on its axis; his ideas were quietly circulated among scholars from about 1530, and first published in 1543; his work began the scientific revolution.

DE VRIES, HUGO MARIE, Feb. 16, 1848 (Netherlands)–May 21, 1935. Dutch botanist. Independently discovered the Mendelian laws of heredity (1900) and found GREGOR MENDEL's original work of a generation earlier; first proposed the theory of mutation, 1901.

DOPPLER, CHRISTIAN JOHANN, Nov. 29, 1803 (Salzburg, Austria)–Mar. 17, 1853. Austrian physicist. The first to explain the Doppler effect, the change in pitch as a sound source approaches and moves away from a listener; correctly predicted a similar effect for light waves.

DUBOIS, MARIE EUGENE FRANÇOIS THOMAS, Jan. 28, 1858 (Netherlands)–Dec. 16, 1940. Dutch paleontologist. The first to discover a "missing link" between ape and man—*Pithecanthropus erectus*, or Java man—1894.

ECCLES, SIR JOHN CAREW, Jan. 27, 1903 (Melbourne, Austrl.). Australian physiologist. Made a major contribution to the study of chemical transfer of nerve impulses across the synapse; knighted, 1958; awarded Nobel Prize in physiology or medicine (with A. L. HODGKIN and A. F. HUXLEY), 1963.

ERATOSTHENES, c.276 B.C. (Cyrene [now in Libya])–c.196 B.C. Greek astronomer. Determined a relatively accurate value for the circumference of the earth that was not bettered until J. Picard's calculations.

ESAKI, LEO, Mar. 12, 1925 (Osaka, Jap.). Japanese physicist. Conducted basic research in electron "tunneling" in semiconductors; discovered the tunnel diode, 1957; awarded Nobel Prize in physics (with I. GIAEVER and B. D. JOSEPHSON), 1973.

EUCLID, fl. 305-285 B.C. Greek mathematician. Compiled and arranged logically the geometrical

SCIENTISTS, PHYSICIANS, AND INVENTORS

knowledge of his time, some number theory, and problems of ratio and proportion. *Elements.*

EULER, LEONHARD, Apr. 15, 1707 (Basel, Switz.)–Sept. 18, 1783. Swiss mathematician. Made major contributions in all areas of mathematics and to the application of mathematics to work in physics; established many of the mathematical notations used today.

EULER, ULF SVANTE VON, Feb. 7, 1905 (Stockholm, Swe.). Swedish physiologist. Noted for his basic research on the action of hormones in the nervous system and the discovery of the key role of noradrenaline as the impulse transmitter in the sympathetic nervous system; awarded Nobel Prize in physiology or medicine (with B. KATZ and J. AXELROD), 1970.

EULER-CHELPIN, HANS KARL AUGUST SIMON, Feb. 15, 1873 (Germany)–Nov. 7, 1964. German-Swedish chemist. Contributed to knowledge of the structure of several vitamins; first to work out the structure of a coenzyme; awarded Nobel Prize in chemistry (with A. HARDEN), 1929.

FERMI, ENRICO, Sept. 29, 1901 (Rome, It.)–Nov. 28, 1954. U.S.-Italian physicist. Pioneer in the study of neutrons and neutron bombardment, beginning in 1932; led the group which achieved the first manmade nuclear chain reaction, Dec. 2, 1942, in Chicago; awarded Nobel Prize in physics, 1938.

FIBONACCI, LEONARDO (or Leonard da Pisa), c.1170 (Pisa, It.)–c.1230. Italian mathematician. Primarily responsible for European adoption of Arabic numerals, which he explained in *Liber Abaci* (1202).

FRANK, ILYA MIKHAYLOVICH, Oct. 23, 1908 (St. Petersburg, Rus. [now Leningrad, USSR]). Soviet physicist. With I. Y. TAMM, explained Cherenkov radiation as caused by the passage of high-energy particles through water or other mediums at a speed greater than light in that medium, 1937; awarded Nobel Prize in physics (with Tamm and P. CHERENKOV), 1958.

FREUD, SIGMUND, May 6, 1856 (Freiburg, Moravia [now Příbor, Czech.])–Sept. 23, 1939. Austrian neurologist. As the founder of psychoanalysis, made an incalculable impact on modern thought with his theories of neuroses stemming from childhood relationships with parents and with his stress on the importance of sexuality in both normal and abnormal development. *Studies in Hysteria,* with J. Breuer, 1895; *The Interpretation of Dreams,* 1900.

FRISCH, KARL VON, Nov. 20, 1886 (Vienna, Austria). Austrian-German zoologist. Discovered that the "dances" of bees convey the direction and distance of food sources (1923) and that bees can orient themselves by the direction of light polarization (1949); awarded Nobel Prize in physiology or medicine (with K. LORENZ and N. TINBERGEN), 1973.

FRISCH, OTTO ROBERT, Oct. 1, 1904 (Vienna, Austria). Austrian-British physicist. Collaborated with his aunt, L. MEITNER, on a paper proposing that changes observed in uranium bombarded with neutrons were caused by fission; before publication (1939), told N. BOHR, who told U.S. physicists, thereby initiating the development of the A-bomb.

GALEN, c.130 (Pergamum [now Bergama, Tur.])–c.200. Greek physician. The leading medical authority in Europe until the 17th cent.; made basic discoveries in anatomy; court physician to MARCUS AURELIUS.

GALILEO, born Galileo Galilei, Feb. 15, 1564 (Pisa, It.)–Jan. 8, 1642. Italian physicist, astronomer. Established mechanics as a science, discovering the law of uniformly accelerated motion (1604) and the law of parabolic fall; invented the astronomical telescope (1609) and discovered four of Jupiter's moons, the period of the sun's rotation, and the phases of Venus; his discoveries ended the influence of ARISTOTLE and PTOLEMY on astronomy; the first to systematically pursue experimentation and quantitative methods; forced by religious authorities to recant Copernican view, June 22, 1633. *Dialogue on the Two Chief World Systems,* 1632; *Discourse concerning Two New Sciences,* 1638.

GALVANI, LUIGI, Sept. 9, 1737 (Bologna, It.)–Dec. 4, 1798. Italian anatomist. Conducted studies of the effects of electric impulses on muscle, from 1771; galvanic electric processes were named after him.

GÖDEL, KURT, Apr. 28, 1906 (Brünn, Aust.-H. [now Brno, Czech.]). Austrian-U.S. mathematician. Author of "Gödel's proof" (1931), showing that no logically certain basis can be established for any logical mathematical system, ending nearly 100 years of search for such a basis and freeing mathematics for greater advances.

GOLDHABER, MAURICE, Apr. 18, 1911 (Austria). Austrian-U.S. physicist. Discovered that the nucleus of deuterium contains a proton and a neutron; discovered the nuclear photoelectric effect, 1934; demonstrated the usefulness of photographic emulsions for particle studies; demonstrated that beta rays are electrons; discovered that beryllium was a good moderator, an essential contribution to nuclear reactor technology, 1940.

GOLGI, CAMILLO, July 7, 1843 (Italy)–Jan. 21, 1926. Italian histologist. Did the basic work on the fine structure of the nervous system, discovering silver nitrate staining, the Golgi cells and the Golgi complex, and demonstrating the existence of the synapses; awarded Nobel Prize in physiology or medicine (with RAMÓN Y CAJAL), 1906.

GUILLAUME, CHARLES EDOUARD, Feb. 15, 1861 (Switzerland)–June 13, 1938. Swiss-French physicist. Dir. of Bureau of Internatl. Weights and Measures, 1915–36; did basic work in increasing precision of measurements; discovered invar, an iron-nickel alloy essential to accurate time measurement, 1896; awarded Nobel Prize in physics, 1920.

HALLER, ALBRECHT VON, Oct. 16, 1708 (Bern, Switz.)–Dec. 12, 1777. Swiss physiologist, poet. Father of experimental physiology and neurology; the first to understand the mechanics of respiration (1747) and to recognize the autonomous operation of the heart and the function of bile; his extensive experiments proved that nerves, not tissues, were the channels of sensation and muscular stimulation, 1766.

HERTZSPRUNG, EJNAR, Oct. 8, 1873 (Denmark)–Oct. 21, 1967. Danish astronomer. Devised the notion of stars' absolute magnitude and related that to their color, devising a scale of stellar types basic to modern astronomy, 1905 and 1907; devised a luminosity scale for Cepheid variable stars, the first step in the process of determining the shape of the galaxy and the sun's place in it.

HEVESY, GEORG, Aug. 1, 1885 (Budapest, Hung.)–July 5, 1966. Hungarian-Danish chemist. The first to use radioactive tracers to study biological processes, 1923; discovered hafnium, 1923; awarded Nobel Prize in chemistry, 1943.

HIPPARCHUS, c.190 B.C. (Nicea [now Iznik, Tur.])–c.120 B.C. Greek astronomer. Often considered the father of trigonometry, which he used to compute the moon's distance with relative accuracy; created an accurate map of over 1,000 stars; established the idea of the latitude and longitude grid on earth; discovered the "precession of the equinoxes"; devised the basic outlines of the present star-magnitude scale; worked out the basic mathematics of the geocentric (Ptolemaic) system of astronomy.

HIPPOCRATES, 460 B.C. (Cos, Gr.)–c.370 B.C. Greek physician. The father of medicine; founded the most famous medical school of the ancient world; established rational, cautious ethical standards for medical practice.

HOUSSAY, BERNARDO ALBERTO, Apr. 10, 1887 (Buenos Aires, Arg.)–Sept. 21, 1971. Argentine physiologist. Demonstrated the importance of the pituitary gland to sugar metabolism; awarded Nobel Prize in physiology or medicine (with CARL F. and GERTY T. CORI), 1947.

HUYGENS, CHRISTIAAN, Apr. 14, 1629 (The Hague, Neth.)–June 8, 1695. Dutch physicist, astronomer, mathematician. Wrote first formal treatise on probability, 1657; discovered first satellite of Saturn and Saturn's rings, 1656; invented the pendulum clock, 1656; the first major advocate of the wave theory of light.

INGENHOUSZ, JAN, Dec. 8, 1730 (Netherlands)–Sept. 7, 1799. Dutch physician, plant physiologist. First to show clearly that green plants consume carbon dioxide and exude oxygen in light and do the opposite in the dark, thus discovering photosynthesis, 1779.

KAMERLINGH-ONNES, HEIKE, Sept. 21, 1853 (Netherlands)–Feb. 21, 1926. Dutch physicist. First to liquefy helium, 1908; discovered superconductivity (loss of electrical resistance in some metals at low temperatures); awarded Nobel Prize in physics, 1912.

KAPITSA, PYOTR LEONIDOVICH, June 26, 1894 (Russia). Soviet physicist. Discovered superfluidity of helium II, 1941; made major contributions to the development of high-powered magnetic fields (1924), to the Soviet space program (1957), and to nuclear fusion studies (1969); awarded Nobel Prize in physics (with A. PENZIAS and R. WILSON), 1978.

KITASATO, SHIBASABURO, BARON, Dec. 20, 1856 (Japan)–June 13, 1931. Japanese bacteriologist. Isolated the causative agents of tetanus (1889), bubonic plague (1894), and dysentery (1898); made a baron, 1924.

KOCHER, EMIL THEODAR, Aug. 25, 1841 (Berne, Switz.)–July 27, 1917. Swiss surgeon. Advanced surgical techniques for many operations; received 1909 Nobel Prize in physiology or medicine for his work on the physiology, pathology, and surgery of the thyroid gland. *Chirurgische Operationslehre,* 1892.

KURCHATOV, IGOR VASILEVITCH, Jan. 12, 1903 (Russia)–Feb. 7, 1960. Soviet physicist. The prime mover of Soviet fission research (1943-60), leading the Soviet groups which developed the A-bomb (1949), H-bomb (1952), and an experimental nuclear-power plant (1954).

LANDAU, LEV DAVIDOVITCH, Jan. 22, 1908 (Baku, Rus.)–Apr. 1, 1968. Soviet physicist. Did fundamental theoretical work in low-temperature

physics, predicting properties for a rare helium isotope that scientists are still trying to verify; awarded Nobel Prize in physics, 1962.

LEEUWENHOEK, ANTON VAN, Oct. 24, 1632 (Delft, Neth.)–Aug. 26, 1723. Dutch biologist. A pioneer in precision lens-grinding and microscopy; discovered protozoa, 1677; described bacteria, 1683.

LENOIR, JEAN JOSEPH ÉTIENNE, Jan. 12, 1822 (Belgium)–Aug. 4, 1900. Belgian inventor. Devised the first workable and commercially successful internal-combustion engine (1859), which he attached to a vehicle for a six-mile trip (1860); also attached his invention to a boat.

LINNAEUS, CAROLUS, born Carl Linné, later von Linné, May 23, 1707 (Sweden)–Jan. 10, 1778. Swedish botanist. Founded modern taxonomy by devising a methodical system of classification (the "two name"—genera and species—method), developing classes and orders, and precisely describing differences between species, 1735; named *Homo sapiens;* the first to use male and female symbols (δ, φ). *Systema Natura,* 1735.

LIPPERSHEY, HANS, 1587 (Netherlands)–1619. Dutch optician who invented the telescope, 1608.

LOMONOSOV, MIKHAIL VASILIEVICH, Nov. 8, 1711 (nr. Archangel, Rus.)–Apr. 4, 1765. Russian chemist, author. The first major Russian scientist, although most of his work remained unknown for decades in the West; with L. EULER, founded U. of Moscow, 1755; wrote poetry, plays; introduced reforms into the Russian language, 1755.

LORENZ, HENDRIK ANTOON, July 18, 1853 (Arnhem, Neth.)–Feb. 4, 1928. Dutch physicist. One of the first to theorize that charged particles in the atom produced visible light, c.1890; first to show that an electron's mass at the speed of light must be infinite (Lorenz transformations, the basis of ALBERT EINSTEIN's special theory of relativity), 1904; awarded Nobel Prize in physics (with P. ZEEMAN), 1902.

LORENZ, KONRAD ZACHARIAS, Nov. 7, 1903 (Vienna, Austria). Austro-German ethologist. The major pioneer of modern ethology, the study of animal behavior; proposed the theory that all animal behavior is explicable in terms of adaptive evolution; awarded Nobel Prize in physiology or medicine (with K. VON FRISCH and N. TINBERGEN), 1973. *On Aggression,* 1966.

LYSENKO, TROFIM DAVIDOVICH, Sept. 29, 1898 (Ukraine, Rus.)–Nov. 20, 1977. Soviet biologist. A major modern proponent of the idea of the inheritance of acquired characteristics, in opposition to mainstream biology and genetics; received strong political support from J. STALIN and was dir. of the Soviet Inst. of Genetics, 1940-65.

MACH, ERNST, Feb. 18, 1838 (Moravia)–Feb. 19, 1916. Austrian physicist. Best known for his studies of airflow and the discovery (1887) of sudden change of airflow over an object moving at close to the speed of sound; the speed of sound in air is named for him.

MALPIGHI, MARCELLO, Mar. 10, 1628 (Italy)–Nov. 30, 1694. Italian physiologist. First to make extensive use of the microscope, 1650s; discovered capillaries, thus filling in the gap between the venous and arterial systems; discovered that blood flows over the lungs; the first to observe many physiological elements of plant and insect life.

MARCONI, GUGLIELMO, MARCHESE, Apr. 25, 1874 (Bologna, Italy)–July 20, 1937. Italian physicist. Invented the radio, 1895-1901; received his first patent, 1896; transmitted signals across the Atlantic, Dec. 12, 1901; made a major contribution to the development of short-wave radio; awarded Nobel Prize in physics (with K. F. Braun), 1909.

MEITNER, LISE, Nov. 7, 1878 (Vienna, Austria)–Oct. 17, 1968. Austrian-Swedish physicist. The first to make public the probability that uranium fission had occurred in the laboratory; worked with O. HAHN for 30 years and collaborated in many achievements credited to him.

MENDEL, GREGOR JOHANN, July 22, 1822 (Lower Silesia, A.-H. [now Czech.])–Jan. 6, 1884. Austrian botanist, monk. Discovered the basic laws of biological inheritance, including the statistical probability of dominant and recessive trait-reproduction, early 1860s; his work explained the mechanisms of natural selection, but was ignored and forgotten by other scientists until discovered by H. M. DEVRIES in 1900.

MENDELEEV, DMITRI IVANOVICH, Feb. 7, 1834 (Siberia, Rus.)–Feb. 2, 1907. Russian chemist. Created the periodic table of elements (1869), leaving gaps in the table to fit his schema and predicting (1871) the gaps would be filled by yet undiscovered elements, three of which he described in detail; all three new elements were discovered by 1885; though he won worldwide acclaim, he missed receiving the 1906 Nobel Prize in chemistry by one vote.

MERCATOR, GERARDUS, born Gerhard Kremer, Mar. 5, 1512 (Flanders)–Dec. 5, 1594. Flemish geographer. Invented the Mercator projection system of mapmaking, still the most common projection for world maps, 1568; a founder of modern geography.

METCHNIKOFF, ÉLIE, born Ilya Ilich Mechnikov, May 15, 1845 (Ukraine, Rus.)–July 15, 1916. Russian-French bacteriologist. Discovered white corpuscles in living cells, identifying them as phagocytes of alien bacteria and an important factor in resistance to disease and infection; succeeded LOUIS PASTEUR as dir. of the Pasteur Inst.; awarded Nobel Prize in physiology or medicine (with P. EHRLICH), 1908.

MONIZ, ANTONIO CAETANO DE ABREU FREIRE EGAS, Nov. 29, 1874 (Portugal)–Dec. 13, 1955. Portuguese surgeon, statesman. Foreign min. of Portugal, 1918–19; invented prefrontal lobotomy for hopelessly disturbed mental patients, thus beginning the field of psychosurgery, 1935; awarded Nobel Prize in physiology or medicine (with W. R. Hess), 1949.

MORGAGNI, GIOVANNI BATTISTA, Feb. 25, 1682 (Italy)–Dec. 6, 1771. Italian anatomist. The father of medical pathology; from early work on anatomy and diseases of the ear (1704), went on to seek the causes of disease through autopsies. *On the Seats and Causes of Diseases,* 1761.

MOTTELSON, BEN RAY, July 9, 1926 (Chicago, Ill.). Danish physicist. With A. BOHR, discovered relationship of motion of parts of the nucleus to motion of the whole, 1950–53; awarded Nobel Prize in physics (with J. RAINWATER and A. BOHR), 1975.

MÜLLER, PAUL, Jan. 12, 1899 (Switzerland)–Oct. 12, 1965. Swiss chemist. Discovered the value of DDT as an insecticide (1939) in time to stop two threatening typhus epidemics (Naples, 1944; Japan, 1945); awarded Nobel Prize in physiology or medicine, 1948.

OERSTED, HANS CHRISTIAN, Aug. 14, 1777 (Denmark)–Mar. 9, 1851. Danish physicist. First to demonstrate a connection between electricity and magnetism, 1819; first to make metallic aluminum, 1825.

PARACELSUS, born Theophrastus Bombastus von Hohenheim, May 1, 1493 (Switzerland)–Sept. 24, 1541. Swiss physician. His work marks the transition from alchemy to chemistry; introduced a questioning, experimental approach to medicine.

PAVLOV, IVAN PETROVICH, Sept. 14, 1849 (Russia)–Feb. 27, 1936. Russian physiologist. Made basic discoveries in the way autonomic nerves control the digestive process, 1889; did basic studies of the nature and development of conditional reflexes, early 1890s; awarded Nobel Prize in physiology or medicine, 1904.

PICCARD, AUGUSTE, Jan. 28, 1884 (Basel, Switz.)–Mar. 24, 1962. Swiss physicist. Developed enclosed balloon gondolas to carry men into the stratosphere, reaching a height of 55,500 ft., 1932; invented the bathyscaphe to carry men to ocean depths, 1946; one of his bathyscaphes reached 35,800 ft., 1960.

PREGL, FRITZ, Sept. 3, 1869 (Laibach, Austria [now Ljubljana, Yugo.])–Dec. 13, 1930. Austrian chemist. The father of microchemistry; developed methods for performing chemical analysis of substances in quantities of only 3 mg; awarded Nobel Prize in chemistry, 1923.

PROKHOROV, ALEKSANDR MIKHAILOVICH, July 11, 1916 (Australia). Soviet physicist. Made basic contributions to the theories that led to the development of the maser and the laser, 1955; awarded Nobel Prize in physics (with N. G. BASOV and C. H. TOWNES), 1955.

PTOLEMY (Claudius Ptolemaeus), c.75 (Egypt)–? Greek or Egyptian astronomer. Using the system of HIPPARCHUS, established the geocentric view of the universe; named 48 constellations; preserved some ancient trigonometry; his views dominated astronomy for 1,400 years. *Megale mathematica syntaxis (Almagest in Arabic)*.

PURKINJE (or Purkyne), **JAN EVANGELISTE,** Dec. 17, 1787 (Bohemia [now Czech.])–July 18, 1869. Czech physiologist. An expert in microscopy, for which he devised several improvements in technique; made many basic discoveries in histology, brain and heart function, and other areas; founded German system of lab training for university students; discovered Purkinje nerve cells in the brain (1837) and the Purkinje nerve fibers in the heart (1839); coined the word *protoplasm,* 1839; remembered in Czechoslovakia more for his poetry, his translations of J. GOETHE and F. SCHILLER, and his nationalism.

PYTHEAS, fl. c.300 B.C. (Massalia [now Marseilles, Fr.]). Greek explorer, astronomer. Explored the western and northern coasts of Europe and the eastern coast of England; discovered that the Pole Star is not precisely at the pole; the first to attribute tidal motion to the moon's influence.

RAMAN, SIR CHANDRASEKHARA VENKATA, Nov. 7, 1888 (Madras, India)–Nov. 21, 1970. Indian physicist. Proved that visible light changed wavelengths when scattered, thus adding to the particle theory of light, 1928; the primary founder of higher education in science in India; awarded Nobel Prize in physics, 1930.

RAMÓN Y CAJAL, SANTIAGO, May 1, 1852 (Spain)–Oct. 17, 1934. Spanish histologist. His basic studies of the nervous system revealed the connection between the cells in the brain and the spinal cord, 1889; worked out the structure of the retina; established the neuron theory of the brain;

THE BOOK OF WHO

awarded Nobel Prize in physiology or medicine (with C. GOLGI), 1906.

REICHSTEIN, TADEUSZ, July 20, 1897 (Poland). Swiss chemist. A synthesizer of vitamin C, 1933; independently of E. C. KENDALL, isolated many corticoid compounds, 1930s; awarded Nobel Prize in physiology or medicine (with Kendall and P. S. HENCH), 1950.

RICCI (-Curbastro), **GREGORIO,** Jan. 12, 1853 (Lugo, It.)–Aug. 7, 1925. Italian mathematician. Primary developer of tensor analysis (absolute differential calculus), and indispensable tool for EINSTEIN's formulation of the theory of general relativity.

SCHEELE, KARL WILHELM, Dec. 9, 1742 (Pomerania [now Pol.])–May 21, 1786. Swedish chemist. Discovered a wide variety of compounds and played a role in the discovery of several elements, including oxygen, which he discovered (1772) before J. PRIESTLEY but failed to announce.

SCHIAPARELLI, GIOVANNI VIRGINIO, Mar. 14, 1835 (Italy)–July 4, 1910. Italian astronomer. The "discoverer" of Mars's "canals," an illusion of a system of straight lines that gave rise to the speculation about life on the planets, 1881.

SCHRÖDINGER, ERWIN, Aug. 12, 1887 (Vienna, Austria)–Jan. 4, 1961. Austrian physicist. His work in wave mechanics put quantum theory on a firm mathematical base and clarified the modern view of atomic structure; awarded Nobel Prize in physics (with P. DIRAC), 1933.

SEMENOV, NIKOLAY NIKOLAEVICH, Apr. 15, 1896 (Saratov, Rus.). Soviet physical chemist. In basic work on chemical chain reactions and thermal explosions, developed the theory of branched chain reactions, 1920s; awarded Nobel Prize in chemistry (with C. N. HINSHELWOOD), 1956.

SIEGBAHN, KARL MANNE GEORG, Dec. 3, 1886 (Sweden)–Sept. 30, 1978. Swedish physicist. The major contributor to the development of X-ray spectroscopy, from 1916; the first to demonstrate X-ray refraction; awarded Nobel Prize in physics, 1924.

SPALLANZANI, LAZZARO, Jan. 12, 1729 (Italy)–Feb. 11, 1799. Italian physiologist. Did basic experiments to disprove ideas of spontaneous generation of life, 1767–68; the first successfully to try artificial insemination, 1785; experimented with tissue regeneration and transplantation, 1767–68.

STEVINUS, SIMON, born Simon Stevin, 1548 (Bruges, Flanders [now Belg.])–1620. Flemish mathematician. Established the use of decimal fractions, 1585; first to demonstrate that all bodies fall at the same rate regardless of weight, 1586; founded modern science of statics, 1586.

SVEDBERG, THEODOR H. E., Aug. 30, 1884 (Sweden)–Feb. 26, 1971. Swedish chemist. Developed the ultracentrifuge to separate colloids and large molecules, particularly proteins, 1923; developed electrophonetic methods to separate proteins; awarded Nobel Prize in chemistry, 1926.

SZENT-GYÖRGYI (von Nagryapolt), **ALBERT,** Sept. 16, 1893 (Budapest, Hung.). Hungarian-U.S. biochemist. First to isolate vitamin C, although he failed to identify it as such, c.1928; did basic research in oxidation of nutrients by cells (1930s) and the chemical processes of muscle contraction (1940s); awarded Nobel Prize in physiology or medicine, 1937.

TAMM, IGOR YEVGENYEVICH, July 8, 1895

(Vladivostok, Rus.)–Apr. 12, 1971. Soviet physicist. With I. M. FRANK, found the explanation for Cherenkov radiation, 1937; suggested the "pinch effect" for magnetic containment of plasma in fusion reactions; awarded Nobel Prize in physics (with Frank), 1958.

TOMONAGA, SIN-ITIRO, Mar. 31, 1906 (Tokyo, Jap.). Japanese physicist. Worked out the basic theory of quantum electrodynamics, making it consistent with A. EINSTEIN'S special theory of relativity, independently of J. S. SCHWINGER and R. P. FEYNMAN; awarded Nobel Prize in physics (with Schwinger and Feynman), 1965.

TORRICELLI, EVANGELISTA, Oct. 15, 1608 (Italy)–Oct. 25, 1647. Italian physicist, mathematician. Invented the barometer and created the first manmade sustained vacuum, 1643; his work in geometry contributed to the development of integral calculus, 1644.

TSAI LUN, c.50 (China)–c.118. Chinese court official. Invented paper, which he made from bamboo pulp, c.105.

TSVETT, MIKHAIL SEMENOVICH, May 14, 1872 (Italy)–May 1920. Russian botanist. Invented chromatography (1906), a technique of separating fine substances in the laboratory (later reinvented by R. Willstätter).

TSIOLKOVSKY, KONSTANTIN EDUARDO-VICH, Sept. 17, 1857 (Russia)–Sept. 19, 1935. Soviet physicist. Father of the Soviet space effort; a pioneer in rocket theory, from 1895.

VAN DER WAALS, JOHANNES DIDERIK, Nov. 23, 1837 (Leiden, Neth.)–Mar. 9, 1923. Dutch physicist. Worked out the mathematics of the actual behavior of gases and liquids under varying temperatures and pressures, making possible modern low-temperature physics studies, 1881; awarded Nobel Prize in physics, 1910.

VAN'T HOFF, JACOBUS HENRICUS, Aug. 30, 1852 (Rotterdam, Neth.)–Mar. 1, 1911. Dutch physical chemist. Explained optical activity and asymmetry of organic compounds in solution by introducing the three-dimensional view of chemical bonds; did basic research on the behavior of materials in solutions, 1886; awarded the first Nobel Prize in chemistry, 1901.

VESALIUS, ANDREAS, Dec. 31, 1514 (Brussels, Flanders [now Belg.])–Oct. 15, 1564. Flemish anatomist. Father of modern anatomy; wrote the first accurate text on human anatomy, with superb illustrations, 1543.

VOLTA, ALESSANDRO GIUSEPPE ANTONIO ANASTASIO, CONTE, Feb. 18, 1745 (Como, It.)–Mar. 5, 1827. Italian physicist. Invented the electric battery, 1800; developed the basic elements for the condenser, 1775.

YUKAWA, HIDEKI, Jan. 23, 1907 (Kyoto, Jap.). Japanese physicist. Predicted the existence of mesons (1935) and the process of "K capture" (1938); awarded Nobel Prize in physics, 1949.

ZEEMAN, PIETER, May 25, 1865 (Netherlands)–Oct. 9, 1943. Dutch physicist. Discovered the Zeeman effect, by which the spectral lines of a light source in a strong magnetic field are split into three components; awarded Nobel Prize in physics (with H. A. LORENZ), 1902.

ZWICKY, FRITZ, Feb. 14, 1898 (Bulgaria)–Feb. 8, 1974. Swiss astronomer. Made basic contributions to the understanding of supernovas; discovered 18 supernovas, 1937–41; invented many essential elements of jet engines.

EXPLORERS

U.S. EXPLORERS

ALDRIN, EDWIN EUGENE, JR. ("Buzz"), Jan. 20, 1930 (Montclair, N.J.). U.S. astronaut. Participated in *Gemini 12* flight (1966) and *Apollo 11* flight (1969); the second man to set foot on the moon, 1969.

ANDREWS, ROY CHAPMAN, Jan. 26, 1884 (Beloit, Wisc.)–Mar. 11, 1960. U.S. naturalist, explorer, author. Led scientific expeditions to Alaska (1909), northern Korea (1911–12), Tibet, southwestern China, and Burma (1916–17), northern China and Outer Mongolia (1919). In Central Asia, discovered first known dinosaur eggs, a skull, and other parts of the Baluchitherium, the largest known land animal, along with other evidence of prehistoric life; director, American Museum of Natural History, 1935–42.

ARMSTRONG, NEIL ALDEN, Aug. 5, 1930 (Wapakoneta, Ohio). U.S. astronaut. Served as command pilot of *Gemini 8,* 1966; on *Apollo 11* mission, became the first man to step on the moon, stating, "That's one small step for a man, one giant leap for mankind," 1969.

AUSTIN, STEPHEN FULLER, Nov. 3, 1793 (Austinville, Va.)–Dec. 27, 1836. U.S. colonizer, public official. Founded English-speaking settlements in Texas in the 1830s; a leader in the fight for Texas independence from Mexico; as Texas secretary of state, laid the groundwork for U.S. recognition of the new republic, 1836.

BALCHEN, BERNT, Oct. 23, 1899 (Tveit, Nor.)–Oct. 17, 1973. Norwegian-U.S. aviator. Piloted the first flight over the South Pole, Nov. 29, 1929; chief pilot for RICHARD BYRD (1928–30) and LINCOLN ELLSWORTH (1933–35) polar expeditions; U.S. Air Force officer in WW II.

BARTLETT, ROBERT ABRAM, Aug. 15, 1875 (Brigus, Nfld.)–Apr. 28, 1946. Canadian-U.S. explorer. Commanded ROBERT PEARY's expedition ship, 1905–09; commanded *Karluk,* which was crushed by ice near Wrangel I., reached Siberia, 1914; headed expeditions to Greenland, Baffin I., and Labrador, 1926–32.

BECKNELL, WILLIAM, c.1796 (Amherst Co., Va.)–Apr. 30, 1865. U.S. fur trader and explorer who blazed the Santa Fe Trail from Franklin, Mo., to Santa Fe, N. M., 1821.

BORMAN, FRANK, Mar. 14, 1928 (Gary, Ind.). U.S. astronaut, airline executive. Made *Gemini 7* flight, 1965; made *Apollo 8* flight, the first manned flight around the moon, 1968; pres. and chief executive officer (1975–76), and chairman of the board (1976–   ), Eastern Airlines.

BYRD, RICHARD EVELYN, Oct. 25, 1888 (Winchester, Va.)–Mar. 11, 1957. U.S. admiral, aviator, explorer. Made first flight over the North Pole (1926) and over the South Pole (1928); conducted five Antarctic exploration expeditions, pioneering the aerial mapping and scientific investigation of the continent, 1928–56.

CARPENTER, MALCOLM SCOTT, May 1, 1925 (Boulder, Col.). U.S. astronaut, oceanographer. Completed three-orbit space flight mission of *Aurora 7,* Project Mercury, 1962; presently engaged in a private oceanographic and energy research business.

CARSON, KIT, born Christopher Carson, Dec. 24, 1809 (Madison Co., Ky.)–May 23, 1868. U.S. fron-

tiersman, soldier, Indian agent. Guided JOHN C. FRÉMONT's expeditions into Wyoming and California, 1842–46; U.S. scout in the Mexican War, 1846–48; Indian agent at Taos, N.M., 1853–60; Union Army officer in the Civil War.

CHISHOLM, JESSE, 1806–c.1868. U.S. frontiersman. Gave his name to the Chisholm Trail, which ran from the Mexican border to Abilene, Kan., and was used for cattle drives from 1867 to the 1880s.

CLARK, WILLIAM, Aug. 1, 1770 (Caroline Co., Va.)–Sept. 1, 1838. U.S. frontiersman, explorer, mapmaker. With MERIWETHER LEWIS, led an expedition to the Pacific Northwest, giving the first comprehensive description of that vast area, 1804–06.

COCHRAN, JACQUELINE, 1910 (Pensacola, Fla.). U.S. aviator, cosmetics executive. Piloted bomber to England, and trained British women for air transport service, 1941; organized Women's Air Force Service, 1943; first woman to exceed the speed of sound, in an F-86 Sabre jet, 1953; holds numerous world speed records; owned her own cosmetics firm, 1935–63.

CODY, WILLIAM FREDERICK ("Buffalo Bill"), Feb. 26, 1846 (Scott Co., Ia.)–Jan. 10, 1917. U.S. buffalo hunter, army scout, Indian fighter, showman. His exploits were fictionalized by dime novelists, including NED BUNTLINE. Starred as himself in Buntline's drama, *The Scouts of the Prairie,* 1872; organized his own Wild West Exhibitions, featuring fancy shooting, a buffalo hunt, ANNIE OAKLEY, and Chief SITTING BULL, from 1883.

COLLINS, MICHAEL, Oct. 31, 1930 (Rome, It.). U.S. astronaut. Copiloted *Gemini 10* space flight, 1966; on *Apollo 11* flight, piloted command module during the first moon landing, 1969.

CONRAD, CHARLES, JR., June 2, 1930 (Philadelphia, Pa.). U.S. astronaut. Copiloted *Gemini 5* space flight, 1962; command pilot of *Gemini 11* space flight, 1966; commander of *Apollo 12* moon flight, 1969.

COOPER, LEROY GORDON, JR., Mar. 6, 1927 (Shawnee, Okla.). U.S. astronaut. Command pilot of *Gemini 5* space flight, 1965.

CROCKETT, DAVEY, born David Crockett, Aug. 17, 1786 (Limestone, Tenn.)–Mar. 6, 1836. U.S. frontiersman, politician. One of the legendary heroes of frontier America. Fought in Creek War (1813–14) under ANDREW JACKSON; elected to Tennessee leg., 1821 and 1823; U.S. rep. (D, Tenn.), 1827–31 and 1833–35; joined Texas independence forces and was killed at the Alamo. *Autobiography* (with Thomas Chilton), 1834.

DU SABLE, JEAN BAPTISTE POINT (also de Sable, de Saible, Sable, Point du Sable), c.1745 (prob. Sainte-Domingue [now Haiti])–Aug. 28, 1818. U.S. pioneer. Called the "Father of Chicago," on whose site he built the first house and opened the first trading post, in the 1770s.

EARHART, AMELIA (married name, Putnam), July 24, 1898 (Atchison, Kan.)–disappeared July 2, 1937. U.S. aviatrix. The first woman to make a solo flight across the Atlantic, May 20–21, 1932; made solo flight from Hawaii to California, 1935; disappeared in the South Pacific while attempting to fly around the world, 1937.

ELLSWORTH, LINCOLN, May 12, 1880 (Chica-

THE BOOK OF WHO

go, Ill.)–May 26, 1951. U.S. polar explorer, scientist. Led first trans-Arctic (1926) and trans-Antarctic (1935) air crossings; with UMBERTO NOBILE, made first crossing of the Polar Basin, a 3,393-mi. journey from Spitsbergen to Alaska, 1926; made an 800-mile canoe trip through central Labrador, 1931; claimed some 300,000 sq. mi. of Antarctic terrain for the U.S.

FREMONT, JOHN CHARLES, Jan. 21, 1813 (Savannah, Ga.)–July 13, 1890. U.S. explorer, public official, Union general, mapmaker. Led three expeditions into the Far West, 1842–46; mapped out the Oregon Trail and the South Pass in the Rockies, helping make possible the western expansion of the mid-19th cent.; first Republican presidential candidate, 1856; territorial governor of Arizona, 1878–81.

GIST, CHRISTOPHER, c.1706 (Maryland)–c.1759. U.S. explorer, scout. The first white American to explore the Ohio Valley, 1750; rescued GEORGE WASHINGTON from drowning, 1753; guided EDWARD BRADDOCK's ill-fated expedition against Ft. Duquesne, 1755.

GLENN, JOHN HERSCHEL, JR., July 18, 1921 (Cambridge, Ohio). U.S. astronaut, politician. The first man to orbit the Earth, Feb. 20, 1962; U.S. senator (D, Ohio), 1975– .

GRAY, ROBERT, May 10, 1755 (Tiverton, R.I.)–1806. U.S. sailor, explorer. Captained the first U.S. ship to circumnavigate the world, 1787–90; discovered the Columbia R. in Oregon, 1792.

GRISSOM, VIRGIL IVAN ("Gus"). Apr. 3, 1926 (Mitchell, Ind.)–Jan. 27, 1967. U.S. astronaut. The third man to enter space, 1961; the first man to return to space, 1965; killed during a simulation of the *Apollo 1* launching, 1967.

HENSON, MATTHEW A., 1866–Mar. 9, 1955. U.S. explorer. Black explorer who accompanied Adm. PEARY on all of his polar expeditions; placed U.S. flag at the North Pole, 1909.

LEWIS, MERIWETHER, Aug. 18, 1774 (Albemarle Co., Va.)–Oct. 11, 1809. U.S. explorer. With WILLIAM CLARK, led expedition into the Pacific Northwest, 1804–06; private secy. to Pres. THOMAS JEFFERSON, 1801–03; the first gov. of the Louisiana Territory, 1807–09.

LINDBERGH, CHARLES AUGUSTUS ("The Lone Eagle"), Feb. 4, 1902 (Detroit, Mich)–Aug. 26, 1974. U.S. aviator. Made the first solo nonstop trans-Atlantic flight, New York–Paris, 1927; his infant son kidnapped and murdered, 1932; spokesman for isolationism, 1939–41; flew combat missions in the Pacific during WW II; awarded Pulitzer Prize for his biography, *The Spirit of St. Louis*, 1953.

LOVELL, JAMES ARTHUR, JR, Mar. 25, 1928 (Cleveland, Ohio). U.S. astronaut. Participated in the following space flights: *Gemini 7*, 1965; *Gemini 12*, 1966; *Apollo 8*, the first flight around the moon, 1968; *Apollo 13*, 1970.

MACMILLAN, DONALD BAXTER, Nov. 10, 1874 (Provincetown, Mass.)–Sept. 7, 1970. U.S. Arctic explorer. Went with ROBERT PEARY on Arctic expedition, 1908–09; led numerous expeditions to Arctic lands, 1913–37.

MCDIVITT, JAMES ALTON, June 10, 1929 (Chicago, Ill.). U.S. astronaut. Commanded *Gemini 4* space flight, 1965; participated in *Apollo 9* flight, 1969.

PALMER, NATHANIEL BROWN, Aug. 8, 1799 (Stonington, Conn.)–June 21, 1877. U.S. explorer, sea captain. Sighted Palmer Peninsula (named in his honor), becoming the first man to lay eyes on

the Antarctic continent, 1820; aided in the discovery of the South Orkney Is., 1822.

PEARY, ROBERT EDWIN, May 6, 1856 (Cresson, Pa.)–Feb. 20, 1920. U.S. Arctic explorer, admiral. Led the first expedition to reach the North Pole (1909), though his claim is still disputed by some; explored the Greenland ice cap, 1886 and 1893–94.

PIKE, ZEBULON MONTGOMERY, Jan. 5, 1779 (Lamberton, N.J.)–Apr. 27, 1813. U.S. Army officer, explorer. Led wilderness expedition into the northern portions of the Louisiana Purchase to seek Mississippi R. headwaters, 1805–06; led journey through Southwest, sighting Pike's Peak (named after him), 1806–07; served in War of 1812, killed during attack on York (now Toronto), Can., 1813.

POST, WILEY, Nov. 22, 1899 (Grand Saline, Tex.)–Aug. 15, 1935. U.S. aviator. Made the first solo around-the-world flight, proving the value of navigation intruments, including the automatic pilot, July 15–22, 1933; killed, with WILL ROGERS, in a plane crash in Alaska, 1935.

SACAGAWEA or **SACAJAWEA** ("Bird Woman"), c.1787 (Montana or Idaho)–1812 or 1884. Shoshone Indian guide. Interpreted for MERIWETHER LEWIS and WILLIAM CLARK on their expedition to the Pacific Northwest, 1804–06; death date in doubt because an old woman claiming to be Sacagawea turned up in 1875 and lived until 1884.

SCHIRRA, WALTER MARTY, JR., Mar. 12, 1923 (Hackensack, N.J.). U.S. astronaut. Manned Mercury *Sigma 7* space flight, 1962; commanded *Gemini 6* (1965) and *Apollo 7* (1968) space flights.

SHEPARD, ALAN BARTLETT, JR., Nov. 18, 1923 (East Derry, N.H.). U.S. astronaut. First U.S. astronaut to travel in space, May 5, 1961; commanded *Apollo 14* space flight, 1971.

SMITH, JEDEDIAH STRONG, Jan. 6, 1799 (Jericho, now Bainbridge, N.Y.)–May 27, 1831. U.S. explorer and fur trader, the leading explorer of the West and Pacific Northwest. Opened South Pass through the Rocky Mts., 1824; crossed Mojave Desert to California, then made first west-to-east crossing over the Sierra Nevadas and Great Salt Desert to Salt Lake, 1826.

STAFFORD, THOMAS PATTEN, Sept. 17, 1930 (Weatherford, Okla.). U.S. astronaut. Participated in the following space flights: *Gemini 6* (1965), *Gemini 9* (1966), and *Apollo 10* (1969).

STEFANSSON, VILHJALMUR, Nov. 3, 1879 (Arnes, Man., Can.)–Aug. 26, 1962. Canadian-U.S. explorer, ethnologist. Explored vast areas of the Canadian Arctic, 1908–12; after adapting himself to the Eskimo way of life, led expedition that discovered new lands in the Arctic archipelago and destroyed many myths about the inhospitality of the Far North, 1913–18.

SUTTER, JOHN AUGUSTUS, born Johann August Suter, Feb. 15, 1803 (Kandern, Ger.)–June 18, 1880. U.S. pioneer. Colonized California, establishing settlement called New Helvetia on the site of present-day Sacramento, 1839; discovery of gold on his land precipitated the California gold rush, 1848.

WHITMAN, MARCUS, Sept. 4, 1802 (Rushville, N.Y.)–Nov. 29, 1847. U.S. Congregational missionary, pioneer, physician. A missionary to the Indians of Washington and Oregon and prominent pioneer in opening up the Pacific Northwest to settlement; along with wife and children, massacred

130

by the Cayuse Indians, which led to early passage of a bill to organize the Oregon Territory (1848).

WILKES, CHARLES, Apr. 3, 1798 (New York, N.Y.)–Feb. 8, 1877. U.S. naval officer, explorer. Led round-the-world expedition that explored Antarctic area now known as Wilkes Land, 1838–42; as a Union Navy officer in the Civil War, stopped a British ship, precipitating the so-called *Trent* Affair, 1861.

WINNEMUCCA, SARAH, c.1844 (Humboldt Sink, Nev.)–Oct. 16, 1891. American Indian scout. A member of the Paiute tribe, she voluntarily scouted more than 100 miles of hostile territory for the U.S. Army, 1878; lectured across the U.S., collecting thousands of signatures requesting the govt. to give land to the Paiutes.

YOUNG, JOHN WATTS, Sept. 24, 1930 (San Francisco, Calif.). U.S. astronaut. Participated in the following space flights: *Gemini 3* (1965), *Gemini 10* (1966), and *Apollo 10* (1969).

FOREIGN EXPLORERS

ADAMS, WILLIAM, 1564 (England)–May 16, 1620. English navigator, adventurer. As the first Englishman in Japan (1600) made a nobleman by the shogun (ruler); prototype for the character Blackthorn in JAMES CLAVELL's novel *Shogun* (1975).

AMUNDSEN, ROALD, July 16, 1872 (Borge, Nor.)–June 1928. Norwegian polar explorer. Commanded the first ship to complete the Northwest Passage, 1903–06; the first man to reach the South Pole, 1911; one of the first to cross the Arctic by air, 1926.

BAFFIN, WILLIAM, c.1584 (England)–Jan. 23, 1622. British navigator who searched for the Northwest Passage and gave his name to Baffin I. and Baffin Bay.

BAKER, SIR SAMUEL WHITE, June 8, 1821 (London, Eng.)–Dec. 30, 1893. British explorer who helped locate the sources of the Nile, 1861–64.

BALBOA, VASCO NÚÑEZ DE, c. 1475 (Extremadura Prov., Sp.)–Jan. 1519. Spanish conquistador, explorer. The first European to sight the Pacific Ocean, Sept. 1513.

BARENTS (or Barentz), WILLEM, c.1550 (Terschelling, Neth.)–June 20, 1597. Dutch navigator. In search of the Northwest Passage, made three voyages, 1594–97, into what would later be called the Barents Sea.

BERING, VITUS JONASSEN, 1681 (Horsens, Den.)–Dec. 19, 1741. Danish navigator. Employed by Russia to discover if N. America and Asia were connected (1725–41), he discovered the Bering Sea and Bering Strait.

BOUGAINVILLE, LOUIS ANTOINE DE, Nov. 11, 1729 (Paris, Fr.)–Apr. 31, 1811. French navigator. Headed the first French naval force to circumnavigate the globe, 1766–69; fought in the latter part of the French and Indian wars; bougainvillaea, a tropical flowering vine, named after him. *Voyage autour du Monde,* 1771.

BRULÉ, ÉTIENNE, c.1592 (Champigny-sur-Marne, Fr.)–c.1632. French explorer. Explored the Great Lakes, 1610–26; interpreted Indian languages for SAMUEL DE CHAMPLAIN; betrayed the French to the British, leading to the capture of Quebec, 1629.

BURTON, SIR RICHARD FRANCIS, Mar. 19, 1821 (Elstree, Eng.)–Oct. 20, 1890. British scholar, explorer. The first European to discover Lake Tanganyika, 1858; the first European to enter the

forbidden city of Harar, in present-day Ethiopia, 1854; wrote 43 volumes on his explorations and translated some 30 volumes of Eastern writings.

CABEZA DE VACA, ÁLVAR NÚÑEZ, c.1490 (Extremadura Prov., Sp.)–c.1560. Spanish explorer. Spent eight years in the gulf region of present-day Texas, 1528–36; his accounts of the legendary Seven Golden Cities of Cibola inspired extensive exploration of U.S. South and Southwest by HERNANDO DE SOTO and FRANCISCO DE CORONADO.

CABOT, JOHN, born Giovanni Caboto, c.1450 (Genoa, It.)–c.1499. Italian navigator, explorer. Employed by the British, he reached North America, laying the groundwork for British claim to Canada, 1497; sailed again for N. America, 1498; details of last voyage are obscure—he may have died at sea or returned to England. (Father of SEBASTIAN CABOT.)

CABOT, SEBASTIAN, c.1476 (Venice, It.)–1557. Italian explorer, cartographer who served England and Spain. His efforts to find a Northwest Passage led to the development of trade between England and Russia. (Son of JOHN CABOT.)

CABRAL, PEDRO ALVAREZ, c.1467 (Belmonte, Port.)–1520. Portuguese navigator who is generally credited with the discovery of Brazil, 1500.

CABRILLO, JUAN RODRÍGUEZ, ?(Portugal)–c.1543. Portuguese soldier-explorer in the employ of Spain. Discovered California, entering San Diego Bay, 1542.

CADILLAC, ANTOINE DE LA MOTHE, Mar. 5, 1658 (Les Laumets, Fr.)–Oct. 15, 1730. French fur trader and explorer who founded Detroit, 1701.

CANO, JUAN SEBASTIÁN DEL, c.1460 (Guetaria, Sp.)–Aug. 4, 1526. Spanish navigator who sailed with F. MAGELLAN, after whose death Cano commanded the first expedition to circumnavigate the globe, 1522.

CARTIER, JACQUES, 1491 (St. Malo, Fr.)–Sept. 1, 1557. French explorer. His explorations (1534–42) of the North American coast and St. Lawrence R. laid the basis for later French claims to Canada (1534–42), although his pessimistic reports discouraged French exploration in North America for over half a century.

CHAMPLAIN, SAMUEL DE, c.1567 (Brouage, Fr.)–Dec. 25, 1635. French explorer. Mapped New England coast as far as Cape Cod, 1605–08; founded Quebec, the first white settlement in New France, 1608; discovered Lake Champlain, 1609; surrendered Quebec to the British, 1629.

COLUMBUS, CHRISTOPHER, born Cristoforo Columbo, c.1451 (Genoa, It.)–May 20, 1506. Italian explorer, navigator. In the service of Spain, made the first historically verifiable European discovery of the New World, sighting San Salvador on Oct. 12, 1492; discovered South America (1498) and Central America (1502); his four voyages to the New World opened the way for European exploration and colonization and changed the course of history.

COOK, JAMES, Oct. 27, 1728 (Marton-in-Cleveland, Eng.)–Feb. 14, 1779. British navigator. Led scientific voyage to Tahiti, 1768–71; surveyed coast of New Zealand, charted eastern coast of Australia, naming it New South Wales, and claimed it for England, 1770; mapped much of the southern hemisphere, sailing farther south than anyone before him, 1772–75; discovered Sandwich (Hawaiian) Is., 1778.

CORONADO, FRANCISCO VÁSQUEZ DE, c.1510 (Salamanca, Sp.)–Sept. 22, 1554. Spanish explorer. Explored the U.S. Southwest, 1540-42; he or his lieutenants discovered many noted physical landmarks, including the Grand Canyon.

CORTES, HERNAN (or Hernando Cortez), 1485 (Medellin, Sp.)-Sept. 2, 1547. Spanish conquistador. Aided in conquest of Cuba, 1511; conquered Aztec Empire in Mexico, 1518-21.

COUSTEAU, JACQUES IVES, June 11, 1910 (Sainte-Andre-de-Cubzac, Fr.). French explorer of the oceans, filmmaker, author. Famed for extensive undersea investigations. Invented the aqualung, making possible the sport of scuba diving, 1943; designed underwater structures that house men for prolonged periods of time. Books: *The Silent World,* 1953; *The Living Sea,* 1963; *Life and Death in a Coral Sea,* 1971. Films: *World Without Sun,* 1964; *Desert Whales,* 1970.

DAMPIER, WILLIAM, c.1652 (East Coker, Eng.)-Mar. 1715. British buccaneer and explorer who was one of the first Englishmen to see Australia, 1686.

DAVIS (or Davys), **JOHN,** c.1550 (Devonshire, Eng.)-Dec. 1605. British navigator, Arctic explorer. Searching for a Northwest Passage, pushed through Davis Strait (named for him) into Baffin Bay, 1587; discovered Falkland Is., 1592.

DE SOTO, HERNANDO, c.1499 (Extremadura Prov., Sp.)-May 21, 1542. Spanish explorer. Explored coastal and interior areas of Central America, 1516-20; helped conquer Nicaragua and Peru; headed an expedition that explored much of southeastern U.S., probably being the first Europeans to sight the Mississippi R., 1539-42.

DRAKE, SIR FRANCIS, c.1540 (Devonshire, Eng.)-Jan. 28, 1596. British admiral, the most renowned seaman of the Elizabethan age. Circumnavigated the globe, 1577-80; played an important role in the defeat of the Spanish Armada, 1588.

ERICSON (also Ericsson, Eriksson), **LEIF,** Norse explorer. Made landfall on North American coast, c.1000, calling landing place Vinland; according to speculation, Vinland could have been present-day Newfoundland, Nova Scotia, or Cape Cod. (Son of ERIC THE RED.)

ERIC THE RED, born Eric Thorvaldson, c.950 (Norway)-c.1000. Norse explorer who established first European settlement on Greenland, c.986. (Father of LEIF ERICSON.)

FROBISHER, SIR MARTIN, 1535 (Yorkshire, Eng.)-Nov. 22, 1594. British navigator. Early explorer of Canada's northeastern coast, 1576-78; played a prominent role in the campaign against the Spanish Armada, 1588.

GAGARIN, YURI ALEKSEYEVICH, Mar. 9, 1934 (nr. Gzhatsk, USSR)-Mar. 27, 1968. Soviet cosmonaut. First man to travel into space, Apr. 12, 1961; awarded Order of Lenin; died in an airplane crash on a routine training flight, 1968.

GAMA, VASCO DA, 1460 (Sines, Port.)-Dec. 24, 1524. Portuguese navigator who led expedition around Africa to India, opening a sea route to Asia, 1497-99.

GILBERT, SIR HUMPHREY, c.1537 (Devon, Eng.)-Sept. 9, 1583. British explorer who attempted to start first English colony in America, at present-day St. John's, Nfld., 1583.

HENRY THE NAVIGATOR, PRINCE OF PORTUGAL, Mar. 4, 1394 (Porto, Port.)-Nov. 13, 1460. Portuguese prince who sponsored voyages that led to the foundation of the Portuguese Empire.

HEYERDAHL, THOR, Oct. 6, 1914 (Larvik, Nor.).

Norwegian ethnologist, adventurer. Led "Kon-Tiki" expedition from South American Pacific coast to Polynesia, establishing the possibility that Polynesians may have originated in South America, 1947; led Ra expedition from Morocco to within 600 miles of Central America, confirming the possibility that pre-Columbian cultures may have been influenced by Egyptian civilization, 1970. *Kon-Tiki,* 1950; *Aku-Aku: The Secret of Easter Island,* 1958; *The Ra Expeditions,* 1971.

HILLARY, SIR EDMUND PERCIVAL, July 20, 1919 (Auckland, N.Z.). New Zealand mountain climber, Arctic explorer. The first, with Tenzing Norgay, to reach the summit of Mt. Everest, May 19, 1953; led the New Zealand group in the British Commonwealth Trans-Antarctic expedition, 1955-58.

HUDSON, HENRY, fl. 1607-1611. English explorer. Explored the Hudson R. for the Dutch East India Co., establishing the basis of Dutch claims to New York, 1609; in the service of England, sailed through Hudson Strait into Hudson Bay and James Bay, where his mutinous crew set him adrift to die, 1610-11.

IBERVILLE, PIERRE LE MOYNE, SIEUR D', July 16, 1661 (Montreal, Can.)-July 9, 1706. French-Canadian soldier, explorer. Founded the first permanent settlement in the French territory of Louisiana, 1699; led West Indian fleet in attacks on Nevis and St. Kitts islands, forcing British surrender, 1706.

JOLLIET (or Joliet), **LOUIS,** Sept. 21, 1645 (Quebec, Can.)-May, 1700. French-Canadian explorer, cartographer. The first white man, with JACQUES MARQUETTE, to traverse the Mississippi R. from its confluence with the Fox R. in present-day Wisconsin to the Arkansas R. in present-day Arkansas, 1673; traveled to Hudson Bay, charted Labrador coast, 1694.

LA SALLE, ROBERT CAVELIER, SIEUR DE, Nov. 21, 1643 (Rouen, Fr.)-Mar. 19, 1687. French explorer, fur trader. Led the first expedition to the mouth of the Mississippi R., establishing France's claim to the Mississippi Valley and Louisiana, 1681-82.

LEONOV, ALEKSEI ARKHIPOVICH, May 30, 1934 (nr. Kemerovo, USSR). Soviet cosmonaut. On the *Voshod 2* space flight, was the first man to climb out of a ship in space, 1965.

LIVINGSTONE, DAVID, Mar. 19, 1813 (Blantyre, Scot.)-May 1, 1873. British missionary, physician, explorer. Accomplished extensive exploration of Africa, then the "dark continent"; attempted to end the slave trade; the famous greeting, "Dr. Livingstone, I presume," addressed to him by HENRY M. STANLEY, who found him on a rescue mission. *Missionary Travels and Researches in Africa,* 1857.

MACKENZIE, SIR ALEXANDER, 1755 (Is. of Lewis, Outer Hebrides)-Mar. 11, 1820. Scottish fur trader, explorer. Journeyed from Ft. Chipewyan along Slave and Mackenzie rivers to the Arctic Ocean, 1789; crossed the Rocky Mts. to the Pacific coast at present-day British Columbia, the first known transcontinental crossing of America north of Mexico, 1793.

MAGELLAN, FERDINAND, 1480 (Porto, Port.)-1521. Portuguese navigator in the service of Spain, often called the first circumnavigator of the globe, although he died before the voyage was completed. Sailed through the strait that was to bear his name, 1520; reached the Philippines (1521), becoming the first European to cross the Pacific from east to west and establishing a new route between Europe and Asia.

MARQUETTE, JACQUES ("Père Marquette"), June 1, 1637 (Laon, Fr.)–May 18, 1675. French Jesuit missionary, explorer. Traveled with LOUIS JOLLIET down the Mississippi R. and reported the first accurate data on its course, 1673; one of the first white men to live near present-day Chicago.

MENDOZA, PEDRO DE, c.1487 (Guadix, Sp.)–1537. Spanish colonizer and explorer who founded the first colony at Buenos Aires, Arg., 1536.

NICOLET, JEAN, 1598 (Cherbourg, Fr.)–Nov. 1, 1642. French explorer. The first European to discover Lake Michigan and the area that now comprises Wisconsin and Michigan, 1634.

NOBILE, UMBERTO, Jan. 24, 1885 (Lauro, It.)–July 29, 1978. Italian aeronautical engineer, pioneer in Arctic aviation. Flew over the North Pole with ROALD AMUNDSEN and LINCOLN ELLSWORTH, from Spitsbergen to Alaska, 1926.

PINZÓN, MARTIN ALONSO, c.1441 (Palos, Sp.)–1493. Spanish explorer. Part-owner of the *Pinta*, and *Niña* of CHRISTOPHER COLUMBUS's 1492 fleet; his suggestion, as commander of the *Pinta*, resulted in landfall in the Bahamas, Oct. 12, 1492. (Brother of VICENTE PINZÓN.)

PINZÓN, VICENTE YAÑEZ, c.1460 (Palos, Sp.)–c.1523. Spanish navigator. Commanded *Niña* in CHRISTOPHER COLUMBUS's expedition, 1492-93; discovered Amazon R. estuary and present-day Costa Rica, c.1500. (Brother of MARTIN ALONSO PINZÓN.)

PIZARRO, FRANCISCO, 1475 (Trujillo, Sp.)–June 26, 1541. Spanish conquistador. Accompanied VASCO BALBOA on his discovery of the Pacific Ocean, 1513; conquered the Inca Empire in Peru, 1531-35; founded city of Lima, Peru, 1535. (Half-brother of GONZALO PIZARRO.)

PIZARRO, GONZALO, c.1502 (Trujillo, Sp.)–Apr. 10, 1548. Spanish explorer. Aided his half-brother FRANCISCO PIZARRO in the conquest of Peru, 1531-35; led anti-royalist forces in Peru, won Battle of Anaquito, 1546; was captured and executed, 1548.

PONCE DE LEÓN, JUAN, 1460 (Tierra de Campos Palencia, Sp.)–1521. Spanish explorer. Sailed with CHRISTOPHER COLUMBUS on his second voyage to the New World, 1493; explored Puerto Rico, founding colony near present-day San Juan, 1508-09; discovered Florida while searching for the mythical fountain of youth, 1513.

PORTOLÁ, GASPAR DE, c.1723 (Catalonia, Sp.)–c.1784. Spanish explorer. Commanded expedition to colonize upper California, 1767-70; honored as founder of San Diego.

RADISSON, PIERRE ESPRIT, c.1636 (St. Malo, Fr.)–c.1710. French explorer, fur trader, in service of England. Explored Hudson Bay and the wilderness west of the Great Lakes; his activities led to formation of the Hudson's Bay Co., 1670.

RIBAUT, JEAN, c.1520 (Dieppe, Fr.)–Sept. 23, 1565. French explorer who founded first French colony in America, at present-day Port Royal, S.C., 1562.

SCOTT, ROBERT FALCON, June 6, 1868 (Devonport [now part of Plymouth], Eng.)–c.Mar. 19, 1912. British Antarctic explorer. As leader of expedition to the South Pole, arrived (Jan. 1912) only to find R. AMUNDSEN had already been there; plagued by sickness and ill weather, entire party died by March.

SHACKLETON, SIR ERNEST HENRY, Feb. 15, 1874 (Kilkee, Ire.)–Jan. 5, 1922. British Antarctic explorer. Made three expeditions to the Antarctic; reached 97 miles from South Pole, sent parties to the summit of Mt. Erebrus, and went to magnetic South Pole, 1909. *Heart of the Antarctic,* 1909; *South,* 1919.

STANLEY, HENRY MORTON, born John Rowlands, Jan. 28, 1841 (Denbighshire, Eng.)–May 10, 1904. English-U.S. journalist. As a journalist for the New York *Herald,* was commissioned to find African explorer DAVID LIVINGSTONE; when he finally reached Livingstone (1871), greeted him with the words, "Dr. Livingstone, I presume?"; led a second expedition, furthering Livingstone's explorations, 1874-77; on third expedition, laid foundation for Congo Free State, 1879-84; on last expedition, relieved Emin Pasha during Mahdist advance in Sudan, 1887-89. *How I Found Livingstone,* 1872; *In Darkest Africa,* 2 vols., 1890.

TABEI, JUNKO, 1940 (nr. Tokyo, Japan). Japanese mountain climber. The first woman to reach the top of Mt. Everest, 1975; part of a 15-member all-female Japanese expedition.

TERESHKOVA, VALENTINA VLADIMIROVNA, Mar. 6, 1937 (Maslennikovo, USSR). Soviet cosmonaut. The first woman to travel into space; completed 48 orbits in 71 hours aboard *Vostok 6,* 1963.

THOMPSON, DAVID, Apr. 30, 1770 (London, Eng.)–Feb. 10, 1857. British-Canadian explorer, geographer. The first European to explore the Columbia R., 1807-11; made the first definitive map of western Canada and portions of northwestern U.S.; served on commission that surveyed the U.S.-Canadian border, 1816-26; died in obscurity, unrecognized until the 20th cent. as one of the great land geographers in history.

THORFINN KARLSEFNI, c.980 (Iceland)–? Scandinavian explorer. Believed to be the first European to attempt colonization of North America, probably on Newfoundland, 1002.

VANCOUVER, GEORGE, June 22, 1757 (King's Lynn, Eng.)–May 10, 1798. British navigator. Surveyed Pacific coast of North America from the vicinity of San Francisco to present-day British Columbia, 1791-94; Vancouver I. and Vancouver, B.C., were named for him.

VÉRENDRYE, PIERRE GAULTIER DE VARENNES, SIEUR DE LA, Nov. 17, 1685 (Trois-Rivières, Que., Can.)–Dec. 5, 1749. French-Canadian fur trader, explorer. Built a string of trading posts from Rainy Lake, Ont., to Winnipeg, Man., breaking the Hudson's Bay Co. monopoly and strengthening French claims in North America 1731-38; pushing farther west than any other previous white man, claimed present-day Pierre, S. D., for France, 1743.

VERRAZANO (or Verazzano), **GIOVANNI DA,** c.1485 (nr. Florence, It.)–c.1528. Italian navigator in the service of France. Explored North American coast from Cape Fear, N.C., to Cape Breton, N.S., becoming the first European to sight New York and Narragansett bays, 1524.

VESPUCCI, AMERIGO, 1454 (Florence, It.)–Feb. 22, 1512. Italian navigator, explorer. Made voyages in the service of Spain (1499-1500) and Portugal (1501-02); explored 6,000 miles of the S. American coast, observing that it was not Asia, but a new continent; Martin Waldseemuller, a geographer, issued a map showing the new continent (now S. America) and proposed naming it after its discov-

THE BOOK OF WHO

erer; in time, name was applied to the N. American continent as well.

WEDDELL, JAMES, Aug. 24, 1787 (Ostend, Belg.)–Sept. 9, 1834. British explorer who penetrated farther south than any previous explorer, reaching present-day Weddell Sea in the Antarctic, 1823.

WILKINS, SIR GEORGE HUBERT, Oct. 31, 1888 (Mount Bryan East, Austrl.)–Dec. 1, 1958. Australian explorer and aviator who advanced use of the

airplane and pioneered use of the submarine for polar research. Captained the submarine *Nautilus,* 1931 and navigated it under the Arctic Ocean; managed Lincoln Ellsworth's Antarctic expedition, 1933–39.

WRANGEL (or Wrangell), FERDINAND PETROVICH, BARON VON, Dec. 29, 1796 (St. Petersburg, Rus.)–June 6, 1870. Russian explorer. Mapped northeastern coast of Siberia, locating present-day Wrangel I., 1820–24.

RULERS, STATESMEN, AND POLITICAL LEADERS

U.S. RULERS, STATESMAN, AND POLITICAL LEADERS

ABZUG, BELLA, née Savitzky, July 14, 1920, (New York, N.Y.). U.S. politician, lawyer. Helped found Women Strike for Peace (1961), and served as its legislative dir., (1961–70); a founder of the New Democratic Coalition, 1968; first Jewish woman elected U.S. rep. (D, N.Y.), 1970–76; a leader of the anti-Vietnam War movement; a leader of the feminist movement.

ACHESON, DEAN G., Apr. 11, 1893 (Middletown, Conn.)–Oct. 12, 1971. U.S. lawyer, statesman. As secy. of state (1949–53), the principal creator of the U.S. foreign policy aimed at containment of communist expansion after WW II; helped create NATO; awarded Pulitzer Prize in history for *Present at the Creation,* 1970

ADAMS, JOHN, Oct. 30, 1735 (Braintree, Mass.)–July 4, 1826. U.S. president, lawyer, diplomat. Helped draft Declaration of Independence, 1776; helped draft Treaty of Paris that ended Revolutionary War, 1783; served as diplomat in France, Netherlands, and Great Britain, 1777–88; v.-pres., 1789–97; as 2nd U.S. pres. (1797–1801), prevented war with France (1798) and approved the Alien and Sedition Acts (1798). (Father of JOHN QUINCY ADAMS; husband of ABIGAIL ADAMS.)

ADAMS, JOHN QUINCY, July 11, 1767 (Braintree, Mass.)–Feb. 23, 1848. U.S. president, lawyer, diplomat, political writer. As U.S. secy. of state under JAMES MONROE, helped prepare Monroe Doctrine, 1823; negotiated Treaty of Ghent, ending War of 1812, 1814; min. to the Netherlands (1794), Prussia (1797–1801), Russia (1809–14), and Great Britain (1815–17); U.S. Rep. (Mass.), 1831–48; 6th U.S. pres., 1825–29. (Son of JOHN and ABIGAIL ADAMS.)

ADAMS, SAMUEL, Sept. 27, 1722 (Boston, Mass.)–Oct. 2, 1803. American Revolutionary patriot, statesman. Helped plan the Boston Tea Party, 1773; pamphleteered against the British and helped organize the Sons of Liberty, early 1770s; member of the Continental Cong., 1774–81; signer of the Declaration of Independence, 1776; gov. of Massachusetts, 1794–97.

ADAMS, SHERMAN, Jan. 8, 1899 (East Dover, Vt.). U.S. politician, lumber-industry exec. U.S. rep. (R, N.H.), 1945–47; gov. (R) of New Hampshire, 1949–53; asst. to Pres. D. D. EISENHOWER, 1953–58.

AGNEW, SPIRO, Nov. 9, 1918 (Baltimore, Md.). U.S. vice-pres., lawyer. Baltimore Co. exec., 1962–67; as Maryland gov. (R), implemented progressive policies, 1967–68; known for outspokenness as U.S. vice-pres. (R, 1969–73); resigned as vice-pres. when faced with federal income-tax charge, 1973.

ALBERT, CARL, May 10, 1908 (McAlester, Okla.). U.S. lawyer, politician. U.S. rep. (D, Okla.), 1947–76; Democrat House whip, 1955–61; House majority leader, 1962–71; House Speaker, 1971–76.

ALDEN (or Aldin), JOHN, 1599? (England)–Sept. 12, 1687. English gov. official in colonial America. One of the Pilgrim Fathers, a founder of Plymouth Colony, serving as assistant gov. intermittently between 1633 and 1686; founded Duxbury, Mass.; married PRISCILLA MULLINS, after, according to legend, failing to win her hand for MILES STANDISH.

ANDRUS, CECIL D., Aug. 25, 1931 (Hood River, Ore.). U.S. politician. Gov. (D) of Idaho, 1971–77; U.S. secy. of int., 1977– .

ARTHUR, CHESTER ALAN, Oct. 5, 1829 (Fairfield, Vt.)–Nov. 18, 1886. U.S. pres., lawyer. Collector of the port of New York, 1871–78; U.S. Vice Pres, 1881; on death of Pres JAMES GARFIELD became 21st pres. (R, 1881–85); supported the Civil Service Reform Act of 1883 and vetoed a Chinese exclusion bill.

ATTUCKS, CRISPUS, c.1723 (Framingham, Mass.)–Mar. 5, 1770. American colonial anti-British agitator. A leader of the demonstration that resulted in the Boston Massacre, in which he died.

BACON, NATHANIEL, Jan. 2, 1647 (Suffolk, Eng.)–Oct. 1676. American colonial leader. An English aristocrat who led angry frontiersmen in the short-lived Bacon's Rebellion in colonial Virginia, 1676.

BAKER, HOWARD HENRY, JR., Nov. 15, 1925 (Huntsville, Tenn.). U.S. politician, lawyer. U.S. sen. (R, Tenn.), 1967– ; Senate minority leader, 1977– ; member of Senate Select Com. on Presidential Activities, Foreign Relations Com., and Public Works Com.

BARKLEY, ALBEN WILLIAM, Nov. 24, 1877 (Graves Co, Ky.)–Apr. 30, 1956. U.S. vice-pres., lawyer. A major contributor to the Democratic New Deal of the 1930s; U.S. sen. (D, Ky.), 1927–49, 1954–56; U.S. vice-pres. (D), 1949–53.

BARTLETT, EDWARD LOUIS ("Bob"), Apr. 20, 1904 (Seattle, Wash.)–Dec. 11, 1968. U.S. politician, gold miner, newspaperman. Alaska's most popular political figure. U.S. rep. (D, Alaska), 1945–59; as U.S. sen. (D, Alaska; 1959–68), came out early (1964) in opposition to the Vietnam War; worked for development of U.S. maritime industry.

BARTLETT, JOSIAH, Nov. 21, 1729 (Amesbury, Mass.)–May 19, 1795. American Revolutionary patriot. A signer of the Declaration of Independence, 1776; chief justice of the New Hampshire state sup. ct., 1788; first gov. of New Hampshire, 1792–94.

BAYH, BIRCH EVANS, Jan. 22, 1928 (Vigo Co. Ind.). U.S. politician, lawyer, farmer. U.S. sen. (D,

134

Ind.), 1963–   ; chm. of Senate Rights of Americans, Transportation Appropriations, and Construction sub coms.

BELL, JOHN, Feb. 1, 1797 (nr. Nashville, Tenn.)–Sept. 10, 1869. U.S. politician, lawyer, iron-works operator. Led the conservative Southern faction that, even though it supported slavery, put the Union first. U.S. Rep. (D–Whig, Tenn.), 1827–41; U.S. sen. (Whig, Tenn.), 1847–59; Constitutional Union party presidential candidate, 1860.

BENTON, THOMAS HART, Mar. 1, 1782 (Harts Mill, N.C.)–Apr. 10, 1858. U.S. politician, lawyer, teacher, editor, author. Vigorous advocate of the opening up of the West and of a hard money (gold over silver) policy, and an opponent of the extension of slavery into the territories. Editor of the *St. Louis Enquirer,* 1818–20; U.S. sen. (D, Mo.), 1821–51; served as Democratic leader in the Senate. *Thirty Years' View,* 1854–56.

BENTSEN, LLOYD MILLARD, JR., Feb. 11, 1921 (Mission, Tex.). U.S. politician, businessman. U.S. rep. (D, Tex.), 1948–54; pres. of Lincoln Consolidated, a financial holding company, and dir. of a number of corporations, 1955–70; U.S. sen. (D, Tex.), 1971–   ; member of Senate Finance, Environment, Public Works, and Joint Economic coms.

BERGLAND, BOB SELMER, July 22, 1928 (Roseau, Minn.). U.S. politician, farmer. Dir. of Midwest Area Agricultural Stablilization and Conservation Service, 1963–68; U.S. rep. (D, Minn.), 1971–76; U.S. secy. of agr., 1977–   .

BERLE, ADOLF A., Jan. 29, 1895 (Boston, Mass.)–Feb. 17, 1971. U.S. lawyer, economist. Early advisor to Pres. F D. ROOSEVELT; helped develop plan for reopening the banks following the bank holiday of March 1933; active in securing passage of the Bankruptcy act of 1933.

BIRCH, JOHN, killed Aug. 25, 1945. U.S. soldier. U.S. intelligence officer in China, killed by the Communist Chinese ten days after V-J Day; name adopted by a U.S. anticommunist political organization, The John Birch Society, which honors him as the first hero of the Cold War.

BIRD, ROSE ELIZABETH, Nov. 2, 1936 (Tucson, Ariz.). U.S. jurist. As California secy. of agric. (1975–77), drafted a controversial farm-labor law that restored peace to California farming; chief justice of California Sup. Ct., 1977–

BIRNEY, JAMES GILLESPIE, Feb. 4, 1792 (Danville, Ky.)–Nov. 25, 1857. U.S. lawyer, author, abolitionist. Organized Kentucky branch of the Anti-Slavery Soc.; persecuted in Cincinnati, Ohio, for his antislavery work; secy. of National Anti-Slavery Soc., 1837–39; Liberty party presidential candidate, 1840 and 1844.

BLACK, HUGO LAFAYETTE, Feb. 27, 1886 (Harlan, Ala.)–Sept. 24, 1971. U.S. jurist, lawyer. U.S. sen. (D, Ala.), 1927–37; as U.S. Sup. Ct. assoc. justice (1937–71), opposed Congressional and state violation of free speech and due process, led activists on the court, advocated court-enforced legislative reapportionment, wrote the opinion forbiding prayers in public schools, worked for procedural simplicity and enforcement of antitrust laws.

BLACKMUN, HARRY ANDREW, Nov. 12, 1908 (Nashville, Ill.). U.S. jurist, lawyer. Federal cir. ct. judge, 1959–70; as U.S. Sup. Ct. assoc. justice (1970–   ), noted for his scholarly opinions, and for his generally conservative stands (except in civil-rights cases).

BLAINE, JAMES GILLESPIE, Jan. 31, 1830 (West Brownsville, Pa.)–Jan. 27, 1893. U.S. politician, newspaper editor. A leading Republican politician during the latter half of the 19th cen., he attempted to foster closer relations with Latin American countries, began the Pan-American movement, originated the idea of reciprocal tariff treaties. U.S. rep. (R, Me.), 1869–75; U.S. sen. (R, Me.), 1876–80; U.S. secy. of state, 1881, 1889–92; Republican presidential candidate, 1884.

BLUMENTHAL, W. MICHAEL, Jan. 3, 1926 (Germany). U.S. economist, businessman. Pres. of Bendix International, 1967–76; amb. and President's deputy special rep. for trade negotiations, 1963–67; U.S secy. of the treas., 1977–79.

BOGGS, CORINNE ("Lindy"), Mar. 13, 1916 (Brunswick Plantation, La.). U.S. politician. Elected U.S. rep. (D, La.) to fill seat vacated by the death of her husband, 1973–   ; member of House Appropriations Com.; chairperson of Democratic National Convention, 1976.

BOHLEN, CHARLES E. ("Chip"), Aug. 30, 1904 (Clayton, N.Y.)–Jan. 2, 1974. U.S. diplomat. Specialist in Soviet affairs; served as Russian interpreter for U.S. presidents at the Teheran (1943) and Yalta (1945) conferences; U.S. amb. to the USSR, 1953–57; U.S. amb. to the Philippines, 1957–59; U.S. amb. to France, 1962–68.

BOND, JULIAN, Jan. 14, 1940 (Nashville, Tenn.). U.S. politician, poet, television commentator. Gained national prominence at the 1968 Democratic National Convention in Chicago, where he cochaired the challenge delegation from Georgia that fought in oppostion to then-gov. LESTER MADDOX's handpicked delegation; Georgia state rep., 1967–74; Georgia state sen., 1975–78.

BORAH, WILLIAM EDGAR, June 29, 1865 (Fairfield, Ill.)–Jan. 19, 1940. U.S. politician, lawyer. U.S. sen. (R, Idaho), 1907–40; an isolationist, he played a major role in preventing the U.S. from joining the League of Nations and the World Court.

BOWLES, CHESTER, Apr. 5, 1901 (Springfield, Mass.). U.S. diplomat, advertising executive. Cofounder of Benton and Bowles advertising agency, 1929; gov. (D) of Connecticut, 1949–51; U.S. amb. to India, 1951–53, 1963–69; U.S. undersecy. of state, 1961–63. *Tomorrow without Fear,* 1946; *Promises to Keep,* 1971.

BRADEMAS, JOHN, Mar. 2, 1927 (Mishawaka, Ind.). U.S politic .n. U.S. rep. (D., Ind.), 1958–   ; House majority whip, 1976–   .

BRADFORD, WILLIAM, Mar. 1590 (Yorkshire, Eng.)–May 9, 1657. English leader in colonial America. A framer of the Mayflower Compact, 1620; as gov. of Plymouth Colony (intermittently 1621–56), played a major role in the colony's survival, dealt cleverly with the economic hardships of the colony, treated the Indians fairly. *History of Plymouth Plantation, 1620–47.*

BRADLEY, BILL, born William Warren Bradley, July 28, 1943 (Crystal City, Mo). U.S. politician, basketball player. A Rhodes scholar from Princeton U., who played professional basketball for the N.Y. Knickerbockers, 1967–77; U.S. sen. (D, N.J.), 1979–   .

BRADLEY, THOMAS, Dec. 29, 1917 (Calvert, Tex.). U.S. politician, lawyer, policeman. A member of the Los Angeles Police Dept., 1940–62; mayor of Los Angeles, 1973–   ; cochairperson of Democratic National Convention, 1976.

BRANDEIS, LOUIS DEMBITZ, Nov. 13, 1856 (Louisville, Ky.)–Oct. 5, 1941. U.S. jurist, lawyer. As assoc. justice of U.S. Sup. Ct., (1916–39) was a judicial liberal; the first to devise a brief in which economic and sociological data are used to buttress legal propositions; fought monopolies and defended individual rights, state legislative power, and economic legislation.

BRECKINRIDGE, JOHN CABELL, Jan. 21, 1821 (nr. Lexington, Ky.)–May 17, 1875. U.S. politician, lawyer, railroad executive, soldier. As U.S. vicepres. (D), he presided over the U.S. Senate during the troublesome years prior to the Civil War, 1857–61; unsuccessfully supported by Southern Democrats for the presidency, 1860; a gen. in the Confederate Army, 1861–65.

BRENNAN, WILLIAM JOSEPH, JR., Apr. 25, 1906 (Newark, N.J.). U.S. jurist, lawyer. As assoc. justice of U.S. Sup. Ct., (1956–), he has written many majority opinions, particularly in the areas of obscenity and antitrust.

BROOKE, EDWARD WILLIAM, Oct. 26, 1919 (Washington, D.C.). U.S. politician, lawyer. U.S. sen. (R, Mass.), 1967–79; served on Senate Banking, Housing and Urban Affairs, and Appropriations coms., and on the Senate Special Com. on aging. *The Challenge of Change,* 1966.

BROWDER, EARL RUSSELL, May 20, 1891 (Wichita, Kan.)–June 27, 1973. U.S. political leader. Led the U.S. Communist party from 1921 to 1946, when he was ousted, then expelled, for being a "right deviationist"; imprisoned for refusing the draft, 1919–20; U.S. Communist party candidate for U.S. pres., 1936 and 1940.

BROWN, EDMUND GERALD ("Pat"), Apr. 21, 1905 (San Francisco, Calif.). U.S. politician, lawyer. California atty. gen. (D), 1950–58; gov. (D) of California, 1958–66; chm. of National Commission for the Reform of Federal Criminal Codes and of the California Council on the Environment and Economic Balance. (Father of EDMUND G. BROWN, JR.)

BROWN, EDMUND G., JR. ("Jerry"), Apr. 7, 1938 (San Francisco, Calif.). U.S. politician, lawyer. Member of Los Angeles Co. Crime Commission, 1969–70; California secy. of state (D), 1971–75; Gov. (D) of California, 1975– . (Son of EDMUND G. BROWN.)

BROWN, HAROLD, Sept. 19, 1927 (New York, N.Y.). U.S. government official, physicist. Pres. of California Inst. of Technology, 1969–77; U.S. delegate to SALT talks, 1969; U.S. secy. of def., 1977– .

BRUCE, DAVID K. E., Feb. 12, 1898 (Baltimore, Md.)–Dec. 4, 1977. U.S. diplomat. U.S. amb. to France (1949–52), West Germany (1957–59), Great Britain (1961–69); headed U.S. delegation to Paris peace talks on Vietnam, 1970–71; head of U.S. liaison office in Peking, 1973–74; U.S. amb. to NATO, 1974–76.

BRYAN, WILLIAM JENNINGS, Mar. 19, 1860 (Salem, Ill.)–July 26, 1925. U.S. politician, orator, lawyer, editor. Political leader of the agrarian and silver forces in the late 19th cent. Won Democratic presidential nomination with his famous "Cross of Gold" speech, 1896 (also received 1900 and 1908 Democratic presidential nominations); established and edited *Commoner,* a weekly political journal, 1900; editor of *Omaha World-Herald,* 1894–96; as U.S. secy. of state, advocated arbitration to prevent war, 1912–15; took part in the prosecution at the Scopes trial, 1925.

BRZEZINSKI, ZBIGNIEW, Mar. 28, 1928 (Warsaw, Pol.). U.S. gov. official, political scientist. Prof. and dir. of research at Inst. for International

Change of Columbia U., 1960–77; dir. of Trilateral Com., 1973–77; asst. to the U.S. pres. for national security affairs, 1977– . *Soviet Bloc: Unity and Conflict,* 1960; *Fragile Blossom: Crisis and Change in Japan,* 1972.

BUCHANAN, JAMES, Apr. 23, 1791 (Cove Gap, Pa.)–June 1, 1868. U.S. pres., lawyer. U.S. sen. (D, Pa.), 1834–45; U.S. secy. of state, 1845–49; U.S. min. to Great Britain, 1853–56; as 15th U.S. pres. (D, 1857–61), attempted to find a compromise in the conflict between the North and the South, but failed to prevent civil war.

BULLITT, WILLIAM CHRISTIAN, Jan. 25, 1891 (Philadelphia, Pa.)–Feb. 15, 1967. U.S. diplomat. As member of the U.S. delegation to the peace talks at the end of WW I, unsuccessfully recommended recognition of the USSR; first U.S. amb. to the USSR, 1933–36; U.S. amb. to France, 1936–42. *It's Not Done,* 1926; *The Great Globe Itself,* 1946.

BUMPERS, DALE, Aug. 12, 1925 (Charleston, Ark.). U.S. politician, lawyer. Gov. (D) of Arkansas, 1971–75; U.S. sen. (D, Ark.), 1975– .

BUNCHE, RALPH, Aug. 7, 1904 (Detroit, Mich.)–Dec. 9, 1971. U.S. diplomat, educator. After teaching political science at Howard U. (from 1928), entered UN as director of the Trusteeship Council, 1946; became principal secy. of UN Palestine Com., 1947; awarded 1950 Nobel Peace Prize for mediating Palestine conflict of 1948–49; U.S. undersecy. for special political affairs, 1958–70; UN special rep. to the Congo, 1960.

BUNDY, WILLIAM PUTNAM, Sept. 24, 1917 (Washington, DC). U.S. gov. official, lawyer. U.S. asst. secy of def. for internal security affairs, 1961–63; U.S. asst. secy. of state for East Asian and Pacific affairs, 1964–69; visiting prof. at M.I.T., 1969–71; editor of *Foreign Affairs,* 1972– .

BUNKER, ELLSWORTH, May 11, 1894 (Yonkers, N.Y.). U.S. diplomat, businessman. Dir. of National Sugar Refining Co., 1927–40; U.S. amb. to India (1956–61), Org. of American States, (1964–66), South Vietnam (1967–73); U.S. amb.-at-large, 1966 and 1973–77.

BURGER, WARREN EARL, Sept. 17, 1907 (St. Paul, Minn.). U.S. jurist, lawyer. Justice of U.S. Ct. of Appeals for the Dist. of Columbia, 1955–69; chief justice of U.S. 1969– ; considered a strict constructionist in criminal law matters.

BURNS, ARTHUR F., Apr. 27, 1904 (Stanislau, Austria). U.S. gov. official, economist. Prof. of economics at Columbia U., 1941–69; pres. of National Bureau of Economic Research, 1957–67; counselor to the U.S. pres., 1969–70; chm. of the board of governors of the Federal Reserve System, 1970–78.

BURR, AARON, Feb. 6, 1756 (Newark, N.J.)–Sept. 14, 1836. U.S. politician. U.S. sen. (D, N.Y.), 1791–97; in 1800 election, lost U.S. presidency to THOMAS JEFFERSON on 36th ballot; U.S. vicepres., 1801–05; after losing 1804 race for New York gov., held ALEXANDER HAMILTON responsible, challenged him to a duel, and killed him, 1804; conspired with Gen. JAMES WILKINSON to invade Mexico and set up an independent gov.; arrested, tried for treason, acquitted, 1807.

BURTON, HAROLD H., June 22, 1888 (Jamaica Plain, Mass.)–Oct. 28, 1964. U.S. jurist, lawyer. Reform mayor of Cleveland, Ohio, 1935–40; U.S. sen. (R, Ohio), 1941–45; as assoc. justice, U.S. Sup. Ct. (1945–58), known as an advocate of judicial restraint, and voted to uphold noncommunist-oath requirement of the Taft-Hartley Act.

BURTON, PHILLIP, June 1, 1926 (Cincinnati, Ohio). U.S. politician, lawyer. U.S. rep. (D, Calif.), 1964-   ; member of House Interior and Insular Affairs, Education, and Labor coms.

BUSH, GEORGE HERBERT WALKER, June 12,1924 (Milton, Mass.). U.S. politician, diplomat. U.S. rep. (R, Tex.), 1966-70; U.S. amb. to the UN, 1971-73; chm. of Republican National Com., 1973-74; chief of U.S. Liaison Office, Peoples' Republic of China, 1974-75; dir. of CIA, 1976-77; chm., of exec. com. of the First International Bank of Houston, Tex. 1977-   ; candidate for 1980 Republican presidential nomination.

BYRD, HARRY FLOOD, Dec. 20, 1914 (Winchester, Va.). U.S. politician. Pres. and editor of Winchester (Va.) *Evening Star,* 1935-   ; U.S. sen. (Ind, Va.), 1965-   ; second person in the hisory of the Senate to be elected as an independent; reelected for third term with largest vote ever given to any Virginia candidate, 1976.

BYRD, ROBERT CARLYLE, born Cornelius Calvin Sale, Nov. 20, 1917 (North Wilkesboro, N.C.). U.S. politician, lawyer. Widely considered one of the most influential political leaders in the U.S.; U.S. rep. (D, W.Va.), 1952-58; U.S. sen. (D, W.Va.), 1958-   ; Senate majority whip, 1971-76; Senate majority leader, 1977-

BYRNES, JAMES FRANCIS, May 2, 1879 (Charleston, S.C.)-Apr. 9, 1972. U.S. politician, lawyer, editor. U.S. sen. (D, S.C.), 1931-41; assoc. justice of U.S. Sup. Ct., 1941-42; during WW II, served as dir. of economic stabilization (1942) and dir. of war mobilization (1943); secy. of state, 1945-47; gov. (D) of South Carolina, 1951-55.

CALHOUN, JOHN CALDWELL, Mar. 16, 1782 (Abbeville Dist., S.C.)-Mar. 31, 1850. U.S. politician, lawyer, political philosopher. A leading Southern politician who championed states' rights, opposed the prohibition of slavery in newly admitted states, defended the interest of the Southern aristocracy, and promoted Southern unity. U.S.rep. (D, S.C.), 1811-17; U.S. secy. of war, 1817-25; U.S. vice-pres. (D), 1824-32; U.S. sen. (D, S.C.), 1833-44, 1845-50.

CALIFANO, JOSEPH ANTHONY, JR., May 15, 1931 (Brooklyn, N.Y.). U.S. govt. official, lawyer. Special asst. to Pres. LYNDON JOHNSON, 1965-69; U.S. secy of HEW, 1977-79. *The Student Revolution,* 1969; *A Presidential Nation,* 1975; *The Media and the Law* (with Howard Simons), 1976.

CANNON, CLARENCE, Apr. 11, 1879 (Elsberry, Mo.)-May 12, 1964. U.S. politician, lawyer, history prof. U.S. rep. (D, Mo.), 1922-64; chm. of powerful House Appropriations Com., 1941-47, 1949-53, 1955-64; a noted parliamentarian.

CANNON, JOSEPH GURNEY ("Uncle Joe"), May 7, 1836 (New Garden, N.C.)-Nov. 12, 1926. U.S. politician, lawyer. U.S. rep., (R, Ill.), 1873-91, 1893-1913, 1915-23; through his chairmanship of the House Rules Com. and then as Speaker of the House (1903-11), ruled that body despotically; noted leader of reactionary Republicans.

CARAWAY, HATTIE WYATT, Feb. 1, 1878 (Bakerville, Tenn.)-Dec. 21, 1950. U.S. politician, teacher. The first woman elected to the U.S. Senate (D, Ark.) and twice reelected, 1932-45; supported Prohibition, antilobbying bills, equal rights for women, and most New Deal legislation.

CARDOZO, BENJAMIN NATHAN, May 24, 1870 (New York, N.Y.)-July 9, 1938. U.S. jurist, lawyer. Judge of the New York Ct. of Appeals, 1914-32; as

assoc. justice of U.S. Sup. Ct. (1932-38), a foremost spokesman for sociological jurisprudence, concerned with the relationship between law and social change; influenced the U.S. appellate toward more involvement in public issues.

CAREY, HUGH LEO, Apr. 11, 1919 (Brooklyn, N.Y.). U.S. politician, lawyer. As U.S. rep. (D, N.Y.; 1960-75), and gov. (D) of New York (1975-   ), has worked to solve the financial difficulties of New York City; holder of Bronze Star and Croix de Guerre with Silver Star war decorations.

CARR, WILBUR JOHN, Oct. 31, 1870 (Hillsboro, Ohio)-June 26, 1942. U.S. diplomat. Called the "Father of the U.S. Foreign Service," in recognition of his role in making it an honorable career based on merit, not political patronage; U.S. asst. secy. of state, 1924-37; U.S. min. to Czechoslovakia, 1937-39.

CARROLL (of Carrollton), **CHARLES,** Sept. 20, 1737 (Annapolis, Md.)-Nov. 14, 1832. American Revolutionary leader. Helped draft Maryland constitution, 1776; U.S. sen. (Fed, Md.), 1789-92; the only Roman Catholic signer of the Declaration of Independence and the last signer to die.

CARTER, JIMMY, born James Earl Carter, Oct. 1, 1924 (Plains, Ga.). U.S. president, peanut farmer, nuclear engineer. Georgia state sen. (D), 1962-66; gov. (D) of Georgia, 1971-74; 39th pres. (D, 1977-   ), the first pres. elected from the deep South since before the Civil War; as pres., initiated a human-rights campaign in foreign policy; negotiated treaty to end U.S. sovereignty over the Panama Canal Zone by the year 2000; led negotiations on Egyptian-Israeli conflict, leading to a major breakthrough, 1978.

CELLER, EMANUEL, May 6, 1888 (Brooklyn, N.Y.). U.S. politician, lawyer. U.S. rep. (D, N.Y.), 1922-72; noted for his support of the New Deal and opposition to Sen. JOSEPH MCCARTHY; served as chairman or ranking party leader on the House Judiciary Com., 1949-72; coauthored Celler-Kefauver Anti-Merger Act of 1950, and numerous civil rights bills.

CHASE, SALMON PORTLAND, Jan. 13, 1808 (Cornish Township, N.H.)-May 7, 1873. U.S. jurist, lawyer, teacher. A determined foe of slavery; active in the Free Soil movement, elected sen. (FS-D, Ohio; 1849-55) and gov. of Ohio (1855-59); as U.S. treas. secy. (1861-64), originated national banking system, 1863; as chief justice of U.S. Sup. Ct. (1864-73), presided over the trial of Pres. ANDREW JOHNSON.

CHASE, SAMUEL, Apr. 17, 1741 (Princess Anne, Md.)-June 19, 1811. U.S. jurist, lawyer. Signer of the Declaration of Independence, 1776; assoc. justice of U.S. Sup. Ct., 1796-1811; his acquittal in an impeachment trial increased the independence of the judiciary, 1805.

CHISHOLM, SHIRLEY, Nov. 30, 1924 (Brooklyn, N.Y.). U.S. politician, nursery-school teacher. New York st. assemblywoman (D), 1964-68; U.S. rep. (D, N.Y.), 1968-   ; candidate for the presidency, 1972. *Unbossed and Unbought,* 1970; *The Good Fight,* 1973.

CHURCH, FRANK, July 25, 1924 (Boise, Idaho). U.S. politician, lawyer. U.S. sen. (D, Ida.), 1956-   ; chm. of Senate Intelligence and Aging coms.; ranking member Senate Foreign Relations Com. and Energy and Natural Resources Com.

CLARK, CHAMP, born James Beauchamp Clark, Mar. 7, 1850 (nr. Lawrenceburg, Ky.)-Mar. 3, 1921. U.S. politician. As U.S. rep. (D, Mo.; 1893-

THE BOOK OF WHO

95 and 1897-1921), became Democratic leader (1907), organized successful fight (1910) against House Speaker JOSEPH CANNON and his arbitrary control of legislative procedure, and served as House Speaker (1911-19).

CLARK, THOMAS CAMPBELL, Sept. 23, 1899 (Dallas, Tex.)-June 13, 1977. U.S. jurist. As assoc. justice of U.S. Sup. Ct. (1949-67), wrote opinion upholding constitutionality of the 1964 Civil Rights Act stipulation requiring desegregation of public accommodations; often upheld the government position in antitrust, internal security, and criminal procedure cases; U.S. Atty. Gen., 1945-49. (Father of RAMSEY CLARK.)

CLARK, (William) RAMSEY, Dec. 18, 1927 (Dallas, Tex.). U.S. lawyer, government official. A strong supporter of civil rights and opponent of the death penalty. Asst. atty. gen., U.S. Justice Dept., 1961-65; U.S. dep. atty. gen. 1965-67; as U.S. atty. gen. (1967-69), refused to use wiretaps except in cases of national security. *Crime in America*, 1970. (Son of THOMAS CLARK.)

CLAY, HENRY, Apr. 22, 1777 (Hanover Co., Va.)-June 29, 1852. U.S politician, lawyer. Influential political figure of the pre-Civil War decades, called the "Great Pacificator" for his role as drafter of the Missouri Compromise (1820); advocated economic expansion, laid the foundations for Pan-Americanism; made significant contribution in attempt to avoid civil war, in the Compromise of1850; U.S. sen. (Ky.), 1806-07, 1810-11, 1831-42, and 1849-52; U.S. rep. (Ky.). 1811-14, 1815-21, 1823-25; speaker (same years, except 1821); U.S. secy. of state, 1825-29; elected to American Hall of Fame, 1900.

CLEVELAND, (Stephen) GROVER. Mar. 18, 1837 (Caldwell, N.J.)-June 24, 1908. U.S. pres., politician. As gov. (D) of New York (1883-84), opposed Tammany Hall; as 22nd and 24th U.S. pres. (D, 1885-89 and 1893-97), attempted to lower the tariff and supported the Civil Service Commission.

CLINTON, DEWITT. Mar. 2, 1769 (Napanock, N.Y.)-Feb. 11, 1828. U.S. political leader, lawyer, historian. Mayor of New York City, 1803-15 (intermittently); gov. of New York, 1817-21, 1825-28; a patron of the arts and supporter of public education; responsible for promoting the idea of an Erie Canal.

CLINTON, GEORGE, July 26, 1739 (Little Britain, N.Y.)-Apr. 2, 1812. U.S. politician, soldier, lawyer. Gov. of New York, 1777-95 and 1800-04; U.S. vice-pres., 1805-12; opposed adoption of the U.S. Constitution as a threat to state power.

COHEN, WILLIAM, Aug. 28, 1940 (Bangor, Me.). U.S. politician, lawyer. U.S. rep. (R, Me.), 1973-77; U.S. sen. (R, Me.), 1979- ; gained national attention during the 1974 impeachment hearings as one of the first Republican members of the House Judiciary committee to call for Pres. R. M. NIXON's ouster.

COLFAX, SCHUYLER, Mar. 23, 1823 (New York, N.Y.)-Jan. 13 1885. U.S. politician, newspaper editor. Editor of St. Joseph Valley (Ind.) *Register*, a Whig paper, 1845-63; U.S. rep. (R, Ind.), 1854-69; U.S. vice-pres. (R) 1869-73; involvement in Credit Mobilier scandal terminated his political career.

COLSON, CHARLES W., Oct. 16, 1931 (Boston, Mass.). U.S lawyer. As special counsel to Pres. R. M. NIXON (1969-73), became involved in the Watergate scandal; assoc. of Fellowship House (Washington, D.C), 1975-

CONKLING, ROSCOE, Oct. 3, 1829 (Albany, N.Y.)-Apr. 18, 1888. U.S. politician. New York

State political boss who controlled federal patronage; U.S. sen. (R, N.Y.) 1867-81; opposed JAMES T. BLAINE for Republican presidential nomination, 1876; resigned Senate seat in protest against policies of Pres. JAMES A. GARFIELD.

CONNALLY, JOHN BOWDEN, Feb. 27, 1917 (Floresville, Tex.). U.S. politician, lawyer. Gov. (D) of Texas, 1963-69; switched to Republican party, 1973; special adviser to pres. R. M. NIXON, 1973; acquitted of bribery charges in effort to raise federal milk price supports, 1975; U.S. secy. of the treas., 1971-72.

COOLIDGE, (John) CALVIN, July 4, 1872 (Plymouth, Vt.)-Jan. 5 1933. U.S pres., lawyer. Gov. (R) of Massachusetts, 1919-20; U.S. vice-pres. (R), 1921-23; succeeded to U.S. presidency upon death of WARREN G. HARDING, 1923; reelected by huge majority, 1924; as 30th pres. (1923-29), twice vetoed farm-relief bills because of their price-fixing features.

COOPER, JOHN SHERMAN, Aug. 23, 1901 (Somerset, Ky.). U.S politician, lawyer. U.S. sen. (D, Ky.), 1946-48, 1952-54, 1956-72; U.S. amb. to India and Nepal (1955-56) and to East Germany (1974-76).

COX, ARCHIBALD, May 17, 1912 (Plainfield, N.J.). U.S. lawyer, professor. Named Watergate special prosecutor, then fired by Pres. R. M. NIXON when he rejected an admin. compromise on the disputed Watergate tapes (Oct. 20, 1973). Prof. at Harvard Law School, 1946- ; U.S. solicitor gen., 1961-65. *The Warren Court*, 1968; *Role of the Supreme Court in American Government,* 1976.

CRANSTON, ALAN MACGREGOR, June 19, 1914 (Palo Alto, Calif.). U.S. politician. U.S. sen. (D, Calif.) 1969- ; member of Senate Budget Com. and Nutrition and Human Needs Com.; chm. of Democratic Credentials Com.

CRITTENDEN, JOHN JORDAN, Sept. 10, 1787 (nr. Versailles, Ky.)-July 26, 1863. U.S. politician, lawyer. U.S. sen. (Whig, Ky.), 1817-19, 1835-41, 1842-48, and 1855-61; gov. of Kentucky, 1848-50; noted for Crittenden Compromise on the slavery issue that he proposed in the Senate prior to the Civil War.

CURTIS, BENJAMIN ROBBINS, Nov. 4, 1809 (Watertown, Mass.)-Sept. 15, 1874. U.S. jurist, lawyer. As assoc. justice of the U.S. Sup. Ct. (1851-57), wrote one of the two dissenting opinions in the Dred Scott case (1857); chief counsel to Pres. ANDREW JOHNSON at his impeachment.

CURTIS, CHARLES, Jan. 25, 1860 (N. Topeka, Kan.)-Feb. 8, 1936. U.S. politician, lawyer. U.S. rep. (R, Kan.), 1893-1907; U.S. sen. (R, Kan.), 1907-13 and 1915-29; Republican whip, 1915-24; majority leader, 1924-29; U.S. vice-pres. (R), 1929-33.

DAVIS, JEFFERSON, June 3, 1808 (Fairview, Ky.)-Dec. 6, 1889. U.S. political leader, soldier-farmer. U.S. sen. (D, Miss.), 1847-51 and 1857-61; U.S. secy. of war, 1853-57; pres. of the Confederate States of America, 1861-65; his firm rule as CSA pres. conflicted with the states'-rights sentiment behind the South's secession; disapproved of Gen. ROBERT E. LEE's surrender; imprisoned and indicted for treason, but case dropped. *Rise and Fall of the Confederate Government,* 1881.

DAWES, CHARLES GATES, Aug. 27, 1865 (Marietta, Ohio)-Apr. 23, 1951. U.S. politician, diplomat, financier. Working for the Allied Reparations Commission, developed Dawes Plan to stabilize post-WW I finances; awarded Nobel Peace Prize, 1925; U.S. vice-pres., 1925-29; U.S. amb. to Great Britain, 1929-1932.

DAYTON, JONATHAN, Oct. 16, 1760 (Elizabethtown [now Elizabeth] N.J.)-Oct. 9, 1824. U.S. politician, lawyer, soldier. Del. to Constitutional Convention and youngest signer of the U.S. Constitution; U.S rep. (Fed, N.J.), 1791-99; U.S. sen. (Fed, N.J.), 1799-1805; indicted (1807) for conspiracy with AARON BURR, but never brought to trial.

DEAN, JOHN WESLEY, 3rd, Oct. 15, 1938 (Akron, Ohio). U.S. lawyer. Counsel to Pres. RICHARD M. NIXON, 1971-73; key prosecution witness in the Watergate hearings. *Blind Ambition,* 1976.

DEANE, SILAS, Dec. 24, 1737 (Groton, Conn.)- Sept. 23 1789. U.S. diplomat, lawyer, merchant. The first American diplomat sent abroad, he procured French aid for the Revolutionary cause, 1776; accused of irregularities, investigated (1778), fled into exile (1780); posthumously vindicated by Congress.

DEWEY, THOMAS EDMUND, Mar. 24, 1902 (Owosso, Mich.)-Mar. 16, 1971. U.S. politician, lawyer. "Racket-busting" prosecuting atty. for New York City, 1935-37; dist. atty. of New York Co., 1938-43; gov. (R) of New York, 1943-55; Republican candidate for president, 1944 and 1948.

DICKINSON, JOHN, Nov. 8, 1732 (Talbot Co., Md.)-Feb. 14, 1808. American patriot, lawyer. Conservative patriot of the American Revolutionary era, called the "Penman of the Revolution." Drafted declaration of rights and grievances of the Stamp Act Congress, 1765; voted against the Declaration of Independence, 1776; member of Constitutional Convention, 1787. *Letters from a Farmer in Pennsylvania,* 1767-68.

DIES, MARTIN, Nov. 5, 1901 (Colorado, Tex.)- Nov. 14, 1972. U.S. politician. U.S. rep. (D, Tex.), 1931-45 and 1953-59; first chm. of the House Com. on Un-American Activities, 1938-45; claimed that the New Deal and the Congress of Industrial Organizations were infiltrated by communists. *The Martin Dies Story,* 1963.

DIGGS, CHARLES COLE, JR., Dec. 2, 1922 (Detroit, Mich). U.S. politician, lawyer, mortician. U.S. rep. (D, Mich.), 1954-   ; founder and chm. of Congressional Black Caucus.

DIRKSEN, EVERETT MCKINLEY, Jan. 4, 1896 (Pekin, Ill.)-Sept. 7, 1969. U.S. politician. U.S. sen. (R, Ill.), 1951-69; Senate Republican minority leader, 1959-69; played a critical role in the passage of the 1965 Voting Rights Act and the 1968 Fair Housing Act; noted as an excellent orator.

DOLE, ROBERT J., July 22, 1923 (Russell, Kan.). U.S. politician, lawyer. U.S. sen. (R, Kan.), 1969-   ; chm. of Republican National Com., 1971-73; Republican vice-presidential candidate, 1976.

DOUGLAS, HELEN, née Gahagan, Nov. 25, 1900 (Boonton, N.J.). U.S. politician, actress. U.S. rep. (D, Cal.), 1945-51; ran against RICHARD M. NIXON for California Senate seat and lost, at which time she was called "the most courageous fighter for Liberalism in Congress" by *The New Republic.* (Wife of MELVYN DOUGLAS.)

DOUGLAS, PAUL HOWARD, Mar. 26, 1892 (Salem, Mass.)-Sept. 24, 1976. U.S. politician, educator. Prof. of economics at U. of Chicago, 1925-39; adviser to the National Recovery Administration, 1930s; as U.S. Sen. (D, Ill.), concentrated on labor, banking, and social security legislation 1948-66. *In the Fullness of Time,* 1972.

DOUGLAS, STEPHEN ARNOLD, Apr. 23, 1813 (Brandon, Vt.)-June 3, 1861. U.S. politician, lawyer. U.S. rep. (D, Ill.), 1843-47; U.S. sen. (D, Ill.), 1847-61; advocated popular sovereignty on the issue of slavery in the territories; as chm. of the Senate com. on territories was instrumental in the passage of the Compromise of 1850 and the Kansas-Nebraska Act of 1854; a great orator noted for his debates with ABRAHAM LINCOLN during 1858 Senate campaign; defeated by Lincoln for the presidency, 1860.

DOUGLAS, WILLIAM ORVILLE, Oct. 16, 1898 (Maine, Minn.)-Jan. 19, 1980. U.S. jurist. As assoc. justice of the U.S. Sup. Ct. (1939-75), advocated a strong interpretation of the Bill of Rights, often voted for a broad exercise of the court's powers; author of many works on business law, outdoor life, and travel, including *Of Men and Mountains* (1950), *Russian Journey* (1956), *A Living Bill of Rights* (1961).

DULLES, ALLEN, Apr. 7, 1893 (Watertown, N.Y.)-Jan. 29, 1969. U.S. govt. official, diplomat, lawyer. Chief of Near Eastern Affairs Div. at U.S. State Dept., 1922-26; chief of Office of Strategic Services in Switzerland and Germany, 1942-45; dir. of CIA, 1953-61. (Brother of JOHN FOSTER DULLES.)

DULLES, JOHN FOSTER, Feb. 25, 1888 (Washington, D.C.)-May 24, 1959. U.S. govt. official, diplomat, lawyer. U.S. del. to the UN Gen. Assembly, 1946-50; U.S. amb.-at-large, 1951; U.S. secy of state, 1953-59; the prime architect of the U.S. policy of containment of communism, he believed in developing military forces to make possible "massive retaliation."(Brother of ALLEN DULLES.)

EAGLETON, THOMAS FRANCIS, Sept. 1929 (St. Louis, Mo.). U.S. politician, lawyer. Atty. gen. (1961-65) and lt. gov. (1965-68) of Missouri (D); U.S. sen. (D, Mo.), 1968-   ; forced to withdraw from Democratic vice-presidential nomination after confirmed reports that he had undergone psychiatric examinations, 1972. *War and Presidential Power: A Chronicle of Congressional Surrender,* 1974.

EASTLAND, JAMES O., Nov. 28, 1904 (Doddsville, Miss.). U.S. politician, lawyer, farmer. U.S. sen. (D, Miss.), 1941-78; pres. pro-tem of the Senate, 1972-78; chm. of Senate Judiciary Com.; member of Senate Agriculture, Nutrition and Forestry Com. and of Democratic Policy Com.

EISENHOWER, DWIGHT DAVID ("Ike"), Oct. 14, 1890 (Denison, Tex.)-Mar. 28, 1969. U.S. pres., soldier. As supreme commander of the Allied Expeditionary Force in Europe during WW II, led the invasion that forced Germany's surrender, 1943-45; U.S. Army chief of staff, 1945-48; pres. of Columbia U., 1948-50; supreme commander of NATO, 1951-52. As 34th U.S. pres. (R, 1953-61), ended the Korean War; sent federal troops to Little Rock, Ark., to force compliance with desegregation orders; suffered difficulties passing domestic legislation; extended aid to S. Vietnam.

EIZENSTAT, STUART E., Jan. 15, 1943 (Chicago, Ill.). U.S. govt. official, lawyer. Aide-de-camp to Georgia Gov. JIMMY CARTER, 1971-74; Pres. Carter's asst. for domestic affairs and policy, 1977-

ELLSBERG, DANIEL, Apr. 7, 1931 (Chicago, Ill.). U.S. govt. official, political activist. Noted for leaking the Pentagon Papers to *The New York Times,* 1971. Staff member at Rand Corp., 1959-64 and 1967-70; member of R. MCNAMARA study group

THE BOOK OF WHO

on the history of U.S. decision-making in Vietnam, 1967-69.

ERLICHMAN, JOHN DANIEL, Mar. 20, 1925 (Tacoma, Wash.). U.S. govt. official, lawyer. As domestic-affairs asst. to Pres. R. M. NIXON (1969-74) and exec. dir. of the Domestic Council, played a major role in the Watergate scandal; convicted (1975), imprisoned (1976), and released (1978). *The Company,* 1976.

ERVIN, SAMUEL JAMES, JR., Sept. 17, 1896 (Morgantown, N.C.). U.S. politician, lawyer. U.S. sen. (D, N.C.), 1954-75; as head of the Senate Select Com. on Presidential Campaign Activities investigating the Watergate scandal, fought Pres. R. M. NIXON's efforts to withhold evidence and testimony on the grounds of executive privilege, 1973-74.

FALL, ALBERT BACON, Nov. 26, 1861 (Frankfort, Ky.)-Nov. 30, 1944. U.S. politician, lawyer, rancher. As U.S. secy. of the int. (1921-23), involved in the Teapot Dome and Elk Hills oil-leasing scandals; convicted (1929) of accepting a $100,000 bribe and jailed (1931-32).

FARLEY, JAMES ALOYSIUS, May 30, 1888 (Grassy Point, NY.)-June 9, 1976. U.S. political leader, businessman. Managed Pres. F. D. ROOSEVELT'S 1932 and 1936 presidential campaigns; chm. of Democratic National Com., 1932-40; U.S. postmaster gen., 1933-40.

FAUBUS, ORVAL, Jan. 7, 1910 (Combs, Ark.). U.S. politician, teacher, editor. Gov. (D) of Arkansas, 1955-67; the only state gov. to serve six times; called out the National Guard to block integration of Little Rock Central High School, 1957.

FERGUSON, MIRIAM ("Ma"), June 13, 1875 (Bell Co., Tex.)-June 25, 1961. U.S. politician. Gov. (D) of Texas, 1925-27 and 1933-35; ran for office to clear the name of her husband, "Farmer" Jim Ferguson, a former gov. convicted of misuse of funds.

FESSENDEN, WILLIAM PITT, Oct. 16, 1806 (Boscarven, N.H.)-Sept. 9, 1869. U.S. politician, lawyer. A Whig politician who played a major role in the founding of the Republican party, 1856; U.S. sen. (Whig-R, Me.), 1854-64 and 1865-69; a great debator, he cast the deciding vote for acquittal of impeached Pres. ANDREW JOHNSON, 1868.

FILLMORE, MILLARD, Jan. 7, 1800 (Locke Township, N.Y.)-Mar. 8, 1874. U.S. pres., lawyer. U.S. vice pres.; 1849-50; upon Pres. Z. TAYLOR'S death became 13th U.S. pres. (Whig, 1850-53); worked for compromise on the slavery issue, but his support of the Fugitive Slave Act of 1850 alienated the North and ruined his political career.

FISH, HAMILTON, Aug. 3, 1808 (New York, N.Y.)-Sept. 6, 1893. U.S. politician, lawyer. As U.S. secy. of state (1869-77), negotiated the Treaty of Washington (1871) with Britain, settling the *Alabama* claims; fought graft in the administration of Pres. U.S. GRANT; opposed intervention on behalf of Cuba against Spain.

FITZGERALD, JOHN ("Honey Fitz"), Feb. 11, 1863 (Boston, Mass.)-Oct. 2, 1950. U.S. newspaper publisher, banker, insurance broker. A power in the Massachusetts Democratic party; U.S. rep. (D, Mass.), 1895-1901; mayor (D) of Boston, 1906, 1907, and 1910-14. (Grandfather of JOHN, ROBERT, and EDWARD KENNEDY.)

FORD, GERALD RUDOLPH J., born Leslie King, Jr., July 14, 1917 (Omaha, Neb.). U.S. pres., politician. U.S. rep. (R, Mich.), 1949-73; appointed vice-pres. by Pres. R. M. NIXON, 1973; became 38th U.S. pres. (R, 1974-76) after Nixon's resignation; attempted to heal the wounds of Watergate by conducting an open administration; in a controversial move, pardoned Nixon, 1974; a fiscal conservative who vetoed many Congressional legislative initiatives.

FORRESTAL, JAMES VINCENT, Feb. 15, 1892 (Beacon, N.Y.)-May 22, 1949. U.S. govt. official. Pres. of Dillon, Read and Co., 1937-40; as undersecy. (1940-43) and secy. (1944-46) of the navy, responsible for meeting the need for the massive deployment of naval power during WW II; first U.S. secy. of def., 1947-49; committed suicide, 1949.

FORTAS, ABE, June 19, 1910 (Memphis, Tenn.). U.S. jurist, lawyer. As assoc. justice of U.S. Sup. Ct., (1965-69), considered a liberal; nominated to be chief justice, but accusations of bribery and political resistance to the nomination forced him to resign from the court, 1969.

FRANKFURTER, FELIX, Nov. 15, 1882 (Vienna, Austria)-Feb. 22, 1965. U.S. jurist. Prof. at Harvard Law School, 1914-39; helped found American Civil Liberties Union, 1920; as assoc. justice of U.S. Sup. Ct. (1939-62), a liberal who advocated judicial restraint; an active U.S. Zionist.

FRANKLIN, BENJAMIN, Jan. 17, 1706 (Boston, Mass.)-Apr. 17, 1790. U.S. statesman, diplomat, inventor, scientist, printer. Published *Poor Richard's Almanack* (1732-57) and the *Pennsylvania Gazette;* helped draft and signed the Declaration of Independence, 1776; min. to France, 1776-85; as a del. to the Federal Constitutional Convention (1787), helped formulate compromise that resulted in the Constitution; proved the existence of electricity in lightning, invented the Franklin stove, bifocal spectacles, and lightning rod.

FULBRIGHT J(ames) WILLIAM, Apr. 9, 1905 (Sumner, Mo.). U.S. politician, lawyer, teacher. As U.S. sen. (D, Ark.), 1945-75; a defender of congressional prerogatives in the conduct of U.S. foreign affairs and an articulate critic of U.S. Vietnam policy; chm. of Senate Foreign Relations Com. (1959-75) and Banking and Currency com. (1955-59); founded the Fulbright scholarship program.

GALLATIN, ALBERT, Jan. 29, 1761 (Geneva, Switz.)-Aug. 12, 1849. U.S. politician, banker, farmer. U.S. secy. of the treasury, 1801-14; played a crucial role in negotiating an end to the War of 1812; U.S. min. to France (1816-23) and Great Britain (1826-27); helped found New York U. and the American Ethnological Soc.

GARFIELD, JAMES ABRAM, Nov. 19, 1831 (nr. Orange, Ohio)-Sept. 9, 1881. U.S. pres., college pres., lay preacher. U.S. rep. (R, Ohio), 1863-80; 20th U.S. pres. (R), Mar. 4-Sept. 19, 1881; shot after only four months in office, he lay ill for 80 days before dying.

GARNER, JOHN NANCE, Nov. 22, 1868 (Red River Co., Tex.)-Nov. 7, 1967. U.S. politician, lawyer. U.S. rep. (D, Tex.) 1903-33; U.S. vice-pres. (D), 1933-41.

GERRY, ELBRIDGE, July 17, 1744 (Marblehead, Mass.)-Nov. 23, 1814. U.S. statesman, exporter/importer. Signer of the Declaration of Independence (1776) and Articles of Confederation (1781); U.S. rep., 1789-93; member of the XYZ diplomatic mission to France; gov. of Massachusetts, 1810-11; U.S. vice-pres., 1812-14; his support of a partisan redistricting bill gave rise to the term *gerrymander.*

GIBSON, KENNETH, May 15, 1932 (Enterprise, Ala.). U.S. politician, engineer. Mayor (D) of Newark, N.J., 1970–

GLASS, CARTER, Jan. 4, 1858 (Lynchburg, Va.)–May 28, 1946. U.S. politician. As U.S. rep. (D, Va.; 1902–19), helped draft Federal Reserve Bank Act of 1913; U.S. treas. secy., 1918–20; as U.S. sen. (D, Va.; 1920–46), was one of the sponsors of the Glass-Steagall Act of 1933, which created the Federal Deposit Insurance Corp.; a determined opponent of most New Deal legislation.

GOLDBERG, ARTHUR JOSEPH, Aug. 8, 1908 (Chicago, Ill.). U.S. govt. official, jurist, lawyer. A prominent labor lawyer who played an important role in the 1955 merger of the CIO and AFL unions and led fight to expel the teamsters from the AFL. U.S. secy. of labor, 1961–62; assoc. justice of U.S. Sup. Ct., 1962–65; U.S. del. to the UN, 1965–68.

GOLDWATER, BARRY MORRIS, Jan. 1, 1909 (Phoenix, Ariz.). U.S. politician. A widely respected conservative Republican leader. U.S. sen. (R, Ariz.), 1952–64 and 1969–   ; as Republican presidential candidate (1964), urged total victory over world communism and a drastic reduction of federal powers. *Conscience of a Conservative,* 1960.

GORE, ALBERT ARNOLD, Dec. 26, 1907 (Granville, Tenn.). U.S. coal-industry exec., politician. U.S. rep. (D, Tenn.), 1939–53; as U.S. sen. (D, Tenn.; 1953–70), principal author of the 1956 Interstate Highways Act; chm. of Creek Coal Co., 1972–

GRANT, ULYSSES SIMPSON, born Hiram Ulysses Grant, Apr. 27, 1822 (Point Pleasant, Ohio)–July 23, 1885. U.S. pres., soldier. As Union Army gen., scored first major Union victory of the Civil War, at Ft. Donelson, Tenn., 1862; as commander of the Army of the Tennessee, conducted a brilliant campaign to capture Vicksburg, 1863; as commander in chief of Union Army (1864–65), he forced and accepted Gen. R. E. LEE's surrender; elected 18th pres. (R, 1869–77), his admin. was characterized by corruption and bitter partisan politics.

GRASSO, ELLA T., May 10, 1919 (Windsor Locks, Conn.). U.S. politician. Connecticut secy. of state (D), 1959–71; U.S. rep. (D, Conn.), 1971–74; gov. (D) of Connecticut, 1975–   ; chairperson of Governors' Commission on the Status of Women.

GRAVEL, MIKE, May 13, 1930 (Springfield, Mass.). U.S. politician. U.S. sen. (D, Alaska), 1969–   ; member of National Transportation Policy Study Commission and Senate Finance, Environment, and Public Works coms. *Citizen Power,* 1972.

GRIFFIN, ROBERT P., Nov. 6, 1923 (Detroit, Mich.). U.S. politician, lawyer. U.S. rep. (R, Mich.), 1957–66; U.S. sen. (R, Mich.), 1966–78; Senate minority whip, 1969–77.

GRIFFITHS, MARTHA, née Wright, ? (Pierre, Mo.). U.S. politician. As U.S. rep. (D, Mich.; 1955–74), devised the strategy that got the Equal Rights Amendment out of com. and through Congress (1972), and was the first woman to serve as a member of both the Joint Economic Com. and the House Ways and Means Com.

GRUENING, ERNEST, Feb. 6, 1887 (New York, N.Y.)–June 26, 1974. U.S. politician, journalist, editor. As gov. (D) of Alaska (1939–53), attempted to develop wisely the state's natural resources; as U.S. sen. (D, Alas.; 1959–69), lobbied for statehood for Alaska.

GUFFEY, JOSEPH FINCH, Dec. 29, 1870 (Guffey's Landing, Pa.)–Mar. 6, 1959. U.S. politician, utilities exec., oil producer. As U.S. sen. (D, Pa.), opposed poll taxes and supported antilynching laws, 1935–47; credited with coining the term "unholy alliance" to describe the alliance of Southern Democrats whose purpose was to defeat New Deal measures.

GWINNETT, BUTTON, c.1735 (Down Hatherley, Eng.)–May 16, 1777. American patriot, planter. Del. to Continental Congress, 1776–77; a signer of the Declaration of Independence, 1776; pres. of the state of Georgia, 1777.

HALDEMAN, H(arry) **R,** Oct. 27, 1926 (Los Angeles, Calif.). U.S. govt. official, advertising exec. Chief of staff of R. M. NIXON's presidential campaign, 1968; asst. to Pres. Nixon, 1969–73; convicted (1975) for his involvement in the Watergate scandal and jailed, 1977–78.

HALLECK, CHARLES A., Aug. 22, 1900 (De Motte, Ind.). U.S. politician. As U.S. rep. (R, Ind.; 1935–68), a leader of the conservative coalition that dominated the House in the 1950s and early 1960s, defeating many J. F. KENNEDY admin. bills; House majority leader, 1947–48 and 1953–54; House minority leader, 1959–68.

HAMILTON, ALEXANDER, Jan. 11, 1755 (Nevis, W.I.)–July 12, 1804. U.S. statesman, lawyer, author. Federalist party leader who coauthored (with JAMES MADISON) the *Federalist* papers. As First secy. of the treas. (1789–95), created the Bank of the United States, 1791; killed by AARON BURR in a duel. Elected to the American Hall of Fame, 1915.

HAMLIN, HANNIBAL, Aug. 27, 1809 (Paris Hill, Me.)–July 4, 1891. U.S. politician, lawyer, farmer. A prominent antislavery advocate who switched from the Democratic to the Republican party over that issue; U.S. sen. (D, Me.), 1848–57; U.S. vice-pres., 1861–65; as U.S. sen. (R, Me.), was a radical reconstructionist, 1869–81.

HANCOCK, JOHN, Jan. 12, 1737 (Quincy, Mass.)–Oct. 8, 1793. American patriot and Revolutionary leader, merchant. Pres. of Continental Congress, 1775–77; the first signer of the Declaration of Independence, 1776; gov. of Massachusetts, 1780–85 and 1787–93.

HANNA, MARCUS ALONZO ("Mark"), Sept. 24, 1837 (New Lisbon [now Lisbon], Ohio)–Feb. 15, 1904. U.S. political leader, businessman, banker. Republican kingmaker who backed WILLIAM MCKINLEY, playing the crucial role in his election to the presidency, 1896; U.S. sen. (R, Ohio), 1897–1904; represented the alliance of big business and politics to further economic policy.

HANSON, JOHN, Apr. 3, 1715 (Mulberry Grove, Md.)–Nov. 15, 1783. U.S. politician, farmer. As first pres. under the Articles of Confederation (1781–82), sometimes considered the first pres. of the U.S.

HARDING, WARREN GAMALIEL, Nov. 2, 1865 (Blooming Grove, Ohio)–Aug. 2, 1923. U.S. president, teacher, newspaperman. U.S. sen. (R, Ohio), 1914–20; as 29th U.S. pres. (R, 1921–23), promised a "return to normalcy"; his administration was plagued by corruption and scandals; died in office.

HARLAN, JOHN MARSHALL, June 1, 1833 (Boyle Co., Ky.)–Oct. 14, 1911. U.S. jurist, lawyer. As assoc. justice of U.S. Sup. Ct. (1877–1911), noted as a great dissenter; supporter of black

THE BOOK OF WHO

rights, which he argued, were guaranteed by the Constitutional amendments passed after the Civil War.

HARRIMAN, W(illiam) AVERELL, Nov. 15, 1891 (New York, N.Y.). U.S. statesman, diplomat, banker. A prominent U.S. diplomat who has served a succession of presidents during his long career. Lend-Lease coordinator, 1941–43; U.S. amb. to USSR (1943–46) and Great Britain (1946); U.S. secy. of commerce, 1946–48; gov. (D) of New York, 1955–58; U.S. amb.-at-large, 1961 and 1965–75; as U.S. undersecy. of state for political affairs, 1963–65, negotiated limited nuclear test ban treaty; conducted Paris peace negotiations with N. Vietnam, 1968–69.

HARRIS, PATRICIA ROBERTS, May 31, 1924 (Mattoon, Ill.). U.S. govt. official, lawyer. Prof. of law at Howard U., 1961–65, 1967–69; U.S. amb. to Luxembourg, 1965–67; U.S. secy. of HUD, 1977–79; U.S. secy. of HEW, 1979–   ; first black woman to reach both ambassadorial and cabinet rank.

HARRISON, BENJAMIN, Aug. 20, 1833 (North Bend, Ohio)–Mar. 13, 1901. U.S. pres., lawyer. U.S. sen. (R, Ind.), 1881–87; as 23rd U.S. pres. (R, 1889–93), oversaw enactment of McKinley Tariff Act (1890) and Sherman Silver Purchase Act (1890). (Grandson of WILLIAM HENRY HARRISON.)

HARRISON, WILLIAM HENRY, Feb. 9, 1773 (Charles City Co., Va.)–Apr. 4, 1841. U.S. pres., soldier. A major gen. in the War of 1812; U.S. sen. (Whig, Ohio), 1825–28; the first to use public relations in a presidential campaign; as 9th U.S. pres. (Whig, 1841), served in office for one month before his death from pneumonia. (Grandfather of BENJAMIN HARRISON.)

HART, PHILIP A., Dec.10, 1912 (Bryn Mawr, Pa.)–Dec. 26, 1976. U.S. politician, lawyer. As U.S. sen. (D, Mich.), 1959–76, worked for civil rights, consumer, and antitrust legislation.

HARTKE, (Rupert) VANCE, May 31, 1919 (Stendal, Ind.). U.S. politician. Mayor (D) of Evansville, Ind., 1956–58; as U.S. sen. (D, Ind.), worked for civil rights and flood-control legislation, 1958–76. *The American Crisis in Vietnam,* 1968; *You and Your Senator,* 1970.

HATCHER, RICHARD G., July 10, 1933 (Michigan City, Ind.). U.S. politician, lawyer. Mayor (D) of Gary, Ind., 1967–   ; co-convenor of National Black Political Convention, 1972; pres. of National Black Political Council, 1973–   .

HATFIELD, MARK O(dom), July 12, 1922 (Dallas, Ore.). U.S. politician, political scientist. Secy. of state (1956–58) and gov. (R) of Oregon, 1959–67; U.S. sen. (R, Ore.), 1967–

HAY, JOHN, Oct. 8, 1838 (Salem, Ind.)–July 1, 1905. U.S. statesman, diplomat, author. Private secy. to ABRAHAM LINCOLN, 1861–65; U.S. amb. to Great Britain, 1897–98; served as U.S. secy. of state (1898-1905) during the critical period when the U.S. emerged as a world power, promoting Open Door policy with China and signing treaties opening the way for the Panama Canal. *Abraham Lincoln: A History,* 1890.

HAYAKAWA, SAMUEL ICHIYE, July 18, 1906 (Vancouver, B.C., Can.). U.S. politician, educator. As Pres. of San Francisco St. C., was noted for his stand against student protesters, 1968–73; U.S. sen. (R, Cal.), 1977–

HAYDEN, CARL TRUMBULL, Oct. 2, 1877 (Hayden's Ferry [now Tempe], Ariz.)–Jan. 25, 1972. U.S. politician who served in the U.S. Con-

gress for 56 years (1912–69), the longest term in the nation's history. U.S. rep. (D, Ariz.), 1912–27; U.S. sen. (D, Ariz.), 1927–69; Senate pres. pro tem, 1957–69; chm. of Senate Appropriations Com., 1957–69.

HAYES, RUTHERFORD BIRCHARD, Oct. 4, 1822 (Delaware, Ohio)–Jan. 17, 1893. U.S. pres., politician. Gov. of Ohio, 1868–72 and 1876–77; as the 19th U.S. pres. (R, 1877–81), ended the Reconstruction period in the South, attempted to establish higher standards of integrity in the government, fought for civil service reform, and sent troops to suppress the railroad strike of 1877.

HELMS, JESSE A., Oct. 18, 1921 (Monroe, N.C.). U.S. politician, newspaper editor. Exec. vice-pres. of WRAL-TV and Tobacco Radio Network, 1960–72; U.S. sen. (R, N.C.), 1972–   ; member of Senate Banking, Housing and Urban Development, and Agriculture and Forestry coms.

HENRY, PATRICK, May 29, 1736 (Studley, Va.)–June 6, 1799. American patriot, lawyer, merchant. Del. to Continental Congress, 1774–76; gov. of Virginia, 1776–79 and 1784–86; great orator of the American Revolution, whose stirring call to arms against the British brought many to the cause; a radical leader who argued against the Stamp Act, advocated individual liberties, opposed to Federal Constitution because he feared it infringed upon states' rights; remembered for his words, ". . . give me liberty or give me death."

HERTER, CHRISTIAN ARCHIBALD, Mar. 28, 1895 (Paris, Fr.)–Dec. 30, 1966. U.S. diplomat, journalist. Gov. (D) of Massachusetts, 1953–57; as U.S. secy. of state (1959–61), backed a firm defense of Berlin and stronger U.S.-European ties; chief U.S. trade negotiator in the J. F. KENNEDY and L. B. JOHNSON admins.

HISS, ALGER, Nov. 11, 1904 (Baltimore, Md.). U.S. public official. The central figure in a sensational spy case, accused by WHITTAKER CHAMBERS of being part of a communist espionage ring in Washington, D.C.; convicted of perjury in 1950, imprisoned for five years, released still claiming his innocence. U.S. State Dept. official, 1936–46; pres. of Carnegie Endowment for Peace, 1946–49.

HOBBY, OVETA CULP, Jan. 19, 1905 (Killeen, Tex.). U.S. govt. official, newspaper publisher. Participated in planning Women's Army Corps, becoming its first dir., 1942; awarded Distinguished Service Medal for her work with WAC; first U.S. secy. of HEW, 1953–55; pres. and editor (1955–   ) and chm. of the board (1965–   ) of the Houston *Post.*

HOLMES, OLIVER WENDELL, JR., Mar. 8, 1841 (Boston, Mass.)–Mar. 6, 1935. U.S. jurist. An assoc. justice of U.S. Sup. Ct. (1902–35), known as the "Great Dissenter"; developed the "clear and present danger" rule of the First Amendment, believed in "judicial restraint," proposed new conceptions of the origin of the nature of law. Elected to American Hall of Fame, 1965. (Son of poet OLIVER WENDELL HOLMES.)

HOLTZMAN, ELIZABETH, Aug. 11, 1941 (Brooklyn, N.Y.). U.S. politician, lawyer. U.S. rep. (D, N.Y.), 1973–   ; member of the House Judiciary Com. who gained national attention during the 1974 Nixon impeachment hearings.

HOOVER, HERBERT CLARK, Aug. 10, 1874 (West Branch, Ia.)–Oct. 20, 1964. U.S. pres., engineer. Head of allied relief operations during WW I; U.S. secy. of commerce, 1921–29; participated in famine relief work in Europe after WW II; as 31st

142

RULERS, STATESMEN, AND POLITICAL LEADERS

U.S. pres. (R, 1929-33), led the U.S. through the early years of the Depression, worked through the Federal Farm Bureau and the Reconstruction Finance Corp. to aid the suffering; defeated for reelection, 1932.

HOOVER, J(ohn) EDGAR, Jan. 1, 1895 (Washington, D.C.)-May 1, 1972. U.S. govt. official, lawyer, criminologist. As dir. of the FBI (1924-72), established a fingerprint file, a scientific crime-detection laboratory, and the FBI National Acad.; contributed greatly to higher standards of police work; freed the FBI from political control; became known for his anticommunist views; criticized toward the end of his career for his authoritarianism and overzealousness.

HOPKINS, HARRY L., Aug. 17, 1890 (Sioux City, Ia.)-Jan. 29, 1946. U.S. govt. administrator, social worker. A close friend and adviser to Pres. F. D. ROOSEVELT. Administrator of Federal Emergency Relief, 1933-35; organized Civil Works Admin.; head of Works Progress Admin., 1935-38; U.S. secy. of commerce, 1938-40; Pres. H.S. TRUMAN's representative to Moscow to settle the Polish question, 1945.

HOPKINS, STEPHEN, Mar. 7, 1707 (Scituate, R.I.)-July 13, 1785. American patriot, farmer, merchant. Signer of the Declaration of Independence, 1776; member of Continental Congress, 1774-80; gov. of Rhode Island, 1755, 1756, 1758-61, 1763, 1764, and 1767. *The Rights of the Colonies Examined,* 1765.

HOPKINSON, FRANCIS, Sept. 21, 1737 (Philadelphia, Pa.)-May 9, 1791. American patriot, lawyer, author. Signer of the Declaration of Independence, 1776; claimed design of the U.S. flag. *Miscellaneous Essays and Occasional Writings,* 1792; *A Pretty Story,* 1774; *The New Roof,* 1787.

HOUSE, EDWARD MANDELL ("Colonel"), July 26, 1858 (Houston, Tex.)-Mar. 28, 1938. U.S. statesman, diplomat. As confidential advisor to Pres. WOODROW WILSON (1913-19), played an important role in peace negotiations at the end of WW I; primarily interested in foreign affairs, he yielded to Allied pressure for harsh measures against Germany following WW I, for which he was dismissed by Wilson.

HOUSTON, SAM(uel), Mar. 2, 1793 (Lexington, Va.)-July 26, 1863. U.S. politician, soldier, lawyer. Leader of the fight with Mexico for control of Texas. A Tennessee politician, he moved to Oklahoma, later Texas; commanded forces of provisional Texas govt. in brilliant victory over SANTA ANA at San Jacinto, 1836; pres. of Rep. of Texas, 1836-38 and 1841-44; after admission of Texas to the Union, served as an antisecessionist Union Democrat U.S. sen. (1846-59) and Texas gov. (1859-61).

HUFSTEDLER, SHIRLEY, Aug. 24, 1925 (Denver, Col.). U.S. jurist. The highest-ranking woman judge in the U.S. Judge of Ct. of Appeals of California, 1966-68; judge of U.S. Ct. of Appeals 1968-79; first U.S. secy. of educ. 1979-

HUGHES, CHARLES EVANS, Apr. 11, 1862 (Glens Falls, N.Y.)-Aug. 27, 1948. U.S. jurist, lawyer. As chief justice of U.S. (1930-41), resisted attempts to "pack" the court with justices favorable to Pres. F. D. ROOSEVELT. Gov. (R) of New York, 1907-10; assoc. justice of U.S. Sup. Ct., 1910-16; Republican presidential nominee, 1916; U.S. secy. of state, 1921-25.

HULL, CORDELL, Oct. 2, 1871 (Byrdstown, Tenn.)-July 23, 1955. U.S. statesman, diplomat, lawyer. As U.S. secy. of state (1933-44), initiated a reciprocal trade program, developed the Good Neighbor policy with Latin America, promoted cooperation with the Soviet Union against Hitler, obtained support in Congress and internationally for starting the UN; awarded Nobel Peace Prize, 1945.

HUMPHREY, HUBERT HORATIO, May 27, 1911 (Wallace, S.D.)-Jan. 13, 1978. U.S. politician, pharmacist. Outstanding liberal and Democratic party leader. Mayor (D) of Minneapolis, 1945-48; as U.S. sen. (D, Minn.; 1949-65 and 1971-78), helped achieve bipartisan support for the Nuclear Test Ban Treaty (1963) and the Civil Rights Act (1964); as U.S. vice-pres. (1965-69), defended U.S. Vietnam policy; Democratic presidential candidate, 1968.

HUNT, E(verette) HOWARD, JR., Oct. 9, 1918 (Hamburg, N.Y.). U.S. govt. official. A 21-year veteran of the CIA, was serving as a consultant to CHARLES W. COLSON when he was caught during the Watergate break-in, 1972; pleaded guilty to all charges, 1973; author of 42 short stories and spy novels under several pseudonyms.

HUTCHINSON, THOMAS, Sept. 9, 1711 (Boston, Mass.)-June 3, 1780. Colonial American administrator. As colonial gov. of Massachusetts (1771-74), resisted the Boston revolutionaries and helped to inflame them; refused to allow tea-laden ships to leave Boston harbor before the tea was unloaded, precipitating the Boston Tea Party, 1773.

INGALLS, JOHN JAMES, Dec. 29, 1833 (Middletown, Mass.)-Aug. 16, 1900. U.S. politician, lawyer, farmer. U.S. sen. (R, Kan.), 1873-91; well-known orator who "waved the bloody shirt" during the Reconstruction era.

INOUYE, DANIEL KEN, Sept. 7, 1924 (Honolulu, Haw.). U.S. politician, lawyer. U.S. rep. (D. Haw.), 1959-62; U.S. sen. (D. Haw.), 1963- ; Senate asst. majority whip, 1963-76; chm. of Senate Select Com. on Intelligence, 1976-

JACKSON, ANDREW ("Old Hickory"), Mar. 15, 1767 (Waxhaw, S.C.)-June 8, 1845. U.S. pres., soldier, lawyer, planter. As 7th U.S. pres. (D., 1829-37), the first to be elected by a mass base of voters, rewarded the men of his Democratic party with jobs, and fought the Bank of the United States. U.S. rep. (D, Tenn.), 1796-97; U.S. sen. (D, Tenn.), 1797-98; a military hero of the War of 1812 for his victory at New Orleans (1815). Elected to American Hall of Fame, 1910.

JACKSON, HENRY MARTIN, May 31, 1912 (Everett, Wash.). U.S. politician, lawyer. Influential Democratic party leader, authority on national defense, supporter of Israel, conservationist. U.S. sen. (D, Wash.), 1952- ; chm. of Senate Energy and Natural Resources Com.; unsuccessfully sought Democratic presidential nomination in 1972 and 1976.

JACKSON, MAYNARD, Mar. 23, 1938 (Dallas, Tex.). U.S. politician, lawyer. Mayor (D) of Atlanta, 1974- ; member of Democratic National Com.

JACKSON, ROBERT HOUGHWOUT, Feb. 13, 1892 (Spring Creek, Pa.)-Oct. 9, 1954. U.S. jurist, lawyer. As assoc. justice of U.S. Sup. Ct. (1941-54), opposed monopolies, believed in judicial restraint, supported civil liberties; U.S. rep. and chief counsel at the Nuremberg war crimes trials, 1945-46.

JARVIS, HOWARD A., 1902 (Magna, Ut.). U.S. tax reformer. A co-sponsor (with Paul Gann) and vocal supporter of Proposition 13, a California primary-

THE BOOK OF WHO

ballot initiative to cut property taxes 57% (passed in June 1978); exec. dir. of Apartment Assn. of Los Angeles Co. and of the United Org. of Taxpayers.

JAVITS, JACOB KOPPEL, May 18, 1904 (New York, N.Y.). U.S. politician, lawyer. U.S. rep. (R, N.Y.), 1946–54; U.S. sen. (R, N.Y.), 1956– ; member of Senate Select Com. on Small Business, Joint Economic Com., Foreign Relations Com., Govt. Operations Com., and Labor and Public Welfare Com.

JAWORSKI, LEON, Sept. 19, 1905 (Waco, Tex.). U.S. lawyer. Dir. of Office of the Watergate Special Prosecution Force, 1973–74; special counsel to House Com. on Standards for Official Conduct, for its investigation of the Korean lobbying scandal, 1977– ; member, President's Commission on the Causes and Prevention of Violence. *The Right and the Power,* 1976.

JAY, JOHN, Dec. 12, 1745 (New York, N.Y.)–May 17, 1829. U.S. jurist, lawyer, statesman. Pres. of Continental Congress, 1778, 1789; negotiated the Treaty of Paris with Great Britain, 1781; negotiated the Jay Treaty, a controversial commercial treaty, 1794; as first chief justice of U.S., played an important role in formation of the court's procedures, 1789–95.

JEFFERSON, THOMAS, Apr. 13, 1743 (Shadwell, Va.)–July 4, 1826. U.S. pres., lawyer, educator, architect. The principal intellectual force behind the founding of the Rep. of the U.S. Author of the Declaration of Independence, 1776; U.S. secy. of state, 1789–93; as 3rd U.S. pres. (1801–09), negotiated Louisiana Purchase for the U.S. (1803), and kept the U.S. out of the Napoleonic Wars; founded the U. of Virginia, 1819. Elected to American Hall of Fame, 1900.

JOHNSON, ANDREW, Dec. 29, 1808 (Raleigh, N.C.)–July 31, 1875. U.S. pres., tailor. Military gov. of Tennessee, 1862–64; succeeded the assassinated ABRAHAM LINCOLN to become 17th U.S. pres. (D), 1865–69; made enemies by executing a mild Reconstruction program; survived impeachment attempt by Congress, 1868.

JOHNSON, HIRAM WARREN, Sept. 2, 1866 (Sacramento, Calif.)–Aug. 6, 1945. U.S. politician, lawyer. A founder of the Progressive party and an isolationist who voted against U.S. entry into WW I and sponsored the Neutrality Acts of the 1930s. Reform gov. of California, 1911–17; U.S. sen. (R, Calif.), 1917–45.

JOHNSON, LYNDON BAINES, Aug. 27, 1908 (Gillespie Co., Tex.)–Jan. 22, 1973. U.S. president, teacher. A protégé of Rep. SAM RAYBURN; as U.S. sen. (D, Tex.), was a highly successful majority leader, 1954–61; succeeded the assassinated Pres. JOHN F. KENNEDY to become 36th U.S. pres., 1963–69; as pres., exercised his political skill in passing legislation, especially in areas of civil rights, tax reduction, antipoverty programs, and conservation; escalated U.S. involvement in South Vietnam; anti–Vietnam War sentiment caused him to decide not to seek renomination in 1968.

JORDAN, BARBARA, Feb. 21, 1936 (Houston, Tex.). U.S. politician, lawyer. As Texas state sen. (D, 1967–72), the first black woman to serve in the Texas leg. in the 20th cent.; U.S. rep. (D, Tex.), 1972–78; as a member of House Judiciary Comm. during 1974 Nixon impeachment hearings, supported Pres. R. M. NIXON's impeachment; as keynote speaker, ignited the 1976 Democratic National Convention.

JORDAN, HAMILTON, Sept. 21, 1944 (Charlotte,

N.C.). U.S. govt. official. Campaign manager during JIMMY CARTER's race for Georgia gov., 1970; exec. secy. to Gov. Carter, 1970–74; asst. to Pres. Carter 1977–79; chief of staff, 1979– .

KEFAUVER, (Carey) ESTES, July 26, 1903 (Monroe Co., Tenn.)–Aug. 10, 1963. U.S. politician, lawyer. U.S. rep. (D, Tenn., 1939–49); U.S. sen. (D, Tenn.), 1949–63; attracted nationwide attention as chm. of Senate com. investigating organized crime, 1950–52; Democratic party nominee for vice-pres., 1956.

KELLEY, CLARENCE M., Oct. 24, 1911 (Kansas City, Mo.). U.S. govt. official. Chief of police in Kansas City, Mo., 1961–73; dir. of FBI, 1973–78.

KELLOGG, FRANK BILLINGS, Dec. 22, 1857 (Potsdam, N.Y.)–Dec. 21, 1937. U.S. politician, diplomat, lawyer. Originally a trustbusting lawyer who helped break up the Standard Oil Co.; U.S. sen. (R, Minn.), 1917–23; U.S. amb. to Great Britain, 1923–25; as U.S. secy. of state (1925–29), negotiated the antiwar Kellogg-Briand Pact (1928); awarded Nobel Peace Prize, 1929.

KENNAN, GEORGE FROST, Feb. 16, 1904 (Milwaukee, Wisc.). U.S. diplomat, historian. Influential in forming the U.S. policy of "containment" of the Soviet Union following WW II; prof. at Inst. for Advanced Study, 1963–74. Awarded 1957 Pulitzer Prize in history for *Russia Leaves the War* (1956) and 1968 Pulitzer Prize in biography for *Memoirs 1925–50* (1967).

KENNEDY, EDWARD MOORE ("Ted"), Feb. 22, 1932 (Brookline, Mass.). U.S. politician, lawyer. As U.S. sen. (D, Mass.), has worked for national health insurance and tax reduction, 1962– ; Senate asst. majority leader, 1968–71. His political future was temporarily blighted when he left the scene of an accident on Chappaquiddick I., 1969. (Brother of JOHN F. and ROBERT F. KENNEDY.)

KENNEDY, JOHN FITZGERALD, May 29, 1917 (Brookline, Mass.)–Nov. 22, 1963. U.S. pres., politician. WW II hero; U.S. rep. (D, Mass.), 1947–53; U.S. sen. (D, Mass.), 1953–60; as 35th U.S. pres. (D, 1961–63), the first Roman Catholic to hold the office; took responsibility for the Bay of Pigs Invasion of Cuba, 1961; started the Alliance for Progress with Latin America and the Peace Corps, 1961; forced the USSR to remove missiles from Cuba, 1962; negotiated a limited test-ban treaty, 1963; assassinated in Dallas, Tex. Awarded 1957 Pulitzer Prize in history for *Profiles in Courage* (1956). (Brother of ROBERT F. and EDWARD M. KENNEDY.)

KENNEDY, ROBERT FRANCIS, Nov. 20, 1925 (Brookline, Mass.)–June 6, 1968. U.S. politician, lawyer. As U.S. atty. gen. (1961–64), aggressive fighter for civil rights and a leading adviser to brother Pres. JOHN F. KENNEDY; U.S. sen. (D, N.Y.), 1965–68; assassinated in the midst of his campaign for the 1968 Democratic presidential nomination. (Brother of EDWARD M. KENNEDY.)

KERR, ROBERT SAMUEL, Sept. 11, 1896 (Ada, Okla.)–Jan. 1, 1963. U.S. politician, oilman. Gov. (D) of Oklahoma, 1943–47; as U.S. Sen. (D, Okla.), 1949–63, a powerful defendant of the domestic oil business and influential in securing passage of much of Pres. JOHN F. KENNEDY's legislation.

KING, RUFUS, Mar. 24, 1755 (Scarborough, Me.)–Apr. 27, 1827. U.S. politician, diplomat, lawyer. Eloquent U.S. sen. (Fed, N.Y., 1789–96 and 1813–25) who argued for a strong central govt. at the 1787 Constitutional Convention; U.S.

min. to Great Britain, 1796–1803 and 1825–26; unsuccessful Federalist candidate for vice-pres. in 1804 and 1808, and for pres. in 1816.

KISSINGER, HENRY, May 27, 1923 (Furth, Ger.). U.S. govt. official, scholar. As adviser for national security affairs (1969–75) and U.S. secy. of state (1973–77), heavily influenced U.S. foreign policy, particularly in the negotiations that ended the U.S. role in Vietnam. Prof. of govt. at Harvard U., 1962–69; initiated the SALT talks, 1969; attempted to negotiate an Arab-Israeli peace agreement, 1973–75; awarded (with LE DUC THO) Nobel Peace Prize, 1973. *Nuclear Weapons and Foreign Policy,* 1957.

KNOWLAND, WILLIAM FIFE, June 26, 1908 (Alameda, Calif.)–Feb. 23, 1974. U.S. politician, publisher. U.S. sen. (R, Calif.), 1945–58; Senate minority leader (1955–58) and majority leader (1953–54); publisher of the Oakland *Tribune,* 1965–74.

KNOX, PHILANDER CHASE, May 6, 1853 (Brownsville, Pa.)–Oct. 12, 1921. U.S. politician, lawyer. U.S. atty gen., 1901–04; U.S. sen. (R, Pa.), 1904–09 and 1917–21. As U.S. secy. of state (1909–13), extended the Monroe Doctrine to include Asian Nations and started "dollar diplomacy."

KOCH, EDWARD IRVING, Dec. 12, 1924 (New York, N.Y.). U.S. politician, lawyer. U.S. rep. (D, N.Y.), 1969–76; mayor (D) of New York City 1977–   .

LA FOLLETTE, PHILIP F., May 8, 1897 (Madison, Wisc.)–Aug. 18, 1965. U.S. politician, lawyer. As gov. (Prog.) of Wisconsin (1931–33 and 1935–39), passed the nation's first unemployment legislation. (Son of R. M. LA FOLLETTE; brother of R. M. LA FOLLETTE, JR.)

LA FOLLETTE, ROBERT MARION, June 14, 1855 (Primrose, Wisc.)–June 18, 1925. U.S. politician, lawyer. Leader of the U.S. Progressive movement, championed the little guy against established interests. U.S. rep. (R, Wisc.), 1885–91; reform gov. (R) of Wisconsin, 1900–06; U.S. sen. (R-Prog., Wisc.), 1907–25; founded *La Follette's Weekly* (later called *The Progressive*), 1909; Progressive party presidential candidate, 1924. (Father of PHILIP F. LA FOLLETTE and ROBERT MARION LA FOLLETTE, JR.)

LA FOLLETTE, ROBERT MARION, JR., Feb. 6, 1895 (Madison, Wisc.)–Feb. 24, 1953. U.S. politician, publishing and broadcasting executive. Like his father, ROBERT LA FOLLETTE, an independent Progressive Republican, elected to succeed his father as U.S. sen. (Wisc.), 1925–47; an isolationist and advocate of unemployment legislation; defeated by JOE MCCARTHY. (Brother of PHILIP F. LAFOLLETTE.)

LAGUARDIA, FIORELLO HENRY ("The Little Flower"), Dec. 11, 1882 (New York, N.Y.)–Sept. 20, 1947. U.S. politician. U.S. rep. (R, N.Y.), 1917–19 and 1922–23; as New York City mayor (1933–45), known for his honesty and nonpartisanship; obtained a new charter for the city (1938), promoted building in the city, and improved the efficiency of city govt.

LAIRD, MELVIN ROBERT, Sept. 1, 1922 (Omaha, Neb.). U.S. politician, govt. official. As U.S. secy. of def. (1967–73), reduced the U.S. armed forces by 1 million men, laid plans for an all-volunteer army, and marshaled support for the continuing presence of U.S. armed forces in Vietnam. U.S. rep. (R, Wisc.), 1953–69; domestic affairs counselor to U.S. pres., 1973–74.

LANCE, (Thomas) BERT(ram), June 3, 1931 (Gainesville, Ga.). U.S. banker, govt. official. Pres. (1963–74) and chm. (1974–77) of Calhoun (Ga.) First National Bank; dir. of U.S. Office of Management and the Budget, 1977; forced to resign because of questionable banking practices.

LANDON, ALF(red), Sept. 9, 1887 (Westmiddlesex, Pa.). U.S. politician, oilman. Gov. (R) of Kansas, 1933–37; Republican presidential candidate, 1936.

LANDRIEU, MOON, July 30, 1930 (New Orleans, La.). U.S. politician, lawyer. Mayor (D) of New Orleans, 1970–77; U.S. secy. of HUD, 1979–   .

LAXALT, PAUL, Aug. 2, 1922 (Reno, Nev.). U.S. politician, lawyer. Gov. (R) of Nevada, 1967–71; U.S. sen. (R, Nev.), 1975–   ; chm. of RONALD REAGAN's presidential campaign, 1976.

LEE, FRANCIS LIGHTFOOT, Oct. 14, 1734 (Westmoreland Co., Va.)–Jan. 11, 1797. U.S. political leader. Member, Virginia House of Burgesses, 1758–76; a signer of the Declaration of Independence, 1776; member, second Continental Congress, 1775–79; fought for ratification of the Constitution.

LEE, RICHARD HENRY, Jan. 20, 1732 (Stratford, Va.)–June 19, 1794. American Revolutionary patriot, lawyer. Proposed a resolution for the independence of the colonies that was passed by the Second Continental Congress, July 2, 1776; a signer of the Declaration of Independence, 1776; U.S. sen. (Va.), 1789–92.

LIDDY, G(eorge) GORDON, Nov. 30, 1930 (New York, N.Y.). U.S. lawyer, govt. official. The most flamboyant of the original defendants in the Watergate break-in, 1972; served as counsel for the Com. to Re-elect the President (1971) and its Finance Com. (1971); convicted on six counts for his involvement, 1973; imprisoned, 1973; 20-year sentence commuted by Pres. J. CARTER, released 1977.

LINCOLN, ABRAHAM, Feb. 12, 1809 (Hardin Co. [now Larue Co.] Ky.)–Apr. 15, 1865. U.S. pres., lawyer. As 16th U.S. pres. (1861–65) led the Union during the Civil War, published the Emancipation Proclamation (1863), delivered the famous Gettysburg Address (1863); widely hailed as the savior of the Union, he was assassinated by J. W. BOOTH. U.S. rep. (Whig, Ill.), 1847–49; joined Republican party and chosen to oppose STEPHEN A. DOUGLAS in the 1858 Senate race, which he lost despite his brilliant performance in debates with Douglas.

LINDSAY, JOHN VLIET, Nov. 24, 1921 (New York, N.Y.). U.S. politician, lawyer, author. U.S. rep. (R, N.Y.), 1959–65; as mayor of New York City (1966–74), the first Republican elected to that post in 20 years, he was plagued with labor unrest, increased crime, and rising welfare costs; switched to Democratic party and unsuccessfully campaigned for presidential nomination in 1972. *The Edge,* 1976.

LIPSHUTZ, ROBERT, Dec. 27, 1921 (Atlanta, Ga.). U.S. lawyer. Treas. of JIMMY CARTER Pres. Campaign Com., 1976; counsel to Pres. Carter, 1977–79.

LIVINGSTON, PHILIP, Jan. 15, 1716 (Albany, N.Y.)–June 12, 1778. American patriot, merchant. A signer of the Declaration of Independence, 1776; played a crucial role in organizing New York's boycott of British goods, 1768; represented New York in the first and second Continental Congresses.

LIVINGSTON, ROBERT R., Nov. 27, 1746 (New York, N.Y.)-Feb. 26, 1813. U.S. diplomat, lawyer. Member of the Com. of Five who drafted the Declaration of Independence, 1776; administered the oath of office to Pres. GEORGE WASHINGTON; partner with ROBERT FULTON in building the first steamboat; as U.S. min. to France (1801-1804), helped negotiate the Louisiana Purchase (1803).

LODGE, HENRY CABOT, May 12, 1850 (Boston, Mass.)-Nov. 9, 1924. U.S. politician, historian. As U.S. sen. (R, Mass.), 1893-1924, led the successful Congressional opposition to U.S. participation in the League of Nations following WW I. *Life and Letters of George Cabot,* 1877. (Grandfather of HENRY CABOT LODGE, JR.)

LODGE, HENRY CABOT, JR., July 5, 1902 (Nahant, Mass.). U.S. politician, diplomat. U.S. sen. (R, Mass.), 1937-44 and 1947-53; U.S. del. to the UN, 1953-60; Rep. vice-presidential candidate, 1960; U.S. amb. to S. Vietnam, 1963-64 and 1965-67; Pres. RICHARD M. NIXON's rep. at the Paris Peace Talks on Vietnam, 1969.

LONG, HUEY PIERCE ("The Kingfish"), Aug. 30, 1893 (Winn Parish, La.)-Sept. 10, 1935. U.S. politician, lawyer. Demagogic political leader in Louisiana politics who commanded a nationwide following in the 1930s. As gov. (D) of Louisiana (1928-32) and U.S. sen. (D, La.; 1932-35), fought established interests for benefits for the poor; assassinated. (Father of RUSSELL B. LONG.)

LONG, RUSSELL BILLIU, Nov. 3, 1918 (Shreveport, La.). U.S. politician, lawyer. U.S. sen. (D, La.), 1948- ; asst. Senate majority leader, 1965-68; chm. of Senate Finance Com., 1966- . (Son of HUEY P. LONG.)

LUCE, CLARE BOOTHE, Apr. 10, 1903 (New York, N.Y.). U.S. politician, journalist, diplomat. Assoc. editor of *Vogue,* 1930; assoc. and managing editor of *Vanity Fair,* 1930-34; U.S. rep. (R, Conn.), 1943-47; keynote speaker at 1944 Republican National Convention; U.S. amb. to Italy, 1953-57. *Stuffed Shirts,* 1931; *The Women,* 1936; *Kiss the Boys Goodbye,* 1938. (Wife of HENRY LUCE.)

LUGAR, RICHARD G., Apr. 4, 1932 (Indianapolis, Ind.). U.S. politician, stockfarmer. Mayor (R) of Indianapolis, Ind., 1968-75; U.S. sen. (R, Ind.), 1977- ; member of National Advisory Commission on Criminal Justice Standards and Goals.

MADDOX, LESTER, Sept. 30, 1915 (Atlanta, Ga.). U.S. politician. Gained notoriety by driving blacks from his Picrick restaurant in defiance of federal civil-rights laws and closing the restaurant rather than desegregating it, 1964; although elected gov. (D) of Georgia (1967-71) as an avowed segregationist with Ku Klux Klan support, was unable to stop desegregation; Ga. lt. gov., 1971-75.

MADISON, JAMES, Mar. 16, 1751 (Port Conway, Va.)-June 28, 1836. U.S. pres., political theorist. Influential in the framing of the Constitution; contributed to the *Federalist* papers; sponsored the first ten amendments (Bill of Rights) to the Constitution; U.S. secy. of state, 1801-09; 4th U.S. pres., 1809-17.

MAGNUSON, WARREN G., Apr. 12, 1905 (Moorhead, Minn.). U.S. politician, lawyer. U.S. sen. (D, Wash.), 1944- ; chm. of Senate Appropriations Com.

MAGRUDER, JEB STUART, Nov. 5, 1934 (Staten I., N.Y.). U.S. govt. official. As dep. dir. of the Committee to Re-elect the President (1971-72), was involved in the Watergate scandal; pleaded guilty,

1974; imprisoned, 1974-75. *An American Life,* 1974.

MANSFIELD, MIKE, Mar. 16, 1903 (New York, N.Y.). U.S. politician, diplomat, engineer. U.S. rep. (D, Mont.), 1943-53; U.S. sen. (D, Mont.), 1953-76; asst. Senate majority leader, 1957-61; Senate majority leader, 1961-76; U.S. amb. to Japan, 1977- .

MARCY, WILLIAM LEARNED, Dec. 12, 1786 (Southbridge, Mass.)-July 4, 1857. U.S. politician. Known as the champion of the "spoils system," credited with the remark, "To the victor belong the spoils of the enemy." U.S. sen. (D, N.Y.), 1831-33; gov. (D) of New York, 1833-39; U.S. secy. of war, 1845-49; U.S. secy. of state, 1853-57.

MARSHALL, F. RAY, Aug. 22, 1928 (Oak Grove, La.). U.S. govt. official, economist. Chm. of Dept. of Economics at U. of Texas, 1970-72; dir. of Center for the Study of Human Resources, 1969-77; U.S. secy. of labor, 1977- . *Role of Unions in the American Economy,* 1976.

MARSHALL, JOHN, Sept. 24, 1755 (Germantown, Va.)-July 6, 1835. U.S. jurist. As 4th chief justice of U.S. (1801-35), influential in molding the Court and establishing its function; founder of the U.S. system of Constitutional law and doctrine of judicial review. Special commissioner to France in the XYZ Affair, 1797-98; U.S. secy. of state, 1800-01.

MARSHALL, THOMAS RILEY, Mar. 14, 1854 (N. Manchester, Ind.)-June 1, 1925. Democratic party wit known for the slogan, "What this country needs is a good five-cent cigar." Gov. of Indiana, 1909-13; U.S. vice-pres., 1913-21.

MARSHALL, THURGOOD, July 2, 1908 (Baltimore, Md.). U.S. jurist, lawyer. As assoc. justice of U.S. Sup. Ct. (1967-), the first black to serve on the Court. Chief of the legal staff of NAACP, 1940-61; argued the case of *Brown vs. Board of Education of Topeka* before the U.S. Sup. Ct., 1954; U.S. solicitor gen., 1965-67.

MARTIN, WILLIAM MCCHESNEY, JR., Dec. 17, 1906 (St. Louis, Mo.). U.S. govt. official, financier. The first salaried pres. of the New York Stock Exchange, 1938-41; dir. of Export-Import Bank, 1945-50; asst. secy. of the U.S. treas., 1949-51; as chm. of Federal Reserve Board (1951-70), favored a "hard money" policy and tight control over the money supply.

MCADOO, WILLIAM GIBBS, Oct. 31, 1863 (nr. Marietta, Ga.)-Feb. 1, 1941. U.S. govt. official, lawyer. As U.S. secy. of the treas. (1913-18), successfully floated $18 billion worth of loans to finance WW I allied forces; a founder and chm. of the Federal Reserve Board, 1913. (Son-in-law of WOODROW WILSON.)

MCCARRAN, PATRICK A., Aug. 8, 1876 (Reno, Nev.)-Sept. 28, 1954. U.S. politician, lawyer, farmer. U.S. sen. (D, Nev.), 1932-54; chm. of Senate Judiciary Com., 1943-46 and 1949-53; sponsored a bill for the registration of communists and an alien immigration act that tightened loyalty regulations (1952).

MCCARTHY, EUGENE, Mar. 29, 1916 (Watkins, Minn.). U.S. politician, teacher. U.S. rep. (D, Minn.), 1949-59; U.S. sen. (D, Minn.), 1959-70; ran against Pres. LYNDON JOHNSON for the Democratic nomination in the 1968 state primaries, calling for disengagement from and negotiated peace in Vietnam.

MCCARTHY, JOSEPH RAYMOND, Nov. 14, 1908 (Grand Chute, Wisc.)-May 2, 1957. U.S. politician, lawyer, farmer. As U.S. sen. (R, Wisc.;

1947-57), conducted highly publicized investigations of alleged communists, using his chairmanship of the Senate Permanent Subcom. on Investigations to pursue his witch hunt; censured by the Senate (1954) for contempt and abuse, after which his influence declined.

MCCLELLAN, JOHN LITTLE, Feb. 25, 1896 (Sheridan, Ark.)-Nov. 27, 1977. U.S. politician, lawyer. U.S. rep. (D, Ark.), 1935-38; U.S. sen. (D, Ark.), 1943-77; chm. of Senate Appropriations Com. 1972-77; as chm. of the Senate Select Com. on Improper Activities in the Labor or Management Field (late 1950s), investigated unions, especially the Teamsters.

MCCLOSKEY, PAUL N., JR., ("Pete"), Sept. 29, 1927 (San Bernardino, Calif.). U.S. politician, lawyer. U.S. rep. (R, Calif.), 1967-   ; ran unsuccessfully for the 1972 Republican presidential nomination.

MCCORD, JAMES WALTER, JR., July 26, 1924 (Texas). U.S. govt. official. CIA employee, 1951-71; was working as security coordinator for the R. M. NIXON reelection com. and Republican Natl. Com. when arrested as one of the burglars in the Watergate break-in (1972); convicted, 1973; imprisoned, March-May 1975.

MCCORMACK, JOHN W., Dec. 21, 1891 (Boston, Mass.). U.S. politician, lawyer. U.S. rep. (D, Mass.), 1928-71; House majority leader, 1940-47, 1949-53, and 1955-61; Speaker of the House, 1962-71.

MCGOVERN, GEORGE STANLEY, July 19, 1922 (Avon, S.D.). U.S. politician, historian. Dir. of Food for Peace Program, 1960-62; U.S. rep. (D, S.D.), 1957-60; U.S. sen. (D, S.D.), 1963-   ; as Democratic presidential candidate in 1972, campaigned for an immediate end to the Vietnam War and a broad program of social change.

MCKINLEY, WILLIAM, Jan. 29, 1843 (Niles, Ohio)-Sept. 14, 1901. U.S. pres., politician. As U.S. rep. (R, Ohio; 1877-83 and 1885-91), advocated tariff protectionism and opposed silver; as 25th U.S. pres. (R, 1897-1901), led the U.S. through the Spanish-American War; assassinated by LEON CZOLGOSZ, an anarchist.

MCMAHON, BRIEN, Oct. 6, 1903 (Norwalk, Conn.)-July 28, 1952. U.S. politician, lawyer. As U.S. sen. (D, Conn; 1944-52), played a major role in the formation of U.S. atomic energy policy; an advocate of civilian control of atomic development, sponsored McMahon Act of 1946 that established the AEC; chm. of Joint Congressional Com. on Atomic Energy, 1948-52.

MCNAMARA, ROBERT STRANGE, June 9, 1916 (San Francisco, Calif.). U.S. govt. official, banker, business executive. Exec. of Ford Motor Co., 1946-60; as U.S. secy. of def. (1961-68), caused controversy by applying modern managerial concepts; pres. of International Bank for Reconstruction and Development, 1968-   .

MILLER, G. WILLIAM, Mar. 9, 1925 (Sapulpa, Okla.). U.S. govt. official, lawyer, business exec. Pres. and chm. of the board (1960-74) of Textron, Inc.; chm. of Federal Reserve Board, 1978-79; U.S. secy. of the treasury, 1979-   .

MINUIT (or Minnewit), **PETER,** 1580 (Wesel, Ger.)-June 1638. Dutch administrator in colonial America. Dir.-gen. of colony of New Netherland, 1626-31; purchased Manhattan I. from the Indians for the equivalent of $24; in the service of Sweden, established New Sweden (later Wilmington, Del.), 1638.

MITCHELL, JOHN NEWTON, Sept. 5, 1913 (Detroit, Mich.). U.S. govt. official, lawyer. As U.S. atty. gen. (1968-72), played a major role in the Watergate scandal; directed Pres. R. M. NIXON's Com. for the Reelection of the President, 1972-73; convicted of conspiracy, obstruction of justice, and perjury (1975)—the first member of any cabinet to be imprisoned, 1977-79.

MONDALE, WALTER FREDERICK ("Fritz"), Jan. 5, 1928 (Ceylon, Minn.). U.S. politician, lawyer. U.S. sen. (D, Minn.), 1964-76; U.S. vice-pres. (D, 1977-   .

MONROE, JAMES, Apr. 28, 1758 (Westmoreland Co., Va.)-July 4, 1831. U.S. pres., diplomat. U.S. sen. (Va.), 1790-94; U.S. min. to France, 1794-96; as special envoy to France (1802-03), participated in negotiations for the Louisiana Purchase; U.S. secy. of state, 1811-17; as fifth U.S. pres. (1817-25), established Monroe Doctrine, warning Europe not to interfere in the Western Hemisphere, and approved the Missouri Compromise (1820).

MORGENTHAU, HENRY, JR., May 11, 1891 (New York, N.Y.)-Feb. 6, 1967. U.S. govt. official, farmer, conservationist. Editor of *American Agriculturist,* 1922-33; head of Farm Credit Admin., 1933; as U.S. secy. of the treas. (1934-45), raised and spent the incredibly large amount of money the New Deal and WW II demanded.

MORRIS, GOUVERNEUR, Jan. 31, 1752 (Morrisania [now part of New York City], N.Y.)-Nov. 6, 1816. American Revolutionary patriot, govt. official. One of the authors of New York's first state constitution, 1776; del. to Continental Congress, 1777-78; as U.S. min. of finance (1781-85), devised the decimal coinage plan; U.S. sen. (Fed, N.Y.), 1800-03. *Observations on the American Revolution,* 1779; *Diary of the French Revolution,* 1939 (edited and published by his great-granddaughter).

MORRIS, ROBERT, Jan. 31, 1734 (Liverpool, Eng.)-May 8, 1806. U.S. financier, Revolutionary patriot. A successful shipper to the W. Indies, 1755-1806; del. to Second Continental Congress and a signer of the Declaration of Independence, 1776; purchasing agent for Continental Army troops, 1778-79; a founder of the Bank of Pennsylvania, first U.S. bank, 1780; founded Bank of North America, 1782; colonial supt. of finance, 1781-1784; personally financed a large part of Revolutionary War effort; del. to Constitutional Congress, 1787; first U.S. sen. from Pennsylvania.

MORSE, WAYNE, Oct. 20, 1900 (Madison, Wisc.)-July 22, 1974. U.S. politician, lawyer. Elected to U.S. Senate (Ore.), as a Republican in 1944; refused to support D. D. EISENHOWER for the presidency (1952) and declared himself an independent; formally became a Democrat, serving as such until 1969; noted for his outspokenness; opposed Vietnam War from the outset.

MORTON, ROGERS C. B., Sept. 19, 1914 (Louisville, Ky.)-Apr. 19, 1979. U.S. politician, farmer, businessman. U.S. rep. (R, Md.), 1962-71; chm. of Republican National Com., 1969-71; U.S. secy. of the int. 1971-75; U.S. secy. of commerce, 1975-76. (Brother of THRUSTON B. MORTON.)

MORTON, THRUSTON BALLARD, Aug. 19, 1907 (Louisville, Ky.). U.S. politician, businessman. U.S. rep. (R, Ky.), 1946-52; U.S. asst. secy. of state, 1953-56; U.S. sen. (R, Ky.), 1957-69. (Brother of ROGERS C. B. MORTON.)

MOSES, ROBERT, Dec. 18, 1888 (New Haven, Conn.). U.S. public official. As a New York state official dominated state politics in his time and

147

built many highways, parks, and public works. NYC parks commissioner, 1934-60; chm. of Consolidated Triborough Bridge and New York Tunnel Authority, 1946-48; chm. of Power Authority of the State of New York, 1954-63.

MOYNIHAN, DANIEL PATRICK, Mar. 16, 1927 (Tulsa, Okla.). U.S. politician, professor. Prof. of education and urban politics at Harvard U., 1966-72 and 1975-   ; U.S. amb. to India (1973-74) and the UN (1975-76); U.S. sen. (D, N.Y.), 1977-   . *Beyond the Melting Pot,* 1963; *Maximum Feasible Misunderstanding,* 1969.

MUHLENBERG, FREDERICK AUGUSTUS CONRAD, Jan. 1, 1750 (New Providence [now Trappe], Pa.)-June 4, 1801. U.S. statesman, Lutheran clergyman. Del. to Continental Congress, 1779-80; first Speaker of the House, 1789-97. (Son of H. M. MUHLENBERG)

MURRAY, WILLIAM HENRY ("Alfalfa Bill"), Nov. 21, 1869 (Grayson Co., Tex.)-Oct. 15, 1956. U.S. politician. Played a major role in Oklahoma's achievement of statehood. House Speaker at first session of the Oklahoma leg., 1907; U.S. rep. (D, Okla.), 1913-17; gov. (D) of Oklahoma, 1931-35.

MUSKIE, EDMUND SIXTUS, Mar. 28, 1914 (Rumford, Me.). U.S. politician, lawyer. Gov. (D.) of Maine, 1955-59; U.S. sen. (D, Me.), 1959-   ; chm. of Senate Budget com., 1975-   ; Democratic vice-presidential candidate, 1968; ran unsuccessfully for Democratic presidential nomination, 1972.

NELSON, GAYLORD A., June 4, 1916 (Clear Lake, Wisc.). U.S. politician. Gov. (D) of Wisconsin, 1958-62; U.S. sen. (D, Wisc.), 1962-   ; chm. of Senate Select Com. on Small Business.

NIXON, RICHARD MILHOUS, Jan. 9, 1913 (Yorba Linda, Calif.). U.S. president, lawyer. U.S. rep. (R, Calif.), 1947-50; U.S. sen. (R, Calif.); U.S. vice-pres. (R), 1953-61; as 37th U.S. pres. (1969-74), reopened relations with the People's Republic of China after a 21-year estrangement (1972), attempted wage and price controls (1971-73), ended U.S. involvement in Vietnam (1973); implicated in the Watergate scandal, became the first president to resign office, Aug. 9, 1974.

NORRIS, GEORGE WILLIAM, July 11, 1861 (Sandusky Co., Ohio)-Sept. 3, 1944. U.S. politician, lawyer. As U.S. rep. (R, Neb.; 1903-13), led fight against absolute control of House Speaker JOSEPH CANNON, 1910; as U.S. sen. (R-Ind., Neb.; 1913-42), wrote the 20th Amendment and was influential in passage of bills creating the Tennessee Valley Authority, 1933.

NORTON, ELEANOR HOLMES, June 13, 1937 (Washington, D.C.). U.S. govt. official, lawyer. Asst. legal dir. of ACLU, 1965-70; exec. asst. to mayor of NYC, 1971-74; chm. of Equal Employment Opportunities Commission, 1977-   .

O'BRIEN, LAWRENCE, July 7, 1917 (Springfield, Mass.). U.S. politician. Prominent political adviser and strategist. Key figure in JOHN F. KENNEDY's Senate (1952 and 1958) and presidential (1960) campaigns; U.S. postmaster gen., 1965-68; chm. of Democratic National Com., 1968-72; commissioner of the National Basketball Assn., 1975-   .

OGLETHORPE, JAMES EDWARD, Dec. 22, 1696 (London, Eng.)-July 1, 1785. English founder of the colony of Georgia in America. A member of Parliament interested in prison reforms, he conceived of founding a colony for debtors; received charter for colony in Georgia, 1732;

founded Savannah; repulsed Spanish attack on Georgia, 1742.

O'NEILL, THOMAS P., JR. ("Tip"), Dec. 9, 1912. U.S. politician. U.S. rep. (D, Mass.), 1952-   ; House majority leader, 1972-76; Speaker of the House, 1976-   .

OTIS, JAMES, Feb. 5, 1725 (W. Barnstable, Mass.)-May 23, 1783. American Revolutionary leader who developed a powerful legal rationale for the rights of the colonies. Argued against British-imposed writs of assistance in the Superior Ct. in Boston, 1761; member of Stamp Act Congress, 1765. *A Vindication of the Conduct of the House of Representatives of the Province of Massachusetts Bay,* 1762.

PASSMAN, OTTO ERNEST, June 27, 1900 (Washington Par., La.). U.S. politician. As U.S. rep. (D, La; 1946-76), worked for the reduction of foreign aid and foreign operations in order to reduce the growing federal debt; chm. of House Subcom. on Foreign Operations for many years.

PATMAN, WRIGHT, Aug. 6, 1893 (Patman's Switch, Tex.)-Mar. 7, 1976. U.S. politician, lawyer. U.S. rep. (D, Tex.), 1928-76; sponsored the legislation that created the Small Business Administration; chm. of House Banking Com., 1963-75.

PELL, CLAIBORNE, Nov. 22, 1918 (New York, N.Y.). U.S. politician, business exec. U.S. sen. (D, R.I.), 1960-   . *Megalopolis Unbound,* 1966; *Power and Policy,* 1972.

PENN, WILLIAM, Oct. 14, 1644 (London, Eng.)-July 30, 1718. An English Quaker leader and champion of religious toleration who founded Pennsylvania. In England, engaged in political campaigns, fighting for religious toleration, 1675-80; received grant in America from Crown, 1681; sailed for America, laid out city of Philadelphia, 1682; returned to England, where he drafted the first plan for a union of American colonies, 1696; returned to Pennsylvania, 1699-1701. *The Great Case of Liberty of Conscience,* 1670.

PERCY, CHARLES HARTING, Sept. 27, 1919 (Pensacola, Fla.). U.S. politician, business exec. Pres. of Bell and Howell, 1949-61; as U.S. sen. (R, Ill.; 1967-   ), suggested appointment of a Watergate special prosecutor (1973) and asked for the end of the U.S. embargo of Cuba (1975).

PERKINS, FRANCES, Apr. 10, 1882 (Boston, Mass.)-May 14, 1965. U.S. govt. official. Member (1923-26) and chm. (1926-29) of New York St. Industrial Board; New York St. industrial commissioner, 1929-33; as U.S. secy. of labor (1933-45), the first woman to serve in a presidential cabinet and an important contributor to New Deal legislation.

PIERCE, FRANKLIN, Nov. 23, 1804 (Hillsborough, N.H.)-Oct. 8, 1869. U.S. pres., lawyer. As 14th U.S. pres. (D, 1853-57), mishandled the sectional controversy over slavery, and oversaw passage of the Kansas-Nebraska Bill (1854) and the Gadsden Purchase (1853).

PINCKNEY, CHARLES, Oct. 26, 1757 (Charleston, S.C.)-Oct. 29, 1824. U.S. politician, diplomat, lawyer. As a delegate to the Constitutional Convention, submitted "Pinckney Draught" (1787), influential plan for the final U.S. Constitution; gov. of South Carolina, 1796-98; U.S. sen. (D, S.C.), 1798-1801; U.S. min. to Spain, 1801-04. (Cousin of CHARLES C. PINCKNEY).

PINCKNEY, CHARLES COTESWORTH, Feb. 25, 1746 (Charleston, S.C.)-Aug. 16, 1825. U.S. statesman, diplomat. Prominent soldier in the American Revolution; active participant in the formation of the Constitution; took part in the XYZ affair with France, 1798; Federal party presidential candidate, 1804 and 1808. (Cousin of CHARLES PINCKNEY.)

POLK, JAMES KNOX, Nov. 2, 1795 (Mecklenburg Co., N.C.)-June 15, 1849. U.S. pres., lawyer. Eleventh U.S. pres. (D, 1845-49), the first "dark horse" candidate to be elected; reluctantly led U.S. in war against Mexico, which resulted in annexation of U.S. Southwest.

POWELL, ADAM CLAYTON, JR., Nov. 29, 1908 (New Haven, Conn.)-Apr. 4, 1972. U.S. politician, minister. Prominent black leader. Min. at Abyssinian Baptist Church of New York City, 1937-71; founder and editor of *The People's Voice,* 1942; U.S. rep. (D, N.Y.), 1945-67 and 1969-70; excluded from the House for alleged improper acts, 1967. *Is This a White Man's War?,* 1942.

POWELL, JOSEPH LESTER, JR., ("Jody"), Sept. 30, 1943 (Cordile, Ga.). U.S. govt. official. Press secy. to Georgia Gov. JIMMY CARTER (1971-75) and for the Carter presidential campaign (1975-76); press secy. to Pres. Carter 1977- .

POWELL, LEWIS F., JR., Sept. 19, 1907 (Suffolk, Va.). U.S. jurist, lawyer. Pres. of American Bar Assn., 1964-65; member of National Commission on Law Enforcement and Admin. of Justice, 1965-67; assoc. justice of U.S. Sup. Ct. 1972- .

PROXMIRE, WILLIAM, Nov. 11, 1915 (Lake Forest, Ill.). U.S. politician. U.S. sen. (D, Wisc.), 1957-   ; chm. Senate Banking, Housing, and Urban Affairs Com. and House-Senate Joint Com. on Defense Production; a critic of bureaucratic waste, periodically awards a "Golden Fleece" to persons or groups he deems guilty of such waste.

RAINEY, JOSEPH HAYNE, June 21, 1832 (Georgetown, S.C.)-Aug. 2, 1887. U.S. politician, banker, broker. The son of slaves who had purchased their freedom, the first black to serve in the U.S. House (R, S.C.), 1870-79.

RANDOLPH, EDMUND JENNINGS, Aug. 10, 1753 (Williamsburg, Va.)-Sept. 12, 1813. U.S. politician, lawyer. Influential in drafting and ratification of U.S. Constitution. The first U.S. atty. gen., 1789-94; served as secy. of state (1794-95), during the negotiations of the Jay Treaty; chief defense counsel at the treason trial of AARON BURR, 1807.

RANDOLPH, JOHN, June 2, 1773 (Prince George Co., Va.)-May 24, 1833. U.S. politician, planter. As U.S. rep. (Va.; 1799-1813, 1815-17, 1819-25 and 1827-29) and U.S. sen. (Va.; 1825-27), a brilliant advocate of states' rights who opposed a national bank and protective tariffs and resisted the Missouri Compromise of 1820.

RANDOLPH, PEYTON, c.1721 (Williamsburg, Va.)-Oct. 22, 1775. American colonial political leader. As a member of the Virginia House of Burgesses (1748-49 and 1752-75), wrote the protest against the proposed Stamp Act, 1764; first pres. of the Continental Congress, 1774.

RANKIN, JEANETTE, June 11, 1880 (nr. Missoula, Mont.)-May 18, 1973. U.S. politician, social worker. First woman U.S. rep. (R, Mont.), 1917-19 and 1941-43; an active suffragist and pacifist who voted against U.S. entrance into both world wars; opposed U.S. involvement in the Vietnam War.

RAY, DIXY LEE, Sept. 3, 1914 (Tacoma, Wash.). U.S. politician, marine biologist. Member (1972-75) and chairperson (1973-75) of AEC; U.S. asst. secy. of state for oceans and international environment and science affairs, 1975; gov. (D) of Washington, 1977-   .

RAYBURN, SAM TALIAFERRO ("Mr. Democrat"), Jan. 6, 1882 (Roane Co., Tenn.)-Nov. 16, 1961. U.S. politician, lawyer. U.S. rep. (D, Tex.), 1913-61; Speaker of the House (1940-46, 1949-53, and 1955-61); a congressional power who was responsible for passage of a great part of the New Deal legislation.

REAGAN, RONALD. Feb. 6, 1911 (Tampico, Ill.). U.S. politician, actor. Co-chm. of Calif. Republicans for Goldwater, 1964; as gov. (R) of California (1967-75) sought to reverse the growth of state govt.; sought Republican presidential nomination, 1968, 1976, and 1980.

REHNQUIST, WILLIAM, Oct. 1, 1924 (Milwaukee, Wisc.). U.S. jurist, lawyer. U.S. asst. atty. gen., 1969-71; assoc. justice of U.S. Sup. Ct., 1972- .

REUSS, HENRY S., Feb. 22, 1912 (Milwaukee, Wisc.). U.S. politician, lawyer. U.S. rep. (D, Wisc.), 1954-   ; chm. of House Banking, Currency, and Housing Com. *Revenue Sharing,* 1970.

REVELS, HIRAM RHODES, Sept. 1, 1822 (Fayetteville, N.C.)-Jan. 16, 1901. U.S. politician, teacher, minister. The first black to be elected to U.S. Senate (R, Miss.), 1870-71; backed legislation to restore the right to vote and hold office to all ex-Confederates.

RHODES, JOHN J., Sept. 18, 1916 (Council Grove, Kan.). U.S. politician, lawyer. U.S. rep. (R, Ariz.), 1952-   ; House minority leader, 1973- .

RIBICOFF, ABRAHAM A., Apr. 9, 1910 (New Britain, Conn.). U.S. politician, lawyer. U.S. rep. (D, Conn.), 1948-52; gov. (D) of Connecticut, 1954-61; U.S. secy. of HEW, 1961-62; U.S. sen. (D, Conn.), 1962-80; chm. of Senate Governmental Affairs com.

RICHARDSON, ELLIOT LEE, July 20, 1920 (Boston, Mass.). U.S. govt. official, diplomat. U.S. secy. of HEW, 1970-73; U.S. secy. of defense, 1973; U.S. atty. gen., 1973; U.S. amb. to Great Britain. 1975-76; U.S. amb.-at-large, 1977-   .

RIVERS, L(ucius) MENDEL, Sept. 28, 1905 (Berkeley Co., S.C.). U.S. politician. U.S. rep. (D, S.C.), 1941-70; chm. of House Armed Services Com., 1965-70.

ROCKEFELLER, JOHN DAVISON, IV ("Jay"), June 18, 1937 (New Yor, N.Y.). U.S. politician, college pres. West Virginia secy. of state, 1969-72, pres. of West Virginia Wesleyan C., 1973-75; gov. (D) of West Virignia, 1977- . (Great-grandson of JOHN D. ROCKEFELLER; grandson of JOHN D. ROCKEFELLER, JR.; and son of John D. Rockefeller III.)

ROCKEFELLER, NELSON ALDRICH, July 8, 1908 (Bar Harbor, Me.)-Jan. 26, 1979. U.S. politician, art patron. As gov. (R) of New York (1959-73), tremendously expanded the state university system and oversaw much public construction; refused to negotiate with inmates involved in the Attica prison uprising, 1971; U.S. vice-pres. (R) 1974-76. (Grandson of JOHN D. ROCKEFELLER; son of JOHN D. ROCKEFELLER, JR.; brother of DAVID, John D. III, LAURANCE, and Winthrop Rockefeller.)

RODINO, PETER WALLACE, JR., June 7, 1909 (Newark, N.J.). U.S. politician, lawyer. U.S. rep. (D, N.J.), 1948-   ; as chm. of the Housing Judiciary com. (1973-   ), chaired the Nixon impeachment hearings, 1974.

RODNEY, CAESAR, Oct. 7, 1728 (Dover, Del.)-

June 26, 1784. American Revolutionary leader. A signer of the Declaration of Independence, 1776; del. to Stamp Act Congress, 1765; pres. of Delaware, 1778-82.

ROOSEVELT, FRANKLIN DELANO, Jan. 30, 1882 (Hyde Park, N.Y.)-Apr. 12, 1945. As 32nd U.S. pres., (1933-45), brought the U.S. out of Depression and led it through WW II; initiated many reforms and expanded the govt.'s powers through New Deal programs aimed at bringing about economic recovery; played a major role in creating an alliance among the U.S., the USSR, and Great Britian during WW II; died in office. Asst. secy. of the Navy, 1913-20; stricken with polio, 1921; gov. (D) of New York, 1929-33.

ROOSEVELT, THEODORE, Oct. 17, 1858 (New York, N.Y.)-Jan. 6, 1919. U.S. pres. Led "Rough Riders" in Cuba during the Spanish-American War, 1898; gov. (R) of New York, 1899-1900; U.S. vice-pres., 1901; as 26th U.S. pres. (1901-09), aggressively broke up trusts and regulated business, attempted to conserve national resources, acquired the Panama Canal Zone (1903), and intervened in Latin American affairs; awarded Nobel Peace Prize, 1906; organized Progressive (or Bull Moose) party and ran as its presidential candidate, 1912.

ROOT, ELIHU, Feb. 15, 1845 (Clinton, N.Y.)-Feb. 7, 1937. U.S. govt. official. U.S. secy. of war, 1899-1904; U.S. secy. of state, 1905-09; U.S. sen. (R, N.Y.), 1909-15; member of Hague Tribunal, 1910; pres. of Carnegie Endowment for International Peace, 1912; awarded Nobel Peace Prize, 1912.

ROSS, NELLIE TAYLOE, 1876 (St. Joseph, Mo.)-Dec. 19, 1977. U.S. politician, govt. official. First woman in U.S. to serve as gov. (D) of a state (Wyoming, 1925-27); dir. of the U.S. Mint (also the first woman to hold the position), 1933-53.

RUSH, BENJAMIN, Dec. 24, 1745 (Byberry, Pa. [now part of Philadelphia])-Apr. 19, 1813. U.S. physician, chemist. First prof. of chemistry at an American university (C. of Philadelphia, 1769); signer for Pennsylvania of the Declaration of Independence, 1776; helped start the Conway Cabal, 1777; established first free dispensary in the U.S., 1786; sometimes considered the father of the Women's Christian Temperance Union.

RUSK, DEAN, Feb. 9, 1909 (Cherokee Co., Ga.). U.S. govt. official. Pres. of Rockefeller Fndn., 1952-60; as U.S. secy. of state (1961-69), became a defender of U.S. involvement in Vietnam.

RUSSELL, RICHARD B., Nov. 2, 1897 (Winder, Ga.)-Jan. 21, 1971. U.S. politician, lawyer. As U.S. sen. (D, Ga.; 1933-71), led the Southern bloc; chm. of Senate Armed Forces Com., 1951-69; pres. pro tem of the Senate, 1969-71.

RUTLEDGE, EDWARD, Nov. 23, 1749 (Charleston, S.C.)-Jan. 23, 1800. U.S. politician. A signer of the Declaration of Independence, 1776; member of S. Carolina leg., 1782-96; gov. of S. Carolina, 1798-1800.

SCHLESINGER, JAMES R., Feb. 15, 1929 (New York, N.Y.). U.S. govt. official, economist. Chm. of AEC, 1971-73; dir. of CIA, 1973; U.S. secy. of defense, 1973-75; U.S. secy. of energy, 1977-79.

SCHMITT, HARRISON ("Jack"), July 3, 1935 (Santa Rita, N.M.). U.S. politician, geologist, astronaut. Scientist at NASA, 1965-73; piloted Apollo 17 lunar module, 1972; U.S. sen. (R, N.M.), 1977- .

SCHULTZE, CHARLES, Dec. 12, 1924 (Alexandria, Va.). U.S. government official; economist. Dir.

of U.S. Bureau of the Budget, 1965-68; senior fellow at Brookings Inst., 1968-   ; chm. of Council of Economic Advisers, 1977-   .

SCHURZ, CARL, Mar. 2, 1829 (Liblar, Prussia)-May 14, 1906. U.S. statesman, orator, writer, lawyer. Political reformer who led the Liberal Republicans and the Mugwumps. U.S. sen. (R, Mo.), 1869-75; U.S. secy. of the int., 1877-81; editor of the New York Evening Post, 1881-84.

SCHWEIKER, RICHARD SCHULTZ, June 1, 1926 (Norristown, Pa.). U.S. politician. U.S. rep. (R, Pa.), 1961-69; U.S. sen. (R, Pa.), 1969-   ; ranking minority member of Senate Labor-HEW Subcom., Labor and Human Resources Com. and its Health Subcom.

SCOTT, HUGH DOGGETT, JR., Nov. 11, 1900 (Fredericksburg, Va.). U.S. politician, lawyer. U.S. rep. (R, Pa.), 1941-45 and 1947-59; chm. of Republican National Com., 1948-49; as U.S. sen. (R, Pa.; 1958-76), served as Senate minority leader (1969-76) and defended Pres. R. M. NIXON's Vietnam policy.

SCRANTON, WILLIAM WARREN, July 19, 1917 (Madison, Conn.). U.S. politician, lawyer, diplomat. Gov. (R) of Pennsylvania, 1963-67; chm. of President's Commission on Campus Unrest, 1970; amb. to the U.S. mission to the UN, 1976.

SEWALL, SAMUEL, Mar. 28, 1652 (Bishopstoke, Eng.)-Jan. 1, 1730. American colonial jurist. Presided over the Salem witchcraft trials (1692), but later publically confessed his error and guilt in the condemnations (1697); chief justice of Mass. Sup. Ct., 1718-28; his diary, Diary: The Selling of Joseph (1700), is an invaluable record of his times.

SEWARD, WILLIAM HENRY, May 16, 1801 (Florida, N.Y.)-Oct. 10, 1872. U.S. politician, statesman. As U.S. secy. of state (1861-69), kept the European nations out of the Civil War and acquired Alaska from Russia. Gov. (Whig) of New York, 1838-42; U.S. sen. (Whig-R, N.Y.), 1849-61; severely wounded in assassination attempt as part of LINCOLN conspiracy, 1865.

SHERMAN, JOHN, May 10, 1823 (Lancaster, Ohio)-Oct. 22, 1900. U.S. politician, govt. official. A leading expert on finance who helped plan the national banking system, opposed free coinage of silver, and supported the Specie Resumption Act (1875). U.S. sen. (R, Ohio), 1861-77 and 1881-97; U.S. secy. of the treas., 1877-81; U.S. secy. of state, 1897-98. (Brother of WILLIAM T. SHERMAN.)

SHERMAN, ROGER, Apr. 19, 1721 (Newton, Mass.)-July 23, 1793. U.S. statesman, lawyer, surveyor. Signer of the Declaration of Independence, Articles of Association, Articles of Confederation, and the Constitution—the only person to sign all four. As del. to the Constitutional Convention (1787), proposed the Connecticut Compromise setting up a bicameral Congress; mayor of New Haven, 1784-93; U.S. sen. (Conn.), 1791-93.

SHRIVER, R. SARGENT, JR., Nov. 9, 1915 (Westminster, Md.). U.S. govt. official, diplomat. Dir. of Peace Corps, 1961-66; dir. of Office of Economic Opportunity, 1964-68; U.S. amb. to France, 1968-70; Democratic vice-presidential candidate, 1972.

SIMON, WILLIAM EDWARD, Nov. 27, 1927 (Paterson, N.J.). U.S. govt. official, financier. Partner in Salomon Bros., 1964-72; administrator of Federal Energy Office, 1973-74; U.S. secy. of the treas., 1974-77; pres. of John M. Olin Foundation, 1977-   .

SIRICA, JOHN J., Mar. 19, 1904 (Waterbury, Conn.). As chief judge of U.S. Dist. Ct., Dist. of Columbia (1971–74), presided over the Watergate scandal trials, 1972–74.

SMITH, ALFRED E(mmanuel), Dec. 30, 1873 (New York, N.Y.)–Oct. 4, 1944. U.S. politician. As gov. (D) of New York (1918–20 and 1922–28), effective in pushing his reform programs through a Republican-controlled leg.; first Roman Catholic to seek the Presidency (as Democratic candidate), 1928.

SMITH, JOHN, 1580 (Lincolnshire, Eng.)–June 1631. English colonist in America. A leader of the first permanent English settlement in N. America, at Jamestown, Va., 1607–09; saved from death by POCAHONTAS; developed trade for corn with Indians; returned to England, 1609; on second voyage, mapped the New England coast, 1614. *A True Relation of ... Virginia Since the First Planting of That Colony,* 1608; *A Description of New England,* 1616.

SMITH, MARGARET CHASE, Dec. 14, 1897 (Skowhegan, Me.). U.S. politician, columnist, U.S. rep. (R, Me.), 1940–49; as U.S. sen. (R, Me.; 1948–72), served longer than any other woman; sought Republican presidential nomination, 1964.

SPARKMAN, JOHN J., Dec. 20, 1899 (Hartselle, Ala.). U.S. politician, lawyer. U.S. rep. (D, Ala) 1937–46; U.S. sen. (D, Ala), 1946–79; as chm. of Senate Banking, Housing, and Urban Affairs com.; supported U.S. military and defense policy in the 1960s.

STANS, MAURICE HUBERT, Mar. 22, 1908 (Shakopee, Minn.). U.S. govt. official. Dir. of Bureau of the Budget, 1958–61; chm. of Nixon for President Com., 1968; as chm. of Finance Com. to Reelect the President (1972), became involved peripherally in the Watergate scandal; U.S. secy. of commerce, 1969–72.

STANTON, EDWIN MCMASTERS, Dec. 19, 1814 (Steubenville, Ohio)–Dec. 24, 1869. U.S. statesman. As U.S. secy. of war (1862–68), competently administered the Union Army during the Civil War; dismissed by Pres. ANDREW JOHNSON for advocating stricter Reconstruction measures than Johnson wanted.

STASSEN, HAROLD EDWARD, Apr. 13, 1907 (W. St. Paul, Minn.). U.S. lawyer, politician. Gov. (R) of Minnesota, 1938–45; pres. of U. of Pa., 1948–53; special asst. to U.S. pres., with cabinet rank, to direct studies of U.S. and world disarmament, 1955–58; unsuccessful candidate for Republican presidential nomination, 1948, 1964, and 1968.

STENNIS, JOHN CORNELIUS, Aug. 3, 1901 (Kemper Co., Miss.). U.S. politician, lawyer. U.S. sen. (D, Miss.), 1947–   ; chm. of Senate Armed Services com., 1969–   ; supporter of a strong national defense.

STEPHENS, ALEXANDER HAMILTON, Feb. 11, 1812 (Crawfordsville, Ga.)–Mar. 4, 1883. U.S. political leader, lawyer. U.S. rep. (Ga.), 1843–59 and 1873–82; as vice-pres. of the Confederacy (1861–65), opposed use of extraordinary war powers by Pres. JEFFERSON DAVIS because of his concern for states' rights and civil liberties. *Constitutional View of the Late War between the States,* 2 vols., 1868–70.

STETTINIUS, EDWARD REILLY, JR., Oct. 22, 1900 (Chicago, Ill.)–Oct. 31, 1949. U.S. statesman, industrialist. Chm. of the board of U.S. Steel, 1938; chm. of War Resources Board, 1939; administrator of Lend-Lease, 1941–43; U.S. secy. of state, 1944–45; an adviser to FDR at the Yalta Confer-

ence, 1945; chm. of U.S. delegation to UN conference in San Francisco and first U.S. del. to UN (1945–46).

STEVENS, JOHN PAUL, Apr. 20, 1920 (Chicago, Ill.). U.S. jurist. Judge of U.S. Ct. of Appeals for the Seventh Cir. (Chicago, Ill.), 1970–75; as assoc. justice of U.S. Sup. Ct. (1975–   ), considered a legal centrist.

STEVENS, THEODORE FULTON, Nov. 18, 1923 (Indianapolis, Ind.). U.S. politician, lawyer. U.S. sen. (R, Alaska), 1968–   ; Senate asst. minority leader, 1977–

STEVENSON, ADLAI EWING, Oct. 23, 1835 (Christian Co., Ky.)–June 14, 1914. U.S. politician. U.S. rep. (D, Ill.), 1875–76 and 1879–80; U.S. vice-pres. (D), 1893–97. (Grandfather of ADLAI E. STEVENSON II.)

STEVENSON, ADLAI EWING II, Feb. 5, 1900 (Los Angeles, Calif.)–July 14, 1965. U.S. statesman, diplomat, lawyer. Participant at foundation of UN at San Francisco Conference, 1946; gov. (D) of Illinois, 1948–52; Democratic presidential candidate, 1952 and 1956; U.S. del. to the UN, 1961–65. (Grandson of ADLAI E. STEVENSON; Father of ADLAI E. STEVENSON III)

STEVENSON, ADLAI EWING III, Oct. 10, 1930 (Chicago, Ill.). U.S. politician, lawyer. Illinois treas. (D), 1967–70; U.S. sen. (D, Ill.), 1970–   . (Son of ADLAI E. STEVENSON II.)

STEWART, POTTER, Jan. 23, 1915 (Jackson, Mich.). U.S. jurist, lawyer. Judge of U.S. Ct. of Appeals, Sixth Cir., 1954–58; as assoc. justice of U.S. Sup. Ct. (1959–   ), known as an independent and a moderate.

STIMSON, HENRY LEWIS, Sept. 21, 1867 (New York, N.Y.)–Oct. 20, 1950. U.S. govt. official. U.S. secy. of war, 1911–13 and 1940–45; U.S. secy. of state, 1929–33; following Japanese invasion of Manchuria (1931) advocated nonrecognition of Japanese rule (the "Stimson Doctrine"); recommended use of the atom bomb on Japan, 1945.

STONE, HARLAN FISKE, Oct. 11, 1872 (Chesterfield, N.H.)–Apr. 22, 1946. U.S. jurist. As assoc. justice (1925–41) and chief justice (1941–46) of U.S. Sup. Ct., a liberal who believed in judicial restraint; contributed to legal thought on the power of the state to regulate interstate commerce and the power of the national govt. to make basic changes in society.

STORY, JOSEPH, Sept. 18, 1779 (Marblehead, Mass.)–Sept. 10, 1845. U.S. jurist. Prof. of Law at Harvard C., 1829–45; a pioneer in founding and directing Harvard Law School; as assoc. justice of U.S. Sup. Ct., (1811–45), wrote opinion putting the highest state courts under the appellate authority of the Sup. Ct. in cases involving federal law; wrote famous series of nine commentaries, 1832–45. Elected to American Hall of Fame, 1900.

STRAUSS, ROBERT SCHWARZ, Oct. 9, 1918 (Lockhart, Tex.). U.S. govt. official, lawyer. Pres. of Strauss Broadcasting Co., 1964–   ; chm. of Democratic National Com. 1972–76; U.S. special rep. for trade negotiations (with rank of amb.) 1977–   ; U.S. amb.-at-large to the Middle East, 1979.

STUYVESANT, Peter (or Petrus), c.1610 (Friesland, Neth.)–Feb. 1672. Dutch colonial gov. in America. Lost his leg in campaign against St. Martin I., 1644; gov. of New Netherland (later New York), 1646–64; aroused great discontent in the colony with his dictatorial rule.

SUMNER, CHARLES, Jan. 6, 1811 (Boston, Mass.)–Mar. 11, 1874. U.S. politician. As U.S. sen.

THE BOOK OF WHO

(D-Free Soil-R, Mass.; 1851-74), a powerful opponent of slavery; attacked Kansas-Nebraska Bill of 1854 with his famous "Crime against Kansas" speech; led radical Republicans in their opposition to Pres. ANDREW JOHNSON's moderate Reconstruction program for the South; chm. of Senate Foreign Relations com., 1861-71.

SYMINGTON, STUART, June 26, 1901 (Amherst, Mass.). U.S. politician, businessman. Pres. of Emerson Electric Manufacturing Co., 1938-45; U.S. secy. of the air force, 1947-50; as U.S. sen. (D, Mo.; 1952-77), opposed waste in the defense budget and the Vietnam War.

TAFT, ROBERT ALPHONSO ("Mr. Republican"), Sept. 8, 1889 (Cincinnati, Ohio)-July 31, 1953. U.S. politician. As U.S. sen. (R, Ohio; 1939-53), advocated isolationism prior to WW II, helped write Taft-Hartley Act (1947), opposed centralization of power in the federal govt., and opposed U.S. membership in NATO; unsuccessfully sought Republican presidential nomination, 1952. (Son of WILLIAM HOWARD TAFT.)

TAFT, WILLIAM HOWARD, Sept. 15, 1857 (Cincinnati, Ohio)-Mar. 8, 1930. U.S. pres., jurist. Pres. of Philippine Commission, 1900-04; U.S. secy. of war, 1904-08; as 27th U.S. pres. (R; 1909-13), vigorously enforced antitrust legislation, began postal savings bank (1910), created dept. of labor (1911); chief justice of U.S. Sup. Ct., 1921-30. (Father of ROBERT A. TAFT.)

TALMADGE, HERMAN EUGENE, Aug. 9, 1913 (McRae, Ga.). U.S. politician, lawyer. Gov. (D) of Georgia, 1948-55; U.S. sen. (D, Ga.), 1957-   ; chm. of Senate Agr., Nutrition, and Forestry Com.

TANEY, ROGER BROOKE, Mar. 17, 1777 (Calvert Co., Md.)-Oct. 12, 1864. U.S. jurist, lawyer. As U.S. atty. gen. (1831-32), fought against the federal bank; as chief justice of U.S. Sup. Ct. (1836-64), upheld federal supremacy over state authorities, but in the Dred Scott case (1857), held that Congress could not forbid slavery in the territories and that slaves were not citizens.

TAYLOR, ZACHARY ("Old Rough and Ready"), Nov. 24, 1784 (Orange Co., Va.)-July 9, 1850. U.S. president, soldier. The hero of the U.S.-Mexican War (1846-48), he commanded army at the Texas border and won Northern Mexico at the Battle of Buena Vista (1847); as 12th pres. (Whig, 1849-50), favored admission of California into the Union, faced charges of corruption in his cabinet; died in office.

THOMPSON, JAMES ROBERT, May 8, 1936 (Chicago, Ill.). U.S. politician, lawyer. U.S. atty. for Northern Illinois Dist., 1971-75; gov. (R) of Illinois, 1977-

THURMOND, (James) STROM, Dec. 5, 1902 (Edgefield, S.C.). U.S. politician, farmer, lawyer. Gov. (D) of South Carolina, 1947-51; States'-Rights presidential candidate, 1948; U.S. sen. (D-R, S.C.), 1954-   ; switched from Democrat to Republican party, 1964; has often been the rallying point for Southern conservatism in the Senate.

TILDEN, SAMUEL JONES, Feb. 9, 1814 (New Lebanon, N.Y.)-Aug. 4, 1886. U.S. politician, lawyer. A leader in the overthrow of the Tweed Ring, 1866-72; gov. (D) of New York, 1874-76; the 1876 Democratic presidential candidate, lost by one electoral vote to R. B. HAYES in a highly disputed election; donated his vast estate to establish a free public library in New York City.

TOWER, JOHN GOODWIN, Sept. 29, 1925 (Houston, Tex.). U.S. politician, political scientist.

U.S. sen. (R, Tex.), 1961-   ; chm. of Senate Republican Policy Com.

TRUMAN, HARRY S., May 8, 1884 (Lamar, Mo.)-Dec. 26, 1972. U.S. pres., politician. U.S. sen. (D, Mo.), 1935-45; as 33rd U.S. pres. (D, 1945-53), made decision to drop the atom bomb on Japan, decided to go to war against Korea, propounded a doctrine of containment of communism.

TRUMBULL, JONATHAN, Oct. 12, 1710 (Lebanon, Conn.)-Aug. 17, 1785. American colonial leader. As gov. of Connecticut (1769-84), the only colonial gov. to advocate the Revolutionary cause.

TWEED, WILLIAM MARCY ("Boss"), Apr. 3, 1823 (New York, N.Y.)-Apr. 12, 1878. U.S. politician. Democratic political boss who plundered New York City of over $30 million. New York St. senator, 1856-57; a sachem (1859) and grand sachem (1868) in Tammany Hall; charged with corruption by *The New York Times* and THOMAS NAST's powerful cartoons, 1870; pursued legally by SAMUEL J. TILDEN, arrested and convicted (1873).

TYDINGS, MILLARD EVANS, Apr. 6, 1890 (Havre de Grace, Md.)-Feb. 9, 1961. U.S. politician, civil engineer. U.S. rep. (D, Md.), 1923-27; as U.S. sen. (D, Md.), 1927-51, opposed much of the New Deal legislation and some of Pres. F. D. ROOSEVELT's foreign policy; headed Senate subcom. investigating Sen. JOSEPH R. MCCARTHY's allegations of communist infiltration in the U.S. State Dept. (1950); the com. cleared the dept. and denounced McCarthy as a liar.

TYLER, JOHN, Mar. 29, 1790 (Charles City Co., Va.)-Jan. 18, 1862. U.S. pres. As 10th U.S. pres. (Whig, 1841-45), twice vetoed a national bank bill, annexed Texas, and reorganized the U.S. navy; the first vice-pres. to attain presidency upon the death of a pres., W.H. HARRISON.

UDALL, MORRIS KING ("Mo"), June 15, 1922 (Saint Johns, Ariz.). U.S. politician, lawyer. U.S. rep. (D, Ariz.), 1961-   ; chm. of House Interior and Insular Affairs Com. and Energy and Environment Subcom.; sought Democratic presidential nomination, 1976. (Brother of STEWART L. UDALL.)

UDALL, STEWART LEE, Jan. 31, 1920 (Saint Johns, Ariz.). U.S. politician, govt. official. U.S. rep. (D, Ariz.), 1954-61. As U.S. secy. of the int. (1961-69), launched Parks for America, establishing many new wildlife refuges and ranges; syndicated columnist, 1970-   . *The Quiet Crisis,* 1963; *National Parks of America,* 1966. (Brother of MORRIS UDALL.)

ULLMAN, AL, Mar. 9, 1914 (Great Falls, Mont.). U.S. politician. U.S. rep. (D, Ore.), 1956-   ; chm. of House Ways and Means Com. (1975-   ) and Joint Com. on Taxation (1975-   ).

VALLANDIGHAM, CLEMENT LAIRD, July 29, 1820 (New Lisbon, Ohio)-June 17, 1871. U.S. politician, lawyer. A leader of the Peace Democrats, or Copperheads, during the Civil War. U.S. rep. (D, Ohio), 1856-62; convicted for alleged treasonable utterances (1863) and banished to the Confederacy; following the Civil War, worked for national unity.

VAN BUREN, MARTIN, Dec. 5, 1782 (Kinderhook, N.Y.)-July 24, 1862. U.S. pres. U.S. sen. (D, N.Y.), 1821-28; U.S. secy. of state, 1829-31; vice-pres., 1833-37; as eighth pres. of the U.S. (1837-41), known for his political cunning; attempting to deal with the Panic of 1837, recommended an independent treas. system.

152

RULERS, STATESMEN, AND POLITICAL LEADERS

VANCE, CYRUS ROBERT, Mar. 27, 1917 (Clarksburg, W. Va.). U.S. govt. official. U.S. secy. of the army, 1962-64; U.S. dep. secy. of def., 1964-67; U.S. negotiator at Paris Peace Conference on Vietnam, 1968-69; U.S. secy. of state, 1977- .

VANDENBERG, ARTHUR HENDRICK, Mar. 22, 1884 (Grand Rapids, Mich.)-Apr. 18, 1951. U.S. politician, editor. As U.S. sen. (R, Mich; 1928-51), progressed from isolationism to a leading backer of Pres. HARRY TRUMAN's anticommunist foreign policy; chm. of Senate Foreign Relations com., 1947-49; played an important role in the formation of the UN; marshaled congressional support for NATO and the Marshall Plan.

VINSON, FREDERICK MOORE, Jan. 22, 1890 (Louisa, Ky.)-Sept. 8, 1953. U.S. politician, jurist. As U.S. rep. (D, Ky.; 1923-29 and 1931-38), became known as a fiscal expert; dir. of Office of Economic Stabilization, 1943-45; dir. of Office of War Mobilization and Reconversion, 1945; as chief justice of U.S. Sup. Ct. (1946-53), frequently upheld the powers of the federal govt. versus individual rights.

VOLSTEAD, ANDREW JOSEPH, Oct. 31, 1860 (Goodhue Co., Minn.)-Jan. 20, 1947. U.S. politician, lawyer. As U.S. rep. (R, Minn.) (1903-23), authored the Volstead Act (1919), which enforced prohibition; chm. of House Judiciary Com., 1919-23.

WAGNER, ROBERT FERDINAND, June 8, 1877 (Nastätten, Ger.)- May 4, 1953. U.S. politician, lawyer. Known as the "Legislative Pilot of the New Deal." As U.S. sen. (D, N.Y.; 1927-49), directed the Congressional career of the National Labor Relations Act (1935) and worked for the extension of federal housing. (Father of ROBERT F. WAGNER, JR.)

WAGNER, ROBERT FERDINAND, JR., Apr. 20, 1910 (New York, N.Y.). U.S. politician, diplomat. As mayor (D) of New York City (1954-66) and pres. of the Borough of Manhattan (1949-53) accomplished significant reforms in education and housing; U.S. amb. to Spain, 1968-69. (Son of ROBERT F. WAGNER.)

WALKER, JAMES JOHN ("Jimmy"), June 19, 1881 (New York, N.Y.)-Nov. 18, 1946. U.S. politician, lawyer. As mayor of New York City (1925-32), developed the transit system, created the Sanitation Dept.; very popular figure, noted as dapper and debonair.

WALLACE, GEORGE CORLEY, Aug. 25, 1919 (Clio, Ala.). U.S. politician, lawyer. Leader of the South's fight against federally ordered racial integration in the 1960s. Gov. (D) of Alabama, 1963-66, 1971-74, and 1975-78; attempted to block enrollment of black students at the U. of Alabama, 1963; American Independent party presidential candidate, 1968; sought Democratic presidential nomination, 1972 and 1976; shot while campaigning and paralyzed from the waist down, 1972.

WALLACE, HENRY AGARD, Oct. 7, 1888 (Adair Co, Ia.)-Nov. 18, 1965. U.S. politician, editor, agricultural expert. As U.S. secy. of agric. (1933-40), led the New Deal farm program; U.S. vice-pres. (D, 1941-45); editor of The New Republic, 1946-47; Progressive party presidential candidate, 1948.

WARNER, JOHN WILLIAM, Feb. 18, 1927 (Washington, D.C.). U.S. politician, lawyer. U.S. secy. of the navy, 1972-74; administrator of American Revolution Bicentennial Adm., 1974-76; U.S. sen. (R, Va.), 1979- . (Husband of ELIZABETH TAYLOR.)

WARNKE, PAUL CULLITON, Jan. 31, 1920 (Webster, Mass.). U.S. govt. official, lawyer. U.S. asst. secy. of def. for internal security affairs, 1967-69; dir. of Arms Control and Disarmament Agency, 1977-78; chief negotiator at SALT talks, 1977-78.

WARREN, EARL, Mar. 18, 1891 (Los Angeles, Calif.)-July 9, 1974. U.S. politician, jurist. Gov. (R) of California, 1943-53; as chief justice of U.S. Sup. Ct. (1953-69), presided over a period of great change in civil rights, wrote the decision regarding school desegregation in Brown v. Board of Education of Topeka, Kans., 1954, led Court to expand the rights of the accused, headed the official investigation into the assassination of Pres. JOHN F. KENNEDY.

WASHINGTON, GEORGE, Feb. 22, 1732 (Westmoreland Co., Va.)-Dec. 14, 1799. U.S. pres., soldier, farmer, surveyor. As commander in chief of the Continental forces during the American Revolution, provided steady and inspirational leadership that kept the Revolutionary Army in being, 1775-83; as first U.S. pres. (1789-97), did much to shape the office, warned against the dangers of party politics and foreign alliances.

WASHINGTON, WALTER E., Apr. 16, 1915 (Dawson, Ga.). U.S. politician, lawyer. Chm. of New York Housing Authority, 1966-67; mayor-commissioner (appointed) of Washington, D.C., 1967-74; mayor of Washington, D.C., 1975- .

WEAVER, ROBERT C., Dec. 29, 1907 (Washington, D.C.). U.S. govt. official, economist. As U.S. secy. of HUD (1966-69), the first black to serve in the U.S. cabinet; prof. of urban affairs at Hunter C., 1970- . Negro Ghetto, 1948.

WEBSTER, DANIEL, Jan. 18, 1782 (Salisbury, N.H.)-Oct. 24, 1852. U.S. politician, lawyer, orator. U.S. rep. (Fed, N.H.), 1813-17 and 1823-27; as U.S. sen. (Whig, Mass; 1827-41 and 1845-50), gained fame as an orator; backed the Compromise of 1850 in his devotion to the survival of the Union; defended the industrial interests of his region; U.S. secy. of state, 1841-43 and 1850-52. Elected to American Hall of Fame, 1900.

WEICKER, LOWELL PALMER, JR., May 16, 1931 (Paris, Fr.). U.S. politician, lawyer. U.S. sen. (R, Conn.), 1971- ; as a member of the Senate Watergate Com., played a prominent role in the investigation of the Watergate scandal, 1973-74.

WELLES, (Benjamin) SUMNER, Oct. 14, 1892 (New York, N.Y.)-Sept. 24, 1961. U.S. diplomat. As U.S. under-secy. of state (1937-43), a major architect of the "Good Neighbor Policy" toward Latin America.

WHEELER, BURTON K., Feb. 27, 1882 (Hudson, Mass.)-Jan. 7, 1975. U.S. politician, lawyer. U.S. sen. (D, Mont.), 1922-46; a leader of the isolationist movement prior to WW II; Progressive party vice-presidential running-mate of ROBERT M. LA FOLLETTE, 1924.

WHIPPLE, WILLIAM, Jan. 14, 1730 (Kittery, Me.)-Nov. 10, 1785. American Revolutionary leader, legislator, soldier. A signer of the Declaration of Independence, 1776; member of Continental Congress, 1776-79; a brigadier gen. in the Revolutionary army.

WHITE, BYRON RAYMOND ("Whizzer"), June 8, 1917 (Ft. Collins, Col.). U.S. athlete, jurist. An All-American football player at U. of Colorado, played professional football with the Pittsburgh Pirates (now Steelers), and with the Detroit Lions; U.S. dep. atty. gen., 1961-62; as assoc. justice of U.S. Sup. Ct. (1962-), a "swing" justice who has

THE BOOK OF WHO

written many dissenting opinions in rights of criminal defendants and the protection of First Amendment guarantees; elected to the Football Hall of Fame, 1954.

WHITE, EDWARD DOUGLAS, Nov. 3, 1845 (Lafourche Par., La.)–May 19, 1921. U.S. jurist. As assoc. justice (1894–1910) and chief justice (1910–21) of U.S. Sup. Ct., read the "rule of reason" into the antitrust laws, made decisions in favor of federal emergency powers, formulated concept of the "incorporation" of territories acquired by the U.S. in 1898.

WHITE, KEVIN, Sept. 25, 1929 (Boston, Mass.). U.S. politician, lawyer. Mayor (D) of Boston, 1968– ; member of Steering Com. of National Urban Coalition, 1972–

WHITNEY, WILLIAM COLLINS, July 5, 1841 (Conway, Mass.)–Feb. 2, 1904. U.S. lawyer, govt. official. Led the fight that broke the Tweed ring; as U.S. secy. of the Navy (1885–89), promoted armor-plated war vessels; a leading sportsman.

WILLKIE, WENDELL LEWIS, Feb. 18, 1892 (Elwood, Ind.)–Oct. 8, 1944. U.S. politician, business exec., lawyer. Pres. of Commonwealth and Southern Corp., 1933–40; a major critic of the New Deal; Republican presidential candidate, 1940; fought isolationism during WW II. *One World,* 1943.

WILSON, (Thomas) WOODROW, Dec. 28, 1856 Staunton, Va.)–Feb. 23, 1924. U.S. pres., political scientist, educator. Pres. of Princeton U., 1902–09; gov. (D) of New Jersey, 1910–12; as 28th U.S. pres. (D, 1913–21), worked for creation of the Federal Reserve System (1913) and the FTC (1914), opposed imperialism, attempted to maintain U.S. neutrality in WW I; after WW I, put forward peace plan based on "Fourteen Points," attended Paris Peace Conference (1919), and labored tirelessly for the League of Nations; awarded Nobel Peace Prize, 1919.

WINTHROP, JOHN, Jan. 12, 1588 (Suffolk, Eng.)–Mar. 26, 1649. American colonial leader. A leader of the Massachusetts Bay Colony, serving as its gov. 12 times between 1629 and 1648; led effort to oust ANNE HUTCHINSON and the Antinomians; attempted to make the colony into a theocratic society.

WITHERSPOON, JOHN, Feb. 5, 1723 (Yester, Scot.)–Nov. 15, 1794. Scottish-U.S. Presbyterian clergyman. Pres., C. of New Jersey (later Princeton U.), 1768–94; a signer of the Declaration of Independence (1776) and delegate to the Continental Congress (1776–82).

WOLCOTT, OLIVER, Nov. 20, 1725 (Windsor, Conn.)–Dec. 1, 1797. American Revolutionary leader. Helped negotiate the neutrality of the pro-British Six Nations Indians prior to the Revolution, 1775; a signer of the Declaration of Independence, 1776; during the Revolution, in charge of the defense of the Connecticut coast against British raids; gov. of Connecticut, 1796–97.

WOODCOCK, LEONARD FREEL, Feb. 15, 1911 (Providence, R.I.). U.S. govt. and labor-union official. Succeeded WALTER REUTHER as pres. of United Automobile Workers, 1970–77; chief of mission, with rank of U.S. amb., to China, 1977–

YOUNG, ANDREW, Mar. 12, 1932 (New Orleans, La.). U.S. politician, minister. As U.S. rep. (D, Ga.), the first black to win a Democratic nomination for Congress from the South in 100 years; U.S. amb. to the UN, 1977–79.

YOUNG, COLEMAN ALEXANDER, May 24, 1918

(Tuscaloosa, Ala.). U.S. politician. Mayor (D) of Detroit, Mich., 1974–

YOUNG, MILTON R., Dec. 6, 1897 (Berlin, N.D.). U.S. politician, farmer. Republican dean of the Senate. U.S. sen. (R, N.D.), 1945– ; as secy. of Senate Republican Conference Com. (1946–71), served for longest period ever in a leadership position in the Senate.

BRITISH RULERS, STATESMEN, AND POLITICAL LEADERS

ALBERT, OF SAXE-COBURG-GOTHA, PRINCE, August 26, 1819 (Rosenau, Ger.)–Dec. 14, 1861. Prince consort of England (from 1857), husband of QUEEN VICTORIA, and her most trusted counselor; upon his death at age 42, mourned by Victoria for the remaining years of her reign.

ALFRED THE GREAT, 849 (Saxony)–Apr. 26, 899. Saxon king, soldier, scholar. As king of the West Saxons (871–99), saved England from Danish conquest; strengthened the English military; led a great revival of learning; translated many major works of the time; organized a court school; issued his own code of laws.

ASQUITH, HERBERT HENRY, EARL OF OXFORD AND ASQUITH, Sept. 12, 1852 (Yorkshire, Eng.)–Feb. 15, 1928. English statesman. As Liberal party prime min. (1908–16), put through the Parliament Act of 1911 limiting the House of Lords, and also enacted much social legislation.

ASTOR, VISCOUNTESS NANCY WITCHER, née Langhorne, May 19, 1879 (Greenwood, Va.)–May 2, 1964. English politician. The first woman to sit in the British House of Commons; advocate of women's rights, temperance; an opponent of socialism. *My Two Countries,* 1923.

ATTLEE, CLEMENT RICHARD, VISCOUNT PRESTWOOD, Jan. 3, 1883 (London, Eng.)–Oct. 8, 1967. English politician. Leader of the Labour party, 1935–55; as prime min. (1945–52), led Great Britain during a period of economic austerity and development of a welfare state.

BALFOUR, ARTHUR JAMES, FIRST EARL OF BALFOUR, July 25, 1848 (East Lothian, Eng.)–Mar. 19, 1930. English statesman. A major force in the Conservative party for 50 years. Prime min., 1902–05; as foreign secy. (1916–19), known for the Balfour Declaration (1917) expressing official British approval of Zionism.

BEAVERBROOK, LORD, born William Maxwell Aitken, May 25, 1879 (Maple, Ont., Can.)–June 9, 1964. British publisher, statesman, financier. As owner of several British newspapers, including the *Daily Express, Sunday Express,* and *Evening Standard,* played a major role in building the popular press in Great Britain; entered govt. during WW II as min. of aircraft production (1940–41) and min. of supply (1941–42).

BEVAN, ANEURIN, Nov. 15, 1897 (Monmouthshire, Eng.)–July 6, 1960. British political leader. Labour Party leader; as min. of health (1945–51), developed the socialized medicine system in Britain; a brilliant orator who opposed German rearmament after WW I and Britain's reliance on the U.S. in foreign affairs.

BEVIN, ERNEST, Mar. 9, 1881 (Somersetshire, Eng.)–Apr. 14, 1951. English statesman, labor leader. Powerful British union leader who merged several unions to form the Transport and General Workers' Union, 1922; as min. of labor (1940–45), mobilized manpower for WW II; as foreign min. (1945–51), helped lay the basis of NATO.

BOLEYN, ANNE, 1507? (England)-1536. English queen (1533-36), second wife of HENRY VIII and mother of ELIZABETH I. Her refusal to be Henry's mistress led him to start proceedings to annul his marriage to Catherine of Aragon; after papal delays, newly appointed archbishop of Canterbury declared marriage invalid; her failure to provide a male heir turned Henry away; beheaded for adultery and incest with her brother, 1536.

BOLINGBROKE, HENRY ST. JOHN, FIRST VISCOUNT, Sept. 16, 1678 (Wilshire?, Eng.)-Dec. 12, 1751. English politician, historian, philosopher. The leading political leader in the reign of Queen Anne, 1702-14. As secy. of state (1710-14), negotiated the Treaty of Utrecht (1713).

BRIGHT, JOHN, Nov. 16, 1811 (Lancashire, Eng.)-Mar. 27, 1889. English politician, orator. A populist reformer who founded the Anti-Corn Law League, 1839; fought for parliamentary reform; opposed the Crimean War.

CALLAGHAN, (Leonard) **JAMES,** Mar. 27, 1912 (Portsmouth, Eng.). English politician. Member of Parliament, 1945-   ; chan. of the exchequer, 1964-67; home secy., 1967-70; as foreign secy. (1974-76), renegotiated the terms for British membership in the European Economic Community; prime min., 1976-79. *A House Divided,* 1973.

CASEMENT, SIR ROGER DAVID, Sept. 1, 1864 (County Dublin, Ire.)-Aug. 3, 1916. British civil servant and Irish martyr for the nationalist cause. As a British official, exposed exploitation in the Congo; joined Irish Nationalists in opposition to Irish participation in WW I; tried and hanged for treason for attempts to seek aid from Germany for Irish cause; verdict remains controversial because of British use of uncertain evidence of his homosexuality.

CECIL, (Edgar Algernon) **ROBERT, FIRST VISCOUNT CECIL OF CHELWOOD,** Sept. 14, 1864 (London, Eng.)-Nov. 24, 1958. English statesman. Collaborator in drafting of the League of Nations Covenant and ardent backer of the league; awarded Nobel Peace Prize, 1937.

CHAMBERLAIN, SIR JOSEPH AUSTEN, Oct. 16, 1863 (Birmingham, Eng.)-Mar. 16, 1937. English statesman. As foreign secy. (1924-25), played a major role in the Locarno Pact (1925); lost political favor after the failure of the Geneva Conference on naval limitations, 1927; awarded Nobel Peace Prize (with CHARLES G. DAWES), 1925.

CHAMBERLAIN, NEVILLE, Mar. 18, 1869 (Birmingham, Eng.)-Nov. 9, 1940. English statesman. As prime min. (1937-40), became symbol of appeasement when he signed the Munich Pact (1938) that granted most of A. HITLER's demands and left Czechoslovakia defenseless.

CHURCHILL, LORD RANDOLPH HENRY SPENCER, Feb. 13, 1849 (Blenheim Palace, Eng.)-Jan. 24, 1895. English politician. Independent Conservative Party leader, advocate of "Tory Democracy"; secy. of state for India (1885-86) during the annexation of Burma; chan. of the exchequer and leader of the House of Commons, 1886. (Father of WINSTON CHURCHILL.)

CHURCHILL, SIR WINSTON, Nov. 30, 1874 (Blenheim Palace, Eng.)-Jan. 24, 1965. English statesman, author. As prime min. (1939-45 and 1951-55), gave Britain inspiring leadership during WW II; visited battlefronts, attended internatl. conferences, and provided stirring oratory for his struggling nation. Secy. of war 1919-21; head of colonial office, 1921-22; knighted, 1953; awarded 1953 Nobel Prize in literature for his *The Second World War* (6 vols., 1948-53). (Son of LORD RANDOLPH CHURCHILL.)

CLIVE, ROBERT, Baron Clive of Plassey, Sept. 29, 1725 (Shropshire, Eng.)-Nov. 22, 1774. English administrator, soldier. Conqueror of Bengal and first British administrator in India. As gov. of British territories in Bengal (1758-59), ran a corrupt admin.; returned to England and honored for his conquests, 1760; serving again as gov. (1765-67), secured East India Co.'s rule over Bengal and Bihar and corrected many abuses; committed suicide after debate in Parliament over his conduct.

CROMWELL, OLIVER, Apr. 25, 1599 (Huntingdonshire, Eng.)-Sept. 3, 1658. English statesman, soldier. Led the parliamentary forces in the English Civil War; waged war against Ireland and Scotland, 1650; dissolved the Parliament, 1653; installed as lord protector of England, Scotland and Ireland, 1653-58; led a war against the Dutch and Spain.

CROMWELL, THOMAS, c. 1485 (London, Eng.)-July 28, 1540. English statesman. As adviser to HENRY VIII (1532-40), drafted the acts that brought the Ref. to England; suppressed the monasteries; negotiated Henry VIII's marriage to Anne of Cleves, 1539; accused of treason and executed.

CURZON, GEORGE NATHANIEL, FIRST BARON AND FIRST MARQUIS CURZON OF KEDLESTON, Jan. 11, 1859 (Kedleston Hall, Eng.)-Mar. 20, 1925. English statesman. As viceroy of India (1898-1905), instituted many reforms and pacified the northern frontier; lord privy seal, 1915-16; foreign secy., 1919-24; presided over the Conference of Lausanne, 1922-23.

DE VALERA, EAMON, Oct. 14, 1882 (New York, N.Y.)-Aug. 29, 1975. Irish statesman. Fought for Irish independence from England in the Easter Rising of 1916; pres. of the Sinn Fein party, 1917-26; prime min., 1937-48, 1951-54, and 1957-59; pres., 1959-73.

DEVLIN, BERNADETTE JOSEPHINE (married name, McAliskey), April 23, 1947 (Cookstown, Ire.). Irish civil-rights leader. Leader of Northern Ireland's civil-rights movement in the late 1960s. At age of 21, youngest woman ever elected to the British Parliament, 1969; imprisoned for four months for her part in Londonderry demonstrations, 1969; defeated for reelection, 1974; member of the Irish Republican Socialist Party.

DISRAELI, BENJAMIN, EARL OF BEACONSFIELD, Dec. 21, 1804 (London, Eng.)-Apr. 19, 1881. British statesman. Founder of the modern Conservative party. Brilliant parliamentarian; elected to House of Commons, 1837; instrumental in passage of Reform Bill of 1867; as prime min. (1868, 1874-80), instituted many reforms in housing, public health, and factory legislation; checked Russian imperialism in Turkey and the Balkans. Novels: *Vivian Grey,* 1826; *Coningsby,* 1844.

EDEN, SIR ANTHONY, FIRST EARL OF AVON, June 12, 1897 (Durham, Eng.)-Jan. 14, 1977. English statesman. Foreign secy., 1935-38, 1940-45, and 1951-55; as prime min. (1955-57), took part in the Indochina settlement in Geneva (1954), helped establish the Southeast Asia Treaty Org., played a key (and controversial) role in the Anglo-French Suez expedition (1956).

EDWARD VIII (after his abdication, **DUKE OF WINDSOR**), June 23, 1894 (Richmond, Eng.)-May 18, 1972. King of Great Britain and Ireland, Jan. 20-Dec. 10, 1936. Abdicated in order to marry the twice-divorced American Mrs. Wallis

THE BOOK OF WHO

Warfield Spencer Simpson (DUCHESS OF WINDSOR); following the abdication, lived mainly in France. *A King's Story,* 1951.

ELIZABETH I, Sept. 7, 1533 (Greenwich, Eng.)-Mar. 23, 1603. Queen of England (1558-1603), who led her country during one of its greatest periods. Instituted the religious settlement of 1559, which enforced the Protestant religion by law and tolerated Catholics for the sake of national unity; restored the currency; encouraged interest in exploration of the New World; fought Spain's world empire, notably defeating the Spanish Armada (1588); passed "poor laws" in an attempt to eradicate widespread poverty; her reign was marked by a brilliant English literary renaissance, led by W. SHAKESPEARE and F. BACON.

ELIZABETH II, born Elizabeth Alexandra Mary, Apr. 21, 1926 (London, Eng.). Queen of Great Britain and Northern Ireland, 1952-   . Trained as a junior subaltern in the women's services during WW II; married Philip Mountbatten, duke of Edinburgh, 1947; as queen, joined Pres. D. D. EISENHOWER in the opening of the St. Lawrence Seaway, 1959; had audience with Pope JOHN XXIII, 1961; allowed televised reports of the royal family's domestic life, 1970.

FOX, CHARLES JAMES, Jan. 24, 1749 (London, Eng.)-Sept. 13, 1806. English statesman, orator. Fought for liberal reform and opposed King GEORGE III's policies, especially his coercive policies against the American colonies; helped to end British slave trade; favored the French Revolution; secured passage of Libel Bill (1792), which upheld full rights of juries in libel cases.

GAITSKELL, HUGH TODD NAYLOR, April 9, 1906 (London, Eng.)-Jan. 18, 1963. British political leader. Entered House of Commons, 1945; min. of state for economic affairs, 1950; chan. of the exchequer, 1950-51; as Labour Party leader (1955-63), persuaded the party to reverse its decision in favor of unilateral disarmament.

GLADSTONE, WILLIAM EWART, Dec. 29, 1809 (Liverpool, Eng.)-May 19, 1898. British statesman. As prime min. (1868-74, 1880-85, 1886, and 1892) and Liberal Party leader, powerfully affected the political life of his era; crusaded for Irish Home Rule, despite its political unpopularity; injected a high moral tone into Victorian politics; reformed the British Civil Service; took anti-imperialist stand; attempted to extend suffrage; reorganized the courts.

GREY, CHARLES, SECOND EARL, Mar. 13, 1764 (Northumberland, Eng.)-July 17, 1845. English statesman. A liberal Whig, part of the opposition to the Tory admin. of WILLIAM PITT; advocate of Catholic Emancipation; foreign secy., 1806-07; as prime min. (1830-34), fought for extension of the franchise, leading to the Reform Act of 1832.

GREY, LADY JANE, Oct. 1537 (Leicestershire, Eng.)-Feb. 12, 1554. Queen of England for nine days in 1553. Put on the throne by unscrupulous politicians; executed for treason under MARY I for her father's participation in Wyatt's Rebellion.

HALIFAX, EARL OF, born Edward Frederick Lindley Wood, Apr. 16, 1881 (Devon, Eng.)-Dec. 23, 1959. English statesman, diplomat. Viceroy of India, 1925-31; as foreign secy. (1938-40), identified with an appeasement policy toward Nazi Germany; amb. to the U.S., 1941-46.

HAROLD II, c. 1020-Oct. 14, 1066. The last Anglo-Saxon king of England. Ruled for nine months until his death at the hands of WILLIAM THE CONQUEROR at the Battle of Hastings.

HASTINGS, WARREN, Dec. 6, 1732 (Oxfordshire, Eng.)-Aug. 22, 1818. English administrator. As the first gov.-gen. of British India (1773-85), revitalized the British presence in India with his aggressive rule; suppressed banditry; involved Britain more deeply in Indian politics, both in conquered and unconquered provinces; impeached (1787) for maladministration and acquitted (1795).

HEATH, EDWARD RICHARD GEORGE, July 9, 1916 (Kent, Eng.) English statesman. As lord privy seal (1960-63), negotiated British entry into the European Economic Community; Conservative party leader, 1965-75; as prime min. (1970-74), his admin. was hurt by bad inflation and a threatened miners' strike.

HENRY VII, Jan. 28, 1457 (Pembrokeshire, Eng.)-Apr. 21, 1509. King of England, 1485-1509. Founded the Tudor dynasty, thereby ending the dynastic War of the Roses; as king, kept England at peace; promoted trade and internal law and order.

HENRY VIII, June 28, 1491 (Greenwich, Eng.)-Jan. 28, 1547. King of England, 1509-47. Played a major role in the break of the English church from Rome and the beginning of Protestantism in England. Wanting to divorce his wife Catherine, fought against the church to gain papal assent; because of continued conflict, with Parliament's backing created a national church separate from the Roman Catholic Church and proclaimed himself its head; confiscated the monasteries; also brought unity to England, built up the navy, and increased parliamentary powers. (Wives: CATHERINE OF ARAGON [1509-1533], ANNE BOLEYN [1533-1536], Jane Seymour [1536-1537], Anne of Cleves [Jan.-July, 1540], Catherine Howard [1540-1542], Catherine Parr [1543-1547].)

HYDE, EDWARD, 1st Earl of Clarendon, Feb. 18, 1609 (Wiltshire, Eng.)-Dec. 9, 1674. English statesman, historian. Entered Parliament, 1640; worked to create a bridge between CHARLES I and Parliament; after English Civil War brought OLIVER CROMWELL to power, followed Prince Charles into exile, 1648; following Cromwell's death, helped negotiate restoration of the monarchy under CHARLES II, 1660; fell from grace for his criticism of king's immorality; lived in France until his death. *History of the Rebellion,* 1670.

JOHN, born John Lackland, Dec. 24, 1167 (Oxford, Eng.)-Oct. 19, 1216. King of England (1199-1216) who was forced by the English barons to sign the Magna Carta (June 1215) after he violated the traditional feudal relationships with the nobility. (Brother of RICHARD I)

LAW, ANDREW BONAR, Sept. 16, 1858 (Kingston, N.B., Can.)-Oct. 30, 1923. British politician. Leader of British Conservative party, 1911-21 and 1922-23; British chan. of the exchequer (1916-18) and prime min. (1922-23); a supporter of tariff reform and an opponent of home rule for Ireland.

LLOYD GEORGE, DAVID, Jan. 17, 1863 (Manchester, Eng.)-Mar. 26, 1945. British statesman. As prime min. (1916-22), laid the foundations of the modern welfare state. Chan. of the exchequer, 1908-14; worked for a nonvindictive treaty at Versailles, 1919; negotiated Irish independence, 1921.

MACBRIDE, SEAN, Jan. 26, 1904 (Paris, Fr.). Irish internatl. civil servant. Secy. gen. of Internatl. Com. of Jurists, 1963-70; UN commander for Namibia, 1973-76; chm. of Amnesty Internatl., 1970-73; awarded Nobel Peace Prize, 1974; Lenin Peace Prize, 1977.

MACMILLAN, HAROLD, Feb. 10, 1894 (London, Eng.). English statesman. Min. to Allied Hq. in N. Africa, 1942–45; chan. of the exchequer, 1955–57; as Conservative party prime min. (1957–63), failed to gain British entry into the European Economic Community and suffered setback of the Profumo scandal; achieved Nuclear Test-Ban Treaty, 1963.

MARY, QUEEN OF SCOTS, born Mary Stuart, Dec. 7, 1542 (Linlithgow, Scot.)–Feb. 8, 1587. Queen of Scotland. Inherited throne at age of six days; queen consort of François II of France, 1559–60; returned to Scotland to rule, 1561; faced hostility because of her Roman Catholicism; married (1565) Lord Darnley, a generally unpopular choice; then allegedly conspired in Darnley's murder, 1567; married Earl of Bothwell, provoking rebellion of Scottish nobles; imprisoned, forced to abdicate, 1567; fled to England, where she was imprisoned by ELIZABETH I; held for 18 years and executed.

MARY I ("Bloody Mary"), Feb. 18, 1516 (Greenwich, Eng.)–Nov. 17, 1558. Queen of England, 1553–58. The first English queen to rule in her own right; persecuted Protestants in an attempt to restore Roman Catholicism in England.

MORE, SIR THOMAS, Feb. 7, 1477 (London, Eng.)–July 6, 1535. English statesman, humanist. A leading humanist whose *Utopia* (1516) formulated an ideal state based on reason. Entered service of HENRY VIII, 1518; knighted, 1521; succeeded Cardinal WOLSEY as lord chan.; 1529–32; enraged Henry by refusing to attend ANNE BOLEYN's crowning, 1533; arrested and imprisoned, 1534; refused to accept Act of Supremacy making Henry head of the Church of England; beheaded for treason. A saint of the Roman Catholic Church.

MOSELY, SIR OSWALD ERNALD, Nov. 16, 1896 (London, Eng.). British fascist leader. Leader of British Union of Fascists (1932–40) and its successor, the Union movement (1948–   ); member of House of Commons, 1918–31; interned, 1940–43.

NICOLSON, SIR HAROLD GEORGE, Nov. 21, 1886 (Teheran, Persia [now Iran])–May 1, 1968. English diplomat, biographer, historian. Served in British foreign service, 1909–29; member of Parliament, 1935–45. *Peacemaking, 1919,* 1933; *The Congress of Vienna,* 1946.

NORTH, FREDERICK, SECOND EARL OF GUILFORD, Apr. 13, 1732 (London, Eng.)–Aug. 5, 1792. English statesman. Served as prime min. during the American Revolution, 1770–82; partially repealed the Townshend Acts, 1770; passed the Intolerable Acts (1774), including the Boston Port Bill; became convinced the king's policy toward the colonies was mistaken and attempted to convince Parliament not to tax the colonies; resigned.

O'CONNELL, DANIEL ("The Liberator"), Aug. 6, 1775 (County Kerry, Ire.)–May 15, 1847. Irish nationalist leader in the British House of Commons, 1829–40 and 1844–47. United Irish Roman Catholics into a league to press for Irish claims; his election to Parliament (1828) forced British govt. to accept Emancipation Act of 1829, which allowed Roman Catholics to sit in Parliament and hold office; lord mayor of Dublin, 1841–43.

PALMERSTON, VISCOUNT, born Henry John Temple ("Pam"), Oct. 20, 1784 (Hampshire, Eng.)–Oct. 18, 1865. English statesman. As foreign min. (1830–34, 1835–41, and 1846–51) and prime min. (1855–58), pursued a highly successful nationalist policy; used the navy to save

Turkey from being conquered by Mohammed Ali of Egypt, 1839–41.

PARNELL, CHARLES STEWART, June 27, 1846 (Avondale, Ire.)–Oct. 6, 1891. Irish nationalist leader. First pres. of Natl. Land League of Ireland, 1879; as member of Parliament, obstructed parliamentary business in order to bring attention to Irish Home Rule; advocated a boycott against landlords and land agents; political career ruined by a scandal involving himself and a colleague's wife, 1889.

PEEL, SIR ROBERT, Feb. 5, 1788 (Lancashire, Eng.)–July 2, 1850. English political leader, a major founder of the Conservative Party. Chief secy. for Ireland, 1812–18; as home secy. (1823–30), founded the London Police Force (1829) and sponsored a bill enabling Roman Catholics to sit in the House of Commons (1829); as British prime min. (1834–35 and 1841–46), reorganized the Bank of England, launched a policy of reform in Ireland (1845) and repealed the Corn Laws (1846) that had restricted grain imports.

PITT (the Elder), WILLIAM, EARL OF CHATHAM, ("The Great Commoner"), Nov. 15, 1708 (Westminster, Eng.)–May 11, 1778. English statesman. As secy. of state (1756–61 and 1766–68), extremely influential in making England into an imperial power. Led England during the Seven Years' War (1756–63), which won vast territory for England, including Canada; worked for conciliation with the American colonies, just short of independence.

PITT, (the Younger), WILLIAM, May 28, 1759 (Kent, Eng.)–Jan. 23, 1806. English statesman. As prime min. (1783–1801), led England during the French Revolutionary wars. Widely considered to be England's greatest prime min.; implemented financial reforms; during French Revolutionary wars, clamped down on radical agitation; worked for Catholic emancipation in Ireland; led England during the initial stages of the Napoleonic wars.

RHODES, CECIL, July 5, 1853 (Hertfordshire, Eng.)–Mar. 26, 1902. English statesman, financier. Based on the fortune he had cleverly amassed in diamonds, built an empire in S. Africa; formed the De Beers Mining Co., 1880; prime min. of Cape Colony, 1890–96; established the Rhodes Scholarships at Oxford U. Rhodesia named for him.

RICHARD I ("The Lion-Heart"), Sept. 8, 1157 (Oxford, Eng.)–Apr. 6, 1199. King of England, 1189–99. Known for his chivalry, the subject of many romantic legends. Started on the Third Crusade, 1189; conquered Cyprus, 1191; recaptured Jaffa from Saladin, 1192; on his return, captured in Austria (1192) and held for ransom; ransomed and returned to England.

RICHARD III, Oct. 2, 1452 (Northamptonshire, Eng.)–Aug. 22, 1485. King of England, 1483–85. On the death of his brother, Edward IV, assumed protectorship of young Edward V; placed Edward and his brother, the duke of York, in the Tower of London, and crowned himself king; the mysterious deaths of the two young princes traditionally has been attributed to Richard, although modern research has cast doubt on his guilt; Henry Tudor (later Henry VII) killed Richard at Bosworth Field, thereby ending War of Roses, 1485.

ROBERT I, or Robert the Bruce, July 11, 1274 (prob. Ayrshire, Scot.)–June 7, 1329. King (1306–29) and liberator of Scotland. Initially paid homage to Edward I of England; crowned king of Scotland, he rebelled but was defeated, 1306; upon returning from refuge in Ireland, recon-

THE BOOK OF WHO

quered most of Scotland from England, 1307-09; defeated Edward II's army at Bannockburn, 1314; fought the English repeatedly until Edward III recognized the independence of Scotland, 1328.

SHAFTESBURY, ANTHONY ASHLEY COOPER, FIRST EARL OF SHAFTESBURY, 1st BARON ASHLEY, July 22, 1621 (Dorset, Eng.)-Jan. 21, 1683. English statesman. A leading politician of his time, served as a cabinet min. both under OLIVER CROMWELL and after the Restoration of Charles II; opposed Charles's pro-Roman Catholic policies.

STRAFFORD, SIR THOMAS WENTWORTH, Apr. 13, 1593 (London, Eng.)-May 11, 1641. English statesman. From an influential family of the north, initially opposed King Charles I, but became one of his chief supporters with appointment as lord pres. of the north (1628) and privy chan. (1629); supported king's authoritarian rule; as lord dep. of Ireland (1633-39), sought to strengthen royal power there; his failed attempt to quell Scottish revolt of 1639-40 brought impeachment by Parliament; executed with consent of Charles.

VICTORIA (in full, Alexandrina Victoria), May 24, 1819 (London, Eng.)-Jan. 22, 1901. Queen of Great Britain and Ireland (1837-1901) and empress of India (1876-1901). Through her long reign, enjoyed great popularity and restored dignity to the crown; very devoted to her husband Prince ALBERT, on whom she conferred the title Prince Consort; had nine children; had great interest in the British colonies, especially India.

WALPOLE, ROBERT, Aug. 26, 1676 (Norfolk, Eng.)-Mar. 18, 1745. English statesman. Regarded as the first British prime min. (1721-42). Made the cabinet system effective and powerful for the first time; successfully handled the South Sea Bubble financial problem, 1720; encouraged trade; cultivated friendship with France; managed Parliament brilliantly, enforcing party discipline.

WILLIAM I ("the Conqueror"), c. 1028 (Normandy, Fr.)-Sept. 9, 1087. King of England (1066-87) and duke of Normandy (1035-87). Conquered England (the Norman Conquest), 1066; replaced old English nobility with his followers; made a survey of England called the Doomsday Book, 1085; established the primacy of loyalty to the king rather than to subordinate lords.

WILSON, SIR (James) **HAROLD,** Mar. 11, 1916 (Yorkshire, Eng.). English statesman, economist. As prime min. (1964-76), attempted unsuccessfully to impose economic sanctions against the white supremacist regime in Rhodesia; plagued by economic problems in England. *New Deal for Coal,* 1945.

WOLSEY, THOMAS, c. 1475 (Suffolk, Eng.)-Nov. 29, 1530. English cardinal, statesman. Dominated the English govt. during the reign of HENRY VIII, 1515-1529. Named lord chancellor, 1515; appointed papal rep., 1515; used his power to amass wealth second only to that of the king; failed in attempt to persuade the pope to annul Henry's marriage to Catherine of Aragon.

FRENCH RULERS, STATESMEN, AND POLITICAL LEADERS

BARRE, RAYMOND, Apr. 12, 1924 (Saint-Denis, Fr.). French politician. Vice-pres. of the Comm. of European Communities, 1967-72; min. of economy and finance, 1976-78; prime min. 1976- . *Economie politique,* 1956.

BRIAND, ARISTIDE, Mar. 28, 1862 (Nantes, Fr.)-Mar. 7, 1932. French statesman. With Jean Jaurès, founded *L'Humanité,* 1904; served as prime min. seven times, 1909-1932; as foreign min. (1925-32), responsible for the Locarno treaties (1925) and the Kellogg-Briand Pact (1927-28) to renounce war; awarded Nobel Peace Prize (with GUSTAVE STRESEMANN), 1926.

CAPET, HUGH, c. 938-Oct. 14, 996. Founder of the Capetian line of French monarchs; battled with Charles, the Carolingian contender, to defend his rule; secured his election as king, 987.

CASSIN, RENE, Oct. 5, 1887 (Bayonne, Fr.)-Feb. 20, 1976. French jurist. As pres. of UN Human Rights Comm. (1946-68), the principal author of the UN Declaration of the Rights of Man (adopted 1948); awarded Nobel Peace Prize, 1968.

CATHERINE DE MEDICIS, Apr. 13, 1519 (Florence, It.)-Jan. 5, 1589. Queen consort of HENRY II of France, then regent of France (1560-74). Deeply involved in the Catholic-Huguenot wars, at first tried to reconcile the two sides, then joined the Catholics; after religious war broke out, helped plan the St. Bartholomew's Day massacre (1572).

CHARLEMAGNE (or Charles the Great, Charles I), Apr. 2, c. 742 (Aachen, now in W. Ger.)-Jan. 28, 814. French ruler. King of the Franks, 768-814; conquered and united almost all of the Christian lands of W. Europe and ruled as emperor (800-814); reformed admin. by the use of personal reps.; nurtured a renaissance in learning; preserved classical literature and established schools; began a monometallic system of currency; introduced the capitulary as a form of legal promulgation, 779.

CHARLES VII, Feb. 22, 1403 (Paris, Fr.)-July 22, 1461. King of France, 1422-61. Inspired and aided by JOAN OF ARC, waged war against the English occupation of northern France; captured Orleans and crowned at Reims, 1429; concluded peace with the Burgundians, 1435; recovered all French lands from the English, except Calais, 1437-53; reorganized admin., undermined the power of the nobility.

CLEMENCEAU, GEORGES, Sept. 28, 1841 (Mouilleron-en-Pareds, Fr.)-Nov. 24, 1929. French statesman. Helped LÉON GAMBETTA in overthrowing the empire of Napoleon III, 1870; a defender of A. DREYFUS; as premier (1906-09 and 1917-20), extended French interests in Morocco and strengthened the alliance with England, then revitalized the French war effort during WW I.

COLBERT, JEAN BAPTISTE, Aug. 29, 1619 (Reims, Fr.)-Sept. 6, 1683. French govt. official, businessman. As finance min. to LOUIS XIV (1665-85), oversaw economic reconstruction of France; followed doctrines of mercantilism; encouraged tariff protection; built French navy, 1669-72; initiated state manufactures.

CORDAY, CHARLOTTE, born Marie Anne Charlotte Corday d'Armont, July 27, 1768 (Normandy, Fr.)-July 17, 1793. French patriot. An aristocrat inspired by the Girondist cause, she assassinated the French revolutionary JEAN PAUL MARAT because she saw him as the persecutor of the Girondists, 1793.

DALADIER, EDOUARD, June 18, 1884 (Carpentras, Fr.)-Oct. 10, 1970. French politician. Member of Chamber of Deputies, 1919-40; as premier (1933-34, 1936, and 1938-40), signed the Munich Pact (1938); imprisoned by Vichy govt., 1940-45.

DANTON, GEORGES JACQUES, Oct. 26, 1759 (Champagne, Fr.)-Apr. 5, 1794. French revolution-

158

ary leader. Led the Cordeliers in the early days of the revolution; participated in the overthrow of the monarchy; dominated the first Com. of Public Safety, 1793; became critical of the revolutionary govt. for its excesses; executed for treason.

ELEANOR OF AQUITAINE, c.1122–Apr. 1, 1204. Queen consort of Louis VII of France (1137–52) and HENRY II of England (1154–89). Went on the Second Crusade, 1147–49; helped her sons, RICHARD I and JOHN, to rule England; a patroness of the arts.

GAMBETTA, LÉON, Apr. 2, 1838 (Cahors, Fr.)–Dec. 31, 1882. French political leader. One of the chief founders of the Third Republic. Pres. of Chamber of Deputies, 1879–81; premier, 1881–82.

DE GAULLE, CHARLES ANDRÉ JOSEPH MARIE, Nov. 22, 1890 (Lille, Fr.)–Nov. 9, 1970. French statesman, soldier. Distinguished himself as a soldier in WW I; leader of the French govt.-in-exile during WW II and symbol of the French Resistance; critical of the Fourth Republic, retired to private life; returned as pres. of the Fifth Republic (1958–69); solved Algerian crisis by granting independence, 1962; attempted to build a powerful France; formed a foreign policy independent of the USSR and the U.S.

GISCARD D'ESTAING, VALÉRY, Feb. 2, 1926 (Coblenz, Ger.). French political leader. Elected to the National Assembly, 1956; to UN Gen. Assembly, 1956–58; leader of Independent Republican party, 1966–   ; min. for finance and economic affairs, 1962–66; pres., 1974–   .

HENRY IV (or Henry of Navarre), Dec. 13, 1553 (Pau, Fr.)–May 14, 1610. King of Navarre (as Henry III) (1572–89) and king of France (1589–1610). The first of the Bourbon line; brought an end to the religious wars in France. Raised a Calvinist, renounced Protestantism for Catholicism when he became king; defeated the Catholic League and other opposition; with the Edict of Nantes (1598), established toleration of the Protestants; encouraged economic prosperity in France.

LAVAL, PIERRE, June 28, 1883 (Chateldon, Fr.)–Oct. 15, 1945. French politician. Leader of the Vichy govt.'s collaboration with the Germans during WW II; executed for treason.

LOUIS XIV ("The Sun King"), Sept. 5, 1638 (Saint-Germain-en-Laye, Fr.)–Sept. 1, 1715. King of France (1643–1715) who made the state an absolute monarchy and led France during a period of greatness. Unified France; made the nobility financially dependent upon him; through wars, expanded France territorially, 1667–97; persecuted the Huguenots; built the palace at Versailles; patron of the arts; military reverses in later wars and the ruinous expenditures on the armed forces left France exhausted and poor at his death.

LOUIS XVI, Aug. 23, 1754 (Versailles, Fr.)–Jan. 21, 1793. King of France (1774–93), the last prior to the French Revolution of 1789. His reforms failed to prevent revolution; once the revolution was underway, he failed to hold the confidence of its leadership; imprisoned, convicted of treason, guillotined.

MACMAHON, COMTE MARIE EDME PATRICE MAURICE DE, July 13, 1808 (Sully, Fr.)–Oct. 17, 1893. French politician, soldier. A marshal of France, monarchist. As pres. of the French Republic (1873–79), suffered a constitutional crisis that resulted in parliamentary rather than presidential control of the republic.

MAGINOT, ANDRÉ, Feb. 17, 1877 (Paris, Fr.)–Jan. 7, 1932. French statesman. As min. of war (1929–31), largely responsible for the construction of the Maginot Line, a defense barrier along the eastern border of France.

MARAT, JEAN PAUL, May 24, 1743 (Boudry, Switz.)–July 13, 1793. French revolutionary. Well-known writer and advocate of extreme violence during the French Revolution; editor of *The Friend of the People,* 1789; del. to the Natl. Convention, 1792; leader of the radical Montagnard faction; helped DANTON and ROBESPIERRE overthrow the Girondists; assassinated by C. CORDAY while in his bath.

MARIE ANTOINETTE (in full, Josephe Jeanne Marie Antoinette), Nov. 2, 1755 (Vienna, Austria)–Oct. 16, 1793. Austrian queen-consort of LOUIS XVI of France, 1774–93. Attempted to strengthen French ties with Austria, an unpopular policy in France; surrounded herself with a dissipated clique; found guilty of treason by French Revolutionary forces and guillotined.

MAZARIN, JULES, born Guilio Mazarini, July 14, 1602 (Peseina, It.)–Mar. 9, 1661. French cardinal, statesman. The successor to RICHELIEU, he continued to strengthen France. Became chief min., 1642; won a war with Austria; defeated the Fronde (revolt of the nobility) with clever diplomacy, 1648–53; negotiated the favorable Peace of the Pyrennees at the end of war with Spain, 1659.

MENDÈS-FRANCE, PIERRE, Jan. 11, 1907 (Paris, Fr.). French political leader, economist. Leader of the Radical-Socialist Party; as premier (1954–55), withdrew France from Indochina and aided the formation of the Western European Union; opposed the return of CHARLES DE GAULLE to power.

NAPOLEON I, born Napoleon Bonaparte, Aug. 15, 1769 (Ajaccio, Corsica)–May 15, 1821. French soldier and emperor. Became an army officer, 1785; fought during the French Revolution; promoted to brig. gen., 1793; commanded the Army of Italy in several victories, 1796–97; defeated in Egypt and Syria, 1798–99; in coup, brought to supreme power as first consul, 1799; made reforms in education and govt., formulating the Napoleonic Code that remains the basis of the French legal system; defeated the Austrians, 1800; went to war against Great Britain, 1803; had himself crowned emperor, 1804; disastrously invaded Russia, 1812; defeated by Allied coalition, 1814; exiled to Elba, 1814; returned, regained power, defeated at Waterloo, 1815; exiled to St. Helena.

POINCARÉ, RAYMOND, Aug. 20, 1860 (Bar-le-Duc, Fr.)–Oct. 15, 1934. French statesman. As prime min. and foreign min. (1912), strove to increase French security, supporting entente with Britain and alliance with Russia; as pres. (1913–20), sought national unity during WW I and pressed for harsher measures for Germany after the war.

POMPADOUR, MADAME DE (Marquise de), born Jeanne Antoinette Poisson, Dec. 29, 1721 (Paris, Fr.)–Apr. 15, 1764. French mistress of Louis XV of France. Exerted much control over French policies; encouraged France's alliance with Austria, which involved France in the Seven Years' War (1756–63); a patron of the anticlerical philosophers; a friend of VOLTAIRE.

POMPIDOU, GEORGES, July 5, 1911 (Montboudif, Fr.)–Apr. 2, 1974. French statesman. WW II aide to CHARLES DE GAULLE; as premier (1962–68), was a prominent negotiator during the 1968 strikes and riots; as pres. of the Fifth Repub-

THE BOOK OF WHO

lic (1969-74), ended France's opposition to Great Britain's entry into the European Common Market.

REYNAUD, PAUL, Oct. 15, 1878 (Barcelonette, Fr.)-Sept. 21, 1966. French statesman. As min. of finance (1938-39), devalued the franc to help pay for a better defense; as prime min. (1940), tried unsuccessfully to save France from German occupation.

RICHELIEU, ARMAND JEAN DU PLESSIS, DUC DE, Sept. 9, 1585 (Poitou, Fr.)-Dec. 4, 1642. French cardinal, statesman. As chief min. to Louis XIII (1624-42), built France into a great power; centralized the govt., suppressing the Huguenots and the great nobles; made alliances with the Netherlands and the German Protestant powers, increasing France's power to the detriment of Spain's.

ROBESPIERRE, MAXIMILIEN FRANÇOIS MARIE ISIDORE DE, May 6, 1758 (Arras, Fr.)-July 28, 1794. French revolutionary leader. Jacobin leader and a major figure of the Reign of Terror of the French Revolution. Elected to the Estates-Gen., 1789; leader of the radical Montagnard faction in the Natl. Convention; dominated the Com. of Public Safety (1793), which ruled during the Reign of Terror; overthrown and killed in the Thermidorian Reaction of 1794.

SCHUMAN, ROBERT, June 29, 1886 (Luxembourg)-Sept. 4, 1963. French statesman. Founder of the European Coal and Steel Community (1952) and proponent of European unity. As French foreign min. (1948-52), proposed the Schuman Plan (1950) for European economic and political unity; pres. of European Parliament Assembly, the consultive arm of the Common Market. 1958-60.

SILHOUETTE, ÉTIENNE DE, 1709-1767. French government official. As controller general of finances (1759), attempted to enforce stringent economies, causing the nobility to apply his name to a mere outline profile drawing, i.e., a "silhouette."

TALLEYRAND-PÉRIGORD, CHARLES MAURICE DE, PRINCE DE BÉNÉVET, Feb. 2, 1754 (Paris, Fr.)-May 17, 1838. French statesman, diplomat. The leading French politician of his time. Min. of foreign affairs under NAPOLEON I, 1797-1807; aided in the restoration of the Bourbons; negotiated the Treaty of Paris; represented France brilliantly at the Congress of Vienna, 1814; helped organize the Quadruple Alliance, 1834.

THIERS, LOUIS ADOLPHE, Apr. 15, 1797 (Marseilles, Fr.)-Sept. 3, 1877. French statesman, historian. A founder and the first pres. of the Third Republic (1871-73). Suppressed the Paris Commune, 1871. *Histoire de la Révolution Française,* 10 vols., 1823-27.

OTHER FOREIGN RULERS, STATESMEN, AND POLITICAL LEADERS

ABU BAKR ("The Upright"), c.573 (Mecca, Arabia)-Aug. 23, 634. First Moslem Caliph (632-35) and successor to MOHAMMED. Father-in-law of Mohammed and his only companion on the hegira; began the amazing expansion of Islam as a world religion.

ADENAUER, KONRAD ("der Alte"), Jan. 5, 1876 (Cologne, Ger.)-Apr. 19, 1967. German statesman. As first chan. of the Federal Republic of Germany (1949-63), responsible for the nation's amazing economic recovery and political independence after WW II. Mayor of Cologne, 1917-33; twice imprisoned by the Nazis, 1934 and 1944.

AKBAR, born Jala ud-Din Mohammed, Oct. 15, 1542 (Umarkot, Sind [now Pakistan])-1605. Greatest of the Indian Moghul emperors. Extended his father's (Humayun) empire to the whole of northern India; instituted administrative and fiscal reforms; encouraged religious toleration; instituted a new religion, Din-i-Ilahi.

ALARIC, c.370 (Peuce I. [now Rumania])-410. Chief of the Visigoths (from 395). Conquered and sacked Rome, 410.

ALEXANDER NEVSKY, 1220 (Vladimir, Rus.)-Nov. 14, 1236. Prince of Kiev, grand prince of Vladimir. Halted the Swedish and Teutonic Knights' invasions of Russia; canonized by the Russian Orthodox Church.

ALEXANDER THE GREAT, or Alexander III, 356 B.C. (Pella, Macedonia)-June 13, 323 B.C. King of Macedonia, 336-323 B.C. Conquered Thrace and Illyria and gained control over all Greece, 335; conquered Persia (334), Tyre, Gaza, occupied Egypt and founded Alexandria (332); died of fever and fatigue at age 33.

ALLENDE GOSSENS, SALVADOR, July 26, 1908 (Valparaiso, Chile)-Sept. 11, 1973. Chilean politician, physician. As the first Marxist pres. of Chile (1970-73), nationalized several foreign-owned industries and pushed agrarian reform; besieged by crippling strikes and economic problems, overthrown by a military coup (1973); reported to have committed suicide.

AMIN DADA, IDI, 1925? (Koboko, Uganda). Ugandan military and political leader. As pres. of Uganda, (1971-79), ordered almost all Asians expelled, 1972; in attempt to purge Lango and Acholi tribes, caused deaths of an estimated 90,000 persons, 1971-74; chaired Org. of African Unity, 1975-76; survived many assassination attempts; ousted by Tanzanian-led invasion, 1979.

ANDREOTTI, GIULIO, Jan. 14, 1919 (Rome, It.). Italian politician, journalist. Editor of *Concretezza,* 1954-76; chm. of Christian Democratic party 1968-72; prime min. 1972-73 and 1976- .

ANTONESCU, MARSHALL ION, June 15, 1882 (Pitesti, Rum.)-June 1, 1946. Rumanian statesman, soldier. As dictator of the pro-German govt. during WW II (1940-44), declared war on the USSR, 1941; initiated domestic reform programs; fostered emergence into power of the fascist Iron Guard, then suppressed it, 1941; lost support with increasing losses on the Russian front and overthrown, 1944.

ANTONY, MARC (in Latin, Marcus Antonius), c.83 B.C.-Aug. 30 B.C. Roman triumver, general. After J. CAESAR's death, formed with Octavian (later AUGUSTUS) and Lepidus the second triumvirate, 43 B.C.; defeated BRUTUS and Cassius at Philippi, 42 B.C.; lived with CLEOPATRA in Alexandria, from c.40 B.C.; committed suicide after naval defeat at Actium by Octavian's forces.

ARAFAT, YASIR, 1929 (Jerusalem, Palestine [now Israel]). Palestinian political and guerrilla leader. Helped found the al-Fatah fedayeen; head of Palestine Liberation Org., 1969- ; addressed UN in historic address seeking recognition of the PLO, 1974.

ASOKA ("the Great"), died c.232 B.C. Indian emperor of the Maurya dynasty (c.273-c.232 B.C.) who united most of India for the first time and spread Buddhism widely, elevating it to a world religion.

ATATÜRK, KEMAL, born Mustafa Kemal, 1881 (Salonika, Gr.)-Nov. 10, 1938. Turkish statesman, reformer, soldier. As founder and first pres. of the Turkish Republic (1923-38), abolished the

RULERS, STATESMEN, AND POLITICAL LEADERS

caliphate, closed religious courts and schools, instituted modern law (1926), decreed use of Latin rather than Arabic letters (1928), and extended the franchise to women (1934).

AUGUSTUS, GAIUS, JULIUS CAESAR OCTAVIANUS (Octavian), Sept. 23, 63 B.C.-Aug. 19, 14. First Roman emperor (27 B.C.-14). The adopted son of JULIUS CAESAR, went to Rome to avenge his death, 44 B.C.; in an alliance with ANTONY and Lepidus (the Second Triumvirate), defeated his enemies. As emperor, centralized power; spread the army throughout the empire; supported the arts; introduced the Pax Romana, an era of peace; made taxation more equitable; accomplished much construction.

AURANGZEB (or Aurungzeb, Aurungzebel), Oct. 24, 1618 (Ahmadnagar)-Mar. 3, 1707. Moghul emperor of India (1658-1707), under whom the empire reached its greatest size; his fanatical devotion to Islam alienated the Hindus and his empire disintegrated after his rule.

BAKUNIN, MIKHAIL, May 30, 1814 (Torzhok, Rus.[now Kalinin, USSR])-July 1, 1876. Russian anarchist. An opponent of KARL MARX; participated in the German revolutions of 1848-49; active in the First Internatl., 1868; believed in complete freedom and that destruction of the existing order was necessary. *God and the State*, 1882.

BANDARANAIKE, SIRIMAVO, Apr. 17, 1916 (Ratnapura, Ceylon [now Sri Lanka]). Ceylonese stateswoman. As prime minister of Ceylon, the world's first woman to hold the position, 1960-65 and 1970-77.

BATISTA Y ZALDIVAR, FULGENCIO, Jan. 16, 1901 (Banes, Cuba)-Aug. 6, 1973. Cuban dictator, soldier. As dictator of Cuba (1933-44), built a strong, efficient govt.; in his second term (1952-59) turned brutal and corrupt; ousted by FIDEL CASTRO, 1959.

BAUDOUIN, KING, Sept. 7, 1930 (Stuyenberg Castle, Belg.). Belgian political leader. King of Belgium, 1951- ; proclaimed the independence of the Belgian Congo (now Zaire), 1960; helped form five coalition govts., 1958-68.

BEGIN, MENACHEM, Aug. 16, 1913 (Brest-Litovsk, Rus.). Israeli political leader. Headed Betar Zionist Youth Movement in Poland, 1939; arrested by Soviet govt. and held in a Siberian concentration camp, 1940-41; in Palestine, took command of underground Irgun Zvai Leumi extremist organization, 1943; founded Herut (Freedom) Movement in Israel, 1948; joint chm. of Likud (Unity) Party, 1973- ; prime min. of Israel, 1977-

BENEŠ, EDUARD, May 28, 1884 (Kožlany, Bohemia [now Czech.])-Sept. 3, 1948. Czechoslovak statesman. A founder of modern Czechoslovakia. Min. of foreign affairs, 1918-35; pres. 1935-38; fled in 1938 to lead a Czech exile regime in London during WW II; returned in 1945 and served as pres. until forced to succumb to communist takeover, 1948.

BEN-GURION, DAVID, born David Gruen, Oct. 16, 1886 (Plonsk, Pol.)-Dec. 1, 1973. Israeli statesman. The first prime min. of Israel (1948-52 and 1954-63), often called the "Father of the Nation." A young Zionist who emigrated to Palestine in 1906; expelled by Turks, but returned when British took over rule; founded Histadrut (General Org. of Jewish Labor), 1920; chaired World Zionist Org. during the struggle to create the state of Israel.

BERIA, LAVRENTI PAVLOVICH, Mar. 29, 1899 (Merkheuli, Rus.)-Dec. 23, 1953. Soviet political-

leader. As head of Soviet internal security (1938-53), purged many of J. STALIN's opponents and administered labor camps; killed in power struggle to succeed Stalin.

BETANCOURT, ROMULO, Feb. 22, 1908 (Guatiré, Ven.). Venezuelan leader. Helped found the Accion Democratia, an anticommunist party, 1941; as pres. (1945-48 and 1959-64), instituted many reforms.

BISMARCK, OTTO VON ("The Iron Chancellor"), Apr. 1, 1815 (Schönhausen, Brandenburg)-July 30, 1898. German statesman. Founder and first chan. of the German Empire. Unified the German states into one empire under Prussian leadership, 1871; developed a common currency, a central bank, and a single code of commercial and civil law; first European statesman to devise a comprehensive scheme of Social Security; presided over the Congress of Berlin, 1878.

BOLIVAR, SIMON ("The Liberator"), July 24, 1783 (Caracas, Ven.)-Dec. 17, 1830. S. American statesman, soldier. Leader in the liberation of northern S. America from Spanish imperial control, leading to independence for Colombia (1819), Venezuela (1821), Peru (1824), and Bolivia (1825). Pres. of Colombia, 1819-30; pres. of Peru, 1824-27; his attempts to form a Hispanic-American union under his control failed.

BORGIA, CESARE, c.1475 (Rome?, It.)-Mar. 12, 1507. Italian leader, soldier. Powerful papal lieutenant who was idealized by N. MACHIAVELLI in *The Prince*. The son of Pope Alexander VI, became duke of Romagna and captain-gen. of the Church; murdered his brother; through intrigue and military victory became lord of large territory in central Italy and spread terror throughout the country.

BORGIA, LUCREZIA, Duchess of Ferrara, Apr. 18, 1480 (Rome, It.)-June 24, 1519. Italian noblewoman. Long associated with crimes and the moral excesses of her father, Rodrigo Borgia (later Pope Alexander VI), and brother CESARE BORGIA, she has been largely cleared by recent research; married three times into prominent families for reasons of political expediency; after her father's death (1503), led an exemplary life, making Ferrara an artistic and literary center of the Italian Renaissance.

BOSCH, JUAN, June 30, 1909 (La Vega, D.R.). Dominican political leader. Elected pres. in first free elections in 38 years, 1932; overthrown by military as too leftist, 1963; attempts at restoration to power failed, 1965; founded Dominican Liberation party, 1973.

BOTHA, LOUIS, Sept. 27, 1862 (nr. Greytown, S.A.)-Aug. 27, 1919. S. African statesman, soldier. Brilliant gen. of the Boer troops in the S. African War; premier of Transvaal, 1907-10; first prime min. of the Union of S. Africa, 1910-19.

BRANDT, WILLY, born Karl Herbert Frahn, Dec. 18, 1913 (Lubeck, Ger.). German politician. Member of Bundestag, 1949-57; mayor of W. Berlin, 1957-65; chan. of Federal Republic of Germany, 1969-74; resigned after a spy scandal; awarded Nobel Peace Prize in 1971 for his work in improving relations between W. Germany and the Soviet Union.

BREZHNEV, LEONID ILYCH, Dec. 19, 1906 (Kamenskoye, Rus. [now Dneprodzerzhinsk, USSR]). Soviet political leader. First Soviet leader to hold simultaneously the posts of secy. gen. of Soviet Communist party (1964-) and chm. of the Presidium of the Supreme Soviet. While in power, has applied scientific management to domestic problems and some forceful measures to foreign-policy problems.

BRIAN BORU (or Boramham, Boraimbe), 940? (County Clare, Ire.)-1014. King of Ireland (963-1014) who increased his territory through conquest and broke Norse power in Ireland forever.

BRUTUS, MARCUS JUNIUS, 85 B.C.-42 B.C. Roman politician, soldier. Remembered chiefly as one of the conspirators who assassinated JULIUS CAESAR, 44 B.C.; his army was defeated by MARK ANTONY, 42 B.C.; committed suicide.

BUKHARIN, NIKOLAI IVANOVICH, Oct. 9, 1888 (Moscow, Rus.)-Mar. 13, 1938. Russian communist leader. A member of the Bolshevik wing of the Social Democratic party who became a member of the Central Com. of the Russian Communist party following the 1917 Revolution; member of the Soviet Politburo, 1924-29; head of Third Internatl., 1926-29; advocated slow agricultural collectivization and industrialization; expelled from party (1929), readmitted (1934), tried for treason and executed (1938).

BULGANIN, NIKOLAI ALEKSANDROVICH, June 11, 1895 (Nizhni-Novgorod, Rus. [now Gorki, USSR])-Feb. 24, 1975. Soviet leader. Mayor of Moscow, 1931-37; chm. of the State Bank, 1937-41; became a full member of the Politburo, 1948; defense min., 1947-49 and 1953-55; premier, 1955-58.

BÜLOW, PRINCE, BERNHARD VON, May 3, 1849 (Klein-Flott-bek, Ger.)-Oct. 28, 1929. German statesman. As chan. (1900-09), aggressively pursued Germany's interests, in the process strengthening the Triple Entente among Great Britain, France, and Russia.

CAESAR, GAIUS JULIUS, July 12, 100 B.C. (Rome, It.)-Mar. 15, 44 B.C. Roman general, statesman, orator, writer. Formed the first triumvirate, with Pompey and Crassus, 60 B.C.; conquered all Gaul (modern France and Belgium), 58-49 B.C.; conquered Britain, 54 B.C., ruled as Roman dictator, 49-44 B.C.; reformed the calendar, 46 B.C.; assassinated by BRUTUS, Cassius and others in the Senate house. *Commentaries (De bello Gallico* and *De bello civili).*

CALIGULA, GAIUS CAESAR, Aug. 31, 12 (Antium [now Anzio], It.)-Jan. 24, 41. Roman emperor, 37-41. After a short period of rule marked by moderation, resorted to cruelty and tyranny; reputed to have suffered from insanity; murdered by a member of the Praetorian Guard.

CARL XVI GUSTAF, Apr. 30, 1946 (Stockholm, Swed.). King of Sweden, 1973-   .

CASTRO, FIDEL, Aug. 13, 1926 (near Birán, Cuba). Cuban political leader. As premier of Cuba (1959-   ), has transformed his nation into the first communist state in the Western Hemisphere. Led the 26th of July Movement, a guerrilla campaign, to overthrow the F. BATISTA regime, 1959; collectivized agriculture, expropriated all native and foreign industry; held absolute authority until Dec. 1976, when assemblies with limited power were created.

CATHERINE II ("The Great"), born Sophia Augusta Frederika, of Anhalt-Zerbst, May 2, 1729 (Stettin, Ger. [now Szczecin, Pol.])-Nov. 17, 1796. Russian empress, 1762-1796. With help of the palace guard, overthrew her husband, Tsar Peter III; extended Russian territory greatly; through her diplomacy, increased Russian power and prestige; annexed Crimea from the Turks, 1783; divided Poland among Russia, Austria, and Prussia, 1795; a patron of the arts who corresponded with VOL-

TAIRE and was a disciple of the French Encyclopedists.

CATHERINE OF ARAGON, Dec. 16, 1485 (Alcala de Henares, Sp.)-Jan. 7, 1536. Spanish princess. First wife of King HENRY VIII of England; Henry wanted a legitimate male successor and after six of Catherine's children died and only one female (Queen Mary) lived, the couple separated, 1531; the annulment of their marriage by the archbishop of Canterbury (1533) brought about the break between Henry and Rome and led to the English Reformation.

CATO, THE ELDER, MARCUS PORCIUS, 234 B.C. (Tusculum, It.)-149 B.C. Roman statesman, soldier, writer. Fought in the Second Punic War (218-201 B.C.) and First Syrian War (192-189 B.C.); crucial in defeat of Antiochus at Thermopylae, 191 B.C.; as Roman censor (elected 184), defended traditional Roman values; the first Latin prose writer of importance. *On Farming,* 160 B.C.

CAVOUR, CAMILLO BENSO, COMTE DE, Aug. 10, 1810 (Turin, It.)-June 6, 1861. Italian statesman. Primarily responsible for the unification of Italy. Founded the liberal daily *Risorgimento,* 1847; as premier of Sardinia (1852-59 and 1860-61), modernized and industrialized the state; with help from the French, liberated Italy from Austrian domination; with diplomatic maneuvering and G. GARIBALDI's military successes, molded a unified Italy, 1861.

CEAUSESCU, NICHOLAE, Jan. 26, 1918 (Oltenia, Rum.). Rumanian political leader. Deputy min. of the Armed Forces, 1950-54; member of Politburo of Rumanian Communist party, 1955; as leader of the Rumanian Communist party (1967-   ), asserted independence of Rumania from Soviet domination; first pres. of the Socialist Republic of Rumania, 1974-   .

CHARLES V, Feb. 24, 1500 (Ghent, Flanders)-Sept. 21, 1558. Holy Roman emperor (1519-56) and (as Charles I) king of Spain (1516-56). Attempted to establish a universal Christian empire; tried to stop the Turkish invasion of Europe; struggled against the Protestant Ref.; hampered by economic problems as well as the new nationalism.

CHARLES XIV JOHN, born Jean Baptiste Jules Bernadotte, Jan. 26, 1763 (Pau, Fr.)-Mar. 8, 1844. French soldier and king of Sweden and Norway, 1818-44. A gen. in the French Army and brilliant administrator under NAPOLEON I; chosen by the Swedish monarchy to succeed an aging king; united Norway with Sweden by marching on Denmark, forcing the Danes to cede Norway, 1814; ruled well, promoting many internal improvements.

CHARLES MARTEL ("The Hammer"), 688-741? Frankish ruler. The mayor of the palace of Austrasia who united the Frankish realm under his rule. Stopped the Moslem invasion of Europe by his victory over the Moors of Spain in the Battle of Tours (or Poitiers), 732; supported missionary efforts directed at the German tribes he conquered.

CHEOPS (Khufu), fl.c.2680 B.C. Egyptian king, second of the fourth dynasty. Builder of the Great Pyramid at Giza.

CHIANG KAI-SHEK, Oct. 31, 1887 (Chekiang Prov., China)-Apr. 5, 1975. Chinese statesman, soldier. Fought against the Manchus (1911) and then joined SUN YAT-SEN; commander in chief of the Revolutionary Army, 1925; established himself as Chinese head of state, 1928-49; fought both

RULERS, STATESMEN, AND POLITICAL LEADERS

the Chinese communists and the Japanese; defeated by communists, 1949; resumed presidency of China in exile on Taiwan, 1949–75.

CHOU EN-LAI, 1898 (Kiangsu Prov., China)–Jan. 8, 1976. Chinese communist leader. Became a communist in France, 1920–24; participated in national revolution in China led by the Kuomintang; succeeded MAO TSE-TUNG as political commissar of the Red Army, 1932; chief negotiator of Chinese Communist party with noncommunist Chinese against Japan and with the U.S. at the end of WW II; foreign min. 1949–58; premier, 1949–76; sided with moderates in the Cultural revolution of the 1960s; normalized relations with the West in the 1970s in face of the growing Soviet threat.

CHU TEH, Dec. 18, 1886 (Szechwan Prov., China)–July 6, 1976. Chinese military leader. Founder of the Communist Chinese army and a great military leader of China. Took part in the Nanking uprising, 1927; led the Red Army through the Long March of 1934–35 and to victory over the Nationalists in 1949; remained in command of the People's Liberation Army until 1954.

CICERO, MARCUS TULLIUS, 106 B.C. (Arpino, It.)–Dec. 7, 43 B.C. Roman statesman, scholar, orator who upheld republican values during the civil wars of the Roman Republic. As consul of Rome (63–58) executed Catiline and his conspirators; exiled by his political enemies, 58; recalled by Pompey, 57; Opposed to JULIUS CAESAR; defended rule of law and constitutional govt. *Philippics; De oratore; De republica; De legibus; De natura deorum.*

CLAUDIUS I, born Tiberius Claudius Drusus Nero Germanicus, Aug. 1, 10 B.C. (Lugdunum [now Lyon, Fr.])–Oct. 13, 54. Roman emperor. Made Britain a Roman province; implemented administrative reforms, including increased reliance on freedmen; extended Roman rule over N. Africa; built many roads; thought to have been killed by his wife Agrippina.

CLEOPATRA VII (or VI), 69 B.C. (Egypt)–30 B.C. Egyptian queen (51–49 and 48–30 B.C.), noted in history and drama as a *femme fatale.* Engaged in civil war with her brother, Ptolemy XIII, over the Egyptian throne for 30 years; after his arrival (48) won over JULIUS CAESAR, who defeated her brother (47); joined Caesar in Rome (c.46), remaining until his death (44;) captivated his successor, MARK ANTONY whom she married (37), ruining his popularity in Rome; defeated with Antony by the Roman Senate, 31; fled to Egypt, committed suicide.

CONSTANTINE I ("the Great"), born Flavius Valerius Aurelius Constantinus c.280 (Naissus [now Nis, Yugo.])–Mar. 22, 337. Roman emperor (306–337) who made Christianity the empire's lawful religion and moved the capitol to Byzantium, which was rebuilt as Constantinople. Converted to Christianity just before the Battle of Milvian Bridge, 312; emerged after civil wars as sole ruler; convened the church council at Nicea; strengthened and unified the empire.

CYRUS THE GREAT, 600? B.C.–529 B.C. Persian king (559–529 B.C.) who conquered much of the Near East and founded the Achaemenid (Persian) empire; noted for respecting the autonomy and local customs of the lands he conquered.

DARIUS I, 550 B.C.–486 B.C. King of Persia, 522–486 B.C. One of the greatest rulers of the Achaemenid dynasty; revised and increased satrapies (territories) in the admin. of his empire;

promoted trade; built great buildings; led numerous military campaigns; noted as a lawgiver; instituted new gold coinage; defeated by the Greeks at the Battle of Marathon, 490 B.C.

DAVID, 11th cent. B.C. (Bethlehem, Israel)–c.973 B.C. Second king of Israel, 1013?–973? B.C. Symbol of the ideal king in the Jewish tradition; successor to SAUL; unified the tribes into a nation; as king of the southern kingdom of Judah, fought for the liberation of the northern tribes from the Philistines; made Jerusalem the capital of the united kingdom; completed the conquest of the Promised Land.

DE GASPERI, ALCIDE, Apr. 3, 1881 (Pieve Tesino, Aus. [now in Italy])–Aug. 19, 1954. Italian politician. As prime min. (1945–53), led the reconstruction of Italy after WW II, brought Italy into NATO (1951), began long-term land reform, helped establish the European Coal and Steel Comm. (1951).

DEMOSTHENES, 384 B.C. (Athens, Gr.)–Oct. 12, 322 B.C. Greek orator, statesman. Greatest of the Greek orators, roused Athens to oppose Philip of Macedon and ALEXANDER the Great; leader of the democratic faction in Athens.

DESAI, MORARJI, Feb. 26, 1896 (Gujarat Prov., India). Indian statesman. A disciple of MAHATMA GANDHI; finance min., 1958–63; deputy prime min., 1967–69; resigned in break with INDIRA GANDHI and the Congress party and formed, with other former Congress leaders, another Congress party; imprisoned by Gandhi for vocal opposition, 1975–77; helped form the Janata party, a new political coalition that he headed; prime min., 1977–79.

DIAZ, PORFIRIO, Sept. 15, 1830 (Oaxaca, Mex.)–July 2, 1915. Mexican statesman. As pres. (1876–80 and 1884–1911), an absolute ruler who brought peace and prosperity to Mexico; played his opponents off one another; welcomed foreign capital.

DIEFENBAKER, JOHN GEORGE, Sept. 18, 1895 (Grey Co., Ont., Can.)–Aug. 16, 1979. Canadian leader of the Progressive Conservative party. As prime min. (1957–63), obtained Agricultural Rehabilitation Development Act (ARDA) of 1961; suffered downfall in crisis over proposed manufacture of nuclear weapons.

DIEM, NGO DINH, Jan. 3, 1901 (Quang Binh Prov., Vietnam)–Nov. 2, 1963. Vietnamese leader. As pres. of the Republic of Vietnam (1954–63), ruled as a dictator, backed by the U.S.; assassinated by his generals in a coup d'état.

DIOCLETIAN, born Gaius Aurelius Valerius Diocletianus, 245 (Salonae, Dalmatia [now Yugo.])–316. Roman emperor, 284–305. Split empire into four administrative divisions and subdivided them; reorganized the army; failed in an attempt to control prices; persecuted Christians.

DOLLFUSS, ENGELBERT, Oct. 4, 1892 (Kirnberg, Austria)–July 25, 1934. Austrian statesman. As chan. and dictator of Austria (1932–34), destroyed the Austrian Republic; obtained support from B. MUSSOLINI; took military action against Austrian socialists; killed by rebelling Austrian Nazis.

DUNANT, JEAN HENRI, May 8, 1828 (Geneva, Switz.)–Oct. 30, 1910. Swiss philanthropist. Founder of the Red Cross, 1864; a founder of the World's Young Men's Christian Assn.; took part in the first Geneva Convention, 1864; awarded first Nobel Peace Prize (with FRÉDÉRIC PASSY), 1901.

DUVALIER, FRANÇOIS ("Papa Doc"), Apr. 14,

THE BOOK OF WHO

1907 (Port-au-Prince, Haiti)–Apr. 21, 1971. Haitian leader. Entered politics as a reformer and black nationalist; as pres. (1957–71), consolidated power into a regime marked by terror and corruption; succeeded by his son, Jean Claude Duvalier.

ECHEVERRIA ALVAREZ, LUIS, 1922 (Mexico). Mexican leader. Member of Institutional Revolutionary party; as secy. of the interior (1964–69), quelled the 1969 student riots in Mexico City; as pres. (1970–76), promoted agricultural technical-assistance programs.

EICHMANN, (Karl) ADOLF, Mar. 19, 1906 (Solingen, Ger.)–May 31, 1962. German Nazi official. The principal technician in the execution of millions of Jews during WW II; seized by Israeli agents in Argentina, 1960; convicted by Israeli court (1961), and executed.

ERHARD, LUDWIG, Feb. 4, 1897 (Fürth, Ger.)–May 5, 1977. German statesman, economist. As federal economics min. (1949–63), the chief architect of West Germany's post-WW II economic recovery; introduced the currency reform (1948) that started West Germany's economic recovery; chan., 1963–66.

FAISAL, 1906? (al-Quaysumah [now Saudi Arabia])–Mar. 25, 1975. King of Saudi Arabia, 1964–75. Worked for Islamic unity and to improve the lot of his people; assassinated by his nephew.

FARUK (or Farouk), Feb. 11, 1920 (Cairo, Egypt)–Mar. 18, 1965. King of Egypt, 1936–52. Clashed with the Wafd party; suffered imposition of a pro-British premier during WW II; met a humiliating defeat in the 1949 Arab-Israeli conflict; toppled by military coup, led by G. NASSER, 1952.

FERDINAND V (of Castile) or Ferdinand II (of Aragon), Mar. 10, 1452 (Sos, Sp.)–Jan. 25, 1516. King of Aragon who brought about the unification of Spain by his marriage to ISABELLA I, queen of Castile, 1469. Expelled Jews from Spain; initiated the search for American gold; converted large agricultural areas into grazing lands for the benefit of the wool industry; began the Spanish Inquisition.

FRANCIS FERDINAND, ARCHDUKE, Dec. 18, 1863 (Graz, Austria)–June 28, 1914. Austrian archduke, and heir to the Austrian throne whose assassination (June 28, 1914) at Sarajevo was the immediate cause of WW I.

FRANCO, FRANCISCO, Dec. 4, 1892 (El Ferrol, Sp.)–Nov. 20, 1975. Spanish dictator. Led the Nationalist forces that overthrew the Spanish democratic republic in the Spanish Civil War; as gen. and dictator of Spain (1936–75), kept Spain neutral during WW II; obtained U.S. economic aid in exchange for allowing U.S. military bases; relaxed his iron grip in the 1950s and 1960s only to reassert it in the 1970s.

FRASER, JOHN MALCOLM, May 21, 1930 (Melbourne, Austrl.). Australian politician. Min. of education and science, 1968–69 and 1971–72; min. of def., 1969–71; prime min., 1975–   ; leader of the Liberal party, 1975–   .

FUKUDA, TAKEO, Jan. 14, 1905 (Ashikado, Jap.). Japanese politician. Implicated in a political scandal (1947), acquitted (1958); secy. gen. of Liberal Democratic party, 1966–68; min. of foreign affairs, 1971–72; min. of finance, 1965–68, 1968–71, and 1973–74; deputy prime min. and dir. of the Economic Planning Agency, 1974–76; prime min. 1976–78.

GANDHI, INDIRA, née Nehru, Nov. 19, 1917 (Allahabad, India). Indian stateswoman. As prime min. (1966–77) and Congress party leader, attempted to hold the two wings of the party together in a coalition; worked for economic planning and social reform; convicted of election-law violation, declared state of emergency and suspended civil liberties, 1975; soundly defeated in elections, 1977; re-elected prime minister, 1980. (Daughter of JAWAHARLAL NEHRU.)

GANDHI, MOHANDAS KARAMCHAND, Oct. 2, 1869 (Porbandar, India)–Jan. 30, 1948. Indian political leader. Leader of Indian nationalist movement against British rule. Espoused a doctrine of nonviolence to achieve political and social progress; led civil disobedience campaign in S. Africa against anti-Hindu discrimination, 1893; in Indian independence movement, called for revival of home industries and the abolition of untouchability; threatened "fasts unto death," which were effective because of his prestige; unified the Indian National Congress, 1925; shot to death by fanatics.

GARIBALDI, GIUSEPPE, July 4, 1807 (Nice, Fr.)–June 2, 1882. Italian military leader in the movement for Italian unification and independence, influenced by GUISEPPE MAZZINI. Conquered the Kingdom of the Two Sicilies (1860), capturing Naples, and thus paving the way for Italian unification (1861); defeated in attempt to capture Rome, 1862 and 1867.

GENGHIS KHAN, born Temujin, c.1162 (nr. Lake Baikal)–Aug. 18, 1227. Mongol conqueror who amassed a huge empire stretching from Eastern Europe to the Sea of Japan. Consolidated tribes in Mongolia and eliminated his enemies; named supreme ruler, 1206; conquered northern China, southern Russia and Iran; administered his wide empire well; in military campaigns, brilliantly used flying horse columns and feigned retreats.

GIEREK, EDWARD, Jan. 6, 1913 (Porabka, Pol.). Polish communist leader. Involved in the Belgian underground during WW II; a specialist in economics and heavy industry; secy. of Central Communist Comm. of Poland, 1970–

GODFREY (Godefroy) DE BOUILLON, c.1060 (Baisy, Brabant)–July 18, 1100. Leader of the First Crusade. Duke of Lower Lorraine; first Latin ruler of Jerusalem (elected 1099); a great hero, the subject of many legends.

GODUNOV, BORIS FYODOROVICH, c.1551–Apr. 23, 1605. Tsar of Russia, 1598–1605. A favorite of Tsar IVAN IV and chief adviser to Fyodor I, Ivan's son, virtually ruling Russia (1584–98); succeeded as tsar; strengthened the power of state officials at the expense of the boyars; recolonized Siberia; made peace with Sweden and Poland; rule undermined by famine.

GOEBBELS, (Paul) JOSEPH, Oct. 29, 1897 (Rheydt, Ger.)–May 1, 1945. German Nazi official. As Nazi min. of propaganda (1928–45), controlled the press, radio, films, publications, theater, and music, and was responsible for creating a favorable image of the Nazi regime to the German people; killed his wife and six children and committed suicide in the Berlin bunker at the end of WW II.

GOERING, HERMANN WILHELM, Jan. 12, 1893 (Rosenheim, Ger.)–Oct. 15, 1946. German Nazi leader. A WW I flying ace who rearmed Germany and built its Air Force in the 1930s; founded the Gestapo (secret police); virtually dictated the German economy until 1943; Hitler's designated successor; committed suicide in jail.

GROTIUS, HUGO (Huig de Groot), Apr. 10, 1583 (Delft, Neth.)–Aug. 28, 1645. Dutch jurist, scholar. Called the "Father of modern internatl. law," made major contributions in the field. *On the Law of Prize and Booty*, 1604; *On the Law of War and Peace*, 1625.

GUEVARA, CHE, born Ernesto Guevara de la Serna, June 14, 1928 (Rosario, Arg.)–Oct. 9, 1967. Latin American guerrilla and revolutionary theoretician and tactician who played a major role in the Cuban Revolution. Became a trusted aide of FIDEL CASTRO and min. of industry; disappeared in 1965, reappeared in Bolivia in 1966, where he established a guerrilla base. *Guerrilla Warfare*, 1961.

GUILLOTIN, JOSEPH IGNACE, May 28, 1738 (Saintes, Fr.)–Mar. 26, 1814. French politician, physician. Dep. of the 1789 Constituent Assembly who is incorrectly credited with the invention of the guillotine; did propose decapitation by machine as the most humane capital punishment.

HADRIAN (or Adrian), born Publius Aelius Hadrianus, Jan. 24, 76 (Spain)–July 10, 138. Roman emperor, 117–138. Although he did not expand the empire, it reached its height during his reign; excellent administrator; strenghened fortifications; did extensive building; reorganized law and civil service; patron of the arts; brutally suppressed a Jewish rebellion.

HAILE SELASSIE ("The Lion of Judah"), born Tafari Makonnen, July 23, 1892 (Harar Prov., Ethiopia)–Aug. 27, 1975. Emperor of Ethiopia, 1930–74. Emancipated the slaves, 1924; led troops against Italian invasion, 1935; fled to Britain but returned (1941) to defeat allies with British help; established Natl. Assembly, 1955; crushed domestic rebellion, 1960; overthrown in military coup, 1974.

HAMMARSKJÖLD, DAG, July 29, 1905 (Jönköping, Swe.)–Sept. 18, 1961. Swedish diplomat political economist. As secy. gen. of UN (1953–61), played an important role in the resolution of the Suez Canal crisis; sent UN troops to suppress civil strife in the Congo, 1960; built up prestige of the UN and established its independence from the U.S.; awarded Nobel Peace Prize, 1961. *Markings*, 1964.

HAMMURABI (or Hammurapi), c.1792 B.C. (Babylon)–1750 B.C. Babylonian ruler. The sixth ruler of the first dynasty of Babylon, 1792–1750 B.C.; known for his set of laws, once considered to be oldest promulgation of laws in history; brought all of Mesopotamia under one rule.

HASSAN II, July 9, 1929 (Rabat, Morocco). King of Morocco, 1961– . Succeeded his father; in foreign affairs, has followed a policy of nonalignment; has attempted to expand education and make it more Arabic; suspended attempts to institute a democratic constitution after riots ensued, 1965.

HEROD, 73? B.C. (Palestine)–4 B.C. King of Judea under the Romans, 47–4 B.C. A tyrannical ruler who expanded Judea; destroyed traditional Jewish institutions; attempted to Hellenize the country; used brutal police methods.

HERZL, THEODOR, May 2, 1860 (Budapest, Hung.)–July 3, 1904. Hungarian-born journalist, founder of Zionism. Correspondent with *Neue Freie Presse* (Vienna), 1891–95; founded Congress of the Zionist Orgs., 1897; established the Zionist newspaper *Die Welt*; negotiated with Turkey and Britain for a mass Jewish settlement in Palestine. *Der Judenstaat* (The Jewish State), 1896.

HEYDRICH, REINHARD, Mar. 7, 1904 (Halle, Ger.)–June 4, 1942. German Nazi official. Nazi

specialist in terror. As dep. chief of Gestapo, involved in June 1934 purges; administered Nazi concentration camps; head of Reich Central Security Office, 1939–42; assassinated by Czech patriots.

HIMMLER, HEINRICH, Oct. 7, 1900 (Munich, Ger.)–May 23, 1945. German Nazi official, the second most powerful man in the Third Reich. Participated in the Munich Putsch, 1923; became head of the SS, 1929; commander of all police forces, 1936; established first concentration camp, at Dachau; organized the extermination camps in Eastern Europe; dismissed by HITLER for his involvement in a conspiracy to succeed him, 1945.

HINDENBURG, PAUL VON, Oct. 2, 1847 (Posen, Prussia [now Poznan, Pol.])–Aug. 2, 1934. German statesman, soldier. As field marshal during WW I, scored some brilliant victories on the Eastern Front; as second pres. of the Weimar Republic (1925–34), his power dwindled as the economy worsened and he was pressured into appointing A. HITLER as chan.

HIROHITO, Apr. 29, 1901 (Tokyo, Jap.). Emperor of Japan, 1926– . Helped convince Japanese govt. to surrender to the Allies, 1945; publicly renounced the idea of imperial divinity, 1946; has attempted to bring the throne close to the people; visited the U.S., 1975; interested in marine biology.

HITLER, ADOLF, Apr. 20, 1889 (Braunau, Austria)–Apr. 30, 1945. German dictator. Leader of the National Socialist Workers' (Nazi) Party (1921–45) and dictator of Germany (1933–45). Gained political power in the early 1930s, playing on people's fears and the worsening economic situation; named chan., 1933; on death of P. HINDENBURG, united offices of pres. and chan., taking title Der Führer; concentrated on territorial expansion; initiated policy of anti-semitism; annexed Austria (1938), the Sudetenland (1938), and Czechoslovakia (1939); invaded Poland, starting WW II, 1939; became poor strategist as war turned against him; committed suicide. *Mein Kampf* (Eng. trans.), 1933.

HO CHI MINH, born Nguyen That Thanh, May 19, 1890 (Hoang Tru, Vietnam)–Sept. 3, 1969. Vietnamese leader; one of the most influential communist leaders in the 20th cent. Joined French Communist party 1920; founded the Communist party of Vietnam, 1930; organized the Vietminh, which fought the Japanese in Vietnam and China (1945); as pres. of Vietnam (1946–54) during the First Indochina War sought negotiations with France, thereby playing an indirect role in the Geneva Accord (1954), which created two Vietnams; pres. of Democratic Republic of Vietnam (North Vietnam), 1954–69.

HORTHY, MIKLOS VON NAGYBANYA, June 18, 1869 (Kenderes, Hung.)–Feb. 9, 1957. Commanded the Austro-Hungarian fleet in WW I; ousted Béla Kun regime and became regent of Hungary (1920–44); during WW II, acquiesced to alliance with the Axis powers, but later rebelled.

HUA KUO-FENG, c.1920 (Shansi Prov., China). Chinese political leader. An ardent Maoist, identified with the moderates. Dep. prime min. and min. of public security, 1975; premier of Chinese People's Republic and first dep. chm. of Chinese Communist party, 1976– .

HUERTA, VICTORIANO, Dec. 23, 1854 (Colotan, Mex.)–Jan. 13, 1916. Mexican revolutionary, politician. Took part in revolution that raised PORFIRIO DIAZ to power; provisional pres. of Mexico, 1913–14.

THE BOOK OF WHO

HUSAK, GUSTAV, Jan. 10, 1913 (Bratislava, Slovakia [now Czech.]). Czechoslovak communist leader. Took part in the Slovak National Rising, 1944; member of Natl. Assembly, 1945–51; following the Soviet invasion of Czechoslovakia (Aug. 1968), succeeded A. Dubcek as gen. secy. of the Czechoslovak Communist party (1969–   .)

HUSSEIN, ABDUL IBN, Nov. 14, 1935 (Amman, Trans Jordan [now Jordan]). As king of Jordan (1953–   ), his generally pro-western policies have met with criticism from the Arab League and Arab refugees from Israeli-occupied territory.

IBARRURI, DELORES ("La Pasionaria"), 1895 (Spain). Spanish communist leader. Joined (1920) the Spanish Communist party and became one of its most influential members; during Spanish Civil War, gave radio speeches urging Spaniards to resist the forces of Gen F. FRANCO; at war's end, fled to Soviet Union to head the exiled Spanish Communist party, 1939; when Communist party was legalized in Spain by King JUAN CARLOS, returned to Spain, 1976.

IBN SAUD, c.1880 (Riyadh, Saudi Arabia)–Nov. 9, 1953. King of Saudi Arabia, 1932–53. Founder of the kingdom of Saudi Arabia. Captured Riyadh, the ancestral capital, 1902; continued to capture and defend his territory until he created Saudi Arabia, 1932; signed the first agreement for oil exploration, 1933; played only a minor role in Arab-Israeli hostilities.

IEYASU (Iyeyasn), 1542 (Okazaki, Jap.)–1616. Japanese dictator, gen. As founder of the Tokugawa shogunate, unified Japan against the feudal barons and the Buddhist monasteries; defeated his rivals in the battle of Sekigahara, 1600; built up and strengthened the state; encouraged foreign trade.

IKHNATON (also called Amenhotep IV), fl. 1379–1362 B.C. Pharaoh of Egypt. Noted for his introduction of a monotheistic form of worship centered on Aten, the sun god; this redirection to sun-irradiated nature encouraged artists to become more naturalistic; founded the new capital of Akhetaton; empire declined due to his negligence.

ISABELLA I ("The Catholic"), Apr. 22, 1451 (Madrigal, Sp.)–Nov. 26, 1504. Queen of Castile (1474–1504) who married Ferdinand II of Aragon and ruled jointly with him as Isabella I and FERDINAND V of Castile and Aragon (1479–1504); Helped unify Spain; reestablished the Inquisition; encouraged the arts; patron of CHRISTOPHER COLUMBUS.

ITO, PRINCE HIROBUMI, Sept. 2, 1841 (Choshu, Jap.)–Oct. 26, 1909. Japanese statesman. An important figure in the emergence of modern Japan. Drafter of the Meiji constitution, 1889; served as prime min. four times, 1886–1901; first pres. of the Seiyuhai party; assassinated by a Korean fanatic.

IVAN IV ("the Terrible"), Aug. 25, 1530 (Moscow, Rus.)–Mar. 17, 1584. Ruler of Russia (1544–84) and tsar of Moscow. Established the tsarist autocracy; surrounded himself with commoners rather than boyars (nobles); started the eastward expansion of Russia; grew gloomy and suspicious, terrorizing the country with murder; killed his son in a fit of fury.

JOHN III SOBIESKI, June 2, 1624 (Olesko, Pol.)–June 17, 1696. King of Poland, 1674–96. Built Poland into a great country in a short period of time; distinguished himself as a soldier in wars against Sweden and Russia; saved Vienna from the Turks, 1683.

JUAN CARLOS I, Jan. 5, 1938 (Rome, It.). King of Spain, 1975–   . Designated by F. FRANCO as his successor, 1969.

JUAREZ, BENITO, Mar. 21, 1806 (San Pablo Guelatao, Mex.)–July 18, 1872. Mexican leader and revolutionary hero. Led the rebellion against SANTA ANNA, 1855; chief justice of Mexican Sup. Ct., 1857; as pres. (1858–59, 1861–63, and 1867–72), fought French and reduced the privileges of the army and the clergy.

JUDAS MACCABAEUS, died c.160 B.C. Jewish patriot. Leader of the Jewish revolt against Antiochus IV, king of Syria; reconsecrated the Temple of Jerusalem (165 B.C.), in memory of which the festival of Hanukkah was instituted.

JUSTINIAN I (the Great), born Flavius Petrus Sabbatius Justinianus, 483 (Tauresium [now in Yugo.])–Nov. 14, 565. Byzantine emperor (527–65) whose reign was the most brilliant of the Eastern empire. Extended the empire in Africa and Italy; insisted on the supremacy of the emperor over the church; commissioned extensive construction, including the rebuilding of Hagia Sophia; codified Roman law into the *Corpus Juris Civillis* (body of civil law).

KARAMANLIS, CONSTANTINE, Feb. 23, 1907 (Prote, Greece). Greek politician. As premier (1955–63 and 1974–   ), has maintained a pro-Western foreign policy; restored the 1952 constitution; granted political amnesty.

KAUNDA, KENNETH DAVID, Apr. 28, 1924 (Chinsali, Zambia). Zambian leader. As the first pres. of Zambia (1964–   ), has supported African unity and pressed economic development. Helped organize the African Natl. Congress (ANC), 1949; assumed leadership of the United Natl. Independence party, 1960.

KENYATTA, JOMO, c.1894 (Ichaweri, Kenya)–Aug. 22, 1978. Kenyan leader. The first pres. of the Republic of Kenya, 1964–78. Pres. of Kenya African Union, 1947; imprisoned for allegedly leading Mau Mau terrorism, 1952–59; helped negotiate Kenya's independence at London Conference, 1962; as pres., attempted to strengthen ties among E. African states.

KERENSKY, ALEXANDER, Apr. 22, 1881 (Simbirsk, Rus. [now Ulyanovsk, USSR])–June 11, 1970. Russian revolutionary leader. A moderate socialist who, following the first Russian Revolution (Feb. 1917), headed the provisional govt. from July to Oct. 1917, when he was overthrown by the Bolsheviks.

KHALID BIN ABDUL AZIZ, 1913 (Riyadh, Saudi Arabia). King of Saudi Arabia, 1975–   . Earlier, as vice-pres. of Council of Ministers (1962–75), represented his nation at various internatl. conferences.

KHOMEINI, RUHOLLA, born Ruhollah Hendi, 1901 (Khumain, Iran). Iranian ayatollah (Moslem religious leader). In exile since 1963, returned to Iran after overthrow of the Shah, and proclaimed new regime, April 1979.

KHRUSHCHEV, NIKITA, Apr. 17, 1894 (Kalinkova, Rus.)–Sept. 11, 1971. Soviet communist leader. As first secy. of the Soviet Communist party (1953–64) and premier (1958–64), initiated a program of destalinization; failed to achieve the sixth five-year plan; enunciated a policy of peaceful coexistence with the Western powers; became involved in an increasingly bitter struggle with China; withdrew missiles from Cuba, 1962; removed from power for failures in agricultural production and other problems.

KIM IL-SUNG, born Kim Sung Chu, Apr. 5, 1912 (nr. Pyongyang, Korea). Korean communist leader. Organized Korean armed resistance to the Japanese occupation in the 1930s; following WW II, with the help of the USSR, took control of the northern part of Korea; attempted to conquer the south, 1950-53; has maintained friendly relations with the USSR.

KING, WILLIAM LYON MACKENZIE, Dec. 17, 1874 (Berlin [now Kitchener], Ont., Can.)-July 22, 1950. Canadian statesman. Leader of the Liberal party, 1919-21; as prime min. (1921-26, 1926-30, and 1935-48), signed an agreement to help the U.S. build up defense production during WW II; signed the Washington Declaration on Nuclear Power, 1945; handled the French-Canadian problem skillfully.

KOSSUTH, LAJOS, Sept. 19, 1802 (Monok, Hung.)-Mar. 20, 1894. Hungarian statesman. Principal figure in the Hungarian revolution of 1848; became pres. of the independent Republic of Hungary (1848), but forced to flee when the insurrection was crushed (1849).

KOSYGIN, ALEXEI NIKOLAEVICH, Feb. 20, 1904 (St. Petersburg, Rus.[now Leningrad, USSR]). Soviet communist leader. As premier (1964-   ), led the Soviet effort at economic modernization in the 1960s, but has receded into the background in the 1970s. Member of the Soviet Communist party, 1927-   ; deputy chm. of Council of Ministers, 1957-64; negotiated India-Pakistan ceasefire, 1966; headed Soviet mission to Czechoslovakia, 1968.

KREISKY, BRUNO, Jan. 22, 1911 (Vienna, Austria). Austrian political leader. Min. of foreign affairs, 1959-66; chm. of Socialist party of Austria, 1967-   ; federal chan. of Austria, 1970-   .

KROPOTKIN, PRINCE PYOTR, Dec. 21, 1842 (Moscow, Rus.)-Feb. 8, 1921. Russian revolutionist, social philosopher, leader and theorist of the anarchist movement. Renounced his aristocratic background to devote himself to the peasants; imprisoned, 1874; fled to Western Europe, settling in England, 1886-1917; returned to Russia but took no part in political life. *Fields, Factories, and Workshops,* 1899; *Modern Science and Anarchism,* 1903; *Terror in Russia,* 1909.

KRÜGER, STEPHANUS JOHANNES PAULUS ("Oom Paul"), Oct. 10, 1825 (Cape Colony)-July 14, 1904. South African leader. Leader of Dutch South African (or Transvaal) movement for independence. A leader of Boer rebellion (1880), helped negotiate peace (1881); pres., South African Republic, 1883-99; fled to Europe during the Boer War, 1900.

KUBLAI KHAN (or Kubla Khan), 1216-1294. Mongol leader. Grandson of GHENGHIS KHAN; subdued northern China (1260s) and by 1279 controlled southern China as well, thus becoming the first foreign conqueror to rule all of China; became famous in the West through accounts of his empire written by MARCO POLO.

LASSALLE, FERDINAND, Apr. 11, 1825 (Breslau, Ger. [now Wroclaw, Pol.])-Aug. 31, 1864. German socialist leader. Founder of the German Social Democratic party. A disciple of KARL MARX, from 1848; propagandist for and champion of the working classes; founded the General German Workers' Assn. to promote use of political power by workers, 1863.

LAURIER, SIR WILFRID, Nov. 20, 1841 (Saint-Lin, Que., Can.)-Feb. 17, 1919. Canadian statesman. The first French-Canadian prime min. of Canada, 1896-1919. Liberal Party leader who worked for national unity, the development of the western territories, the building of the railroads, and tariff arrangements.

LENIN, VLADIMIR ILYICH (original surname, Ulyanov), May 4, 1870 (Simbirsk, Rus. [now Ulyanovsk, USSR])-Jan. 21, 1924. Russian communist leader, founder of Bolshevism, and architect of the first Soviet state. Converted to Marxism, 1889; exiled to Siberia, 1897; went to Switzerland (1900), where he founded *Iskra* (Spark), a revolutionary journal; split Russian Socialist party into two factions, taking up leadership of Bolshevik faction, 1903; returned to Russia after Feb. 1917 revolution, assumed control of revolutionary movement, and overthrew the provisional government (Nov. 1917); declared all power to be vested in the Soviets; became premier (1918-24), establishing the dictatorship of the proletariat; led Russia through civil war with counter-revolutionaries, 1918-21; eliminated all opposition; instituted far-reaching social and economic reforms; founded the Third Internatl., 1919. *What Is to Be Done?,* 1902; *The State and the Revolution,* 1917.

LEONE, GIOVANNI, Nov. 3, 1908 (Naples, It.). Italian politician, professor. Pres. of Chamber of Deputies, 1955-63; prime min., 1963 and 1968; pres., 1971-   .

LESSEPS, FERDINAND DE, Nov. 19, 1805 (Versailles, Fr.)-Dec. 7, 1894. French diplomat, engineer. Best known as the builder of the Suez Canal; persuaded Egyptian viceroy to allow construction of the canal, 1854; organized the Suez Canal Co., raised necessary capital, and oversaw the construction, 1859-69; headed French co. formed to build Panama Canal, but gave up the project because of financial difficulties, 1881-88.

LIE, TRYGVE, July 16, 1896 (Oslo, Nor.)-Dec. 30, 1968. Norwegian govt. official. As first secy.-gen. of the UN (1946-52), dealt with Arab intervention in Israel, N. Korea's invasion of S. Korea, and accusations that the UN employed U.S. communists.

LIEBKNECHT, KARL, Aug. 13, 1871 (Leipzig, Ger.)-Jan. 15, 1919. German socialist leader. Founder of the Spartacus Union, the precursor to the German Communist party; elected to Reichstag, 1912; played an important role in the Spartacist Revolt, 1919; arrested (with ROSA LUXEMBURG) and killed.

LI HUNG-CHANG, Feb. 25, 1823 (Hofei, China)-Nov. 7, 1901. Chinese diplomat. Leading diplomat of the late 19th cent. who advocated the self-strengthening of China. Negotiated peace treaty (1895) that ended first Sino-Japanese war (1894); prime min. 1895-98; negotiated with foreigners in the Boxer Rebellion, 1900.

LILUOKALANI, LYDIA KAMEKEHA, Sept. 2, 1938 (Honolulu, Haw.)-Nov. 11, 1917. Hawaiian queen (1891-93), the last sovereign to rule before the annexation of the islands. Composed "Aloha Oe."

LIN PIAO, Dec. 5, 1908 (Hupeh Prov., China)-Sept. 12, 1971. Chinese communist military leader. Pres. of the Red Acad., 1936; field commander of the Red Army against Japan and the Nationalist Chinese; def. min., 1959; supporter of the Cultural Revolution, 1966-69; disappeared mysteriously in a plane crash.

LOPEZ PORTILLO, JOSÉ, June 16, 1920 (Mexico City, Mex.). Mexican leader. Gen. dir. of Electricity Federal Com., 1972-73; secy. for finances and public credit, 1973-75; pres., 1976-   .

167

THE BOOK OF WHO

LUMUMBA, PATRICE, July 2, 1925 (Oualua, Belgian Congo [now Zaire])–Jan. 1961. Congolese leader. As the first prime min. of the Congo (1960), a national hero. Founded Congolese Natl. Movement, 1958; fled following the Jan. 1959 uprising against the Belgians; a leading negotiator with Belgium for independence; as premier, met opposition over his determination to end Belgian-backed secession of Katanga Prov.; removed from office and killed.

LUTHULI, ALBERT JOHN, 1898 (nr. Bulawayo, Rhodesia)–July 21, 1967. S. African reformer. Member of African Natl. Congress, 1945; led passive-resistance campaign against apartheid, 1952; arrested, 1956; awarded Nobel Peace Prize for his nonviolent opposition to racial discrimination, 1960. *Let My People Go,* 1962.

LUXEMBURG, ROSA, Dec. 25, 1870 (Zamosc, Pol.)–1919. German socialist revolutionary. Took part in the Russian Revolution of 1905; cofounder (with KARL LIEBKNECHT), of the Spartacus Union; advocated the general strike as a revolutionary weapon; involved in Spartacist uprising (1919), arrested, and killed on the way to prison.

MACDONALD, SIR JOHN ALEXANDER, Jan. 11, 1815 (Glasgow, Scot.)–June 6, 1891. Canadian statesman. A powerful figure in the unification of the British N. American provinces. As first prime min. of Canada (1867–73 and 1878–91), advocated reciprocal trade agreements with the U.S., worked for strong bonds with Great Britain, oversaw building of the Canadian Pacific RR.

MACHIAVELLI, NICCOLÒ, May 3, 1469 (Florence, It.)–June 22, 1527. Italian statesman, writer. Best known for *The Prince* (1513), a work outlining his pragmatic theory of govt. and maxims of practical statecraft. *The Discourses on the First Ten Books of Livy,* 1519; *The Art of War,* 1519–20.

MAKARIOS III, born Mikhail Khristodolou Mouskos, Aug. 13, 1913 (Panagia, Cyprus)–Aug. 13, 1977. Cypriot leader. The first pres. of Cyprus (1960–74), and archbishop of the Orthodox Church of Cyprus (1950–77). Led the struggle for *enosis* (union) with Greece during the British occupation, in the 1950s; as pres., worked for the integration of the Greek and Turkish communities on Cyprus; following Turkish invasion (1974), resisted partition of the island.

MAO TSE-TUNG, Dec. 26, 1893 (Hunan Prov., China)–Sept. 9, 1976. Chinese communist leader and prime theorist of Chinese communism. Organized peasant and industrial unions in the 1920s; broke with CHIANG KAI-SHEK and led the Red Army on the Long March, 1934–35; fought the Nationalists and Japanese, winning control of China, 1949; became chm. of the Chinese Communist party (1949–76) and chm. of the People's Republic of China (1949–59); attempted to decentralize the economy with the Great Leap Forward, 1957; reasserted control through the Cultural Revolution, 1966–69.

MARCOS, FERDINAND EDRALIN, Sept. 11, 1917 (Sarrat, Philippines). Philippine leader. As pres. of the Philippines (1966–   ), supported U.S. policy in Vietnam, imposed martial law to quell mounting internal disturbances in the 1970s, established diplomatic relations with communist nations.

MARCOS, IMELDA, née Romualdez, July 2, 1931 (Leyte, Philippines). Philippine political leader. The wife of Philippine Pres. FERDINAND MARCOS and second-most powerful figure in the country. Escaped assassination attempt, 1972; appointed gov. of metropolitan Manila; named to head Dept. of Ecology and Human Settlements, responsible for the planning and development of the country's 1,500 cities and towns, 1978–   .

MARIA THERESA, May 13, 1717 (Vienna, Austria)–Nov. 29, 1780. Empress of Austria (1740–80), archduchess of Austria, queen of Hungary and Bohemia. Ousted the pretender Charles VII and crowned queen, 1742; obtained election of husband Francis I as Roman emperor and coregent, 1745; fought Seven Year's War with FREDERICK THE GREAT of Prussia, 1756–63; known for her diplomatic skill; instituted governmental reforms affecting taxes and fiscal matters, and enlarged central admin. of the Austrian Empire.

MARTI, JOSÉ, Jan. 28, 1853 (Havana, Cuba)–May 19, 1895. Cuban poet, patriot. Leader of the Cuban struggle for independence and noted Spanish-American writer. Deported for his political activities on behalf of independence, 1871 and 1879; helped organize the Cuban Revolutionary party, 1892; led an invasion of Cuba, in which he died, 1895. *Neustra América,* 1891; *Bolivar,* 1893.

MASARYK, JAN GARRIGUE, Sept. 14, 1886 (Prague, Czech.)–Mar. 10, 1948. Czech statesman, Min. to Great Britain, 1925–38; foreign min., 1940–48; vice-premier of Czechoslovak Provisional Govt. in London, 1941–45; allegedly committed suicide after the communist takeover of Czechoslovakia. (Son of T. G. MASARYK.)

MASARYK, THOMAS GARRIGUE, Mar. 7, 1850 (Hodonin, Moravia [now Czech.])–Sept. 14, 1937. Czech statesman, philosopher. Chief founder and first pres. (1918–35) of the Czechoslovak Republic. Prof. of philosophy at Charles U., 1882–1911; member of Austrian Parliament, 1891–93 and 1907–14; formed Czechoslovak national council in Paris during WW I; as pres., instituted extensive land reform, brought minorities together, and tried to reconcile church and state. (Father of J. G. MASARYK.)

MAXIMILIAN (in full, Ferdinand Maximilian Joseph), July 6, 1832 (Vienna, Austria)–June 19, 1867. Austrian archduke, emperor of Mexico (1864–67). Given the Mexican throne by Mexican conservatives and French Emperor Napoleon III, he ruled poorly, alienating many with his liberal plans; with withdrawal of French troops, his empire collapsed and he was killed.

MAZZINI, GIUSEPPE, June 22, 1805 (Genoa, It.)–Mar. 10, 1872. Italian patriot, revolutionary. Fought for Italian unity and independence, even though in exile much of his life. Founded Giovini Italia (young Italy), a secret revolutionary society, in exile, 1832; returned during the upheavals of 1848, and became a member of the Republic of Rome (1849), but returned to exile with reestablishment of papal control; took part in various rebellions and aided in organizing G. GARIBALDI's revolutionary expeditions, 1860, 1862, and 1867.

MBOYA, TOM, Aug. 15, 1930 (Central Province, Kenya)–July 5, 1969. Kenyan political leader. A leader in the Kenyan struggle for independence. Gen. secy., Kenya Federation of Labour (KLF); founder-member, Kenya African National Union party, 1960; Kenyan min. for economic planning, 1964–67; assassinated.

MEDICI, COSIMO I DI ("the Great"), June 12,

RULERS, STATESMEN, AND POLITICAL LEADERS

1519-Apr. 21, 1574. Florentine statesman. As grand duke of Tuscany (1569-74) and duke of Florence (1537-69), guided Florence to the peak of its political importance and prosperity; a cruel but effective tyrant; conquered Siena, 1555.

MEDICI, LORENZO DI ("the Magnificent"), Jan. 1, 1449 (Florence, It.)-Apr. 8, 1492. Florentine statesman, merchant prince, patron of the arts. As ruler of Florence (1469-92), a major figure in the Italian Ren.; engaged in a struggle with supporters of the pope, with whom he made peace, 1480; though his rule was tyrannical, Florence prospered under him.

MEIR, GOLDA, née Mabovitch, May 3, 1898 (Kiev, Rus.)-Dec. 8, 1978. Israeli stateswoman. The first woman premier of Israel, 1969-74. Emigrated to Palestine from Milwaukee, Wisc., where she had grown up, 1921; worked with the Histadruth (Federation of Labor); a leader in the fight for a state of Israel, 1948; min. of labor (1949-56) and foreign affairs (1956-66); as premier, worked to achieve a peace with the Arabs through diplomacy, but eruption of the fourth Arab-Israeli War (1973) eroded her support.

MENES, fl. 3100 B.C. First king of the first dynasty of Egypt. Unified Upper and Lower Egypt into a single monarchy; founded the capitol of Memphis; tomb discovered at Negadr, 1897.

METAXAS, JOANNES, Apr. 12, 1871 (Ithaca, Greece)-Jan. 29, 1941. Greek statesman, general. As dictator of Greece (1936-41), led Greece into war with Italy and Germany. A royalist, he distinguished himself in the Balkan wars.

METTERNICH, KLEMENS WENZEL NEPOMUK LOTHAR VON, May 15, 1773 (Coblenz, Ger.)-June 11, 1859. Austrian diplomat, statesman. As min. of foreign affairs (1809-48), made Austria a leading power and built a stable internatl. order in Europe. A voice of conservatism; one of the leaders of the Allies against Napoleon; the dominant influence at the Congress of Vienna, 1814-15; the years 1815-1848 have been called the Age of Metternich because of his role in maintaining a balance of power during that era.

MIRANDA, FRANCISCO ANTONIO GABRIEL, Mar. 28, 1750 (Caracas, Ven.)-July 14, 1816. Venezuelan revolutionist. A precursor of the Latin American independence struggles. Gained support from many foreign leaders for the liberation of S. and Central America from Spanish domination; became dictator of Venezuela when it gained independence, 1811; fought in vain against royalists, forced to sign treaty ceding control, imprisoned (1812).

MOLOTOV, VYACHESLAV MIKHAILOVICH, Mar. 9, 1890 (Kukarka, Rus.) Soviet communist leader. Editor and cofounder of *Pravda,* 1912; chm. of Council of People's Commissars, 1930-41; as foreign min. (1939-49 and 1953-56), negotiated the German-Soviet Nonaggression Pact (1939).

MORO, ALDO, Sept. 23, 1916 (Maglie, It.)-May 9, 1978. Italian statesman. Secy. of Christian Democratic party, 1959-63; as prime min. (1963-68 and 1974-76), brought about a coalition between Socialists and Christian Democrats for the first time; kidnapped and killed by the *Brigata Rossa,* Italian leftist terrorists, 1978.

MUAWIYAH I (or Moawiyah), c.602 (Mecca, Arabia)-680. First ruler of Islam (661-80) after the legitimate caliphs. Founder of the Umayyad dynasty; governor of Syria; centralized admin.;

made continual raids beyond his borders; practiced religious toleration within conquered provinces.

MUNOZ, MARIN LUIS, Feb. 18, 1898 (San Juan, P.R.). Puerto Rican statesman. Founder of the Commonwealth of Puerto Rico. Gov. of Territory of Puerto Rico (1948-52) and Commonwealth of Puerto Rico (1952-65); senator-at-large, 1932 and 1965-72; initially an advocate of Puerto Rican independence, later worked for progress under U.S. governance.

MUSSOLINI, BENITO, July 29, 1883 (Predappio, It.)-Apr. 28, 1945. Italian fascist leader. Founded the Italian Fascist Party, in Milan, 1919; led fascists in march on Rome, 1922; when cabinet resigned, was asked to form a government; as prime min. (1922-43), assured fascist control of govt., assuming dictatorial powers; attacked Ethiopia, 1935; made an alliance with A. HITLER, 1939; entered WW II with the fall of France, June 1940; after Allied invasion of Italy, lost support, dismissed by King, arrested, rescued by Germans, 1943; killed by Italian partisans.

MUTSUHITO (reign name, Meiji), Nov. 3, 1852 (Kyoto, Jap.)-July 30, 1912. Emperor of Japan, 1867-1912. A unifying symbol during a period of great transformations, delegating much authority and allowing change while standing for traditional values; oversaw many reforms, including the abolition of feudalism; granted a constitution, 1889.

NAGY, IMRE, June 7, 1896 (Kaposvar, Hung.)-June 16, 1958. Hungarian communist leader. As premier (1953-55), forced out of office, denounced for "Titoism" as his "new course" loosened controls and he became increasingly critical of Soviet control; recalled as premier of the new govt. in the Hungarian revolution, 1956; as revolution began to fail, appealed to West for help; when revolution was crushed, arrested, tried, and executed.

NASSER, GAMAL ABDEL, Jan. 15, 1918 (Alexandria, Egypt)-Sept. 28, 1970. Egyptian leader. As the first pres. of Egypt (1956-58) and of the United Arab Republic (1958-70), a symbol of Arab nationalism and an advocate of Arab unity. Led the coup d'état against King Faruk, 1952; as pres., began construction of the Aswan Dam, forced Britain to evacuate its troops from the Suez Canal (1956), accepted Soviet arms, lost war with Israel (1967), inaugurated land reform.

NEBUCHADNEZZAR II, c.605-562 B.C. King of Babylonia. Made many conquests; built the city of Babylon, constructing its famous hanging gardens; destroyed Jerusalem (586 B.C.) and deported many of the survivors into the 70 Years' Captivity.

NEHRU, JAWAHARLAL, Nov. 14, 1889 (Allahabad, India)-May 27, 1964. Indian statesman. The first prime min. of independent India, 1947-64. Associated with M. GANDHI and the Indian Natl. Congress, of which he became pres. in 1929; imprisoned frequently for civil disobedience in opposition to British colonialism; as prime min., attempted to pursue a policy of nonalignment in foreign affairs; loved by the Indian people, but criticized for his handling of Communist China.

NKRUMAH, KWAME, Sept. 1909 (Nkroful, Gold Coast [now Ghana])-Apr. 27, 1972. Ghanian leader. The first prime min. of Ghana, 1957-66. Formed Convention People's party to fight for self-government of Gold Coast, 1949; elected prime min. of Gold Coast, 1952; after indepen-

169

dence, pursued a pan-African policy, increasingly suppressed dissent; overthrown; awarded Lenin Peace Prize, 1962.

OLAV V, July 2, 1903 (Sandringham, Eng.). King of Norway, 1957–   . Headed Norwegian armed forces, 1944; spent WW II in exile in England.

PADEREWSKI, IGNACE JAN, Nov. 18, 1860 (Kurylowka, Pol.)–June 29, 1941. Polish statesman, pianist, composer. Leader of the movement to restore Poland as a nation. As Polish rep. to U.S. during WW I, influenced Pres. W. WILSON to include Polish independence as one of his "14 Points"; prime min. of Poland, 1919; a master pianist.

PAHLAVI, MOHAMMED REZA, Oct. 26, 1919 (Teheran, Persia [now Iran]). Shah of Iran, 1941–79. Pursued a course of rapid industrialization that led to unrest and his eventual overthrow. In early 1950s, struggled with Premier Mohammed Mosaddeq, a zealous nationalist, for control; when Mosaddeq was overthrown, assumed control, 1953; implemented land reform; developed dam and irrigation projects; tolerated no political opposition, causing thousands to be arrested in the 1970s; under attack from Moslem rightists, he was forced into exile.

PARK CHUNG HEE, Sept. 30, 1917 (Sangmo, Korea)–Oct. 26, 1979. S. Korean leader, military officer. Led coup d'état that overthrew the Second Republic, 1961; as S. Korean pres. (1963–79), maintained close relations with the U.S., grew more dictatorial, declared martial law (1972), altered constitution to give himself unlimited power, assassinated.

PEARSON, LESTER BOWLES, Apr. 23, 1897 (Toronto, Ont., Can.)–Dec. 27, 1972. Canadian statesman, diplomat. Headed Canadian delegation to the UN, 1948–57; awarded 1957 Nobel Peace Prize for his work on the Suez Crisis of 1956; prime min., 1963–68.

PEDRO I, DOM, (or Pedro IV of Portugal), born Dom Antonio Pedro de Alcantara Bourbon, Oct. 12, 1798 (Lisbon, Port.)–Sept. 24, 1834. Portuguese founder of the Brazilian Empire and first emperor of Brazil (1822–31). Fled to Brazil when NAPOLEON conquered Portugal; made Brazilian regent, 1821; sided with Brazilians against Portuguese reactionary policy; declared Brazilian independence, crowned emperor, 1822; proclaimed king of Portugal in 1826, but ousted in 1828; abdicated as Brazilian emperor, 1831.

PERON, EVA DUARTE DE ("Evita"), May 7, 1919 (Los Toldos, Arg.)–July 26, 1952. Argentine political figure. As a teenager, one of the most popular radio and film stars in Argentina; married JUAN PERÓN (1945), and campaigned actively for his election as Argentine pres., (1946); virtually cogoverned during the first six years of Peron's admin.; credited with the introduction of compulsory religious education in Argentina; amassed a large popular following; died of cancer.

PERON, JUAN DOMINGO, Oct. 8, 1895 (Lobos, Arg.)–July 1, 1974. Argentine political leader. As pres. (1946–55 and 1973–74), a strongly nationalistic leader who attempted to make Argentina self-sufficient economically; repressed opposition; overthrown and forced into exile, 1955; his popularity, fostered by a Peronista movement, continued; returned following victory of his party in gen. elections; succeeded by his wife, ISABEL PERÓN.

PERON, (Maria Estela) ISABEL (Martinez) DE, Feb. 6, 1931 (La Rioja Prov., Arg.). Argentine polit-

ical leader, dancer. Succeeded her husband, JUAN PERÓN, as pres. of Argentina, 1974–76; deposed in a military coup.

PETER I ("the Great"), June 9, 1672 (Moscow, Rus.)–Feb. 8, 1725. Tsar (1682–1725) and emperor (1721–25) of Russia. Through wars with Turkey (1695–96) and Sweden (1700–21), obtained access for Russia to the Baltic and Black seas; brought Russia closer to Europe by pushing modernization; reformed the calendar; formed a regular army; created a navy; established technical schools; moved the capitol to a new city he built as a "window to the West," St. Petersburg (now Leningrad).

PIECK, WILHELM, Jan. 3, 1876 (Guben, Ger.)–Sept. 1960. German communist leader. One of the foremost communist leaders of Europe; a leader in Spartacist movement, the forerunner of the German Communist party; pres. of the German Democratic Republic (E. Germany), 1949–60.

PILATE, PONTIUS. Roman procurator of Judea (26–36) under TIBERIUS; handed JESUS CHRIST over to Jewish authorities to be crucified.

PILSUDSKI, JOSEPH, Dec. 5, 1867 (Zulow, Pol. [now USSR])–May 12, 1935. Polish statesman. Poland's first chief of state (1918–22) and virtual dictator (1926–28 and 1930). Fought against Russian domination, arrested, exiled to Siberia (1887); joined Polish Socialist party, 1892; fought against Germany during WW I.

PINOCHET UGARTE, AUGUSTO, Nov. 11, 1915 (Valparaiso, Chile). Chilean leader, military officer. Army chief of staff, 1972; leader of the military junta that overthrew the Socialist govt. of Pres. SALVADOR ALLENDE, 1973; pres., 1973–   .

PLEKHANOV, GEORGI, Dec. 11, 1856 (Tambob Prov., Rus.)–May 30, 1918. Russian revolutionist, social philosopher, founder of Russian Marxism. Broke with Land and Liberty Org. because of his opposition to political terror, 1879; fled to Geneva and helped found the League for the Emancipation of Labor, 1883; started *Iskra*, a revolutionary journal (with V. I. LENIN), 1900; in Russian Socialist party split (1903), his political thinking provided basis of the Menshevik faction. *Socialism and Political Struggle*, 1883.

EL-QADDAFI (or al-Quaddafi, al-Khadafy), MUAMMAR, 1942 (Misratah, Libya). Libyan leader. Led a military coup against King Idris, 1969; as prime min. (1970–   ), removed U.S. and British military bases (1970), nationalized foreign-owned petroleum assets (1973); has supported Palestinian, Pan-Arab, and revolutionary causes.

QUEZON Y MOLINA, MANUEL LUIS, Aug. 19, 1878 (Tayabas Prov., Philippines)–Aug. 1, 1944. Philippine statesman. First pres. of the Commonwealth of the Philippines, 1935–44. Fought for independence from the U.S., 1899; resident commissioner for the Philippines to the U.S. Congress, 1909–16; as pres., expanded his power and strengthened defense; went into exile in the U.S. during the Japanese occupation.

QUIDDE, LUDWIG, Mar. 23, 1858 (Bremen, Ger.)–Mar. 5, 1941. German peace activist. Leader of the German peace movement. Pres. of German Peace Soc., 1914–29; awarded Nobel Peace Prize (with F. E. Buisson), 1927.

QUISLING, VIDKUN, July 18, 1887 (Fyresdal, Nor.)–Oct. 24, 1945. Norwegian politician. Formed the fascist National Union party, 1933; collaborated in German conquest of Norway,

1940; head of state during German occupation during WW II, 1942–45; tried for treason, executed; name has become synonymous with "traitor."

RASPUTIN, GRIGORI EFIMOVICH, c.1873 (Pokrovskoye, Rus.)–Dec. 30/31, 1916. Russian monk. A powerful figure at the court of Emperor Nicholas II and Empress Alexandra; notorious for his debauchery; interfered in church and secular politics; his influence at court led to incompetency in the govt.; killed by a conspiracy of nobles.

RAZIN, (Stepan Timofeyevich) STENKA, ? (Zimoveysky, Rus.)–June 16, 1671. Russian rebel leader. Leader of a major Cossack and peasant rebellion on Russia's southeastern frontier, 1670–71; executed (quartered) by loyalist Cossacks in Red Square in Moscow; regarded as a hero, his exploits were immortalized in many folk songs and legends.

RHEE, SYNGMAN, Apr. 26, 1875 (Whanghae, Korea)–July 19, 1965. Korean statesman. Pres., of Korean provisional govt. in exile, 1919–39. As the first pres. of the Republic of Korea (S. Korea), ruled dictatorially, 1948–60; forced out of office by popular uprising sparked by election fraud and other abuses.

RIBBENTROP, JOACHIM VON, Apr. 30, 1893 (Wesel, Ger.)–Oct. 16, 1946. German diplomat. Amb. to Great Britain, 1936–38; as foreign min. (1938–45), negotiated the German-Soviet Nonaggression Pact of 1939; played key roles in forming the Rome-Berlin Axis and planning the German attack on Poland that started WW II.

RURIK, died 879. Reputed founder of the Russian empire. A prince of the Scandinavian Vikings; probably conquered Novgorod, c.862; the Rurik dynasty reigned until 1598.

SAAVEDRA LAMAS, CARLOS DE, Nov. 1, 1878 (Buenos Aires, Arg.)–May 5, 1959. Argentine statesman. As foreign min. (1932–38), helped end the Chaco War (1932–35) between Bolivia and Paraguay; awarded Nobel Peace Prize, 1936.

EL-SADAT, (Mohamed) ANWAR, Dec. 25, 1918 (Talah Minufiya, Egypt). Egyptian leader. Served time in prison for antigovt. activities, 1940s; participated in the overthrow of King FARUK, 1952; served in the govt. under G. NASSER; as pres. (1970–   ), ousted Soviet advisers and technicians (1972), attacked the Israelis across the Suez Canal (1973), traveled to Israel to promote peace (1977), and signed a peace agreement with Israel (1979).

SALADIN (in full, Salah-al-Din Yusuf ibn Ayyub), c.1138 (Tilsrit [now Iraq])–Mar. 1193. Sultan of Egypt and Syria, from c. 1174. Tried to drive the Christians from Palestine; after forestalling RICHARD I's attempt to conquer Jerusalem, negotiated a truce with the Crusaders, 1192.

SALAZAR, ANTONIO DE OLIVEIRA, Apr. 28, 1889 (Vimieiro, Port.)–July 27, 1970. Portuguese leader. Prof. of economics at U. of Coimbra, 1918–26; helped form the Catholic Center Party; min. of finance, 1928; as prime min. (1932–68), ruled ruthlessly as virtual dictator, was chiefly responsible for draft of a new constitution (1932), improved public finances, and made alliance with Spain (1942).

SAN MARTIN, JOSÉ DE, Feb. 25, 1778 (Yapeyu, now in Arg.)–Aug. 17, 1850. S. American statesman, soldier. With SIMON BOLIVAR, leader of S. America's independence movement. Served as an officer in the Spanish army for 20 years; trained guerrillas in Argentina, 1812; led an army over the Andes (1817), defeating the Spanish at Chaca-buco and Maipo (1818); established independence of Chile; won over Peruvians, taking Lima (1821) and proclaiming an independent Peru; proclaimed the Protector of Peru.

SANTA ANNA, ANTONIO LÓPEZ DE, Feb. 21, 1794 (Jalapa, Mex.)–June 21, 1876. Mexican statesman, army officer. Led several revolts against Spanish rule, 1822–32; pres. of Mexico, 1833–36 and 1846–47; in attempt to crush Texan Revolution, seized Alamo but was defeated at San Jacinto and captured by SAM HOUSTON, 1836; commanded Mexican Army against U.S., 1846–47; defeated at Buena Vista, Cerro Gordo, and Puebla; exiled, 1848; recalled and made pres., 1853–55; exiled, 1855.

SATO, EISAKO, Mar. 27, 1901 (Tabuse, Jap.)–June 3, 1975. Japanese statesman. Worked as lawyer in the ministry of railways, 1924–47; elected as a Liberal Democrat to Diet, 1948; min. of finance, 1958–60; as prime min. (1964–72), signed treaty with U.S. returning Okinawa to Japan (1969) and oversaw the increasing prosperity of Japan; awarded Nobel Peace Prize (with SEAN MACBRIDE), 1974.

SAUL, fl.1025–1000 B.C. First king of Israel, c.1021–1000 B.C. Anointed king by Samuel; reigned over the hill country of Judah; defended Israel against the Philistines; killed by the Philistines in battle of Mount Gilboa and succeeded by DAVID.

SCHMIDT, HELMUT, Dec. 23, 1918 (Hamburg, Ger.). German political leader. Defense min. 1972–74; finance min. 1972–74; chanc., 1974–

SEYSS-INQUART, ARTHUR, July 22, 1892 (Stannern, Bohemia [now Czech.])–Oct. 16, 1946. Austrian Nazi leader. Austrian chan. (1938–39), after Austria was annexed by Germany (1938); German high commissioner of the Netherlands, 1940–45; executed as a war criminal.

SHAH JEHAN, born Prince Khurram, Jan. 5, 1592 (Lahore, India [now Pak.])–Jan. 22, 1666. Mogul emperor in India (1628–58) and builder of the Taj Mahal; restored Islam as a state religion; conquered much of S. India; carried Mogul empire to the height of its wealth and glory.

SHIH HUANG TI (or Ch'in Shih Huang Ti), c.259 B.C. (Ch'in, China)–210 B.C. Chinese emperor (c.247–210 B.C.), the fourth ruler of the Ch'in dynasty. Created the first unified Chinese empire; built a system of roads and canals; developed a centralized admin.; standardized coinage and weights and measures; connected local walls into the Great Wall of China; ordered the burning of all books in China to suppress dissent, 213.

SMITH, IAN DOUGLAS, Apr. 8, 1919 (Selukwe, Southern Rhodesia). Rhodesian political leader. Elected to Southern Rhodesian assembly, 1948; founded right-wing Rhodesian Front, 1961; as prime min. of Rhodesia (1964–79), unilaterally declared his nation's independence rather than negotiate a constitution that would have given power to the black majority, 1965; after elections giving blacks majority rule (1979), remained in cabinet as min. without portfolio.

SMUTS, JAN CHRISTIAAN, May 24, 1870 (Cape Colony [now S.A.])–Sept. 11, 1950. South African statesman, soldier. Boer guerrilla leader in the S. African War, 1899–1902; played a major role in the formation of the Union of S. Africa as a self-governing part of the British Empire, 1910; as prime min. of the S. African Union (1919–24 and 1939–48), aided in the British-Irish problem, supported the League of Nations, and took part in the organization of the UN.

SOARES, MARIO, Dec. 7, 1924 (Lisbon, Port.). Portuguese political leader. A Socialist who was imprisoned 12 times on political grounds under Portugal's repressive govt.; in exile in Paris, 1970–74; returned following the April 1974 coup; min. of foreign affairs, 1974–75; prime min., 1976–78.

SOMOZA, ANASTASIO, Feb. 1, 1896 (San Marcos, Nicar.)–Apr. 13, 1967. Nicaraguan leader. As pres. (1937–47 and 1950–56), ruled harshly, amassed a fortune, exiled most of his opponents, was assassinated. (Father of ANASTASIO SOMOZA-DEBAYLE.)

SOMOZA-DEBAYLE, ANASTASIO, Dec. 5, 1925 (Leon, Nicar.). Nicaraguan political leader. Leader of the Liberal National party; pres., 1967–72 and 1974–79; forced to resign by Sandinist rebels after a protracted civil war and went into exile in the U.S., 1979.

SPAAK, PAUL HENRI, Jan. 25, 1899 (Schaerbeek, Belg.)–July 31, 1972. Belgian statesman. Premier, 1938–39, 1946, and 1947–49; first pres. of UN Gen. Assembly, 1946; participated in formation of the European Coal and Steel Community; Belgian foreign min., 1954–57 and 1961–66; secy. gen. of NATO, 1957–61.

SPINOLA, ANTONIO DE, Apr. 11, 1910 (Estremoz, Port.). Portuguese leader, army officer. Leader of the military junta that overthrew Portugal's repressive govt, 1974; served as provisional pres., May–Sept., 1974. *Portugal and the Future,* 1974.

STALIN, JOSEPH, born Iosif Vissarionovich Dzhugashvili, Dec. 21, 1879 (Gori, Rus.)–Mar. 5, 1953. Soviet political leader. As the virtual dictator of the Soviet Union (1929–53), built the nation into a world power. Joined the Social Democratic party, 1896; became a close advisor of V. I. LENIN; eliminated his rivals to become Lenin's successor, using his position as secy. gen. of Central Com. of the Soviet Communist Party as a power base; as unopposed ruler, started intensive industrialization, forced collectivization of agric., purged the party several times during the 1930s, concluded a nonaggression pact with Germany (1939); took control of the military after Hitler invaded; was a key figure in the post-WW II Cold War.

STRESEMANN, GUSTAV, May 10, 1878 (Berlin, Ger.)–Oct. 3, 1929. German statesman. As foreign min. (1923–29) and chan. (1923) of the Weimar Republic, improved Germany's prestige after WW I; formed the German People's party, 1918; brought Germany into the League of Nations; signed the Kellogg-Briand Pact, 1928; awarded Nobel Peace Prize, with A. BRIAND), 1926.

SUAREZ GONZALES, ADOLFO, Sept. 25, 1932 (Cebreros, Sp.). Spanish political leader. Civil gov. of Segovia, 1968–69; Spanish prime min. and pres. of the council of ministers, 1976–   ; leader of Union Centro Democrátio (UCD), 1977–   .

SUCRE, ANTONIO JOSÉ DE, Feb. 3, 1795 (Cumana, Ven.)–June 4, 1830. S. American leader, soldier. Leader of the Latin American wars of independence from Spain; the liberator of Ecuador. Appointed gen. by SIMON BOLIVAR at the age 26; won victories at Pichincha (1822), Junin (1824), and Ayacucho (1829); helped set up Bolivia and served as its first pres. (1826–28); assassinated.

SUHARTO, RADEN, June 8, 1921 (Batavia [now Djakarta], Indonesia). Indonesian leader, military officer. As a major-gen. in charge of army strate-

gic command, put down an alleged communist coup d'etat and overthrew Pres. SUKARNO; as pres. (1967–   ), has worked for economic progress and a cooperative foreign policy.

SUI WEN TI, born Yang Chien, 541 (China)–604. Chinese emperor (581–604), founder of Sui dynasty, who reunified China after it had been divided for hundreds of years. Laid foundations for the great T'ang dynasty; started construction of the Grand Canal, which connects China's two greatest rivers; instituted civil-service examinations for the selection of govt. officials.

SUKARNO, June 6, 1901 (Surabaja, Indonesia)–June 21, 1970. Indonesian statesman. Leader of the Indonesian independence movement and his nation's first pres. (1949–65). Helped found the Indonesian Nationalist party, 1928; exiled, 1933–42; led struggle against the Dutch, 1945–49; as pres., ignored economic problems in a quest for internatl. prestige, worked for friendly relations with China, opposed U.S. influence; toppled by a military coup, 1965.

SUN YAT-SEN, Nov. 12, 1866 (Kwangtung Prov., China)–Mar. 12, 1925. Chinese revolutionary leader and national hero. Worked to overthrow the Ch'ing dynasty; in exile (1895–1911), organized the Revolutionary Alliance, 1905; participated in several abortive uprisings; planned revolution against Manchus, finally accomplishing it in 1911; formed Kuomintang, or Nationalist party (1912) and served as provisional Chinese pres. for two months; disagreed with dictatorial policies of his successor Yuan Shi-k'ai, elected head of self-proclaimed S. Chinese Republic, 1921; fought to conquer and unite China.

TANAKA, KAKUEI, May 4, 1918 (Nishiyama, Jap.). Japanese statesman. Rose through the ranks of the Liberal Democratic party to min. of finance (1962–64) and min. of international trade (1971); as prime min. (1972–74), established diplomatic relations with Communist China; forced to leave office amid charges he had used it to amass a personal fortune.

TENG HSIAO-PING, 1904 (Szechwan Prov., China). Chinese political leader. Although only vice-chm. of the Chinese Communist party central com. and vice-premier, seems to be China's real administrator. Took part in the Long March, 1934–35; appointed gen. secy. of Chinese Communist party, 1949; vice-premier, 1956; purged during Cultural Revolution (1966–69) for revisionism; returned (1973), then purged again by radical "gang of four" as a "capitalist roader," 1976; reemerged after MAO TSE-TUNG's death and purge of "gang of four," 1976.

THANT, U, Jan. 22, 1909 (Pantanaw, Burma)–Nov. 25, 1974. Burmese diplomat. Chairman of Burmese delegation to UN, 1947–52; rep. to UN, 1953–61; as secy.-gen. of UN (1962–72), deeply involved in internatl. peacekeeping and led UN into concentrating on social and economic development of Third World countries.

TIBERIUS, in full Tiberius Claudius Nero Caesar, Nov. 16, 42 B.C. (Rome, It.)–Mar. 16, 37. Second Roman emperor, 14–37. Succeeding to principate on the death of his stepfather AUGUSTUS, ruled with moderation, strengthening the principate and leaving the state stronger than when he inherited it; vilified by Roman historians as a vicious tyrant.

TITO, born Josip Broz, May 7, 1892 (Kumrovec, now in Yugo.). Yugoslav communist leader, creator of the Yugoslav state. Led the Yugoslav partisans against the German invaders in WW II, assuming military control by war's end; as Yugoslav prime min. (1943-53), was first communist national leader to defy Soviet control, 1948; as pres. (1953–   ), developed relations with Western nations, attempted to form a neutralist bloc with Egypt and India, worked for conciliation of Yugoslavia's different nationalities.

TOGLIATTI, PALMIRO, Mar. 26, 1893 (Genoa, It.)-Apr. 21, 1964. Italian political leader. A leader of the Italian Communist party from 1924 until his death; worked for a national, democratically-oriented communism. Became a member of Central com. of the Italian Communist party, 1924; vice-premier of Italy, 1945; the Soviet city of Stavrapol was renamed after him, 1964.

TOJO, HIDEKI, Dec. 30, 1884 (Tokyo, Jap.)-Dec. 23, 1948. Japanese leader, military officer. As prime min. (1941-44), ordered the attack on Pearl Harbor, pushed the Japanese offensive in China, Southeast Asia, and the Pacific; hanged as a war criminal.

TORRIJOS-HERRERA, OMAR, Feb. 13, 1929 (Santiago, Pan.). Panamanian leader, soldier. As pres. (1969–   ), pushed Panama's claim to the Canal Zone, resulting in an agreement with the U.S. for its gradual release (1977); has worked for social and economic reform.

TOUSSAINT L'OUVERTURE, FRANÇOIS, 1749 (Saint-Dominque [now Haiti]). Haitian liberator, soldier. Leader of the Haitian independence movement during the French Revolution. Joined a slave revolt, 1791; formed his own guerrilla band to fight against the Spanish and British; gained control over the entire island and freed the slaves, 1801; surrendered to French invaders, died in prison.

TRAJAN, born Marcus Alpius Trajanus, Sept. 15?, 53 (Italica [now Santiponce, Sp.])-Aug. 8, 117. Roman emperor, 98-117. Led the last major expansion of the Roman Empire; conquered Dacia (modern Rumania) and most of the Parthian empire; an excellent ruler and administrator.

TROTSKY, LEON, Oct. 26, 1879 (Yanovka, Rus.)-Aug. 20, 1940. Soviet communist leader, one of the founders of the Soviet state. Collaborated with V. I. LENIN on the revolutionary journal *Iskra* in Switzerland; returned to Russia during the Revolution of 1905; advocated theory of permanent revolution; a leader in the October Revolution, 1917; commissar of foreign affairs and of war, 1917-25; engaged in power struggle with J. STALIN; banished from the Soviet Union, 1929; lived in exile, writing against Stalin; assassinated in Mexico.

TRUDEAU, PIERRE ELLIOTT, Oct. 18, 1919 (Montreal, Que., Can.). Canadian political leader. As prime min. (1968-79), took a strong stand against terrorists of the Front de Liberation du Quebec (1970); led Canada to recognize Communist China, 1970; presented anti-inflationary budgets; oversaw the institution of French and English as dual official languages in federal offices.

TRUJILLO MOLINA, RAFAEL LEONIDAS, Oct. 24, 1891 (San Cristobal, D.R.)-May 30, 1961. Dominican political leader, army officer. Seized power in a revolt against Pres. Horacio Vasquez, 1930; ruled with absolute power as dictator (1930-61), placing family members in office; stabilized his nation; assassinated by military officers.

TSHOMBE, MOISE KAPENDA, Nov. 10, 1919 (Musumba, Belgian Congo [now Zaire])-June 29, 1969. Congolese political leader. Worked for a loose federation within the Congo after its independence (1960); when he failed, declared his province of Katanga independent; served as pres. of the secessionist state, 1960-1963; finally forced to capitulate (1963) by UN forces and went into exile; returned to be premier in a govt. of national reconciliation, 1965; exiled again after charges of treason, 1965.

TUTANKHAMEN, fl.1350 B.C. Egyptian pharaoh. His reign witnessed the return of traditional religion and art following Akhenaton's "revolution"; his intact tomb was discovered by Howard Carter, 1922.

ULBRICHT, WALTER, June 30, 1893 (Leipzig, Ger.)-Aug. 1, 1973. E. German Communist party leader. Joined German Communist party in the 1920s; fled to Soviet Union under the Third Reich; influential in the formation of the E. German state after WW II; as chm. of the council of state (1960-71), ruled ruthlessly, suppressing opposition and keeping E. Germany a close ally of the USSR.

VARGAS, GETULIO DORNELES, Apr. 19, 1883 (São Borja, Braz.)-Aug. 24, 1954. Brazilian leader. As pres. (1930-45 and 1951-54), ruled Brazil as a benevolent dictator; centralized fiscal control; enfranchised laborers and women; enacted social-security laws; reformed education; overthrown by democratic movement, 1945; returned (1950) as pres., but following govt. scandal, committed suicide.

VENIZELOS, ELEUTHERIOS, Aug. 23, 1864 (Mournies, Crete)-Mar. 18, 1936. Greek statesman, diplomat. Played a major role in Crete's uprising against Ottoman rule, 1897; as prime min. of Greece (1910-15, 1917-20, 1924, 1928-32), doubled the area and population of the state during the Balkan Wars and led Greece into WW I on the allied side, opposed the royalists.

VERWOERD, HENDRIK FRENSCH, Sept. 8, 1901 (Amsterdam, Neth.)-Sept. 6, 1966. South African leader, educator. As min. of native affairs (1950-57), responsible for pushing through much of the apartheid legislation; as prime min. (1958-66), vigorously applied apartheid policy and led South Africa out of the Commonwealth of Nations, 1961; assassinated.

VLADIMIR II, Monomachus (Monomakh), 1053 (Kiev, Rus.)-May 19, 1125. Grand duke of Kiev, 1113-25. Won many campaigns against the Germans; led Kiev to the peak of its power; founded the city of Vladimir.

VORSTER, BALTHAZAR JOHANNES, Dec. 13, 1915 (Jamestown, S.A.). S. African political leader. Imprisoned for his opposition to the Allies in WW II, 1942-44; as min. of justice (1961-66), repressed opponents of apartheid; as prime min. (1966-78), developed a more conciliatory foreign policy and personified Afrikaaner values of determination and rectitude; pres., 1978-79; resigned on charges of previous irregularities.

WEIZMANN, CHAIM, Nov. 27, 1874 (Motol, Rus.)-Nov. 9, 1952. Zionist leader, biochemist. Participated in the negotiations leading to the Balfour Declaration of 1917; pres. of World Zionist Org., 1920-29 and 1935-46; first pres. of Israel, 1949-52. As biochemist, discovered a process of synthesizing acetone that aided British munitions during WW I.

WITTE, COUNT SERGEI YULEVICH, June 29, 1849 (Tiflis, Rus. [now Tbilisi, USSR])-Mar. 13, 1915. Russian political leader. A great exponent of Russian modernization as the first constitutional prime min. of tsarist Russia, 1905-06.

THE BOOK OF WHO

XERXES, c.519 B.C.–465 B.C. King of Persia, 486–465 B.C. Son of DARIUS THE GREAT; invaded Greece; defeated Leonidas and his 300 Spartans at Thermopylae, 480 B.C.; occupied Athens; his fleet destroyed at Salamis, 480 B.C.

ZAPATA, EMILIANO, Aug. 8, 1883 (Anenecuilco, Mex.)–Apr. 10, 1919. Mexican leader. Revolutionary leader of a Mexican agrarian movement. Supported Francisco Madero's overthrow of PORFIRIO DIAZ, 1911; seized land with an army of Indians; outlined the Plan of Ayala (1911) for agrarian reform and dropped support of Madero; occupied Mexico City three times, 1914–15; assassinated.

ZHDANOV, ANDREI ALEXANDROVICH, Feb. 14, 1896 (probably Marivpol, Rus. [now Zhdanov, USSR]). Soviet govt. and Communist party official. A close associate of J. STALIN, directed the post-WW II Cold War policy called Zhdanovism, which severely restricted cultural activities and promoted an anti-Western bias in policy.

ZINOVIEV, GRIGORI EVSEVICH, born Ovsel Gershon Aronov Radomylsky, Sept. 11, 1883 (Yelizavetgrad, Rus. [now Kirovgrad, USSR])–Aug. 25, 1936. Soviet political leader. Worked closely with V. I. LENIN in the Bolshevik party before the 1917 revolution; following Lenin's death (1924), briefly involved in a ruling triumvirate with J. STALIN and L. Kamenev; a victim of Stalin's Great Purge.

MILITARY AND NAVAL LEADERS

U.S. MILITARY AND NAVAL LEADERS

ABRAMS, CREIGHTON WILLIAMS, Sept. 15, 1914 (Springfield, Mass.)–Sept. 4, 1974. U.S. Army general. As a WW II tank commander, broke through German lines to relieve U.S. troops at Bastogne, 1944; commanded U.S. forces in Vietnam, 1968–72; chief of staff, U.S. Army, 1972–74.

ALLEN, ETHAN, Jan 21, 1738 (Litchfield, Conn.)–Feb. 12, 1789. American Revolutionary soldier, politician. Commanded the "Green Mountain Boys"; captured Ft. Ticonderoga, 1775; taken prisoner by the British and held in captivity, 1775–78.

ANDREWS, FRANK MAXWELL, Feb. 3, 1884 (Nashville, Tenn.)–May 3, 1943. U.S. Army Air Force general who was an early advocate of strategic air power. Credited with development of Boeing B-17 bomber; commander, U.S. forces in Europe, Feb.–May 1943.

ARNOLD, BENEDICT, Jan. 14, 1741 (Norwich, Conn.)–June 14, 1801. American Revolutionary general best known as traitor during American Revolution. Fought with Ethan Allen at Ft. Ticonderoga, 1775; failed to capture Quebec, 1775; played a major role in American victory at Saratoga, 1777; attempted to surrender West Point to the British for £20,000, 1780; led British forces in raids in Virginia and Connecticut, 1780–81.

ARNOLD, HENRY HARLEY ("Hap"), June 25, 1886 (Gladwyne, Pa.)–Jan. 15, 1950. U.S. Army Air Force general. As commanding general, U.S. Army Air Force (1941–46), built world's largest air force; planned strategic bombing of Germany and Japan in WW II.

BANKS, NATHANIEL PRENTISS, Jan. 30, 1816 (Waltham, Mass.)–Sept. 1, 1894. Union Army general, public official. Served as U.S. rep. nine times in period 1852–88; gov. of Massachusetts, 1858–61; captured Port Hudson on the Mississippi R., 1863; led disastrous Red River campaign, 1864.

BARRY, JOHN, 1745 (Co. Wexford, Ire.)–Sept. 13, 1803. American Revolutionary naval officer. Often called the "Father of the U.S. Navy"; won numerous sea battles during the Revolution.

BEAUREGARD, PIERRE GUSTAVE TOUTANT, May 28, 1818 (St. Bernard Par., La.)–Feb. 20, 1893. Confederate Army general. Ordered bombardment of Ft. Sumter to open Civil War; victorious at the First Battle of Bull Run, 1861.

BLACK HAWK (a.k.a. Makataimeshekiakiak or Black Sparrow Hawk), 1767 (Ill.)–Oct. 3, 1838. Algonquian Indian leader. His defeat at Bad Axe R. (1832) led to first Indian cession of lands in Iowa.

BOWIE, JAMES, 1796 (Burke Co., Ga.)–Mar. 6, 1836. U.S. frontiersman, soldier. Popular hero of the Texas Revolution; killed at the Alamo, 1836; his name is associated with the Bowie knife, invented by James or his brother, Rezin.

BRADLEY, OMAR NELSON, Feb. 12, 1893 (Clark, Mo.). U.S. general of the army (appointed 1950). Commander, U.S. II Corps, North Africa and Sicily, 1943; led U.S. ground troops in the Normandy invasion, 1944; commander, 12th Army Group, 1944–45; chairman, Joint Chiefs of Staff, 1949–50.

BRAGG, BRAXTON, Mar. 22, 1817 (Warrenton, N.C.)–Sept. 27, 1876. Confederate Army general. Victorious at Chickamauga, 1863; defeated at Chattanooga, 1863; Confederate commander-in-chief, 1864–65.

BROWN, GEORGE SCRATCHLEY, Aug. 17, 1918 (Montclair, N.J.)–Dec. 5, 1978. U.S. Air Force general. U.S. Air Force chief of staff, 1973–74; chairman, Joint Chiefs of Staff, 1974–78; sparked controversy by suggesting that U.S. Jews exert undue influence in U.S. affairs (1974), and by calling Israel a "burden" to U.S. (1976); awards include Silver Star, Legion of Merit, and Distinguished Flying Cross.

BUCKNER, SIMON BOLIVAR, Apr. 1, 1823 (nr. Munfordville, Ky.)–Jan. 8, 1914. Confederate Army general, politician. Surrendered Ft. Donelson, Tenn., to Gen. U. S. Grant, 1862; gov. of Kentucky, 1887–91.

BUCKNER, SIMON BOLIVAR, JR., July 18, 1886 (Mundfordville, Ky.)–June 18, 1945. U.S. Army general. Led successful invasion of Japanese-held Ryukyu Is., 1945.

BUFORD, JOHN, Mar. 4, 1826 (Woodford, Ky.)–Dec. 16, 1863. Union Army general. Led cavalry of the Army of the Potomac, 1862–63; fought at Antietam (1862), Gettysburg (1863).

BURNSIDE, AMBROSE EVERETT, May 23, 1824 (Liberty, Ind.)–Sept. 13, 1881. Union Army general, political leader. Credited with originating side whiskers (sideburns). Defeated at Fredericksburg, 1862; mishandled operations at Petersburg, Va., 1864, and forced to resign; gov. of Rhode Island, 1866–69; U.S. senator (R, R.I.), 1875–81.

BUTLER, BENJAMIN FRANKLIN, Nov. 5, 1818 (Deerfield, N.H.)–Jan. 11, 1893. Union Army general, public official. As military gov. of New Orleans (1862) outraged public sensibilities by his dictatorial rule and was recalled by Pres. LINCOLN; U.S. rep. (R, Mass.), 1867–75, 1877–79; led impeachment movement against ANDREW JOHNSON, 1868; Greenback Party presidential candidate, 1884.

CARLSON, EVANS FORDYCE, Feb. 26, 1896 (Sidney, N.Y.)–May 27, 1947. U.S. Marine Corps general. Led commando force known as Carlson's Raiders, whose battle cry was "Gung Ho," during WW II.

CHAFFEE, ADNA ROMANZA, Apr. 14, 1842 (Orwell, Ohio)–Nov. 1, 1914. U.S. Army officer. His career extended from the Civil War through the Boxer Rebellion (1900), in which he commanded U.S. contingent; U.S. Army chief of staff, 1904–06. (Father of A.R. CHAFFEE, JR.)

CHAFFEE, ADNA ROMANZA, JR., Sept. 23, 1884 (Junction City, Kan.)–Aug. 22, 1941. U.S. Army officer who was a prime mover behind the development of the U.S. armored force. (Son of A.R. CHAFFEE.)

CHENNAULT, CLAIRE LEE, Sept. 6, 1890 (Commerce, Tex.)–July 27, 1958. U.S. Army Air Force general who created and led "Flying Tigers" in China in WW II.

CLARK, GEORGE ROGERS, Nov. 19, 1752 (nr. Charlottesville, Va.)–Feb. 13, 1818. U.S. frontiersman, army general. Captured Vincennes, 1779; saved St. Louis, 1780.

CLARK, MARK WAYNE, May 1, 1896 (Madison Barracks, N.Y.) U.S. Army general. Commanded 5th Army in Italy, 1943–44; commanded United Nations forces in Korea, 1952–53.

CLAY, LUCIUS DU BIGNON, Apr. 23, 1897 (Marietta, Ga.)–Apr. 16, 1978. U.S. Army general. Commander-in-chief, U.S. forces in Europe, 1947–49; administered Berlin airlift, 1948–49.

COCHISE, c.1812 (probably Ariz.)–June 9, 1874. Apache leader. Led war against white settlers in Southwest, 1861–72.

CRAZY HORSE (Indian name: Ta-Sunko-Witko), c.1840 (nr. Rapid City, S.D.)–Sept. 15, 1877. Oglala Sioux chief who led resistance against white encroachments in Black Hills. One of the Indian leaders in the victory at the Little Bighorn, 1876.

CROOK, GEORGE, Sept. 23, 1829 (Dayton, Ohio)–Mar. 21, 1890. U.S. Army general, Indian fighter. Fought in Civil War and Sioux War, 1876; captured GERONIMO, 1882.

CUSTER, GEORGE ARMSTRONG, Dec. 5, 1839 (Harrison Co., Ohio)–June 25, 1876. U.S. cavalry officer. Outstanding record in the Civil War; defeated and killed at Battle of Little Bighorn (1876), the worst defeat in the Indian campaigns, often called Custer's Last Stand.

DAVIS, BENJAMIN OLIVER, July 1, 1877 (Wash., D.C.)–Nov. 26, 1970. U.S. Army general. First black general in U.S. Army, 1940; lieut., Spanish-Amer. War, 1898; U.S. military attaché in Liberia, 1911–12. (Father of B. O. DAVIS, JR.)

DAVIS, BENJAMIN OLIVER, JR., 1912 (Wash., D.C.). U.S. Air Force general. First black graduate of West Point, 1936; WW II pilot. First black general in the Air Force, 1954. (Son of B. O. DAVIS.)

DECATUR, STEPHEN, Jan. 5, 1779 (Sinepuxent, Md.)–Mar. 22, 1820. U.S. naval commodore. Hero of the Barbary Wars, 1801–05, 1815; fought in War of 1812; famed for toast, "Our country, right or wrong."

DEWEY, GEORGE, Dec. 26, 1837 (Montpelier, Vt.)–Jan. 16, 1917. U.S. admiral. Defeated Spanish fleet at Manila Bay during the Spanish-American War, 1898.

DONOVAN, WILLIAM JOSEPH ("Wild Bill"), Jan. 1, 1883 (Buffalo, N.Y.)–Feb. 8, 1959. U.S. Army general, public official. Director, Office of Strategic Services, 1942–45.

DOOLITTLE, JAMES HAROLD, Dec. 14, 1896 (Alameda, Calif.). U.S. Army Air Corps general who led first U.S. WW II bombing raid on Tokyo, 1942.

EARLY, JUBAL ANDERSON, Nov. 3, 1816 (Franklin Co., Va.)–Mar. 2, 1894. Confederate Army general. Raided Washington, D.C., causing panic and forcing Gen. U.S. GRANT to divert forces to repel him, 1864.

EDMONDS, SARAH EMMA EVELYN, née Edmonson, or Edmondson, a.k.a. Frank Thompson), Dec. 1841 (New Brunswick, Can.)–Sept. 5, 1898. Union Army soldier. Disguised as a man, fought at the First Battle of Bull Run (1861), the Peninsular campaign (1862), and Fredericksburg (1862); spied behind Confederate lines "disguised" as a woman; granted a veteran's pension by Congress.

FARRAGUT, DAVID GLASGOW, July 5, 1801 (Knoxville, Tenn.)–Aug. 14, 1870. Union admiral, the first admiral in U.S. history. Seized New Orleans, 1862; captured Mobile Bay, 1864, bellowing, "Damn the torpedos: full speed ahead!"

FLETCHER, FRANK JACK, Apr. 29, 1885 (Marshalltown, Ia.)–Apr. 25, 1973. U.S. admiral who led naval forces in Pacific in WW II.

FORREST, NATHAN BEDFORD, July 13, 1821 (Chapel Hill, Tenn.)–Oct. 29, 1877. Confederate cavalry general. Noted for daring cavalry raids that disrupted Union supply lines; first Grand Wizard of the original Ku Klux Klan (disbanded, 1869).

GATES, HORATIO, c.1728 (Maldon, Eng.)–Apr. 10, 1806. American Revolutionary general. As a British soldier, engaged in French and Indian War, 1754–63; moved to America (1772) and joined Continental Army; won the Battle of Saratoga, 1777; blamed for disastrous defeat at Camden (1780), and relieved of command.

GAVIN, JAMES MAURICE, Mar. 22, 1907 (Brooklyn, N.Y.). U.S. Army general, diplomat. Engaged at Normandy and the Battle of the Bulge during WW II; U.S. ambassador to France, 1960–62; critic of U.S. military strategy during the Vietnam War. *On to Berlin,* 1978.

GERONIMO (Indian name: Goyathlay, "One Who Yawns"), June 1829 (Ariz.)–Feb. 17, 1909. Apache Indian chief. Led raids in Mexico and U.S.; surrendered to U.S. troops, 1886.

GREENE, NATHANAEL, Aug. 7, 1742 (Potowomut [now Warwick] R.I.)–June 19, 1786. American Revolutionary general who ranked second to Gen. GEORGE WASHINGTON. Defeated British in Southern campaign, 1780–81.

GROVES, LESLIE RICHARD, Aug. 17, 1896 (Albany, N.Y.)–July 13, 1970. U.S. Army general who headed Manhattan Project, which developed the atomic bomb, 1942–47.

HAIG, ALEXANDER MEIGS, JR., Dec. 2, 1914 (Philadelphia, Pa.). U.S. Army general, presidential assistant. Chief of White House staff, 1973–74; NATO Supreme Allied Commander, Europe, 1974–79.

HALE, NATHAN, June 6, 1755 (Coventry, Conn.)–Sept. 22, 1776. American Revolutionary hero. Hanged by British as a spy, he gained immortality with his last words: "I only regret that I have but one life to lose for my country."

HALLECK, HENRY WAGER, Jan. 16, 1815 (Westernville, N.Y.)–Jan. 9, 1872. U.S. military officer. General in chief of the Union Army, 1862–64; known as an excellent administrator but poor strategist.

HALSEY, WILLIAM FREDERICK, JR., ("Bull"), Oct. 30, 1882 (Elizabeth, N.J.)–Aug. 16, 1959. U.S. admiral. South Pacific theater commander during WW II; helped turn back Japanese at Guadalcanal, 1942; played a major role in the destruction of the

THE BOOK OF WHO

Japanese battle fleet at Battle of Leyte Gulf (the largest sea battle in history), 1944; directed final major operations of WW II, around Okinawa, 1945.

HAMPTON, WADE, Mar. 28, 1818 (Charleston, S.C.)–Apr. 11, 1902. Confederate cavalry general, public official. Fought at Antietam (1862), Gettysburg (1863); governor of South Carolina, 1877–79; U.S. senator (D, S.C.), 1879–81.

HANCOCK, WINFIELD SCOTT, Feb. 14, 1824 (Montgomery Co., Pa.)–Feb. 9, 1886. Union Army general. Served in Peninsular campaign, 1862; prepared defensive positions on Cemetery Ridge at Gettysburg, 1863; Democratic presidential candidate, 1880.

HERKIMER, NICHOLAS, 1728 (Herkimer, N.Y.)–Aug. 6, 1777. American Revolutionary general. Led militiamen at Battle of Oriskany, where he was mortally wounded; hometown named in his honor.

HERSHEY, LEWIS BLAINE, Sept. 12, 1893 (Steuben Co., Ind.). U.S. Army general. Directed Selective Service System under six presidents, overseeing the draft of some 14.5 million Americans, 1941–70.

HODGES, COURTNEY HICKS, Jan. 5, 1887 (Perry, Ga.)–Jan. 16, 1966. U.S. Army general. Commanded 1st Army, the first to enter Paris and to cross the Siegfried Line, 1944.

HOOD, JOHN BELL, June 1, 1831 (Owingsville, Ky.)–Aug. 30, 1879. Confederate general. One of the South's bravest generals, wounded at Gettysburg and Chickamauga; as commander, Army of Tennessee, failed to repel the forces of Gen. WILLIAM T. SHERMAN at Atlanta, 1864; suffered disastrous defeat at Battle of Nashville, Dec. 1864.

HOOKER, JOSEPH ("Fighting Joe"), Nov. 13, 1814 (Hadley, Mass.)–Oct. 31, 1879. Union Army general. Commander, Army of the Potomac, 1863; defeated at Battle of Chancellorsville, May 2–4, 1863.

HOPKINS, ESEK, Apr. 26, 1718 (Scituate, R.I.)–Feb. 26, 1802. American Revolutionary naval commander. Commanded Continental Navy, 1775–77; suspended from command following his defeat on Long Island Sound.

HOWARD, OLIVER OTIS, Nov. 8, 1830 (Leeds, Me.)–Oct. 26, 1909. U.S. Army general, educator. Engaged in the First Battle of Bull Run (1861), Peninsular campaign (1862), Antietam (1862), and Fredericksburg (1862) during the Civil War; founder and first pres., Howard U., 1867; negotiated peace with CHIEF JOSEPH, 1877.

HULL, ISAAC, Mar. 9, 1773 (Derby, Conn.)–Feb. 13, 1843. U.S. naval commodore. Commanded U.S.S. *Constitution* (nick-named "Old Ironsides") in victory over British frigate *Guerriere,* (1812), a battle that helped unite the nation behind the war effort.

HULL, WILLIAM, June 24, 1753 (Derby, Conn.)–Nov. 29, 1825. U.S. Army general. Surrendered Detroit to British with no resistance, 1812; court-martialed and sentenced to death for cowardice; sentence remitted by Pres. JAMES MADISON.

INGERSOLL, ROYAL EASON, June 20, 1883 (Washington, D.C.)–May 20, 1976. U.S. admiral. Commander of the Atlantic Fleet, 1942–44.

JACKSON, THOMAS JONATHAN ("Stonewall"), Jan. 21, 1824 (Clarksburg, Va., now in W.Va.)–May 10, 1863. Confederate Army general. Won acclaim at the First Battle of Bull Run (1861), when another general shouted, "There stands Jackson like a stone wall"; victorious in Shenandoah campaign, 1862; his flanking movement led

to Confederate victory at Chancellorsville, where he was mortally wounded, 1863.

JOHNSTON, JOSEPH EGGLESTON, Feb. 3, 1807 (nr. Farmville, Va.)–Mar. 21, 1891. Confederate Army general. Helped win first important Southern victory at the First Battle of Bull Run, 1861; commander, Army of No. Virginia, 1861–62; failed to stop Gen. W. T. SHERMAN's advance on Atlanta, 1864.

JONES, JOHN PAUL, born John Paul, July 6, 1747 (Kirkcudbright, Scot.)–July 18, 1792. Scottish naval hero of the American Revolution. Captured eight British ships, sank eight others, 1776; commanded *Bonhomme Richard* in celebrated victory over *Serapis* (when asked to surrender, replied, "Sir, I have not yet begun to fight"), 1779; as admiral in Russian navy, won victories over Turks, 1788; died in Paris; remains transferred to U.S. Naval Acad. at Annapolis, 1913.

JOSEPH (Chief Joseph; Ind. name; Hinmatonyalatkit), c. 1840 (Oregon)–Sept. 21, 1904. Nez Percé Indian leader. Led his band in flight to Canada, traveling 1,600 miles through Idaho and Montana and fighting brilliant rearguard action before surrender, 1877.

KEARNY, STEPHEN WATTS, Aug. 30, 1794 (Newark, N.J.)–Oct. 31, 1848. U.S. Army general. Commanded Army of the West in the Mexican War, 1846–48; captured New Mexico, helped win California.

KENNEY, GEORGE CHURCHILL, Aug. 6, 1889 (Yarmouth, N.S., Can.)–U.S. Army Air Force general. Headed Gen. DOUGLAS MACARTHUR's air forces in the Pacific during WW II.

KIMMEL, HUSBAND EDWARD, Feb. 26, 1882 (Henderson, Ky.)–May 14, 1968. U.S. admiral. Commander of Pearl Harbor naval base at the time of the Japanese attack, 1941; was relieved of his command 10 days later, charged with errors of judgement.

KING, ERNEST JOSEPH, Nov. 23, 1878 (Lorain, Ohio)–June 25, 1956. U.S. admiral. Commander-in-chief of U.S. Fleet (1941–45) and chief of Naval Operations (1942–45), the first to hold both jobs at the same time; principal architect of the Allied victory at sea in WW II.

KIRBY-SMITH, EDMUND, May 16, 1824 (St. Augustine, Fla.)–Mar. 28, 1893. Confederate Army officer. Last Confederate commander to surrender, 1865. Pres. of U. of Nashville, 1875–93.

KRUEGER, WALTER, Jan. 26, 1881 (Flatow, W. Prussia, now Pol.)–Aug. 20, 1967. U.S. Army general. Headed Southern Defense Command, 1941–43; commander, 6th Army, 1943–46; his troops invaded New Britain, occupied Hollandia; advanced 2,000 miles to the Philippine Islands, occupied Japan.

LAWRENCE, JAMES, Oct. 1, 1781 (Burlington, N.J.)–June 1, 1813. U.S. naval captain. Commander of the U.S.S. *Chesapeake* when it was defeated by the British frigate *Shannon* in battle off Boston, 1813; famed for his dying words, uttered during the battle: "Don't give up the ship."

LEAHY, WILLIAM DANIEL, May 6, 1875 (Hampton, Ia.)–July 20, 1959. U.S. admiral. Served as personal chief of staff for Pres. FRANKLIN D. ROOSEVELT during WW II.

LEE, CHARLES, 1731 (Dernhall, Eng.)–Oct. 2, 1782. American Revolutionary general. Held captive by the British, 1776–78 (letters found in 1858 in papers of WILLIAM HOWE indicated Lee had treasonable negotiations with the British during his captivity); failed at the Battle of Monmouth, 1778;

176

court-martialed and suspended, dismissed after writing an insulting letter to Congress, 1780.

LEE, HENRY ("Light-Horse Harry"), Jan. 29, 1756 (Prince William Co., Va.)–Mar. 25, 1818. American Revolutionary cavalry officer, public official. Captured British post at Paulus Hook, N.J., 1779; engaged in Carolina campaign; served in Continental Congress, 1785–88; governor of Virginia, 1792–95. (Father of ROBERT E. LEE.)

LEE, ROBERT EDWARD, Jan. 19, 1807 (Stratford, Va.)–Oct. 12, 1870. Confederate Army general, the South's outstanding military leader. Supt., U.S. Military Academy, 1852–55; refused command of Union armies, resigned U.S. commission, 1861; military adviser to JEFFERSON DAVIS, 1861–62; led Army of Northern Virginia, 1862–65; commander-in-chief of all Confederate armies, 1865; victorious at Seven Days' Battle (1862), Second Bull Run (1862), Fredericksburg (1862), Chancellorsville (1863); defeated at Gettysburg, 1863; surrendered at Appomattox Courthouse, 1865. (Son of HENRY LEE.)

LEMAY, CURTIS EMERSON, Nov. 15, 1906 (Columbus, Ohio). U.S. Air Force general, pioneer of strategic bombing concepts in WW II. Commander in chief, Strategic Air Command, 1957–61; chief of staff, U.S. Air Force, 1961–65; American Independent Party v.-pres. candidate (ran with GEORGE WALLACE), 1968.

LEMNITZER, LYMAN, Aug. 29, 1899 (Honesdale, Pa.). U.S. Army general. Engaged in WW II and Korean War; chief of staff, U.S. Army, 1959–60; chairman, Joint Chiefs of Staff, 1960–62; commander, U.S. forces in Europe, 1962; Supreme Allied Commander, 1963.

LONGSTREET, JAMES, Jan. 8, 1821 (Edgefield Dist., S.C.)–Jan. 2, 1904. Confederate Army general. Held important commands at the First and Second battles of Bull Run (1861, 1862), Peninsular campaign (1862), Antietam (1862), Fredericksburg (1862), Gettysburg (1863), Chickamauga (1863), and the Wilderness campaign (1864); made a scapegoat in the South after the war for the defeat at Gettysburg, partly because he joined the Republican party.

MACARTHUR, ARTHUR, June 2, 1845 (Chicopee Falls, Mass.)–Sept. 5, 1912. U.S. Army officer. Engaged for the Union in the Civil War, winning the Congressional Medal of Honor for heroism at Battle of Missionary Ridge; in Spanish-American War, helped capture Manila, 1898; ranking officer in the U.S. Army at retirement, 1909. (Father of DOUGLAS MACARTHUR.)

MACARTHUR, DOUGLAS, Jan. 26, 1880 (nr. Little Rock, Ark.)–Apr. 5, 1964. U.S. Army officer. Commander of 42nd (Rainbow) Division, WW I; supt. of West Point, 1919–22; army chief of staff and military advisor to Philippines prior to WW II; retired, 1937; recalled, 1941; withdrawn from Corregidor, fled 3,000 miles to Australia, saying, "I have come through, I shall return," 1941; made supreme allied commander in SW Pacific (1941), launched counterattack; liberated Philippines, 1944–45; accepted Japanese surrender, 1945; commander of occupation forces in Japan, 1945–50; commander in chief of UN forces in Korea, 1950–51; dismissed when he publicly challenged Pres. TRUMAN's conduct of the war; returned to U.S. to hero's welcome, saying "Old soldiers never die, they just fade away." (Son of ARTHUR MACARTHUR)

MAHAN, ALFRED THAYER, Sept. 27, 1840 (West Point, N.Y.)–Dec. 1, 1914. U.S. admiral, naval historian and theorist. Wrote some 20 books on naval history and global strategy, which were instrumental in shaping the policies of the great powers in the late-19th and early-20th cent., his doctrines influenced the enlargement of the U.S. Navy after 1880, the annexation of Hawaii, and the digging of the Panama Canal.

MARION, FRANCIS ("The Swamp Fox"), c. 1732 (Winyah, S.C.)–Feb. 27, 1795. American Revolutionary general. Led guerrilla actions against British in South Carolina, 1780–81.

MARSHALL, GEORGE CATLETT, Dec. 31, 1880 (Uniontown, Pa.)–Oct. 16, 1959. U.S. Army general, statesman. As U.S. Army chief of staff in WW II, was the principal organizer of the U.S. war effort, 1939–45; presidential envoy to China, 1945–47; U.S. secretary of state, 1947–49; U.S. secretary of defense, 1950–51; authored Marshall Plan for postwar European relief, for which he won the Nobel Peace Prize, 1953.

MCAULIFFE, ANTHONY CLEMENT, July 2, 1898 (Washington, D.C.)–Aug. 11, 1975. U.S. Army general famed for his reply to German surrender demand at Bastogne, 1941—"Nuts!"

MCCAULEY, MARY, ("Molly Pitcher") née Ludwig, Oct. 13, 1754 (Trenton, N.J.)–Jan. 22, 1832. American Revolutionary heroine who carried water and fired cannon at Battle of Monmouth, 1778.

MCCLELLAN, GEORGE BRINTON, Dec. 3, 1826 (Philadelphia, Pa.)–Oct. 29, 1885. Union Army general, public official. Commander, Army of the Potomac, 1861–62; his indecisiveness led to Union defeats in the Peninsular campaign and Seven Days' Battles and to the bloody draw at Antietam, 1862; relieved of command, 1862; Democratic presidential candidate, 1864; gov. of New Jersey, 1878–81.

MEADE, GEORGE GORDON, Dec. 31, 1815 (Cadiz, Sp.)–Nov. 6, 1872. Union Army general. Commander, Army of the Potomac 1863–65; victor at Gettysburg, 1863.

MILES, NELSON APPLETON, Aug. 8, 1839 (Westminster, Mass.)–May 15, 1925. U.S. Army general most noted for his role in wars with the Western Indians. Drove SITTING BULL into Canada, 1876; captured CHIEF JOSEPH, 1877; put down the Ghost Dance disturbances that ended with Battle of Wounded Knee, 1890; led invasion of Puerto Rico, 1898.

MITCHELL, WILLIAM ("Billy"), Dec. 29, 1879 (Nice, Fr.)–Feb. 19, 1936. U.S. Army Air Corps general, aviation pioneer. WW I aviation hero; an ardent advocate of air power who warned of inadequate U.S. defenses in regard to Japan; his attack against the Navy and War departments for their neglect of air power led to guilty verdict in court-martial for insubordination, 1925; resigned his commission, 1926; vindicated by events of WW II.

MITSCHER, MARC ANDREW, Jan. 26, 1887 (Hillsboro, Wisc.)–Feb. 3, 1947. U.S. admiral. Commanded U.S.S. *Hornet* in the Battle of Midway, 1942; commanded Task Force 58, the principal carrier strike force in the Pacific; led successful air strikes in the battles of the Philippine Sea, Leyte Gulf, Iwo Jima, and Okinawa, 1944–45.

MONTGOMERY, RICHARD, 1738 (Ire.)–Dec. 1775. American Revolutionary general. Commanded Quebec campaign for Continental Army; killed during assault on Quebec, 1775.

MOORER, THOMAS HINMAN, Feb. 9, 1912 (Mount Willing, Ala.). U.S. admiral. Chief of Naval

THE BOOK OF WHO

Operations, 1967-70; chairman, Joint Chiefs of Staff, 1970-74.

MORGAN, DANIEL, 1736 (Hunterdon Co., N.J.)-July 6, 1802. American Revolutionary general. Engaged at Quebec, Saratoga, 1777; victorious at Battle of Cowpens, 1781.

MOULTRIE, WILLIAM, Dec. 4, 1730 (Charleston, S.C.)-Sept. 27, 1805. American Revolutionary general. Held fort on Sullivan's I., near Charleston, S.C., against heavy British attack, 1776; surrendered at Charleston, 1780.

MUHLENBERG, JOHN PETER GABRIEL, Oct. 1, 1746 (Trappe, Pa.)-Oct. 1, 1807. American Revolutionary general, clergyman, congressman. Engaged at Brandywine, Monmouth, Yorktown; served three times as U.S. rep. from Pennsylvania, 1789-1801. (Son of Lutheran leader HEINRICH M. MUHLENBERG.)

NIMITZ, CHESTER WILLIAM, Feb. 24, 1885 (Fredericksburg, Tex.)-Feb. 20, 1966. U.S. admiral. Commanded U.S. naval forces in the Pacific during WW II; directed the battles of Coral Sea and Midway, 1942; directed the landings on the Solomons, Gilberts, Marshalls, Marianas, Philippines, Iwo Jima, and Okinawa, 1942-45; chief of Naval Operations, 1945-47.

O'HARE, EDWARD HENRY ("Butch"), Mar. 13, 1914 (St. Louis, Mo.)-Nov. 27, 1943 (killed in action). U.S. Navy officer, aviator. Credited with saving U.S.S. *Lexington* in heroic air battle, shooting down five Japanese bombers and damaging three others, 1942; Chicago's O'Hare Airport named in his honor.

PATTON, GEORGE SMITH, JR. ("Old Blood and Guts"), Nov. 11, 1885 (San Gabriel, Calif.)-Dec. 21, 1945. U.S. army officer, armored-warfare tactician. Led U.S. Army II Corps in N. Africa, 1942-43; led 7th Army assault on Sicily, 1943; caused home-front furor by slapping a hospitalized GI and cursing others as malingerers in Sicilian field hospital, 1943; led 3rd Army invasion of German occupied Europe, 1944; made political statements that often embarrassed superiors and was relieved of command, 1945.

PERRY, MATTHEW CALBRAITH, Apr. 10, 1794 (So. Kingston, R.I.)-Mar. 4, 1858. U.S. Navy commodore. Helped capture Veracruz, 1847; helped prepare first curriculum for the U.S. Naval Academy; negotiated Treaty of Kanagawa, which opened U.S. trade with Japan, 1853-54. (Brother of OLIVER HAZARD PERRY.)

PERRY, OLIVER HAZARD, Aug. 20, 1785 (So. Kingston, R.I.)-Aug. 23, 1819. U.S. Navy captain. Won the decisive Battle of Lake Erie in the War of 1812, 1813. (Brother of MATTHEW PERRY.)

PERSHING, JOHN JOSEPH ("Black Jack"), Sept. 13, 1860 (Laclede, Mo.)-July 15, 1948. U.S. Army general. Commanded Mexican border campaign, 1916-17; commanded American Expeditionary Force in Europe in WW I; named by Congress general of the armies, 1919; chief of staff, U.S. Army, 1921-24; won 1932 Pulitzer Prize in history for *My Experiences in the World War,* 1931.

PICKETT, GEORGE EDWARD, Jan. 25, 1825 (Richmond, Va.)-July 30, 1875. Confederate Army general whose name is linked with disastrous Pickett's Charge at Gettysburg, although he did not command the overall attack.

PONTIAC, c.1720 (Ohio)-Apr. 20, 1769. Ottawa Indian tribal chief. Forged an alliance of 18 Indian tribes; led uprising against the British following the French surrender in the French and Indian War;

laid siege to Detroit; victorious at Battle of Bloody Run, 1763; signed peace treaty, 1766.

POPE, JOHN, Mar. 16, 1822 (Louisville, Ky.)-Sept. 23, 1892. Union Army general who suffered disastrous defeat at the Second Battle of Bull Run, 1862.

PORTER, DAVID, Feb. 1, 1780 (Boston, Mass.)-Mar. 3, 1843. U.S. Navy commodore. Commanded frigate *Essex* during War of 1812, capturing numerous British whaling vessels in the Pacific; captured, 1814; headed Mexican Navy, 1826-29; U.S. chargé d'affaires, minister to Turkey, 1831-43. (Father of DAVID DIXON PORTER; adopted DAVID FARRAGUT.)

PORTER, DAVID DIXON, June 8, 1813 (Chester, Pa.)-Feb. 13, 1891. U.S. admiral. Helped seize New Orleans (1862), Vicksburg (1863), and Ft. Fisher (1865) for the Union during the Civil War; headed Naval Academy, 1865-69. (Son of DAVID PORTER; foster brother of DAVID FARRAGUT.)

PORTER, FITZ-JOHN, Aug. 31, 1822 (Portsmouth, N.H.)-May 21, 1901. Union Army general. Engaged in Peninsular campaign; court-martialed and cashiered for disobedience at Second Battle of Bull Run, 1862; later vindicated.

POWERS, FRANCIS GARY, Aug. 17, 1929 (Jenkins, Ky.)-Aug. 1, 1977. U.S. pilot. Precipitated major diplomatic incident when his high-altitude reconnaissance plane (U-2) was shot down over the USSR and he was imprisoned, 1960; exchanged for Soviet spy RUDOLF ABEL, 1962.

PRESCOTT, WILLIAM, Feb. 20, 1726 (Groton, Mass.)-Oct. 13, 1775. American Revolutionary officer who is remembered as the hero of the Battle of Bunker Hill, 1775.

PULLER, LEWIS BURWELL ("Chesty"), June 26, 1898 (West Point, Va.)-Oct. 11, 1971. U.S. Marine Corps general. Won four Navy Crosses in WW II; led first Marine regiment ashore at Inchon, Korea, 1950; won fifth Navy Cross in Korean War.

PUTNAM, ISRAEL, Jan. 7, 1718 (Salem Village, Mass.)-May 29, 1790. American Revolutionary general. Helped plan the fortifications for the Battle of Bunker Hill, where he warned his troops as the British approached, "Don't fire until you see the whites of their eyes."

QUANTRILL, WILLIAM CLARKE (a.k.a. Charley Hunt), July 31, 1839 (Dover, Ohio)-June 6, 1865. Confederate Army guerrilla leader who led Aug. 21, 1863, raid on Lawrence, Kan., razing the town and killing 150 persons.

RADFORD, ARTHUR WILLIAM, Feb. 27, 1896 (Chicago, Ill.)-Aug. 17, 1973. U.S. admiral. Engaged in campaigns in Gilbert and Marshall Is.; chairman, Joint Chiefs of Staff, 1953-57.

REVERE, PAUL, Jan. 1, 1735 (Boston, Mass.)-May 10, 1818. American patriot, silversmith. An organizer of the Boston Tea Party, 1773; famed for his ride to warn of the British march on Concord, 1775; commanded Boston fortress, 1778-79; designed and printed first Continental money.

RICKENBACKER, EDWARD VERNON ("Eddie"), Oct. 8, 1890 (Columbus, Ohio)-July 23, 1973. U.S. aviator, airline executive. The most celebrated U.S. air ace in WW I, in which he won Medal of Honor; headed Eastern Airlines, 1938-63; while touring military bases in the South Pacific during WW II, his plane crashed at sea and he spent over three weeks in a life raft before being rescued.

RICKOVER, HYMAN GEORGE, Jan. 27, 1900 (Makov, Pol.). U.S. admiral, educator. Called "Father of the atomic submarine," he supervised construction of the first nuclear submarine, U.S.S.

Nautilus, 1947–54; helped develop first U.S. full-scale experimental nuclear power plant, 1956–57; influential in upgrading U.S. education in mathematics and science.

RIDGWAY, MATTHEW BUNKER, Mar. 3, 1895 (Ft. Monroe, Va.). U.S. Army general. Directed U.S. airborne assaults on Sicily (1943) and Europe (1944–45); commander, UN forces in Korea, 1951–52; supreme commander, Allied Forces in Europe, 1952–53; chief of staff, U.S. Army, 1953–55.

ROGERS, ROBERT, c.1727 (Dunbarton, N.H.)–May 18, 1795. Colonial military officer. Led Rogers' Rangers, forerunners of modern commandos, during French and Indian War, 1755–63.

ROSECRANS, WILLIAM STARKE, Sept. 6, 1819 (Kingston Township, Ohio)–Mar. 11, 1898. Union Army general. Victorious at Stones River, 1862–63; drove Confederates out of central Tennessee, 1863; defeated at Chickamauga and relieved, 1863.

ST. CLAIR, ARTHUR, April 3, 1737 (Thurso, Scot.)–Aug. 31, 1818. American Revolutionary general, public official. Abandoned Ft. Ticonderoga, 1777; served in Continental Congress, 1785–87 (pres., 1787); gov. of the Northwest Territory, 1787–1802; defeated by Miami Indians, 1791.

SCOTT, WINFIELD ("Old Fuss and Feathers"), June 13, 1786 (Petersburg, Va.)–May 29, 1866. U.S. Army general. Defeated British at Chippewa, 1814; general in chief, U.S. Army, 1841–61; led U.S. forces in Mexican War, 1846–48; Whig party presidential candidate, 1852.

SEMMES, RAPHAEL, Sept. 27, 1809 (Charles Co., Mo.)–Aug. 30, 1877. Confederate naval commander whose raider, *Alabama,* seized or sank over 80 Union vessels during the Civil War.

SHAYS, DANIEL, c.1747 (Hopkinton, Mass.)–Sept. 29, 1825. American Revolutionary soldier who served at Bunker Hill, Ticonderoga, and Saratoga, his name is associated with "rebellion" at Springfield, Mass., in which he played a prominent part, 1786–87.

SHERIDAN, PHILIP HENRY, Mar. 6, 1831 (Albany, N.Y.)–Aug. 5, 1888. Union Army general. Commanded Army of the Shenandoah, 1864–65; cut off GEN. ROBERT E. LEE's line of retreat at Appomattox, 1865.

SHERMAN, WILLIAM TECUMSEH, Feb. 8, 1820 (Lancaster, Ohio)–Feb. 14, 1891. Union Army general. Held important commands at Shiloh (1862), Vicksburg (1863), Chattanooga (1863); led advance on Atlanta and the "March to the Sea," 1864; commanding general of the army, 1869–83; known for observation, "War is hell"; halted Republican party attempt (1883) to nominate him for the presidency by saying, "If nominated I will not run. If elected I will not serve." (Brother of JOHN SHERMAN.)

SIGSBEE, CHARLES DWIGHT, Jan. 16, 1845 (Albany, N.Y.)–July 19, 1923. U.S. admiral. Commander of the U.S.S. *Maine* when it was sunk at Havana harbor, 1898; "Remember the *Maine*" became the catch phrase of the Spanish-American War.

SIMS, WILLIAM SOWDEN, Oct. 15, 1858 (Port Hope, Ont., Can.)–Sept. 28, 1936. U.S. admiral. Promoted convoy system that contributed to Allied victory in WW I; won Pulitzer Prize for history for *The Victory at Sea,* 1920.

SITTING BULL (Ind. name: Tatanka Iyotake), c.1831 (S.D.)–Dec. 15, 1890. Hunkpapa Sioux In-

dian leader, medicine man. Organized resistance leading to the Battle of Little Bighorn (made medicine, took no part in fighting), 1876; toured with BUFFALO BILL's Wild West show; a leader in Ghost Dance agitation leading to Battle of Wounded Knee, 1890.

SMITH, HOLLAND MCTYEIRE ("Howlin' Mad Smith"), Apr. 20, 1882 (Seale, Ala.)–Jan. 12, 1967. U.S. Marine Corps general who helped plan WW II Marine assaults on Gilbert and Marshall Is., Saipan, Guam, Iwo Jima, and Okinawa, 1943–45.

SPAATZ, CARL, June 28, 1891 (Boyertown, Pa.)–July 14, 1974. U.S. Air Force general. As commander of U.S. Strategic Air Forces in Europe, directed strategic bombing of Germany, and later Japan, in WW II; chief of staff, U.S. Air Force, 1947–48.

SPRUANCE, RAYMOND AMES, Jan. 3, 1886 (Baltimore, Md.)–Dec. 13, 1969. U.S. admiral. Victor at Midway Island, 1942; commanded U.S. 5th Fleet in the Pacific, 1944–45; headed Naval War College, 1945–48; U.S. ambassador to the Philippines, 1952–55.

STANDISH, MILES (or MYLES), c.1584 (Lancashire, Eng.)–Oct. 3, 1656. British officer. Military leader of Plymouth Colony, 1620–25; his role in HENRY WADSWORTH LONGFELLOW's poem "The Courtship of Miles Standish" is not based on historical evidence.

STARK, JOHN, Aug. 28, 1728 (Londonderry, N.H.)–May 8, 1822. American Revolutionary general. Engaged at Bunker Hill, 1775; defeated Hessians at Bennington, 1777; played an important role in the victory at Saratoga, 1777.

STEWART, CHARLES, July 18, 1778 (Philadelphia, Pa.)–Nov. 6, 1869. U.S. naval officer who commanded U.S.S. *Constitution* during the War of 1812.

STILWELL, JOSEPH WARREN ("Vinegar Joe"), Mar. 19, 1883 (Palatka, Fla)–Oct. 12, 1946. U.S. Army general. Commanded U.S. forces in the China-Burma-India theater during WW II; also served as chief of staff to Chinese pres. CHIANG KAI-SHEK; his disagreement with Chiang over the role of Chinese forces led to his being relieved of command by Pres. FRANKLIN D. ROOSEVELT, 1944.

STUART, JEB (James) **EWELL BROWN,** Feb. 6, 1833 (Patrick Co., Va)–May 12, 1864. Confederate cavalry commander. Played a major role in numerous Southern victories; killed at Yellow Tavern, 1864.

TAYLOR, MAXWELL DAVENPORT, Aug. 26, 1901 (Keytesville, Md.). U.S. general, diplomat. Commanded 101st Airborne Division in WW II; supt., U.S. Military Academy, 1945–49; commanded U.S. 8th Army in Korean War; chairman, Joint Chiefs of Staff, 1962–64; U.S. ambassador to South Vietnam, 1964–65.

TECUMSEH (Tecumtha or Tikamthi), Mar. 1768 (Greene Co., Ohio)–Oct. 5, 1813. Shawnee Indian chief. Tried to unite tribes to resist westward expansion of the white man; thwarted by U.S. victory at Tippecanoe, 1811; allied with British forces in War of 1812; killed at Battle of the Thames, 1813.

THAYER, SULVANIUS, June 9, 1785 (Braintree, Mass.)–Sept. 7, 1872. U.S. general, educator. As supt. of U.S. Military Academy (1817–33), upgraded training and curriculum.

THOMAS, GEORGE HENRY ("The Rock of Chickamauga"), July 31, 1816 (Southhampton Co., Va.)–Mar. 28, 1870. Union Army general. Saved Union Army of the Tennessee at Chickarnauga, 1863; victorious at Battle of Nashville, 1864.

TRAVIS, WILLIAM BARRAT, Aug. 9, 1809 (Red Banks, S.C.)-Mar. 6, 1836. Texas Revolutionary army officer, lawyer. Commanded forces that defended the Alamo, 1836.

TURNER, STANSFIELD, Feb. 1, 1923 (Chicago, Ill.). U.S. admiral. Commander, U.S. 2nd Fleet, 1974-75; commander-in-chief, Allied Forces, Southern Europe (NATO), 1975-77; director, Central Intelligence Agency, 1977- .

TWINING, NATHAN FARRAGUT, Oct. 11, 1897 (Monroe, Wis.). U.S. Air Force general. Directed air assaults against Solomon Islands and New Guinea in WW II; chairman, Joint Chiefs of Staff, 1957-60.

UNCAS, c.1588 (?)-c.1683. Pequot Indian sachem. Fought Narragansett tribe, 1643-47; attacked Massasoit, 1661.

VANDEGRIFT, ALEXANDER ARCHER, Mar. 13, 1887 (Charlotteville, Va.)-May 8, 1973. U.S. Marine Corps general who distinguished himself at Guadalcanal, 1942.

WAINWRIGHT, JONATHAN MAYHEW ("Skinny"), Aug. 23, 1883 (Walla Walla, Wash.)-Sept. 2, 1953. U.S. Army general. Defended Corregidor, forced to surrender, and taken as prisoner of war, 1942; rescued in Manchuria, 1945.

WALKER, WALTON HARRIS, Dec. 3, 1899 (Belton, Tex.)-Dec. 23, 1950. U.S. army officer. Commanding U.S. Army Corps, captured Reims and liberated Buchenwald concentration camp, 1944-45; led S. Korean and UN forces in Korea, 1950.

WARREN, JOSEPH, June 10, 1741 (Roxbury, Mass.)-June 17, 1775. American Revolutionary general. Sent PAUL REVERE and William Dawes on their famous ride, killed at Bunker Hill, 1775.

WAYNE, ANTHONY ("Mad Anthony"), Jan. 1, 1745 (nr. Paoli, Pa.)-Dec. 15, 1796. American Revolutionary general. Captured Stony Point, 1779; defeated Indians at the Battle of Fallen Timbers, which helped open the Northwest Territory to settlement, 1794.

WESTMORELAND, WILLIAM CHILDS, Mar. 26, 1914 (Spartanburg Co., S.C.). U.S. Army general. Commanded U.S. forces in Vietnam, 1964-68; chief of staff, U.S. Army, 1968-72.

WHEELER, EARLE GILMORE, Jan. 13, 1908 (Washington, D.C.)-Dec. 18, 1975. U.S. Army general. Chairman, Joint Chiefs of Staff, 1964-70; directed secret bombings over Cambodia on orders of Pres. RICHARD M. NIXON, 1969-70.

WHEELER, JOSEPH ("Fighting Joe"), Sept. 10, 1836 (Augusta, Ga.)-Jan. 25, 1906. U.S. and Confederate Army general (the only man to serve as corps commander in both armies). Engaged for the Confederacy at Chattanooga and Chickamauga (1863), and in the Atlanta campaign (1864); served as U.S. rep. (D, Ala.), 1881-99; engaged at San Juan and Las Guasimas during the Spanish-American War.

WILKINSON, JAMES, 1757 (Calvert Co., Md.)-Dec. 28, 1825. U.S. Revolutionary general, double-agent intriguer. Involved in "Conway Cabal" against GEORGE WASHINGTON and forced to resign his commission, 1778; appointed clothier-general of Continental Army, but forced to resign because of irregularity in his accounts, 1781; agent of Spain, 1787-1806; implicated in AARON BURR conspiracy, 1805-07, but acquitted by court-martial, 1811; mishandled Montreal expedition, but acquitted by court-martial, 1813.

WILSON, JAMES HARRISON, Sept. 2, 1837 (Shawneetown, Ill.)-Feb. 23, 1925. Union Army general. Captured Selma, Montgomery, Columbus, Macon, and CSA Pres. JEFFERSON DAVIS, 1865; engaged in the Spanish-American War (1898-99) and the Boxer Rebellion (1900).

WOOD, LEONARD, Oct. 9, 1860 (Winchester, N.H.)-Aug. 7, 1927. U.S. Army general. A close friend of THEODORE ROOSEVELT, helped raise and organize the Rough Riders, 1898; chief of staff, U.S. Army, 1910-14; governor-general of the Philippines, 1921-27.

YORK, ALVIN CULLUM, Dec. 13, 1887 (Pall Mall, Tenn.)-Dec. 2, 1964. U.S. soldier. One of the most decorated heroes of WW I, received 50 medals, including the Congressional Medal of Honor; film *Sergeant York,* his story, won an Academy Award for GARY COOPER.

ZUMWALT, ELMO RUSSELL, JR., Nov. 29, 1920 (Tulare, Cal.). U.S. admiral. Commanded U.S. naval forces in Vietnam, 1968-70; chief of Naval Operations, 1970-74.

FOREIGN MILITARY AND NAVAL LEADERS

ABEL, RUDOLF IVANOVICH, c.1902 (Moscow, Rus.)-Nov. 15, 1971. Soviet intelligence officer. Convicted in U.S. for conspiring to transmit military secrets to the USSR, 1957; exchanged for FRANCIS GARY POWERS, 1962.

ABERCROMBY, SIR RALPH, Oct. 7, 1734 (Tullibody, Eng.)-Mar. 28, 1801. British Army general who defeated French army at Alexandria, Egypt, where he was mortally wounded, 1801.

ABERCROMBIE (or Abercromby), **JAMES,** 1706 (Scot.)-Apr. 28, 1781. British Army general. Commanded forces in N. America during the French and Indian War; defeated at Ticonderoga, 1758.

ALEXANDER, HAROLD RUPERT LEOFRIC GEORGE, 1st EARL ALEXANDER OF TUNIS ("Alex"), Dec. 10, 1891 (Slough, Eng.)-June 16, 1969. British Army general. Commanded British forces at Dunkirk, supervising the evacuation of 300,000 troops, 1940; commander in chief, Allied forces in Italy, 1943-45; gov.-gen. of Can la 1946-52.

ALLENBY, EDMUND HENRY HYNMAN, 1st VISCOUNT ALLENBY OF MEGIDDO, Apr. 23, 1861 (Brackenhurst, Eng.)-May 14, 1936. British field marshal. Served in Boer War and WW I; led Egyptian Expeditionary Force, capturing Gaza and Jerusalem (1917) and Megiddo (1918).

ALVARADO, PEDRO DE, c.1485 (Badajoz, Sp.)-1541. Spanish conquistador who helped conquer Mexico and Central America for Spain, 1519-34.

AMHERST, JEFFREY, BARON AMHERST, Jan. 29, 1717 (Sevenoaks, Eng.)-Aug. 3, 1797. British Army commander. Captured Canada for Great Britain, 1758-60; commander in chief of British Army, 1772-95; Amherst College and several U.S. towns are named after him.

ANDRÉ, JOHN, May 2, 1750 (London, Eng.)-Oct. 2, 1780. British Army officer who negotiated with BENEDICT ARNOLD for surrender of West Point; captured with incriminating papers and executed, 1780.

ATTILA, KING OF THE HUNS, c.406 (Central Asia)-453. Barbarian ruler known as the Scourge of God. Attacked the Roman Empire, destroying towns and cities, 441-43; invaded Gaul, conducting campaign against Romans and Visigoths, 451; invaded Italy, 452.

BAGRATION, PRINCE PYOTR IVANOVICH, 1765 (Kizlyar, Rus.)-Sept. 12, 1812. Russian Army general, hero of the Napoleonic Wars. Captured Brescia, 1799; captured Aaland I., 1808; killed at Borodino, 1812.

BALBO, ITALO, June 6, 1896 (nr. Ferrar, It.)–June 28, 1940. Italian air marshal and fascist leader who developed BENITO MUSSOLINI's air force.

BELISARIUS, c.505 (Germania, now in Greece)–Mar. 565. Byzantine general who was the leading military figure in the time of Byzantine emperor Justinian I.

BLIGH, WILLIAM, Sept. 9, 1754 (Cornwall, Eng.)–Dec. 7, 1817. British admiral. As captain of the H.M.S. *Bounty* at the time of the celebrated mutiny, Apr. 28, 1789, cast adrift with 18 others in an open boat and sailed nearly 4,000 miles, reaching Timor, East Indies, June 14; as captain of H.M.S. *Director,* again put ashore in a mutiny, 1797.

BLÜCHER VON WAHLSTATT, GEBHARD LIBERECHT, Dec. 16, 1742 (Rostock, Mecklenburg-Schwerin, now E. Ger.)–Sept. 12, 1819. Prussian field marshal. Victorious at the Battle of Leipzig, 1813; played an important role in the defeat of Napoleon at Waterloo, 1815.

BRADDOCK, EDWARD, 1695 (Perthshire, Scot.)–July 13, 1755. British general. Commanded British forces in North America during early stages of French and Indian War, 1755; on expedition against Ft. Duquesne (Pittsburgh, Pa.), surprised by French and their Indian allies and mortally wounded, 1755.

BRAUCHITSCH, HEINRICH ALFRED WALTHER VON, Oct. 4, 1881 (Berlin, Ger.)–Oct. 18, 1948. German field marshal. As commander in chief of German Army, directed campaigns against Poland, the Netherlands, Belgium, France, the Balkans, and USSR, 1938–41; made the scapegoat for German failure to capture Moscow and removed from command, 1941.

BROOKE, ALAN FRANCIS, 1st VISCOUNT ALANBROOKE, (a.k.a. Alanbrooke or Allenbrooke) July 23, 1883 (Bagneres-de-Bigorre, Fr.)–June 17, 1963. British Army field marshal. Principal military adviser to WINSTON CHURCHILL during WW II.

BUDENNY, SIMON MIKHAILOVICH, 1883 (Voronezh Province, Rus.)–Oct. 27, 1973. Soviet Army marshal. Commanded Soviet cavalry corps during the Russian civil war; defeated by Germans at Kiev, 1941.

BURGOYNE, JOHN ("Gentleman Johnny"), 1722 (Sutton, Eng.)–Aug. 4, 1792. British Army general, dramatist, fashion leader. Recaptured Ft. Ticonderoga, 1777; defeated at Saratoga (Oct. 1777), and returned to England to face severe criticism.

CANARIS, WILHELM FRANZ, Jan. 1, 1887 (Westphalia, Ger.)–Apr. 9, 1945. German admiral. Chief of military intelligence (ABWEHR) (1935–44), and a leader among anti-Hitler conspirators; executed by SS, 1945.

CARRANZA, VENUSTIANO, Dec. 29, 1859 (Coahuila, Mex.)–May 21, 1920. Mexican revolutionist, political leader. Played a leading role in civil war following overthrow of PROFIRIO DIAZ, 1911; successfully opposed VICTORIANO HUERTA (1914), and proclaimed "first chief"; provisional pres., 1915–17; elected pres., 1917–20.

CHAUVIN, NICOLAS, French soldier whose simpleminded devotion to Napoleon and all things military led to the coining of the word *chauvinism.*

CHUIKOV, VASILII IVANOVICH, 1900 (Russia). Soviet field marshal. Military adviser to CHIANG KAI-SHEK, 1941–42; in command of the 62nd

Soviet Army, defended Stalingrad, 1942; led his army to recapture Odessa (1944) and in the assault on Berlin (1945); became commander of Soviet occupation forces in Germany. *The Beginning of the Road,* 1962.

CHURCHILL, JOHN, 1st DUKE OF MARLBOROUGH, May 26, 1650 (Ashe, Eng.)–June 16, 1722. British general, political figure. Supported William of Orange in the Glorious Revolution, 1688; led British and Allied armies against Louis XIV in the War of the Spanish Succession, gaining victories at Blenheim (1704) Ramillies (1706), Oudenaarde (1708), and Malplaquet (1709).

CID, EL, born Rodrigo Diaz de Vivar, c.1043 (Vivar, Sp.)–July 10, 1099. Spanish military leader and national hero whose role in history is the subject of much controversy among historians.

CINCINNATUS, LUCIUS QUINCTIUS, c.519 B.C.–?. Roman general, statesman. Supported the patricians in the struggle against the plebians, 462–454 B.C.; appointed dictator, defeated the Aequians, and resigned, all in the span of 16 days, 458 B.C.

CLAUSEWITZ, KARL MARIA VON, June 1, 1780 (Burg, Ger.)–Nov. 16, 1831. Prussian Army general, military strategist whose books on the philosophy of war influenced military events up to the nuclear age.

CLINTON, SIR HENRY, 1738 (Newfld., Can.)–Dec. 11, 1795. British Army general. Commander in chief, British forces in America, 1778–1781; developed British strategy in the successful Southern campaign, 1780.

COLLINS, MICHAEL, Oct. 16, 1890 (County Cork, Ire.)–Aug. 22, 1922. Irish revolutionary and military leader. Pioneered modern urban guerrilla warfare in the Anglo-Irish War, 1919–21; commanded Free State Army during Irish civil war, 1921–22.

CONWAY, THOMAS, Feb. 27, 1735 (Ire.)–c.1800. Irish soldier who served in American Revolution. Fought at Brandywine and Germantown, 1777; name associated with "Conway Cabal" against GEORGE WASHINGTON (1777–78), although he was its least culpable participant.

CORNWALLIS, CHARLES, 1st MARQUIS, Dec. 31, 1738 (London, Eng.)–Oct. 5, 1805. British Army general. Victorious at Brandywine (1777) and Guilford Courthouse (1781); surrendered at Yorktown, 1781; as gov.-gen. of India, established many legal and administrative reforms, 1786–93; viceroy of Ireland, 1798–1801.

DAYAN, MOSHE, May 20, 1915 (Deganya, Pal., now Israel). Israeli general, public official. Led invasion of Sinai Pen., 1956; agriculture minister 1959–64; defense minister, 1964–74; led forces to victory in Six Day War, 1967; foreign minister, 1977–79.

DENIKIN, ANTON IVANOVICH, Dec. 16, 1872 (Nr. Warsaw, Pol.)–Aug. 8, 1947. Russian general who led White (anti-Bolshevik) forces on the Southern front during Russian civil war, 1918–20.

DOENITZ, KARL, Sept. 16, 1891 (Grünau, Ger.). German admiral. As commander-in-chief of the German Navy (1943–45), led the U-boat offensive against Allied shipping during WW II; as chan. of Germany after A. HITLER's death (1945), surrendered unconditionally to the Allies.

DOWDING, HUGH CASWALL TREMENHEERE, 1st BARON DOWDING, Apr. 24, 1882 (Moffat, Eng.)–Feb. 15, 1970. British air chief marshal. Headed Fighter Command, 1936–42; defeated German Luftwaffe in the Battle of Britain, 1940.

DREYFUS, ALFRED, Oct. 19, 1859 (Mulhouse,

Fr.)–July 11, 1935. French Army officer of Jewish parentage. The center of a political controversy tied to anti-Semitism, anticlericism, and antirepublicanism under the Third Republic of France. Convicted of treason (1894) and imprisoned on Devil's I. (1895); investigation (1898), following massive campaign, led chiefly by EMILE ZOLA, proved evidence had been forged; retried and again found guilty, 1899; conviction set aside, 1906; awarded Legion of Honor, promoted to major, 1906.

ESTERHAZY, MARIE CHARLES FERDINAND WALSIN, COMTE DE VOILEMENT, 1847 (Aus.)–May 21, 1923. Austrian officer in the French Army who, as a German spy, forged documents that incriminated ALFRED DREYFUS.

FABIUS MAXIMUS VERRUCOSUS, QUINTUS ("Cuncator" [The Delayer]), d. 203 B.C. Roman soldier. Best known as the opponent of HANNIBAL. Used "Fabian" tactics (a waiting policy), keeping his army always near, never attacking, but continually harassing Hannibal; relieved (216) from command, leading to Hannibal's great victory at Cannae.

FOCH, FERDINAND, Oct. 2, 1851 (Tarbes, Fr.)–Mar. 20, 1929. French Army marshal. Helped win the First Battle of the Marne, 1914; commander in chief of the Allied armies, 1918.

FREDERICK II (Frederick the Great), Jan. 24, 1712 (Berlin, Ger.)–Aug. 17, 1786. Prussian king, military leader. Led Prussia in the Seven Years' War, 1756–63.

FULLER, JOHN FREDERICK CHARLES, Sept. 1, 1878 (W. Sussex, Eng.)–Feb. 10, 1966. British soldier and military theoretician. Recognized the importance of mechanized warfare during WW I; his ideas, published in *Tanks in the Great War* (1920) and *On Future Warfare* (1928), had a great influence on military thinking in Europe, particularly in Germany and the USSR.

GAGE, THOMAS, 1721 (Firle, Eng.)–Apr. 2, 1787. British general. Colonial gov. in America, 1763–74; military gov. of Massachusetts, 1774–75.

GORDON, CHARLES GEORGE ("Chinese Gordon"; "Gordon of Khartoum"), Jan. 28, 1833 (Woolwich, Eng.)–Jan. 26, 1885. British general. Became a national hero for his exploits in China, 1859–65; killed at the siege of Khartoum, 1885.

GRASSE, FRANÇOIS JOSEPH PAUL DE, MARQUIS DE GRASSE-TILLY, Sept. 13, 1722 (Alpes-Maritimes, Fr.)–Jan. 11, 1788. French admiral who reinforced French and American forces at Yorktown and won Battle of Chesapeake Bay, 1781.

GUDERIAN, HEINZ WILHELM, June 17, 1888 (Kulm, Prussia)–May 15, 1954. German Army general and tank theorist, a principal architect of armored and "blitzkrieg" warfare. Led panzer forces in Poland (1939), France (1940), and Russia (1941–42) during WW II; chief of German Army general staff, 1944–45.

GUSTAVUS II, known as Gustavus Adolphus ("Lion of the North"; "Snow King"), Dec. 9, 1594 (Stockholm, Swe.)–Nov. 16, 1632. King of Sweden, 1611–32. Instituted sweeping legal, administrative and educational reforms, including the establishment of secondary schools; ended war with Denmark (1613) and Russia (1617); hoping to increase Sweden's control of the Baltic, entered Thirty Years' War; defeated A. WALLENSTEIN at Lützen, but died in the battle, 1632.

HANNIBAL, 247 B.C. (N. Africa)–183 B.C. Carthaginian soldier. One of the foremost military commanders in history. Took command of Car-

thaginian forces in Spain, 221 B.C.: with 35,000 select troops, plus elephants, crossed the Alps into Italy; won brilliant victories at Ticinus and Trebia, 218; in his greatest victory, wiped out Roman forces at Cannae, 216; lacking support from Carthage, was unable to take Rome; recalled to Carthage, 203; defeated by SCIPIO AFRICANUS at Zama, 202; governed Carthage, c.202–196; forced to flee by enemies; committed suicide.

HAIG, DOUGLAS, 1st EARL HAIG OF BEMERSYDE, June 19, 1861 (Edinburgh, Scot.)–Jan. 29, 1928. Scottish field marshal in British Army. His strategy as commander in chief of the British armies in France (1915–18), resulted in huge British casualties.

HAWKINS (or Hawkyns), **SIR JOHN,** 1532 (Plymouth, Eng.)–Nov. 12, 1595. British naval commander, administrator. The foremost seaman of 16th-cent. England; chief shaper of the Elizabethan navy.

HOWE, RICHARD, EARL HOWE, Mar. 8, 1726 (London, Eng.)–Aug. 5, 1799. British admiral. Commanded British forces in N. America, 1776–78; commanded Channel fleet in "Glorious First of June" victory against the French, 1794. (Brother of WILLIAM HOWE.)

HOWE, WILLIAM, 5th VISCOUNT HOWE, Aug. 10, 1729 (Plymouth, Eng.)–July 12, 1814. British Army general. Distinguished himself in the French and Indian War, 1754–63; commander in chief of the British army in N. America, 1776–78; occupied New York, but failed to destroy GEORGE WASHINGTON's crippled army, 1776; victorious at Brandywine and Germantown and occupied Philadelphia, 1777. (Brother of RICHARD HOWE.)

JODL, ALFRED, May 10, 1890 (Wurzburg, Ger.)–Oct. 16, 1946. German Army general. Headed armed forces operations staff, 1939–45; helped plan most of Germany's WW II military campaigns; signed surrender of German armed forces, May 7, 1945; convicted as a war criminal at Nuremberg trials and executed, 1946.

JOFFRE, JOSEPH JACQUES CÉSAIRE, Jan. 12, 1852 (Pyrénées-Prientales, Fr.)–Jan. 3, 1931. French Army marshal. Commander in chief of French armies on the Western Front in WW I, 1914–16; victorious in the First Battle of the Marne, 1914.

KEITEL, WILHELM, Sept. 22, 1882 (Helmscherode, Ger.)–Oct. 16, 1946. German Army field marshal. Headed armed forces high command during WW II; generally considered a weak officer who served as ADOLF HITLER's lackey; convicted and executed as a war criminal, 1946.

KESSELRING, ALBERT, Nov. 20, 1885 (Markstedt, Ger.)–July 16, 1960. German Air Force field marshal. Commanded air fleets in Poland, France, and the Battle of Britain, 1939–41; helped direct North African campaign, 1941–42; directed defensive action in Italy that prevented Allied victory for over a year, 1943–45; commander in chief, Western Front, 1945.

KITCHENER, HORATIO HERBERT, 1st EARL KITCHENER OF KHARTOUM, June 24, 1850 (County Kerry, Ire.)–June 5, 1916. British Army field marshal, imperial administrator. Commander in chief of the Egyptian Army, 1892–1900; won Battle of Omdurman and occupied Khartoum, 1898; broke power of Boer guerrillas, 1900–01; commander in chief in India, 1902–09; ruled Egypt and the Sudan, 1911–14; secy. of state for war, 1914–16.

KLUCK, ALEXANDER VON, May 20, 1846 (Münster, Ger.)–Oct. 19, 1934. German Army general. Headed 1st Army in siege of Paris, 1914; lost First Battle of the Marne, 1914.

KOLCHAK, ALEKSANDR VASILIEVICH, 1873 (St. Petersburg, Rus.)–Feb. 7, 1920. Russian admiral. Ruled the White (counter-revolutionary) forces in Russia, 1918–20; captured and executed by the Bolsheviks, 1920.

KORNILOV, LAVRENTI GEORGIEVICH, July 30, 1870 (Siberia, Rus.)–Apr. 13, 1918. Russian Army general. Commander in chief of the Russian Army, 1917; led counter-revolutionary march on Petrograd, 1917; led makeshift army in assault on Ekaterinodar, mortally wounded, 1918.

KOSCIUSZKO, TADEUSZ ANDRZEI BONAWNTURA, Feb. 4, 1746 (Mereczowszczyzna, Pol., now Belorussian SSR)–Oct. 15, 1817. Polish general and national hero. Served rebels in American Revolution; fortified West Point, 1778–80; chief engineer in Gen. NATHANAEL GREENE's Southern campaign, 1780–81; led unsuccessful uprising against Russian, Prussian, and Austrian occupiers of Poland, 1794; promoted Poland's cause for independence in the U.S. and Europe, 1797–1817.

KUTUZOV, PRINCE MIKHAIL ILLARIONOVICH GOLENISHCHEV, Sept. 16, 1745 (St. Petersburg, Rus.)–Apr. 28, 1813. Russian Army field marshal. Engaged in Russo-Turkish war, 1787–91; victorious over French at Durrenstein, defeated at Austerlitz, 1805; commander in chief of Russian forces at Battle of Borodino, defeated and withdrew, allowing NAPOLEON to enter Moscow, 1812.

LAFAYETTE, MARIE JOSEPH PAUL IVES ROCH GILBERT DU MOTIER DE, MARQUIS DE LAFAYETTE, Sept. 6, 1757 (Chavaniac, Fr.)–May 20, 1834. French soldier, statesman, hero of the American Revolution. Engaged at Brandywine, 1777; wintered at Valley Forge, 1777–78; negotiated French military support for the American cause, 1779; aided victory at Yorktown, 1781.

LAWRENCE, THOMAS EDWARD ("Lawrence of Arabia"), Aug. 15, 1888 (Tremadoc, Eng.)–May 19, 1935. British archeologist, military strategist, author. Aided Arab revolt against Turks during WW I; led Arab army to assist Gen. EDMUND ALLENBY in conquest of Palestine, 1918; agitated for Arab independence after WW I; his reputation as a military genius is the subject of much controversy. *The Seven Pillars of Wisdom*, 1926.

LEONIDAS I, fl. early 5th century B.C.. King of Sparta, 490?–480 B.C. Remembered for his defense of the pass of Thermopylae against a vast Persian army; refused to flee, killed with all his men; evoked as the epitome of bravery against overwhelming odds.

LUDENDORFF, ERICH FRIEDRICH WILHELM, Apr. 9, 1865 (Kruszewnia, Prussian Pol.)–Dec. 20, 1937. German Army general. Victorious at Tannenberg, 1914; with PAUL VON HINDENBURG, directed German war effort, 1916–18; launched unlimited submarine warfare that drew U.S. into the war, 1917; formulated the German-Russian treaties of Brest-Litovsk, 1918; marched with ADOLF HITLER in Munich Putsch, 1923.

MANNERHEIM, CARL GUSTAV EMIL, BARON VON, June 4, 1867 (Villnas, Fin.)–Jan. 27, 1951. Finnish field marshal, public official. Commanded White (counter-revolutionary) forces in suppression of Finnish Workers' Republic, 1918; directed first Winter War against USSR, 1939–40; pres. of Finland, 1944–46.

MASSÉNA, ANDRÉ, PRINCE D'ESSLING, DUC

DE RIVOLI, May 6, 1758 (Nice, Fr.)–Apr. 4, 1817. French Army marshal. A leading figure in the French Revolutionary and Napoleonic wars. Victor at Zurich, 1799; blamed for French defeat in the Peninsular War, 1808–14.

MEDINA-SIDONIA, 7th DUQUE DE, born Alonso Perez de Guzman, 1550?–1619? Spanish admiral. Commanded the Spanish Armada when it was destroyed by the British, 1588; responsible for the loss of Cadiz (1596) and Gibraltar (1606).

MOLTKE, HELMUTH JOHANNES LUDWIG, GRAF VON ("Moltke the Younger"), May 25, 1848 (Gersdorff, Ger.)–June 18, 1916. German Army general. Chief of general staff, 1906–14; replaced after defeat at the First Battle of the Marne, 1914. (Nephew of HELMUTH K. B. VON MOLTKE.)

MOLTKE, HELMUTH KARL BERNARD, GRAF VON, Oct. 26, 1800 (Parchim, Mecklenburg)–Apr. 24, 1891. Prussian field marshal. As head of general staff (1858–88), reorganized Prussian Army; victorious in war against Denmark (1864), the Austro-Prussian War (1866), and Franco-Prussian War (1870–71), paving the way for German unification. (Uncle of HELMUTH J. L. VON MOLTKE.)

MONTCALM, LOUIS JOSEPH DE, MARQUIS DE SAINT-VÉRAN, Feb. 28, 1712 (Chateau de Candiac, Fr.)–Sept. 14, 1759. French Army general. Commander in chief of French forces in Canada, 1756–59; captured Ft. Oswego, 1756; successfully defended Ft. Ticonderoga, 1758; killed defending Quebec, 1759.

MONTGOMERY, BERNARD LAW, 1st VISCOUNT OF ALAMEIN, Nov. 17, 1887 (London, Eng.)–Mar. 24, 1976. British Army field marshal. Defeated Gen. ERWIN ROMMEL at El Alamein, 1942; forced Axis surrender in Tunisia, 1943; aided successful Allied invasion of Sicily, 1943; commanded Allied landings in Normandy, 1944; led Allied forces across northern France, Belgium, the Netherlands, and Germany, 1944–45.

MOREAU, JEAN VICTOR MARIE, Feb. 14, 1763 (Morlaix, Fr.)–Sept. 2, 1813. French Revolutionary general. Participated in French Revolution, 1792–99; became bitter opponent of Napoleon.

MURAT, JOACHIM, Mar. 25, 1767 (La Bastide-Fortunière, Fr.)–Oct. 13, 1815. French cavalry leader, marshal. Instrumental in NAPOLEON's victories at Marengo (1800), Austerlitz (1805), and Jena (1806); in Russian campaign, distinguished himself at Borodino, 1812; made significant contribution to foundation of Italian unity as king of Naples, 1808–15.

NAGANO, OSAMI, 1880 (Kochi, Jap.)–Jan. 5, 1947. Japanese admiral. Naval chief of staff, 1941–44; planned and ordered attack on Pearl Harbor, 1941.

NAGUMO, CHUICHI, 1886?–June 1944. Japanese admiral. Commanded carrier fleet that carried out attack on Pearl Harbor, 1941; his defeat at Midway reversed the balance of naval power in the Pacific, 1942.

NAPIER, ROBERT CORNELIS, 1st BARON NAPIER OF MAGDALA, Dec. 6, 1810 (Colombo, Ceylon)–Jan. 14, 1890. British Army field marshal, administrator. Engaged in Sikh Wars, 1845–51; commanded military expeditions to Abyssinia and China; commander in chief in India, 1870–76; gov. of Gibraltar, 1876–82.

NELSON, VISCOUNT HORATIO, Sept. 29, 1758 (Norfolk, Eng.)–Oct. 21, 1805. British naval commander. Served in wars with Revolutionary and Napoleonic France; defeated French in Battle of the Nile, 1798; attacked Copenhagen, 1801; killed

183

THE BOOK OF WHO

during the Battle of Trafalgar, in which the French fleet was destroyed; his long romance with Lady Emma Hamilton caused scandal.

NEY, MICHEL, DUC D'ELCHINGEN, PRINCE DE LA MOSKOWA, Jan. 10, 1769 (Sarrelouis, Fr.)-Dec. 7, 1815. French Army marshal. The most famous of NAPOLEON's marshals, he served with Napoleon in Switzerland, Austria, Germany, Spain, and Russia; helped induce Napoleon to abdicate, 1814; rejoined Napoleon after his return from Elba, and shared in defeat at Waterloo, 1815; executed for treason by the Bourbon regime, 1815.

PAULUS, FRIEDRICH, Sept. 23, 1890 (Breitenau, Ger.)-Feb. 1, 1957. German field marshal. Commanded 6th Army on the Eastern Front, 1942-1943; surrounded by Russians at Stalingrad, surrendered, 1943.

PÉTAIN, HENRI PHILIPPE OMER, Apr. 24, 1856 (Cauchy-a-la-Tour, Fr.)-July 23, 1951. French Army marshal, chief of state. His defense of Verdun made him a national hero, 1916; as French premier in 1940, negotiated armistice with Germany; headed Vichy government of unoccupied France until 1944; imprisoned as a collaborator after the war.

PLUMER, HERBERT CHARLES ONSLOW, 1st VISCOUNT PLUMER, Mar. 13, 1857 (Torquay, Eng.)-July 16, 1932. British Army field marshal. Led successful offensive on Messines Ridge, 1917; gov. of Malta, 1919-25; high commissioner for Palestine, 1925-28; the model for cartoonist David Low's "Colonel Blimp."

PULASKI, COUNT CASIMIR, Mar. 4, 1747 (Winiary, Pol.)-Oct. 11, 1779. Polish cavalry general in the American Revolution. Aide to Gen. GEORGE WASHINGTON at Brandywine and Valley Forge, 1777-78; killed leading a cavalry charge near Savannah, Ga., 1779.

RADETZKY, JOSEPH WENZEL, COUNT RADETZKY VON RADETZ, Nov. 2, 1766 (Trebnice, now Czech.)-Jan. 5, 1858. Austrian field marshal, national hero. Engaged in Turkish and French Revolutionary wars; helped plan Allied Leipzig campaign, 1813; invaded France, 1814; put down Italian revolt, 1848-49.

RAEDER, ERICH, Apr. 24, 1876 (Wandsbek, Ger.)-Nov. 6, 1960. German admiral. Naval commander-in-chief, 1928-43; in the 1930s, advocated construction of submarines and fast cruisers in contravention of Versailles Treaty; planned and executed invasion of Denmark and Norway, 1940.

RAGLAN, FITZROY JAMES HENRY SOMERSET, 1st BARON RAGLAN, Sept. 30, 1788 (Badminton, Eng.)-June 28, 1855. British Army field marshal. As commander in chief of British forces during the Crimean War (1853-55), criticized for his uninspired leadership; his ambiguous order at Battle of Balaklava led to the disastrous "Charge of the Light Brigade," 1854; his improvisation with slit potato sacks to provide uniforms for this troops gave rise to a sleeve style that follows the natural contours of the shoulder—now called the raglan sleeve.

RAMSEY, SIR BERTRAM HOME, Jan. 20, 1883 (Hampton, Eng.)-Jan. 2, 1945. British admiral. Directed Dunkirk evacuation, 1940; planned invasion of N. Africa, 1942; led British naval task force in assault on Sicily, 1943; Allied naval commander in chief for Normandy invasion, 1944.

RICHTHOFEN, MANFRED FREIHERR VON ("The Red Baron"; "The Red Knight"), May 2, 1892 (Breslau, Ger., now Wroclaw, Pol.)-Apr. 21, 1918. German aviator, national hero. As WW I

fighter ace, shot down 80 enemy aircraft; killed in action, 1918.

ROCHAMBEAU, JEAN BAPTISTE DONATIEN DE VIMEUR, COMTE DE, July 1, 1725 (Vendôme, Fr.)-May 10, 1807. French Army marshal who in American Revolution commanded French forces that helped defeat the British at Yorktown, 1781.

RÖHM, ERNST, Nov. 28, 1887 (Munich, Ger.)-June 30, 1934. German Army officer, Nazi leader. Headed ADOLF HITLER's storm troops, the SA or"Brownshirts"; murdered on Hitler's orders, 1934.

ROKOSSOVSKI, KONSTANTIN KONSTANTINOVICH, 1896 (Warsaw, Pol.)-Aug. 3, 1968. Soviet Army marshal. Commanded victorious forces at Stalingrad, 1942-43; led Russian armies through Poland, 1944-45.

ROMMEL, ERWIN JOHANNES EUGIN ("The Desert Fox"), Nov. 15, 1891 (Heidenheim, Ger.)-Oct. 14, 1944. German Army field marshal. Led Afrika Korps to numerous victories, 1941-42; defeated by Gen. BERNARD MONTGOMERY at El Alamein, 1942; took poison to avoid public trial when suspected of being in contact with anti-Hitler conspirators, 1944.

RUNDSTEDT, KARL RUDOLF VON, Dec. 12, 1875 (Aschersleben, Ger.)-Feb. 24, 1953. German Army field marshal. Led forces in Poland (1939), France (1940), and USSR (1941); directed Battle of the Bulge, 1944.

SAMSONOV, ALEKSANDR VASILEVICH, 1859?-Aug. 29, 1914. Russian WW I general who was defeated at Tannenberg, 1914.

SCHLIEFFEN, ALFRED, GRAF VON, Feb. 28, 1833 (Berlin, Ger.)-Jan. 4, 1913. German Army field marshal. As chief of general staff (1891-1905), developed the Schlieffen Plan, used, with modifications, in invasion of Belgium and France at the outbreak of WW I.

SCIPIO AFRICANUS, PUBLIUS CORNELIUS, 237 B.C. (Rome, It.)-183 B.C. Roman soldier. Commanded the Roman invasion of Carthage; his successes necessitated the recall of HANNIBAL, whom he defeated in the Battle of Zama (202), ending the Second Punic War.

SLIM, WILLIAM JOSEPH, 1st VISCOUNT SLIM, Aug. 6, 1891 (Bristol, Eng.)-Dec. 14, 1970. British Army field marshal. Repelled Japanese invasion of India, 1944; defeated Japanese in Burma, 1945; gov.-gen. of Australia, 1953-60.

SPEE, MAXIMILIAN JOHANNES MARIA HUBERT, GRAF VON, June 22, 1861 (Copenhagen, Den.)-Dec. 8, 1914. German admiral. Commanded German forces in battles of Coronel and the Falkland Islands, 1914.

STEUBEN, BARON FRIEDRICH WILLIAM AUGUSTUS, Sept. 17, 1730 (Magdeburg, Prussia)-Nov. 28, 1794. German-born American Revolutionary general who trained Continental Army troops.

SUVOROV, ALEKSANDR VASILIEVICH, COUNT SUVOROV RIMNIKSY, PRINCE ITOLSKY, Nov. 13, 1729 (Moscow, Rus.)-May 6, 1800. Russian field marshal. Noted for his achievements during the Russo-Turkish War, 1787-92, and in the French Revolutionary wars, 1798-99.

TEDDER, ARTHUR WILLIAM, 1st BARON TEDDER, July 11, 1890 (Glenguin, Eng.)-June 3, 1967. British air marshal. Contributed to German defeat in N. Africa 1942-43; played key role in successful Allied landings in Sicily (1943), Italy (1943), and Normandy (1944).

THEMISTOCLES, c. 524 B.C.?-c.460 B.C. Athenian naval strategist. Enlarged Athenian fleet; induced Sparta and other Peloponnesian communities to adopt his naval strategy; responsible for Greek victory over King Xerxes I's Persian fleet off Salamis, 480 B.C.

TIMOSHENKO, SEMYON KONSTANTINO-VICH, 1895 (Ukrainian SSR)–Mar. 31, 1970. Soviet Army marshal. Engaged in Russo-Finnish war, 1939–40; failed to halt the German advance into the Crimea and toward Stalingrad, 1942.

TIRPITZ, ALFRED VON, Mar. 19, 1849 (Kustrin, Prussia, now Kostrzyn, Pol.)–Mar. 6, 1930. German admiral. Naval secy., 1897–1916; created formidable High Seas Fleet.

TOGO, COUNT HEIHACHIRO, 1846 (Satsuma, now Kagoshima Pref., Jap.)–1934. Japanese admiral who won naval victories in Russo-Japanese war. Blocked Port Arthur, forcing its surrender, 1904; destroyed Russian fleet in the Tsushima Strait, ending the war, 1905.

TORSTENSON, COUNT LENNART, Aug. 17, 1603 (Forstena, Swe.)–Apr. 7, 1651. Swedish field marshal. Called the "Father of Field Artillery," he won important victories in the Thirty Years' War (1618–48), and Sweden's war against Denmark (1643–44).

TRENCHARD, HUGH MONTAGUE, 1st VISCOUNT TRENCHARD, Feb. 3, 1873 (Taunton, Eng.)–Feb. 10, 1956. British air marshal. The principal organizer of the Royal Air Force, 1918.

TURENNE, HENRI DE LA TOUR D'AUVERGNE, VICOMTE DE, Sept. 11, 1611 (Sedan, Fr.)–July 27, 1675. French Army marshal. Distinguished himself in the Thirty Years' War (1618–48), the civil war of the Fronde (1648–53), the Franco-Spanish war (1650s), and the Third Dutch War (1672–78).

VAUBAN, SEBASTIEN LE PRESTRE DE, May 15, 1633 (St.-Leger-Vauban, Fr.)–Mar. 30, 1707. French military engineer and theorist who revolutionized the art of defensive fortifications.

VILLA, FRANCISCO ("Pancho Villa"), born Doroteo Arango, June 5, 1878 (San Juan del Rio, Mex.)–June 20, 1923. Mexican guerrilla leader, revolutionary. Executed 16 Americans in Mexico, attacked Columbus, N.M., provoking the U.S. government to send a military expedition under Gen. JOHN PERSHING in an unsuccessful attempt to arrest him, 1916.

VOROSHILOV, KLIMENT YEFREMOVICH, Feb. 4, 1881 (Ukraine)–Dec. 3, 1969. Soviet Army marshal, political leader. Engaged in the Russian civil war, Winter War with Finland (1939–40), and WW II; as a leader in an unsuccessful attempt to oust NIKITA KHRUSHCHEV from power, 1957; pres. of the USSR, 1953–60.

WALLENSTEIN, ALBRECHT EUSEBIUS WEN-

SOCIAL REFORMERS

ZEL VON, DUKE OF FRIEDLAND AND MECKLENBURG, PRINCE OF SAGAN, Sept. 24, 1583 (Hermanice [now in Czech.])–Feb. 25, 1634. Loyalty to Holy Roman Emperor Ferdinand II during the Bohemian rebellion (1618–23) led to high appointments; generalissimo during the Thirty Years War, 1625–30 and 1632–34; defeated by GUSTAVUS ADOLPHUS at Lützen, 1632; his ambitions for power brought charges of treason; murdered.

WAVELL, ARCHIBALD PERCIVAL, 1st EARL WAVELL, May 5, 1883 (Colchester, Eng.)–May 24, 1950. British Army field marshal. Commander in chief for Middle East, 1938–41; destroyed Italian armies in N. Africa and E. Africa, 1940–41; as commander in chief in S.E. Asia, lost Malaya, Singapore, and Burma, 1941–43; viceroy of India, 1943–47.

WELLINGTON, ARTHUR WELLESLEY, 1st DUKE OF, May 1, 1769 (Dublin, Ire.)–Sept. 14, 1852. British Army field marshal, public official. Successful in Peninsular War against the French, 1808–14; defeated NAPOLEON at Waterloo, 1815; British prime minister, 1928–30.

WINGATE, ORDE CHARLES, Feb. 26, 1903 (India)–Mar. 24, 1944. British Army general. Led "Chindits," or "Wingate's Raiders," against Japanese Army in northern Burma during WW II.

WOLFE, JAMES, Jan. 2, 1727 (Westerham, Eng.)–Sept. 13, 1759. British Army general. Commanded army at capture of Quebec from French, the victory that led to British supremacy of Canada, 1759.

WRANGEL, BARON PETR NIKOLAYEVICH, Aug. 27, 1878 (Lith.)–Apr. 25, 1928. Russian Army general who led White (counter-revolutionary) forces, 1920.

YAMAGATA, ARITOMO, June 14, 1838 (Choshu, Jap.)–Feb. 1, 1922. Japanese Army general who played a major role in Japan's emergence as a military power at the beginning of the 20th century.

YAMASHITA, TOMOYUKI, Nov. 8, 1885 (Kochi Pref., Jap.)–Feb. 23, 1946. Japanese Army general. Conquered Malaya and Singapore, 1941–42; hanged as a war criminal, 1946.

YAMAMOTO, ISOROKU, Apr. 4, 1884 (Nagaoka, Jap.)–Apr. 18, 1943. Japanese admiral who planned and led attack on Pearl Harbor, 1941.

ZHUKOV, GEORGI KONSTANTINOVICH, 1896 (Kaluga Province, Rus.)–June 18, 1974. Soviet Army marshal, political figure. Directed defense of Moscow, 1941; commanded final assault on Berlin, 1945; minister of defense, 1955–57; the first military figure to become a member of the Presidium, 1957.

SOCIAL REFORMERS

ABBOTT, GRACE, Nov. 17, 1878 (Grand I., Neb.)–June 19, 1939. U.S. social worker, public administrator. Attacked exploitation of immigrants in newspaper articles and books; as dir. of U.S. Children's Bureau, worked for a constitutional amendment against child labor; a close assoc. of JANE ADDAMS. The *Child and the State*, 2 vols., 1938.

ABEL, I(orwith) W(ilbur), Aug. 11, 1908 (Magnolia, Ohio). U.S. labor leader. A leading union organizer of the steel industry. Staff member of Steel Workers Organizing Com. (later, United Steel Workers of America), 1937–   ; dist. dir., 1942–52; secy.-treasurer, 1953–65; pres., 1965–   ; vice-pres. of AFL-CIO, 1965–   .

ABERNATHY, RALPH, Mar. 11, 1926 (Linden, Ala.). U.S. civil-rights leader, clergyman. A deputy of MARTIN LUTHER KING, JR., in the Southern Christian Leadership Conference, of which he became pres. after King's assassination, 1968–   . With King, organized Montgomery Improvement Assn. (1955), initiated Montgomery bus boycott (1955), and organized the SCLC (1957).

ADDAMS, JANE, Sept. 6, 1869 (Cedarville, Ill.)–May 21, 1935. U.S. social reformer, social worker. With Ellen Gates Starr, founded Hull House, in Chicago, one of the first social settlements in N. America, 1889; active in the pacifist and woman-suffrage movements; worked for social reforms, including the first juvenile-court law, factory inspection, and workmen's compensation. Awarded Nobel Peace Prize (with NICHOLAS MURRAY BUTLER), 1931; named to Hall of Fame for Great Americans, 1965. *The Spirit of Youth and the City Streets*, 1909; *Twenty Years at Hull House*, 1910.

ALINSKY, SAUL DAVID, Jan. 30, 1909 (Chicago, Ill.)-June 12, 1972. U.S. social activist. A self-termed "professional radical" who organized poor communities to use picketing, sitdowns, strikes, and boycotts to exert pressure on the business establishment, landlords, and local political machines. *John L. Lewis, A Biography*, 1949; *The Professional Radical* (with Marion K. Sanders), 1970; *Rules for Radicals*, 1971.

ANTHONY, SUSAN BROWNELL, Feb. 15, 1820 (Adams, Mass.)-Mar. 13, 1906. U.S. social reformer and pioneer crusader for woman suffrage. Pres. of Natl. Woman Suffrage Assn., 1892-1900; organized Internatl. Council of Women (1888) and Internatl. Woman Suffrage Alliance (1904); with E. STANTON, secured first laws in New York State guaranteeing women rights over their children and control of property and wages; named to Hall of Fame for Great Americans, 1950. *The History of Woman Suffrage* (with Stanton and M. J. Gage), 3 vols., 1881-86.

BADEN-POWELL, ROBERT STEPHENSON SMYTH, FIRST BARON BADEN-POWELL OF GILWELL, Feb. 22, 1857 (London, Eng.)-Jan. 8, 1941. English founder of the Boy Scouts, 1907; with sister Agnes, founded Girl Guides, 1910 (in U.S. called Girl Scouts, from 1912); founded Wolf Cubs, 1916 (in U.S. called Cub Scouts, from 1916). National hero for his part in defense of Mafeking in the Boer War of 1899-1902. *Scouting for Boys*, 1908; *Scouting and Youth Movements*, 1929.

BALCH, EMILY GREEN, Jan. 8, 1867 (Jamaica Plain[now Boston], Mass.)-Jan. 9, 1961. U.S. economist, social scientist, pacifist. Prof. of economics and sociology at Wellesley C., 1896-1918; a founder and internatl. secy. of Women's Internatl. League for Peace and Freedom, 1919-22; helped found Boston's Denison House Settlement, Women's Trade Union League; awarded Nobel Peace Prize (with J. MOTT), 1946. *Public Assistance of the Poor in France*, 1893; *Toward Human Unity*, 1952.

BALDWIN, ROGER NASH, Jan. 21, 1884 (Wellesley, Mass.). U.S. lawyer, reformer. Dir. of American Civil Liberties Union, 1917-50; ACLU natl. chm., 1950-55. *Liberty under the Soviets*, 1928.

BARTON, CLARA, born Clarissa Harlowe Barton, Dec. 25, 1821 (Oxford, Mass.)-Apr. 12, 1912. U.S. humanitarian, founder of the American Red Cross. Called "Angel of the Battlefield" during Civil War for establishing a service of supplies for soldiers in army camps and on the battlefield; worked for U.S. signing of the Geneva Agreement for care of war wounded, 1882; founded American Red Cross and served as its pres., 1881-1904. *History of the Red Cross*, 1882; *The Red Cross in Peace and War*, 1899.

BEARD, DAN(iel Carter), June 21, 1850 (Cincinnati, Ohio)-June 11, 1941. U.S. illustrator, naturalist. A founder of the Boy Scouts in America (1910), he served as national scout commissioner until his death. Illustrated many books, including the first edition of M. TWAIN's *A Connecticut Yankee at King Arthur's Court* (1889). *The America Boys' Handy Book*, 1882; *American Boys' Book of Wild Animals*, 1921.

BEECHER, HENRY WARD, June 24, 1813 (Litchfield, Conn.)-Mar. 8, 1887. U.S. clergyman, abolitionist. Famed as orator and leader in the antislavery movement; an advocate of woman suffrage; sued for adultery by Theodore Tilton (1874), exonerated by two church tribunals, but civil trial ended in jury disagreement. Named to Hall of Fame for Great Americans, 1900. *Seven Lectures to Young Men*, 1844; *Evolution and Religion*, 1855. (Son of LYMAN BEECHER; brother of H. B. STOWE and C. E. Beecher.)

BEECHER, LYMAN, Oct. 12, 1775 (New Haven, Conn.)-Jan. 10, 1863. U.S. Presbyterian clergyman. Influential abolitionist and anti-Roman Catholic theologian; pres. of Theological Seminary of Cincinnati, 1832-50. (Father of CATHERINE ESTHER BEECHER, HARRIET BEECHER STOWE, and HENRY WARD BEECHER.)

BISSELL, EMILY PERKINS, May 31, 1861 (Wilmington, Del.)-Mar. 8, 1948. U.S. welfare worker. Headed the first Christmas seal drive (to aid tubercular children) in the U.S., designing, printing and selling the seals, 1907.

BLACK, JAMES, Sept. 23, 1823 (Lewisburg, Pa.)-Dec. 16, 1893. U.S. temperance advocate. The first Natl. Prohibition Party presidential candidate, winning over 5,000 votes, 1872; owned world's largest collection of temperance literature, now in New York Public Library. *The Necessity for the Prohibition Party*, 1876; *The History of the National Prohibition Party*, 1893.

BLACKWELL, ANTOINETTE LOUISA, May 20, 1825 (Henrietta, N.Y.)-Nov. 5, 1921. U.S. clergywoman. First ordained woman min. in the U.S. (Congregational; later, Unitarian), 1853. One of first U.S. women to receive a college education; active feminist, abolitionist, temperance advocate. *The Sexes Throughout Nature*, 1875. (Sister-in-law of HENRY B. BLACKWELL and ELIZABETH BLACKWELL.)

BLACKWELL, HENRY BROWNE, May 4, 1825 (Bristol, Eng.)-Sept. 7, 1909. U.S. social reformer. Distinguished activist in the woman-suffrage movement. With wife LUCY STONE, helped organize American Woman Suffrage Assn., 1869; campaigned for suffrage in over 25 states; editor of *Woman's Journal*, 1870-1909.

BLANC, (Jean Joseph Charles) LOUIS, Oct. 29, 1811 (Madrid, Sp.)-Dec. 6, 1882. French utopian socialist who is considered the founder of state socialism. Founded *Revue de Progrès* (1839), in which he published his seminal work, "The Organization of Labor" (1839); influential in the "banquet" campaign for political reform, 1847; member of provisional govt. of the Second Republic, following 1848 Revolution; after defeat of workers' revolt, lived in exile in England, 1848-70.

BLOOMER, AMELIA, née Jenks, May 27, 1818 (Homer, N.Y.)-Dec. 30, 1894. U.S. social reformer. Campaigned for temperance and women's rights; published biweekly paper, *The Lily*, 1849-54; recommended and adopted full trousers (introduced by Elizabeth Smith Miller) that became known as "bloomers."

BOOTH, BALLINGTON, July 28, 1859 (Brighouse, Eng.)-Oct. 5, 1940. British-U.S. reformer. Son of WILLIAM BOOTH, founder of the Salvation Army; following rift with his father, founded a similar body, the Volunteers of America, 1896. (Brother of E. C. BOOTH.)

BOOTH, EVANGELINE CORY, Dec. 25, 1865 (London, Eng.)-July 17, 1950. English social reformer. The daughter of W. BOOTH, founder of the Salvation Army; was a leader in the move-

SOCIAL REFORMERS

ment's work in England; credited with winning repeal of bylaws forbidding open-air preaching; commander of U.S.S.A., 1904–34; elected gen. of international org., 1934. *The War Romance with the Salvation Army* (with G. L. Hill), 1919. (Sister of BALLINGTON BOOTH.)

BOOTH, WILLIAM, Apr. 10, 1829 (Nottingham, Eng.)–Aug. 20, 1912. English social reformer. Founder (1878) and first gen. of the Salvation Army. An ordained minister of the Methodist New Connexion (1852), resigned (1861) to become an itinerant evangelist; with wife, founded mission (1865) that became S.A. *Darkest England and the Way Out* (with W. T. Stead), 1890. (Father of E. C. and BALLINGTON BOOTH.)

BRECKINRIDGE, SOPHONISBA PRESTON, Apr. 1, 1866 (Lexington, Ky.)–July 30, 1948. U.S. social reformer, social worker, educator. Prominent activist for woman suffrage, child welfare, prison reform, labor legislation, internatl. peace; assisted J. LATHROP in organizing the Chicago School of Civics and Philanthropy, 1907. *Marriage and the Civic Rights of Women,* 1931; *Women in the Twentieth Century: A Study of their Political, Social and Economic Activities,* 1933.

BRENT, MARGARET, c.1600 (Gloucester, Eng.)–c.1671. American colonial lawyer. The first woman lawyer in the colonies and probably the first feminist. Through family connections, received the first land grant ever vested in a woman; through other acquisitions, became one of the largest landowners in the colonies, earning title of Lord, right to conduct business and sign contracts; acted as attorney for friends and neighbors.

BROWN, JOHN, May 9, 1800 (Torrington, Conn.)–Dec. 2, 1859. U.S. abolitionist. With 21 followers, raided federal arsenal at Harper's Ferry, Va., 1859; captured and tried for treason; his dignity and high moral tone in court won Northern sympathy; when convicted and hanged, became martyr to the antislavery cause.

BROWNMILLER, SUSAN, Feb. 15, 1935 (New York, N.Y.). U.S. feminist. Noted as the author of *Against Our Will: Men, Women and Rape* (1975), a comprehensive study of rape.

CARMICHAEL, STOKELY, June 29, 1941 (Port-of-Spain, Trinidad). U.S. black militant. As chm. of Student Nonviolent Coordinating Com. (1966), responsible for the controversial Black Power concept; resigned (1967) to become prime min. of the Black Panther Party; resigned and moved to Guinea, 1969. *Black Power* (with Charles V. Hamilton), 1967.

CATT, CARRIE CHAPMAN, née Lane, Jan. 9, 1859 (Ripon, Wisc.)–Mar. 9, 1947. U.S. women's-rights leader. A leader in the campaign for woman suffrage for more than 25 years, culminating in adoption of the 19th Amendment (1920). Reorganized Natl. Woman Suffrage Assn. (1905–15), and served as its pres. (1915–47), later transformed it into the League of Women Voters; also founded the Internatl. Woman Suffrage Alliance (1902) and Com. on the Cause and Cure of War (1925). *Woman Suffrage and Politics, the Inner Study of the Suffrage Movement,* (with N. R. Shuler), 1923.

CHAVEZ, CESAR ESTRADA, Mar. 31, 1927 (Yuma, Ariz.). U.S. labor-union organizer. Founder and first pres. of United Farm Workers, AFL-CIO, the first viable agricultural union in the U.S.; used nonviolent tactics, including fasts, marches, long-term strikes, and boycotts.

COXEY, JACOB SECHLER, Apr. 16, 1854 (Selinsgrove, Pa.)–May 18, 1951. U.S. reformer.

Leader of the famous 1894 march of the unemployed on Washington, D.C., from Massillon, Ohio; remained one of the nation's most colorful personalities, perennially a candidate for offices ranging from mayor to U.S. pres.; only elective office held was as mayor of Massillon, Ohio, 1931–33.

DAVIS, ANGELA YVONNE, Jan. 26, 1944 (Birmingham, Ala.). U.S. black militant, communist activist. Acting prof. of philosophy at U. of California at Los Angeles; acquitted on charges of kidnapping, murder, and conspiracy in connection with the 1970 shootout at Marin Co. (Calif.) courthouse, 1972.

DAY, DOROTHY, Nov. 8, 1897 (New York, N.Y.). U.S. reformer. A founder (with Peter Maurin), and head of the pacifist Catholic Worker movement, 1933; publisher of *Catholic Worker,* 1933–   ; jailed numerous times in the 1950s for protests against preparations for nuclear war. *From Union Square to Rome,* 1938; *House of Hospitality,* 1939; *The Long Loneliness,* 1952.

DEBS, EUGENE VICTOR, Nov. 5, 1855 (Terre Haute, Ind.)–Oct. 20, 1926. U.S. socialist leader, labor organizer. First pres. of the American Railway Union, which gained natl. fame with its successful strike against the Great Northern RR (1894), and participated in the Pullman strike (1894); as Socialist party presidential candidate five times(1900–20), received his highest popular vote in 1920, while imprisoned for criticizing the govt. "Unionism and Socialism," 1904; *Walls and Bars,* 1927.

DIX, DOROTHEA LYNDE, Apr. 4, 1802 (Hampden, Me.)–July 17, 1887. U.S. social reformer. Pioneer in the movement for specialized treatment of the insane; her crusades resulted in the establishment of state hospitals for the insane in more than 15 states and Canada.

DOUGLASS, FREDERICK, born Frederick Augustus Washington Bailey, c. 1817 (Tuckahoe, Md.)–Feb. 29, 1895. U.S. abolitionist, orator, journalist. Born into slavery, escaped to Massachusetts (1838) where he joined Massachusetts Anti-Slavery Society; British admirers bought his freedom and raised money for him to start an abolitionist weekly, *North Star* (1847); aided in recruiting black troops for the Union Army. *Narrative of the Life of Frederick Douglass,* 1845.

DUBINSKY, DAVID, Feb. 22, 1892 (Brest-Litovsk, Pol.). U.S. labor leader. Pres. of Internatl. Ladies Garment Workers' Union, 1932–66; a founder of the Labor party in New York State, 1936; resigned party when it came under communist influence; helped organize Liberal party, 1942.

DUBOIS, W(illiam) E(dward) B(urghardt), Feb. 23, 1868 (Great Barrington, Mass.)–Aug. 27, 1963. U.S. civil-rights leader, author. Advocate of civil, political, and economic equality. A founder of the Natl. Negro Com., later the Natl. Assn. for the Advancement of Colored People, 1909; editor of *Crisis,* NAACP magazine, 1910–32. Prof. of economics and history at Atlanta U., 1897–1910 and 1932–44; joined Communist party (1961), moved to Ghana and renounced U.S. citizenship. *The Souls of Black Folk,* 1903.

ENGELS, FRIEDRICH, Nov. 28, 1820 (Barmen, Ger.)–Aug. 5, 1895. German philosopher, businessman. Cofounder (with KARL MARX), of modern communism. With Marx, coauthored *The Communist Manifesto* (1848); played a leading role in the First and Second Internatls. *The Condition of the Working Class in England in 1844,* 1845; *The Origin of the Family, Private Property and the State,* 1884.

THE BOOK OF WHO

EVERS, JAMES CHARLES, Sept. 11, 1922 (Decatur, Miss.). U.S. political, civil-rights leader. Led a biracial coalition that unseated an all-white Mississippi delegation at the 1968 Democratic National Convention; first black to run for gov. of Mississippi, 1971; mayor of Fayette, Miss., 1969–   .

FARMER, JAMES LEONARD, Jan. 12, 1920 (Marshall, Tex.). U.S. civil-rights activist, union organizer, lecturer. Helped found (1942) Congress of Racial Equality, which he served as natl. dir. (1961–66); leader of 1961 Freedom Ride; U.S. asst. secy. of HEW, 1969–70 and 1972–75. *Freedom—When?*, 1965.

FLANAGAN, EDWARD JOSEPH, July 13, 1886 (Roscommon, Ire.)–May 15, 1948. U.S. Roman Catholic priest. Founder of Boys Town, 1922; attempted to develop character in the boys by supplementing vocational training with religious and social education.

FLYNN, ELIZABETH GURLEY, Aug. 7, 1890 (Concord, N.H.)–Sept. 5, 1964. U.S. communist leader. Took part in the bitter textile strikes at Lawrence, Mass. (1912), and Paterson, N.J. (1913); joined U.S. Communist party in 1937; became chairperson of the party's National Com. in 1961, the first woman to hold that post; a founder and board member of the American Civil Liberties Union, expelled (1940) for being a communist.

FOSTER, WILLIAM ZEBULON, Feb. 25, 1881 (Taunton, Mass.)–Sept. 1, 1961. U.S. political leader. U.S. communist leader; took part in organizing steelworkers for the strike of 1919; U.S. Communist party presidential candidate in 1924, 1928, and 1932. *Towards Soviet America, From Bryan to Stalin*, 1937.

FOURIER, (François Marie) CHARLES, Apr. 7, 1772 (Besancon, Fr.)–Oct. 10, 1837. French social theorist. Propounded a type of utopian socialism in which agrarian society would be reorganized into communal groups of producers known as *phalanges* (phalanxes); failed to produce any such assns. himself, although his followers attempted to do so in the U.S.

FRIEDAN, BETTY, Feb. 4, 1921 (Peoria, Ill.). U.S. feminist, writer. As author of *The Feminine Mystique* (1963), helped revive the feminist movement in the U.S.; a founder and pres. of Natl. Org. for Women, 1966–70. *It Changed My Life: Writings on the Women's Movement*, 1976.

FULLER, SARAH MARGARET, MARCHIONESS OSSOLI, May 23, 1810 (Cambridgeport, Mass.)–July 19, 1850. U.S. journalist, writer, educator. Often called the first professional U.S. newspaperwoman. An advocate of women's rights; leader of classes of "conversations" for women on various topics; editor of *Dial*, 1840–42; literary critic with the *New York Herald-Tribune*, 1844–46; covered Italy (from 1848–49), becoming first U.S. woman foreign correspondent; married Marquis Angelo Ossoli, with whom she took part in Italian Revolution of 1848.

GARDNER, JOHN WILLIAM, Oct. 8, 1912 (Los Angeles, Calif.). U.S. psychologist, educator, public official. Founder and chm. of Common Cause, a nonpartisan citizen's lobby, 1970–77. Pres. of Carnegie Fndn. for the Advancement of Teaching, 1955–56; U.S. secy. of HEW, 1965–68; chm. of Urban Coalition, 1968–70.

GARRISON, WILLIAM LLOYD, Dec. 10, 1805 (Newburyport, Mass.)–May 24, 1879. U.S. journalist. Abolitionist leader who published *The Liberator* (1831–65), in which he advocated his uncompromising opposition to slavery; active in organizing the New England Anti-Slavery Soc.,

1831; believed that moral persuasion, rather than force or the ballot, was the method needed to achieve abolition; also campaigned for woman suffrage and Prohibition.

GARVEY, MARCUS, Aug. 17, 1887 (St. Ann's Bay, Jamaica)–June 10, 1940. U.S. black nationalist leader. Advocated separatism and racial pride; promoted a "Back to Africa" movement; established the Universal Negro Improvement Assn., 1914; editor of *Negro World*, 1918–23.

GEORGE, HENRY, Sept. 2, 1839 (Philadelphia, Pa.)–Oct. 29, 1897. U.S. economist, journalist. Famed as the proponent of a single tax. Shocked by the inequalities of wealth in New York, he attempted to find a fair means of redistribution; enjoyed such immense popularity that he nearly won the 1886 New York City mayoral election; his *Poverty and Progress* (1879) greatly increased interest in economics.

GODWIN, MARY, née Wollstonecraft, Apr. 27, 1759 (nr. London, Eng.)–Sept. 10, 1797. English writer, feminist. An early advocate of women's rights, noted as the author of *Vindicaiton of the Rights of Women* (1792). (Wife of WILLIAM GODWIN; mother of MARY SHELLEY.)

GOMPERS, SAMUEL, Jan. 27, 1850 (London, Eng.)–Dec. 13, 1924. U.S. labor leader. A founder and the first pres. of the AFL, 1886–1924; stressed business unionism, craft autonomy, and voluntarism; marshalled labor support for WW I.

GRIMKÉ, ANGELINA EMILY, Feb. 20, 1805 (Charleston, S.C.)–Oct. 26, 1879; and her sister **SARAH MOORE GRIMKÉ,** Nov. 26, 1792 (Charleston, S.C.)–Dec. 23, 1873. U.S. reformers, abolitionists. Worked in abolition movement, 1835–38; also lectured and wrote on behalf of women's rights.

GUESDE, JULES, born Mathieu Basile, Nov. 11, 1845 (Paris, Fr.)–July 18, 1922. French socialist. Leader of the Marxist wing of the French labor movement; founded *L'Egalité*, a Socialist weekly, 1877; member of the Chamber of Deputies, 1893–98 and 1906–22.

HAMER, FANNIE LOU, 1917 (Montgomery Co., Miss.)–Mar. 14, 1977. U.S. civil-rights leader. As a field worker and leader of Student Nonviolent Coordinating Com. (1962–77), helped found the black-led Mississippi Freedom Democratic party; spoke before the 1964 Democratic Convention.

HAYNES, GEORGE EDMUND, May 11, 1880 (Pine Bluff, Ark.)–Jan. 8, 1960. U.S. sociologist, civil-rights leader. Cofounder and first exec. dir. of Natl. Urban League, 1910–16; developed the Interracial Clinic, whose methods for dealing with racial tensions were put into effect in more than 30 U.S. cities; organized social science dept. of Fisk U., 1910–12; first black to receive a Ph.D. at Columbia U., 1912.

HILLMAN, BESSIE, née Abramowitz, May 15, 1889 (Grodno, Rus.)–Dec. 23, 1970. U.S. labor leader. A founder of the Amalgamated Clothing Workers of America, 1914; for 20 years, the only female union leader in the clothing industry; led a strike against Hart, Schaffner, and Marx (Chicago), 1910. (Wife of SIDNEY HILLMAN.)

HILLMAN, SIDNEY, Mar. 23, 1887 (Zagare, Lith.)–July 10, 1946. U.S. labor leader. First pres. of Amalgamated Clothing Workers of America, 1914–46; a founder of the CIO; an advisor to Pres. F. D. ROOSEVELT, held several posts in New Deal orgs. (Husband of BESSIE ABRAMOVITZ HILLMAN.)

HOWE, SAMUEL GRIDLEY, Nov. 10, 1801 (Boston, Mass.)–Jan. 9, 1876. U.S. humanitarian, physician, educator. First dir. of Perkins School for the Blind, 1832-76; a pioneer in printing books for the blind; established first U.S. school for the mentally retarded.

HUERTA, DOLORES, 1930 (Dawson, N.M.). U.S. labor leader. With CESAR CHAVEZ, worked to unionize farm workers and to prevent takeover of the union by the Teamsters; vice-pres. of United Farm Workers, 1977- . Organized Community Service Org., 1955-62.

JACKSON, JESSE, Oct. 8, 1941 (Greenville, N.C.). U.S. civil-rights leader, Baptist clergyman. A founder of Operation Breadbasket and its national dir., 1966-71; founder and exec. dir. of, Operation PUSH, 1971- .

JOHNSON, WILLIAM EUGENE ("Pussyfoot Johnson"), Mar. 25, 1862 (Coventry, N.Y.)-Feb. 2, 1945. U.S. reformer. A militant Prohibitionist; chief special officer of the Indian Service, 1908-11; known as "Pussyfoot" for his methods of pursuing lawbreakers in the Indian Ter.; managing editor for Anti-Saloon League publications, 1912-16; publicity dir. of league, 1916-18.

JONES, MARY, née Harris ("Mother Jones"), May 1, 1830 (Cork, Ire.)-Nov. 30, 1930. U.S. labor leader. Gained fame as an agitator for Appalachian coal miners; led a children's march from Kensington, Pa., to Sagamore Hill, the N.Y. home of Pres. T. ROOSEVELT, to dramatize the evils of child labor, 1903.

JORDAN, VERNON EULION, JR., Aug. 15, 1935 (Atlanta, Ga.). U.S. civil-rights leader, lawyer. Dir. of Voter Education Project, Southern Regional Council, 1964-68; exec. dir. of United Negro College Fund, 1970-71; exec. dir. of National Urban League, 1972- .

JOUHAUX, LEON, July 1, 1879 (Paris, Fr.)-Apr. 28, 1954. French Socialist and labor leader. Secy.-gen. of Gen. Confederation of Labor, 1909-47; attempted an antimilitaristic pact with German labor leaders prior to WW I; a founder of the Internatl. Labor Org.; his split with the communist majority in his union (1947) is considered to have saved French labor unions from communism; awarded Nobel Peace Prize, 1951.

KELLER, HELEN, June 27, 1880 (Tuscumbia, Ala.)-June 1, 1968. U.S. educator, author. As a deaf and blind woman who graduated from college, became a public figure as an example of achievement in spite of handicaps; taught by ANNE SULLIVAN MACY, via manual alphabet pressed into her hand; traveled and spoke widely on behalf of the physically handicapped. *The Story of My Life,* 1903.

KENNEDY, THOMAS, Nov. 2, 1887 (Lansford, Pa.)-Jan. 19, 1963. U.S. labor leader. As a leader of the United Mine Workers of America (1925-62), led the fight to force the AFL to endorse Social Security and government responsibility for unemployment.

KING, CORETTA, née Scott, Apr. 27, 1927 (Marion, Ala.). U.S. civil-rights leader, lecturer, writer, concert singer. The widow of MARTIN LUTHER KING, JR., she has continued his work for social justice; pres. of Martin Luther King, Jr., Center for Social Change; chairperson of Commission on Economic Justice for Women; cochairperson of Natl. Com. on Full Employment.

KING, MARTIN LUTHER, JR., Jan. 15, 1929 (Atlanta, Ga.)-Apr. 4, 1968. U.S. civil-rights leader, clergyman. Leader of the U.S. civil-rights movement from mid-1950s until his death. Led black boycott in Montgomery, Ala., against segregated city bus lines, 1955; advocated nonviolent resis-

tance; organized Southern Christian Leadership Conference, 1957; organized massive civil-rights march on Washington D.C., 1963; announced a "Poor People's Campaign," 1968; assassinated in Memphis, Tenn.; awarded Nobel Peace Prize, 1964. *Stride Toward Freedom,* 1958; *Why We Can't Wait,* 1964.

KRUPSKAYA, NADEZHDA KONSTANTINOVA, Feb. 23, 1869 (St. Petersburg, Rus. [now Leningrad, USSR])-Feb. 27, 1939. Russian revolutionary, educator. Secy. of Bolshevik faction of the Social Democratic party, 1901-17; married V. I. LENIN, after whose death she exerted great influence in matters of education.

KUHN, MARGARET ("Maggie"), 1905 (Buffalo, N.Y.). U.S. social worker. Organizer of the Gray Panthers, a group dedicated to improving conditions for senior citizens, 1970.

LATHROP, JULIA CLIFFORD, June 29, 1858 (Rockford, Ill.)-Apr. 15, 1932. U.S. social worker. First chief of the U.S. Children's Bureau, 1912-21; surveyed the problem of infant mortality; worked for legal protection of children born out of wedlock.

LEARY, TIMOTHY FRANCIS, Oct. 22, 1920 (Springfield, Mass.). U.S. psychologist, educator, drug cult leader. A leader of the 1960s drug culture; an advocate of the ingestion of LSD; dismissed as prof. at Harvard U. for involving students in drug experiments. *Politics of Ecstasy,* 1968.

LEWIS, JOHN LLEWELLYN, Feb. 12, 1880 (nr. Lucas, Ia.)-June 11, 1969. U.S. labor leader. As pres. of United Mine Workers of America (1920-60), built that union into one of the most powerful in the U.S.; successfully organized mass-production industries, but broke with the AFL to form the CIO, which he served as pres. (1936-40).

MALCOLM X, born Malcolm Little, May 19, 1925 (Omaha, Neb.)-Feb. 21, 1965. U.S. militant black leader who spoke for racial pride and black nationalism in the early 1960s. Joined Black Muslims and rose to a position of leadership; suspended (1964) for an inflammatory statement; he formed his own Org. for Afro-American Unity; assassinated. *The Autobiography of Malcolm X* (with ALEX HALEY), 1965.

MARX, KARL, May 5, 1818 (Trier, Ger.)-Mar. 14, 1883. German social philosopher. Chief theorist of modern socialism and communism; also a founder of economic history and sociology. Spent the majority of his life studying in the British Museum (London), from 1849; joined the Communist League (1847) and with F. ENGELS wrote its *Communist Manifesto* (1848); after failure of the revolutions of 1848, worked for formation of revolutionary parties; helped found Internatl. Workingmen's Assn., 1864. *Das Kapital,* 3 vols., 1867, 1885, and 1895.

MCBRIDE, F(rancis) **SCOTT,** July 29, 1872 (Carroll Co., Ohio)-Apr. 23, 1955. U.S. temperance leader. As gen. supt. of the Anti-Saloon League of America (1924-32), led the temperance forces in their fight to prevent repeal of the 18th Amendment.

MCNICHOLS, JOHN TIMOTHY, Dec. 15, 1877 (County Mayo, Ire.)-Apr. 22, 1950. U.S. Roman Catholic archbishop. Founder of the Natl. Legion of Decency (1934) to boycott motion pictures considered immoral or obscene. Archbishop of Cincinnati, Ohio, 1925-50.

MEANY, GEORGE, Aug. 16, 1894 (New York, N.Y.)-Jan. 10, 1980. U.S. labor leader. Pres. of AFL-CIO, 1955-79. Helped reunify the U.S. labor movement by bringing together the AFL and CIO;

led the fight after WW II to keep U.S. labor out of the Soviet-dominated World Federation of Trade Unions; has worked against labor corruption; awarded Presidential Medal of Freedom, 1964.

MILLETT, KATE (Katherine) **MURRAY** Sept. 14, 1934 (St. Paul, Minn.). U.S. feminist, sculptor, teacher. Lectures and writes extensively on behalf of women's liberation. *Sexual Politics*, 1970; *Flying*, 1974.

MITCHELL, JOHN, Feb. 4, 1870 (Braidwood, Ill.)–Sept. 9, 1919. U.S. labor leader. Played a major role in the United Mine Workers' first successful national strike, 1897; as UMW pres. (1898–1908), organized a 1902 strike of anthracite miners that gained him reputation as greatest labor leader of his time; vice-pres. of American Federation of Labor, 1899–1914.

MORRIS, ESTHER HOBART MCQUIGG SLACK, Aug. 8, 1814 (Tioga Co., N.Y.)–Apr. 2, 1902. U.S. suffragist. Instrumental in winning the right for women to vote in Wyoming (1869), the first state to provide for women's suffrage in its constitution; as justice of the peace in South Pass City, Wyo., the first woman in the U.S. to hold the post, 1870; her statue stands in Statuary Hall of the U.S. Capitol.

MOTT, LUCRETIA, Jan. 3, 1793 (Nantucket, Mass.)–Nov. 11, 1880. U.S. abolitionist, feminist, Quaker minister. Refused recognition by the World Anti-Slavery Convention in London (1840), along with all other women delegates; lectured widely for the rights of women; with E. STANTON, a founder of the organized women's-rights movement in the U.S., at Seneca Falls, N.Y., 1848; made her home a sanctuary for runaway slaves.

MURRAY, PHILIP, May 25, 1886 (Blantyre, Ire.)–Nov. 9, 1952. U.S. labor leader. As pres. of CIO (1940–52), led the expulsion of several communist-dominated unions, 1949–50; helped organize the steelworkers; pres. of United Steelworkers of America, 1942–52.

NATION, CARRY AMELIA, née Moore, Nov. 25, 1846 (Garrard Co., Ky.)–June 9, 1911. U.S. temperance advocate. Famed for entering saloons and wrecking them with a hatchet; lectured widely; supported woman suffrage; was an imposing figure at six ft. and 175 lbs.

OWEN, ROBERT, May 14, 1771 (Newtown, Wales)–Nov. 17, 1858. Welsh manufacturer, socialist. As a manager of a cotton mill, attempted to improve the lot of his employees, leading to the development of a social philosophy; developed a socialist theory in which work and the enjoyment of its results would be shared; believed man's character is molded by his environment; set up two social communities based on his plan. *A New View of Society*, 1813. (Father of ROBERT D. OWEN.)

OWEN, ROBERT DALE, Nov. 9, 1801 (Glasgow, Scot.)–June 24, 1877. U.S. social reformer. A founder of *The Free Enquirer*, a Socialist publication, 1827; as U.S. rep. (D, Ind.; 1843–47), instrumental in founding the Smithsonian Inst. (1845); an active abolitionist and spiritualist. (Son of ROBERT OWEN.)

PANKHURST, EMMELINE, July 4, 1858 (Manchester, Eng.)–June 14, 1928. English suffragist. A militant suffragist who founded her own movement, the Women's Social and Political Union, 1903; imprisoned numerous times, conducted hunger strikes in her cell; tactics of her group included window-smashing, arson, and bombings. *My Own Story*, 1914.

PARKS, ROSA, Feb. 4, 1913. U.S. civil-rights leader. Initiated the bus boycott in Montgomery, Ala., thereby sparking the beginning of the concerted civil-rights movement, 1955; a staff asst. to U.S. rep. John Conyers (D. Mich.), 1965–   .

PAUL, ALICE, Jan. 11, 1885 (Moorestown, N.J.)–July 9, 1977. U.S. feminist, lawyer. A leader of the woman-suffrage movement and then the Equal Rights Amendment movement, early 1900s; natl. chairperson of Natl. Woman's Party, 1942; a founder of World Women's Party; known for her radical, confrontation tactics.

POTOFSKY, JACOB SAMUEL, Nov. 16, 1894 (Radomisl, Rus.)–Aug. 5, 1979. U.S. labor leader. Took part in the historic garment strike (1910) that led to the formation of the Amalgamated Clothing Workers of America, which he served as pres. (1946–72).

PROUDHON, PIERRE JOSEPH, July 15, 1809 (Besancon, Fr.)–Jan. 16, 1865. French social theorist. The first to formulate the doctrines of philosophical anarchism; condemned the abuses of private property; attempted to found a bank with the goal of abolishing interest and ending capital, 1849; prosecuted and tried for his revolutionary opinions. *What is Property?*, 1840.

RANDOLPH, A. PHILIP, Apr. 15, 1889 (Crescent City, Fla.)–May 16, 1979. U.S. black labor leader. Organized the Brotherhood of Sleeping Car Porters (1925) and continued to work for job rights for blacks; persuaded Pres. F. D. ROOSEVELT to issue a fair-employment-practices exec. order, 1941; directed the massive 1963 civil-rights march on Washington, D.C.

REUTHER, WALTER PHILIP, Sept. 1, 1907 (Wheeling, W.Va.)–May 9, 1970. U.S. labor leader. As pres. of the United Auto Workers (1946–70) and pres. of the CIO (1952–55), an effective negotiator; a leading labor anticommunist; an architect of the 1955 merger of the AFL and the CIO.

RIIS, JACOB AUGUST, May 3, 1849 (Ribe, Den.)–May 26, 1914. U.S. journalist, reformer, author. Crusader for urban reforms. As police reporter for the New York *Tribune* (1877–88), gained wide attention with his exposes of city slums and life among the urban poor. *How the Other Half Lives*, 1890; *The Making of an American*, 1901; *Children of the Tenements*, 1903.

RIPLEY, GEORGE, Oct. 3, 1802 (Greenfield, Mass.)–July 4, 1880. U.S. journalist, social reformer. Pastor of Purchase St. Church in Boston, Mass., 1826–41; founded *Dial*, the prototypical little magazine, 1840; organized and directed Brook Farm, the famous utopian community, 1841–47; literary editor of the New York *Tribune*, 1849–80; founder of *Harper's New Monthly Magazine*, 1850.

RUSTIN, BAYARD, Mar. 17, 1910 (West Chester, Pa.). U.S. civil-rights activist. Special asst. to Dr. MARTIN LUTHER KING, JR., 1955–60; organized March on Washington for Jobs and Freedom, 1963; pres. of A. Philip Randolph Inst. 1966–   . *Down the Line*, 1971; *Strategies for Freedom*, 1976.

SAKHAROV, ANDREI, May 21, 1921 (Moscow, USSR.). Soviet political dissident, physicist. A leader of the dissident movement in the Soviet Union; author of an essay advocating atomic disarmament and intellectual freedom in the USSR; awarded Nobel Peace Prize, 1975. *My Country and the World*, 1975.

SANGER, MARGARET HIGGINS, Sept. 14, 1883 (Corning, N.Y.)– Sept. 6, 1966. Founder of the birth-control movement in the U.S. Founded the National Birth Control League, 1914; opened the nation's first birth-control clinic, in Brooklyn, N.Y., 1916; organized the first American Control Conference, New York City, 1921; served as first pres. of the Internatl. Planned Parenthood Fnd. (founded 1953).

SAVONAROLA, GIROLAMO, Sept. 21, 1452 (Ferrara, It.)–May 23, 1498. Italian reformer, Dominican monk. Preached against church and state corruption; became the spiritual leader of Florence (1494) and defied the pope; excommunicated (1497), but continued to rule; tried for sedition and heresy, tortured and hanged.

SCHLAFLY, PHYLLIS, Aug. 15, 1924 (St. Louis, Mo.). U.S. political activist, author. Chairwoman of Stop ERA, 1972–   ; author of a monthly newsletter, *Phyllis Schlafly Report,* 1967–   . *A Choice, Not an Echo,* 1964; *Safe—Not Sorry,* 1967; *The Power of the Positive Woman,* 1977.

SCHNEIDERMAN, ROSE, 1884 (Poland)–Aug. 11, 1972. U.S. labor leader. One of the best-known U.S. trade unionists. Only eastern organizer of the Women's Trade Union League, 1917–19; elected natl. pres. of Natl. Women's Trade Union League, 1928; secy. of New York State Dept. of Labor, 1937–44.

SCHWEITZER, ALBERT, Jan. 14, 1875 (Kayerberg, Alsace |now France|)–Sept. 4, 1965. French theologian, musician, medical missionary. An inspiring figure who gave up the life of a brilliant scholar and musician to become a medical missionary in Africa; set up a native hospital at Lambarene in French Equatorial Africa, 1913; espoused a philosophy of "reverence for life"; a great organist who wrote a biography of J. S. BACH.

SCOTT, DRED, 1795?–1858. U.S. black slave who sued for his freedom (1846), claiming that his residence in a free state and a free territory had made him a free man; U.S. Sup. Ct. ruled against him in a decision that made slavery legal in the territories and inflamed passions on both sides of the issue.

SEQUOYA (or Sequoyah), a.k.a. George Guess, c. 1770 (Taskigi, Tenn.)–Aug. 1843. American Indian scholar. Created the Cherokee syllabary (85 characters) that enabled many Cherokees to read and write; sequoia tree and Sequoia Natl. Park are named after him.

SIEYES, EMMANUEL JOSEPH, called Abbé Sieyes, May 3, 1748 (Frejus, Fr.)–June 20, 1836. French Revolutionary leader. Author of "What Is the Third Estate?" (1789), delineating a concept of popular sovereignty that fueled the bourgeois revolt; one of the chief organizers of the coup d'etat that brought NAPOLEON BONAPARTE to power, 1799.

SMEAL, ELEANOR CUTRI, Jan. 30, 1939 (Ashtabula, Ohio). U.S. housewife. Pres. of National Org. of Women (NOW), 1977–   ; the organization's first salaried pres.

SMITH, ROBERT HOLBROOK, Aug. 8, 1879 (St. Johnsbury, Vt.)–Nov. 6, 1950. U.S. reformer. With WILLIAM G. WILSON, founded Alcoholics Anonymous, a self-help organization, 1935.

SPARTACUS, ? (Thrace)–71 B.C. Roman slave. Leader of the Gladiatorial War (73–71 B.C.), in which he gathered an army of slaves and overran southern Italy, before he was finally defeated and killed.

STANTON, ELIZABETH CADY, Nov. 12, 1815 (Johnstown, N.Y.)–Oct. 26, 1902. U.S. reformer. A leader of the woman-suffrage movement who helped organize the Seneca Falls, N.Y., convention (1848), the first ever dealing with women's rights; insisted that suffrage was the key to all other rights

for women; editor of *Revolution,* a militant feminist publication, 1868–70; pres. of Natl. Woman Suffrage Assn., 1868–70; associated with L. MOTT and S. B. ANTHONY.

STEINEM, GLORIA, Mar. 25, 1934 (Toledo, Ohio). U.S. feminist, writer, lecturer. A founder of the Women's Political Caucus (1971) and Women's Active Alliance (1970); a founder and editor of *Ms.* magazine, 1972–   .

STONE, LUCY, Aug. 13, 1818 (W. Brookfield, Mass.)–Oct. 18, 1893. U.S. reformer. A leader in the women's-rights movement; lectured widely against slavery; helped establish the American-Woman Suffrage Assn., whose strategy was to gain suffrage for women by state legislation, 1869; founded *Woman's Journal,* 1870; refused to give up her name when she married. (Wife of HENRY BROWNE BLACKWELL.)

SZOLD, HENRIETTA, Dec. 21, 1860 (Baltimore, Md.)–Feb. 13, 1945. U.S. Zionist leader. Founding pres. of Hadassah, a U.S. women's Zionist org. dedicated to health work in Palestine (now Israel) and the largest women's org. in the U.S. today.

TAYLOR, GRAHAM, May 2, 1851 (Schenectady, N.Y.)–Sept. 26, 1938. U.S. clergyman, sociologist. Innovator in social work in Chicago, Ill.; founded the forerunner of the U. of Chicago School of Social Work; professor of social economics, Chicago Theological Seminary; founded Chicago Commons, an early social settlement, 1894.

TERRELL, MARY CHURCH, Sept. 23, 1863 (Memphis, Tenn.)–July 24, 1954. U.S. educator, civil-rights leader. The first black woman to serve on the Dist. of Columbia Board of Ed., 1895–1911; first pres. of National Assn. of Colored Women, 1896–1901; challenged several discriminatory organizations, including American Assn. of U. Women, opening them up to blacks.

THOMAS, NORMAN MATTOON, Nov. 20, 1884 (Marion,Ohio)–Dec. 19, 1968. U.S. socialist leader, reformer, editor, minister. Codir. of League for Industrial Democracy, 1922–23; helped found ACLU, 1920; socialist candidate for pres., 1928, 1932, 1936, 1940, 1944, and 1948; a pacifist. *America's Way Out—A Program for Democracy,* 1930.

TOBIN, DANIEL JOSEPH, Apr. 1875 (County Clare, Ire.)–Nov. 14, 1955. U.S. labor leader. As pres. of Internatl. Brotherhood of Teamsters, Chauffeurs, Warehousemen and Helpers of America (1907–52), oversaw massive growth of the union into the largest in the U.S.; worked for labor reunification; prominent in the AFL and Democratic party.

TOWNSEND, FRANCIS EVERETT, Jan 13, 1867 (Fairbury, Ill.)–Sept. 1, 1960. Originator and head of Old-Age Revolving Pensions, Inc. (1934), an old-age pension plan that gained immense popular support and helped win support for a federal Social Security program.

TOWNSEND, WILLARD SAXBY, Dec. 4, 1895 (Cincinnati, Ohio)–Feb. 3, 1957. U.S. labor leader. As international pres. of United Transport Service Employees of America (1940–57), was the first black on the CIO exec. board and first black exec. of a national union that included whites.

TRUTH, SOJOURNER, legally, Isabella Van Wagener, c.1797 (Ulster Co., N.Y.)–Nov. 26, 1883. U.S. abolitionist, reformer. A freed slave, she traveled widely in the North preaching emancipation and women's rights; a moving orator who claimed divine inspiration; renamed herself Sojourner Truth as a reflection of the message she preached.

TUBMAN, HARRIET, c.1820 (Dorchester Co., Md.)–Mar. 10, 1913. U.S. abolitionist. Called the "Moses of Her People," a black slave who became a prominent abolitionist prior to the Civil War; as a leader of the "Underground RR," helped more than 300 slaves to escape.

WALD, LILLIAN D., Mar. 10, 1867 (Cincinnati, Ohio)–Sept. 1, 1940. U.S. social worker, nurse. The founder of New York City's Henry Street Settlement, 1893; initiated the first city school-nurse service, 1902; encouraged establishment of U.S. Children's Bureau (founded 1912). *The House on Henry Street,* 1915; *Windows on Henry Street,* 1934.

WEBB, BEATRICE, née Potter, Jan. 22, 1858 (Gloucester, Eng.)–Apr. 30, 1943, and husband **SIDNEY JAMES WEBB,** 1st Baron Passfield, July 13, 1859 (London, Eng.)–Oct. 13, 1947. English socialists, economists. Coauthored many works on labor history and economics; founded the London School of Economics, 1895; founded the *New Statesman,* 1913; leaders of the Fabian Soc. and the Labor movement. *The Cooperative Movement in Great Britain* (Beatrice alone), 1891; *Facts for Socialists* (Sidney alone), 1887; *The History of Trade Unionism,* 1894; *Industrial Democracy,* 1897.

WHITE, WALTER FRANCIS, July 1, 1893 (Atlanta, Ga.)–Mar. 21, 1955. U.S. black leader, author. As exec. secy. of NAACP (1931–55), waged a long campaign against lynching of blacks by white mobs. *Five in the Flint,* 1924; *Rope and Faggot: A Biography of Judge Lynch,* 1929; *A Man Called White,* 1948.

WILKINS, ROY, Aug. 30, 1901 (St. Louis, Mo.). U.S. civil rights leader. Considered the senior statesman of the U.S. civil-rights movement; as exec. dir. of NAACP (1965–77), sought equal rights via legal redress.

WILLARD, FRANCES ELIZABETH CAROLINE, Sept. 28, 1839 (Churchville, N.Y.)–Feb. 18, 1898. U.S. reformer. Pres. of Women's Christian Temperance Union, 1879–98; founder and first pres. of World's Women's Christian Temperance Union, 1883; a leader of the Natl. Prohibition Party.

WILSON, WILLIAM GRIFFITH, Nov. 26, 1895 (E. Dorset, Vt.)–Jan. 24, 1971. U.S. reformer.

Cofounded (with ROBERT HOLBROOK SMITH), Alcoholics Anonymous, a self-help organization, 1935; his wife, Lois Burnham Wilson, founded Al-Anon for spouses of alcoholics and Alateen for children of alcoholics.

WITTENMYER, ANNIE TURNER, Aug. 26, 1827 (Sandy Springs, Ohio)–Feb. 2, 1906. U.S. social reformer. Headed Union Army kitchens during the Civil War and ministered to the sick and wounded; established and edited *The Christian Woman,* 1871–82; first pres. of the Natl. Woman's Christian Temperance Union, 1874–79. *History of the Woman's Temperance Crusade,* 1882.

WOLD, EMMA, Sept. 29, 1871 (Norway, S.D.)–July 21, 1950. U.S. lawyer, reformer. Women's-rights activist, affiliated with the National Woman's Party from 1920; authority on women's rights in the Americas. *A Comparison of the Political and Civil Rights of Men and Women in the United States,* 1936.

WOODHULL, VICTORIA, née Claflin, Sept. 23, 1838 (Homer, Ohio)–June 10, 1927. U.S. social reformer. An unconventional reformer, claimed to experience visions (from 1841), gave spiritualistic exhibitions in Ohio; with her sister Tennessee, opened stock-brokerage office supported by CORNELIUS VANDERBILT, 1868; founded *Woodhull & Claflin's Weekly* advocating equal rights for women, free love, and single moral standard, 1870; first woman candidate for U.S. pres. (Equal Rights party), 1872. *Origin, Tendencies and Principles of Government,* 1871; *The Human Body; The Temple of God,* 1890.

WRIGHT, FRANCES ("Fanny"), Sept. 6, 1795 (Dundee, Scot.)–Dec. 13, 1852. Scottish-U.S. reformer. Noted as the author of one of the most celebrated travel memoirs of the 19th cent., *Views of Society and Manners in America* (1821); a close friend of the MARQUIS DE LAFAYETTE, whom she joined in a triumphal 1824–25 tour of the U.S.; first woman lecturer in the U.S.

YOUNG, WHITNEY MOORE, JR., July 31, 1921 (Lincoln Ridge, Ky.)–Mar. 11, 1971. U.S. civil-rights leader. As exec. dir. of the Natl. Urban League (1961–1971), promoted its programs to improve opportunities for blacks in housing, employment, and social welfare.

BUSINESS LEADERS

ALLERTON, SAMUEL WATERS, May 26, 1828 (Amenia, N.Y.)–Feb. 22, 1914. U.S. financier. With John B. Sherman, founded Chicago Union Stockyards, 1865; a leader in the development of modern Chicago.

ANDERSON, ROBERT ORVILLE, Apr. 13, 1917 (Chicago, Ill.). U.S. oil-industry exec. Chm. of the board and chief exec. officer of Atlantic Richfield Co., a major oil concern, 1963– .

ANDERSON, SWAN FRITEAF, Jan. 2, 1879 (Tedaholm, Swe.)–Mar. 12, 1963. U.S. manufacturer and inventor. As exec. with Anderson Bros. Mfg. Co. (1915–63), developed dairy-product packaging machinery, including a machine for producing Eskimo Pies.

ARDEN, ELIZABETH, born Florence Nightingale (married name, Graham), 1887 (Ontario, Can.)–Oct. 18, 1966. U.S. cosmetics exec. Founder and sole owner of Elizabeth Arden, Inc.; operated salons throughout the U.S., Canada, and Europe; sought to improve the safety of cosmetics.

ARKWRIGHT, SIR RICHARD, Dec. 23, 1732

(Preston, Eng.)–Aug. 3, 1792. English textile manufacturer. Through his use of power-driven machinery, developed cotton-cloth manufacture as principal industry in northern England in late 1770s; invented machinery for spinning cotton yarn that revolutionized textile industry.

ARMOUR, PHILIP DANFORTH, May 16, 1832 (Stockbridge, N.Y.)–Jan. 6, 1901. U.S. meat-packing exec. Pres. of Armour & Co. of Chicago, 1875–1901; introduced on-premise slaughtering and utilization of animal waste; one of first to use refrigerator cars to transport meat cross-country and to make canned-meat products.

ASTOR, JOHN JACOB, July 17, 1763 (Heidelberg, Ger.)–Mar. 29, 1848. U.S. businessman. Founder of an American financial and social dynasty; after emigration to U.S. in 1784, amassed a fortune trading furs all over North America; at his retirement (1834), the richest man in the U.S.

AUSTIN, HERBERT, 1866 (Little Missenden, Eng.)–May 23, 1941. English automaker. Worked in Australia as an engineer, 1883–90; returned to

England and formed the auto-making concern that would become Austin-Healey, makers of sports cars, 1905.

AYER, FRANCIS WAYLAND, Feb. 4, 1848 (Lee, Mass.)-Mar. 5, 1923. U.S. advertising pioneer. Founded advertising firm N.W. Ayer, 1869; first to do market research for clients; pioneer in use of trademarks, slogans, and ad copy.

AYER, HARRIET, née Hubbard, June 27, 1849 (Chicago, Ill.)-Nov. 23, 1903. U.S. manufacturer, writer. After collapse of her husband's business, began to manufacture her own skin cream, Recamier, for which she wrote advertising using testimonials from well-known entertainers and socialites; in plot by financial backers to discredit her and seize business, she was sued, slandered, and kept in an insane asylum; upon release, lectured on "14 Months in a Madhouse"; wrote beauty column for newspapers. *Harriet Hubbard Ayer's Book of Health and Beauty,* 1902.

BACHE, HAROLD LEOPOLD, June 17, 1894 (New York, N.Y.)-Mar. 14, 1968. U.S. stockbroker. Senior partner in J. S. Bache and Co., 1945-68.

BAER, GEORGE FREDERICK, Sept. 26, 1842 (Somerset, Pa.)-Apr. 26, 1914. U.S. railroad exec. Close financial adviser to J. P. MORGAN; pres. of Reading Railway Co. and Central Railway Co., from 1901; prominent figure in 1902 coal strike, the first test of the nascent United Mine Workers.

BAMBERGER, LOUIS, May 15, 1855 (Baltimore, Md.)-Mar. 11, 1944. U.S. retailer. Founded L. Bamberger & Co. dept. stores (now a division of Macy's) in Newark, N.J., 1892; founded New York City radio station WOR, 1922; founded Princeton U.'s Inst. for Advanced Study, 1933.

BARTON, BRUCE, Aug. 5, 1886 (Robbins, Tenn.)-July 5, 1967. U.S. advertising exec. A founder of Batten, Barton, Durstine and Osborne (1918), which he built into an industry leader; as U.S. rep. (R, N.Y.; 1937-41), a leader of opposition to Pres. F. D. ROOSEVELT's New Deal policies. *The Man Nobody Knows,* 1925; *The Book Nobody Knows,* 1926.

BARTON, ENOS MELANCTHON, Dec. 2, 1842 (Lorraine, N.Y.)-May 3, 1916. U.S. manufacturer. With Elisha Gray and Anson Stager, founded Western Electric Co., 1872.

BARUCH, BERNARD MANNES, Aug. 19, 1870 (Camden, S.C.)-June 20, 1965. U.S. financier, public official. Made fortune in stock market (1889-1913), then devoted himself to public service; respected adviser to every president from W. WILSON to J. F. KENNEDY; author of the Baruch Plan for international development and control of atomic energy, 1946.

BASSETT, HARRY HOXIE, Sept. 11, 1875 (Utica, N.Y.)-Oct. 17, 1926. U.S. auto manufacturer. As pres. of Buick Motor Co. (1920-26), developed firm into number two automaker in the U.S.

BAY, JOSEPHINE HOLT, née Perfect, Aug. 10, 1900 (Anamosa, Idaho). U.S. stockbroker. In 1956, as pres. and chm. of A. M. Kidder and Co., became first woman ever to head member firm of NYSE.

BEECH, OLIVE ANN, née Mellor, Sept. 25, 1903 (Waverly, Kan.). U.S. aircraft industry exec. With husband WALTER H. BEECH, founded Beech Aircraft Corp., 1932; following her husband's death (1950), became pres., board chm., and chief exec. officer of Beech; under her guidance, sales rose from $74 million in 1963 to $267 million in 1975; retired since 1968, remains active in day-to-day operations.

BEECH, WALTER HERSCHEL, Jan. 30, 1891 (Pulaski, Tenn.)-Nov. 29, 1950. U.S. manufacturer. Founder and pres. of Beech Aircraft Corp. (1936-50), which manufactures planes for commercial and private use. (Husband of OLIVE ANN BEECH.)

BEHN, SOSTHENES, Jan. 30, 1882 (St. Thomas, V. I.)-June 6, 1957. U.S. telephone exec. Founder, pres., and chm. of the board of ITT, 1920-56.

BELMONT, AUGUST, Feb. 18, 1853 (New York, N.Y.)-Dec. 10, 1924. U.S. banker. Through family banking firm, financed much of construction of New York City's IRT subway system, 1900; financed Cape Cod Canal, 1914; a renowned horseman, owned illustrious horses including MAN O' WAR; Belmont Stakes and Belmont Racetrack named in his family's honor.

BENDIX, VINCENT, Aug. 12, 1882 (Moline, Ill.)-Mar. 27, 1945. U.S. inventor, industrialist. Pioneer automotive and aviation manufacturer; invented an automobile self-starter; founder, Bendix Aviation Corp., 1929; founder of the Transcontinental Air Race (1931) and donor of the Bendix Trophy.

BERNBACH, WILLIAM, Aug. 31, 1911 (New York, N.Y.). U.S. advertising exec. Principal in Doyle-Dane-Bernbach advertising agency, 1949- ; credited with introducing low-pressure, uncluttered advertising; responsible for Avis Rent-a-Car slogan, "When you're only number two, you try harder."

BICH, MARCEL, July 29, 1914 (Turin, It.). U.S. manufacturer. Founder, pres., and chm. of the board of Bic Pen Corp., manufacturers of inexpensive ballpoint pens and lighters, 1950- .

BIDDLE, NICHOLAS, Jan. 8, 1786 (Philadelphia, Pa.)-Feb. 27, 1844. U.S. financier. After pursuing careers as lawyer, diplomat, and publisher, appointed (1819) by Pres. JAMES MONROE as a dir. of the U.S. Bank, which he served as pres. (1823-39) during period when the government withdrew its deposits (1833), setting off banking "war."

BIGELOW, ERASTUS BRIGHAM, Apr. 2, 1814 (W. Boylston, Mass.)-Dec. 6, 1879. U.S. textile manufacturer, inventor. Invented several types of power looms for specialty work, especially the manufacture of carpets; founded Bigelow carpet mills, c.1850; a founder of MIT.

BIRCH, STEPHEN, Mar. 24, 1872 (New York, N.Y.)-Dec. 29, 1940. U.S. mining exec. As pres. of Kennecott Copper Corp. (1915-33), developed firm into one of the world's largest mining concerns.

BIRDSEYE, CLARENCE, Dec. 9, 1886 (New York, N.Y.)-Oct. 7, 1956. U.S. businessman, inventor. Invented a quick-freeze process, an infrared heat lamp, and other items; founded Gen. Seafoods, later Gen. Foods Corp.

BISHOP, HAZEL GLADYS, Aug. 17, 1906 (Hoboken, N.J.). U.S. chemist, cosmetics manufacturer. Founded Hazel Bishop, Inc., and marketed first "no-smear" lipstick, 1950; financial analyst of cosmetic and health-related stocks, 1968- ; head, cosmetic marketing program, Fashion Institute of Technology, 1978- ; first to occupy Revlon Chair, FIT, 1979.

BISSELL, GEORGE HENRY, Nov. 8, 1821 (Hanover, N.H.)-Nov. 19, 1884. U.S. oil man. Organized Pennsylvania Rock Oil Co., first oil company in the U.S., to develop Pennsylvania's Oil Creek region, 1854; the first to suggest drilling for oil, rather than surface mining.

BISSELL, RICHARD MERVIN, June 8, 1862 (Chicago, Ill.)-July 18, 1941. U.S. insurance exec. Organized more successful insurance companies than anyone else in the industry (Aetna, Connecticut Gen.); pres. of Hartford Insurance Co., 1913-41; a founder of Chicago Symphony Orchestra, 1891.

BLOOMINGDALE, JOSEPH BERNARD, Dec. 22, 1842 (New York, N.Y.)–Nov. 21, 1904. U.S. merchant. With his brother, founded Bloomingdale's dept. store, 1872; a progressive turn-of-the-cent. employer, he instituted a 10-hour workday and a half-day off per week.

BLOUGH, ROGER M., Jan. 19, 1904 (Riverside, Pa.). U.S. corp. lawyer, steel exec., philanthropist. Chm. of the board and chief exec. officer of U.S. Steel Corp., 1955-69; member of U.S. Steel Corp. exec. comm., 1956-76.

BOUTELLE, RICHARD SCHLEY, July 4, 1898 (Vincennes, Ind.)–Jan. 15, 1962. U.S. aircraft exec. At Fairchild Aviation, originated the WW II C-82 "Flying Boxcar" airplane, 1944.

BOYLE, W(illiam) A(nthony) ("Tony"), Dec. 1, 1904 (Bald Butte, Mont.). U.S. labor leader. A protégé of JOHN L. LEWIS; pres. of United Mine Workers, 1963-72; convicted of 1969 murders of union opponent JOSEPH YABLONSKI, his wife, and his daughter, 1974.

BRADY, JAMES BUCHANAN ("Diamond Jim"), Aug. 12, 1856 (New York, N.Y.)–Apr. 13, 1917. U.S. financier and bon vivant, noted for his ample girth and lavish life-style. As exclusive agent for Fox Pressed Steel Car Truck Co., amassed a fortune in commissions in 1888; organized Pressed Steel Car Co. and Standard Steel Car Co.

BRECK, JOHN HENRY, June 5, 1877 (Holyoke, Mass.)–Feb. 16, 1965. U.S. cosmetics manufacturer. Researched hair and scalp conditions to produce shampoos and other hair-care products sold through John H. Breck Co., founded 1908.

BROOKINGS, ROBERT SOMERS, Jan. 22, 1850 (Cecil Co., Md.)–Nov. 15, 1932. U.S. manufacturer, philanthropist. In woodenware business, St. Louis, 1867-96; a benefactor of Washington U. and pres. of the corporation, 1897-1928; provided funds that led to creation of the Brookings Inst. for research in public affairs, 1926.

BROWN, JOHN Y., Dec. 28, 1933 (Lexington, Ky.). U.S. restaurateur. Instrumental in founding Kentucky Fried Chicken, Inc., served as pres. (1964-71) and chm. of the bd. (1971-74); also owns Lum's and Ollie's Trolley restaurants; owner, Boston Celtics, 1978-79; gov. of Kentucky, 1979- .

BRYANT, LANE, born Lena Himmelstein, Dec. 1, 1879 (Lithuania)–Sept. 26, 1951. U.S. merchant. Began as seamstress of maternity clothes and lingerie; opened store that became flagship of Lane Bryant chain, first to sell ready-to-wear stout-women's and maternity clothes, 1904.

BUDD, RALPH, Aug. 20, 1879 (Waterloo, Iowa)–Feb. 2, 1962. U.S. railroad exec. Introduced first diesel-powered, streamlined passenger trains, 1935; pres. of both Great Northern and Burlington RRs.

BULOVA, ARDE, Oct. 24, 1889 (New York, N.Y.)–Mar. 19, 1958. U.S. manufacturer. Developed family-owned Bulova Watch Co.; standardized numerous aspects of watchmaking process; began manufacturing portable radios in early 1930s; originated spot advertising on radio, 1926.

BURPEE, DAVID, Apr. 5, 1893 (Philadelphia, Pa.). U.S. seed-products exec. Chief exec. officer of family-owned Atlee Burpee Seed Co., 1915-70; as plant breeder, created and introduced numerous new hybrid flowers and vegetables, including Ford-

hook lima beans, Spencer sweet peas, and Dutch tulip bulbs. (Son of WASHINGTON A. BURPEE.)

BURPEE, WASHINGTON ATLEE, Apr. 5, 1858 (Sheffield, N.B., Can.)–Nov. 26, 1915. U.S. seed-products exec. Founded first successful mail-order seed business, 1878; first to introduce bush lima beans, 1890; responsible for developing cultivation of many new hybrid vegetables and flowers. (Father of DAVID BURPEE.)

BUSCH, ADOLPHUS, July 10, 1839 (Mainz, Ger.)–Oct. 10, 1913. U.S. brewery exec. With father-in-law Eberhard Anheuser, founded Anheuser-Busch brewery in St. Louis, 1861; pioneered pasteurization of beer, making long-distance unrefrigerated shipping possible.

CANDLER, ASA GRIGGS, Dec. 30, 1851 (nr. Villa Rica, Ga.)–Mar. 12, 1929. U.S. businessman. Originally a pharmacist, he purchased formula for Coca-Cola, introduced some changes in the process, and sold it to soda fountains; its phenomenal success allowed him by 1890 to concentrate full-time on Coca-Cola, which grew to be one of most prosperous companies in the South; mayor of Atlanta, Ga., 1917-18; a major benefactor of Emory U.

CARLAN, BOGART, Mar. 28, 1904 (Minneapolis, Minn.)–Feb. 12, 1979. U.S. advertising exec. Associated with several major advertising agencies including J. Walter Thompson, and Foote, Cone, Belding, and Ted Bates & Co., 1925-66; originated "Umm, umm good" slogan for Campbell's Soup, among other product slogans.

CARLTON, RICHARD PAUL, Dec. 20, 1893 (Minneapolis, Minn.)–June 17, 1953. U.S. manufacturer. Rose through ranks of Minnesota Mining & Manufacturing to become pres., 1949-53; helped introduce Scotch tape, Scotch magnetic tape, and Scotchlite reflector tape.

CARNEGIE, ANDREW, Nov. 25, 1835 (Dunfermline, Scot.)–Aug. 11, 1919. U.S. industrialist, philanthropist. Though poor and poorly educated, rose quickly from position as a Pittsburgh telegraph-office messenger to superintendent of the Pennsylvania RR; formed Keystone Bridge Co., 1865; became chief owner of Homestead Steel Works (1888) and controlled seven other steel manufacturers, all of which he consolidated into Carnegie Steel Co., 1899; sold out to U.S. Steel, for $250 million, 1901; endowed over 2,800 libraries, Carnegie Fndn. (1905), Carnegie Endowment (1910), and Carnegie Corp. (1911). *Wealth,* 1889.

CESSNA, CLYDE VERNON, Dec. 5, 1879 (Hawthorne, Ia.)–Nov. 20, 1954. U.S. aircraft manufacturer. Built first cantilever airplane, 1927; founded Cessna Airplane Co., 1927; supplied airplanes to Curtiss Flying Service, an early airline.

CHENEY, BENJAMIN PIERCE, Aug. 12, 1815 (Hillsboro, N.H.)–July 23, 1895. U.S. business exec. Beginning as a New England stagecoach driver in 1830s, parlayed an express-company run between Boston and Montreal into a business that grew into the American Express Co., 1879.

CHILDS, SAMUEL SHANNON, Apr. 4, 1863 (Basking Ridge, N.J.)–Mar. 17, 1925. U.S. restaurateur. With only $1,600 in capital, founded nationwide Childs Restaurant chain, 1888; introduced such innovations as waitresses and calorie-counts on menus.

CHRYSLER, WALTER PERCY, Apr. 2, 1875 (Wamego, Kan.)–Aug. 18, 1940. U.S. industrialist. By introducing (1924) a six-cylinder auto, turned the economically-troubled Maxwell Car Co. into the highly prosperous Chrysler Corp.; built Chrysler Bldg. in New York City, 1930.

COFFIN, CHARLES ALBERT, Dec. 30, 1844 (Somerset Co., Me.)–July 14, 1926. U.S. manufacturer. In 1892, merged two firms to create Gen. Electric, which he headed until 1922; credited with development of electrical industry in U.S.

COHEN, OTTO, 1883 (New York, N.Y.)–Apr. 25, 1979. U.S. cosmetics exec. One of the founders of the Charles of the Ritz Cosmetics Co., 1927; credited with being the first to put quality cosmetics into dept. stores, and with creating special training for salespeople to promote the cosmetics.

COLGATE, WILLIAM, Jan. 25, 1783 (Hollingbourn, Eng.)–Mar. 25, 1857. U.S. manufacturer, philanthropist. Founded soap-and-perfume firm that became the Colgate-Palmolive Co., 1806; one of the founders of the American Bible Union, 1850; contributed land to Madison U, which was renamed Colgate U. (1890) in honor of his family.

COLLIER, BARRON GIFT, Mar. 23, 1873 (Memphis, Tenn.)–Mar. 13, 1939. U.S. business exec., financier. Founder of Barron G. Collier, Inc., advertising agency, 1900; first to place advertising placards in subways in major cities; leader in reclamation of Florida Everglades swampland and completion of the Tamiami Trail.

COOKE, JAY, Aug. 10, 1821 (Sandusky, Ohio)–Feb. 18, 1905. U.S. financier. Partner in Philadelphia investment-banking firm, 1842-58; formed Jay Cooke & Co. banking house, 1861; floated $3 million Civil War loan to Pennsylvania; sold a $500 million U.S. bond issue (1862) and an $830 million U.S. bond issue (1865), to aid Union in the Civil War; his financial failure in 1873 precipitated severe financial panic; recouped fortune in Utah mining investments.

COOPER, PETER, Feb. 12, 1791 (New York, N.Y.)–Apr. 4, 1883. U.S. inventor, manufacturer, philanthropist. Built (1828) Canton ironworks in Baltimore, Md., where he designed and constructed first U.S. steam locomotive, the "Tom Thumb," 1830; built first rolling mill, in New York City, 1836; made first iron structural beams, at Trenton, N.J., mill, 1854; first to use Bessemer process, 1856; active in laying first transatlantic cable; founded Cooper Union educational institution, 1859.

COREY, WILLIAM ELLIS, May 4, 1866 (Braddock, Pa.)–May 11, 1934. U.S. industrialist. Second pres. of U.S. Steel Corp., 1903-11; instrumental in building city of Gary, Ind., and making U.S. Steel the largest steel-producer in the U.S.

CORMACK, GEORGE, June 17, 1870 (Aberdeen, Scot.)–Sept. 26, 1953. U.S. cereal manufacturer. As head miller at Washburn Crosby Co., (predecessor of Gen. Mills), invented Wheaties, 1924.

CORNELL, EZRA, Jan. 11, 1807 (Westchester Landing, N.Y.)–Dec. 9, 1874. U.S. capitalist, philanthropist. Organized Western Union Telegraph Co., 1855; founded Cornell U., 1862.

COWEN, JOSHUA LIONEL, Aug. 25, 1880 (New York, N.Y.)–Sept. 8, 1965. U.S. business exec., inventor. Invented toy electric train, 1900; headed Lionel Corp., 1945-65; invented the flashlight, a detonator, and one of the first dry-cell batteries.

CROCKER, CHARLES, Sept. 16, 1822 (Troy, N.Y.)–Aug. 14, 1888. U.S. railroad exec. Sought gold in California, 1849-50; joined LELAND STANFORD, Collis P. Huntington, and MARK HOPKINS to head construction of California Pacific RR, 1863-69; pres. of Southern Pacific RR, 1871-88; effected merger of California Pacific and Southern Pacific RRs, 1884.

CROSLEY, POWEL, JR., Sept. 18, 1886 (Cincinnati, Ohio)–Mar. 28, 1961. U.S. industrialist. Manufactured the vacuum-tube socket, the first popularly-priced piece of radio equipment; invented and manufactured Crosley autos; pres., The Crosley Corp., 1921-45; pres., Crosley Motors, 1945-52.

CUDAHY, EDWARD ALOYSIUS, Feb. 1, 1859 (Milwaukee, Wisc.)–Oct. 18, 1941. U.S. meat packer. Associated with his brother MICHAEL CUDAHY in Armour & Co. 1875-87; pres. (1887-1926) and chm. (1926-41) of Cudahy Packing Co.

CUDAHY, MICHAEL, Dec. 7, 1841 (Callan, Ire.)–Nov. 27, 1910. U.S. meat-packer. Partner in Armour & Co., 1875; instrumental in first use of refrigeration in meat-packing industry; formed Armour-Cudahy (1887), which became Cudahy Packing Co. (1890) when it parted from Armour. (Brother of EDWARD CUDAHY.)

CULLEN, HUGH ROY, July 3, 1881 (Denton Co., Tex.)–July 4, 1957. U.S. oilman. Discovered and developed much of the oil resources in the Houston, Tex. (including the fabulously rich Thompson field, 1930), area for Humble Oil, Gulf Oil, and other companies.

CUNARD, SIR SAMUEL, Nov. 21, 1787 (Halifax, N.S., Can.)–Apr. 28, 1865. Canadian shipowner. Founded British steamship company bearing his name, 1839; inaugurated first regular trans-Atlantic mail service, 1840; created baronet, 1859.

CURRAN, JOSEPH EDWIN, Mar. 1, 1906 (New York, N.Y.). U.S. labor leader. Organizer and first pres. of the National Maritime Union, 1937–

DALY, MARCUS, Dec. 5, 1841 (Ireland)–Nov. 12, 1900. U.S. mining exec. His discovery of copper (c.1876) in Anaconda silver mine led to formation of Anaconda Mining Co.; a major figure in Montana politics, 1888-1909.

DAMON, RALPH SHEPARD, July 6, 1897 (Franklin, N.H.)–Jan. 4, 1956. U.S. airline exec. Pres. of Curtiss-Wright Airplane Co., 1935; pres. of Trans World Airlines, 1949-56; developed the Condor airplane, the first "skysleeper," 1933.

DAWES, HENRY MAY, Apr. 22, 1877 (Marietta, Ohio)–Sept. 29, 1952. U.S. oil exec. U.S. comptroller of the currency, 1921-28; pres. and chm. of Pure Oil Co., 1924-52. (Brother of CHARLES G. DAWES.)

DODGE, HORACE ELGIN, May 17, 1868 (Niles, Mich.)–Dec. 10, 1920. U.S. manufacturer. Engineering genius of the Dodge Co., he is credited with developing the first midrange, midprice automobile. (Brother of JOHN F. DODGE.)

DODGE, JOHN FRANCIS, Oct. 25, 1864 (Niles, Mich.)–Jan. 14, 1920. U.S. manufacturer. The business and organizational genius behind the creation of the Dodge Co., 1901. (Brother of HORACE E. DODGE.)

DODGE, JOSEPH MORRELL, Nov. 18, 1890 (Detroit, Mich.)–Dec. 2, 1964. U.S. banker, govt. official. As financial adviser to U.S. military govt. in Germany, initiated plans for reform of German currency and establishment of a West German central bank, 1945-46; in a similar capacity, helped rebuild and reorganize Japan's economy.

DOHENY, EDWARD LAWRENCE, Aug. 10, 1856 (Fond du Lac, Wisc.)–Sept. 8, 1935. U.S. oilman. A major figure in Teapot Dome oil leasing scandal of 1921-24; with HARRY SINCLAIR of Sinclair Oil, obtained a lease of public lands in Wyoming and drilled for oil for their own benefit; Secy. of Interior ALBERT FALL was forced to resign as a result of granting the lease.

DOHERTY, HENRY LATHAM, May 15, 1870

195

THE BOOK OF WHO

(Columbus, Ohio)–Dec. 26, 1939. U.S. industrialist. In 1910, created Cities Service Co., which eventually controlled the oil, natural gas, and electric-power properties in 33 states and several foreign countries.

DONNELLEY, THOMAS ELLIOT, Aug. 18, 1867 (Chicago, Ill.)–Feb. 6, 1955. U.S. printer. Developed family firm R. R. Donnelley & Sons into major printing firm, introducing an apprentice-training program, incentives for employees, and the first cost-accounting system in the U.S. printing industry.

DOUGLAS, DONALD WILLIS, Apr. 6, 1892 (Brooklyn, N.Y.). U.S. aircraft manufacturer. Founded Douglas Aircraft, 1920; produced the Cloudster, the first streamlined plane and the first plane featuring gas-dump valves and an effective instrument panel, 1920; produced the DC series for commercial airlines and bombers for U.S. govt.

DOW, HERBERT HENRY, Feb. 26, 1866 (Belleville, Ont., Can.)–Oct. 15, 1930. U.S. chemist. Founded the Dow Chemical Co. (1890) upon developing a new method for manufacturing bromine from brine.

DRAKE, EDWIN LAURENTINE, Mar. 29, 1819 (Greenville, N.Y.)–Nov. 8, 1880. U.S. oil-industry pioneer. Became first person to tap an oil reservoir by drilling when he struck oil at 69 ft. in Titusville, Pa., Aug. 27, 1859.

DREYFUS, PIERRE, Nov. 18, 1907 (Paris, Fr.). French industrialist. Pres. of Regie Nationale des Usine Renault, manufacturers of Renault automobiles, 1949–

DUKE, BENJAMIN NEWTON, Apr. 27, 1855 (Durham, N.C.)–Jan. 8, 1929. U.S. tobacco-products manufacturer, philanthropist. Principal exec. of W. Duke & Sons (1885–1929) and American Tobacco Co. (1890–1929); a major benefactor of Duke U. (Brother of JAMES BUCHANAN DUKE.)

DUKE, JAMES BUCHANAN, Dec. 23, 1856 (nr. Durham, N.C.)–Oct. 10, 1925. U.S. tobacco-products manufacturer. With his brother BENJAMIN NEWTON DUKE, founded tobacco-manufacturing firms that became (1890) American Tobacco Co., which he served as pres. from 1890 until 1911, when U.S. Supr. Ct. ordered break-up of the huge combine; a major benfactor of Duke U.

DU PONT, ÉLEUTHÈRE IRÉNÉE, June 24, 1771 (Paris, Fr.)–Oct. 31, 1834. French-U.S. manufacturer. Worked under ANTOINE LAVOISIER at French royal gunpowder works in Essone, 1788–91; operated family publishing house, 1788–91; built E. I. Du Pont de Nemours, a gunpowder manufacturing plant, nr. Wilmington, Del., 1802; sold his first gunpowder in 1804 and thereafter was extremely successful; chief powdermaker for U.S. in War of 1812 and after. (Son of PIERRE S. DU PONT DE NEMOURS; great grandfather of THOMAS C. DU PONT and PIERRE S. DU PONT.)

DU PONT, PIERRE SAMUEL, Jan. 15, 1870 (Wilmington, Del.)–Apr. 5, 1954. U.S. industrialist. Pres. (1915–19) and chm. of the board (1919–40) of E. I. Du Pont de Nemours; codeveloper of smokeless shotgun powder, 1893. (Great grandson of E. I. DU PONT.)

DU PONT, THOMAS COLEMAN, Dec. 11, 1863 (Louisville, Ky.)–Nov. 11, 1930. U.S. manufacturer. Consolidated all companies controlled by E. I Du Pont de Nemours into one corp. (1902–07), developing it into one of the largest trusts in the U.S. (Great grandson of E. I. DU PONT.)

DURANT, THOMAS CLARK, Feb. 6, 1820 (Lee, Mass.)–Oct. 5, 1885. U.S. railroad magnate. Constructed Michigan Southern RR and other Midwest lines; a chief organizer of the Union Pacific RR, (1862), which he served as pres. until his involvement in Credit Mobilier stock scandal forced him from office in 1867 and off the board of directors in 1869.

DURANT, WILLIAM CRAPO, Dec. 8, 1861 (Boston, Mass.)–Mar. 17, 1947. U.S. auto manufacturer. A founder of Durant-Dort Carriage Co., 1886; organized Buick Motor Co. (1905), Gen. Motors Co. (1908), and Chevrolet (1915); held controlling interest in GM, 1915–20; founded Durant Motors, Inc., 1921.

EATON, CYRUS STEPHEN, Dec. 27, 1883 (Pugwash, N.S., Can.)–May 9, 1979. U.S. industrialist. Protégé of JOHN D. ROCKEFELLER: parlayed a Canadian power-plant franchise into a fortune; developed Continental Gas and Electric, 1912; entered steel industry, taking over Trumbull Steel (1925) and helping to bring about the formation of Republic Steel (1930); lost $100 million of his personal fortune in stock-market crash of 1929; known for his strong advocacy of friendly relations with USSR and other communist countries for business purposes and to maintain world peace.

ECCLES, MARRINER STODDARD, Sept. 9, 1890 (Logan, Utah)–Dec. 18, 1977. U.S. financier, govt. official. Headed family-owned investment firm in Utah, 1929–71; member (1936–51) and chm. (1936–48) of Federal Reserve Board.

FARGO, WILLIAM GEORGE, May 20, 1818 (Pompey, N.Y.)–Aug. 3, 1881. U.S. transportation exec. Founder of American Express Co. (1844) and Wells Fargo & Co. (1851).

FERGUSON, HOMER LENOIR, Mar. 6, 1873 (Waynesville, N.C.)–Mar. 14, 1952. U.S. shipbuilder. As pres. of Newport News Shipbuilding and Dry Dock Co., built many famous ships, including S.S. *America,* S.S. *United States,* and the carriers U.S.S. *Yorktown,* U.S.S. *Ticonderoga,* U.S.S. *Hornet,* U.S.S. *Midway,* and U.S.S. *Forrestal.*

FERRARI, ENZO, Feb. 20, 1898 (Modena, It.). Italian auto manufacturer. As a sports-car racer, associated with Alfa-Romeo; founded his own auto-making firm, 1940; has produced some of the world's fastest racers and fanciest sports cars.

FIELD, CYRUS WEST, Nov. 30, 1819 (Stockbridge, Mass.)–July 12, 1892. U.S. businessman, science promoter. Spent his fortune laying the first transatlantic cable, 1866.

FIELD, MARSHALL, Aug. 18, 1834 (Conway, Mass.)–Jan. 16, 1906. U.S. merchant, philanthropist. Founder of Marshall Field & Co., Chicago's premier dept. store, 1881; introduced first in-store restaurant for customers; left a large part of his $125 million estate to U. of Chicago and the Field Museum of Natural History. (Grandfather of MARSHALL FIELD III.)

FILENE, EDWARD ALBERT, Sept. 3, 1860 (Salem, Mass.)–Sept. 26, 1937. U.S. merchant, philanthropist. With his brother Lincoln, developed family store into Filene's, a leading Boston dept. store; founded Massachusetts Credit Union Assn. (1917) and the Twentieth Century Fund (1919); with THOMAS A. EDISON, developed simultaneous translating device.

FIRESTONE, HARVEY SAMUEL, Dec. 20, 1868 (Columbiana Co., Ohio)–Feb. 7, 1938. U.S. tire manufacturer. Founded Firestone Tire & Rubber Co. in 1900, and served as its pres. and chm. until 1938; pioneered a method of making tires in continuous lengths; made first detachable tire rims; started auto supply/service chain, 1928.

FITZSIMMONS, FRANK, Apr. 7, 1908. U.S. labor leader. Vice-pres. (1961-67), gen. vice-pres. (1967-71), and pres. and chm. of the negotiating comm. (1971-   ) of Internatl. Brotherhood of Teamsters.

FLECK, SIR ALEXANDER, Nov. 11, 1889 (Glasgow, Scot.)-Aug. 6, 1968. Scottish industrialist. Chm. of Imperial Chemical Industries, Ltd., a major British chemical manufacturing concern, 1953-60; instrumental in developing polyethylene and Dacron.

FOLGER, HENRY CLAY, June 18, 1857 (New York, N.Y.)-June 11, 1930. U.S. industrialist, philanthropist. An exec. with Standard Oil Co. of New York and New Jersey, 1923-28; a collector of Shakespeariana, he built the Folger Shakespeare Library in Washington, D.C., to house his vast collection.

FOLSOM, FRANCIS MARION (Frank), May 14, 1894 (Sprague, Wash.). U.S. electronics exec. As pres. of RCA (1949-57), presided over much of firm's development in color-TV manufacture and in broadcasting.

FORD, EDSEL BRYANT, Nov. 6, 1893 (Detroit, Mich.)-May 26, 1943. U.S. auto exec. The only child of HENRY FORD, he served as president of Ford Motor Co. from 1919 to 1943; the ill-fated Edsel automobile was named after him. (Father of HENRY FORD III.)

FORD, HENRY, July 30, 1863 (Wayne Co. Mich.)-Apr. 7, 1947. U.S. auto manufacturer, the father of the mass-produced automobile. Started career as a machinist and engineer; organized Detroit Automobile Co., 1899; organized Ford Motor Co., 1903; introduced Model T, 1908; using mass-production technique, produced a car that sold for $500, 1913; bought out stockholders, becoming sole owner of Ford Motor Co., 1917; introduced Model A, 1927; introduced first V-8 engine, 1932; signed first union-shop contract in auto industry, 1941. *My Life and Work,* 1922. (Father of EDSEL B. FORD; grandfather of HENRY FORD II.)

FORD, HENRY II, Sept. 4, 1917 (Detroit, Mich.). U.S. auto exec. Chief exec. officer of Ford Motor Co., 1960-   . (Grandson of HENRY FORD; son of EDSEL B. FORD.)

FREER, CHARLES LANG, Feb. 25, 1856 (Kingston, N.Y.)-Sept. 25, 1919. U.S. industrialist, philanthropist. Made his fortune manufacturing railroad cars; retired, 1899; collected art, chiefly Chinese, amassing a collection of some 8,000 pieces that he donated to Smithsonian Inst. for display in the Freer Gallery of Art, 1906; patron of painter JAMES ABBOT MCNEILL WHISTLER.

FRICK, HENRY CLAY, Dec. 19, 1849 (W. Overton, Pa.)-Dec. 2, 1919. U.S. industrialist. Chm. of the Carnegie Steel Co. during Homestead Strike of 1892, when he was shot and stabbed by a laborer; made a fortune through stock options when he left Carnegie and doubled it when U.S. Steel Corp. absorbed Carnegie in 1901; endowed Frick Museum of Art (once his home).

FRUEHAUF, HARVEY CHARLES, Dec. 15, 1896 (Detroit, Mich.)-Oct. 14, 1968. U.S. manufacturer. A founder (1916) of Fruehauf Trailer Co., builders of one of the first "semi" trailers for hauling cargo.

FUGGER, JAKOB II ("Jakob the Rich"), 1459 (Augsburg, Ger.)-1525. German financier. Scion of the German family that owned the largest trading, mining, and banking house in 15th and 16th cent. Europe; chief financial supporter of German Emperor Maximilian I, 1490; made large loan to Henry VII of England, 1516.

FULLER, ALFRED CARL, Jan. 13, 1885 (Kings Co., N.S., Can.)-Dec. 4, 1973. U.S. manufacturer. Founder of Fuller Brush Co., 1910; invented the "twisted wire" brush and the door-to-door sales approach that made his firm a leader in the industry.

GAMBLE, JAMES NORRIS, Aug. 9, 1836 (Cincinnati, Ohio)-July 2, 1932. U.S. business exec. Became partner in family-owned Procter & Gamble Co. in 1862, later serving as a vice-pres., 1890-1932; responsible for development of Ivory soap, the first floating soap.

GARVIN, CLIFTON CANTER, JR., Dec. 22, 1921 (Portsmouth, Va.). U.S. oil exec. Chm. and chief exec. officer of Exxon Corp., 1975-   .

GARY, ELBERT HENRY, Oct. 8, 1846 (Wheaton, Ill.)-Aug. 15, 1927. U.S. lawyer, financier. An organizer of U.S. Steel Corp., 1901; Gary, Ind., the industrial city built (1906-08) by U.S. Steel, was named in his honor.

GERBER, DANIEL F., May 6, 1898 (Fremont, Mich.)-Mar. 16, 1974. U.S. manufacturer. Pres. and chm. of Gerber Products, a family-owned baby-food manufacturing firm, 1945-64; introduced strained baby food into U.S. (Son of FRANK GERBER.)

GERBER, FRANK, Jan. 12, 1873 (Douglas, Mich.)-Oct. 7, 1952. U.S. manufacturer. Pres. (1917-1945) and chm. (1945-52) of the firm that became Gerber Products (1941); entered the baby-food business, 1928. (Father of DANIEL F. GERBER.)

GETTY, J(ean) P(aul), Dec. 15, 1892 (Minneapolis, Minn.)-June 6, 1976. U.S. oil man. With his father, George Franklin Getty, formed the Getty Oil Co. of Oklahoma, 1916; during Depression, purchased shares of other oil companies, including Skelly Oil Co. and Tidewater Oil; negotiated oil concessions in Saudi Arabia and Kuwait, 1950; merged holdings into Getty Oil Co., 1956; reputed to be world's richest man, leaving over $1 billion at his death.

GIANNINI, AMADEO PETER, May 6, 1870 (San Jose, Calif.)-June 3, 1949. U.S. banker. Organized California's Bank of America, 1904; a pioneer in branch-banking system; founded Transamerica Corp., 1928. (Father of L. M. GIANNINI.)

GIANNINI, LAWRENCE MARIO, Nov. 25, 1894 (San Francisco, Calif.)-Aug. 19, 1952. U.S. banker. The son of AMADEO PETER GIANNINI, he worked for the Bank of America from 1918 to 1952, serving as pres. from 1936 to 1952; built the internatl. div. of the bank; pres. of Transamerica Corp., 1930-32.

GILLETTE, KING CAMP, Jan. 5, 1855 (Fond du Lac, Wisc.)-July 9, 1932. U.S. inventor, manufacturer. Invented the safety razor and blade, c.1900; founded the Gillette Co., 1901.

GIMBEL, BERNARD FEUSTMAN, Apr. 10, 1885 (Vincennes, Ind.)-Sept. 29, 1966. U.S. retailer. As pres. (1927-53) and chm. (1931-66) of Gimbel Bros., responsible for the store's growth to nationwide chain; responsible for purchase of Sak's Fifth Avenue, 1925.

GOLDBERG, SOL HARRY, Apr. 20, 1880 (Cincinnati, Ohio)-June 4, 1940. U.S. manufacturer. Devised "humps" for hairpins to help them grip the hair; produced and sold the hairpins, beginning in 1913, through his Hump Hairpin Mfg. Co.; bobbie-pin industry pioneer.

THE BOOK OF WHO

GOODRICH, BENJAMIN FRANKLIN, Nov. 4, 1841 (Ripley, N.Y.)–Aug. 3, 1888. U.S. manufacturer. Founded (1876) B. F. Goodrich Rubber Co., the makers of the first solid rubber tires and first pneumatic auto tires.

GOODRICH, DAVID MARTIN, June 22, 1876 (Akron, Ohio)–May 17, 1950. U.S. manufacturer. The son of B. F. GOODRICH; active in research into rubber, he directed the B. F. Goodrich Rubber Co.'s research in synthetic rubber in the 1930s.

GOULD, JAY, born Jason Gould, May 27, 1836 (Roxbury, N.Y.)–Dec. 2, 1892. U.S. financier, railroad exec. A shrewd and unscrupulous investor whose speculation in gold caused the Black Friday panic of Sept. 24, 1869; invested in Erie RR in struggle for control against CORNELIUS VANDERBILT; invested in Union Pacific and Missouri Pacific RRs; controlled Western Union Telegraph Co. and the New York Elevated Railways.

GRACE, EUGENE GIFFORD, Aug. 27, 1876 (Bethlehem, Pa.)–July 25, 1960. U.S. industrialist. As pres. (1916–57) and chm. (1945–57) of Bethlehem Steel Corp., expanded firm into a major supplier of munitions, ships, and steel to the U.S. military.

GRACE, JOSEPH PETER, May 25, 1913 (Manhasset, N.Y.). U.S. business exec. Pres. (1945–   ) of W. R. Grace & Co., a major U.S. manufacturer and processor of chemicals and owner of a major shipping line (Grace Line).

GROSS, ROBERT ELLSWORTH, May 11, 1897 (Boston, Mass.)–Sept. 3, 1961. U.S. industrialist. Purchased Lockheed Aircraft Corp. in 1932 for $40,000, and developed it into huge manufacturer of passenger and military aircraft and missiles; introduced jet power for commercial aviation; developed Polaris missile.

GROSSINGER, JENNIE, June 16, 1892 (Austria)–Nov. 20, 1972. U.S. hotelier. With her parents, founded Grossinger's Hotel in the Catskill Mts. of New York (1914), and developed it into an internationally known resort.

GRUMMAN, LEROY RANDLE, Jan. 4, 1895 (Huntington, N.Y.). U.S. aircraft manufacturer. Built his airplane-repair shop into Grumman Aircraft Engineering Corp., a major manufacturer of U.S. military aircraft, particularly amphibious flying craft.

GUGGENHEIM, DANIEL, July 9, 1856 (Philadelphia, Pa.)–Sept. 28, 1930. U.S. industrialist. A founder (1901) of American Smelting & Refining Co., one of the world's largest mining operations; endowed the Daniel Guggenheim Fund for Promotion of Aeronautics, 1926. (Son of MEYER GUGGENHEIM.)

GUGGENHEIM, MEYER, Feb. 1, 1828 (Langnau, Switz.)–Mar. 15, 1905. U.S. industrialist. Formed (1881) M. Guggenheim's Sons, a smelting and mining operation that in 1901 joined the Smelter Fund, which Guggenheim headed. (Father of DANIEL GUGGENHEIM.)

GUTT, CAMILLE ADOLPH, Nov. 14, 1884 (Brussels, Belg.)–June 7, 1971. Belgian internatl. banker. As head of the Internatl. Monetary Fund (1946–51), one of the originators of the Benelux customs union and responsible for putting Belgium on a sound financial basis after WW II.

HAAS, WALTER ABRAHAM, 1889 (San Francisco, Calif.). U.S. manufacturer. Credited with transforming the family-owned Levi-Strauss Co. into a major clothing manufacturer, which he served as pres. (1928–56), chm. (1956–70), and chm. emeritus, 1970–

HALABY, NAJEEB, Nov. 19, 1915 (Dallas, Tex.). U.S. business exec., lawyer. Administrator of FAA, 1961–65; pres. (1968–72) and chm. (1969–72) of Pan American Airways; his daughter, Lisa, married KING HUSSEIN of Jordan in 1978.

HALL, JOYCE CLYDE, Aug. 29, 1891 (David City, Neb.). U.S. manufacturer. Founder (1913), pres. (1913–66), and chm. of the board (1913–   ) of Hallmark Cards, Inc., foremost greeting-card maker in U.S.

HAMMER, ARMAND, May 21, 1898 (New York, N.Y.). U.S. oil exec., art patron. Chm. and chief exec. officer of Occidental Petroleum Corp., Los Angeles-based oil firm, 1957–   ; renowned art collector; coowner of New York City's Knoedler Gallery, 1971–   ; owner of Hammer Galleries, Inc. 1930–   ; organized Soviet exhibition of modern French painting that toured U.S., 1972–73.

HARMSWORTH, ALFRED CHARLES WILLIAM, VISCOUNT NORTHCLIFFE, July 15, 1865 (County Dublin, Ire.)–Aug. 14, 1922. Irish newspaper publisher. With brother HAROLD SIDNEY HARMSWORTH, founded British newspaper empire that included *Answers* (1888), *London Evening News* (1894), *London Daily Mail* (1896), *Daily Mirror* (1903), and the *Times* (1908).

HARMSWORTH, HAROLD SIDNEY, VISCOUNT ROTHMERE, Apr. 26, 1868 (Hampstead, Eng.)–Nov. 26, 1940. Irish newspaper publisher. With brother ALFRED HARMSWORTH, founded British newspaper empire that included the *London Daily Mail* (1896) and *Times* (1908); British air min., 1917–18; endowed chairs at Oxford and Cambridge to honor his sons, who were killed in WW I.

HARRIMAN, EDWARD HENRY, Feb. 25, 1848 (Hempstead, N.Y.)–Sept. 9, 1909. U.S. railroad magnate. Owner and dir. of Union Pacific, Illinois Central, Delaware & Hudson, Erie, Georgia Central, Northern Pacific, and other railroads; lost out to J. P. MORGAN and J. J. HILL in epic struggle to control Burlington RR, a battle that set off the stock-market panic of 1901; organized first Boys Club, 1876. (Father of diplomat W. A. HARRIMAN.)

HAVEMEYER, HENRY OSBORNE, Oct. 18, 1847 (New York, N.Y.)–Dec. 4, 1907. U.S. business exec., art collector. With his brother, Theodore Havemeyer, merged 15 New York City and Brooklyn refining plants into Sugar Refineries Co. (later American Refinery Co.), 1887; produced one half of all sugar used in the U.S. by 1907; bequeathed his art collection to New York City's Metropolitan Museum of Art.

HEINZ, HENRY JOHN, Oct. 11, 1844 (Pittsburgh, Pa.)–May 14, 1919. U.S. food-products manufacturer. Founded H. J. Heinz Co., 1876 (incorporated 1905); coined slogan "57 varieties" to describe his products, 1896. (Father of H. J. HEINZ II.)

HEINZ, HENRY JOHN II, July 10, 1908 (Sewickley, Pa.). U.S. food-products manufacturer. Pres. (1941–59) and board chm. (1959–   ) of H. J. Heinz Co. (Son of H. J. HEINZ).

HERSHEY, MILTON SNAVELY, Sept. 13, 1857 (Derry Twp., Pa.)–Oct. 13, 1945. U.S. manufacturer. Founded Hershey Chocolate Corp., world's largest firm devoted solely to the manufacture of cocoa and chocolate, 1893; built Hershey, Pa., out of his factory and surrounding property, from 1903.

HEWITT, ABRAM STEVENS, July 31, 1822 (Haverstraw, N.Y.)–Jan. 18, 1903. U.S iron-works operator, politician. Introduced first open-hearth furnace in U.S. (1862) and made first U.S.-made steel (1870); mayor of New York City, 1886–88; U.S. rep. (D, N.Y.), 1875–79 and 1881–86.

HIGGINS, ANDREW JACKSON, Aug. 28, 1886 (Columbus, Neb.)–Aug. 1, 1952. U.S. shipbuilder. His company, Higgins Industries (founded 1930), served as largest manufacturer of PT boats and landing craft for U.S. military during WW II.

HILL, JAMES JEROME, Sept. 16, 1838 (Guelph, Ont., Can.)–May 29, 1916. U.S. railroad magnate. Organized system that became the Great Northern RR, 1878; reorganized the Northern Pacific RR (1893) and the Chicago, Burlington & Quincy RR (after epic battle with E. H. HARRIMAN), 1901; his attempt, along with Harriman and J. P. MORGAN, to combine all three railroads under the Northern Securities Co. was broken up when the U.S. Sup. Ct. invoked the Sherman Anti-trust Act, 1904.

HILTON, CONRAD NICHOLSON, Dec. 25, 1887 (San Antonio, N.M.)–Jan. 3, 1979. U.S. hotelier. Began buying hotels in 1918 and founded Hilton Hotels Corp. in 1946; at his death, his corp. owned 125 hotels worldwide, valued at $500 million.

HIRSHHORN, JOSEPH HERMAN, Aug. 11, 1899 (Mitau, Latvia). U.S. financier, art collector. Speculator in securities and uranium; donated his art collection to the U.S. govt. in 1966, leading to the building of the Hirshhorn Museum of the Smithsonian Inst. in Washington, D.C.

HOBBS, LEONARD SINCLAIR ("Luke"), Dec.20, 1896 (Carbon, Wisc.)–Nov. 1, 1977. U.S. aircraft manufacturer, engineer. Engineer and exec. with Pratt-Whitney Aircraft, 1927–44; exec. with United Aircraft Corp., 1944–58; developed J-57 split-compressor turbojet engine (first with 10,000-pound thrust), 1948–52; awarded Collier Trophy, presented by Pres. D. D. EISENHOWER for the development of the J-57 jet engine, 1952.

HOFFA, JAMES RIDDLE, Feb. 14, 1913 (Brazil, Ind.)–disappeared July 30, 1975, presumed dead. U.S. labor leader. During his tenure as pres. of Internatl. Teamsters Union (1957–71), extensive corruption was uncovered in union, leading to its expulsion from the AFL-CIO (1957); indicted for accepting illegal payments from a trucking concern, case ended in mistrial; convicted of jury tampering and fraud in union benefits, 1964; imprisoned until sentence commuted by Pres. R. M. NIXON, 1967–71; worked for prison reform, 1971–75; last seen in parking lot of a Michigan restaurant prior to lunch with three alleged mob figures.

HOLLEY, GEORGE MALVIN, Apr. 14, 1878 (Port Jervis, N.Y.)–June 27, 1963. U.S. industrialist. His Holley Motor Co. manufactured the first practical motorcycle (1899) and was a major supplier of carburetors for the Model A Ford and many other autos.

HOMER, ARTHUR BARTLETT, Apr. 14, 1896 (Belmont, Mass.)–June 18, 1972. U.S. industrialist. Beginning in 1919 in Bethlehem Steel Corp.'s shipbuilding subsidiary became Bethlehem's pres. and chief exec. officer, 1945–64; led Bethlehem during the U.S. govt.'s temporary takeover of steel companies, 1952.

HOPKINS, JOHN JAY, Oct. 15, 1893 (Santa Ana, Calif.)–May 3, 1957. U.S. business exec. During his tenure as pres. and board chm. of Gen. Dynamics Corp. (1947–57), built the *Nautilus*, the first nuclear-powered submarine.

HOPKINS, MARK, Sept. 1, 1813 (Henderson, N.Y.)–Mar. 29, 1878. U.S. capitalist. An organizer and treasurer of Central Pacific RR, 1861–78; prominent in California gold rush politics.

HORLICK, WILLIAM, Feb. 23, 1846 (Ruardean, Eng.)–Sept. 25, 1936. U.S. manufacturer. Discovered and produced malted milk as pres. and gen. mgr. of Horlick's Malted Milk Corp., 1883–1936.

HORMEL, GEORGE ALBERT, Dec. 4, 1860 (Buffalo, N.Y.)–June 5, 1946. U.S. meat packer. As founder and pres. (1892–1928) of Geo. A. Hormel & Co., produced first canned hams in the U.S.

HOUSER, THEODORE V., Sept. 8, 1892 (Kansas City, Mo.)–Dec. 17, 1963. U.S. retail-industry exec. As an exec. with Sears, Roebuck & Co. (from 1928), directed firm's entry into retail stores (1928) and insurance (1931); developed Sears-owned "brands"; Sears chm. of the board, 1954–58.

HOVING, WALTER, Dec. 2, 1897 (Stockholm, Swe.). U.S. retailer. Served as exec. with Macy's, Montgomery Ward, Lord & Taylor, and Bonwit Teller; chm. of the board of Tiffany & Co., 1955– .

HUGHES, HOWARD ROBARD, JR., Dec. 24, 1905 (Houston, Tex.)–Apr. 5, 1976. U.S. industrialist, considered during his lifetime to be one of the world's richest men. Inherited (1925) patent rights to an oil tool drill, which, manufactured by Hughes Tool Co., laid the basis for his financial empire; founded Hughes Aircraft Co.; went to Hollywood to produce films, including *Two Arabian Nights* (AA, 1928), *Hell's Angels* (AA, 1930), *Scarface* (1932), and *The Outlaw* (1941); designed and flew airplanes, setting world land-speed record (352.46 mph) on Sept. 12, 1935, and transcontinental flight record on Jan. 19, 1937; went into seclusion, 1950; sold his 78% share of Trans World Airlines stock for $500 million, 1966; bought hotels and casinos in Las Vegas, Nev.

HUMPHREY, GEORGE MAGOFFIN, Mar. 8, 1890 (Cheboygan, Mich.)–Jan. 20, 1970. U.S. manufacturer, govt. official. Exec. with M. A. Hanna Co., an iron-ore firm, 1918–53; U.S. secy. of the treas., 1953–57.

HUNT, H(aroldson) **L**(afayette), Feb. 17, 1889 (Vandalia, Ill.)–Nov. 29, 1974. U.S. oilman considered during his lifetime to be one of the richest men in the world. Drilled first major East Texas oilfield, 1930; a conservative advocate of free enterprise, he financed *Life Line* (previously *Facts Forum*), an anticommunist radio program.

HUNTINGTON, HENRY EDWARDS, Feb. 27, 1850 (Oneonta, N.Y.)–May 23, 1927. U.S. capitalist. Organized and financed the Los Angeles transit system and Pacific Light & Power Co., c.1892–1903; renowned book collector.

INGERSOLL, CHARLES HENRY, Oct. 29, 1865 (Delta, Mich.)–Sept. 21, 1948. U.S. manufacturer. With brother ROBERT H. INGERSOLL, founded Robert H. Ingersoll & Bro. Watch Co., makers of the famous one-dollar Ingersoll watch, 1887.

INGERSOLL, ROBERT HAWLEY, Dec. 26, 1859 (Delta, Mich.)–Sept. 4, 1928. U.S. manufacturer. With brother CHARLES HENRY INGERSOLL, founded Robert H. Ingersoll & Bro. Watch Co., makers of the famous one-dollar Ingersoll watch, 1887.

JACK, WILLIAM SAUNDERS, Nov. 24, 1888 (Cleveland, Ohio). U.S. industrialist. As head of Jack & Heinz (founded 1939), manufacturers of aircraft parts, made large profits on WW II contracts, which he distributed in extraordinary employee benefits.

JOHNSON, TOM LOFTIN, July 18, 1854 (Blue Spring, Ky.)–June 10, 1911. U.S. manufacturer, govt. official. A public transportation-system developer who invented the transparent fare-box,

1873; U.S. rep. (D, Ohio), 1890–94; reform mayor of Cleveland, Ohio, 1901–09.

KAHN, OTTO HERMANN, Feb. 21, 1867 (Mannheim, Ger.)–Mar. 29, 1934. U.S. banker, philanthropist. Partner in Kuhn, Loeb & Co., 1897–1934; a noted patron of the arts.

KAISER, HENRY JOHN, May 9, 1882 (Sprout Brook, N.Y.)–Aug. 24, 1967. U.S. industrialist. As pres. of Bridge Builders, Inc., built S.F. Bay Bridge (1933), Bonneville Dam (1934), and Grand Coulee Dam (1939); turning to shipbuilding, bought yards (1942) in California and Oregon and developed prefabrication and assembly methods that greatly reduced ship construction time; built some 1,460 ships during WW II, most of them the famed Liberty-class cargo vessels; to facilitate getting steel for construction, built first steel plant on the Pacific coast, 1942; established Permanente (later Kaiser) Foundation, a non-profit health plan and facilities for his workers.

KALMUS, HERBERT THOMAS, Nov. 9, 1881 (Chelsea, Mass.)–July 11, 1963. U.S. business exec. One of the developers of the Technicolor process for making color movies, 1914; head of Technology, Inc., 1922–63.

KEITH, MINOR COOPER, Jan. 19, 1848 (Brooklyn, N.Y.)–June 14, 1929. U.S. financier. Constructed cross-Costa Rica railroad, 1871–1890; through his extensive holdings in banana plantations in Costa Rica, became leader in Central American banana trade by 1899; merged with his chief rival, Boston Fruit Co., to form United Fruit Co., 1899.

KELLOGG, JOHN HARVEY, Feb. 26, 1852 (Tyrone, Mich.)–Dec. 14, 1943. U.S. physician. As dir. of a sanitarium, his experiments with health foods and dry breakfast cereals inspired brother WILL KELLOGG to found the W. K. Kellogg Co., 1906.

KELLOGG, WILL KEITH, Apr. 7, 1860 (Battle Creek, Mich.)–Oct. 6, 1951. U.S. food-products manufacturer. Founded W. K. Kellogg Co., manufacturer of cereal products, and introduced cornflakes, 1906. (Brother of JOHN HARVEY KELLOGG.)

KENNEDY, JOSEPH PATRICK, Sept. 6, 1888 (Boston, Mass.)–Nov. 18, 1969. U.S. financier, diplomat, who founded the Kennedy political dynasty. First chm. of SEC, 1934–35; U.S. amb. to Great Britain, 1937–40. (Father of JOHN F. KENNEDY, ROBERT F. KENNEDY and EDWARD M. KENNEDY.)

KING, HENRIETTA MARIA MORSE, née Chamberlain, July 21, 1832 (Boonville, Mo.)–Mar. 31, 1925. U.S. cattlewoman, ranch owner. Married RICHARD KING (1854), and upon his death in 1885, inherited and ran King Ranch; added to holdings, building ranch to size of Delaware by the time of her death.

KING, RICHARD, July 10, 1825 (Orange Co., N.Y.)–Apr. 14, 1885. U.S. cattleman. Acquired some 500,000 acres of land near Corpus Christi, Tex., thus creating the King Ranch, a major cattle-producing operation in Texas, 1852–85; ran steamboats on the Rio Grande R., 1850–72; built San Diego, Corpus Christi, and Rio Grande RRs, 1876–80. (Husband of HENRIETTA KING.)

KIRBY, FRED MORGAN, Oct. 30, 1861 (Jefferson Co., N.Y.)–Oct. 16, 1940. U.S. merchant. His chain of 96 Kirby "five-and-ten cent" stores (founded 1887) merged with F. W. Woolworth Co. in 1912 to form a reorganized and enlarged chain.

KRAFT, CHARLES HERBERT, Oct. 17, 1880 (Ft. Erie, Ont., Can.)–Mar. 25, 1952. U.S. food-products manufacturer. Joined brother in 1906 in Chicago cheese-sales firms and instituted manufacture of cheese; his firm became J. L. Kraft Co. in 1909 and Kraft Foods in 1945; a pioneer in development of blended and pasteurized cheese.

KRESS, SAMUEL HENRY, July 23, 1863 (Cherryville, Pa.)–Sept. 22, 1955. U.S. merchant, philanthropist. Founded S. H. Kress & Co. dime-store chain, 1907; established Samuel H. Kress Fndn. for purchase and donation of great works of art to museums, 1929.

KREUGER, IVAR, Mar. 2, 1880 (Kalmar, Swe.)–Mar. 12, 1932. Swedish financier. Originally a building contractor, became involved in the manufacture of matches, 1907; by the end of WW I controlled three-quarters of the world's matches; made govt. loans in exchange for monopolies; committed suicide after it was discovered that he had looted his vast trust, 1932.

KROC, RAY A., Oct. 5, 1902 (Chicago, Ill.). U.S. restauranteur. Founded (1955) McDonald's Corp., a pioneering fast-food hamburger chain, which he has served as pres. (1955–68) and board chm. (1968–); owner of the San Diego Padres baseball team, 1974– .

KROGER, BERNARD HENRY, Jan. 24, 1860 (Cincinnati, Ohio)–July 21, 1938. U.S. grocer. Founded the business that became the Kroger grocery-store chain, first to operate its own bakeries and meat-packing operations, 1884; pres. and chm. of Provident Savings Bank and Trust Co. of Cincinnati, 1901–38.

KRUPP, ALFRED, Apr. 26, 1812 (Essen, Ger.)–July 14, 1887. German armaments manufacturer. Considered the father of modern armaments. Converted family cast-steel manufacturing firm to the manufacture of weapons; Krupp cast-steel cannon highlighted London's Crystal Palace Exhibition, 1851; during Franco-Prussian War of 1870–71, supplied field guns to Prussians, aiding them in winning the war; by 1887, supplied armaments to 46 nations.

LANE, SIR ALLEN, born Allen Lane Williams, Sept. 21, 1902 (Bristol, Eng.)–July 7, 1970. English publisher. With his two brothers, founded Penguin Books, Ltd., the first British publishers of paperback books, 1935–36.

LASKER, ALBERT DAVIS, May 1, 1880 (Freiburg, Ger.)–May 30, 1952. U.S. advertising exec. As owner of the Lord & Thomas advertising agency (1908–42), credited with being the first to create ads telling consumers why they should buy products; founder, with his wife, of Albert and Mary Lasker Fndn., 1942.

LAWRENCE, ABBOTT, Dec. 16, 1792 (Groton, Mass.)–Aug. 18, 1855. U.S. manufacturer, govt. official. Associated with brother A. A. LAWRENCE in Lowell, Mass., cotton mill and other ventures; U.S. representative (Whig-Mass.), 1834–36 and 1839–40; settled northeast Mass. (Maine) boundary dispute with British, 1842; U.S. amb. to Great Britain, 1849–52.

LAWRENCE, AMOS ADAMS, July 31, 1814 (Groton, Mass.)–Aug. 22, 1886. U.S. merchant, philanthropist. With brother ABBOTT LAWRENCE, made fortune in textile manufacture; established Lawrence Co. in Appleton, Wisc., 1847; contributed to settlement of Kansas, where town of Lawrence is named in his honor; founded U. of Kansas.

LAWRENCE, MARY GEORGENE, née Wells, May 25, 1928 (Youngstown, Ohio). U.S. advertising exec. Cofounder of Wells, Rich, and Greene, Inc., an innovative New York City advertising agency,

1966; best known for complete remake of the Braniff Airlines image—painting the planes in wild colors and dressing the stewardesses in uniforms designed by EMILIO PUCCI.

LAWSON, THOMAS WILLIAM, Feb. 26, 1857 (Charleston, Mass.)–Feb. 8, 1925. U.S. financier, author. A financial wizard who amassed a personal fortune of $10 million before age 30; participated in merger of Anaconda and other companies in Amalgamated Copper Co., 1897; wrote *Frenzied Finance,* an exposé of shady dealings in the Amalgamated merger, 1904.

LEFRAK, SAMUEL J., Feb. 12, 1918 (New York, N.Y.). U.S. real-estate exec. Pres. and board chm. of Lefrak Org., builders of Lefrak City apartment development in New York City, 1948–   .

LEIGH, DOUGLAS, May 24, 1907 (Anniston, Ala.). U.S. advertising exec. Pioneer in neon-sign field; his oversized creations adorned the Times Square area of New York City, most notably the Coca-Cola weather sign (1937) and the smoking-man sign for Camel cigarettes (1941).

LELAND, HENRY MARTYN, Feb. 16, 1843 (Danville, Vt.)–Mar. 26, 1932. U.S. manufacturer, auto-industry pioneer. As pres. and gen. mgr. of Cadillac Motor Co. (1902-17) and Lincoln Motor Co. (1917–22), responsible for development of the Cadillac and Lincoln motor cars; with Charles Kettering, developed first electric starter, 1911; developed first eight-cylinder motor, 1914.

LETOURNEAU, ROBERT GILMOUR, Nov. 30, 1888 (Richford, Vt.)–June 1, 1969. U.S. business exec. A heavy-equipment manufacturer whose R. G. LeTourneau, Inc. (founded 1929) supplied over 70% of all earth-moving equipment for the U.S. armed forces during WW II.

LEVER, WILLIAM HESKETH, FIRST VISCOUNT LEVERHULME, Sept. 19, 1851 (Lancashire, Eng.)–May 7, 1925. English manufacturer. With brother James Darcy Lever, leased a financially-ailing soap factory, 1884; began to make Sunlight soap from vegetable oil, 1885; the enterprise, Lever Brothers, Inc., began to expand to cover the country; built model town called Port Sunlight, 1888; started many employee-benefits programs.

LEVITT, WILLIAM JAIRD, Feb. 11, 1907 (Brooklyn, N.Y.). U.S. building exec. Founder and chm. of Levitt & Sons, Inc. (1929–   ), home builders who created the developed communities of Levittown, N.Y. (1947), and Levittown, Pa., among others.

LEWISOHN, ADOLPH, May 27, 1849 (Hamburg, Ger.)–Aug. 17, 1938. U.S. financier, philanthropist. A metals broker active in Montana copper; noted for philanthropies, chiefly Lewisohn Stadium at City C. of New York (dedicated 1915), and his devotion to child labor reform and prison reform; founded ORT, a Jewish welfare org., 1922.

LILLY, ELI, Apr. 1, 1885 (Indianapolis, Ind.)–Jan. 24, 1977. U.S. drug manufacturer, philanthropist. Pres. (1932-48) and board chm. (1948-66) of Eli Lilly & Co., the pharmaceutical firm founded by his grandfather; founded (1937) Lilly Endowment, which had donated over $250 million to charity by the time of his death.

LIPTON, SIR THOMAS JOHNSTONE, May 10, 1850 (Glasgow, Scot.)–Oct. 2, 1931. British merchant. Opened a small grocery store in Glasgow that became the basis for Thomas J. Lipton Co., tea and other foods merchants, 1898; maintained his own tea, coffee, and cocoa plantations to provide inexpensive products for his shops.

LITCHFIELD, PAUL WEEKS, July 26, 1875 (Boston, Mass.)–Mar. 18, 1959. U.S. industrialist. As-

sociated with Goodyear Tire & Rubber Co. from 1900, he developed the first "straight-side" tire, first airplane tire, and the first pneumatic truck tire; Goodyear chm. of the board, 1930-64.

LOEB, CARL MORRIS, Sept. 28, 1875 (Frankfurt-am-Main, Ger.)–Jan. 3, 1955. U.S. investment banker. Pres. of American Metal Co., 1917–29; founded Carl M. Loeb, Rhoades & Co., one of the largest brokerage houses in the U.S., 1931.

LOVE, JAMES SPENCER, July 6, 1896 (Cambridge, Mass.)–Jan. 20, 1962. U.S. textile exec. Developed small, family-owned cotton mill into Burlington Industries, Inc., founded 1923; first manufacturer of rayon, 1924.

LUCE, CHARLES FRANKLIN, Aug. 29, 1917 (Platteville, Wisc.). U.S. utilities exec. Chm. and chief exec. officer of Consolidated Edison Co. of New York, 1967–   .

MACK, JOSEPH SANFORD, Nov. 27, 1870 (Mount Cobb, Pa.)–July 25, 1953. U.S. manufacturer. A silk manufacturer who joined with brothers Augustus, William, and John M. to form Mack Bros. Wagon Co., 1889; built first successful gas-powered bus and truck, 1900; formed company that manufactured Mack trucks, 1911.

MARCUS, HAROLD STANLEY, Apr. 20, 1905 (Dallas, Tex.). U.S. retailer. Joined family firm, Nieman-Marcus Co., in 1926 and served as pres. from 1950 to 1972; originated fashion shows for which the store became famous, 1926; originated Nieman-Marcus fashion awards, 1938. *Minding the Store,* 1974.

MARRIOTT, JOHN WILLARD, Sept. 17, 1900 (Marriott, Utah.). U.S. hotel and restaurant exec. From a small chain of Marriott Hot Shoppes restaurants, developed and founded Marriott hotel and restaurant chain, 1928; Marriott's pres. (1928-64) and board chm. (1964–   ); a leading conservative Republican and R. M. NIXON supporter.

MARTIN, GLENN LUTHER, Jan. 17, 1886 (Macksburg, Ia.)–Dec. 4, 1955. U.S. aircraft manufacturer. His Glenn L. Martin Co. (founded 1918) manufactured the first successful twin-engine plane, the Martin Bomber, 1918; manufactured the first American metal monoplane, 1922.

MAYER, OSCAR FERDINAND, Mar. 29, 1859 (Kaesingen, Württemberg)–Mar. 11, 1955. U.S. meat-packer. Converted a small Chicago meat market and sausage shop into a major meatpacking firm, Oscar Mayer & Co., 1888 (incorporated 1919); pres. and board chm. of Oscar Mayer, 1919-55.

MAYTAG, ELMER HENRY, Sept. 18, 1883 (Newton, Ia.)–July 20, 1940. U.S. manufacturer. Converted a family-owned farm-implement business into a major manufacturer of washing machines, the Maytag Co., which produced its first machines in 1907; pres., treasurer, and board chm. of Maytag, 1926-40. (Son of FREDERICK L. MAYTAG.)

MAYTAG, FREDERICK LOUIS, July 14, 1857 (Elgin, Ill.)–Mar. 26, 1937. U.S. manufacturer. Co-founder (1893) of Parson Band Cutter and Self-Feeder Co., the company that became the Maytag Co. (1907), washing-machine manufacturers. (Father of ELMER HENRY MAYTAG.)

MCELROY, NEIL HOSLER, Oct. 30, 1904 (Berea, Ohio)–Nov. 30, 1972. U.S. manufacturer. Pres. (1948-57) and board chm. (1959-72) of Procter & Gamble; instrumental in firm's introduction of "Prell" shampoo, as well as "Dreft" (the first synthetic detergent), "Joy", "Cheer", and "Lilt" products; U.S. secy. of def., 1957-59.

MCGILL, JAMES, Oct. 6, 1744 (Glasgow, Scot.)–

THE BOOK OF WHO

Dec. 19, 1813. Scottish-Canadian fur trapper, philanthropist. Based in Montreal as a fur trader from 1774; left the bulk of his estate to found McGill U. (opened 1829).

MCNEELY, EUGENE JOHNSON, Nov. 1, 1900 (Jackson, Mo.)–Dec. 27, 1973. U.S. communications exec. Associated with AT&T since 1922, serving as pres. from 1961 to 1964; instrumental in development of Telstar, the first communications satellite, 1962.

MELLON, ANDREW WILLIAM, Mar. 24, 1855 (Pittsburgh, Pa.)–Aug. 26, 1937. U.S. financier, govt. official, philanthropist. Joined his father in family banking business, 1874; founded Union Trust Co. (Pittsburgh), which became the center of his financial activities, 1889; developed extensive interests in coal, coke, railroads, steel, oil, water power; as U.S. secy. of the treas. (1921-32), substantially reduced natl. debt; U.S. amb. to Great Britain, 1932-33; donated the first building to house Natl. Gallery of Art, Washington, D.C., along with his art collection, 1937. (Father of PAUL MELLON.)

MELLON, PAUL, June 11, 1907 (Pittsburgh, Pa.). U.S. philanthropist. Son and heir of ANDREW W. MELLON; art connoisseur; pres. and trustee of Natl. Gallery of Art; trustee of Mellon Fndn.; received Natl. Inst. of Arts and Letters award for distinguished service to the arts, 1962.

MERRILL, CHARLES EDWARD, Oct. 19, 1885 (Green Cove Springs, Fla.)–Oct. 6, 1956. U.S. investment banker. As founder (1914) of the firm that became Merrill-Lynch brokers, pioneered the stockbroking business; first to pay brokers with salaries rather than commissions; first in brokerage business to provide financial counseling; first to advertise in popular publications, aiming at the small investor.

MILLER, ARNOLD RAY, Apr. 25, 1923 (Leewood, W. Va.). U.S. labor leader. A coal miner who rose to the presidency of the embattled United Mine Workers, 1972–

MOORE, WILLIAM HENRY, Oct, 25, 1848 (Utica, N.Y.)–Jan. 11, 1923. U.S. financier. Formed Natl. Biscuit Co. from several competing firms, 1898; organized and consolidated several early steel firms that grew into U.S. Steel Corp., 1901; acquired Rock Island RR, 1901.

MORGAN, JOHN PIERPONT, Apr. 7, 1837 (Hartford, Conn.)–Mar. 31, 1913. U.S. financier, philanthropist. Partner (1871) in Drexel, Morgan & Co. (J. P. Morgan and Co. from 1895), which he built into one of the world's most influential banking firms; formed syndicate that ended JAY COOKE's monopoly of treasury notes, 1873; entered railroad reorganization field, 1879; averted financial crisis by forming syndicate to restore depleted gold to U.S. Treas., 1895; financed several companies that became U.S. Steel, 1898; financed Internatl. Harvester Co., 1902; donated art collection to New York City's Metropolitan Museum of Art, 1918.

MORTON, JOY, Sept. 27, 1855 (Detroit, Mich.)–May 9, 1934. U.S. manufacturer. Founder (1885) and pres. (1885-1934) of the Morton Salt Co. (incorporated 1910).

NASH, CHARLES WILLIAM, Jan. 28, 1864 (DeKalb Co., Ill.)–June 6, 1948. U.S. manufacturer. Automotive pioneer. Pres. of Buick Motor Co. (1910-16) and Gen. Motors (1912-16); founded Nash Motor Co., 1916; merged with Kelvinator Corp. (appliance manufacturers) in 1937, and ran the merged corp., Nash-Kelvinator Corp., until his death.

NECKER, JACQUES, Sept. 30, 1732 (Geneva, Switz.)–Apr. 9, 1804. Swiss banker. A dir. of the French East India Co.; min. of finance for King LOUIS XVI of France, 1788-90; attempted unsuccessful fiduciary reforms to save France from bankruptcy.

NIARCHOS, STAVROS SPYROS, July 3, 1909 (Athens, Gr.). Greek shipping exec. Founded (1939) Niarchos Group Cos., which eventually became the world's largest privately-owned fleet of tankers; brother-in-law of ARISTOTLE ONASSIS; renowned art collector.

NICHOLS, WILLIAM HENRY, Jan. 9, 1852 (Brooklyn, N.Y.)–Feb. 22, 1930. U.S. manufacturer, chemist. In 1871, founded firm that became (1905) Nichols Copper Co., one of the largest copper refiners in the world; formed (1899) Gen. Chemical Co., a leading manufacturer of heavy chemicals that introduced catalytic method of sulphuric-acid manufacture.

NOBEL, ALFRED BERNHARD, Oct. 21, 1833 (Stockholm, Swe.)–Dec. 10, 1896. Swedish industrialist, inventor, philanthropist. Discovered and perfected dynamite, 1867; developed blasting gelatin, 1876; left the bulk of his estate for establishment of Nobel prizes for peace, literature, physics, chemistry, and medicine (first prizes awarded in 1901).

NOBLE, EDWARD JOHN, Aug. 8, 1882 (Gouverneur, N.Y.)–Dec. 28, 1958. U.S. business exec. Bought Life Savers candy from its inventor in 1913, and sold it nationwide; merged Life Savers, Inc. with Beech-Nut, Inc., 1956; bought Blue Network from RCA in 1943, and when it became ABC, Inc., continued as principal stockholder and chm. of the board until 1958.

NORDHOFF, HEINZ, born Heinrich Nordhoff, Jan. 6, 1889 (Hildesheim, Ger.)–Apr. 12, 1968. German auto executive. Chosen to head Volkswagen Co. by British occupation authorities in Germany, 1948; developed firm into one of world's major automakers; introduced Volkswagen in U.S., 1952; headed firm until 1968.

NORTHRUP, JOHN KNUDSEN, Nov. 10, 1895 (Newark, N.J.). U.S. aircraft manufacturer. An aircraft engineer who formed Lockheed Aircraft, 1927; formed Northrup Corp., 1938 (became Northrup Aircraft, 1939); designed many pioneering planes, including Vega (1927), Alpha (1930), Flying Wing (1940), and Black Widow (1940).

NORTON, OLIVER WILLCOX, Dec. 17, 1839 (Allegany Co., N.Y.)–Oct. 1, 1920. U.S. manufacturer. With his brothers, founded Norton Bros., first manufacturer of tin cans for food preservation, 1890; an organizer of the American Can Co., which bought out Norton Bros. in 1901.

OBICI, AMEDEO, July 15, 1877 (Oderzo, It.)–May 21, 1942. U.S. manufacturer. With partner Mario Reruzzi, established (1907) Planters Nut & Chocolate Co. (later the Planters Co.), makers of Planters nuts, peanut candies, and chocolate-covered peanut products; discovered process of roasting peanuts so that they could be skinned without breaking in half.

OGILVY, DAVID MACKENZIE, June 23, 1911 (W. Horsley, Eng.). U.S. advertising exec. A founder of Hewitt, Ogilvy, Benson, and Mather (later Ogilvy & Mather) advertising agency, 1948; created Hathaway Shirt man with eyepatch and Commander Whitehead of Schweppes, among other advertising characters.

OLDS, RANSON ELI, June 3, 1864 (Geneva, Ohio)–Aug. 26, 1950. U.S. inventor, auto manufacturer. Began designing automobiles, 1886; manufactured first Oldsmobile in 1895 and second, more successful Oldsmobile in 1897; his firm became Olds Motor Works in 1899, featuring first U.S. factory especially designed for automaking and first assembly line.

OLIN, JOHN MERRILL, Nov. 10, 1892 (Alton, Ill.). U.S. manufacturer. Credited with a number of innovations in manufacture of ammunition and guns; head (1944-54) and board chm. (1954-57) of Olin-Matheson Chemical Corp.

ONASSIS, ARISTOTLE SOCRATES, Jan. 15, 1906 (Smyrna, Turk.)-Mar. 15, 1975. Greek shipping exec. At age 16 sent to Buenos Aires with $60; by age 25 made his first $1 million in the tobacco business; bought first six ships, 1932; started in oil tanker business, 1935; built large fleet of cargo and passenger ships; operated Olympic Airways, 1956-68; married JACQUELINE BOUVIER KENNEDY, 1968.

PACKARD, JAMES WARD, Nov. 5, 1863 (Warren, Ohio)-Mar. 20, 1928. U.S. manufacturer. Designed and built first Packard auto, 1899; with brother William Doud Packard, organized Packard Motor Car Co., 1902.

PALMER, POTTER, May 20, 1826 (Albany Co., N.Y.)-May 4, 1902. U.S. merchant. Founded (1852) Chicago dept. store that became Marshall Field & Co. in 1881; originated many retailing firsts, including allowing a customer to return or exchange goods and to try goods on approval at home; from 1867 on, devoted his talents to real estate, building, and speculation; credited with shifting business-center of Chicago to State Street.

PARKER, GEORGE SWINNERTON, Dec. 12, 1866 (Salem, Mass.)-Sept. 26, 1952. U.S. games manufacturer. Founder (1888), pres. (1901-33), and board chm. (1933-52) of Parker Bros.; popularized many games, notably Monopoly.

PATIÑO, SIMÓN ITURRI, June 1, 1862 (Cochabamba, Bol.)-Apr. 20, 1947. Bolivian mining exec. Pioneer in Bolivian tin mining; began in 1897 with the small Espíritu Santo mine and developed numerous concessions in the same area, eventually finding 46 main and 1,000 branch veins in the area, making it the world's richest tin mine.

PATTERSON, JOHN HENRY, Dec. 13, 1844 (nr. Dayton, Ohio)-May 7, 1922. U.S. manufacturer. At age 40, bought a cash-register company for $6,500; through an innovative sales technique, built firm into the National Cash Register Co., which he served as pres., 1884-1922; credited with instigating the widespread use of cash registers in business.

PEABODY, GEORGE, Feb. 18, 1795 (S. Danvers, Mass.)-Nov. 4, 1869. U.S. merchant, philanthropist. Partner in Baltimore dry-goods business, 1815-37; negotiated $8 million loan from Great Britain to save Maryland from bankruptcy, 1835; founded and operated (1837-64) Geo. Peabody & Co., a London banking firm that became the basis of J. P. MORGAN's financial empire; funded Peabody Inst. (Baltimore), Peabody museums at Yale and Harvard, and Peabody Education Fund; birthplace, S. Danvers, was renamed Peabody in his honor, 1868.

PEABODY, GEORGE FOSTER, July 27, 1852 (Columbus, Ga.)-Mar. 4, 1938. U.S. banker, philanthropist. Dir. of Federal Reserve Bank of New York, 1914-21; donated his estate, Yaddo, at Saratoga Springs, N.Y., for an arts center, 1926; Peabody Awards for excellence in broadcasting were named in his memory.

PENNEY, JAMES CASH, Sept. 16, 1875 (Hamilton, Mo.)-Feb. 12, 1971. U.S. merchant. In 1907 purchased a store in Kemperer, Wyo., that became the J. C. Penney Co., a nationwide chain of dept. stores; served as pres. (1913-17) board chm., (1917-58) and a dir. (1958-71) of what is now J.C. Penney Co., Inc.

PHILLIPS, FRANK, Nov. 28, 1873 (Scotia, Neb.)-Aug. 23, 1950. U.S. oilman. In partnership with his brothers, formed (1917) Phillips Petroleum Co.; as pres. (1917-1938) and board chm. (1938-49), expanded Phillips's operations into refining.

PHIPPS, HENRY, Sept. 27, 1839 (Philadelphia, Pa.)-Sept. 22, 1930. U.S. manufacturer, philanthropist. A manufacturer of iron products, he associated himself with ANDREW CARNEGIE in 1867 to form Union Iron Mills; dir. of U.S. Steel Corp., 1901-30; benefactor of several medical research clinics.

PILLSBURY, CHARLES ALFRED, Dec. 3, 1842 (Warner, N.H.)-Sept. 17, 1899. U.S. milling executive. Founder (1872) of Charles A. Pillsbury & Co., which built largest mills in the world; sold to English syndicate, 1889, and helped organize the Washburn-Pillsbury Mills (later the Pillsbury Company) in partnership.

PINKERTON, ALLAN, Aug. 25, 1819 (Glasgow, Scot.)-July 1, 1884. U.S. detective-agency founder. Spurred to detective work by a chance discovery of a nest of counterfeiters, 1846; worked for the Kane Co. and Cook Co., Ill., sheriffs, 1846-51; founded Pinkerton National Detective Agency to catch railway thieves, 1850; responsible for plan that got Pres. A. LINCOLN safely to his 1861 inauguration; founded first secret service for U.S. govt., 1861.

PIPER, WILLIAM THOMAS, Jan. 8, 1881 (Knapps Creek, N.Y.)-Jan. 15, 1970. U.S. aircraft manufacturer. Turned a failing aircraft firm into the Piper Aircraft Corp., the first successful mass-producer of small, inexpensive airplanes; designed the Piper Cub airplane, 1931.

PITCAIRN, JOHN, Jan. 10, 1841 (Johnstone, Scot.)-July 22, 1916. U.S. manufacturer. As a young telegraph clerk, was put in charge of the train that secretly carried Abraham Lincoln to his 1861 inauguration after rumors of an assassination conspiracy; after a career as an oil producer and railwayman, organized Pittsburgh Plate Glass Co., 1883; founded Swedenborgian community at Bryn Athyn, Pa.

POST, CHARLES WILLIAM, Oct. 26, 1854 (Springfield, Ill.)-May 9, 1914. U.S. food-products manufacturer. While an invalid for eight years (1884-91), developed Grape-Nuts breakfast cereal; founded Postum Cereal Co., 1897; developed Postum beverage.

POWERS, JOHN ROBERT, Sept. 14, 1896 (Easton, Pa.)-July 19, 1977. U.S. model-agency pioneer. Founded John Robert Powers Agency, 1921; started chain of modeling schools, 1929.

PRATT, CHARLES, Oct. 2, 1830 (Watertown, Mass.)-May 4, 1891. U.S. oilman, philanthropist. One of the first oil operators in the rich Pennsylvania oil fields; sold his refining firm to Standard Oil, 1874; founded Pratt Inst. in Brooklyn, N.Y., 1887.

PRINCE, WILLIAM HENRY WOOD, Feb. 7, 1914 (St. Louis, Mo.). U.S. business exec. Heir to Prince manufacturing fortune. Responsible for $2 million revitalization of Chicago Union Stockyards (1949-57) and $3 million reconstruction of Chicago's Internatl. Amphitheatre (1952); pres. (1957-61) and board chm. (1961-) of Armour & Co. meat packers (a major family holding).

THE BOOK OF WHO

PROCTER, WILLIAM COOPER, Aug. 25, 1862 (Glendale, Ohio)–May 2, 1934. U.S. manufacturer. Pres. (1907-30) and board chm. (1930-34) of Procter & Gamble Co.; one of the first employers to give one-half day off on Saturdays and to institute profit-sharing.

PULLMAN, GEORGE MORTIMER, Mar. 3, 1831 (Brocton, N.Y.)–Oct. 19, 1897. U.S. manufacturer. Constructed first "palace" (e.g., one that could be used night and day) sleeping car, "The Pioneer," 1863; organized Pullman Palace Car Co. (later the Pullman Co.), 1867; founded and built Pullman City, a company town in Chicago, Ill., for his employees, 1880.

QUANT, MARY, Feb. 11, 1934 (Blackheath, Eng.). English fashion designer. Credited with developing the "Chelsea look" in fashion in the 1960s; designed line of clothes and cosmetics that developed into multimillion-dollar internatl. fashion empire; named officer of the Order of the British Empire (first woman fashion designer to be so honored), 1966.

QUEENY, JOHN FRANCIS, Aug. 17, 1859 (Chicago, Ill.)–Mar. 19, 1933. U.S. chemicals manufacturer. Founded Monsanto Chemical Co., 1901; first to manufacture phenol (carbolic acid) in U.S. and to develop other coal-tar products.

RACKMIL, MILTON R., Feb. 12, 1903 (New York, N.Y.). U.S. business exec. A founder of Decca Records, Inc. (1934), he served Decca as treasurer (1934-45, vice-pres. (1945-49) and pres. 1949-52; when Decca bought Universal Pictures in 1951, served as pres. of Universal Pictures, 1952-72.

RAND, JAMES HENRY, May 29, 1859 (Tonawanda, N.Y.)–Sept. 15, 1944. U.S. business-equipment manufacturer. Devised first visible-ledger system; formed company that became Remington-Rand, Inc., 1890.

RATHENAU, EMIL, Dec. 11, 1838 (Berlin, Ger.)–June 20, 1915. German industrialist. Founded Deutsche Edison-Gesellschaft, manufacturer of electrical products based on Edison patents, 1883; firm eventually became (in partnership with WERNER VON SIEMENS) Telefunken, the leading electronic manufacturer in Germany, 1903; first to produce aluminum in Germany.

REMINGTON, ELIPHALET, Oct. 28, 1793 (Sheffield, Conn.)–Aug. 12, 1861. U.S. manufacturer. With his father, began to manufacture rifles and other guns, 1828; formed E. Remington & Sons, which manufactured a cultivator for farming as well as weapons, 1856.

REUTER, BARON PAUL JULIUS VON, born Israel Beer Josaphat, 1816 (Kassell, Ger.)–Feb. 25, 1899. German media executive. Founded a telegraph and carrier-pigeon bureau that collected and sent news between Germany and France, 1849; expanded service to London, 1851; extended operation (now called the Reuters News Agency) to the U.S., 1865.

REVSON, CHARLES HASKELL, Oct. 11, 1906 (Boston, Mass.)–Aug. 24, 1975. U.S. cosmetics manufacturer. With a $300 investment, founded (1932) Revlon, Inc., the world's largest cosmetics and fragrance manufacturer, which he served as pres. (1932-62) and chm. and chief exec. officer (1962-75).

RICE, WILLIAM MARSH, Mar. 14, 1816 (Springfield, Mass.)–Sept. 23, 1900. U.S. merchant, philanthropist. Settled in Houston, Tex., where he amassed a considerable fortune as a dry-goods merchant, importer, and land speculator; left endowment for a higher-education

institution founded as Rice Inst. (later Rice U.), 1912.

ROCKEFELLER, DAVID, June 12, 1915 (New York, N.Y.). U.S. banker, philanthropist. An exec. with Chase Natl. Bank of New York from 1948 until 1955, when it merged to form Chase Manhattan Bank; with CMB, served as exec. vice-pres. (1955-57), vice-chm. of the board (1957-61), pres. and chm. of exec. com. (1961-69), and chief exec. officer (1969-   ); serves as trustee of the Rockefeller Bros. Fund, Rockefeller Center, and Rockefeller Family Fund. (Son of JOHN D. ROCKEFELLER, JR.; brother of John D. III, LAURANCE, NELSON A., and Winthrop Rockefeller.)

ROCKEFELLER, JOHN DAVISON, July 9, 1839 (Richford, N.Y.)–May 23, 1937. U.S. financier, philanthropist, founder of the political and financial dynasty that bears his name. Founded an oil-refining business (1860) that became Standard Oil of Ohio in 1870; consolidated firm with many others to form Standard Oil Trust, 1882; Ohio Sup. Ct. deemed illegal and dissolved the trust, 1892; founded U. of Chicago, 1890; founded Rockefeller Fndn., 1913. (Father of J. D. ROCKEFELLER, JR. and EDITH ROCKEFELLER MCCORMICK.)

ROCKEFELLER, JOHN DAVISON, JR., Jan. 29, 1874 (Cleveland, Ohio)–May 11, 1960. U.S. philanthropist. Son of JOHN D. ROCKEFELLER, he devoted his life to philanthropic use of family fortune; philanthropies included Rockefeller Inst. for Medical Research (1901), Gen. Education Board (1902), Rockefeller Foundation (1910), and Internatl. Education Board (1923); built Rockefeller Center (1931-39) and Radio City in New York City; also gave major financial support to Sleepy Hollow Restorations, Inc., Cmdr. RICHARD BYRD's Arctic and Antarctic expeditions, the Cloisters (1938), restoration of Colonial Williamsburg, Va. (1926-60) and Lincoln Center for the Performing Arts, New York City. (Father of DAVID, John D. III, LAURANCE, NELSON A. and Winthrop Rockefeller.)

ROCKEFELLER, LAURANCE SPELMAN, May 26, 1910 (New York, N.Y.). U.S. exec., conservationist. Chm. of Rockefeller Center, Inc., 1953-56 and 1958-66; pres. of Rockresorts, Inc.; chm. of Citizen's Advisory Commission on Environmental Quality, 1969-73. (Son of J. D. ROCKEFELLER, JR.; brother of DAVID, John D. III, NELSON A., and Winthrop Rockefeller.)

ROGERS, HENRY HUTTLESTON, Dec. 29, 1839 (Mattapoisett, Mass.)–May 19, 1909. U.S. financier. Standard Oil of New Jersey exec., 1892-1909; organized Amalgamated Copper Co., which consolidated copper industry (including Anaconda mines), 1898; managed MARK TWAIN's finances and financed HELEN KELLER's education.

ROLLS, CHARLES STEWART, 1877 (?)–July 27, 1910. English automaker, aviator. With Sir FREDERICK HENRY ROYCE, formed Rolls-Royce, Ltd., 1906; first aviator to fly across the English Channel, 1910; one month later, became first English air fatality.

ROTHSCHILD, LIONEL NATHAN, Nov. 22, 1808 (London, Eng.)–June 3, 1879. English banker. First Jewish member of Parliament, 1858-74; made Irish famine loan (1847) and Crimean War loans (1856). (Son of N. M. ROTHSCHILD; grandson of MAYER ROTHSCHILD.)

ROTHSCHILD, MAYER (or Meyer) **ANSELM** (or Amschel), Feb. 23, 1743 (Frankfurt, Ger.)–Sept. 19, 1812. German banker, financier. Founded the

House of Rothschild financial dynasty; began as a money lender in Jewish ghetto of Frankfurt; became a banker and as financial agent (from 1801) for William, Elector of Hesse-Cassell, preserved William's sizable fortune from the 1806 French invasion; in gratitude for his efforts, was allowed free use of the money for a time and, thereby, laid the cornerstone for his own fortune. (Father of N. M. ROTHSCHILD; grandfather of L. N. ROTHSCHILD.)

ROTHSCHILD, NATHAN MAYER (Meyer) **1ST BARON**, Sept. 16, 1777 (Frankfurt, Ger.)–July 28, 1836. German-British financier.. The son of MAYER ANSELM ROTHSCHILD, extended family financial operation to England; opened business firm, 1805; subsidized much of British action against NAPOLEON I; made loans to govts. in Europe and S. America; raised £15 million for British govt. to compensate West Indies slave owners, 1835 (Father of L. N. ROTHSCHILD.)

ROTHSCHILD, WALTER NATHAN, Apr. 28, 1892 (New York, N.Y.)–Oct. 8, 1960. U.S. merchant. Entered family firm, Abraham & Straus dept. store, 1913; as pres. (1937-55) and chm. (1955-60) of A&S, directed expansion of store into chain; a founder and exec. of Federated Dept. Stores, a nationwide group that includes A&S, Filene's, Foley's, Bloomingdale's, and Lazarus dept. stores, 1929-60.

ROYCE, SIR FREDERICK HENRY, Mar. 27, 1863 (Alwalton, Eng.)–Apr. 22, 1933. English automaker. Built three experimental cars in 1904 and interested CHARLES STEWART ROLLS, a car dealer, in selling them; their firms merged to form Rolls-Royce, Ltd., 1906.

RUBICAM, RAYMOND, June 16, 1892 (Brooklyn, N.Y.). U.S. advertising exec. Copywriter at N. W. Ayer & Sons, 1919-23; with John Orr Young, organized (1923) Young & Rubicam advertising agency, which he served as chief exec. officer until his retirement in 1944; first in advertising to engage GEORGE GALLUP to conduct market research, 1932.

RUBINSTEIN, HELENA, 1872 (Cracow, Pol.)–Apr. 1, 1965. U.S. cosmetics exec. Entered beauty business in Australia, 1902; by 1918, her cosmetics line was renowned in the U.S.; founder and pres. of Helena Rubinstein, Inc.

RUPPERT, JACOB, Aug. 5, 1867 (New York, N.Y.)–Jan. 13, 1939. U.S. brewery exec. Pres. of Jacob Ruppert Brewery (founded by his father, 1867), 1915-39; owner of the New York Yankees baseball team, 1914-39.

RUSSELL, WILLIAM HEPBURN, Jan. 31, 1812 (Burlington, Vt.)–Sept. 10, 1872. U.S. pioneer in express business. Organized several freight lines in the West; founded Pony Express between St. Joseph, Mo., and Sacramento, Calif., 1860.

RYAN, JOHN DENIS, Oct. 10, 1864 (Hancock, Mich.)–Feb. 11, 1933. U.S. industrialist. An organizer of Amalgamated Copper Co., 1899; as head of Anaconda copper div. (1903-33), developed it into world's foremost copper producer; in 1912, merged several firms to form Montana Power Co., which he served as pres. until his death.

RYAN, THOMAS FORTUNE, Oct. 17, 1851 (Nelson Co., Va.)–Nov. 23, 1928. U.S. financier. Formed first holding company in the U.S. with his promotion of the New York City transit system, 1886; one of the organizers of the American Tobacco Co., 1890; controlled many banks, 1898-1928.

SAGE, MARGARET OLIVIA, née Slocum, Sept. 8, 1828 (Syracuse, N.Y.)–Nov. 4, 1918. U.S. philanthropist. Widow of financier RUSSELL SAGE, she founded Russell Sage Findn. (1907) with $10 million for the purpose of improving social and living conditions; founded Russell Sage C. for Women, 1916; her vast gifts to charities have been attributed to an attempt to counteract her husband's reputation as a skinflint.

SAGE, RUSSELL, Aug. 4, 1816 (Verona Twp., N.Y.)–July 22, 1906. U.S. financier. Operated successful grocery in Troy, N.Y., 1839-57; U.S. rep. (Whig, N.Y.), 1853-57; went to New York City to engage in stock speculation, 1863; became associated with JAY GOULD in the control of several Western railroads; left his fortune to his wife, MARGARET OLIVIA SAGE.

SCHACHT, HJALMAR, Jan. 22, 1877 (Tingleff, Ger.)–June 4, 1970. German financier. Financial expert noted for stopping the terrible inflation in the Weimar Republic, 1922-23; pres. of Reichsbank, 1923-30; min. of economics under the Third Reich, 1934-37.

SCHAEFER, RUDOLPH JAY, Feb. 21, 1863 (New York, N.Y.)–Nov. 9, 1923. U.S. brewery exec. Joined family-owned F & M Schaefer Brewing Co., 1882; introduced first bottled beer, 1891.

SCHICK, JACOB, Sept. 16, 1877 (Des Moines, Iowa)–July 3, 1937. U.S. manufacturer. Invented and manufactured Pencilaid pencil sharpener (1921), Schick magazine razor (1923), and "Schick dry shaver," the first successful electric shaver (1924).

SCHNERING, OTTO YOUNG, Oct. 9, 1891 (Chicago, Ill.)–Jan. 19, 1953. U.S. manufacturer. Established small candymaking firm (became Curtiss Candy Co., 1919), 1917; pioneer of "nickel" candy bars; first to present brand-name, individually-wrapped candy bars, including "Baby Ruth" and "Butterfingers."

SCHWAB, CHARLES MICHAEL, Feb. 18, 1862 (Williamsburg, Pa.)–Sept. 18, 1939. U.S. manufacturer. "Boy wonder" of the steel industry; pres. of Carnegie Steel Corp., 1897-1901; first pres. of U.S. Steel Corp., 1901-03; as pres. (1903-1913) and chm. of the bd. (1913-39) of Bethlehem Steel Corp., moved firm to major leadership role in metals manufacture.

SCRANTON, GEORGE WHITFIELD, May 11, 1811 (Madison, Conn.)–Mar. 24, 1861. U.S. manufacturer. Developed manufacturing process to smelt iron ore with anthracite coal, 1842; Scranton, Pa., named in his honor.

SEARS, RICHARD W., Dec. 7, 1863 (Stewartville, Minn.)–Sept. 28, 1914. U.S. merchant. Pioneered mail-order business; founded Sears, Roebuck & Co., 1893; Sears pres., 1893-1909.

SELFRIDGE, HARRY GORDON, Jan. 11, 1864 (Ripon, Wisc.)–May 8, 1947. U.S.-British merchant. Partner in Marshall Field & Co. (to 1904); went to London and founded Selfridge & Co., Ltd., a major British dept. store, 1909.

SHEDD, JOHN GRAVES, July 20, 1850 (Alstead, N.H.)–Oct. 22, 1926. U.S. merchant. Became partner of MARSHALL FIELD, 1893; as pres. of Marshall Field & Co. (1906-22), developed firm into retail chain; first Chicago merchant to give half-day holiday on Saturday to employees; endowed Shedd Aquarium in Chicago's Grant Park.

SHIELD, LANSING PETER, Apr. 8, 1896 (Linlithgo, N.Y.)–Jan. 6, 1960. U.S. business exec. Associated with Jones Bros. Tea Co., which merged to form Grand Union Co. grocery chain; pres. of Grand Union, 1947-60; invented Food-O-Mat food dispensing system, 1947.

SHREVE, HENRY MILLER, Oct. 21, 1785 (Burlington Co., N.J.)–Mar. 6, 1851. U.S. river-transport

205

pioneer. Started first trade by water between Philadelphia and St. Louis, 1807; pioneer of Mississippi R. transport, 1810–15; U.S. supt. of Western river improvements, 1827–41; Shreveport, La., named for him, 1839.

SIEMENS, ERNST WERNER VON, Dec. 13, 1816 (Lenthe, Ger.)–Dec. 6, 1892. German manufacturer, inventor. Invented the dial telegraph, 1846; founded Siemens and Halske, manufacturer of electrical equipment, 1847; built the first telegraph line in Germany, 1848; proposed Siemens unit of electrical resistance.

SINCLAIR, HARRY FORD, July 6, 1876 (Wheeling, W. Va.)–Nov. 10, 1956. U.S. oilman. Founder of Sinclair Oil Corp., 1901 (incorporated 1916); a major figure in Teapot Dome scandal, 1923–24.

SKODA, EMIL VON, Nov. 19, 1839 (Pilsen, Bohemia [now Czech.])–Aug. 8, 1900. Czech industrialist. Took over family-owned machine works in Pilsen and developed it into the Skoda Works, famed for the manufacture of munitions, 1869 (incorporated, 1899).

SLATER, SAMUEL, June 9, 1768 (Belper, Eng.)–Apr. 21, 1835. U.S. manufacturer. Manufactured first American-made yarn and founded American cotton-spinning industry, 1790; founded S. Slater Sons, textile manufacturers, 1798; built cotton mills all over New England.

SLOAN, ALFRED PRITCHARD, JR., May 23, 1875 (New Haven, Conn.)–Feb. 17, 1966. U.S. auto exec. Worked for Hyatt Roller Bearing (1895–1916) until it merged into United Motors Corp., which he served as pres. until 1918, when United Motors became part of Gen. Motors Co.; GM pres. (1923–37), and board chm. (1937–56); founded Alfred P. Sloan Fndn., which started Sloan-Kettering Inst. for Cancer Research, 1945.

SPIEGEL, MODIE JOSEPH, Jan. 29, 1901 (Chicago, Ill.). U.S. merchandising exec. Board chm. and chief exec. officer (1932–72) of Spiegel, Inc., the giant Chicago mail-order merchandise firm founded by his grandfather.

STANFORD, A(masa) LELAND, Mar. 9, 1824 Watervliet, N.Y.)–June 21, 1893. U.S. financier, philanthropist, major California pioneer. Financed and constructed Central Pacific RR, 1863–69; CP pres. and dir. 1863–93; gov. of California, 1861–63; U.S. sen. (R, Cal.), 1885–93; pres. of Southern Pacific RR, 1885–90; founded Stanford U. in memory of his son, 1885.

STEINWAY, HENRY ENGELHARD, Feb. 15, 1797 (Wolfshagen, Ger.)–Feb. 7, 1871. German-U.S. manufacturer. Made pianos in Germany, 1825–48; founded Steinway and Sons piano manufacturers, 1853. (Father of WILLIAM STEINWAY.)

STEINWAY, WILLIAM, Mar. 5, 1836 (Seesen, Ger.)–Nov. 30, 1896. U.S. manufacturer. With his father and two brothers, founded Steinway & Sons piano makers, 1853; a skilled piano-maker, oversaw financial and business matters for the firm. (Son of H. E. STEINWAY.)

STONE, AMASA, Apr. 27, 1818 (Charlton, Mass.)–May 11, 1883. U.S. philanthropist, builder. Formed partnership with Azariah Boody to build bridges and railroads; built Cleveland, Columbus & Cincinnati RR, 1846; built Chicago & Milwaukee RR, 1858; endowed Western Reserve C.

STRAUS, JACK ISIDOR, Jan. 13, 1900 (New York, N.Y.). U.S. merchant. The third generation of his family to be associated with the R. H. Macy & Co. dept. stores, serving as pres. (1939–56), chm. of the board and chief exec. officer (1956–68), chm. of exec. com. (1968–76), and honorary chm.

and dir. emeritus (1976–   ). (Son of JESSE ISIDOR STRAUS; nephew of PERCY SELDEN STRAUS.)

STRAUS, JESSE ISIDOR, June 25, 1872 (New York, N.Y.)–Oct. 4, 1936. U.S. merchant. Joined R. H. Macy Co., 1896; became partner when his father, ISIDOR STRAUS, a senior partner, went down on the *Titanic*, 1912; as pres. (1919–33), developed Macy's into "world's largest store"; U.S. amb. to France, 1933–36. (Father of JACK ISIDOR STRAUS.)

STRAUS, ISIDOR, Feb. 6, 1845 (Otterberg, Ger.)–Apr. 15, 1912. U.S. merchant. With his brother, NATHAN STRAUS, became an owner of R. H. Macy Co. dept. store, 1896; U.S. rep. (D, N.Y.), 1894–95; went down with the *Titanic*. (Father of JESSE ISIDOR and PERCY SELDEN STRAUS.)

STRAUS, NATHAN, Jan. 31, 1848 (Otterberg, Ger.)–Jan. 11, 1931. U.S. merchant. With his brother, ISIDOR STRAUS, became an owner of R. H. Macy & Co. dept. store, 1896; a prominent Zionist; initiated campaign for compulsory pasteurization of milk, 1892.

STRAUS, PERCY SELDEN, June 27, 1876 (New York, N.Y.)–Apr. 6, 1944. U.S. merchant. Associated with R. H. Macy dept. store from 1897, serving as pres. (1933–39) and board chm. (1939–44); responsible for flagship store's move to present Herald Sq. location in New York City, 1902. (Son of ISIDOR STRAUS; brother of JESSE ISIDOR STRAUS.)

STRAUSS, LEVI, c.1829 (?)–1902. U.S. manufacturer. Little known about his life; left New York City for California to prospect for gold, c.1850; sold cloth to earn money for prospecting; used a spare bolt of canvas to create pants for a miner who had complained about the cheapness of cloth, thus inventing "denim jeans"; founded Levi-Strauss Co. in San Francisco and manufactured Levi pants until his death.

STUART, ELBRIDGE AMOS, Sept. 10, 1856 (Guilford Co., N.C.)–Jan. 14, 1944. U.S. manufacturer. Established and ran a Texas wholesale and retail grocery business, 1881–93; organized firm that produced Carnation evaporated milk (later the Carnation Co.), 1899; Carnation pres. (1899–1932) and board chm. (1932–44).

STUBER, WILLIAM GEORGE, Apr. 9, 1864 (Louisville, Ky.)–June 17, 1959. U.S. business exec. Succeeded GEORGE EASTMAN as pres. of Eastman Kodak Co., 1925–34; EK board chm., 1934–41; made many technical advances in Kodak's sensitized products, including X-ray film (introduced 1914).

STUDEBAKER, CLEMENT, Mar. 12, 1831 (nr. Gettysburg, Pa.)–Nov. 27, 1901. U.S. manufacturer. Cofounder of H. and C. Studebaker blacksmith and wagon-making firm, 1852; firm became Studebaker Bros. Manufacturing Co., 1868; as pres. (1868–1901), made Studebaker the largest wagon and carriage manufacturer in U.S.; firm later made Studebaker autos.

SWIFT, GUSTAVUS FRANKLIN, June 24, 1839 (Sandwich, Mass.)–Mar. 29, 1903. U.S. meat packer. Started as a butcher in Massachusetts, moved to Chicago; instrumental in development of refrigerated railroad car, 1875; incorporated Swift & Co. meat-packing firm, 1885.

THOMPSON, J(ames) WALTER, Oct. 28, 1847 (Pittsfield, Mass.)–Oct. 16, 1928. U.S. advertising exec. Started as advertising-space salesman for William J. Carlton, 1867; bought out Carlton and formed J. Walter Thompson advertising agency,

1878; brought respectability to advertising industry; famous clients included Pabst Breweries, Kodak, and Prudential Insurance; sold his agency and retired, 1916.

THOMSON, ROY HERBERT, LORD THOMSON OF FLEET, June 5, 1894 (Toronto, Ont., Can.)–Aug. 4, 1976. Canadian-British publishing exec. Parlayed a small Ontario radio station into one of the world's largest media empires, the Thomson Organization, Ltd.; acquired controlling interest in *The Times* of London, 1967. *Baron of the Realm,* 1964.

THYSSEN, FRITZ, Nov. 9, 1873 (Mülheim, Ger.)–Feb. 8, 1951. German industrialist. An early supporter of ADOLF HITLER; controlled 15% of Vereingte Stahlwerke, the world's largest mining trust; had major falling out with Nazis, fled to Switzerland, losing all his money and property, 1933.

TIFFANY, CHARLES LEWIS, Feb. 15, 1812 (Killingly, Conn.)–Feb. 18, 1902. U.S. merchant. Founded (1837) a business that became (1868) Tiffany & Co. jewelers.

TILYOU, GEORGE CORNELIUS, Feb. 3, 1862 (New York, N.Y.)–Nov. 30, 1914. U.S. amusement-park operator. A real-estate pioneer in the Coney Is., N.Y., area; beginning with Tilyou's Surf Theatre in 1890, built an amusement-park empire that included the Coney Is. boardwalk and Steeplechase amusement park.

TREES, JOE CLIFTON, Nov. 10, 1869 (Trees Mills, Pa.)–May 19, 1943. U.S. oilman. In partnership with Michael L. Benedum (1896–1943), discovered more oil than any individual or group in history, including first oil in Illinois (1899), the Caddo pool in Louisiana (1909), and the Big Lake field in western Texas (1924).

TRIPPE, JUAN TERRY, June 27, 1899 (Seabright, N.J.). U.S. aviation exec. A WW I naval aviator who formed Long Island Airways, 1922; a founder of Colonial Air Transport (New York City–Boston), one of first domestic carriers, 1927; a founder of airline that became Pan American Airways, Inc., in 1928; as Pan Am pres. (1927–68) and honorary chm. (1968–), started first U.S. internatl. air mail service, using Pan Am planes (1927) and started first transatlantic passenger service (1939).

VAIL, THEODORE NEWTON, July 16, 1845 (Minerva, Ohio)–Apr. 16, 1920. U.S. communications exec. Launched U.S. govt.'s fast mail service, 1875; gen. mgr. of Bell Telephone Co., 1878–85; founded Western Union Telegraph Co., 1881; pres. of A.T. & T., 1885–87 and 1907–19; as pres. of Western Union (1909–13), revitalized firm; influential in laying first transcontinental telephone cable, 1915.

VAN CAMP, GILBERT C., Dec. 25, 1817 (Brookville, Ind.)–Apr. 4, 1900. U.S. food-products exec. While associated with an Indianapolis grocery firm, built first cold-storage warehouse in U.S.; originated process of canning foods and organized (1862) Van Camp Packing Co., serving as pres. until 1898.

VANDERBILT, CORNELIUS ("Commodore"), May 27, 1794 (Staten Is., N.Y.)–Jan. 4, 1877. U.S. financier, transport exec. Started ferry service between Staten Is. and Manhattan, 1810; in association with Thomas Gibbons, captained ferry line between New Brunswick, N.J. and New York City; formed his own Hudson R. steamboat line in 1829, and by 1846 was a millionaire; owned a New York–to–California steamship line, 1850–58; bought controlling interest in New York and Harlem RR, New York Central RR, and Hudson R. RR,

1862–63; left $100 million at his death. (Father of W. H. VANDERBILT; grandfather of W. K. VANDERBILT.)

VANDERBILT, WILLIAM HENRY, May 8, 1821 (New Brunswick, N.J.)–Dec. 8, 1885. U.S. financier. Oldest son of the Commodore CORNELIUS VANDERBILT; succeeded his father as pres. of New York Central RR in 1877 and expanded holdings to include Chicago, Northwestern, and Nickel Plate RRs; donated $100,000 for erection of Cleopatra's Needle in New York City's Central Park.

VANDERBILT, WILLIAM KISSAM, Dec. 12, 1849 (New Dorp, N.Y.)–July 12, 1920. U.S. financier. Grandson of the Commodore CORNELIUS VANDERBILT; financed many railroad consolidations and expansions; pres. of New York & Harlem RR, 1899–1920; a philanthropist who bequeathed his collections of paintings to New York City's Metropolitan Museum of Art, 1920.

VAUCLAIN, SAMUEL MATTHEW, May 18, 1856 (Philadelphia, Pa.)–Feb. 4, 1940. U.S. manufacturer, inventor. Associated with Baldwin Locomotive works, 1883–1940; invented first compound locomotive (1889), wrought iron center for railroad tracks (1889), and rack and adhesion locomotive, 1895.

VILLARD, HENRY, born Ferdinand Heinrich Gustav Hilgard, Apr. 10, 1835 (Speyer, Bavaria)–Nov. 12, 1900. U.S. railroad magnate. Fled Bavaria to avoid military service; worked as journalist in New York City, 1858–63; formed (1881) a pool that bought the Northern Pacific RR, which he served as pres. (1881–84) and board chm. (1888–93); gave financial support to THOMAS A. EDISON; founded Edison Gen. Electric Co., 1889.

WALLER, FREDERIC, Mar. 10, 1886 (Brooklyn, N.Y.)–May 18, 1954. U.S. manufacturer, inventor. Through his firm, which manufactured and designed optical equipment for movies, invented and developed the Cinerama process, 1938–54.

WANAMAKER, JOHN, July 11, 1838 (Philadelphia, Pa.)–Dec. 12, 1922. U.S. merchant, govt. official. Cofounder of Oak Hall, a Philadelphia clothing store, 1861; founded in 1869 a men's store bearing his name, converting it to a dept. store in 1877; U.S. postmaster gen., 1889–93.

WARBURG, FELIX MORITZ, Jan. 14, 1871 (Hamburg, Ger.)–Oct. 20, 1937. U.S. financier, philanthropist. Partner in Kuhn, Loeb & Co., internatl. bankers, 1897–1937; helped secure first legislation for probation for juvenile offenders, 1902; worked with Henry St. Settlement House in New York City, 1919–37; founded and served as officer with several Jewish charities, including Jewish Relief Com. (1914) and Council of the Jewish Agency for Palestine (1929). (Uncle of J. P. WARBURG.)

WARBURG, JAMES PAUL, Aug. 18, 1896 (Hamburg, Ger.)–June 3, 1969. U.S. banker, govt. official, author. A member of Pres. F. D. ROOSEVELT's "Brain Trust," 1932–34. *The Money Muddle,* 1934; *Our War and Our Peace,* 1941; *Germany—Bridge or Battleground,* 1947. (Nephew of F. M. WARBURG.)

WARD, MONTGOMERY, Feb. 17, 1844 (Chatham, N.J.)–Dec. 7, 1913. U.S. merchant. In partnership with George P. Thorne, founded Montgomery Ward & Co., first U.S. mail-order house, 1872.

WARNER, ALBERT, July 23, 1884 (Poland)–Nov. 26, 1967. U.S. film exec. Founded Warner Bros. Pictures, Inc., with his brothers Harry M., Sam, and JACK L. WARNER, 1923; Warner's vice-pres. and treasurer, 1923-56; known for his honesty in business.

WARNER, JACK L., Aug, 2, 1892 (London, Ont., Can.)-Sept. 9, 1978. U.S. movie exec. With his brothers, Harry, Sam, and ALBERT WARNER, founded Warner Brothers Pictures, Inc., 1923; introduced first film with soundtrack, 1926; introduced first film with spoken sound, 1927; as head of production for the studio, credited with discovery of many stars and directors and with instituting a development program for contract players.

WASHBURN, WILLIAM DREW, Jan. 14, 1831 (Livermore, Me.)-July 29, 1912. U.S. manufacturer, govt. official. Founded Minneapolis & St. Louis RR, 1870; founded Pillsbury-Washburn flour mills, 1874; U.S. rep. (R, Minn.), 1879-1885; U.S. sen. (R, Minn.), 1889-95.

WATSON, THOMAS JOHN, Feb. 17, 1874 (Campbell, N.Y.)-June 19, 1956. U.S. industrialist. Converted financially ailing Computing-Tabulating-Recording Co., makers of business machines, into an international giant, Internatl. Business Machines Corp. (named changed to IBM, 1924); introduced many firsts, including printing tabulator (1920), electric typewriter (1935-41), electronic calculator (1948), and electronic data-processing system (1952); pres. and dir. (1914-49) and chm. bd. and chief exec. off. (1949-56), IBM. (Father of T. J. WATSON, JR.)

WATSON, THOMAS JOHN, JR., Jan. 8, 1914 (Dayton, Ohio). U.S. business exec. Son of THOMAS J. WATSON, the founder of IBM, which he joined as junior salesman, 1937; succeeded his father as pres., 1952-79; U.S. amb. to the USSR, 1979-

WELLS, HENRY WILLIAM DWIGHT, Dec. 12, 1805 (Thetford, Vt.)-Dec. 10, 1878. U.S. transportation exec. In partnership with WILLIAM G. FARGO, established Western Express, 1844; firm consolidated with other companies to form American Express Co., 1850; American Express pres., 1850-68; also with Fargo, formed Wells Fargo & Co., 1852.

WHARTON, JOSEPH, Mar. 3, 1826 (Philadelphia, Pa.)-Jan. 11, 1909. U.S. metals producer. First producer of nickel in U.S., 1873; founded Bethlehem Steel Corp., 1873; founded Wharton School of Finance and Political Economy at U. of Pennsylvania, 1881.

WHITE, ALFRED TREDWAY, May 28, 1846 (Brooklyn, N.Y.)-Jan. 29, 1921. U.S. merchant, philanthropist. Associated with family firm, W. A. & A. M. White, merchants, 1865-1921; in 1872, built Tower & Homes tenements in Brooklyn, N.Y., the first planned, decent low-income housing in U.S., which spurred tenement reform.

WHITE, WILLIAM, Feb. 3, 1897 (Midland, N.J.)-Apr. 6, 1967. U.S. railroad exec. Often called the "railroader's railroader"; pres. of Delaware, Lackawanna & Western RR, 1941-52; pres. of New York Central RR, 1952-54; pres. of Delaware & Hudson RR, 1954-63, chmn., 1963-67; pres. of Erie-Lackawanna RR, 1963-67.

WICKMAN, CARL ERIC, Aug. 7, 1887 (Vamhus, Swe.)-Feb. 5, 1954. U.S. transportation exec. Pioneered bus lines in Minnesota, 1914-25; formed holding company for several Midwest bus lines, Motor Transit Corp., 1926; company name changed to Greyhound Corp., 1930; as pres. (1930-46) and board chm. (1946-51), developed Greyhound into nationwide bus system.

WIDENER, PAUL ARRELL BROWN, Nov. 13, 1834 (Philadelphia, Pa.)-Nov. 6, 1915. U.S. finan-

cier, philanthropist. With William L. Elkins, purchased Philadelphia street-car lines, 1864; developed Philadelphia and New York City transit systems, 1886-93; well-known art collector, chiefly of Chinese porcelain.

WILLARD, DANIEL, Jan. 28, 1861 (North Hartland, Vt.)-July 6, 1942. U.S. railroad exec. As pres. of Baltimore & Ohio RR, (1910-41), expanded and improved service, encouraged development of labor unions; effectively headed off a nationwide rail strike, 1917; negotiated temporary 10% industrywide worker layoffs to save U.S. railroads an estimated $400 million at the height of the Depression, 1932.

WILLYS, JOHN NORTH, Oct. 25, 1873 (Canandaigua, N.Y.)-Aug. 26, 1935. U.S. manufacturer, diplomat. In 1908, reorganized failing Overland Auto Co. into Willys-Overland, which he served as pres., 1908-29 and 1935; U.S. amb. to Poland, 1930-32.

WILSON, CHARLES ERWIN, July 18, 1890 (Minerva, Ohio)-Sept. 26, 1961. U.S. industrialist, govt. official. As an engineer with the Westinghouse Corp. (1909-19), designed firm's first auto starter (1912); joined Gen. Motors Co., 1919; GM pres., 1941-53; U.S. secretary of def., 1953-57.

WILSON, KEMMONS, Jan. 5, 1913 (Osceola, Ark.). U.S. hotelier. A Memphis, Tenn., realtor since 1945, opened his first Holiday Inn motel there, 1952; founded Holiday Inn chain, 1953; chm. of the board of Holiday Inns, Inc., 1953-79.

WINSTON, HARRY, Mar. 1, 1896 (New York, N.Y.)-Dec. 8, 1978. U.S. jeweler. Founded the renowned gem dealership Harry Winston, Inc., 1932; purchased many famous jewels, including the Hope Diamond, which he gave to the Smithsonian Inst., 1958.

WITTEMANN, CHARLES R., Sept. 15, 1884 (Staten I., N.Y.)-July 8, 1967. U.S. manufacturer, aviation pioneer. Designed and developed first commercially-sold biplane-type gliders, 1903; designed and built Baldwin Red Devil airplane, 1908; developed first automatic-pilot systems for aircraft, 1916-18.

WOOD, ROBERT ELKINGTON, June 13, 1879 (Kansas City, Mo.)-Nov. 6, 1969. U.S. merchant, soldier. Served with distinction in WW I; vice-pres. of Montgomery Ward, 1919-24; joined Sears, Roebuck & Co. in 1924, serving as pres. (1928-39) and board chm. (1939-54); developed Sears from strictly mail-order to retail business; a leader of America First movement prior to WW II.

WOOLWORTH, FRANK WINFIELD, Apr. 13, 1852 (Rodman, N.Y.)-Aug. 8, 1919. U.S. merchant. Founded F. W. Woolworth Co., 1879; opened his first successful store, selling only five-and ten-cent merchandise, in Lancaster, Pa., June 1879; built network of over 1,000 stores in North America by the time of his death; built Woolworth Bldg. in New York City, 1913.

WRIGLEY, P(hillip) K(night), Dec. 5, 1894 (Chicago, Ill.)-Apr. 12, 1977. U.S. manufacturer. Pres. (1925-61) and chm. of the bd. of dirs. (1961-77), William Wrigley & Co., world's largest chewing-gum manufacturer; owner of the Chicago Cubs baseball team. (Son of W. WRIGLEY, JR.)

WRIGLEY, WILLIAM, JR., Sept. 30, 1861 (Philadelphia, Pa.)-Jan. 26, 1932. U.S. manufacturer. Founded the Chicago-based chewing-gum firm bearing his name, 1891; served as pres. until 1932. (Father of P. K. WRIGLEY.)

WRISTON, WALTER BIGELOW, Aug. 3, 1919 (Middletown, Conn.). U.S. banker. Rose through ranks of First Natl. City Bank (now Citibank, N.A.) to become pres. (1967-70) and board chm. (1970-   ).

WURF, JERRY, May 18, 1919 (New York, N.Y.). U.S. labor leader. Organizer for the American Federation of State, County, and Municipal Employees, 1947-58; internatl. pres. of the union, 1964-   .

WURLITZER, RUDOLPH, Jan. 31, 1831 (Schoneck, Ger.)-Jan. 14, 1914. U.S. manufacturer. Began making trumpets and drums in Cincinnati, Ohio in 1860, branching out into pianos in 1868; introduced first automatically-played, electric, coin-operated instruments, 1892.

YABLONSKI, JOSEPH, 1910 (Pittsburgh, Pa.)-Jan. 5, 1970. U.S. union official. Began working as coal miner in 1925; lost election for presidency of United Mine Workers in bitter dispute with the in-

cumbent W. A. "TONY" BOYLE, 1969; found slain with his wife and daughter; Boyle and four others were indicted and convicted of the murders.

YALE, ELIHU, 1649 (Boston, Mass.)-July 8, 1721. U.S. philanthropist. Made fortune with British East India Co., 1671-99; gov. of Madras, 1687-92; donated monetary gifts and books (1714-18) to Collegiate School, which became Yale C. in 1745.

ZECKENDORF, WILLIAM, June 30, 1905 (Paris, Ill.)-Sept. 30, 1976. U.S. business exec. Noted for his interests in urban development; joined Webb & Knapp, Inc., internatl. realtors in 1939, rising to pres. and chm. of the board, 1942-65; sold property for UN headquarters to JOHN D. ROCK-EFELLER, JR. 1946; managed Astor family holdings, 1941-46; built business developments in Los Angeles (Century City) and L'Enfant Plaza in Washington, D.C.

SPORTS PERSONALITIES

AARON, HENRY LOUIS, Feb. 5, 1934 (Mobile, Ala.). U.S. baseball player. Milwaukee/Atlanta Braves (1954-74), Milwaukee Brewers (1975-76) outfielder; holds major-league record for most career home runs (755), RBIs (2,297), games played (3,298), at bats (12,364), total bases (6,856); NL batting champ, 1956, 1959; NL home-run leader, 1957, 1963, 1966, and 1967; NL RBI leader, 1957, 1960, 1963, and 1966; holds record for most NL career hits (3,771).

ABDUL-JABBAR, KAREEM, born Lew Alcindor, Apr. 16, 1947 (New York, N.Y.). U.S. basketball player. Led UCLA to three consecutive NCAA titles 1967-69; NBA scoring leader 1971, 1972; NBA MVP 1971, 1972, 1974, 1976, 1977.

ADRIAN, ANSON ("Cap"), Apr. 17, 1851 (Marshalltown, Ia.)-Apr. 14, 1922. U.S. baseball player. Pioneer baseball player/manager with Chicago Cubs, 1876-98 (manager, 1879-98); led NL in batting, 1881, 1888; elected to Baseball Hall of Fame, 1939.

ALBRIGHT, TENLEY EMMA (Mrs. Tudor Gardiner), July 18, 1935 (Newton Center, Mass.). U.S. figure skater. First U.S. woman to win world amateur figure-skating championship (1953) and Olympic gold medal (1956); first to win world, N. American, and U.S. championships in one year, 1953.

ALEXANDER, GROVER CLEVELAND, Feb. 26, 1887 (Elba, Neb.)-Nov. 4, 1950. U.S. baseball pitcher. Won 374 major-league games; elected to Baseball Hall of Fame, 1938.

ALI, MUHAMMAD, born Cassius Clay, Jan. 18, 1942 (Louisville, Ky.). U.S. boxer. First boxer to hold heavyweight title three times, 1964-67, 1974-78, 1978-79. Light-heavyweight gold medalist, 1960 Olympics; stripped of pro title by World Boxing Assn. and other groups after refusing military induction (1967), then reinstated after U.S. Sup. Ct. ruling (1971); leader in Black Muslim faith; known for poetic predictions before fights.

ALLEN, GEORGE, Apr. 29, 1922 (Detroit, Mich.). U.S. football coach. Head coach of L.A. Rams, 1966-70 and 1978; head coach of Washington Redskins, 1970-78; took Redskins to Super Bowl, 1973.

ALLEN, MEL, Feb. 14, 1913 (Birmingham, Ala.). U.S. sports broadcaster. Broadcasted for N.Y. Yankees, 1939-64; Fox *Movietone News* commentator, 1946-64; elected to National Sportswriters and Broadcasters Hall of Fame, 1972.

ALLISON, BOBBY, Dec. 3, 1937 (Hueytown, Ala.). U.S. auto racer. Won Daytona 500 race, 1978.

ALSTON, WALTER, Dec. 1, 1911 (Butler Co., Ohio). U.S. baseball manager. Managed Brooklyn/L.A. Dodgers, 1954-76; team won seven NL titles and four World Series (1955, 1959, 1963, 1965).

ALWORTH, LANCE, Aug. 3, 1940 (Houston, Tex.). U.S. football player. Pass receiver with AFL San Diego Chargers (1962-70) and NFL Dallas Cowboys (1971-72); led AFL in receptions, 1966, 1968-69; scored 85 pro TDs on pass receptions; named to *Sporting News* AFL All-Star team, 1963-69; elected to Football Hall of Fame, 1978.

ANDRETTI, MARIO GABRIEL, Feb. 28, 1940 (Trieste, Italy). U.S. auto racer. American Automobile Assn. champ., 1965, 1966, 1969. Won Indy 500, 1969; World Grand Prix champion, 1978.

ANTHONY, EARL, Apr. 27, 1938 (Tacoma, Wash.). U.S. bowler. Won record $110,833 on pro tour, 1976; Bowler of the Year, 1974-76.

ARCARO, EDDIE, born George Edward Arcaro, Feb. 19, 1916 (Cincinnati, Ohio). U.S. jockey. Won 4,779 races in career, including five Kentucky Derbies, six Preaknesses, six Belmont Stakes; rode Triple Crown winners Whirlaway (1941) and Citation (1948).

ARMSTRONG, HENRY, born Henry Jackson, Dec. 12, 1912 (Columbus, Miss.). U.S. boxer. Held feather-, bantam-, and lightweight titles simultaneously, 1937-38; elected to Boxing Hall of Fame, 1954.

ASHE, ARTHUR, July 10, 1943 (Richmond, Va.). U.S. tennis player. First black to make top rank in men's competition. U.S. singles champion, 1968; Wimbledon champion, 1975.

AUSTIN, TRACY, Dec. 2, 1962 (Rolling Hills, Calif.). U.S. tennis player. National junior champion, 1977 and 1978; youngest U.S. champ, 1979.

BALUKAS, JEAN, 1959 (Brooklyn, N.Y.). U.S. pool player. U.S. women's champion, 1972-   .

BANKS, ERNIE, born Ernest Banks, Jan. 31, 1931 (Dallas, Tex.). U.S. baseball player. Led NL in home runs, 1958 and 1960; led NL in RBIs, 1958 and 1960; NL MVP, 1958 and 1959; elected to Baseball Hall of Fame, 1977; spent entire career (1953-71) with Chicago Cubs.

BANNISTER, ROGER, Mar. 23, 1929 (Harrow,

Eng.). British athlete, physician. First to run a mile in under four minutes (3:59.4), May 6, 1954.

BARBER, RED, born Walter Barber, Feb. 17, 1908 (Columbus, Miss.). U.S. sports broadcaster. Covered Brooklyn Dodgers and N.Y. Yankees baseball games from 1930s to 1960s.

BARRY, RICK, Mar. 28, 1944 (Elizabeth, N.J.). U.S. basketball player. NCAA scoring leader, 1965; NBA Rookie of the Year, 1966; NBA scoring leader, 1967; ABA scoring leader, 1969.

BAUGH, SAMUEL ("Slingin' Sammy"), Mar. 17, 1914 (Temple, Tex.). U.S. football player. Held numerous NFL passing and punting records at 1952 retirement, after 16 pro seasons; elected to Football Hall of Fame, 1963.

BAYI, FILBERT, June 23, 1953 (Karratu, Tanganyika). Tanzanian runner. Set 1,500-m world record (3:32.2) in 1974, (broken in 1979 by SEBASTIAN COE); ran 3:51 mile, 1975.

BAYLOR, ELGIN, Sept. 16, 1934 (Washington, D.C.). U.S. basketball player, coach. A 10-time NBA All-Star; elected to Basketball Hall of Fame, 1976; head coach of New Orleans Jazz, 1974-79.

BELIVEAU, JEAN, Aug. 31, 1931 (Three Rivers, Que., Can.). Canadian hockey player. As Montreal Canadiens center (1953-71) scored 507 goals; NHL leading scorer, 1956; NHL MVP, 1956 and 1964.

BENCH, JOHNNY, Dec. 7, 1947 (Oklahoma City, Okla.). U.S. baseball player. Cincinnati Reds catcher; NL Rookie of the Year, 1968; NL home-run leader, 1970 and 1972; NL RBI leader, 1970, 1972 and 1974; NL MVP, 1970 and 1972.

BERG, PATTY, Feb. 13, 1918 (Minneapolis, Minn.). U.S. golfer. Won over 80 tournaments; Female Athlete of the Year, 1938, 1943, 1955.

BERGEY, BILL, Feb. 9, 1945 (S. Dayton, N.Y.). U.S. football player. Philadelphia Eagles linebacker; played in Pro Bowl, 1974 and 1976-78.

BERRA, YOGI, born Lawrence Peter Berra, May 12, 1925 (St. Louis, Mo.). U.S. baseball player, manager, coach. As N.Y. Yankees catcher (1946-63), played in 14 World Series; AL MVP, 1951, 1954, and 1955; managed N.Y. Yankees to AL pennant, 1964.

BERRY, RAY(mond), Feb. 27, 1933 (Corpus Christi, Tex.). U.S. football player. Baltimore Colts receiver who caught 631 career passes, good for 9,275 yds.

BING, DAVE, Nov. 24, 1943 (Washington, D.C.). U.S. basketball player. NBA leading scorer, 1968; averaged over 20 points per game during career (1967-78).

BLALOCK, JANE, Sept. 19, 1945 (Portsmouth, N.H.). U.S. golfer. Has won over $500,000 on pro tour during career; LPGA Rookie of the Year, 1969.

BLANDA, GEORGE, Sept. 17, 1927 (Youngwood, Pa.). U.S. football player. Quarterback-kicker for Chicago Bears (1949-58), Houston Oilers (1960-66) and Oakland Raiders (1967-69 and 1970-74); scored record 2,002 points in 26-year pro career.

BLANKERS-KOEN, FANNY, 1918 (Amsterdam, Neth.). Dutch track star. Won four gold medals at 1948 Olympics: 100-meter run, 200-meter run, 80-meter hurdles, and 400-meter relay.

BLUE, VIDA ROCHELLE, July 28, 1949 (Mansfield, La.). U.S. baseball player. Pitcher for Oakland A's, S.F. Giants; 20-game winner three times; AL MVP, 1971; won AL Cy Young Award, 1971.

BORG, BJORN, June 6, 1956 (Södertalje, Swe.).

Swedish tennis player. Led Sweden to first Davis Cup win, 1975; Wimbledon champ, 1976, 1977, 1978, 1979.

BOROS, JULIUS, Mar. 3, 1920 (Fairfield, Conn.). U.S. golfer. U.S. Open champion, 1952 and 1963; PGA champion, 1968.

BOSSY, MIKE, Jan. 22, 1957 (Montreal, Que., Can.). Canadian hockey player. N.Y. Islanders right wing, 1977- . Scored NHL record 53 rookie goals, 1978; led NHL in goals, 1979.

BOSTOCK, LYMAN, Nov. 22, 1950 (Birmingham, Ala.)-Sept. 24, 1978. U.S. baseball player. As Minn. Twins and Calif. Angels outfielder, one of highest-paid baseball players in 1978; shot dead in Gary, Ind.

BOUDREAU, LOU(is), July 17, 1917 (Harvey, Ill.)-U.S. baseball player, manager. Shortstop for Clev. Indians (1938-50) and Boston Red Sox (1951-52); AL MVP, 1948; managed Clev. Indians to World Series win, 1948; now a sportscaster for the Chicago Cubs.

BOUTON, JIM, born James Alan Bouton, Mar. 8, 1939 (Newark, N.J.). U.S. baseball player. Controversial pitcher principally for N.Y. Yankees (1962-68) who wrote "tell-all" book *Ball Four* (1970) after leaving game; made news with attempted comeback, 1978.

BOWA, LARRY, Dec. 6, 1945 (Sacramento, Calif.). U.S. baseball player. As Philadelphia Phillies shortstop, (1970-), one of the best fielders of the 1970s.

BRABHAM, JACK, Apr. 2, 1926 (Sydney, Austrl.). Australian auto racer, builder. Grand Prix champ, 1959, 1960, 1966.

BRADSHAW, TERRY, Sept. 12, 1948 (Shreveport, La.). U.S. football player. Quarterback for Pittsburgh Steelers, whom he led to Super Bowl championships in 1975, 1976, 1979 and 1980.

BRETT, GEORGE, May 15, 1953 (Moundsville, W. Va.). U.S. baseball player. K.C. Royals third baseman (1973-); had .333 batting average to win AL batting title, 1976.

BROCK, LOU, June 18, 1939 (El Dorado, Ark.). U.S. baseball player. Chicago Cubs (1961-64), St. Louis Cardinals (1964-79) outfielder; stole record 118 bases, 1974; has led NL in stolen bases eight times; broke record for all-time major-league bases stolen, surpassing W. R. Hamilton's record of 937, 1978; stroked 3,000th hit, 1979.

BROWN, JIM, Feb. 17, 1936 (St. Simon's, Ga.). U.S. football player, actor. As Cleveland Browns fullback (1957-65), rushed for record 12,312 career yards (5.2 yds./carry); had record 106 career touchdowns; rushed for 100 yds. or more record 58 times during career; named NFL Player of the Year, 1958 and 1963; now a film actor, mostly in action films.

BROWN, MORDECAI PETER CENTENNIAL ("Three Finger"), Oct. 19, 1876 (Nyesville, Ind.)-Feb. 14, 1948. U.S. baseball player. Pitcher, chiefly with Chicago Cubs, (1904-13 and 1916); 20-game winner five times; led NL in ERA, 1906; had 2.06 career ERA; elected to Baseball Hall of Fame, 1949.

BROWN, PAUL, July 9, 1908 (Norwalk, Ohio). U.S. football coach, executive. One of the most innovative football coaches of all time. Coached Cleveland Browns, 1946-62; coached Cincinnati Bengals, 1968-76; elected to Pro Football Hall of Fame, 1967.

BRUNDAGE, AVERY, Sept. 28, 1887 (Detroit, Mich.)-May 8, 1975. U.S. sports figure. Pres. of

U.S. Olympic Assoc., 1929–53; pres. of International Olympic Com., 1952–72.

BRYANT, PAUL ("Bear"), Sept. 11, 1913 (Kingsland, Ark.). U.S. football coach. Coach of U. of Alabama, 1958–   ; Amer. Football Coaches Assn. Coach of the Year, 1961, 1972, and 1973.

BUDGE, DON, June 13, 1915 (Oakland, Calif.). U.S. tennis player. Won tennis Grand Slam, 1938; inducted into Tennis Hall of Fame, 1964.

BUENO, MARIA, Oct. 11, 1939 (São Paulo, Braz.). Brazilian tennis player. U.S. singles champ, 1959, 1963, 1964, 1966; Wimbledon champ three times.

BUNNING, JIM, Oct. 23, 1931 (Southgate, Ky.). U.S. baseball pitcher. Played chiefly with Detroit Tigers (1955–63) and Phillies (1964–69 and 70–71); led AL in strikeouts, 1959–60; led NL in strikeouts, 1967; pitched 2 no-hitters, including perfect game against N.Y. Mets, June 21, 1964.

BURTON, MIKE, July 3, 1947 (Des Moines, Ia.). U.S. swimmer. Olympic gold medalist in 1,500-m freestyle, 1968 and 1972.

BUTKUS, DICK, Dec. 9, 1942 (Chicago, Ill.). U.S. football player. Chicago Bears linebacker, 1965–73; chosen best NFL defensive player in 1969 and 1970.

BUTTON, DICK, July 18, 1929 (Englewood, N.J.). U.S. figure skater, broadcaster. Olympic gold medalist in figure skating, 1948 and 1952; world titlist, 1948–52; now sports commentator for ABC.

CAMP, WALTER CHAUNCEY, Apr. 17, 1859 (New Britain, Conn.)–Mar. 14, 1925. U.S. football player, coach, athletic director. Often called the father of American football, developed game and established many rules; promoted All-American designations.

CAMPANELLA, ROY, Nov. 19, 1921 (Philadelphia, Pa.). U.S. baseball player. Brooklyn Dodgers catcher, 1948–57; NL MVP, 1951, 1953, and 1955; inducted into Baseball Hall of Fame, 1969; crippled in accident, 1958.

CAMPBELL, EARL, Mar. 29, 1955 (Tyler, Tex.). U.S. football player. As U. of Texas running back, awarded 1977 Heisman Trophy; with NFL Houston Oilers, Rookie of Year, 1978; AFC's leading rusher, MVP, 1978, 1979.

CAREW, ROD, Oct. 1, 1945 (Gatun, Panama). U.S. baseball player. Infielder for the Minnesota Twins (1964–78) and Calif. Angels (1979–   ); AL batting champ seven times; .335 lifetime batting avg.; 200 or more hits, four times; hit .388 in 1977; AL MVP, 1977.

CARLTON, STEVE(n Thomas), Dec. 22, 1944 (Miami, Fla.). U.S. baseball player. As St. Louis Cardinals (1965–71) and Phila. Phillies (1972–   ) pitcher, a four-time 20-game winner; led NL with 27 wins, 310 strikeouts, 1.98 ERA in 1972; NL Cy Young Award, 1972 and 1977.

CARNER, JOANNE, née Gunderson, 1939(?). U.S. golfer. U.S. Women's Open champ, 1971 and 1976; U.S. Women's Amateur champ, 1957, 1960, 1962, 1966, and 1968.

CARTER, DON, July 29, 1930 (Miami, Fla.). U.S. professional bowler. PBA Bowler of the Year 1953, 1954, 1957, 1958, 1960, and 1962.

ČASLAVSKA, VERA, 1942 (Czechoslovakia). Czech gymnast. Won four gold (in all-around, long horse vault, uneven parallel bars, and floor exercise) and two silver medals in 1968 Olympics.

CASPER, BILLY, June 24, 1931 (San Diego, Calif.). U.S. golfer. U.S. Open champ, 1959 and 1966; PGA Player of the Year, 1966, 1968, and 1970.

CASPER, DAVE, born David John, Sept. 26, 1951 (Bemidji, Minn.). U.S. football player. As Notre Dame U. tight end, All-American in 1973; with NFL Oakland Raiders (1974–   ), All-Pro, 1976–78.

CAULKINS, TRACY, Jan. 11, 1963 (Winona, Minn.). U.S. swimmer. Set world records in 200- and 400-m individual medley, 1978; Sullivan Award winner, 1978.

CAUTHEN, STEVE, May 1, 1960 (Covington, Ky.). U.S. jockey. His mounts won a record $6,151,750 in 1977; rode Triple Crown winner Affirmed, 1978.

CHADWICK, FLORENCE, May, 1918 (San Diego, Calif.). U.S. distance swimmer. The first woman to swim the English Channel in both directions, from France to England (1950) and from England to France (1951); first woman to swim 21-mile Catalina Channel, off Long Beach, Calif., breaking all speed records, 1952; swam Bosporus, the Dardanelles, and Straits of Gibraltar, 1953.

CHAMBERLAIN, WILT ("The Stilt"), born Wilton Norman Chamberlain, Aug. 21, 1936 (Philadelphia, Pa.). U.S. basketball player. Center with Phila./S.F. Warriors (1960–68) and L.A. Lakers (1969–73); NBA scoring leader, 1960–66; scored NBA career-record 31,419 points; record 100 points in one game, Mar. 2, 1962; scored a record 50.4 points per game, 1962; holds NBA career records of 30.1 points per game and 23,924 rebounds; now active in pro volleyball.

CHINAGLIA, GIORGIO, Jan. 24, 1947 (Carrara, It.). Italian soccer player. Star of the N.Y. Cosmos team, 1976–   ; leading scorer of N. American Soccer League, 1976, 1978, 1979.

CLARK, JIM, Mar. 4, 1936 (Duns, Eng.)–Apr. 7, 1968. English auto racer. Won Indianapolis 500, 1965; World Grand Prix champ, 1963, and 1965.

CLARKE, BOBBY, Aug. 13, 1949 (Flin Flon, Man., Can.). Canadian hockey player. Center for the Philadelphia Flyers, 1969–   ; led team to Stanley Cup championship in 1975 and 1976; named NHL MVP, 1973, 1975, and 1976.

CLEMENTE, ROBERTO, Aug. 18, 1934 (Carolina, P.R.)–Dec. 31, 1972. Puerto Rican baseball player. Pittsburgh Pirates outfielder, 1955–72; NL batting champ, 1961, 1964, 1965, and 1967; compiled lifetime batting avg. of .317; inducted into Baseball Hall of Fame, 1973; killed in plane crash.

COBB, TY(rus Raymond) ("Georgia Peach"), Dec. 18, 1886 (Narrows, Ga.)–July 17, 1961. U.S. baseball player. As Detroit Tigers (1905–26) and Philadelphia A's (1927–28) outfielder, often called the greatest player in baseball history; held major-league career records for batting avg. (.367), hits (4,191), most batting titles won (12), most consecutive batting titles won (nine, 1907–15); inducted into Baseball Hall of Fame, 1936.

COE, SEBASTIAN, Sept. 29, 1956 (Yorkshire, Eng.). British runner. Set three world records in 1979: 800-m (1:42.4), mile (3:49) and 1,500-m (3:32.1).

COMANECI, NADIA, Nov. 12, 1961 (Onesti, Rum.). Rumanian gymnast. Petite winner of three gold medals in 1976 Olympics, where she earned seven perfect scores.

CONCEPCION, DAVE, June 17, 1948 (Aragua, Ven.). Venezuelan baseball player. Shortstop for Cincinnati Reds, 1970–   ; played in four World Series.

CONN, BILLY, Oct. 8, 1917 (Pittsburgh, Pa.). U.S. boxer. Light-heavyweight champ, 1939–41; KO'd

THE BOOK OF WHO

by JOE LOUIS in heavyweight title bout, 1941; inducted into Boxing Hall of Fame, 1965.

CONNOLLY, MAUREEN ("Little Mo"), Sept. 17, 1934 (San Diego, Calif.)-June 21, 1969. U.S. tennis player. U.S. singles champ, 1951-53; won tennis Grand Slam, 1953; Wimbledon champ, 1952-54; AP Woman Athlete of the Year, 1952-54.

CONNORS, JIMMY, Sept. 2, 1952 (E. St. Louis, Ill.). U.S. tennis player. U.S. singles champ, 1974, 1976, and 1978; Wimbledon champ, 1974; won record $922,657 in 1977.

CORBETT, JAMES J. ("Gentleman Jim"), Sept. 1, 1866 (San Francisco, Calif.)-Feb. 18, 1933. U.S. boxer. Credited with being first scientific boxer, he was heavyweight champ from 1892 to 1897.

CORDERO, ÁNGEL, JR., May 8, 1942 (Santurce, P.R.). Puerto Rican jockey. Rode Kentucky Derby winners Cannonade (1974) and Bold Forbes (1976); leading money-winning jockey, 1976.

COUBERTIN, PIERRE, BARON DE, Jan. 1, 1863 (Paris, France)-Sept. 1, 1937; French sportsman. Revived Olympic Games, 1894; pres. of the Internatl. Olympic Com., 1894-1925.

COURT, MARGARET, née Smith, July 16, 1942 (Albury, Austrl.). Australian tennis player. U.S. singles champ, 1962, 1965, 1969, 1970, and 1973; Wimbledon champ, 1963, 1965, and 1970.

COUSY, BOB, born Robert Joseph Cousy, Aug. 9, 1928 (New York, N.Y.). U.S. basketball player, coach. As Boston Celtics guard (1951-1963), led team to six NBA championships; 10-time NBA all-star; inducted into Basketball Hall of Fame, 1970.

COWENS, DAVE, Oct. 25, 1948 (Newport, Ky.). U.S. basketball player, coach. Boston Celtics center (1970-   ), and player-coach (1979); NBA MVP, 1973.

CSONKA, LARRY, Dec. 25, 1946 (Stow, Ohio). U.S. football player. Rushed for over 7,000 yds. in his career with Miami Dolphins (1968-74, and 1979-   ) and N.Y. Giants (1976-78).

CULP, CURLEY, Mar. 10, 1946 (Yuma, Ariz.). U.S. football player. Defensive lineman with K.C. Chiefs (1968-69 and 1970-74), Houston Oilers (1974-   ); named NFL outstanding defensive player, 1973; played in Pro Bowl, 1971, 1975, 1976, 1977, and 1978.

CUNNINGHAM, GLENN, 1909 (Topeka, Kan.). U.S. runner. A top miler in the 1930s; set the world mile record (4:06.8), 1934.

DAVIS, WALTER, Sept. 9, 1954 (Pineville, N.C.). U.S. basketball player. U. of North Carolina All-American forward, 1977; with NBA Phoenix Suns (1977-   ) named NBA Rookie of the Year, 1978.

DAWSON, LEN, June 20, 1935 (Alliance, Ohio). U.S. football player, broadcaster. As K.C. Chiefs quarterback (1963-75) passed for 28,711 career yds. Now a commentator for NBC sports.

DEAN, DIZZY, born Jerome Dean, Jan. 16, 1911 (Lucas, Ark.)-July 17, 1974. U.S. baseball player, broadcaster. Known for zany antics. Pitcher for St. L. Cardinals (1930-37), Chicago Cubs (1938-41); won 30 games, 1934; NL MVP, 1934; inducted into Baseball Hall of Fame, 1953.

DEBUSSCHERE, DAVE, Oct. 16, 1940 (Detroit, Mich.). U.S. basketball player and executive, baseball player. Basketball forward for Detroit Pistons (1964-68) and N.Y. Knicks (1968-74); NBA All-Defensive team, 1969-74; ABA commissioner, 1975-76; prof. baseball pitcher for Chicago White Sox, 1962-63.

DEMPSEY, JACK ("The Manassa Mauler"), June 24, 1895 (Manassa, Colo.). U.S. boxer. Heavyweight champ, 1919-26; lost title to GENE TUNNEY.

DEVINE, DAN, Dec. 23, 1924 (Augusta, Wisc.). U.S. football coach. Head coach at U. of Missouri (1958-70); NFL Green Bay Packers (1971-75); Notre Dame U., (1975-   ).

DIMAGGIO, JOE ("The Yankee Clipper," "Jolting Joe"), born Joseph Paul DiMaggio, Nov. 25, 1914 (Martinez, Calif.). U.S. baseball player. Famed N.Y. Yankees outfielder, 1936-51; batted safely in record 56 consecutive games, 1941; AL batting champ, 1939-40; AL home-run leader, 1937 and 1948; career batting avg. of .325; inducted into Baseball Hall of Fame, 1955. (Married to MARILYN MONROE, 1954-55.)

DORSETT, TONY, Apr. 7, 1954 (Rochester, Pa.). U.S. football player. As U. of Pittsburgh running back, awarded 1976 Heisman Trophy and rushed for NCAA record, 6,082 career yds.; with NFL Dallas Cowboys, 1977-   .

DOUBLEDAY, ABNER, June 26, 1819 (Ballston Spa, N.Y.)-Jan. 26, 1893. U.S. sportsman, soldier. Credited for many years with inventing baseball (now considered untrue); Baseball Hall of Fame established where he attended school, in Cooperstown, N.Y.; commanded Ft. Sumter gunners who fired first shots of Civil War.

DREW, JOHN, Sept. 30, 1954 (Vredenburgh, Ala.). U.S. basketball player. With NBA Atlanta Hawks, has scored over 20 points per game in 1976-79.

DRYSDALE, DON(ald Scott), July 23, 1936 (Van Nuys, Calif.). U.S. baseball player. Brooklyn, L.A. Dodgers pitcher, 1956-69; pitched record 58 consecutive scoreless innings, 1968; led NL in strikeouts, 1959, 1960, and 1962; Cy Young Award winner, 1962.

DURAN, ROBERTO, June 16, 1951 (Panama City, Panama). Panamanian boxer. World lightweight champ, 1972-79; defeated only once in over 65 fights, through mid-1979; now fighting in welter-weight class.

DUROCHER, LEO ERNEST ("The Lip"), July 27, 1906 (W. Springfield, Mass.). U.S. baseball player, manager. Outspoken manager famed for comment "Nice guys finish last"; played for 17 years and managed several National League teams for 25 years; managed N.Y. Giants to World Series win, 1954.

EDERLE, GERTRUDE, Oct. 23, 1906 (New York, N.Y.). U.S. swimmer. Caused a sensation in 1926, when she became first woman to swim the English Channel.

EMERSON, ROY, Nov. 3, 1936 (Kingsway, Austrl.). Australian tennis player. U.S. singles champ, 1961 and 1964; Wimbledon champ, 1964 and 1965.

ERVING, JULIUS ("Dr. J."), Feb. 22, 1950 (Roosevelt, N.Y.). U.S. basketball player. ABA leading scorer, 1973, 1974, and 1976; NBA all-star, 1977 and 1978.

ESPOSITO, PHIL, Feb. 20, 1942 (Sault Ste. Marie, Can.). Canadian hockey player. Center for the Chicago Black Hawks, (1964-67); Boston Bruins, (1968-76); N.Y. Rangers (1976-   ); scored record 76 goals, 1971; record 152 points, 1971; NHL leading scorer five times; led NHL in goals six times; led NHL in assists three times; scored 50 or more goals per season five times; NHL MVP, 1969 and 1974.

EVERT, CHRIS (married name: Lloyd), Dec. 21, 1954 (Ft. Lauderdale, Fla.). U.S. tennis player. U.S.

singles champion, 1975-78; Wimbledon champion, 1974 and 1976; AP Female Athlete of the Year, 1974, 1975, and 1977.

EWBANK, WEEB, May 6, 1907 (Richmond, Ind.). U.S. football coach. Head coach, Baltimore Colts, 1954-62; as head coach (1963-73) led N.Y. Jets to Super Bowl championship in 1969.

EWRY, RAY, Oct. 14, 1873 (Lafayette, Ind.)-Sept. 29, 1937. U.S. athlete. Track-and-field standout who won eight gold medals in 1900, 1904, and 1908 Olympics.

FAIRBANKS, CHUCK, June 10, 1933 (Detroit, Mich.). U.S. football coach. Head coach at U. of Oklahoma (1967-73), NFL New England Patriots (1973-78), and U. of Colorado (1979-   ).

FANGIO, JUAN, June 24, 1911 (nr. Balcarce, Arg.). Argentine auto racer. World Grand Prix champ, 1951 and 1954-57.

FELLER, ROBERT WILLIAM ANDREW ("Rapid Robert"), Nov. 3, 1918 (Van Meter, Ia.). U.S. baseball player. As pitcher for Cleveland Indians (1936-56), a six-time 20-game winner; struck out 348 batters, 1946; AL strikeout leader seven times; pitched three no-hitters and 12 one-hitters; won 266 games; inducted into Baseball Hall of Fame, 1962.

FINGERS, ROLLIE, born Roland Glen Fingers, Aug. 25, 1946 (Steubenville, Ohio). U.S. baseball player. One of game's premier relief pitchers with the Oakland A's (1968-76) and S.D. Padres (1977-   ).

FINLEY, CHARLES, O., Feb. 22, 1918 (Birmingham, Ala.). U.S. baseball executive. Colorful owner of the Oakland A's (1960-   ), known for feuds with the commissioner, other owners, and players; built A's team that won three consecutive World Series, 1972-74.

FISCHER, ROBERT JAMES ("Bobby"), Mar. 9, 1943 (Chicago, Ill.). U.S. chess player. Noted as the first American to hold the world chess title, defeating Boris Spassky in 1972 (held title through 1975); U.S. champion, 1958-61 and 1963-67. *Games of Chess,* 1959; *My Sixty Memorable Games,* 1969; *Bobby Fischer Teaches Chess,* 1972.

FLEISCHER, NAT, Nov. 3, 1887 (New York, N.Y.)-June 25, 1972. U.S. boxing expert, publisher, author. Founded *The Ring* magazine, 1922; wrote over 50 books on boxing and wrestling.

FLEMING, PEGGY, July 27, 1948 (San Jose, Calif.). U.S. figure skater. Olympic gold medalist, 1968; world champion, 1966-68.

FLOOD, CURT(is) **CHARLES,** Jan. 18, 1938 (Houston, Tex.). U.S. baseball player. Played as an outfielder for the St. Louis Cardinals, 1958-69; led the fight to end baseball's reserve clause.

FORD, WHITEY, born Edward Charles Ford, Oct. 21, 1928 (New York, N.Y.) U.S. baseball player. As N.Y. Yankees pitcher (1950-67), won 10 World Series games; career 2.74 ERA; Cy Young Award winner, 1961; inducted into Baseball Hall of Fame, 1974.

FOREMAN, GEORGE, Jan. 10, 1949 (Marshall, Tex.). U.S. boxer. Olympic heavyweight champ, 1968; world pro heavyweight champ, 1973-74.

FOSBURY, DICK, Mar. 6, 1947 (Portland, Ore.). U.S. high jumper. Won 1968 Olympic gold medal; developed "Fosbury Flop" maneuver.

FOSTER, GEORGE, Dec. 1, 1948 (Tuscaloosa, Ala.). U.S. baseball player. Outfielder for S.F. Giants (1969-71) and Cincinnati Reds (1971-   ); led NL in home runs, 1977-78; NL RBI leader, 1976-78; NL MVP, 1977.

FOX, NELLIE, born Jacob Nelson Fox, Dec. 25, 1927 (St. Thomas, Pa.)-Dec. 1, 1975. U.S. baseball player. Infielder for Philadelphia A's (1947-49), Chicago White Sox (1950-63), and Houston Astros (1964-65); led AL in hits four times; AL MVP, 1959.

FOXX, JIMMY ("Double X"), born James Emory Foxx, Oct. 22, 1907 (Sudlersville, Md.)-July 21, 1967. U.S. baseball player. As outfielder for Philadelphia A's (1925-35), Boston Red Sox (1936-42), others, hit 534 home runs and compiled a .325 career batting avg.; won AL Triple Crown, 1933; AL batting champ, 1933 and 1938; AL home run leader, 1932, 1933, 1935, and 1939; hit 58 home runs in 1932; inducted into Baseball Hall of Fame, 1951.

FOYT, A(nthony) **J**(ames), Jan. 16, 1935 (Houston, Tex.). U.S. auto racer. Won Indianapolis 500 in 1961, 1964, 1967, and 1977; USAC champion six times.

FRANCIS, RUSS, born Ross Francis, Apr. 3, 1953 (Seattle, Wash.). U.S. football player. Tight end for New England Patriots, 1975-   ; played in Pro Bowl, 1976, 1977, and 1978.

FRASER, DAWN, Sept. 4, 1937 (Balmain, Austrl.). Australian swimmer. Won Olympic gold medals in 100-m freestyle in 1956, 1960, and 1964.

FRAZIER, WALT ("Clyde"), born Walter Frazier, Mar. 29, 1945 (Atlanta, Ga.). U.S. basketball player. Guard for N.Y. Knicks (1967-77) and Cleveland Cavaliers (1977-79); key player on Knicks championship teams of 1970 and 1973.

FRICK, FORD, Dec. 19, 1894 (Wawaka, Ind.)-Apr. 8, 1978. U.S. baseball executive. Pro baseball commissioner, 1951-65.

FRISCH, FRANKIE ("The Fordham Flash"), born Frank Francis Frisch, Sept. 9, 1898 (New York, N.Y.)-Mar. 12, 1973. U.S. baseball player. With N.Y. Giants (1919-26) and St. Louis Cardinals (1927-37); .316 career batting avg.; hit over .300 13 times; named NL MVP, 1931; elected to Baseball Hall of Fame, 1947.

GAINEY, BOB, Dec. 13, 1953 (Peterborough, Ont., Can.). Canadian hockey player. Forward-defenseman with Montreal Canadiens, 1973-   ; won Selke Trophy (outstanding defensive forward), 1978, 1979; won Smythe Trophy (MVP in playoffs), 1979.

GARVEY, STEVE PATRICK, Dec. 22, 1948 (Tampa, Fla.). U.S. baseball player. First baseman for L.A. Dodgers, 1969-   ; NL MVP, 1974.

GEHRIG, (Henry) LOU(is), June 19, 1903 (New York, N.Y.)-June 2, 1941. U.S. baseball player. N.Y. Yankees great (1923-39) who played a major-league record 2,130 consecutive games; career .340 batting avg.; AL batting champ, 1934; AL home-run champ, 1931, 1934, and 1936; AL MVP, 1927, 1931, 1934, and 1936; inducted into Baseball Hall of Fame, 1936; died of muscle wasting disease that bears his name.

GERVIN, GEORGE ("The Iceman"), Apr. 27, 1952 (Detroit, Mich.). U.S. basketball player. Guard for San Antonio Spurs, 1974-   ; NBA scoring leader, 1978 and 1979.

GIBSON, ALTHEA, Aug. 25, 1927 (Silver, S.C.). U.S. tennis player. First black player to win a major tournament. U.S. singles champ, 1957 and 1958; Wimbledon champ, 1957 and 1958.

GIBSON, BOB, born Robert Gibson, Nov. 9, 1935 (Omaha, Neb.). U.S. baseball player. As St. L. Cardinals pitcher (1959-75), struck out NL record 3,117 batters; compiled NL single-season record

ERA of 1.12, 1968; NL Cy Young Award winner, 1968 and 1970; NL MVP, 1968.

GIBSON, JOSH, Dec. 21, 1911 (Buena Vista. Ga.)-Jan. 20, 1947. U.S. baseball player. Legendary slugger in Negro leagues; inducted into Baseball Hall of Fame, 1972.

GIFFORD, FRANK, Aug. 16, 1930 (Santa Monica, Calif.). U.S. football player, broadcaster. Running back and kicker for the NFL N.Y. Giants, 1952-65; NFL MVP, 1956; with HOWARD COSELL, DON MEREDITH, and others, broadcast *Monday Night Football* games, 1971- . Elected Football Hall of Fame, 1975.

GILMORE, ARTIS, Sept. 21, 1949 (Chipley, Fla.). U.S. basketball player. Center with ABA Kentucky Colonels (1972-76) and Chicago Bulls (1976-); has averaged over 1,000 rebounds each pro season.

GONZALEZ, RICHARD ALONZO ("Pancho"), May 9, 1928 (Los Angeles, Calif.). U.S. tennis player, coach. Won U.S. clay court and lawn singles titles, 1948-49; member of U.S. teams that won Wimbledon and Davis Cup, 1949; turned pro, 1949; world pro tennis champion eight times.

GOOLAGONG, EVONNE (Mrs. Roger Cawley), July 31, 1951 (Barallan, Austl.). Australian tennis player. Wimbledon champ, 1971.

GOWDY, CURT(is), 1919 (Green River, Wyo.). U.S. sportscaster. Broadcast N.Y. Yankee (1949-51) and Boston Red Sox (1951-66) games; all-purpose sports announcer for NBC; named sportscaster of the year, 1965 and 1967.

GRAHAM, OTTO EVERETT, JR., Dec. 6, 1921 (Waukegan, Ill.). U.S. football player, coach. Quarterback with Cleveland Browns, 1946-55; inducted into Pro Football Hall of Fame, 1965.

GRANGE, HAROLD EDWARD ("Red", "The Galloping Ghost"), June 13, 1903 (Folksville, Pa.). U.S. football player. All-American running back at U. of Ill., 1923-25; played for NFL Chicago Bears, 1925-35; inducted into Pro Football Hall of Fame, 1963.

GRANT, HAROLD ("Bud"), May 20, 1927 (Superior, Wisc.). U.S. football coach. Played with Minn. Lakers, 1949-51; coach, Winnipeg (CFL), 1957-66; coach, Minn. Vikings, 1969- ; led team to Super Bowl four times and lost each time. 1970, 1974-75 and 1977.

GREENBERG, HANK, Jan. 1, 1911 (New York, N.Y.). U.S. baseball player. First baseman, outfielder for the Detroit Tigers, 1930-46; led AL in homers, 1935, 1938, 1940, and 1946; led AL in RBIs, 1935, 1937, 1940 and 1946; .313 career batting average; 331 career homers; elected to Baseball Hall of Fame, 1956.

GREENE, JOE ("Mean Joe Greene"), Sept. 24, 1946 (Temple, Tex.). U.S. football player. Defensive lineman with Pittsburgh Steelers, 1969- ; named NFL's outstanding defensive player, 1972 and 1974.

GRIESE, BOB, Feb. 3, 1945 (Evansville, Ind.). U.S. football player. All-American quarterback at Purdue U.; with NFL Miami Dolphins 1967- ; league's leading passer in 1971 and 1977; NFL MVP, 1971.

GRIFFIN, ARCHIE MASON, Aug. 21, 1954 (Columbus, Ohio). U.S. football player. While playing running back for Ohio St. U., was the only player ever to win the Heisman Trophy twice (1974, 1975); with the NFL Cincinnati Bengals, 1976- .

GRIFFITH, EMILE, Feb. 3, 1938 (Virgin Is.). U.S.

boxer. Welterweight champ three times in period 1961-66; middleweight champ twice in period 1966-68.

GROVE, LEFTY, born Robert Moses Grove, Mar. 6, 1900 (Lonaconing, Md.)-May 23, 1975. U.S. baseball player. As Philadelphia A's (1925-33) and Boston Red Sox (1934-41) pitcher, won 300 games in career; had a 31-4 record in 1931; 20-game winner eight times; lowest AL ERA nine times; inducted into Baseball Hall of Fame, 1947.

GROZA, LOU ("The Toe"), Jan. 25, 1924 (Martin's Ferry, Ohio). U.S. football player. Defensive lineman and placekicker with the Cleveland Browns (1946-67) who scored 1,608 points in his NFL career.

GUIDRY, RON(ald Ames). Aug. 28, 1950 (Carencero, La.). U.S. baseball player. Pitcher for N.Y. Yankees (1975-); had 25-3 record with 1.74 ERA in 1978; AL Cy Young Award winner, 1978.

GUTHRIE, JANET, Mar. 7, 1938 (Iowa City, Ia.). U.S. auto racer. The first woman to qualify for and race in the Indianapolis 500, 1977.

GUY, WILLIAM RAY, Dec. 22, 1949 (Swainsboro, Ga.). U.S. football player. Punter with Oakland Raiders, 1973- ; played in Pro Bowl, 1973-79.

HAGEN, WALTER, Dec. 21, 1892 (Rochester, N.Y.)-Oct. 5, 1969. U.S. golfer. PGA champ, 1921 and 1924-27; British Open champ, 1922, 1924, 1928, and 1929.

HALAS, GEORGE, Feb. 2, 1895 (Chicago, Ill.). U.S. football player, coach, executive. Founder-coach of Chicago Bears and one of the founders of the NFL; as Bears coach, he won five NFL championships and 320 NFL games; inducted into Pro Football Hall of Fame, 1963.

HARRIS, CLIFF, Nov. 12, 1948 (Fayetteville, Ark.). U.S. football player. Defensive back for Dallas Cowboys, 1970- ; played in Pro Bowl, 1974-78.

HARRIS, FRANCO, Mar. 7, 1950 (Ft. Dix, N.J.). U.S. football player. As Pittsburgh Steelers running back (1972-), has rushed for 8,563 career yards (through 1979); played in Pro Bowl, 1972-79.

HARTACK, BILL, Dec. 9, 1932 (Colver, Pa.). U.S. jockey. Rode record five Kentucky Derby winners, 1957, 1960, 1962, 1964, 1969.

HAUGHTON, BILL, Nov. 2, 1923 (Gloversville, N.Y.). U.S. harness-racing driver. Drove Hambletonian winner, 1974 and 1976-77; drove Little Brown Jug winner four times, 1955, 1964, 1968, and 1969.

HAVLICEK, JOHN, Apr. 8, 1940 (Martin's Ferry. Ohio). U.S. basketball player. Boston Celtics forward-guard, 1962-78; played in NBA record 1,188 games; scored 25,073 career points; first-team NBA All-Star four times.

HAYES, ELVIN, Nov. 17, 1945 (Rayville, La.). U.S. basketball player. With Baltimore/Washington Bullets, 1972- ; NBA leading scorer, 1969; has averaged nearly 25 points per game during career.

HAYES, WAYNE WOODROW ("Woody"), Feb. 14, 1913 (Clifton, Ohio). U.S. football coach. Controversial head coach of Ohio State U. football team, 1951-79.

HAYNES, MIKE, born Michael James Haynes, July 1, 1953 (Denison, Tex.). U.S. football player. Defensive back for New England Patriots, 1976- ; played in Pro Bowl, 1976-78; AFC Rookie of the Year, 1976.

HEDBERG, ANDERS, Feb. 25, 1951 (Ornskoldsvik, Swe.). Swedish hockey player. WHA rookie of the year, 1975; led WHA in goals, 1977; signed multiyear contract with N.Y. Rangers, 1978.

HEIDEN, ERIC, June 14, 1958 (La Crosse, Wisc.). U.S. speed skater. World All-Around Speed-Skating champion, 1977-79; won five gold medals in Olympics, 1980.

HENIE, SONJA, Apr. 8, 1912 (Oslo, Norway)-Oct. 12, 1969. U.S. figure skater. Olympic gold medalist, 1928, 1932, and 1936; world champion, 1927-36; leading box-office attraction in 10 movies, 1937-45.

HILL, GRAHAM, Feb. 15, 1929 (London, Eng.)-Nov. 29, 1975. British auto racer. Won Grand Prix championship 1962, 1968; won Indianapolis 500, 1966; won 14 Grand Prix events during his career before his death in a plane crash.

HODGES, GIL(bert Raymond), Apr. 4, 1924 (Princeton, Ind.)-Apr. 2, 1972. U.S. baseball player, manager. As first baseman with Brooklyn/L.A. Dodgers (1943-61) and N.Y. Mets (1962-63), hit 370 career home runs; managed N.Y. Mets to World Series win, 1969.

HOGAN, (William) **BEN**(jamin), Aug. 13, 1912 (Dublin, Tex.). U.S. golfer. Winner of U.S. Open, 1948, 1950, 1951, and 1953; Masters champ, 1951 and 1953; PGA champ, 1946 and 1948; inducted into PGA Hall of Fame, 1953.

HOLMAN, NAT, Feb. 1, 1896 (New York, N.Y.). U.S. basketball player/coach. Star of the original Celtics team, which won 720 of 795 games, 1921-30; coach of City College of New York basketball team, 1920-52 and 1955-60; elected to Hall of Fame, 1964.

HOLMES, LARRY, Nov. 3, 1949 (Cuthbert, Ga.). U.S. boxer. Defeated KEN NORTON to become World Boxing Council heavyweight champ, 1978.

HOLZMAN, RED, born William Holzman, Aug. 10, 1920 (New York, N.Y.). U.S. basketball coach. Coached (1967-77) and led N.Y. Knickerbockers to NBA championships in 1970 and 1973; NBA Coach of the Year, 1970. Knick coach 1979-

HOPPE, WILLIE, Oct. 11, 1887 (Cornwall-on-the-Hudson, N.Y.)-Feb. 1, 1959. U.S. billiards player. Won some 50 world billiard titles.

HORNSBY, ROGERS ("The Rajah"), Apr. 27, 1896 (Winters, Tex.)-Jan. 5, 1963. U.S. baseball player. Infielder with several teams, principally the St. L. Cardinals (1915-26) and Chicago Cubs (1929-33); batted record .424 in 1924; won NL Triple Crown, 1922 and 1925; NL batting champ, 1920-25 and 1928; .358 lifetime batting avg.; inducted into Baseball Hall of Fame, 1942.

HORNUNG, PAUL ("The Golden Boy"), Dec. 23, 1935 (Louisville, Ky.). U.S. football player, broadcaster. An All-American at Notre Dame U., 1957; runner-placekicker with NFL Green Bay Packers, 1957-66; scored NFL record 176 points in 1960.

HOWE, GORDIE, Mar. 31, 1928 (Floral, Sask., Can.). Canadian hockey player. Forward with the Detroit Red Wings [NHL] (1947-71), Houston Aeros [WHA] (1974-77), New England Whalers (1978-); NHL-record career goals (786); NHL-record career points (1,809); NHL leading scorer, 1951-54, 1957, 1963; led NHL in goals five times, assists three times; played in 19 Stanley Cup playoffs; NHL first team all-star 12 times; received Lester Patrick Award for outstanding service to U.S. hockey, 1967; still playing at age 50 in NHL, 1979-80 season.

HRABOSKY, AL(an) ("The Mad Hungarian"), July 21, 1949 (Oakland, Calif.). U.S. baseball player. One of game's premier relief pitchers

with St. L. Cardinals (1973-77), K. C. Royals (1978-79), Atlanta Braves (1980-   ).

HUBBARD, CAL, Oct. 31, 1900 (Keytesville, Mo.)-Oct. 17, 1977. U.S. football lineman, baseball umpire. Only man inducted into both Pro Football (1963) and Baseball (1976) halls of fame.

HUBBELL, CARL ("King Carl, "The Meal Ticket"), June 22, 1903 (Carthage, Mo.). U.S. baseball player. As N.Y. Giants pitcher (1928-43), won 253 games; won at least 20 games per season, 1933-37; compiled lowest ERA in NL three times, 1933, 1934, 1936; inducted into Baseball Hall of Fame, 1947.

HUGGINS, MILLER, Mar. 27, 1879 (Cincinnati, Ohio)-Dec. 25, 1929. U.S. baseball manager. As N.Y. Yankees manager (1918-29), won six AL pennants and three World Series, 1923, 1927, 1928; inducted into Baseball Hall of Fame, 1964.

HULL, BOBBY, Jan. 3, 1939 (Point Anne, Ont., Can.). Canadian hockey player. Forward with the Chicago Black Hawks [NHL] (1958-72) and Winnipeg Jets [WHA] (1973-80); NHL leading scorer, 1960, 1962, 1966; led NHL in goals seven times; scored 77 WHA goals, 1975; NHL MVP, 1965 and 1966; WHA MVP, 1973 and 1975.

HUNTER, JAMES ("Catfish"), Apr. 8, 1946 (Hertford, N.C.). U.S. baseball player. Pitcher with K.C./Oakland A's (1965-74) and N.Y. Yankees (1975-79); pitched perfect game against Minnesota Twins on May 8, 1968; a 20-game winner, 1971-75; AL Cy Young Award winner, 1974.

HUTSON, DON, Jan. 31, 1913 (Pine Bluff, Ark.). U.S. football player. With the Green Bay Packers, 1935-45; led NFL in scoring, 1940-44; led NFL in pass receiving eight times; led NFL in touchdowns, 1935-38 and 1941-44; inducted into Pro Football Hall of Fame, 1963.

IRWIN, HALE, June 3, 1945 (Joplin, Mo.). U.S. golfer. U.S. Open champion, 1974 and 1979.

ISSEL, DAN, Oct. 25, 1948 (Batavia, Ill.). U.S. basketball player. Center with ABA Kentucky Colonels (1971-75) and NBA Denver Nuggets (1976-   ); ABA Rookie of the Year and leading scorer, 1971.

JACKSON, REGGIE, born Reginald Jackson, May 18, 1946 (Wyncote, Pa.). U.S. baseball player. Outfielder with K.C./Oakland A's (1967-75), Baltimore Orioles (1976), and N.Y. Yankees (1977-   ); led AL in home runs, 1973, 1975; hit five World Series home runs, 1977 (3 in one game); AL MVP, 1973; candy bar named after him.

JACOBS, HELEN HULL, Aug. 6, 1908 (Globe, Ariz.). U.S. tennis player, writer. U.S. singles champ, 1932-35; Wimbledon champ, 1936; author of children's books, historical novels, and books on tennis.

JENKINS, FERGUSON ("Fergie"), Dec. 13, 1943 (Chatham, Ont., Can.). Canadian baseball player. Pitcher chiefly with Chicago Cubs, 1966-73; won at least 20 games per season, 1967-72; NL Cy Young Award, 1971.

JENNER, BRUCE, Oct. 28, 1949 (Mt. Kisco, N.Y.). U.S. athlete. Winner of decathlon in 1976 Olympics; Sullivan Trophy winner, 1976; AP Athlete of the Year, 1976.

JOHN, TOMMY, born Thomas Edward John, May 22, 1943 (Terre Haute, Ind.). U.S. baseball player. Pitcher with Cleveland Indians (1963-64), Chicago White Sox (1965-71), L.A. Dodgers (1972-78), and N.Y. Yankees (1979-   ); noted mainly for miraculous comeback from 1974 injury, with a rebuilt pitching arm.

JOHNSON, JACK, Mar. 31, 1878 (Galveston, Tex.)–June 10, 1946. U.S. boxer. First black to hold world heavyweight title, 1908–1915.

JOHNSON, RAFER, Aug. 18, 1935 (Hillsboro, Tex.). U.S. athlete. Winner of decathlon in 1960 Olympics; one of persons who captured assassin of ROBERT KENNEDY, 1968.

JOHNSON, WALTER PERRY ("The Big Train"), Nov. 6, 1887 (Humboldt, Kan.)–Dec. 10, 1946. U.S. baseball player. As a pitcher with the Washington Senators (1907–27), won 413 career games and struck out a major-league record 3,499 batters; 20-game winner, 1910–19 and 1924–25; pitched 110 career shutouts; inducted into Baseball Hall of Fame, 1936.

JONES, BERT (ram) **HAYES,** Sept. 7, 1951 (Rustin, La.). U.S. football player. An All-American at LSU; quarterback for the Baltimore Colts, 1973– ; completed record 17 consecutive passes against N.Y. Jets, 1974; NFL MVP, 1976.

JONES, BOBBY, Mar. 17, 1902 (Atlanta, Ga.)–Dec. 18, 1971. U.S. golfer. The dominant force in golf in the 1920s; won Grand Slam, 1930; won four U.S. Opens (1923, 1926 and 1929–30), five U.S. Amateurs (1924–25, 1927–28, 1930) and three British Opens (1926–27 and 1930); helped found the Masters Tournament, 1934.

JONES, DAVID ("Deacon"), Dec. 9, 1938 (Eatonville, Fla.). U.S. football player. Defensive lineman with L.A. Rams, 1961–71; named NFL outstanding defensive player, 1967 and 1968.

JONES, ED ("Too Tall"), Feb. 23, 1951 (Jackson, Tenn.). U.S. football player. Defensive lineman with Dallas Cowboys, 1974–1978; All-American at Tennessee State, 1973; quit football for boxing career, 1979.

JUANTORENA, ALBERTO, Dec. 3, 1951 (Santiago, Cuba). Cuban runner. Gold medalist in the 400- and 800-m races in Olympics; held world record at 800-m (1:43.43), set 1977.

JURGENSON, SONNY, born Christian Adolf Jurgenson III, Aug. 23, 1934 (Wilmington, N.C.). U.S. football player. Quarterback for the Philadelphia Eagles (1957–64) and Washington Redskins (1964–74); led NFL in passing, 1967, 1969, and 1974; completed an NFL record 288 passes, 1967.

KAHANAMOKU, DUKE, Aug. 26, 1890 (Waikiki, Haw.)–Jan. 22, 1968. Hawaiian swimmer. Olympic champion in 100-m freestyle, 1912 and 1920.

KALINE, AL, Dec. 19, 1934 (Baltimore, Md.). U.S. baseball player. Played with Detroit Tigers, 1953–74; .297 career batting avg.; led AL in batting, 1955; inducted into Baseball Hall of Fame, 1980.

KARRAS, ALEX, July 15, 1935 (Gary, Ind.). U.S. football player, broadcaster. Defensive lineman for Detroit Lions, 1958–71; named All-Pro, 1960–61, 1963, and 1965; Outland Award, 1957.

KEELER, WILLIE ("Wee Willie"), born William Henry Keeler, March 3, 1872 (Brooklyn, N.Y.)–Jan. 1, 1923. U.S. baseball player. Played chiefly with Baltimore (1894–98), Brooklyn (1899–1902) and New York (1903–10); .341 career batting avg.; led NL in batting, 1897–98; credited with saying, "I hit 'em where they ain't"; elected to Baseball Hall of Fame, 1939.

KILLEBREW, HARMON CLAYTON ("Killer"), June 29, 1936 (Payette, Idaho). U.S. baseball player. Outfielder-infielder with Washington Senators/Minnesota Twins (1954–74) and K.C. Royals (1975); led AL in home runs, 1959, 1962–64, 1967, and 1969; AL MVP, 1969; hit 573 career home runs.

KILLY, JEAN-CLAUDE, Aug. 30, 1943 (St. Cloud, Fr.). French skier. Olympic champ in downhill, slalom, giant slalom, 1968; World Cup champ, 1967, 1968.

KINER, RALPH MCPHERRAN, Oct. 27, 1922 (Santa Rita, N.M.). U.S. baseball player, broadcaster. Outfielder, principally with the Pittsburgh Pirates, 1946–53; led NL in home runs, 1946–52; hit 54 home runs, 1954; inducted into Baseball Hall of Fame, 1977.

KING, BILLIE JEAN, née Moffitt, Nov. 22, 1943 (Long Beach, Calif.). U.S. tennis player. U.S. singles champ, 1967, 1971–72, and 1974; Wimbledon champ, 1966–68, 1972–73, and 1975; beat BOBBY RIGGS in so-called "Match of the Century," 1973; AP Female Athlete of the Year, 1967 and 1973.

KNIEVEL, EVEL, born Robert Craig Knievel, Oct. 17, 1938 (Butte, Mont.). U.S. stunt motorcyclist. Attempted sky-cycle jump of Snake River Canyon, Idaho, 1974.

KORBUT, OLGA, May 16, 1955 (Grodno, USSR). Soviet gymnast. Petite gold medalist (three medals) in 1972 Olympics; credited with popularizing gymnastics in U.S.

KOUFAX, SANDY, born Sanford Koufax, Dec. 30, 1935 (Brooklyn, N.Y.). U.S. baseball player. Pitched with Brooklyn/L.A. Dodgers, 1955–66; pitched perfect game against Chicago, 1965; pitched four no-hitters; lowest NL ERA, 1962–65; won 27 games with 1.73 ERA, 1966; struck out 382 batters, 1965; NL MVP, 1963; Cy Young Award winner, 1963, 1965, 1966; inducted into Baseball Hall of Fame, 1972.

KRAMER, JACK, Aug. 1, 1921 (Las Vegas, Nev.). U.S. tennis player, promoter. U.S. singles champ, 1946–47; Wimbledon champ, 1947; organized pro tours, from 1948.

KUBEK, TONY, born Anthony Christopher Kubek, Oct. 12, 1936 (Milwaukee, Wisc.). U.S. baseball player, broadcaster. Shortstop with N.Y. Yankees, 1957–65; played in six World Series; now an NBC sports broadcaster.

KUHN, BOWIE, Oct. 28, 1926 (Tacoma Park, Md.). U.S. sports executive. Commissioner of baseball, 1969– .

KUTS, VLADIMIR, 1927 (Aleskino, USSR)–Aug. 16, 1975. Soviet runner. Distance runner who won 5,000- and 10,000-m events at 1956 Olympics.

LAFLEUR, GUY, Sept. 20, 1951 (Thurso, Que., Can.). Canadian hockey player. Forward with Montreal Canadiens, 1972– ; NHL leading scorer, 1976–78; NHL MVP, 1977 and 1978; first team all-star, 1975–79; MVP in 1978 playoffs.

LAJOIE, NAPOLEON, Sept. 5, 1875 (Woonsocket, R.I.)–Feb. 7, 1959. U.S. baseball player. Infielder with several teams, chiefly the Cleveland Indians, 1903–14; won AL batting crown, 1901–03; had 3,242 career hits for a .338 batting avg.; inducted into Baseball Hall of Fame, 1937.

LAMBEAU, CURLY, born Earl Louis Lambeau, Apr. 9, 1898 (Green Bay, Wisc.)–June 1, 1965. U.S. football coach. Founder of Green Bay Packers (1919), whom he led to six NFL championships, 1929, 1930–31, 1936, 1939, 1944; inducted into Pro Football Hall of Fame, 1963; Green Bay Packers home field is named after him.

LAMBERT, JACK, July 8, 1952 (Mantua, Ohio). U.S. football player. Linebacker with Pittsburgh Steelers, 1974– ; played in Pro Bowl, 1975–79.

LANDIS, JUDGE KENESAW MOUNTAIN, Nov. 20, 1866 (Millville, Ohio)–Nov. 25, 1944. U.S. jurist, sports executive. First baseball commissioner, 1920-44; inducted into Baseball Hall of Fame, 1944.

LANDRY, TOM, Sept. 11, 1924 (Mission, Tex.). U.S. football coach. Head coach of NFL Dallas Cowboys, 1960-   ; led team to Super Bowl victory in 1972, 1978.

LANIER, BOB, Sept. 10, 1948 (Buffalo, N.Y.). U.S. basketball player. Center with the NBA Detroit Pistons, 1972-80; has career scoring avg. of over 20 points per game.

LARRIEU-LUTZ, FRANCIE, Nov. 28, 1952 (Palo Alto, Calif.). U.S. runner. Top woman miler; won one-mile and two-mile races, AAU Indoor Nationals, 1977; 1980 Olympic hopeful.

LARSEN, DON(ald James), Aug. 7, 1929 (Michigan City, Ind.). U.S. baseball player. While pitching for the N.Y. Yankees, hurled the only perfect game in World Series history, against Brooklyn Dodgers on Oct. 8, 1956.

LAUDA, NIKI, Feb. 22, 1949 (Austria). Austrian auto racer. World Grand Prix champ, 1977.

LAVER, ROD, Aug. 9, 1938 (Rockhampton, Austrl.). Australian tennis player. Won tennis Grand Slam, 1962 and 1969; U.S. singles champ, 1962, 1969; Wimbledon champ, 1961-62, 1968-69; world professional champ, 1964-67, 1970.

LEFLORE, RON(ald), June 16, 1952 (Detroit, Mich.). U.S. baseball player. Learned to play baseball in prison; outfielder with Detroit Tigers (1974-79) and Montreal Expos (1980-   ); compiled a .325 batting avg., 1977.

LEMON, BOB, born Robert Granville Lemon, Sept. 22, 1920 (San Bernardino, Calif.). U.S. baseball player, manager. As Cleveland Indians pitcher (1941-58), won 20 or more games six times; managed N.Y. Yankees to World Series victory, 1978; inducted into Baseball Hall of Fame, 1976.

LENGLEN, SUZANNE, May 24, 1899 (Compiègne, Fr.)-July 4, 1938. French tennis player. Called the "Pavlova of Tennis," she won singles and doubles six times each and mixed doubles three times at Wimbledon; French champion in singles, doubles, and mixed doubles, 1919-23 and 1925-26.

LEONARD, RAY ("Sugar Ray"), May 17, 1956 (Wilmington, N.C.). U.S. boxer. Won Olympic lt.-welterweight gold medal, 1976; WBC welterweight champ, 1979-   .

LILLY, BOB ("Tiger"), July 26, 1939 (Olney, Tex.). U.S. football player. Defensive lineman with Dallas Cowboys, 1961-75; rated as a top defensive lineman; earned all-pro honors seven times at defensive tackle; never missed a game in 14 years.

LINDSAY, TED, July 29, 1925 (Renfrew, Ont., Can.). Canadian hockey player. Forward with Detroit Red Wings, 1944-57 and 1964-65; leading NHL scorer, 1950; inducted into Hockey Hall of Fame, 1966; now Detroit Red Wings exec.

LIQUORI, MARTY, born Martin William Liquori, Jr., Sept. 11, 1949 (Montclair, N.J.). U.S. athlete. Leading miler and distance runner; commentator, ABC-TV, 1971-   ; designer and promotional dir., Brooks Shoe Co. (Hanover, Pa.), 1974-   .

LOMBARDI, VINCE, June 11, 1913 (Brooklyn, N.Y.)-Sept. 3, 1970. U.S. football coach. As Green Bay Packers head coach (1959-67), led team to 141-39-4 record; won Super Bowl championships, 1967 and 1968; won NFL championships, 1961, 1962, 1965-67; inducted into Pro Football Hall of Fame, 1971.

LONGDEN, JOHNNY, Feb. 14, 1907 (Wakefield, Eng.). British jockey. Rode 6,032 winners, becoming first to ride over 5,000 winners; rode Count

Fleet to Triple Crown, 1943; inducted into Racing Hall of Fame, 1958.

LOPEZ, NANCY, Jan. 1, 1957 (Torrance, Calif.). U.S. golfer. Won an unprecedented five consecutive tournaments on LPGA circuits, 1978; LPGA leading money winner, 1978, 1979.

LOUIS, JOE ("The Brown Bomber"), born Joseph Louis Barrow, May 13, 1914 (Lexington, Ala.). U.S. boxer. World heavyweight champ, 1937-49 (longest reign in history); successfully defended title 25 times; inducted into Boxing Hall of Fame, 1954.

LUCKMAN, SID, Nov. 21, 1916 (Brooklyn, N.Y.). U.S. football player. Quarterback for Chicago Bears, 1939-50; led team to NFL championships, 1940-41, 1943, and 1946; passed for seven touchdowns in one game, 1943; inducted into Pro Football Hall of Fame, 1965.

LUZINSKI, GREG(ory Michael), Nov. 22, 1950 (Chicago, Ill.). U.S. baseball player. Philadelphia Phillies outfielder, 1970-   ; led NL in RBIs, 1975; batted .300 or better, 1975-77.

LYLE, ALBERT ("Sparky"), July 22, 1944 (DuBois, Pa.). U.S. baseball player. Relief pitcher with the Boston Red Sox (1967-71), N.Y. Yankees (1972-78) and Texas Rangers (1978-   ). The Bronx Zoo, 1979.

LYNN, FRED(rick Michael), Feb. 3, 1952 (Chicago, Ill.). U.S. baseball player. Outfielder with Boston Red Sox, 1974-   ; AL Rookie of the Year, and MVP, 1975; AL batting champ, 1979.

MACK, CONNIE, born Cornelius McGillicuddy, Dec. 22, 1862 (E. Brookfield, Mass.)-Feb. 8, 1956. U.S. baseball owner, manager. Owned and managed Philadelphia A's, 1901-50; won nine AL pennants, five world championships; inducted into Baseball Hall of Fame, 1937.

MADLOCK, BILL, Jan. 12, 1951 (Memphis, Tenn.). U.S. baseball player. As infielder with the Chicago Cubs, led NL in batting, 1975 and 1976; has hit over .300, 1974-78; with Pittsburgh Pirates 1979-   .

MALONE, MOSES, Mar. 23, 1954 (Petersburg, Va.). U.S. basketball player. Recruited from ABA directly from high school, 1974; avg. 15 rebounds per game, 1978; playing for the Houston Rockets, named NBA MVP, 1979.

MANNING (Elisha) **ARCHIE,** May 19, 1949 (Drew, Miss.). U.S. football player. All-American quarterback at U. of Mississippi, 1969; N.O. Saints quarterback, 1971-   .

MANTLE, MICKEY, Oct. 20, 1931 (Spavinaw, Okla.). U.S. baseball player. N.Y. Yankees outfielder-first baseman who hit 536 career home runs; won AL triple crown, 1956; led AL in home runs, 1955-56, 1958, 1960; hit 54 home runs in 1961; hit record 18 World Series home runs; AL MVP, 1956-57, 1962; inducted into Baseball Hall of Fame, 1974.

MARAVICH, PETER ("Pistol Pete"), June 22, 1948 (Aliquippa, Pa.). U.S. basketball player. Guard who averaged an NCAA record 44.2 points per game at Louisiana St. U., 1968-70; played with NBA Atlanta Hawks (1970-74) and N.O. Utah Jazz (1974-80); led NBA in scoring, 1977.

MARBLE, ALICE, Sept. 28, 1913 (Plumas Co., Calif.). U.S. tennis player. U.S. singles champ, 1936, 1938-40; Wimbledon singles champ, 1939.

MARCIANO, ROCKY, born Rocco Marchegiano, Sept. 1, 1923 (Brockton, Mass.)-Aug. 31, 1969. U.S. boxer. World heavyweight champ, 1952-56; retired undefeated after 49 pro fights; inducted into Boxing Hall of Fame, 1959; killed in plane crash.

217

MARIS, ROGER, born Roger Eugene Maras, Sept. 10, 1934 (Hibbing, Minn.). U.S. baseball player. As N.Y. Yankee outfielder (1960–66), hit record 61 home runs in 1961; AL MVP, 1960–61.

MARSHALL, MIKE, born Michael Grant Marshall, Jan. 15, 1943 (Adrian, Mich.). U.S. baseball player. Premier relief pitcher with several teams; as L.A. Dodger, won NL Cy Young Award, 1974.

MARTIN, BILLY, born Alfred Manuel Pesano, May 16, 1928. (Berkeley, Calif.). U.S. baseball player and manager famed for brawls, feuds, and firings; after playing career as an infielder, chiefly with the N.Y. Yankees (1950–57), managed Minnesota Twins (1969), Detroit Tigers (1971–73), and Texas Rangers (1973–75); as N.Y. Yankees manager (1975–78), won pennants in 1976 and 1977 and World Series in 1977; fired by Yankees, 1978; re-hired by Yankees, mid-1979; fired again at the end of 1979 season; mgr., Oakland A's, 1980–.

MARTIN, HARVEY, Nov. 16, 1950 (Dallas, Tex.). U.S. football player. Defensive lineman with NFL Dallas Cowboys, 1973– ; named NFL outstanding defensive player, 1977.

MATHEWS, EDDIE, born Edwin Lee Mathews, Oct. 13, 1931 (Texarkana, Tex.). U.S. baseball player. Chiefly with the Milwaukee/Atlanta Braves 1953–66; led NL in home runs, 1953 and 1959; hit 512 career homers; elected to Baseball Hall of Fame, 1978.

MATHEWSON, CHRISTY ("Big Six"), born Christopher Mathewson, Aug. 12, 1880 (Factoryville, Pa.)-Oct. 7, 1925. U.S. baseball player. As N.Y. Giants (1900–16) and Cincinnati Reds (1916) pitcher, won 373 games in career; won 30 or more games, 1904–05, 1908; inducted into Baseball Hall of Fame, 1936.

MATHIAS, BOB, born Robert Bruce Mathias, Nov. 17, 1930 (Tulare, Calif.). U.S. athlete. Winner of decathlon in 1948 and 1952 Olympics; U.S. rep. (R. Calif.), 1967–73.

MAYS, WILLIE HOWARD ("Say Hey Kid"), May 6, 1931 (Fairfield, Ala.). U.S. baseball player. As N.Y./S.F. Giants (1951–72) and N.Y. Mets (1972–73) outfielder, hit 660 career home runs; led NL in home runs, 1955, 1962, and 1964–5; NL MVP, 1954, 1965; NL leading batter, 1954; inducted into Baseball Hall of Fame, 1979.

MCADOO, BOB, Sept. 25, 1951 (Greensboro, N.C.). U.S. basketball player. Forward-center with several NBA teams: with Buffalo (1972–76) and New York Knicks (1977–79); leading scorer in NBA, 1974–76; NBA MVP, 1975.

MCCOVEY, WILLIE LEE ("Stretch"), Jan. 10, 1938 (Mobile, Ala.). U.S. baseball player. First baseman with S.F. Giants (1959–73, 1978–) and S.D. Padres (1974–77); led NL in home runs, 1963 and 1968–69; led NL in RBIs, 1968–69; has 520 career home runs.

MCENROE, JOHN, Feb. 16, 1959 (New York, N.Y.). U.S. tennis player. NCAA singles champ at Stanford U., 1978; U.S. singles and doubles champ, 1979.

MCGINNIS, GEORGE, Aug. 12, 1950 (Indianapolis, Ind.). U.S. basketball player. With Indiana Pacers (1971–75; 1980–), Philadelphia 76ers (1975–78) and Denver Nuggets (1978–1980), leading scorer in ABA, 1975.

MCGRAW, JOHN JOSEPH ("Little Napoleon"), Apr. 7, 1873 (Truxton, N.Y.)-Feb. 25, 1934. U.S. baseball player, manager. As N.Y. Giants manager (1902–32), led team to ten pennants and three world championships, 1905, 1921, and 1922; inducted into Baseball Hall of Fame, 1937.

MCGRAW, TUG, born Frank Edwin McGraw, Aug. 30, 1944 (Martinez, Calif.). U.S. baseball player. Star relief pitcher with N.Y. Mets (1969–74) and Philadelphia Phillies (1975–).

MCGUIRE, AL, Sept. 7, 1931 (New York, N.Y.). U.S. basketball player, coach, broadcaster. Coached Marquette U., 1964–77; won NCAA championship, 1977.

MCKAY, JIM, Sept. 24, 1921 (Philadelphia, Pa.). U.S. sportscaster-commentator. Host of ABC's *Wide World of Sports,* 1961– ; covered Olympics, 1960, 1964, 1968, 1972, 1976; George Polk Award winner, 1973; six Emmy awards.

MCKAY, JOHN, July 5, 1923 (Everettsville, W. Va.). U.S. football coach. As head coach at U. of S. Cal., led team to five Rose Bowl wins in eight outings, 1960–75; coach, Tampa Bay NFL team, 1976–.

MEDWICK, JOE ("Ducky"), born Joseph Michael Medwick, Nov. 24, 1911 (Carteret, N.J.)-Mar. 21, 1975. U.S. baseball player. Outfielder with several teams, chiefly St. L. Cardinals (1932–40; 1947–48); won NL Triple Crown, 1937; hit NL record 64 doubles, 1936; career batting avg. of .324; inducted into Baseball Hall of Fame, 1968.

MEREDITH, DON ("Dandy Don"), Apr. 10, 1938 (Mt. Vernon, Tex.). U.S. football player, sportscaster. Dallas Cowboys quarterback, 1960–69; fixture on ABC *Monday Night Football,* 1970–73 and 1977– .

MEYER, DEBBIE, Aug. 14, 1952 (Haddonfield, N.J.). U.S. swimmer. Won gold medals in 200-, 400-, and 800-m freestyle at 1968 Olympics.

MIKAN, GEORGE LAWRENCE, June 18, 1924 (Joliet, Ill.). U.S. basketball player, executive. Played with Minneapolis Lakers, 1946–55; NBA scoring leader, 1949–51; selected by AP (1950) as greatest basketball player of the era 1900–50; ABA commissioner, 1967–69.

MIKITA, STAN, May 20, 1940 (Sokolce, Czech.). Canadian hockey player. Center with Chicago Black Hawks, 1959–80; NHL leading scorer, 1964–65, 1967–68; NHL leader in assists three times; NHL MVP, 1967–68; won NHL Lady Byng Trophy (for sportsmanship), 1967–68.

MILLER, JOHNNY, Apr. 29, 1947 (San Francisco, Calif.). U.S. golfer. U.S. Open champ, 1973; leading PGA money-winner ($353,201), 1974.

MITTERMAIER, ROSI, 1950 (West Germany). German skier. Gold medalist in the downhill and slalom in 1976 Olympics; World Cup winner, 1976.

MONROE, EARL ("The Pearl"), Nov. 21, 1944 (Philadelphia, Pa.). U.S. basketball player. Played with Baltimore Bullets (1967–72) and New York Knicks (1972–); averaged over 20 points per game, 1968–71 and 1975–76.

MOORE, ARCHIE, born Archibald Lee Wright, Dec. 13, 1913 (Benoit, Miss.). U.S. boxer. World light-heavyweight champion, 1952–62.

MORENZ, HOWIE, 1902 (Mitchell, Ont., Can.)-Mar. 8, 1937. Canadian hockey player. Played with the Montreal Canadiens, 1924–34; NHL MVP, 1928, 1931–32; chosen in Canadian Press Poll as outstanding hockey player of first half of century, 1950.

MORGAN, JOE, born Joseph Leonard Morgan, Sept. 19, 1943 (Bonham, Tex.). U.S. baseball player. Second baseman for Houston Astros (1963–71; 1980–) and Cincinnati Reds (1972–79); NL MVP, 1975 and 1976.

MORPHY, PAUL, June 22, 1837 (New Orleans, La.)-July 10, 1884. U.S. chessmaster. Defeated world's best players, 1857; first to rely on principle of development before attack.

MOSCONI, WILLIE, June 21, 1913 (Philadelphia, Pa.). U.S. billiards player. World pocket billiards champ, 1941, 1944-45, 1947-48, 1950-53, and 1955.

MOSES, EDWIN, Aug. 31, 1955 (Dayton, Ohio). U.S. hurdler. Won Olympic gold medal in 400-m hurdles, 1976; set world record in his event (47.45 sec.), 1977.

MOTTA, (John) RICHARD, Sept. 3, 1931 (Salt Lake City, Utah). U.S. basketball coach. Coached Chicago Bulls (1969-76) and Washington Bullets, 1976-   ; led Bullets to NBA championship, 1978.

MUNSON, THURMAN, June 7, 1947 (Akron, Ohio)-Aug. 2, 1979. U.S. baseball player. Catcher with N.Y. Yankees, 1969-79; AL Rookie of the Year, 1970; hit .300 five times; AL MVP, 1976; killed in plane crash.

MURPHY, CALVIN, May 9, 1948 (Norwalk, Conn.). U.S. basketball player. A 5'9" guard who has been with the Houston Rockets in NBA since 1971.

MUSIAL, STAN ("The Man"), born Stanley Frank Musial, Nov. 21, 1920 (Donora, Pa.). U.S. baseball player. St. Louis Cardinals outfielder, 1941-63; NL batting leader, 1943, 1946, 1948, 1950-52, 1957; hit 475 career homers; had .331 career batting avg. and NL record 3,630 career hits; NL MVP, 1943, 1946, 1948; inducted into Baseball Hall of Fame, 1969.

NAGURSKI, BRONISLAW ("Bronko"), Nov. 3, 1908 (Rainy River, Ont., Can.). Canadian football player. Fullback and tackle with Chicago Bears, 1930-37; gained over 4,000 yards rushing, 1930-37; inducted into Football Hall of Fame, 1963.

NAISMITH, JAMES, Nov. 6, 1861 (Almonte, Ont., Can.)-Nov. 28, 1939. Canadian educator. Teacher of phys. ed. who is credited with inventing basketball, 1891.

NAMATH, JOE ("Broadway Joe"), born Joseph William Namath, May 31, 1943 (Beaver Falls, Pa.). U.S. football player, actor. Quarterback with the New York Jets (1965-77) and Los Angeles Rams (1977-78); passed for record 4,007 yds., 1967; led N.Y. Jets to Super Bowl victory, 1969.

NASTASE, ILIE ("Nasty"), July 19, 1946 (Bucharest, Rum.). Rumanian tennis player. Famed for on-court temper tantrums; U.S. singles champ, 1972.

NAVRATILOVA, MARTINA, Oct. 10, 1956 (Prague, Czech.). Czech-U.S. tennis player. Wimbledon champ, 1978 and 1979.

NELSON, BYRON, Feb. 4, 1912 (Ft. Worth, Tex.). U.S. golfer. Won 11 consecutive tournaments, 1945; Masters champ, 1937, 1942; U.S. Open champ, 1939; PGA champ, 1940, 1945; inducted into Golf Hall of Fame, 1953; now a TV commentator.

NETTLES, GRAIG, Aug. 20, 1944 (San Diego, Calif.). U.S. baseball player. Third baseman with Minnesota Twins (1967-69), Cleveland Indians (1969-72), and N.Y. Yankees (1973-   ); led AL in home runs, 1976; noted for fielding prowess.

NEVERS, ERNIE, June 11, 1903 (Willow River, Minn.)-May 3, 1976. U.S. football and baseball player. Chosen by Football Writers Assn. as greatest college (Stanford U.) fullback of era 1919-69; pitched for St. Louis Browns, 1926-28.

NEWCOMBE, JOHN, May 23, 1943 (Sydney, Austrl.). Australian tennis player. U.S. singles champ,

1967, 1973; Wimbledon champ, 1967, 1970, and 1971.

NICKLAUS, JACK ("The Golden Bear"), Jan. 21, 1940 (Columbus, Ohio). U.S. golfer. Ranked by many as the greatest golfer of all time, he has won over $3 million in career. U.S. Open champ, 1962, 1967, 1972; Masters champ, 1963, 1965-66, 1972, 1975; PGA champ, 1963, 1971, 1973, 1975; leading PGA Tour money-winner seven times.

NILSSON, ULF, May 11, 1950 (Nynashamn, Swe.). Swedish hockey player. Led WHA in assists, 1977-78; signed multiyear contract with N.Y. Rangers, 1978.

NOLL, CHUCK, 1931 (Cleveland, Ohio). U.S. football coach. Head coach of Pittsburgh Steelers, 1969-   ; led team to Super Bowl championships, 1975, 1976, 1979, and 1980.

NORTON, KEN, Aug. 9, 1945 (Jacksonville, Ill.). U.S. boxer. Defeated MUHAMMAD ALI 1973; World Boxing Council heavyweight champion, 1978; occasionally seen as film actor.

NURMI, PAAVO ("The Flying Finn"), June 13, 1897 (Turku, Fin.)-Oct. 2, 1973. Finnish distance runner. Won six Olympic Gold Medals, 1920, 1924, and 1928; held world record for mile, 1923-31.

OERTER, AL, Sept. 19, 1936 (New York, N.Y.). U.S. discus thrower. Won gold medal at four consecutive Olympics, 1956-68.

OH, SADAHARU, May 20, 1940 (Tokyo, Jap.). Japanese baseball player. Known as the "Babe Ruth of Japan"; has hit over 800 home runs.

OLDFIELD, BARNEY, Jan. 29, 1878 (Wauseon, Ohio)-Oct. 4, 1946. U.S. auto racer. First to travel at the speed of a mile a minute, 1903.

OLIVA, TONY, born Antonio Pedro Oliva, July 20, 1940 (Pinar del Rio, Cuba). U.S. baseball player. Outfielder with Minnesota Twins, 1962-76; led AL in batting, 1964-65 and 1971; AL Rookie of the Year, 1964.

OLIVER, AL(bert), Oct. 14, 1946 (Portsmouth, Ohio). U.S. baseball player. Outfielder with Pittsburgh Pirates (1968-77) and Texas Rangers (1978-   ); has batted over .300 five times.

OLSEN, MERLIN JAY, Sept. 15, 1940 (Logan, Ut.). U.S. football player. Defensive lineman with L.A. Rams, 1962-76; now a broadcaster and actor.

ORR, BOBBY, Mar. 20, 1948 (Parry Sound, Ont., Can.). Canadian hockey player. Defenseman with Boston Bruins (1967-76) and Chicago Black Hawks (1977-1979); NHL Rookie of the Year, 1967; first defenseman to be NHL leading scorer, 1970 and 1975; NHL first team all-star, 1968-75; won Norris Trophy (best defenseman), 1968-75; scored record (for defenseman) 46 goals, 1975; career shortened by five knee operations.

OTT, MEL(vin Thomas), Mar. 2, 1909 (Gretna, La.)-Nov. 21, 1958. U.S. baseball player. N.Y. Giants outfielder, 1926-47; first to hit 500 home runs in NL; led NL in home runs, 1932, 1934, 1936-38, and 1942; inducted into Baseball Hall of Fame, 1951.

OWENS, JESSE, born James Cleveland Owens, Sept. 12, 1913 (Danville, Ala.). U.S. athlete. Won four gold medals in track and field at 1936 Olympics in Berlin.

PAGE, ALAN, Aug. 7, 1945 (Canton, Ohio). U.S. football player. All-American defensive lineman at Notre Dame U., 1966; with Minnesota Vikings (1967-76), and Chicago Bears (1977-   ); played in Pro Bowl eight times; named NFL's outstanding defensive player, 1973.

PAIGE, LEROY ("Satchel"), July 7, 1906 (Mobile,

THE BOOK OF WHO

Ala.). U.S. baseball player. Legendary pitcher in Negro leagues; joined Cleveland Indians, 1948; inducted into Baseball Hall of Fame, 1971.

PALMER, ARNOLD, Sept. 10, 1929 (Youngstown, Pa.). U.S. golfer. First $1 million-winner in game; Master's champ, 1958, 1960, 1962, and 1964; U.S. Open champ, 1960.

PALMER, JIM, born James Alvin, Oct. 15, 1945 (New York, N.Y.). U.S. baseball player. Baltimore Orioles pitcher, 1965-   ; 20-game winner eight times; most AL games won, 1975-77; lowest AL ERA, 1973, 1975; AL Cy Young Award winner, 1973, 1975-76.

PARK, BRAD, July 6, 1948 (Toronto, Ont., Can.). Canadian hockey player. Defenseman for N.Y. Rangers (1969-76) and Boston Bruins (1976-   ); NHL first team all-star, 1972, 1974, and 1976.

PARKER, DAVE, June 9, 1951 (Jackson, Miss.). U.S. baseball player. With the Pittsburgh Pirates, 1973-   ; led NL in batting, 1977-78; named NL MVP, 1978.

PARSEGHIAN, ARA RAOUL, May 21, 1923 (Akron, Ohio). U.S. football coach. Coached Northwestern U., 1956-63; coached Notre Dame U.(1964-75), leading it to a national championship, 1966.

PATERNO, JOSEPH VINCENT, Dec. 21, 1926 (Brooklyn, N.Y.). U.S. football coach. Head coach of Pennsylvania St. U., 1966-   .

PATTERSON, FLOYD, Jan. 4, 1935 (Waco, N.C.). U.S. boxer. Olympic light-heavyweight champion, 1952; world heavyweight champion, 1956-59 and 1960-62—first to regain title after losing it.

PAYTON, WALTER, July 25, 1954 (Columbia, Miss.). U.S. football player. Chicago Bears running back, 1976-   ; rushed for NFL record 275 yards against Minnesota, Nov. 20, 1977; NFL MVP, 1977; NFL leading rusher, 1977-78.

PEARSON, DAVID, Dec. 22, 1934 (Spartanburg, S.C.). U.S. auto racer. Three-time NASCAR champion, 1966, 1968, and 1969; won Daytona 500 in 1976.

PELÉ, born Edson Arantes Do Nascimento, Oct. 23, 1940 (Tres Coracoes, Braz.). Brazilian soccer player. Led Brazilian National team to three World Cup championships, 1958, 1962, and 1970; moved to N.Y. Cosmos (1975-77) where he was credited with aiding U.S. soccer growth.

PERRY, GAYLORD, Sept. 15, 1938 (Williamston, N.C.). U.S. baseball player. Pitcher with several teams, chiefly S.F. Giants (1962-71); has led both NL (1970 and 1978) and AL (1972) in wins; AL Cy Young Award winner, 1972; NL Cy Young award winner, 1978. *Me and the Spitter: An Autobiographical Confession,* 1974.

PETTIT, BOB, Dec. 2, 1932 (Baton Rouge, La.). U.S. basketball player. As a forward with the St. Louis Hawks, was the first player to score 20,000 points in the NBA; led NBA scoring, 1956, 1959; NBA MVP, 1956, 1959; inducted into Basketball Hall of Fame, 1970.

PETTY, RICHARD, July 2, 1937 (Randleman, N.C.). U.S. auto racer. Won Daytona 500 in 1964, 1966, 1971, 1973, 1974, and 1979; NASCAR champ in 1964, 1967, 1972, 1974-75.

PHELPS, RICHARD ("Digger"), July 4, 1941 (Beacon, N.Y.). U.S. basketball coach. Coach of Fordham U., 1970-71; coach of Notre Dame U., 1971-

PINCAY, LAFFIT, JR., 1946 (Panama). Panamanian jockey. Leading money-winning jockey, 1970-74, 1979.

PLANTE, JACQUES, Jan. 17, 1929 (Shawinigan Falls, Que., Can.). Canadian hockey player. Goalie, principally with Montreal Canadiens, 1953-63; first goalie to wear a mask in a game; NHL MVP, 1962; won Vezina Trophy (best goalie), 1956-60, 1962, and 1969.

PLAYER, GARY, Nov. 1, 1935 (Johannesburg, S.A.). S. African golfer. PGA champ, 1962 and 1972; U.S. Open champ, 1965; British Open champ, 1959 and 1968; Master's champ, 1974 and 1978.

POTVIN, DENIS, Oct. 29, 1953 (Hull, Ont., Can.). Canadian hockey player. Defenseman with N.Y. Islanders, 1973-   ; NHL Rookie of the Year, 1974; won Norris Trophy (best defenseman), 1976, 1978, and 1979; NHL first team all-star, 1975-79.

PROELL, ANNEMARIE (married name: Moser), Mar. 27, 1953 (Kleinarl, Austria). Austrian skier. Won World Cup championship five consecutive years, 1971-75, 1979.

RANKIN, JUDY, née Torluemke, Feb. 18, 1945 (St. Louis, Mo.). U.S. golfer. Leading money-winner on the LPGA circuit, 1976-77.

REED, WILLIS, June 25, 1942 (Hico, La.). U.S. basketball player, coach. With N.Y. Knickerbockers as a player (1964-74) and as coach (1977-79); named NBA Rookie of the Year, 1965; named MVP in NBA playoffs, 1970 and 1973.

RICE, (Henry) GRANTLAND, Nov. 1, 1880 (Murfreesboro, Tenn.)–July 13, 1954. U.S. sportswriter. As sportswriter at the New York *Tribune* (1914-30), earned reputation as one of the nation's finest; syndicated columnist, 1930-47; selected All-American football teams for *Collier's* magazine; named football's "Four Horsemen," 1924.

RICE, JIM, born James Edward Rice, Mar. 8, 1953 (Anderson, S.C.). U.S. baseball player. An outfielder with the Boston Red Sox, 1974-   ; led AL in home runs, 1977-78; led AL in RBIs, 1978; named AL MVP, 1978.

RICHARD, MAURICE ("Rocket"), Aug. 14, 1924 (Montreal, Que., Can.). Canadian hockey player. Forward with Montreal Canadiens, 1942-60; scored 544 career goals, plus 82 in playoffs; NHL MVP, 1947.

RICKEY, BRANCH WESLEY, Dec. 20, 1881 (Stockdale, Ohio)–Dec. 9, 1965. U.S. baseball executive. Instituted farm system, 1919; as pres. of the Brooklyn Dodgers (1942-49), signed JACKIE ROBINSON to one of the Dodgers' farm teams, thus breaking baseball color barrier, 1946.

RIGGS, BOBBY, Feb. 25, 1918 (Los Angeles, Calif.). U.S. tennis player. U.S. singles champ, 1939 and 1941; Wimbledon champ, 1939; lost "Match of Century" to BILLIE JEAN KING, 1973.

ROBERTSON, OSCAR ("Big O"), Nov. 24, 1938 (Charlotte, Tenn.). U.S. basketball player. A three-time All-American at the U. of Cincinnati, 1958-60; played in NBA for Cincinnati (1960-70) and Milwaukee (1970-74); averaged 25.7 points per game in career; NBA record 9,887 career assists; named NBA MVP, 1964; first team All-Star nine times.

ROBINSON, BROOKS, May 18, 1937 (Little Rock, Ark.). U.S. baseball player. Rated one of game's best-fielding third basemen; with Baltimore Orioles, 1955-77; played in four World Series; named AL MVP, 1964.

ROBINSON, FRANK, Aug. 31, 1935 (Beaumont, Tex.). U.S. baseball player, manager. Played with

SPORTS PERSONALITIES

Cincinnati Reds (1956-65) and Baltimore Orioles (1966-71); won AL Triple Crown, 1966; first black to manage major league team (Cleveland Indians), 1975; hit 586 career home runs; named NL MVP, 1961; named AL MVP, 1966.

ROBINSON, JACK(ie) **ROOSEVELT,** Jan. 31, 1919 (Cairo, Ga.)-Oct. 24, 1972. U.S. baseball player. First black to enter major leagues with the Brooklyn Dodgers, (1947), breaking pro sports color line; played with Dodgers until 1956; NL leading batter, 1949; named NL MVP, 1949; .311 lifetime batting average; inducted into Hall of Fame, 1962; in later years, a civil-rights activist.

ROBINSON, ("Sugar") **RAY,** born Walker Smith, May 3, 1920 (Detroit, Mich.). U.S. boxer. Welterweight champ, 1946-51; middleweight champ five times, 1951-60.

ROCKNE, KNUTE, Mar. 4, 1888 (Voss, Nor.)-Mar. 31, 1931. U.S. football coach. As coach (1918-31), built Notre Dame into a football powerhouse; in 13 seasons, team won 105 games, lost 12, tied 5 and went undefeated in 1919, 1920, 1924, 1929, and 1930 seasons.

RODGERS, BILL, Dec. 23, 1947 (Hartford, Conn.). U.S. distance runner. Won Boston Marathon, 1975, 1978-79; won New York Marathon, 1976-79.

ROONEY, ART, Jan. 27, 1901 (Coulter, Pa.). U.S. football exec. Founder of the NFL Pittsburgh Steelers, 1933; inducted into Football Hall of Fame, 1964.

ROSE, PETE, born Edward Peter Rose, Apr. 14, 1941 (Cincinnati, Ohio). U.S. baseball player. Played with Cincinnati Reds (1963-78) and Philadelphia Phillies (1979-   ); named NL rookie of the year, 1963; NL leading batter, 1968, 1969, 1973; hit safely in NL record 44 consecutive games, 1978; has led NL in hits six times; named NL MVP, 1973; signed by Phillies for $800,000 per year, 1978.

ROSEWALL, KEN, Nov. 2, 1934 (Sydney, Austrl.). Australian tennis player. U.S. singles champ, 1956 and 1970.

ROTH, MARK, Apr. 10, 1951 (New York, N.Y.). U.S. bowler. Leading money-winner on the professional tour, 1977-1979.

ROZELLE, ALVIN RAY ("Pete"). March 1, 1926 (South Gate, Calif.). U.S. football exec. Gen. mgr. of NFL Los Angeles Rams, 1957-60; NFL commissioner, 1960-   .

RUDOLPH, WILMA, June 23, 1940 (St. Bethlehem, Tenn.). U.S. sprinter. Won three gold medals in 1960 Olympics, in the 100- and 200-meter dashes and the 400-meter relay.

RUPP, ADOLPH FREDERICK, Sept. 2, 1901 (Halstead, Kan.)-Dec. 10, 1977. U.S. basketball coach. Coached Kentucky U. (1930-77) to record 879 wins and national championships in 1948, 1949, 1951, and 1958; named national coach of the year by AP and UPI, 1951, 1959, and 1966; inducted into Basketball Hall of Fame, 1968.

RUSSELL, BILL, born William Felton Russell, Feb. 12, 1934 (Monroe, La.). U.S. basketball player, coach. First black to coach major pro sports team (Boston Celtics), 1965-69; playing for Boston (1956-69), five-time NBA MVP, 1958, 1961-63, 1965; revolutionized game by stressing defensive play; inducted into Basketball Hall of Fame, 1974.

RUTH, GEORGE HERMAN ("Babe," "Sultan of Swat," "The Bambino"), Feb. 6, 1895 (Baltimore, Md.)-Aug. 16, 1948. U.S. baseball player. Played with Boston Red Sox (1914-19), New York Yankees (1920-34) and Boston Braves (1935) helped save baseball after Black Sox scandal of 1919-20; led AL in homers 11 times; hit AL record 708 home runs (714 in career); had .342 lifetime batting avg.; played in ten World Series; led AL in RBIs eight times; held over 50 records on retirement; inducted into Baseball Hall of Fame, 1936.

RYAN, NOLAN, born Lynn Nolan Ryan, Jan. 31, 1947 (Refugio, Tex.). U.S. baseball player. Pitcher with the New York Mets (1966-71), California Angels (1972-79); and Houston Astros (1980-   ). Struck out record 383 batters, 1973; pitched no-hitters in 1973, 1974, 1975, and 1977.

RYUN, JIM, Apr. 29, 1947 (Wichita, Kan.). U.S. runner. Set world records (since broken) in the mile (3:51.3) and 1,500-m races, 1967.

SARAZEN, GENE, Feb. 27, 1901 (Harrison, N.Y.). U.S. golfer. U.S. Open champ, 1922 and 1932; PGA champ, 1922-23, 1933; developer of the sand wedge.

SAWCHUCK, TERRY, Dec. 28, 1929 (Winnipeg, Man., Can.)-May 31, 1970. Canadian hockey player. Goalie, principally with Detroit Red Wings 1949-55, 1957-64, and 1968-69; NHL Rookie of the Year, 1951; won Vezina Trophy (best goalie), 1952, 1953, and 1965; NHL-record 103 career shutouts.

SAYERS, GALE, May 30, 1943 (Wichita, Kan.). U.S. football player. Running back with the NFL Chicago Bears, 1965-71; led NFC in rushing, 1966 and 1969; inducted into Football Hall of Fame, 1977.

SCHMELING, MAX, Sept. 28, 1905 (Brandenburg, Ger.). German boxer. World heavyweight champ, 1930-32; KO'd JOE LOUIS, 1936; KO'd by Louis, 1937.

SCHMIDT, MIKE, born Michael Jack Schmidt, Sept. 27, 1949 (Dayton, Ohio). U.S. baseball player. Infielder with the Philadelphia Phillies, 1972-   ; led NL in home runs, 1974-76.

SCULLY, VIN(cent) **EDWARD,** Nov. 29, 1927 (Bronx, N.Y.). U.S. sportscaster. Announcer for Brooklyn/L.A. Dodgers, 1950-   ; named Sportscaster of the Year, 1965; with CBS-TV, 1975-   .

SEAVER, (George) THOMAS, Nov. 17, 1944 (Fresno, Calif.). U.S. baseball player. Pitcher with New York Mets (1967-77) and Cincinnati Reds (1977-   ); 20-game winner five times; named NL rookie of the year, 1967; won NL Cy Young Award, 1969, 1973, 1975; NL lowest ERA, 1970-71, 1973; led NL in strikeouts five times; struck out record 19 in one game, 1970.

SHERO, FRED, Oct. 23, 1924 (Winnipeg, Man., Can.). Canadian hockey coach. Led Philadelphia Flyers (1971-78) to Stanley Cup championships, 1974 and 1975; coach, New York Rangers, 1979-   .

SHOEMAKER, WILLIE, Aug. 19, 1931 (Fabens, Tex.). U.S. jockey. Rode Kentucky Derby winner, 1955, 1959, 1965; rode Belmont Stakes winner five times; first jockey to ride over 7,000 winners; leading money-winning jockey ten times.

SHORE, EDDIE, 1902 (Ft. Qu'appelle, Sask., Can.). Canadian hockey player. Defenseman with Boston Bruins, 1926-40; NHL MVP, 1933, 1935, 1936, and 1938; first team all-star seven times; inducted into Hockey Hall of Fame, 1945.

SHORTER, FRANK, Oct. 31, 1947 (Munich, Ger.). U.S. distance runner. Won gold medal in marathon at 1972 Olympics; won Sullivan Award, 1972; has his own line of running clothing; currently an attorney in Colorado.

SHULA, DON, Jan. 4, 1930 (Grand River, Ohio).

221

THE BOOK OF WHO

U.S. football coach. As coach of the NFL Miami Dolphins (1970–), led team to Super Bowl championships in 1973 and 1974.

SIMMONS, AL, born Aloys Szymanski, May 22, 1902 (Milwaukee, Wis.)–May 26, 1956. U.S. baseball player. Outfielder with many teams, the longest with Philadelphia Athletics, 1924–32, 1940–41, and 1944; led AL in batting, 1930–31; had .334 career batting average; inducted into Baseball Hall of Fame, 1953.

SIMPSON, O(renthal) J(ames), July 9, 1947 (San Francisco, Calif.). U.S. football player, actor. Running back with NFL Buffalo Bills (1969–77), and S.F. 49ers (1978–79); rushed for NFL record 2,003 yds., 1973; rushed for 100 or more yds. a record 11 times, 1973; named NFL MVP, 1973; AFC leading rusher, 1972–73 and 1975–76; actor in action films, including *The Towering Inferno* (1974).

SISLER, GEORGE ("Gorgeous George"), Mar. 24, 1893 (Manchester, Ohio)–Mar. 26, 1973. U.S. baseball player. Played with St. Louis, 1915–27; AL leading batter, 1920 and 1922; had .420 batting avg., 1922; had record 257 hits, 1920; had .340 lifetime batting avg.; inducted into Baseball Hall of Fame, 1939.

SMITH, WALTER WELLESLEY ("Red"), Sept. 25, 1905 (Green Bay, Wisc.). U.S. sports columnist. With Philadelphia *Record*, 1936–45; with N.Y. *Herald-Tribune*, 1945–66; with *The New York Times*, 1971– .

SNEAD, ("Slammin' ") **SAM,** May 27, 1912 (Hot Springs, Va.). U.S. golfer. PGA champ, 1942, 1949, 1951; Master's champ, 1949, 1952, 1954; inducted into Golf Hall of Fame, 1953.

SNELL, PETER, Dec. 17, 1938 (Opunake, N.Z.). New Zealand runner. 800-m gold medalist in 1960 and 1964 Olympics; held world record for mile, 1962–65.

SNYDER, JIMMY ("The Greek"), born Demetrios George Synodinos, 1919 (Steubenville, Ohio). U.S. sports figure. Noted oddsmaker, analyst, and columnist.

SPAHN, WARREN, Apr. 23, 1921 (Buffalo, N.Y.). U.S. baseball player. Pitcher with the Boston/Milwaukee Braves (1942–64) and S.F. Giants (1965); won NL record 363 games; 20-game winner 13 times; led NL in strikeouts, 1949–53; won Cy Young Award, 1957; inducted into Baseball Hall of Fame, 1972.

SPASSKY, BORIS, Jan. 30, 1937 (Leningrad, USSR). Soviet chessmaster. World champion, 1969–72; lost to BOBBY FISCHER in highly-publicized match, 1972.

SPEAKER, TRIS(tram) E., Apr. 4, 1888 (Hubbard, Tex.)–Dec. 8, 1958. U.S. baseball player. Outfielder with Boston Red Sox (1907–15) and Cleveland Indians (1916–26); had .344 career batting avg.; led AL in batting, 1916; inducted into Baseball Hall of Fame, 1937.

SPITZ, MARK, Feb. 10, 1950 (Modesto, Calif.). U.S. swimmer. First athlete to win seven gold medals in a single Olympic games, 1972; won two gold medals in 1968 Olympics; won Sullivan Award, 1971.

STABLER, KEN, Dec. 25, 1945 (Foley, Ala.). U.S. football player. Quarterback with the NFL Oakland Raiders, 1970– ; AFC leading passer, 1973, 1976; named NFL MVP, 1974.

STAGG, AMOS ALONZO, Aug. 16, 1862 (W. Orange, N.J.)–Mar. 17, 1965. U.S. football coach. Coach of the U. of Chicago football team for 41 years 1892–1932; had five undefeated seasons;

introduced huddle, man-in-motion, end-around plays; elected to Football Hall of Fame, 1951.

STARGELL, WILLIE, Mar. 6, 1941 (Earlsboro, Okla.). U.S. baseball player. Outfielder/first baseman with Pittsburgh Pirates 1962– ; led NL in home runs, 1971, 1973; 461 career home runs through 1979; NL and World Series MVP, 1979.

STARR, BART, born Bryan Starr, Jan. 9, 1934 (Montgomery, Ala.). U.S. football player, coach. Quarterback with the NFL Green Bay Packers, 1956–71; NFL leading passer, 1962, 1964, 1966; named NFL MVP, 1966; named Super Bowl MVP, 1967–8; inducted into Football Hall of Fame. 1977.

STAUBACH, ROGER ("The Dodger"), Feb. 5, 1942 (Cincinnati, Ohio). U.S. football player. Quarterback, with the NFL Dallas Cowboys, 1969– ; NFC leading passer, 1971, 1973, 1977, 1978, 1979; won 1963 Heisman Trophy while playing for Navy.

STEINBRENNER, GEORGE, July 4, 1930 (Rocky River, Ohio). U.S. baseball executive. A shipbuilder by profession; owner of N.Y. Yankees, 1973– ; signed free agents to help team win championships in 1977 and 1978.

STENGEL, CASEY, born Charles Dillon Stengel, July 30, 1891 (Kansas City, Mo.)–Sept. 30, 1975. U.S. baseball player, manager. A highly colorful former player who managed the N.Y. Yankees to 10 pennants (1949–53, 1955–58, and 1960), winning seven World Series; managed N.Y. Mets during their infancy; known for his "Stengelese" (fractured sentences); elected to Baseball Hall of Fame, 1966.

STENMARK, INGEMAR, Mar. 18, 1956 (Tarnaby, Swe.). Swedish skier. Won World Cup championship, 1976–78.

STEWART, JACKIE, June 11, 1939 (Dunbartonshire, Scot.). Scottish auto racer, sportscaster. World Grand Prix champ, 1969, 1971, and 1973; retired with record 27 Grand Prix victories; now a TV commentator on auto racing.

STONES, DWIGHT, Dec. 6, 1953 (Los Angeles, Calif.). U.S. high jumper. Set indoor and outdoor world records several times in 1970s; controversial, colorful athlete.

SULLIVAN, JOHN L(awrence), Oct. 15, 1858 (Boston, Mass.)–Feb. 2, 1918. U.S. boxer. Last bareknuckle heavyweight champion, 1882–92; lost to JAMES CORBETT.

SUTTON, DON, born Donald Howard Sutton, Apr. 2, 1945 (Clio, Ala.). U.S. baseball pitcher. With the L.A. Dodgers, 1966– ; has won 209 career games, as of 1979 season.

SWANN, LYNN, Mar. 7, 1952 (Alcoa, Tenn.). U.S. football player. Wide receiver with the Pittsburgh Steelers, 1974– ; named Super Bowl MVP, 1975.

TARKENTON, FRAN(cis), Feb. 3, 1940 (Richmond, Va.). U.S. football player. Quarterback with the N.Y. Giants (1967–71) and Minnesota Vikings (1961–66 and 1974–79); passed for NFL record 47,003 career yds. (342 TDs); named NFL MVP, 1975; retired from football, 1979.

THOENI, GUSTAVO, Feb. 28, 1951 (Trafoi, It.). Italian skier. Won giant slalom gold medal in 1972 Olympics; World Cup champ, 1971–73 and 1975.

THOMAS, KURT, Mar. 29, 1956 (Terre Haute, Ind.). U.S. gymnast. First U.S. male to win gold medal in world championship competition (for floor exercise), 1978; Sullivan Award, 1979.

THOMPSON, DAVID, July 13, 1954 (Shelby, N.C.). U.S. basketball player. With the NBA Denver Nuggets, 1975– ; averaged over 24 points per game, 1977–79.

SPORTS PERSONALITIES

THORPE, JAMES FRANCIS ("Jim"), May 28, 1888 (Prague, Okla.)-Mar. 28, 1953. U.S. athlete, executive. Won pentathlon and decathlon at 1912 Olympics, but was stripped of medals when he was declared not to be amateur; football All-American at Carlisle (Pa.) Indian School 1911-12; played pro baseball with New York Giants (1913-15 and 1917-19) and Cincinnati Reds (1915-17); played pro football with several teams, 1915-26; first pres. of the NFL; elected to Football Hall of Fame, 1963; ranked as outstanding athlete of 20th cent. by AP, 1950.

TIANT, LUIS CLEMENTE, Nov. 23, 1940 (Havana, Cuba). Cuban-U.S. baseball player. Pitcher with the Cleveland Indians (1964-69), Minnesota Twins (1970), Boston Red Sox (1972-78) and New York Yankees (1979-); lowest AL ERA, 1968 and 1972; 20-game winner, 1968, 1973, 1974, 1976.

TICKNER, CHARLES, Nov. 13, 1953 (Oakland, Calif.). U.S. figure skater. World champion, 1978; U.S. champ, 1977-79 won Olympic bronze medal, 1980.

TILDEN, WILLIAM ("Big Bill"), Feb. 10, 1893 (Germantown, Pa.)-June 5, 1953. U.S. tennis player. U.S. singles champ, 1920-25 and 1930; Wimbledon champ, 1921 and 1930; played on 11 Davis Cup teams; voted by AP greatest tennis player of first half of the 20th cent., 1950.

TITTLE, Y(elberton) A(braham), ("The Bald Eagle"), Oct. 24, 1926 (Marshall, Tex.). U.S. football player. Quarterback with NFL Baltimore Colts (1948-50), S.F. 49ers (1951-60), and N.Y. Giants (1961-64), passed for 33,070 yds. in career; named NFL MVP, 1961 and 1963; elected to Football Hall of Fame, 1971.

TOMJANOVICH, RUDY, Nov. 24, 1948 (Hamtramck, Mich.). U.S. basketball player. Forward; All-American at U. of Mich., 1970; averaged over 18 PPG in NBA career with the San Diego/Houston Rockets, 1971- ; missed part of the 1978 season after being injured in courtside brawl; awarded over $3 million in damages, 1979.

TORRE, JOE, born Joseph Paul Torre, July 18, 1940 (Brooklyn, N.Y.). U.S. baseball player, manager. Played with Milwaukee/Atlanta Braves (1960-68), St. Louis Cardinals (1969-74), and New York Mets (1975-76); led NL in batting, 1971; named NL MVP, 1971; manager of N.Y. Mets, 1977- .

TREVINO, LEE, Dec. 1, 1939 (Dallas, Tex.). U.S. golfer. U.S. Open champ, 1968 and 1971; PGA champ, 1974; British Open champ, 1971 and 1972.

TUNNEY, GENE, May 25, 1898 (New York, N.Y.)-Nov. 7,1978. U.S. boxer. World heavyweight champion, 1926-28; twice defeated JACK DEMPSEY.

TURCOTTE, RON, 1950 (Grand Falls, N.B., Can.). Canadian jockey. Rode Triple Crown winner Secretariat, 1973; accident in race ended career, 1978.

TURISCHEVA, LUDMILLA, 1952 (USSR). Soviet gymnast. World champion, 1970, 1972, 1974, and 1976; won two gold medals at the 1972 Olympics.

TURNER, TED, born Robert Edward Turner, Nov. 19, 1938 (Cincinnati, Ohio). U.S. yachtsman, sports exec. Won America's Cup on yacht *Courageous,* 1977; owner of NL Atlanta Braves and NBA Atlanta Hawks.

TYUS, WYOMIA, Aug. 29, 1945 (Griffin, Ga.). U.S. sprinter. Won 100-m. dash gold medal in 1964 and 1968 Olympics.

UNITAS, JOHN, May 7, 1933 (Pittsburgh, Pa.).

U.S. football player. Quarterback with Baltimore Colts (1956-72) and San Diego Chargers (1973); passed for TDs in 47 consecutive games, 1957-60; passed for 40,239 career yds.; named NFL MVP, 1957 and 1967.

UNSELD, WES(ley). Mar. 14, 1946 (Louisville, Ky.). U.S. basketball player. Center with the NBA Baltimore/Capitol/Washington Bullets, 1968- ; named NBA Rookie of the Year, 1969; named NBA MVP, 1969; named MVP in NBA playoffs, 1978.

UNSER, AL, May 29, 1939 (Albuquerque, N.M.). U.S. auto racer. Won Indianapolis 500 in 1970, 1971, and 1978; U.S. Auto Club champion, 1970. (Brother of BOBBY UNSER.)

UNSER, BOBBY, Feb. 20, 1934 (Albuquerque, N.M.). U.S. auto racer. Won Indianapolis 500 in 1968 and 1975; U.S. Auto Club champ, 1968 and 1974. (Brother of AL UNSER.)

VAN BROCKLIN, NORM, ("The Dutchman"), Mar. 15, 1926 (Eagle Butte, S.D.). U.S. football player, coach. Quarterback with Los Angeles Rams (1949-57) and Philadelphia Eagles (1958-60); passed for single-game-record 554 yds., 1951; named NFL MVP, 1960; head coach of Minnesota Vikings (1961-66) and Atlanta Falcons (1968-76).

VANDER MEER, JOHNNY ("Double No-Hit"), Nov. 2, 1914 (Prospect Park, N.J.). U.S. baseball player. Pitcher with the Cincinnati Reds (1937-50) and Cleveland Indians (1951); pitched two consecutive no-hitters, 1938.

VARE, GLENNA, née Collett, June 20, 1903 (New Haven, Conn.). U.S. golfer. Dominated women's golfing in the 1920s; U.S. Women's Amateur champ, 1922, 1925, 1928, 1929, 1930, and 1935; French champ, 1925; represented U.S. in Curtis Cup, 1932, 1936, 1938, and 1948. Vare Trophy, named after her, is awarded annually to the woman professional golfer with the best scoring average.

VILAS, GUILLERMO, Aug. 17, 1952 (Mar del Plata, Arg.). Argentine tennis player. U.S. singles champ, 1977; won over $800,000, 1977.

WADE, VIRGINIA, July 10, 1945 (Bournemouth, Eng.). English tennis player. Wimbledon champ, 1977.

WAGNER, HONUS ("The Flying Dutchman"), born John Peter Wagner, Feb. 24, 1874 (Mansfield, Pa.)-Dec. 6, 1955. U.S. baseball player. Infielder with the Pittsburgh Pirates, 1900-17; led NL in batting, 1900, 1903-04, 1906-09, and 1911; hit career .327; led NL in doubles seven times, RBIs four times; had 3,415 career hits, 722 stolen bases; inducted into Baseball Hall of Fame, 1936.

WALCOTT, JERSEY JOE, born Arnold Raymond Cream, Jan. 31, 1914 (Merchantville, N.J.). U.S. boxer. World heavyweight champion, 1951-52.

WALKER, JOHN, Jan. 12, 1952 (Papukura, N.Z.). New Zealand runner. Set record (3:49.4) for mile, 1975; ran record 2,000 m (4:51.45), 1976; 1,500-m gold medalist in 1976 Olympics.

WALKER, MICKEY ("Toy Bulldog"), born Edward Walker, July 13, 1901 (Elizabeth, N.J.). U.S. boxer. World welterweight champ, 1922-26; world middleweight champ, 1926-31.

WALSH, STELLA, born Stanislawa Walasiewicz, Apr. 11, 1911 (Poland). U.S. athlete. Won some 40 U.S. track-and-field titles; set many world records; won gold medal in 100-m run at the 1932 Olympics.

WALTON, BILL, Nov. 5, 1952 (La Mesa, Calif.). U.S. basketball player. Center with Portland

Trail Blazers (1975–78) and S. D. Clippers (1979–   ); won Sullivan Trophy, 1973; named NBA MVP, 1978; named MVP in NBA playoffs, 1977; known for his unusual dress and radical political views.

WARFIELD, PAUL, Nov. 28, 1942 (Warren, Ohio). U.S. football player. Receiver with NFL Cleveland Browns (1964–69 and 1976–77) and Miami Dolphins (1970–74); named All-Pro, 1964, 1968–72, and 1974; caught career 427 passes, averaging 20.1 yds. per catch.

WATSON, TOM, Sept. 4, 1949 (Kansas City, Mo.). U.S. golfer. Won Masters, 1977; British Open champ, 1975 and 1977; named PGA Player of Year, 1977; leading money-winner, 1977–1979.

WEAVER, EARL, Aug. 14, 1930 (St. Louis, Mo.). U.S. baseball manager. Manager of the Baltimore Orioles, 1968–   ; has won four pennants (1969–71, 1979) and one World Series (1970).

WEISSMÜLLER, JOHNNY, June 2, 1903 (Windber, Pa.). U.S. swimmer, actor. Won 52 national championships and set 67 world records; won five gold medals at the 1924 and 1928 Olympics; played Tarzan in 19 movies of 1930s and 1940s.

WEST, JERRY, May 28, 1938 (Chelyan, W.Va.). U.S. basketball player. Guard with the NBA L.A. Lakers, 1960–74; NBA leading scorer, 1970; averaged 27 points per game in career; scored 25,192 career points; named first-team All-Star ten times; coach of L.A. Lakers, 1976–79.

WHITE, RANDY, Jan. 15, 1953 (Wilmington, Del.). U.S. football player. Defensive lineman with NFL Dallas Cowboys, 1975–   ; won Outland Award, 1974; named to Pro Bowl, 1977–78 seasons.

WHITWORTH, KATHY, Sept. 27, 1939 (Monahans, Tex.). U.S. golfer. LPGA leading money-winner, 1965–69 and 1970–73; named AP Woman Athlete of the Year, 1965 and 1966.

WILLIAMS, TED ("The Thumper"; "The Splendid Splinter"), born Theodore Samuel Williams, Aug. 31, 1918 (San Diego, Calif.). U.S. baseball player. Outfielder with Boston Red Sox, 1939–60; last major leaguer to hit .400 (.406 in 1941); .344 career batting avg.; led AL in batting, 1941–42, 1947–48, 1957–58; led AL in homers four times; led AL in RBIs four times; hit 521 career homers; inducted into Baseball Hall of Fame, 1966.

WILLS, HELEN, Oct. 6, 1905 (Centerville, Calif.). U.S. tennis player. U.S. champ, 1923–25, 1927–29, and 1931; Wimbledon champ, 1927–30, 1932-33, 1935, and 1938.

WOODEN, JOHN ROBERT, Oct. 14, 1910 (Martinsville, Ind.). U.S. basketball coach. Coached (1948–75) UCLA to ten NCAA championships,

1964, 1965, 1967–73, and 1975; elected to Basketball Hall of Fame as player (1960) and coach (1970); U.S. Basketball Writers Coach of Year, 1964, 1967, 1969, 1970, 1972, and 1973.

WRIGHT, MICKEY, born Mary Wright, Feb. 14,1935 (San Diego, Calif.). U.S. golfer. Won Women's Open, 1958–59, 1961, and 1964; LPGA leading money-winner, 1961–64.

WYNN, EARLY, Jan. 6, 1920 (Hartford, Ala.). U.S. baseball player. Pitcher with the Washington Senators (1939–48), Cleveland Indians (1949–57 and 1963) and Chicago White Sox (1958–62); won 300 major league games; led AL in wins, 1954 and 1959; won Cy Young Award, 1959; 20-game winner five times.

YARBOROUGH, CALE(b), Mar. 27, 1940 (Timmonsville, S.C.). U.S. auto racer. NASCAR champ, 1976–78; won Daytona 500, 1977.

YASTRZEMSKI, CARL ("Yaz"), Aug. 22, 1939 (Southampton, N.Y.). U.S. baseball player. Outfielder/first baseman with Boston Red Sox, 1961–   ; won AL Triple Crown, 1967; AL batting champ, 1963, 1967–68; named AL MVP, 1967; first AL player ever to achieve lifetime 400 home runs and 3,000 hits, 1979.

YOUNG, CY, born Denton True Young, Mar. 29, 1867 (Gilmore, Ohio)-Nov. 4, 1955. U.S. baseball player. Pitcher in NL with Cleveland (1890-98) and St. Louis (1899-1900) and in AL with Boston (1901-08) and Cleveland (1909-11); won record 511 games; pitched perfect game, 1904; 20-game winner 16 times; 30-game winner five times; inducted into Baseball Hall of Fame, 1937; best pitcher of the year award named for him.

YOUNG, SHEILA (married name: Ochowicz), Oct. 14, 1950 (Detroit, Mich.). U.S. speed skater. Won gold medal in 500-m. speed skating at 1976 Olympics; also silver in 1500-meter and bronze in 1000-meter, becoming first American, male or female, to win three medals in a single Winter Olympics; also a bicycle racer.

YOUNGBLOOD, JACK, born Herbert John Youngblood, Jan. 26, 1950 (Monticello, Fla.). U.S. football player. Defensive lineman with L.A. Rams, 1971–   ; named to Pro Bowl, 1973–79.

ZAHARIAS, BABE, born Mildred Ella Didrikson, June 26, 1914 (Port Arthur, Tex.)-Sept. 27, 1956. U.S. athlete. All-around athlete who won javelin and 80-m hurdles gold medals at 1932 Olympics; won U.S. Open golf championship, 1948, 1950, and 1954; named AP Woman Athlete of the Century, 1950.

ZATOPEK, EMIL, 1922 (N. Moravia, Czech.). Czech runner. Won 5,000- and 10,000-m events and the marathon in 1952 Olympics.

ENTERTAINERS

U.S. ACTORS

ADAMS, DON, Apr. 19, 1927 (New York, N.Y.). U.S. actor, comedian. Best known as inept spy on TV series Get Smart (1965-70), for which he won an Emmy in 1967.

ADAMS, EDIE, Apr. 16, 1929 (Kingston, Pa.). U.S. actress. Best known for TV work, especially on husband ERNIE KOVACS' TV show (1951-53 and 1956) and cigar commercials.

ADAMS, MAUDE, born Maude Kiskadden, Nov. 11, 1872 (Salt Lake City, Utah)-July 17, 1953. U.S. actress. Made stage debut at the age of nine

months in The Lost Child; first real success in The Masked Ball, 1892; most widely known for role as Lady Babbie in The Little Minister, 1897-98.

ADLER, LUTHER, born Lutha Adler, May 4, 1903 (New York, N.Y.). U.S. character actor. Plays: Golden Boy, 1938; Merchant of Venice, 1956; View from the Bridge, 1957.

AHERNE, BRIAN DELACY, May 2, 1902 (Worcestershire, Eng.). U.S. actor. "British gentleman" figure of U.S. stage and screen. Films: Shooting Stars, 1928; The Great Garrick, 1937; Juarez, 1939; Lancelot and Guinevere, 1963.

AKINS, CLAUDE, May 25, 1918 (Nelson, Ga.).

U.S. actor. Film career as "heavy"; star of TV series *Movin' On*, 1974-75.

ALBERT, EDDIE, born Edward Albert Heimberger, April 22, 1908 (Rock Island, Ill.). U.S. actor. Known for "nice guy" film roles; received National Film Critics Award, 1972. Films: *Oklahoma*, 1955; *Attack!*, 1956; *Heartbreak Kid*, 1972. TV: *Green Acres* (series), 1965-70.

ALBERTSON, JACK, June 16, 1910 (Malden, Mass.). U.S. actor. A burlesque straight man and a character actor in films; film career capped by *The Subject Was Roses* (best supporting actor AA), 1968; star of TV series *Chico and the Man* (1974-78), for which he received an Emmy award, 1976.

ALBRIGHT, LOLA, July 20, 1925 (Akron, Ohio). U.S. actress. Tough-talking leading lady. Films: *Tender Trap*, 1956; *Love Cage*, 1965. TV: *Peter Gunn* (series), 1958-61.

ALDA, ALAN, Jan. 28, 1936 (New York, N.Y.). U.S. actor. Films: *Paper Lion*, 1968; *To Kill a Clown*, 1972; *The Seduction of Joe Tynan*, 1979. TV: *M*A*S*H** (Emmy award, 1974), 1972-   . (Son of ROBERT ALDA.)

ALDA, ROBERT, born Alphonso d'Abruzzo, Feb. 26, 1914 (New York, N.Y.). U.S. actor. Moved from radio and stage to films. Stage: *Guys and Dolls* (Best Actor Tony), 1951. Films: *Rhapsody in Blue*, 1945; *April Showers*, 1948; *Imitation of Life*, 1959. (Father of ALAN ALDA.)

ALEXANDER, JANE, born Jane Quigley, Oct. 28, 1939 (Boston, Mass.). U.S. actress. Principally a stage actress, she won 1969 Tony award for her work in *The Great White Hope*.

ALLISON, FRAN, ? (La Porte, Ia.). U.S. actress. Best known for role opposite puppets on TV series *Kukla, Fran and Ollie*, 1948-57.

ALLYSON, JUNE, born Ella Geisman, Oct. 7, 1923 (Lucerne, N.Y.). U.S. actress. Played girl-next-door roles in films of the 1940s and 1950s, including *Two Girls and a Sailor* (1944), *High Barbaree* (1947), *Little Women* (1949), and *The Glenn Miller Story* (1954). (One-time wife of DICK POWELL.)

AMECHE, DON, born Dominic Felix Amici, May 31, 1908 (Kenosha, Wisc.). U.S. actor. Popular leading man in 1930s and 1940s films, including *The Three Musketeers* (1939) and *Heaven Can Wait* (1943).

AMES, ED, 1929 (Boston, Mass.). U.S. singer, actor. Best known as a member of the Ames Brothers; gained fame as a solo with "My Cup Runneth Over". TV: Mingo on *Daniel Boone*, 1964-68.

AMES, LEON, born Leon Waycoff, Jan. 20, 1903 (Portland, Ore.). U.S. character actor. Best known as star of TV series *Life with Father*, 1953-55.

ANDERSON, GILBERT ("Bronco Billy"), born Max Aronson, 1882-1972. Produced and starred in 400 one-reel silent westerns up to 1920.

ANDREWS, DANA, born Carver Daniel Andrews, Jan. 1, 1909 (Collins, Miss.). U.S. actor. A leading man in films of the 1940s and 1950s. Films: *Laura*, 1944; *Best Years of Our Lives*, 1946; *Boomerang*, 1947.

ANN-MARGRET, born Ann Margret Olsson, Apr. 28, 1941 (Stockholm, Swe.). U.S. dancer, singer, actress. Adding to early sex-symbol status, she won reputation as a film actress and nightclub star. Films: *Bye Bye Birdie*, 1962; *Carnal Knowledge*, 1971; *Magic*, 1978. (Wife of ROGER SMITH.)

ARDEN, EVE, born Eunice Quedens, Apr. 30, 1912 (Mill Valley, Calif.). U.S. comedic actress. Known as wise-cracking second lead. Films: *Stage Door*, 1937; *Mildred Pierce*, 1945. TV: *Our Miss Brooks* (series), 1952-55 (previously on radio, 1948-51).

ARKIN, ALAN WOLF, Mar. 26, 1935 (New York, N.Y.). U.S. actor, director. Films: *The Russians Are Coming . . .*, 1966; *Little Murders* (also directed), 1971; *The In-Laws*, 1979.

ARNAZ, DESI, born Desiderio Alberto Arnaz y de Acha, Mar. 2, 1917 (Santiago, Cuba). Cuban-U.S. singer, bandleader, comic actor. Starred in the TV series *I Love Lucy*, 1951-61. (One-time husband of LUCILLE BALL; father of DESI ARNAZ, JR., and LUCIE ARNAZ.)

ARNAZ, DESI, JR., Jan. 19, 1953 (Los Angeles, Calif.). U.S. actor. Films: *Red Sky at Morning*, 1971; *Marlo*, 1973. (Son of LUCILLE BALL and DESI ARNAZ; brother of LUCIE ARNAZ.)

ARNAZ, LUCIE, 1951 (Hollywood, Calif.). U.S. actress. Stage: *They're Playing Our Song*, 1979. (Daughter of LUCILLE BALL and DESI ARNAZ; sister of DESI ARNAZ, JR.)

ARNESS, JAMES, born James Aurness. May 26, 1923 (Minneapolis, Minn.). U.S. actor. Played Marshal Dillon in long-running TV series *Gunsmoke*, 1955-75. TV: *How the West Was Won*, (series), 1978. (Brother of PETER GRAVES.)

ARNOLD, EDWARD, born Guenther Schneider, Feb. 18, 1890 (New York, N.Y.)-Apr. 26, 1956. U.S. actor. A lead actor in 1930s films; later did character roles. Films: *Diamond Jim*, 1935; *Mr. Smith Goes to Washington*, 1939; *Dear Ruth*, 1947.

ARTHUR, BEATRICE, born Bernice Frankel, May 13, 1926 (New York, N.Y.). U.S. comedic actress. After Broadway career, starred in the TV series *Maude*, 1972-78.

ARTHUR, JEAN, born Gladys Greene, Oct. 17, 1908 (New York, N.Y.). U.S. actress. Squeaky-voiced leading lady in 1930s-1950s films, including *Mr. Deeds Goes to Town* (1936), *Talk of the Town* (1942), *Shane* (1953).

ASHLEY, ELIZABETH, born Elizabeth Cole, Aug. 30, 1941 (Ocala, Fla.). U.S. actress. Films: *The Carpetbaggers*, 1964; *Ship of Fools*, 1965; *Marriage of a Young Stockbroker*, 1971; *The Face of Fear* (TV), 1971; *One of My Wives is Missing* (TV), 1974. (One-time wife of GEORGE PEPPARD.)

ASNER, EDWARD, Nov. 15, 1929 (Kansas City, Mo.). U.S. actor. TV: *Mary Tyler Moore Show* (series), 1972-77; *Lou Grant* (series), 1977-   ; *Roots* (movie), 1977.

ASTIN, JOHN ALLEN, Mar. 30, 1930 (Baltimore, Md.). U.S. actor, director. Starred in the TV series *The Addams Family*, 1964-66. (Husband of PATTY DUKE.)

ASTOR, MARY, born Lucille Langehanke, May 5, 1906 (Quincy, Ill.). U.S. actress. A leading lady in 1920s-40s films, including *Dodsworth* (1936), *The Maltese Falcon* (1941), *Meet Me in St. Louis* (1944), *Act of Violence* (1949), and *Little Women* (1949).

AYRES, LEW, Dec. 28, 1908 (Minneapolis, Minn.). U.S. actor. Leading man in films of the 1930s; made eight "Dr. Kildare" features, 1938-41. Films: *The Kiss*, 1929; *All Quiet on the Western Front*, 1930; *State Fair*, 1933; *Last Train from Madrid*, 1937; *Holiday*, 1938; *Advise and Consent*, 1961; *The Carpetbaggers*, 1964.

BACALL, LAUREN, born Betty Joan Perske, Sept.

THE BOOK OF WHO

16, 1924 (New York, N.Y.). U.S. actress. Films: *To Have and Have Not*, 1944; *The Big Sleep*, 1946; *Key Largo*, 1948. Plays: *Applause* (Tony award), 1969. (One-time wife of HUMPHREY BOGART and JASON ROBARDS.)

BACKUS, JIM, born James Gilmore Backus, Feb. 25, 1913 (Cleveland, Ohio). U.S. actor. Known for the voice of Mr. Magoo in the 1950s cartoon series; starred in TV series *Gilligan's Island*, 1964-67. Films: *Rebel without a Cause*, 1955; *It's a Mad Mad Mad Mad World*, 1963.

BAER, MAX ADELBERT, JR., Dec. 4, 1937 (Oakland, Calif.). U.S. actor, producer, director. Starred in the TV series *The Beverly Hillbillies*, 1962-71; produced and directed the film *Ode to Billy Joe*, 1976.

BAIN, BARBARA, 1934 (Chicago, Ill.). U.S. actress. Appeared in the TV series *Mission Impossible* (1966-69) and *Space 1999*. (Wife of MARTIN LANDAU.)

BAINTER, FAY, 1891 (Los Angeles, Calif.)-Apr. 16, 1968. U.S. character actress. Films: *Jezebel*, 1937; *Our Town*, 1940; *Children's Hour*, 1962.

BAIO, SCOTT, Sept. 22, 1961 (New York, N.Y.). U.S. actor. Has appeared in TV series *Happy Days* (1977-) and in other juvenile roles.

BAKER, CARROLL, May 28, 1931 (Johnstown, Pa.). U.S. actress. Sultry leading lady of the 1950s and 1960s. Films: *Baby Doll*, 1956; *The Carpetbaggers*, 1964; *Harlow*, 1965.

BALL, LUCILLE, Aug. 6, 1911 (Jamestown, N.Y.). U.S. comedic actress. After prolific film career, largely in B-grade movies, starred in *I Love Lucy* TV series (1950-61); received Emmys in 1952, 1955, 1967, 1968. Films: *Stage Door*, 1937; *Du Barry Was a Lady*, 1943; *Sorrowful Jones*, 1949; *Fancy Pants*, 1950; *Yours, Mine, and Ours*, 1968; *Mame*, 1973. (One-time wife of DESI ARNAZ, mother of LUCIE and DESI ARNAZ JR.)

BALSAM, MARTIN HENRY, Nov. 4, 1919 (New York, N.Y.). U.S. actor. Films: *Twelve Angry Men*, 1957; *Psycho*, 1960; *A Thousand Clowns* (Best Supporting Actor AA), 1965.

BANCROFT, ANNE, born Anna Maria Italiano, Sept. 17, 1931 (New York, N.Y.). U.S. actress. After early film roles, won two Tonys for *Two for the Seesaw* (1958) and *The Miracle Worker* (1959); won best actress AA for lead role in film of *The Miracle Worker*, 1962. Other films: *The Graduate*, 1968; *Young Winston*, 1972; *The Prisoner of Second Avenue*, 1975; *The Turning Point*, 1977. (Wife of MEL BROOKS.)

BANKHEAD, TALLULAH BROCKMAN, Jan. 31, 1903 (Huntsville, Ala.)-Dec. 12, 1968. U.S. actress. Renowned for gravel voice, wit. Plays: *Little Foxes* (Critics' Circle Award), 1939; *Skin of Our Teeth*, 1944. Films: *Lifeboat*, 1943.

BARA, THEDA, born Theodosia Goodman, July 20, 1890 (Cincinnati, Ohio)-Apr. 7, 1955. Silent-screen star in "vamp" (femme fatale) roles in films such as *A Fool There Was* (1916); retired in 1926.

BARRY, GENE, born Eugene Klass, June 4, 1922 (New York, N.Y.). U.S. actor. Starred in the TV series *Bat Masterson* (1959-61), *Burke's Law* (1963-65), *Name of the Game* (1969-70).

BARRYMORE, ETHEL, Aug. 15, 1879 (Philadelphia, Pa.)-June 18, 1959. U.S. actress. Called the "First Lady of American theater," 1900-1940s. Films: *None but the Lonely Heart* (Best supporting Actress AA), 1944; *Farmer's Daughter*, 1947; *Pinky*, 1949. (Sister of JOHN and LIONEL BARRYMORE.)

BARRYMORE, JOHN ("The Great Profile"), Feb. 15, 1882 (Philadelphia, Pa.)-May 29, 1942. U.S. actor. Played Shakespearean stage roles, romantic film leads through the 1930s; later known for dissolute life and film roles. Films: *Dr. Jekyll and Mr. Hyde*, 1920; *Grand Hotel*, 1932; *Dinner at Eight*, 1933. (Brother of ETHEL and LIONEL BARRYMORE.)

BARRYMORE, LIONEL, Apr. 28, 1878 (Philadelphia, Pa.)-Nov. 15, 1954. U.S. actor. Made over 100 films in 30-year career as the leading U.S. character actor, often in sentimental roles; in wheelchair from 1938, played Dr. Gillespie in "Dr. Kildare" film series, 1938-41. Films: *A Free Soul*, 1931; *Grand Hotel*, 1932; *You Can't Take It with You*, 1938; *It's a Wonderful Life*, 1946; *Duel in the Sun*, 1946. (Brother of ETHEL and JOHN BARRYMORE.)

BASEHART, RICHARD, Aug. 31, 1919 (Zanesville, Ohio). U.S. actor. Films: *He Walked by Night*, 1948; *Moby Dick*, 1956. TV: *Voyage to the Bottom of the Sea* (series), 1964-68.

BAXTER, ANNE, May 7, 1923 (Michigan City, Ind.). U.S. actress. A Hollywood leading lady of the 1940s. Films: *The Magnificent Ambersons*, 1942; *The Razor's Edge* (Best Supporting Actress AA), 1946; *All about Eve*, 1950.

BEATTY, WARREN, Mar. 30, 1938 (Richmond, Va.). U.S. actor, director, screenwriter. Films: *Splendor in the Grass*, 1961; *Bonnie and Clyde*, 1967; *Shampoo* (also cowrote), 1975; *Heaven Can Wait* (also directed and cowrote), 1978. (Brother of SHIRLEY MACLAINE.)

BEDELIA, BONNIE, Mar. 25, 1948 (New York, N.Y.). U.S. actress. TV: *The New Land* (movie), 1974. Films: *Lovers and Other Strangers*, 1970; *They Shoot Horses, Don't They?*, 1970.

BEERY, NOAH, JR., Aug. 10, 1916 (New York, N.Y.). U.S. actor. Has played character roles in films since childhood. TV: *Rockford Files* (series), 1974- .

BEERY, WALLACE, c.1886 (Kansas City, Mo.)-Apr. 15, 1949. U.S. actor. Character actor in films from 1916; best remembered for roles as tough, thick heavy. Films: *Min and Bill*, 1930; *The Champ* (Best Actor AA), 1931; *Grand Hotel*, 1932; *Dinner at Eight*, 1933; *Tugboat Annie*, 1933; *Viva Villa*, 1934; *Slave Ship*, 1937; *Barbary Coast Gent*, 1944.

BEGLEY, ED, 1901 (Hartford, Conn.)-Apr. 28, 1970. U.S. actor. Likeable, blustery character actor on stage and in films. Films: *Patterns*, 1956; *Twelve Angry Men*, 1957; *Sweet Bird of Youth* (Best Supporting Actor AA), 1962.

BEL GEDDES, BARBARA, Oct. 31, 1922 (New York, N.Y.). U.S. actress. Known for dramatic lead in plays, some films. Plays: *The Moon Is Blue*, 1952; *Cat on a Hot Tin Roof*, 1955; *Mary, Mary*, 1961. TV: *Dallas* (series), 1978- .

BELLAMY, RALPH, June 17, 1904 (Chicago, Ill.). U.S. actor. Played in over 100 films, several TV series, and many plays. Films: *The Awful Truth*, 1937; *His Girl Friday*, 1940. Plays: *Sunrise at Campobello* (Tony award), 1958.

BENDIX, WILLIAM, 1906 (New York, N.Y.)-Dec. 14, 1964. U.S. actor. Character actor, usually playing amiable tough guy in numerous 1940s and 1950s films; starred in the TV series *The Life of Riley*, 1953-58.

BENJAMIN, RICHARD, May 22, 1938 (New York, N.Y.). U.S. actor. Films: *Good-bye Columbus*, 1968; *Diary of a Mad Housewife*, 1970. (Husband of PAULA PRENTISS.)

BENNETT, CONSTANCE, 1904 (New York, N.Y.)–July 24, 1965. U.S. actress. A leading lady of 1930s films, including *Moulin Rouge* (1933) and *Topper* (1937). (Sister of JOAN BENNETT.)

BENNETT, JOAN, Feb. 27, 1910 (Palisades, N.J.). U.S. actress. A leading lady in many 1930s and 1940s films, including *Private Worlds* (1935) and *The Macomber Affair* (1947); has played in many TV soap operas. (Sister of CONSTANCE BENNETT.)

BENSON, ROBBY, 1957 (Dallas, Tex.). U.S. actor. Films: *One on One,* 1977; *Ice Castles,* 1979.

BERG, GERTRUDE, born Gertrude Edelstein, Oct. 3, 1899 (New York, N.Y.)–Sept. 14, 1966. U.S. comedic actress, writer. Wrote and starred (as Molly Goldberg) in *The Goldbergs* radio and TV series, 1929–54; won 1959 Tony award for her role in *A Majority of One.*

BERGEN, CANDICE, May 9, 1946 (Beverly Hills, Calif.). U.S. actress. Films: *The Group,* 1966; *Carnal Knowledge,* 1971; *The Wind and the Lion,* 1977. (Daughter of EDGAR BERGEN.)

BERGEN, POLLY, born Nellie Bergen, July 14, 1930 (Knoxville, Tenn.). U.S. actress, beauty executive. Leading lady in such films as *Cape Fear* (1962), *Move Over, Darling* (1963), and *Kisses for My President* (1964); currently heads own cosmetic firm.

BERGMAN, INGRID, Aug. 29, 1915 (Stockholm, Swe.). Swedish-U.S. actress. Has had a long and distinguished career as dramatic leading actress. Films: *Casablanca,* 1943; *Gaslight* (Best Actress AA), 1944; *Joan of Arc,* 1948; *Anastasia* (Best Actress AA), 1956; *Murder on the Orient Express* (Best Supporting Actress AA), 1974; *Autumn Sonata,* 1978.

BERNARDI, HERSCHEL, 1923 (New York, N.Y.). U.S. character actor. Often seen as a cop or gangster. Films: *Crime, Inc,* 1945; *A Cold Wind in August,* 1961; *Irma La Douce,* 1963. TV: *Peter Gunn,* 1958–61.

BICKFORD, CHARLES, 1889 (Cambridge, Mass.)–Nov. 9, 1967. U.S. actor. Rough-edged character actor. Films: *Of Mice and Men,* 1940; *The Big Country,* 1958.

BISSET, JACQUELINE, Sept. 13, 1946 (Weybridge, Eng.). U.S. actress. Films: *The Grasshopper,* 1970; *The Greek Tycoon,* 1977.

BIXBY, BILL, Jan. 22, 1934 (San Francisco, Calif.). U.S. actor. TV: *My Favorite Martian* (series), 1963–65; *The Incredible Hulk* (series), 1978–

BLACK, KAREN, born Karen Zeigler, July 1, 1942 (Park Ridge, Ill.). U.S. actress. Films: *Easy Rider,* 1969; *Five Easy Pieces,* 1970; *Nashville,* 1975.

BLACKMER, SIDNEY, July 13, 1898 (Salisbury, N.C.)–Oct. 5, 1973. U.S. actor. Suave character actor in some 200 films, 40 Broadway plays, and numerous TV dramas; won 1950 Tony award for his performance in *Come Back Little Sheba.*

BLAIR, LINDA DENISE, Jan. 22, 1959 (St. Louis, Mo.). U.S. actress. Films: *The Exorcist,* 1973; *The Exorcist, Part 2,* 1977.

BLAKE, AMANDA, born Beverly Neill, Feb. 20, 1931 (Buffalo, N.Y.). U.S. actress. Famed for her portrayal of Kitty in the TV series *Gunsmoke,* 1955–74.

BLAKE, ROBERT, born Michael Gubitosi, Sept. 18, 1938 (Nutley, N.J.). U.S. actor. Began as child actor. Films: *The Treasure of the Sierra Madre,* 1948; *In Cold Blood,* 1968. TV: *Baretta* (series), 1974–78.

BLONDELL, JOAN, Aug. 30, 1909 (New York,

N.Y.)–Dec. 25, 1979. U.S. comedic actress. Wisecracking lead or support in 1930s films; later played character roles in movies and TV. Films: *Footlight Parade,* 1933; *A Tree Grows in Brooklyn,* 1945; *The Cincinnati Kid,* 1965. (One-time wife of DICK POWELL and MIKE TODD.)

BLYTH, ANN, Aug. 16, 1928 (Mt. Kisco, N.Y.). U.S. actress. A film singer, then a dramatic lead. Films: *Mildred Pierce,* 1945; *Rose Marie,* 1954; *The Helen Morgan Story,* 1957.

BOGART, HUMPHREY, Dec. 25, 1899 (New York, N.Y.)–Jan. 14, 1957. U.S. actor. His 1940s and 1950s screen persona as cynical but good-hearted tough guy had top box-office appeal. Films: *Petrified Forest,* 1936; *Dead End,* 1937; *The Maltese Falcon,* 1941; *Casablanca,* 1943; *To Have and Have Not,* 1943; *The Big Sleep,* 1946; *The Treasure of the Sierra Madre,* 1947; *Key Largo,* 1948; *African Queen* (Best Actor AA), 1952; *The Caine Mutiny,* 1954; *The Barefoot Contessa,* 1954. (Husband of LAUREN BACALL.)

BOND, WARD, 1903 (Denver, Col.)–Nov. 5, 1960. U.S. actor. Character actor in many westerns, from 1930; starred in the TV series *Wagon Train,* 1957–60.

BOONE, RICHARD ALLEN, June 18, 1917 (Los Angeles, Calif.). U.S. actor. Familiar for rugged face and outlook in dozens of films. TV: *Medic* (series), 1954–56; *Have Gun, Will Travel* (series), 1957–63.

BOOTH, EDWIN, Nov. 13, 1833 (Belair, Md.)–June 7, 1893. U.S. actor. One of greatest 19th-cent. American stage actors, famous for his Hamlet. (Brother of JOHN WILKES BOOTH.)

BOOTH, SHIRLEY, born Thelma Booth Ford, Aug. 30, 1907 (New York, N.Y.). U.S. actress. Noted for distinguished stage career (won 1953 Tony award for *Time of the Cuckoo*), film appearances (won 1953 Best Actress AA for *Come Back Little Sheba*), and TV roles (won 1963 Emmy for her role in the series *Hazel,* 1961–66).

BORGNINE, ERNEST, born Ermes Borgnino, Jan. 24, 1917 (Hamden, Conn.). U.S. actor. Strong character actor in many films, including *From Here to Eternity* (1953), *Marty,* (1955; Best Actor AA), and *The Dirty Dozen* (1967); starred in TV sitcom *McHale's Navy,* 1962–65.

BOSLEY, TOM, Oct. 1, 1927. U.S. actor. Plays: *Fiorello* (Tony award), 1959. Films: *Debbie,* 1969. TV: *Happy Days* (series), 1974–

BOTTOMS, TIMOTHY, 1951 (Santa Barbara, Calif.). U.S. actor. Lead actor in youth roles. Films: *Last Picture Show,* 1971; *The Paper Chase,* 1972; *The White Dawn,* 1974; *The Crazy World of Julius Vrooder,* 1974.

BOW, CLARA, Aug. 6, 1905 (New York, N.Y.)–Sept. 26, 1965. U.S. actress. The "It" girl who personified the flapper in 1920s silents. Films: *Mantrap,* 1926; *It,* 1927.

BOYD, WILLIAM, 1895 (Cambridge, Ohio)–Sept. 12, 1972. U.S. actor. Renowned as Hopalong Cassidy in scores of second features and TV episodes.

BOYLE, PETER, 1933 (Philadelphia, Pa.). U.S. actor. Films: *Joe,* 1970; *Young Frankenstein,* 1974; *Taxi Driver,* 1976.

BRACKEN, EDDIE, Feb. 7, 1920 (New York, N.Y.). U.S. comedic actor. Played many character roles, often as rural type, in films such as *The Miracle of Morgan's Creek* (1943).

BRAND, NEVILLE, Aug. 13, 1921 (Kewanee, Ill.). U.S. actor. Tough-talking character actor in films, on TV; starred in the TV series *Laredo,* 1965–67.

BRANDO, MARLON, Apr. 3, 1924 (Omaha,

227

THE BOOK OF WHO

Neb.). U.S. actor. "Method actor" in stage dramatic roles such as *Streetcar Named Desire*, 1947; developed persona of brooding, tough sex symbol. Films: *The Men*, 1950; *Julius Caesar*, 1953; *On the Waterfront* (Best Actor AA), 1954; *Guys and Dolls*, 1955; *Mutiny on the Bounty*, 1962; *The Godfather—Part 1* (Best Actor AA), 1972; *Last Tango in Paris*, 1973; *Apocalypse Now*, 1979.

BRENNAN, EILEEN, 1937 (Los Angeles, Calif.). U.S. actress. Mostly on Broadway. Films: *Divorce, American Style*, 1967; *The Last Picture Show*, 1971; *At Long Last Love*, 1975; *Murder by Death*, 1976.

BRENNAN, WALTER, July 25, 1894 (Lynn, Mass.)-Sept. 21, 1974. Character actor in over 100 films, including *Come and Get It* (1936; Best Supporting Actor AA), *Kentucky* (1938; Best Supporting Actor AA), *The Westerner* (Best Supporting Actor AA); star of *Real McCoys* TV series, 1957-63.

BRENT, GEORGE, born George Brent Nolan, Mar. 15, 1904 (Dublin, Ire.)-May 26, 1979. U.S. actor. Films: *Forty-second Street*, 1933; *Jezebel*, 1938; *The Spiral Staircase*, 1945.

BRIDGES, BEAU, Dec. 4, 1941 (Hollywood, Calif.). U.S. actor. Films: *Force of Evil*, 1968; *Gaily Gaily*, 1969; *The Landlord*, 1970; *The Other Side of the Mountain*, 1975. (Son of LLOYD BRIDGES.)

BRIDGES, LLOYD, Jan. 15, 1913 (San Leandro, Calif.). U.S. actor. In films from 1941 *(Home of the Brave*, 1949; *Goddess*, 1958); most famous as star of the TV series *Sea Hunt*, 1957-61. (Father of BEAU BRIDGES.)

BRODERICK, HELEN, 1891 (Philadelphia, Pa.)-Sept. 25, 1959. U.S. comedic actress. Films: *Top Hat*, 1935; *Swing Time*, 1936; *No, No, Nanette*, 1940. (Mother of BRODERICK CRAWFORD.)

BROLIN, JAMES, July 10, 1942 (Los Angeles, Calif.). U.S. actor. TV: *Marcus Welby* (series), 1969-76. Films: *Westworld*, 1973; *Gable and Lombard*, 1976.

BRONSON, CHARLES, born Charles Buchinsky, Nov. 13, 1922 (Ehrenfeld, Pa.). U.S. actor. International box-office star in 1970s action films. Films: *The Magnificent Seven*, 1960; *The Dirty Dozen*, 1967; *Death Wish*, 1974; *Breakheart Pass*, 1976; *Telefon*, 1979.

BRUCE, VIRGINIA, born Helen Virginia Briggs, 1910 (Minneapolis, Minn.). U.S. actress. A leading lady in 1930s films, including *Jane Eyre* (1934).

BRYNNER, YUL, born Youl Bryner, July 11, 1920 (Sakhalin, Jap.). U.S. actor. His bald head and accent led to success in "exotic" roles; starred in stage, TV, and film versions of *The King and I* (Best Actor AA, 1956). Other films: *Anastasia*, 1956; *The Magnificent Seven*, 1960; *Westworld*, 1973.

BUCHANAN, EDGAR, Mar. 20, 1903 (Humansville, Mo.)-Apr. 4, 1979. U.S. character actor. Has appeared in many film westerns; starred in the TV series *Petticoat Junction*, 1963-69.

BUONO, VICTOR, 1938 (Los Angeles, Calif.). U.S. character actor. Films: *Whatever Happened to Baby Jane?*, 1962; *Hush, Hush, Sweet Charlotte*, 1965.

BURGHOFF, GARY, May 24, ? (Bristol, Conn.). U.S. actor. Received 1977 supporting actor Emmy award for his work as Radar O'Reilly in the TV series *M*A*S*H** (1972-79).

BURKE, BILLIE MARY, Aug. 7, 1885 (Wash., D.C.)-May 14, 1970. U.S. stage and film actress. Films: *Dinner at Eight*, 1933, *The Wizard of Oz*,

1939; *The Man Who Came to Dinner*, 1941. (One-time wife of FLORENZ ZIEGFELD.)

BURSTYN, ELLEN, born Edna Rae Gillooly, Dec. 7, 1932 (Detroit, Mich.). U.S. actress. Films: *The Last Picture Show*, 1971; *The Exorcist*, 1973; *Harry and Tonto*, 1974; *Alice Doesn't Live Here Anymore* (Best Actress AA), 1974; *Same Time, Next Year*, 1978.

BUSHMAN, FRANCIS XAVIER, Jan. 10, 1883 (Baltimore, Md.)-Aug. 23, 1966. U.S. silent-screen actor. Made over 400 films, 1911-18; his fans deserted him after his divorce to marry his favorite leading lady Beverly Bayne in 1918; played bit parts in 1960s movies.

BUTTERWORTH, CHARLES, 1896 (South Bend, Ind.)-June 13, 1946. U.S. comedic actor. Usually played the role of the shy upper-class bachelor. Films: *Love Me Tonight*, 1932; *Baby Face Harrington*, 1935; *Every Day's a Holiday*, 1937.

BUTTONS, RED, born Aaron Schwatt, Feb. 5, 1919 (New York, N.Y.). U.S. vaudeville comedian, actor. A supporting actor in numerous films, including *Sayonara*, (1957), for which he won supporting actor AA. TV: *Red Buttons Show*, 1952-55.

BYINGTON, SPRING, Oct. 17, 1893 (Colorado Springs, Col.)-Sept. 7, 1971. U.S. actress. Films: *Little Women*, 1933; *You Can't Take It with You*, 1938. TV: *December Bride* (series), 1954-58.

CAAN, JAMES, Mar. 26, 1939 (New York, N.Y.). U.S. actor. Films: *Games*, 1967; *The Godfather—Part 1*, 1972; *The Gambler*, 1974; *The Godfather—Part 2*, 1974; *Funny Lady*, 1975; *Rollerball*, 1975; *Silent Movie*, 1976. TV: *Brian's Song* (movie), 1971.

CABOT, BRUCE, 1905 (Carlsbad, N.M.)-May 3, 1972. U.S. actor. Played the hero in many 1930s action films; later often played Western film villains. Films: *King Kong*, 1933; *Wild Bill Hickok Rides*, 1942; *Angel and the Badmen*, 1947; *John Paul Jones*, 1959; *Diamonds Are Forever*, 1971.

CAGNEY, JAMES, July 17, 1899 (New York, N.Y.). U.S. actor, dancer. His distinctive mannerisms and staccato delivery are much imitated. Films: *A Midsummer Night's Dream*, 1935; *Yankee Doodle Dandy* (Best Actor AA), 1942; *Mister Roberts*, 1955; *Man of a Thousand Faces*, 1957; *Shake Hands with the Devil*, 1959; *The Gallant Hours*, 1960. Received American Film Inst. Life Achievement award, 1974.

CALHERN LOUIS, born Carl Henry Vogt, Feb. 19, 1895 (New York, N.Y.)-May 12, 1956. U.S. stage and film actor who generally played supporting roles in 1940s and 1950s.

CALHOUN, RORY, born Francis Timothy Durgin, Aug. 8, 1922 (Los Angeles, Calif.). U.S. actor. A leading man in 1950s action films. Films: *With a Song in My Heart*, 1952; *How to Marry a Millionaire*, 1953.

CANNON, DYAN, born Samile Diane Friesen, Jan. 4, 1937 (Tacoma, Wash.). U.S. actress. Films: *Bob & Carol & Ted & Alice*, 1969; *The Love Machine*, 1971; *Such Good Friends*, 1971; *The Last of Sheila*, 1973. (One-time wife of CARY GRANT.)

CAREY, MACDONALD, Mar. 15, 1913 (Sioux City, Ia.). U.S. actor. Appeared in numerous films, 1940-50s; received two Emmys (1974 and 1975) for best actor in daytime drama, *Days of Our Lives*.

CARLISLE, KITTY, born Catherine Holzman, Sept. 3, 1915 (New Orleans, La.). U.S. singer, actress. Starred in a few movies, most notably *Night*

at the Opera (1935); mainstay of TV's To Tell the Truth quiz show; wife of playwright MOSS HART; member of N.Y. State Comm. on the Arts, 1976- .

CARNEY, ART(hur), Nov. 4, 1918 (Mt. Vernon, N.Y.). U.S. actor. Featured for many years with Jackie Gleason in TV series The Honeymooners; winner of four Emmys. Films: Harry and Tonto (Best Actor AA), 1974; The Late Show, 1977. Stage: The Odd Couple, 1965; The Prisoner of Second Avenue, 1972.

CARRADINE, DAVID, 1937 (Hollywood, Calif.). U.S. actor. Best known as the star of TV series Kung Fu 1972-75. (Son of JOHN CARRADINE; brother of KEITH CARRADINE.)

CARRADINE, JOHN, born Richmond Reed Carradine, Feb. 5, 1906 (New York, N.Y.). U.S. character actor. Films: Jesse James, 1939; Five Came Back, 1939; Stagecoach, 1939; The Grapes of Wrath, 1940; Bluebeard, 1944. (FATHER OF DAVID and KEITH CARRADINE.)

CARRADINE, KEITH, 1950 (San Mateo, Calif.). U.S. actor, songwriter. Films: Nashville, 1975; Old Boyfriends, 1979. Song: "I'm Easy" (1975 AA). (Son of JOHN CARRADINE; brother of DAVID CARRADINE.)

CARRILLO, LEO, 1880 (Los Angeles, Calif.)-Sept. 10, 1961. U.S. character actor in numerous films. Films: The Gay Desperado, 1936; History Is Made at Night, 1937.

CARROLL, NANCY, born Ann Veronica LaHiff, 1905 (New York, N.Y.)-Aug. 6, 1965. U.S. actress. A leading lady in musical films and light dramas of the 1930s. Films: The Shopworn Angel, 1929; Laughter, 1930.

CARSON, JACK, 1910 (Canada)-Jan. 2, 1963. Canadian comedian, supporting actor. Films: Stage Door, 1937; Mildred Pierce, 1945; A Star Is Born, 1954.

CARTER, MRS. LESLIE, born Caroline Louise Dudley, June 10, 1862 (Lexington, Ky.)-Nov. 13, 1937. U.S. stage actress. Often called the "American Sarah Bernhardt."

CARTER, LYNDA, ? (Phoenix, Ariz.). U.S. actress. Star of TV series Wonder Woman, 1977-79.

CASSAVETES, JOHN, Dec. 9, 1929 (New York, N.Y.). U.S. actor, director, screenwriter. Films: Edge of the City, 1957; Rosemary's Baby, 1968; Husbands, 1970. Films (dir.): Shadows, 1960. Films (writer/dir.): Faces, 1968. Films (writer/dir./producer): A Woman under the Influence, 1974. (Husband of GENA ROWLANDS.)

CASSIDY, JACK, Mar. 5, 1927 (New York, N.Y.)-Dec. 12, 1976. U.S. actor, singer. Best known for theater and TV appearances. (Father of DAVID and Shaun Cassidy; one-time husband of SHIRLEY JONES.)

CASTELLANO, RICHARD, Sept. 4, 1933 (New York, N.Y.). U.S. character actor. Films: Lovers and Other Strangers, 1969; The Godfather—Part 1, 1972.

CHAMBERLAIN, RICHARD, Mar. 31, 1935 (Beverly Hills, Calif.). U.S. actor. Best known for his starring role in the TV series Dr. Kildare, 1961-65. Films: The Music Lovers, 1970; Lady Caroline Lamb, 1972; The Last Wave, 1979.

CHANEY, LON, Apr. 1, 1883 (Colorado Springs, Col.)-Aug. 26, 1930. U.S. silent-screen actor. Known as the "Man of a Thousand Faces." Films: The Miracle Man, 1919; The Hunchback of Notre Dame, 1923; The Phantom of the Opera, 1925.

CHAPLIN, GERALDINE, 1944 (Santa Monica, Calif.). U.S. actress. Films: Doctor Zhivago, 1965;

Nashville, 1975; Welcome to L.A., 1977. (Daughter of CHARLIE CHAPLIN; granddaughter of EUGENE O'NEILL.)

CHATTERTON, RUTH, Dec. 24, 1893 (New York, N.Y.)-Nov. 24, 1961. U.S. actress. Hollywood leading lady of the 1920s and 1930s. Films: Madame X, 1929; Dodsworth, 1936.

CHRISTIE, JULIE, Apr. 14, 1941 (India). British actress. Films: Billy Liar, 1963; Darling (Best Actress AA), 1965; Doctor Zhivago, 1965; McCabe and Mrs. Miller, 1971; Don't Look Now, 1974; Shampoo, 1975.

CLAIRE, INA, born Ina Fagan, Oct. 15, 1892 (Washington, D.C.). U.S. actress. Vaudeville appearances; in the Ziegfeld Follies, 1915-16. Plays: The Gold Diggers, 1919; Once Is Enough, 1938. Films: The Royal Family of Broadway, 1931; The Greeks Had a Word for Them, 1932.

CLARK, DANE, born Bernard Zanville, Feb. 18, 1915 (New York, N.Y.). U.S. actor. A popular leading man in 1940s action films.

CLAYBURGH, JILL, 1945 (Los Angeles, Calif.). U.S. actress. Film actress, with stage experience. Films: Gable & Lombard, 1976; Semi-Tough, 1977; An Unmarried Woman, 1978; Luna, 1979; Starting Over, 1979. Stage: Pippin, 1970.

CLAYTON, JAN, 1925 (Tularosa, N.M.). U.S. actress. Film and TV actress, best known as the original mother on the Lassie TV series, 1954-57.

CLIFT, MONTGOMERY, Oct. 17, 1920 (Omaha, Neb.)-July 23, 1966. U.S. actor. Films: The Search, 1948; Red River, 1948; A Place in the Sun, 1951; From Here to Eternity, 1953; The Young Lions, 1959; The Misfits, 1960; Freud, 1963.

COBB, LEE J., Dec. 8, 1911 (New York, N.Y.)-Feb. 11, 1976. U.S. actor. Best known for the lead role of Willy Loman in the play Death of a Salesman, 1949. Films: Golden Boy, 1939; On the Waterfront, 1954; Twelve Angry Men, 1957. TV: The Virginian (series), 1962-1966.

COBURN, CHARLES, June 19, 1877 (Savannah, Ga.)-Aug. 30, 1961. U.S. character actor. Films: Bachelor Mother, 1939; The Lady Eve, 1941; The Devil and Miss Jones, 1941; Heaven Can Wait, 1943; Knickerbocker Holiday, 1945; Monkey Business, 1952.

COBURN, JAMES, Aug. 31, 1928 (Laurel, Neb.). U.S. actor; Films: The Magnificent Seven, 1960; The Great Escape, 1963; Our Man Flint, 1966; A Fistful of Dynamite, 1971; Billy the Kid, 1973; The Last of Sheila, 1973; Hard Times, 1975; Midway, 1976; Cross of Iron, 1977.

COCO, JAMES, Mar. 21, 1930 (New York, N.Y.). U.S. stage, film, TV actor. Films: A New Leaf, 1971; Man of La Mancha, 1972; Murder by Death, 1976. TV: Calucci's Department, 1973; The Dumplings, 1976.

COLBERT, CLAUDETTE, born Lily Claudette Chauchoin, Sept. 18, 1905 (Paris, Fr.). U.S. actress. Best known for her role opposite CLARK GABLE in It Happened One Night (1934), for which she won Best Actress AA. Other films: Imitation of Life, 1934; Since You Went Away, 1944; The Egg and I, 1947. Play: The Kingfisher, 1978.

COLEMAN, GARY, Feb. 8, 1968 (Zion, Ill.). U.S. child actor. Star of the TV series Diff'rent Strokes, 1978- .

COLLINS, RAY, 1890 (Sacramento, Calif.)-1965. U.S. character actor. Films: Citizen Kane, 1941; The Magnificent Ambersons, 1942. TV: Perry Mason (series), 1958-65.

CONNORS, CHUCK, born Kevin Joseph Connors, Apr. 10, 1921 (New York, N.Y.). U.S. actor, athlete. Professional baseball player with Brooklyn Dodgers (1949), and Chicago Cubs (1951); best known as actor for role in the TV series *The Rifleman,* 1957–62. TV: *Roots* (movie), 1977.

CONRAD, ROBERT, born Conrad Robert Falk, Mar. 1, 1935 (Chicago, Ill.). U.S. actor. Best known for leading roles in the TV series *Hawaiian Eye* (1959–63), *Wild, Wild West* (1965–69), *Baa, Baa, Black Sheep* (1976) and *A Man Called Sloane,* (1979–   ).

CONRAD, WILLIAM, Sept. 27, 1920 (Louisville, Ky.). U.S. actor. Radio: *Gunsmoke* (series), 1949–60. TV: *Cannon* (series), 1971–76.

CONREID, HANS, born Frank Foster, Apr. 1, 1915 (Baltimore, Md.). U.S. character actor.

CONSTANTINE, MICHAEL, born Constantine Efstration, May 22, 1927 (Reading, Pa.). U.S. character actor. Best known for role in the TV series *Room 222* (1968–74), for which he won 1969 Supporting Actor Emmy award.

CONTE, RICHARD, born Nicholas Conte, 1918 (New York, N.Y.)–Apr. 15, 1975. U.S. actor. Films: *The Purple Heart,* 1944; *A Walk in the Sun,* 1946; *Call Northside 777,* 1948; *The Brothers Rico,* 1957; *Tony Rome,* 1967.

COOGAN, JACKIE, born John Leslie, Oct. 26, 1914 (Los Angeles, Calif.). U.S. actor. As child actor, appeared in such silent films as *The Kid* (1920) and *Oliver Twist* (1921); as adult actor, best known for role in the TV series *The Addams Family,* 1963–65.

COOPER, GARY, born Frank James Cooper, May 7, 1901 (Helena, Mont.)–May 13, 1961. U.S. actor. Best known for his screen portrayals of strong, laconic heroes. Films: *A Farewell to Arms,* 1932; *Lives of a Bengal Lancer,* 1935; *Mr. Deeds Goes to Town,* 1936; *Beau Geste,* 1939; *Sergeant York* (Best Actor AA), 1941; *High Noon* (Best Actor AA), 1952; *Love in the Afternoon,* 1956. Received special AA, 1960.

COOPER, JACKIE, Sept. 15, 1922 (Los Angeles, Calif.). U.S. actor, TV director, producer. As child actor, starred in *Our Gang* film shorts (1927–28), *The Champ* (1931), *The Bowery* (1933), and *Treasure Island* (1934); adult work includes the TV series *People's Choice* (1955–58) and *Hennessey* (1959–60); director of many episodes of TV comedy series such as M*A*S*H* (1972–   ).

CORBY, ELLEN, born Ellen Hansen, 1913 (Racine, Wisc.). U.S. character actress. Best known for her role as Grandma in the TV series *The Waltons* (1972–   ).

COREY, WENDELL, 1914 (Dracut, Mass.)–Nov. 8, 1968. U.S. film and TV actor. Often played solid, dependable characters.

CORNELL, KATHERINE, Feb. 16, 1898 (Berlin, Ger.)–June 8, 1974. U.S. stage actress. A celebrated leading lady, 1921–61.

COTTON, JOSEPH, 1905 (Petersburg, Va.). U.S. actor. Films: *Citizen Kane,* 1941; *The Magnificent Ambersons,* 1942; *Duel in the Sun,* 1946; *The Farmer's Daughter,* 1947; *Portrait of Jenny,* 1948; *The Third Man,* 1949; *Hush, Hush, Sweet Charlotte,* 1964; *Petulia,* 1968; *Tora! Tora! Tora!,* 1971.

CRABBE, BUSTER, born Clarence Linden Crabbe, Feb. 7, 1908 (Oakland, Calif.). U.S. actor, swimmer. Gold medalist in the 400-m freestyle, 1932 Olympics; star of 1930s and 1940s film series as Flash Gordon, Tarzan, Buck Rogers; star of 1950s TV series as Captain Gallant of the Foreign Legion.

CRAIN, JEANNE, May 25, 1925 (Barstow, Calif.). U.S. actress. A leading lady of the 1940s. Films: *State Fair,* 1945; *Margie,* 1946; *A Letter to Three Wives,* 1949; *Pinky,* 1949.

CRAWFORD, BRODERICK, Dec. 9, 1911 (Philadelphia, Pa.). U.S. actor. Won Best Actor AA for *All the King's Men* (1949); star of the TV series *Highway Patrol,* 1955–59. (Son of HELEN BRODERICK.)

CRAWFORD, JOAN, born Lucille Le Sueur, Mar. 23, 1908 (San Antonio, Tex.)–Feb. 14, 1977. U.S. actress, dancer. Films: *Our Dancing Daughters,* 1928; *Grand Hotel,* 1932; *Rain,* 1932; *A Woman's Face,* 1941; *Mildred Pierce* (Best Actress AA), 1945; *Humoresque,* 1946; *Whatever Happened to Baby Jane?,* 1962. Books: *A Portrait of Joan,* 1962; *My Way of Life,* 1971.

CRENNA, RICHARD, Nov. 30, 1927 (Los Angeles, Calif.). U.S. actor. Star of the TV series *Our Miss Brooks* (1952–55), *The Real McCoys* (1957–63), and *Slattery's People* (1964–65).

CRYSTAL, BILLY, 1947 (New York, N.Y.). U.S. actor. Star of the TV series *Soap,* 1977–   .

CULP, ROBERT, Aug. 16, 1930 (Oakland, Calif.). U.S. actor. Best known for his role in the TV series *I Spy,* 1965–68. Films: *Bob & Carol & Ted & Alice,* 1969; *Hickey and Boggs,* 1972; *Breaking Point,* 1976.

CUMMINGS, CONSTANCE, born Constance Halverstadt, May 15, 1910 (Seattle, Wash.). U.S. stage and film actress. Films: *Blithe Spirit,* 1945; *The Battle of the Sexes,* 1959.

CUMMINGS, ROBERT, June 9, 1910 (Joplin, Mo.). U.S. actor. A leading man in 1940s films. Films: *King's Row,* 1941; *Saboteur,* 1942; *The Bride Wore Boots,* 1946; *The Chase,* 1946; *Sleep My Love,* 1948. TV: *The Bob Cummings Show,* 1955–59.

CURTIS, TONY, born Bernard Schwartz, June 3, 1925 (New York, N.Y.). U.S. actor. Films: *Houdini,* 1953; *Trapeze,* 1956; *Sweet Smell of Success,* 1957; *The Vikings,* 1958; *Some Like It Hot,* 1959; *Spartacus,* 1960; *The Great Race,* 1965; *The Boston Strangler,* 1968. TV: *Vegas,* 1978–   . (One-time husband of JANET LEIGH.)

DAHL, ARLENE, Aug. 11, 1928 (Minneapolis, Minn.) U.S. actress, beauty columnist, model. A leading lady in films of the 1950s and early 1960s.

DAILEY, DAN, Dec. 12, 1917 (New York, N.Y.)–Oct. 17, 1978. U.S. actor. A song-and-dance man in 1940s and 1950s musicals. Films: *Mother Wore Tights,* 1947; *Give My Regards to Broadway,* 1948; *When My Baby Smiles at Me,* 1948; *Chicken Every Sunday,* 1949; *When Willie Comes Marching Home,* 1950; *Pride of St. Louis,* 1951; *It's Always Fair Weather,* 1955.

DALY, JAMES, Oct. 23, 1918 (Wisconsin Rapids, Wisc.)–July 3, 1978. U.S. actor. Best known for supporting role in the TV series *Medical Center* (1970–76), for which he won 1966 Emmy.

DANDRIDGE, DOROTHY, 1923 (Cleveland, Ohio)–Sept. 8, 1965. U.S. actress. Films: *Carmen Jones,* 1954; *Island in the Sun,* 1957; *Porgy and Bess,* 1959.

DANNER, BLYTHE KATHERINE, ? (Philadelphia, Pa.). U.S. actress. Won 1971 Tony for her performance in the play *Butterflies Are Free.* TV: *The Seagull* (movie), 1975; *Eccentricities of a Nightingale* (movie), 1976; *Too Far To Go,* 1979. Films: *1776,* 1972; *Futureworld,* 1976.

DANTON, RAY, Sept. 19, 1931 (New York, N.Y.). U.S. actor. Films: *Too Much Too Soon,* 1958; *The*

Rise and Fall of Legs Diamond, 1959; The George Raft Story, 1961.

DARNELL, LINDA, born Manetta Eloisa Darnell, 1921 (Dallas, Tex.)–Apr. 10, 1965. U.S. actress. Films: Anna and the King of Siam, 1946; My Darling Clementine, 1946; Forever Amber, 1947; A Letter to Three Wives, 1948.

DARREN, JAMES, born James Ercolani, June 8, 1936 (Philadelphia, Pa.). U.S. actor, singer. Films: Gidget, 1959; The Guns of Navarone, 1961. TV: Time Tunnel (series), 1966-67.

DARWELL, JANE, born Patti Woodward, 1879 (Palmyra, Mo.)–Aug. 13, 1967. U.S. character actress. Films: Jesse James, 1939; The Grapes of Wrath (Best Supporting Actress AA), 1940; Captain Tugboat Annie, 1946; The Last Hurrah, 1958; Mary Poppins, 1964.

DA SILVA, HOWARD, born Howard Silverblatt, May 4, 1909 (Cleveland, Ohio). U.S. actor, theater director. Films: The Lost Weekend, 1945; Two Years before the Mast, 1946; David and Lisa, 1962; 1776, 1972.

DAVIES, MARION, Jan. 1, 1900 (New York, N.Y.)–Sept. 1961. U.S. actress. A protégé of WILLIAM RANDOLPH HEARST, who was determined to make her a star, in films, 1917-36.

DAVIS, BETTE, born Ruth Elizabeth Davis, Apr. 5, 1908 (Lowell, Mass.). U.S. actress. One of the foremost dramatic actresses in film history. Films: Of Human Bondage, 1934; Dangerous (Best Actress AA), 1935; The Petrified Forest, 1936; Jezebel (Best Actress AA), 1938; The Great Lie, 1941; A Stolen Life, 1946; All about Eve, 1950; A Pocketful of Miracles, 1961; Whatever Happened to Baby Jane, 1962; Hush, Hush, Sweet Charlotte, 1964; The Nanny, 1965. Received American Film Inst. Life Achievement Award, 1977.

DAVIS, OSSIE, Dec. 18, 1917 (Cogdell, Ga.). U.S. actor, director. Films: The Hill, 1965; The Scalphunters, 1968; Malcolm X, 1972.

DAWSON, RICHARD, Nov. 20, ? (Hampshire, Eng.). British actor, TV game-show host. TV: Hogan's Heroes (series), 1965-71; Family Feud (game show), 1976–

DAY, DORIS, born Doris von Kappelhoff, Apr. 3, 1924 (Cincinnati, Ohio). U.S. singer, dancer, actress. Films: Young Man with a Horn, 1950; Tea for Two, 1950; I'll See You in My Dreams, 1951; Young at Heart, 1955; The Pajama Game, 1957; Pillow Talk, 1959; Midnight Lace, 1960; The Glass Bottom Boat, 1966; With Six You Get Egg Roll, 1968. TV: The Doris Day Show (series), 1970-73.

DAY, LARAINE, born Laraine Johnson, Oct. 13, 1920 (Roosevelt, Utah). U.S. actress. A popular film star of the 1940s best known for her work in the "Dr. Kildare" series of films.

DEAN, JAMES, born James Byron, Feb. 8, 1931 (Marion, Ind.)–Sept. 30, 1955. U.S. actor. A cult figure who epitomized restless youth of the early 1950s. Films: East of Eden, 1955; Rebel without a Cause, 1955; Giant, 1956.

DEE, RUBY, born Ruby Ann Wallace, Oct. 27, 1924 (Cleveland, Ohio). U.S. actress. Plays: Raisin in the Sun, 1959; Purlie Victorious, 1961. Films: Raisin in the Sun, 1961. Winner of Obie award in 1971 and Drama Desk Award in 1974.

DEE, SANDRA, born Alexandra Zuck, Apr. 23, 1942 (Bayonne, N.J.). U.S. actress. Films: Gidget, 1959; Imitation of Life, 1959; A Summer Place, 1959; Tammy and the Doctor, 1963; Take Her, She's Mine, 1964; That Funny Feeling, 1965.

DE HAVILLAND, OLIVIA, July 1, 1916 (Tokyo, Jap.). English-U.S. actress. Films: A Midsummer Night's Dream, 1935; Gone with the Wind, 1939; To Each His Own (Best Actress AA), 1946; The Heiress (Best Actress AA), 1949; The Light in the Piazza, 1962; Hush, Hush, Sweet Charlotte, 1964. (Sister of JOAN FONTAINE.)

DEL RIO, DOLORES, born Dolores Asunsolo, Aug. 3, 1908 (Durango, Mex.). Mexican-U.S. actress. A leading lady of 1920s and 1930s films.

DEMAREST, WILLIAM, Feb. 27, 1892 (St. Paul, Minn.). U.S. character actor. Appeared in numerous films, from 1927. TV: Wells Fargo (series), 1956-58; My Three Sons (series), 1967-73.

DE NIRO, ROBERT, 1945 (New York, N.Y.). U.S. actor. Films: Bang the Drum Slowly, 1973; The Godfather—Part 2 (Best Supporting Actor AA), 1974; The Last Tycoon, 1976; Taxi Driver, 1976; New York, New York, 1977; The Deer Hunter, 1978.

DENNING, RICHARD, born Louis Denninger, Mar. 27, 1914 (Poughkeepsie, N.Y.). U.S. actor. Star of 1940s and 1950s B-grade films. TV: Mr. and Mrs. North (series), 1953-54.

DENNIS, SANDY, Apr. 27, 1937 (Hastings, Neb.). U.S. actress. Films: Who's Afraid of Virginia Woolf? (Best Supporting Actress AA), 1965; Up the Down Staircase, 1967; The Fox, 1967; Sweet November, 1968; The Out-Of-Towners, 1969. Plays: A Thousand Clowns (Tony award), 1963; Any Wednesday (Tony award), 1964.

DENVER, BOB, 1935, (New Rochelle, N.Y.). U.S. comedic actor. TV: Dobie Gillis (series), 1959-62; Gilligan's Island (series), 1964-66.

DEREK, JOHN, born Derek Harris, 1926 (Hollywood, Calif.). U.S. actor. Films: Knock on Any Door, 1949; All the King's Men, 1949; Prince of Players, 1955; The Ten Commandments, 1956; Exodus, 1960. (One-time husband of URSULA ANDRESS.)

DERN, BRUCE, June 4, 1936 (Chicago, Ill.). U.S. actor. Films: Silent Running, 1972; King of Marvin Gardens, 1972; The Great Gatsby, 1974; Smile, 1975; Won Ton Ton, 1976; Black Sunday, 1977; Coming Home, 1978.

DEVANE, WILLIAM, 1937 (Albany, N.Y.). U.S. actor. Films: The Marathon Man, 1977; Yanks, 1979. TV: From Here to Eternity (movie), 1979.

DEVINE, ANDY, Oct. 7, 1905 (Flagstaff, Ariz.)–Feb. 18, 1977. U.S. squeaky-voiced character actor who appeared in over 300 films, 1928-77; remembered for playing Wild Bill Hickock's sidekick in the 1950's TV series.

DEWHURST, COLLEEN, June 6, 1926 (Montreal, Que., Can.). Canadian actress. Plays: All the Way Home (Tony award), 1961; A Moon for the Misbegotten (Tony Award), 1974. (One-time wife of GEORGE C. SCOTT.)

DICKINSON, ANGIE, born Angeline Brown, Sept. 30, 1931 (Kulm, N.D.). U.S. actress. Films: Rio Bravo, 1959; Point Blank, 1968; Pretty Maids All in a Row, 1971. TV: Police Woman (series), 1974-78. (One-time wife of BURT BACHARACH.)

DILLMAN, BRADFORD, Apr. 14, 1930 (San Francisco, Calif.). U.S. actor. Films: A Certain Smile, 1958; Compulsion, 1959; Francis of Assisi, 1961; Escape from the Planet of the Apes, 1971.

DIXON, IVAN, Apr. 6, 1931 (New York, N.Y.). U.S. actor. Films: Raisin in the Sun, 1959; A Patch of Blue, 1965; Car Wash, 1976. TV: Hogan's Heroes (series), 1965-71.

DONAHUE, TROY, born Merle Johnson, Jan. 27, 1936 (New York, N.Y.). U.S. actor. Films: Parrish,

1961; *Susan Slade*, 1961; *A Summer Place*, 1962. TV: *Surfside Six* (series), 1960-62.

DOUGLAS, KIRK, born Issur Danielovitch Demsky, Dec. 9, 1918 (Amsterdam, N.Y.). U.S. actor. Films: *Champion*, 1949; *Young Man with a Horn*, 1950; *The Glass Menagerie*, 1951; *Detective Story*, 1952; *Gunfight at the OK Corral*, 1957; *Paths of Glory*, 1957; *Spartacus*, 1960; *Lonely Are the Brave*, 1962; *Seven Days in May*, 1964; *Cast a Giant Shadow*, 1966; *Once Is Not Enough*, 1973. (Father of MICHAEL DOUGLAS.)

DOUGLAS, MELVYN, born Melvyn Hesselberg, Apr. 5, 1901 (Macon, Ga.). U.S. actor. Films: *Captains Courageous*, 1937; *Ninotchka*, 1939; *Hud* (Best Supporting Actor AA), 1963; *Hotel*, 1967; *I Never Sang for My Father*, 1969.

DOUGLAS, MICHAEL, 1945 (New Brunswick, N.J.). U.S. actor, producer. Films: *Hail Hero*, 1970; *One Flew Over the Cuckoo's Nest* (co-producer only), 1975; *Running*, 1979. TV: *The Streets of San Francisco* (series), 1972-76. (Son of KIRK DOUGLAS.)

DOUGLAS, PAUL, Apr. 11, 1907 (Philadelphia, Pa.)-Sept. 11, 1959. U.S. actor. Character leading man in films. Films: *A Letter to Three Wives*, 1948; *Fourteen Hours*, 1951; *Executive Suite*, 1954; *Joe Macbeth*, 1955; *The Solid Gold Cadillac*, 1956.

DREYFUSS, RICHARD STEPHEN, Oct. 29, 1947 (New York, N.Y.). U.S. actor. Films: *American Graffiti*, 1972; *Jaws*, 1975; *Close Encounters of the Third Kind*, 1976; *The Good-Bye Girl*, (Best Actor AA), 1977; *The Big Fix*, 1977.

DRU, JOANNE, born Joanne La Cock, Jan. 31, 1923 (Logan, W.Va.). U.S. actress. A leading lady in 1940s films. Films: *Abie's Irish Rose*, 1946; *Red River*, 1948; *All the King's Men*, 1949.

DUFF, HOWARD, Nov. 24, 1917 (Bremerton, Wash.). U.S. actor. Films: *Brute Force*, 1947; *All My Sons*, 1948. TV: *Mr. Adams and Eve* (series), 1956-57; *Felony Squad* (series), 1966-68. (Husband of IDA LUPINO.)

DUKE, PATTY, born Anna Marie Duke, Dec. 14, 1946 (New York, N.Y.). U.S. actress. Films: *The Miracle Worker* (Best Supporting Actress AA), 1962; *Valley of the Dolls*, 1967; *My Sweet Charlie*, 1970. TV: *Patty Duke Show* (series), 1963-64. Plays: *The Miracle Worker*, 1959. Received Emmy award for *Captains and Kings*, 1977. (Wife of JOHN ASTIN.)

DULLEA, KEIR, May 30, 1936 (Cleveland, Ohio). U.S. actor. Films: *David and Lisa*, 1962; *Bunny Lake Is Missing*, 1965; *2001: A Space Odyssey*, 1969. Plays: *Butterflies Are Free*, 1969.

DUNAWAY, FAYE, Jan. 14, 1941 (Bascom, Fla.). U.S. actress. Films: *Hurry Sundown*, 1967; *Bonnie and Clyde*, 1967; *The Thomas Crown Affair*, 1968; *Oklahoma Crude*, 1973; *Chinatown*, 1974; *The Voyage of the Damned*, 1976; *Network* (Best Actress AA), 1976; *The Champ*, 1979.

DUNCAN, SANDY, Feb. 20, 1946 (Henderson, Tex.). U.S. actress, singer, dancer. TV: *The Sandy Duncan Show* (series), 1972. Stage: *Peter Pan*, 1979. Films: *Star Spangled Girl*, 1971.

DUNN, JAMES, Nov. 2, 1905 (Santa Monica, Calif.)-1967. U.S. actor. Won Best Supporting Actor AA for his role in *A Tree Grows in Brooklyn*, 1945.

DUNNE, IRENE, Dec. 20, 1904 (Louisville, Ky.). U.S. actress. Films: *Cimarron*, 1931; *Back Street*, 1932; *Show Boat*, 1936; *The Awful Truth*, 1937; *My Favorite Wife*, 1940; *Anna and the King of Siam*, 1946; *Life with Father*, 1947; *I Remember Mama*, 1948.

DUNNOCK, MILDRED, Jan. 25, 1906 (Baltimore, Md.). U.S. stage and film actress, often seen in motherly roles.

DURBIN, DEANNA, born Edna Mae Durbin, Dec. 4, 1922 (Winnipeg, Man., Can.). U.S. singer, actress. Popular teenage star in films in 1930s and 1940s; special AA, 1938. *Three Smart Girls*, 1936; *Mad About Music*, 1938; *That Certain Age*, 1938; *It Started with Eve*, 1941; *Can't Help Singing*, 1944.

DURYEA, DAN, 1907 (White Plains, N.Y.)-June 7, 1968. U.S. character actor. Films: *The Little Foxes*, 1941; *The Woman in the Window*, 1944; *Black Angel*, 1946; *Another Part of the Forest*, 1948; *The Flight of the Phoenix*, 1965.

DUVALL, ROBERT, 1931 (San Diego, Calif.). U.S. actor. Films: *True Grit*, 1969; *The Godfather—Part 1*, 1972; *The Conversation*, 1974; *The Godfather—Part 2*, 1974; *Network*, 1976; *The Seven Per Cent Solution*, 1976; *The Betsy*, 1978; *Apocalypse Now*, 1979.

DUVALL, SHELLEY, 1949 (Houston, Tex.). U.S. actress. Gawky film actress, frequently featured in films by ROBERT ALTMAN. Films: *Thieves Like Us*, 1974; *Nashville*, 1975; *Three Women*, 1977.

EAGELS, JEANNE, 1894 (Kansas City, Mo.)-1929. U.S. actress. A leading lady in 1920s films. Led a highly-publicized private life; portrayed by KIM NOVAK in a 1957 film biography.

EASTWOOD, CLINT, May 31, 1930 (San Francisco, Calif.). U.S. actor. Sprang into prominence as the tight-lipped hero of low-budget "spaghetti" westerns. Films: *A Fistful of Dollars*, 1964; *For a Few Dollars More*, 1965; *The Good, the Bad and the Ugly*, 1966; *Hang 'Em High*, 1968; *Coogan's Bluff*, 1968; *Paint Your Wagon*, 1969; *Play Misty for Me*, 1971; *Dirty Harry*, 1971; *Magnum Force*, 1973; *The Eiger Sanction*, 1975; *Every Which Way but Loose*, 1978. TV: *Rawhide* (series), 1958-65.

EBSEN, BUDDY, born Christian Rudolf Ebsen, Apr. 2, 1908 (Belleville, Ill.). U.S. actor, dancer. Originally a song-and-dance man in 1930s films. TV: *Davy Crockett* (series), 1954-55; *The Beverly Hillbillies* (series), 1962-71; *Barnaby Jones* (series), 1973-   .

EDEN, BARBARA, born Barbara Huffman, 1934 (Tucson, Ariz.). U.S. actress. Best known for her role in the TV series *I Dream of Jeannie*, 1965-69.

EDWARDS, VINCENT, born Vincent Edward Zorio, July 7, 1928 (Brooklyn, N.Y.). U.S. actor. Best known as star of the TV series *Ben Casey*, 1960-65.

ELDRIDGE, FLORENCE, born Florence McKechnie, Sept. 5, 1901 (Brooklyn, N.Y.). U.S. actress. Many theater appearances, often with husband FREDRIC MARCH.

ERICKSON, LEIF, born William Anderson, Oct. 27, 1911 (Alameda, Calif.). U.S. actor. TV: *High Chaparral* (series), 1967-69.

ERWIN, STUART, 1903 (Squaw Valley, Calif.)-Dec. 21, 1967. U.S. character actor. Often played leading man's sidekick in 1930s-50s films. TV: *The Stu Erwin Show*, 1950-55.

ESTRADA, ERIK, Mar. 16, 1949 (New York, N.Y.). U.S. actor. Teen-age heartthrob. TV: *CHIPS* (series), 1977-   .

EVANS, DALE, born Francis Smith, Oct. 31, 1912 (Uvalde, Tex.). U.S. singer, actress. A film star in 1940s westerns, she is best known for her role opposite husband ROY ROGERS in TV series, *The Roy Rogers Show*, 1951–57.

EVERETT, CHAD, born Raymond Lee Cramton, June 11, 1937 (South Bend, Ind.) U.S. actor. Best known as star of the TV series *Medical Center*, 1969–75.

EWELL, TOM, born Yewell Tomkins, Apr. 29, 1909 (Owensboro, Ky.). U.S. comedic actor. Films: *Adam's Rib*, 1949; *The Seven Year Itch*, 1955; *State Fair*, 1962. TV: *Baretta* (series), 1975–78.

FAIRBANKS, DOUGLAS, born Douglas Ullman, May 23, 1883 (Denver, Col.)–Dec. 12, 1939. U.S. actor. A silent-screen star, first of great swashbuckling screen heros; a founder of United Artists Corp., 1919; honored with posthumous AA for his contribution to motion pictures, 1939. Films: *The Mark of Zorro*, 1920; *The Three Musketeers*, 1921; *Robin Hood*, 1921; *The Thief of Baghdad*, 1923. (One-time husband of MARY PICKFORD; father of DOUGLAS FAIRBANKS, JR.)

FAIRBANKS, DOUGLAS, JR., Dec. 9, 1909 (New York, N.Y.). U.S. actor, TV producer. Films: *Dawn Patrol*, 1930; *Morning Glory*, 1933; *The Prisoner of Zenda*, 1937; *Gunga Din*, 1939; *Sinbad the Sailor*, 1947. (Son of DOUGLAS FAIRBANKS)

FALK, PETER, Sept. 16, 1927 (New York, N.Y.). U.S. actor. Best known as star of TV series *Columbo* (1971–78), for which he received 1972 Emmy award. Films: *Murder, Inc.*, 1960; *Luv*, 1967; *Husbands*, 1970; *Murder by Death*, 1976; *The Cheap Detective*, 1978; *The In-Laws*, 1979.

FARMER, FRANCES, 1915 (Seattle, Wash.)–Aug. 1, 1970. U.S. actress. Actress of late 1930s-early 1940s; her career ended with her commitment to a mental institution, 1943; in her autobiography, *Will There Ever Be A Morning*, gave an account of her nearly 30-years battle with mental illness and alcoholism, 1972. Stage: *Golden Boy*, 1937. Film: *Come and Get It*, 1936.

FARRELL, MIKE, Feb. 6, ? (St. Paul, Minn.). U.S. actor. TV: *M*A*S*H* (series), 1975– .

FARROW, MIA, Feb. 9, 1945 (Los Angeles, Calif.). U.S. actress. Films: *Rosemary's Baby*, 1968; *John and Mary*, 1969; *The Great Gatsby*, 1973. TV: *Peyton Place* (series), 1964–67. (Daughter of MAUREEN O'SULLIVAN; one-time wife of ANDRE PREVIN and FRANK SINATRA.)

FAWCETT, FARRAH, Feb. 2, 1947 (Corpus Christi, Tex.). U.S. actress. Sex symbol of the 1970s. TV: *Charlie's Angels* (series), 1976–77. Films: *Sunburn*, 1979. (One-time wife of LEE MAJORS.)

FAYE, ALICE, born Alice Leppert, May 5, 1915 (New York, N.Y.). U.S. singer, actress. Films: *In Old Chicago*, 1938; *Alexander's Ragtime Band*, 1938; *Rose of Washington Square*, 1939; *Lillian Russell*, 1940; *State Fair*, 1962. (Wife of PHIL HARRIS.)

FELDON, BARBARA, Mar. 12, 1941 (Pittsburgh, Pa.). U.S. actress. Best known for her role in the TV series *Get Smart*, 1965–70.

FELL, NORMAN, Mar. 24, 1925 (Philadelphia, Pa.). U.S. actor. TV: *Three's Company* (series), 1977–79; *The Ropers* (series), 1979– .

FERRER, MEL, Aug. 25, 1917 (Elberon, N.J.). U.S. actor. Films: *Lost Boundaries*, 1949; *Scaramouche*, 1952; *War and Peace*, 1956; *Fraulein*, 1958. (One-time husband of AUDREY HEPBURN.)

FIELD, BETTY, Feb. 8, 1918 (Boston, Mass.)–Sept. 13, 1973. U.S. actress. Films: *Of Mice and Men*, 1939; *King's Row*, 1942; *The Southerner*, 1945; *Picnic*, 1957.

FIELD, SALLY, 1946 (Pasadena, Calif.). U.S. actress. TV: *Gidget* (series), 1965; *The Flying Nun* (series), 1967–68; *The Girl with Something Extra* (series), 1973. Films: *Smokey and the Bandit*, 1977; *Norma Rae*, 1979.

FISHER, CARRIE, 1956 (Beverly Hills, Calif.). U.S. actress. Films: *Star Wars*, 1977. (Daughter of DEBBIE REYNOLDS and EDDIE FISHER.)

FLEMING, RHONDA, born Marilyn Louis, 1923 (Hollywood, Calif.). U.S. actress. A leading lady in 1940s and 1950s films. Films: *Spellbound*, 1945; *The Spiral Staircase*, 1945; *Gunfight at the OK Corral*, 1957.

FLETCHER, LOUISE, 1936 (Birmingham, Ala.). U.S. actress. Films: *One Flew over the Cuckoo's Nest* (Best Actress AA), 1975; *Exorcist II*, 1977.

FLYNN, ERROL, June 20, 1909 (Hobart, Tasmania, Austrl.)–Oct. 14, 1959. U.S. actor. A great star of action-adventure films of the 1930s and 1940s. Films: *Captain Blood*, 1935; *The Charge of the Light Brigade*, 1936; *The Adventures of Robin Hood*, 1938; *Elizabeth and Essex*, 1939; *They Died with Their Boots On*, 1941; *Gentleman Jim*, 1942; *The Sun Also Rises*, 1957. Autobiography: *My Wicked, Wicked Ways*, 1959.

FONDA, HENRY, May 16, 1905 (Grand Island, Neb.). U.S. actor. Best known for his portrayal of upright, reasonable heroes. Films: *Jezebel*, 1938; *Young Mr. Lincoln*, 1939; *The Grapes of Wrath*, 1940; *Chad Hanna*, 1940; *The Ox-Bow Incident*, 1942; *My Darling Clementine*, 1946; *Ft. Apache*, 1948; *Mr. Roberts*, 1955; *Twelve Angry Men*, 1957; *Fail Safe*, 1964; *Welcome to Hard Times*, 1967; *Yours, Mine and Ours*, 1968; *The Cheyenne Social Club*, 1970; *The Swarm*, 1977. Received special Tony award, 1979. (Father of JANE and PETER FONDA)

FONDA, JANE, Dec. 21, 1937 (New York, N.Y.). U.S. actress, social activist. Films: *Tall Story*, 1960; *Cat Ballou*, 1965; *Barefoot in the Park*, 1967; *Barbarella*, 1968; *They Shoot Horses, Don't They?*, 1969; *Klute* (Best Actress AA), 1971; *Steelyard Blues*, 1973; *A Doll's House*, 1973; *Fun with Dick and Jane*, 1977; *Julia*, 1977; *Coming Home* (Best Actress AA), 1978. (Daughter of HENRY FONDA; sister of PETER FONDA.)

FONDA, PETER, Feb. 23, 1939 (New York, N.Y.). U.S. actor. Best known as the writer, coproducer, and star of the film *Easy Rider*, 1969. Other films: *The Trip*, 1967; *Futureworld*, 1976; *Outlaw Blues*, 1977. (Son of HENRY FONDA; brother of JANE FONDA.)

FONTAINE, JOAN, born Joan de Havilland, Oct. 22, 1917 (Tokyo, Jap.). English-U.S. actress. Films: *Gunga Din*, 1938; *Rebecca*, 1940; *Suspicion* (Best Actress AA), 1941; *Jane Eyre*, 1943; *Letter from an Unknown Woman*, 1948; *A Certain Smile*, 1958. (Sister of OLIVIA DE HAVILLAND.)

FORD, GLENN, born Gwyllyn Ford, May 1, 1916 (Quebec, Can.). Canadian-U.S. actor. Films: *The Adventures of Martin Eden*, 1942; *Gilda*, 1946; *The Blackboard Jungle*, 1955; *The Sheepman*, 1958; *Is Paris Burning?*, 1966. TV: *Cade's County* (series), 1971.

FORD, HARRISON, 1942 (Chicago, Ill.). U.S. actor. Films: *American Graffiti*, 1974; *Star Wars*, 1977; *Heroes*, 1977; *Hanover Street*, 1979; *1941*, 1979.

FORD, PAUL, 1901 (Baltimore, Md.)–Apr. 12,

THE BOOK OF WHO

1976. U.S. character actor. Films: *Teahouse of the August Moon*, 1956; *The Matchmaker*, 1958; *Never Too Late*, 1965. TV: *The Phil Silvers Show* (series), 1955-59.

FORSYTHE, JOHN, born John Freund, Jan. 29, 1918 (Penns Grove, N.J.). U.S. actor. Best known as star of the TV series *Bachelor Father* (1957-62) and *Charlie's Angels* (1976-   ).

FOSTER, JODIE, 1962 (Los Angeles, Calif.). U.S. actress. Films: *Alice Doesn't Live Here Anymore*, 1975; *Taxi Driver*, 1976; *Bugsy Malone*, 1976; *The Little Girl Who Lives down the Lane*, 1977.

FOSTER, PRESTON, 1904 (Orange City, N.J.)-July 14, 1970. U.S. actor. Films: *The Last Mile*, 1931; *The Informer*, 1935; *Northwest Mounted Police*, 1940. TV: *The Waterfront* (series), 1954-60; *Gunslinger* (series), 1960.

FRANCIOSA, ANTHONY, born Anthony Papaleo, Oct. 25, 1928 (New York, N.Y.). U.S. actor. TV: *Valentine's Day* (series), 1964-65; *The Name of the Game* (series), 1968-72; *Search* (series), 1972-73; *Matt Helm* (series), 1975-76.

FRANCIS, ARLENE, born Arlene Kazanjian, Oct. 20, 1908 (Boston, Mass.). U.S. actress, radio and TV personality. TV: *What's My Line* (game show), 1950-67. (Wife of MARTIN GABEL.)

FRANCIS, KAY, born Katherine Gibbs, Jan. 13, 1905 (Oklahoma City, Okla.)-Aug. 26, 1968. U.S. actress. A leading lady in 1930s "women's" films. Films: *Street of Chance*, 1930; *One Way Passage*, 1932; *Trouble in Paradise*, 1932; *First Lady*, 1937; *Charley's Aunt*, 1941.

FRANCISCUS, JAMES, Jan. 31, 1934 (Clayton, Mo.). U.S. actor. Films: *Youngblood Hawke*, 1964; *Marooned*, 1969. TV: *Mr. Novak* (series), 1963-64; *Longstreet* (series), 1971.

FRANKLIN, BONNIE GAIL, Jan. 6, 1944 (Santa Monica, Calif.). U.S. actress, dancer. Play: *Applause*, 1970. TV: *One Day at a Time* (series) 1975-   .

FRAWLEY, WILLIAM, 1893 (Burlington, Ia.)-Mar. 3, 1966. U.S. comedic actor. TV: *I Love Lucy* (series), 1951-60; *My Three Sons* (series), 1960-63.

FUNICELLO, ANNETTE, 1942 (Utica, N.Y.). U.S. entertainer. One of Disney Mouseketeers in 1950s; later starred in family and "beach party" films.

GABEL, MARTIN, 1912 (Philadelphia, Pa.). U.S. stage and film actor. Received Tony award for *Big Fish, Little Fish* (1961). (Husband of ARLENE FRANCIS.)

GABLE, (William) CLARK, Feb. 1, 1901 (Cadiz, Ohio)-Nov. 16, 1960. U.S. actor. Extremely popular "he-man" hero of romance-adventure films. Films: *It Happened One Night* (Best Actor AA), 1934; *Mutiny on the Bounty*, 1935; *Call of the Wild*, 1935; *Gone with the Wind*, 1939; *The Hucksters*, 1947; *Command Decision*, 1948; *Teacher's Pet*, 1958; *Run Silent, Run Deep*, 1958; *The Misfits*, 1960. (One-time husband of CAROLE LOMBARD.)

GABOR, EVA, 1919? (Hungary). Hungarian-U.S. actress. TV: *Green Acres* (series), 1965-71. (Sister of ZSA ZSA GABOR.)

GABOR, ZSA ZSA, born Sari Gabor, 1921? (Hungary). Hungarian-U.S. actress. Miss Hungary, 1936. Autobiography: *My Story*, 1961 (Sister of EVA GABOR.)

GARDNER, AVA, born Lucy Johnson, Dec. 24, 1922 (Smithfield, N.C.). U.S. actress. Films: *The Killers*, 1946; *The Hucksters*, 1947; *Show Boat*, 1951; *Mogambo*, 1953; *The Barefoot Contessa*,

1954; *The Sun Also Rises*, 1957; *The Naked Maja*, 1959; *On the Beach*, 1959; *55 Days at Peking*, 1963; *The Night of the Iguana*, 1964. (One-time wife of MICKEY ROONEY, ARTIE SHAW, FRANK SINATRA.)

GARFIELD, JOHN, born Julius Garfinkle, 1913 (New York, N.Y.)-May 21, 1952. U.S. actor. Known for powerful dramatic performances in films. Films: *They Made Me a Criminal*, 1939; *The Sea Wolf*, 1941; *The Fallen Sparrow*, 1943; *Destination Tokyo*, 1944; *Pride of the Marines*, 1945; *The Postman Always Rings Twice*, 1946; *Humoresque*, 1946; *Body and Soul*, 1947; *Gentlemen's Agreement*, 1948, *Force of Evil*, 1949.

GARGAN, WILLIAM, July 17, 1905 (Brooklyn, N.Y.)-Feb. 17, 1979. U.S. actor. A leading man in 1930s and 1940s films and star of the 1950s TV series *Martin Kane, Private Eye*. After his larynx was removed (1960), taught speech to those similarly afflicted; wrote autobiography titled *Why Me?*, 1969.

GARNER, JAMES, born James Baumgardner, Apr. 7, 1928 (Norman, Okla.). U.S. actor. Best known as star of TV series *Maverick*, (1957-61) and *Rockford Files* (1975-   ). Films: *Cash McCall*, 1959; *The Thrill of It All*, 1963; *Grand Prix*, 1966; *The Skin Game*, 1971; *They Only Kill Their Masters*, 1973.

GAYNOR, JANET, born Laura Gainer, Oct. 6, 1906 (Philadelphia, Pa.). U.S. actress. Films: *Seventh Heaven* (Best Actress AA), 1927; *Daddy Longlegs*, 1931; *State Fair*, 1933; *A Star Is Born*, 1937.

GAZZARA, BEN, Aug. 28, 1930 (New York, N.Y.). U.S. actor. Received Drama Critics award, as most promising young actor of the season for *End As a Man*, 1953. Stage: *Cat on a Hot Tin Roof*, 1955; *Hatful of Rain*, 1955. Films: *The Young Doctors*, 1961; *Husbands*, 1969; *Al Capone*, 1974; *Voyage of the Damned*, 1976; *Saint Jack*, 1979. TV: *Run for Your Life* (series), 1965-68.

GEER, WILL, Mar. 9, 1902 (Frankfort, Ind.)-Apr. 22, 1978. U.S. character actor. Best known for the role of the grandfather on the TV series *The Waltons*, for which he received a 1975 Emmy award.

GHOSTLEY, ALICE, Aug. 14, 1926 (Eve, Mo.). U.S. comedic actress. Received Tony Award for best supporting actress for *The Sign in Sidney Brustein's Window*, 1965.

GIBSON, HOOT, born Edward Gibson, 1892 (Tememah, Neb.)-Aug. 23, 1962. U.S. silent-film actor, principally in cowboy roles.

GILBERT, JOHN, born John Pringle, July 10, 1897 (Logan, Utah)-Jan. 9, 1936. U.S. silent-screen actor whose high-pitched voice brought his career to an end when talkies superseded silent films.

GILFORD, JACK, July 25, 1907 (New York, N.Y.). U.S. comedic actor. Films: *A Funny Thing Happened on the Way to the Forum*, 1966; *Catch 22*, 1971; *Save the Tiger*, 1973. Plays: *The World of Sholom Aleichem*, 1953; *Once Upon a Mattress*, 1959; *A Funny Thing Happened on the Way to the Forum*, 1966.

GISH, DOROTHY, born Dorothy de Guiche, Mar. 11, 1898 (Massillon, Ohio)-June 4, 1968. U.S. silent-screen actress. Star of numerous D.W. GRIFFITH films. (Sister of LILLIAN GISH.)

GISH, LILLIAN, born Lillian de Guiche, Oct. 14, 1896 (Springfield, Ohio). U.S. silent-screen actress. Films: *Birth of a Nation*, 1914; *Intolerance*, 1916; *Way Down East*, 1920; *Orphans of the Storm*,

1927; *Duel in the Sun*, 1946; *Night of the Hunter*, 1958. (Sister of DOROTHY GISH.)

GLEASON, JAMES, May 23, 1886 (New York, N.Y.)-Apr. 12, 1959. U.S. character actor, writer, director. Actor in films such as *Here Comes Mr. Jordan* (1941), *Once Upon a Time* (1944), and *Suddenly* (1954).

GODDARD, PAULETTE, born Marion Levy, June 3, 1915 (Great Neck, N.Y.). U.S. actress. Leading lady in 1940s films, including *The Ghost Breakers* (1940), *The Great Dictator* (1940), *Kitty* (1945), *The Diary of a Chambermaid* (1946). (One-time wife of CHARLIE CHAPLIN, BURGESS MEREDITH, and ERICH MARIA REMARQUE.)

GORCEY, LEO, 1917 (New York, N.Y.)-June 2, 1969. U.S. actor. Films: *Dead End*, 1937; *Angels with Dirty Faces*, 1938; numerous second-feature "Bowery Boys" films of the 1930s.

GORDON, RUTH, born Ruth Gordon Jones, Oct. 30, 1896 (Wollaston, Mass.). U.S. stage and film actress, screenwriter. Films, (actress): *Rosemary's Baby* (Best Supporting Actress AA), 1968; *Where's Poppa?*, 1970; *Harold and Maude*, 1971; *Every Which Way but Loose*, 1978. Films (writer, with husband GARSON KANIN): *A Double Life* (1948), *Adam's Rib* (1949), *Pat and Mike* (1952). Wrote autobiography titled *My Side*, 1976.

GOULD, ELLIOTT, born Elliot Goldstein, Aug. 29, 1938 (New York, N.Y.). U.S. actor. Films: *Bob & Carol & Ted & Alice*, 1969; *M*A*S*H**, 1970; *I Love My Wife*, 1970; *Little Murders*, 1971; *The Long Goodbye*, 1972. (One-time husband of BARBRA STREISAND.)

GRABLE, BETTY, 1916 (St. Louis, Mo.)-July 2, 1973. U.S. actress. Pin-up girl of WW II. Films: *Million Dollar Legs*, 1939; *Moon Over Miami*, 1941; *I Wake up Screaming*, 1941; *Pin Up Girl*, 1944; *Diamond Horseshoe*, 1945; *The Dolly Sisters*, 1945; *Mother Wore Tights*, 1947; *How to Marry a Millionaire*, 1953. (One-time wife of HARRY JAMES.)

GRANGER, FARLEY, July 1, 1925 (San Jose, Calif.). U.S. actor. Films: *Rope*, 1948; *Strangers on a Train*, 1951; *Hans Christian Anderson*, 1952; *The Girl in the Red Velvet Swing*, 1955.

GRANT, LEE, born Loyova Haskell Rosenthal, Oct. 10, 1931 (New York, N.Y.). U.S. actress. Won Supporting Actress AA for *Shampoo* (1975), Emmy awards for best supporting actress in *Peyton Place* (1966) and for single performance by a leading lady in *The Neon Ceiling* (1971).

GRAVES, PETER, born Peter Aurness, Mar. 18, 1926 (Minneapolis, Minn.). U.S. actor. Leading man in B-grade films; starred as James Phelps in TV series *Mission Impossible*, 1967-75. (Brother of JAMES ARNESS.)

GREENE, LORNE, Feb. 12, 1915 (Ottawa, Ont., Can.). Canadian actor. Star of TV series *Bonanza* (1959-73) and *Battlestar Galactica* (1978-79).

GREY, JOEL, born Joe Katz, Apr. 11, 1932 (Cleveland, Ohio). U.S. actor. Originally a Broadway song-and-dance man. Plays: *Cabaret* (1967 Tony award); *Grand Tour*, 1979. Films: *Cabaret* (Best Supporting Actor AA), 1972; *Man on a Swing*, 1974; *The Seven Per Cent Solution*, 1976.

GRIFFITH, ANDY, June 1, 1926 (Mt. Airy, N.C.). U.S. actor. Best known as star of the TV series *The Andy Griffith Show*, 1960-69. Films: *A Face in the Crowd*, 1957; *No Time for Sergeants*, 1958.

GRIMES, TAMMY, Jan. 30, 1936 (Lynn, Mass.). U.S. actress, singer. Principally a stage actress. Plays: *The Unsinkable Molly Brown*, 1961 (Tony award); *Private Lives* (Tony award), 1970.

GRIZZARD, GEORGE, Apr. 1, 1928 (Roanoke Rapids, N.C.). U.S. actor. Principally a stage actor. Stage: *Who's Afraid of Virginia Woolf*, 1962. Films: *From the Terrace*, 1960; *Advise and Consent*, 1962; *Happy Birthday, Wanda June*, 1971.

GRODIN, CHARLES, Apr. 21, 1935 (Pittsburgh, Pa.). U.S. actor. Films: *The Heartbreak Kid*, 1973; *King Kong*, 1977.

HACKETT, JOAN, Mar. 1, 1933 (New York, N.Y.). U.S. actress. Stage, TV, and film appearances. Films: *The Group*, 1966; *Support Your Local Sheriff*, 1969; *The Last of Sheila*, 1973.

HACKMAN, GENE, Jan. 30, 1931 (San Bernardino, Calif.). U.S. actor. Films: *Bonnie and Clyde*, 1967; *I Never Sang for My Father*, 1969; *The French Connection* (Best Actor AA), 1972; *The Poseidon Adventure*, 1972; *The Conversation*, 1974; *The French Connection II*, 1975; *Night Moves*, 1975; *The Domino Principle*, 1977.

HAGMAN, LARRY, 1931 (Ft. Worth, Tex.). U.S. actor. Star of the TV series *I Dream of Jeannie* (1965-68) and *Dallas* (1978–   ). (Son of MARY MARTIN.)

HALEY, JACK, born John Joseph Haley, Aug. 10, 1899 (Boston, Mass.)-June 6, 1979. U.S. comedic actor. Best known for role as the Tin Man in the film, *The Wizard of Oz*, 1939.

HAMILTON, GEORGE, Aug. 12, 1939 (Memphis, Tenn.). U.S. actor. Films: *The Light in the Piazza*, 1962; *Act One*, 1963; *Your Cheating Heart*, 1965; *Evel Knievel*, 1972; *Love at First Bite*, 1979.

HARLOW, JEAN, born Harlean Carpentier, Mar. 3, 1911 (Kansas City, Mo.)-June 7, 1937. U.S. actress. Known for her sexy roles in 1930s films. Films: *Hell's Angels*, 1930; *Public Enemy*, 1931; *Red Dust*, 1932; *Dinner at Eight*, 1933; *China Seas*, 1935.

HARPER, ETHEL, 1904-Mar. 31, 1979. U.S. entertainer. Appeared in 1930s black Broadway shows such as *The Hot Mikado* and *The Negro Follies*; known as "Aunt Jemima," in pancake advertising campaign of 1950s.

HARPER, VALERIE, Aug. 22, 1940 (Suffern, N.Y.). U.S. comedic actress. Rose to prominence on the TV series *Mary Tyler Moore Show*, 1970-74; star of the TV series *Rhoda*, 1974-78.

HARRIS, BARBARA, 1935 (Evanston, Ill.). U.S. actress. Plays: *Oh Dad, Poor Dad . . .*, 1962; *Mother Courage and Her Children*, 1963; *On a Clear Day You Can See Forever*, 1965. Films: *A Thousand Clowns*, 1965; *Who is Harry Kellerman . . . ?*, 1971; *Nashville*, 1975; *The Seduction of Joe Tynan*, 1979.

HARRIS, JULIE, Dec. 2, 1925 (Grosse Pointe Park, Mich.). U.S. actress. A Broadway star since 1950. Plays: *The Member of the Wedding*, 1950; *Forty Carats* (Tony Award), 1969; *The Last of Mrs. Lincoln*, 1973; *The Belle of Amherst* (Tony Award), 1976.

HART, WILLIAM S., Dec. 6, 1870 (Newburgh, N.Y.)-June 23, 1946. U.S. actor. A leading star of silent-screen westerns.

HAWN, GOLDIE, Nov. 21, 1945 (Washington, D.C.). U.S. actress. Rose to prominence as giddy commedienne on the TV comedy show *Laugh-In*, 1968-70. Films: *Cactus Flower* (Best Supporting Actress AA), 1969; *There's a Girl in My Soup*, 1970; *Butterflies Are Free*, 1971; *The Sugarland Express*, 1974; *Shampoo*, 1975; *Foul Play*, 1978.

HAYDEN, STERLING, born John Hamilton, 1916 (Montclair, N.J.). U.S. actor, novelist. Films: *The Asphalt Jungle*, 1950; *The Killing*, 1956; *Dr.*

235

THE BOOK OF WHO

Strangelove, 1963; *The Godfather,* 1972. Novel: *Voyage,* 1975.

HAYES, GABBY, born George Hayes, May 7, 1885 (Wellesville, N.Y.)–Feb. 9, 1969. U.S. character actor. Appeared in over 200 westerns, 1929–69.

HAYES, HELEN, born Helen Brown, Oct. 10, 1900 (Washington, D.C.). U.S. actress. Considered the first lady of the American stage. Recipient of 1958 Tony award for *Time Remembered* and 1953 Emmy award for best actress. Films: *The Sin of Madelon Claudet,* 1931; *Arrowsmith,* 1931; *A Farewell to Arms,* 1932; *My Son John,* 1951; *Anastasia,* 1956; *Airport* (Best Supporting Actress AA), 1970. (Mother of JAMES MACARTHUR.)

HAYWARD, SUSAN, born Edythe Marrener, June 30, 1919 (Brooklyn, N.Y.)–Mar. 14, 1975. U.S. actress. Films: *Smash-Up,* 1947; *Tap Roots,* 1948; *My Foolish Heart,* 1949; *With a Song in My Heart,* 1952; *I'll Cry Tomorrow,* 1955; *I Want to Live* (Best Actress AA), 1958.

HAYWORTH, RITA, born Margarita Carmen Cansino, Oct. 17, 1918 (New York, N.Y.). U.S. actress, dancer. Films: *Only Angels Have Wings,* 1939; *The Strawberry Blonde,* 1941; *My Gal Sal,* 1942; *Cover Girl,* 1944; *Gilda,* 1946; *The Lady from Shanghai,* 1948; *Miss Sadie Thompson,* 1953; *Pal Joey,* 1957; *Separate Tables,* 1958. (Onetime wife of ORSON WELLES.)

HECKART, EILEEN, Mar. 29, 1919 (Columbus, Ohio). U.S. character actress. Appears chiefly on the stage; received Emmy for *Save Me a Place at Forest Lawn,* 1967.

HEFLIN, VAN, born Emmett Evan Heflin, Dec. 13, 1910 (Walters, Okla.)–July 23, 1971. U.S. actor. Films: *Tap Roots,* 1948; *Shane,* 1953; *Patterns,* 1956; *Airport,* 1969.

HEPBURN, AUDREY, born Audrey Hepburn-Ruston, May 4, 1929 (Brussels, Belg.). U.S. actress. Films: *Roman Holiday* (Best Actress AA), 1953; *Funny Face,* 1957; *Love in the Afternoon,* 1957; *The Nun's Story,* 1959; *Breakfast at Tiffany's,* 1961; *The Children's Hour,* 1962; *Charade,* 1963; *My Fair Lady,* 1964; *Two for the Road,* 1966; *Wait until Dark,* 1967; *Bloodline,* 1979.

HEPBURN, KATHARINE, Nov. 8, 1909 (Hartford, Conn.). U.S. actress. Best known for her leading roles opposite long-time good friend SPENCER TRACY in fast-paced film comedies. Films: *A Bill of Divorcement,* 1932; *Morning Glory* (Best Actress AA), 1933; *Stage Door,* 1937; *Bringing Up Baby,* 1938; *The Philadelphia Story,* 1940; *Woman of the Year,* 1942; *The African Queen,* 1951; *Pat and Mike,* 1952; *The Rainmaker,* 1956; *Long Day's Journey into Night,* 1962; *Guess Who's Coming to Dinner?* (Best Actress AA), 1967; *The Lion in Winter* (Best Actress AA), 1968; *Rooster Cogburn,* 1975.

HESTON, CHARLTON, Oct. 4, 1924 (Evansville, Ill.). U.S. actor. Best known for leading roles in high-budget film spectaculars; pres., Screen Actors Guild, 1966–71. Films: *The Greatest Show on Earth,* 1952; *The Naked Jungle,* 1954; *Ben Hur* (Best Actor AA), 1959; *Major Dundee,* 1965; *The Agony and the Ecstasy,* 1965; *Khartoum,* 1966; *Planet of the Apes,* 1967; *Julius Caesar,* 1970; *The Three Musketeers,* 1973; *Two Minute Warning,* 1976.

HILL, ARTHUR, 1922 (Medfort, Sask., Can.). U.S. actor. Stage: *Who's Afraid of Virginia Woolf* (Best Actor Tony), 1962. TV (series): *Owen Marshall, Counselor at Law,* 1971–74.

HINGLE, PAT, July 19, 1924 (Denver, Colo.). U.S. character actor. Stage: *Cat on a Hot Tin Roof,* 1955; *Dark at the Top of the Stairs,* 1957; *The Odd Couple,* 1966; *The Price,* 1968; *That Championship Season,* 1973. Films: *On the Waterfront,* 1954; *The Ugly American,* 1963.

HIRSCH, JUDD, 1935 (New York, N.Y.). U.S. actor. Star of the TV series *Taxi,* 1978–

HODIAK, JOHN, 1914 (Pittsburgh, Pa.)–Oct. 19, 1955. U.S. actor. Films: *Sunday Dinner for a Soldier,* 1944; *A Bell for Adano,* 1945; *The Harvey Girls,* 1946.

HOFFMAN, DUSTIN, Aug. 8, 1937 (Los Angeles, Calif.). U.S. actor. Films: *The Graduate,* 1967; *Midnight Cowboy,* 1969; *Little Big Man,* 1971; *Straw Dogs,* 1972; *Papillon,* 1973; *Lenny,* 1974; *All the President's Men,* 1975; *Marathon Man,* 1976; *Straight Time,* 1978; *Kramer vs. Kramer,* 1979.

HOLBROOK, HAL, born Harold Rowe Holbrook, Feb. 17, 1925 (Cleveland, Ohio). U.S. actor. Principally a stage and TV actor; received Vernon Rice award, 1959; received Tony award and N.Y. Drama Critics special citation for one-man play *Mark Twain Tonight,* 1966; winner of three Emmy awards.

HOLDEN, WILLIAM, born William Beedle, Apr. 17, 1918 (O'Fallon, Ill.). U.S. actor. Films: *Golden Boy,* 1939; *Born Yesterday,* 1950; *Stalag 17* (Best Actor AA), 1953; *Executive Suite,* 1954; *Love Is a Many Splendored Thing,* 1955; *The Bridge on the River Kwai,* 1957; *The Counterfeit Traitor,* 1962; *The Wild Bunch,* 1969; *Network,* 1976.

HOLLIDAY, JUDY, born Judith Tuvim, 1923 (New York, N.Y.)–June 7, 1965. U.S. actress. Films: *Born Yesterday* (Best Actress AA), 1950; *The Solid Gold Cadillac,* 1956; *Bells Are Ringing,* 1960.

HOLLOWAY, STERLING, 1905 (Cedartown, Ga.). U.S. actor. The voice of many WALT DISNEY characters.

HOLM, CELESTE, Apr. 29, 1919 (New York, N.Y.). U.S. actress. Films: *Gentlemen's Agreement,* (Best Supporting Actress AA), 1947; *Come to the Stable,* 1949; *All about Eve,* 1950.

HOPKINS, MIRIAM, Oct. 18, 1902 (Savannah, Ga.)–1973. U.S. actress. Films: *Becky Sharp,* 1935; *Barbary Coast,* 1935; *Old Acquaintance,* 1943.

HOPPER, DENNIS, May 17, 1936 (Dodge City, Kan.). U.S. actor, director. Best known for his role in the film *Easy Rider,* 1969.

HORTON, EDWARD EVERETT, 1888 (Brooklyn, N.Y.)–Sept. 29, 1970. U.S. comedic actor in numerous films since 1922. Films: *Holiday,* 1930; *Trouble in Paradise,* 1932; *Alice in Wonderland,* 1933; *The Gay Divorcee,* 1935; *Here Comes Mr. Jordan,* 1941; *Pocketful of Miracles,* 1961.

HOUSEMAN, JOHN, born Jacques Haussman, Sept. 22, 1902 (Bucharest, Rum.). U.S. actor, producer, director. Has produced plays and films since 1934; as actor, starred in the 1974 film *The Paper Chase* (Best Supporting Actor AA), as well as the TV series of the same name (1978–79).

HOWARD, KEN, Mar. 28, 1944 (El Centro, Calif.). U.S. actor. Received Tony award for *Child Play,* 1970; star of the TV series *The White Shadow,* 1978–

HOWARD, RON, Mar. 1, 1954 (Duncan, Okla.). U.S. actor. Began as a child actor in TV series *The Andy Griffith Show,* 1960–68; star of TV series

ENTERTAINERS

Happy Days, 1974– . Films: *American Graffiti,* 1974; *The Shootist,* 1976.

HUDSON, ROCK, born Roy Fitzgerald, Nov. 17, 1925 (Winnetka, Ill.). U.S. actor. Films: *Magnificent Obsession,* 1954; *Giant,* 1956; *Written on the Wind,* 1956; *A Farewell to Arms,* 1957; *Pillow Talk,* 1959; *Seconds,* 1966; *Ice Station Zebra,* 1968; *Darling Lili,* 1969. TV: *McMillan and Wife* (series), 1971–77.

HULL, JOSEPHINE, born Josephine Sherwood, Jan. 3, 1886 (Newtonville, Mass.)–Mar. 12, 1957. U.S. actress. Best known for her stage work. Films: *Arsenic and Old Lace,* 1944; *Harvey* (Best Supporting Actress AA), 1950.

HUNNICUT, GAYLE, Feb. 6, 1943 (Ft. Worth, Tex.). U.S. actress. Leading lady in 1960s–70s films. Films: *Eye of the Cat,* 1969; *Legend of Hell House,* 1973; *The Sellout,* 1976.

HUNTER, JEFFREY, born Henry H. McKinnies, Nov. 25, 1925 (New Orleans, La.)–May 27, 1969. U.S. actor, popular in 1950s and 1960s films, including *King of Kings* (1961).

HUNTER, KIM, born Janet Cole, Nov. 12, 1922 (Detroit, Mich.). U.S. actress. Films: *A Streetcar Named Desire* (Best Supporting Actress AA), 1951; *Planet of the Apes* series, 1974.

HUNTER, TAB, born Art Gelien, July 11, 1931 (New York, N.Y.). U.S. actor. A teenage favorite in 1950s films. Films: *Track of the Cat,* 1954; *Damn Yankees,* 1958; *The Pleasure of his Company,* 1960; *Judge Roy Bean,* 1972.

HUSSEY, RUTH, born Ruth Carol O'Rourke, Oct. 30, 1917 (Providence, R.I.). U.S. actress. A leading lady in 1940s films. Films: *Fast and Furious,* 1939; *The Philadelphia Story,* 1940; *H.M. Pulham Esq.,* 1941.

HUTTON, BETTY, born Betty Jane Thornburg, Feb. 26, 1921 (Battle Creek, Mich.). U.S. singer, dancer, actress. Films: *Incendiary Blonde,* 1943; *Red Hot and Blue,* 1949; *Annie Get Your Gun,*1950.

INGRAM, REX, 1895 (Cairo, Ill.)–Sept. 19, 1969. U.S. actor. Films: *The Emperor Jones,* 1933; *Green Pastures,* 1936; *Cabin in the Sky,* 1943.

IVES, BURL, born Burl Icle Ivanhoe, June 14, 1909 (Hull, Ill.). U.S. folk singer, character actor. Films: *Cat on a Hot Tin Roof,* 1957; *The Big Country* (Best Supporting Actor AA), 1959. TV: *The Bold Ones* (series), 1970–72.

JACKSON, ANNE, Sept. 3, 1936 (Allegheny, Pa.). U.S. actress. Principally a stage actress, often playing opposite husband ELI WALLACH. Plays: *Luv,* 1964; *The Waltz of the Toreadors,* 1973. Films: *The Secret Life of an American Wife,* 1968; *Lovers and Other Strangers,* 1970.

JACKSON, KATE, Oct. 29, 1949 (Birmingham, Ala.). U.S. actress. TV: *Dark Shadows* (series), 1966–71; *The Rookies* (series), 1972–76; *Charlie's Angels* (series), 1976–79.

JAFFE, SAM, Mar. 10, 1891 (New York, N.Y.). U.S. character actor. Stage actor since 1916, in films since 1933. Films: *Lost Horizon,* 1937; *Gunga Din,* 1939. TV: *Ben Casey* (series), 1960–64.

JAGGER, DEAN, born Dean Jeffries, Nov. 7, 1905 (Columbus Grove, Ohio). U.S. character actor. Films: *Brigham Young,* 1940; *Twelve O'Clock High,* 1949; *Executive Suite,* 1954; *Elmer Gantry,* 1960. TV: *Mr. Novak* (series), 1963–65.

JANSSEN, DAVID, born David Meyer, Mar. 27, 1930 (Naponee, Neb.)–Feb. 13, 1980. U.S. actor. TV: *Richard Diamond* (series), 1957–60; *The Fugitive* (series), 1963–67; *Harry-O* (series), 1974–76.

JEFFREYS, ANNE, 1923 (Goldsboro, N.C.). U.S. actress. A leading lady in 1940s films; star of the TV series *Topper,* 1953–56.

JOHNSON, VAN, Aug. 20, 1916 (Newport, R.I.). U.S. actor. Films: *A Guy Named Joe,* 1943; *Thirty Seconds over Tokyo,* 1944; *Weekend at the Waldorf,* 1945; *High Barbaree,* 1946; *Battleground,* 1950; *The Caine Mutiny,* 1954; *The Last Time I Saw Paris,* 1955; *Miracle in the Rain,* 1956.

JONES, BUCK, born Charles Gebhardt, 1889 (Vincennes, Ind.)–Nov. 30, 1942. U.S. actor. Known for film westerns such as *Straight from the Shoulder* (1920), *The Lone Rider* (1930), *When a Man Sees Red* (1934), and *Riders of Death Valley* (1941); died in fire at Boston's Coconut Grove nightclub.

JONES, CAROLYN, Apr. 28, 1933 (Amarillo, Tex.). U.S. actress. Starred in the TV series *The Addams Family,* 1964–66.

JONES, DEAN, Jan. 25, 1935 (Morgan Co., Ala). U.S. actor. Films: *Under the Yum-Yum Tree,* 1964; *The Love Bug,* 1969.

JONES, JAMES EARL, Jan. 17, 1931 (Tate Co., Miss.). U.S. actor. Noted for stage roles, he received 1969 Tony award for his work in *The Great White Hope.* Films: *The Great White Hope,* 1970; *Claudine,* 1973; *Swashbuckler,* 1976; *The Greatest,* 1977.

JONES, JENNIFER, born Phyllis Isley, Mar. 2, 1919 (Tulsa, Okla.). U.S. actress. Films: *The Song of Bernadette* (Best Actress AA), 1943; *Love Letters,* 1945; *Duel in the Sun,* 1946; *Portrait of Jennie,* 1948; *Carrie,* 1951; *Love is a Many Splendored Thing,* 1955; *A Farewell to Arms,* 1958. (One-time wife of DAVID O. SELZNICK and ROBERT WALKER.)

KAHN, MADELINE, Sept. 29, 1942 (Boston, Mass.). U.S. comedic actress. Films: *Paper Moon,* 1973; *Blazing Saddles,* 1974; *Young Frankenstein,* 1975; *High Anxiety,* 1977; *The Cheap Detective,* 1978.

KAYE, DANNY, born David Daniel Kaminsky, Jan. 18, 1913 (New York, N.Y.). U.S. actor, comedian. Received special AA, for service to the industry and the American people, 1954; received Emmy award, 1963; received Peabody Award, 1963. Films: *Up in Arms,* 1944; *The Secret Life of Walter Mitty,* 1947; *Hans Christian Anderson,* 1952; *Knock on Wood,* 1953; *Merry Andrew,* 1958.

KEACH, STACY, June 2, 1941 (Savannah, Ga.). U.S. actor. Received a 1967 Obie award and the 1967 Vernon Rice award for his work on stage. Films: *The Heart Is a Lonely Hunter,* 1968; *The New Centurions,* 1972.

KEATON, DIANE, 1949 (Santa Ana, Calif.). U.S. actress. Films: *Play It Again Sam,* 1972; *The Godfather—Part I,* 1972; *The Godfather—Part 2,* 1974; *Love and Death,* 1975; *Annie Hall* (Best Actress AA), 1977; *Looking for Mr. Goodbar,* 1977; *Interiors,* 1978; *Manhattan,* 1979.

KEEL, HOWARD, born Harold Keel, Apr. 13, 1919 (Gillespie, Ill.). U.S. actor. Virile leading man in musical comedy films of the 1950s. Films: *Annie Get Your Gun,* 1950; *Showboat,* 1951; *Calamity Jane,* 1953; *Kiss Me, Kate,* 1953; *Seven Brides for Seven Brothers,* 1954.

KEITEL, HARVEY, 1947 (New York, N.Y.). U.S. actor. Films: *Alice Doesn't Live Here Anymore,* 1975; *Taxi Driver,* 1976; *Welcome to L.A.,* 1977; *The Duelists,* 1978.

KEITH, BRIAN, born Robert Keith, Jr., Nov. 14,

THE BOOK OF WHO

1921 (Bayonne, N.J.). U.S. actor. Best known as star of the TV series *Family Affair*, 1966–71.

KELLERMAN, SALLY, June 2, 1937 (Long Beach, Calif.). U.S. actress. Films: *M*A*S*H*,* 1969; *Last of the Red Hot Lovers,* 1972; *The Big Bus,* 1976.

KELLY, GRACE (Princess Grace of Monaco), Nov. 12, 1929 (Philadelphia, Pa.). U.S. actress. Retired from career to marry Prince Rainier of Monaco, Apr. 19, 1956. Films: *High Noon,* 1952; *Dial M for Murder,* 1954; *Rear Window,* 1954; *The Country Girl* (Best Actress AA), 1954; *High Society,* 1956.

KELLY, PATSY, born Sarah Veronica Rose Kelly, Jan. 12, 1910 (Brooklyn, N.Y.). U.S. comedic actress. Appeared in many films in the 1930s and 1940s. TV: *Valentine's Day* (series), 1964. Play: *No, No, Nanette* (Tony award), 1971.

KENDALL, KAY, born Justine McCarthy, 1926–Sept. 6, 1959. British actress. Films: *Les Girls,* 1957; *The Reluctant Debutante,* 1958. (One-time wife of REX HARRISON.)

KENNEDY, ARTHUR, Feb. 17, 1914 (Worcester, Mass.). U.S. actor. Films: *Champion,* 1949; *The Glass Menagerie,* 1950; *Peyton Place,* 1957; *Lawrence of Arabia,* 1962.

KERR, JOHN, Nov. 15, 1931 (New York, N.Y.). U.S. actor, lawyer. Films: *Tea and Sympathy,* 1956; *South Pacific,* 1958.

KERT, LARRY, born Frederick Lawrence Kert, Dec. 5, 1930 (Los Angeles, Calif.). U.S. actor/singer. Musical comedy performer on Broadway and in touring productions. Plays: *West Side Story,* 1957; *I Can Get It For You Wholesale,* 1962; *Company,* 1970; *Side by Side by Sondheim,* 1977.

KEYES, EVELYN, 1925 (Port Arthur, Tex.). U.S. actress, dancer. Appeared in 1940s films, including *The Jolson Story* (1946); wrote autobiography titled *Scarlett O'Hara's Younger Sister,* 1977. (One-time wife of JOHN HUSTON and ARTIE SHAW.)

KILEY, RICHARD, Mar. 21, 1922 (Chicago, Ill.). U.S. actor, singer. Plays: *Redhead,* (Tony award), 1958; *The Man of La Mancha* (Tony award), 1966.

KIRBY, DURWOOD, Aug. 24, 1912 (Covington, Ky.). U.S. radio and TV announcer, comedic actor. Associated with GARRY MOORE, 1940s–70s.

KLEMPERER, WERNER, Mar. 22, 1920 (Cologne, Ger.). U.S. actor. Best known for role in the TV series *Hogan's Heroes,* 1965–71. (Son of OTTO KLEMPERER.)

KLUGMAN, JACK, Apr. 27, 1922 (Philadelphia, Pa.). U.S. actor. Character actor in many films, including *Twelve Angry Men* (1957); starred in the TV series *Harris against the World* (1964–65), *The Odd Couple,* (1970–75), and *Quincy,* (1976–   ); winner of Emmy awards in 1963, 1971, and 1973.

KNIGHT, TED, born Tadeus Wladyslaw Konopka, Dec. 7, 1923 (Terryville, Conn.). U.S. comedic actor. Best known for role as Ted Baxter in the TV series *Mary Tyler Moore Show,* 1970–77.

KRISTOFFERSON, KRIS, June 22, 1936 (Brownsville, Tex.). U.S. actor, singer, songwriter. Films: *Alice Doesn't Live Here Anymore,* 1974; *A Star Is Born,* 1976; *Semi-Tough,* 1977. Musical compositions: "Sunday Morning Comin' Down," "Help Me Make It through the Night," "Me and Bobby McGee," "For the Good Times."

KRUGER, OTTO, Sept. 6, 1885 (Toledo, Oh.)–Sept. 6, 1974. U.S. actor. Appeared in over 100 films. Films: *Chained,* 1934; *Dracula's Daughter,*

1936; *The Housemaster,* 1938; *Saboteur,* 1942; *Murder, My Sweet,* 1944.

LADD, ALAN, Sept. 3, 1913 (Hot Springs, Ark.)–Jan. 29, 1964. U.S. actor. Films: *This Gun for Hire,* 1942; *The Glass Key,* 1942; *Salty O'Rourke,* 1945; *Two Years before the Mast,* 1946; *The Great Gatsby,* 1949; *Shane,* 1953; *The Carpetbaggers,* 1964.

LADD, CHERYL, née Stoppelmoor, July 2, 1951 (Huron, S. D.). U.S. actress, singer. Best known for role on TV series *Charlie's Angels,* 1977–   .

LAKE, VERONICA, born Constance Ockleman, Nov. 14, 1919 (Lake Placid, N.Y.)–July 7, 1973. U.S. actress. A leading lady in 1940s films; her long, straight hairstyle set a national trend. Films: *I Wanted Wings,* 1941; *This Gun for Hire,* 1942; *I Married a Witch,* 1942; *The Blue Dahlia,* 1946.

LAMARR, HEDY, born Hedwig Kiesler, 1915 (Vienna, Austria). Austrian-U.S. actress. A 1930s sex symbol. Films: *Ecstasy,* 1933; *Algiers,* 1938; *Ziegfeld Girl,* 1941; *White Cargo,* 1942; *Samson and Delilah,* 1949; *My Favorite Spy,* 1951.

LAMOUR, DOROTHY, born Dorothy Kaumeyer, Oct. 10, 1914 (New Orleans, La.). U.S. actress. A leading lady in 1930s and 1940s films; known for "Road" films with BING CROSBY and BOB HOPE.

LANCASTER, BURT, Nov. 2, 1913 (New York, N.Y.). U.S. actor. Known for lead roles as athletic, tough hero. Films: *The Killers,* 1946; *Sorry Wrong Number,* 1948; *From Here to Eternity,* 1953; *The Rainmaker,* 1957; *Gunfight at the OK Corral,* 1957; *Separate Tables,* 1958; *Elmer Gantry* (Best Actor AA), 1960; *Judgment at Nuremberg,* 1961; *Birdman of Alcatraz,* 1962; *Airport,* 1969; *Scorpio,* 1973.

LANDAU, MARTIN, 1934 (New York, N.Y.). U.S. actor. Star of the TV series *Mission Impossible,* (1966–69) and *Space 1999* (1977–   ). (Husband of BARBARA BAIN.)

LANDON, MICHAEL, born Eugene Maurice Orowitz, Oct. 21, 1937 (New York, N.Y.). U.S. actor. Star of the TV series *Bonanza* (1959–72; star, director, exec. producer, writer of the TV series) and *Little House on the Prairie* (1974–   ).

LANGE, HOPE, Nov. 28, 1933 (Redding Ridge, Conn.). U.S. actress. Films: *Bus Stop,* 1956; *Peyton Place,* 1957; *A Pocketful of Miracles,* 1961. TV: *The Ghost and Mrs. Muir* (series), 1968–70; *The New Dick Van Dyke Show* (series), 1971–74. (One-time wife of DON MURRAY.)

LANGELLA, FRANK, Jan. 1, 1946 (Bayonne, N.J.). U.S. actor. Films: *Diary of a Mad Housewife,* 1970; *The Twelve Chairs,* 1970; *Dracula,* 1979. Plays: *Seascape* (Tony award), 1975; *Dracula,* 1977.

LANSBURY, ANGELA, Oct. 16, 1925 (London, Eng.). English-U.S. actress. Star of several Broadway musicals including *Dear World* (1969), *Mame* (1972), *Gypsy* (1973), *Sweeney Todd* (1979); won Tony awards in 1966, 1969, 1979.

LASSER, LOUISE, 1941 (New York, N.Y.). U.S. actress. Best known as star of TV series *Mary Hartman, Mary Hartman,* 1976. Films: *What's New Pussycat?,* 1965; *Take the Money and Run,* 1969; *Bananas,* 1971. (One-time wife of WOODY ALLEN.)

LAVIN, LINDA, Oct. 15, 1937 (Portland, Maine). U.S. actress. Star of the TV series *Alice,* 1976–   .

LEACHMAN, CLORIS, 1926 (Des Moines, Ia.). U.S. actress. Films: *The Last Picture Show* (Supporting Actress AA), 1971; *Young Frankenstein,*

1976; *High Anxiety,* 1978. TV: *Mary Tyler Moore Show* (series), 1970–75; *Phyllis* (series), 1975–77. Has won four Emmy awards.

LEARNED, MICHAEL, Apr. 9, 1939 (Washington, D.C.). U.S. actress. Star of the TV series *The Waltons* (1972–   ), for which she won Emmy awards in 1973, 1974, and 1976.

LEIGH, JANET, born Jeanette Morrison, July 6, 1927 (Merced, Calif.). U.S. actress. Films: *The Romance of Rosy Ridge,* 1947; *Houdini,* 1953; *Prince Valiant,* 1954; *My Sister Eileen,* 1955; *The Vikings,* 1958; *Psycho,* 1960; *Harper,* 1966. (One-time wife of TONY CURTIS.)

LEMMON, JACK, Feb. 8, 1925 (Boston, Mass.). U.S. actor. Light-comedy leading actor. Films: *Mister Roberts* (Best Supporting Actor AA), 1955; *Some Like It Hot,* 1959; *The Apartment,* 1960; *The Great Race,* 1965; *The Odd Couple,* 1968; *The Out-of-Towners,* 1969; *Save the Tiger* (Best Actor AA), 1973; *The Entertainer,* 1975; *Airport '77,* 1977.

LEONTOVICH, EUGENIE, Mar. 21, 1894 (Moscow, Rus.). Russian-U.S. actress, dramatic coach. Stage career from 1922. Plays: *Grand Hotel,* 1930–32; *Twentieth Century,* 1932; *Tovarich,* 1935, 1937–38; *Anastasia,* 1954. Founder of the Actors' Workshop, Los Angeles (1953) and New York City (1973).

LESLIE, JOAN, born Joan Brodell, Jan. 26, 1925 (Detroit, Mich.). U.S. actress. Films: *Sergeant York,* 1941; *Yankee Doodle Dandy,* 1942; *Rhapsody in Blue,* 1945.

LEVANT, OSCAR, Dec. 27, 1906 (Pittsburgh, Pa.)–Aug. 14, 1972. U.S. concert pianist, comedic actor. Films: *Rhapsody in Blue,* 1945; *You Were Meant for Me,* 1947; *The Barclays of Broadway,* 1949; *An American in Paris,* 1951; *The Band Wagon,* 1953. Autobiographies: *A Smattering of Ignorance* (1944) and *Memoirs of an Amnesiac* (1965).

LEVENE, SAM(uel), Aug. 28, 1905 (Russia). U.S. stage and film actor. Films: *Three Men on a Horse,* 1936; *Crossfire,* 1947; *Boomerang,* 1947; *Such Good Friends,* 1971.

LINDEN, HAL, born Harold Lipshitz, Mar. 20, 1931 (New York, N.Y.). U.S. singer, actor. Star of the TV series *Barney Miller,* 1975–   ; won 1971 Tony award for his work in the play *The Rothschilds.*

LINDSAY, MARGARET, born Margaret Kies, 1910 (Dubuque, Ia.). U.S. actress. Films: *West of Singapore,* 1932; *The House of the Seven Gables,* 1940; *No Place for a Lady,* 1943; *Emergency Hospital,* 1956; *Tammy and the Doctor,* 1963.

LITTLE, CLEAVON, June 1, 1939 (Chickasha, Okla.). U.S. actor. Plays: *Purlie* (Tony award), 1970. Films: *Blazing Saddles,* 1974, *Greased Lightning,* 1977.

LIVINGSTONE, MARY, 1909 (Seattle, Wash.). U.S. actress. Wife of JACK BENNY, she appeared on his radio and TV programs, 1930s–65.

LOCKHART, JUNE, June 25, 1925 (New York, N.Y.). U.S. actress. Best known as star of the TV series *Lassie* (1958–64) and *Lost in Space,* (1965–68).

LOMBARD, CAROLE, born Jane Peters, 1909 (Ft. Wayne, Ind.)–Jan. 16, 1942. U.S. actress. Best known for her roles in "screwball" film comedies of the 1930s. Films: *No Man of Her Own,* 1932; *My Man Godfrey,* 1936; *They Knew What They Wanted,* 1940. (One-time wife of CLARK GABLE.)

LONDON, JULIE, born Julie Peck, Sept. 26, 1926 (Santa Rosa, Calif.). U.S. actress, singer. Best known as a star of the TV series *Emergency,*

1972–77; also did several films. (One-time wife of JACK WEBB.)

LORD, JACK, born John Joseph Ryan, Dec. 30, 1930? (New York, N.Y.). U.S. actor. Best known as star of the TV series *Stony Burke* (1962–63) and *Hawaii Five-O* (1968–   ).

LORNE, MARION, born Marion MacDougal, Aug. 12, 1888 (Pennsylvania)–May 9, 1968. U.S. character actress. Best known for the TV series *Bewitched,* 1964–68.

LOUDON, DOROTHY, Sept. 17, 1933 (Boston, Mass.). U.S. actress, singer. Principally as stage actress; received Tony award for her role in *Annie,* 1977.

LOUISE, ANITA, born A. L. Fremault, 1917 (New York, N.Y.)–Apr. 25, 1970. U.S. actress. A leading lady in 1930s and 1940s films; star of the TV series *My Friend Flicka,* 1956–58.

LOWE, EDMUND, Mar. 3, 1892 (San Jose, Calif.)–1971. U.S. actor. Films: *What Price Glory?,* 1926; *In Old Arizona,* 1929; *Dinner at Eight,* 1933.

LOY, MYRNA, born Myrna Williams, Aug. 2, 1905 (Helena, Mont.). U.S. actress. Films: "The Thin Man" series of the 1930s–40s; *The Rains Came,* 1939; *The Best Years of Our Lives,* 1946; *Mr. Blandings Builds His Dream House,* 1948; *Cheaper by the Dozen,* 1950.

LUCKINBILL, LAURENCE GEORGE, Nov. 21, 1934 (Ft. Smith, Ark.). U.S. actor. Has appeared in numerous Broadway plays and TV dramas. TV: *The Delphi Bureau* (series), 1972–73. Stage: *A Man for All Seasons,* 1963; *The Boys in the Band,* 1968; *The Shadow Box,* 1975.

LUGOSI, BELA, born B. L. Blasko, Oct. 20, 1884 (Lugos, Hung.)–Aug. 16, 1956. Hungarian-U.S. actor. Best known for horror films, especially *Dracula* (1930). Other films: *Island of Lost Souls,* 1933; *The Black Cat,* 1934; *The Raven,* 1935; *Son of Frankenstein,* 1939; *Frankenstein Meets the Wolf Man,* 1943; *The Body Snatcher,* 1945.

LUKAS, PAUL, May 26, 1891 (Budapest, Hung.)–Aug. 15, 1971. Hungarian-U.S. actor. Films: *Little Women,* 1933; *Dodsworth,* 1936; *Watch on the Rhine* (Best Actor AA), 1943.

LUKE, KEYE, 1904 (Canton, China). Chinese-U.S. actor. Popular in 1930s films as Charlie Chan's No. 2 son; appeared in the TV series *Kung Fu,* 1972–75.

LUNT, ALFRED, Aug. 19, 1892 (Milwaukee, Wisc.)–Aug. 3, 1977. U.S. actor. Known for stage performances for over 40 years; appeared with wife LYNN FONTANNE in 27 Broadway plays; films include *The Guardsman* (1931).

LYNLEY, CAROL, Feb. 13, 1942 (New York, N.Y.). U.S. actress. Films: *Blue Denim,* 1959; *The Cardinal,* 1963; *Bunny Lake Is Missing,* 1965.

LYON, BEN, Feb. 6, 1901 (Atlanta, Ga.)–Mar. 22, 1979. U.S. actor, executive. Dashing leading man in 72 films of the 1920s–30s; as talent dir. for Twentieth-Century-Fox in the 1940s, credited with discovering MARILYN MONROE.

MACARTHUR, JAMES, Dec. 8, 1937 (Los Angeles, Calif.). U.S. actor. Appeared in many WALT DISNEY movies; best known as costar of the TV series *Hawaii Five-0,* 1968–   . (Son of HELEN HAYES.)

MACGRAW, ALI, Apr. 1, 1939 (Pound Ridge, N.Y.). U.S. model, actress. Films: *Goodby Columbus,* 1969; *Love Story,* 1971; *Players,* 1978. (One-time wife of Robert Evans, STEVE MCQUEEN.)

MACLAINE, SHIRLEY, born Shirley Beaty, Apr.

24, 1934 (Richmond, Va.). U.S. dancer, actress, author. Plays: *Pajama Game*, 1954. Films: *Can-Can*, 1959; *The Apartment*, 1959; *Irma La Douce*, 1963; *Sweet Charity*, 1968; *The Turning Point*, 1977. Books: *Don't Fall off the Mountain*, 1970; *You Can Get There from Here*, 1975. (Sister of WARREN BEATTY.)

MACMURRAY, FRED(erick) **MARTIN**, Aug. 30, 1908 (Kankakee, Ill.). U.S. actor. A leading man in films from the late 1930s to the 1960s. Films: *The Trail of the Lonesome Pine*, 1936; *Double Indemnity*, 1944; *The Caine Mutiny*, 1954; *The Shaggy Dog*, 1959; *The Absent-Minded Professor*, 1961. TV: *My Three Sons* (series), 1960-72.

MACRAE, GORDON, Mar. 12, 1921 (E. Orange, N.J.). U.S. singer, actor. Films: *The Daughter of Rosie O'Grady*, 1950; *West Point Story*, 1951; *By the Light of the Silvery Moon*, 1953; *Oklahoma*, 1955; *Carousel*, 1956. (One-time husband of SHEILA MACRAE; father of MEREDITH MACRAE.)

MACRAE, MEREDITH, 1945 (Houston, Tex.). U.S. actress. Star of the TV series *Petticoat Junction*, 1966-70. (Daughter of GORDON and SHEILA MACRAE.)

MACRAE, SHEILA, née Stephens, Sept. 24, 1924 (London, Eng.). U.S entertainer, singer, radio actress. (One-time wife of GORDON MACRAE; mother of MEREDITH MACRAE.)

MACY, BILL, born William Macy Garber, May 18, 1922 (Revere, Mass.). U.S. actor. Numerous Broadway stage appearances, 1958-71. Films: *The Late Show*, 1977. TV: *Maude* (series), 1972-78.

MAIN, MARJORIE, Feb. 24, 1890 (Acton, Ia.)-Apr. 10, 1975. U.S. actress. Films: *The Women*, 1939; *Meet Me in St. Louis*, 1944; *The Harvey Girls*, 1945; *The Egg and I*, 1947; "*Ma and Pa Kettle*" series, 1949-56.

MAJORS, LEE, Apr. 23, 1940 (Wyandotte, Mich.). U.S. actor. Starred in the TV series *The Big Valley* (1965-69), and *The Six Million Dollar Man* (1974-78). (One-time husband of FARRAH FAWCETT.)

MALDEN, KARL, born Malden Sekulovich, Mar. 22, 1913 (Chicago, Ill.). U.S. actor. Plays: *Golden Boy*, 1938; *A Streetcar Named Desire*, 1950; Films: *A Streetcar Named Desire* (Best Supporting Actor AA), 1952; *On the Waterfront*, 1954. TV: *Streets of San Francisco* (series), 1972-77.

MALONE, DOROTHY, June 30, 1925 (Chicago, Ill.). U.S. actress. Films: *Written on the Wind*, (Best Supporting Actress AA) 1956; *Too Much Too Soon*, 1958. TV: *Peyton Place*, (series), 1964-69.

MANSFIELD, JAYNE, born Vera Jane Palmer, Apr. 19, 1932 (Bryn Mawr, Pa.)-June 29, 1967. U.S. actress. Films: *Will Success Spoil Rock Hunter?* 1957; *The Wayward Bus*, 1957.

MANSFIELD, RICHARD, May 24, 1854 (Helgoland, Ger.)-Aug. 30, 1907. U.S. actor. Noted both as a tragedian and comedian; played H. IBSEN and G. B. SHAW roles; most famous for his performances as Beau Brummell and Cyrano.

MARCH, FREDRIC, born Frederic McIntyre Bickel, Aug. 31, 1897 (Racine, Wisc.)-Apr. 14, 1975. U.S. actor. A leading man in stage and film dramas, 1930s-1960s. Plays: *The Royal Family*, 1930; *The Skin of Our Teeth*, 1944; *Long Day's Journey into Night* (Tony award), 1956. Films: *Dr. Jekyll and Mr Hyde* (Best Actor AA), 1932; *Death Takes a Holiday*, 1934; *Les Miserables*, 1935; *A Star Is Born*, 1937; *The Best Years of Our Lives* (Best Actor AA), 1944; *Inherit the Wind*, 1960; *Seven Days in May*, 1964.

MARGO, born Maria Marguerita Guadelupe Boldao y Castilla, May 10, 1918 (Mexico City, Mex.). Mexican-U.S. actress, dancer. Films: *Lost Horizon*, 1937; *Behind the Rising Sun*, 1963. (Wife of EDDIE ALBERT.)

MARGOLIN, JANET, 1943 (New York, N.Y.). U.S. actress. Best known for her roles in the films *David and Lisa* (1962) and *Take the Money and Run* (1970).

MARLOWE, HUGH, born Hugh Hipple, 1914 (Philadelphia, Pa.). U.S. actor. Films: *Meet Me in St. Louis*, 1944; *Twelve O'Clock High*, 1950; *All about Eve*, 1950; *Earth versus Flying Saucers*, 1956.

MARSHALL, E(verett) **G.**, June 18, 1910 (Owatonna, Minn.). U.S. actor. Plays: *The Iceman Cometh*, 1946; *Waiting for Godot*, 1956; *The Gin Game*, 1978. Films: *12 Angry Men*, 1957; *The Bachelor Party*, 1957. TV: *The Defenders* (series), 1961-65; *The Bold Ones* (series), 1969-73.

MARSHALL, PENNY, Oct. 15, 1943 (New York, N.Y.). U.S. actress. Regular appearances on the TV series *The Odd Couple*, 1972-74; star of the TV series *Laverne and Shirley*, 1976- . (Wife of ROB REINER.)

MARSHALL, TULLY, born William Phillips, Apr. 13, 1864 (Nevada City, Calif.)-1943. U.S. silent-film actor. Films: *Intolerance*, 1915; *Oliver Twist*, 1916; *The Hunchback of Notre Dame*, 1923; *The Merry Widow*, 1925; *The Red Mill*. 1929.

MARTIN, DEAN, June 17, 1917 (Steubenville, Ohio). U.S. actor, singer, entertainer. Comedy act with JERRY LEWIS, 1946-56; TV host for celebrity "roasts," 1970s. Films: *The Young Lions*, 1958; *Bells Are Ringing*, 1960; *Robin and the Seven Hoods*, 1964; *Kiss Me, Stupid*, 1964; *Sons of Katie Elder*, 1965; *The Silencers*, 1966. TV: *The Dean Martin Show*, 1965-74.

MARTIN, MARY, Dec. 1, 1913 (Weatherford, Tex.). U.S. actress, singer. Principally a stage actress in musicals, best known for her performance in *Peter Pan*, 1954-56 (on stage and TV). Other plays: *Leave It to Me*, 1938; *South Pacific*, 1949; *The Skin of Our Teeth*, 1955; *The Sound of Music*, 1959; *Hello Dolly*, 1965; *I Do, I Do*, 1968; *Do You Turn Somersaults?* 1977. Autobiography: *My Heart Belongs*, 1976. (Mother of LARRY HAGMAN.)

MARTIN, ROSS, born Martin Rosenblatt, Mar. 22, 1920 (Grodek, Pol.). U.S. actor. Best known for his role as Artemis Gordon on the TV series *Wild, Wild West*, 1965-70.

MARTIN, STROTHER, 1920 (Kokomo, Ind.). U.S. actor. Best known for roles in film westerns, including *True Grit* (1969) and *Butch Cassidy and the Sundance Kid* (1969).

MARVIN, LEE, Feb. 19, 1924 (New York, N.Y.). U.S. actor. Films: *Attack*, 1957; *The Man Who Shot Liberty Valance*, 1962; *The Killers*, 1964; *Cat Ballou* (AA Best Actor), 1965; *The Dirty Dozen*, 1967; *Paint Your Wagon*, 1969; *The Iceman Cometh*, 1973. TV: *M Squad* (series), 1958-60. Involved in landmark "palimony" case, 1979.

MASON, MARSHA, Apr. 3, 1942 (St. Louis, Mo.). U.S. actress. Films: *Cinderella Liberty*, 1974; *The Goodbye Girl*, 1977; *Chapter Two*, 1979. (Wife of playwright NEIL SIMON.)

MASSEY, RAYMOND, Aug. 30, 1896 (Toronto, Ont., Can.). Canadian-U.S. actor, director. Plays: *Saint Joan*, 1929; *Idiot's Delight*, 1938; *Abe Lincoln in Illinois*, 1938. Films: *The Scarlet Pimpernel*, 1934; *The Prisoner of Zenda*, 1937; *Arsenic* *and Old Lace,* 1944; *East of Eden,* 1955. TV: *Dr. Kildare* (series), 1961-66.

MATTHAU, WALTER, Oct. 1, 1920 (New York, N.Y.). U.S. actor. Films: *A Face in the Crowd,* 1957; *Charade,* 1963; *The Fortune Cookie,* (Best Supporting Actor AA), 1966; *A Guide for the Married Man,* 1967; *The Odd Couple,* 1968; *Hello Dolly,* 1969; *Pete 'n' Tillie,* 1972; *The Bad News Bears,* 1975; *The Sunshine Boys,* 1975; *House Calls,* 1978.

MATURE, VICTOR, Jan. 29, 1916 (Louisville, Ky.). U.S. actor. Known for well-developed pectoral muscles. Films: *My Darling Clementine,* 1946; *Samson and Delilah,* 1949; *The Robe,* 1953.

MAY, ELAINE, Apr. 21, 1932 (Philadelphia, Pa.). U.S. entertainer. Improvisational comic act with MIKE NICHOLS, 1955-62; screenwriter and dir. of *A New Leaf* (1972) and *The Heartbreak Kid* (1973).

MAYO, VIRGINIA, born Virginia Jones, 1920 (St. Louis, Mo.). U.S. actress. A leading lady in 1940s and 1950s films, including *The Princess and the Pirate* (1944) and *The Secret Life of Walter Mitty* (1947).

MCARDLE, ANDREA, Nov. 4, 1963 (Philadelphia, Pa.). U.S. actress. The original Annie in the musical *Annie,* 1976.

MCCAMBRIDGE, MERCEDES, Mar. 17, 1918 (Joliet, Ill.). U.S. actress. Films: *All the King's Men* (Best Supporting Actress AA), 1950; *Giant,* 1956; *The Exorcist* (as the voice of the devil), 1973.

MCCARTHY, KEVIN, 1915 (Seattle, Wash.). U.S. actor. Stage performances include *Death of a Salesman,* 1952; starred in the 1956 film *Invasion of the Body Snatchers,* and had a cameo role in 1978 remake; frequent guest star on TV shows. (Brother of MARY MCCARTHY.)

MCCLURE, DOUG(las), May 11, 1938 (Glendale, Calif.). U.S. actor. Star of the TV series *Checkmate* (1960-62) and *The Virginian* (1962-71).

MCCORD, KENT, 1942 (Los Angeles, Calif.). U.S. actor. Costarred in the TV series *Adam-12,* 1968-75.

MCCREA, JOEL, Nov. 5, 1905 (Los Angeles, Calif.). U.S. actor. A leading man in action-adventure films of the 1930s and 1940s. Films: *The Most Dangerous Game,* 1932; *Barbary Coast,* 1935; *Dead End,* 1937; *Union Pacific,* 1939; *Foreign Correspondent,* 1940; *The Palm Beach Story,* 1942.

MCDANIEL, HATTIE, 1895 (Wichita, Kan.)-Oct. 26, 1952. U.S. actress. Film career, 1933-52; won Best Supporting Actress AA for her role in *Gone with the Wind,* 1939; a former radio singer.

MCFARLAND, GEORGE EMMETT ("Spanky"), 1928 (Dallas, Tex.). U.S. actor. Child actor, best known as the fat boy in the "Our Gang" film comedy series.

MCGAVIN, DARREN, May 7, 1922 (Spokane, Wash.). U.S. actor. Films: *The Man with the Golden Arm,* 1956; *Beau James,* 1957. TV: *Riverboat* (series), 1959-61; *The Outsider* (series), 1968-69; *The Night Stalker* (series), 1974-75.

MCGIVER, JOHN, 1913 (New York, N.Y.)-Sept. 9, 1975. U.S. actor. Films: *Breakfast at Tiffany's,* 1961; *The Manchurian Candidate,* 1962; *Midnight Cowboy,* 1969.

MCGOOHAN, PATRICK, Mar. 19, 1928 (Queens, N.Y.). U.S. actor. Has performed mostly in Great Britain; star of U.S. TV series *Secret Agent,* 1965-66; star of British TV series *The Prisoner,* 1967.

MCGUIRE, DOROTHY, June 14, 1919 (Omaha,

Neb.). U.S. actress. Films: *A Tree Grows in Brooklyn,* 1944; *The Spiral Staircase,* 1945; *Three Coins in the Fountain,* 1954; *The Dark at the Top of the Stairs,* 1960. TV: *Rich Man, Poor Man* (movie), 1976.

MCLAUGHLIN, EMILY, Dec. 1, ? (White Plains, N.Y.). U.S. actress. Best known for the role of Jessie on TV soap opera *General Hospital,* 1963-

MCQUEEN, BUTTERFLY, born Thelma McQueen, Jan. 7, 1911 (Tampa, Fla.). U.S. actress. Best known for roles as eccentric servant in films such as *Gone with the Wind* (1939).

MCQUEEN, STEVE, Mar. 24, 1930 (Indianapolis, Ind.). U.S. actor. Top box-office star of action-adventure films of the 1960s and 1970s. Films: *The Magnificent Seven,* 1960; *The Great Escape,* 1963; *Love with the Proper Stranger,* 1963; *Cincinnati Kid,* 1965; *Bullitt,* 1968; *The Reivers,* 1970; *Papillon,* 1973; *Towering Inferno,* 1974; *An Enemy of the People,* 1976. (One-time husband of ALI MACGRAW.)

MEADOWS, AUDREY, 1924 (Wu Chang, China). U.S. actress. Best known for role of Alice Kramden on *The Jackie Gleason Show* (1952-55) and the TV series, *The Honeymooners,* 1955-56. (Sister of JAYNE MEADOWS.)

MEADOWS, JAYNE, Sept. 27, 1926 (Wu Chang, China). U.S. actress. Regular panelist on TV game show *I've Got a Secret,* 1952-58. (Wife of STEVE ALLEN; sister of AUDREY MEADOWS.)

MEARA, ANNE, 1929 (Brooklyn, N.Y.). U.S. comedienne, actress. Stand-up comedy act with husband JERRY STILLER, 1963- ; TV, stage, and film appearances.

MEEKER, RALPH, born Ralph Rathgeber, Nov. 21, 1920 (Minneapolis, Minn.). U.S. actor. Appeared on stage in *Mr. Roberts* (1947) and *Picnic* (1956). Films: *Kiss Me Deadly,* 1955; *Paths of Glory,* 1957; *The Detective,* 1968.

MENJOU, ADOLPHE, Feb. 18, 1890 (Pittsburgh, Pa.)-Oct. 29, 1963. U.S. actor. Films: *Forbidden Paradise,* 1924; *The Front Page,* 1931; *Morning Glory,* 1933; *Little Miss Marker,* 1934; *A Star Is Born,* 1937; *Roxie Hart,* 1942; *State of the Union,* 1948; *Paths of Glory,* 1957.

MEREDITH, BURGESS, Nov. 16, 1909 (Cleveland, Ohio). U.S. actor. Plays: *Winterset,* 1936; *High Tor,* 1937; *Liliom,* 1940; *Teahouse of the August Moon,* 1955. Films: *Winterset,* 1937; *Of Mice and Men,* 1939; *That Uncertain Feeling,* 1941; *The Story of G.I. Joe,* 1945; *Advise and Consent,* 1962; *Day of the Locust,* 1974; *Rocky,* 1977; *Foul Play,* 1978; *Rocky—Part 2,* 1979.

MERIWETHER, LEE, May 27, 1935 (Los Angeles, Calif.). U.S. actress. Miss America, 1955; costar of the TV series *Barnaby Jones,* 1973-   .

MERMAN, ETHEL, born Ethel Zimmerman, Jan. 16, 1909 (Astoria, N.Y.). U.S. singer, actress. Famed for her booming voice in Broadway musicals. Plays: *Girl Crazy,* 1930; *George White's Scandals,* 1931; *Anything Goes,* 1934; *Red Hot and Blue,* 1936; *Dubarry Was a Lady,* 1939; *Panama Hattie,* 1940; *Annie Get Your Gun,* 1946; *Call Me Madam,* 1950 (film, 1953); *Gypsy,* 1959; *Hello Dolly,* 1970. Received N.Y. Drama Critics award, 1943, 1946, and 1959; received Tony awards, 1951, 1972; received Drama Desk award, 1970.

MERRILL, DINA, born Nedenia Hutton, Dec. 9, 1925 (New York, N.Y.). U.S. actress. An heiress to the Post Cereal fortune; stage, film, TV career. (Wife of CLIFF ROBERTSON.)

THE BOOK OF WHO

MERRILL, GARY, 1915 (Hartford, Conn). U.S. actor. Films: *Twelve O'Clock High*, 1949; *All About Eve*, 1950; *Phone Call from a Stranger*, 1953. (One-time husband of BETTE DAVIS.)

MILES, VERA, born Vera Ralston, Aug. 23, 1930 (Boise City, Okla.). U.S. actress. Films: *The Searchers*, 1956; *The Wrong Man*, 1957; *Psycho*, 1960.

MILLAND, RAY(mond) **ALTON,** Jan. 3, 1908 (Glamorganshire, Wales). U.S. actor. Films: *The Jungle Princess*, 1936; *Beau Geste*, 1939; *Arise My Love*, 1941; *Lady in the Dark*, 1944; *Ministry of Fear*, 1944; *The Lost Weekend* (Best Actor AA), 1945; *Alias Nick Beal*, 1949; *Dial M for Murder*, 1954; *Love Story*, 1970. Autobiography: *Wide-Eyed in Babylon*, 1974.

MILLER, MARILYN, born Mary Ellen Reynolds, Sept. 1, 1898 (Findlay, Ohio?/Evansville, Ind.?)-Apr. 7, 1936. U.S. actress, dancer. Made New York stage debut in *The Passing Show of 1914*; also appeared in The Ziegfeld Follies and in *Peter Pan* (1924).

MILNER, MARTIN, Dec. 28, 1931 (Detroit, Mich.). U.S. actor. Star of the TV series *Route 66* (1960-64) and *Adam 12* (1968-75).

MIMIEUX, YVETTE, Jan. 8, 1942 (Los Angeles, Calif.). U.S. actress. Films: *Where the Boys Are*, 1961; *The Light in the Piazza*, 1962; *Skyjacked*, 1972; *Jackson County Jail*, 1976.

MINEO, SAL, Jan. 10, 1939 (New York, N.Y.)-Feb. 12, 1976. U.S. actor. Films: *Rebel without a Cause*, 1955; *Giant*, 1956; *Exodus*, 1960; *Escape from the Planet of the Apes*, 1971.

MITCHELL, CAMERON, Apr. 11, 1918 (Dallastown, Pa.), U.S. actor. Best known for roles in the film *Death of a Salesman* (1952) and the TV series *The High Chaparral* (1967-71).

MITCHELL, THOMAS, July 11, 1892 (Elizabeth, N.J.)-Dec. 17, 1962. U.S. actor. A former news reporter, in films from 1936; received Best Supporting Actor AA for his role in *Stagecoach* (1939);

MITCHUM, ROBERT, Aug. 6, 1917 (Bridgeport, Conn.). U.S. actor. Films: *The Story of G.I. Joe*, 1945; *Night of the Hunter*, 1955; *The Sundowners*, 1960; *Ryan's Daughter*, 1971; *Farewell My Lovely*, 1975.

MIX, TOM, born Thomas Edwin Mix, Jan. 6, 1880 (El Paso, Tex.)-Oct. 12, 1940. U.S. actor. Appeared in over 400 film westerns, both silent and sound.

MONROE, MARILYN, born Norma Jean Baker, June 1, 1926 (Los Angeles, Calif.)-Aug. 5, 1962. U.S. actress. The sex symbol of the 1950s. Films: *The Asphalt Jungle*, 1950; *All About Eve*, 1950; *Niagara*, 1952; *Gentlemen Prefer Blondes*, 1953; *How to Marry a Millionaire*, 1953; *The Seven-Year Itch*, 1955; *Some Like It Hot*, 1959. (One time wife of ARTHUR MILLER and JOE DiMAGGIO.)

MONTALBAN, RICARDO, Nov. 25, 1920 (Mexico City, Mex.). U.S. actor. Star of the TV series *Fantasy Island*, 1978-   . Films: *Battleground*, 1950; *Sayonara*, 1957; *Sweet Charity*, 1968.

MONTGOMERY, ELIZABETH, Apr. 15, 1933 (Los Angeles, Calif.). U.S. actress. Best known for her role as Samantha on the TV series *Bewitched*, 1964-72. (Daughter of ROBERT MONTGOMERY.)

MONTGOMERY, ROBERT, May 21, 1904 (Beacon, N.Y.). U.S. actor, producer. In films since 1930s, including *Busman's Holiday* (1940) and *Here Comes Mr. Jordan* (1941); consultant to Pres. D. D. EISENHOWER on radio and TV appearances, 1952-60. (Father of ELIZABETH MONTGOMERY.)

MOORE, MARY TYLER, Dec. 29, 1937 (Brooklyn, N.Y.). U.S. actress. Star of the TV series *Dick Van Dyke Show* (1961-66) and *Mary Tyler Moore Show* (1970-77); head of MTM Enterprises production co.; received Emmy awards in 1964, 1965, 1973, 1974, and 1976.

MOORE, VICTOR, Feb. 24, 1876 (Hammonton, N.J.)-July 23, 1962. U.S. actor. On stage, from 1893; in films, from 1934. Plays: *Oh Kay*, 1926; *Funny Face*, 1927; *Of Thee I Sing*, 1931. Films: *Louisiana Purchase*, 1941; *The Seven-Year Itch*, 1955.

MOOREHEAD, AGNES, Dec. 6, 1906 (Boston, Mass.)-Apr. 30, 1974. U.S. actress. TV: *Bewitched* (series), 1964-72. Films: *Citizen Kane*, 1941; *The Magnificent Ambersons*, 1942; *The Lost Moment*, 1947; *The Woman in White*, 1948; *The Bat*, 1959; *Hush, Hush, Sweet Charlotte*, 1964.

MORGAN, DENNIS, born Stanley Morner, Dec. 10, 1920 (Prentice, Wisc.). U.S. singer, actor. Singing career in theaters, opera houses, and on radio. Films: *Kitty Foyle*, 1940; *My Wild Irish Rose*, 1947.

MORGAN, FRANK, born Frank Wupperman, June 1, 1890 (New York, N.Y.)-Sept. 18, 1949. U.S. comedic character actor. Best known for title role in the film *The Wizard of Oz*, 1939. Other films: *The Shop around the Corner*, 1940; *Boom Town*, 1940; *The Human Comedy*, 1943; *Summer Holiday*, 1948.

MORGAN, HARRY, born Harry Bratsburg, Apr. 10, 1915 (Detroit, Mich.). U.S. character actor. Star of the TV series *December Bride* (1954-61), *Dragnet* (1967-70), and "M*A*S*H" (1975-   ).

MORGAN, HELEN, 1900 (Danville, Ill.)-Oct. 8, 1941. U.S. singer, actress. Originally cafe singer; known for her role in the film *Show Boat*, 1936.

MORIARTY, MICHAEL, Apr. 5, 1941 (Detroit, Mich.). U.S. actor. Films: *Bang the Drum Slowly*, 1973. Plays: *Find Your Way Home* (Tony award), 1974. TV: *The Glass Menagerie* (movie), 1973; *Holocaust* (movie), 1978. Received Emmy award, 1973.

MORRIS, CHESTER, Feb. 16, 1901 (New York, N.Y.)-Sept. 11, 1970. U.S. actor. Appeared in many 1930s and 1940s films, notably the "Boston Blackie" series (1941-49).

MORRIS, GREG, 1934 (Cleveland, Ohio). U.S. actor. Best known for the role on the TV series *Mission Impossible*, 1966-73.

MORRIS, WAYNE, born Bert de Wayne Morris, Feb. 17, 1914 (Los Angeles, Calif.)-Sept. 14, 1959. U.S. actor. Films: *Kid Galahad*, 1937; *The Time of Your Life*, 1947; *Paths of Glory*, 1957.

MORSE, ROBERT ALAN, May 18, 1931 (Newton, Mass.). U.S. actor. Best known for starring role in *How to Succeed in Business without Really Trying* (play, 1961; film, 1967); received Tony award, 1961.

MOSTEL, ZERO, born Sam Mostel, Feb. 28, 1915 (Brooklyn, N.Y.)-Sept. 8, 1977. U.S. comedic actor. Best known for his portrayal of Tevye in the play, *The Fiddler on the Roof*, 1964-66. Other plays: *Rhinoceros*, 1961; *A Funny Thing Happened on the Way to the Forum*, 1962. Films: *The Producers*, 1968. Received Tony awards in 1961, 1962, and 1964.

MUNI, PAUL, born Muni Weisenfreund, Sept. 22, 1895 (Lemberg, Austria)-Aug. 25, 1967. U.S. actor. A leading star of the Yiddish theater, 1918-26.

242

ENTERTAINERS

Films: *I Am a Fugitive from a Chain Gang*, 1932; *The Story of Louis Pasteur* (Best Actor AA), 1936; *The Good Earth*, 1937; *The Life of Emile Zola*, 1937; *A Song to Remember*, 1944.

MURPHY, AUDIE, June 20, 1924 (Kingston, Tex.)–May 28, 1971. U.S. soldier, actor. U.S.'s most decorated WW II hero. Films: *The Red Badge of Courage*, 1951; *Destry*, 1955; *To Hell and Back*, 1955; *The Quiet American*, 1958.

MURPHY, GEORGE, July 4, 1902 (New Haven, Conn.). U.S. actor, politician. Song-and-dance man in films of the 1930s and 1940s. U.S. senator (R, Calif.), 1964–71.

MURRAY, DON, July 31, 1929 (Hollywood, Calif.). U.S. actor. Best known for his role in the films *The Hoodlum Priest* (1961) and *Advise and Consent* (1962). (One-time husband of HOPE LANGE).

MURRAY, KEN, born Don Court, July 14, 1903 (New York, N.Y.). U.S. comedic actor. Film, radio, TV and stage career; motion-picture industry historian; received special AA for *Bill and Coo* (1947), a film fantasy using live birds as actors, 1947.

NABORS, JIM, June 12, 1933 (Sylacauga, Ala.). U.S. actor, singer. Best known for his role in *The Andy Griffith Show* (1963–64) and the TV series *Gomer Pyle, U.S.M.C.*, 1964–70; later a club singer.

NAGEL, CONRAD, Mar. 16, 1896 (Keokuk, Ia.)–Feb. 24, 1970. U.S. character actor. Films: *Little Women*, 1919; *Quality Street*, 1927; *Bad Sister*, 1931; *East Lynne*, 1931.

NAISH, J. CARROLL, Jan. 21, 1900 (New York, N.Y.)–Jan. 24, 1973. U.S. character actor. *Beau Geste*, 1939; *Blood and Sand*, 1941; *A Medal for Benny*, 1945; *Annie Get Your Gun*, 1950. TV: *Life with Luigi* (series), 1954; *Guestward Ho!* (series), 1960.

NATWICK, MILDRED, June 19, 1908 (Baltimore, Md.). U.S. character actress. Plays: *Blithe Spirit*, 1941; *Candida*, 1937, 1942, 1946. Films: *The Trouble with Harry*, 1955; *The Court Jester*, 1956; *Barefoot in the Park*, 1967; *If It's Tuesday, This Must Be Belgium*, 1969.

NEAL, PATRICIA, Jan. 20, 1926 (Packard, N.Y.). U.S. actress. Films: *The Fountainhead*, 1949; *The Hasty Heart*, 1950; *A Face in the Crowd*, 1957; *Hud* (Best Actress AA), 1963; *The Subject Was Roses*, 1968; *The Homecoming*, 1971.

NEGRI, POLA, born Appolonia Chalupek, 1899 (Lipno, Pol.). U.S. actress. A silent-screen star; best known as star of the film *Forbidden Paradise*, 1924.

NELSON, BARRY, 1920 (San Francisco, Calif.). U.S. actor. Plays: *The Moon Is Blue*, 1951; *Mary, Mary*, 1960; *Cactus Flower*, 1965; *The Norman Conquests*, 1975; *The Act*, 1977. Films: *Airport*, 1970; *Pete 'n' Tillie*, 1972.

NELSON, HARRIET, née Hilliard, July 18, 1914 (Des Moines, Ia.). U.S. actress. Big Band singer with husband OZZIE NELSON's band; appeared on the TV series, *Ozzie and Harriet*, 1952–65. (Wife of Ozzie Nelson; mother of David and RICK NELSON.)

NELSON, OZZIE, born Oswald George Nelson, Mar. 20, 1907 (Jersey City, N.J.)–June 3, 1975. U.S. bandleader, actor. Formed dance band, 1930; appeared in the TV series *Ozzie and Harriet*, 1952–65. (Husband of HARRIET NELSON, father of David and RICK NELSON.)

NELSON, RICK(y), May 8, 1940 (Teaneck, N.J.). U.S. singer, actor, songwriter. Appeared on the TV series *Ozzie and Harriet*, 1952–65; later a singer and songwriter of pop-rock tunes. (Son of OZZIE and HARRIET NELSON.)

NEWMAN, BARRY FOSTER, Nov. 7, 1938 (Boston, Mass.). U.S. actor. Films: *The Lawyers*, 1969; *Vanishing Point*, 1971. TV: *Petrocelli* (series) 1974–75; received Emmy award, 1975.

NEWMAN, PAUL, Jan. 26, 1925 (Cleveland, Ohio). U.S. actor. Leading male sex symbol of 1960s and 1970s films. Films: *The Long Hot Summer*, 1958; *Cat on a Hot Tin Roof*, 1958; *Exodus*, 1960; *Hud*, 1963; *Cool Hand Luke*, 1967; *Butch Cassidy and the Sundance Kid*, 1969; *Judge Roy Bean*, 1972; *The Sting*, 1973; *The Towering Inferno*, 1974; *Quintet*, 1979. (Husband of JOANNE WOODWARD.)

NEWMAN, PHYLLIS, Mar. 19, 1935 (Jersey City, N.J.). U.S. actress. TV: panelist on the game shows *To Tell the Truth* (1964–66) and *What's My Line?* (1966–68). Plays: *Subways Are for Sleeping*, 1961; *The Madwoman of Central Park West*, 1979. (Wife of ADOLPH GREEN.)

NICHOLSON, JACK, Apr. 28, 1937 (Neptune, N.J.). U.S. actor. Star of offbeat films of the 1960s–1970s. Films: *Easy Rider* (Best Supporting Actor AA), 1969; *Five Easy Pieces*, 1970; *Carnal Knowledge*, 1971; *Chinatown*, 1974; *One Flew over the Cuckoo's Nest*, (Best Actor AA), 1975; *The Last Tycoon*, 1976.

NIELSEN, LESLIE, Feb. 11, 1926 (Saskatchewan, Can.). U.S. actor. A former disc jockey in Canada.

NIMOY, LEONARD, Mar. 26, 1931 (Boston, Mass.). U.S. actor. Best known for his roles on the TV series *Star Trek* (1966–69) and *Mission Impossible* (1967–71).

NOLAN, KATHY, 1934 (St. Louis, Mo.). U.S. actress, union leader. Starred in the TV series *The Real McCoys*, (1957–62) and *Broadside* (1964–65); presently pres. of Screen Actor's Guild.

NOLAN, LLOYD, Aug. 11, 1902 (San Francisco, Calif.). U.S. character actor. Films: *A Tree Grows in Brooklyn*, 1944; *The House on 92nd Street*, 1945; *Peyton Place*, 1958; *Ice Station Zebra*, 1968; *Airport*, 1969; *Earthquake*, 1974.

NOLTE, NICK, 1940 (Omaha, Neb.). U.S. actor. Rose to prominence via starring role in TV miniseries *Rich Man, Poor Man*, 1976–77. Films: *Return to Macon County*, 1975; *The Deep*, 1977; *Who'll Stop the Rain*, 1978; *North Dallas Forty*, 1979.

NORTON-TAYLOR, JUDY, Jan. 29, 1958 (Santa Monica, Calif.). U.S. actress. Best known for her role as Mary Ellen Walton Willard on the TV series *The Waltons*, 1972–

NOVAK, KIM, born Marilyn Novak, Feb. 18, 1933 (Chicago, Ill.). U.S. actress. Films: *The Man with the Golden Arm*, 1956; *Picnic*, 1965; *Jeanne Eagels*, 1957; *Vertigo*, 1958; *Bell, Book and Candle*, 1958; *Pal Joey*, 1958.

NOVARRO, RAMON, Feb. 6, 1899 (Durango, Mex.)–Oct. 31, 1968. Mexican-U.S. actor. First of Hollywood's Latin lovers. Films: *Scaramouche*, 1923; *The Arabs*, 1924; *Ben Hur*, 1925; *The Student Prince*, 1928; *Mata Hari*, 1931.

OAKIE, JACK, born Lewis D. Offield, Nov. 12, 1903 (Sedalia, Mo.)–Jan. 23, 1978. U.S. comedic actor. Best known for his "double take"; did over 100 films, including *The Great Dictator* (1940), *It Happened Tomorrow* (1944), and *Around the World in Eighty Days* (1956).

O'BRIAN, HUGH, Apr. 19, 1930 (Rochester, N.Y.). U.S. actor. Best known as star of the TV series *The*

243

Life and Legend of Wyatt Earp, 1955-61; founder of The Thalians, an actors' group that sponsors a clinic for the retarded.

O'BRIEN, EDMOND, Sept. 10, 1915 (New York, N.Y.). U.S. actor. Films: *The Killers*, 1946; *D.O.A.*, 1949; *The Barefoot Contessa*, 1954; *1984*, 1955; *The Third Voice*, 1959; *Seven Days in May*, 1964.

O'BRIEN, MARGARET, born Angela Maxine O'Brien, Jan. 15, 1937 (Los Angeles, Calif.). U.S. actress. Began as child star. Films: *Journey for Margaret*, 1942; *Lost Angel*, 1943; *Meet Me in St. Louis*, 1944; *Our Vines Have Tender Grapes*, 1945; *Little Women*, 1949.

O'BRIEN, PAT, Nov. 11, 1899 (Milwaukee, Wisc.). U.S. actor. Films: *The Front Page*, 1931; *Bombshell*, 1933; *Page Miss Glory*, 1935; *Boy Meets Girl*, 1938; *Angels with Dirty Faces*, 1938; *Knute Rockne, All American*, 1941; *The Last Hurrah*, 1958; *Some Like It Hot*, 1959.

O'CONNELL, ARTHUR, Mar. 29, 1908 (New York, N.Y.). U.S. character actor. Films: *Citizen Kane*, 1941; *Naked City*, 1948; *Picnic*, 1955; *The Man in the Gray Flannel Suit*, 1956; *Anatomy of a Murder*, 1959.

O'CONNOR, CARROLL, Aug. 2, 1924 (New York, N.Y.). U.S. actor. Best known for his role as Archie Bunker on TV series *All in the Family*, 1971-79.

O'CONNOR, DONALD, Aug. 28, 1925 (Chicago, Ill.). U.S. actor, singer, dancer. Films: *Tom Sawyer, Detective*, 1938; *Mister Big*, 1943; *Chip off the Old Block*, 1944; *Patrick the Great*, 1945; *Francis*, 1949; *Singin' in the Rain*, 1952; *Call Me Madam*, 1953; *There's No Business like Show Business*, 1954; *The Buster Keaton Story*, 1957.

O'KEEFE, DENNIS, born Edward Flanagan, 1908 (Ft. Madison, Ia.)-Aug. 31, 1968. U.S. actor. Films: *Topper Returns*, 1941; *Up in Mabel's Room*, 1944; *The Affairs of Susan*, 1945; *Mr. District Attorney*, 1947.

OLAND, WARNER, Oct. 3, 1880 (Umea, Swe.)-Aug. 6,1938. U.S. actor. Appeared in 16 feature films as Charlie Chan, 1931-38.

OLIVER, EDNA MAY, Nov. 9, 1883 (Boston, Mass.)-Nov. 9, 1942. U.S. character actress. Best known for film roles in *David Copperfield* (1934), *Romeo and Juliet* (1936), and *Pride and Prejudice* (1940).

O'NEAL, PATRICK, Sept 26, 1927 (Ocala, Fla.). U.S. character actor. Plays: *The Ginger Man*, 1963. Films: *King Rat*, 1965, *The Kremlin Letter*, 1970. With family, part-owner of a group of New York City restaurants.

O'NEAL, RYAN, Apr. 20, 1941 (Los Angeles, Calif.). U.S. actor. TV: *Peyton Place* (series), 1964-69. Films: *Love Story*, 1970; *What's Up Doc?*, 1972; *Paper Moon*, 1973; *Oliver's Story*, 1978; *The Main Event*, 1979. (Father of TATUM O'NEAL.)

O'NEAL, TATUM, Nov. 5, 1963 (Los Angeles, Calif.). U.S. child actress. Films: *Paper Moon* (Best Supporting Actress AA), 1973; *The Bad News Bears*, 1976; *International Velvet*, 1978. (Daughter of RYAN O'NEAL.)

O'NEILL, JAMES, Nov. 15, 1849 (Kilkenny, Ire.)-Aug. 10, 1920. U.S. actor. Stage career, from 1867; best known for role in *The Count of Monte Cristo*, which he played over 6,000 times. (Father of playwright EUGENE O'NEILL.)

ORBACH, JERRY, Oct. 20, 1935 (New York, N.Y.). U.S. actor. Best known for lead role in the play *The Fantasticks*, 1961; received Tony award for *Promises, Promises*, 1968.

O'SULLIVAN, MAUREEN, May 17, 1911 (Bayle,

Ire.). U.S. actress. Best known for her role as Jane in the "Tarzan" film series, 1932-42. Other films: *The Barretts of Wimpole Street*, 1934; *Pride and Prejudice*, 1940; *Never Too Late*, 1965. (Mother of MIA FARROW.)

OUSPENSKAYA, MARIA, July 29, 1876 (Tula, Rus.)-Dec. 3, 1949. Russian-U.S. actress. As Russian stage actress (1911-23), known for her roles in Chekhov plays. Films: *Love Affair*, 1939; *The Rains Came*, 1939; *The Wolf Man*, 1941; *Kings Row*, 1942; *A Kiss in the Dark*, 1949.

OWEN, REGINALD, Aug. 5, 1887 (Wheathampstead, Eng.)-Nov. 5, 1972. U.S. character actor. Film career, 1929-72. Films: *Trouble for Two*, 1936; *Mrs. Minniver*, 1942; *Kitty*, 1945.

PACINO, AL(fred), Apr. 25, 1940 (New York, N.Y.). U.S. actor. A versatile leading man of 1970s films. Plays: *The Indian Wants the Bronx*, 1968; *Does the Tiger Wear a Necktie?* 1969; *The Basic Training of Pavlo Hummel*, 1972 and 1978. Films: *The Godfather—Parts 1 and 2*, 1972, 1974; *Serpico*, 1973; *Dog Day Afternoon*, 1975. Received 1968 Obie award and 1969 Tony award.

PAGE, GERALDINE, Nov. 22, 1924 (Kirksville, Mo.). U.S. actress. Plays: *The Immoralist*, 1954; *The Rainmaker*, 1954-57; *Separate Tables*, 1957-58; *Sweet Bird of Youth*, 1959-61; *Absurd Person Singular*, 1974-75. Films: *Hondo*, 1954.

PALANCE, JACK, born Walter Palanuik, Feb. 18, 1920 (Lattimer Mines, Pa.). U.S. actor. Best known as a film "heavy." Films: *Shane*, 1953; *The Big Knife*, 1955; *Barabbas*, 1962; *Ché*, 1969; *Chato's Land*, 1972; *Dracula*, 1973.

PALILLO, RON, Apr. 2, ? (New Haven, Conn.). U.S. actor. Gained fame playing Arnold Horshack, one of the Sweathogs on the TV series *Welcome Back, Kotter*, 1975-79.

PALMER, LILLI, May 24, 1914 (Posen, Ger.). U.S. actress, author. Plays: *No Time for Comedy*, 1940; *Caesar and Cleopatra*, 1950; *Bell, Book and Candle*, 1951. Films: *The Rake's Progress*, 1945; *My Girl Tesa*, 1947; *The Pleasure of His Company*, 1961. Memoirs: *Change Lobsters and Dance*, 1975. Novel: *The Red Raven*, 1979. (One-time wife of REX HARRISON.)

PARKER, ELEANOR, June 26, 1922 (Cedarville, Ohio). U.S. actress. Films: *The Voice of the Turtle*, 1947; *Detective Story*, 1951; *Interrupted Melody*, 1955; *The Sound of Music*, 1965; *The Oscar*, 1966.

PARKER, FESS, Aug. 16, 1925 (Fort Worth, Tex.). U.S. actor. Best known for his portrayal of Davy Crockett in the film by the same name and its two sequels, 1955. TV: *Daniel Boone* (series), 1964-70.

PARKS, LARRY, born Samuel Klausman Parks, 1914 (Olathe, Kan.)-Apr. 13, 1975. U.S. actor. Best known for his portrayal of Al Jolson in *The Jolson Story*, 1946; forced out of Hollywood after admitting he had once been a member of the U.S. Communist party.

PARSONS, ESTELLE, Nov. 20, 1927 (Lynn, Mass.). U.S. actress. Plays: *Mrs. Dally Has a Lover*, 1962; *Ready When You Are, C.B.*, 1964; *And Miss Reardon Drinks a Little*, 1974; *The Norman Conquests*, 1975-76; *Miss Margarida's Way*, 1977-78. Films: *Bonnie and Clyde*, 1967.

PAVAN, MARISA, born Marisa Pierangeli, June 19, 1932 (Caligari, Sardinia). U.S. actress. Films: *What Price Glory?*, 1952; *The Rose Tattoo*, 1955; *The Man in the Gray Flannel Suit*, 1956; *John Paul Jones*, 1959; *Solomon and Sheba*, 1959.

PAYNE, JOHN, 1912 (Roanoke, Va.). U.S. actor. Films: *Tin Pan Alley*, 1940; *The Great American*

ENTERTAINERS

Broadcast, 1941; The Dolly Sisters, 1945; Miracle on 34th Street, 1947; The Boss, 1956.

PECK, GREGORY, Apr. 5, 1916 (La Jolla, Calif.). U.S. actor. Hollywood leading man for over 30 years. Films: The Keys of the Kingdom, 1944; Spellbound, 1945; Duel in the Sun, 1946; Gentleman's Agreement, 1947; Twelve O'Clock High, 1949; The Man in the Gray Flannel Suit, 1956; The Guns of Navarone, 1961; To Kill a Mockingbird, 1963; The Omen, 1976; MacArthur, 1977; The Boys from Brazil, 1978.

PEPPARD, GEORGE, Oct. 1, 1928 (Detroit, Mich.). U.S. actor. Films: Breakfast at Tiffany's, 1961; The Blue Max, 1966; Rough Night in Jericho, 1967. TV: Banacek (series), 1972–74. (One-time husband of ELIZABETH ASHLEY.)

PERKINS, ANTHONY, Apr. 4, 1932 (New York, N.Y.). U.S. actor. Films: Desire under the Elms, 1957; Psycho, 1960; Pretty Poison, 1968; WUSA, 1970, Remember My Name, 1978. Plays: Equus, 1975.

PERRINE, VALERIE, Sept. 3, 1943 (Galveston, Tex.). U.S. actress. Films: Slaughterhouse Five, 1972; Lenny, 1975; W. C. Fields and Me, 1976; Superman, 1978; best actress award, Cannes Film Festival of 1975; best supporting actress award, N.Y. Film Critics, 1975.

PERSOFF, NEHEMIAH, Aug. 14, 1920 (Jerusalem, Palestine [now Israel]). U.S. character actor. Films: On the Waterfront, 1954; This Angry Age, 1957; Some Like It Hot, 1959; Fate Is the Hunter, 1964; Red Sky at Morning, 1971.

PETERS, BERNADETTE, born Bernadette Lazzara, Feb. 28, 1948 (Queens, N.Y.). U.S. musical-comedy actress. Plays: George M!, 1968; Dames at Sea, 1968; Mack and Mabel, 1974. TV: All's Fair (series), 1976–77.

PETERS, BROCK, July 2, 1927 (New York, N.Y.). U.S. actor, singer. Plays: South Pacific, 1943; Anna Lucasta, 1944–45; Great White Hope, 1970. Films: To Kill a Mockingbird, 1962; The L-Shaped Room, 1962; Heavens Above, 1963; The Incident, 1968.

PETERS, JEAN, Oct. 15, 1926 (Canton, Ohio). U.S. actress. Films: Viva Zapata, 1952; Three Coins in the Fountain, 1954; A Man Called Peter, 1955. (One-time wife of HOWARD HUGHES.)

PICKENS, SLIM, born Louis Bert Lindley, June 29, 1919 (Kingsberg, Calif.). U.S. character actor. Principally in western films, from the 1940s.

PICKFORD, MARY, born Gladys Marie Smith, Apr. 9, 1893 (Toronto, Can.)–May 29, 1979. U.S. actress. A leading lady of the silent screen; then talkies; in 1919, established United Artists Corp. with (husband) DOUGLAS FAIRBANKS, CHARLIE CHAPLIN, and D. W. GRIFFITH. Films: Pollyanna, 1919; Little Lord Fauntleroy, 1921; Tess of the Storm Country, 1922; Coquette (Best Actress AA), 1929.

PICON, MOLLY, Feb. 28, 1898 (New York, N.Y.). U.S. actress. Star of Yiddish theater, from 1904. Plays: A Majority of One, 1960; Milk and Honey, 1961; Dear Me, The Sky Is Falling, 1965.

PITTS, ZASU, Jan. 3, 1898 (Parsons, Kan.)–Jun. 7, 1963. U.S. comedic character actress. Films: Mrs. Wiggs of the Cabbage Patch, 1934; Life with Father, 1947. TV: The Gale Storm Show (series, later syndicated as Oh Susanna), 1956–60.

PLESHETTE, SUZANNE, Jan. 31, 1937 (New York, N.Y.). U.S. actress. Films: The Birds, 1963; Fate Is the Hunter, 1964; If It's Tuesday, This Must Be Belgium, 1969. TV: The Bob Newhart Show (series), 1972–78.

POITIER, SIDNEY, Feb. 20, 1927 (Miami, Fla.). U.S. actor. The first black actor to win Best Actor AA. Films: A Raisin in the Sun, 1961; Porgy and Bess, 1959; Lilies of the Field (Best Actor AA), 1963; The Bedford Incident, 1965; In the Heat of the Night, 1967; Guess Who's Coming to Dinner?, 1967; To Sir with Love, 1967; Buck and the Preacher, 1972.

POSTON, TOM, Oct. 17, 1927 (Columbus, Ohio). U.S. comedic character. TV: The Steve Allen Show, 1956–59 and 1961.

POWELL, DICK, born Richard E. Powell, Nov. 14, 1904 (Mt. View, Ark.)–Jan. 3, 1963. U.S. actor, producer, director. Films: 42nd Street, 1933; Dames, 1934; On the Avenue, 1937; Christmas in July, 1940; Murder My Sweet, 1944. Founder of the Four Star Television production firm. (One-time husband of JOAN BLONDELL and JUNE ALLYSON.)

POWELL, JANE, born Suzanne Burce, Apr. 1, 1929 (Portland, Ore.). U.S. actress, singer. A leading lady in 1940s-1950s films, including Seven Brides for Seven Brothers (1954); played the lead role in Broadway musical Irene, 1972.

POWELL, WILLIAM, July 29, 1892 (Pittsburgh, Pa.). U.S. actor. Best known for "The Thin Man" film series, 1934–47. Other films: The Canary Murder Case, 1929; Street of Chance, 1930; One-Way Passage, 1932; The Great Ziegfeld, 1936; My Man Godfrey, 1936; Life with Father, 1947; Mister Roberts, 1955.

POWER, TYRONE EDMUND, May 5, 1913 (Cincinnati, Ohio)–Nov. 15, 1958. U.S. actor. Handsome leading man of 1940s and 1950s films. Films: Lloyds of London, 1937; In Old Chicago, 1938; Alexander's Ragtime Band, 1938; Rose of Washington Square, 1939; Jesse James, 1939; Zorro, 1940; The Black Swan, 1942; The Sun Also Rises, 1957.

PRENTISS, PAULA, born Paula Ragusa, Mar. 4, 1939 (San Antonio, Tex.). U.S. actress. Films: Man's Favorite Sport, 1964; In Harm's Way, 1965; What's New, Pussycat?, 1965; The Stepford Wives, 1975. (Wife of RICHARD BENJAMIN.)

PRESTON, ROBERT, June 8, 1918 (Newton Highlands, Mass.). U.S. actor. Best known for lead role in The Music Man (play, 1957; film, 1962). Plays: The Tender Trap, 1954; Ben Franklin in Paris, 1964; I Do, I Do, 1966; Sly Fox, 1977. Films: Union Pacific, 1938; The Dark at the Top of the Stairs, 1960; How the West Was Won, 1963; Semi-Tough, 1977.

PRICE, VINCENT, May 27, 1911 (St. Louis, Mo.). U.S. stage and screen actor. Best known for his roles in horror movies, particularly those based on Edgar Allan Poe stories; a gourmet cook and famed art collector who has written several books on these subjects.

PROVINE, DOROTHY, Jan. 20, 1937 (Deadwood, S.D.). U.S. actress. Film and TV career; best known for her role in the TV series The Roaring Twenties, 1960–62.

QUINN, ANTHONY RUDOLPH, Apr. 21, 1915 (Chihuahua, Mex.). U.S. actor. Specializes in ethnic characters. Films: Viva Zapata (Best Supporting Actor AA), 1952; La Strada, 1954; Lust for Life (Best Supporting Actor AA), 1956; Guns of Navarone, 1961; Requiem for a Heavyweight, 1963; Zorba the Greek, 1964; The Shoes of the Fisherman, 1968; Mohammed, 1976.

RAFT, GEORGE, 1895 (New York, N.Y.). U.S. actor. Best known for film roles as gangsters. Films:

THE BOOK OF WHO

Scarface, 1932; The Bowery, 1933; Bolero, 1934; Rumba, 1935; The Glass Key, 1935; Souls at Sea, 1937; Each Dawn I Die, 1939.

RAINER, LUISE, Jan. 12, 1912 (Vienna, Austria). U.S. actress. Retired from film industry after having received Best Actress AA, for The Great Ziegfeld (1936) and The Good Earth (1937).

RAINS, CLAUDE, Nov. 10, 1889 (London, Eng.)–May 30, 1967. British-U.S. character actor. Films: The Invisible Man, 1933; Crime without Passion, 1934; The Adventures of Robin Hood, 1938; Mr. Smith Goes to Washington, 1939; King's Row, 1941; Casablanca, 1942; Mr. Skeffington, 1944; Notorious, 1946; Lawrence of Arabia, 1962.

RAITT, JOHN EMMET, Jan. 29, 1917 (Santa Ana, Calif.). U.S. actor, singer. A leading man in the musical theatre; best known for starring roles in Oklahoma (natl. tour, 1944), Carousel (1945), The Pajama Game (1954), and Zorba (natl. tour, 1969).

RAMBEAU, MARJORIE, July 15, 1889 (San Francisco, Calif.)–July 7, 1970. U.S. character actress. Stage career, from 1901; film career, from 1916. Films: Her Man, 1930; Primrose Path, 1940; Tugboat Annie Sails Again, 1941; Tobacco Road, 1941; Torch Song, 1953; The Man with a Thousand Faces, 1957.

RANDALL, TONY, Feb. 26, 1920 (Tulsa, Okla.). U.S. actor. Best known for his role as Felix Unger in the TV series The Odd Couple, 1970–75. Films: Will Success Spoil Rock Hunter?, 1957; Pillow Talk, 1959; Send Me No Flowers, 1964; Seven Faces of Dr. Lao, 1964.

RATHBONE, BASIL, June 13, 1892 (Johannesburg, S.A.)–1967. English actor. Best known for his role as Sherlock Holmes in a series of 1930s-1940s films. Films: David Copperfield, 1935; Anna Karenina, 1935; Captain Blood, 1935; The Adventures of Robin Hood, 1938; Hound of the Baskervilles, 1939; Spider Woman, 1944. Autobiography: In and Out of Character, 1962.

RAY, ALDO, born Aldo da Re, Sept. 25, 1926 (Pen Argul, Pa.). U.S. actor. Beefy character-actor in films. Films: The Marrying Kind, 1951; Pat and Mike, 1952; God's Little Acre, 1958; What Did You Do in the War, Daddy?, 1966.

RAYE, MARTHA, born Maggie Yvonne O'Reed, Aug. 27, 1916 (Butte, Mont.). U.S. actress. Has played vaudeville, clubs, radio, TV; in films since 1936. Films: The Boys from Syracuse, 1940; Hellzapoppin', 1942; Monsieur Verdoux, 1947; Jumbo, 1962. Plays: Annie Get Your Gun, 1952; Calamity Jane, 1961; Call Me Madam, 1963; Hello Dolly, 1967; No, No Nanette, 1972.

RAYMOND, GENE, born Raymond Guion, Aug. 13, 1908 (New York, N.Y.). U.S. actor. Films: Zoo in Budapest, 1933; Flying Down to Rio, 1933; Mr. and Mrs. Smith, 1941; Smilin' Through, 1941; The Locket, 1946; Hit the Deck, 1955; The Best Man, 1964. (Husband of JEANETTE MACDONALD.)

REDFORD, ROBERT, Aug. 18, 1937 (Santa Monica, Calif.). U.S. actor. Handsome leading man of 1960s-1970s movies; also known for his interest in ecology. Films: The Chase, 1966; Barefoot in the Park, 1967; Butch Cassidy and the Sundance Kid, 1969; The Candidate, 1972; The Way We Were, 1973; The Sting, 1973; Three Days of Condor, 1975; All the President's Men, 1976. Book: The Outlaw Trail, 1978.

REED, DONNA, born Donna Mullenger, Jan. 27, 1921 (Denison, la.). U.S. actress. Known for TV series The Donna Reed Show, 1958–66. Films:

From Here to Eternity (Best Supporting Actress AA), 1953; a leader in anti-Vietnam war movement.

REED, ROBERT, 1932 (Highland Park, Ill.). U.S. actor. Best known for roles in the TV series The Defenders (1961–65) and The Brady Bunch (1969–74).

REGAN, PHIL, May 28, 1908 (Brooklyn, N.Y.). U.S. actor, singer. Film musicals: Dames, 1934; Sweet Adeline, 1935; We're in the Money, 1935; Go into Your Dance, 1935; Sweet Rosie O'Grady, 1940s.

REID, WALLACE, Apr. 15, 1890 (St. Louis, Mo.)–Jan. 18, 1923. U.S. actor. A leading man in silent films, including Birth of a Nation (1915).

REILLY, CHARLES NELSON, Jan. 13, 1931 (New York, N.Y.). U.S. comedic actor. Plays: How to Succeed in Business without Really Trying (Tony award), 1962; Belle of Amherst (director), 1977. TV: The Ghost and Mrs. Muir (series), 1968–79; Match Game (game show).

REINER, ROB, Mar. 6, 1945 (New York, N.Y.). U.S. actor. Best known for role as Mike Stivic in the TV series All in the Family, 1971–78. (Son of CARL REINER; husband of PENNY MARSHALL.)

REMICK, LEE, Dec. 14, 1935 (Quincy, Mass.). U.S. actress. Films: The Anatomy of a Murder, 1959; Experiment in Terror, 1962; Days of Wine and Roses, 1963; No Way to Treat a Lady, 1968; The Omen, 1976. TV: QB VII (movie), 1974; Jennie (miniseries), 1975.

REYNOLDS, BURT, Feb. 11, 1936 (Waycross, Ga.). U.S. actor, director. Films: Deliverance, 1972; White Lightning, 1973; The Longest Yard, 1974; Lucky Lady, 1975; Smokey and the Bandit, 1977; Semi-Tough, 1977. TV: Dan August (series), 1970–75. (One-time husband of JUDY CARNE.)

REYNOLDS, DEBBIE, born Mary Frances Reynolds, Apr. 1, 1932 (El Paso, Tex.). U.S. actress, singer, dancer. Films: Singin' in the Rain, 1952; The Unsinkable Molly Brown, 1964. Plays: Irene, 1973. (One-time wife of EDDIE FISHER; mother of CARRIE FISHER.)

RICH, IRENE, born Irene Luther, Oct. 13, 1897? (Buffalo, N.Y.). U.S. actress. A silent-film leading lady, later in talkies. Films: Stella Maris, 1918; Craig's Wife, 1928; Lady Windermere's Fan, 1928.

RITTER, JOHN(athan) Sept. 17, 1948 (Burbank, Calif.). U.S. actor. Best known for his lead role in the TV series Three's Company, 1977-   . (Son of country singer TEX RITTER.)

RITTER, THELMA, Feb. 14, 1905 (Brooklyn, N.Y.)–Feb. 5, 1969. U.S. character actress. Films: Miracle on 34th Street, 1947; All about Eve, 1950; The Model and the Marriage Broker, 1951; Pickup on South Street, 1953; The Misfits, 1961; How the West Was Won, 1962.

ROBARDS, JASON NELSON, JR., July 22, 1922 (Chicago, Ill.). U.S. actor. Best known for his roles in EUGENE O'NEILL's plays. Plays: Stalag 17, 1951; The Iceman Cometh, 1956; Long Day's Journey into Night, 1956, 1976; A Thousand Clowns, 1962; After the Fall, 1964; A Moon for the Misbegotten, 1973; Touch of the Poet, 1977. Films: A Thousand Clowns, 1966; All the President's Men (Best Supporting Actor AA), 1976; Julia, 1977. (One-time husband of LAUREN BACALL.)

ROBERTSON, CLIFF, Sept. 9, 1925 (La Jolla, Calif.). U.S. actor, director. Films: Picnic, 1955; P.T. 109, 1963; The Best Man, 1964; The Honey Pot, 1967; Charly, (Best Actor AA), 1968; J. W.

Coop (also directed and wrote), 1972; *Three Days of the Condor*, 1976; *Obsession*, 1976.

ROBERTSON, DALE, July 14, 1923 (Oklahoma City, Okla.). U.S. actor. In many cowboy films, 1950s–60s; starred in the TV series *Tales of Wells Fargo*, 1957–62.

ROBINSON, EDWARD G., born Emanuel Goldenburg, Dec. 12, 1893 (Bucharest, Hung.)–Jan. 26, 1973. U.S. actor. Rose to prominence in 1930s gangster films, later played a variety of dramatic roles. Films: *Little Caesar*, 1930; *Five Star Final*, 1931; *The Whole Town's Talking*, 1934; *A Slight Case of Murder*, 1938; *Brother Orchid*, 1940; *The Sea Wolf*, 1941; *Double Indemnity*, 1944; *All My Sons*, 1948; *The Cincinnati Kid*, 1965.

ROBSON, MAY, born Mary Robison, Apr. 19, 1865 (Melbourne, Austrl.)–Oct. 20, 1942. U.S. character actress. Films: *If I Had a Million*, 1932; *Lady for a Day*, 1933; *Dinner at Eight*, 1933; *A Star Is Born*, 1937; *Bringing Up Baby*, 1938.

"ROCHESTER," born Eddie Anderson, Sept. 18, 1905 (Oakland, Calif.)–Feb. 28, 1977. U.S. character actor best known for his role as Rochester, JACK BENNY's butler, on TV and radio, 1953–65. Films: *Green Pastures*, 1936; *You Can't Take It with You*, 1938; *Gone with the Wind*, 1939; *Cabin in the Sky*, 1943.

ROGERS, CHARLES ("Buddy"), Aug. 13, 1904 (Olathe, Kan.). U.S. actor. A silent-screen star best known for his performance in *Wings* (1928), the first film to win an AA. (One-time husband of MARY PICKFORD.)

ROGERS, ROY, born Leonard Slye, Nov. 5, 1912 (Cincinnati, Ohio). U.S. actor, singer. Starred in cowboy films 1935–53; formed music group, Sons of the Pioneers, 1932–38; developed Roy Rogers Roast Beef fast-food restaurants; costarred with wife DALE EVANS in the TV series *The Roy Rogers Show*, 1951–57.

ROLAND, GILBERT, born Luis Damaso de Alonso, Dec. 11, 1905 (Chihuahua, Mex.). Mexican-U.S. actor. A former bullfighter; in U.S. films since the mid-1930s.

ROLLE, ESTHER, Nov. 8, ? (Pompano Beach, Fla.). U.S. actress. Best known for role as Florida Evans in the TV series *Maude* (1972–74) and *Good Times* (1974–77 and 1978–79).

ROMERO, CESAR, Feb. 15, 1907 (New York, N.Y.). U.S. actor. In a long film and TV career, best known for his role in the "Cisco Kid" film series of the 1930s and 1940s.

ROONEY, MICKEY, born Joe Yule, Jr., Sept. 23, 1920 (Brooklyn, N.Y.). U.S. actor. Began as a child actor in vaudeville, 1922–32. Films: *A Midsummer Night's Dream*, 1935; "Andy Hardy" series, 1937–46; *Ah Wilderness*, 1935; *Boys Town*, 1938; *Babes in Arms*, 1939; *Strike up the Band*, 1940; *The Human Comedy*, 1943; *The Bold and the Brave*, 1956; *Breakfast at Tiffany's*, 1961; *The Domino Principle*, 1977. (One-time husband of AVA GARDNER.)

ROSE MARIE, (New York, N.Y.). U.S. actress. Former child actress; best known for her role as Sally Rogers on the TV series *The Dick Van Dyke Show*, 1961–66.

ROSS, KATHARINE, Jan. 29, 1943 (Hollywood, Calif.). U.S. actress. Films: *The Graduate*, 1967; *Tell Them Willie Boy Is Here*, 1969; *Butch Cassidy and the Sundance Kid*, 1969; *The Stepford Wives*, 1975; *The Betsy*, 1978.

ROUNDTREE, RICHARD, July 9, 1942 (New Rochelle, N.Y.). U.S. actor. Former actor with The Negro Ensemble Co.; best known as star of the film *Shaft* (1971) and its two sequels.

ROWLANDS, GENA, June 19, 1936 (Cambria, Wisc.). U.S. actress. Films: *Faces*, 1968; *Minnie and Moscowitz*, 1971; *A Woman under the Influence*, 1974. (Wife of JOHN CASSAVETES.)

RUGGLES, CHARLES, 1886 (Los Angeles, Calif.)–Dec. 23, 1970. U.S. comedic character actor. Films: *Charley's Aunt*, 1930; *Love Me Tonight*, 1932; *Trouble in Paradise*, 1932; *Ruggles of Red Gap*, 1935; *Bringing Up Baby*, 1938; *The Farmer's Daughter*, 1940; *It Happened on 5th Avenue*, 1947; *Look for the Silver Lining*, 1949; *The Pleasure of His Company*, 1961.

RULE, JANICE, Aug. 15, 1931 (Norwood, Ohio). U.S. actress. Films: *Bell, Book and Candle*, 1958; *The Chase*, 1966; *Kid Blue*, 1973. (One-time wife of BEN GAZZARA.)

RUSH, BARBARA, Jan. 4, 1930 (Denver, Colo.). U.S. actress. A leading lady in 1950s and 1960s films; best known for her role in the film *Come Blow Your Horn*, 1963.

RUSSELL, JANE, June 21, 1921 (Bemidji, Minn.). U.S. actress. A former model; a leading lady in 1940s–1950s films; best known for her role in *The Outlaw*, 1943.

RUSSELL, ROSALIND, June 4, 1911 (Waterbury, Conn.)–Nov. 28, 1976. U.S. actress. Films: *Night Must Fall*, 1937; *The Citadel*, 1938; *The Women*, 1939; *His Girl Friday*, 1940; *My Sister Eileen*, 1942; *Auntie Mame*, 1958; *Gypsy*, 1962; *Mrs. Pollifax—Spy*, 1970.

RUTHERFORD, ANN, 1924 (Toronto, Ont., Can.). U.S. actress. Originally a child actress, became a leading lady in 1940s films. Films: *Gone with the Wind*, 1939; *The Secret Life of Walter Mitty*, 1947.

RYAN, IRENE, 1903–Apr. 26, 1973. U.S. actress. Best known for her role as Granny in the TV series *The Beverly Hillbillies*, 1962–71. Films: *Melody for Three*, 1941; *Diary of a Chambermaid*, 1945; *Meet Me after the Show*, 1951; *Spring Reunion*, 1957.

RYAN, PEGGY, Aug. 28, 1924 (Long Beach, Calif.). U.S. comedic actress. In many 1940s–1950s films; appeared in the TV series *Hawaii Five-O*, 1969–76.

RYAN, ROBERT, Nov. 11, 1909 (Chicago, Ill.)–July 11, 1973. U.S. actor. A leading man in action films since the mid-1940s. Films: *Crossfire*, 1947; *The Set-Up*, 1949; *Clash By Night*, 1952; *God's Little Acre*, 1958; *Odds Against Tomorrow*, 1959; *Billy Budd*, 1962; *The Dirty Dozen*, 1967; *The Wild Bunch*, 1969; *The Iceman Cometh*, 1973.

SAINT, EVA MARIE, July 4, 1924 (Newark, N.J.). U.S. actress. Films: *On the Waterfront* (Best Supporting Actress AA), 1954; *A Hatful of Rain*, 1957; *North By Northwest*, 1959; *Exodus*, 1960; *The Russians Are Coming...*, 1966.

ST. JAMES, SUSAN, born Susan Miller, Aug. 14, 1946 (Los Angeles, Calif.). U.S. actress. Best known for TV series *The Name of the Game* (1968–71) and *McMillan and Wife* (1971–77).

ST. JOHN, JILL, Aug. 19, 1940 (Los Angeles, Calif.). U.S. actress. Began career at age six, on radio. Films: *Who's Minding the Store?*, 1962; *The Oscar*, 1966; *Tony Rome*, 1967; *Diamonds are Forever*, 1971.

SAND, PAUL, born Pablo Sanchez, Mar. 5, 1935 (Santa Monica, Calif.). U.S. actor. Began career as a dancer; in Second City Improvisation Group, Chicago, 1960–63; best known for his adaptation and direction of, and performance in the play *Story Theatre* (Tony award), 1970.

SANDERS, GEORGE, July 3, 1906 (St. Petersburg, Rus. |now Leningrad, USSR|)–Apr. 25,

THE BOOK OF WHO

1972. U.S. actor. Films: *Rebecca*, 1940; *The Picture of Dorian Gray*, 1945; *Forever Amber*, 1947; *All about Eve* (Best Supporting Actor AA), 1950; *The Kremlin Letter*, 1970.

SANDS, DIANA, 1934 (New York, N.Y.)–Sept. 21, 1973. U.S. actress. Best known for her roles in the films *A Raisin in the Sun* (1961) and *The Landlord* (1971).

SANFORD, ISABEL GWENDOLYN, Aug. 29, ? (New York, N.Y.). U.S. actress. Best known for her role as Louise Jefferson on the TV series *The Jeffersons*, 1975–

SAVALAS, TELLY, born Aristotle Savalas, Jan. 21, 1927. U.S. actor. Film and TV actor noted for his bald head; star of the TV series *Kojak*, 1973–78. Films: *The Battle of the Bulge*, 1965; *The Scalphunters*, 1968.

SAXON, JOHN, born Carmen Orrico, Aug. 5, 1935 (Brooklyn, N.Y.). U.S. actor. Films: *The Cardinal*, 1963; *The Appaloosa*, 1966; *Enter the Dragon*, 1973; *Mitchell*, 1975.

SCHEIDER, ROY RICHARD, Nov. 10, 1935 (Orange, N.J.). U.S. actor. Best known for roles in the films *Jaws* (1975) and *Jaws II* (1978). Other films: *The French Connection*, 1971; *Marathon Man*, 1976; *All That Jazz*, 1979.

SCOTT, GEORGE C(ampbell), Oct. 18, 1927 (Wise, Va.). U.S. actor, dir. Films: *Anatomy of a Murder*, 1959; *The Hustler*, 1962; *The List of Adrian Messenger*, 1963; *Dr. Strangelove*, 1963; *Patton*, (Best Actor AA), 1970; *The Hospital*, 1972; *Hardcore*, 1979.

SCOTT, LIZABETH, born Emma Matzo, 1923 (Scranton, Pa.). U.S. actress. Leading lady of the 1940s, known for her blond hair, defiant expression, and stiff upper lip. Films: *The Strange Love of Martha Ivers*, 1946; *I Walk Alone*, 1947.

SCOTT, MARTHA, Sept. 22, 1914 (Jamesport, Mo.). U.S. actress. Films: *Our Town*, 1940; *The Desperate Hours*, 1955; *The Ten Commandments*, 1956; *Ben Hur*, 1959; *Airport '75*, 1974.

SCOTT, RANDOLPH, born Randolph Crance, Jan. 23, 1903 (Orange County, Va.). U.S. actor. Films: *She*, 1935; *Last of the Mohicans*, 1936; *Virginia City*, 1940; *Western Union*, 1941; *Ride the High Country*, 1962.

SCOTT, ZACHARY, 1914–Oct. 3, 1965. U.S. actor. Noted for playing suave cads. *The Mask of Dimitrios*, 1944; *The Southerner*, 1945; *Mildred Pierce*, 1946.

SCOURBY, ALEXANDER, 1913 (New York, N.Y.). U.S. stage and film character actor. Appeared in *The Web* on CBS-TV, 1957. Films: *The Big Heat*, 1953; *Giant*, 1956; *Confessions of a Counterspy*, 1960.

SEGAL, GEORGE, Feb. 13, 1934 (Great Neck, N.Y.). U.S. actor. Best known for comedy roles. Films: *King Rat*, 1965; *Who's Afraid of Virginia Woolf?*, 1966; *The Owl and the Pussycat*, 1970; *Where's Poppa?*, 1970; *A Touch of Class*, 1973.

SHATNER, WILLIAM, Mar. 22, 1931 (Montreal, Que., Can.). U.S. actor. Best known for his role as Capt. James Kirk in the TV series *Star Trek*, (1966–69) and movie (1979); played repertory theater in Canada, 1952–56.

SHEARER, NORMA, 1904 (Montreal, Que., Can.). U.S. actress. A leading lady of 1930s films. Films: *The Trial of Mary Dugan*, 1929; *The Divorcee*, 1929; *Private Lives*, 1931; *Strange Interlude*, 1931; *The Barretts of Wimpole Street*, 1934; *Romeo and Juliet*, 1936; *The Women*, 1939. (Wife of IRVING THALBERG.)

SHEEN, MARTIN, born Ramon Estevez, Aug. 3,

1940 (Dayton, Ohio). U.S. actor. Stage, film, TV career. Plays: *The Subject Was Roses*, 1964 (film, 1968). Films: *Badlands*, 1973; *Apocalypse Now*, 1979. TV: *That Certain Summer* (movie), 1973; *The Execution of Private Slovik* (movie), 1974; *The Missiles of October* (movie), 1974.

SHEPHERD, CYBILL, 1950 (Memphis, Tenn.). U.S. actress, model. Films: *The Last Picture Show*, 1971; *The Heartbreak Kid*, 1972; *Taxi Driver*, 1976.

SHERIDAN, ANN, born Clara Lou Sheridan, 1915 (Denton, Tex.)–Jan. 21, 1967. U.S. actress. Films: *Angels with Dirty Faces*, 1938; *Torrid Zone*, 1940; *They Drive By Night*, 1940; *King's Row*, 1941; *The Man Who Came to Dinner*, 1941; *Shine on Harvest Moon*, 1944; *Come Next Spring*, 1956.

SHIELDS, BROOKE, May 31, 1965 (New York, N.Y.). U.S. actress. A model, as Ivory Snow baby, at age 11 months. Films: *Pretty Baby*, 1978; *King of the Gypsies*, 1978; *Just You and Me Kid*, 1979.

SHIRE, TALIA, Apr. 25, 1946 (Jamaica, N.Y.). U.S. actress. Best known for her role in *Rocky*, 1976. Other films: *Godfather—Part 1*, 1972; *Godfather—Part 2*, 1974. (Sister of FRANCIS FORD COPPOLA.)

SIDNEY, SYLVIA, born Sophia Koskow, Aug. 8, 1910 (New York, N.Y.). U.S. actress. Films: *City Streets*, 1931; *Street Scene*, 1931; *An American Tragedy*, 1931; *You Only Live Once*, 1937; *Summer Wishes, Winter Dreams*, 1973; *I Never Promised You a Rose Garden*, 1978. Author of two bestselling books on needlepoint, 1968 and 1975.

SILVERS, PHIL, May 11, 1912 (Brooklyn, N.Y.). U.S. comedic actor. Best known as star of the TV series *The Phil Silvers Show: You'll Never Get Rich*, 1955–59. Films: *You're in the Army Now*, 1942; *Cover Girl*, 1944; *It's a Mad, Mad, Mad, Mad World*, 1963; *A Funny Thing Happened on the Way to the Forum*, 1966. Plays: *High Button Shoes*, 1947; *Top Banana*, 1951; *Do-Re-Mi*, 1960.

SKELTON, RED, born Richard Skelton, July 18, 1913 (Vincennes, Ind.). U.S. comedian, actor. A master of pantomime and slapstick comedy. TV: *The Red Skelton Show*, 1951–71. Films: *Whistling in the Dark*, 1941; *Whistling in Dixie*, 1942; *DuBarry Was a Lady*, 1943; *Three Little Words*, 1950.

SKINNER, CORNELIA OTIS, May 30, 1901 (Chicago, Ill.)–July 9, 1979. U.S. actress, author. Best known for one-woman shows and monogues, 1925–61; cowrote and starred in the play *The Pleasure of His Company*, 1958. Books: *Our Hearts were Young and Gay*, 1942; *Elegant Wits and Grand Horizontals*, 1962; *Life with Lindsay and Crouse*, 1976. (Daughter of OTIS SKINNER.)

SKINNER, OTIS, June 28, 1858 (Cambridge, Mass.)–Jan. 4, 1942. U.S. stage actor. Best known for his Shakespearean roles in *Hamlet* (1896), *The Merry Wives of Windsor* (1927) and *The Merchant of Venice* (1931). (Father of CORNELIA OTIS SKINNER.)

SLEZAK, WALTER, May 3, 1902 (Vienna, Austria). U.S. actor. Noted as a character actor. Films: *Once Upon a Honeymoon*, 1942; *Lifeboat*, 1944; *The Inspector General*, 1949; *Call Me Madam*, 1953; *Emil and the Detectives*, 1964. Autobiography: *What Time's the Next Swan?*, 1962. (Son of LEO SLEZAK.)

SMITH, ALEXIS, June 8, 1921 (Penticton, B.C., Can.). U.S. actress. Films: *Gentleman Jim*, 1942;

The Constant Nymph, 1942; *Of Human Bondage,* 1946; *Any Number Can Play,* 1950; *Once Is Not Enough,* 1975. Plays: *Follies,* 1971.

SMITH, JACLYN, Oct. 26, 1948 (Houston, Tex.). U.S. model, actress. Best known for her role in the TV series *Charlie's Angels,* 1976–

SMITH, ROGER, Dec. 18, 1932 (South Gate, Calif.). U.S. actor. Best known as star of the TV series *77 Sunset Strip,* 1958–1963; manages career of wife ANN-MARGRET.

SNODGRESS, CARRIE, Oct. 27, 1946 (Chicago, Ill.). U.S. actress. Began career with Goodman Theater of Chicago. Films: *Rabbit Run,* 1971; *Diary of a Mad Housewife,* 1972; *The Fury,* 1978.

SOMERS, SUZANNE, born Suzanne Mahoney, Oct. 16, 1946 (San Bruno, Calif.). U.S. actress, model. Star of the TV series *Three's Company,* 1977–

SOMMER, ELKE, born Elke Schletz, Nov. 5, 1941 (Berlin, Ger.). U.S. actress. Films: *The Prize,* 1963; *A Shot in the Dark,* 1964; *The Oscar,* 1966; *Boy, Did I Get a Wrong Number,* 1966; *The Wrecking Crew,* 1969; *Zeppelin,* 1971.

SOO, JACK, born Goro Suzuki, 1917 (Oakland, Calif.)–Jan. 11, 1979. U.S. actor. Oriental character actor in films and on TV, best known as Nick Yemana on the TV series *Barney Miller,* 1975–79.

SORVINO, PAUL, 1939 (Brooklyn, N.Y.). U.S. actor. Films: *I Will, I Will—For Now,* 1976; *Bloodbrothers,* 1978; *Slow Dancing in the Big City,* 1979.

SOTHERN, ANN, born Harriette Lake, Jan. 22, 1912 (Valley City, N.D.). U.S. comedic actress. Films: "Maisie" series, 1939–47; *A Letter to Three Wives,* 1949. TV: *Private Secretary* (series), 1953–57; *The Ann Sothern Show* (series), 1958–61.

SOUL, DAVID, born David Solberg, Aug. 28, ? (Chicago, Ill.). U.S. actor. Best known as star of the TV series *Starsky and Hutch,* 1975–

SPACEK, SISSY, born Mary Elizabeth Spacek, 1950 (Quitman, Tex.). U.S. actress. A leading lady in 1970s films such as *Badlands* (1973), *Carrie* (1976), *Three Women* (1977), and *Welcome to L.A.* (1977).

SPENCER, DANIELLE, June 24, 1965 (Bronx, N.Y.). U.S. actress. Best known for her role as Dee Thomas in the TV series *What's Happening?,* 1976–79.

STACK, ROBERT LANGFORD, Jan. 13, 1919 (Los Angeles, Calif.). U.S. actor. Films: *Written on the Wind,* 1956; *John Paul Jones,* 1959. TV: *The Untouchables* (series), 1959–63; *The Name of the Game* (series), 1968–71.

STALLONE, SYLVESTER ENZIO, July 6, 1946 (New York, N.Y.). U.S. actor, writer. Best known as star and writer of the film *Rocky* (1976). Other films: *F.I.S.T.,* 1978; *Paradise Alley,* 1978; *Rocky—Part II,* 1979.

STANLEY, KIM, born Patricia Kimberly Reid, Feb. 11, 1925 (Tularosa, N.M.). U.S. actress. Stage and film career; best known for her role in the play *Bus Stop,* 1955; films include *The Goddess,* 1958.

STANWYCK, BARBARA, born Ruby Stevens, July 16, 1907 (Brooklyn, N.Y.). U.S. actress. A leading lady, usually in dramatic roles, in films of the 1930s and 1940s. Films: *The Bitter Tea of General Yen,* 1933; *Stella Dallas,* 1937; *Baby Face,* 1941; *Double Indemnity,* 1944; *The Strange Love of Martha Ivers,* 1946; *Sorry, Wrong Number,* 1948; *Executive Suite,* 1954. TV: *The Big Valley* (series), 1965–69.

STAPLETON, JEAN, born Jeanne Murray, Jan. 19, 1923 (New York, N.Y.). U.S. actress. After a long stage career, became widely known for her role as Edith Bunker on the TV series *All in the Family,* 1971–79.

STAPLETON, MAUREEN, June 21, 1925 (Troy, N.Y.). U.S. character actress. Stage and film career. Plays: *The Rose Tattoo,* 1951, 1966; *The Crucible,* 1953; *The Seagull,* 1954; *27 Wagons Full of Cotton,* 1955; *The Glass Menagerie,* 1965, 1975; *Plaza Suite,* 1968; *The Gingerbread Lady,* 1970; *The Gin Game,* 1978. Received Tony awards in 1951 and 1970.

STEIGER, ROD, Apr. 14, 1925 (Westhampton, N.Y.). U.S. actor. Versatile leading man in films since the mid-1950s. Films: *On the Waterfront,* 1954; *The Harder They Fall,* 1956; *Al Capone,* 1958; *The Pawnbroker,* 1965; *In the Heat of the Night* (Best Actor AA), 1967; *The Sergeant,* 1968; *The Illustrated Man,* 1969; *W. C. Fields and Me,* 1976; *F.I.S.T.,* 1978. (One-time husband of CLAIRE BLOOM.)

STERLING, JAN, born Jane Sterling Adriance, Apr. 3, 1923 (New York, N.Y.). U.S. actress. Films: *Johnny Belinda,* 1948; *Ace in the Hole,* 1951; *The High and the Mighty,* 1954; *The Female on the Beach,* 1955; *1984,* 1956.

STEVENS, CONNIE, born Concetta Ingolia, Aug. 8, 1938 (Brooklyn, N.Y.). U.S. singer, actress. Starred in the series *Hawaiian Eye,* 1959–63; Las Vegas club singer, 1969–76; (One-time wife of EDDIE FISHER.)

STEVENS, STELLA, born Estelle Eggleston, Oct. 1, 1936 (Yazoo City, Miss.). U.S. actress. Films: *Lil' Abner,* 1959; *The Courtship of Eddie's Father,* 1963; *The Silencers,* 1966; *How to Save a Marriage,* 1967; *The Poseidon Adventure,* 1972.

STEWART, JAMES MAITLAND, May 20, 1908 (Indiana, Pa.). U.S. actor. A leading man, usually in comedic roles, in films since the mid 1930s. Films: *Seventh Heaven,* 1937; *You Can't Take It with You,* 1938; *Mr. Smith Goes to Washington,* 1939; *Destry Rides Again,* 1939; *The Shop around the Corner,* 1939; *Philadelphia Story* (Best Actor AA), 1940; *It's a Wonderful Life,* 1946; *Harvey,* 1950; *Anatomy of a Murder,* 1959; *Mr. Hobbs Takes a Vacation,* 1962; *Shenandoah,* 1965; *Airport '77,* 1977.

STICKNEY, DOROTHY HAYES, June 21, 1900 (Dickinson, N.D.). U.S. stage actress. Best known for her role as the mother in the play *Life with Father,* 1939; played one-woman show about EDNA ST. VINCENT MILLAY, 1958. (Wife of HOWARD LINDSAY.)

STOCKWELL, DEAN, Mar. 5, 1936 (Hollywood, Calif.). U.S. actor. Films: *The Green Years,* 1946; *The Boy with Green Hair,* 1948; *Compulsion,* 1959; *Sons and Lovers,* 1960; *Long Day's Journey into Night,* 1962; *The Dunwich Horror,* 1970.

STONE, LEWIS, Nov. 15, 1879 (Worcester, Mass.)–Sept. 12, 1953. U.S. actor. Character actor in both silent films and talkies; best known for his role as Judge Hardy in the "Andy Hardy" film series, 1937–47.

STORCH, LARRY, Jan. 8, 1925 (New York, N.Y.). U.S. comedic character actor. Films: *Captain Newman, M.D.,* 1963; *Wild and Wonderful,* 1964. TV: *F Troop* (series), 1965–67.

STORM, GALE, born Josephine Cottle, Apr. 5, 1922 (Bloomington, Tex.). U.S. actress. In films, 1930s–50s; best known for her role as Margie Albright in the TV series *My Little Margie,* 1952–55.

STRAIGHT, BEATRICE, born Beatrice Whitney Dickerman, Aug. 2, 1918 (Old Westbury, N.Y.). U.S. actress. Distinguished Broadway stage career; won Best Supporting Actress AA for her performance in the film *Network,* 1976.

STRASBERG, SUSAN, May 22, 1938 (New York, N.Y.). U.S. actress. Created the title role in stage production of *The Diary of Anne Frank,* 1955. Films: *Picnic,* 1955; *In Praise of Older Women,* 1979. TV: *Toma* (series), 1973-74. (Daughter of LEE STRASBERG.)

STRAUSS, PETER, 1947 (Croton-on-Hudson, N.Y.). U.S. actor. Best known for starring role in the TV miniseries *Rich Man, Poor Man,* 1976-77. Films: *Soldier Blue,* 1971; *The Last Tycoon,* 1976; *The Jericho Mile* (TV), 1979.

STREISAND, BARBRA, born Barbara Joan Streisand, Apr. 24, 1942 (Brooklyn, N.Y.). U.S. actress, singer. Achieved Broadway stardom as Fanny Brice in *Funny Girl,* 1964 (Best Actress AA for film, 1968). Films: *Hello Dolly,* 1969; *The Owl and the Pussycat,* 1970; *What's Up, Doc?,* 1972; *The Way We Were,* 1973; *Funny Lady,* 1975; *A Star Is Born,* 1977. Record albums: *People,* 1965; *Color Me Barbra,* 1966; *Superman,* 1977; *Wet,* 1979. (One-time wife of ELLIOTT GOULD.)

STRITCH, ELAINE, Feb. 2, 1925 (Detroit, Mich.). U.S. actress, singer. In a long musical stage career, best known for her role in *Company* (1970).

STRUTHERS, SALLY ANNE, July 28, 1948 (Portland, Ore.). U.S. actress. Best known for her role as Gloria in the TV series *All in the Family,* 1971-78; received Emmy award, 1972.

SULLAVAN, MARGARET BROOKE, May 16, 1911 (Norfolk, Va.)-Jan. 1, 1960. U.S. actress. Plays: *Coquette,* 1934; *Stage Door,* 1936; *The Voice of the Turtle,* 1943. Films: *Only Yesterday,* 1933; *The Shopworn Angel,* 1938; *The Shop around the Corner,* 1940; *Back Street,* 1941

SULLIVAN, BARRY, born Patrick Barry Sullivan, Aug. 29, 1912 (New York, N.Y.). U.S. actor. Plays: *The Man Who Came to Dinner,* 1940; *The Caine Mutiny,* 1954. Films: *Earthquake,* 1974; *Oh God,* 1977.

SUMMERVILLE, SLIM, born George J. Summerville, 1892 (Albuquerque, N.M.)-Jan. 5, 1946. U.S. character actor. Associated with MACK SENNETT in Keystone comedies. Other films: *All Quiet on the Western Front,* 1930; *Rebecca of Sunnybrook Farm,* 1938; *Tobacco Road,* 1941.

SWANSON, GLORIA MAY JOSEPHINE, Mar. 27, 1899 (Chicago, Ill.). U.S. actress. Films: *Male and Female,* 1919; *The Affairs of Anatol,* 1921; *Sadie Thompson,* 1928; *Queen Kelly,* 1928; *Sunset Boulevard,* 1950; *The Killer Bees,* 1973; *Airport 1975,* 1974. Broadway stage career includes role in *Butterflies Are Free,* 1970. Known for her interest in fashion and nutrition.

SWEET, BLANCHE, June 18, 1895 (Chicago, Ill.). U.S. actress. A silent-screen star, 1908-30. Films: *The Secret Sin,* 1915; *Anna Christie,* 1923; *Tess of the D'Urbervilles,* 1924.

SWIT, LORETTA, Nov. 4, ? (Passaic, N.J.). U.S. actress. Best known for her role as "Hot Lips" Houlihan in the TV series *M*A*S*H,* 1972- .

TALBOT, LYLE, Feb. 8, 1904 (Pittsburgh, Pa.). U.S. actor. Films: *Love Is a Racket,* 1932; *Up in Arms,* 1944; *There's No Business like Show Business,* 1954; *Sunrise at Campobello,* 1960.

TALBOT, NITA, 1930 (New York, N.Y.). U.S. actress, comedienne. Films: *Bundle of Joy,* 1956; *Once Upon a Horse,* 1958; *Very Special Favor,* 1965; *The Cool Ones,* 1967. TV: *Hot off the Wire* (movie), 1961; *Here We Go Again* (movie), 1972.

TALMADGE, NORMA, 1893 (Brooklyn, N.Y.)-Dec. 24, 1957. U.S. actress. A silent-film heroine. Films: *Battle Cry of Peace,* 1914; *Going Straight,* 1915; *Forbidden City,* 1918; *The Sign on the Door,* 1921; *Camille,* 1927; *The Dove,* 1928; *Dubarry—Woman of Passion,* 1930.

TAMIROFF, AKIM, 1899 (Russia)-Sept. 17, 1972. Russian-U.S. character actor. In U.S. films, from 1923. Films: *Sadie McKee,* 1934; *The General Died at Dawn,* 1936; *The Great Gambini,* 1937; *The Way of All Flesh,* 1940; *For Whom the Bell Tolls,* 1943.

TASHMAN, LILYAN, 1899-Mar. 21, 1934. U.S. actress. A silent-screen star. Films: *Experience,* 1921; *Manhandled,* 1924; *Don't Tell the Wife,* 1927; *New York Nights,* 1929; *Murder by the Clock,* 1931; *Scarlet Dawn,* 1932; *Frankie and Johnny,* 1933.

TAYLOR, ELIZABETH, Feb. 27, 1932 (London, Eng.). English-U.S. actress. Glamorous leading lady of films; began as a child actress. Films: *National Velvet,* 1944; *Life with Father,* 1947; *Little Women,* 1949; *Father of the Bride,* 1950; *A Place in the Sun,* 1951; *Giant,* 1956; *Cat on a Hot Tin Roof,* 1958; *Butterfield 8* (Best Actress AA), 1960; *Cleopatra,* 1962; *Who's Afraid of Virginia Woolf?,* (Best Actress AA), 1966; *A Little Night Music,* 1977. (One-time wife of MICHAEL WILDING, MICHAEL TODD, EDDIE FISHER, RICHARD BURTON; wife of JOHN WARNER.)

TAYLOR, ESTELLE, born Estelle Boylan, 1899-April 4, 1958. U.S. stage and film actress. Films: *While New York Sleeps,* 1922; *The Ten Commandments,* 1923; *Don Juan,* 1926; *The Whip Woman,* 1927.

TAYLOR, KENT, born Louis Weiss, May 11, 1907 (Nashua, Ia.). U.S. actor. Films: *I'm No Angel,* 1933; *Bomber's Moon,* 1943; *Ghost Town,* 1956; *Harbor Lights,* 1964; *Smashing the Crime Syndicate,* 1973. TV: *Boston Blackie* (series), 1951-52.

TAYLOR, ROBERT, born Spangler Arlington Brugh, Aug. 5, 1911 (Filley, Neb.)-June 8, 1969. U.S. actor. Films: *Magnificent Obsession,* 1935; *Knights of the Round Table,* 1953; *Devil May Care,* 1968; *The Glass Sphinx,* 1968. TV: *The Detectives* (series), 1959-62.

TAYLOR, ROD, Jan. 11, 1930 (Sydney, Austrl.). U.S. actor. Films: *The Time Machine,* 1960; *The Birds,* 1964; *Sunday in New York,* 1966; *The Glass Bottom Boat,* 1966; *Hotel,* 1967. TV: *Hong Kong* (series), 1960-61; *The Oregon Trail* (series), 1977.

TEARLE, CONWAY, born Frederick Levy, 1878 (New York, N.Y.)-Oct. 1, 1938. U.S. actor. A silent-film star. Films: *Stella Mavis,* 1918; *Gold Diggers of Broadway,* 1929; *Vanity Fair,* 1932; *Klondike Annie,* 1936; *Romeo and Juliet,* 1936.

TEMPLE, SHIRLEY (Mrs. Charles A. Black), Apr. 23, 1928 (Santa Monica, Calif.). U.S. actress, diplomat. A child film star. Films: *Stand Up and Cheer,* 1934; *Bright Eyes* (awarded special AA), 1934; *Our Little Girl,* 1935; *Wee Willie Winkie,* 1937; *Rebecca of Sunnybrook Farm,* 1938; *Little Miss Broadway,* 1938; *The Blue Bird,* 1940; *That Hagen Girl,* 1947. TV: *Shirley Temple's Storybook* (series), 1959-61. U.S. rep. to the UN, 1969-70; U.S. amb. to Ghana, 1974-76; White House protocol chief, 1976-77.

THOMAS, DANNY, born Amos Jacobs, Jan. 6, 1914 (Deerfield, Mich.). U.S. actor. Films: *Call Me Mister,* 1948; *Jazz Singer,* 1952. TV: *The Danny Thomas Show* (series), 1953-65, 70-71; received special Emmy awards (1953-64) and humanitarian awards; founder of St. Jude's Children's Research Hospital in Memphis, Tenn. (Father of MARLO THOMAS.)

THOMAS, MARLO, Nov. 21, 1943 (Detroit, Mich.). U.S. actress. Best known for her role in *That Girl* TV series, 1966-71. Plays: *Thieves,* 1974; *Barefoot in the Park,* (London), 1974. Wrote the TV special *Free to Be ... You and Me,* which won Emmy award for Best Children's Show, 1977. (Daughter of DANNY THOMAS.)

THOMAS, RICHARD, June 13, 1951 (New York, N.Y.). U.S. actor. Best known for starring role in TV series *The Waltons,* 1972-79. Films: *Winning,* 1969; *Last Summer,* 1969; *The Red Badge of Courage,* 1974; *The Silence,* 1975. Poetry: *Poems by Richard Thomas,* 1974.

THOMPSON, SADA CAROLYN, Sept. 27, 1929 (Des Moines, Ia.). U.S. actress. Plays: *The Clandestine Marriage,* 1954; *Much Ado about Nothing,* 1957. Films: *Desperate Characters,* 1971. TV: *Family* (series), 1976-   ; received Tony award, 1972.

TIERNEY, GENE, Nov. 20, 1920 (Brooklyn, N.Y.). U.S. actress. Films: *Return of Frank James,* 1940; *Hudson's Bay,* 1940; *Tobacco Road,* 1941; *Belle Star,* 1941; *Sundown,* 1941; *Son of Fury,* 1942; *Heaven Can Wait,* 1943; *The Razor's Edge,* 1946; *The Ghost and Mrs. Muir,* 1947; *The Left Hand of God,* 1954; *Advise and Consent,* 1962; published autobiog., *Gene Tierney by Gene Tierney,* 1979.

TOBIAS, GEORGE, -1901 (New York, N.Y.)-Feb. 27, 1980. U.S. actor. Films: *Between Two Worlds,* 1944; *Sinbad the Sailor,* 1947; *The Glenn Miller Story,* 1953; *Seven Little Foys,* 1955; *The Glass Bottom Boat,* 1966. TV: *Bewitched* (series), 1964-72.

TODD, THELMA, 1905-1935. U.S. actress. Films: *Fascinating Youth,* 1926; *Aloha,* 1930; *Monkey Business,* 1931; *Horse Feathers,* 1932; *Two for Tonight,* 1935.

TOLER, SIDNEY, Apr. 28, 1874 (Warrensburg, Mo.)-Feb. 12, 1947. U.S. character actor. Played the title role in 25 episodes in the "Charlie Chan" film series. Other films: *Wide Open Faces,* 1938; *White Savage,* 1943; *The Scarlet Clue,* 1945.

TOMLIN, LILY, 1939 (Detroit, Mich.). U.S. actress, comedienne. Rose to prominence in the TV series *Rowan and Martin's Laugh-In,* 1970-73; won two Emmy awards for her TV special, 1972. Films: *Nashville,* 1975; *The Late Show,* 1977; *Moment by Moment,* 1979. Records: *This Is a Recording, And That's the Truth, Modern Scream, On Stage* (1977).

TONE, FRANCHOT, Feb. 27, 1906 (Niagara Falls, N.Y.)-Sept. 18, 1968. U.S. actor. Stage and film career. Films: *The Wiser Sex,* 1932; *They Gave Him a Gun,* 1937; *Five Graves to Cairo,* 1943; *Phantom Lady,* 1944; *Advise and Consent,* 1962; *In Harm's Way,* 1965.

TOOMEY, REGIS, Aug. 13, 1902 (Pittsburgh, Pa.). U.S. character actor. Films: *Alibi,* 1929; *The Big Sleep,* 1946; *Guys and Dolls,* 1955; *Peter Gunn,* 1967. TV: *Burke's Law* (series), 1963-65.

TORN, RIP, born Elmore Torn, Jr., Feb. 6, 1931 (Temple, Tex.). U.S. actor. Plays: *Cat on a Hot Tin Roof,* 1955; *Sweet Bird of Youth,* 1959. Films: *The Cincinnati Kid,* 1965; *Crazy Joe,* 1974; *The Man Who Fell to Earth,* 1976.

TRACY, LEE, Apr. 14, 1898 (Atlanta, Ga.)-Oct. 18, 1968. U.S. actor. Films: *She Got What She Wanted,* 1930; *Liliom,* 1930; *Dinner at Eight,* 1933; *The Lemon Drop Kid,* 1934; *The Best Man,* 1964.

TRACY, SPENCER, Apr. 5, 1900 (Milwaukee,

Wisc.)-June 10, 1967. U.S. actor. A leading man in over 80 films, often with KATHARINE HEPBURN. Films: *Captains Courageous* (Best Actor AA), 1937; *Boys' Town,* (Best Actor AA), 1938; *Northwest Passage,* 1940; *Adam's Rib,* 1949; *Father of the Bride,* 1950; *Bad Day at Black Rock,* 1954; *Inherit the Wind,* 1962; *Guess Who's Coming to Dinner,* 1967.

TRAVOLTA, JOHN, Feb. 18, 1954 (Englewood, N.J.). U.S. actor. A 1970s teen idol. TV: *Welcome Back Kotter* (series), 1975-79. Films: *Carrie,* 1976; *Saturday Night Fever,* 1978; *Grease,* 1978. *Moment by Moment,* 1979.

TREVOR, CLAIRE, born Claire Wemlinger, Mar. 8, 1909 (New York, N.Y.) U.S. actress. Films: *Stagecoach,* 1939; *Murder, My Sweet,* 1944; *Key Largo* (Best Supporting Actress AA), 1948; *How to Murder Your Wife,* 1965.

TRUEX, ERNEST, Sept. 19, 1889 (Kansas City, Mo.)-June 27, 1973. U.S. actor. Began career in silent films, then did talkies. Films: *Whistling in the Dark,* 1933; *The Warrior's Husband,* 1933; *The Adventures of Marco Polo,* 1938.

TUCKER, FORREST, Feb. 12, 1919 (Plainfield, Ind.). U.S. actor. Star of the TV series *F Troop,* 1965-67. Films: *The Yearling,* 1947; *Sands of Iwo Jima,* 1950; *The Wild Blue Yonder,* 1952; *The Abominable Snowman,* 1957; *The Night They Raided Minsky's,* 1968.

TURNER, LANA, Feb. 8, 1920 (Wallace, Idaho). U.S. actress. The original "sweater girl." Films: *Love Finds Andy Hardy,* 1938; *Ziegfeld Girl,* 1941; *Somewhere I'll Find You,* 1942; *Weekend at the Waldorf,* 1947; *Cass Timberlane,* 1947; *Imitation of Life,* 1959; *Madame X,* 1966. TV: *The Survivors,* 1969-70.

TURPIN, BEN, Sept. 17, 1869 (New Orleans, La.)-July 1, 1940. U.S. comedic actor. Best known for his cross-eyed expression; in films, 1907-40.

TYSON, CICELY, Dec. 19, ? (New York, N.Y.). U.S. actress. Film and TV career; cofounder of the Dance Theatre of Harlem. Films: *Sounder,* 1972. TV: *The Autobiography of Miss Jane Pitman* (movie, Emmy award), 1973; *Roots* (miniseries), 1977.

UMEKI, MIYOSHI, 1929 (Hokkaido, Jap.). U.S. actress. Films: *Sayonara,* (Best Supporting Actress AA), 1957; *Flower Drum Song,* 1961. TV: *The Courtship of Eddie's Father* (series), 1969-72.

VACCARO, BRENDA, Nov. 18, 1939 (Brooklyn, N.Y.). U.S. actress. Stage, film, TV career. Films: *Midnight Cowboy,* 1969; *Airport '77,* 1977. Plays: *Cactus Flower,* 1965; *How, Now, Dow Jones,* 1968.

VALENTINO, RUDOLPH, May 6, 1895 (Castellaneta, It.)-Aug. 23, 1926. U.S. actor. Romantic idol of the 1920s. Films: *The Four Horsemen of the Apocalypse,* 1921; *The Sheik,* 1921; *Blood and Sand,* 1922; *Monsieur Beaucaire,* 1924; *The Eagle,* 1925; *Son of the Sheik,* 1926.

VANCE, VIVIAN, July 26, 1912 (Cherryvale, Kan.)-Aug. 17, 1979. U.S. actress. Stage and TV career; best known for her role as Ethel Mertz on the TV series *I Love Lucy,* 1951-61; received Emmy award, 1953.

VAN CLEEF, LEE, Jan. 9, 1925 (Somerville, N.J.). U.S. actor. A former accountant. Films: *For a Few Dollars More,* 1967; *The Good, the Bad and the Ugly,* 1967; *The Magnificent Seven Ride,* 1972.

VAN DEVERE, TRISH, 1943 (Tenafly, N.J.). U.S. actress. Films: *Where's Poppa?,* 1970; *The Day of the Dolphins,* 1973; *The Savage Is Loose,* 1976. (Wife of GEORGE C. SCOTT.)

VAN DOREN, MAMIE, born Joan Lucille Olander,

Feb. 6, 1933 (Rowena, S.D.). U.S. actress. Best known for her appearances in "bombshell" roles in films of the 1950s and 1960s. Films: *Running Wild*, 1955; *The Girl in the Black Stockings*, 1956; *Teacher's Pet*, 1958.

VAN DYKE, DICK, Dec. 13, 1925 (West Plains, Mo.). U.S. actor, singer, dancer. TV: *The Dick Van Dyke Show* (series), 1961-66; *The New Dick Van Dyke Show* (series), 1971-74. Films: *Mary Poppins*, 1965; *Chitty Chitty Bang Bang*, 1968. Plays: *Bye Bye Birdie*, 1960. (Brother of JERRY VAN DYKE.)

VAN DYKE, JERRY, 1932 (Danville, Ill.). U.S. actor. Star of the TV series *My Mother the Car* (1965-66) and *13 Queens Blvd.* (1979). (Brother of DICK VAN DYKE.)

VAN FLEET, JO, 1922 (Oakland, Calif.). U.S. actress. Films: *East of Eden*, 1954; *Gunfight at the O.K. Corral*, 1956. Plays: *The Trip to Bountiful*, 1953; *Look Homeward, Angel*, 1958; *Oh Dad, Poor Dad...*, 1962.

VAN PATTEN, DICK VINCENT Dec. 9, 1928 (Kew Gardens, N.Y.). U.S. actor. Stage and TV career; best known for his role as Tom Bradford in the TV series *Eight is Enough*, 1977-   .

VARSI, DIANE, 1938 (San Francisco, Calif.). U.S. actress. Films: *Peyton Place*, 1957; *Ten North Frederick*, 1958; *Wild in the Streets*, 1968; *Johnny Got His Gun*, 1971.

VAUGHN, ROBERT FRANCIS, Nov. 22, 1932 (New York, N.Y.). U.S. actor. Best known for role as Napoleon Solo in the TV series *The Man from U.N.C.L.E.*, 1964-68.

VIGODA, ABE, Feb. 24, 1922 (New York, N.Y.). U.S. actor. Sad-faced character actor who gained fame as Detective Phil Fish on the TV series *Barney Miller*, 1975-77; starred in the TV series *Fish*, 1977-78.

VINCENT, JAN-MICHAEL, July 15, 1944 (Ventura, Calif.). U.S. actor. Films: *The World's Greatest Athlete*, 1973; *Buster and Billie*, 1974; *Bite the Bullet*, 1974; *Baby Blue Marine*, 1976; *Big Wednesday*, 1978.

VOIGHT, JON, Dec. 29, 1938 (Yonkers, N.Y.). U.S. actor. Films: *Midnight Cowboy*, 1969; *Catch-22*, 1970; *Deliverance*, 1972; *Conrack*, 1974; *Coming Home*, (Best Actor AA), 1978.

VON FÜRSTENBERG, BETSY, Aug. 16, 1932 (Neiheim Heusen, Ger.). U.S. stage actress. Plays: *Oh, Men!, Oh Women!*, 1953; *The Chalk Garden*, 1955; *Mary, Mary*, 1961; *The Paisley Convertible*, 1967; *The Gingerbread Lady*, 1970; *Absurd Person Singular*, 1976.

VON ZELL, HARRY, July 11, 1906 (Indianapolis, Ind.). U.S. actor. Best known as the announcer and friend of the family on *The George Burns and Gracie Allen Show*, 1951-58; also announced for EDDIE CANTOR, FRED ALLEN, and DINAH SHORE.

WAGGONER, LYLE WESLEY, Aug. 13, 1935 (Kansas City, Kan.). U.S. actor. Regular on the TV variety show, *The Carol Burnett Show* (1967-74), and series *Wonder Woman*, (1976-79).

WAGNER, LINDSAY J., June 22, 1949 (Los Angeles, Calif.). U.S. actress. Star of the TV series *The Bionic Woman*, 1976-78. Films: *Two People*, 1972; *The Paper Chase*, 1973.

WAGNER, ROBERT, Feb. 10, 1930 (Detroit, Mich.). U.S. actor. TV: *It Takes a Thief* (series), 1968-70; *Switch* (series), 1975-78. Films: *All the Fine Young Cannibals*, 1959; *The Longest Day*, 1962; *The Towering Inferno*, 1976. (Husband of NATALIE WOOD.)

WAITE, RALPH, June 22, 1929 (White Plains, N.Y.). U.S. actor. Best known for his role as John Walton in the TV series *The Waltons*, 1972-   ; appeared in the TV miniseries *Roots*, 1977; founder of the Los Angeles Actors Theatre, 1975.

WALKER, CLINT, May 30, 1927 (Hartford, Ill.). U.S. actor. Best known for starring role in the TV series *Cheyenne*, 1955-63.

WALKER, NANCY, born Ann Myrtle Swoyer, May 10, 1921 (Philadelphia, Pa.). U.S. actress. Plays: *Best Foot Forward*, 1941; *On the Town*, 1944; *Do-Re-Mi*, 1960. TV: *McMillan and Wife* (series), 1971-74; *Rhoda* (series), 1974-78.

WALKER, ROBERT, Oct. 13, 1914 (Utah)-Aug. 28, 1951. U.S. actor. Film career, 1939-51. Films: "Private Hargrove" series, 1940s; *One Touch of Venus*, 1948; *Strangers on a Train*, 1951. (One-time husband of JENNIFER JONES.)

WALLACH, ELI, Dec. 7, 1915 (Brooklyn, N.Y.). U.S. actor. Plays: *Rose Tattoo*, (Best Actor Tony) 1950; *Teahouse of the August Moon*, 1954; *Rhinoceros*, 1961; *The Waltz of the Toreadors*, 1973; *Diary of Anne Frank*, 1979. Films: *The Tiger Makes Out*, 1967; *The Good, the Bad, and the Ugly*, 1967; *The Sentinel*, 1977. (Husband of ANNE JACKSON.)

WALTHALL, HENRY B., Mar. 16, 1878 (Shelby City, Ala.)-June 17, 1936. U.S. actor. Pioneer of the silent screen. Films: *Birth of a Nation*, 1915; *The Scarlet Letter*, 1926.

WARDEN, JACK, Sept. 18, 1920 (Newark, N.J.). U.S. actor. Starred in the TV series *N.Y.P.D.*, 1967-69. Plays: *Golden Boy*, 1964; *A View from the Bridge*, 1965; *The Man in the Glass Booth*, 1968. Films: *From Here to Eternity*, 1953; *Twelve Angry Men*, 1957; *The Bachelor Party*, 1957; *Shampoo*, 1975.

WATSON, LUCILE, May 27, 1879 (Quebec, Can.)-June 24, 1962. U.S. character actress. Stage and film career. Films: *The Women*, 1939; *Waterloo Bridge*, 1940; *The Great Lie*, 1941; *Watch on the Rhine*, 1943.

WAYNE, DAVID, born Wayne James McMeekan, Jan. 30, 1914 (Traverse City, Mich.). U.S. actor. Plays: *Finian's Rainbow*, 1947; *Mr. Roberts*, 1948; *Teahouse of the August Moon*, 1953. Films: *Adam's Rib*, 1949; *My Blue Heaven*, 1950; *With a Song in My Heart*, 1952; *The Apple Dumpling Gang*, 1975.

WAYNE, JOHN, born Marion Michael Morrison, May 26, 1907 (Winterset, Iowa)-June 11, 1979. U.S. actor. Began career as a stunt man, 1926-28; known for leading roles in film westerns. Films: *Stagecoach*, 1939; *Red River*, 1946; *Sands of Iwo Jima*, 1949; *The Quiet Man*, 1951; *Horse Soldiers*, 1959; *The Longest Day*, 1961; *Sons of Katie Elder*, 1965; *True Grit* (Best Actor AA), 1968; Congressional Medal, 1979.

WEAVER, DENNIS, June 4, 1924 (Joplin, Mo.). U.S. actor. Best known for roles in the TV series *Gunsmoke* (1955-64) and *McCloud* (1970-77).

WEAVER, FRITZ WILLIAM, Jan. 19, 1926 (Pittsburgh, Pa.). U.S. actor. Stage, film and TV career. Plays: *White Devil*, 1955; *A Shot in the Dark*, 1962; *Baker Street*, 1965. Films: *Marathon Man*, 1976; *Demon Seed*, 1977. TV: *Holocaust* (miniseries), 1979.

WEBB, CLIFTON, born Webb Parmelee Hallenbeck, Nov. 19, 1896 (Indianapolis, Ind.)-Oct. 13, 1966. U.S. character actor. Films: *Laura*, 1944; *The Razor's Edge*, 1946; *Sitting Pretty*, 1947; *Cheaper by the Dozen*, 1950; *Dreamboat*, 1952; *Three Coins in the Fountain*, 1954.

WEBB, JACK, Apr. 2, 1920 (Santa Monica, Calif.). U.S. actor, producer. Starred as Sgt. Joe Friday in the TV series *Dragnet,* 1952–70; produced the TV series *Adam-12* (1968–75) and *Emergency* (1972–77). (One-time husband of JULIE LONDON.)

WELCH, RAQUEL, Sept. 5, 1942 (Chicago, Ill.). U.S. actress. A sex symbol of the 1960s–70s. Films: *Myra Breckenridge,* 1970; *Kansas City Bomber,* 1972; *The Three Musketeers,* 1974; *Mother, Jugs and Speed,* 1976.

WELD, TUESDAY, born Susan Ker Weld, Aug. 27, 1943 (New York, N.Y.). U.S. actress. Films: *The Five Pennies,* 1959; *Return to Peyton Place,* 1961; *Lord Love a Duck,* 1966; *Pretty Poison,* 1968; *I Walk the Line,* 1970.; *Looking for Mr. Goodbar,* 1977.

WEST, MAE, Aug. 17, 1892 (Brooklyn, N.Y.). U.S. actress. Stage career, from 1897; a sex symbol in films since the early 1930s. Films: *She Done Him Wrong,* 1933; *I'm No Angel,* 1933; *Go West, Young Man,* 1936; *My Little Chickadee,* 1940; *Myra Breckenridge,* 1969.

WHITE, BETTY, Jan. 17, ? (Oak Park, Ill.). U.S. actress. Stage, film, TV career. TV: *The Mary Tyler Moore Show* (series), 1973–77; *The Betty White Show* (series), 1977–78.

WHITE, JESSE, born Jesse Marc Weidenfeld, Jan. 3, 1919 (Buffalo, N.Y.). U.S. character actor. Plays: *Harvey,* 1944; *Born Yesterday,* 1949. Films: *Harvey,* 1950; *Death of a Salesman,* 1951; *The Bad Seed,* 1956. TV: *The Danny Thomas Show* (series), 1955–57.

WHITE, PEARL, Mar. 4, 1889 (Green Ridge, Mo.)–Aug. 4, 1938. U.S. actress. A silent-film star best known for her role in *The Perils of Pauline,* 1914.

WHITMAN, STUART, Feb. 1, 1926 (San Francisco, Calif.). U.S. actor. Films: *When Worlds Collide,* 1952; *Ten North Frederick,* 1958; *The Mark,* 1962; *Those Magnificent Men in Their Flying Machines,* 1965.

WHITMORE, JAMES ALLEN, Oct. 1, 1921 (White Plains, N.Y.). U.S. actor. Best known for stage impersonations of famous people. Plays: *Command Decision* (Tony award), 1947; *Will Rogers, USA,* 1973. Films: *Black like Me,* 1962; *Give 'em Hell, Harry* (film and play), 1974.

WIDMARK, RICHARD, Dec. 26, 1914 (Sunrise, Minn.). U.S. actor. Films: *Yellow Sky,* 1948; *Halls of Montezuma,* 1950; *Judgment at Nuremberg,* 1961; *How the West Was Won,* 1962; *Cheyenne Autumn,* 1963; *Murder on the Orient Express,* 1974.

WILDE, CORNEL, Oct, 13, 1918 (New York, N.Y.). U.S. actor. Films: *A Song to Remember,* 1944; *The Bandit of Sherwood Forest,* 1946; *The Greatest Show on Earth,* 1953; *Woman's World,* 1954.

WILDER, GENE, born Jerry Silberman, June 11, 1935 (Milwaukee, Wisc.). U.S. comedic actor. Films: *The Producers,* 1968; *Start the Revolution without Me,* 1969; *Willy Wonka and the Chocolate Factory,* 1971; *Blazing Saddles,* 1973; *The World's Greatest Lover* (also wrote and directed), 1977.

WILLIAMS, CINDY, Aug. 22, 1948 (Van Nuys, Calif.). U.S. actress. Best known for her role as Shirley in the TV series *Laverne and Shirley,* 1976–   . Films: *American Graffiti,* 1973; *The Conversation,* 1974.

WILLIAMS, ESTHER, Aug. 8, 1923 (Los Angeles, Calif.). U.S. actress. A former swimming champion. Films: *Bathing Beauty,* 1944; *Take Me Out to the Ball Game,* 1948; *Dangerous When Wet,* 1953.

WILLIAMS, ROBIN, July 21, 1955 (Edinburgh, Scotland). U.S. comedic actor. Star of the TV series *Mork and Mindy,* 1978–

WILLS, CHILL, July 18, 1902 (Seagoville, Tex.)–Dec. 15, 1978. U.S. character actor. Best known as the voice of Francis the Talking Mule in the film series of the same name, 1940s–50s.

WILSON, DEMOND, ? (Valdosta, Ga.). U.S. actor. Best known for role on TV series *Sanford and Son,* 1972–77.

WILSON, MARIE, born Katherine Elizabeth White, Dec. 30, 1917 (Anaheim, Calif.)–Nov. 23, 1972. U.S. actress. Best known for her role in *My Friend Irma* (film, 1949; TV series, 1952–54).

WINDOM, WILLIAM, Sept. 28, 1923 (New York, N.Y.). U.S. actor. Film and TV career; played lead roles in the TV series *The Farmer's Daughter* (1963–66) and *My World and Welcome to It* (1969–72).

WINFIELD, PAUL EDWARD, May 22, 1941 (Los Angeles, Calif.). U.S. actor. A leading black film actor. Films: *The Lost Man,* 1969; *Sounder,* 1972; *Conrack,* 1974; *Damnation Alley,* 1977.

WINKLER, HENRY FRANKLIN, Oct. 30, 1945 (New York, N.Y.). U.S. actor. Best known for his role as "The Fonz" in the TV series *Happy Days,* 1973–   . Films: *The Lords of Flatbush,* 1972; *Heroes,* 1977; *The One and Only,* 1977.

WINNINGER, CHARLES, May 26, 1884 (Athens, Wisc.)–Jan. 1969. U.S. character actor. Films: *Show Boat,* 1936; *Destry Rides Again,* 1939; *Ziegfeld Girl,* 1941; *State Fair,* 1945; *Give My Regards to Broadway,* 1948; *The Sun Shines Bright,* 1954.

WINTERS, JONATHAN, Nov. 11, 1925 (Dayton, Ohio). U.S. comedian. Numerous TV and film appearances; a regular on TV game show *Hollywood Squares,* 1975–   ; known for zany characters, especially "Maudie Frickett."

WINTERS, SHELLEY, Aug. 18, 1922 (St. Louis, Mo.). U.S. actress. Films: *The Diary of Anne Frank* (Best Supporting Actress AA), 1958; *Lolita,* 1962; *Patch of Blue,* 1965; *Alfie,* 1965; *The Poseidon Adventure,* 1972; *Next Stop Greenwich Village,* 1976.

WITHERS, JANE, 1927 (Atlanta. Ga.). U.S. actress. A child star of the 1930s. Films: *Bright Eyes,* 1934; *Ginger,* 1935; *Giant,* 1956. Also known for TV commercials as Josephine the Plumber.

WONG, ANNA MAY, born Lu Tsong Wong, Jan. 3, 1907 (Los Angeles, Calif.)–Feb. 3, 1961. U.S. actress. Film career, 1919–60. Films: *Piccadilly,* 1929; *Chu Chin Chow,* 1933; *Java Head,* 1934.

WOOD, NATALIE, born Natasha Gurdin, July 20, 1938 (San Francisco, Calif.). U.S. actress. Films: *Miracle on 34th Street,* 1947; *Rebel without a Cause,* 1953; *West Side Story,* 1961; *Sex and the Single Girl,* 1964; *Bob and Carol and Ted and Alice,* 1969. (Wife of ROBERT WAGNER.)

WOOD, PEGGY, Feb. 9, 1892 (Brooklyn, N.Y.).–Mar. 18, 1978. U.S. character actress. A former opera singer; played the title role in the TV series *Mama,* 1949–56; films include *The Sound of Music,* 1965.

WOODWARD, JOANNE GIGNILLIAT, Feb. 27, 1930 (Thomasville, Ga.). U.S. actress. Films: *Three Faces of Eve* (Best Actress AA), 1957; *Long Hot Summer,* 1958; *Rachel, Rachel,* 1968; *Summer Wishes, Winter Dreams,* 1973. (Wife of PAUL NEWMAN.)

WOOLLEY, MONTY, born Edgar Montillion Woolley, Aug. 17, 1888 (New York, N.Y.)–May 6, 1963. U.S. actor, director. Plays, dir.: *The New Yorkers*, 1930; *50 Million Frenchmen*, 1929; *Jubilee*, 1935. Films, actor: *The Man Who Came to Dinner*, 1941 (also on stage, 1939); *Holy Matrimony*, 1943; *Night and Day*, 1946; *Miss Tatlock's Millions*, 1948.

WORTH, IRENE, June 23, 1916 (Nebraska). U.S. stage actress. Plays: *Toys in the Attic*, 1960; *Sweet Bird of Youth*, 1975; *The Cherry Orchard*, 1977.

WRAY, FAY, Sept. 10, 1907 (Alberta, Can.). U.S. actress. A leading lady in 1930s films; best known for her screams in *King Kong*, 1933; other films include *The Most Dangerous Game*, 1932.

WRIGHT, TERESA, Oct. 27, 1918 (New York, N.Y.). U.S. actress. Films: *The Little Foxes*, 1941; *Mrs. Miniver* (Best Supporting Actress AA), 1942; *Shadow of a Doubt*, 1943; *The Best Years of Our Lives*, 1946; *The Men*, 1950; *The Search for Bridey Murphy*, 1956.

WYATT, JANE, Aug. 12, 1912 (Campgaw, N.J.). U.S. actress. Stage and film career, 1930–   . TV: *Father Knows Best* (series), 1954–63. Films: *Lost Horizon*, 1934. Received Emmy awards in 1958, 1959, and 1960.

WYMAN, JANE, born Sarah Jane Fulks, Jan. 4, 1914 (St. Joseph, Mo.). U.S. actress. Films: *My Man Godfrey*, 1936; *The Lost Weekend*, 1945; *Johnny Belinda* (Best Actress AA), 1948; *The Magnificent Obsession*, 1954. (One-time wife of RONALD REAGAN.)

WYNN, ED, born Isaiah Edwind Leopold, 1886 (Philadelphia, Pa.)–June 19, 1966. U.S. comedic actor. Vaudeville and stage star. Star of the radio show *The Texaco Fire Chief*. Films: *The Great Man*, 1956; *The Diary of Anne Frank*, 1959; *Mary Poppins*, 1964. (Father of KEENAN WYNN.)

WYNN, KEENAN, July 27, 1916 (New York, N.Y.). U.S. actor. Best known for appearances in WALT DISNEY features, 1962–76. (Son of ED WYNN.)

YOUNG, ALAN, born Angus Young, Nov. 19, 1919 (North Shield, Eng.). U.S. actor. Star of the TV series *Mr. Ed*, 1961–65. Films: *Androcles and the Lion*, 1953; *The Time Machine*, 1959. Now devotes time to the promotion of the Church of Christ.

YOUNG, CLARA KIMBALL, 1890 (Chicago, Ill.)–Oct. 15, 1960. U.S. actress. A silent-screen heroine. Films: *Cardinal Wolsey*, 1912; *Beau Brummell*, 1913; *Lying Wives*, 1925.

YOUNG, GIG, born Byron Barr, Nov. 4, 1917 (St. Cloud, Minn.)–Oct. 19, 1978. U.S. actor. Films: *Come Fill the Cup*, 1951; *Teacher's Pet*, 1958; *They Shoot Horses, Don't They?* (Best Supporting Actor AA), 1969; *Lovers and Other Strangers*, 1970.

YOUNG, LORETTA, born Gretchen Young, Jan. 6, 1913 (Salt Lake City, Utah). U.S. actress. TV: *The Loretta Young Show* (series), 1953–61. Films: *The Story of Alexander Graham Bell*, 1939; *Along Came Jones*, 1946; *The Farmer's Daughter* (Best Actress AA), 1947; *Come to the Stable*, 1949.

YOUNG, ROBERT, Feb. 22, 1907 (Chicago, Ill.). U.S. actor. Starred in the TV series *Father Knows Best* (1954–63) and *Marcus Welby, M.D.* (1969–76). Films: *Strange Interlude*, 1931; *The Bride Wore Red*, 1937; *Northwest Passage*, 1940; *And Baby Makes Three*, 1950.

ZIMBALIST, EFREM, JR. Nov. 30, 1923 (New York, N.Y.). U.S. actor. Starred in the TV series 77 *Sunset Strip* (1958–64) and *The F.B.I.* (1965–74). (Son of EFREM ZIMBALIST.)

FOREIGN ACTORS

AIMÉE, ANOUK, born Françoise Sorya, 1932 (Paris, Fr.). French actress. Leading lady in 1960s films, including *A Man and A Woman* (1966) and *Justine* (1969).

ANDERSON, DAME JUDITH, born Frances Margaret Anderson, Feb. 10, 1898 (Adelaide, Austrl.). Australian actress. Films: *Rebecca*, 1940; *Cat on a Hot Tin Roof*, 1958; *A Man Called Horse*, 1970.

ANDERSSON, BIBI, Nov. 11, 1935 (Stockholm, Swe.). Swedish actress. Success in INGMAR BERGMAN films led to international career. Films: *Wild Strawberries*, 1957; *The Kremlin Letter*, 1970.

ANDRESS, URSULA, 1936 (Switzerland). Swiss actress. Leading film sex symbol of the 1960s. Films: *She*, 1964; *What's New Pussycat?*, 1965. (One-time wife of JOHN DEREK.)

ARLISS, GEORGE, born Augustus George Andrews, Apr. 10, 1868 (London, Eng.)–Feb. 5, 1946. English actor. After long stage career, became international star of historical films, including *Disraeli* (Best Actor AA), 1929.

ATTENBOROUGH, RICHARD, Aug. 29, 1923 (Cambridge, Eng.). English actor, producer, director. Films, actor: *Sand Pebbles*, 1966; Films, dir.: *Young Winston*, 1972; *A Bridge Too Far*, 1975.

AUMONT, JEAN-PIERRE, born Jean-Pierre Salomons, Jan. 5, 1913 (Paris, Fr.). French actor, in U.S. since 1941. Films: *Hotel du Nord*, 1938; *Lili*, 1953; *Day for Night*, 1973.

BADDELEY, HERMIONE, Nov. 13, 1906 (Shropshire, England). British character actress. Long stage and film career in Great Britain. TV: *Maude* (series), 1974–77.

BAIN, CONRAD STAFFORD, Feb. 4, 1923 (Lethbridge, Alta., Can.). Canadian actor. Played supporting role in the TV series *Maude*, 1971–78; star of the TV series *Diff'rent Strokes*, 1978–

BARDOT, BRIGITTE, c.1933–35 (Paris, Fr.). French actress. Billed as "sex kitten." Films: *And God Created Woman*, 1956; *Please, Not Now*, 1961; *Love on a Pillow*, 1962; *Viva Maria*, 1965.

BARTHOLOMEW, FREDDIE, born Frederick Llewellyn, Mar. 28, 1924 (London, Eng.). English actor. Famed as Hollywood child actor. Films: *David Copperfield*, 1935; *Little Lord Fauntleroy*, 1936; *Kidnapped*, 1938; *Tom Brown's Schooldays*, 1940.

BATES, ALAN, Feb. 17, 1934 (Allestree, Eng.). English actor. Stage: *Long Day's Journey Into Night*, 1958; *The Caretaker*, 1960–61; *Poor Richard*, 1965; *Butley*, 1971–72; *Otherwise Engaged*, 1975. Films: *Zorba the Greek*, 1965; *Women in Love*, 1969; *An Unmarried Woman*, 1977.

BELMONDO, JEAN-PAUL, Apr. 9, 1933 (Neuilly-sur-Seine, Fr.). French actor. Off-beat French film lead. Films: *Breathless*, 1959; *That Man from Rio*, 1964; *Pierrot le Fou*, 1965; *The Mississippi Mermaid*, 1969; *Borsalino*, 1970; *Stavisky*, 1974.

BERNHARDT, SARAH ("The Divine Sarah"), born Henriette Rosine Bernard, Oct. 22/23, 1844 (Paris, Fr.)–Mar. 26, 1923. French actress. Revered stage tragedienne, world-renowned for dramatic life on- and off-stage; made nine U.S. tours.

BLOOM, CLAIRE, born Claire Blume, Feb. 15,

ENTERTAINERS

1931 (London, Eng.). English actress. Respected for dramatic roles on London and Broadway stage. Films: *Limelight*, 1952; *The Spy Who Came in from the Cold*, 1966. (One-time wife of ROD STEIGER.)

BOGARDE, DIRK, born Derek van den Bogaerd, Mar. 28, 1921 (London, Eng.). English actor. Successful in comic, dramatic, and character roles. Films: *Quartet*, 1948; *A Tale of Two Cities*, 1958; *Servant*, 1963; *Darling*, 1965; *The Damned*, 1969; *Death in Venice*, 1970.

BOYD, STEPHEN, born William Millar, July 4, 1928 (Belfast, N. Ire.)–June 2, 1977. Irish actor. Leading man in international films. Films: *Ben Hur* (as Messala), 1959; *The Fall of the Roman Empire*, 1964.

BOYER, CHARLES, Aug. 28, 1899 (Figeac, Fr.)–Aug. 26, 1978. French actor. World-famous romantic lead. Films: *History Is Made at Night*, 1937; *All This and Heaven Too*, 1940; *Gaslight*, 1944; *Happy Time*, 1952; *Fanny*, 1962; *Barefoot in the Park*, 1968.

BRAZZI, ROSSANO, Sept. 18, 1916 (Bologna, It.). Italian actor. A romantic lead in films such as *Three Coins in the Fountain* (1954), *Summertime* (1955), and *South Pacific* (1958).

BRUCE, NIGEL, Feb. 4, 1895 (Mexico)–Oct. 8, 1953. British actor. In numerous films, often playing an amiable upper-class buffoon; played Dr. Watson in "Sherlock Holmes" film series.

BUCHHOLZ, HORST, Dec. 4, 1933 (Berlin, Ger.). German actor. Occasionally stars in U.S. films, including *The Magnificent Seven* (1960), *One, Two, Three* (1961), *Fanny* (1961).

BUJOLD, GENEVIEVE, July 1, 1942 (Montreal, Que., Can.). French-Canadian actress. Films: *Anne of the Thousand Days*, 1970; *Obsession*, 1976.

BURR, RAYMOND, May 21, 1917 (New Westminster, B.C., Can.). Canadian actor. Best known for his starring roles in the TV series *Perry Mason* (1957–66) and *Ironside* (1967–75); won Emmy awards in 1961 and 1962.

BURTON, RICHARD, born Richard Jenkins, Nov. 10, 1925 (Pontrhydfen, Wales.) Welsh actor. Known for his commanding dramatic presence and stentorian voice; played Hamlet, many other roles, with Old Vic Company, from 1953; greatest fame came with Broadway *Hamlet*, 1961. Musical: *Camelot*, 1960. Films: *The Robe*, 1953; *Look Back in Anger*, 1959; *Becket*, 1964; *Who's Afraid of Virginia Woolf?*, 1966; *Equus*, 1978. (Twice married to ELIZABETH TAYLOR.)

CABOT, SEBASTIAN, July 6, 1918 (London, Eng.)–Aug. 23, 1977. British character actor. Featured in the TV series *Checkmate* (1960–62) and *Family Affair* (1966–71). Films: *Kismet*, 1955; *The Family Jewels*, 1965.

CAINE, MICHAEL, born Maurice Micklewhite, Mar. 14, 1933 (London, Eng.). British actor. Films: *The Ipcress File*, 1965; *Alfie*, 1966; *Funeral in Berlin*, 1966; *Sleuth*, 1972.

CALDWELL, ZOE, Sept. 14, 1933 (Melbourne, Austrl.). Australian stage actress. Plays: *The Prime of Miss Jean Brodie*, 1968; *Colette*, 1970; *The Creation of the World and other Business*, 1972; *The Dance of Death*, 1975.

CAMPBELL, MRS. PATRICK, born Beatrice Stella Tanner, Feb. 9, 1865 (London, Eng.)–Apr. 9, 1940. British stage actress. G. B. SHAW created the role of Eliza Doolittle in *Pygmalion* for her.

CARMICHAEL, IAN, June 18, 1920 (Hull, Eng.).

British actor. Leading man in light 1950s and 1960s films, including *I'm All Right, Jack* (1959); featured as Lord Peter Wimsey in the BBC-TV series of DOROTHY SAYERS's mysteries.

CARNE, JUDY, 1939 (Northampton, Eng.). British actress, entertainer. The "Sock it to me" girl in TV's *Laugh-In* series of the 1960s. (One-time wife of BURT REYNOLDS.)

CARON, LESLIE, July 1, 1931 (Boulogne, Fr.). French actress, dancer. Films: *An American in Paris*, 1951; *Lili*, 1953; *Gigi*, 1958; *Fanny*, 1961; *The L-Shaped Room*, 1962; *Is Paris Burning?*, 1968.

CARROLL, LEO G., 1892 (Weedon, Eng.)–Oct. 16, 1972. English character actor. Films: *Rebecca*, 1940; *Spellbound*, 1945; *North by Northwest*, 1959. TV: *Topper* (series), 1953–55; *The Man From U.N.C.L.E.* (series), 1964–67.

CARROLL, MADELEINE, born Marie Madeleine Bernadette O'Carroll, Feb. 26, 1906 (W. Bromwich, Eng.). English actress. Leading lady in 1930s and 1940s films, including *The 39 Steps* (1935), *The Prisoner of Zenda* (1937), and *My Favorite Blonde* (1942).

COLMAN, RONALD, Feb. 9, 1891 (Richmond, Eng.)–May 19, 1958. British actor. A leading man in romantic-adventure films of the 1930s. Films: *Beau Geste*, 1926; *Arrowsmith*, 1931; *A Tale of Two Cities*, 1935; *Lost Horizon*, 1937; *The Prisoner of Zenda*, 1937; *A Double Life* (Best Actor AA), 1948.

CONNERY, SEAN, born Thomas Connery, Aug. 25, 1930 (Edinburgh, Scot.). Scottish actor. Best known for his role as James Bond in *Dr. No* (1962), *From Russia with Love* (1963), *Goldfinger* (1964), and other spy thrillers. Other films: *The Longest Day*, 1964; *The Anderson Tapes*, 1971; *The Man Who Would Be King*, 1976; *The Great Train Robbery*, 1979.

COOPER, GLADYS, Dec. 18, 1891 (Lewisham, Eng.)–Nov. 17, 1971. English actress. Stage, film, TV career for 60 years.

COURTENAY, TOM, Feb. 25, 1937 (Hull, Eng.). British actor. London stage career, from 1960; Films: *Billy Liar*, 1963; *The Loneliness of the Long Distance Runner*, 1962; *Doctor Zhivago*, 1965; *One Day in the Life of Ivan Denisovitch*, 1971.

CRISP, DONALD, 1880 (London, Eng.)–May 26, 1974. British character actor. Films: *Wuthering Heights*, 1939; *How Green Was My Valley* (Supporting Actor AA), 1941; *National Velvet*, 1944; *Pollyanna*, 1960.

CRONYN, HUME, born Hume Blake, July 18, 1911 (London, Ont., Can.). Canadian character actor. Best known for stage appearances with wife JESSICA TANDY, most notably in *The Gin Game*, 1978.

DECARLO, YVONNE, born Peggy Middleton, Sept. 1, 1924 (Vancouver, B.C., Can.). Canadian actress. Films: *Salome, Where She Danced*, 1945; *Song of Scheherezade*, 1947; *Casbah*, 1948. TV: *The Munsters* (series), 1964–66.

DELON, ALAIN, Nov. 8, 1935 (France). French actor. Films: *Rocco and His Brothers*, 1960; *Is Paris Burning?*, 1966; *The Sicilian Clan*, 1970; *Airport 1979—The Concorde*, 1979.

DENEUVE, CATHERINE, born Catherine DeDorleac, Oct. 22, 1943 (Paris, Fr.). French actress. Films: *Belle du Jour*, 1967; *April Fools*, 1968; *Hustle*, 1975; *March or Die*, 1977.

DIETRICH, MARLENE, born Maria Magdalena

von Losch, 1901/02 (Berlin, Ger.). German-U.S. actress, singer. Films: *The Blue Angel*, 1930; *Shanghai Express*, 1932; *Destry Rides Again*, 1939; *The Spoilers*, 1942; *A Foreign Affair*, 1948; *Witness for the Prosecution*, 1957; *Judgment at Nuremberg*, 1961. Received special Tony award, 1968.

DONAT, ROBERT, March. 18, 1905 (Manchester, Eng.)–June 9, 1958. English actor. Films: *The Count of Monte Cristo*, 1934; *The Ghost Goes West*, 1936; *The Citadel*, 1938; *Goodbye Mr. Chips* (Best Actor AA), 1939; *The Young Mr. Pitt*, 1942; *The Winslow Boy*, 1948.

DONLEVY, BRIAN, 1903 (Ireland)–Apr. 5, 1972. Irish actor. Films: *Barbary Coast*, 1935; *Beau Geste*, 1939; *Destry Rides Again*, 1939; *The Great McGinty*, 1940; *Two Years before the Mast*, 1944; *The Virginian*, 1945; *Kiss of Death*, 1947.

DORS, DIANA, born Diana Fluck, Oct. 23, 1931 (Gwindon, Eng.). English actress. Played "blonde bombshell" types in 1940s and 1950s films.

D'ORSAY, FIFI, 1908 (Montreal, Que., Can.). Canadian actress. A leading lady in 1930s films.

DRESSLER, MARIE, born Leila von Koerber, Nov. 9, 1869 (Coburg, Ont., Can.)–July 28, 1934. Canadian actress. Worked in silent films, then in 1930s comedies. Films: *Tillie's Punctured Romance*, 1915; *Anna Christie*, 1930; *Min and Bill* (Best Actress AA), 1930; *Tugboat Annie*, 1933; *Dinner at Eight*, 1933.

DUSE, ELEANORA, Oct. 3, 1858 (nr. Vigevano, It.)–Apr. 21, 1924. Italian stage actress of legendary emotional power. The great rival of SARAH BERNHARDT.

EGGAR, SAMANTHA, Mar. 5, 1929 (London, Eng.). British actress. Films: *The Collector*, 1965; *Walk, Don't Run*, 1966; *Doctor Doolittle*, 1967; *Light at the Edge of the World*, 1972.

EKLAND, BRITT, 1942 (Stockholm, Swe.). Swedish actress. Films: *After the Fox*, 1966; *The Night They Raided Minsky's*, 1969. (One-time wife of PETER SELLERS.)

EVANS, DAME EDITH, Feb. 8, 1888 (London, Eng.)–Oct. 14, 1976. English stage and film actress. Known principally for stage appearances, especially Shakespearean roles. Made a Dame of the British Empire, 1946.

EVANS, MAURICE, June 3, 1901 (Dorchester, Eng.). English actor. Brought to U.S. by KATHARINE CORNELL to play Romeo to her Juliet, 1936. Distinguished career as producer/actor, Broadway, TV, films.

FELDMAN, MARTY, 1933 (England). English comedic actor. Films: *Young Frankenstein*, 1974; *The Adventures of Sherlock Holmes' Smarter Brother*, 1976; *Silent Movie*, 1976; *Beau Geste* (also cowriter and codirector), 1977.

FERRER, JOSÉ, born José Vincente Ferrer y Centron, Jan. 8, 1912 (Santurce, P.R.). Puerto Rican actor, director, producer. Films: *Cyrano de Bergerac* (Best Actor AA), 1950; *Moulin Rouge*, 1952; *Miss Sadie Thompson*, 1953; *The Caine Mutiny*, 1954; *The Shrike*, 1955. Received Tony awards (as actor) in 1947 and 1952.

FINCH, PETER, born William Mitchell, Sept. 28, 1916 (Kensington, Eng.)–Jan. 14, 1977. English actor. Films: *The Nun's Story*, 1959; *Far from the Madding Crowd*, 1967; *Sunday, Bloody Sunday*, 1971; *Lost Horizon*, 1973; *Network* (Best Actor AA), 1976.

FINNEY, ALBERT, May 9, 1936 (Salford, Eng.). En-

glish actor. Films: *Saturday Night and Sunday Morning*, 1960; *Tom Jones*, 1963; *Night Must Fall*, 1963; *Two for the Road*, 1967; *Charlie Bubbles*, 1968; *Murder on the Orient Express*, 1974.

FITZGERALD, BARRY, born William Joseph Shields, Mar. 10, 1888 (Dublin, Ire.)–Jan. 4, 1961. Irish character actor. Films: *The Plough and the Stars*, 1936; *The Long Voyage Home*, 1940; *How Green Was My Valley*, 1941; *Going My Way* (Best Supporting Actor AA), 1944; *And Then There Were None*, 1945; *The Naked City*, 1948; *The Quiet Man*, 1952.

FITZGERALD, GERALDINE, Nov. 24, 1914 (Dublin, Ire.). Irish actress. Films: *Dark Victory*, 1939; *Wuthering Heights*, 1939; *Wilson*, 1944; *The Pawnbroker*, 1965.

FOCH, NINA, Apr. 20, 1924 (Leyden, Neth.). Dutch actress who appeared in films of the 1940s and 1950s. Films: *My Name is Julia Ross*, 1946; *An American in Paris*, 1951.

FONTANNE, LYNN, Dec. 6, 1887 (London, Eng.). English-U.S. actress. Made London debut in 1909, New York debut in 1910. With husband, ALFRED LUNT, most famous couple in American theater. Co-starred with husband in numerous plays, including *The Guardsman, Design for Living, The Taming of the Shrew, There Shall Be No Night, The Visit*.

GABIN, JEAN, born Alexis Moncourge, May 17, 1904 (Paris, Fr.)–Nov. 15, 1976. French actor. Films: *Pepe Le Moko*, 1936; *La Grande Illusion*, 1937; *Quai des Brumes*, 1938; *La Bête Humaine*, 1938; *Le Jour Se Lève*, 1939; *Touchez Pas au Grisbi*, 1953.

GARBO, GRETA, born Greta Lovisa Gustafsson, Sept. 18, 1905 (Stockholm, Swe.). Swedish actress. Famed for her matchless beauty and reclusive personality. Films: *The Torrent*, 1926; *Flesh and the Devil*, 1927; *Anna Christie*, 1930; *Grand Hotel*, 1932; *Queen Christina*, 1933; *Anna Karenina*, 1935; *Camille*, 1936; *Ninotchka*, 1939; received special AA, for her "unforgettable screen performances," 1954.

GARSON, GREER, Sept. 29, 1908 (County Down, Ire.). Irish actress. Films: *Pride and Prejudice*, 1940; *Mrs. Miniver* (Best Actress AA), 1942; *Random Harvest*, 1942; *Madam Curie*, 1943; *Mrs. Parkington*, 1944; *That Forsyte Woman*, 1949; *Sunrise at Campobello*, 1960.

GASSMAN, VITTORIO, Sept. 1, 1922 (Genoa, It.). Italian actor. A leading man in U.S. and European films since 1946. Films: *Bitter Rice*, 1948; *War and Peace*, 1956; *Barabbas*, 1962; *The Devil in Love*, 1966.

GIANNINI, GIANCARLO, Aug. 1, 1942 (Spezia, It.). Italian actor. Films: *Love and Anarchy*, 1974; *The Seduction of Mimi*, 1974; *Swept Away . . .*, 1975; *Seven Beauties*, 1976.

GIELGUD, SIR JOHN, Apr. 14, 1904 (London, Eng.). British actor, director. Long, distinguished career, particularly as Shakespearean actor. Gained first fame as Hamlet with Old Vic Co., 1929; greatest early success was in the title role in *Richard II*, which he also directed; knighted, 1953. Plays: *Constant Nymph, Love for Love, The Seagull, Tiny Alice*. Films: *Julius Caesar*, 1953; *Murder on the Orient Express*, 1974.

GINGOLD, HERMIONE, Dec. 12, 1897 (London, Eng.). English actress. Films: *Pickwick Papers*, 1952; *Gigi*, 1958; *The Music Man*, 1961.

GRANGER, STEWART, born James Stewart, May 6, 1913 (London, Eng.). British actor. Films: *Captain *Boycott*, 1947; *King Solomon's Mines*, 1950; *Scaramouche*, 1952; *Beau Brummell*, 1954.

GRANT, CARY, born Archibald Leach, Jan. 18, 1904 (Bristol, Eng.). English actor. Peerless lightcomedy actor, a film star since the mid 1930s. Films: *The Awful Truth*, 1937; *Bringing Up Baby*, 1938; *Gunga Din*, 1939; *My Favorite Wife*, 1940; *The Philadelphia Story*, 1940; *Suspicion*, 1941; *Night and Day*, 1945; *To Catch a Thief*, 1955; *An Affair to Remember*, 1957; *Houseboat*, 1958; *North by Northwest*, 1959; *Charade*, 1963; *Walk Don't Run*, 1966. Received special AA, 1969. (One-time husband of DYAN CANNON and BARBARA HUTTON.)

GREENE, RICHARD, 1918 (England). English actor. Starred in 165 episodes of the 1950s TV series *Robin Hood*.

GREENSTREET, SYDNEY, Dec. 27, 1879 (Kent, Eng.)–Jan. 18, 1954. English actor. After a full career on stage, became a film star at age 62. Films: *The Maltese Falcon*, 1941; *Across the Pacific*, 1942; *Casablanca*, 1942; *Passage to Marseilles*, 1944; *The Mask of Dimitrios*, 1944; *Three Strangers*, 1946; *The Hucksters*, 1947.

GRIFFITH, HUGH, May 30, 1912 (Wales). Welsh actor. A former bank clerk, noted for his flamboyant acting style. Films: *The Titfield Thunderbolt*, 1953; *Lucky Jim*, 1957; *Ben Hur* (Best Supporting Actor AA), 1959; *Tom Jones*, 1963.

GUINNESS, SIR ALEC, Apr. 2, 1914 (London, Eng.). English actor. On stage since 1934. Films: *Oliver Twist*, 1948; *Kind Hearts and Coronets*, 1949; *The Lavender Hill Mob*, 1951; *The Man in the White Suit*, 1951; *Father Brown*, 1954; *The Bridge on the River Kwai* (Best Actor AA), 1957; *Our Man in Havana*, 1959; *Tunes of Glory*, 1960; *A Majority of One*, 1961; *Lawrence of Arabia*, 1962; *Hotel Paradiso*, 1966; *The Comedians*, 1967; *Scrooge*, 1970; *Hitler: The Last Ten Days*, 1973. Knighted, 1959.

GUTHRIE, (William) TYRONE, July 2, 1900 (Tunbridge Wells, Eng.)–May 15, 1971. English theater director. Influenced 20th-cent. revival of interest in traditional theater.

GWENN, EDMUND, Sept. 26, 1875 (London, Eng.)–Sept. 6, 1959. English actor. Films: *Pride and Prejudice*, 1940; *Lassie Come Home*, 1943; *Miracle on 34th Street* (Best Supporting Actor AA), 1946; *Pretty Baby*, 1950; *Them*, 1954; *The Trouble with Harry*, 1955.

HAGEN, UTA, June 12, 1919 (Gottingen, Ger.). German actress, teacher. Has had a long and distinguished stage career; received Tony award, for *Who's Afraid of Virginia Woolf?*, 1963; received London Critics Award for 1963-64 season, for the same play.

HAMPSHIRE, SUSAN, May 12, 1942 (London, Eng.). English actress. Star of BBC-TV series *The Forsyte Saga* (1967), and *The Pallisers* (1977).

HARDWICKE, SIR CEDRIC, Feb. 19, 1893 (Worcestershire, Eng.)–Aug. 6, 1964. British actor. A stage actor, he settled in Hollywood, from 1926. Films: *Nell Gwyn*, 1934; *King Solomon's Mines*, 1937; *On Borrowed Time*, 1939; *Stanley and Livingstone*, 1939; *Tom Brown's Schooldays*, 1940; *Nicholas Nickleby*, 1947; *Richard III*, 1955.

HARRIS, RICHARD, Oct. 1, 1933 (County Limerick, Ire.). Irish actor. Films: *Mutiny on the Bounty*, 1962; *This Sporting Life*, 1963; *Camelot*, 1967; *The Molly Maguires*, 1969; *A Man Called Horse*, 1976.

HARRISON, REX, born Reginald Carey, Mar. 5, 1908 (Huyton, Eng.). English stage and film actor. Starred on Broadway in *My Fair Lady* (1956). Films: *Major Barbara*, 1940; *Blithe Spirit*, 1945; *Anna and the King of Siam*, 1946; *The Foxes of Harrow*, 1947; *The Reluctant Debutante*, 1958; *Midnight Lace*, 1960; *Cleopatra*, 1962; *My Fair Lady* (Best Actor AA), 1964; *The Agony and the Ecstasy*, 1965; *Dr. Dolittle*, 1967.

HARVEY, LAURENCE, born Larushka Mischa Skikne, Oct. 1, 1928 (Joniskis, Lithuania)–Nov. 25, 1973. Lithuanian-British actor. Films: *Room at the Top*, 1959; *Expresso Bongo*, 1959; *Butterfield 8*, 1961; *A Walk on the Wild Side*, 1962; *The Manchurian Candidate*, 1962; *Darling*, 1965; *A Dandy in Aspic*, 1968.

HAVOC, JUNE, born June Hovick, 1916 (Vancouver, B.C., Can.). Canadian actress. Autobiography: *Early Havoc*, 1960. (Sister of GYPSY ROSE LEE.)

HAWKINS, JACK, Sept. 14, 1910 (London, Eng.)–July 18, 1973. English actor. Films: *The Fallen Idol*, 1948; *The Cruel Sea*, 1952; *The Bridge on the River Kwai*, 1957; *Gideon's Day*, 1958; *Lawrence of Arabia*, 1962; *Young Winston*, 1972.

HAYAKAWA, SESSUE, 1890 (Chiba, Jap.)–Nov. 23, 1973. Japanese actor. A silent-film star who later played character roles; best known for role in the film *The Bridge on the River Kwai*, 1957.

HEMMINGS, DAVID, Nov. 2, 1941 (Guilford, Eng.). English actor. Films: *Blow Up*, 1966; *The Charge of the Light Brigade*, 1968; *Barbarella*, 1968; *The Love Machine*, 1971.

HENREID, PAUL, born Paul von Hernried, Jan. 10, 1908 (Trieste, A.-H. [now Italy]). Austrian actor. Films: *Now, Voyager*, 1942; *Casablanca*, 1942; *The Spanish Main*, 1945; *Of Human Bondage*, 1946.

HILLER, WENDY, Aug. 15, 1912 (Stockport, Eng.). English actress. Films: *Pygmalion*, 1938; *Major Barbara*, 1940; *Separate Tables*, 1958; *Sons and Lovers*, 1960; *A Man for All Seasons*, 1966.

HOLLOWAY, STANLEY, Oct. 1, 1890 (London, Eng.). English entertainer, singer, actor. Best known for role as Alfred P. Doolittle in play (1956) and film *My Fair Lady* (1964).

HOMOLKA, OSCAR, Oct. 12, 1898 (Vienna, Austria)–Jan. 27, 1978. Austrian character actor. Films: *Rhodes of Africa*, 1936; *Sabotage*, 1937; *Ebb Tide*, 1937; *I Remember Mama*, 1948; *War and Peace*, 1956; *Billion Dollar Brain*, 1968.

HOPKINS, ANTHONY, Dec. 31, 1937 (Port Talbot, Wales). Welsh actor. Films: *Young Winston*, 1972; *Audrey Rose*, 1977; *Magic*, 1978. TV: *War and Peace* (BBC series), 1972; Emmy award for "The Lindbergh Kidnapping Case," 1976. Play: *Equus*, 1974.

HOWARD, LESLIE, born Leslie Stainer, Apr. 3, 1893 (London, Eng.)–June 1, 1943. English actor. Films: *Berkeley Square*, 1933; *The Scarlet Pimpernel*, 1935; *The Petrified Forest*, 1936; *Pygmalion*, 1938; *Gone with the Wind*, 1939; *Intermezzo*, 1939.

HOWARD, TREVOR, Aug. 29, 1916 (Kent, Eng.). English actor. Films: *Brief Encounter*, 1946; *The Third Man*, 1949; *The Heart of the Matter*, 1953; *Sons and Lovers*, 1960; *Mutiny on the Bounty*, 1962; *Von Ryan's Express*, 1965; *Ryan's Daughter*, 1970.

HUSTON, WALTER, born Walter Houghston, Apr. 6, 1884 (Toronto, Ont., Can.)–Apr. 7, 1950. Canadian character actor. Introduced "September Song," on stage, 1950. Films: *Rain*, 1932; *Dodsworth*, 1936; *Yankee Doodle Dandy*, 1942; *Mission to Moscow*, 1942; *The Treasure of Sierra*

Madre (Best Supporting Actor AA), 1947. (Father of JOHN HUSTON.)

HYDE-WHITE, WILFRED, 1903 (England). English character actor in numerous films, 1937– . Films: *The Third Man,* 1949; *North-West Frontier,* 1959; *My Fair Lady,* 1964.

IRELAND, JOHN, Jan. 30, 1915 (Vancouver, B.C., Can.). Canadian film actor. Best known for his role in the film *All the King's Men,* 1949.

IRVING, SIR HENRY, born John Henry Brodribb, Feb. 6, 1838 (Somerset, Eng.)-Oct. 13, 1905. English actor. First English actor ever knighted (1895); known for partnership with ELLEN TERRY; U.S. tour, 1883.

JACKSON, GLENDA, May 9, 1936 (Cheshire, Eng.). English actress. Films: *Women in Love* (Best Actress AA), 1970; *Sunday, Bloody Sunday,* 1971; *Mary, Queen of Scots,* 1971; *A Touch of Class* (Best Actress AA), 1973; *Nasty Habits,* 1976.

JANNINGS, EMIL, born Theodor Emil Janenz, July 26, 1886 (Brooklyn, N.Y.)-Jan. 2, 1950. German-U.S. actor. Films: *The Way of All Flesh* (first Best Actor AA), 1928; *The Blue Angel,* 1930.

JOHNS, GLYNIS, Oct. 5, 1923 (Durban, S. Africa). S. African stage and film actress. Films: *Perfect Strangers,* 1945; *Miranda,* 1947; *The Card,* 1952; *The Court Jester,* 1956; *The Chapman Report,* 1962.

JORY, VICTOR, Nov. 23, 1902 (Dawson, Yukon, Can.). Canadian character actor. In films since 1932, often as a villain. Films: *The Adventures of Tom Sawyer,* 1938; *The Miracle Worker,* 1963. TV: *Manhunt* (series), 1959-61.

JOURDAN, LOUIS, born Louis Gendre, June 19, 1921 (Marseilles, Fr.). French actor. U.S. and European film career, including *Three Coins in the Fountain* (1954), *Gigi* (1958), and *Can-Can* (1960).

KARLOFF, BORIS, born William Henry Pratt, Nov. 23, 1887 (London, Eng.)-Feb. 3, 1969. English actor. Best known for horror-film roles. Films: *Frankenstein* (as the monster), 1931; *The Raven,* 1935; *Tower of London,* 1939; *The Body Snatcher,* 1945. TV: hosted anthology series *Thriller,* 1960-62.

KELLAWAY, CECIL, Aug. 22, 1894 (Capetown, S. Africa)-Feb. 28, 1973. English character actor. Films: *I Married a Witch,* 1942; *Portrait of Jennie,* 1948; *Harvey,* 1950; *Guess Who's Coming to Dinner?,* 1967.

KERR, DEBORAH, born Deborah Kerr-Trimmer, Aug. 30, 1921 (Helensburgh, Scot.). Scottish actress. Films: *The Hucksters,* 1947; *Quo Vadis,* 1951; *From Here to Eternity,* 1953; *The King and I,* 1956; *Tea and Sympathy,* 1956; *An Affair to Remember,* 1957; *Separate Tables,* 1958; *The Sundowners,* 1960; *The Innocents,* 1961; *The Night of the Iguana,* 1964.

LANCHESTER, ELSA, born Elizabeth Sullivan, Oct. 28, 1902 (London, Eng.). English character actress. Films: *The Bride of Frankenstein,* 1935; *Rembrandt,* 1937; *Witness for the Prosecution,* 1957. (Wife of CHARLES LAUGHTON.)

LANGTRY, LILLIE, born Emilie Charlotte Le Breton, Oct. 13, 1853 (Isle of Jersey, G.B.)-Feb. 12, 1929. British actress. First society woman to go on stage, 1881; made U.S. tours; Langtry, Tex., was named for her.

LAUGHTON, CHARLES, July 1, 1899 (Scarborough, Eng.)-Dec. 15, 1962. English actor. One of the great dramatic actors in film history. Films:

The Sign of the Cross, 1932; *The Private Life of Henry VIII* (Best Actor AA), 1933; *Les Miserables,* 1935; *Mutiny on the Bounty,* 1935; *The Hunchback of Notre Dame,* 1939; *The Canterville Ghost,* 1944; *The Paradine Case,* 1948; *Witness for the Prosecution,* 1957. (Husband of ELSA LANCHESTER.)

LAWFORD, PETER, Sept. 7, 1923 (London, Eng.). English actor. Films: *Easter Parade,* 1948; *Little Women,* 1949; *Royal Wedding,* 1952; *Salt and Pepper,* 1968; *Won Ton Ton,* 1976. TV: *Dear Phoebe* (series), 1954-56; *The Thin Man* (series), 1957-59.

LAWRENCE, GERTRUDE, born Alexandra Dagmar Lawrence-Klasen, July 4, 1898 (London, Eng.)-Sept. 6, 1952. British actress, revue star. Associated with NOEL COWARD; best-known roles were in *Private Lives* (1931), *Lady in the Dark* (1943), *Blithe Spirit* (1945), *Pygmalion* (1946). Film: *The Glass Menagerie,* 1950.

LEGALLIENNE, EVA, Jan. 11, 1899 (London, Eng.). English actress. Founder (1926), director of New York's Civic Repertory Theater; cofounder (1946) of American Repertory Theater; appeared on London and N.Y. stage, from 1915; won a special Tony award, 1964.

LEIGH, VIVIEN, born Vivien Hartley, Nov. 5, 1913 (Darjeeling, India)-July 8, 1967. English film and stage actress. Best known for her AA-winning performance as Scarlett O'Hara in the film *Gone with the Wind* (1939). Films: *A Yank at Oxford,* 1938; *Lady Hamilton,* 1941; *Anna Karenina,* 1948; *A Streetcar Named Desire* (Best Actress AA), 1951; *The Roman Spring of Mrs. Stone,* 1961; *Ship of Fools,* 1965. (One-time wife of LAURENCE OLIVIER.)

LEIGHTON, MARGARET, Feb. 26, 1922 (Barnt Green, Eng.)-Jan. 14, 1976. British actress. Films: *The Waltz of the Toreadors,* 1961; *The Go-Between,* 1970; *Lady Caroline Lamb,* 1972. Received Tony awards for her performances in the plays *Separate Tables* (1956) and *The Night of the Iguana* (1962).

LINDFORS, VIVECA, Dec. 29, 1920 (Uppsala, Swe.). Swedish-U.S. actress. On the stage since 1938, in films since 1941.

LOCKWOOD, MARGARET, born Margaret Day, Sept. 15, 1916 (Karachi, India). British actress. In films since 1935; also many stage and TV appearances. Films: *The Lady Vanishes,* 1938; *Night Train to Munich,* 1940; *The Man in Grey,* 1943; *The Wicked Lady,* 1945; *Cast a Dark Shadow,* 1957.

LOLLOBRIGIDA, GINA, July 4, 1928 (Subiaco, It.). Italian actress. Films: *Bread, Love and Dreams,* 1953; *Trapeze,* 1956; *Solomon and Sheba,* 1959; *Buona Sera, Mrs. Campbell,* 1968.

LOM, HERBERT, 1917 (Prague, Czech.). Czech-British actor. Films: *The Young Mr. Pitt,* 1941; *The Seventh Veil,* 1945; *The Pink Panther,* film series, 1964–

LOREN, SOPHIA, born Sophia Scicoloni, Sept. 20, 1934 (Rome, It.). Italian actress. Known for her beauty and powerful dramatic performances. Films: *Boy on a Dolphin,* 1957; *Houseboat,* 1958; *Two Women* (Best Actress AA), 1961; *Yesterday, Today and Tomorrow,* 1963; *Marriage Italian Style,* 1964; *Lady L,* 1966; *A Special Day,* 1977. Autobiography: *Sophia,* 1979.

LORRE, PETER, born Laszlo Loewenstein, June 26, 1904 (Rosenberg, Hung.)-Mar. 23, 1964. Hungarian character actor. Films: *M,* 1931; "Mr.

Moto" series, 1930s; *The Maltese Falcon*, 1941; *Casablanca*, 1942; *The Mask of Dimitrios*, 1944; *The Beast with Five Fingers*, 1946.

LUPINO, IDA, Feb. 4, 1918 (London, Eng.). British actress, director, producer. Films: *They Drive by Night*, 1940; *High Sierra*, 1941; *Devotion*, 1946; *Roadhouse*, 1948. (One-time wife of HOWARD DUFF.)

MAGNANI, ANNA, Mar. 7, 1908 (Alexandria, Egypt)–Sept. 26, 1973. Italian actress. In films since 1934. Films: *The Open City*, 1945; *The Rose Tattoo* (Best Actress AA), 1955; *The Fugitive Kind*, 1959.

MARCEAU, MARCEL, Mar. 22, 1923 (Strasbourg, Fr.). French mime. Best known mime of his age; created the character Bip, a white-faced clown.

MARSH, JEAN LYNDSEY TARREN, July 1, 1934 (London, Eng.). English actress, writer. Best known for creating and starring in BBC and PBS TV series *Upstairs/Downstairs*, 1975–76; received Emmy award, 1975.

MARSHALL, HERBERT, May 23, 1890 (London, Eng.)–Jan. 22, 1966. British actor. Films: *Angel*, 1937; *Foreign Correspondent*, 1940; *The Letter*, 1940; *The Little Foxes*, 1941; *The Moon and Sixpence*, 1942; *Stage Struck*, 1957; *The List of Adrian Messenger*, 1963.

MASON, JAMES, May 15, 1909 (Huddersfield, Eng.). English actor. Made Broadway debut in *The Faith Healer*, 1979. Films: *The Seventh Veil*, 1945; *20,000 Leagues under the Sea*, 1954; *A Star Is Born*, 1954; *Journey to the Center of the Earth*, 1959; *Lolita*, 1962; *Heaven Can Wait*, 1978; *The Boys from Brazil*, 1978.

MASTROIANNI, MARCELLO, Sept. 28, 1924 (Fontane Liri, It.). Italian actor. A romantic leading man in Italian films. Films: *White Nights*, 1957; *Days of Love*, 1958; *La Dolce Vita*, 1959; *Bell' Antonio*, 1960; *Divorce Italian Style*, 1962; *Yesterday, Today and Tomorrow*, 1963; *A Place for Lovers*, 1969; *The Priest's Wife*, 1975; *A Special Day*, 1977; *Wifemistress*, 1979.

MCDOWELL, MALCOLM, June 19, 1943 (Leeds, Eng.). English actor. Known for roles in controversial films, including *If* (1969), *A Clockwork Orange* (1971), and *O Lucky Man* (1973).

MCDOWALL, RODDY, Sept. 17, 1928 (London, Eng.). English actor. Films: *How Green Was My Valley*, 1941; *My Friend Flicka*, 1943; *Lassie Come Home*, 1943; *The Loved One*, 1965; "Planet of the Apes" series, 1967–73.

MCKENNA, SIOBHAN, May 24, 1922 (Belfast, Ire.). Irish actress. Dublin's Abbey Players, 1943–46; best known for roles in *Saint Joan* and *The Playboy of the Western World*.

MCLAGLEN, VICTOR, Dec. 11, 1883 (London, Eng.)–Nov. 7, 1959. English-U.S. actor. A former boxer. Films: *What Price Glory?*, 1926; *Dick Turpin*, 1933; *The Informer* (Best Actor AA), 1935; *Gunga Din*, 1939; *She Wore a Yellow Ribbon*, 1949; *The Quiet Man*, 1952.

MERCOURI, MELINA, born Maria Amalia Mercouri, Oct. 18, 1925 (Athens, Gr.). Greek actress, political activist. Best known for her role in the film *Never on Sunday*, 1960.

MILES, SARAH, Dec. 31, 1943 (Ingatestone, Eng.). English actress. Films: *Blow Up*, 1966; *Ryan's Daughter*, 1970; *Lady Caroline Lamb*, 1972; *The Sailor Who Fell from Grace with the Sea*, 1976.

MILLS, HAYLEY, Apr. 18, 1946 (London, Eng.). English actress. Received special AA, 1960. Films:

Tiger Bay, 1959; *Pollyanna*, 1960; *The Parent Trap*, 1961; *The Chalk Garden*, 1964. (Daughter of JOHN MILLS.)

MILLS, SIR JOHN, Feb. 22, 1908 (Suffolk, Eng.). English actor. Films: *Those Were the Days*, 1934; *Cottage to Let*, 1941; *Great Expectations*, 1946; *Hobson's Choice*, 1953; *Tiger Bay*, 1959; *The Swiss Family Robinson*, 1961; *The Wrong Box*, 1966; *Ryan's Daughter*, 1971. (Father of HAYLEY MILLS.)

MIRANDA, CARMEN, 1913 (Marco Canauezes, Port.)–Aug. 5, 1955. Brazilian singer, actress. Began as cafe entertainer in South America, starred in camp films of the 1940s and 1950s.

MONTAND, YVES, born Ivo Levi, Oct. 31, 1921 (Monsummano, It.). French actor. A romantic leading man in French and American films. Films: *The Wages of Fear*, 1953; *Let's Make Love*, 1960; *My Geisha*, 1962; *Is Paris Burning?*, 1966; *'Z,'* 1968; *On a Clear Day You Can See Forever*, 1969; *State of Siege*, 1973. (Husband of SIMONE SIGNORET.)

MOORE, ROGER GEORGE, Oct. 14, 1927 (London, Eng.). English actor. Star of the TV series *The Saint*, 1967–69; best known in films for his role as James Bond in *Live and Let Die* (1973), *The Man with the Golden Gun* (1974), *The Spy Who Loved Me* (1977), and *Moonraker* (1979).

MOREAU, JEANNE, 1929 (Paris, Fr.). French actress. Films: *The Lovers*, 1959; *Jules et Jim*, 1961; *Diary of a Chambermaid*, 1964; *Viva Maria*, 1965; *Mr. Klein*, 1976.

MORENO, RITA, Dec. 11, 1931 (Humacao, P. R.). Puerto Rican actress. Best known for roles in the film *West Side Story* (Best Supporting Actress AA; 1961) and the play *The Ritz* (Tony award; 1975).

MORLEY, ROBERT, May 26, 1908 (Wiltshire, Eng.). English character actor. Known as TV spokesman for British Airways. Plays: *Oscar Wilde*, 1936; *Pygmalion*, 1937. Films: *Major Barbara*, 1940; *Gilbert and Sullivan*, 1953; *Beat the Devil*, 1953; *Oscar Wilde*, 1960; *Who Is Killing the Great Chefs of Europe?*, 1978.

MULHARE, EDWARD, 1923 (Ireland). Irish actor. Best known for his role as the ghost in the TV series *The Ghost and Mrs. Muir*, 1968–70.

NAZIMOVA, ALLA, June 4, 1879 (Yalta, Rus.)–July 13, 1945. Russian-U.S. actress. Leading dramatic actress on the stage in Russia, from 1904; noted for her IBSEN roles in the U.S. and abroad, especially as *Hedda Gabler* (1906) and Mrs. Alving in *Ghosts* (1937); starred in early silent films, 1916–23.

NEFF, HILDEGARDE, Dec. 28, 1925 (Ulm, Ger.). German actress. A former cartoon artist for a Berlin studio; starred in films such as *The Snows of Kilimanjaro* (1952) and *Mozambique* (1965). Autobiography: *The Gift Horse*, 1971.

NESBIT, CATHLEEN, Nov. 24, 1889 (Cheshire, Eng.). English actress. In a long stage career (began 1910), developed a repertoire of character roles.

NEWLEY, ANTHONY, Sept. 24, 1931 (Hackney, Eng.). English actor, singer. Best known for appearances in stage musicals, notably *Stop the World I Want to Get Off* (1961) and *The Roar of the Greasepaint, the Smell of the Crowd* (cowrote and cocomposed with Leslie Bricusse, 1963). Films: *Dr. Dolittle*, 1967; *Hieronymus Merkin*, 1969.

NEWTON, ROBERT, June 1, 1905 (Dorset, Eng.)–Mar. 25, 1956. English character actor

THE BOOK OF WHO

Films: *Jamaica Inn*, 1939; *Gaslight*, 1940; *Major Barbara*, 1940; *Oliver Twist*, 1948; *Treasure Island*, 1950; *Androcles and the Lion*, 1953; *Around the World in Eighty Days*, 1956.

NIVEN, DAVID, Mar. 1, 1910 (Kirriemuir, Scot.). Scottish-U.S. actor. Debonair leading man in films since 1935. Films: *Dodsworth*, 1936; *The Prisoner of Zenda*, 1937; *Bachelor Mother*, 1939; *Around the World in Eighty Days*, 1956; *Separate Tables* (Best Actor AA), 1958; *Guns of Navarone*, 1961; *Casino Royale*, 1967; *Murder by Death*, 1976. Memoirs: *The Moon's a Balloon* (1971) and *Bring on the Empty Horses* (1975).

NOVELLO, IVOR, born Ivor Davies, Jan. 15, 1893 (Cardiff, Wales)–May. 6, 1951. Welsh actor. Musical-comedy stage career, 1921–51. Films: *The Man Without Desire*, 1923; *The Rat*, 1925; *The Lodger*, 1926.

OBERON, MERLE, Feb. 19, 1911 (Tasmania)–Nov. 23, 1979. British actress. Began as a dance-hall hostess. Films: *The Scarlet Pimpernel*, 1934; *The Divorce of Lady X*, 1938; *Wuthering Heights*, 1939; *A Song to Remember*, 1945; *Hotel*, 1967.

O'CONNOR, UNA, born Agnes Teresa McGlade, 1893 (Belfast, Ire.)–Feb. 4, 1959. Irish actress. Stage career, from 1911; in films, from 1929. Films: *The Invisible Man*, 1933; *The Barretts of Wimpole Street*, 1934; *Bride of Frankenstein*, 1935; *Witness for the Prosecution*, 1957.

O'HARA, MAUREEN, born Maureen Fitzsimons, Aug. 17, 1921 (Dublin, Ire.). Irish-U.S. actress. Stage career with Dublin's Abbey Theatre. Films: *The Hunchback of Notre Dame*, 1939; *The Black Swan*, 1942; *Miracle on 34th Street*, 1947; *Rio Grande*, 1950; *The Quiet Man*, 1952; *The Long Gray Line*, 1955.

O'HERLIHY, DAN, 1919 (Wexford, Ire.). Irish actor. Associated with Dublin's Abbey Theatre. Films: *Odd Man Out*, 1946; *The Adventures of Robinson Crusoe*, 1952; *The Cabinet of Caligari*, 1961; *Fail-Safe*, 1964; *The Tamarind Seed*, 1974.

OLIVIER, LAURENCE KERR, BARON, May 22, 1907 (Dorking, Eng.). English stage and film actor. Known for his large repertoire and particularly his Shakespearean heroes; often cited as the best modern actor; received special AA, 1979. Knighted, 1947; created a baron, 1970 (the first actor to be awarded a life peerage). Films: *The Divorce of Lady X*, 1938; *Wuthering Heights*, 1939; *Rebecca*, 1940; *Pride and Prejudice*, 1940; *Henry V*, 1944; *Hamlet* (Best Actor AA), 1948; *Richard III*, 1956; *The Devil's Disciple*, 1959; *The Entertainer*, 1960; *Marathon Man*, 1976; *The Boys from Brazil*, 1978. (Husband of JOAN PLOWRIGHT; one-time husband of VIVIEN LEIGH.)

O'TOOLE, PETER, Aug. 2, 1932 (Connemara, Ire.). Irish actor. Films: *Lawrence of Arabia*, 1962; *Becket*, 1964; *Lord Jim*, 1965; *The Lion in Winter*, 1968; *Goodbye, Mr. Chips*, 1969; *The Ruling Class*, 1971.

PAPAS, IRENE, 1926 (Corinth, Gr.). Greek actress. Known for her interpretations of classical roles. Films: *Electra*, 1962; *Zorba the Greek*, 1964; *'Z,'* 1968; *The Trojan Women*, 1971.

PAXINOU, KATINA, 1900 (Piraeus, Gr.)–Feb. 22, 1973. Greek actress. International film career. Films: *For Whom the Bell Tolls* (Best Supporting Actress AA), 1943; *Mourning Becomes Electra*, 1947.

PIDGEON, WALTER, Sept. 23, 1898 (New Brunswick, Can.). Canadian actor. Films: *Society Lawyer*, 1939; *Man Hunt*, 1941; *Blossoms in the Dust*, 1941; *How Green Was My Valley*, 1941; *Mrs. Miniver*, 1942; *Madame Curie*, 1943; *That Forsyte Woman*, 1949; *Executive Suite*, 1954; *Forbidden Planet*, 1956; *Advise and Consent*, 1962; *Funny Girl*, 1968.

PLEASANCE, DONALD, Oct. 5, 1919 (Worksop, Eng.). English actor. Best known for his offbeat, sinister roles in films such as *The Caretaker*, 1964.

PLOWRIGHT, JOAN ANNE, Oct. 28, 1929 (Scunthorpe, Eng.). English actress. Long associated with Britain's National Theatre. (Wife of LORD LAURENCE OLIVIER.)

PLUMMER, CHRISTOPHER, Dec. 13, 1929 (Toronto, Ont., Can.). Canadian actor. Films: *The Sound of Music*, 1965; *Waterloo*, 1970; *The Return of the Pink Panther*, 1975; *Murder by Decree*, 1979.

QUAYLE, (John) ANTHONY, Sept. 7, 1913 (Lancashire, Eng.). English actor, director. Known for roles in Shakespearean plays; director of The Shakespeare Memorial Theatre, Stratford, Eng., 1948– . Plays: *The Rivals*, 1945; *Sleuth*, 1970.

REDGRAVE, LYNN, Mar. 8, 1943 (London, Eng.). English actress. With National Theatre of Great Britain, 1963–66. Plays: *Black Comedy*, 1967; *My Fat Friend*, 1974; *Mrs. Warren's Profession*, 1975; *California Suite*, 1977; *St. Joan*, 1977. Films: *Tom Jones*, 1963; *Georgy Girl*, 1966; *The Happy Hooker*, 1975. (Daughter of SIR MICHAEL REDGRAVE; sister of VANESSA REDGRAVE.)

REDGRAVE, SIR MICHAEL, Mar. 20, 1908 (Bristol, Eng.). English actor. From childhood, distinguished stage career. Films: *The Lady Vanishes*, 1938; *Kipps*, 1941; *Mourning Becomes Electra*, 1947; *The Importance of Being Earnest*, 1952; *The Quiet American*, 1958; *Oh What a Lovely War*, 1969; *The Go-Between*, 1971. (Father of VANESSA and LYNN REDGRAVE.)

REDGRAVE, VANESSA, Jan. 30, 1937 (London, Eng.). English actress. Also known for her espousal of radical causes. Films: *Morgan*, 1966; *Camelot*, 1967; *Isadora*, 1968; *Mary, Queen of Scots*, 1972; *Murder on the Orient Express*, 1974; *Julia*, 1977; *Agatha*, 1979. (Daughter of SIR MICHAEL REDGRAVE; sister of LYNN REDGRAVE.)

REED, (Robert) OLIVER, Feb. 13, 1938 (London, Eng.). English actor. Films: *The Damned*, 1962; *The Jokers*, 1967; *Women in Love*, 1969; *The Devils*, 1971; *The Three Musketeers*, 1973; *Tommy*, 1975; *Burnt Offerings*, 1976.

RENNIE, MICHAEL, 1909 (Bradford, England)–June 10, 1971. English-U.S. actor. Best known for leading roles in such science-fiction films as *The Day the Earth Stood Still* (1952) and *The Lost World* (1960).

RICHARDSON, SIR RALPH DAVID, Dec. 19, 1902 (Cheltenham, Eng.). English character actor. Distinguished stage and film career; best known for Shakespearean roles; codirector of the Old Vic Theatre, 1944–47.

RIGG, DIANA, July 20, 1938 (Doncaster, Eng.). English actress. Associated with Royal Shakespeare Co., (1959–71) and the National Theatre (1972–); best known for role as Emma Peel in the TV series *The Avengers*, 1966–68.

RITCHARD, CYRIL, Dec. 1, 1897 (Sydney, Austrl.)–Dec. 18, 1977. Australian actor, director. Best known for his role as Captain Hook in *Peter Pan* (stage, 1954; TV show, 1956). Other plays: *Side by Side by Sondheim*, 1977.

RUTHERFORD, DAME MARGARET (Taylor),

May 11, 1892 (London, Eng.)–May 22, 1972. English comedic character actress. Long stage and film career; best known for appearances as Miss Marple in films based on AGATHA CHRISTIE books. Films: *Blithe Spirit*, 1945; *The Importance of Being Earnest*, 1952; *The VIPs* (Best Supporting Actress AA), 1963.

SANDA, DOMINIQUE, born Dominique Varaigne, Mar. 1951 (Paris, Fr.). French actress. A leading lady in international films of the 1970s. Films: *The Garden of the Finzi-Continis*, 1971; *The Conformist*, 1971.

SARRAZIN, MICHAEL, May 22, 1940 (Quebec, Can.). Canadian actor. Films: *The Flim-Flam Man*, 1967; *The Eye of the Cat*, 1968; *They Shoot Horses, Don't They?*, 1969; *The Reincarnation of Peter Proud*, 1975.

SCHELL, MARIA, 1926 (Vienna, Austria). Austrian actress. Films: *So Little Time*, 1952; *The Brothers Karamazov*, 1958; *The Odessa File*, 1974. (Sister of MAXIMILIAN SCHELL.)

SCHELL, MAXIMILIAN, Dec. 8, 1930 (Vienna, Austria). Austrian actor. Films: *Judgment at Nuremberg* (Best Actor AA), 1961; *Five-Finger Exercise*, 1962; *Topkapi*, 1964; *The Passenger* (producer, dir.), 1973; *Julia*, 1977. (Brother of MARIA SCHELL.)

SCHILDKRAUT, JOSEPH, Mar. 22, 1896 (Vienna, Austria)–Jan. 21, 1964. Austrian actor. A silent-screen star who also enjoyed an extensive career as a supporting actor in talkies. *King of Kings*, 1927; *Show Boat*, 1929; *The Life of Emile Zola* (Best Supporting Actor AA), 1937; *The Cheaters*, 1945; *The Diary of Anne Frank*, 1959.

SCHNEIDER, ROMY, born Rosemarie Albach-Retty, Sept. 23, 1938 (Austria). Austrian actress. Films: *The Cardinal*, 1963; *Good Neighbor Sam*, 1964; *What's New Pussycat?*, 1968; *The Assassination of Trotsky*, 1972.

SCOFIELD, PAUL, Jan. 21, 1922 (Hurst, Eng.). English stage and film actor. Best known for roles in Shakespearean plays. Films: *A Man for All Seasons* (Best Actor AA), 1966.

SELLERS, PETER, Sept. 8, 1925 (Southsea, Eng.). English comedic actor. Films: *The Mouse That Roared*, 1959; *I'm All Right, Jack*, 1959; *The Pink Panther*, 1963; *Dr. Strangelove*, 1963; *A Shot in the Dark*, 1964; *What's New Pussycat?*, 1965; *Murder by Death*, 1976; *The Pink Panther Strikes Again*, 1977.

SHARIF, OMAR, born Michel Shalhouz, Apr. 10, 1932 (Alexandria, Egypt). Egyptian actor. Films: *Lawrence of Arabia*, 1962; *Dr. Zhivago*, 1965; *Funny Girl*, 1968; *Che!*, 1969; *Juggernaut*, 1974; *Funny Lady*, 1975.

SHAW, ROBERT, Aug. 9, 1927 (Westhoughton, Eng.)–Aug. 28, 1978. English actor, playwright. Films: *From Russia with Love*, 1963; *The Luck of Ginger Coffey*, 1964; *A Man for All Seasons*, 1966; *The Sting*, 1973; *Jaws*, 1975; *Black Sunday*, 1977; *Force Ten From Navarone*, 1978. Play (author): *The Man in the Glass Booth*.

SIDDONS, SARAH, born Sarah Kemble, July 5, 1756 (Brecknock, Wales)–June 8, 1831. Welsh actress. Best known for her tragic-heroine roles as Isabella in *The Fatal Marriage* (1782) and as Lady Macbeth (1785); with the Covent Garden Theatre repertory co., 1803–12.

SIGNORET, SIMONE, born Simone-Henriette-Charlotte Kaminker, Mar. 25, 1921 (Wiesbaden, Ger.). French actress. Films: *Casque d'Or*, 1951; *Les Diaboliques*, 1954; *Room at the Top* (Best Actress awards in U.S., Britain, Cannes, Germany),

1959; *Ship of Fools*, 1965; *Le Chat*, 1974. (Wife of YVES MONTAND.)

SIM, ALISTAIR, Oct. 9, 1900 (Edinburgh, Scot.)–Aug. 20, 1976. Scottish comedic actor. Films: *The Happiest Days of Your Life*, 1951; *Laughter in Paradise*, 1951; *A Christmas Carol*, 1951; *An Inspector Calls*, 1954; *The Belles of St. Trinian's*, 1954; *The Ruling Class*, 1971.

SIMMONS, JEAN, Jan. 31, 1929 (London, Eng.). English actress. Films: *Great Expectations*, 1946; *Black Narcissus*, 1946; *Hamlet*, 1948; *The Robe*, 1953; *Elmer Gantry*, 1960; *The Grass Is Greener*, 1961; *The Happy Ending*, 1969.

SMITH, SIR C(harles) **AUBREY,** July 21, 1863 (England)–Dec. 20, 1948. English character actor. Long stage and film career. Films: *Love Me Tonight*, 1932; *Morning Glory*, 1933; *Lives of a Bengal Lancer*, 1935; *And Then There Were None*, 1945.

SMITH, MAGGIE, Dec. 28, 1934 (Ilford, Eng.). English actress. Distinguished stage and film career in both Great Britain and U.S. Films: *The VIPs*, 1963; *The Honey Pot*, 1967; *The Prime of Miss Jean Brodie* (Best Actress AA), 1968; *Murder by Death*, 1976; *California Suite* (Best Supporting Actress AA), 1978.

STAMP, TERENCE, 1940 (London, Eng.). English actor. A leading man in 1960s films such as *Billy Budd* (1962), *The Collector* (1965), *Modesty Blaise* (1966) and *Far From the Madding Crowd* (1967).

SUTHERLAND, DONALD, July 17, 1934 (St. John, N.B., Can.). Canadian actor. Films: *The Dirty Dozen*, 1967; *Start the Revolution without Me*, 1969; *M*A*S*H*, 1970; *Little Murders*, 1970; *Klute*, 1971; *Day of the Locust*, 1976; *Invasion of the Body Snatchers*, 1978.

TANDY, JESSICA, June 7, 1909 (London, Eng.). English actress. Known for long stage career especially with husband, HUME CRONYN. Received best actress Tony (1948) for *A Streetcar Named Desire* (1947). Films: *The Seventh Cross*, 1944; *Rommel, The Desert Fox*, 1951; *The Birds*, 1963.

TEARLE, SIR GODFREY, Oct. 12, 1884 (New York, N.Y.)–June 9, 1953. English actor. Principally a stage career; occasional films, including *If Youth but Knew* (1930), *The 39 Steps* (1935), *One of Our Aircraft Is Missing* (1935), and *The Titfield Thunderbolt* (1953). (Half-brother of CONWAY TEARLE.)

TEMPEST, DAME MARIE, born Marie Susan Etherington, 1864 (London, England)–Oct. 15, 1942. English stage and film actress. Films: *Moonlight Sonata*, 1937; *Yellow Sands*, 1938.

TERRY, ELLEN ALICE, Feb. 27, 1847 (Coventry, Eng.)–July 21, 1928. English stage actress. Famous for "paper courtship" with GEORGE BERNARD SHAW; performed in some of his plays.

TERRY-THOMAS, born Thomas Terry Hoar-Stevens, July 14, 1911 (London, Eng.). English actor. Films: *Private's Progress*, 1956; *Tom Thumb*, 1958; *Carleton Browne of the FO*, 1958; *I'm All Right, Jack*, 1959; *It's a Mad, Mad, Mad, Mad, World*, 1963; *Those Magnificent Men in Their Flying Machines*, 1965.

THORNDIKE, DAME SYBIL, Oct. 24, 1882 (Gainsborough, Eng.)–June 9, 1976. English actress. U.S. and British stage career, from 1904; in films, from 1921; became a Dame Commander of the British Empire, 1931.

THULIN, INGRID, Jan. 27, 1929 (Solleftea, Swe.). Swedish actress. Films: *Wild Strawberries*, 1957;

Winter Light, 1962; *The Silence*, 1963; *Return from Ashes*, 1965; *The Damned*, 1969; *Cries and Whispers*, 1972.

TODD, RICHARD, June 11, 1919 (Dublin, Ire.). English actor. With the British Repertory Theatre, 1937-   ; in U.S. and British films, 1948-   . Films: *Robin Hood*, 1952; *A Man Called Peter*, 1955; *The Dam Busters*, 1955; *The Longest Day*, 1962.

TOMLINSON, DAVID, May 17, 1917 (Scotland). Scottish actor. Films: *Name, Rank and Number*, 1938; *The Way to the Stars*, 1945; *Miranda*, 1948; *The Chiltern Hundreds*, 1949; *Three Men in a Boat*, 1955; *Mary Poppins*, 1964; *The Love Bug*, 1969; *Bedknobs and Broomsticks*, 1971.

TREACHER, ARTHUR, July 23, 1894 (Brighton, Eng.)-Dec. 14, 1975. English actor. Films: *Anything Goes*, 1936; *Thank You, Jeeves*, 1936; *Step Lively, Jeeves*, 1937; *Heidi*, 1937; *National Velvet*, 1940; *Mary Poppins*, 1964. Announcer on TV talk show *The Merv Griffin Show*, 1969-72; Fish-and-chips fast-food franchise firm bears his name.

TREE, SIR HERBERT DRAPER BEERBOHM, Dec. 17, 1853 (London, Eng.)-July 2, 1917. English actor, producer, playwright. Shakespearean actor on the British stage, 1878-1917; founder of the Royal Acad. of Dramatic Art, London; mgr. and producer of the Haymarket Theatre, London, 1887-96. (Half-brother of SIR MAX BEERBOHM.)

TRINTIGNAUT, JEAN-LOUIS, Dec. 11, 1930 (Aix-en-Provence, Fr.). French actor. Films: *A Man and a Woman*, 1966; *'Z'*, 1969; *The Conformist*, 1970; *My Night at Maud's*, 1971.

TUSHINGHAM, RITA, 1942 (Liverpool, Eng.). English actress. Films: *A Taste of Honey*, 1961; *The Leather Boys*, 1965; *The Knack*, 1965; *Doctor Zhivago*, 1965.

ULLMANN, LIV, Dec. 16, 1939 (Tokyo, Japan). Norwegian actress. A leading lady in INGMAR BERGMAN films, from 1966. Films: *Persona*, 1966; *The Passion of Anna*, 1970; *Cries and Whispers*, 1972; *Face to Face*, 1976; *Scenes from a Marriage*, 1974; *Autumn Sonata*, 1978. Autobiography: *Changing*, 1977. Plays: *I Remember Mama*, 1979.

USTINOV, PETER ALEXANDER, Apr. 16, 1921 (London, Eng.). English actor, producer, writer. Films: *Quo Vadis*, 1951; *Spartacus* (Best Supporting Actor AA), 1960; *Romanoff and Juliet*, 1961; *Billy Budd*, 1962; *Topkapi*, 1964; *Logan's Run*, 1976. Book: *Dear Me*, 1977.

VEIDT, CONRAD, June 22, 1893 (Berlin, Ger.)-Apr. 3, 1943. German character actor. U.S. and German film and stage career. Films: *The Cabinet of Dr. Caligari*, 1921; *Thirteen Men and a Girl*, 1930; *Dark Journey*, 1937; *Casablanca*, 1942.

VENTURA, LINO, born L. Barrini, 1918 (Italy). Italian actor. A former boxer. Films: *Crooks in Clover*, 1963; *The Valachi Papers*, 1972; *La Bonne Année*, 1973.

VON SYDOW, MAX CARL ADOLF, Apr. 10, 1929 (Lund, Swe.). Swedish actor. Best known for roles in INGMAR BERGMAN films. Films: *The Seventh Seal*, 1956; *The Virgin Spring*, 1959; *The Hour of the Wolf*, 1968; *The Greatest Story Ever Told*, 1963; *The Passion of Anna*, 1971; *The Immigrants*, 1971; *The Emigrants*, 1972.

WARD, SIMON, 1941 (London, Eng.). English actor. Films: *If*, 1967; *Young Winston*, 1972; *The Three Musketeers*, 1974. Plays: *A Meeting by the River*, 1979.

WARNER, H(erbert) B(ryan), Oct. 26, 1876 (London, Eng.)-Dec. 24, 1958. English actor. Stage and film career in U.S. and Great Britain. Films: *King of Kings*, 1927; *Mr. Deeds Goes to Town*, 1936; *Lost Horizon*, 1937; *Victoria the Great*, 1937; *Sunset Boulevard*, 1950.

WERNER, OSKAR, Nov. 13, 1922 (Vienna, Austria). Austrian actor. U.S. film career. Films: *Decision before Dawn*, 1951; *Jules et Jim*, 1961; *Ship of Fools*, 1965; *Fahrenheit 451*, 1966; *Voyage of the Damned*, 1976.

WHITTY, DAME MAY, June 19, 1865 (Liverpool, Eng.)-May 29, 1948. British character actress; D.B.E.,1918. Stage career, from1881; in U.S. films, 1937-48. Films: *Night Must Fall*, 1937; *The Lady Vanishes*, 1938; *Mrs. Miniver*, 1942; *Gaslight*, 1944; *My Name Is Julia Ross*, 1945.

WILDING, MICHAEL, July 23, 1912 (Essex, Eng.)-July 8, 1979. English actor. Began career as stage actor. Films: *In Which We Serve*, 1942; *Stage Fright*, 1950; *The World of Suzie Wong*, 1960; *Lady Caroline Lamb*, 1972.

WILLIAMS, EMLYN, Nov. 26, 1905 (Mostyn, Wales). Welsh actor, playwright. Plays: *The Citadel*, 1938; *Hatter's Castle*, 1941; *The Last Days of Dolwyn*, 1948; *Three Husbands*, 1950; *The Deep Blue Sea*, 1956. Autobiographies: *George*, 1972; *Emlyn*, 1974.

WILLIAMSON, NICOL, Sept. 14, 1938 (Hamilton, Scot.). Scottish actor. Best known for his Shakespearean roles, particularly in *Hamlet* (stage and film, 1969-70).

WINWOOD, ESTELLE, born Estelle Goodwin, Jan. 24, 1883 (Lee, Eng.). English actress. Films: *Quality Street*, 1937; *The Swan*, 1956; *Camelot*, 1967; *The Producers*, 1968; *Murder by Death*, 1976.

YORK, MICHAEL, born Michael York-Johnson, Mar. 27, 1942 (Fulmer, Eng.). English actor. Plays: *Hamlet*, 1970; *Outcry*, 1973. Films: *Taming of the Shrew*, 1966; *Romeo and Juliet*, 1967; *Lost Horizon*, 1972; *Great Expectations*, 1974; *The Last Remake of Beau Geste*, 1977.

YORK, SUSANNAH, Jan. 9, 1942 (London, Eng.). English actress. Films: *A Man for All Seasons*, 1966; *They Shoot Horses, Don't They?*, 1969; *The Battle of Britain*, 1969; *Happy Birthday, Wanda June*, 1971.

YOUNG, ROLAND KEITH, Nov. 11, 1887 (London, Eng.)-June 5, 1953. English character actor. Best known for his role in the "Topper" film series, 1930s-40s. Other films: *One Hour With You*, 1932; *David Copperfield*, 1934; *The Young in Heart*, 1939; *The Philadelphia Story*, 1940.

ZETTERLING, MAI, May 24, 1925 (Sweden). Swedish actress, director. Films, actress: *Quartet*, 1948; *Only Two Can Play*, 1962. Films, dir.: *The Loving Couples*, 1964; *Night Games*, 1966.

DANCERS

ASTAIRE, ADELE, born Adele Austerlitz, Sept. 10, 1898 (Omaha, Neb.). U.S. dancer. Toast of vaudeville in dance team with brother FRED ASTAIRE, 1916-32; appeared with him in musical shows, notably *Lady Be Good* (1926), *The Band Wagon* (1931) and *Funny Face* (1927); retired from show business in 1932.

ASTAIRE, FRED, born Frederick Austerlitz, May 10, 1899 (Omaha, Neb.). U.S. dancer, actor. Leading dance star of his generation on stage (with sister ADELE, 1916-32) and screen (frequently partnered with GINGER ROGERS); in later years, has appeared as character actor in films and on TV. Films: *Gay Divorcee* (1934), *Roberta* (1935), *Top Hat* (1935), *Story of Vernon and Irene Castle* (1939), *Holiday Inn* (1942), *Easter Parade* (1948), *Daddy Long Legs* (1955), *Funny Face* (1957), and *Silk Stockings* (1957).

BAKER, JOSEPHINE, June 3, 1906 (St. Louis, Mo.)–Apr. 10, 1975. U.S.-French dancer. The "Dark Star" of the Folies-Bergère, who made her Parisian debut in 1925 in La Revue Nègre; starred in her own Paris revues, from 1930; made triumphal return to New York City stage in 1973, although she had been semiretired since 1950.

BOLGER, RAY, Jan. 10, 1904 (Boston, Mass.). U.S. dancer, actor. Began in vaudeville, 1923; starred in Broadway shows from 1925; moved on to films, in which his best-known role was the Scarecrow in *The Wizard of Oz* (1939). Plays: *Geo. White's Scandals,* 1931; *Life Begins at 8:40,* 1934; *By Jupiter,* 1942; *Where's Charley?,* 1948. Films: *The Harvey Girls,* 1946; *Look for the Silver Lining,* 1949; *Where's Charley?,* 1952; *April in Paris,* 1952.

BUBBLES, JOHN, 1902 (Louisville, Ky.). U.S. dancer. Teamed with Fred "Buck" Washington to form dance team "Buck and Bubbles," a top vaudeville act of 1920s and 1930s; starred as Sportin' Life in 1935 film *Porgy and Bess;* acted in other films; retired 1955, except for 1964 nightclub act with ANNA MARIA ALBERGHETTI.

CASTLE, IRENE, née Foote, Apr. 7, 1893 (New Rochelle, N.Y.)–Jan. 25, 1969. U.S. dancer. With husband VERNON CASTLE, formed popular dance team, 1912–17; a number of dances are credited to them, including the Turkey Trot, the One-step and the Castle Walk; her appearance popularized bobbed hair and the natural figure; made films, 1917–22; in later years, was a leader in the antivivisection movement.

CASTLE, VERNON, born Vernon Castle Blythe, May 2, 1887 (Norwich, Eng.)–Feb. 15, 1918. U.S. dancer. With wife IRENE CASTLE, the dancing sensation of pre-World War I cabarets; elegance in ballroom dancing their trademark; with wife, wrote *The Modern Dance,* 1914; killed in airplane crash.

CHAMPION, MARGE, born Marjorie Celeste Belcher, Sept. 2, 1923 (Los Angeles, Calif.). U.S. dancer, actress. Teamed with her then-husband GOWER CHAMPION in several film musicals; solo film appearances included *The Story of Vernon and Irene Castle* (1939); later appeared as character actress and choreographed for TV, where she won 1975 Emmy Award for *Queen of the Stardust Ballroom* (movie).

CHARISSE, CYD, born Tula Ellice Finklea, Mar. 8, 1923 (Amarillo, Tex.). U.S. dancer. Stylish, long-legged star of 1950s musicals; occasionally teamed with FRED ASTAIRE. Films: *The Bandwagon,* 1953; *Silk Stockings,* 1957. Autobiography with husband TONY MARTIN: *The Two of Us,* 1978.

THE DOLLY SISTERS: ROSIE, Oct. 25, 1892 (Hungary)–Feb. 1, 1970; and **JENNY,** Oct. 25, 1892 (Hungary)–June 1, 1941. Twins who formed one of most popular dance acts in history of vaudeville, from 1909; in Ziegfeld Follies, 1911; starred in long list of musical comedies and revues in 1920s; Jenny committed suicide.

FULLER, LOIE, born Marie Louise Fuller, Jan. 15, 1862 (Fullersburg, Ill.)–Jan. 1, 1928. U.S. dancer. Achieved fame for innovations in theatrical lighting;

invented the "serpentine" dance; appeared in burlesque, vaudeville, Buffalo Bill's Wild West Show, and the Folies-Bergère.

GAYNOR, MITZI, born Francesca Mitzi von Gerber, Sept. 4, 1931 (Chicago, Ill.). U.S. dancer. Best remembered for leading roles in films such as *There's No Business like Show Business* (1954), *Les Girls* (1957), and *South Pacific* (1958); has recently done one-woman concert tours.

GENNARO, PETER, 1924 (Metaire, La.). U.S. dancer, choreographer. Professional since 1949, in Broadway shows; choreographer for many plays, films, and TV shows.

GRAY, GILDA, born Marianna Michalska, 1901 (Pol.)–Dec. 22, 1959. U.S. dancer. Popular dancer of the 1920s; credited with inventing the "shimmy."

HANEY, CAROL, Dec. 24, 1924 (New Bedford, Mass.)–May 10, 1964. U.S. dancer, choreographer. Achieved stardom as dancer in the Broadway show *Pajama Game,* 1954; former assistant to GENE KELLY. Films: *Kiss Me Kate,* 1953; *Invitation to the Dance,* 1954. Plays: *Funny Girl* (choreographer), 1964.

HEATHERTON, JOEY, Sept. 14, 1944 (Rockville Centre, N.Y.). U.S. dancer. Former child stage performer who has appeared in several films; a frequent nightclub performer, often seen on TV.

KEELER, RUBY, born Ethel Keeler, Aug. 25, 1910 (Halifax, N.S., Can.). U.S. dancer, actress. Broadway musical star who gained greatest fame in BUSBY BERKELEY films of 1930s; revived career as star of play *No, No, Nanette,* 1970.

KELLY, GENE CURRAN, Aug. 23, 1912 (Pittsburgh, Pa.). U.S. dancer, choreographer. Carefree, athletic dancer of Hollywood musicals of the 1940s and 1950s; turned to direction when musicals went out of style. Films: *For Me and My Gal,* 1942; *Anchors Aweigh,* 1945; *The Pirate,* 1948; *On the Town,* 1949; *An American in Paris,* 1951; *Singin' in the Rain,* 1952; *Brigadoon,* 1954. Plays: *Pal Joey,* 1941.

KIDD, MICHAEL, Aug. 12, 1919 (Brooklyn, N.Y.). U.S. dancer, choreographer. Appeared with several ballet companies (including Ballet Theatre, 1942–47) before becoming choreographer and dir. for a number of Broadway productions. Plays choreographed: *Finian's Rainbow,* 1947; *Guys and Dolls,* 1950; *Can-Can,* 1953; *Li'l Abner,* 1956; *Destry Rides Again,* 1959. Received Tony Awards for all of the abovementioned plays.

McKECHNIE, DONNA RUTH, Nov. 16, 1942 (Pontiac, Mich.). U.S. dancer. Fluid, powerful dancer; Broadway star since 1960 debut in *How to Succeed in Business without Really Trying.* Plays: *Promises, Promises,* 1968; *Company,* 1970; *A Chorus Line* (Tony Award), 1975.

MILLER, ANN, born Lucille Ann Collier, Apr. 12, 1923 (Houston, Tex.). U.S. dancer. Tap dancer in films and on stage and TV. Films: *You Can't Take It with You,* 1939; *Easter Parade,* 1949; *On the Town,* 1950; *Hit the Deck,* 1952; *Kiss Me Kate,* 1953.

MONTEZ, LOLA, born Marie Dolores Eliza Rosana Gilbert, 1818 (Limerick, Ire.)–Jan. 17, 1861. Irish dancer, courtesan. "Spanish" dancer and adventuress, known more for her liaison with King Louis I of Bavaria than for her dancing.

MORENO, RITA, born Rosita Dolores Alverio, Dec. 11, 1931 (Humacao, P.R.). Puerto Rican-U.S. dancer, actress. Spanish dancer since childhood; nightclub entertainer who has performed in stage productions and films. Plays: *The Sign in Sidney Brustein's Window,* 1964; *Gantry,* 1969; *The*

THE BOOK OF WHO

Last of the Red Hot Lovers, 1970; The National Health, 1975; The Ritz, 1975. Films: West Side Story (Best Supporting Actress AA, 1961).

POWELL, ELEANOR, Nov. 21, 1912 (Springfield, Mass.). U.S. dancer. Vivacious, long-legged tap-dancing star of musical films in 1930s and 1940s. Films: Born to Dance, 1936; Rosalie, 1938.

PROWSE, JULIET, 1937 (Bombay, India). British dancer. Appeared in movies in the 1950s and 1960s; frequent performer in clubs and on TV in U.S. and Great Britain.

RAND, SALLY, born Helen Beck, Jan. 2, 1904 (Elkton, Mo.).–Aug. 31, 1979. U.S. dancer. Sensation of 1933 World's Fair in Chicago, with her exotic dances, especially the Fan Dance; picked her name from the Rand-McNally Atlas; performed in clubs across U.S. until her death.

RIVERA, CHITA, Jan. 23, 1933 (Washington, D.C.). U.S. dancer, actress. Studied at School of American Ballet (with G. BALANCHINE); star of musicals on Broadway, where she created role of Anita in West Side Story (1957). Plays: Mr. Wonderful, 1956; Bye, Bye, Birdie, 1960; Chicago, 1975.

ROBINSON, BILL ("Bojangles"), born Luther Robinson, May 25, 1878 (Richmond, Va.)–Nov. 25, 1949. U.S. dancer. A popular vaudeville tap dancer, best known for his stairway dance and his appearances in several SHIRLEY TEMPLE films.

ROGERS, GINGER, born Virginia Katherine McMath, July 16, 1911 (Independence, Mo.). U.S. dancer, actress. Star of movie musicals, many as partner of FRED ASTAIRE. Films: Flying Down to Rio, 1933; The Gay Divorcee, 1934; Roberta, 1934; Top Hat, 1935; Shall We Dance?, 1937; Stage Door, 1938; The Story of Vernon and Irene Castle, 1939; Kitty Foyle (Best Actress AA) 1940; Roxie Hart, 1942; Lady in the Dark, 1943.

TUNE, TOMMY, Feb. 28, 1939 (Wichita Falls, Tex.). U.S. dancer, choreographer. Featured in films and on Broadway, came to prominence as choreographer-director of the musicals Seesaw (1973) and The Best Little Whorehouse in Texas (1978).

VERDON, GWEN, born Gwyneth Evelyn Verdon, Jan. 13, 1925 (Los Angeles, Calif.). U.S. dancer, actress. Red-haired musical-comedy star on Broadway and in films. Plays: Can-Can, 1953; Damn Yankees, 1955; New Girl in Town, 1957; Red Head, 1958; Sweet Charity, 1966; Chicago, 1975. Won Tony Awards for the first four listed above.

VEREEN, BEN, Oct. 10, 1946 (Miami, Fla.). U.S. dancer, actor. Prominent in Broadway musicals of the 1960s and 1970s; achieved stardom with role on TV miniseries Roots (1977) and with dynamic nightclub and TV variety-show act.

SINGERS

ALBERGHETTI, ANNA MARIA, May 15, 1936 (Pesaro, It.). Italian-U.S. singer. Operatic soprano who specializes in light classics and musical shows, plus films; won Tony award for Broadway musical Carnival, 1962.

ANDERSON, IAN, Aug. 10, 1947 (Blackpool, Eng.). British rock musician. Singer and guitarist; leader of Jethro Tull rock group since 1967; eight Gold Albums.

ANDREWS, JULIE, born Julia Wells, Oct. 1, 1935 (Walton, Eng.). British singer, actress. Original Eliza in musical My Fair Lady (stage); starred in wholesome films, including Mary Poppins (Best Actress AA; 1964), The Sound of Music (1965) and Star (1968); numerous TV specials.

THE ANDREWS SISTERS: LAVERNE, 1915 (Minneapolis, Minn.)–May 8, 1967; **MAXINE,** 1918 (Minneapolis, Minn.); **PATTY,** 1920 (Minneapolis, Minn.). U.S. singers. Formed popular singing group in the 1940s, with several hit records and film appearances. Songs: "Don't Sit Under the Apple Tree with Anyone Else but Me"; "Bei Mir Bist Du Schön"; "Boogie-Woogie Bugle Boy from Company B."

ANKA, PAUL, July 30, 1941 (Ottawa, Ont., Can.). Canadian singer, composer. Popular singer from 1956, when he was teen idol. Compositions: "Diana," "Put Your Head on My Shoulder," "Tonight Show Theme."

ARNOLD, EDDY, May 15, 1918 (Henderson, Tex.) U.S. singer. Country-and-western star, with numerous hits since 1944; elected to Country Music Hall of Fame, 1966.

AUTRY, (Orvon) **GENE,** Sept. 29, 1907 (Tioga, Tex.). U.S. singer, executive. The "Singing Cowboy," he made 82 movie Westerns, 1934-54; wrote over 250 songs, including "Here Comes Santa Claus"; chm., Calif. Angels baseball team.

AVALON, FRANKIE, born Francis Avallone, Sept. 8, 1940 (Philadelphia, Pa.). U.S. singer. Teen heartthrob of 1960s, made series of "beach party" films, often with ANNETTE FUNICELLO.

AZNAVOUR, CHARLES, born Varenagh Aznavourian, May 22, 1924 (Paris, Fr.). French singer. Singer of romantic ballads and sometime actor. Films: Shoot the Piano Player,1960; Candy, 1968.

BAEZ, JOAN, Jan. 9, 1941 (New York, N.Y.). U.S. singer, political activist. Folksinger active in civil rights and antiwar movements of 1960s; founder of the Inst. for the Study of Non-Violence, 1965.

BAILEY, PEARL MAE, Mar. 29, 1918 (Newport News, Va.). U.S. singer. Star of stage, films, TV; most noted for lead in play Hello Dolly (1967), and work as special U.S. rep. to the UN; played in films Carmen Jones (1954), Porgy & Bess (1959), The Landlord (1969).

BASSEY, SHIRLEY, Jan. 8, 1937 (Cardiff, Wales). English singer. Noted for her dynamic style. Considered one of the best post-WW II female vocalists produced by England. Songs: "As I Love You," 1958; "Kiss Me, Honey, Kiss Me," 1959; "As Long as He Needs Me," 1960; "Something," 1970.

BEE GEES, THE: BARRY GIBB, Sept. 1, 1946 (Douglas, Isle of Man, Eng.); **MAURICE GIBB,** Dec. 22, 1949 (Manchester, Eng.); **ROBIN GIBB,** Dec. 22, 1949 (Manchester, Eng.). British singers. Leading 1960s rock group; gained new prominence as disco group in 1970s; wrote and performed score for the film Saturday Night Fever, 1977. Songs: "Lonely Days," "How Can You Mend a Broken Heart," "Stayin' Alive," "Jive Talkin'."

BELAFONTE, HARRY, Mar. 1, 1927 (New York, N.Y.). U.S. singer, actor. Noted for calypso songs; his films include Carmen Jones (1954), Island in the Sun (1957), Odds against Tomorrow (1959), and Uptown Saturday Night (1974).

BENNETT, TONY, born Anthony Benedetto, Aug. 3, 1926 (New York, N.Y.). U.S. singer. Popular crooner in concert, nightclubs, TV since early 1950s.

BERRY, CHUCK, born Charles Edward Anderson Berry, Jan. 15, 1926 (San Jose, Calif.). U.S. singer, songwriter. Among first to shape big-beat blues into rock-and-roll; composer of "Maybellene," "Roll over Beethoven," "Johnny B. Goode," "Rock 'n' Roll Music."

BIKEL, THEODORE, May 2, 1924 (Vienna, Austria). U.S. singer, actor. Popular Yiddish and Hebrew folksinger; was original Capt. Von Trapp in play *Sound of Music*, 1959-61.

BONO, SONNY, born Salvatore Bono, Feb. 16, 1940 (Detroit, Mich.). U.S. singer. Teamed with ex-wife CHER (1964-74) in popular singing duo.

BOONE, PAT, born Charles Eugene Boone, June 1, 1934 (Jacksonville, Fla.). U.S. singer. Top pop singer in 1950s, noted for clean-cut image and white buck shoes; sings now with wife and family, particularly daughter Debby Boone. Films: *Bernardine*, 1957; *April Love*, 1957; *Mardi Gras*, 1958; *State Fair*, 1962. Books: *Twixt Twelve and Twenty*, 1958; *Care and Feeding of Parents*, 1967; *Joy*, 1973.

BOWIE, DAVID, born David Robert Jones, Jan. 8, 1947 (London, Eng.). British musician, actor. Androgynous rock star with many successful albums, including *Hunky Dory, Diamond Dogs*, and *Station to Station;* starred in the film *The Man Who Fell to Earth*, 1976.

BREWER, TERESA, May 7, 1931 (Toledo, Ohio). U.S. singer. Pop singer of such 1950s song hits as "Music, Music, Music" and "Ricochet Romance."

BROWN, JAMES, June 17, 1928 (Pulaski, Tenn.). U.S. singer. Often called the "King of Soul Music"; records include "Please, Please, Please," "Papa's Got a Brand New Bag," and "Don't Be a Dropout."

BROWNE, JACKSON, Oct. 9, c.1948 (Heidelberg, Ger.). U.S. musician. Pop-rock songwriter-singer, his late 1960s songs were sung by many other people; became solo performer, 1971. Songs: "Doctor My Eyes," 1972; "Rock Me on the Water," 1972; "Take It Easy," 1972; "Red Neck Friend," 1974; "Ready or Not."

BRYANT, ANITA JANE, Mar. 25, 1940 (Barnsdale, Okla.). U.S. singer. Runner-up Miss America, 1959; recorded several religious albums; spokeswoman for Coca-Cola and Florida Citrus Comm. since 1968; leader of "Save Our Children" antihomosexual crusade, 1977-   .

BUCHANAN, JACK, 1891 (Scotland)-Oct. 13, 1957. British entertainer. Song-and-dance man of the stage and films. Films: *The Gang's All Here*, 1939; *The Bandwagon*, 1953.

CAMPBELL, GLEN, Apr. 22, 1938 (Billstown, Ark.). U.S. singer. Country-rock recording star; records include "Gentle on My Mind," "Wichita Lineman," "By the Time I Get to Phoenix," "Rhinestone Cowboy"; star of TV show *Glen Campbell Good Time Hour*, 1969-71; starred in film *True Grit*, 1969; winner of four Grammys, five Country Music Assn. awards.

THE CARPENTERS: KAREN ANNE, Mar. 2, 1950 (New Haven, Conn.); **RICHARD LYNN,** Oct. 15, 1946 (New Haven, Conn.). U.S. singers. Mellow pop-rock singers of hits such as "Close to You," "Goodbye to Love," "Top of the World," "Only Yesterday"; winners of three Grammys.

CARR, VIKKI, born Florencia Bisenta de Casillas Martinez Cardona, July 19, 1942 (El Paso, Tex.). U.S. singer. Pop songstress who frequently sings multilingually; records include "It Must Be Him" and "With Pen in Hand."

CARROLL, DIAHANN, born Carol Diahann Johnson, July 17, 1935 (New York, N.Y.). U.S. singer, actress; won Tony award for Broadway musical *No Strings*, 1962. Films: *Paris Blues*

(1961), *Hurry Sundown* (1967), *Claudine* (1972); first black woman to star in a TV series, *Julia* (1968-69).

CARTER, JUNE, June 23, 1929 (Maces Spring, Va.). U.S. singer. Member of famed country-and-western Carter Family group. (Wife of JOHNNY CASH.)

CASH, JOHNNY, Feb. 26, 1932 (Kingsland, Ark.). U.S. singer. Country-and-western superstar; singer-composer of "I Walk the Line," "Folsom Prison Blues," "Don't Take Your Guns to Town"; starred in own TV series, 1969-71. (Husband of JUNE CARTER.)

CASSIDY, DAVID, Apr. 12, 1950 (New York, N.Y.). U.S. singer. Rose to teenybopper idol status through appearances on TV series *The Partridge Family* in early 1970s. (Son of JACK CASSIDY; stepson of SHIRLEY JONES.)

CHANNING, CAROL, Jan. 31, 1923 (Seattle, Wash.). U.S. actress, singer. Vivacious blond who created lead in *Hello Dolly* on Broadway, 1964; also starred in *Gentlemen Prefer Blondes* (1949), *Wonderful Town* (1953), *Lorelei* (1974).

CHARLES, RAY, born Ray Charles Robinson, Sept. 23, 1930 (Albany, Ga.). U.S. singer, composer. Blind star of jazz, soul, pop, country-and-western genres; winner of 10 Grammys.

CHECKER, CHUBBY, born Ernest Evans, Oct. 3, 1941 (Philadelphia, Pa.). U.S. singer. Helped popularize the Twist dance craze of early 1960s.

CHER, born Cherilyn La Pierre, May 20, 1946 (El Centro, Calif.). U.S. singer. Vaulted to prominence in a singing duo with husband SONNY BONO, 1964-74; now a successful solo act.

CHEVALIER, MAURICE, Sept. 12, 1888 (Paris, Fr.)-Jan. 1, 1972. French singer. Musical comedy star; starred in many films, including *The Love Parade* (1930), *Folies Bergère* (1935), *Love in the Afternoon* (1957), *Gigi* (1958); known for his straw hat and charming manner.

CLARK, PETULA, Nov. 15, 1934 (Ewell, Eng.). English singer. Pop singer, from the early 1960s. Songs: "Downtown," "I Know a Place," "Don't Sleep in the Subway, Darling."

CLARK, ROY, Apr. 15, 1933 (Meherrin, Va.). U.S. country-and-western singer, musician. Star of *Hee-Haw* TV show; named Entertainer of the Year by the Country Music Assn., 1963.

COLE, NATALIE, Feb. 6, 1950 (Los Angeles, Calif.). U.S. singer. Disco-rock singer; daughter of NAT "KING" COLE.; won Grammy awards in 1975, 1976. Songs: "This Will Be," 1975.

COLE, NAT "KING", born Nathaniel Adams Coles, Mar. 17, 1919 (Montgomery, Ala.)-Feb. 15, 1965. U.S. singer, pianist. Pop singer of numerous hits, including "Straighten Up and Fly Right," "Too Young," "Nature Boy," "Route 66," "Unforgettable," "Ramblin' Rose."(Father of NATALIE COLE.)

COLLINS, DOROTHY, born Marjorie Chandler, Nov. 18, 1926 (Windsor, Ont., Can.). U.S. singer. Popular on TV's *Hit Parade*, early 1950s.

COLLINS, JUDY MARJORIE, May 1, 1939 (Seattle, Wash.). U.S. folksinger. Has recorded many successful albums, including "Golden Apples in the Sun" (1962), "In My Life" (1967), "Wildflowers" (1968), "Recollections" (1969), and "Living" (1971); as filmmaker, produced and directed *Antonia* (1976), which received Acad. Award nomination as best documentary.

COMO, PERRY, born Pierino Como, May 18, 1912 (Cannonsburg, Pa.). U.S. singer. Easygoing crooner who had a very popular TV show, 1948-

THE BOOK OF WHO

63; his hit records include "Prisoner of Love," "If," "It's Impossible"; named Variety Club Personality of the Year, 1956.

COOKE, SAM, Jan. 22, 1935 (Chicago, Ill.)-Dec. 11, 1964. U.S. singer. Pioneer in soul and rhythm-and-blues movements, began as gospel singer; shot to death in bizarre incident in L.A. Songs: "I'll Come Running Back to You," 1957; "Forever," 1957; "You Send Me," 1958; "Summertime," 1958; "Chain Gang," 1960; "Twistin' the Night Away," 1962; "Shake," 1964.

COOPER, ALICE, Feb. 4, 1948 (Detroit, Mich.). U.S. singer. Bizarre 1970's rock star whose songs often dealt with violent themes and were frequently performed with violent staging. Songs: "Sun Arise," "Caught in a Dream"; "Eighteen"; "The Ballad of Dwight Fry"; "No More Mr. Nice Guy"; "Killer"; "Under My Wheels"; "School's Out"; "Be My Lover."

CROCE, JIM, Jan. 10, 1942 (Philadelphia, Pa.)-Sept. 20, 1973. U.S. musician. Singer, guitarist, songwriter of folk-rock music in late 1960s and early 1970s; was just becoming a star when he died in private plane crash. Songs: "You Don't Mess Around with Jim," 1972; "Operator," 1972; "Bad, Bad Leroy Brown," 1973; "I've Got a Name," 1973; "Time in a Bottle," 1973.

CROSBY, BING, born Harry Lillis Crosby, May 2, 1903 (Tacoma, Wash.)-Oct. 14, 1977. U.S. singer, actor. Leading crooner of the 1930s and 1940s; radio star, 1931-57; starred in a number of films, including *Anything Goes* (1936), *Pennies From Heaven* (1936), *Going My Way* (AA, 1944), *The Bells of St. Mary's* (1945), *White Christmas* (1954), *High Society* (1956) and six "road" pictures with BOB HOPE; founded Bing Crosby Golf Tournament at Pebble Beach, Calif.

CULLUM, JOHN, Mar. 2, 1930 (Knoxville, Tenn.). U.S. singer, actor, director. Star of stage musicals *Shenandoah* (1976-77) and *On the 20th Century* (1978-79); has recently turned to directing.

DAMONE, VIC, born Vito Farinola, June 12, 1928 (Brooklyn, N.Y.). U.S. singer. Club and recording star who appeared in some films in 1950s.

DARIN, BOBBY, born Walden Robert Cassotto, May 14, 1936 (New York, N.Y.)-Dec. 20, 1973. U.S. singer. Major star of rock-and-roll era, with recordings such as "Mack the Knife" and "Splish Splash."

DAVIDSON, JOHN, 1943 (White Plains, N.Y.). U.S. singer, actor. Handsome, wholesome pop star of 1960s; frequent guest host on TV's *The Tonight Show;* starred in sitcom *The Girl with Something Extra,* 1973-74.

DAVIS, MAC, Jan. 21, 1942 (Lubbock, Tex.). U.S. country-and-western singer, composer. Had summer variety shows on TV, 1974-76. Songs: "A Little Less Conversation"; "In the Ghetto"; "Friend, Lover, Woman, Wife"; "Daddy's Little Man"; "I Believe in Music".

DAVIS, SAMMY, JR., Dec. 8, 1925 (New York, N.Y.). U.S. singer, actor. In vaudeville, clubs with Will Mastin Trio, 1930-48; star of Broadway shows *Mr. Wonderful* (1956), *Golden Boy* (1964); films include *Porgy and Bess* (1959), *Ocean's 11* (1960), *Sweet Charity* (1968); numerous TV appearances as singer, actor; author of autobiography, *Yes I Can* (1965).

DEAN, JIMMY, Aug. 10, 1928 (Plainview, Tex.). U.S. country-and-western singer. Numerous county-fair and TV appearances, recordings. Best known for "Big Bad John."

DENVER, JOHN, born Henry John Deutschendorf, Jr., Dec. 31, 1943 (Roswell, N.M.). U.S. singer, composer, actor. Many hit songs, including "Leaving on a Jet Plane," "Rocky Mountain High," "Take Me Home, Country Roads"; made film debut in *Oh God!,* 1977; active in environmental, world hunger movements.

DIAMOND, NEIL, Jan. 24, 1941 (Brooklyn, N.Y.). U.S. singer, songwriter. Rock star who wrote and recorded such hits as "Kentucky Woman," "Sweet Caroline," "Young Girl," "Song Sung Blue"; many concert appearances; wrote score for film *Jonathan Livingston Seagull,* 1973.

DIDDLEY, BO, born Elias McDaniel, Dec. 30, 1928 (McComb, Miss.). U.S. musician. Pioneer in rock-and-roll; a singer/songwriter who combined jazz and blues with rock. Songs: "Bo Diddley," 1955; "I'm a Man," 1955; "Say Man," 1959; "Road Runner," 1960; "You Can't Judge a Book by Its Cover," 1962; "Ooh Baby," 1967.

DION, born Dion Dimucci, July 18, 1939 (Bronx, N.Y.). U.S. musician. With backup group The Belmonts was popular star of late 1950s-early 1960s; solo act, 1960-   . Songs: "A Teenager in Love," 1959; "A Lover's Prayer," 1960; "Where or When," 1960; "Runaround Sue," 1961; "The Wanderer," 1961; "Ruby Baby," 1963; "Drip Drop," 1964; "Abraham, Martin and John," 1968.

DOMINO, FATS, born Antoine Domino, Feb. 26, 1928 (New Orleans, La.). U.S. pianist, singer, songwriter. Popular in 1950s boogie-woogie era, with songs such as "Blueberry Hill" and "Ain't That a Shame."

DONOVAN, born Donovan Leitch, May 10, 1946 (Glasgow, Scot.). Scottish singer. Leading exponent of "flower power" rock in 1960s, with songs such as "Sunshine Superman" and "Mellow Yellow."

DRAKE, ALFRED, born Alfred Capurro, Oct. 7, 1914 (New York, N.Y.). U.S. singer, actor. Star of musical comedies, including *Kiss Me, Kate* (1948) and *Kismet* (1954; Tony award for best starring role in a musical).

DYLAN, BOB, born Robert Zimmerman, May 24, 1941 (Duluth, Minn.). U.S. singer, songwriter. His "Blowin' in the Wind" and "Times They Are A-Changin'" were anthems of the 1960s civil-rights movement; other hits include "Mr. Tambourine Man," "Gates of Eden."

EBERLE, RAY, 1919-Aug. 25, 1979. U.S. band singer. Best known as vocalist with GLENN MILLER band (1938-44); with Tex Beneke band, and as part of Modernaires singing group; later had own band. Songs: "Serenade in Blue," "Midnight Cocktail."

EDDY, NELSON, 1901 (Providence, R.I.)-Mar. 6, 1967. U.S. singer, actor. Famed for series of operetta films with JEANETTE MACDONALD, including *Naughty Marietta* (1935), *Rose Marie* (1936), *May Time* (1937), *Sweethearts* (1939), *New Moon* (1940).

ELLIOTT, CASS(andra), Sept. 19, 1941 (Baltimore, Md.)-July 29, 1974. U.S. singer. Rotund, sweet-voiced pop-rock singer who was part of The Mamas and the Papas, 1963-67; successful solo act, 1967-74. Songs: "Dream a Little Dream of Me" and "Disney Girls."

ETTING, RUTH, 1898 (David City, Neb.)-Sept. 24, 1978. U.S. singer. Torch singer popular on radio and in films in the 1930s; subject of film biography *Love Me or Leave Me* (1955).

THE EVERLY BROTHERS: DON, Feb. 1, 1937 (Brownie, Ky.); and **PHIL,** Jan. 19, 1938 (Brownie, Ky.). U.S. singers. Popular stars of late 1950s-early

1960s, with hits such as "Bye Bye Love" and "Wake Up, Little Susie."

FABIAN, born Fabian Forte, Feb. 6, 1943 (Philadelphia, Pa.). U.S. singer. Teenage idol in the 1950s; appeared in a series of B movies in the 1960s.

FABRAY, NANETTE, born Nanette Fabares, Oct. 27, 1920 (San Diego, Calif.). U.S. singer, actress. Began as child actress in "Our Gang" film shorts; in Broadway and film musicals including *High Button Shoes* (1947), *Love Life* (1949); *The Bandwagon* (1953). Winner of Donaldson Award (1947), Tony Award (1949), Emmy Awards, (1953, 1956).

FELICIANO, JOSÉ, Sept. 10, 1945 (Larez, P.R.). Puerto Rican singer, composer, guitarist. Blind performer who has won two Grammys and recorded over 30 Gold Albums.

FIELDS, GRACIE, born Grace Stansfield, Jan. 9, 1898 (Rochdale, Eng.)-Sept. 27, 1979. English singer, comedienne. Popular music-hall performer. Films: *Sally in Our Alley,* 1931; *Sing as We Go,* 1934; *Holy Matrimony,* 1943.

THE FIFTH DIMENSION: Billy Davis, Jr., June 26 (St. Louis, Mo.); Florence LaRue, Feb. 4, 1944 (Plainfield, N.J.); Marilyn McCoo, Sept. 30 ? (Jersey City, N.J.); LaMonte McLemore, Sept. 17 ? (St. Louis, Mo.); Ron Townson, Jan. 20 ? (St. Louis, Mo.). U.S. singers. Mellow soft-rock singing group of mid-1960s and early 1970s; after group broke up (1973) McCoo and Davis (who were married) became a separate act. Songs: "Up, Up and Away," 1967; "Stoned Soul Picnic," 1968; "Sweet Blindness," 1968; "Wedding Bell Blues," 1969; "Aquarius," 1969.

FISHER, EDDIE, born Edwin Jack Fisher, Aug. 10, 1928 (Philadelphia, Pa.). U.S. singer. Very popular in 1950s, with many hit records. (Husband of DEBBIE REYNOLDS, ELIZABETH TAYLOR, and CONNIE STEVENS.)

FITZGERALD, ELLA, Apr. 25, 1918 (Newport News, Va.). U.S. jazz singer. Began with Chick Webb Orchestra, 1934; winner of numerous jazz popularity polls; has won eight Grammy awards.

FLACK, ROBERTA, Feb. 10, 1939 (Black Mountain, N.C.). U.S. singer. Former schoolteacher turned rock performer; hit songs include "The First Time Ever I Saw Your Face" (1972) and "Killing Me Softly" (1973).

FOLEY, RED, born Clyde Julian Foley, June 17, 1910 (Blue Lick, Ky.)-Sept. 19, 1968. U.S. country-and-western singer. Popular radio and recording artist of the 1940s-50s; one of the first to record in Nashville.

FORD, TENNESSEE ERNIE, born Ernest Jennings Ford, Feb. 13, 1919 (Bristol, Tenn.). U.S. singer. Country singer who had own TV show (1955-61 and 1962-65); "16 Tons" best-known record.

FRAMPTON, PETER, Apr. 22, 1950 (Beckenham, Eng.). English rock singer. Teen idol, with many hit records; member of the groups Humble Pie (1968-71) and Frampton's Camel (1971-74); solo since 1974.

FRANCIS, CONNIE, born Constance Franconero, Dec. 12, 1938 (Newark, N.J.). U.S. singer, actress. Popular in late 1950s-early 1960s; film credits include *Where the Boys Are* (1963), *Follow the Boys* (1964).

FRANKLIN, ARETHA, Mar. 25, 1942 (Memphis, Tenn.). U.S. singer. Rhythm-and-blues star of records, concerts, TV; winner of Grammys in 1972, 1973.

GARFUNKEL, ART(hur), Oct. 13, 1942 (New York, N.Y.). U.S. singer, songwriter. With PAUL SIMON, formed one of 1960s major folk-rock teams; solo since 1973; hits include "The Sounds of Silence," "Homeward Bound," "59th Street Bridge Song," "Scarborough Fair," "Mrs. Robinson," "Bridge Over Troubled Water"; starred in film *Carnal Knowledge* (1971).

GARLAND, JUDY, born Frances Gumm, June 10, 1922 (Grand Rapids, Minn.)-June 22, 1969. U.S. singer, actress. Legendary singer of 1940s-1960s and star of many memorable films; gained fame as Dorothy in *The Wizard of Oz,* 1939; also starred in *Babes in Arms* (1939), *Meet Me in St. Louis* (1944), *The Clock,* (1945), *The Harvey Girls* (1946), *Easter Parade* (1948), *A Star Is Born* (1954), *Judgment at Nuremberg* (1960); worldwide concert appearances in 1950s and 1960s. (One-time wife of VINCENTE MINNELLI; mother of LIZA MINNELLI.)

GATES, DAVID, Dec. 11, ? (Tulsa, Okla.). U.S. musician. Singer/songwriter; founder of the softrock group Bread, 1970; after group broke up (1977), became solo act. Songs: "Make It with You," 1970; "Let Your Love Go," 1971; "Baby, I'm-a Want You," 1971; "Sweet Surrender," 1972; "Diary," 1972; "It Don't Matter to Me"; "Guitar."

GAYE, MARVIN, Apr. 2, 1939 (Washington, D.C.). U.S. musician. Rhythm-and-blues/soul singer, associated with Motown Records since 1962, credited with doing much to advance popularity of rhythm-and-blues; partnered with Tammi Terrell (1967-70) in many hits. Songs: "Stubborn Kind of Fellow," 1962; "How Sweet It Is to Be Loved by You," 1965; "Little Darling," 1967; "Ain't No Mountain High Enough," 1967; "Ain't Nothing like the Real Thing," 1968; "I Heard It through the Grapevine," 1968; "Mercy Mercy Me," 1971.

GENTRY, BOBBY, July 27, 1944 (Chickasaw Co., Miss.). U.S. singer, songwriter. Wrote and recorded "Ode to Billy Joe" (1968), which won three Grammys and was the subject of a film, 1976.

GIBB, ANDY, Mar. 5, 1958 (Manchester, Eng.). English singer. One of the Gibb Brothers (see BEE GEES); a teen disco idol. Songs: "Shadow Dancing," "I Just Want to Be Your Everything," "Love Is Thicker Than Water."

GOLDSBORO, BOBBY, Jan. 11, 1944 (Marianna, Fla.). U.S. singer, songwriter. Country-and-western performer; Country Music Assn. Star of Year, 1968; hits include "Honey," "The Straight Life."

GORE, LESLEY, May 2, 1946 (Tenafly, N.J.). U.S. singer. Rock singer of early 1960s who gave up show business to enter college (1965). Songs: "It's My Party," 1963; "Judy's Turn to Cry," 1963; "Sunshine, Lollipops and Rainbows," 1964; "That's the Way Boys Are," 1964.

GORME, EYDIE, 1932 (New York, N.Y.). U.S. singer. Often appears with husband STEVE LAWRENCE in clubs and on TV; won Grammy, 1967.

GOULET, ROBERT, Nov. 26, 1933 (Lawrence, Kan.). U.S. singer, actor. Pop singer and star of Broadway musicals; made Broadway debut in *Camelot* (1960). (One-time husband of CAROL LAWRENCE.)

GRAYSON, KATHRYN, born Zelma Hedrick, Feb. 9, 1923 (Winston-Salem, N.C.). U.S. singer, actress. Leading lady in musical films of 1940s and 1950s, including *Anchors Aweigh* (1945), *Two Sisters from Boston* (1945), *Showboat* (1951), *Kiss Me Kate* (1953), *The Vagabond King* (1955).

THE BOOK OF WHO

GUTHRIE, ARLO, July 10,1947 (New York, N.Y.). U.S. folk-rock singer. Composed and recorded the hit song "Alice's Restaurant," 1969. (Son of WOODY GUTHRIE.)

GUTHRIE, WOODY, born Woodrow Wilson Guthrie, July 14, 1912 (Okemah, Okla.)-Oct. 3, 1967. U.S. folksinger, composer. Folk spokesman for populist and labor movements of the 1930s; his "This Land Is Your Land" was adopted by civil-rights movement of 1960s; other songs include "So Long, It's Been Good to Know You," "Hard Traveling," "Blowing Down This Old Dusty Road."

HAGGARD, MERLE RONALD, Apr. 6, 1937 (Bakersfield, Calif.). U.S. singer, songwriter. Country-and-western winner of five Gold Albums, one Platinum.

HALEY, BILL, born William John Clifton Haley, Mar., 1927 (Highland Park, Mich.). U.S. musician. Singer/songwriter/guitarist whose The Comets was a pioneering rock-and-roll group of the early 1950s; his musical style influenced ELVIS PRESLEY and paved the way for the combining of country-and-western with rock. Songs: "Shake, Rattle and Roll," 1954; "Rock around the Clock," 1955; "See You Later Alligator," 1956.

HARRISON, GEORGE, Feb. 25, 1943 (Liverpool, Eng.). British singer. Member of The Beatles, 1963-70; had some solo success after group split up.

HAYMES, DICK, 1918 (Buenos Aires, Arg.). U.S. singer. Popular in the Big Bands of the 1940s; appeared in some films, including *Irish Eyes Are Smiling* (1944), *State Fair* (1945), and *Up in Central Park* (1948).

HENDERSON, FLORENCE, Feb. 14, 1934 (Dale, Ind.). U.S. singer, actress. Stage and TV performer; best known as star of TV sitcom *The Brady Bunch,* 1969-74.

HENDRIX, JIMI, born James Marshall Hendricks, Nov. 27, 1942 (Seattle, Wash.)-Sept. 18, 1970. U.S. singer, guitarist. Leading exponent of 1960s "acid rock"; died of drug overdose, 1970.

HILDEGARDE, born Loretta Sell, Feb. 1, 1906 (Adell, Wis.). U.S. singer. "Incomparable" cabaret singer.

HOLIDAY, BILLIE ("Lady Day"), born Eleanora Holiday, Apr. 7, 1915 (Baltimore, Md.)-July 17, 1959. U.S. singer. Stellar jazz-blues singer of late 1930s and early 1940s; during her last years she struggled with heroin addiction; her autobiography, *Lady Sings the Blues* (1956), inspired 1972 film of same name.

HOLLY, BUDDY, born Charles Harden Holley, Sept. 7, 1936 (Lubbock, Tex.)-Feb. 2, 1959. U.S. singer, guitarist. Major influence in early rock-and-roll; leader of The Crickets; hits included "That'll Be the Day," "Maybe Baby," "Peggy Sue," "It Doesn't Matter Anymore."

HOPKINS, SAM ("Lightnin'"), Mar. 15, 1912 (Leon County, Tex.). U.S. singer/songwriter. Southwestern blues singer, whose style influenced 1970s rock-and-roll.

HORNE, LENA, June 30, 1917 (Brooklyn, N.Y.). U.S. singer. Beauteous star of nightclubs, TV; appeared in 1940s black musicals. Films: *Panama Hattie,* 1942; *Cabin in the Sky,* 1943; *Stormy Weather,* 1943; *Death of a Gunfighter,* 1969.

HORTON, JOHNNY, Apr. 3, 1929 (Tyler, Tex.)-Nov. 5, 1960. U.S. musician. Singer/songwriter/guitarist of early country-and-western music; best known for 1959 hit "Battle of New Orleans" and the posthumous hit "Sleepy-Eyed John" (1961).

HUMPERDINCK, ENGELBERT, born Arnold George Dorsey, May 3, 1936 (Madras, India). English singer. Many hit records, including "Release Me," "The Last Waltz," "After the Lovin'."

IAN, JANIS, May 7, 1950 (New York, N.Y.). U.S. singer/songwriter. Folk-rock star at 16, with her hit "Society's Child" (1966); left show business, 1967-71; now making club and concert appearances, writing songs. Songs: "Seventeen," 1977.

JACKSON, MAHALIA, Oct. 29, 1911 (New Orleans, La.)-Jan. 27, 1972. U.S. singer. Gospel singer, a prime example of link between religious and secular roots of jazz.

THE JACKSON 5: (All Jackson, all born in Gary, Ind.). Jackie (born Sigmund Esco), 1952; Jermaine (born Jermaine LaJune), 1956; Marlon (David), 1959; Michael Joe, 1960; Tito (born Toriano Adaryll), 1955. U.S. musicians. Family vocal-instrumental rock and soul group of late 1960s and 1970s; Michael made it as a solo performer and was featured in film *The Wiz* (1978).

JAGGER, MICK, born Michael Philip Jagger, July 26, 1943 (Dartford, Eng.). English rock singer. Leader of The Rolling Stones group since 1962; wrote many of group's hits, including "Ruby Tuesday," "Brown Sugar," and "Jumpin' Jack Flash"; known for flamboyant on-stage mannerisms.

JEFFERSON, BLIND LEMON, c.1897 (Texas)-1930. U.S. blues singer and guitarist.

JOEL, BILLY, May 9, 1949 (Bronx, N.Y.). U.S. singer, songwriter. Exponent of urban rock and roll; writes original, varied middle-class ballads. Songs: "Piano Man," "Just The Way You Are," "My Life," "Honesty."

JOHN, ELTON, born Reginald Kenneth Dwight, Mar. 25, 1947 (Pinner, Eng.). English musician. Rock star of 1960s and 1970s. Songs: "Goodbye, Yellow Brick Road," "Don't Let the Sun Go Down on Me," "Rocket Man," "Daniel," "Don't Go Breaking My Heart."

JOLSON, AL, born Asa Yoelson, May 26, 1886 (Srednick, Rus.)-Oct. 23, 1950. U.S. singer, actor. Musical comedy star (often in blackface); starred in *The Jazz Singer,* the first talking film (1927). (One-time husband of RUBY KEELER.)

JONES, ALLAN, 1907 (Scranton, Pa.). U.S. singer. Leading man in films of 1930s, including *A Night at the Opera* (1935), *Rose Marie* (1936), and *Firefly* (1937). (Father of JACK JONES.)

JONES, JACK, 1938 (Hollywood, Calif.). U.S. singer. Popular singer of 1960s and 1970s. (Son of ALLAN JONES.)

JONES, SHIRLEY, Mar. 31, 1934 (Smithtown, Pa.). U.S. singer, actress. Star of musical comedy films *Oklahoma* (1955), *Carousel* (1956), *The Music Man* (1962); received AA for best supporting actress in *Elmer Gantry* (1960); star of *The Partridge Family* TV series, 1970-74. (One-time wife of JACK CASSIDY; mother of Shaun Cassidy; stepmother of DAVID CASSIDY.)

JONES, TOM, born Thomas Jones Woodward, June 7, 1940 (Pontypridd, Wales). Welsh singer. Sexy, gyrating pop singer of 1960s and 1970s.

JOPLIN, JANIS, Jan. 19, 1943 (Port Arthur, Tex.)-Oct. 4, 1970. U.S. singer. Whiskey-voiced rock superstar; lead vocalist with Big Brother and the Holding Company, 1966-68; hits included "Down on Me," "Me and Bobby McGee," "Mercedes Benz," "Ball and Chain."

KAZAN, LAINIE, born Lainie Levine, May 15, 1942 (Brooklyn, N.Y.). U.S. singer. Frequent performer in clubs and on TV; has own lounges in Playboy Clubs, 1978-

268

KING, B.B., born Riley B. King, Sept. 16, 1925 (Itta Bena, Miss.). U.S. singer, guitarist. Leading exponent of rhythm-and-blues style; many recordings, concert appearances; received Grammy award, 1970.

KING, CAROLE, Feb. 9, 1942 (Brooklyn, N.Y.). U.S. musician. As singer/songwriter, a popular folk-rock performer of 1970s; with then-husband Gerry Goffin, wrote hit songs in the 1960s recorded by other groups (most notably "The Locomotion" for Little Eva and "Hi-De-Ho" for BLOOD, SWEAT and TEARS); now semi-retired. Songs: "So Far Away," "Where You Lead," "Tapestry," "It's Too Late," "You've Got a Friend."

KITT, EARTHA, Jan. 26, 1928 (North, S.C.). U.S. singer, actress. Feline singer in clubs since 1949, in U.S. and Europe; featured in the shows *New Faces of 1952* (1952), *Shinbone Alley* (1957) and *Timbuktu!* (1978).

KNIGHT, GLADYS, May 28, 1944 (Atlanta, Ga.). U.S. singer. With soul group The Pips, has performed in concerts, and on TV, since 1953; received two Grammy Awards, 1973.

LABELLE, PATTI, May 24, 1944 (Philadelphia, Pa.). U.S. singer. With her group The Bluebells, an early exponent of the "Philadelphia Sound" in 1960s rock; in the 1970s, led rock-disco singing group LaBelle; solo performer, from 1978. Songs: "Down the Aisle," 1963; "I Sold My Heart to the Junkman," 1964; "You Never Walk Alone," 1964; "All or Nothing," 1966; "Lady Marmalade," 1974.

LAINE, FRANKIE, born Frank Paul Lo Vecchio, Mar. 30, 1913 (Chicago, Ill.). U.S. singer. Popular in 1950s. Songs: "That's My Desire," "Mule Train," "The Wild Goose."

LANE, ABBE, 1932 (Brooklyn, N.Y.). U.S. singer. Sultry songstress, chiefly of Latin music; came to prominence as singer with XAVIER CUGAT's band (when she and Cugat were married).

LANZA, MARIO, born Alfredo Arnold Cocozza, Jan. 31, 1921 (Philadelphia, Pa.)–Oct. 7, 1959. U.S. singer, actor. Tenor who starred in MGM musicals in 1950s. Films: *The Great Caruso,* 1951; *Because You're Mine,* 1952; *The Student Prince* (voice only), 1954; *Serenade,* 1956; *Seven Hills of Rome,* 1958.

LAWRENCE, CAROL, Sept. 5, 1934 (Melrose Park, Ill.). U.S. singer. Has appeared in Broadway musicals, in nightclubs, and on TV, frequently with one-time husband ROBERT GOULET.

LAWRENCE, STEVE, born Sidney Leibowitz, July 8, 1935 (Brooklyn, N.Y.). U.S. singer. Has appeared in nightclubs, on TV, often with wife EYDIE GORME; received Emmy award, 1976.

LEDBETTER, HUDDIE ("Leadbelly"), c.1888 (Louisiana)–Dec. 6, 1949. U.S. blues singer, guitarist. Composed the song "Good Night, Irene."

LEE, MICHELE, born Michele Dusiak, 1942 (Los Angeles, Calif.). U.S. singer, actress. TV, club, and Broadway career. Films: *How to Succeed in Business . . .,* 1967; *The Love Bug,* 1969. Stage: *Seesaw,* 1973.

LEE, PEGGY, born Norma Egstrom, May 26, 1920 (Jamestown, S.D.). U.S. singer. Began with BENNY GOODMAN band, 1941–43; appeared in some films; frequent appearances in concerts, clubs. Records: "You Was Right Baby," "Fever," "It's a Good Day," "Manana," "Is That All There Is?"

LENNON, JOHN, Oct. 9, 1940 (Liverpool, Eng.). English singer, composer. Member of The Beatles, 1960–71; wrote (with PAUL McCARTNEY) many of the group's songs. Films: *A Hard Day's Night,* 1964; *Help!,* 1965.

THE LENNON SISTERS: DIANNE, born 1939 (Los Angeles, Calif.); **JANET,** born 1946 (Culver City, Calif.); **KATHY,** born 1944 (Santa Monica, Calif.); **PEGGY,** born 1941 (Los Angeles, Calif.). U.S. singers. Wholesome family act; came to prominence on the LAWRENCE WELK TV show, late 1950s.

LENYA, LOTTE, born Karoline Blamauer, Oct. 18, 1900 (Vienna, Aus.). Austrian cabaret singer, character actress. The wife of KURT WEILL, known for his interpretations of his songs; fled Germany with Weill (1933) to U.S., where she appeared in the plays *The Threepenny Opera, Brecht on Brecht, Mahagonny,* and *Cabaret.* Films: *The Roman Spring of Mrs. Stone,* 1961; *From Russia with Love,* 1961.

LEWIS, JERRY LEE, Sept. 29, 1935 (Ferriday, La.). U.S. musician. As singer/pianist/songwriter, one of the first rockers to incorporate sexually provocative physical behavior into his act; known for hard-driving style; one of few rock pioneers still popular today, with more country flavor to his music; caused scandal in 1958 by marrying 13-year-old cousin. Songs: "Great Balls of Fire," 1957; "Whole Lotta Shakin' Goin' On," 1958.

LIGHTFOOT, GORDON, 1939 (Orillia, Ont., Can.). Canadian musician. Singer/songwriter of folk-rock music in 1960s and 1970s; many of his songs were recorded by other performers; known for haunting lyrics and sad melodies. Songs: "Early Morning Rain"; "If You Could Read My Mind."

LITTLE RICHARD, born Richard Penniman, 1935 (Macon, Ga.). U.S. rock-and-roll singer. His frenetic style influenced the styles of many rock-and-roll artists; left profession to become a minister. Songs: "Tutti Frutti," "Long Tall Sally," "Good Golly Miss Molly," "Whole Lotta Shakin' Goin' On," "Slippin' and Slidin'."

LLOYD, MARIE, born Matilda Alice Victoria Wood, Feb. 12, 1870 (London, Eng.)–Oct. 7, 1922. English entertainer. The foremost star of the English musical halls in the late 19th century.

LOGGINS, KENNY, Jan. 7, 1948 (Everett, Wash.). U.S. singer, songwriter. With JIM MESSINA formed country rock duo, 1970–74; solo performer, from 1974. Songs: "Your Mama Don't Dance," 1972; "Thinking of You," 1973; "Ain't Gonna Change My Music," 1974.

LYNN, LORETTA, born Loretta Webb, Jan. 14, 1932 (Butcher Hollow, Ky.). U.S. singer. Country-and-western singing star; numerous Gold Records; named Country Music Assn. female vocalist of year, 1967, 1972–73. Autobiography: *Coal Miner's Daughter,* 1977.

MACDONALD, JEANETTE, June 18, 1907 (Philadelphia, Pa.)–Jan 14, 1965. U.S. singer, actress. With NELSON EDDY, made a series of films of operettas (1935–42), including *Naughty Marietta* (1935), *Rose Marie* (1936), and *San Francisco* (1936). (Wife of GENE RAYMOND.)

MACKENZIE, GISELE, Jan. 10, 1927 (Winnipeg, Man., Can.). U.S. singer, actress. Appeared on TV show *Your Hit Parade,* 1953–57.

MAKEBA, MIRIAM, Mar. 4, 1932 (Prospect, S. A.). S. African singer. Began in church choir; first prominent for role in African opera *King Kong,* 1959; leading singer in African-jazz music scene. (One-time wife of STOKELY CARMICHAEL.)

MANILOW, BARRY, June 17, 1946 (New York, N.Y.). U.S. singer, songwriter. Pop-rock singing star who began writing advertising jingles and serving as BETTE MIDLER's accompanist/arranger.

THE BOOK OF WHO

Songs: "At the Copa," "Mandy," "Can't Smile Without You."

MARTIN, TONY, Dec. 25, 1913 (San Francisco, Calif.). U.S. singer. Big Band–era singer who made transition to films; he and wife CYD CHARISSE wrote best-selling memoir, *The Two of Us* (1977).

MARTINO, AL, born Alfred Cini, Oct. 7, 1927 (Philadelphia, Pa.). U.S. pop singer. Popular in the 1950s, made a comeback in the mid-1960s. Songs: "Here in My Heart," 1952; "I Love You Because," 1962; "Mary in the Morning," 1967; "Love Theme from *The Godfather*," 1972.

MATHIS, JOHNNY, Sept. 30, 1935 (San Francisco, Calif.). U.S. singer. Mellow-voiced pop singer of ballads; most popular songs include "A Certain Smile," "Misty," "Chances Are," and "The Shadow of Your Smile."

MAYALL, JOHN, c.1934 (Manchester, Eng.). English musician. Singer, songwriter, instrumentalist of blues-jazz rock; had own bands from 1950s; known as "Grandfather of British rock"; very popular in late 1960s with his band Bluesbreakers (1963–73), featuring his harmonica playing.

McCARTNEY, PAUL, June 18, 1942 (Walton Park, Eng.). English musician. Lead singer and songwriter for The Beatles, 1962–70; with Wings, 1970–   . Compositions (with J. LENNON): "Yesterday," "Michelle," "Hey Jude," "And I Love Her," "Eleanor Rigby." Compositions (solo): "Wings Wild Life," "My Love," "Band on the Run."

McGUIRE SISTERS: CHRISTINE, born 1928 (Middletown, Ohio); **DOROTHY,** born 1930 (Middletown, Ohio); **PHYLLIS,** born 1931 (Middletown, Ohio). U.S. singers. Formed an extremely popular vocal trio in the 1940s and 1950s; performed with bands, on stage; numerous TV appearances, especially on *Arthur Godfrey and His Friends* (1952–57).

McLEAN, DON, Oct. 2, 1945 (New Rochelle, N.Y.). U.S. musician. Singer, songwriter, guitarist of folk-rock who achieved greatest success in 1970s as soloist, after working with PETE SEEGER and other artists. Songs: "American Pie," 1972; "Vincent," 1972.

MELANIE, born Melanie Sofka, Feb. 3, 1948 (New York, N.Y.). U.S. singer, songwriter. Pop-folk-rock singer of the late 1960s and early 1970s. Songs: "Peace Will Come," 1970; "Lay Down," 1971; "Leftover Wine," 1971; "Brand New Key," 1971.

MIDLER, BETTE ("The Divine Miss M"), Dec. 1, c.1945 (Paterson, N.J.). U.S. singer. Musical comedy actress, 1966–69; became solo performer and major star of 1970s, starting career in gay bathhouse in New York City; first album, "The Divine Miss M," 1972; starred in one-woman Broadway shows in 1973 and 1975; made film debut in *The Rose*, 1979.

MILLER, ROGER DEAN, Jan. 2, 1936 (Ft. Worth, Tex.). U.S. singer, songwriter. Country-and-western performer, very popular in 1960s; hits include "Dang Me," "England Swings," "King of the Road."

MILSAP, RONNIE, Jan. 16 ? (Robinsville, N.C.). U.S. singer. Blind country-and-western singer; voted Entertainer of the Year by the Country Music Assn., 1977.

MINNELLI, LIZA, Mar. 12, 1946 (Los Angeles, Calif.). U.S. singer, actress. Daughter of JUDY GARLAND and VINCENTE MINNELLI; successful stage, film and TV career. Stage: *Flora and the Red Menace* (Tony Award), 1967; *The Act* (Tony Award), 1977. Films: *The Sterile Cuckoo,* 1969; *Cabaret* (Best Actress AA), 1972; *New York, New York,* 1977.

MITCHELL, JONI, born Roberta Joan Anderson, Nov. 7, 1943 (Macleod, Alta., Can.). Canadian singer, songwriter. Began as folksinger in Toronto coffeehouses, 1964; gained fame with song "Both Sides Now," 1968; many albums and songs since.

THE MONKEES: Mickey Dolenz, Mar. 8, 1945 (Los Angeles, Calif.); David Jones, Dec. 30, 1946 (Manchester, Eng.); Michael Nesmith, Dec. 30, 1942 (Houston, Tex.); Peter Tork, Feb. 13, 1944 (Washington, D.C.). U.S. musicians. Manufactured TV-rock group, formed 1965 to star in sitcom; group broke up in 1969; only Nesmith made it as soloist afterward. Songs: "Last Train to Clarksville," 1966; "I'm a Believer," 1966.

MOORE, MELBA, Oct. 29, 1945 (New York, N.Y.). U.S. singer, actress. Musical-comedy star of *Hair* (1968) and *Purlie* (1970); now a solo performer, with disco hits "You Stepped into My Life" and "Pick Me Up, I'll Dance."

MORGAN, JANE, 1920 (Boston, Mass.). U.S. singer. Popular in the 1950s, especially for her rendition of "Fascination."

MORRISON, JIM, Dec. 8, 1943 (Melbourne, Fla.)–July 3, 1971. U.S. musician. Leading rock vocalist of 1960s, as part of supergroup The Doors 1965–71; victim of drug overdose; one of first '60s rock sex symbols. Songs: "Light My Fire," 1966; "People are Strange," 1967; "Hello, I Love You," 1968; "Love Her Madly," 1971.

MURRAY, ANNE, June 20, c.1946 (Spring Hill, N.S., Can.). Canadian singer. Folksinger who hit the big time with 1970 rendition of "Snowbird."

NEWMAN, RANDY, Nov. 28, 1943 (Los Angeles, Calif.). U.S. singer, songwriter. Pop-rock singer/composer of such songs as "Mama Told Me Not to Come," "I Think It's Going to Rain Today," "Love Story," "Short People."

NEWTON, WAYNE, Apr. 3, 1942 (Norfolk, Va.). U.S. singer. Boyish pop singer, extremely popular on Las Vegas show circuit.

NEWTON-JOHN, OLIVIA, Sept. 26, 1948 (Cambridge, Eng.). British singer. Rock star who ventured into acting in film *Grease,* 1978.

NILSSON, HARRY, born Harry Edward Nelson III, June 5, 1941 (New York, N.Y.). U.S. singer, songwriter. Popular troubador of late 1960s and the 1970s, in the folk-rock genre. Songs: "Everybody's Talkin'," 1970; "Theme for *The Courtship of Eddie's Father,*" 1969; "The Point," 1971.

NYRO, LAURA, 1947 (Bronx, N.Y.). U.S. singer, songwriter. Pop-rock composer of the late 1960s and early 1970s, known for her urbanized rock; now sings own songs in concert and on records. Compositions: "Stoned Soul Picnic," 1968; "Blowin' Away," 1972.

O'CONNELL, HELEN, 1920 (Lima, Ohio). U.S. singer. Big Band–era singer; currently involved in a nightclub act *Four Girls Four,* with ROSE MARIE, ROSEMARY CLOONEY, and MARGARET WHITING.

O'DAY, ANITA, ? (Chicago, Ill.). U.S. singer. Best known for stint with GENE KRUPA band, 1941–43 and STAN KENTON, 1944–45; now solo, on cabaret circuit. Songs: "Let Me Off Uptown," "That's What You Think," "And Her Tears Flowed Like Wine."

ODETTA, born Odetta Felious Gordon, Dec. 31, 1930 (Birmingham, Ala.). U.S. singer. Leading folksinger of the 1950s and 1960s, known for mellow style and African motifs.

ORBISON, ROY, Apr. 23, 1936 (Wink, Tex.). U.S. musician. Singer/composer of rock and roll in 1950s, credited with creating mass market for the music; career floundered in middle 1960s. Songs: "Claudette," 1956; "Ooby-Dooby," 1956; "Running Scared," 1961; "Crying," 1961.

ORLANDO, TONY, born Michael Anthony Orlando Cassavitis, Apr. 3, 1944 (New York, N.Y.). U.S. singer. Pop singer of "Tie a Yellow Ribbon 'round the Old Oak Tree," "Knock Three Times," "Candida," with Dawn back-up group; had TV variety show, "Tony Orlando and Dawn," 1974-76.

OSMOND, DONALD CLARK ("Donny"), Dec. 9, 1957 (Ogden, Utah). U.S. singer. With Osmond Family group since 1961; solo, 1971-   ; with sister MARIE, star of a top-rated TV variety show, 1976-79.

OSMOND, MARIE, Oct. 13, 1959 (Ogden, Utah). U.S. singer. With family group, 1966-   ; solo act, 1973; starred with brother DONNY on TV variety show, 1976-79.

OWENS, BUCK, born Alvis Edgar Owens, Jr., Aug. 12, 1929 (Sherman, Tex.). U.S. singer, guitarist. Leader of Buckaroos band, since 1960; star of *Hee-Haw* TV series, 1969-71.

PAGE, PATTI, born Clara Anne Fowler, Nov. 8, 1927 (Claremore, Okla.). U.S. singer. Began on radio, 1946; popular in 1950s and 1960s; hits include "How Much Is That Doggy in the Window?," "In Old Cape Cod," "Hush, Hush, Sweet Charlotte."

PARTON, DOLLY, Jan. 19, 1946 (Seiverville, Tenn.). U.S. singer. Country-and-western singing star who bridged gap into pop; known for blond tresses and ample bosom; teamed with PORTER WAGONER; hits include "Dumb Blonde," "Something Fishy," "I'm in No Condition," "Friends Tell Me," "The Company You Keep," "Here You Come Again."

PEARL, MINNIE, born Sarah Ophelia Colley Cannon, Oct. 25, 1912 (Centerville, Tenn.). U.S. singer, comedienne. Known for her outlandish clothes and straw hat with price tag hanging on it; a fixture at Nashville's Grand Ole Opry since 1940.

PIAF, EDITH, born Edith Giovanna Gassion, Dec. 1915 (Paris, Fr.)-Oct. 11, 1963. French singer. Legendary international cabaret star who began as a street singer in Paris, 1930; known for her emotional, powerful voice and delivery, especially in the songs "Milord," "Non, Je Ne Regrette Rien," and "La Vie en Rose."

PICKETT, WILSON, Mar. 18, 1941 (Prattville, Ala.). U.S. singer/songwriter. Rhythm and blues singer, originally with The Falcons. "If You Need Me," 1963; "Don't Fight It" 1965; "Land of a Thousand Dances," 1966; "Funky Broadway," 1967; "Sugar Sugar," 1970.

PITNEY, GENE, Feb. 17, 1941 (Hartford, Conn.). U.S. musician. Former rock songwriter who switched to performing in 1960s; sang several songs written by BURT BACHRACH and HAL DAVID as Western movie themes. Songs: "Town without Pity," 1961; "24 Hours from Tulsa," 1962; "The Man Who Shot Liberty Valance," 1963; "Only Love Can Break a Heart," 1964; "Looking through the Eyes of Love," 1965.

PRESLEY, ELVIS, Jan. 8, 1935 (Tupelo, Miss.)-Aug. 16, 1977. U.S. singer, actor. Pelvis-grinding king of rock-and-roll in the 1950s and 1960s; in addition to many records, also made musical movies. Songs: "Love Me Tender," "Hound Dog," "Blue Suede Shoes," "Heartbreak Hotel, "In the Ghetto," "Don't Be Cruel." Films: *Love Me Tender,* 1956; *Jailhouse Rock,* 1957; *King Creole,* 1958; *Girls, Girls, Girls,* 1962; *Viva Las Vegas,* 1964; many others.

PRICE, (Noble) **RAY,** Jan. 12, 1926 (Perryville,

Tex.). U.S. singer. Country-and-western singer whose greatest hits have been "Crazy Arms," "Release Me," "Danny Boy," "For the Good Times."

PRIDE, CHARLEY, Mar. 18, 1939 (Sledge, Miss.). U.S. singer. One of first blacks in country-and-western field; recorded "Let the Chips Fall," "Kiss an Angel Good Morning," "I'd Rather Love You," "She Made Me Go."

RAINEY, MA, born Gertrude Melissa Nix Pridgett, Apr. 26, 1886 (Columbus, Ga.)-Dec. 22, 1939. U.S. musician. Jazz singer, who began in cabarets and then appeared in black vaudeville shows; her blues recordings of 1923-29 are considered major historical items; BESSIE SMITH was her protégé.

RAWLS, LOU, Dec. 1, 1935 (Chicago, Ill.). U.S. singer. Started as gospel singer, became leading exponent of rhythm-and-blues singing in late 1960s and the 1970s; won Grammy, 1978.

RAY, JOHNNIE, born John Alvin Ray, Jan. 10, 1927 (Dallas, Ore.). U.S. singer. Pop singer best known for 1951 hits "Cry" and "The Little White Cloud That Cried."

REDDING, OTIS, 1941 (Macon, Ga.)-Dec. 10, 1967. U.S. singer. Leading rhythm-and-blues soul singer of 1960s; became a superstar only with posthumous release of his "Dock of the Bay," 1968.

REDDY, HELEN, Oct. 25, 1941 (Melbourne, Austrl.). Australian singer, songwriter. Pop star in her native land, came to U.S. (1966). Songs: "I Don't Know How to Love Him," 1971; "I Am Woman," 1972; "Leave Me Alone," 1973; "Ruby," 1976.

REED, JERRY ("Guitar Man"), Mar. 20, 1937 (Atlanta, Ga.). U.S. singer, guitarist. Country-rock performer, known for his slightly offbeat songs (many of which he wrote); solo performer, 1965-   ; hits include "Guitar Man," "U.S. Male," "Amos Moses," "When You're Hot, You're Hot," "Lord, Mr. Ford."

REED, LOU, Mar. 20, c.1940 (New York, N.Y.). U.S. musician. Bizarre singer/songwriter/guitarist who achieved some fame with group Velvet Underground (1966-71), but had greatest success as solo performer who presaged punk rock with his hard-driving style. Song: "Walk on the Wild Side," 1973.

REESE, DELLA, born Delloreese Patricia Early, July 6, 1932 (Detroit, Mich.). U.S. jazz singer. Former cabdriver who sang with MAHALIA JACKSON, 1945-49; nightclub and concert soloist, 1957-   ; appears frequently on TV.

RICH, CHARLIE ("The Silver Fox"), born Charles Allan Rich, Dec. 14, 1932 (Forrest City, Ark.). U.S. singer. Country-and-western singer; won Grammy, 1973; recorded hits "Behind Closed Doors," "The Most Beautiful Girl."

RICHMAN, HARRY, Aug. 10, 1895 (Cincinnati, Ohio)-Nov. 3, 1972. U.S. singer. Vaudeville sensation, noted for his elegant manner and the song "Puttin' on the Ritz"; one of the highest-paid entertainers of the 1930s.

RIPERTON, MINNIE, Nov. 8, 1947 (Chicago, Ill.)-July 12, 1979. U.S. singer. Pop-soul singer of the 1970s, known for her 5-1/2 octave range; back-up singer, 1963-70; with group Rotary Connection, 1966-70; after a mastectomy (1976) spent much of her time lecturing for American Cancer Society. Major hit: "Loving You," 1973.

RITTER, TEX, born Woodward Maurice Ritter, Jan. 12, 1907 (Murvaul, Tex.)-Jan. 2, 1974. U.S. singer, songwriter. Singing cowboy of stage, screen and broadcasting; starred in 60 films,

THE BOOK OF WHO

1936-45; first country singer to sign with Capitol Records, 1942; won AA for singing title song to *High Noon*, 1952; with Grand Ole Opry, 1965-73; ran unsuccessfully for U.S. Senate, 1970; elected to Country Music Hall of Fame, 1965. (Father of JOHN RITTER.)

RIVERS, JOHNNY, born John Ramistella, Nov. 7, 1942 (New York, N.Y.). U.S. musician. Singer/guitarist/songwriter influenced by Southern country music and rock; Alan Freed gave him his name and started his career, 1960; was popular headliner at Whiskey-a-Go-Go discotheque in Los Angeles, where many of his records were taped. Songs: "Memphis," 1964; "Seventh Son," 1965; "Secret Agent Man," 1966.

ROBBINS, MARTY, born Martin David Robinson, Sept. 26, 1925 (Glendale, Ariz.). U.S. singer. Country-and-western singer with Grand Ole Opry, 1954- ; pres. of own record label, 1960-

RODGERS, JIMMIE ("The Singing Brakeman"), Sept. 8, 1897 (Meridian, Miss.)-May 26, 1933. U.S. singer, songwriter. Former railroadman, first hillbilly-country music star, known for his "blue yodels," 13 songs with distinctive yodel ending.

ROGERS, KENNY, 1941 (Houston, Tex.). U.S. singer. Country-rock singer whose roots were in folk music (was with the New Christy Minstrels, 1965-67); formed The First Edition, 1967, a popular late 1960s-1970s group; has had solo act since 1974. Songs: "Ruby," "Lucille."

RONSTADT, LINDA, July 15, 1946 (Tucson, Ariz.). U.S. singer. Pop-rock superstar who began as lead singer with Stone Poneys group, 1964-68; solo performer since 1968. Albums: *Long Long Time*, 1970; *Very Lovely Woman*, 1971; *Rock Me on the Water*, 1972; *Hasten Down the Wind*, 1976; *Simple Dreams*, 1977.

ROSS, DIANA, Mar. 26, 1944 (Detroit, Mich.). U.S. singer, actress. With two friends, formed The Supremes (1958), a leading 1960s soul group; solo since 1969; star of films *Lady Sings the Blues* (1972) and *Mahogany* (1974).

ROTH, LILLIAN, born Lillian Rutstein, Dec. 13, 1910 (Boston, Mass.). U.S. singer. Torch singer of 1920s and 1930s; retired young as result of personal problems; her story was filmed as *I'll Cry Tomorrow* (1955), with SUSAN HAYWARD.

RUNDGREN, TODD, c.1950 (Philadelphia, Pa.). U.S. singer/guitarist. Rock bandleader of late 1960s (The Nazz, 1968-70) and later a frequent producer of sessions for other rock groups; now a solo act. Songs: "Hello, It's Me," 1969; "We Got to Get You a Woman," 1970; "A Long Way to Go," 1971; "Couldn't I Just Tell You," 1972; "I Saw the Light," 1972.

RUSHING, JIMMY ("Mr. Five by Five"), Aug. 26, 1903 (Oklahoma City, Okla.). U.S. musician. Jazz-blues singer with bands in 1920s, but most famous as singer with COUNT BASIE, 1935-50; solo since 1952; known for "shouting" blues style.

RUSSELL, LILLIAN, born Helen Louise Leonard, Dec. 4, 1861 (Clinton, Ia.)-June 6, 1922. U.S. entertainer. Stage beauty of the gaslight era; appeared as a singer with Tony Pastor's shows (from 1880) and with the Weber and Fields Burlesque Co. (1899-1904).

RYDELL, BOBBY, born Robert Ridarelli, Apr. 26, 1942 (Philadelphia, Pa.). U.S. singer. Teen idol of the late 1950s-early 1960s; hits include "Kissin' Time" (1959), "We Got Love" (1959), "Wild One" (1960), "Volare" (1960), "The Cha-Cha-Cha" (1962), "Forget Him" (1964).

SAINTE-MARIE, BUFFY, Feb. 20, 1941 (Piaput Reservation, Sask., Can.). Canadian singer,

songwriter. Amerind folksinger specializing in songs about her heritage and the cause of peace. Compositions: "It's My Way," 1964; "Little Wheel Spin and Spin," 1966; "Universal Soldier"; "Until It's Time for You to Go."

SEBASTIAN, JOHN B., Mar. 17, 1944 (New York, N.Y.). U.S. musician. Pop-rock singer/instrumentalist; a major influence in late '60s music for combination of rock, jazz, folk and blues; founded and led Lovin' Spoonful group, 1965-67; solo performer, 1967- . Songs: "Do You Believe in Magic?," 1965; "You Didn't Have to Be So Nice," 1965; "Did You Ever Have to Make Up Your Mind?," 1966; "Welcome Back," 1976.

SEDAKA, NEIL, Mar. 13, 1939 (New York, N.Y.). U.S. singer, songwriter. Pop-rock star since the 1950s; recorded "Stupid Cupid," "Calendar Girl," "Stairway to Heaven," "Love Will Keep Us Together," "Breaking Up Is Hard to Do."

SEEGER, PETE, May 3, 1919 (New York, N.Y.). U.S. singer, composer. Dean of American folksingers; collaborator with WOODY GUTHRIE; organizer of The Weavers group, 1948; associated with radical-left politics; sang and composed "Where Have All the Flowers Gone?," "If I Had a Hammer," "Turn, Turn, Turn," "Kisses Sweeter Than Wine."

SEVILLE, DAVID, born Ross Bagdasarian, Jan. 27, 1919 (Fresno, Calif.)-Jan. 1972. U.S. entertainer. Music industry executive; created "The Chipmunks," a singing trio, by speeding up three tracks of his voice on a tape recorder; "The Chipmunks" became animated cartoon TV series, 1965-67. Songs: "Witch Doctor," 1958; "Chipmunk Song," 1958; "Alvin's Harmonica," 1959.

SHANNON, DEL, born Charles Westover, c.1940 (Grand Rapids, Mich.). U.S. musician. Rock singer popular in the 1960s; in the 1970s became record producer. Songs: "Runaway"; "Hats Off to Larry"; "Keep Searchin'."

SHORE, DINAH, born Frances Rose Shore, Mar. 1, 1921 (Winchester, Tenn.). U.S. singer, talk-show hostess. Pop singer with bands, on radio and TV in the 1940s and 1950s; hostess of TV talk shows *Dinah's Place* (1970-74) and *Dinah!* (1974-). (One-time wife of actor George Montgomery.)

SHORT, BOBBY, born Robert Waltrip Short, Sept. 15, 1924 (Danville, Ill.). U.S. singer, pianist. Nightclub and concert pop singer-pianist, 1956- ; specializes in interpretations of COLE PORTER songs; performed White House concert, 1970.

SIMON, CARLY, June 25, 1945 (New York, N.Y.). U.S. singer. Rock singer and composer since 1971; recorded albums include *Anticipation* (1972), *No Secrets* (1973), *Hotcakes* (1974), *Playing Possum* (1975). (Wife of JAMES TAYLOR.)

SIMON, PAUL, Nov. 13, 1941 or 42 (New York, N.Y.). U.S. singer, composer. Teamed with ART GARFUNKEL, 1964-70; solo performer since 1970; hits include "The Dangling Conversation," "Scarborough Fair," "Sounds of Silence," "Bridge over Troubled Water," "The Boxer," "Me and Julio down by the Schoolyard."

SIMONE, NINA, born Eunice Wayman, Feb. 12, 1933 (Tryon, N.C.). U.S. singer, pianist. Jazz artist, composer since 1954; recorded "The Other Woman," "I Don't Want Him, You Can Have Him," "Black Is the Color," "Children, Go Where I Send You," "Nina's Blues."

SINATRA, FRANK, born Francis Albert Sinatra, Dec. 12, 1915 (Hoboken, N.J.). U.S. singer, actor. Teen heartthrob of 1940s Big Band era; major pop

ENTERTAINERS

singer ever since; notable film career. Songs: "Night and Day," 1943; "Love and Marriage," 1955; "Chicago," 1957; "Strangers in the Night," 1968; "My Way," 1969. Films: *On the Town*, 1949; *From Here to Eternity* (Best Supporting Actor AA), 1953; *High Society*, 1956; *Pal Joey*, 1957; *The Manchurian Candidate*, 1962; *The Detective*, 1968.

SLICK, GRACE, née Wing, Oct. 30, 1939 (Chicago, Ill.). U.S. singer. Rock star as lead vocalist with Jefferson Airplane (1966-72) and Jefferson Starship (1974-   ).

SMITH, BESSIE ("The Empress of the Blues"), Apr. 15, 1894 (Chattanooga, Tenn.)-Sept. 26, 1937. U.S. singer. Legendary blues singer of 1920s-1930s; most prolific time was 1924-27, when she sang in vaudeville and recorded with most major jazz groups of day; after 1930, her career declined because of alcoholism; bled to death in car wreck.

SMITH, KATE, ("Songbird of the South"), May 1, 1909 (Greenville, Va.). U.S. singer. Rotund popular songstress, especially in the 1930s, when she had a top-rated weekly radio program; beloved for her rendition of "God Bless America."

SMITH, KEELY, born Dorothy Jacqueline Keely Smith, Mar. 9, 1932 (Norfolk, Va.). U.S. singer. Jazz-pop singer with LOUIS PRIMA Band since 1948; married Prima, 1953; "That Old Black Magic" her most famous tune.

SMITH, PATTI, c.1946 (Chicago, Ill.). U.S. musician. As singer/songwriter, a leading force in the "New Wave" of rock of the late 1970s; one of the first punk stars. Songs: "Piss Factory," 1974; "Hey Joe," 1974.

THE SMOTHERS BROTHERS: TOM, Feb. 2, 1937 (New York, N.Y.); and **DICK,** Nov. 20, 1938 (New York, N.Y.). U.S. singers. A major folksinging duo in the 1960s, noted as much for their satiric comedy as their singing; their highly rated TV show was cancelled in 1968 after a censorship row with CBS; starred in Broadway show *I Love My Wife*, 1978.

SNOW, HANK, May 9, 1914 (Liverpool, N.S., Can.). Canadian singer, guitarist. Country-and-western performer; with Grand Ole Opry since 1950.

SPRINGFIELD, DUSTY, born Mary O'Brien, Apr. 16, 1939 (Hampstead, Eng.). English pop singer. A leading pop songstress of the 1960s. Songs: "Silver Threads and Golden Needles," 1963; "I Only Want to Be with You," 1964; "Son of a Preacher Man," 1969.

SPRINGSTEEN, BRUCE, Sept. 23, 1949 (Freehold, N.J.). U.S. musician. As singer/songwriter/guitarist, a late-1970s leader of the "New Wave" in rock music; known for the insistent images and macho posturings of his music.

STAFFORD, JO, 1918 (Coalinga, Calif.). U.S. singer. Big Band-era singer; with Stafford Sisters, 1935-41; joined the TOMMY DORSEY band, 1941; was featured as soloist and lead singer with the Pied Pipers; known for her pure distinctive tone and timbre. Songs: "Temptation," "Shrimp Boats," "You Belong to Me," "Make Love to Me."

STARR, RINGO, born Richard Starkey, July 7, 1940 (Liverpool, Eng.). English musician. Drummer for The Beatles, 1962-70; solo since 1970, branching out into singing and songwriting; acted in several "counterculture" films.

STEVENS, CAT, born Steven Georgiou, July, 1948 (London, Eng.). English singer, songwriter. Rock singer in Britain until 1968, when serious ill-

ness led him to change his style to folk-rock; five Gold Albums.

STEWART, ROD(erick David), Jan. 10, 1945 (Scotland). Scottish singer. Rock singer with Jeff Beck group (1968-69) and Faces (1969-75); came into own as solo performer, 1975-   ; named Rock Star of the Year, 1975; many world tours.

STONE, SLY, born Sylvester Stewart, Mar. 15, 1944 (Dallas, Tex.). U.S. musician. Dynamic exponent of psychedelic rock in the late 1960s, with his group Sly and the Family Stone. Songs: "Hot Fun in the Summertime," 1968; "Everyday People," 1969; "Thank You," 1970; "I Want to Take You Higher," 1970.

SUMMER, DONNA, born LaDonna Andrea Gaines, Dec. 31, 1949 (Boston, Mass.). U.S. singer. Disco music's leading lady. Songs: "I Feel Love," "Hot Stuff," "Last Girls," "Bad Girls."

TAYLOR, JAMES, Mar. 12, 1948 (Boston, Mass.). U.S. musician. Rock singer, guitarist and composer; won Grammy, 1978. (Husband of CARLY SIMON.)

THE TEMPTATIONS: Dennis Edwards, Feb. 3, 1943 (Birmingham, Ala.); Melvin Franklin, Oct. 12, 1942 (Montgomery, Ala.); Eddie Kendricks, Dec. 17, 1939 (Birmingham, Ala.); Otis Williams, Oct. 30, 1941 (Texarkana, Tex.); Paul Williams, July 2, 1939 (Birmingham, Ala.). U.S. singing group. With DAVID RUFFIN (Edwards joined group in 1965), formed the soul group that was the male equivalent to THE SUPREMES, 1963-   .

TENNILLE, TONI, May 8, 1943 (Montgomery, Ala.); and **DARYL DRAGON,** Aug. 27, 1942 (Los Angeles, Calif.). U.S. musicians. Husband and wife pop-rock singing duo, The Captain and Tennille; skyrocketed to fame with 1975 hit "Love Will Keep Us Together"; hosted TV variety show, 1976-78.

TINY TIM, born Herbert David Khoury, Apr. 12, 1932? (New York, N.Y.). U.S. singer. His falsetto voice and bizarre appearance tickled the nation in the late 1960s; his wedding to "Miss Vicky" took place on TV's *The Tonight Show*, 1969. Songs: "Tiptoe through the Tulips."

TORME, MEL(vin Howard), Sept. 13, 1925 (Chicago, Ill.). U.S. singer, author. Toured with CHICO MARX band, 1942-43; led Mel-Tones group, 1943-47; solo since 1947; composed, among others, "The Christmas Song"; author of *The Other Side of the Rainbow*, about the later years of JUDY GARLAND.

TRAPP, MARIA AUGUSTA VON, Jan. 26, 1905 (Vienna, Austria). U.S. musician. The inspiration for *The Sound of Music*, she organized Trapp Family Singers and toured world, 1938-56; family fled Nazis (1939), settling in U.S.; managed Trapp Family Lodge in Vermont, 1956-67.

TUCKER, SOPHIE ("The Last of the Red Hot Mamas"), born Sophia Abuza, Jan. 13, 1884 (Russia)-Feb. 10, 1966. U.S. singer. Vaudeville star, from 1906; kept active on stage, in clubs, films, and TV until her death. Autobiography: *Some of These Days* (the title of her theme song), 1945.

TURNER, BIG JOE, May 18, 1911 (Kansas City, Mo.). U.S. singer. Sang in Kansas City for many years before coming to New York City in 1938; one of great blues "shouters"; "Chains of Love" is his most famous song.

TURNER, IKE, Nov. 5, 1932 (Clarksdale, Miss.). U.S. musician. With wife TINA TURNER, has rock-soul group, Ike and Tina Turner Revue; won Grammy, 1972.

TURNER, TINA, born Annie Mae Bullock, Nov. 25,

273

THE BOOK OF WHO

1941 (Brownsville, Tenn.). U.S. singer. With husband IKE TURNER, has rock-soul group Ike and Tina Turner Revue; won Grammy, 1972.

TWITTY, CONWAY, Sept. 1, 1933 (Friarspoint, Miss.). U.S. singer. Country-and-western performer; composer of "I've Already Loved You in My Mind" (1977) and "Games Daddies Play" (1977).

UGGAMS, LESLIE, May 25, 1943 (New York, N.Y.). U.S. singer, actress. First gained fame as singer on *Sing Along with Mitch* TV show, 1961–64; star of *Hallelujah Baby* musical, 1967; as TV actress, starred in *Roots* (1977) and *Backstairs at the White House* (1979).

VALE, JERRY, 1931 (New York, N.Y.). U.S. singer. Pop vocalist in the vein of FRANK SINATRA and TONY BENNETT; easily recognizable by his full head of gray hair.

VALENTI, CATERINA, Jan. 14, 1932 (Paris, Fr.). French-German singer. International singing star best known for her ability to sing in many languages and for her big U.S. hit, "Malagueña."

VALLEE, RUDY, born Hubert Prior Vallee, July 28, 1901 (Island Pond, Vt.). U.S. singer. Leading crooner of the 1920s, with his band, The Connecticut Yankees; popular on radio and concerts; trademark is a megaphone.

VALLI, FRANKIE, born Frank Castelluccio, May 3, 1937 (Newark, N.J.). U.S. singer. With The Four Seasons (1962–   ), as well as solo; recorded "Sherry," "Big Girls Don't Cry," "Walk Like a Man."

VAUGHAN, SARAH LOU, Mar. 27, 1924 (?). U.S. singer. Jazz vocalist who sang with EARL "FATHA" HINES and Billy Eckstine bands; recorded "Lover Man," "Sometimes I'm Happy," "Broken-Hearted Melody," "A Foggy Day in London Town."

VINTON, BOBBY, born Robert Stanley Vinton, Apr. 16, 1935 (Canonsburg, Pa.). U.S. singer. Pop-rock singer; star of own TV show, 1975–   ; recorded the hits "Blue on Blue," "Blue Velvet," "Roses Are Red," "Mr. Lonely."

WAGONER, PORTER, Aug. 12, 1927 (West Plains, Mo.). U.S. singer. With Grand Ole Opry, 1957–   ; formerly teamed with DOLLY PARTON, with whom he won several awards.

WARFIELD, WILLIAM CAESAR, Jan. 22, 1920 (West Helena, Ark.). U.S. singer. Best known for roles in the musicals *Showboat* (1951) and *Porgy and Bess* (1952). (Husband of LEONTYNE PRICE.)

WARWICK, DIONNE, Dec. 12, 1941 (E. Orange, N.J.). U.S. singer. Pop star known particularly for her renderings of songs by BURT BACHRACH, including "Alfie," "Do You Know the Way to San Jose?," "What the World Needs Now."

WASHINGTON, DINAH ("Queen of the Blues"), born Ruth Jones, Aug. 29, 1924 (Tuscaloosa, Ala.)–Dec. 14, 1963. U.S. singer. Rose to fame in LIONEL HAMPTON band (1943–46), then became a solo performer; known for gutsy blues style, which she adapted to pop songs as her career went on.

WATERS, ETHEL, Oct. 31, 1900 (Chester, Pa.)–Sept. 1, 1977. U.S. actress, singer. Stage and film career. Traveled as a singer on BILLY GRAHAM's crusades. Films: *Cabin in the Sky,* 1943; *Pinky,* 1949; *Member of the Wedding,* 1952. Autobiography: *His Eye Is on the Sparrow,* 1953.

WHITE, BARRY, Sept. 12, 1944 (Galveston, Tex.). U.S. musician. Singer/songwriter/orchestra leader of late 1970s pop-soul music; known for his saccharine love songs sung in a deep baritone, frequently backed up by his symphony-sized Love Unlimited Orchestra.

WHITING, MARGARET ("Madcap Maggie"), July 22, 1924. U.S. singer. Big Band-era singer, best known for her renditions of "Moonlight in Vermont" (1944), "A Tree in the Meadow" (1948), and "Slippin' Around" (1949); recently has appeared in a *Four Girls Four* stage act with ROSE MARIE, HELEN O'CONNELL, and ROSEMARY CLOONEY, 1977–   .

WILLIAMS, ANDY, Dec. 3, 1930 (Wall Lake, Ia.). U.S. singer. Began as singer in Williams Bros. Quartet, 1938–52; regular on TV's *Tonight Show,* 1953–55; hits include "Moon River," "Born Free," "Happy Heart," "The Days of Wine and Roses." TV: *The Andy Williams Show,* 1958–71.

WILLIAMS, PAUL, Sept. 19, 1940 (Omaha, Neb.). U.S. singer, composer. Successful pop-rock performer-writer of songs such as "We've Only Just Begun" (1970) and "Rainy Days and Mondays" (1971); won Grammy, 1978, best song AA for "Evergreen," 1976.

WONDER, STEVIE, born Stevland Morris, May 13, 1950 (Saginaw, Mich.). U.S. singer, composer. Blind from birth, a child prodigy, now rock-blues singer and songwriter; has won eight Grammys, 1974–77; hits include "I Wish," "You Are the Sunshine of My Life," "Superstition," "My Cherie Amour," "Reggae Woman."

WYNETTE, TAMMY, May 5, 1942 (Red Bay, Ala.). U.S. singer. Country-and-western singer; regular on Grand Ole Opry, 1968–   ; Country Music Assn. Female Vocalist of Year, 1968–70; hits include "D-I-V-O-R-C-E," "Stand By Your Man," "We're Gonna Hold On."

YARROW, PETER, May 31, 1938 (New York, N.Y.). U.S. singer. Folksinging member of Peter, Paul and Mary group, 1962–70; solo performer since 1970; won Grammy, 1963.

YOUNG, NEIL, Nov. 12, 1945 (Toronto, Ont., Can.). Canadian musician. Leader of rock groups Buffalo Springfield and Crosby, Stills, Nash & Young; currently a solo performer.

ZAPPA, FRANK, Dec. 21, 1940 (Baltimore, Md.). U.S. singer. Founder and leader of the Mothers of Invention rock group; also writes songs for group.

ZIMMER, NORMA, ? (Larsen, Idaho). U.S. singer. Rocketed to fame as LAWRENCE WELK's "Champagne Lady" on his TV show, 1960–71; a born-again Christian, now performs almost exclusively at the BILLY GRAHAM crusades. Autobiography: *Norma,* 1976.

COMEDIANS

ABBOTT, BUD, born William Abbott, Oct. 2, 1895 (Asbury Park, N.J.)–Apr. 24, 1974. U.S. comedian. "Straight man" of comedy team of Abbott and COSTELLO; numerous films in 1940s and 1950s.

ALLEN, FRED, born John Florence Sullivan, May 31, 1894 (Cambridge, Mass.)–Mar. 17, 1956. U.S. comedian. Former vaudeville juggler; star of highly rated radio program featuring *Allen's Alley* (1932–49), which had 20 million listeners at its peak; known for his "Down East" humor, zany characters, and his "feud" with JACK BENNY. Autobiography: *Treadmill to Oblivion,* 1954.

ALLEN, GRACIE, born Grace Ethel Cecile Rosalie Allen, July 26, 1906 (San Francisco, Calif.)–Aug. 27, 1964. U.S. comedienne. With husband GEORGE BURNS, starred for 30 years on radio, in films, and on TV, portraying a lovable scatterbrain.

ALLEN, STEVE, born Stephen Valentine Patrick William Allen, Dec. 26, 1921 (New York, N.Y.). U.S. humorist, composer. Originated TV's *Tonight*

Show, 1950; host of several talk-variety TV shows; composed some 2,000 songs; starred in the film *The Benny Goodman Story*, 1955; conceived, wrote, hosted TV series *Meeting of Minds*, 1977.

ALLEN, WOODY, born Allen Stewart Konigsberg, Dec. 1, 1935 (New York, N.Y.). U.S. comedian, filmmaker. Began as comedy writer; stand-up comic, 1953–66; writer, producer, dir. of and actor in the films *Bananas* (1971), *Play It Again, Sam* (1972), *Love & Death* (1975), *The Front* (actor only; 1976), *Annie Hall* (Best Picture AA, Best Writer and Director AA 1977), *Manhattan* (1979); writer and director of the film *Interiors*, 1978.

AMSTERDAM, MOREY, Dec. 14, 1914 (Chicago, Ill.). U.S. comedian. Nightclub and TV comic; regular on TV's *Dick Van Dyke Show*, 1961–66; wrote the songs "Rum and Coca-Cola" and "Yuk a Puk."

ARBUCKLE, FATTY, born Roscoe Conkling Arbuckle, Mar. 24, 1887 (Smith Center, Kan.)–June 29, 1933. U.S. comedian. Slapstick star of silent films whose career was ruined in 1921 scandal after death of starlet at a party he gave.

BELUSHI, JOHN, Jan. 24, ? (Chicago, Ill.) comedian. Actor in, writer for *The National Lampoon Show*; regular, NBC-TV's *Saturday Night Live*, 1975–79; starred in the film *Animal House*, 1978.

BENNY, JACK, born Benjamin Kubelsky, Feb. 14, 1894 (Chicago, Ill.)–Dec. 26, 1974. U.S. comedian. Famed for his reputed stinginess and deadpan delivery; radio show, 1932–55; TV show, 1955–65; played violin with symphony orchestras for charity; made several films.

BERGEN, EDGAR, born John Edgar Bergren, Feb. 16, 1903 (Chicago, Ill.)–Sept. 30, 1978. U.S. ventriloquist. With dummies Charlie McCarthy and Mortimer Snerd, had top-rated radio show, 1937–47; appeared in films with dummies, later as character actor. (Father of CANDICE BERGEN.)

BERLE, MILTON ("Uncle Miltie"), born Milton Berlinger, July 12, 1908 (New York, N.Y.). U.S. comedian. First TV superstar, 1948–67; came to TV from vaudeville, radio, and films.

BERMAN, SHELLEY, Feb. 3, 1926 (Chicago, Ill.). U.S. comedian. Stand-up comic and actor who was very popular in nightclubs and on records in 1960s.

BISHOP, JOEY, born Joseph Abraham Gottlieb, Feb. 3, 1918 (New York, N.Y.). U.S. comedian. Stand-up comic whose late-night TV show unsuccessfully competed with the *Tonight Show*, 1967–69.

BLUE, BEN, born Benjamin Bernstein, Sept. 12, 1901 (Montreal, Que., Can.)–Mar. 7, 1975. U.S. comedian. Rubber-limbed vaudevillian; in films, from 1933.

BORGE, VICTOR, Jan. 3, 1909 (Copenhagen, Den.). U.S. comedian. Comedic piano player; has had numerous one-man TV specials and stage shows around world; guest artist with major symphony orchestras.

BRENNER, DAVID, 1945 (Philadelphia, Pa.). U.S. comedian. Stand-up comic; frequent *Tonight Show* (TV) guest host; named Las Vegas Entertainer of the Year, 1977.

BRICE, FANNY, born Fannie Borach, Oct. 29, 1891 (New York, N.Y.)–May 29, 1951. U.S. singer, comedienne. Long associated with the Ziegfeld Follies; played "Baby Snooks" on radio show, 1938–51; play and film *Funny Girl* based on her life.

BROOKS, MEL, born Melvin Kaminsky, 1926 (New York, N.Y.). U.S. filmmaker, comedian.

Writer-dir. of several popular films, including *The Producers* (1968), *The Twelve Chairs* (1971), *Blazing Saddles* (1974), *Young Frankenstein* (1975), and *Silent Movie* (1978). (Husband of ANNE BANCROFT.)

BROWN, JOE E., July 28, 1892 (Helgate, Ohio)–July 6, 1973. U.S. comedian. Known for his wide-mouthed appearance, in films such as *You Said a Mouthful* (1932), *Alibi Ike* (1935), *A Midsummer Night's Dream* (1935), and *Show Boat* (1951).

BRUCE, LENNY, born Leonard Alfred Schneider, 1926 (Mineola, N.Y.)–Aug. 3, 1966. U.S. comedian, satirist. Known for off-color material; 1974 film *Lenny* based on his career.

BURNETT, CAROL, April 26, 1936 (San Antonio, Tex.). U.S. comedienne. Regular on TV's *Garry Moore Show*, 1959–62; star of TV's *Carol Burnett Show*, 1967–78; won five Emmys; received Peabody Award, 1963; in some films, made TV drama debut in *Friendly Fire* (movie), 1979.

BURNS, GEORGE, born Nathan Birnbaum, Jan. 20, 1896 (New York, N.Y.). U.S. comedian, actor. With wife GRACIE ALLEN, formed comedy team (1923) that was success in vaudeville, radio, films, TV; best known for TV's *Burns and Allen Show* (1950–58) and movie roles in *The Sunshine Boys* (Best Supporting Actor AA; 1975) and *Oh God!* (1977).

BUZZI, RUTH, July 24, 1936 (Westerly, R.I.). U.S. comedienne. Vaulted to fame as regular on *Rowan and Martin's Laugh-In* TV show 1968–72.

CAESAR, SID, Sept. 8, 1922 (Yonkers, N.Y.). U.S comedian. Mostly on TV, notably *Your Show of Shows* (1950–54) and *Caesar's Hour* (1954–57); on Broadway in musical *Little Me*, 1962; won Emmy award, 1956.

CALLAS, CHARLIE, Dec. 20, ? (New York, N.Y.). U.S. comedian. Stand-up comic in clubs and on TV; turned to acting with regular role on TV's *Switch* (1975–78).

CAMBRIDGE, GODFREY, Feb. 26, 1933 (New York, N.Y.)–Nov. 29, 1976. U.S. comedian, actor. Leading black stand-up comic of 1960s; turned actor in the films *Watermelon Man* (1970) and *Cotton Comes to Harlem* (1971).

CANTOR, EDDY, born Edward Israel Iskowitz, Jan. 31, 1892 (New York, N.Y.)–Oct. 10, 1964. U.S. comedian, song-and-dance man. Appeared in several Ziegfeld Follies; starred in musicals *Kid Boots* (1923) and *Whoopee* (1928); starred in films and on radio in 1930s; on TV in 1950s; received special AA for film service, 1956.

CARSON, JOHNNY, Oct. 23, 1925 (Corning, Ia.). U.S. comedian. Stand-up comic who entered TV as emcee for quiz show *Who Do You Trust?*, 1958–63; host of TV's *Tonight Show*, 1962– .

CARTER, JACK, born Jack Chakrin, June 24, 1923 (New York, N.Y.). U.S. comedian, actor. As a comic, played most major nightclubs; debuted on Broadway in *Call Me Mister*, 1947; on TV, starred in *The Jack Carter Show*, 1950–51.

CHAPLIN, SIR CHARLES SPENCER, Apr. 16, 1889 (London, Eng.)–Dec. 25, 1977. U.S. comedian. Beloved "Little Tramp" of the silent-film era; made many feature films, including *The Kid* (1920), *The Gold Rush* (1924), *City Lights* (1931), *Modern Times* (1936), *The Great Dictator* (1940) and *Limelight* (1952); paternity scandal drove him from U.S., 1944; received special AA for film achievements, 1971.

CHASE, CHEVY, born Cornelius Crane Chase,

Oct. 8, 1943 (New York, N.Y.). U.S. comedian. Regular on NBC-TV's *Saturday Night Live*, 1975-76; particularly noted for his imitation of Pres. GERALD FORD. Films: *Foul Play*, 1978.

CHEECH & CHONG: Tommy Chong, May 24, ? (Edmonton, Alta., Can.); Cheech Marin (born Richard), ? (Los Angeles, Calif.). U.S. comedians. First of the rock-culture comedians, known for their zany routines on long hair, drugs, police, etc., since 1970; made and starred in the highly-successful film *Up In Smoke*, 1978.

CONWAY, TIM, Dec. 15, 1933 (Willoughby, Ohio). U.S. comedian. TV: *McHale's Navy* (series), 1962-66; *The Tim Conway Show* (variety show), 1970; *The Carol Burnett Show* (variety show), 1975-78.

CORRELL, CHARLES, Feb. 2, 1890 (Peoria, III.)-Sept. 26, 1972. U.S. comedic actor. Best known for role as Andy in radio show *Amos 'n' Andy,* in the 1930s.

COSBY, BILL, July 12, 1937 (Philadelphia, Pa.). U.S. comedian, actor. Popular stand-up comic of 1960s; first black to star in a TV series (*I Spy*, 1966-68); had own TV show in 1969 and 1972-73; has won four Emmy awards and six Grammy awards.

COSTELLO, LOU, born Louis Cristillo, Mar. 6, 1906 (Paterson, N.J.)-Mar. 3, 1959. U.S. comedian. With partner BUD ABBOTT, made numerous comedy films in 1940s and 1950s.

COX, WALLY, Dec. 6, 1924 (Detroit, Mich.)-Feb. 15, 1973. U.S. comedian. Meek-appearing actor in films, TV and on stage; starred in *Mr. Peepers* TV series, 1952-55; regular on *Hollywood Squares* TV quiz show.

DANGERFIELD, RODNEY, 1921 (Babylon, N.Y.). U.S. comedian. Stand-up comic who "gets no respect"; has own restaurant and nightclub in New York City.

DE LUISE, DOM, Aug. 1, 1933 (Brooklyn, N.Y.). U.S. comedian. Films: *The Twelve Chairs*, 1971; *Blazing Saddles*, 1974; *Sherlock Holmes' Smarter Brother*, 1977; *The Cheap Detective*, 1978; *The End*, 1978.

DE WOLFE, BILLY, born William Andrew Jones, 1907 (Wollaston, Mass.)-Mar. 5, 1974. U.S. comedian. Actor in 1940s and 1950s films.

DILLER, PHYLLIS, née Driver, July 17, 1917 (Lima, Ohio). U.S. comedienne. Fright-wigged, gravel-voiced stand-up comic in clubs, on TV; makes appearances as concert pianist with symphony orchestras.

DURANTE, JIMMY ("Schnozzola"), Feb. 10, 1893 (New York, N.Y.)-Jan. 29, 1980. U.S. comedian. Vaudeville performer in partnership with Eddie Jackson, Lou Clayton, 1916-30; numerous film, stage, and TV appearances, from 1930s; singer of such memorable songs as "Ink-a-Dink-a-Doo," "You Gotta Start Off Each Day With a Song"; signature was "Good night, Mrs. Calabash . . ."

ELLIOT, ROBERT B. ("Bob"), Mar. 26, 1923 (Boston, Mass.). U.S. comedian. With partner, RAY GOULDING, formed comedy team that played radio, TV, and stage, since 1951.

FIBBER MCGEE AND MOLLY: Jordan, Jim, Nov. 6, 1896 (Peoria, III.); and Jordan, Marian, Apr. 15, 1897 (Peoria, III.)-Apr. 7, 1961. U.S. entertainers. Husband-and-wife team, formed popular radio comedy duo in the 1930s and 1940s; the show featured the front hall closet, crammed with junk, which fell down at least once per show.

FIELDS, TOTIE, May 7, 1930 (Hartford, Conn.)-Aug. 2, 1978. U.S. comedienne. Portly comic in clubs, on TV.

FIELDS, W. C., born William Claude Dukenfield, Jan. 29, 1880 (Philadelphia, Pa.)-Dec. 25, 1946. U.S. comedian. Vaudeville, stage, film and radio performer of considerable eccentricity; noted for red nose, gravel voice, aversion to children and pets, hard drinking; starred in many memorable films, including *David Copperfield* (1934), *Poppy* (1936), *You Can't Cheat an Honest Man* (1939), *My Little Chickadee* (1940), *The Bank Dick* (1940), and *Never Give a Sucker an Even Break,* (1941).

FONTAINE, FRANK, 1920 (Cambridge, Mass.)-Aug. 4, 1978. U.S. comedian. Known for his character "Crazy Guggenheim", who appeared on TV shows, most notably *The Jackie Gleason Show,* 1962-66.

FOSTER, PHIL, Mar. 29, 1914 (Brooklyn, N.Y.). U.S. comedian. Stand-up comic in nightclubs. TV: *Laverne and Shirley* (series), 1976- .

FOXX, REDD, born John Elroy Sanford, Dec. 9, 1922 (St. Louis, Mo.). U.S. comedian. In nightclubs since 1941; known for his comedy "party" records; star of TV series *Sanford and Son,* 1972-77.

FRYE, DAVID, 1934 (Brooklyn, N.Y.). U.S. comedian. Stand-up comic in clubs and on TV; best known for his impression of Pres. R. M. NIXON.

GLEASON, JACKIE, Feb. 26, 1916 (Brooklyn, N.Y.). U.S. comedian, actor. Starred in the TV series *The Life of Riley* (1949-50), and *The Jackie Gleason Show* (1952-55, 1957-59, and 1966-70), often featuring his character Ralph Kramden. Films: *The Hustler,* 1961; *Gigot,* 1962; *Requiem for a Heavyweight,* 1962; *Papa's Delicate Condition,* 1963.

GOSDEN, FREEMAN F., May 5, 1899 (Richmond, Va.). U.S. radio comedian. Played Amos in *Amos 'n' Andy* radio show, 1926-58. Films: *Check and Double Check,* 1930; *The Big Broadcast of 1936,* 1936.

GOULDING, RAY WALTER, Mar. 20, 1922 (Lowell, Mass.). U.S. comedian. With partner BOB ELLIOTT, formed comedy team that played radio, TV, and stage, since 1951.

GREGORY, DICK, Oct. 12, 1932 (St. Louis, Mo.). U.S. comedian, political activist. Stand-up comic in clubs, on TV, on stage, plus many records; civil-rights leader. Books: *From the Back of the Bus,* 1964; *Up from Nigger,* 1976.

HACKETT, BUDDY, born Leonard Hucker, Aug. 31, 1924 (Brooklyn, N.Y.). U.S. comedian. Rotund comic who appears in clubs, on TV; in a few films.

HARDY, OLIVER, Jan. 18, 1892 (Atlanta, Ga.)-Aug. 7, 1957. U.S. comedian. Joined with STAN LAUREL to form memorable early film team, 1926; in over 200 shorts and features, many of which became classics.

HOPE, BOB, born Leslie Townes Hope, May 29, 1903 (Eltham, Eng.). U.S. comedian, actor. Long stage, radio, TV, and film career; master of quick delivery and one-liners; noted for charitable ventures, especially entertaining servicemen overseas (from 1940); has received numerous awards, including Presidential Medal of Freedom, Hersholt Award, Emmy award, four special AAs; star of many films, including famous "Road" pictures with BING CROSBY; numerous TV specials, from 1950.

JOHNSON, CHIC, born Harold Johnson, Mar. 5, 1892 (Chicago, III.)-Feb. 26, 1962. U.S. comedian. Worked with OLE OLSON in vaudeville, on Broadway, in films; known for role in *Hellzapoppin* (play, 1939; film, 1941).

KAPLAN, GABE, Mar. 31, 1945 (Brooklyn, N.Y.). U.S. comedian, actor. A stand-up comic who created and starred in the TV sit-com *Welcome Back, Kotter*, 1975-1979.

KEATON, BUSTER, born Joseph Francis Keaton, Oct. 4, 1895 (Piqua, Kan.)-Feb. 1, 1966. U.S. comedian, actor. One of leading stars of silent-screen comedy, invariably as a deadpan character, often wearing a porkpie hat; in two-reelers and features from 1917; career declined with advent of talkies. Autobiography: *My Wonderful World of Slapstick*, 1962.

KELLY, EMMETT, Dec. 8, 1898 (Sedan, Kan.)-Mar. 28, 1979. U.S. clown. A fixture of the circus world for generations, beloved for his Willie the Tramp character; in a few films.

KING, ALAN, Dec. 26, 1927 (Brooklyn, N.Y.). U.S. comedian. Stand-up comic in clubs and concerts; has done several TV specials; appeared in the films *Bye-Bye Braverman* (1968) and *The Anderson Tapes* (1971); author of *Help! I'm a Prisoner in a Chinese Bakery* (1964) and other books.

KLEIN, ROBERT, Feb. 8, 1942 (New York, N.Y.). U.S. comedian, actor. Concert, nightclub, TV, and recording career; star of Broadway musical *They're Playing Our Song*, 1979.

KNOTTS, DON, July 21, 1924 (Morgantown, W. Va.). U.S. actor. Comic character actor, best known as Barney Fife on TV's *Andy Griffith Show*, 1960-68; a frequent star in WALT DISNEY films.

KORMAN, HARVEY, Feb. 15, 1927 (Chicago, Ill.). U.S. comedian. A popular TV comic on *The Danny Kaye Show* (1963-67) and *The Carol Burnett Show* (1967-78); has won four Emmy awards.

KOVACS, ERNIE, Jan. 23, 1919 (Trenton, N.J.)-Jan. 13, 1962. U.S. comedian. First major comedy star of TV's "Golden Age," with weekly program for "Muriel Cigars," 1952-53 and 1956. Films: *Operation Mad Ball*, 1957; *Wake Me When It's Over*, 1960. (Husband of EDIE ADAMS.)

LAHR, BERT, born Irving Lahrheim, Aug. 13, 1895 (New York, N.Y.)-Dec. 4, 1967. U.S. comedian. Beloved performer in vaudeville and on radio, he is best remembered as the Cowardly Lion in the film *The Wizard of Oz* (1939); in later years, turned to serious acting in stage productions of *Waiting for Godot* and Aristophanes's plays.

LAUREL, STAN, born Arthur Stanley Jefferson, June 16, 1890 (Ulverston, Eng.)-Feb. 23, 1965. English comedian. Joined with OLIVER HARDY to form first great film comedy-team, 1926; made over 200 films, many of them classics; received special AA for pioneering work in film comedy, 1960.

LEVENSON, SAM(uel), Dec. 28, 1911 (New York N.Y.). U.S. comedian, author. Former New York City schoolteacher, 1934-46; known for his gentle satire on everyday life, on TV panel shows during 1950s and 1960s; bestselling author of *Sex and the Single Child* (1969) and *In One Era and Out the Other* (1973).

LEWIS, JERRY, born Joseph Levitch, Mar. 16, 1926 (Newark, N.J.). U.S. comedian, actor. Burst onto comedy scene in zany partnership with DEAN MARTIN, 1946-56; on his own, appeared in a series of nutty movies in 1950s and 1960s; has raised millions with annual telethon for Muscular Dystrophy Assn. Films: *Geisha Boy*, 1958; *The Bellboy*, 1960; *The Nutty Professor*, 1963; *The Patsy*, 1964.

LEWIS, JOE E., 1902 (New York, N.Y.)-June 4, 1971. U.S. comedian. Fixture in nightclubs with stand-up comedy routine; FRANK SINATRA played him in film bio *The Joker Is Wild*, 1958.

LILLIE, BEATRICE, born Constance Sylvia Munston, May 29, 1894 (Toronto, Ont., Can.). English-Can. comedienne, actress. Made her debut in London (1914), where she became popular actress-singer-comedienne in plays and revues—notably those of André Charlot, in which she starred with NOEL COWARD, GERTRUDE LAWRENCE, and others; in a few films. Autobiography: *Every Other Inch a Lady*, 1972.

LITTLE, RICH, Nov. 26, 1938 (Ottawa, Ont., Can.). Canadian comedian. Impressionist (his RICHARD M. NIXON is famous) in clubs, on stage and TV; frequent guest and host of TV's *Tonight Show.*

LLOYD, HAROLD, Apr. 20, 1893 (Burchard, Neb.)-Mar. 8, 1971. U.S. comedian, actor. The highest-paid film star of the 1920s, known for his thrill-comedy films, often featuring him in "cliff-hanging" situations from 1916; received special AA for contributions to film comedy, 1952.

LYNDE, PAUL EDWARD, June 13, 1926 (Mt. Vernon, Ohio). U.S. actor, comedian. Films: *Bye Birdie*, 1963; *Beach Blanket Bingo*, 1965; *How Sweet It Is*, 1968. TV: *Hollywood Squares* (game show), 1966-1979; *The Paul Lynde Show* (series), 1972-73.

MARTIN, DICK, 1923 (Detroit, Mich.). U.S. comedian. Comic partner of DAN ROWAN, from 1952; cohost of TV show *Laugh-In*, 1967-72.

MARX, ARTHUR ("Harpo"), Nov. 21, 1888 (New York, N.Y.)-Sept. 28, 1964. U.S. comedian. Silent, harp-playing, blond-chasing member of MARX Bros.; in real life, talkative and intelligent. Autobiography: *Harpo Speaks*, 1961.

MARX, HERBERT ("Zeppo"), Feb. 25, 1901 (New York, N.Y.)-Nov. 30, 1979. U.S. comedian. Played romantic relief in early MARX Bros. films; left act to become an agent, 1933.

MARX, JULIUS ("Groucho"), Oct. 2, 1890 (New York, N.Y.)-Aug. 20, 1977. U.S. comedian. Mustachioed, cigar-smoking member of the MARX Bros. comedy team; after act broke up (1949), he went on to fame as star of TV quiz show *You Bet Your Life* (1947-62). Films: *Coconuts*, 1929; *Animal Crackers*, 1930; *Monkey Business*, 1931; *Horse Feathers*, 1932; *Duck Soup*, 1935; *A Day at the Races*, 1937. Books: *Groucho and Me*, 1959; *The Groucho Letters*, 1967.

MARX, LEONARD ("Chico"), Mar. 26, 1887 (New York, N.Y.)-Oct. 11, 1961. U.S. comedian. The fractured-speaking, piano-playing member of the MARX Bros.; appeared in all the team's films.

MARX, MILTON ("Gummo"), 1897 (New York, N.Y.)-Apr. 21, 1977. U.S. comedian. Joined with other MARX Bros. and their mother in vaudeville act called The Six Musical Mascots, 1904-18; left act to become their agent and business manager.

MURRAY, JAN, 1917 (New York, N.Y.). U.S. comedian. Stand-up comic; one of the pioneers of "insult humor"; frequently seen on TV.

NEWHART, BOB, Sept. 5, 1929 (Oak Park, Ill.). U.S. comedian, actor. Stand-up comic very popular in 1960s; turned to acting as star of the TV series *The Bob Newhart Show*, 1972-78.

OLSEN, OLE, born John Sigurd Olsen, Nov. 6, 1892 (Peru, Ind.)-Jan. 26, 1963. U.S. comedian. Formed comedy team with CHIC JOHNSON, 1915; appeared in vaudeville and in stage shows, notably *Hellzapoppin'* (play, 1939; film, 1941).

PAULSEN, PAT, ? (South Bend, Wash.). U.S. comedian. Sad-faced comic; regular on TV's *The Smothers Brothers Show*, 1967-68; "ran" for U.S. pres., 1968.

PENNER, JOE, born Joseph Pinter, Nov. 11, 1905 (Budapest, Hung.)-Jan. 10, 1941. U.S. comedian. In vaudeville, on radio, in films; famous catchphrase "Wanna buy a duck?"

PRINZE, FREDDIE, June 22, 1954 (New York,

N.Y.)–Jan. 29, 1977. U.S. comedian. Stand-up comic who skyrocketed to fame as star of the TV series *Chico and the Man*, 1974–77; died of self-inflicted gunshot wound.

PRYOR, RICHARD, Dec. 1, 1940 (Peoria, Ill.). U.S. comedian/actor. Stand-up comic popular on TV and in concert for his irreverent humor. Films: *Lady Sings the Blues*, 1972; *California Suite*, 1978.

RAGLAND, JOHN MORGAN ("Rags"), 1905 (Louisville, Ky.)–Aug. 20, 1946. U.S. comedian. A former boxer who appeared in burlesque musicals, vaudeville, and films; his biggest success was *Panama Hattie* (play, 1940; film, 1942). Films: *Girl Crazy*, 1943; *Anchors Aweigh*, 1945.

RICKLES, DON, May 8, 1926 (Long Island, N.Y.). U.S. comedian. Stand-up comic known for extremely insulting humor; has appeared in films and had own TV series.

RIVERS, JOAN, 1937 (Brooklyn, N.Y.). U.S. comedienne, filmmaker. Stand-up comic, 1960– ; with Second City (Chicago) improvisation troupe, 1961–62; frequent guest and host of TV's *Tonight Show*, 1965– ; cowrote and directed the film *Rabbit Test*, 1977. Author: *Having a Baby Can Be a Scream*, 1974.

ROWAN, DAN HALE, July 2, 1922 (Beggs, Okla.). U.S. comedian. Comic partner of DICK MARTIN, from 1952; cohosted TV series *Laugh-In*, 1968–72.

RUSSELL, NIPSEY, 1924 (Atlanta, Ga.). U.S. comedian. Known for improvised comic poetry recitations; frequent TV quiz-show guest.

SAHL, MORT(on Lyon), May 11, 1927 (Montreal, Que., Can.). Canadian comedian. Iconoclast whose satires on current events were very popular in 1950s; nightclub and TV performer, 1953– .

SALES, SOUPY, 1926 (Franklinton, N.C.). U.S. comedian. Slapstick comic on TV children's shows; host of TV's *Jr. Almost Anything Goes*, 1976–77.

SHAWN, DICK, born Richard Schulefand, Dec. 1, 1929 (Buffalo, N.Y.). U.S. comedian. Zany film actor in *It's a Mad, Mad, Mad, Mad World* (1963) and *The Producers* (1968), among other films.

SHERMAN, ALLAN, Nov. 30, 1924 (Chicago, Ill.)–Nov. 20, 1973. U.S. comedian. Best known for satiric songs he composed, especially "Hello Muddah, Hello Faddah."

SHRINER, HERB, May 29, 1918 (Toledo, Ohio)–Apr. 23, 1970. U.S. comedian. Dry wit and Hoosier humor were his trademark in comedy routines; early TV host, from 1948.

STEINBERG, DAVID, Aug. 9, 1942 (Winnipeg, Man., Can.). Canadian comedian. Stand-up comic of intellectual bent in clubs and on TV; frequent host of TV's *Tonight Show*.

STILLER, JERRY, June 8, ? (New York, N.Y.). U.S. comedian, actor. With wife ANNE MEARA, part of a comedy team, 1961– . Films: *Airport '75*, 1975; *Nasty Habits*, 1976; play: *The Ritz*, 1975.

WALKER, JIMMY, June 25, ? (New York, N.Y.). U.S. comedian, actor. A stand-up comic who gained fame as the irrepressible J. J. on the CBS-TV sitcom *Good Times*, 1974–79.

WEAVER, CHARLIE, born Cliff Arquette, Dec. 28, 1905 (Toledo, Ohio)–Sept. 23, 1974. U.S. comedian. Regularly appeared as "down-home" character on TV quiz show *Hollywood Squares*.

WILSON, FLIP, Dec. 8, 1933 (Jersey City, N.J.). U.S. comedian. Stand-up comic, most noted for impersonation of character Geraldine Jones; had own TV variety show, 1970–74.

YOUNGMAN, HENNY, 1906 (Liverpool, Eng.).

U.S. comedian. TV, radio, and club stand-up comic, noted for his violin playing and equally corny one-liners ("Take my wife—please!").

U.S. PRODUCERS AND DIRECTORS

ABBOTT, GEORGE, June 25, 1887 (Forestville, N.Y.). U.S. producer/director/playwright. An institution on American stage for over 60 years; still active, he produced his 119th show in 1978; cowrote many of musical theater's greatest hits. Plays: *The Boys from Syracuse*, 1938; *Where's Charley?*, 1948; *The Pajama Game*, 1954; *Damn Yankees*, 1955; *Fiorello*, 1959 (1960 Pulitzer Prize in drama).

ALTMAN, ROBERT, Feb. 20, 1925 (Kansas City, Mo.). U.S. producer/director. Films: *M*A*S*H**, 1970; *The Long Goodbye*, 1973; *Nashville*, 1975; *Three Women*, 1977; *A Wedding*, 1978; *Quintet*, 1979.

BELASCO, DAVID, July 25, 1853 (San Francisco, Calif.)–May 14, 1931. U.S. producer, playwright. Theatrical giant who made major innovations in techniques and staging; preferred working with little-knowns, whom he developed; connected with 374 plays, three of which became G. PUCCINI operas.

BOGDANOVICH, PETER, July 30, 1939 (Kingston, N.Y.). U.S. film critic, director, producer, screenwriter. Films: *The Last Picture Show*, 1971; *Nickelodeon*, 1976; *What's Up, Doc?*, 1972; *Paper Moon*, 1973; *Saint Jack*, 1979.

BORZAGE, FRANK, Apr. 23, 1895 (Salt Lake City, Utah)–June 19, 1962. U.S. film director. Films: *Seventh Heaven*, 1927; *History Is Made at Night*, 1937; *Stage Door Canteen*, 1943; *The Spanish Main*, 1945; *The Big Fisherman*, 1959.

CAPRA, FRANK, May 18, 1897 (Palermo, Italy). U.S. director. Leading film director of 1930s and 1940s, known for his comedies and stories of the common man. Films: *Platinum Blonde*, 1932; *It Happened One Night* (AA), 1934; *Mr. Deeds Goes to Town*, 1936; *Lost Horizon*, 1937; *You Can't Take It with You* (AA), 1938; *Mr. Smith Goes to Washington*, 1939; *Meet John Doe*, 1941; *Arsenic and Old Lace*, 1944; *It's a Wonderful Life*, 1946; *State of the Union*, 1948.

CHAMPION, GOWER, June 22, 1921 (Geneva, Ill.). U.S. director. Choreographer-dancer turned director of stage musicals. *Bye, Bye Birdie*, 1960; *Hello Dolly*, 1964; *The Happy Time*, 1968.

COHEN, ALEXANDER H., July 24, 1920 (New York, N.Y.). U.S. producer. In New York City and London, since 1941; producer of TV's *Tony Awards* shows, 1967– . Plays: *At the Drop of a Hat*, 1959; *Little Murders*, 1967; *Come As You Are*, 1970; *Anna Christie*, 1977; *I Remember Mama*, 1979.

COPPOLA, FRANCIS FORD, Apr. 7, 1939 (Detroit, Mich.). U.S. film director, producer, writer. Wrote, produced, and directed films *The Godfather* (AA; 1972); *The Godfather Part II* (3AAs; 1974); *The Conversation* (1974). Other films: *Finian's Rainbow* (writer), 1968; *Patton* (writer), 1970; *The Great Gatsby* (writer), 1974; *Apocalypse Now* (writer/director), 1979. (Brother of TALIA SHIRE.)

CUKOR, GEORGE, July 7, 1899 (New York, N.Y.). U.S. film director. A favorite of the 1930s and 1940s; still active. Films: *Little Women*, 1933; *The Philadelphia Story*, 1940; *A Double Life*, 1947; *Adam's Rib*, 1949; *Born Yesterday*, 1950; *A Star is Born*, 1954; *My Fair Lady* (AA), 1964.

DEMILLE, CECIL B(lount), Aug. 12, 1881

ENTERTAINERS

(Ashfield, Mass.)–Jan. 21, 1959. U.S. director, producer. Hollywood pioneer, most noted for his biblical spectacles. Films: *The Squaw Man*, 1913; *The Ten Commandments*, 1923, 1956; *King of Kings*, 1927; *Sign of the Cross*, 1932; *The Crusades*, 1935; *The Plainsman*, 1936; *Union Pacific*, 1939; *Samson and Delilah*, 1949; *The Greatest Show on Earth* (AA), 1952.

EDWARDS, BLAKE, born William Blake McEdwards, July 26, 1922 (Tulsa, Okla.). U.S. film director. Best known as the writer/director/producer of Pink Panther film series. Films: *Breakfast at Tiffany's*, 1961; *Days of Wine and Roses*, 1962; *Darling Lili*, 1969. (Husband of JULIE ANDREWS.)

EDWARDS, RALPH LIVINGSTONE, 1913 (Merino, Col.). U.S. producer, TV host. Producer of many radio-TV shows, including *Truth or Consequences* (radio, 1940–51) and *This is Your Life* (radio, 1948–50; TV, 1952–61, 1970–73).

FORD, JOHN, born Sean O'Feeney, Feb. 1, 1895 (Cape Elizabeth, Me.)–Aug. 31, 1973. U.S. film director. Directed over 125 films, won 5 AAs; known for action-adventure and Western films. Films: *The Informer* (AA), 1935; *Stagecoach*, 1939; *The Grapes of Wrath* (AA), 1940; *The Long Voyage Home*, 1940; *Tobacco Road*, 1941; *How Green Was My Valley* (AA), 1941; *She Wore a Yellow Ribbon*, 1949; *The Quiet Man* (AA), 1952; *Mr. Roberts*, 1955; *The Searchers*, 1956; *The Man Who Shot Liberty Valance*, 1962.

FOSSE, BOB, June 23, 1927 (Chicago, Ill.). U.S. director/choreographer. Directed films, stage and TV. Stage: *Pajama Game*, 1956; *Damn Yankees*, 1957; *Redhead*, 1959; *Sweet Charity*, 1966; *Pippin*, 1972; *Chicago*, 1975; *Dancin'*, 1978. Film: *Cabaret* (AA), 1972.

FRANKENHEIMER, JOHN, Feb. 19, 1930 (New York, N.Y.). U.S. director. Experienced in stage and TV, best known for his films. Films: *The Manchurian Candidate*, 1962; *The French Connection II*, 1975; *Black Sunday*, 1977. TV: *Studio One*, *Playhouse 90* programs, 1954–59.

GOLDWYN, SAMUEL, born Samuel Goldfish, Aug. 27, 1884 (Warsaw, Pol.)–Jan. 31, 1974. U.S. film producer. Pioneer in film industry, founded Goldwyn Pictures, 1917; merged to form MGM, 1924; independent after that; known for fractured English. Films: *Barbary Coast*, 1935; *Dodsworth*, 1936; *Wuthering Heights*, 1939; *The Little Foxes*, 1941; *The Best Years of Our Lives*, 1946; *Guys and Dolls*, 1955.

GRIFFITH, D(avid) W(ark), Jan. 22, 1875 (Floydsfork, Ky.)–July 23, 1948. U.S. film producer, director. Pioneer in industry from 1908, when he joined Biograph Pictures as actor; credited with major innovations, including mobile camera, flashbacks, fades; one of founders of United Artists; made some 200 silent films; never adapted to talkies. Films: *The Birth of a Nation*, 1915; *Intolerance*, 1916; *Way Down East*, 1920; *Orphans of the Storm*, 1922.

HAMMERSTEIN, OSCAR, May 8, 1847 (Stettin, Ger. [now Szczecin, Pol.])–Aug. 1, 1919. U.S. producer. Pioneer opera impresario, with several houses in New York City, including Manhattan Opera House (1906); sold interests in 1910 to Metropolitan Opera Co.; invented several cigarmaking machines. (Grandfather of composer OSCAR HAMMERSTEIN II.)

HAWKS, HOWARD, May 30, 1896 (Goshen, Ind.)–Dec. 26, 1977. U.S. director. Noted equally for his deft film comedies and his action dramas. Films: *Scarface*, 1932; *Twentieth Century*, 1934;

Bringing Up Baby, 1938; *To Have and Have Not*, 1944; *The Big Sleep*, 1946; *Red River*, 1948; *Rio Bravo*, 1958.

HAYWARD, LELAND, Sept. 15, 1902 (Nebraska City, Neb.)–Mar. 18, 1971. U.S. producer, agent. Producer of stage plays, notably *Mister Roberts* (1948) and *South Pacific* (1949); agent for many of leading stars of stage and screen in 1930s–1960s.

HUNTER, ROSS, born Martin Fuss, May 6, 1926 (Cleveland, Ohio). U.S. film producer. Specializes in remakes. Films: *Magnificent Obsession*, 1954; *Pillow Talk*, 1958; *Imitation of Life*, 1959; *Tammy Tell Me True*, 1961; *Madame X*, 1966; *Thoroughly Modern Millie*, 1967; *Airport*, 1969; *Lost Horizon*, 1973.

HUROK, SOL, Apr. 9,1888 (Pogar, Russ.).–Mar. 5, 1974. U.S. impresario.For 65 years, brought to U.S. the greatest stars of performing arts,including A. SEGOVIA, A. RUBINSTEIN, A.PAVLOVA, R. NUREYEV, the Bolshoi Ballet, etc.

HUSTON, JOHN, Aug. 5, 1906 (Nevada, Mo.). U.S. film director, actor. Films as director: *The Maltese Falcon*,1941; *The Treasure of the Sierra Madre* (AA), 1947; *Key Largo*, 1948; *The African Queen*, 1952; *The Misfits*, 1960; *The Bible*, 1966. Films as actor: *The Cardinal*, 1963; *The Bible*, 1966; *Chinatown*, 1974.(Son of WALTER HUSTON).

KANIN, GARSON, Nov. 24, 1912 (Rochester, N.Y.). U.S. playwright, director, author, screenwriter. A Ren. man of theater and screen; with wife RUTH GORDON, wrote screenplays for the films *A Double Life* (1948) and *Adam's Rib* (1949); wrote and directed the play *Born Yesterday* (1946); directed the plays *The Diary of Anne Frank* (1955), and *Funny Girl* (1964); author of bestselling books, including *Tracy and Hepburn* (1971).

KAZAN, ELIA, born Elia Kazanjoglous, Sept. 7, 1909 (Constantinople [now Istanbul], Turk.). U.S. director, producer, author. A cofounder of the Actors' Studio; directed films and stage productions; author of several popular books. Films: *A Tree Grows in Brooklyn*, 1945; *Gentlemen's Agreement* (AA), 1947; *A Streetcar Named Desire*, 1951; *Viva Zapata*, 1952; *On the Waterfront* (AA), 1954; *East of Eden*, 1955.

KRAMER, STANLEY, Sept. 29, 1913 (New York, N.Y.). U.S. producer, director. Films produced: *Home of the Brave*, 1949; *Death of a Salesman*, 1951; *High Noon*, 1952; *The Caine Mutiny*, 1954. Films produced and directed: *On the Beach*, 1959; *Inherit the Wind*, 1960; *Judgment at Nuremberg*, 1961; *Ship of Fools*, 1965; *Guess Who's Coming to Dinner?*, 1967.

KUBRICK, STANLEY, July 26, 1928 (New York, N.Y.). U.S. filmmaker. Innovative writer, producer, director. Films: *Paths of Glory* (writer-dir.), 1958; *Spartacus* (dir.), 1960; *Lolita* (dir.), 1962; *Dr. Strangelove* (dir.), 1963; *2001* (dir.), 1969; *A Clockwork Orange* (dir.), 1971; *Barry Lyndon* (dir.), 1975.

LEAR, NORMAN, July 27, 1922 (New Haven, Conn.). U.S. producer, director. His TV shows blazed new trails in comedy and openness. TV series: *All in the Family*, *Maude*, *The Jeffersons*, *Sanford and Son*, *Good Times*.

LEONARD, SHELDON, Feb. 22, 1907 (New York, N.Y.). U.S. TV producer and director, actor. Appeared on Broadway stage (1930–39) and in such films as *Guys and Dolls* (1955) and *Pocketful of Miracles* (1961); producer-dir. of the TV series *The Andy Griffith Show* (1960–68), *The Dick Van Dyke Show* (1961–66), and *I Spy* (1965–68);

279

THE BOOK OF WHO

won Emmy awards for best TV director (1957 and 1961) and for best comedy producer (1970).

LE ROY, MERVYN, Oct. 10, 1900 (San Francisco, Calif.). U.S. director. In films since 1924. Films: *Little Caesar,* 1930; *I Am a Fugitive from a Chain Gang,* 1932; *Tugboat Annie,* 1932; *Anthony Adverse,* 1936; *Random Harvest,* 1942; *Quo Vadis,* 1951; *No Time for Sergeants,* 1958; *The FBI Story,* 1959; *Gypsy,* 1962.

LESTER, RICHARD, Jan. 19, 1932 (Philadelphia, Pa.). U.S. film director. Films: *A Hard Day's Night,* 1964; *Petulia,* 1968; *The Three Musketeers,* 1973; *The Four Musketeers,* 1975; *Robin and Marian,* 1976; *The Ritz,* 1976.

LOGAN, JOSHUA, Oct. 5, 1908 (Texarkana, Tex.). U.S. producer, director. Producer-dir. of many Broadway shows. Coauthor, producer, and dir. of the plays *Mr. Roberts, South Pacific,* and *Fanny;* dir. of the films *Picnic* (1955), *Bus Stop* (1956), *South Pacific* (1958), and *Paint Your Wagon* (1969). Autobiography: *Josh,* 1976.

LOSEY, JOSEPH, Jan. 14, 1909 (La Crosse, Wisc.). U.S. film director. Films: *The Servant,* 1963; *Accident,* 1967; *The Go-Between,* 1971; *A Doll's House,* 1973.

LUMET, SIDNEY, June 25, 1924 (Philadelphia, Pa.). U.S. director. Directed over 200 plays for TV's *Playhouse 90,* 1956–61. Films: *Twelve Angry Men,* 1957; *The Pawnbroker,* 1965; *The Group,* 1966; *Serpico,* 1974; *Dog Day Afternoon,* 1975; *Network,* 1976; *Equus,* 1978.

MANKIEWICZ, JOSEPH L(eo), Feb. 11, 1909 (Wilkes-Barre, Pa.). U.S. writer, director. Writer: *A Letter for 3 Wives,* 1949; *All about Eve,* 1950; *The Barefoot Contessa,* 1954. Director: *Cleopatra,* 1963; *Sleuth,* 1972.

MAYER, LOUIS B., July 4, 1885 (Minsk, Russ.)-Oct. 29, 1957. U.S. film producer, executive. Founded Metro Pictures Corp. (1915), parlaying a chain of theaters into a major studio (MGM, 1924); created the star system; led the industry until 1951 retirement.

MAZURSKY, PAUL, Apr. 25, 1930 (Brooklyn, N.Y.). U.S. director, writer. Wrote and directed some of most popular films of 1970s. Films: *Bob and Carol and Ted and Alice,* 1969; *Harry and Tonto,* 1973; *Next Stop Greenwich Village,* 1976; *An Unmarried Woman,* 1978.

MCCAREY, (Thomas) **LEO,** Oct. 3, 1898 (Los Angeles, Calif.)-July 5, 1969. U.S. producer, director. Producer/director of many popular films of the 1930s and 1940s. Films: *Duck Soup,* 1933; *Ruggles of Red Gap,* 1935; *The Awful Truth* (AA), 1937; *Love Affair* (AA), 1939; *Going My Way* (AA), 1944.

MERRICK, DAVID, born David Margulies, Nov. 27, 1912 (New York, N.Y.). U.S. producer. Plays: *Fanny,* 1954; *Gypsy,* 1958; *Becket,* 1960; *Stop the World, I Want to Get Off,* 1962; *Oliver,* 1962; *Hello Dolly,* 1964; *Cactus Flower,* 1965; *Marat/Sade,*1965; *I Do, I Do,* 1966; *Rosencrantz and Guildenstern Are Dead,* 1967; *Promises, Promises,* 1969; *Travesties,* 1975.

MINNELLI, VINCENTE, Feb. 28, 1910 (Chicago, Ill.). U.S. film director. Noted for direction of MGM musicals. Films: *Cabin in the Sky,* 1943; *Meet Me in St. Louis,* 1944; *The Clock,* 1944; *Father of the Bride,* 1950; *An American in Paris,* 1951; *The Band Wagon,* 1953; *Brigadoon,* 1954; *Gigi* (AA), 1958; *Bells Are Ringing,* 1960. (One-time husband of JUDY GARLAND; father of LIZA MINNELLI.)

NICHOLS, MIKE, born Michael Igor Peschowsky, Nov. 6, 1931 (Berlin, Ger.). U.S. director. Comedy

partner of ELAINE MAY; directs for films and stage. Films: *Who's Afraid of Virginia Woolf?,* 1966; *The Graduate,* 1967; *Carnal Knowledge,* 1971. Plays: *Barefoot in the Park,* 1963; *The Odd Couple,* 1965; *Plaza Suite,* 1968; *The Prisoner of Second Avenue,* 1971; *Streamers,* 1976; *The Gin Game,* 1977.

PAPP, JOSEPH, June 22, 1921 (Brooklyn, N.Y.). U.S. producer/director. Founder (1953) and head of New York Shakespeare Festival; founded the Public Theatre, 1966; credited with producing many of major stage presentations of 1960s and 1970s. Plays: *Hair,* 1967; *Two Gentlemen of Verona,* 1971; *Sticks and Bones,*1971;*That Championship Season* (1972); *The Cherry Orchard,* 1973; *A Chorus Line,* 1975; *Streamers,* 1977.

PASTERNAK, JOSEPH, Sept. 19, 1901 (Silagy-Somlyo, Rum. [now Hung.]). U.S. producer. Film producer, with Universal Studios since 1923. Films: *One Hundred Men and a Girl,* 1937; *Destry Rides Again,* 1939; *The Great Caruso,* 1951; *Please Don't Eat the Daisies,* 1960; *Jumbo,* 1962.

PECKINPAH, (David) **SAM**(uel), Feb. 21, 1925 (Fresno, Calif.). U.S. film director. Known for violent, beautifully photographed films. Films: *Ride the High Country,* 1962; *The Wild Bunch,* 1969; *Straw Dogs,* 1971; *Pat Garrett and Billy the Kid,* 1973; *The Killer Elite,* 1976; *Cross of Iron,* 1977.

PENN, ARTHUR, Sept. 27, 1922 (Philadelphia, Pa.). U.S. film director. Films: *The Miracle Worker,* 1962; *Mickey One,* 1965; *Bonnie and Clyde,* 1967; *Alice's Restaurant,* 1969; *Little Big Man,* 1970.

PORTER, EDWIN STANTON, 1870 (Pittsburgh, Pa.)-Apr. 30, 1941. U.S. film pioneer. Associated with T. A. EDISON in the invention and perfection of the motion-picture camera; produced the first "story" film, *The Life of an American Fireman* (1899); produced *The Great Train Robbery* (1903), one of the most influential films of all time.

PREMINGER, OTTO, Dec. 5, 1906 (Vienna, Austria). U.S. film director. Films: *Laura,* 1944; *Forever Amber,* 1947; *The Moon Is Blue,* 1953; *Carmen Jones,* 1954; *The Man with the Golden Arm,* 1956; *Anatomy of a Murder,* 1959; *Exodus,* 1960; *Advise and Consent,* 1961; *The Cardinal,* 1963.

PRINCE, HAROLD STERN, Jan. 30, 1928 (New York, N.Y.). U.S. producer-director. Responsible for some of Broadway's biggest hits. Plays: *Pajama Game,* 1954; *Damn Yankees,* 1955; *West Side Story,* 1957; *Fiorello!,* 1959; *A Funny Thing Happened on the Way to the Forum,* 1962; *Fiddler on the Roof,* 1964; *Cabaret,* 1966; *Company,* 1970; *A Little Night Music,* 1973; *On the 20th Century,* 1978; *Sweeney Todd,* 1978.

REINER, CARL, Mar. 20, 1922 (Bronx, N.Y.). U.S. director, writer, actor. Versatile comedian, on stage and in TV; achieved greatest fame as creator/writer/director of TV's *Dick Van Dyke Show,* 1961–66; formed comedy team with MEL BROOKS, with whom he created famous "2000-year-old-man" character; directs films. (Father of ROB REINER.)

ROSE, BILLY, born William Samuel Rosenberg, Sept. 6, 1899 (New York, N.Y.)-Feb. 10, 1966. U.S. entrepreneur. A shorthand whiz at age 18, taught to take dictation at 350 wpm; songwriter, 1920–30; produced his first play, 1930; owned several theaters and night clubs in New York City. Shows produced: *Billy Rose's Crazy Quilt,* 1931; *Jumbo,* 1935; *Aquacade,* 1939–40; *Carmen Jones,* 1943; *Seven Lively Arts,* 1944.

280

ENTERTAINERS

ROSSEN, ROBERT, Mar. 16, 1908 (New York, N.Y.)–Feb. 18, 1966. U.S. screenwriter. After stage experience, came to Hollywood in 1936. Films written include *The Roaring Twenties* (1939), *A Walk in the Sun* (1945), *All the King's Men* (also produced and directed; AA, 1949), and *The Hustler* (also produced and directed; 1961).

SAKS, GENE MICHAEL, Nov. 8, 1921 (New York, N.Y.). U.S. director. Actor turned theater and film director. Plays: *Half a Sixpence,* 1962; *Mame,* 1964; *Same Time, Next Year,* 1975. Films: *The Odd Couple,* 1967; *Barefoot in the Park,* 1967; *Cactus Flower,* 1970; *The Prisoner of 2nd Avenue,* 1974; *Mame,* 1974.

SCHARY, DORE, Aug. 31, 1905 (Newark, N.J.). U.S. producer, director, writer. Film producer/director, head of production at RKO (1945–48) and MGM (1948–56); independent since 1956. Films: *Boys' Town* (AA),1938; *Sunrise at Campobello,* 1958 (play), 1960 (film).

SCORSESE, MARTIN, Nov. 17, 1942 (Flushing, N.Y.). U.S. film director. Films: *Mean Streets,* 1973; *Alice Doesn't Live Here Anymore,* 1974; *Taxi Driver,* 1976; *New York, New York,* 1977.

SELZNICK, DAVID O., May 10, 1902 (Pittsburgh, Pa.)–June 22, 1965. U.S. film producer. Associated with Paramount (1928–32) and RKO (1932–33), but most noted for career at MGM (1933–36) and as head of Selznick International (1936–65). Most famous film: *Gone with the Wind* (Best picture AA, special AA for Selznick), 1939.

SENNETT, MACK, born Michael Sinnott, Jan. 17, 1880 (Richmond, Que., Can.)–Nov. 5, 1960. U.S. film producer, actor. Known as "King of Comedy" of silent screen, for the two-reel comedies he produced; formed Keystone Co. studio (1912), created Keystone Kops; first feature-length comedy was *Tillie's Punctured Romance,* 1914; gave starts to many famous actors and directors; Special Academy Award, 1937.

SERLIN, OSCAR, Jan. 30, 1901 (Yalowka, Rus. [now Grudnow, USSR])–Feb. 27, 1971. U.S. producer, director. From "super" in Chicago opera, became Broadway producer/director; originated idea for play version of *Life With Father* (1937), which played a record 3,213 performances.

SHUBERT, LEE, Mar. 15, 1875 (Syracuse, N.Y.)–Dec. 25, 1953. U.S. theatrical producer. With his brothers, Sam and Jacob, built up a theatrical empire that at its peak controlled or owned six theaters; started in Syracuse managing touring companies; first to stage the modern revues; pres. of Shubert Co., 1907–31.

STEVENS, GEORGE, Dec. 18, 1904 (Oakland, Calif.)–Mar. 8, 1975. U.S. film director. Films: *Alice Adams,* 1934; *Gunga Din,* 1939; *Woman of the Year,* 1941; *A Place in the Sun* (AA), 1951; *Shane,* 1953; *Giant* (AA), 1956; *Diary of Anne Frank,* 1959.

STRASBERG, LEE, Nov. 17, 1901 (Budzanow, Austria). U.S. theatrical director, teacher, actor. A cofounder of the Group Theatre (1931–37), where he started training in the STANISLAVSKY method; a foremost teacher of acting, has long been associated with the Actors' Studio, as dir. from 1950. (Father of SUSAN STRASBERG.)

SUSSKIND, DAVID HOWARD, Dec. 19, 1920 (New York, N.Y.). U.S. producer, TV host. Producer of many TV shows, movies, and stage shows through his firm, Talent Assoc., 1952–   ; host of syndicated talk show featuring "adult" discussion, 1967–

THALBERG, IRVING GRANT, May 30, 1899 (Brooklyn, N.Y.)–Sept. 14, 1936. U.S. movie executive. As number-two man under LOUIS B. MAYER (1923–36), controlled the artistic policies of MGM; worked to develop studio contract directors; produced many films, including *Greed* (1923), *Freaks* (1932), *A Night at the Opera* (1935), *Naughty Marietta* (1935), *The Good Earth* (1937); thought to be the model for F. SCOTT FITZGERALD's *The Last Tycoon.* (One-time husband of NORMA SHEARER.)

TODD, MICHAEL, born Avron Hirsch Golbogen, June 2, 1909 (Minneapolis, Minn.)–Mar. 22, 1958. U.S. producer. After producing on Broadway (1936–45) entered films; formed company that developed Todd A-O and Cinerama widescreen processes; produced *Around the World in 80 Days* (AA), 1957; killed in plane crash. (Husband of JOAN BLONDELL and ELIZABETH TAYLOR.)

VON STROHEIM, ERICH, born Erich Oswald Hans Carl Maria von Nordenwall, Sept. 22, 1885 (Vienna, Austria)–May 12, 1957. U.S-Austrian director, actor. One of silent screen's greatest director/actors, whose career waned with the talkies. Films: *Blind Husbands,* 1919; *Foolish Wives,* 1921; *Greed,* 1923; *The Great Gabbo* (actor only), 1930; *The Grand Illusion* (actor only), 1937; *Sunset Boulevard* (actor only), 1950.

WALD, JEROME IRVING ("Jerry"), Sept. 16, 1911 (Brooklyn, N.Y.)–July 13, 1962. U.S. film producer. Films: *George Washington Slept Here,* 1942; *Mildred Pierce,* 1945; *Johnny Belinda,* 1948; *Peyton Place,* 1957; *Sons and Lovers,* 1960.

WALLIS, HAL B(rent), Sept. 14, 1898 (Chicago, Ill.). U.S. film producer. With Warner Bros., 1923–44; independent since then. Films: *Little Caesar,* 1930; *Casablanca,* 1942; *Gunfight at the OK Corral,* 1957; *Barefoot in the Park,* 1967; *True Grit,* 1969; *Anne of the Thousand Days,* 1970.

WANGER, WALTER, born Walter Feuchtwanger, July 11, 1894 (San Francisco, Calif.)–Nov. 18, 1968. U.S. film producer. An independent who worked for many studios. Films: *You Only Live Once,* 1937; *Stagecoach,* 1939; *Foreign Correspondent,* 1940; *Scarlet Street,* 1945; *Invasion of the Body Snatchers,* 1955; *Cleopatra,* 1962.

WELLES, ORSON, May 6, 1915 (Kenosha, Wisc.). U.S. actor, director, producer. Founder of Mercury Theater (1937) under whose aegis he directed and acted in plays on stage, radio, film; best known for directing, starring in and cowriting (AA) *Citizen Kane* (1941). Films: *The Magnificent Ambersons,* 1946; *Macbeth,* 1947. (One-time husband of RITA HAYWORTH.)

WELLMAN, WILLIAM AUGUSTUS, Feb. 29, 1896 (Brookline, Mass.)–Dec. 9, 1975. U.S. film director. Specialized in action-adventure genre. Films: *Wings,* 1927; *Public Enemy,* 1931; *A Star Is Born* (AA), 1937; *The Ox-Bow Incident,* 1942; *Roxie Hart,* 1942; *The High and the Mighty,* 1954.

WILDER, BILLY, June 22, 1906 (Austria). U.S. film director/writer. Films: *Ninotchka,* 1939; *Double Indemnity,* 1941; *The Lost Weekend* (AA), 1945; *Sunset Boulevard* (AA), 1950; *Stalag 17,* 1953; *Some Like It Hot,* 1959; *The Seven Year Itch,* 1959; *The Apartment* (2 AAs), 1960.

WISE, ROBERT, Sept. 10, 1914 (Winchester, Ind.). U.S. director, producer. Films: *Run Silent Run Deep,* 1958; *West Side Story* (AA), 1961; *The Haunting,* 1963; *The Sound of Music* (AA), 1965; *The Sand Pebbles,* 1966; *The Andromeda Strain,* 1970.

WYLER, WILLIAM, July 1, 1902 (Mulhouse, Fr.). U.S. film director. Films: *Jezebel,* 1938; *Mrs. Miniver* (AA), 1943; *The Best Years of Our Lives*

281

THE BOOK OF WHO

(AA), 1947; *The Desperate Hours*, 1955; *The Children's Hour*, 1962; *Funny Girl*, 1968.

YORKIN, BUD, born Alan Yorkin, Feb. 22, 1926 (Washington, Pa.). U.S. producer, director. Partner with NORMAN LEAR in Tandem Productions, 1959– . Producer of the TV series *All in the Family* (1969-79), *Sanford and Son* (1971-78), *Maude* (1972-78), and *Good Times* (1973-79). Films, dir.: *Divorce American Style*, 1967; *Inspector Clouseau*, 1968.

ZANUCK, DARRYL F(rancis), Sept. 5, 1902 (Wahoo, Neb.). Dec. 22, 1979. U.S. film producer, executive. Pres. (1962-69) and chm. and chief exec. officer (1971-79) of 20th Century-Fox Corp.; received Irving Thalberg Award, 1937, 1944, 1950; produced many of greatest U.S. films.

ZIEGFELD, FLORENZ, Mar. 21, 1869 (Chicago, Ill.)-July 22, 1932. U.S. producer. His extravagant stage shows, *Ziegfeld Follies*, glorified the American "girl", 1907-30; also produced other stage shows, notably *Show Boat* (1927), *Rio Rita* (1927) and *Bitter Sweet* (1929). (Husband of BILLIE BURKE.)

ZINNEMANN, FRED, Apr. 29, 1907 (Vienna, Austria). U.S. film director. Established neorealist movement in U.S. cinema. Films: *High Noon* (AA), 1951; *The Member of the Wedding*, 1952; *From Here to Eternity*, 1953; *The Nun's Story*, 1958; *A Man for All Seasons* (AA), 1966.

ZUKOR, ADOLPH, Jan. 7, 1873 (Riese, Hung.)-June 10, 1976. U.S. film executive. Founded Engadine Corp. (1912), which through mergers became Famous Players Lasky Corp. (1916) and then Paramount (1927); pres. (1916-35), chm. and chm. emeritus, (1935-76) of Famous Players/Paramount.

FOREIGN PRODUCERS AND DIRECTORS

ANTONIONI, MICHELANGELO, Sept. 29, 1912 (Ferrara, It.). Italian film director, scriptwriter. Films: *L'Avventura*, 1959; *The Red Desert*, 1964; *Blow-up*, 1966; *Zabriskie Point*, 1969.

BERGMAN, (Ernst) **INGMAR,** July 14, 1918 (Uppsala, Swe.). Swedish film director, screenwriter. Perhaps the most influential contemporary filmmaker, famed for his psychologically penetrating works. Films: *Smiles of a Summer Night*, 1955; *The Seventh Seal*, 1956; *Wild Strawberries*, 1957; *The Virgin Spring*, 1960; *Through a Glass Darkly*, 1961; *Winter Light*, 1962; *The Silence*, 1963; *Persona*, 1966; *Cries and Whispers*, 1972; *Scenes from a Marriage*, 1974; *The Magic Flute*, 1975; *Face to Face*, 1976; *Autumn Sonata*, 1978.

BERTOLUCCI, BERNARDO, Mar. 16, 1940 (Parma, It.). Italian film director. Films: *Before the Revolution*, 1965; *The Spider's Stratagem*, 1969; *Last Tango in Paris*, 1972; *1900*, 1978.

BROOK, PETER, Mar. 21, 1925 (London, Eng.). English director. Director of stage and film, especially renowned for his interpretations of Shakespeare. Plays: *King Lear*, 1962 (film, 196 , *Marat/Sade*, 1964; *Midsummer Night's Dream*, 1970. Films: *Lord of the Flies*, 1969.

BUÑUEL, LUIS, 1900 (Calanda, Spain). Spanish film director. Worked in France in 1920s-30s, then in Mexico (1945-60), before returning to France; known for surreal films that mock hypocrisy and religion. Films: *Un Chien Andalou*, 1928; *L'Age d'Or*, 1930; *Los Olvidados*, 1950; *Robinson Crusoe*, 1952; *Viridiana*, 1961; *The Exterminating Angel*, 1962; *Belle de Jour*, 1966; *The Discreet Charm of the Bourgeoisie*, 1972.

CHABROL, CLAUDE, June 24, 1930 (Paris, Fr.) French film director. Credited with starting the "new wave" in French films. Films: *Le Beau Serge*, 1958; *The Beast Must Die*, 1969; *The Butcher*, 1970; *Ophelia*, 1973.

CLOUZOT, HENRI-GEORGES, Nov. 20, 1907 (Niort, Fr.)-Jan. 12, 1977. French film director, writer. Noted for his suspense melodramas. Films: *Le Corbeau*, 1943; *Quai des Orfevres*, 1947; *The Wages of Fear*, 1953; *Les Diaboliques*, 1954.

COSTA-GAVRAS, born Konstantinos Gavras, 1933 (Athens. Gr.). Greek film director. Films: *The Sleeping Car Murders*, 1966; *'Z'* (AA), 1969; *State of Siege*, 1973.

DE BROCA, PHILIPPE CLAUDE ALEX, Mar. 15, 1933 (Paris, Fr.). French film director, producer. Films: *That Man From Rio*, 1963; *King of Hearts*, 1966; *Mademoiselle Mimi*, 1967; *The Devil by the Tail*, 1968; *Give Her the Moon*, 1969; *Chère Louise*, 1972.

DE LAURENTIIS, DINO, Aug. 8, 1919 (Torre Annunziata, It.). Italian film producer. Known for big-budget productions. Films: *Bitter Rice*, 1952; *La Strada*, 1956; *Nights of Cabria*, 1957; *The Bible*, 1966; *Serpico*, 1974; *Death Wish*, 1974; *King Kong*, 1976; *Hurricane*, 1979.

DE SICA, VITTORIO, July 7, 1901 (Sora, It.)-Nov. 13, 1974. Italian film director. Known both for his social realism and his comedies. Films: *Shoeshine*, 1946; *The Bicycle Thief*, 1948; *Miracle in Milan*, 1951; *Umberto D.*, 1952; *Madame De*, 1952; *Two Women*, 1961; *Yesterday, Today and Tomorrow* (AA), 1965; *The Garden of the Finzi-Continis*, 1971; *The Voyage*, 1973.

EISENSTEIN, SERGEI MIKHAYLOVICH, Jan. 23, 1898 (Riga, Latvia [now USSR])-Feb. 11, 1948. Soviet film director. Major influence in world cinema for his theories on film direction. Films: *The Battleship Potemkin*, 1925; *Alexander Nevsky*, 1938; *Ivan the Terrible*, 1944, 1958.

FELLINI, FEDERICO, Jan. 20, 1920 (Rimini, It.). Italian film director. Major influence on post-WW II Italian cinema; occasionally appears in his own films. Films: *La Strada*, 1954; *La Dolce Vita*, 1959; *8½*, 1963; *Juliet of the Spirits*, 1965; *Satyricon*, 1969; *The Clowns*, 1970; *Roma*, 1972; *Casanova*, 1977.

GODARD, JEAN-LUC, Dec. 3, 1930 (Paris, Fr.). French film director. A leader of the French "new wave" cinema. Films: *Breathless*, 1960; *Les Carbiniers*, 1963; *Alphaville*, 1965; *Pierrot Le Fou*, 1966; *Weekend*, 1967; *Symphony for the Devil*, 1970; *Tout va Bien*, 1972.

HITCHCOCK, ALFRED JOSEPH, Aug. 13, 1899 (London, Eng.). English director. Known for suspense/thriller films: Films: *The 39 Steps*, 1935; *Suspicion*, 1941; *Saboteur*, 1942; *Lifeboat*, 1943; *Spellbound*, 1945; *Notorious*, 1946; *Strangers on a Train*, 1951; *Dial M for Murder*, 1954; *Rear Window*, 1954; *Vertigo*, 1958; *North by Northwest*, 1959; *Psycho*, 1960; *The Birds*, 1963; *Frenzy*, 1972; *Family Plot*, 1976. TV: *Alfred Hitchcock Presents*, 1955-65.

KORDA, SIR ALEXANDER, born Sandor Corda, Sept. 16, 1893 (Turkeye, Hung.)-Jan. 23, 1956. Anglo-Hungarian film producer, director. A major figure in the British film industry. Films: *The Private Life of Henry VIII*, 1932; *The Scarlet Pimpernel*, 1934; *The Thief of Baghdad*, 1940; *The Third Man*, 1949.

LANG, FRITZ, Dec. 12, 1890 (Vienna, Austria)-Aug. 2, 1976. Austrian director. Leading film dir. in Europe and Hollywood. Films: *M*, 1931; *Western*

Union, 1941; *Cloak and Dagger*, 1946; *The Big Heat*, 1953.

LEAN, DAVID, Mar. 25, 1908 (Croydon, Eng.). English director. Film dir. in England and Hollywood. Films: *Brief Encounter*, 1946; *Great Expectations*, 1946; *Oliver Twist*, 1948; *The Bridge on the River Kwai* (AA), 1957; *Lawrence of Arabia* (AA), 1962; *Ryan's Daughter*, 1970.

LELOUCH, CLAUDE, Oct. 30, 1937 (Paris. Fr.). French film director. Internationally popular in the mid-1960s; known for his lush visual style. Films: *Un Homme et Une Femme*, 1966; *Vivre Pour Vivre*, 1967; *La Bonne Année*, 1973.

LUBITSCH, ERNST, Jan. 29, 1892 (Berlin, Ger.)–Nov. 30, 1947. Ger.-U.S. director. Noted for his sophisticated comedy films of the 1930s and 1940s. Films: *The Love Parade*, 1929; *Trouble in Paradise*, 1932; *Ninotchka*, 1939; *To Be or Not To Be*, 1942; *Heaven Can Wait*, 1943.

MALLE, LOUIS, Oct. 30, 1932 (Thumeries, Fr.). French film director. One of the "new wave" of French film dirs. Films: *The Lovers*, 1958; *Zazie dans la Metro*, 1961; *Le Feu Follet*, 1963; *Souffle au Coeur*, 1971; *Lucien-Lacombe*, 1975.

MILLER, JONATHAN WOLFE, July 21, 1934 (London, Eng.). English director, actor, writer, physician. Forsook medicine for the theater; coauthor of and actor in the play *Beyond the Fringe*, 1961; directed films and TV for the BBC, 1964–67; directed plays, including *Danton's Death*, *The School for Scandal* and *The Merchant of Venice* (all three for the National Theatre, London), 1957–70; research fellow, history of medicine, at the U. College, 1970– .

OPHÜLS, MARCEL, Nov. 1, 1927 (Frankfurt, Ger.). German producer/director. Produced and directed documentary films. Films: *The Sorrow and The Pity*, 1971; *Memory of Justice*, 1976.

POLANSKI, ROMAN, Aug. 18, 1933 (Paris, Fr.). French film director. Acted in several of his own films; fled U.S. in 1978, to avoid further prosecution on a morals charge. Films: *Two Men and a Wardrobe*, 1958; *Knife in the Water*, 1961; *Repulsion*, 1965; *Rosemary's Baby*, 1968; *Chinatown*, 1974. (Husband of the late Sharon Tate.)

PONTI, CARLO, Dec. 11, 1913 (Milan, It.). Italian film producer. Credited with discovering SOPHIA LOREN, whom he later married. Films: *War and Peace*, 1956; *Marriage—Italian Style*, 1965; *Operation Crossbow*, 1965; *The Passenger*, 1974.

PUDOVKIN V(sevolod), 1893 (Rus.)–July 1, 1953. Soviet director. Films: *Mother*, 1926; *The End of St. Petersburg*, 1927; *Storm over Asia*, 1928; *The Deserter*, 1933; *General Suvorov*, 1941.

REED, SIR CAROL, Dec. 30, 1906 (London, Eng.)–Apr. 25, 1976. English film director. Active mostly in Britain. Films: *Kipps*, 1941; *Odd Man Out*, 1946; *The Third Man*, 1949; *The Agony and the Ecstasy*, 1965; *Oliver* (AA), 1968.

RENOIR, JEAN, Sept. 15, 1894 (Paris. Fr.)–Feb. 12, 1979. French film director. Leading force in world cinema, most remembered for monumental antiwar film *La Grande Illusion* (1937). (Son of PIERRE AUGUSTE RENOIR.)

RESNAIS, ALAIN, June 3, 1922 (Vannes, Fr.). French film director. A founder of the French "new wave" of cinema of the 1950s and 1960s. Films: *Hiroshima Mon Amour*, 1959; *Last Year at Marienbad*, 1961; *La Guerre est fini*, 1966; *Je t'aime*, 1969; *Stavisky*, 1974.

RICHARDSON, TONY, June 5, 1928 (Shipley, Eng.). English director. Film director, who occasionally directs on the stage. Films: *A Taste of Honey*, 1961; *The Loneliness of the Long Distance Runner*, 1963; *Tom Jones*, 1963; *The Loved One*, 1965; *Joseph Andrews*, 1978.

RIEFENSTAHL, LENI, Aug. 22, 1902 (Berlin, Ger.). German film director. Major propagandist for the Nazis, through her documentaries. Films: *Triumph of the Will*, 1934; *Olympische Spiele*, 1936.

ROHMER, ERIC, born Jean-Marie Maurice Schere, Mar. 21, 1920 (Tulle, Fr.). French director. Disciple of Alfred Hitchcock; former assistant for *Cahiers du Cinema* journal. Films: *My Night at Maud's, 1969; Claire's Knee, 1970; Chloe in the Afternoon, 1972; The Marquis of O, 1975; Percival, 1978.*

ROSSELLINI, ROBERTO, May 3, 1906 (Rome, It.). Italian film director. Directed *Open City* (1945), *Paisan* (1946), *Stromboli* (1949). (One-time husband of INGRID BERGMAN.)

RUSSELL, KEN, July 3, 1927 (Southampton, Eng.). English director. Documentary filmmaker for the BBC; known for his bizarre, controversial and lavishly produced films, often biographies of famous artists. Films: *Women in Love*, 1969; *The Music Lovers*, 1970; *The Boy Friend*, 1971; *The Devils*, 1971; *Tommy*, 1975; *Lisztomania*, 1975; *Valentino*, 1977.

STANISLAVSKY, KONSTANTIN, Jan. 7, 1863 (Moscow, Rus.)–Aug. 7, 1938. Russian actor, director. Noted as the creator of the system or theory of acting called the "method"; cofounder and dir. of Moscow Art Theater, 1898–1938.

TRUFFAUT, FRANÇOIS, Feb. 6, 1932 (Paris, Fr.). French filmmaker. Producer, director, writer and actor, from 1957. Films: *The 400 Blows*, 1957; *Shoot the Piano-player*, 1960; *Jules et Jim*, 1961; *Fahrenheit 451*, 1966; *The Wild Child*, 1969; *The Story of Adele H.*, 1975; *Small Change*, 1976.

VADIM, (Plemmianikov) **ROGER,** 1928 (Paris, Fr.). French director. Responsible for BRIGITTE BARDOT's beginnings in film (he was also her husband); was married to JANE FONDA and featured her in his film *Barbarella* (1967).

VISCONTI, LUCHINO, Nov. 2, 1906 (Milan, It.)–Mar. 17, 1976. Italian film director. Father of Italian neorealist school; noted for the sinister beauty of his films. Films: *Ossessione*, 1942; *Senso*, 1952; *Rocco and His Brothers*, 1960; *The Leopard*, 1964; *The Damned*, 1970; *Death in Venice*, 1971; *The Innocent*, 1978.

WERTMULLER, LINA ? (Rome, It.). Italian film director/writer. Began in 1962 as production asst. to FEDERICO FELLINI; wrote and directed popular films. Films: *The Seduction of Mimi*, 1974; *Love and Anarchy*, 1974; *Swept Away . . .*, 1975; *Seven Beauties*, 1976; *A Night Full of Rain*, 1977.

ZEFFIRELLI, FRANCO, Feb. 12, 1923 (Florence, It.). Italian director, designer. Began as a stage designer in Italy, then moved into designing-directing for opera. Films: *Romeo and Juliet* (1968); *Brother Sun and Sister Moon*, 1973.

MUSICIANS

ADDERLEY, CANNONBALL, born Julian Edwin Adderley, Sept. 15, 1928 (Tampa, Fla.)–Aug. 8, 1975. U.S. musician. Leading jazz saxophonist.

ADLER, LARRY, Feb. 10, 1914 (Baltimore, Md.). U.S. harmonica player. Generally considered to be the world's best harmonica player; has played for over 50 years, from 1928.

ALLEN, RED, born Henry Allen, Jan. 1, 1900 (Algiers, La.)–Apr. 17, 1967. U.S. musician. Dixie-land-jazz trumpet player.

ALLMAN, DUANE, Nov. 20, 1946 (Nashville, Tenn.)–Oct. 29, 1971. U.S. musician. Lead guitarist, also frequent back-up for ERIC CLAPTON; noted for slide guitar style; with brother GREGG, formed Allman Bros. band, a popular 1970s rock group; died in motorcycle accident. Songs: "Statesboro Blues"; "In Memory of Elizabeth Reed."

ALLMAN, GREGG, Dec. 8, 1947 (Nashville, Tenn.). U.S. musician. With brother DUANE, formed Allman Bros. rock band, 1969; organist and lead vocals; after Duane's death, regrouped band; noted for successful kicking of drug habit and brief marriage to CHER. Songs: "Ramblin' Man"; "Blue Skies"; "Midnight Rider."

ALPERT, HERB, Mar. 1, 1935 (Los Angeles, Calif.). U.S. musician. Trumpeter who founded and leads Tijuana Brass ensemble 1962– ; founder of A&M Records, a leading pop-jazz recording label.

ARMSTRONG, (Daniel) **LOUIS** ("Satchmo"), July 4, 1900 (New Orleans, La.)–July 6, 1971. U.S. musician. Leading trumpeter in jazz history; made 1,500 jazz recordings, many classics; originated the "scat" vocal; made numerous film, television, concert appearances; in later years, associated most often with song "Hello, Dolly."

ATKINS, CHET, born Chester B. Atkins, June 20, 1924 (Luttrell, Tenn.). U.S. musician. Country-and-western guitarist; performs with Grand Ole Opry; record company exec. (RCA); received Grammy Award, 1967.

BAKER, GINGER, born Peter Baker, Aug. 19, 1940 (Lewisham, Eng.). English musician. Drummer for the legendary rock group Cream, 1966–68; cofounder of Blind Faith band, 1969–70.

BASIE, COUNT, born William Basie, Aug. 21, 1904 (Red Bank, N.J.). U.S. musician. A pianist/composer who has led big jazz bands from 1935. "One O'Clock Jump"; "Two O'Clock Jump"; "Basie Boogie"; "I Left My Baby."

THE BEACH BOYS: Brian Wilson, June 20, 1942 (Hawthorne, Calif.); Alan Jardine, Sept. 3, 1942 (Lima, Ohio); Mike Love, Mar. 15, 1941 (Los Angeles, Calif.); Dennis Wilson, Dec. 4, 1944 (Hawthorne, Calif.); Carl Wilson, Dec. 21, 1946 (Hawthorne, Calif.). U.S. rock group. The epitome of "California-style" rock in the early 1960s, the group foundered in late 1960s and early 1970s, only to resurrect itself into a popular pop-rock group again in late 1970s.

BECHET, SIDNEY, May 14, 1897 (New Orleans, La.)–May 14, 1959. U.S. musician. Early jazz innovator on the soprano saxophone.

BEIDERBECKE, BIX, born Leon Bismarck Beiderbecke, Mar. 10, 1903 (Davenport, Ia.)–Aug. 7, 1931. U.S. musician. Jazz cornetist/composer; first white musician to be considered major innovator in jazz.

BERIGAN, BUNNY, born Roland Bernard Berigan, Nov. 2, 1909–June 2, 1942. U.S. trumpet player. Bandleader of 1930s swing era; theme song: "I Can't Get Started with You."

BLAKEY, ART, Oct. 11, 1919 (Pittsburgh, Pa.). U.S. jazz drummer. Bandleader, 1940s–70s.

BLANTON, JIMMY, c.1921 (Chattanooga, Tenn.)–July 30, 1942. U.S. jazz bass player. Played with DUKE ELLINGTON's band, 1939–42.

BLOCH, RAY, Aug. 3, 1902 (Alsace-Lorraine). U.S. conductor. Conductor, composer, arranger on radio and TV; best known as long-time conductor for ED SULLIVAN's TV show.

BLOOD, SWEAT & TEARS: David Clayton-Thomas, Sept. 13, 1941 (Surrey, Eng.); Bobby Colomby, Dec. 20, 1944 (New York, N.Y.); Steve Katz, May 9, 1945 (Brooklyn, N.Y.); Jim Fielder, Oct. 4, 1947 (Denton, Tex.); Dick Halligan, Aug. 29, 1943 (Troy, N.Y.); Fred Lipsius, Nov. 19, 1944 (New York, N.Y.); Lew Soloff, Feb. 20, 1944 (Brooklyn, N.Y.); Chuck Winfield, Feb. 5, 1943 (Monessen, Pa.); and Jerry Hyman, May 19, 1947 (Brooklyn, N.Y.). U.S. jazz-rock group. With AL KOOPER, established the rock instrumental group in 1968 that became one of most popular of all time and continues successfully today; one of the first rock groups to make use of many instruments other than guitars and drums.

BOLDEN, BUDDY, born Charles Bolden, 1868? (New Orleans, La.)–Oct. 4, 1931. U.S. musician. Cornetist who formed first jazz band in the U.S., 1895; his standard numbers included "If You Don't Like My Potatoes, Why Do You Dig So Deep," "Make Me a Pallet on the Floor," and "Bucket's Got a Hole in It."

BROONZY, BIG BILL, June 26, 1893 (Scott, Miss.)–Aug. 14, 1958. U.S. musician. Blues singer and guitarist.

BROWN, LES, Mar. 14, 1912 (Reinerton, Pa.). U.S. musician. Led his Band of Renown since 1938, often appearing with BOB HOPE; wrote the song "Sentimental Journey."

BRUBECK, DAVE, born David Warren Brubeck, Dec. 6, 1920 (Concord, Calif.). U.S. musician. Leading force in contemporary jazz, came to prominence in 1950s as pianist/composer; had own quartet, 1951–67. Compositions: *The Light in the Wilderness* (oratorio); *La Fiesta de la Posada* (cantata); *They All Sang Yankee Doodle* (symphony); *Points on Jazz* (ballet).

BURDON, ERIC, Apr. 5, 1941 (Newcastle-on-Tyne, Eng.). English musician. Founder of British rock group The Animals, 1963–68; founded black rock group War (1969) with which he performed until 1971. Songs: "Spill the Wine," 1970.

BYRD, CHARLIE, born Charles Lee Byrd, Sept. 16, 1925 (Suffolk, Va.). U.S. guitarist. Jazz guitarist, 1936– ; named *Playboy* guitarist of year, 1964–67.

THE BYRDS: Roger McGuinn, born James McGuinn, July 13, 1942 (Chicago, Ill.); Chris Hillman, Dec. 4, 1942 (Los Angeles, Calif.); Gene Clark, Nov. 17, 1941 (Tipton, Mo.); Mike Clarke, June 3, 1944. U.S. musicians. With David Crosby, the original members of the popular 1960s band, one of first in the folk-rock genre, 1964–73. Songs: "Mr. Tambourine Man," 1964; "Turn, Turn, Turn," 1965; "Mr. Spaceman," 1966; "My Back Pages," 1967.

CALLOWAY, CAB(ell), Dec. 25, 1907 (Rochester, N.Y.). U.S. musician. Has led own band since 1928 in appearances on stage, in films; starred in film *Stormy Weather*, 1943; wrote "Minnie the Moocher"; his autobiography, *Of Minnie the Moocher and Me*, was a best-seller.

CARTER, BENNY, born Bennett Lester Carter, Aug. 8, 1907 (New York, N.Y.). U.S. musician. Jazz performer (alto saxophone, clarinet, trumpet), composer, band leader; had his own band, 1932–35 and 1938–46; composed music for films, including *Stormy Weather* (1943), *Snows of Kilimanjaro* (1952), *Guns of Navarone* (1961).

CATLETT, SIDNEY ("Big Sid"), Jan 17, 1910 (Evansville, Ind.)–Mar. 25, 1951. U.S. musician. A leading jazz drummer of the 1930s–40s.

CLAPTON, ERIC, Mar. 30, 1945 (England). English guitarist and vocalist. With GINGER BAKER and Jack Bruce, formed rock trio Cream (1966-

68), a major influence in rock music; also founded Derek and The Dominoes, 1970–72; member of Blind Faith band, 1969–70.

CLARK, DAVE, Dec. 15, 1942 (London, Eng.). English musician, lead singer. With four others, formed the Dave Clark Five, a major 1960s rock group, 1964–73. Songs: "Glad All Over," 1964; "Because," 1964; "I Like It like That," 1965; "Over and Over," 1965.

COCKER, JOE, born John Cocker, May 20, 1944 (Sheffield, Eng.). English musician. Singer-drummer of blues-rock in 1960s.

COLE, COZY, born William Randolph Cole, Oct. 17, 1909 (E. Orange, N.J.). U.S. jazz drummer. A leading musician of the Big Band era; continued career into the 1970s with own group.

COLEMAN, ORNETTE, Mar. 19, 1930 (Ft. Worth, Tex.). U.S. musician. Jazz saxophonist associated with the avant-garde school.

COLTRANE, JOHN, Sept. 23, 1926 (Hamlet, N.C.)–July 17, 1967. U.S. musician. Jazz saxophonist who worked with DIZZY GILLESPIE and MILES DAVIS.

CROSBY, BOB, Aug. 23, 1913 (Spokane, Wash.). U.S. musician. Bandleader (Bob Crosby and His Bobcats) popular during 1940s and 1950s; appeared in several films. (Brother of BING CROSBY.)

CUGAT, XAVIER, Jan. 1, 1900 (Barcelona, Sp.). U.S. musician. Latin bandleader, extremely popular during rhumba, cha-cha, and mambo dance crazes of the 1940s and 1950s.

DAVIS, MILES DEWEY, JR., May 25, 1926 (Alton, Ill.). U.S. musician. Leading figure in jazz since the 1940s; trumpet player and composer who has his own quintet; ushered in the "birth of cool"; albums include *Milestones, Musings of Miles, At Carnegie Hall, Sorcerer,* and *Bitches' Brew.*

DEFRANCO, BUDDY, born Boniface Ferdinand Leonardo DeFranco, Feb. 17, 1933 (Camden, N.J.). U.S. musician. A clarinetist who performed with GENE KRUPA, TOMMY DORSEY, Charlie Barnet, 1941–46; winner, *Down Beat* poll, 1945–54; featured with GLENN MILLER orchestra, 1966– ; *Down Beat* Critics Award, 1953–54.

DESMOND, PAUL, born Paul Breitenfeld, Nov. 25, 1924 (San Francisco, Calif.)–May 30, 1977. U.S. jazz alto saxophonist. Associated with DAVE BRUBECK's Quartet, 1951–67.

DORSEY, JIMMY, Feb. 29, 1904 (Shenandoah, Pa.)–June 12, 1957. U.S. musician. Important leader of the Big Band era; played clarinet, alto sax; had own band, also played with brother TOMMY DORSEY.

DORSEY, TOMMY, Nov. 19, 1905 (Shenandoah, Pa.)–Nov. 26, 1956. U.S. musician. Key figure in Big Band era; played trombone (noted for sweet tone) and trumpet, often with brother JIMMY DORSEY; had own band.

DUCHIN, EDDY, born Edwin Frank Duchin, 1909 (Cambridge, Mass.)–Feb. 9, 1951. U.S. pianist. Beloved by "high society," played for important balls and social functions; died of leukemia. (Father of PETER DUCHIN.)

DUCHIN, PETER OELRICHS, July 28, 1937 (New York, N.Y.). U.S. musician. Pianist and orchestra leader, popular with "beautiful people" of the 1960s and 1970s. (Son of EDDY DUCHIN.)

EDDY, DUANE, Apr. 26, 1938 (Corning, N.Y.). U.S. musician. Rock-and-roll guitarist/songwriter whose use of the "twang" effect earned him a place in music history; played with backup group The Rebels. Songs: "Rebel Rouser," 1958; Cannonball," 1958; "Because They're Young," 1960.

ELDRIDGE, ROY, Jan. 30, 1911 (Pittsburgh, Pa.). U.S. musician. Jazz trumpeter; bandleader since 1927; joined GENE KRUPA, 1941; with Jazz at the Philharmonic, 1945–51.

ELLINGTON, DUKE, born Edward Kennedy Ellington, Apr. 29, 1899 (Washington, D.C.)–May 24, 1974. U.S. musician. Composer, pianist, jazz orchestra leader; a major jazz influence who led his own orchestra, 1923–74. "Mood Indigo"; "Don't Get Around Much Anymore"; "Satin Doll."

FLATT, LESTER, June 19, 1914 (Overton Co., Tenn.)–May 11, 1979. U.S. guitarist. Country-and-western star who for 25 years was partner with EARL SCRUGGS in popular duo.

GARCIA, JERRY, born Jerome John Garcia, Aug. 1, 1942 (San Francisco, Calif.). U.S. musician. Lead guitarist and a founder (1965) of The Grateful Dead, an acid-rock band of the 1960s.

GARNER, ERROLL, May 15, 1921 (Pittsburgh, Pa.)–Jan. 2, 1977. U.S. musician. Jazz pianist; composer of hit tune "Misty."

GETZ, STAN, Feb. 2, 1927 (Philadelphia, Pa.). U.S. musician. Jazz saxophonist; *Metronome* poll winner, 1950–55; *Down Beat* Award, 1950–54; Grammy award, 1962 and 1964.

GILLESPIE, DIZZY, born John Birks Gillespie, Oct. 21, 1917 (Cheraw, N.C.). U.S. musician. Jazz trumpeter and composer who is credited with developing "bop" style of music.

GOODMAN, BENNY ("The King of Swing"), born Benjamin David Goodman, May 30, 1909 (Chicago, Ill.). U.S. musician. Clarinetist who has led his own orchestra since 1933; conducted swing concerts all over the world; appeared on numerous TV and radio programs and in some films; frequent guest-soloist with bands and symphony orchestras.

HACKETT, BOBBY, Jan. 31, 1915 (Providence, R.I.)–June 7, 1976. U.S. cornetist. Performed with Big Bands 1930s–40s; featured soloist on JACKIE GLEASON albums, 1950s.

HAMPTON, LIONEL, Apr. 12, 1913 (Birmingham, Ala.). U.S. musician. Jazz vibraphonist and bandleader who performed with Benny Goodman Quartet, 1936–40; has led his own band ever since.

HARRIS, PHIL, June 24, 1906 (Linton, Ind.). U.S. bandleader. Had own Big Band; known for long association with JACK BENNY on radio and TV. (Husband of ALICE FAYE.)

HAWKINS, COLEMAN, Nov. 21, 1904 (St. Joseph, Mo.)–May 19, 1969. U. S. musician. Jazz tenor saxophonist; his 1939 recording of "Body and Soul" considered a classic.

HAYES, ISAAC, Aug. 20, 1942 (Covington, Ky.). U.S. musician. Soul singer and composer most noted for score to film *Shaft,* 1971. Albums: *Hot Buttered Soul; Soul Man; Juicy Fruit.*

HENDERSON, (James) **FLETCHER,** Dec. 18, 1898 (Cuthbert, Ga.)–Dec. 29, 1952. U.S. musician. First jazzman to use written arrangements, pioneering the regimented jazz bands and dance bands of the 1930s; bandleader and arranger.

HERMAN, WOODY, born Woodrow Charles, May 16, 1913 (Milwaukee, Wisc.). U.S. musician. Orchestra leader since 1936; Grammy award, 1963 and 1973–74. Compositions: "Apple Honey," "Northwest Passage," "Blowin' Up a Storm," "Blues on Parade."

HIGGINBOTHAM, JAY C., May 11, 1906 (Atlanta, Ga.)–May 26, 1973. U.S. jazz trombonist, singer. Appeared and recorded with such artists as FLETCHER HENDERSON, LOUIS ARMSTRONG, and RED ALLEN, from the 1930s.

THE BOOK OF WHO

HINES, EARL ("Fatha"), Dec. 28, 1905 (Duquesne, Pa.). U.S. musician. Jazz pianist, bandleader, and composer; leading influence in development of swing.

HIRT, AL, Nov. 7, 1922 (New Orleans, La.). U.S. musician. Rotund jazz trumpeter whose career began in 1940; many records, club, concert, TV appearances; played at Pres. Kennedy's inaugural ball, 1961; part-owner of New Orleans Saints football team.

HODGES, JOHNNY, born John Cornelius Hodges, July 25, 1906 (Cambridge, Mass.)–May 11, 1970. U.S. jazz alto saxophonist. Popular in 1930s and 1940s; appeared with DUKE ELLINGTON for 40 years.

JACKSON, MILT, Jan. 1, 1923 (Detroit, Mich.). U.S. musician. Jazz vibraphonist, pianist and guitarist; with WOODY HERMAN, 1949–50; with Modern Jazz Quartet, 1953–74.

JAMES, HARRY, Mar. 15, 1916 (Albany, Ga.). U.S. musician. Trumpeter, bandleader, at peak of his popularity in the 1930s and 1940s. (One-time husband of BETTY GRABLE.)

JAN AND DEAN: Jan Berry, Apr. 3, 1941 (Los Angeles, Calif.); and Dean Torrance, Mar. 10, 1940 (Los Angeles, Calif.). U.S. musicians. The epitome of California surfer-rock of the 1960s, this vocal duo had many hits until 1967, when act disbanded after Jan was seriously injured in auto accident. Songs: "Linda," 1961; "Surf City," 1963; "Dead Man's Curve," 1963; "The Little Old Lady (From Pasadena)," 1964; "Ride the Wild Surf," 1964.

JOHNSON, BUNK, born William Geary Johnson, Dec. 27, 1879 (New Orleans, La.)–July 7, 1949. U.S. jazz musician. Cornet and trumpet player of traditional New Orleans jazz style.

JOHNSON, J. J., Jan. 22, 1924 (Indianapolis, Ind.). U.S. musician. Jazz trombonist and composer; with COUNT BASIE, 1945–47; headed own quintet and sextet, 1957–61; with MILES DAVIS group, 1961– .

JONES, QUINCY, Mar. 14, 1933 (Chicago, Ill.). U.S. musician. Composer, arranger, conductor; composed film scores, including *Banning* (1967), *Cactus Flower* (1969) and *The Anderson Tapes* (1971); arranged for many singers, including SARAH VAUGHAN and PEGGY LEE.

JONES, SPIKE, born Lindley Armstrong Jones, Dec. 14, 1911 (Long Beach, Calif.)–May 1, 1965. U.S. musician. Bandleader whose forte was zany variations on popular songs, often with odd instruments and sound effects.

KAYE, SAMMY, Mar. 13, 1913 (Lakewood, Ohio). U.S. bandleader. Most famous for his "So you want to lead a band?" audience-participation routine; brought his "swing-and-sway" music to TV on *The Sammy Kaye Show*, 1950–59.

KENTON, STAN, Feb. 19, 1912 (Wichita, Kan.)–Aug. 25, 1979. U.S. musician, arranger. Led own jazz orchestra since 1941; music characterized by the screaming "walls of brass"; worldwide concert appearances; theme songs were "Artistry in Rhythm" and "Eager Beaver."

KING, WAYNE, ("The Waltz King"), Feb. 16, 1901 (Savannah, Ill.). U.S. dance-band leader popular in 1930s and 1940s.

KOOPER, AL, Feb. 5, 1944 (Brooklyn, N.Y.). U.S. musician. Guitarist/singer best known as founder of two important rock groups: The Blues Project, (1965) and BLOOD, SWEAT & TEARS (1967); recorded famous "super session" with STEPHEN STILLS and Mike Bloomfield (1968), before turning his energies to solo work and record-producing.

KRUPA, GENE, Jan. 15, 1909 (Chicago, Ill.)–Oct. 16, 1973. U.S. drummer, bandleader. Played with BENNY GOODMAN, 1935; led own band, 1938–51.

LADNIER, TOMMY, May 28, 1900 (Mandeville, La.)–June 4, 1939. U.S. jazz cornetist. Appeared with KING OLIVER, FLETCHER HENDERSON, Noble Sissle.

LED ZEPPELIN: John Bonham, May 31, 1947 (Birmingham, Eng.); John Paul Jones, Jan. 3, 1946 (London, Eng.); Jimmy Page, Jan. 9, 1944 (Middlesex, Eng.); Robert Plant, Aug. 20, 1947 (Birmingham, Eng.). English musicians. Formed leading hard-rock group in 1968, which survived through the 1970s; performed at Woodstock, 1969. Songs: "Whole Lotta Love," 1969.

LEWIS, RAMSEY, May 27, 1935 (Chicago, Ill.). U.S. musician. Pianist/songwriter who formed jazz trio (1956) that became very popular after record "The In Crowd," 1965; re-formed trio in 1970.

LEWIS, TED, born Theodore Leopold Friedman, June 6, 1892 (Circleville, Ohio)–Aug. 25, 1971. U.S. bandleader. Clarinetist, singer, and bandleader whose trademark was phrase, "Is everybody happy?"; vaudeville, club, and film appearances.

LOMBARDO, GUY, June 19, 1902 (London, Ont., Can.)–Nov. 5, 1977. Can.-U.S. bandleader. Led his band, The Royal Canadiens, from 1929, into musical history, playing "the sweetest music this side of heaven"; his annual New Year's Eve performance became national event, via radio and TV.

LUNCEFORD, JIMMIE, June 6, 1902 (Fulton, Miss.)–July 13, 1947. U.S. musician. Jazz bandleader and saxophonist; with FLETCHER HENDERSON orch., 1920; formed own band, 1929.

MANN, HERBIE, born Herbert Jay Solomon, Apr. 16, 1930 (Brooklyn, N.Y.). U.S. musician. Jazz flutist, first came to prominence in Matt Mathews Quintet, 1953–54; formed own Afro-jazz sextet, 1959; exponent of the bossa nova; incorporated rhythm-and-blues, disco, reggae into music. "Comin' Home Baby," 1962; "Hi Jack," 1975; "I Got a Woman," 1976.

MANNE, SHELLY, June 11, 1920 (New York, N.Y.). U.S. musician. Big Band jazz drummer; since 1939, with several orchestras, including STAN KENTON, WOODY HERMAN; led own band, 1955– ; owner of The Manne-Hole, a Hollywood jazz club, 1960– .

MARLEY, BOB, c.1946 (Kingston, Jamaica). W. Indian musician. With his group The Wailers, leading exponent of *reggae* music in the 1960s and 1970s. Songs: "Rude Boy," 1967; "I Can See Clearly Now," 1973; "I Shot the Sheriff," 1974; "Catch a Fire," 1975; "Natty Dread," 1976.

MCDONALD, "COUNTRY" JOE, Jan. 1, 1942 (El Monte, Calif.). U.S. singer, bandleader. With his group The Fish, extremely popular protest-rock singer of late 1960s; vaulted to fame with anti-Vietnam War song "I Feel Like I'm Fixin' to Die Rag" (1965); one of performers at Woodstock, 1969.

MCPARTLAND, JIMMY, born James Duigald McPartland, Mar. 15, 1907 (Chicago, Ill.). U.S. musician. Leading cornetist in tradition of BIX BEIDERBECKE; often plays with wife MARIAN; one of the "Chicago-style" jazzmen.

MCPARTLAND, MARIAN MARGARET, née Turner, Mar. 20, 1920 (Windsor, Eng.). U.S. musician. Jazz pianist/composer who has had own trio since 1951; known for subtle shadings of music at slow tempos.

MENDES, SERGIO, Feb. 11, 1941 (Niteroi, Braz.). Brazilian musician. Formed Brasil '66 (later called

286

ENTERTAINERS

Brasil '77), Latin pop-rock group that was very popular in late 1960s and 1970s; known for distinctive arrangements of tunes from COLE PORTER, THE BEATLES, others. Songs: "Constant Rain," 1966; "Mas Que Nada," 1967; "Night and Day," 1967; "Fool on the Hill," 1968; "Scarborough Fair," 1969; "Pais Tropical," 1971.

MESSINA, JIM, Dec. 5, 1947 (Maywood, Calif.). U.S. musician. With KENNY LOGGINS, formed Loggins and Messina country-rock band, popular in the 1970s; previously with 1960s groups Buffalo Springfield (1967–68) and Poco (1968–70).

MILLER, GLENN, Mar. 1, 1904 (Clarinda, Ia.)–Dec. 16, 1944. U.S. bandleader, trombonist. A prime force in the Big Band era of the 1930s and 1940s; noted for producing the "Glenn Miller" sound, a blending of clarinets and saxophones to produce a mellow tone.

MINGUS, CHARLES, Apr. 22, 1922 (Nogales, Ariz.)–Jan. 12, 1979. U.S. musician. Jazz bass player and a major figure in jazz of the 1950s and 1960s; renowned as teacher; first to exploit bass as solo instrument; led Jazz Workshop Bands, 1959–1977; semi-retired after 1965 because of ill health. "The Black Saint and the Sinner Lady"; "Thrice Upon a Theme"; "Revelations."

MONK, THELONIOUS SPHERE, Oct. 10, 1918 (Rocky Mount, N.C.). U.S. musician. Pianist/composer and pioneer of "bop"; played with John B. Crosby, DIZZY GILLESPIE, and CHARLIE PARKER, among others.

MONROE, VAUGHN, Oct. 7, 1911 (Akron, Ohio)–May 21, 1973. U.S. musician. Bandleader of his own group, from 1940; as singer, known for the "muscular" quality of his voice. Compositions: "Racing with the Moon" (theme song), "Something Sentimental," "Dance, Ballerina, Dance."

MONTGOMERY, WES, born John Leslie Montgomery, Mar. 6, 1925 (Indianapolis, Ind.)–June 15, 1968. U.S. musician. Jazz guitarist, first prominent as member of the Mastersounds, 1958; has led own trio since; developed parallel-octaves style of playing that is much imitated.

MORTON, JELLY ROLL, born Ferdinand Morton, Sept. 20, 1885 (New Orleans, La.)–July 10, 1941. Considered to be one of the inventors of jazz. Got his start playing piano in the bordellos of New Orleans' notorious Storyville; traveled U.S., playing and studying ragtime and jazz styles, from 1907; began recording with New Orleans Rhythm Kings, 1923; formed and recorded with his own band, The Red Hot Peppers, 1926–30. Compositions: "King Porter Stomp," 1924; "Jelly Roll Blues," 1915.

MULLIGAN, GERRY, born Gerald Joseph Mulligan, Apr. 6, 1927 (New York, N.Y.). U.S. musician. Baritone saxophonist/arranger with a number of jazz groups and bands; leader of own quartet, 1951–

NASH, GRAHAM, 1942 (Lancashire, Eng.). English musician. Guitarist, singer, songwriter, with NEIL YOUNG, David Crosby, and STEPHEN STILLS formed 1960s rock group Crosby, Stills, Nash and Young (1968–70).

NAVARRO, THEODORE ("Fats," "Fat Girl"). Sept. 24, 1923 (Key West, Fla.)–July 7, 1950. U.S. musician. Jazz trumpeter of the bop persuasion, noted for clean, pure tone; played with Andy Kirk (1943–44), Billy Eckstine (1944–46), Todd Dameron (1948–49).

NICHOLS, RED, born Ernest Loring Nichols, May 8, 1905 (Ogden, Utah)–June 28, 1965. U.S. musician. Cornetist and bandleader known for slick style; his group, The Five Pennies (really 10

people) was very popular in 1930s and 1940s; famous Pennies include JIMMY DORSEY, BENNY GOODMAN, GLENN MILLER.

NOONE, JIMMIE, Apr. 23, 1895 (Cut-Off, La.)–Apr. 19, 1944. U. S. musician. Clarinetist who led own group from 1927, when group appeared at Chicago's Apex Club; known for blending of New Orleans and swing. "Sweet Lorraine"; "I Know That You Know"; "Sweet Sue"; "Four or Five Times"; "Apex Blues."

NORVO, RED, Mar. 31, 1908 (Beardstown, Ill.). U.S. musician. Pioneer of use of xylophone and vibraphone in jazz; with PAUL WHITEMAN (1924–34), then on own with various-sized groups.

OLIVER, KING, born Joseph Oliver, 1885? (Abend, La.)–Apr. 8, 1938. U.S. musician. Trumpeter in many New Orleans jazz bands, 1907–19; formed the Creole Jazz Band (1922), which gave LOUIS ARMSTRONG his start and was the first black jazz group to record (1923).

ORY, KID, born Edward Ory, Dec. 25, 1886 (La Place, La.)–Jan. 23, 1973. U.S. musician. Leading exponent of New Orleans jazz; trombonist known for "tailgate" style; led own band, 1919–24; worked Chicago scene, 1925–29; retired in 1930, but came back in 1942; "Muskrat Ramble" his most famous piece.

PARKER, CHARLIE ("Bird," "Yardbird"), born Charles Christopher Parker, Jr., Aug. 29, 1920 (Kansas City, Kan.)–Mar. 12, 1955. U.S. musician. Legendary jazz alto saxophonist; co-creator of bebop, 1945; leading force in 52nd Street jazz scene in New York City; arrested and hospitalized for drug abuse, 1946. "Now's the Time"; "Yardbird Suite"; "Confirmation"; "Relaxin' at Camarillo."

PETERSON, OSCAR EMANUEL, Aug. 15, 1925 (Montreal, Que., Can.). Canadian pianist. Leading jazz pianist; has led own trio since 1950; *Down Beat magazine awards,* 1950–54, 1960–63, 1965.

PETTIFORD, OSCAR, Sept. 30, 1922 (Okmulgee, Okla.)–Sept. 8, 1960. U.S. musician. Jazz bass player/composer who pioneered use of pizzicato jazz cello. "Swingin' til the Girls Come Home"; "Black-Eyed Peas and Collard Greens"; "Tricrotism."

POWELL, BUD, Sept. 27, 1924 (New York, N.Y.)–July 31, 1966. U.S. musician. Considered founder of modern jazz piano technique (bebop); associated with Minton's Play House group in New York City and Cootie Williams band.

PRIMA, LOUIS, Dec. 7, 1912 (New Orleans, La.)–Aug. 24, 1978. U.S. musician. Trumpet-player and singer who led his own band since 1940.

RICH, BUDDY, born Bernard Rich, June 30, 1917 (Brooklyn, N.Y.). U.S. musician. Child prodigy on drums, playing in vaudeville at age four; played with many Big Bands and jazz bands, from 1938; *Down Beat* awards: 1941–42, 1944, 1947, 1967 and 1970–72.

RIDDLE, NELSON SMOCK, June 1, 1921 (Hackensack, N.J.). U.S. musician. Bandleader and composer of music for TV and films; music dir., Reprise Records, 1963–   ; guest conductor, Hollywood Bowl, 1954–60.

ROACH, MAX (well Lemuel), Jan. 10, 1924 (Elizabeth City, N.C.). U.S. musician. Jazz percussionist who adapted jazz to tympani; with M'Boom Le group since 1972; prof. of music at Amherst C., 1972–

ROGERS, SHORTY, born Milton M. Rogers, Apr. 14, 1924 (Great Barrington, Mass.). U.S. musician. Trumpeter in several jazz bands in 1940s and

287

1950s; arranger and composer, chiefly for STAN KENTON; frequent back-up on recordings.

ROLLINS, SONNY, born Theodore Walter Rollins, Sept. 7, 1929 (New York, N.Y.). U.S. musician. Tenor saxophonist known for hard bop style; credited by some as first to improvise a complete, overall pattern in solo.

RUGOLO, PETE(r), Dec. 25, 1916 (San Piero Patti, Sicily). U.S. musician. Jazz-pop composer who rose to prominence as arranger for STAN KENTON, 1945–49; composed scores for TV series, including *Richard Diamond,* 1958–60; *Thriller,* 1962; *The Fugitive,* 1963–65; *Run for Your Life,* 1965–66.

RUSSELL, PEE WEE, born Charles Ellsworth Russell, Mar. 27, 1906 (St. Louis, Mo.)–Feb. 15, 1969. U.S. musician. Jazz clarinetist, part of New York City's 52nd Street jazz scene in the '30s; Dixieland player who branched out into swing and other styles; made comeback in 1951 after near-fatal illness.

SEVERINSEN, DOC, born Carl H. Severinsen, July 7, 1927 (Arlington, Ore.). U.S. musician. Trumpeter/bandleader best known as musical director of *Tonight Show* since 1967.

SHAW, ARTIE, born Arthur Arshawsky, May 23, 1910 (New York, N.Y.). U.S. musician. Bandleader and clarinetist; formed one of most popular Big Bands, 1936; known for swing and Latin music. "Begin the Beguine" (1940) most popular song.

SHEARING, GEORGE, Aug. 13, 1919 (London, Eng.). British musician. Blind since birth, a major force in jazz piano since 1950s; became popular in U.S. as pianist at Birdland in New York City; has led quintet since 1947.

SILVER, HORACE WARD MARTIN TAVARES, Sept. 2, 1928 (Norwalk, Conn.). U.S. jazz musician, pianist, composer. Leader of the Horace Silver Quintet, 1955– . Compositions: "Senor Blues," 1956; "Sister Sadie," 1959; "Blowin' the Blues Away," 1959; "Que Pasa?," 1965.

SINGLETON, ZUTTY, born Arthur James Singleton, May 14, 1898 (Bunkier, La.)–July 14, 1975. U.S. musician. Pioneer in New Orleans-style jazz drumming; played with most great bands of 1920s–1960s; most famous as member of LOUIS ARMSTRONG's Hot Five.

SMITH, JOE, June 1902 (Ohio)–Dec. 2, 1937. U.S. musician. Jazz trumpeter in FLETCHER HENDERSON's Black Swan Jazz Masters group; played for ETHEL WATERS, BESSIE SMITH, many others in 1920s and 1930s.

SMITH, PINETOP, born Clarence Smith, June 11, 1904 (Troy, Ala.)–Mar. 14, 1929. U.S. musician. Pioneered the boogie-woogie style of piano playing, developing "8-to-a-bar"; on the MA RAINEY vaudeville circuit; killed in a brawl.

SMITH, WILLIE ("The Lion"), born William Henry Joseph Berthel Bonaparte Bertholoff, Nov. 25, 1897 (Goshen, N.Y.)–Apr. 18, 1973. U.S. musician. Major influence in 1920s as ragtime-stride pianist; branched out into jazz, making many recordings.

SPANIER, MUGGSY, born Francis Joseph Spanier, Nov. 9, 1906 (Chicago, Ill.)–Feb. 12, 1967. U.S. musician. Cornetist who was central figure in Dixieland jazz scene; with Ted Lewis band, 1929–36; led own band, 1941–43; best known for use of plunger mute.

SPITALNY, PHIL, 1890 (Romanoff, Rus.)–Oct. 11, 1970. U.S. bandleader. Conducted an all-girl orchestra on the *Hour of Charm* radio show, and on TV and the concert stage, 1935–55.

STILLS, STEPHEN, Jan. 3, 1945 (Dallas, Tex.).

U.S. musician. Major influence in pop-rock from 1966; cofounder of Buffalo Springfield rock group, 1966–7; joined with GRAHAM NASH and DAVID CROSBY to form Crosby, Stills & Nash group, 1968–70; solo performer since 1970. Songs: "Change Partners"; "Blue Bird"; "Suite: Judy Blue Eyes"; "Love the One You're With"; "49 Bye-Byes."

STITT, SONNY, born Edward Stitt, Feb. 2, 1924 (Boston, Mass.). U.S. musician. Tenor/alto saxophonist noted for bop work in the 1940s and 1950s; disciple of CHARLIE PARKER; associated with DIZZY GILLESPIE groups, 1945–46 and 1958.

TATUM, ART, Oct. 3, 1910 (Toledo, Ohio)–Nov. 4, 1956. U.S. musician. Partially sighted pianist known for highly original technique and harmonic variations; led trio, 1943–55.

TAYLOR, BILLY, born William Edward Taylor, July 24, 1921 (Greenville, N.C.). U.S. musician. Jazz pianist with orchestras, jazz bands; music dir. of DAVID FROST's TV show, 1969; composer of the musical, *Your Arms Too Short to Box with God,* 1977.

TEAGARDEN, JACK WELDON LEE, Aug. 20, 1905 (Vernon, Tex.)–Jan. 15, 1964. U.S. trombonist, orchestra leader. Played with Pete Kelly, RED NICHOLS (1928–33) and PAUL WHITEMAN (1934–38) bands; had his own orchestra, 1939–46; collaborated with GLENN MILLER on the lyrics for "Basin Street Blues."

WALKER, JUNIOR, c.1942 (South Bend, Ind.). U.S. musician. Saxophonist; leader of the group "The All Stars"; a major force in 1960s rhythm-and-blues music.

WALLER, FATS, born Thomas Waller, May 21, 1904 (New York, N.Y.)–Dec. 15, 1943. U.S. musician. Leading jazz pianist; got his start (1919) playing in cabarets; accompanied BESSIE SMITH (and others); began recording, 1934; as stride pianist, refined technique; first to use jazz organ; "Ain't Misbehavin'"; "Honeysuckle Rose"; "Keepin' Out of Mischief Now"; "Squeeze Me."

WARING, FRED M., June 9, 1900 (Tyrone, Pa.). U.S. conductor. His chorus, The Pennsylvanians, has sung on numerous tours and radio and TV shows, 1923– .

WEATHERFORD, TEDDY, Oct. 11, 1903 (Bluefield, W. Va.)–Apr. 25, 1945. U.S. musician. Pianist and leading exponent of "Chicago-style" jazz in 1920s; went to the Far East, (1926), becoming a fixture at the Grand Hotel in Calcutta, India, where he played until his death.

WEBB, CHICK, born William Webb, Feb. 10, 1909 (Baltimore, Md.)–June 16, 1939. U.S. musician. Drummer and leader of Harlem Stompers band featured at the Savoy Ballroom in Harlem, 1927–39; introduced ELLA FITZGERALD as vocalist, 1935.

WELK, LAWRENCE, Mar. 11, 1903 (Strasburg, N.D.). U.S. musician. An accordionist, he started own band in 1927; his TV show, featuring wholesome soloists, was a big hit on network TV (1955–71) and is still thriving in syndication.

WHITEMAN, PAUL SAMUEL ("The King of Jazz"), Mar. 28, 1891 (Denver, Col.)–Dec. 29, 1967. U.S. musician. Jovial, rotund bandleader noted for giving many famous performers their starts; introduced Ferde Grofe's *Grand Canyon Suite* and GEORGE GERSHWIN's *Rhapsody in Blue* in concert.

WILLIAMS, CHARLES MELVIN ("Cootie"), July 24, 1908. U.S. musician. Jazz trumpeter who played with Eagle Eye Shields band (1925-26), DUKE ELLINGTON (1929-40), BENNY GOODMAN, many others.

WILLIAMS, ROGER, Oct. 1, 1926 (Omaha, Neb.). U.S. pianist/composer. Started as hotel pianist; appeared in concerts and on TV and made numerous records.

YARBOROUGH, GLENN, Jan. 12, 1930 (Milwaukee, Wis.). U.S. musician. Began as folksinger/guitarist in Limeliters group, 1959-63; now a solo performer in country-and-western field; formed Stanyan Music Co. with ROD MCKUEN, 1968.

YOUNG, LESTER ("Prez"), Aug. 27, 1909 (Woodville, Miss.)-Mar. 15, 1959. U.S. musician. Jazz saxophonist with the COUNT BASIE, KING OLIVER and Andy Kirk bands; had his own sextette, from 1942; composed several songs, including "Tickle Toe."

OTHER ENTERTAINERS

ACUFF, ROY, Sept. 15, 1903 (Maynardsville, Tenn.). U.S. country-and-western entertainer, record company exec. Known as the "King of Country Music."

ARLEN, HAROLD, Feb. 15, 1905 (Buffalo, N.Y.). U.S. composer. Composed Broadway scores, film musicals (notably, The Wizard of Oz, 1939) and many pop standards. Songs: "Get Happy"; "I Love a Parade"; "Stormy Weather"; "Blues in the Night"; "That Old Black Magic"; "One for My Baby"; "The Man That Got Away."

BACHARACH, BURT, May 12, 1929 (Kansas City, Mo.). U.S. composer, pianist. Wrote many popular songs, often with Hal David; composed score for Broadway musical Promises, Promises (1969). Songs: "What the World Needs Now"; "I'll Never Fall in Love Again"; "The Look of Love"; "Raindrops Keep Falling on My Head" (AA, 1970); "Close to You"; "One Less Bell to Answer." (One-time husband of ANGIE DICKINSON.)

BAIRD, BIL, born William Britton Baird, Aug. 15, 1904 (Grand I. Neb.). U.S. puppeteer. With wife Cora, led 20th-cent. revival of the puppet theater; ardent advocate of planned parenthood who used his puppets to aid the movement.

BALL, ERNEST, July 22, 1878 (Cleveland, Ohio)-May 3, 1927. U.S. composer. Wrote many popular turn-of-the-century sentimental songs, including "Mother Machree," "A Little Bit of Heaven," "Let the Rest of the World Go By," and "When Irish Eyes Are Smiling."

BARNUM, P(hineas) T(aylor), July 5, 1810 (Bethel, Conn.)-Apr. 7, 1871. U.S. showman. Entrepreneur extraordinaire in entertainment; operated New York City museum (1842-68) featuring freaks, wonders and midget Tom Thumb, who attracted 82 million visitors; brought JENNY LIND, the "Swedish Nightingale," to U.S. for concert tour; formed Barnum and Bailey Circus, 1871; reputedly said, "There's a sucker born every minute."

BERLIN, IRVING, born Israel Baline, May 11, 1888 (Russia). U.S. composer. Has written more than 800 pop songs, as well as scores for Broadway musicals; received Congressional Gold Medal for song "God Bless America." Songs: "Alexander's Ragtime Band"; "A Pretty Girl Is like a Melody"; "All by Myself"; "Easter Parade"; "Cheek to Cheek"; "White Christmas" (AA). Plays scored include Annie Get Your Gun (1946) and Call Me Madam (1950).

BERNSTEIN, ELMER, Apr. 4, 1922 (New York,

N.Y.) U.S. composer. Has written scores for numerous films; received 1968 AA for score of the film Thoroughly Modern Millie.

BLANC, MEL, May 30, 1908 (San Francisco, Calif.). U.S. entertainer. Voice of many cartoon characters, including Bugs Bunny, Porky Pig, Daffy Duck.

BOCK, JERRY, born Jerrold Lewis Bock, Nov. 23, 1928 (New Haven, Conn.). U.S. composer. Composed many Broadway show scores. Plays scored: Mr. Wonderful, 1956; Fiorello! (Tony), 1959; She Loves Me, 1963; Fiddler on the Roof, 1964; The Apple Tree, 1966; The Rothschilds, 1972.

BOWES, MAJOR EDWARD, 1874 (San Francisco, Calif.)-June 13, 1946. U.S. radio personality. Originated the Major Bowes Amateur Hour (1934), which became (on his death) Ted Mack's Original Amateur Hour.

BREL, JACQUES, Apr. 8, 1929 (Brussels, Belg.)-Oct. 9, 1978. Belgian composer, singer. Best known in U.S. for musical based on his lyrics, Jacques Brel Is Alive and Well and Living in Paris, 1968.

BURKE, JOHNNY, Oct. 3, 1908 (Antioch, Calif.)-Feb. 25, 1964. U.S. songwriter. Wrote popular songs such as "Pennies from Heaven," "Moonlight Becomes You," and "Swinging on a Star" (AA, 1944).

CARMICHAEL, HOAGY, born Hoagland Howard Carmichael, Nov. 22, 1899 (Bloomington, Ind.). U.S. composer, pianist, singer. Wrote many hits and appeared as actor in some films; regular on the TV series Laramie, 1959-63. Songs: "Georgia on My Mind"; "Rockin' Chair"; "Nearness of You"; "Stardust"; "Two Sleepy People"; "In the Cool, Cool, Cool of the Evening" (AA, 1951).

CARTE, (Richard) D'OYLY, May 3, 1844 (London, Eng.)-Apr. 3, 1901. English impresario. Formed Comedy Opera Company Ltd., which introduced the works of Lecocq and OFFENBACH to England, 1876; founded the Savoy Theatre, home of GILBERT and SULLIVAN productions and London's first theater to use electric lighting, 1881.

CAVETT, DICK, Nov. 19, 1936 (Gibbon, Neb.). U.S. entertainer. Former comedy writer and performer turned talk-show host; shows on ABC in competition with Tonight Show were not successful; since 1978, host of daily talk show on PBS.

COHAN, GEORGE M(ichael), July 3, 1878 (Providence, R.I.)-Nov. 5, 1942. U.S. entertainer. Best known personality of his day, a versatile actor, singer, dancer, songwriter, and producer; starred in numerous musicals. Songs: "I'm a Yankee Doodle Dandy"; "Give My Regards to Broadway"; "You're a Grand Old Flag"; "Mary's a Grand Old Name"; "Over There."

COMDEN, BETTY, May 3, 1919 (New York, N.Y.). U.S. lyricist, singer. Began as performer in Greenwich Village nightclubs; wrote book and lyrics for many Broadway hits, with partner ADOLPH GREEN. Plays: On the Town, 1944; Wonderful Town, 1953; Bells Are Ringing, 1956; Subways Are For Sleeping, 1961.

CROSS, MILTON JOHN, Apr. 16, 1897 (New York, N.Y.)-Jan. 3, 1975. U.S. radio announcer. Best known for his Saturday afternoon broadcasts from the Metropolitan Opera, 1931-74.

CULLEN, WILLIAM LAWRENCE ("Bill"), Feb. 18, 1920 (Pittsburgh, Pa.). U.S. game show personality. Host and guest on many TV game shows; best known as panelist on To Tell the Truth and as a host of The Price is Right and $25,000 Pyramid.

DALY, JOHN CHARLES, JR., Feb. 20, 1914

(Johannesburg, S.A.). U.S. broadcaster. A radio and TV news correspondent best known as moderator of TV's long-running *What's My Line?*, 1950–67.

DESYLVA, B(uddy) G(eorge Gard), Jan. 27, 1895 (New York, N.Y.)–July 11, 1950. U.S. composer, librettist. Wrote, often in partnership with Lew Brown and Ray Henderson, several scores for Broadway and films.

DIETZ, HOWARD, Sept. 8, 1896 (New York, N.Y.). U.S. lyricist. In collaboration with ARTHUR SCHWARTZ, wrote scores for Broadway shows and songs. Songs: "I Love Louisa"; "Dancing in the Dark"; "You and the Night and the Music"; "By Myself"; "That's Entertainment."

DISNEY, WALTER ELIAS, Dec. 5, 1901 (Chicago, Ill.)–Dec. 15, 1966. U.S. film producer. Leader in movie animation; introduced Mickey Mouse in his first cartoon, *Steamboat Willie* (1928); produced first feature-length cartoon, *Snow White*, 1937; produced first live-action animated film, *The Reluctant Dragon*, 1941; built Disneyland, 1955; awarded numerous Acad. Awards. Movies: *Pinocchio*, 1940; *Fantasia*, 1940; *Bambi*, 1942; *The Shaggy Dog*, 1959; *Pollyanna*, 1960; *Davy Crockett*, 1955; *Mary Poppins*, 1964.

DONALDSON, WALTER, Feb. 15, 1893 (Brooklyn, N.Y.)–July 13, 1947. U.S. composer. Wrote music for many Broadway shows and composed songs. Songs: "The Daughter of Rosie O'Grady"; "How Ya Gonna Keep 'em Down on the Farm?"; "My Buddy"; "Carolina in the Morning"; "Yes Sir, That's My Baby"; "My Blue Heaven"; "Little White Lies."

DOUGLAS, MIKE, born Michael Dowd, Aug. 11, 1925 (Chicago, Ill.). U.S. TV personality. A former Big Band-era singer, has his own talk show; won Emmy award.

DOWNS, HUGH MALCOLM, Feb. 14, 1921 (Akron, Ohio). U.S. TV personality. Announcer of TV's *Jack Paar Show* (later, *Tonight Show*), 1957–62; host of TV's *Today Show*, 1962–72; host of TV game show *Concentration*, 1958–68; host of *Over Easy*, PBS series on aging (1978).

EDWARDS, CLIFF ("Ukelele Ike"), 1897 (Hannibal, Mo.)–July 17, 1971. U.S. entertainer. Performed in vaudeville and appeared in some films; was voice of Jiminy Cricket in Disney movie *Pinocchio* (1940) and in subsequent features and shorts.

EDWARDS, GUS, Aug. 18, 1879 (Hohensaliza, Ger.)–Nov. 7, 1945. U.S. composer, producer. Vaudeville and stage-show producer who discovered EDDIE CANTOR, GEORGE JESSEL, ELEANOR POWELL, RAY BOLGER, among others; wrote the songs "School Days" and "By the Light of the Silvery Moon."

EMMETT, DANIEL DECATUR, Oct. 29, 1815 (Mt. Vernon, Ohio)–June 28, 1904. U.S. minstrel, songwriter. Organized the first "Negro Minstrel show," 1843; composed "Dixie."

EPSTEIN, BRIAN, Sept. 19, 1934 (Liverpool, Eng.)–Aug. 27, 1967. English music-group mgr. Managed the Beatles from humble beginnings in 1961 to rock superstardom by the time he died, in swimming pool accident.

FAIN, SAMMY, June 17, 1902 (New York, N.Y.). U.S. composer. Wrote Broadway musicals, numerous film scores. Songs: "Secret Love" (AA), 1953; "Love Is a Many-Splendored Thing" (AA), 1955; "Let a Smile Be Your Umbrella"; "When I Take My Sugar to Tea"; "That Old Feeling"; "April Love."

FALKENBURG, JINX, Jan. 21, 1919 (Barcelona, Sp.). U.S. radio and TV commentator. With TEX MCCRARY, formed a husband-and-wife radio and TV team; the first Miss Rheingold (1941), at which time she was the highest-paid model in the U.S.

FIELDS, DOROTHY, July 15, 1905 (New York, N.Y.)–Mar. 28, 1974. U.S. lyricist. With brother Herbert, wrote many Broadway musicals and other songs. Musicals: *Up in Central Park*, 1945; *Annie Get Your Gun*, 1946. Songs: "I Can't Give You Anything But Love" (with JIMMY MCHUGH); "The Way You Look Tonight" (AA), 1936.

FOSTER, STEPHEN COLLINS, July 4, 1826 (Lawrenceville, Pa.)–Jan. 13, 1864. U.S. composer. Wrote classic minstrel songs and popular ballads of the mid-19th cent. Songs: "My Old Kentucky Home"; "Oh, Susanna"; "Old Folks at Home"; "Camptown Races"; "Old Black Joe"; "Beautiful Dreamer"; "Jeannie with the Light Brown Hair."

FOY, EDDIE, born Edward Fitzgerald, Mar. 9, 1857 (New York, N.Y.)–Feb. 16, 1928. U.S. entertainer. Appeared in song-and-dance act in vaudeville with "The Seven Little Foys," his children; impersonated in films by his son Eddie, Jr., and BOB HOPE.

FREED, ALAN, Dec. 15, 1922 (Johnstown, Pa.)–Jan. 20, 1965. U.S. entertainer. Radio disc jockey of 1940s and 1950s who coined the phrase *rock-and-roll* and was responsible for introducing performers of rhythm-and-blues to general audiences, on long-running WINS (New York City) radio show, 1954–60; emcee of many rock-and-roll concerts nationwide.

FRIML, (Charles) RUDOLF, Dec. 7, 1879 (Prague, Czech.)–Nov. 12, 1972. U.S.–Czech. composer. Composed several popular operettas. *The Firefly*, 1912; *Rose Marie*, 1924; *The Vagabond King*, 1925.

FROST, DAVID PARRADINE, Apr. 7, 1939 (Tenterden, Eng.). English TV personality. First came to notice in U.S. on satirical prime-time show *That Was the Week That Was*, 1962–63; had own talk shows in Great Britian, U.S.; made news with series of interviews with former Pres. R. M. NIXON, 1977.

FUNT, ALLEN, Sept. 16, 1914 (New York, N.Y.). U.S. TV personality. Creator and host of TV's *Candid Camera* program, from early 1950s; produced film *What Do You Say to a Naked Lady?*, 1970.

GARROWAY, DAVE, July 13, 1913 (Schenectady, N.Y.). U.S. TV personality. Popular in 1950s; host of *Garroway at Large*, 1949–54; frequently appeared on the *Today Show* in the company of a chimpanzee named J. Fred Muggs.

GERSHWIN, IRA, Dec. 6, 1896 (New York, N.Y.). U.S. lyricist. Collaborator with brother GEORGE GERSHWIN on Broadway scores; after brother's death, worked with many of the 20th cent.'s most famous composers of theatrical and film music. Musicals: *Lady Be Good*, 1924; *Strike Up the Band*, 1929; *Girl Crazy*, 1930; *Of Thee I Sing* (Pulitzer), 1932; *Porgy and Bess*, 1935.

GODFREY, ARTHUR, Aug. 31, 1903 (New York, N.Y.). U.S. broadcaster. Began as newsman; quickly established himself on radio (then on TV) with folksy variety program that was one of the staples of the 1940s and 1950s (although it continued into the 1960s); appeared in some films.

GORDY, BERRY, JR., Nov. 28, 1929 (Detroit, Mich.). U.S. recording-co. exec. Founder and pres. of Motown Records (1959–   ), the nation's first successful record co. to feature rhythm-and-blues and soul music; responsible for making famous SMOKEY ROBINSON, THE SUPREMES, THE TEMPTATIONS, MARVIN GAYE, STEVIE

WONDER, among others; the music he produced called "Motown Sound."

GRAHAM, BILL, born Wolfgang Grajonca, 1931 (Berlin, Ger.). U.S. entrepreneur. His Fillmore concert halls in San Francisco (opened 1965) and New York City (opened 1968) vaulted rock groups such as Jefferson Airplane, Quicksilver Messenger Service and the Grateful Dead to national prominence; he closed both halls in 1971, after complaining about the commercialization of the rock-music industry.

GRAZIANO, ROCKY, June 7, 1922 (New York, N.Y.). U.S. boxer, TV personality. World middleweight boxing champ, 1947-48; numerous appearances on TV as both guest and pitchman for various products.

GREEN, ADOLPH, Dec. 2, 1915 (New York, N.Y.). U.S. actor, playwright, lyricist. Has collaborated on numerous Broadway hit shows with BETTY COMDEN, including On the Town (1944), Wonderful Town (1953), and Subways Are For Sleeping (1962). Awarded Tonys for cowriting music and lyrics for Hallelujah Baby (1967) and cowriting score for Applause (1967). (Husband of PHYLLIS NEWMAN.)

GRIFFIN, MERV, July 6, 1925 (San Mateo, Calif.). U.S. entertainer, talk-show host. Radio show host in San Francisco, Calif., 1945-48; host of TV's The Merv Griffin Show, 1962-63, 1965-69, and 1969-72; host of syndicated talk show 1972-   .

HALL, MONTY, 1925 (Winnipeg, Man., Can.). U.S. TV personality. Creator, producer, and host of popular TV game show Let's Make a Deal, 1963-   .

HAMMERSTEIN, OSCAR II, July 12, 1895 (New York, N.Y.)-Aug. 23, 1960. U.S. lyricist. Chiefly known for collaboration with RICHARD RODGERS on Broadway musicals, although he also worked with RUDOLF FRIML, JEROME KERN and SIGMUND ROMBERG. Musicals: Rose Marie, 1924; Showboat, 1927; New Moon, 1928; Oklahoma (Pulitzer), 1943; Carousel, 1945; South Pacific (Pulitzer), 1949; The King and I, 1951; Flower Drum Song, 1958; The Sound of Music, 1959.

HARBURG, E(dgar) Y. ("Yip"), Apr. 8, 1896 (New York, N.Y.). U.S. lyricist, librettist. Wrote lyrics for Broadway musicals and films. Plays: Ziegfeld Follies, 1934; Hold on to Your Hats, 1940; Bloomer Girl, 1941. Films: Wizard of Oz, 1938 (AA for "Over the Rainbow"); Kismet, 1944; Stage Struck, 1946. Songs: "Brother Can You Spare a Dime?," "Happiness is a Thing Called Joe."

HART, LORENZ MILTON ("Larry"), May 2, 1895 (New York, N.Y.)-Nov. 22, 1943. U.S. lyricist. Noted for witty, literate, expressive lyrics and his long, successful collaboration with RICHARD RODGERS on musical scores for plays such as Connecticut Yankee (1927), The Boys from Syracuse (1938), Pal Joey (1940), and By Jupiter (1942). Songs: "Manhattan," "Blue Moon," "The Lady Is a Tramp," "My Funny Valentine," "Falling in Love with Love," "I Didn't Know What Time It Was."

HARTMAN, DAVID DOWNS, May 19, 1935 (Pawtucket, R.I.). U.S. actor, TV host. Acted on several TV series (The Virginian [1968-69], The Bold Ones [1969-73] and Lucas Tanner [1974-75]) before becoming host of ABC's "Good Morning, America" show, 1975-

HAYS, WILL H., born William Harrison Hays, Nov. 5, 1879 (Sullivan, Ind.)-Mar. 7, 1954. U.S. politician, motion-picture exec. Chm. of Republican Natl. Com.; 1918-21; U.S. postmaster gen., 1921-22; as pres. (1922-45) of Motion Picture Producers and Distributors of America, administered so-called "Hays Code," the motion-picture morals code, promulgated in 1934.

HENSON, JAMES MAURY ("Jim"), Sept. 24, 1936 (Greenville, Miss.). U.S. puppeteer, TV producer. Creator of the Muppets, 1954; creator of Sesame Street muppets, 1969-   ; Muppet Show, 1976-   ; Muppet Movie, 1979; awarded Emmys for Outstanding Individual Achievement in Children's Programming, 1973-74 and 1975-76.

HERMAN, JERRY, July 10, 1932 (New York, N.Y.). U.S. composer, lyricist. Wrote Broadway musicals. Shows: Milk and Honey, 1961; Hello Dolly, 1964 (Tony award); Mame, 1966; The Grand Tour, 1979.

HOUDINI, HARRY, born Ehrich Weiss, Apr. 6, 1874 (Appleton, Wisc.)-Oct. 31, 1926. U.S. magician. A superstar of magic and an escape artist, many of whose tricks have not been unraveled to-date; noted for escapes from shackles, ropes, handcuffs, and locked containers; campaigned against fake mediums; in some silent films.

HUTTON, LAUREN, 1944 (Charleston, S.C.). U.S. model. Leading cover girl and high-fashion model of the 1970s, noted for her clean, fresh look; closely associated with Revlon, Inc.; has acted in several films.

JESSEL, GEORGE, Apr. 3, 1898 (New York, N.Y.). U.S. entertainer. In vaudeville from childhood; appeared on Broadway first in 1918; called "Toastmaster General of the U.S." for his frequent emcee role at charity affairs.

JOHNSON, HOWARD E., 1888? (Waterbury, Conn.)-May 1, 1941. U.S. songwriter. Wrote lyrics for "When the Moon Comes over the Mountain"; wrote music and lyrics for "M-O-T-H-E-R ("put 'em all together . . .")," and "There's a Broken Heart for Every Light on Broadway."

KEESHAN, ROBERT, June 27, 1927 (Lynbrook, N.Y.). U.S. TV personality. Appeared as Clarabelle the Clown on TV's Howdy Doody Show, 1947-52; best known as creator/producer/star of long-running Captain Kangaroo children's show 1955-

KERN, JEROME, Jan. 27, 1885 (New York, N.Y.)-Nov. 11, 1945. U.S. composer. Composer of over 50 Broadway shows and numerous songs. Shows: Leave It to Jane, 1917; Sally, 1920; Showboat, 1927; Roberta, 1933. Songs: "Look for the Silver Lining"; "Smoke Gets in Your Eyes"; "All the Things You Are"; "The Last Time I Saw Paris."

LAUDER, SIR HARRY, Aug. 4, 1870 (Edinburgh, Scot.)-Feb. 26, 1950. Scottish entertainer. A beloved star of British music hall and American vaudeville, known for his recitations while dressed in traditional kilt; appeared in a few films.

LEE, GYPSY ROSE, born Rose Louise Hovick, Jan. 9, 1914 (Seattle, Wash.)-Apr. 26, 1970. U.S. entertainer. Queen of U.S. burlesque in the 1940s, famed for her "intellectual" striptease act; musical play and film Gypsy based on her life; hosted TV talk show, 1969-70. (Sister of JUNE HAVOC.)

LEGRAND, MICHEL, 1932 (Paris, Fr.). French composer, conductor. Writer, arranger, conductor for over 50 film scores.

LERNER, ALAN JAY, Aug. 31, 1918 (New York, N.Y.). U.S. playwright, lyricist. Noted for his collaborations with F. LOEWE on Broadway musical comedies. Plays: Brigadoon, 1947; Paint Your Wagon, 1951; My Fair Lady (Tony), 1956; Camelot, 1960; On a Clear Day You Can See Forever, 1965. Screenplays: An American in Paris (AA), 1951; Gigi (AA), 1958.

THE BOOK OF WHO

LEWIS, SHARI, born Shari Hurwitz, Jan. 17, 1934 (New York, N.Y.). U.S. entertainer. Ventriloquist and puppeteer, she and her famous "Lambchop" entertained children on TV since 1950s; won five Emmys; won Peabody Award, 1960; had adult nightclub act; author of several children's books.

LIBERACE, born Wladziu Valentino, May 16, 1919 (W. Allis, Wisc.). U.S. entertainer. Toothy, flamboyant pianist; a sensation in nightclubs and on TV, beginning in the 1950s; won two Emmy awards.

LINKLETTER, ART, July 17, 1912 (Moose Jaw, Sask., Can.). Can.-U.S. broadcaster. Popular on radio and TV with several shows (House Party, People Are Funny, etc.) in 1950s and 1960s; author of several books, including Kids Say the Darndest Things.

LOESSER, FRANK, June 29, 1910 (New York, N.Y.)-July 28, 1961. U.S. composer. Composer of Broadway shows and many songs. Musicals scored: Where's Charley?, 1948; Guys and Dolls (Tony), 1951; The Most Happy Fella, 1956; How to Succeed in Business (Pulitzer), 1962.

LOEWE, FREDERICK, June 10, 1901 (Berlin, Ger.). U.S. composer. Noted for collaboration with A. J. LERNER on Broadway musical comedies. Musicals scored: Brigadoon, 1947; Paint Your Wagon, 1951; My Fair Lady (Tony), 1956; Camelot, 1960.

MANCINI, HENRY, April 16, 1924 (Cleveland, Ohio). U.S. composer. Pianist/composer of many songs and film scores; frequently collaborated with JOHNNY MERCER. Film scores: The Glenn Miller Story, 1953; Breakfast at Tiffany's, 1961; The Pink Panther, 1963. Songs: "Moon River"; "The Days of Wine and Roses"; "Charade"; "Dear Heart."

MARSHALL, PETER, born Pierre La Cock, ? (Huntington, W.Va.). U.S. TV host. Worked as a comedian in partnership with Tommy Noonan; host of the TV game show Hollywood Squares, 1966- .

MCBRIDE, MARY MARGARET, Nov. 16, 1899 (Paris, Mo.)-Apr. 7, 1976. U.S. radio commentator. Conducted a long series of daytime talk shows, featuring her homespun advice and interviews with most of the famous people of her day, 1934-54.

MCCRARY, TEX, born John Reagan McCrary, Oct. 13, 1910. U.S. radio and TV commentator. With JINX FALKENBURG, formed a husband-and-wife radio and TV team; previously worked as a reporter and editorial writer for the New York Mirror.

MCHUGH, JIMMY, July 10, 1894 (Boston, Mass.)-May 23, 1969. U.S. composer. Wrote scores for musical films and shows, as well as over 500 pop songs. Songs: "I Can't Give You Anything but Love, Baby"; "I Feel a Song Comin' On"; "On the Sunny Side of the Street"; "Lovely to Look At."

MCMAHON, ED(ward Leo Peter, Jr.), Mar. 6, 1923 (Detroit, Mich.). U.S. TV announcer. Best known as the announcer for JOHNNY CARSON, first on the game show Who Do You Trust? (from 1958) and then on the Tonight Show (1962-   ).

MERCER, JOHNNY, born John H. Mercer, Nov. 18, 1909 (Savannah, Ga.)-June 25, 1976. U.S. lyricist. Wrote many popular songs; an organizer of Capitol Records, 1942. Songs: "Goody-Goody"; "I'm an Old Cowhand"; "Hooray for Hollywood"; "Jeepers Creepers;" "Blues in the Night"; "On the Atchison, Topeka & Santa Fe"; "In the Cool, Cool, Cool of the Evening"; "Moon River"; "Days of Wine and Roses."

MIELZINER, JO, Mar. 19, 1901 (Paris, Fr.)-Mar. 15, 1976. U.S. stage designer. Has designed sets for more than 350 stage productions, including Hamlet, Carousel, Annie Get Your Gun, A Streetcar Named Desire, and Death of a Salesman; introduced the transparent skeletal framework setting to allow separate times and places to be shown simultaneously; with EERO SAARINEN, designed the Vivian Beaumont Theater, New York City.

MOORE, GARRY, born Thomas Garrison Morfit, Jan. 31, 1915 (Baltimore, Md.). U.S. TV personality. His show was one of most popular variety shows in history of the medium, 1950-64; emcee of I've Got a Secret (1953-64) and To Tell the Truth (1969-77).

MORGAN, HENRY, Mar. 31, 1915 (New York, N.Y.). U.S. entertainer. Known for regular TV appearances on quiz and panel shows, especially the TV series, I've Got a Secret, 1952-76.

NERO, PETER, May 22, 1934 (New York, N.Y.). U.S. pianist. Pop pianist with wide experience in clubs and on concert stage; many records; began professional career on tour with PAUL WHITEMAN, 1953-57.

OAKLEY, ANNIE, born Phoebe Anne Oakley Mozee, Aug. 13, 1860 (Patterson Twp., Ohio)-Nov. 3, 1926. U.S. entertainer. A marksman with rifle and shotgun, she joined BUFFALO BILL's Wild West Show in 1885 and was its star attraction for 17 years.

PAAR, JACK, May 1, 1918 (Canton, Ohio). U.S. TV personality. Former radio announcer; one of the pioneers of the TV talk show as host of the nightly Tonight Show (1957-62) and subsequent Jack Paar Show (1962-65, 1973).

PARKS, BERT, Dec. 30, 1914 (Atlanta, Ga.). U.S. TV personality. Ubiquitous emcee, best known for his annual hosting of the Miss America Pageant and his singing of the Miss America theme song, 1954-79.

PORTER, COLE, June 9, 1892 (Peru, Ind.)-Oct. 15, 1964. U.S. composer, lyricist. Witty lyricist and prolific composer known for the sophistication of his work. Started writing songs while at Yale U., 1916; crippled after a riding accident, 1937. Shows: 50 Million Frenchmen, 1929; The Gay Divorce, 1932; Anything Goes, 1934; DuBarry Was a Lady, 1939; Panama Hattie, 1940; Kiss Me Kate, 1948; Can-Can, 1953; Silk Stockings, 1955. Songs: "I Get a Kick Out of You"; "Begin the Beguine"; "I've Got You under My Skin"; "Night and Day."

RAYBURN, GENE, Dec. 22?, 1917 (Christopher, Ill.). U.S. broadcaster. Host on radio and TV. Radio: NBC Monitor, 1963-71. TV: Dough, Re, Mi, 1958-61; Tonight Show, 1954-59; Match Game, 1962-69 and 1972-

RINGLING, JOHN NICHOLAS, 1866 (Baraboo, Wisc.)-Dec. 3, 1936. U.S. circus owner. With his brother Charles, founded and operated the Ringling Bros. circus, 1884-1907; merged with Barnum & Bailey to form the "Greatest Show on Earth," 1907.

RODGERS, RICHARD, June 28, 1902 (New York, N.Y.)-Dec. 30, 1979. U.S. composer. Leading composer of American musical theater, noted for his collaborations with LORENZ HART and OSCAR HAMMERSTEIN II. Shows scored: Jumbo, 1935; Babes in Arms, 1937; The Boys from Syracuse, 1938; Pal Joey, 1940; Oklahoma, (Pulitzer), 1943; Carousel, 1945; South Pacific (Tony, Pulitzer), 1949; Flower Drum Song, 1958; The King and I (Tony), 1951; The Sound of Music, 1960; No Strings (Tony), 1962; I Remember Mama, 1979.

ROGERS, WILL(iam Penn Adair), Nov. 4, 1879

(Oologah, Indian Terr. [now Okla.])–Aug. 15, 1935. U.S. humorist. Homespun philosopher/humorist of the 1920s and 1930s; a "comedy roper" in Ziegfeld Follies, from 1914; wrote syndicated column, 1926–35; appeared in films, killed with WILEY POST in Alaska plane crash at height of his popularity.

ROME, HAROLD JACOB, May 27, 1908 (Hartford, Conn.). U.S. composer. Noted composer and lyricist of the musical theater. Plays scored: *Pins and Needles*, 1937; *Wish You Were Here*, 1952; *Fanny*, 1954; *I Can Get It for You Wholesale*, 1962.

RUBY, HARRY, born Harry Rubinstein, Jan. 27, 1895 (New York, N.Y.)–Feb. 23, 1974. U.S. songwriter. With Bert Kalmar, wrote music and lyrics for Broadway shows and films, many of them associated with the Marx Brothers, including *Animal Crackers* (1928) and *Duck Soup* (1933); GROUCHO MARX used many of Ruby's songs in his act (e.g., "Lydia the Tattooed Lady").

SCHWARTZ, ARTHUR, Nov. 25, 1900 (Brooklyn, N.Y.). U.S. composer. Wrote for Broadway, most notably in collaboration with HOWARD DIETZ. Shows scored: *The Little Show*, 1929; *The Band Wagon*, 1931; *Stars in Yours Eyes*, 1939; *A Tree Grows in Brooklyn*, 1951.

SHANKAR, RAVI, Apr. 7, 1920 (India). Indian musician. A sitar player who gained popularity in the west during the 1960s.

SMITH, BOB ("Buffalo Bob"), 1917 (Buffalo, N.Y.). U.S. entertainer. Best known for creating and starring in children's TV series, *The Howdy Doody Show*, in the 1950's.

SONDHEIM, STEPHEN JOSHUA, Mar. 22, 1930 (New York, N.Y.). U.S. composer, lyricist. Leading figure in Broadway musical theater; known for innovative shows on unconventional subjects. Lyrics for shows: *West Side Story*, 1957; *Gypsy*, 1959. Music and lyrics for shows: *A Funny Thing Happened on the Way to the Forum*, 1962; *Anyone Can Whistle*, 1964; *Company*, 1970; *Follies*, 1971; *A Little Night Music*, 1973; *Pacific Overtures*, 1976; *Sweeney Todd*, 1979.

SOUSA, JOHN PHILIP ("The March King"), Nov. 6, 1854 (Washington, D.C.)–Mar. 6, 1932. U.S. bandmaster, composer. Led U.S. Marine Band, 1880–92; formed own band, 1892; composed 140 marches. Compositions: "Stars and Stripes Forever," 1897; "Semper Fidelis," 1888; "The Washington Post," 1889; "The Liberty Bell," 1893; "El Capitán," 1896.

SPECTOR, PHIL, Dec. 26, 1940 (Bronx, N.Y.). U.S. recording exec. Began as a songwriter, 1957; formed own record company (Philles Records) in 1962 and served as consultant for a number of 1960s rock stars and their groups, including THE BEATLES, the Righteous Brothers, the Crystals, the Ronettes, etc.

SPIVAK, LAURENCE EDMUND, June 11, 1900 (New York, N.Y.). U.S. TV moderator. Cofounder and moderator of long-running news show *Meet the Press* (radio, 1945–47; TV, 1947–75).

STEINER, MAX, May 10, 1888 (Vienna, Austria)–Dec. 28, 1971. U.S.-Austrian composer. One of Hollywood's most important composers. Film scores: *King Kong*, 1933; *Gone With the Wind*, 1939; *The Letter*, 1940; *The Great Lie*, 1941; *Now, Voyager*, 1942; *Casablanca*, 1942; *The Treasure of the Sierra Madre*, 1947; *The Caine Mutiny*, 1954.

STROUSE, CHARLES, June 7, 1928 (New York, N.Y.). U.S. composer. Wrote several popular musical comedies, winning Tony awards for *Bye Bye Birdie* (1959), *Applause* (1970), and *Annie* (1977).

STYNE, JULE, born Julius Kerwin Stein, Dec. 31, 1905 (London, Eng.). U.S. composer, producer. An important composer of the American musical theater. A frequent collaborator with BETTY COMDEN and ADOLPH GREEN. Shows scored: *High Button Shoes*, 1947; *Gentlemen Prefer Blondes*, 1949; *Bells Are Ringing*, 1959; *Gypsy*, 1959; *Funny Girl*, 1964; *Hallelujah Baby*, 1967; *Sugar*, 1972.

SUESSE, DANA ("The Girl Gerswhin"), Dec. 3, 1911 (Shreveport, La.). U.S. musician. A child-prodigy pianist and composer; wrote pop and semiclassical songs and instrumentals; associated with PAUL WHITEMAN as a pianist and composer, from 1933; known for her rapid composition skills. Compositions: "Syncopated Love Song"; "Ho Hum"; "You Ought to Be in Pictures"; "Concerto in Three Rhythms," 1933; "Valses for Piano and Orchestra," 1933.

SULLIVAN, ED(ward Vincent), Sept. 28, 1902 (New York, N.Y.)–Oct. 13, 1974. U.S. TV personality, newspaper columnist. Stone-faced emcee of the popular CBS-TV program *The Ed Sullivan Show* (originally *Toast of the Town*), 1948–71; columnist with the *New York Daily News*, 1932–74.

SWING, RAYMOND GRAM, Mar. 25, 1887 (Cortland, N.Y.)–Dec. 22, 1968. U.S. radio commentator. Had five million listeners in the 1930s; from 1945, harrassed for his liberal views by House Committee on Un-American Activities, and his popularity declined; political commentator for Voice of America, 1951–53 and 1959–64. *Forerunners of American Fascism*, 1938; *How War Came*, 1940; *Good Evening: A Professional Memoir*, 1964.

TILLSTROM, BURR, Oct. 13, 1917 (Chicago, Ill.). U.S. puppeteer. Creator of Kukla, Ollie, and an assortment of other lovable puppets which have appeared on TV (often with human Fran Allison) since 1947; won Peabody Awards in 1949 and 1964; won Emmy awards in 1953, 1965, and 1971.

VALENTI, JACK JOSEPH, Sept. 5, 1921 (Houston, Tex.). U.S. film exec. Special asst. to Pres. L.B. JOHNSON, 1963–66; pres. of Motion Picture Assn. of America, 1966–   ; leading figure in establishing rating system for U.S. films.

VAN HEUSEN, JIMMY, born Edward Chester Babcock, Jan. 26, 1913 (Syracuse, N.Y.). U.S. composer. Author of pop songs and film and stage scores. Scores: "Road" pictures of B. HOPE and B. CROSBY; *Going My Way*, 1944. Songs: "Swinging on a Star"; "High Hopes"; "The Second Time Around"; "Love and Marriage".

VON TILZER, HARRY, born Harry Gumm, July 8, 1872 (Detroit, Mich.)–Jan. 10, 1946. U.S. composer. Music publisher, in partnership with his brothers, 1902–46. Compositions: "A Bird in a Gilded Cage"; "In the Sweet Bye and Bye"; "Wait Till the Sun Shines Nellie"; "I Want a Girl Just like the Girl Who Married Dear Old Dad"; "When My Baby Smiles at Me."

WILLIAMS, HANK, Sept. 15, 1923 (Georgiana, Ala.)–Jan. 1, 1953. U.S. country-music singer, songwriter. Although he could not read music, composed 125 songs, many of them country-and-western standards; with the Grand Ole Opry, 1949–53. Songs: "Lovesick Blues"; "I'll Never Get Out of This World Alive"; "Your Cheatin' Heart"; "Wedding Bells"; "Jambalaya"; "Long-gone Lonesome Blues."

THE BOOK OF WHO

WILLIAMS, JOHN, Feb. 8, 1932 (Flushing, N.Y.). U.S. composer. Films scored: *Valley of the Dolls,* 1967; *The Poseidon Adventure,* 1972; *Jaws,* 1975; *Star Wars,* 1977; *Close Encounters of the Third Kind,* 1977.

WILLSON, MEREDITH, May 18, 1902 (Mason City, Ia.). U.S. composer, lyricist. Created the musicals *The Music Man* (1957; Tony and Grammy awards), *The Unsinkable Molly Brown* (1960), and *Here's Love* (1963).

WILSON, DON, 1900 (Lincoln, Neb.). U.S. entertainer. Radio and TV announcer best known for his role as the announcer/straight man on JACK BENNY'S radio and TV shows; advertising spokesman for Western Union Candygrams.

WINCHELL, PAUL, Dec. 21, 1922 (New York, N.Y.). U.S. ventriloquist. Known for his famous dummies, Jerry Mahoney (1936) and Knucklehead Smith (1950); does voices for TV cartoon shows.

YELLEN, JACK, born Selig Yellen, July 6, 1892 (Razcki, Pol.). U.S. lyricist, playwright. Lyricist since 1913; wrote lyrics or lyrics and book for several Broadway shows, including *The Scandals* (1934) and *The Follies* (1943); formed his own music publishing co., 1922. Songs: "Hard-Hearted Hannah," 1923; "Ain't She Sweet?" 1924; "My Yiddishe Mama," 1924; "Happy Days Are Here Again."

YOUMANS, VINCENT MILLIE, Sept. 27, 1898 (New York, N.Y.)–Apr. 5, 1946. U.S. composer. Collaborated with the greatest names in American musical theatre. *Hit the Deck,* 1915; *No, No Nanette,* 1925. Songs: "I Want to Be Happy"; "Tea for Two"; "The Carioca"; "Great Day".

OTHER NOTED OR NOTORIOUS PERSONALITIES

ADAMS, ABIGAIL, née Smith, Nov. 11, 1744 (Weymouth, Mass.)–Oct. 28, 1818. U.S. First Lady, author of letters. Wife of JOHN ADAMS and mother of JOHN QUINCY ADAMS. *New Letters of Abigail Adams, 1788–1801; The Adams-Jefferson Letters,* 1959.

BAILEY, F(rancis) LEE, June 10, 1933 (Waltham, Mass.). U.S. lawyer. Celebrated criminal lawyer. Won acquittal of Dr. Samuel H. Sheppard at his retrial of conviction in the 1954 murder of his wife; defended Albert DeSalvo, the confessed Boston Strangler; won acquittal of Capt. Ernest L. Medina, accused of killing S. Vietnamese civilians at My Lai; defended PATRICIA HEARST. *The Defense Never Rests* (with Harvey Aronson), 1972; *Cleared for the Approach,* 1977.

BALENCIAGA, CRISTÓBAL, Jan. 21, 1895 (Guetaria, Sp.)–Mar. 24, 1972. Spanish fashion designer. First leading couturier in Spain; later designed in Paris; designed elegant gowns, dresses, suits; helped to popularize capes and flowing clothes in 1950s.

BALMAIN, PIERRE ALEXANDRE, May 18, 1914 (Saint-Jean-Maurienne, Fr.). French fashion designer. With DIOR and BALENCIAGA, launched the "New Look" of the late 1940s, emphasizing low hemlines, narrow shoulders, and small waists.

BARKER, KATE ("Ma"), born Arizona Donnie Clark, 1872 (nr. Springfield, Mo.)–Jan. 16, 1935. U.S. outlaw. Masterminded robberies, kidnappings, and murders committed by her sons, Lloyd (1896–1949), Arthur (1899–1939), and Fred (1894–1927); the brains of the Barker-Karpis gang, the last of the outlaw bands; accumulated at least $3 million.

BARNHART, CLARENCE LEWIS, Dec. 30, 1900 (nr. Plattsburg, Mo.). U.S. lexicographer, editor. Founder and editor of Thorndike-Barnhart dictionaries, 1935– . *U.S. Army Terms,* 1943; *New Century Cyclopedia of Names,* 3 vols., 1954; *New Century Handbook of English Literature,* 1956 and 1967; *The World Book Encyclopedia Dictionary,* 1963.

BARROW, CLYDE, Mar. 24, 1909 (Teleco, Tex.)–May 23, 1934. U.S. outlaw. Called "Public Enemy No. 1 of the Southwest." With companion BONNIE PARKER, accused of 12 murders during a two-year robbery spree in the Southwest; ambushed and shot to death by Texas Rangers and sheriff's deputies.

BEAN, ROY ("Judge"), c.1825 (Mason Co., Ky.)–Mar. 16, 1903. U.S. judge, saloonkeeper, teamster, trader. Legendary American frontier judge, known as "The Law West of the Pecos"; set up a saloon at a construction camp (now Langtry, Tex.) for the Southern Pacific RR, and became the justice of the peace.

BEARD, JAMES, May 5, 1903 (Portland, Ore.). U.S. cookbook author. *James Beard's Treasury of Outdoor Cooking,* 1960; *The James Beard Cookbook,* 1961; *Beard on Bread,* 1973; *The Cook's Catalogue,* 1975.

BELLI, MELVIN MOURON, July 29, 1907 (Sonora, Calif.). U.S. lawyer. Flamboyant attorney who has defended LENNY BRUCE, Martha Mitchell, and JACK RUBY. *Modern Trials and Modern Damages,* 6 vols., 1954; *Malpractice,* 1955; *The Law Revolt,* 2 vols., 1968; *Melvin Belli: My Life on Trial,* 1976.

BILLY THE KID, born William H. Bonney, Nov. 23, 1859 (New York, N.Y.)–July 15, 1881. U.S. outlaw. Gunman in Lincoln Co., Ariz., range war, 1878; rustler, 1878–80; accused of 21 murders; shot by Pat Garrett.

BLASS, BILL, born William Blass, June 22, 1922 (Ft. Wayne, Ind.). U.S. fashion designer. Noted for designing feminine clothes for the tailored woman, using clean, classic all-American lines; also designs menswear, furs, luggage, linens, and men's grooming products.

BLY, NELLIE (pseud. of Elizabeth Cochrane Seaman), May 5, 1867 (Cochran's Mills, Pa.)–Jan. 27, 1922. U.S. journalist. As a reporter for the New York *World,* traveled around the world in 72 days, 6 hours, 11 minutes, beating the fictional record set by Phileas Fogg; feigned madness to expose conditions in Blackwell's Is. Asylum.

BOCUSE, PAUL, 1926 (Collonges, Fr.). French chef, restauranteur. Owner of a Michelin "three-star" restaurant in Collonges-au-Mont d'Or, a suburb of Lyon, Fr.; associated with "the new cuisine," which emphasizes freshness and simplicity. *Paul Bocuse's French Cooking,* 1977.

BOOTH, JOHN WILKES, May 10, 1838 (Bel Air, Md.)–Apr. 26, 1865. U.S. actor, assassin. Killed Pres. ABRAHAM LINCOLN at the Ford's Theatre in Washington, D.C., on Apr. 14, 1865; shot dead while resisting arrest. (Brother of EDWIN BOOTH.)

BORDEN, LIZZIE ANDREW, July 19, 1860 (Fall River, Mass.)–June 1, 1927. U.S. alleged ax murderess. As a 32-year-old spinster, accused of killing her stepmother and father by hacking them with an ax, Aug, 4, 1892; tried and found not guilty, but was popularly believed to be guilty; became

OTHER NOTED OR NOTORIOUS PERSONALITIES

the subject of plays, novels, a ballet, an opera, and a musical revue.

BOYCOTT, CHARLES CUNNINGHAM, Mar. 12, 1832 (Norfolk, Eng.)–June 19, 1897. English land-estate manager. A land agent in County Mayo, Ire., became subject (1880) of economic and social isolation when he attempted to collect harsh rents; his name came to be applied to the tactic of isolating one's opponent.

BRADY, MATHEW B., c.1823 (nr. Lake George, N.Y.)–Jan. 15, 1896. U.S. photographer. Photographed every U.S. president from J. Q. ADAMS through WILLIAM MCKINLEY (except W. H. HARRISON); during the Civil War, hired 20 photographers to record the events; himself photographed battlefields at Bull Run, Antietam, and Gettysburg.

BRAILLE, LOUIS, Jan. 4, 1809 (Coupvray, Fr.)–Jan. 6, 1852. French musician, teacher. Invented the raised-dot system of writing used by the blind, 1829; was blinded himself at age three.

BRAUN, EVA, Feb. 6, 1912 (Bavaria)–Apr. 30, 1945. German mistress of ADOLF HITLER. Never seen in public with Hitler; had no political influence on him; married Hitler on the eve of their joint suicide.

BRINKLEY, JOHN RICHARD, born John Romulus Brinkley, July 8, 1885 (Jackson Co., N.C.)–May 26, 1942. U.S. medical quack, radio entrepreneur. Transplanted goat gonads into aging men, from 1917; founded KFKB, the first radio station in Kansas, to push mail-order drugs; revocation (1930) of the KFKB license established the FCC's right to judge program content; established a powerful transmitter (XERA) in Mexico and resumed broadcasting but was silenced by the Mexican government (1937); made millions of dollars.

BRUCE, AILSA, née Mellon, 1901 (Pittsburgh, Pa.)–Aug. 25, 1969. U.S. philanthropist. At the time of her death, considered the richest woman in the U.S.; in 1968 *Fortune* estimated her personal wealth at $500 million; with brother PAUL MELLON, donated $20 million for construction of an annex to the Natl. Gallery of Art, Washington, D.C., 1968; her Avalon Fndn. gave $2.8 million to Lincoln Center for the Performing Arts, 1958. (Daughter of ANDREW W. MELLON; wife of DAVID K. E. BRUCE.)

BRUMMELL, GEORGE BRYAN ("Beau"), June 7, 1778 (London, Eng.)–Mar. 30, 1840. English dandy and wit. An intimate of the Prince of Wales (later George IV); the center of fashionable London society, influenced men toward simplicity and moderation in dress; credited with inventing trousers to replace breeches.

BUCHALTER, LOUIS ("Lepke"), Feb. 1897 (New York, N.Y.)–Mar. 4, 1944. U.S. mobster. Ran Murder, Inc., and New York City garment center rackets, c.1930–1940; executed at Ossining Prison (Sing Sing).

BURKE, MARTHA JANE, née Cannary ("Calamity Jane"), May 1, 1852? (Princeton, Mo.)–Aug. 1, 1903. U.S. frontier adventuress. Noted for dressing, drinking, and cursing like the toughest of men; drifted through construction camps and cow towns from Missouri to Wyoming, working as a dance-hall girl and often involved in prostitution; many legends of her exploits as an Indian fighter and army scout were probably begun in order to promote her as a star in a traveling "dime museum."

BURNS, WILLIAM JOHN, Oct. 19, 1861 (Baltimore, Md.)–Apr. 14, 1931. U.S. detective. Formed his own detective agency in New York City, 1909; established branches all over the U.S.; attracted natl. attention through investigation of sensational murders; dir. of Bureau of Investigation (now FBI), 1921–24.

CAGLIOSTRO, COUNT ALESSANDRO, June 2, 1743 (Palermo, Sicily)–Aug. 26, 1795. Italian charlatan. With his wife, Lorenza Feliciani, traveled to London, The Hague, Strasbourg, Lyon, Toulouse, Germany, and Russia, posing as an alchemist, medium, soothsayer, necromancer; sold love philters, elixirs of youth; in Paris, imprisoned in Bastille, then released, for implication in the "Affair of the Diamond Necklace," 1785–86; in Rome, condemned to death as a heretic and freemason; sentence commuted to life imprisonment, 1789.

CAPONE, AL(phonse) ("Scarface Al"), Jan. 17, 1899 (Naples, It.)–Jan. 25, 1947. U.S. gangster. Dominated organized crime in Chicago and the surrounding area, 1925–31; imprisoned for federal income tax evasion, 1931–39.

CARDIN, PIERRE, July 7, 1922 (Venice, It.). French fashion designer. From 1957, creator of elegantly cut clothes for women; introduced first collection for men by a top designer, featuring bias cut, soft semifitted lines, and lavish color, 1960; leader in ready-to-wear for both sexes.

CARTER, ROSALYNN, née Smith, Aug. 18, 1927 (Plains, Ga.). U.S. First Lady. One of Pres. JIMMY CARTER's most influential advisors; special interests include mental-health programs and passage of the Equal Rights Amendment; honorary chairperson of President's Com. on Mental Health.

CARTER, WILLIAM ALTON CARTER III ("Billy"), Mar. 29, 1937 (Plains, Ga.). U.S. peanut farmer. The brother of Pres. JIMMY CARTER, a self-proclaimed Georgia "redneck"; sold his name to a brewing company that made "Billy" beer; voluntarily committed himself to a hospital to overcome alcohol abuse, 1979.

CAXTON, WILLIAM, c.1422 (Kent, Eng.)–1491. English printer, translator, publisher. First English printer. Published first book printed in England, *The Recuyell of the Historyes of Troye,* translated from French; and first illustrated English book, 1481; printed most of English literature available at the time.

CAYCE, EDGAR, Mar. 18, 1877 (Hopkinsville, Ky.)–Jan. 3, 1945. U.S. rural healer, seer. Worked from trances that yielded diagnoses and prescriptions for patients, as well as glimpses into the past and future; reputed to have predicted the 1929 stock market crash and WW II.

CHANEL, GABRIELLE BONHEUR ("Coco"), Aug. 19, 1883 (nr. Issoire, Fr.)–Jan. 10, 1971. French fashion designer. One of the most influential couturiers of the 20th cent., she revolutionized women's fashions after WW I with the straight, simple lines of the "Chanel look." The subject of the Broadway musical *Coco* (1969).

CHAPMAN, JOHN (Johnny Appleseed), Sept. 26, 1774 (Leominster, Mass.)–Mar. 1845. U.S. patron saint of orchards and conservation. Planted many apple nurseries from the Alleghenies to central Ohio and beyond, from 1800; sold and gave away thousands of seedlings to pioneers.

CHESSMAN, CARYL WHITTIER ("Red Light Bandit"), born Carol Whittier Chessman, May 27, 1921 (St. Joseph, Mo.)–May 2, 1960. U.S. criminal. Convicted of 17 counts of robbery, kidnapping, sexual abuse, and attempted rape during a three-day crime spree in California, 1948; electrocuted after eight stays of execution during a 12-year fight

295

THE BOOK OF WHO

for his life, during which he wrote four books and smuggled them out of prison; won support from thousands, including ALBERT SCHWEITZER, ALDOUS HUXLEY, BRIGITTE BARDOT; maintained his innocence to the end. *Cell 2455, Death Row*, 1954; *Trial by Ordeal*, 1955; *The Face of Justice*, 1957.

CHILD, JULIA, née McWilliams, Aug. 15, 1912 (Pasadena, Calif.). U.S. author, TV personality. Noted as the author of several popular cookbooks, beginning with the best-selling *Mastering the Art of French Cooking* (with Louisette Bertholle and Simone Beck, 1961); star of *The French Chef*, a TV show on cooking, 1963– . *The French Chef Cookbook*, 1968; *From Julia Child's Kitchen*, 1975.

CHIPPENDALE, THOMAS, baptized June 5, 1718 (Yorkshire, Eng.)–Nov. 1779. English cabinetmaker, furniture designer. Popularized the Anglicized rococo style in furniture. *The Gentleman and Cabinet-Maker's Director*, 1754.

CLAIBORNE, CRAIG, Sept. 4, 1920 (Sunflower, Miss.). U.S. writer. Food editor of *The New York Times*, 1957– . *The New York Times Cook Book*, 1961; *The New York Times International Cookbook*, 1971; *Craig Claiborne's Favorites from The New York Times*, 1975.

CROWLEY, ALEISTER, born Edward Alexander Crowley, 1875 (England)–Dec. 1, 1947. English magician, author, poet. The self-proclaimed "worst man in the world," allegedly practiced black magic and blood sacrifice. *The Diary of a Drug Fiend*, 1970; *Moonchild*, 1970; *The Confessions of Aleister Crowley: An Autohagiography*, 1970; *Magick without Tears*, 1973; *Magick in Theory and Practice*, 1974.

CULBERTSON, ELY, July 22, 1891 (Poiana de Verbilao, Rum.)–Dec. 17, 1955. U.S. bridge expert. Invented system of contract bridge, in early 1930s, helped establish it as a leading card game; pres. of The Bridge World, Inc., 1929–55; devoted his later years to working for world peace. *Contract Bridge Complete*, 1936; *Total Peace*, 1943.

CZOLGOSZ, LEON F., 1873 (Detroit, Mich.)–Oct. 29, 1901. U.S. assassin, anarchist. Fatally wounded Pres. WILLIAM MCKINLEY at the Pan-American Exposition in Buffalo, N.Y., Sept. 6, 1901; electrocuted at Auburn, N.Y.

DARE, VIRGINIA, Aug. 18, 1587 (Roanoke I., Va. [now in N. C.])–c.1587. American colonial child, the first child born in America of English parents. Granddaughter of Gov. John White, the founder and governor of colony on Roanoke I. (1587); known to have lived at least nine days, until Aug. 27, when White sailed to England for supplies; upon his return, he found no remains of settlers, 1591.

DARROW, CLARENCE SEWARD, Apr. 18, 1857 (nr. Kinsman, Ohio)–Mar. 13, 1938. U.S. labor and criminal lawyer. Served as defense counsel in many dramatic criminal trials. Defended EUGENE DEBS, pres. of the American Railway Union, and other union leaders arrested on contempt charges arising from the 1894 Pullman strike; saved RICHARD LOEB and NATHAN LEOPOLD from the death sentence in the sensational Bobby Franks murder case, 1924; defended JOHN SCOPES, 1925. *Crime: Its Cause and Treatment*, 1922; *The Story of My Life*, 1932.

DAVIS, (Daisie) ADELLE, Feb. 25, 1904 (Lizton, Ind.)–May 31, 1974. U.S. nutritionist, author. Natural-foods crusader and expert on vitamin supplements. *Let's Cook It Right*, 1947; *Let's Have Healthy Children*, 1951; *Let's Eat Right to Keep Fit*, 1954; *Let's Get Well*, 1965.

DE LA RENTA, OSCAR, July 22, 1932 (Santo Domingo, D.R.). U.S. fashion designer. Noted for his elegant, sexy clothes for women, especially his lavish, romantic ball gowns for such clients as Mrs. William S. Paley and the DUCHESS OF WINDSOR.

DIAMOND, JOHN THOMAS ("Legs"), c.1898 (Philadelphia, Pa.)–Dec. 18, 1931. U.S. mobster. Ran some New York City rackets, 1928–31; shot dead in bed, probably on the orders of "DUTCH" SCHULTZ.

DILLINGER, JOHN, 1902 (Mooresville, Ind.)–July 22, 1934. U.S. bank robber. With "PRETTY BOY" FLOYD and "BABY FACE" NELSON, terrorized North-Central states in 1933; gunned down by law officers in front of the Biograph Theater, Chicago, Ill.; gang responsible for 16 murders.

DIONNE quintuplets (Marie, Emilie, Yvonne, Annette, and Cecile), May 28, 1934 (Callander, Ont., Can.). Born to Elzire Dionne, a farmer, and his wife Oliva, age 24 and already the mother of six; cared for by Dr. Allan Roy Dafoe, a local gen. practitioner; provided with nursing care by the Canadian Red Cross; made wards of Ontario to avoid exploitation; educated at home until they entered Nicolet C., 1952. Marie died Feb. 27, 1970; Emilie died Aug. 5, 1954.

DIOR, CHRISTIAN, Jan. 21, 1905 (Granville, Fr.)–Oct. 24, 1957. French fashion designer. Created the "New Look" popular after WW II; emphasized long hemlines and full skirts; introduced the sack dress, 1950s.

DOHRN, BERNADINE RAE, Jan. 12, 1942 (Chicago, Ill.). U.S. radical activist. Leader of the Weathermen, the militant faction of Students for a Democratic Soc.; disappeared late Feb. or Mar. 1970; indicted for unlawful flight to avoid prosecution for mob action, and for conspiracy to violate federal antiriot laws and to bomb buildings, 1970; indictments dismissed, 1973 and 1974.

DU BARRY, COMTESSE, born Marie Jeanne Bécu, Aug. 19, 1743 (Valcouleurs, Fr.)–Dec. 8, 1793. French mistress of Louis XV, 1769–74. Of lower-middle-class origins, became mistress of Jean du Barry, a procurer for royalty, 1764–68; to make her suitable as a royal mistress, du Barry married her to his brother Guillaume, Count du Barry; retired from court following king's death; arrested by ROBESPIERRE, 1793; executed.

EARP, WYATT, 1848 (Monmouth, Ill.)–Jan. 13, 1929. U.S. law officer, gunfighter. Involved with his brothers and Doc Holliday, in the controversial shootout at the O.K. Corral, 1881.

EISENHOWER, (Dwight) DAVID II, Apr. 1, 1948 (West Point, N.Y.). U.S. grandson of Pres. DWIGHT D. EISENHOWER, son-in-law of Pres. RICHARD M. NIXON. The presidential retreat, Camp David, is named for him.

ESCOFFIER, GEORGES AUGUSTE, Oct. 28, 1846 (Villeneuve-Loubet, Fr.)–Feb. 12, 1935. French chef. Famous Parisian chef known as the "King of Cooks"; served as chef at the Reine Blanche in Paris, the Savoy, Carlton, and Ritz hotels in London, and the Grand Hotel in Monte Carlo.

FARMER, FANNIE MERRITT ("Mother of Level Measurements"), Mar. 23, 1857 (Boston, Mass.)–Jan 15, 1915. U.S. cookery expert. Established Miss Farmer's School of Cookery, 1902; one of the first to stress the importance of following recipes exactly and using standard, level measurements.

OTHER NOTED OR NOTORIOUS PERSONALITIES

Boston Cooking School Cook Book, 1896; A New Book of Cookery, 1912.

FAWKES, GUY, 1570 (York, Eng.)–Jan. 31, 1606. English conspirator. Involved in the unsuccessful Gunpowder Plot (1604–05) to blow up the Parliament building while James I was meeting within with his chief ministers, to avenge the enforcing of penal laws against Catholics; captured and executed; Nov. 5 is celebrated as Guy Fawkes Day in Great Britain.

FLOYD, CHARLES ARTHUR, a.k.a. Pretty Boy, c.1904 (nr. Sallisaw, Okla.)–Oct. 22, 1934. U.S. bank robber. Member of the JOHN DILLINGER gang; killed in a gun battle with law officers.

FORD, ELIZABETH, née Bloomer, Apr. 8, 1918 (Chicago, Ill.). U.S. First Lady, the wife of Pres. GERALD R. FORD. A dancer with the MARTHA GRAHAM Concert Group, 1939–41; as First Lady and later, much admired for her candor, especially about her hospitalization for alcohol and drug abuse (1978).

FORD, ROBERT, ?–June 24, 1892. U.S. outlaw. As a new recruit to the James Gang, killed JESSE JAMES, Apr. 3, 1882, earning $10,000 reward; drifted through West; opened saloon in Creede, Col., where he was gunned down.

FRANK, ANNE, June 12, 1929 (Frankfurt-am-Main, Ger.)–March 1945. German Jewish girl, a victim of Nazi anti-Semitism. Her The Diary of a Young Girl (1952), written during two years of hiding, gained wide popularity.

FROMME, LYNETTE ALICE ("Squeaky"), 1948 (California?). U.S. follower of CHARLES MANSON. Attempted to assassinate Pres. GERALD R. FORD in Sacramento, Calif., 1975; convicted, serving a life sentence at the San Diego Metropolitan Correctional Center.

FURSTENBERG, DIANE SIMONE MICHELLE VON, Dec. 31, 1946 (Brussels, Belg.). U.S. fashion designer. Beginning in 1971, parlayed a one-woman dress-designing business into a multimillion-dollar internatl. concern marketing ready-to-wear clothes, plus handbags, shoes, sunglasses, cosmetics, and scarves; started the trend toward the simple, sexy, body-hugging jersey shirt-dress. Diane von Furstenberg's Book of Beauty, 1976.

GALLUP, GEORGE HORACE, Nov. 18, 1901 (Jefferson, Ia.). U.S. public-opinion statistician. Famous as the originator of the Gallup Poll. Founded the American Inst. of Public Opinion (1935) and the Audience Research Inst. (1939); first gained fame with his accurate prediction of the 1936 presidential election. Guide to Public Opinion Polls, 1944.

GELLER, URI, Dec. 20, 1946 (Tel Aviv, Pal.). Israeli mentalist. Known for his claims to psychic powers, such as the ability to bend metal spoons with the power of his mind; has been the subject of various scientific attempts to verify or discredit his feats. My Story, 1976.

GERNREICH, RUDI, Aug. 8, 1922 (Vienna, Austria). U.S. fashion designer. Made waves with his topless bathing suits and nightgowns; introduced plastic fabrics in futuristic modes. Founder and pres. of GR Designs, Inc. (name changed to Rudi Gernreich, 1964), 1960– .

GIVENCHY, HUBERT DE, Feb. 21, 1927 (Beauvais, Fr.). French fashion designer. Parisian designer noted for his separate skirts and tops, unusual printed and embroidered fabrics, tubular evening dresses, sumptuous ball gowns; designer of AUDREY HEPBURN's clothes and film costumes.

GONNE, MAUDE (married name: MacBride), Dec. 20, 1865 (London?, Eng.)–Apr. 27, 1953. Irish nationalist. Hailed in her time as the Irish Joan of Arc; a celebrated beauty, she was an impassioned advocate of Irish freedom; pursued unsuccessfully by WILLIAM BUTLER YEATS; term maudgonning means agitating for a cause in a reckless, flamboyant fashion.

GOREN, CHARLES HENRY, Mar. 4, 1901 (Philadelphia, Pa.). U.S. bridge expert, author. Noted bridge player and writer whose point-count bidding system has gained wide popularity; winner of two world bridge championships and 26 U.S. titles; author of "Goren on Bridge," syndicated daily column. Point Count Bidding, 1950; New Contract Bridge in a Nutshell, 1959.

GREEN, HENRIETTA HOWLAND ("Hetty"), née Robinson, Nov. 21, 1834 (New Bedford, Mass.)–July 3, 1916. U.S. financier. Through shrewd investment in railroads, real estate, and govt. bonds, increased family fortune of over $5 million; reputed to have been richest woman in U.S. at her death, with assets estimated at $100 million; her eccentricities (i.e., wearing rags and living in flea-bag hotels), earned her the name the Witch of Wall Street.

GUGGENHEIM, PEGGY, Aug. 26, 1898 (New York, N.Y.)–Dec. 23, 1979. U.S. art patron and collector. Noted for having backed some of the most notable modern artists, such as JACKSON POLLOCK; directed her own New York City gallery, Art of This Century, 1943–47; exhibited her private collection all over Europe, from 1951.

GUINAN, TEXAS, born Mary Louise Cecilia, Jan. 12, 1884 (Waco, Tex.)–Nov. 5, 1933. U.S. actress, night club hostess. The quintessence of the 1920s flapper, acted as hostess for several popular speakeasies in New York City, from 1924; greeted patrons from her high stool at the door with the phrase, "Hello, sucker."

GWYN (or Gwynne), **NELL,** born Eleanor Gwyn, Feb. 2, 1650 (Hereford, Eng.)–Nov. 13, 1687. English actress. Leading comedienne of the King's company, 1664–69; mistress of Charles II, from 1668.

HALSTON, born Roy Halston Frowick, Apr. 23, 1932. U.S. fashion designer. Designer at Bergdorf Goodman, 1959–68; designer at the boutique Halston Ltd., 1968–76; designer and pres., Halston Originals, 1972–75; pres. of Halston Enterprises, 1975–

HARRIS, EMILY, née Schwartz, Feb. 11, 1947 (Baltimore, Md.); and husband **WILLIAM HARRIS,** Jan. 22, 1945 (Ft. Sill, Okla.). U.S. revolutionaries. Members of the Symbionese Liberation Army; Held PATRICIA HEARST in hiding after the rest of the SLA was killed in a siege (1974), and eluded capture until 1976; tried, convicted, imprisoned.

HAUPTMANN, BRUNO RICHARD, 1899 (Germany)–Apr. 3, 1936. U.S. carpenter who was convicted (1935) in a sensational trial of the kidnapping and murder of the son of CHARLES and ANNE MORROW LINDBERGH.

HEAD, EDITH, ? (Los Angeles, Calif.). U.S. fashion designer. Chief designer for Paramount Pictures Corp. since the 1930s; currently with Universal City Studios; awarded costume-design AA for The Heiress (1949), All About Eve (1950), Samson and Delilah (1951), A Place in the Sun (1952), Roman Holiday (1954), Sabrina (1954), The Facts of Life (1960), The Sting (1973).

HEARST, PATRICIA CAMPBELL (married name: Shaw), a.k.a. Tania, Feb. 20, 1954 (San Francisco, Calif.). U.S. kidnap victim, revolutionary. Kidnapped by the Symbionese Liberation Army, a radical terrorist organization, 1974; allegedly joined her abductors in criminal activities as the revolutionary "Tania"; captured by the FBI, 1975; convicted of bank robbery charges, 1976; released after serving 22 months of a seven-year term under an executive clemency order issued by Pres. JIMMY CARTER; married her bodyguard, 1979. (Granddaughter of WILLIAM RANDOLPH HEARST.)

HELOÏSE, c.1098–May 15, 1164. French abbess. The famous lover of the philosopher PIERRE ABELARD; became his illicit wife and bore his child; outraged relatives had Abelard castrated and placed her in a convent; became abbess at the convent of Paraclete, founded by Abelard.

HEPPLEWHITE, GEORGE, died 1786. English cabinetmaker and furniture designer. Associated with the Neoclassical style; gained fame as the author of *Cabinet-Maker and Upholsterer's Guide* (1788).

HICKOK, JAMES BUTLER ("Wild Bill"), May 27, 1837 (Troy Grove, Ill.)–Aug. 2, 1876. U.S. scout, frontier marshal. Served as a Union scout and spy during the Civil War; dep. U.S. marshal, Fort Riley, Kan., 1866–67; U.S. marshal, Hays City, Kan. (1869–71), and Abilene, Kan. (1871); toured with BUFFALO BILL, 1872–73; shot dead from the rear while playing poker, in Deadwood, Dakota Terr.

HINES, DUNCAN, Mar. 26, 1880 (Bowling Green, Ky.)–Mar. 15, 1959. U.S. gourmet. With *Adventures in Good Eating* (1935), a list of 160 superior eating places, plus several other books on restaurants and hotels, built the rating "Recommended by Duncan Hines" to one treasured and displayed by some 10,000 establishments.

HOLLANDER, XAVIERA, ? (Indonesia). Dutch madam in New York City. *The Happy Hooker* (with Robin Moore and Yvonne Dunleavy), 1972; *Xaviera on the Best Part of a Man,* 1975; *Xaviera's Supersex,* 1976.

HUTTON, BARBARA ("The Poor Little Rich Girl"), Nov. 14, 1912 (New York, N.Y.)–May 11, 1979. U.S. heiress. Granddaughter of F. W. WOOLWORTH and heir to family fortune; married seven times, including Prince Alexis Mdivani, CARY GRANT, and Porfirio Rubirosa; a virtual recluse in later years, plagued by ill health and unhappiness.

ICHAZO, OSCAR, 1931 (Bolivia). Bolivian founder of the Arica system of thought and instruction, 1971. Studied Oriental philosophies and occult practices before creating his own system. *The Human Process for Enlightenment and Freedom,* 1977.

JACK THE RIPPER. Pseudonym of a murderer who terrorized London's East End in 1888–89, killing at least seven women, all of them prostitutes, in the Whitechapel dist.; murders remain one of the greatest unsolved mysteries of all time.

JAMES, JESSE WOODSON, Sept. 5, 1847 (nr. Kearney [then Centerville], Mo.)–Apr. 3, 1882. U.S. outlaw. With his gang executed daring bank and train robberies in the Midwest, from 1866; murdered by one of his gang, ROBERT FORD, in St. Joseph, Mo.

JOHNSON, CLAUDIA ALTA ("Ladybird"), née Taylor, Dec. 22, 1912 (Karnack, Tex.). U.S. First Lady, wife of Pres. LYNDON B. JOHNSON. As First Lady, worked for environmental causes and national beautification projects; a successful businesswoman, she built and owned the Texas Broadcasting Corp., Inc., 1943–73.

JONES, JAMES WARREN ("Jim"), born May 13, 1931 (Lynn, Ind.)–Nov. 18, 1978. U.S. leader of the People's Temple, an agrarian-socialist cult. Ordered the more than 900 members of the People's Temple commune in Guyana to commit suicide by drinking a cyanide-laced concoction, 1979; died of a bullet wound in the head.

JUDD, WINNIE RUTH, née McKinnell, Jan. 29, 1905 (Oxford, Ind.). U.S. murderer. Killed two people (1932), dismembered the bodies, tried to ship them in a trunk from Arizona to Los Angeles; turned herself in; found guilty and committed to a mental hospital; tried to escape seven times, and was once at large for eight years; declared sane and imprisoned, 1969; paroled, 1971.

KELLY, GEORGE ("Machine Gun"), 1897 (Tennessee)–July 18, 1954. U.S. gangster. "Society" bootlegger, kidnapper, robber; best known for his machine-gun marksmanship and for coining the term *G-men* for FBI agents; died of a heart attack in Alcatraz Prison while serving a life sentence for kidnapping.

KENNEDY, ROSE, née Fitzgerald, July 22, 1890 (Boston, Mass.). U.S. matriarch of a political dynasty. The mother of a president, JOHN F. KENNEDY, and two senators, ROBERT F. KENNEDY and EDWARD M. KENNEDY; noted for the strength she has shown in the face of multiple tragedies, the loss of her eldest son in WW II, the assassinations of John and Robert, death of a daughter in an air crash, and mental retardation of another daughter.

KIDD, WILLIAM ("Captain Kidd"), c. 1645 (Greenock, Scot.)–May 23, 1701. Scottish pirate. Commissioned as a privateer to defend English ships against pirates, turned pirate himself because of the threat of mutiny and failure to take prizes; charged with piracy, returned to London to defend himself, convicted and hanged.

KUNSTLER, WILLIAM, July 7, 1919 (New York, N.Y.). U.S. lawyer. Radical atty. noted for his defense of political activists, including STOKELY CARMICHAEL, the Chicago 7, and the Catonsville 9, during the 1960s. *The Case for Courage: The Stories of Ten Famous American Attorneys who Risked Their Careers in the Cause of Justice,* 1962; *Deep in My Heart,* 1966.

LAFFITE (or Lafitte), **JEAN,** 1780? (France)–1825. U.S. privateer, smuggler. Fought heroically for the U.S. in the War of 1812; rejected British attempts at bribery, warning New Orleans of the impending attack instead.

LANE, MARK, Feb. 24, 1927 (New York, N.Y.). U.S. lawyer, author. Controversial attorney who defended Marguerite Oswald, the wife of LEE HARVEY OSWALD, at the Warren Commission hearings, 1964; became an anti-Vietnam War activist; with WILLIAM KUNSTLER, chief defense attorney of militant Indian leaders of the 1973 Wounded Knee, S.D., occupation; as the attorney for People's Temple cult, accompanied Rep. LEO J. RYAN to Guyana (1978), but escaped the mass suicide. *Rush to Judgement,* 1966; *Conversations with Americans,* 1970.

LANVIN, JEANNE, 1867?–July 6, 1946. French designer, dressmaker. The founder of La Maison de Couture, a small Paris fashion group that along with a few other designers, set the mode for the world.

LEOPOLD, NATHAN, JR., c.1905 (Chicago, Ill.)–Aug. 30, 1971; and **LOEB, RICHARD,** c.1906 (Chicago, Ill.)–Jan. 28, 1936. U.S. criminals. In the "Crime of the Century," kidnapped and murdered 14-year-old Bobby Franks in Chicago, 1924; weal-

OTHER NOTED OR NOTORIOUS PERSONALITIES

thy and brilliant, the boys became the focus of enormous publicity; their defense attorney, CLARENCE DARROW, saved them from the death penalty; Leopold was released from prison in 1958; Loeb was killed in prison by another inmate. MEYER LEVIN's book *Compulsion* (1956) was based on the case.

LEWIS, ROSA, born Rosa Ovenden, Sept. 27, 1867 (London, Eng.)–Nov. 29, 1952. English hotelkeeper. Celebrated society caterer and owner of the Cavendish Hotel in the heyday of Edwardian England; her clients included Edward VII and the CHURCHILL family. The BBC-TV series *The Duchess of Duke Street* (1978) was based on her life.

LUCCHESE, GAETANO, a.k.a. Three-Finger Brown, 1900 (Sicily)–July 13, 1967. U.S. mobster. Reputedly the boss of one of "Five Families" of New York City, 1953–67; "Three-finger" nickname used by police and press only.

LUCIANO, CHARLES, a.k.a. Lucky Luciano and Charles Ross, born Salvatore Lucania, Nov. 11, 1896 (nr. Palermo, Sicily)–Jan. 26, 1962. Italian-U.S. mobster. Allegedly the major architect of modern Mafia organization; reputed boss of New York City crime family, 1931–46; imprisoned, 1936; deported, 1946.

MADISON, DOLLEY, née Payne, May 20, 1772 (Guilford Co., N.C.)–July 12, 1849. U.S. First Lady, wife of Pres. JAMES MADISON. Famous as a Washington, D.C., hostess while her husband was U.S. secy. of state (1801–09) and pres. (1809–17).

MAINBOCHER, born Main Rousseau Bocher, Oct. 24, 1890 (Chicago, Ill.). U.S. fashion designer. Noted for his expensive, elegant evening clothes. Editor of *French Vogue,* 1923–29; founder and pres. of Mainbocher, Paris, 1930–39; founder and pres. of Mainbocher Inc., New York City, 1940–   ; designed uniforms for WAVES (1942), Girl Scouts (1946), Red Cross (1948), and SPARS (1951).

MALLON, MARY ("Typhoid Mary"), 1870–1938. U.S. cook. A carrier of typhoid fever, she knowingly spread her illness around the New York City area, causing at least 53 cases of typhoid and three deaths, from c.1905 to 1915.

MANDELBAUM, FREDERICKA ("Marm"), 1818–1889. U.S. criminal. One of the most successful fences of all time; living quietly in New York City from 1862 sold nearly $4 million in stolen goods and became a millionaire; taught other female criminals how to improve their trade, and youngsters how to pick pockets, burgle, and blackmail.

MAN O'WAR ("Big Red"), Mar. 29, 1917–Nov. 1, 1947. U.S. thoroughbred horse. Raced for only two years, winning 20 of 21 races and setting five world records, 1919–20; bred by AUGUST BELMONT near Lexington, Ky.; one of the leading sires of all time.

MANSON, CHARLES MILLES, Nov. 12, 1934 (Cincinnati, Ohio). U.S. leader of a California "family" of drifters. Convicted, with four young female followers, of murder in the first degree in the 1969 deaths of actress Sharon Tate and six others, 1971 (Charles "Tex" Watson later also convicted); sentenced to death, but capital punishment voided in California, 1972.

MATA HARI (pseud. of Margaretha Geertruida Macleod, née Zelle), Aug. 7, 1876 (Leeuwarden, Neth.)–Oct. 15, 1917. Dutch dancer, courtesan, spy. As a dancer in Paris, joined German Secret Service; betrayed important military secrets she learned from high Allied officers with whom she

was intimate; arrested, convicted, and executed by the French, 1917.

MESTA, PEARL, née Skirvin, Oct. 12, 1889 (Sturgis, Mich.)–Jan. 11, 1975. U.S. diplomat, hostess. The foremost unofficial hostess in Washington, D.C., during the 1940s; U.S. envoy to Luxembourg, 1949–53. The inspiration of IRVING BERLIN's musical *Call Me Madam.*

MOORE, SARA JANE, Feb. 15, 1930 (Charleston, W.Va.). U.S. radical. Attempted to assassinate Pres. GERALD R. FORD, 1975; convicted and sentenced to life imprisonment, 1976.

MORGAN, MARABEL, June 25, 1937 (Crestline, Ohio). U.S. author. A fervent believer in the virtues of middle-class monogamy, gained fame as author of *The Total Woman* (1973) and *Total Joy* (1976); pres. of Total Woman, Inc., 1970–

MORRIS, c.1961 (Chicago, Ill.)–July 7, 1978. U.S. cat, TV performer. Veteran of dozens of TV commercials; best known for 9 Lives cat-food commercials in which he was presented as "finicky."

MULLENS (Mullins or Mullines), **PRISCILLA.** American pilgrim woman. Daughter of one of the signers of the Mayflower Compact; married JOHN ALDEN, 1621 or 1623. Her role in H.W. LONGFELLOW's poem, *The Courtship of Miles Standish* (1858) is not based on historical fact.

MUMTAZ MAHAL (or Mahall), born Arjumand Banu, 1592–1631. Favorite wife of Mogul emperor Shah Jahan, who built the famous Taj Mahal at Agra as her mausoleum.

MÜNCHHAUSEN, KARL FRIEDRICH HIERONYMOUS, BARON VON, May 11, 1720 (Bodenwerder, Ger.)–Feb. 22, 1797. German soldier, huntsman. A great storyteller of his life as a soldier, hunter and sportsman, whose fame was established by Rudolph Raspe's *Adventures of Baron Munchhausen* (1793); his name is now proverbially associated with absurdly exaggerated tales.

MURRAY, ARTHUR, Apr. 4, 1895 (New York, N.Y.); and his wife **KATHRYN MURRAY,** Sept. 15, 1906 (Jersey City, N.J.). U.S. dancing teachers. Originated the Arthur Murray School of Dancing, a chain of some 450 dance schools throughout the U.S. Producer and hostess of TV's *Arthur Murray Dance Party,* 1950–60.

NADER, RALPH, Feb. 27, 1934 (Winsted, Conn.). U.S. lawyer, consumer advocate, author. A leading advocate of consumer affairs in the U.S. Founded the Center for the Study of Responsive Law, 1969; attained natl. attention for his indictment of the auto industry for its poor safety standards. *Unsafe at Any Speed,* 1965.

NELSON, GEORGE ("Baby Face"), born Lester N. Gillis, Dec. 6, 1908 (Chicago, Ill.)–Nov. 28, 1934. U.S. bank robber. Member of the JOHN DILLINGER gang; killed in a gun battle with law officers.

NESBIT, EVELYN ("The Girl on the Red Velvet Swing"), 1884 (Pennsylvania)–Jan. 17, 1967. U.S. showgirl. The mistress of millionaire architect STANFORD WHITE, she married multimillionaire HARRY K. THAW; Thaw, tormented by jealousy, murdered White at New York City's Madison Square Garden, 1906.

NESS, ELIOT, Apr. 19, 1903 (Chicago, Ill.)–May 7, 1957. U.S. govt. agent. Best known as the special FBI agent who headed the investigation of AL CAPONE, in Chicago, 1929–32.

NIXON, (Thelma Catherine) **PATRICIA,** née Ryan, Mar. 16, 1912 (Ely, Nev.). U.S. First Lady. Wife of U.S. Pres. R. M. NIXON; decorated with Grand Cross Order of Sun for relief work at the time of Peruvian earthquake, 1971; named in George Gallup polls as among the most admired women, in 1957, 1968, 1969, 1970 and 1971.

NIZER, LOUIS, Feb. 6, 1902 (London, Eng.). U.S. lawyer, author. A founding member (1926) and later senior partner of Phillips, Nizer, Benjamin and Krim, a law firm specializing in cases in the entertainment field. *What to Do with Germany,* 1944; *My Life in Court,* 1962; *The Jury Returns,* 1966.

NORELL, NORMAN, 1900 (Noblesville, Ind.)–Oct. 25, 1972. U.S. designer. One of leading designers in U.S. for over 30 years; began as designer with Hattie Carnegie, 1927; showed first collection, with Traina-Norell (New York City), 1941.

ONASSIS, JACQUELINE BOUVIER KENNEDY, July 28, 1929 (Southampton, N.Y.). U.S. First Lady, wife of Pres. JOHN F. KENNEDY. As First Lady, planned and conducted the restoration of the White House décor; married Greek shipping magnate ARISTOTLE ONASSIS, 1968; consulting editor at Viking Press, 1975–77; editor at Doubleday & Co., 1977– .

OSWALD, LEE HARVEY, Oct. 18, 1939 (New Orleans, La.)–Nov. 24, 1963. U.S. assassin. Alleged killer of U.S. Pres. JOHN F. KENNEDY in Dallas, Tex., on Nov. 22, 1963. A former U.S. marine, lived in the USSR (1959–62) and was Cuban communist sympathizer; shot two days after the Kennedy assassination by JACK RUBY.

PARKER, BONNIE, Oct. 1, 1910 (Rowena, Tex.)–May 23, 1934. U.S. outlaw. With CLYDE BARROW, formed the famous duo that robbed and killed on their way across Texas, New Mexico, and Missouri, c.1932; ambushed and shot to death by Texas Rangers and sheriff's deputies.

PARNIS, MOLLIE, Mar. 18, 1905 (New York, N.Y.). U.S. fashion designer. Particularly successful in the 1950s with her simple full-skirted dresses; started, with her husband, Parnis-Livingston, Inc., 1933.

PAYSON, JOAN WHITNEY, Feb. 5, 1903 (New York, N.Y.)–Oct. 4, 1975. U.S. philanthropist, sportswoman. Extended her interests to horse racing, baseball (New York Mets), the arts (a founder of the Museum of Modern Art), and philanthropy (pres. of Helen Hay Whitney Fndn.); co-owner of Greentree Stud, Inc., (1945–75) and Greentree Stable (1945–75).

PERRY, NANCY LING, 1947 (Santa Rosa, Calif.). U.S. revolutionary. The spiritual and doctrinal leader of the Symbionese Liberation Army. Once a Goldwater supporter, turned to radical politics while at Berkeley U.; lived with Russell Little, a philosophy graduate and prison-reform activist; their home became the first SLA hq.

PINKHAM, LYDIA ESTES, Feb. 9, 1819 (nr. Lynn, Mass.)–May 17, 1883. U.S. patent-medicine proprietor. Invented the famous home remedy, "Vegetable Compound," first marketed in 1876; sales peaked at $3.8 million, 1925; compound was a concoction of roots and seeds, plus a generous dose of alcohol as a solvent and preservative.

POCAHONTAS (Ind. name: Matoaka), c.1595 (Virginia)–Mar. 1617. American Indian woman. Daughter of Powhatan; saved the life of Capt. JOHN SMITH; helped maintain peace between the native Americans and the English colonists at Jamestown, Va.; married John Rolfe, converted to Christianity, and was christened Rebecca.

POLO, MARCO, 1254 (Venice)–1324. Medieval Italian traveler whose account of his journeys to Asia was the chief source of information on the East during the Ren. Traveled to Asia with his father and uncle, 1271; a favorite of KUBLAI KHAN for 16 years; upon his return to Venice (1295), wrote his celebrated account, in which he described paper currency, asbestos, coal, and other phenomena unknown to Europe.

PRINCIP, GAVRILLO, July 25, 1895 (Bosnia)–Apr. 28, 1918. Serbian assassin of Archduke FRANCIS FERDINAND and his wife at Sarajevo, 1914.

PUCCI, EMILIO, Nov. 20, 1914 (Naples, It.). Italian fashion designer. Noted for his use of brilliant colors in elegant sportswear, silk blouses, scarves, underclothes.

RALEIGH, SIR WALTER, 1552? (Devonshire, Eng.)–Oct. 29, 1618. English adventurer, statesman, man of letters. A favorite of ELIZABETH I of England; became captain of the queen's guard, 1587; received grants of monopolies and estates from queen; sent expeditions to Virginia; connected with poetic group known as School of Might; attempted to find the fabled El Dorado, 1595; imprisoned after Elizabeth's death, 1603–16; wrote his *History of the World,* 1614; released, went on ill-fated mission to find gold; eventually beheaded for insubordination.

REBOZO, CHARLES ("Bebe"), Nov. 17, 1912. (Tampa, Fla.). U.S. banker. As a friend of Pres. RICHARD M. NIXON, provided him a refuge from the many demands of public office at Key Biscayne, Fla., home; chm. of Key Biscayne (Fla.) Bank, 1964–

ROMBAUER, IRMA S., c.1876 (St. Louis, Mo.)–Oct. 14, 1962. U.S. cook-book author. Best known as author of one of the all-time best-selling cookbooks, *The Joy of Cooking,* first published in 1931 at her own expense; *The New Joy of Cooking* (revised ed., 1951) was written with daughter Marion Rombauer Becker.

ROOSEVELT, ANNA ELEANOR, Oct. 11, 1884 (New York, N.Y.)–Nov. 7, 1962. U.S. First Lady, writer, lecturer. As the wife of Pres. F. D. ROOSEVELT, called "The First Lady of the World." Extremely active in the political affairs of her day. *It's Up to the Women,* 1933; *This Is My Story,* 1937; *The Moral Basis of Democracy,* 1940.

ROSENBERG, JULIUS, May 12, 1918 (New York, N.Y.)–June 19, 1953; and his wife **ETHEL ROSENBERG,** née Greenglass, Sept. 28, 1915 (New York, N.Y.)–June 19, 1953. The first U.S. civilians to be executed for espionage. Dedicated communists who were convicted of turning over to the USSR military secrets that had come into their possession.

ROSS, BETSY, née Griscom, Jan. 1, 1752 (Philadelphia, Pa.)–Jan. 30, 1836. American patriot. According to legend, made the first American flag (1776) at the request of a committee headed by GEORGE WASHINGTON; however, no historical support for this claim exists.

RUBY, JACK, born Jacob Rubenstein c.1911–Jan. 3, 1967. U.S. nightclub owner (Dallas, Tex.) and slayer of LEE HARVEY OSWALD (1963). Said to have been an ardent supporter of Pres. JOHN F. KENNEDY; convicted of murder, 1964; sentence reversed, 1966; died while awaiting retrial; all charges dismissed, 1967.

SACCO, NICOLA, Apr. 22, 1891 (Apulia, It.)–Aug. 23, 1927. Italian-U.S. radical, factory worker. With BARTOLOMEO VANZETTI, tried and convicted of a 1920 robbery and shooting in S. Braintree, Mass., 1921; doubt as to their guilt led to worldwide support and protest; became martyrs to those who believed in their innocence; vindicated

OTHER NOTED OR NOTORIOUS PERSONALITIES

July 19, 1977, by proclamation of Mass. Gov. Dukakis.

ST. LAURENT, YVES MATHIEU, Aug. 1, 1936 (Oran, Algeria). French fashion designer. A protégé of CHRISTIAN DIOR; used leather and fur in introducing the "chic beatnik" look, 1960; introduced the "little boy look" in the mid-60s.

SASSOON, VIDAL, Jan. 17, 1928 (London, Eng.). English hair stylist. Founded a network of schools and salons in New York, London, and San Francisco. *A Year of Health and Beauty,* 1976.

SCHIAPARELLI, ELSA, Sept. 10, 1896 (Rome, It.)–Nov. 13, 1972. Italian-French fashion designer. Noted for her flamboyant, daring innovations; used brilliant colors such as "shocking pink"; introduced the padded shoulder, 1932; by 1935, a leader in *haute couture. Shocking Life,* 1954.

SCHULTZ, DUTCH, born Arthur Flegenheimer, Aug. 6, 1902 (New York, N.Y.)–Oct. 24, 1934. U.S. mobster. Ran bootlegging and other rackets in the Bronx and Harlem, c.1925–34; shot to death, probably on LUCKY LUCIANO's orders.

SHAPIRO, JACOB, a.k.a. Jake Gurrah, May 5, 1897 (Minsk, Rus.)–June 9, 1947. U.S. mobster. Partner of LEPKE BUCHALTER in Murder, Inc.; died of natural causes in Ossining Prison (Sing Sing). (Gurrah is short for *gerarah,* as in New York slang phrase "gerarah here, kid"—i.e., "get out of here, kid.")

SHERATON, THOMAS, 1751 (Durham, Eng.)–Oct. 22, 1806. English furniture designer, cabinetmaker. With his *Cabinet-Maker and Upholsterer's Drawing Book* (1791) popularized his emphasis on straight, vertical lines and his delicate, simple style; a leading exponent of neoclassicism.

SIMPSON, ADELE, née Smithline, Dec. 8, 1908 (New York, N.Y.). U.S. fashion designer. Designer of women's clothes sold through Adele Simpson, Inc.; received Nieman-Marcus Fashion Award, 1946; received Coty Award, 1947.

SIRHAN, SIRHAN BISHARA, 1945 (Jerusalem [now in Israel]). Palestinian assassin. Convicted of first-degree murder in the June 1968 killing of Sen. R. F. KENNEDY; sentenced to death, 1969; a resident-alien, he objected to Kennedy's pro-Israel stance.

SOBEL, MORTON, Apr. 11, 1917 (New York, N.Y.). U.S. alleged spy. Worked as an engineer for U.S. Navy on top-secret U.S. radar and electronic devices, 1942–47; a codefendant with JULIUS and ETHEL ROSENBERG, convicted of being a member of a spy ring that passed atomic secrets to the USSR, 1951; sentenced to 30 years in prison; released, 1969.

STARR, BELLE, born Myra Belle Shirley, Feb. 5, 1848 (Carthage, Mo.)–Feb. 3, 1889. U.S. outlaw. Hard-living, hard-loving woman who led a band of cattle rustlers and horse thieves that made regular raids on Oklahoma ranches; sheltered JESSE JAMES, 1881.

SURRATT, JOHN H., 1844 (Prince George Co., Md.)–Apr. 21, 1916. U.S. conspirator with J. W. BOOTH in the assassination of Pres. ABRAHAM LINCOLN; arrested (1866), tried (1867), but released (1868) when govt. failed to obtain an indictment. (Son of MARY E. SURRATT.)

SURRATT, MARY E., May 1820 (Prince George Co., Md.)–July 7, 1865. U.S. boardinghouse keeper in Washington, D.C. and an alleged conspirator in the assassination of Pres. ABRAHAM LINCOLN; kept the house where J. W. BOOTH lived and met with the other conspirators; hanged for her complicity, probably on insufficient evidence.

THAW, HARRY KENDALL, c.1872 (Pittsburgh, Pa.)–Feb. 22, 1947. U.S. murderer. The playboy son of a Pittsburgh railroad and coke magnate; shot and killed architect STANFORD WHITE in Madison Square Garden (1906), apparently motivated by jealousy over his wife, EVELYN NESBIT Thaw, a former chorus girl; judged insane.

TOKYO ROSE (pseud. of Iva Toguri d'Aquino), July 4, 1916 (Los Angeles, Calif.). U.S. typist, WW II commentator for Radio Tokyo. The only one of the "Tokyo Roses" who broadcast anti-U.S. propaganda during WW II to be imprisoned for treason. Arrested and brought to U.S. from occupied Japan, 1948; charged with eight counts of treason, found guilty on one; sentenced to 10 years in prison, fined $10,000, and deprived of U.S. citizenship; released, 1956; received presidential pardon, 1977.

TSCHIRKY, OSCAR MICHEL, Sept. 28, 1866 (Locle, Switz.)–Nov. 6, 1950. U.S. hotelier. Known as "Oscar of the Waldorf," a famous maître d'hôtel at the Waldorf Hotel, 1893–1943; credited with creation of the Waldorf salad. *Oscar of the Waldorf's Cookbook,* 1903.

TURNER, NAT, Oct. 2, 1800 (Southampton Co., Va.)–Nov. 11, 1831. U.S. slave. Leader of the Southampton Insurrection (1831), the only effective slave revolt in U.S. history. Believing he was divinely called to do so, gathered about 60 followers and killed 55 white people; quickly caught and hanged.

TWIGGY, born Leslie Hornby, Sept. 19, 1949 (Neasden, Eng.). English model, actress, singer. The number-one fashion model of the late 1960s, in the U.S. and Great Britain; earned $240 an hour during her highly-publicized 1967 tour of the U.S.; nick-named "Twiggy" for her 5'6", 92-lb. frame.

VANZETTI, BARTOLOMEO, July 11, 1888 (Villafalletto, It.)–Aug. 23, 1927. Italian fish peddler, anarchist. With NICOLA SACCO, convicted and executed for the murders of a factory paymaster and guard during a robbery in South Braintree, Mass., 1920; doubt as to their guilt created a worldwide storm of protest; the controversial trial sparked numerous plays, novels, poems, and radio and TV productions; vindicated July 19, 1977, by proclamation of Mass. Gov. Dukakis.

VON DÄNIKEN, ERICH, Apr. 14, 1935 (Zofingen, Switz.). Swiss author. In series of best-sellers, postulated that in the remote past extra-terrestrial space travelers visited earth and "seeded" great-ape forefathers with intelligence via artificial mutation. *Chariots of the Gods?* 1970; *Gods from Outer Space,* 1971; *The Gold of the Gods,* 1973; *In Search of Ancient Gods,* 1974.

WARFIELD, (Bessie) WALLIS, DUCHESS OF WINDSOR, June 19, 1896 (Blue Ridge Summit, Pa.). U.S. divorcee for whom EDWARD VIII of England abdicated the throne. *The Heart Has Its Reasons,* 1956.

WEDGWOOD, JOSIAH, baptized July 12, 1730 (Staffordshire, Eng.)–Jan. 3, 1795. English potter. Known for his jasper ware and queen's ware; a leading scientific thinker; invented a pyrometer for measuring temperature.

WILEY, ROLAND HENRY, May 30, 1904 (Avoca, Iowa). U.S. lawyer, farmer. District attorney, Las Vegas, Nev., 1939–43; builder of Cathedral Canyon, Hidden Hills Ranch, Pahrump Valley, Nev., 1973. *Hoover Dam,* 1932.

THE BOOK OF WHO

WILLIAMS, EDWARD BENNETT, May 31, 1920 (Hartford, Conn.). U.S. lawyer. Top criminal lawyer who has defended many controversial figures, including ADAM CLAYTON POWELL, JIMMY HOFFA, and SEN. JOSEPH MCCARTHY. *One Man's Freedom,* 1962.

WILLIAMSONS ("The Terrible Williamsons"; also eight to ten other pseudonyms, including McDonald and Stewart). Clan of about 2,000 "gyp artists" descended from Robert Logan Williamson, a Scotsman who came to the U.S. around the turn of the century; the police have adopted "Williamsons" as generic name for itinerant hustlers.

WORTH, CHARLES FREDERICK, 1825 (Lincolnshire, Eng.)–Mar. 10, 1895. British fashion designer. Left England (1845) for Paris, where he founded (1858) his own ladies' tailor shop, which he developed into a leading fashion house; first to prepare and show a collection in advance; the first prominent man in women's fashions; the founder of Parisian *haute couture.*

ZANGARA, GIUSEPPE, Sept. 1900 (Calabria, It.)–Mar. 20, 1933. Italian-U.S. bricklayer. An anarchist, he hated capitalists and kings; attempted to assassinate Pres. FRANKLIN D. ROOSEVELT, in Miami, Fla., on Feb. 15, 1933; Roosevelt escaped, but Chicago Mayor A. J. Cermak was killed and five others were wounded; executed.

RULERS OF ENGLAND AND GREAT BRITAIN

Name	England	Began	Died
Saxons and Danes			
Egbert	King of Wessex, won allegiance of all English	829	839
Ethelwulf	Son, King of Wessex, Sussex, Kent, Essex	839	858
Ethelbald	Son of Ethelwulf, displaced father in Wessex	858	860
Ethelbert	2d son of Ethelulf, united Kent and Wessex	860	866
Ethelred I	3d son, King of Wessex, fought Danes	866	871
Alfred	The Great, 4th son, defeated Danes, fortified London	871	899
Edward	The Elder, Alfred's son, united English, claimed Scotland	899	924
Athelstan	The Glorious, Edward's son, King of Mercia, Wessex	924	940
Edmund I	3d son of Edward, King of Wessex, Mercia	940	946
Edred	4th son of Edward	946	955
Edwy	The Fair, eldest son of Edmund, King of Wessex	955	959
Edgar	The Peaceful, 2d son of Edmund, ruled all English	959	975
Edward	The Martyr, eldest son of Edgar, murdered by stepmother	975	978
Ethelred II	The Unready, 2d son of Edgar, married Emma of Normandy	978	1016
Edmund II	Ironside, son of Ethelred II, King of London	1016	1016
Canute	The Dane, gave Wessex to Edmund, married Emma	1016	1035
Harold I	Harefoot, natural son of Canute	1035	1040
Hardecanute	Son of Canute by Emma, Danish King	1040	1042
Edward	The Confessor, son of Ethelred II (Canonized 1161)	1042	1066
Harold II	Edward's brother-in-law, last Saxon King	1066	1066
House of Normandy			
William I	The Conqueror, defeated Harold at Hastings	1066	1087
William II	Rufus, 3d son of William I, killed by arrow	1087	1100
Henry I	Beauclerc, youngest son of William I	1100	1135
House of Blois			
Stephen	Son of Adela, daughter of William I, and Count of Blois	1135	1154
House of Plantagenet			
Henry II	Son of Geoffrey Pantagenet (Angevin) by Matilda, dau. of Henry I	1154	1189
Richard I	Coeur de Lion, son of Henry II, crusader	1189	1199
John	Lackland, son of Henry II, signed Magna Carta, 1215	1199	1216
Henry III	Son of John, acceded at 9, under regency until 1227	1216	1272
Edward I	Longshanks, son of Henry III	1272	1307
Edward II	Son of Edward I, deposed by Parliament, 1327	1307	1327
Edward III	Of Windsor, son of Edward II	1327	1377
Richard II	Grandson of Edw. III, minor until 1389, deposed 1399	1377	1400
House of Lancaster			
Henry IV	Son of John of Gaunt, Duke of Lancaster, son of Edw. III	1399	1413
Henry V	Son of Henry IV, victor of Agincourt	1413	1422
Henry VI	Son of Henry V, deposed 1461, died in Tower	1422	1471
House of York			
Edward IV	Great-great-grandson of Edward III, son of Duke of York	1461	1483
Edward V	Son of Edward IV, murdered in Tower of London	1483	1483
Richard III	Crookback, bro. of Edward IV, fell at Bosworth Field	1483	1485
House of Tudor			
Henry VII	Son of Edmund Tudor, Earl of Richmond, whose father had married the widow of Henry V; descended from Edward III through his mother, Margaret Beaufort via John of Gaunt. By marriage with dau. of Edward IV he united Lancaster and York	1485	1509
Henry VIII	Son of Henry VII by Elizabeth, dau. of Edward IV	1509	1547
Edward VI	Son of Henry VIII, by Jane Seymour, his 3d queen. Ruled under regents. Was forced to name Lady Jane Grey his successor. Council of State proclaimed her queen July 10, 1553. Mary Tudor won Council, was proclaimed queen July 19, 1553. Mary had Lady Jane Grey beheaded for treason, Feb., 1554	1547	1553
Mary I	Daughter of Henry VIII, by Catherine of Aragon	1553	1558
Elizabeth I	Daughter of Henry VIII, by Anne Boleyn	1558	1603
Great Britain			
House of Stuart			
James I	James VI of Scotland, son of Mary, Queen of Scots. *First to call himself King of Great Britain. This became official with the Act of Union, 1707*	1603	1625
Charles I	Only surviving son of James I; beheaded Jan. 30, 1649	1625	1649

303

THE BOOK OF WHO

Commonwealth, 1649–1660
Council of State, 1649; Protectorate, 1653

The Cromwells	Oliver Cromwell, Lord Protector	1653	1658
....	Richard Cromwell, son, Lord Protector, resigned May 25, 1659	1658	1712

House of Stuart (Restored)

Charles II	Eldest son of Charles I, died without issue	1660	1685
James II	2d son of Charles I. Deposed 1688. Interregnum Dec 11, 1688, to Feb. 13, 1689	1685	1701
William III	Son of William, Prince of Orange, by Mary, dau. of Charles I .	1689	1702
and Mary II	Eldest daughter of James II and wife of William III		1694
Anne	2d daughter of James II	1702	1714

House of Hanover

George I	Son of Elector of Hanover, by Sophia, grand-dau. of James I	1714	1727
George II	Only son of George I, married Caroline of Brandenburg ...	1727	1760
George III	Grandson of George II, married Charlotte of Mecklenburg .	1760	1820
George IV	Eldest son of George III, Prince Regent, from Feb., 1811 ..	1820	1830
William IV	3d son of George III, married Adelaide of Saxe-Meiningen .	1830	1837
Victoria	Dau. of Edward, 4th son of George III; married (1840) Prince Albert of Saxe-Coburg and Gotha, who became Prince Consort	1837	1901

House of Saxe-Coburg and Gotha

Edward VII	Eldest son of Victoria, married Alexandra, Princess Denmark	1901	1910

House of Windsor
Name Adopted July 17, 1917

George V	2d son of Edward VII, married Princess Mary of Teck	1910	1936
Edward VIII	Eldest son of George V; acceded Jan. 20, 1936, abdicated Dec. 11	1936	1972
George VI	2d son of George V; married Lady Elizabeth Bowes-Lyon ..	1936	1952
Elizabeth II	Elder daughter of George VI, acceded Feb. 6, 1952	1952	—

British Prime Ministers

Prime Minister	Party	Served
Sir Robert Walpole	Whig	1721–42
Earl of Wilmington	Whig	1742–43
Henry Pelham	Whig	1743–54
Duke of Newcastle	Whig	1754–56
Duke of Devonshire	Whig	1756–57
Duke of Newcastle	Whig	1757–62
Earl of Bute	Tory	1762–63
George Grenville	Whig	1763–65
Marquess of Rockingham	Whig	1765–66
Earl of Chatham	Whig	1766–67
Duke of Grafton	Whig	1767–70
Lord North	Tory	1770–82
Marquess of Rockingham	Whig	1782
Earl of Shelburne	Whig	1782–83
Duke of Portland	Coalition	1783
William Pitt	Tory	1783–1801
Henry Addington	Tory	1801–04
William Pitt	Tory	1804–06
Lord Grenville	Whig	1806–07
Duke of Portland	Tory	1807–09
Spencer Perceval	Tory	1809–12
Earl of Liverpool	Tory	1812–27
George Canning	Tory	1827
Viscount Goderich	Tory	1827–28
Duke of Wellington	Tory	1828–30
Earl Grey	Whig	1830–34
Viscount Melbourne	Whig	1834
Sir Robert Peel	Tory	1834–35
Viscount Melbourne	Whig	1835–41
Sir Robert Peel	Tory	1841–46
Lord John Russell	Whig	1846–52

Earl of Derby	Tory	1852
Earl of Aberdeen	Peelite	1852-55
Viscount Palmerston	Liberal	1855-58
Earl of Derby	Conservative	1858-59
Viscount Palmerston	Liberal	1859-65
Earl Russell	Liberal	1865-66
Earl of Derby	Conservative	1866-68
Benjamin Disraeli	Conservative	1868
W. E. Gladstone	Liberal	1868-74
Benjamin Disraeli	Conservative	1874-80
W. E. Gladstone	Liberal	1880-85
Marquess of Salisbury	Conservative	1885-86
W. E. Gladstone	Liberal	1886
Marquess of Salisbury	Conservative	1886-92
W. E. Gladstone	Liberal	1892-94
Earl of Rosebery	Liberal	1894-95
Marquess of Salisbury	Conservative	1895-1902
A. J. Balfour	Conservative	1902-05
Sir H. Campbell-Bannerman	Liberal	1905-08
H. H. Asquith	Liberal	1908-15
H. H. Asquith	Coalition	1915-16
D. Lloyd-George	Coalition	1916-22
A. Bonar Law	Conservative	1922-23
S. Baldwin	Conservative	1923-24
J. R. MacDonald	Labour	1924
S. Baldwin	Conservative	1924-29
J. R. MacDonald	Labour	1929-31
J. R. MacDonald	Coalition	1931-35
S. Baldwin	Coalition	1935-37
N. Chamberlain	Coalition	1937-40
W. S. Churchill	Coalition	1940-45
W. S. Churchill	Conservative	1945
C. R. Atlee	Labour	1945-51
Sir W. S. Churchill	Conservative	1951-55
Sir A. Eden	Conservative	1955-57
H. MacMillan	Conservative	1957-63
Sir A. Douglas-Home	Conservative	1963-64
Harold Wilson	Labour	1964-70
Edward Heath	Conservative	1970-74
Harold Wilson	Labour	1974-76
James Callaghan	Labour	1976-79
Margaret Thatcher	Conservative	1979-

RULERS OF SCOTLAND

Kenneth I MacAlpin was the first Scot to rule both Scots and Picts, 846 AD.

Duncan I was the first general ruler, 1034. Macbeth seized the kingdom 1040, was slain by Duncan's son, Malcolm III MacDuncan (Canmore), 1057.

Malcolm married Margaret, Saxon princess who had fled from the Normans. Queen Margaret introduced English language and English monastic customs. She was canonized, 1250. Her son Edgar, 1097, moved the court to Edinburgh. His brothers Alexander I and David I succeeded. Malcolm IV, the Maiden, 1153, grandson of David I, was followed by his brother, William the Lion, 1165, whose son was Alexander II, 1214. The latter's son, Alexander III, 1249, defeated the Norse and regained the Hebrides. When he died, 1286, his granddaughter, Margaret, child of Eric of Norway and grandniece of Edward I of England, known as the Maid of Norway, was chosen ruler, but died 1290, aged 8.

John Baliol, 1292-1296. (Interregnum, 10 years.)

Robert Bruce (The Bruce), 1306-1329, victor at Bannockburn, 1314.

David II, only son of Robert Bruce, ruled 1329-1371.

Robert II, 1371-1390, grandson of Robert Bruce, son of Walter, the Steward of Scotland, was called The Steward, first of the so-called Stuart line.

Robert III, son of Robert II, 1390-1406.

James I, son of Robert III, 1406-1437.

James II, son of James I, 1437-1460.

James III, eldest son of James II, 1460-1488.

James IV, eldest son of James III, 1488-1513.

James V, eldest son of James IV, 1513-1542.

Mary, daughter of James V, born 1542, became queen when one week old; was crowned 1543. Married, 1558, Francis, son of Henry II of France, who became king 1559, died 1560. Mary ruled Scots 1561 until abdication, 1567. She also married (2) Henry Stewart, Lord Darnley, and (3) James, Earl of Bothwell. Imprisoned by Elizabeth I, Mary was beheaded 1587.

James VI, 1567-1625, son of Mary and Lord Darnley, became King of England on death of Elizabeth in 1603. Although the thrones were thus united, the legislative union of Scotland and England was not effected until the Act of Union, May 1, 1707.

RULERS OF FRANCE: KINGS, QUEENS, PRESIDENTS

Caesar to Charlemagne

Julius Caesar subdued the Gauls, native tribes of Gaul (France) 57 to 52 BC. The Romans ruled 500 years. The Franks, a Teutonic tribe, reached the Somme from the East c. 250 AD. By the 5th century the Merovingian Franks ousted the Romans. In 451 AD, with the help of Visigoths, Burgundians and others, they defeated Attila and the Huns at Chalons-sur-Marne.

Childeric I became leader of the Merovingians 458 AD. His son Clovis I (Chlodwig, Ludwig, Louis), crowned 481, founded the dynasty. After defeating the Alemanni (Germans) 496, he was baptized a Christian and made Paris his capital. His line ruled until Childeric III was deposed, 751.

The West Merovingians were called Neustrians, the eastern Austrasians. Pepin of Herstal (687–714) major domus, or head of the palace, of Austrasia, took over Neustria as dux (leader) of the Franks. Pepin's son, Charles, called Martel (the Hammer) defeated the Saracens at Tours-Poitiers, 732; was succeeded by his son, Pepin the Short, 741, who deposed Childeric III and ruled as king until 768.

His son, Charlemagne, or Charles the Great (742–814), became king of the Franks, 768, with his brother Carloman, who died 771. He ruled France, Germany, parts of Italy, Spain, Austria, and enforced Christianity. Crowned Emperor of the Romans by Pope Leo III in St. Peter's, Rome, Dec. 25, 800 AD. Succeeded by son, Louis I the Pious, 814. At death, 840, Louis left empire to sons, Lothair (Roman emperor); Pepin I (king of Aquitaine); Louis II (of Germany); Charles the Bald (France). They quarreled and by the peace of Verdun, 843, divided the empire.

AD Name, Year of accession

The Carolingians

843 Charles I (the Bald), Roman Emperor, 875
877 Louis II (the Stammerer), son
879 Louis III (died 882) and Carloman, brothers
885 Charles II (the Fat), Roman Emperor, 881
888 Eudes (Odo) elected by nobles
898 Charles III (the Simple), son of Louis II, defeated by
922 Robert, brother of Eudes, killed in war
923 Rudolph (Raoul) Duke of Burgundy
936 Louis IV, son of Charles III
954 Lothair, son, aged 13, defeated by Capet
986 Louis V (the Sluggard), left no heirs

The Capets

987 Hugh Capet, son of Hugh the Great
996 Robert II (the Wise), his son
1031 Henry I, his son, last Norman
1060 Philip I (the Fair), son
1108 Louis VI (the Fat), son
1137 Louis VII (the Younger), son
1180 Philip II (Augustus), son, crowned at Reims
1223 Louis VIII (the Lion), son
1226 Louis IX, son, crusader; Louis IX (1214–1270) reigned 44 years, arbitrated disputes with English King Henry III; led crusades, 1248 (captured in Egypt 1250) and 1270, when he died of plague in Tunis. Canonized 1297 as St. Louis.
1270 Philip III (the Hardy), son
1285 Philip IV (the Fair), son, king at 17
1314 Louis X (the Headstrong), son. His posthumous son, John I, lived only 7 days
1316 Philip V (the Tall), brother of Louis X
1322 Charles IV (the Fair), brother of Louis X

House of Valois

1328 Philip VI (of Valois), grandson of Philip III
1350 John II (the Good), his son, retired to England
1364 Charles V (the Wise), son
1380 Charles VI (the Beloved), son
1422 Charles VII (the Victorious), son. In 1429 Joan of Arc (Jeanne d'Arc) promised Charles to oust the English, who occupied northern France. Joan won at Orleans and Patay and had Charles crowned at Reims July 17, 1429. Joan was captured May 24, 1430, and executed May 30, 1431, at Rouen for heresy. Charles ordered her rehabilitation, effected 1455.
1461 Louis XI (the Cruel), son, civil reformer
1483 Charles VIII (the Affable), son
1498 Louis XII, great-grandson of Charles V
1515 Francis I, of Angouleme, nephew, son-in-law. Francis I (1494–1547) reigned 32 years, fought 4 big wars, was patron of the arts, aided Cellini, del Sarto, Leonardo da Vinci, Rabelais, embellished Fontainebleau.
1547 Henry II, son, killed at a joust in a tournament. He was the husband of Catherine de Medicis (1519–1589) and the lover of Diane de Poitiers (1499–1566). Catherine was born in Florence, daughter of Lorenzo de Medicis. By her marriage to Henry II she became the mother of Francis II, Charles IX, Henry III and Queen Margaret (Reine Margot) wife of Henry IV. She persuaded Charles IX to order the massacre of Huguenots on the Feast of St. Bartholomew, Aug. 24, 1572, the day her daughter was married to Henry of Navarre.
1559 Francis II, son. In 1548, Mary, Queen of Scots since infancy, was betrothed when 6 to Francis, aged 4. They were married 1558. Francis died 1560, aged 16; Mary ruled Scotland, abdicated 1567.
1560 Charles IX, brother
1574 Henry III, brother, assassinated

House of Bourbon

1589 Henry IV, of Navarre, assassinated. Henry IV made enemies when he gave tolerance to Protestants by Edict of Nantes, 1598. He was grandson of Queen Margaret of Navarre, literary patron. He married Margaret of Valois, daughter of Henry II and Catherine de Medicis; was divorced; in 1600 married Marie de Medicis, who became Regent of France, 1610–17 for her son, Louis XIII, but was exiled by Richelieu, 1631.

1610 Louis XIII (the Just), son. Louis XIII (1601-1643) married Anne of Austria. His ministers were Cardinals Richelieu and Mazarin.

1643 Louis XIV (The Grand Monarch), son. Louis XIV was king 72 years. He exhausted a prosperous country in wars for thrones and territory. By revoking the Edict of Nantes (1685) he caused the emigration of the Huguenots. He said: "I am the state."

1715 Louis XV, great-grandson. Louis XV married a Polish princess; lost Canada to the English. His favorites, Mme. Pompadour and Mme. Du Barry, influenced policies. Noted for saying "After me, the deluge."

1774 Louis XVI, grandson; married Marie Antoinette, daughter of Empress Maria Therese of Austria. King and queen beheaded by Revolution, 1793. Their son, called Louis XVII, died in prison, never ruled.

First Republic

1792 National Convention of the French Revolution

1795 Directory, under Barras and others

1799 Consulate, Napoleon Bonaparte, first consul. Elected consul for life, 1802.

First Empire

1804 Napoleon I, emperor. Josephine (de Beauharnais) empress, 1804-09; Marie Louise, empress, 1810-1814. Her son, François (1811-1832), titular King of Rome, later Duke de Reichstadt and "Napoleon II," never ruled. Napoleon abdicated 1814, died 1821.

Bourbons Restored

1814 Louis XVIII king; brother of Louis XVI.

1824 Charles X, brother; reactionary; deposed by the July Revolution, 1830.

House of Orleans

1830 Louis-Philippe, the "citizen king."

Second Republic

1848 Louis Napoleon Bonaparte, president, nephew of Napoleon I. He became:

Second Empire

1852 Napoleon III, emperor; Eugenie (de Montijo) empress. Lost Franco-Prussian war, deposed 1870. Son, Prince Imperial (1856-79), died in Zulu War. Eugenie died 1920.

Third Republic—Presidents

1871 Thiers, Louis Adolphe (1797-1877)
1873 MacMahon, Marshall Patrice M. de (1808-1893)
1879 Grévy, Paul J. (1807-1891)
1887 Sadi-Carnot, M. (1837-1894), assassinated
1894 Casimir-Périer, Jean P. P.(1847-1907)
1895 Faure, François Félix (1841-1899)
1899 Loubet, Émile (1838-1929)
1906 Fallières, C. Armand (1841-1931)
1913 Poincaré, Raymond (1860-1934)
1920 Deschanel, Paul (1856-1922)
1920 Millerand, Alexandre (1859-1943)
1924 Doumergue, Gaston (1863-1937)
1931 Doumer, Paul (1857-1932), assassinated
1932 Lebrun, Albert (1871-1950), resigned 1940
1940 Vichy govt. under German armistice. Henri Philippe Petain (1856-1951) Chief of State, 1940-1944.
Provisional govt. after liberation: Charles de Gaulle (1890-1970) Oct. 1944-Jan. 21, 1946; Felix Gouin (1884-1977) Jan. 23, 1946; Georges Bidault (1899-   ) June 24, 1946.

Fourth Republic—Presidents

1947 Auriol, Vincent (1884-1966)
1954 Coty, René (1882-1962)

Fifth Republic—Presidents

1959 de Gaulle., Charles André J. M. (1890-1970)
1969 Pompidou, Georges (1911-1974)
1974 Giscard d'Estaing, Valéry (1926-   )

RULERS OF MIDDLE EUROPE; RISE AND FALL OF DYNASTIES

Carolingian Dynasty

Charles the Great, or Charlemagne, ruled France, Italy, and Middle Europe; established Ostmark (later Austria); crowned Roman emperor by pope in Rome, 800 AD; died 814.
Louis I (Ludwig) the Pious, son; crowned by Charlemagne 814, d. 840.
Louis II, the German, son; succeeded to East Francia (Germany) 843-876.
Charles the Fat, son; inherited East Francia and West Francia (France) 876, reunited empire, crowned emperor by pope, 881, deposed 887.
Arnulf, nephew, 887-899. Partition of empire.

Louis the Child, 899-911, last direct descendant of Charlemagne.
Conrad I, duke of Franconia, first elected German king, 911-918, founded House of Franconia.

Saxon Dynasty; First Reich

Henry I, the Fowler, duke of Saxony, 919-936.
Otto I, the Great, 936-973, son; crowned Holy Roman Emperor by pope, 962.
Otto II, 973-983, son; failed to oust Greeks and Arabs from Sicily.
Otto III, 983-1002, son; crowned emperor at 16.
Henry II, the Saint, duke of Bavaria, 1002-1024, great-grandson of Otto the Great.

THE BOOK OF WHO

House of Franconia

Conrad II, 1024–1039, elected king of Germany.
Henry III, the Black, 1039–1056, son; deposed 3 popes; annexed Burgundy.
Henry IV, 1056–1106, son; regency by his mother, Agnes of Poitou. Banned by Pope Gregory VII, he did penance at Canossa.
Henry V, 1106–1125, son; last of Salic House.
Lothair, duke of Saxony, 1125–1137. Crowned emperor in Rome, 1134.

House of Hohenstaufen

Conrad III, duke of Swabia, 1138–1152. In 2d Crusade.
Frederick I, Barbarossa, 1152–1190; Conrad's nephew.
Henry VI, 1190–1197, took lower Italy from Normans. Son became king of Sicily.
Philip of Swabia, 1198–1208, brother.
Otto IV, of House of Welf, 1198–1215; deposed.
Frederick II, 1215–1250, son of Henry VI; king of Sicily; crowned king of Jerusalem; in 5th Crusade.
Conrad IV, 1250–1254, son; lost lower Italy to Charles of Anjou.
Conradin (1252–1268) son, king of Jerusalem and Sicily, beheaded. Last Hohenstaufen.
Interregnum, 1254–1273, Rise of the Electors.

Transition

Rudolph I of Hapsburg, 1273–1291, defeated King Ottocar II of Bohemia. Bequeathed duchy of Austria to eldest son, Albert.
Adolph of Nassau, 1292–1298, killed in war with Albert of Austria.
Albert I, king of Germany, 1298–1308, son of Rudolph.
Henry VII, of Luxemburg, 1308–1313, crowned emperor in Rome. Seized Bohemia, 1310.
Louis IV of Bavaria (Wittelsbach), 1314–1347. Also elected was Frederick of Austria, 1314–1330 (Hapsburg). Abolition of papal sanction for election of Holy Roman Emperor.
Charles IV, of Luxemburg, 1347–1378, grandson of Henry VII, German emperor and king of Bohemia, Lombardy, Burgundy; took Mark of Brandenburg.
Wenceslaus, 1378–1400, deposed.
Rupert, Duke of Palatine, 1400–1410.

Hungary

Stephen I, house of Arpad, 997–1038. Crowned king 1000; converted Magyars; canonized 1083. After several centuries of feuds Charles Robert of Anjou became Charles I, 1308–1342.
Louis I, the Great, son, 1342–1382; joint ruler of Poland with Casimir III, 1370. Defeated Turks.
Mary, daughter, 1382–1395, ruled with husband.
Sigismund of Luxemburg, 1387–1437, also king of Bohemia. As bro. of Wenceslaus he succeeded Rupert as Holy Roman Emperor, 1410.
Albert II, 1438–1439, son-in-law of Sigismund; also Roman emperor (see under Hapsburg).
Ulaszlo I (of Poland), 1440–1444.
Ladislas V, posthumous son of Albert II, 1444–1457. John Hunyadi (Hunyadi Janos) governor (1446–1452), fought Turks, Czechs; died 1456.
Matthias I (Corvinus) son of Hunyadi, 1458–1490. Shared rule of Bohemia, captured Vienna, 1485, annexed Austria, Styria, Carinthia.

Ladislas II (king of Bohemia), 1490–1516.
Louis II, son, aged 10, 1516–1526. Wars with Suleiman, Turk. In 1527 Hungary was split between Ferdinand I, Archduke of Austria, bro.-in-law of Louis II, and John Zapolya of Transylvania. After Turkish invasion, 1547, Hungary was split between Ferdinand, Prince John Sigismund (Transylvania) and the Turks.

House of Hapsburg

Albert V of Austria, Hapsburg, crowned king of Hungary, Jan. 1438, Roman emperor, March, 1438, as Albert II; died 1439.
Frederick III, cousin, 1440–1493. Fought Turks.
Maximilian I, son, 1493–1519. Assumed title of Holy Roman Emperor (German), 1493.
Charles V, grandson, 1519–1556. King of Spain with mother co-regent; crowned Roman emperor at Aix, 1520. Confronted Luther at Worms; attempted church reform and religious conciliation; abdicated 1556.
Ferdinand I, king of Bohemia, 1526, of Hungary, 1527; disputed. German king, 1531. Crowned Roman emperor on abdication of brother Charles V, 1556.
Maximilian II, son, 1564–1576.
Rudolph II, son, 1576–1612.
Matthias, brother, 1612–1619, king of Bohemia and Hungary.
Ferdinand II of Styria, king of Bohemia, 1617, of Hungary, 1618, Roman emperor, 1619. Bohemian Protestants deposed him, elected Frederick V of Palatine, starting Thirty Years War.
Ferdinand III, son, king of Hungary, 1625, Bohemia, 1627, Roman emperor, 1637. Peace of Westphalia, 1648, ended war. Leopold I, 1658–1705; Joseph I, 1705–1711; Charles VI, 1711–1740.
Maria Theresa, daughter, 1740–1780. Archduchess of Austria, queen of Hungary; ousted pretender, Charles VII, crowned 1742; in 1745 obtained election of her husband Francis I as Roman emperor and co-regent (d. 1765). Fought Seven Years' War with Frederick II (the Great) of Prussia. Mother of Marie Antoinette, queen of France.
Joseph II, son 1765–1790, Roman emperor, reformer; powers restricted by Empress Maria Theresa until her death, 1780. First partition of Poland. Leopold II, 1790–1792.
Francis II, son, 1792–1835. Fought Napoleon. Proclaimed first hereditary emperor of Austria, 1804. Forced to abdicate as Roman emperor, 1806; last use of title. Ferdinand I, son, 1835–1848, abdicated during revolution.

Austro-Hungarian Monarchy

Francis Joseph I, nephew, 1848–1916, emperor of Austria, king of Hungary. Dual monarchy of Austria-Hungary formed, 1867. After assassination of heir, Archduke Francis Ferdinand, June 28, 1914, Austrian diplomacy precipitated World War I.
Charles I, grand-nephew, 1916–1918, last emperor of Austria and king of Hungary. Abdicated Nov. 11–13, 1918, died 1922.

Rulers of Prussia

Nucleus of Prussia was the Mark of Brandenburg. First margrave was Albert the Bear (Albrecht), 1134–1170. First Hohenzollern margrave was Frederick, burgrave of Nuremberg, 1417–1440.

Frederick William, 1640–1688, the Great Elector. Son, Frederick III, 1688–1713, was crowned King Frederick of Prussia, 1701.

Frederick William I, son, 1713–1740.

Frederick II, the Great, son, 1740–1786, annexed Silesia part of Austria.

Frederick William II, nephew, 1786–1797.

Frederick William III, son, 1797–1840. Napoleonic wars.

Frederick William IV, son, 1840–1861. Uprising of 1848 and first parliament and constitution.

Second and Third Reich

William I, 1861–1888, brother. Annexation of Schleswig and Hanover; Franco-Prussian war, 1870–71, proclamation of German Reich, Jan. 18, 1871, at Versailles; William, German emperor (Deutscher Kaiser), Bismarck, chancellor.

Frederick III, son, 1888.

William II, son, 1888–1918. Led Germany in World War I, abdicated as German emperor and king of Prussia, Nov. 9, 1918. Died in exile in Netherlands June 4, 1941. Minor rulers of Bavaria, Saxony, Wurttemberg also abdicated.

Germany proclaimed a republic at Weimar, July 1, 1919. Presidents: Frederick Ebert, 1919–1925, Paul von Hindenburg-Beneckendorff, 1925, reelected 1932, d. Aug. 2, 1934. Adolf Hitler, chancellor, chosen successor as Leader-Chancellor (Fuehrer & Reichskanzler) of Third Reich. Annexed Austria, March, 1938. Precipitated World War II, 1939–1945. Committed suicide April 30, 1945.

RULERS OF DENMARK, SWEDEN, NORWAY

Denmark

Earliest rulers invaded Britain; King Canute, who ruled in London 1016–1035, was most famous. The Valdemars furnished kings until the 15th century. In 1282 the Danes won the first national assembly, Danehof, from King Erik V.

Most redoubtable medieval character was Margaret, daughter of Valdemar IV, born 1353, married at 10 to King Haakon VI of Norway. In 1376 she had her first infant son Olaf made king of Denmark. After his death, 1387, she was regent of Denmark and Norway. In 1388 Sweden accepted her as sovereign. In 1389 she made her grandnephew, Duke Erik of Pomerania, titular king of Denmark, Sweden, and Norway, with herself as regent. In 1397 she effected the Union of Kalmar of the three kingdoms and had Erik VII crowned. In 1439 the three kingdoms deposed him and elected, 1440, Christopher of Bavaria king (Christopher III). On his death, 1448, the union broke up.

Succeeding rulers were unable to enforce their claims as rulers of Sweden until 1520, when Christian II conquered Sweden. He was thrown out 1522, and in 1523 Gustavus Vasa united Sweden. Denmark continued to dominate Norway until the Napoleonic wars, when Frederick VI, 1808–1839, joined the Napoleonic cause after Britain had destroyed the Danish fleet, 1807. In 1814 he was forced to cede Norway to Sweden and Helgoland to Britain, receiving Lauenburg. Successors Christian VIII, 1839; Frederick VII, 1848; Christian IX, 1863; Frederick VIII, 1906; Christian X, 1912; Frederick IX, 1947; Margrethe II, 1972.

Sweden

Early kings ruled at Uppsala, but did not dominate the country. Sverker, c.1130–c.1156, united the Swedes and Goths. In 1435 Sweden obtained the Riksdag, or parliament. After the Union of Kalmar, 1397, the Danes either ruled or harried the country until Christian II of Denmark conquered it anew, 1520. This led to a rising under Gustavus Vasa, who ruled Sweden 1523–1560, and established an independent kingdom. Charles IX, 1599–1611, crowned 1604, conquered Moscow. Gustavus II Adolphus, 1611–1632, was called the Lion of the North. Later rulers: Christina, 1632; Charles X, Gustavus 1654; Charles XI, 1660; Charles XII (invader of Russia and Poland, defeated at Poltava, June 28, 1709), 1697; Ulrika Eleanora, sister, elected queen 1718; Frederick I (of Hesse), her husband, 1720; Adolphus Frederick, 1751; Gustavus III, 1771; Gustavus IV Adolphus, 1792; Charles XIII, 1809. (Union with Norway began 1814.) Charles XIV John, 1818. He was Jean Bernadotte, Napoleon's Prince of Ponte Corvo, elected 1810 to succeed Charles XIII. He founded the present dynasty: Oscar I, 1844; Charles XV, 1859; Oscar II, 1872; Gustavus V, 1907; Gustav VI Adolf, 1950; Carl XVI Gustaf, 1973.

Norway

Overcoming many rivals, Harald Haarfager, 872–930, conquered Norway, Orkneys, and Shetlands; Olaf I, great-grandson, 995–1000, brought Christianity into Norway, Iceland, and Greenland. In 1035 Magnus the Good also became king of Denmark. Haakon V, 1299–1319, had married his daughter to Erik of Sweden. Their son, Magnus became ruler of Norway and Sweden at 6. His son, Haakon VI, married Margaret of Denmark; their son Olaf IV became king of Norway and Denmark, followed by Margaret's regency and the Union of Kalmar, 1397.

In 1450 Norway became subservient to Denmark. Christian IV, 1588–1648, founded Christiania, now Oslo. After Napoleonic wars, when Denmark ceded Norway to Sweden, a strong nationalist movement forced recognition of Norway as an independent kingdom united with Sweden under the Swedish kings, 1814–1905. In 1905 the union was dissolved and Prince Carl of Denmark became Haakon VII. He died Sept. 21, 1957, aged 85; succeeded by son, Olav V, b. July 2, 1903.

RULERS OF THE NETHERLANDS AND BELGIUM

The Netherlands (Holland)

William Frederick, Prince of Orange, led a revolt against French rule, 1813, and was crowned King of the Netherlands, 1815. Belgium seceded Oct. 4, 1830, after a revolt, and formed a separate government. The change was ratified by the two kingdoms by treaty Apr. 19, 1839.

Succession: William II, son, 1840; William III, son, 1849; Wilhelmina, daughter of William III and his 2d wife Princess Emma of Waldeck, 1890; Wilhelmina abdicated, Sept. 4, 1948, in favor of daughter, Juliana. Juliana abdicated Apr. 30, 1980, in favor of daughter Beatrix.

Belgium

A national congress elected Prince Leopold of Saxe-Coburg king; he took the throne July 21, 1831, as Leopold I. Succession: Leopold II, son 1865; Albert I, nephew of Leopold II, 1909; Leopold III, son of Albert, 1934; Prince Charles, Regent 1944; Leopold returned 1950, yielded powers to son Baudouin, Prince Royal, Aug. 6, 1950, abdicated July 16, 1951. Baudouin I took throne July 17, 1951.

ROMAN RULERS

From Romulus to the end of the Empire in the West. Rulers of the Roman Empire in the East sat in Constantinople and for a brief period in Nicaea, until the capture of Constantinople by the Turks in 1453, when Byzantium was succeeded by the Ottoman Empire.

BC	Name

The Kingdom

753	Romulus (Quirinus)
716	Numa Pompilius
673	Tullus Hostilius
640	Ancus Marcius
616	L. Tarquinius Priscus
578	Servius Tullius
534	L. Tarquinius Superbus

The Republic

509	Consulate established
509	Quaestorship instituted
498	Dictatorship introduced
494	Plebeian Tribunate created
494	Plebeian Aedileship created
444	Consular Tribunate organized
435	Censorship instituted
366	Praetorship established
366	Curule Aedileship created
362	Military Tribunate elective
326	Proconsulate introduced
311	Naval Duumvirate elective
217	Dictatorship of Fabius Maximus
133	Tribunate of Tiberius Gracchus
123	Tribunate of Gaius Gracchus
82	Dictatorship of Sulla
60	First Triumvirate formed (Caesar, Pompeius, Crassus)
46	Dictatorship of Caesar
43	Second Triumvirate formed (Octavianus, Antonius, Lepidus)

BC	The Empire
27	Augustus (Gaius Julius Caesar Octavianus)

AD	
14	Tiberius I
37	Gaius Caesar (Caligula)
41	Claudius I
54	Nero
68	Galba
69	Galba; Otho, Vitellius
69	Vespasianus
79	Titus
81	Domitianus
96	Nerva
98	Trajanus
117	Hadrianus

138	Antoninus Pius
161	Marcus Aurelius and Lucius Verus
169	Marcus Aurelius (alone)
180	Commodus
193	Pertinax; Julianus I
193	Septimius Severus
211	Caracalla and Geta
212	Caracalla (alone)
217	Macrinus
218	Elagabalus (Heliogabalus)
222	Alexander Severus
235	Maximinus I (the Thracian)
238	Gordianus I and Gordianus II; Pupienus and Balbinus
238	Gordianus III
244	Philippus (the Arabian)
249	Decius
251	Gallus and Volusianus
253	Aemilianus
253	Valerianus and Gallienus
258	Gallienus (alone)
268	Claudius II (the Goth)
270	Quintillus
270	Aurelianus
275	Tacitus
276	Florianus
276	Probus
282	Carus
283	Carinus and Numerianus
284	Diocletianus
286	Diocletianus and Maximianus
305	Galerius and Constantius I
306	Galerius, Maximinus II, Severus I
307	Galerius, Maximinus II, Constantinus I, Licinius, Maxentius
311	Maximinus II, Constantinus I, Licinius, Maxentius
314	Maximinus II, Constantinus I, Licinius
314	Constantinus I and Licinius
324	Constantinus I (the Great)
337	Constantinus II, Constans I, Constantius II
340	Constantinus II and Constans I
350	Constantinus II
361	Julianus II (the Apostate)
363	Jovianus

West (Rome) and East (Constantinople)

364	Valentinianus I (West) and Valens (East)
367	Valentinianus I with Gratianus (West) and Valens (East)
375	Gratianus with Valentinianus II (West) and Valens (East)

378	Gratianus with Valentinianus II (West) Theodosius I (East)	456	Avitus (West), Marcianus (East)
383	Valentinianus II (West) and Theodosius I (East)	457	Majorianus (West), Leo I (East)
		461	Severus II (West), Leo I (East)
394	Theodosius I (the Great)	467	Anthemius (West), Leo I (East)
395	Honorius (West) and Arcadius (East)	472	Olybrius (West), Leo I (East)
408	Honorius (West) and Theodosius II (East)	473	Glycerius (West), Leo I (East)
423	Valentinianus III (West) and Theodosius II (East)	474	Julius Nepos (West), Leo II (East)
		475	Romulus Augustulus (West) and Zeno (East)
450	Valentinianus III (West) and Marcianus (East)	476	End of Empire in West; Odovacar, King, drops title of Emperor; murdered by King Theodoric of Ostrogoths 493 AD
455	Maximus (West), Avitus (West); Marcianus (East)		

RULERS OF MODERN ITALY

After the fall of Napoleon in 1814, the Congress of Vienna, 1815, restored Italy as a political patchwork, comprising the Kingdom of Naples and Sicily, the Papal States, and smaller units. Piedmont and Genoa were awarded to Sardinia, ruled by King Victor Emmanuel I of Savoy.

United Italy emerged under the leadership of Camillo, Count di Cavour (1810–1861), Sardinian prime minister. Agitation was led by Giuseppe Mazzini (1805–1872) and Giuseppe Garibaldi (1807–1882), soldier; Victor Emmanuel I abdicated 1821. After a brief regency for a brother, Charles Albert was king 1831–1849, abdicating when defeated by the Austrians at Novara. Succeeded by Victor Emmanuel II, 1849–1861.

In 1859 France forced Austria to cede Lombardy to Sardinia, which gave rights to Savoy and Nice to France. In 1860 Garibaldi led 1,000 volunteers in a spectacular campaign, took Sicily and expelled the king of Naples. In 1860 the House of Savoy annexed Tuscany, Parma, Modena, Romagna, the Two Sicilies, the Marches, and Umbria. Victor Emmanual assumed the title of king of Italy at Turin Mar. 17, 1861. In 1866 he allied with Prussia in the Austro-Prussian War, with Prussia's victory received Venetia. On Sept. 20, 1870, his troops under Gen. Raffaele Cardorna entered Rome and took over the Papal States, ending the temporal power of the Roman Catholic Church.

Succession: Umberto I, 1878, assassinated 1900; Victor Emmanuel III, 1900, abdicated 1946, died 1947; Umberto II, 1946, ruled a month. In 1921 Benito Mussolini (1883–1945) formed the Fascist party and became prime minister Oct. 31, 1922. He made the king emperor of Ethiopia, 1937; entered World War II as ally of Hitler. He was deposed July 25, 1943.

At a plebiscite June 2, 1946, Italy voted for a republic; Premier Alcide de Gasperi became chief of state June 13, 1946. On June 28, 1946, the Constituent Assembly elected Enrico de Nicola, Liberal, provisional president. Successive presidents: Luigi Einaudi, elected May 11, 1948; Giovanni Gronchi, Apr. 29, 1955; Antonio Segni, May 6, 1962; Giuseppe Saragat, Dec. 28, 1964; Giovanni Leone, Dec. 29, 1971; Alessandro Pertini, July 8, 1978.

RULERS OF SPAIN

From 8th to 11th centuries Spain was dominated by the Moors (Arabs and Berbers). The Christian reconquest established small competing kingdoms of the Asturias, Aragon, Castile, Catalonia, Leon, Navarre, and Valencia. In 1474 Isabella (Isabel), b. 1451, became Queen of Castile & Leon. Her husband, Ferdinand, b. 1452, inherited Aragon 1479, with Catalonia, Valencia, and the Balearic Islands, became Ferdinand V of Castile. By Isabella's request Pope Sixtus IV established the Inquisition, 1478. Last Moorish kingdom, Granada, fell 1492. Columbus opened New World ot colonies, 1492. Isabella died 1504, succeeded by her daughter, Juana "the Mad," but Ferdinand ruled until his death 1516.

Charles I, b. 1500, son of Juana and grandson of Ferdinand and Isabella, and of Maximilian I of Hapsburg; succeeded later as Holy Roman Emperor, Charles V, 1520; abdicated 1556. Philip II, son, 1556–1598, inherited only Spanish throne; conquered Portugal, fought Turks, persecuted non-Catholics, sent Armada against England. Was briefly married to Mary I of England, 1554–1558. Succession: Philip III, 1598–1621; Philip IV, 1621–1665; Charles II, 1665–1700, left Spain to Philip of Anjou, grandson of Louis XIV, who as Philip V, 1700–1746, founded Bourbon dynasty. Ferdinand VI, 1746–1759; Charles III, 1759–1788; Charles IV, 1788–1808, abdicated.

Napoleon now dominated politics and made his brother Joseph king of Spain 1808, but the Spanish ousted him finally in 1813. Ferdinand VII, 1808, 1814–1833, lost American colonies; succeeded by daughter Isabella II, aged 3, with wife Maria Christina of Naples regent until 1843. Isabella deposed by revolution 1868. Elected king by the Cortes, Amadeo of Savoy, 1870; abdicated 1873. First republic, 1873–1874. Alphonso XII, son of Isabella, 1875–1885. His posthumous son was Alphonso XIII, with his mother, Queen Maria Christina regent; Spanish-American war, Spain lost Cuba, gave up Puerto Rico, Philippines, Sulu Is., Marianas. Alphonso took throne 1902, aged 16, married British Princess Victoria Eugenia of Battenberg. The dictatorship of Primo de Rivera, 1923–30, precipitated the revolution of 1931. Alphonso agreed to leave without formal abdication. The monarchy was abolished and the second republic established, with strong socialist backing. Presidents were Niceto Alcala Zamora, to 1936, when Manuel Azaña was chosen.

In July, 1936, the army in Morocco revolted

311

against the government and General Francisco Franco led the troops into Spain. The revolution succeeded by Feb. 1939, when Azaña resigned. Franco became chief of state, with provisions that if he was incapacitated the Regency Council by two-thirds vote may propose a king to the Cortes, which must have a two-thirds majority to elect him. Alphonso XIII died in Rome Feb. 28, 1941, aged 54. His property and citizenship had been restored.

A succession law restoring the monarchy was approved in a 1947 referendum. Prince Juan Carlos, son of the pretender to the throne, was designated by Franco and the Cortes in 1969 as the future king and chief of state. Upon Franco's death, Nov. 20, 1975, Juan Carlos was proclaimed king, Nov. 22, 1975.

LEADERS IN THE SOUTH AMERICAN WARS OF LIBERATION

Simon Bolivar (1783-1830), José Francisco de San Martin (1783-1850), and Francisco Antonio Gabriel Miranda (1750-1816), are among the heroes of the early 19th century struggles of South American nations to free themselves from Spain. All three, and their contemporaries, operated in periods of intense factional strife, during which soldiers and civilians suffered.

Miranda, a Venezuelan, who had served with the French in the American Revolution and commanded parts of the French Revolutionary armies in the Netherlands, attempted to start a revolt in Venezuela in 1806 and failed. In 1810, with British and American backing, he returned and was briefly a dictator, until the British withdrew their support. In 1812 he was overcome by the royalists in Venezuela and taken prisoner, dying in a Spanish prison in 1816.

San Martin was born in Argentina and during 1789-1811 served in campaigns of the Spanish armies in Europe and Africa. He first joined the independence movement in Argentina in 1812 and then in 1817 invaded Chile with 4,000 men over the high mountain passes. Here he and General Bernardo O'Higgins (1778-1842) defeated the Spaniards at Chacabuco, 1817, and O'Higgins was named Liberator and became first director of Chile, 1817-1823. In 1821 San Martin occupied Lima and Callao, Peru, and became protector of Peru.

Bolivar, the greatest leader of South American liberation from Spain, was born in Venezuela, the son of an aristocratic family. His organizing and administrative abilities were superior and he foresaw many of the political difficulties of the future. He first served under Miranda in 1812 and in 1813 captured Caracas, where he was named Liberator. Forced out next year by civil strife, he led a campaign that captured Bogota in 1814. In 1817 he was again in control of Venezuela and was named dictator. He organized Nueva Granada with the help of General Francisco de Paula Santander (1792-1840). By joining Nueva Granada, Venezuela, and the present terrain of Panama and Ecuador, the republic of Colombia was formed with Bolivar president. After numerous setbacks he decisively defeated the Spaniards in the second battle of Carabobo, Venezuela, June 24, 1821.

In May, 1822, Gen. Antonio José de Sucre, Bolivar's trusted lieutenant, took Quito. Bolivar went to Guayaquil to confer with San Martin, who resigned as protector of Peru and withdrew from politics. With a new army of Colombians and Peruvians Bolivar defeated the Spaniards in a saber battle at Junin in 1824 and cleared Peru.

De Sucre organized Charcas (Upper Peru) as Republica Bolivar (now Bolivia) and acted as president in place of Bolivar, who wrote its constitution. De Sucre defeated the Spanish faction of Peru at Ayacucho, Dec. 19, 1824.

Continued civil strife finally caused the Colombian federation to break apart. Santander turned against Bolivar, but the latter defeated him and banished him. In 1828 Bolivar gave up the presidency he had held precariously for 14 years. He became ill from tuberculosis and died Dec. 17, 1830. He was honored as the great liberator and is buried in the national pantheon in Caracas.

RULERS OF RUSSIA; PREMIERS OF THE USSR

First ruler to consolidate Slavic tribes was Rurik, leader of the Russians who established himself at Novgorod, 862 AD. He and his immediate successors had Scandinavian affiliations. They moved to Kiev after 972 AD and ruled as Dukes of Kiev. In 988 Vladimir was converted and adopted the Byzantine Greek Orthodox service, later modified by Slav influences. Important as organizer and lawgiver was Yaroslav, 1019-1054, whose daughters married kings of Norway, Hungary, and France. His grandson, Vladimir II (Monomachos), 1113-1125, was progenitor of several rulers, but in 1169 Andrew Bogolubski overthrew Kiev and began the line known as Grand Dukes of Vladimir.

Of the Grand Dukes of Vladimir, Alexander Nevsky, 1246-1263, had a son, Daniel, first to be called Duke of Muscovy (Moscow) who ruled 1294-1303. His successors became Grand Dukes of Muscovy. After Dmitri III Donskoi defeated the Tartars in 1380, they also became Grand Dukes of all Russia. Independence of the Tartars and considerable territorial expansion were achieved under Ivan III, 1462-1505.

Tsars of Muscovy—Ivan III was referred to in church ritual as Tsar. He married Sofia, niece of the last Byzantine emperor. His successor, Basil III, died in 1533 when Basil's son Ivan was only 3. He became Ivan IV, "the Terrible"; crowned 1547 as Tsar of all the Russias, ruled till 1584. Under the weak rule of his son, Feodor I, 1584-1598, Boris Godunov had control. The dynasty died, and after years of tribal strife and intervention by Polish and Swedish armies, the Russians united under 17-year-old Michael Romanov, distantly related to the first wife of Ivan IV. He ruled 1613-1645 and established the Romanov line. Fourth ruler after Michael was Peter I.

Tsars, or Emperors of Russia (Romanovs)— Peter I, 1682-1725, known as Peter the Great, took title of Emperor in 1721. His successors and dates of accession were: Catherine, his widow, 1725; Peter II, his grandson, 1727-1730; Anne, Duchess of Courland, 1730, daughter of Peter the Great's brother, Tsar Ivan V; Ivan VI, 1740-1741, great-grandson of Ivan V, child, kept in prison and murdered 1764; Elizabeth, daughter of Peter I, 1741; Peter III, grandson of Peter I, 1761, deposed 1762 for his consort, Catherine II, former princess of Anhalt Zerbst (Germany) who is known as Catherine the Great, 1762-1796; Paul I, her son, 1796, killed 1801; Alexander I, son of Paul, 1801-1825, defeated Napoleon; Nicholas I, his brother, 1825; Alexander II, son of Nicholas, 1855, assassinated 1881 by terrorists; Alexander III, son, 1881-1894.

Nicholas II, son, 1894-1917, last Tsar of Russia, was forced to abdicate by the Revolution that followed losses to Germany in WWI. The Tsar, the Empress, the Tsarevich (Crown Prince) and the Tsar's four daughters were murdered by the Bolsheviks in Ekaterinburg, July 16, 1918.

Provisional Government—Prince Georgi Lvov and Alexander Kerensky, premiers, 1917.

Union of Soviet Socialist Republics

Bolshevik Revolution, Nov. 7, 1917, displaced Kerensky; council of People's Commissars formed, Lenin (Vladimir Ilyich Ulyanov), premier. Lenin died Jan. 21, 1924. Aleksei Rykov (executed 1938) and V. M. Molotov held the office, but actual ruler was Joseph Stalin (Joseph Vissarionovich Djugashvili), general secretary of the Central Committee of the Communist party. Stalin became president of the Council of Ministers (premier) May 7, 1941, died Mar. 5, 1953. Succeeded by Georgi M. Malenkov, as head of the Council and premier and Nikita S. Khrushchev, first secretary of the Central Committee. Malenkov resigned Feb. 8, 1955, became deputy premier, was dropped July 3, 1957. Marshal Nikolai A. Bulganin became premier Feb. 8, 1955; was demoted and Khrushchev became premier Mar. 27, 1958. Khrushchev was ousted Oct. 14-15, 1964, replaced by Leonid I. Brezhnev as first secretary of the party and by Aleksei N. Kosygin as premier. On June 16, 1977, Brezhnev took office as president.

U.S. LEADERS

Presidents of the U.S.

No.	Name	Politics	Born	in	Died	at age
1	George Washington	Fed.	1732, Feb. 22	Va.	1799, Dec. 14	67
2	John Adams	Fed.	1735, Oct. 30	Mass.	1826, July 4	90
3	Thomas Jefferson	Dem.-Rep.	1743, Apr. 13	Va.	1826, July 4	83
4	James Madison	Dem.-Rep.	1751, Mar. 16	Va.	1836, June 28	85
5	James Monroe	Dem.-Rep.	1758, Apr. 28	Va.	1831, July 4	73
6	John Quincy Adams	Dem.-Rep.	1767, July 11	Mass.	1848, Feb. 23	80
7	Andrew Jackson	Dem.	1767, Mar. 15	S.C.	1845, June 8	78
8	Martin Van Buren	Dem.	1782, Dec. 5	N.Y.	1862, July 24	79
9	William Henry Harrison	Whig	1773, Feb. 9	Va.	1841, Apr. 4	68
10	John Tyler	Whig	1790, Mar. 29	Va.	1862, Jan. 18	71
11	James Knox Polk	Dem.	1795, Nov. 2	N.C.	1849, June 15	53
12	Zachary Taylor	Whig	1784, Nov. 24	Va.	1850, July 9	65
13	Millard Fillmore	Whig	1800, Jan. 7	N.Y.	1874, Mar. 8	74
14	Franklin Pierce	Dem.	1804, Nov. 23	N.H.	1869, Oct. 8	64
15	James Buchanan	Dem.	1791, Apr. 23	Pa.	1868, June 1	77
16	Abraham Lincoln	Rep.	1809, Feb. 12	Ky.	1865, Apr. 15	56
17	Andrew Johnson	(1)	1808, Dec. 29	N.C.	1875, July 31	66
18	Ulysses Simpson Grant	Rep.	1822, Apr. 27	Oh.	1885, July 23	63
19	Rutherford Birchard Hayes	Rep.	1822, Oct. 4	Oh.	1893, Jan. 17	70
20	James Abram Garfield	Rep.	1831, Nov. 19	Oh.	1881, Sept. 19	49
21	Chester Alan Arthur	Rep.	1829, Oct. 5	Vt.	1886, Nov. 18	57
22	Grover Cleveland	Dem.	1837, Mar. 18	N.J.	1908, June 24	71
23	Benjamin Harrison	Rep.	1833, Aug. 20	Oh.	1901, Mar. 13	67
24	Grover Cleveland	Dem.	1837, Mar. 18	N.J.	1908, June 24	71
25	William McKinley	Rep.	1843, Jan. 29	Oh.	1901, Sept. 14	58
26	Theodore Roosevelt	Rep.	1858, Oct. 27	N.Y.	1919, Jan. 6	60
27	William Howard Taft	Rep.	1857, Sept. 15	Oh.	1930, Mar. 8	72
28	Woodrow Wilson	Dem.	1856, Dec. 28	Va.	1924, Feb. 3	67
29	Warren Gamaliel Harding	Rep.	1865, Nov. 2	Oh.	1923, Aug. 2	57
30	Calvin Coolidge	Rep.	1872, July 4	Vt.	1933, Jan. 5	60
31	Herbert Clark Hoover	Rep.	1874, Aug. 10	Ia.	1964, Oct. 20	90
32	Franklin Delano Roosevelt	Dem.	1882, Jan. 30	N.Y.	1945, Apr. 12	63
33	Harry S. Truman	Dem.	1884, May 8	Mo.	1972, Dec. 26	88
34	Dwight David Eisenhower	Rep.	1890, Oct. 14	Tex.	1969, Mar. 28	78
35	John Fitzgerald Kennedy	Dem.	1917, May 29	Mass.	1963, Nov. 22	46
36	Lyndon Baines Johnson	Dem.	1908, Aug. 27	Tex.	1973, Jan. 22	64
37	Richard Milhous Nixon (2)	Rep.	1913, Jan. 9	Cal.		
38	Gerald Rudolph Ford	Rep.	1913, July 14	Neb.		
39	Jimmy (James Earl) Carter	Dem.	1924, Oct. 1	Ga.		

(1) Andrew Johnson—a Democrat, nominated vice president by Republicans and elected with Lincoln on National Union ticket. (2) Resigned Aug. 9, 1974.

THE BOOK OF WHO

Vice Presidents of the U.S.

The numerals given vice presidents do not coincide with those given presidents, because some presidents had none and some had more than one.

	Name	Birthplace	Year	Residence	Inaug.	Politics	Died	Age
1	John Adams	Quincy, Mass	1735	Mass. ...	1789	Fed. ...	1826	90
2	Thomas Jefferson	Shadwell, Va.	1743	Va. ...	1797	Rep. ...	1826	83
3	Aaron Burr	Newark, N.J.	1756	N.Y. ...	1801	Rep. ...	1836	80
4	George Clinton	Ulster Co., N.Y.	1739	N.Y. ...	1805	Rep. ..	1812	73
5	Elbridge Gerry	Marblehead, Mass.	1744	Mass. ...	1813	Rep. ..	1814	70
6	Daniel D. Tompkins	Scarsdale, N.Y.	1774	N.Y. ...	1817	Rep. ..	1825	51
7	John C. Calhoun (1)	Abbeville, S.C.	1782	S.C. ...	1825	Rep. ...	1850	68
8	Martin Van Buren	Kinderhook, N.Y.	1782	N.Y. ...	1833	Dem...	1862	79
9	Richard M. Johnson	Louisville, Ky.	1780	Ky. ...	1837	Dem...	1850	70
10	John Tyler	Greenway, Va.	1790	Va. ...	1841	Whig ..	1862	71
11	George M. Dallas	Philadelphia, Pa.	1792	Pa. ...	1845	Dem...	1864	72
12	Millard Fillmore	Summerhill, N.Y.	1800	N.Y. ...	1849	Whig ..	1874	74
13	William R. King	Sampson Co., N.C.	1786	Ala. ...	1853	Dem...	1853	67
14	John C. Breckinridge	Lexington, Ky.	1821	Ky. ...	1857	Dem...	1875	54
15	Hannibal Hamlin	Paris, Me.	1809	Me. ...	1861	Rep. ..	1891	81
16	Andrew Johnson	Raleigh, N.C.	1808	Tenn. ...	1865	(2) ...	1875	66
17	Schuyler Colfax	New York City, N.Y.	1823	Ind. ...	1869	Rep. ..	1885	62
18	Henry Wilson	Farmington, N.H.	1812	Mass. ...	1873	Rep. ..	1875	63
19	William A. Wheeler	Malone, N.Y.	1819	N.Y. ...	1877	Rep. ..	1887	68
20	Chester A. Arthur	Fairfield, Vt.	1830	N.Y. ...	1881	Rep. ..	1886	56
21	Thomas A. Hendricks	Muskingum Co., Oh.	1819	Ind. ...	1885	Dem...	1885	66
22	Levi P. Morton	Shoreham, Vt.	1824	N.Y. ...	1889	Rep. ..	1920	96
23	Adlai E. Stevenson (3)	Christian Co., Ky.	1835	Ill. ...	1893	Dem...	1914	78
24	Garret A. Hobart	Long Branch, N.J.	1844	N.J. ...	1897	Rep. ..	1899	55
25	Theodore Roosevelt	New York City, N.Y.	1858	N.Y. ...	1901	Rep. ..	1919	60
26	Charles W. Fairbanks	Unionville Centre, Oh.	1852	Ind. ...	1905	Rep. ..	1918	66
27	James S. Sherman	Utica, N.Y.	1855	N.Y. ...	1909	Rep. ..	1912	57
28	Thomas R. Marshall	N. Manchester, Ind.	1854	Ind. ...	1913	Dem...	1925	71
29	Calvin Coolidge	Plymouth, Vt.	1872	Mass. ...	1921	Rep. ..	1933	60
30	Charles G. Dawes	Marietta, Oh.	1865	Ill. ...	1925	Rep. ..	1951	85
31	Charles Curtis	Topeka, Kan.	1860	Kan. ...	1929	Rep. ..	1936	76
32	John Nance Garner	Red River Co., Tex.	1868	Tex. ...	1933	Dem...	1967	98
33	Henry Agard Wallace	Adair County, Ia.	1888	Iowa ...	1941	Dem...	1965	77
34	Harry S. Truman	Lamar, Mo.	1884	Mo. ...	1945	Dem...	1972	88
35	Alben W. Barkley	Graves County, Ky.	1877	Ky. ...	1949	Dem...	1956	78
36	Richard M. Nixon	Yorba Linda, Cal.	1913	Cal. ...	1953	Rep. ..		
37	Lyndon B. Johnson	Johnson City, Tex.	1908	Tex. ...	1961	Dem...	1973	64
38	Hubert H. Humphrey	Wallace, S.D.	1911	Minn. ...	1965	Dem...	1978	66
39	Spiro T. Agnew	Baltimore, Md.	1918	Md. ...	1969	Rep. ..		
40	Gerald R. Ford	Omaha, Neb.	1913	Mich. ...	1973	Rep. ..		
41	Nelson A. Rockefeller	Bar Harbor, Me.	1908	N.Y. ...	1974	Rep. ..	1979	70
42	Walter F. Mondale	Ceylon, Minn.	1928	Minn. ...	1977	Dem...		

(1) John C. Calhoun resigned Dec. 28, 1832, having been elected to the Senate to fill a vacancy. (2) Andrew Johnson—a Democrat nominated by Republicans and elected with Lincoln on the National Union Ticket. (3) Adlai E. Stevenson, 23d vice president, was grandfater of Democratic candidate for president, 1952 and 1956.

Wives of the Presidents

Listed in order of presidential administrations.

Name	State	Born	Married	Died
Martha Dandridge Custis Washington	Va.	1732	1759	1802
Abigail Smith Adams	Mass.	1744	1764	1818
Martha Wayles Skelton Jefferson	Va.	1748	1772	1782
Dorothea "Dolley" Payne Todd Madison	N.C.	1768	1794	1849
Elizabeth Kortright Monroe	N.Y.	1768	1786	1830
Louise Catherine Johnson Adams	Md.(1)	1775	1797	1852
Rachel Donelson Robards Jackson	Va.	1767	1791	1828
Hannah Hoes Van Buren	N.Y.	1783	1807	1819
Anna Symmes Harrison	N.J.	1775	1795	1864
Letitia Christian Tyler	Va.	1790	1813	1842
Julia Gardiner Tyler	N.Y.	1820	1844	1889
Sarah Childress Polk	Tenn.	1803	1824	1891
Margaret Smith Taylor	Md.	1788	1810	1852
Abigail Powers Fillmore	N.Y.	1798	1826	1853

Name	State			
Caroline Carmichael McIntosh Fillmore	N.J.	1813	1858	1881
Jane Means Appleton Pierce	N.H.	1806	1834	1863
Mary Todd Lincoln	Ky.	1818	1842	1882
Eliza McCardle Johnson	Tenn.	1810	1827	1876
Julia Dent Grant	Mo.	1826	1848	1902
Lucy Ware Webb Hayes	Oh.	1831	1852	1889
Lucretia Rudolph Garfield	Oh.	1832	1858	1918
Ellen Louise Axson Wilson	Va.	1837	1859	1880
Frances Folsom Cleveland	N.Y.	1864	1886	1947
Caroline Lavinia Scott Harrison	Oh.	1832	1853	1892
Mary Scott Lord Dimmick Harrison	Pa.	1858	1896	1948
Ida Saxton McKinley	Oh.	1847	1871	1907
Alice Hathaway Lee Roosevelt	Mass.	1861	1880	1884
Edith Kermit Carow Roosevelt	Conn.	1861	1886	1948
Helen Herron Taft	Oh.	1861	1886	1943
Ellen Louise Axson Wilson	Ga.	1860	1885	1914
Edith Bolling Galt Wilson	Va.	1872	1915	1961
Florence Kling De Wolfe Harding	Oh.	1860	1891	1924
Grace Anna Goodhue Coolidge	Vt.	1879	1905	1957
Lou Henry Hoover	Ia.	1875	1899	1944
Anna Eleanor Roosevelt Roosevelt	N.Y.	1884	1905	1962
Bess Wallace Truman	Mo.	1885	1919	....
Mamie Geneva Doud Eisenhower	Ia.	1896	1916	1979
Jacqueline Lee Bouvier Kennedy	N.Y.	1929	1953	....
Claudia "Lady Bird" Alta Taylor Johnson	Tex.	1912	1934	....
Thelma Catherine Patricia Ryan Nixon	Nev.	1912	1940	....
Elizabeth Bloomer Warren Ford	Ill.	1918	1948	....
Rosalynn Smith Carter	Ga.	1927	1946	....

James Buchanan, 15th president, was unmarried. (1) Born London, father a Md. citizen.

THE ALFRED B. NOBEL PRIZE WINNERS

Alfred B. Nobel, inventor of dynamite, bequeathed $9,000,000, the interest to be distributed yearly to those who had most benefited mankind in physics, chemistry, medicine-physiology, literature, and peace. The first Nobel Memorial Prize in Economics was awarded in 1969. No awards given for years omitted. In 1979, each prize was worth approximately $190,000.

Physics

1979 Steven Weinberg, Sheldon L. Glashow, both
   U.S.; Abdus Salam, Pakistani
1978 Pyotyr Kapitsa, USSR
   Robert Wilson, U.S.
   Arno Penzias, U.S.
1977 John H. Van Vleck, Philip W.
   Anderson, both U.S.; Nevill F. Mott, British
1976 Burton Richter, U.S.
   Samuel C.C. Ting, U.S.
1975 L. James Rainwater, U.S.
   Ben Mottelson, U.S.-Danish
   Aage Bohr, Danish
1974 Martin Ryle, British
   Antony Hewish, British
1973 Ivar Giaever, U.S.
   Leo Esaki, Jap.
   Brian D. Josephson, British
1972 John Bardeen, U.S.
   Leon N. Cooper, U.S.
   John R. Schrieffer, U.S.
1971 Dennis Gabor, British
1970 Louis Néel, French
   Hannes Alfvén, Swedish
1969 Murray Gell-Mann, U.S.
1968 Luis W. Alvarez, U.S.
1967 Hans A. Bethe, U.S.
1966 Alfred Kastler, French
1965 Richard P. Feynman, U.S.
   Julian S. Schwinger, U.S.
   Shinichiro Tomonaga, Japanese
1964 Nikolai G. Basov, USSR

Aleksander M. Prochorov, USSR
Charles H. Townes, U.S.
1963 Maria Goeppert-Mayer, U.S.
   J. Hans D. Jensen, German
   Eugene P. Wigner, U.S.
1962 Lev D. Landau, USSR
1961 Robert Hofstadter, U.S.
   Rudolf L. Mössbauer, German
1960 Donald A. Glaser, U.S.
1959 Owen Chamberlain, U.S.
   Emilio G. Segrè, U.S.
1958 Pavel Cerenkov, Ilya Frank,
   Igor H. Tamm, all USSR
1957 Tsung-Yao Lee,
   Chen Ning Yang, both U.S.
1956 John Bardeen, U.S.
   Walter H. Brattain, U.S.
   William Shockley, U.S.
1955 Polykarp Kusch, U.S.
   Willis E. Lamb, U.S.
1954 Max Born, British
   Walter Bothe, German
1953 Frits Zernike, Dutch
1952 Felix Bloch, U.S.
   Edward M. Purcell, U.S.
1951 Sir John D. Cockroft, British
   Ernest T. S. Walton, Irish
1950 Cecil F. Powell, British
1949 Hideki Yukawa, Japanese
1948 Patrick M. S. Blackett, British
1947 Sir Edward V. Appleton, British

THE BOOK OF WHO

1946 Percy Williams Bridgman, U.S.
1945 Wolfgang Pauli, U.S.
1944 Isidor Isaac Rabi, U.S.
1943 Otto Sern, U.S.
1939 Ernest O. Lawrence, U.S.
1938 Enrico Fermi, U.S.
1937 Clinton J. Davisson, U.S.
     Sir George P. Thomson, British
1936 Carl D. Anderson, U.S.
     Victor F. Hess, Austrian
1935 Sir James Chadwick, British
1933 Paul A. M. Dirac, British
     Erwin Schrödinger, Austrian
1932 Werner Heisenberg, German
1930 Sir Chandrasekhara V. Raman, Indian
1929 Prince Louis-Victor de Broglie, French
1928 Owen W. Richardson, British
1927 Arthur H. Compton, U.S.
     Charles T. R. Wilson, British
1926 Jean B. Perrin, French
1925 James Franck,
     Gustav Hertz, both German
1924 Karl M. G. Siegbahn, Swedish
1923 Robert A. Millikan, U.S.
1922 Niels Bohr, Danish

1921 Albert Einstein, Ger.-U.S.
1920 Charles E. Guillaume, French
1919 Johannes Stark, German
1918 Max K. E. L. Planck, German
1917 Charles G. Barkla, British
1915 Sir William H. Bragg, British
     William L. Bragg, British
1914 Max von Laue, German
1913 Heike Kamerlingh-Onnes, Dutch
1912 Nils G. Dalén, Sweden
1911 Wilhelm Wein, German
1910 Johannes D. van der Waals, Dutch
1909 Carl F. Braun, German
     Guglielmo Marconi, Italian
1908 Gabriel Lippmann, French
1907 Albert A. Michelson, U.S.
1906 Sir Joseph J. Thomson, British
1905 Philipp E. A. von Lenard, German
1904 Lord Rayleigh (John W. Strutt), British
1903 Antoine Henri Becquerel,
     Marie and Pierre Curie, all French
1902 Hendrik A. Lorentz,
     Pieter Zeeman, both Dutch
1901 Wilhelm C. Roentgen, German

Chemistry

1979 Herbert C. Brown, U.S.
     Georg Wittig, W. German
1978 Peter Mitchell, British
1977 Ilya Prigogine, Belgian
1976 William L. Lipscomb, U.S.
1975 John Cornforth, Austral.-Brit.,
     Vladimir Prelog, Yugo.-Switz.
1974 Paul J. Flory, U.S.
1973 Ernst Otto Fischer, W. German
     Geoffrey Wilkinson, British
1972 Christian B. Anfinsen, U.S.
     Stanford Moore, U.S.
     William H. Stein, U.S.
1971 Gerhard Herzberg, Canadian
1970 Luis F. Leloir, Argentinian
1969 Derek H. R. Barton, British
     Odd Hassel, Norwegian
1968 Lars Onsager, U.S.
1967 Manfred Eigen, German
     Ronald G. W. Norrish, British
     George Porter, British
1966 Robert S. Mulliken, U.S.
1965 Robert B. Woodward, U.S.
1964 Dorothy C. Hodgkin, British
1963 Giulio Natta, Italian
     Karl Ziegler, German
1962 John C. Kendrew, British
     Max F. Perutz, British
1961 Melvin Calvin, U.S.
1960 Willard F. Libby, U.S.
1959 Jaroslav Heyrovsky, Czech
1958 Frederick Sanger, British
1957 Sir Alexander R. Todd, British
1956 Sir Cyril N. Hinshelwood, British
     Nikolai N. Semenov, USSR
1955 Vincent du Vigneaud, U.S.
1954 Linus C. Pauling, U.S.
1953 Hermann Staudinger, German
1952 Archer J. P. Martin, British
     Richard L. M. Synge, British
1951 Edwin M. McMillan, U.S.
     Glenn T. Seaborg, U.S.
1950 Kurt Adler, German
     Otto P. H. Diels, German
1949 William F. Giauque, U.S.
1948 Arne W. K. Tiselius, Swedish

1947 Sir Robert Robinson, British
1946 James B. Sumner, John H.
     Northrop, Wendell M. Stanley, all U.S.
1945 Artturi I. Virtanen, Finnish
1944 Otto Hahn, German
1943 Georg de Hevesy, Hungarian
1939 Adolf F. J. Butenandt, German
     Leopold Ruzicka, Swiss
1938 Richard Kuhn, German
1937 Walter N. Haworth, British
     Paul Karrer, Swiss
1936 Peter J. W. Debye, Dutch
1935 Frédéric Joliot-Curie, French
     Irene Joliot-Curie, French
1934 Harold C. Urey, U.S.
1932 Irving Langmuir, U.S.
1931 Friedrich Bergius, German
     Karl Bosch, German
1930 Hans Fischer, German
1929 Sir Arthur Harden, British
     Hans von Euler-Chelpin, Swedish
1928 Adolf O. R. Windaus, German
1927 Heinrich O. Wieland, German
1926 Theodor Svedberg, Swedish
1925 Richard A. Zsigmondy, German
1923 Fritz Pregl, Austrian
1922 Francis W. Aston, British
1921 Frederick Soddy, British
1920 Walter H. Nernst, German
1918 Fritz Haber, German
1915 Richard M. Willstätter, German
1914 Theodore W. Richards, U.S.
1913 Alfred Werner, Swiss
1912 Victor Grignard, French
     Paul Sabatier, French
1911 Marie Curie, French
1910 Otto Wallach, German
1909 Wilhelm Ostwald, German
1908 Ernest Rutherford, British
1907 Eduard Buchner, German
1906 Henri Moissan, French
1905 Adolf von Baeyer, German
1904 Sir William Ramsay, British
1903 Svante A. Arrhenius, Swedish
1902 Emil Fischer, German
1901 Jacobus H. van't Hoff, Dutch

316

NOBEL PRIZE WINNERS

Physiology or Medicine

1979 Allan MacLeod Cormack, U.S.
Godfrey Newbold Hounsfield, British
1978 Daniel Nathans, U.S.
Hamilton O. Smith, U.S.
Werner Arber, Swiss
1977 Rosalyn S. Yallow, Roger C. L.
Guillemin, Andrew V. Schally, all
U.S.
1976 Baruch S. Blumberg, U.S.
Daniel Carleton Gajdusek, U.S.
1975 David Baltimore, Howard Temin,
both U.S.; Renato Dulbecco,
Ital.-U.S.
1974 Albert Claude, Lux.-U.S.; George
Emil Palade, Rom.-U.S.; Christian
Rene de Duve, Belg.
1973 Karl von Frisch, Ger.; Konrad
Lorenz, Ger.-Austrian; Nikolaas
Tinbergen, Brit.
1972 Gerald M. Edelman, U.S.
Rodney R. Porter, British
1971 Earl W. Sutherland Jr., U.S.
1970 Julius Axelrod, U.S.
Sir Bernard Katz, British
Ulf von Euler, Swedish
1969 Max Delbrück,
Alfred D. Hershey,
Salvador Luria, all U.S.
1968 Robert W. Holley,
H. Gobind Khorana,
Marshall W. Nirenberg, all U.S.
1967 Ragnar Granit, Swedish
Haldan Keffer Hartline, U.S.
George Wald, U.S.
1966 Charles B. Huggins,
Francis Peyton Rous, both U.S.
1965 François Jacob, André Lwoff,
Jacques Monod, all French
1964 Konrad E. Bloch, U.S.
Feodor Lynen, German
1963 Sir John C. Eccles, Australian
Alan L. Hodgkin, British
Andrew F. Huxley, British
1962 Francis H. C. Crick, British
James D. Watson, U.S.
Maurice H. F. Wilkins, British
1961 George von Bekesy, U.S.
1960 Sir F. MacFarlane Burnet,
Australian
Peter B. Medawar, British
1959 Arthur Kornberg, U.S.
Severo Ochoa, U.S.
1958 George W. Beadle, U.S.
Edward L. Tatum, U.S.
Joshua Lederberg, U.S.
1957 Daniel Bovet, Italian
1956 Andre F. Cournand, U.S.
Werner Forssmann, German
Dickinson W. Richards, Jr., U.S.
1955 Alex H. T. Theorell, Swedish
1954 John F. Enders,
Frederick C. Robbins,
Thomas H. Weller, all U.S.

1953 Hans A. Krebs, British
Fritz A. Lipmann, U.S.
1952 Selman A. Waksman, U.S.
1951 Max Theiler, U.S.
1950 Philip S. Hench,
Edward C. Kendall, both U.S.
Tadeus Reichstein, Swiss
1949 Walter R. Hess, Swiss
Antonio Moniz, Portuguese
1948 Paul H. Müller, Swiss
1947 Carl F. Cori,
Gerty T. Cori, both U.S.
Bernardo A. Houssay, Arg.
1946 Hermann J. Muller, U.S.
1945 Ernst B. Chain, British
Sir Alexander Fleming, British
Sir Howard W. Florey, British
1944 Joseph Erlanger, U.S.
Herbert S. Gasser, U.S.
1943 Henrik C. P. Dam, Danish
Edward A. Doisy, U.S.
1939 Gerhard Domagk, German
1938 Corneille J. F. Heymans, Belg.
1937 Albert Szent-Györgyi, U.S.
1936 Sir Henry H. Dale, British
Otto Loewi, U.S.
1935 Hans Spemann, German
1934 George R. Minot, Wm. P. Murphy,
G. H. Whipple, all U.S.
1933 Thomas H. Morgan, U.S.
1932 Edgar D. Adrian, British
Sir Charles S. Sherrington, Brit.
1931 Otto H. Warburg, German
1930 Karl Landsteiner, U.S.
1929 Christiaan Eijkman, Dutch
Sir Frederick G. Hopkins, British
1928 Charles J. H. Nicolle, French
1927 Julius Wagner-Jauregg, Aus.
1926 Johannes A. G. Fibiger, Danish
1924 Willem Einthoven, Dutch
1923 Frederick G. Banting, Canadian
John J. R. Macleod, British
1922 Archibald V. Hill, British
Otto F. Meyerhof, German
1920 Schack A. S. Krogh, Danish
1919 Jules Bordet, Belgian
1914 Robert Bárány, Austrian
1913 Charles R. Richet, French
1912 Alexis Carrel, French
1911 Allvar Gullstrand, Swedish
1910 Albrecht Kossel, German
1909 Emil T. Kocher, Swiss
1908 Paul Ehrlich,German
Elie Metchnikoff, French
1907 Charles L. A. Laveran, French
1906 Camillo Golgi, Italian
Santiago Roman y Cajal, Sp.
1905 Robert Koch, German
1904 Ivan P. Pavlov, Russian
1903 Niels R. Finsen, Danish
1902 Sir Ronald Ross, British
1901 Emil A. von Behring, German

Literature

1979 Odysseus Elytis, Greek
1978 Isaac Bashevis Singer, U.S.
1977 Vicente Aleixandre, Spanish
1976 Saul Bellow, U.S.
1975 Eugenio Montale, Italian

1974 Eyvind Johnson, Harry Edmund
Martinson, both Swedish
1973 Patrick White, Australian
1972 Heinrich Böll, W. German
1971 Pablo Neruda, Chilean

1970 Alexander I. Solzhenitsyn, Russ.
1969 Samuel Beckett, Irish
1968 Yasunari Kawabata, Japanese
1967 Miguel Angel Asturias, Guate.
1966 Samuel Joseph Agnon, Israeli
　　 Nelly Sachs, Swedish
1965 Mikhail Sholokhov, Russian
1964 Jean Paul Sartre, French
　　 (Prize declined)
1963 Giorgos Seferis, Greek
1962 John Steinbeck, U.S.
1961 Ivo Andric, Yugoslavian
1960 Saint-John Perse, French
1959 Salvatore Quasimodo, Italian
1958 Boris L. Pasternak, Russian
　　 (Prize declined)
1957 Albert Camus, French
1956 Juan Ramón Jiménez,
　　 Puerto Rican-Span.
1955 Halldór K. Laxness, Icelandic
1954 Ernest Hemingway, U.S.
1953 Sir Winston Churchill, British
1952 François Mauriac, French
1951 Pär F. Lagerkvist, Swedish
1950 Bertrand Russell, British
1949 William Faulkner, U.S.
1948 T. S. Eliot, British
1947 André Gide, French
1946 Hermann Hesse, Swiss
1945 Gabriela Mistral, Chilean
1944 Johannes V. Jensen, Danish
1939 Frans E. Sillanpää, Finnish
1938 Pearl S. Buck, U.S.
1937 Roger Martin du Gard, French
1936 Eugene O'Neill, U.S.

1934 Luigi Pirandello, Italian
1933 Ivan A. Bunin, French
1932 John Galsworthy, British
1931 Erik A. Karlfeldt, Swedish
1930 Sinclair Lewis, U.S.
1929 Thomas Mann, German
1928 Sigrid Undset, Norwegian
1927 Henri Bergson, French
1926 Grazia Deledda, Italian
1925 George Bernard Shaw, British
1924 Wladyslaw S. Reymont, Polish
1923 William Butler Yeats, Irish
1922 Jacinto Benavente, Spanish
1921 Anatole France, French
1920 Knut Hamsun, Norwegian
1919 Carl F. G. Spitteler, Swiss
1917 Karl A. Gjellerup, Danish
　　 Henrik Pontoppidan, Danish
1916 Verner von Heidenstam, Swed.
1915 Romain Rolland, French
1913 Rabindranath Tagore, Indian
1912 Gerhart Hauptmann, German
1911 Maurice Maeterlinck, Belgian
1910 Paul J. L. Heyse, German
1909 Selma Lagerlöf, Swedish
1908 Rudolf C. Eucken,German
1907 Rudyard Kipling, British
1906 Giosuè Carducci, Italian
1905 Henryk Sienkiewicz, Polish
1904 Frédéric Mistral, French
　　 José Echegaray, Spanish
1903 Björnsterne Björnson, Norw.
1902 Theodor Mommsen, German
1901 René F. A. Sully Prudhomme,
　　 French

Peace

1979 Mother Teresa of Calcutta, Yugo-Ind.
1978 Anwar Sadat, Egyptian
　　 Menachem Begin,
　　 Israeli
1977 Amnesty International
1976 Mairead Corrigan, Betty Williams,
　　 N. Irish
1975 Andrei Sakharov, USSR
1974 Eisaku Sato, Jap., Sean MacBride,
　　 Irish
1973 Henry Kissinger, U.S.
　　 Le Duc Tho, N. Vietnamese
　　 (Tho declined)
1971 Willy Brandt, W. German
1970 Norman E. Borlaug, U.S.
1969 Intl. Labor Organization
1968 René Cassin, French
1965 U.N. Children's Fund (UNICEF)
1964 Martin Luther King Jr., U.S.
1963 International Red Cross,
　　 League of Red Cross Societies
1962 Linus C. Pauling, U.S.
1961 Dag Hammarskjöld, Swedish
1960 Albert J. Luthuli, South African
1959 Philip J. Noel-Baker, British
1958 Georges Pire, Belgian
1957 Lester B. Pearson, Canadian
1954 Office of the U.N. High
　　 Commissioner for Refugees
1953 George C. Marshall, U.S.
1952 Albert Schweitzer, French
1951 Leon Jouhaux, French
1950 Ralph J. Bunche, U.S.
1949 Lord John Boyd Orr of Brechin
　　 Mearns, British

1947 Friends Service Council, Brit.
　　 Amer. Friends Service Com.
1946 Emily G. Balch,
　　 John R. Mott, both U.S.
1945 Cordell Hull, U.S.
1944 International Red Cross
1938 Nansen International Office
　　 for Refugees
1937 Viscount Cecil of Chelwood, Brit.
1936 Carlos de Saavedra Lamas, Arg.
1935 Carl von Ossietzky, German
1934 Arthur Henderson, British
1933 Sir Norman Angell, British
1931 Jane Addams, Nicholas
　　 Murray Butler, both U.S.
1930 Nathan Söderblom, Swedish
1929 Frank B. Kellogg, U.S.
1927 Ferdinand E. Buisson, French
　　 Ludwig Quidde, German
1926 Aristide Briand, French
　　 Gustav Stresemann, German
1925 Sir J. Austen Chamberlain, Brit.
　　 Charles G. Dawes, U.S.
1922 Fridtjof Nansen, Norwegian
1921 Karl H. Branting, Swedish
　　 Christian L. Lange, Norwegian
1920 Léon V. A. Bourgeois, French
1919 Woodrow Wilson, U.S.
1917 International Red Cross
1913 Henri La Fontaine, Belgian
1912 Elihu Root, U.S.
1911 Tobias M. C. Asser, Dutch
　　 Alfred H. Fried, Austrian
1910 Permanent International Peace Bureau
1909 Auguste M. F. Beernaert, Belg.

PULITZER PRIZE WINNERS

Paul H. B. B. d'Estournells de Constant, French
1908 Klas P. Arnoldson, Swedish
Fredrik Bajer, Danish
1907 Ernesto T. Moneta, Italian
Louis Renault, French
1906 Theodore Roosevelt, U.S.
1905 Baroness Bertha von Suttner,

Austrian
1904 Institute of International Law
1903 Sir William R. Cremer, British
1902 Élie Ducommun, Charles A. Gobat, both Swiss
1901 Jean H. Dunant, Swiss
Frédéric Passy, French

Economics

1979 Sir Arthur Lewis, British
Theodore W. Schultz, U.S.
1978 Herbert A. Simon, U.S.
1977 Bertil Ohlin, Swedish
James E. Meade, British
1976 Milton Friedman, U.S.
1975 Tjalling Koopmans, Dutch-U.S., Leonid Kantorovich, USSR
1974 Gunnar Myrdal, Swed.,

Friedrich A. von Hayek, Austrian
1973 Wassily Leontief, U.S.
1972 Kenneth J. Arrow, U.S.
John R. Hicks, British
1971 Simon Kuznets, U.S.
1970 Paul A. Samuelson, U.S.
1969 Ragnar Frisch, Norwegian
Jan Tinbergen, Dutch

PULITZER PRIZES IN LETTERS AND MUSIC

LETTERS

Fiction

For fiction in book form by an American author, preferably dealing with American life.
1918—Ernest Poole, His Family.
1919—Booth Tarkington, The Magnificent Ambersons.
1921—Edith Wharton, The Age of Innocence.
1922—Booth Tarkington, Alice Adams.
1923—Willa Cather, One of Ours.
1924—Margaret Wilson, The Able McLaughlins.
1925—Edna Ferber, So Big.
1926—Sinclair Lewis, Arrowsmith. (Refused prize.)
1927—Louis Bromfield, Early Autumn.
1928—Thornton Wilder, Bridge of San Luis Rey.
1929—Julia M. Peterkin, Scarlet Sister Mary.
1930—Oliver LaFarge, Laughing Boy.
1931—Margaret Ayer Barnes, Years of Grace.
1932—Pearl S. Buck, The Good Earth.
1933—T. S. Stribling, The Store.
1934—Caroline Miller, Lamb in His Bosom.
1935—Josephine W. Johnson, Now in November.
1936—Harold L. Davis, Honey in the Horn.
1937—Margaret Mitchell, Gone with the Wind.
1938—John P. Marquand, The Late George Apley.
1939—Marjorie Kinnan Rawlings, The Yearling.
1940—John Steinbeck, The Grapes of Wrath.
1942—Ellen Glasgow, In This Our Life.
1943—Upton Sinclair, Dragon's Teeth.
1944—Martin Flavin, Journey in the Dark.
1945—John Hersey, A Bell for Adano.
1947—Robert Penn Warren, All the King's Men.
1948—James A. Michener, Tales of the South Pacific.
1949—James Gould Cozzens, Guard of Honor.
1950—A. B. Guthrie Jr., The Way West.
1951—Conrad Richter, The Town.
1952—Herman Wouk, The Caine Mutiny.
1953—Ernest Hemingway, The Old Man and the Sea.
1955—William Faulkner, A Fable.
1956—MacKinlay Kantor, Andersonville.

1958—James Agee, A Death in the Family.
1959—Robert Lewis Taylor, The Travels of Jaimie McPheeters.
1960—Allen Drury, Advise and Consent.
1961—Harper Lee, To Kill a Mockingbird.
1962—Edwin O'Connor, The Edge of Sadness.
1963—William Faulkner, The Reivers.
1965—Shirley Ann Grau, The Keepers of the House.
1966—Katherine Anne Porter, Collected Stories of Katherine Anne Porter.
1967—Bernard Malamud, The Fixer.
1968—William Styron, The Confessions of Nat Turner.
1969—N. Scott Momaday, House Made of Dawn.
1970—Jean Stafford, Collected Stories.
1972—Wallace Stegner, Angle of Repose.
1973—Eudora Welty, The Optimist's Daughter.
1975—Michael Shaara, The Killer Angels.
1976—Saul Bellow, Humboldt's Gift.
1978—James Alan McPherson, Elbow Room.
1979—John Cheever, The Stories of John Cheever.

Drama

For an American play, preferably original and dealing with American life.
1918—Jesse Lynch Williams, Why Marry?
1920—Eugene O'Neill, Beyond the Horizon.
1921—Zona Gale, Miss Lulu Bett.
1922—Eugene O'Neill, Anna Christie.
1923—Owen Davis, Icebound.
1924—Hatcher Hughes, Hell-Bent for Heaven.
1925—Sidney Howard, They Knew What They Wanted.
1926—George Kelly, Craig's Wife.
1927—Paul Green, In Abraham's Bosom.
1928—Eugene O'Neill, Strange Interlude.
1929—Elmer Rice, Street Scene.
1930—Marc Connelly, The Green Pastures.
1931—Susan Glaspell, Alison's House.
1932—George S. Kaufman, Morrie Ryskind and Ira Gershwin, Of Thee I Sing.
1933—Maxwell Anderson, Both Your Houses.
1934—Sidney Kingsley, Men in White.
1935—Zoe Akins, The Old Maid.

THE BOOK OF WHO

1936—Robert E. Sherwood, Idiot's Delight.
1937—George S. Kaufman and Moss Hart, You Can't Take It With You.
1938—Thornton Wilder, Our Town.
1939—Robert E. Sherwood, Abe Lincoln in Illinois.
1940—William Saroyan, The Time of Your Life.
1941—Robert E. Sherwood, There Shall Be No Night.
1943—Thornton Wilder, The Skin of Our Teeth.
1945—Mary Chase, Harvey.
1946—Russel Crouse and Howard Lindsay, State of the Union.
1948—Tennessee Williams, A Streetcar Named Desire.
1949—Arthur Miller, Death of a Salesman.
1950—Richard Rodgers, Oscar Hammerstein II, and Joshua Logan, South Pacific.
1952—Joseph Kramm, The Shrike.
1953—William Inge, Picnic.
1954—John Patrick, Teahouse of the August Moon.
1955—Tennessee Williams, Cat on a Hot Tin Roof.
1956—Frances Goodrich and Albert Hackett, The Diary of Anne Frank.
1957—Eugene O'Neill, Long Day's Journey Into Night.
1958—Ketti Frings, Look Homeward, Angel.
1959—Archibald MacLeish, J. B.
1960—George Abbott, Jerome Weidman, Sheldon Harnick and Jerry Bock, Fiorello.
1961—Tad Mosel, All the Way Home.
1962—Frank Loesser and Abe Burrows, How To Succeed In Business Without Really Trying.
1965—Frank D. Gilroy, The Subject Was Roses.
1967—Edward Albee, A Delicate Balance.
1969—Howard Sackler, The Great White Hope.
1970—Charles Gordone, No Place to Be Somebody.
1971—Paul Zindel, The Effect of Gamma Rays on Man-in-the-Moon Marigolds.
1973—Jason Miller, That Championship Season.
1975—Edward Albee, Seascape.
1976—Michael Bennett, James Kirkwood, Nicholas Dante, Marvin Hamlisch, Edward Kleban, A Chorus Line.
1977—Michael Cristofer, The Shadow Box.
1978—Donald L. Coburn, The Gin Game.
1979—Sam Shepard, Buried Child.

History

For a book on the history of the United States.
1917—J. J. Jusserand, With Americans of Past and Present Days.
1918—James Ford Rhodes, History of the Civil War.
1920—Justin H. Smith, The War with Mexico.
1921—William Sowden Sims, The Victory at Sea.
1922—James Truslow Adams, The Founding of New England.
1923—Charles Warren, The Supreme Court in United States History.
1924—Charles Howard McIlwain, The American Revolution: A Constitutional Interpretation.
1925—Frederick L. Paxton, A History of the American Frontier.
1926—Edward Channing, A History of the U.S.
1927—Samuel Flagg Bemis, Pinckney's Treaty.
1928—Vernon Louis Parrington, Main Currents in American Thought.

1929—Fred A. Shannon, The Organization and Administration of the Union Army, 1861-65.
1930—Claude H. Van Tyne, The War of Independence.
1931—Bernadotte E. Schmitt, The Coming of the War, 1914.
1932—Gen. John J. Pershing, My Experiences in the World War.
1933—Frederick J. Turner, The Significance of Sections in American History.
1934—Herbert Agar, The People's Choice.
1935—Charles McLean Andrews, The Colonial Period of American History.
1936—Andrew C. McLaughlin, The Constitutional History of the United States.
1937—Van Wyck Brooks, The Flowering of New England.
1938—Paul Herman Buck, The Road to Reunion, 1865-1900.
1939—Frank Luther Mott, A History of American Magazines.
1940—Carl Sandburg, Abraham Lincoln: The War Years.
1941—Marcus Lee Hansen, The Atlantic Migration, 1607-1860.
1942—Margaret Leech, Reveille in Washington.
1943—Esther Forbes, Paul Revere and the World He Lived In.
1944—Merle Curti, The Growth of American Thought.
1945—Stephen Bonsal, Unfinished Business.
1946—Arthur M. Schlesinger Jr., The Age of Jackson.
1947—James Phinney Baxter 3d, Scientists Against Time.
1948—Bernard De Voto, Across the Wide Missouri.
1949—Roy F. Nichols, The Disruption of American Democracy.
1950—O. W. Larkin, Art and Life in America.
1951—R. Carlyle Buley, The Old Northwest: Pioneer Period 1815-1840.
1952—Oscar Handlin, The Uprooted.
1953—George Dangerfield, The Era of Good Feelings.
1954—Bruce Catton, A Stillness at Appomattox.
1955—Paul Horgan, Great River: The Rio Grande in North American History.
1956—Richard Hofstadter, The Age of Reform.
1957—George F. Kennan, Russia Leaves the War.
1958—Bray Hammond, Banks and Politics in America—From the Revolution to the Civil War.
1959—Leonard D. White and Jean Schneider, The Republican Era; 1869-1901.
1960—Margaret Leech, In the Days of McKinley.
1961—Herbert Feis, Between War and Peace: The Potsdam Conference.
1962—Lawrence H. Gibson, The Triumphant Empire: Thunderclouds Gather in the West.
1963—Constance McLaughlin Green, Washington: Village and Capital, 1800-1878.
1964—Sumner Chilton Powell, Puritan Village: The Formation of A New England Town.
1965—Irwin Unger, The Greenback Era.
1966—Perry Miller, Life of the Mind in America.
1967—William H. Goetzmann, Exploration and Empire: the Explorer and Scientist in the Winning of the American West.
1968—Bernard Bailyn, The Ideological Origins of the American Revolution.
1969—Leonard W. Levy, Origin of the Fifth Amendment.

PULITZER PRIZE WINNERS

1970—Dean Acheson, Present at the Creation: My Years in the State Department.
1971—James McGregor Burns, Roosevelt: The Soldier of Freedom.
1972—Carl N. Degler, Neither Black Nor White.
1973—Michael Kammen, People of Paradox: An Inquiry Concerning the Origins of American Civilization.
1974—Daniel J. Boorstin, The Americans: The Democratic Experience.
1975—Dumas Malone, Jefferson and His Time.
1976—Paul Horgan, Lamy of Santa Fe.
1977—David M. Potter, The Impending Crisis.
1978—Alfred D. Chandler, Jr., The Visible Hand: The Managerial Revolution in American Business.
1979—Don E. Fehrenbacher, The Dred Scott Case: Its Significance in American Law and Politics.

Biography or Autobiography

For a distinguished biography or autobiography by an American author, preferably on an American subject.
1917—Laura E. Richards and Maude Howe Elliott, assisted by Florence Howe Hall, Julia Ward Howe.
1918—William Cabell Bruce, Benjamin Franklin, Self-Revealed.
1919—Henry Adams, The Education of Henry Adams.
1920—Albert J. Beveridge, The Life of John Marshall.
1921—Edward Bok, The Americanization of Edward Bok.
1922—Hamlin Garland, A Daughter of the Middle Border.
1923—Burton J. Hendrick, The Life and Letters of Walter H. Page.
1924—Michael Pupin, From Immigrant to Inventor.
1925—M. A. DeWolfe Howe, Barrett Wendell and His Letters.
1926—Harvey Cushing, Life of Sir William Osler.
1927—Emory Holloway, Whitman: An Interpretation in Narrative.
1928—Charles Edward Russell, The American Orchestra and Theodore Thomas.
1929—Burton J. Hendrick, The Training of an American: The Earlier Life and Letters of Walter H. Page.
1930—Marquis James, The Raven (Sam Houston).
1931—Henry James, Charles W. Eliot.
1932—Henry F. Pringle, Theodore Roosevelt.
1933—Allan Nevins, Grover Cleveland.
1934—Tyler Dennett, John Hay.
1935—Douglas Southall Freeman, R. E. Lee
1936—Ralph Barton Perry, The Thought and Character of William James.
1937—Allan Nevins, Hamilton Fish: The Inner History of the Grand Administration.
1938—Divided between Odell Shepard, Pedlar's Progress; Marquis James, Andrew Jackson.
1939—Carl Van Doren, Benjamin Franklin.
1940—Ray Stannard Baker, Woodrow Wilson, Life and Letters.
1941—Ola Elizabeth Winslow, Jonathan Edwards.
1942—Forrest Wilson, Crusader in Crinoline.
1943—Samuel Eliot Morison, Admiral of the Ocean Sea (Columbus).

1944—Carleton Mabee, The American Leonardo: The Life of Samuel F. B. Morse.
1945—Russell Blaine Nye, George Bancroft; Brahmin Rebel.
1946—Linny Marsh Wolfe, Son of the Wilderness.
1947—William Allen White, The Autobiography of William Allen White.
1948—Margaret Clapp, Forgotten First Citizen: John Bigelow.
1949—Robert E. Sherwood, Roosevelt and Hopkins.
1950—Samuel Flag Bemis, John Quincy Adams and the Foundations of American Foreign Policy.
1951—Margaret Louise Colt, John C. Calhoun: American Portrait.
1952—Merlo J. Pusey, Charles Evans Hughes.
1953—David J. Mays, Edmund Pendleton, 1721–1803.
1954—Charles A. Lindbergh, The Spirit of St. Louis.
1955—William S. White, The Taft Story.
1956—Talbot F. Hamlin, Benjamin Henry Latrobe.
1957—John F. Kennedy, Profiles in Courage.
1958—Douglas Southall Freeman (decd. 1953), George Washington, Vols. I-VI; John Alexander Carroll and Mary Wells Ashworth, Vol. VII.
1959—Arthur Walworth, Woodrow Wilson: American Prophet.
1960—Samuel Eliot Morison, John Paul Jones.
1961—David Donald, Charles Sumner and The Coming of the Civil War.
1963—Leon Edel, Henry James: Vol. II. The Conquest of London, 1870–1881; Vol. III, The Middle Years, 1881–1895.
1964—Walter Jackson Bate, John Keats.
1965—Ernest Samuels, Henry Adams.
1966—Arthur M. Schlesinger Jr., A Thousand Days.
1967—Justin Kaplan, Mr. Clemens and Mark Twain.
1968—George F. Kennan, Memoirs (1925–1950).
1969—B. L. Reid, The Man from New York: John Quinn and his Friends.
1970—T. Harry Williams, Huey Long.
1971—Lawrence Thompson, Robert Frost: The Years of Triumph, 1915–1938.
1972—Joseph P. Lash, Eleanor and Franklin.
1973—W. A. Swanberg, Luce and His Empire.
1974—Louis Sheaffer, O'Neill, Son and Artist.
1975—Robert A. Caro, The Power Broker: Robert Moses and the Fall of New York.
1976—R.W.B. Lewis, Edith Wharton: A Biography.
1977—John E. Mack, A Prince of Our Disorder, The Life of T. E. Lawrence.
1978—Walter Jackson Bate, Samuel Johnson.
1979—Leonard Baker, Days of Sorrow and Pain: Leo Baeck and the Berlin Jews.

American Poetry

Before this prize was established in 1922, awards were made from gifts provided by the Poetry Society: 1918—Love Songs, by Sara Teasdale. 1919—Old Road to Paradise, by Margaret Widemer; Corn Huskers, by Carl Sandburg.
1922—Edwin Arlington Robinson, Collected Poems.
1923—Edna St. Vincent Millay, The Ballad of the

321

Harp-Weaver; A Few Figs from Thistles; Eight Sonnets in American Poetry, 1922; A Miscellany.
1924—Robert Frost, New Hampshire: A Poem with Notes and Grace Notes.
1925—Edwin Arlington Robinson, The Man Who Died Twice.
1926—Amy Lowell, What's O'Clock.
1927—Leonora Speyer, Fiddler's Farewell.
1928—Edwin Arlington Robinson, Tristram.
1929—Stephen Vincent Benet, John Brown's Body.
1930—Conrad Aiken, Selected Poems.
1931—Robert Frost, Collected Poems.
1932—George Dillon, The Flowering Stone.
1933—Archibald MacLeish, Conquistador.
1934—Robert Hillyer, Collected Verse.
1935—Audrey Wurdemann, Bright Ambush.
1936—Robert P. Tristram Coffin, Strange Holiness.
1937—Robert Frost, A Further Range.
1938—Marya Zaturenska, Cold Morning Sky.
1939—John Gould Fletcher, Selected Poems.
1940—Mark Van Doren, Collected Poems.
1941—Leonard Bacon, Sunderland Capture.
1942—William Rose Benet, The Dust Which Is God.
1943—Robert Frost, A Witness Tree.
1944—Stephen Vincent Benet, Western Star.
1945—Karl Shapiro, V-Letter and Other Poems.
1947—Robert Lowell, Lord Weary's Castle.
1948—W. H. Auden, The Age of Anxiety.
1949—Peter Viereck, Terror and Decorum.
1950—Gwendolyn Brooks, Annie Allen.
1951—Carl Sandburg, Complete Poems.
1952—Marianne Moore, Collected Poems.
1953—Archibald MacLeish, Collected Poems.
1954—Theodore Roethke, The Waking.
1955—Wallace Stevens, Collected Poems.
1956—Elizabeth Bishop, Poems, North and South.
1957—Richard Wilbur, Things of This World.
1958—Robert Penn Warren, Promises: Poems 1954-1956.
1959—Stanley Kunitz, Selected Poems 1928-1958.
1960—W. D. Snodgrass, Heart's Needle.
1961—Phyllis McGinley, Times Three: Selected Verse from Three Decades.
1962—Alan Dugan, Poems.
1963—William Carlos Williams, Pictures From Breughel.
1964—Louis Simpson, At the End of the Open Road.
1965—John Berryman, 77 Dream Songs.
1966—Richard Eberhart, Selected Poems.
1967—Anne Sexton, Live or Die.
1968—Anthony Hecht, The Hard Hours.
1969—George Oppen, Of Being Numerous.
1970—Richard Howard, Untitled Subjects.
1971—William S. Merwin, The Carrier of Ladders.
1972—James Wright, Collected Poems.
1973—Maxine Winokur Kumin, Up Country.
1975—Gary Snyder, Turtle Island.
1976—John Ashbery, Self-Portrait in a Convex Mirror.
1977—James Merrill, Divine Comedies.
1978—Howard Nemerov, Collected Poems.
1979—Robert Penn Warren, Now and Then: Poems 1976-1978.

General Non-Fiction

For best book by an American, not eligible in any other category.

1962—Theodore H. White, The Making of the President 1960.
1963—Barbara W. Tuchman, The Guns of August.
1964—Richard Hofstadter, Anti-Intellectualism in American Life.
1965—Howard Mumford Jones, O Strange New World.
1966—Edwin Way Teale, Wandering Through Winter.
1967—David Brion Davis, The Problem of Slavery in Western Culture.
1968—Will and Ariel Durant, Rousseau and Revolution.
1969—Norman Mailer, The Armies of the Night; and Rene Jules Dubos, So Human an Animal: How We Are Shaped by Surroundings and Events.
1970—Eric H. Erikson, Gandhi's Truth.
1971—John Toland, The Rising Sun.
1972—Barbara W. Tuchman, Stilwell and the American Experience in China, 1911-1945.
1973—Frances FitzGerald, Fire in the Lake: The Vietnamese and the Americans in Vietnam; and Robert Coles, Children of Crisis, Volumes II and III.
1974—Ernest Becker, The Denial of Death.
1975—Annie Dillard, Pilgrim at Tinker Creek.
1976—Robert N. Butler, Why Survive? Being Old in America.
1977—William W. Warner, Beautiful Swimmers.
1978—Carl Sagan, The Dragons of Eden.
1979—Edward O. Wilson, On Human Nature.

Music

For composition by an American (before 1977, by a composer resident in the U.S.), in the larger forms of chamber, orchestra or choral music or for an operatic work including ballet. A special posthumous award was granted in 1976 to Scott Joplin.

1943—William Schuman, Secular Cantata No. 2, A Free Song.
1944—Howard Hanson, Symphony No. 4, Op. 34.
1945—Aaron Copland, Appalachian Spring.
1946—Leo Sowerby, The Canticle of the Sun.
1947—Charles E. Ives, Symphony No. 3.
1948—Walter Piston, Symphony No. 3.
1949—Virgil Thomson, Louisiana Story.
1950—Gian-Carlo Menotti, The Consul.
1951—Douglas Moore, Giants in the Earth.
1952—Gail Kubil, Symphony Concertante.
1954—Quincy Porter, Concerto for Two Pianos and Orchestra.
1955—Gian-Carlo Menotti, The Saint of Bleecker Street.
1956—Ernest Toch, Symphony No. 3.
1957—Norman Dello Joio, Meditations on Ecclesiastes.
1958—Samuel Barber, Vanessa.
1959—John La Montaine, Concerto for Piano and Orchestra.
1960—Elliott Carter, Second String Quartet.
1961—Walter Piston, Symphony No. 7.
1962—Robert Ward, The Crucible.
1963—Samuel Barber, Piano Concerto No. 1.
1966—Leslie Bassett, Variations for Orchestra.
1967—Leon Kirchner, Quartet No. 3.
1968—George Crumb, Echoes of Time and The River.
1969—Karel Husa, String Quartet No. 3.
1970—Charles W. Wuorinen, Time's Encomium.

1971—Mario Davidovsky, Synchronisms No. 6.
1972—Jacob Druckman, Windows.
1973—Elliott Carter, String Quartet No. 3.
1974—Donald Martino, Notturno. (Special citation) Roger Sessions.
1975—Dominick Argento, From the Diary of Virginia Woolf.

1976—Ned Rorem, Air Music.
1977—Richard Wernick, Visions of Terror and Wonder.
1978—Michael Colgrass, Deja Vu for Percussion and Orchestra.
1979—Joseph Schwantner, Aftertones of Infinity.

MOTION PICTURE ACADEMY AWARDS (OSCARS)

1927-28
Actor: Emil Jannings, The Way of All Flesh
Actress: Janet Gaynor, Seventh Heaven
1928-29
Actor: Warner Baxter, In Old Arizona
Actress: Mary Pickford, Coquette
1929-30
Actor: George Arliss, Disraeli
Actress: Norma Shearer, The Divorcee
1930-31
Actor: Lionel Barrymore, A Free Soul
Actress: Marie Dressler, Min and Bill
1931-32
Actor: Wallace Beery, The Champ
    Fredric March, Dr. Jekyll and Mr. Hyde
Actress: Helen Hayes, The Sin of Madelon Claudet
1932-33
Actor: Charles Laughton, The Private Life of Henry VIII
Actress: Katharine Hepburn, Morning Glory
1934
Actor: Clark Gable, It Happened One Night
Actress: Claudette Colbert, It Happened One Night
1935
Actor: Victor McLaglen, The Informer
Actress: Bette Davis, Dangerous
1936
Actor: Paul Muni, The Story of Louis Pasteur
Actress: Luise Rainer, The Great Ziegfeld
Supp. Actor: Walter Brennan, Come and Get It
Supp. Actress: Gale Sondergaard, Anthony Adverse
1937
Actor: Spencer Tracy, Captains Courageous
Actress: Luise Rainer, The Good Earth
Supp. Actor: Joseph Schildkraut, The Life of Emile Zola
Supp. Actress: Alice Brady, In Old Chicago
1938
Actor: Spencer Tracy, Boys Town
Actress: Bette Davis, Jezebel
Supp. Actor: Walter Brennan, Kentucky
Supp. Actress: Fay Bainter, Jezebel
1939
Actor: Robert Donat, Goodbye, Mr. Chips
Actress: Vivien Leigh, Gone with the Wind
Supp. Actor: Thomas Mitchell, Stagecoach
Supp. Actress: Hattie McDaniel, Gone with the Wind
1940
Actor: James Stewart, The Philadelphia Story
Actress: Ginger Rogers, Kitty Foyle
Supp. Actor: Walter Brennan, The Westerner
Supp. Actress: Jane Darwell, The Grapes of Wrath
1941
Actor: Gary Cooper, Sergeant York
Actress: Joan Fontaine, Suspicion
Supp. Actor: Donald Crisp, How Green Was My Valley

Supp. Actress: Mary Astor, The Great Lie
1942
Actor: James Cagney, Yankee Doodle Dandy
Actress: Greer Garson, Mrs. Miniver
Supp. Actor: Van Heflin, Johnny Eager
Supp. Actress: Teresa Wright, Mrs. Miniver
1943
Actor: Paul Lukas, Watch on the Rhine
Actress: Jennifer Jones, The Song of Bernadette
Supp. Actor: Charles Coburn, The More the Merrier
Supp. Actress: Katina Paxinou, For Whom the Bell Tolls
1944
Actor: Bing Crosby, Going My Way
Actress: Ingrid Bergman, Gaslight
Supp. Actor: Barry Fitzgerald, Going My Way
Supp. Actress: Ethel Barrymore, None But the Lonely Heart
1945
Actor: Ray Milland, The Lost Weekend
Actress: Joan Crawford, Mildred Pierce
Supp. Actor: James Dunn, A Tree Grows in Brooklyn
Supp. Actress: Anne Revere, National Velvet
1946
Actor: Fredric March, The Best Years of Our Lives
Actress: Olivia de Havilland, To Each His Own
Supp. Actor: Harold Russell, The Best Years of Our Lives
Supp. Actress: Anne Baxter, The Razor's Edge
1947
Actor: Ronald Colman, A Double Life
Actress: Loretta Young, The Farmer's Daughter
Supp. Actor: Edmund Gwenn, Miracle on 34th Street
Supp. Actress: Celeste Holm, Gentleman's Agreement
1948
Actor: Laurence Olivier, Hamlet
Actress: Jane Wyman, Johnny Belinda
Supp. Actor: Walter Huston, The Treasure of the Sierre Madre
Supp. Actress: Claire Trevor, Key Largo
1949
Actor: Broderick Crawford, All the King's Men
Actress: Olivia de Havilland, The Heiress
Supp. Actor: Dean Jagger, Twelve O'Clock High
Supp. Actress: Mercedes McCambridge, All the King's Men
1950
Actor: José Ferrer, Cyrano de Bergerac
Actress: Judy Holliday, Born Yesterday
Supp. Actor: George Sanders, All About Eve
Supp. Actress: Josephine Hull, Harvey
1951
Actor: Humphrey Bogart, The African Queen
Actress: Vivien Leigh, A Streetcar Named Desire
Supp. Actor: Karl Malden, A Streetcar Named Desire
Supp. Actress: Kim Hunter, A Streetcar Named Desire

THE BOOK OF WHO

1952
Actor: Gary Cooper, High Noon
Actress: Shirley Booth, Come Back, Little Sheba
Supp. Actor: Anthony Quinn, Viva Zapata!
Supp. Actress: Gloria Grahame, The Bad and The Beautiful
1953
Actor: William Holden, Stalag 17
Actress: Audrey Hepburn, Roman Holiday
Supp. Actor: Frank Sinatra, From Here to Eternity
Supp. Actress: Donna Reed, From Here to Eternity
1954
Actor: Marlon Brando, On the Waterfront
Actress: Grace Kelly, The Country Girl
Supp. Actor: Edmond O'Brien, The Barefoot Contessa
Supp. Actress: Eva Marie Saint, On the Waterfront
1955
Actor: Ernest Borgine, Marty
Actress: Anna Magnani, The Rose Tattoo
Supp. Actor: Jack Lemmon, Mister Roberts
Supp. Actress: Jo Van Fleet, East of Eden
1956
Actor: Yul Brynner, The King and I
Actress: Ingrid Bergman, Anastasia
Supp. Actor: Anthony Quinn, Lust for Life
Supp. Actress: Dorothy Malone, Written on the Wind
1957
Actor: Alec Guinness, The Bridge on the River Kwai
Actress: Joanne Woodward, The Three Faces of Eve
Supp. Actor: Red Buttons, Sayonara
Supp. Actress: Miyoshi Umeki, Sayonara
1958
Actor: David Niven, Separate Tables
Actress: Susan Hayward, I Want to Live
Supp. Actor: Burl Ives, The Big Country
Supp. Actress: Wendy Hiller, Separate Tables
1959
Actor: Charlton Heston, Ben-Hur
Actress: Simone Signoret, Room at the Top
Supp. Actor: Hugh Griffith, Ben-Hur
Supp. Actress: Shelley Winters, The Diary of Anne Frank
1960
Actor: Burt Lancaster, Elmer Gantry
Actress: Elizabeth Taylor, Butterfield 8
Supp. Actor: Peter Ustinov, Spartacus
Supp. Actress: Shirley Jones, Elmer Gantry
1961
Actor: Maximilian Schell, Judgment at Nuremberg
Actress: Sophia Loren, Two Women
Supp. Actor: George Chakiris, West Side Story
Supp. Actress: Rita Moreno, West Side Story
1962
Actor: Gregory Peck, To Kill a Mockingbird
Actress: Anne Bancroft, The Miracle Worker
Supp. Actor: Ed Begley, Sweet Bird of Youth
Supp. Actress: Patty Duke, The Miracle Worker
1963
Actor: Sidney Poitier, Lilies of the Field
Actress: Patricia Neal, Hud
Supp. Actor: Melvyn Douglas, Hud
Supp. Actress: Margaret Rutherford, The V.I.P.s
1964
Actor: Rex Harrison, My Fair Lady
Actress: Julie Andrews, Mary Poppins

Supp. Actor: Peter Ustinov, Topkapi
Supp. Actress: Lila Kedrova, Zorba the Greek
1965
Actor: Lee Marvin, Cat Ballou
Actress: Julie Christie, Darling
Supp. Actor: Martin Balsam, A Thousand Clowns
Supp. Actress: Shelley Winters, A Patch of Blue
1966
Actor: Paul Scofield, A Man for All Seasons
Actress: Elizabeth Taylor, Who's Afraid of Virginia Woolf?
Supp. Actor: Walter Matthau, The Fortune Cookie
Supp. Actress: Sandy Dennis, Who's Afraid of Virginia Woolf?
1967
Actor: Rod Steiger, In the Heat of the Night
Actress: Katharine Hepburn, Guess Who's Coming to Dinner?
Supp. Actor: George Kennedy, Cool Hand Luke
Supp. Actress: Estelle Parsons, Bonnie and Clyde
1968
Actor: Cliff Robertson, Charly
Actress: Katharine Hepburn, The Lion in Winter
Barbra Streisand, Funny Girl
Supp. Actor: Jack Albertson, The Subject Was Roses
Supp. Actress: Ruth Gordon, Rosemary's Baby
1969
Actor: John Wayne, True Grit
Actress: Maggie Smith, The Prime of Miss Jean Brodie
Supp. Actor: Gig Young, They Shoot Horses, Don't They?
Supp. Actress: Goldie Hawn, Cactus Flower
1970
Actor: George C. Scott, Patton
Actress: Glenda Jackson, Women in Love
Supp. Actor: John Mills, Ryan's Daughter
Supp. Actress: Helen Hayes, Airport
1971
Actor: Gene Hackman, The French Connection
Actress: Jane Fonda, Klute
Supp. Actor: Ben Johnson, The Last Picture Show
Supp. Actress: Cloris Leachman, The Last Picture Show
1972
Actor: Marlon Brando, The Godfather
Actress: Liza Minnelli, Cabaret
Supp. Actor: Joel Grey, Cabaret
Supp. Actress: Eileen Heckart, Butterflies Are Free
1973
Actor: Jack Lemmon, Save the Tiger
Actress: Glenda Jackson, A Touch of Class
Supp. Actor: John Houseman, The Paper Chase
Supp. Actress: Tatum O'Neal, Paper Moon
1974
Actor: Art Carney, Harry and Tonto
Actress: Ellyn Burstyn, Alice Doesn't Live Here Anymore
Supp. Actor: Robert DeNiro, The Godfather, Part II
Supp. Actress: Ingrid Bergman, Murder on the Orient Express
1975
Actor: Jack Nicholson, One Flew Over the Cuckoo's Nest
Actress: Louise Fletcher, One Flew Over the Cuckoo's Nest
Supp. Actor: George Burns, The Sunshine Boys

Supp. Actress: Lee Grant, Shampoo
1976
Actor: Peter Finch, Network
Actress: Faye Dunaway, Network
Supp. Actor: Jason Robards, Jr., All the President's Men
Supp. Actress: Beatrice Straight, Network
1977
Actor: Richard Dreyfuss, The Goodbye Girl

Actress: Diane Keaton, Annie Hall
Supp. Actor: Jason Robards, Jr., Julia
Supp. Actress: Vanessa Redgrave, Julia
1978
Actor: Jon Voight, Coming Home
Actress: Jane Fonda, Coming Home
Supp. Actor: Christopher Walken, The Deer Hunter
Supp. Actress: Maggie Smith, California Suite

MISS AMERICA WINNERS

Prior to 1950 the selection of Miss America was for the year in which she was selected. Starting with 1950 she became Miss America of the following year, as a result was no Miss America for 1950. No contest was held from 1928 to 1932 and in 1934.

Year	Winner	Year	Winner
1921	Margaret Gorman, Washington, D.C.	1956	Sharon Ritchie, Denver, Colorado
1922-23	Mary Campbell, Columbus, Ohio	1957	Marian McKnight, Manning, S.C.
1924	Ruth Malcolmson, Philadelphia, Pa.	1958	Marilyn Van Derbur, Denver, Colorado
1925	Fay Lanphier, Oakland, California	1959	Mary Ann Mobley, Brandon, Miss.
1926	Norma Smallwood, Tulsa, Oklahoma	1960	Lynda Lee Mead, Natchez, Miss.
1927	Lois Delaner, Joliet, Illinois	1961	Nancy Fleming, Montague, Michigan
1933	Marion Bergeron, West Haven, Conn.	1962	Maria Fletcher, Asheville, N.C.
1935	Henrietta Leaver, Pittsburgh, Pa.	1963	Jacquelyn Mayer, Sandusky, Ohio
1936	Rose Coyle, Philadelphia, Pa.	1964	Donna Axum, El Dorado, Arkansas
1937	Bette Cooper, Bertrand Island, N.J.	1965	Vonda Kay Van Dyke, Phoenix, Ariz.
1938	Marilyn Meseke, Marion, Ohio	1966	Deborah Irene Bryant, Overland Park, Kansas
1939	Patricia Donnelly, Detroit, Michigan		
1940	Frances Marie Burke, Philadelphia, Pa.	1967	Jane Anne Jayroe, Laverne, Oklahoma
1941	Rosemary LaPlanche, Los Angeles, Calif.	1968	Debra Dene Barnes, Moran, Kansas
1942	Jo-Carroll Dennison, Tyler, Texas	1969	Judith Anne Ford, Belvidere, Ill.
1943	Jean Bartel, Los Angeles, Calif.	1970	Pamela Anne Eldred, Birmingham, Mich.
1944	Venus Ramey, Washington, D.C.		
1945	Bess Myerson, New York City, N.Y.	1971	Phyllis Ann George, Denton, Texas
1946	Marilyn Buferd, Los Angeles, Calif.	1972	Laurie Lea Schaefer, Columbus, Ohio
1947	Barbara Walker, Memphis, Tennessee	1973	Terry Anne Meeuwsen, DePere, Wisconsin
1948	BeBe Shopp, Hopkins, Minnesota		
1949	Jacque Mercer, Litchfield, Arizona	1974	Rebecca Ann King, Denver, Colorado
1951	Yolande Betbeze, Mobile, Alabama (Postdated)	1975	Shirley Cothran, Fort Worth, Texas
		1976	Tawney Elaine Godin, Yonkers, N.Y.
1952	Colleen Kay Hutchins, Salt Lake City, Utah	1977	Dorothy Benham, Edina, Minn.
		1978	Susan Perkins, Columbus, Ohio
1953	Neva Jane Langley, Macon, Ga.	1979	Kylene J. Barker, Galax, Va.
1954	Evelyn Margaret Ay, Ephrata, Pa.	1980	Cheryl Prewitt, Ackerman, Miss.
1955	Lee Meriwether, San Francisco, Calif.		

NAME INDEX

NAME INDEX

Benes, Eduard, *161*
Benét, Stephen Vincent, *10*
Benét, William Rose, *10*
Ben-Gurion, David, *161*
Benjamin, Richard, *226, 245*
Benn, Gottfried, *37*
Bennett, Arnold, *24*
Bennett, Constance, *227*
Bennett, Joan, *227*
Bennett, Tony, *264*
Benny, Jack, *247, 274, 275*
Benson, Robby, *227*
Benson, Sally, *10*
Bensten, Lloyd M., Jr., *135*
Bentham, Jeremy, *85*
Benton, Thomas Hart, *57*
Benton, Thomas Hart, *135*
Benz, Karl F., *117*
Berdyaev, Nikolai Aleksandrovich, *85*
Berg, Alban, *74*
Berg, Gertrude, *227*
Berg, Patty, *210*
Bergen, Candice, *227, 275*
Bergen, Edgar, *227, 275*
Bergen, Polly, *227*
Bergey, Bill, *210*
Bergius, Friedrich K., *117*
Bergland, Bob S., *135*
Bergman, Ingmar, *282*
Bergman, Ingrid, *227, 283*
Bergson, Henri, *85*
Beria, Lavrenti Pavlovich, *161*
Berigen, Bunny, *284*
Bering, Vitus J., *131*
Beriosova, Svetlana, *74*
Berkeley, Anthony, *45*
Berkeley, George, *85*
Berle, Adolf A., *135*
Berle, Milton, *275*
Berlin, Irving, *289*
Berliner, Emile, *102*
Berlioz, Hector, *74*
Berman, Shelley, *275*
Bernadette, Saint, *85*
Bernadotte, Jean B. J. (see Charles XIV John)
Bernardi, Herschel, *227*
Bernbach, William, *193*
Bernhardt, Sarah, *254, 256*
Bernini, Giovanni Lorenzo, *62*
Bernoulli, Daniel, *124*
Bernstein, Carl, *50, 56*
Bernstein, Elmer, *289*
Bernstein, Leonard, *69*
Berra, Yogi, *210*
Berry, Chuck, *264*
Berry, Ray, *210*
Berryman, John, *10*
Berthelot, Pierre E. M., *121*
Bertolucci, Bernardo, *282*
Berzelius, Baron Jöns J., *124*
Besant, Annie, *86*
Bessel, Friedrich W., *117*
Bessemer, Sir Henry, *111*
Betancourt, Romulo, *161*
Bethe, Hans A., *117*
Bethune, Mary McLeod, *99*
Betjeman, John, *24*
Bettelheim, Bruno, *93*
Bevan, Aneurin, *154*
Bevin, Ernest, *154*
Bich, Marcel, *193*
Bickford, Charles, *227*
Biddle, John, *86*
Biddle, Nicholas, *193*
Bierce, Ambrose, *10*
Bigelow, Erastus B., *193*
Biggers, Earl Derr, *45*
Biggs, E. Power, *69*
Bikel, Theodore, *265*
Billy the Kid (William H. Bonney), *294*
Binet, Alfred, *121*
Bing, Dave, *210*

Bing, Sir Rudolf, *74*
Bingham, George Caleb, *57*
Birch, John, *135*
Birch, Stephen, *193*
Bird, Rose Elizabeth, *135*
Birdseye, Clarence, *193*
Birney, James Gillespie, *135*
Bishop, Hazel G., *193*
Bishop, Jim, *50*
Bishop, Joey, *275*
Bismarck, Otto von, *161*
Bissel, George H., *193*
Bissell, Emily P., *186*
Bissell, Richard M., *193*
Bisset, Jacqueline, *227*
Bixby, Bill, *227*
Bizet, Georges, *34, 74*
Bjerknes, Jacob A. B., *102*
Björling, Jussi, *74*
Bjørnson, Bjørnstjerne, *37*
Black, Hugo L., *135*
Black, James, *186*
Black, Karen, *227*
Black, Shirley Temple (see Temple, Shirley)
Blackett, Patrick M. S., *111*
Black Hawk, *174*
Blackmer, Sidney, *227*
Blackmun, Harry A., *135*
Blackstone, Sir William, *93*
Blackwell, Antoinette Louisa, *186*
Blackwell, Elizabeth, *102, 110, 186*
Blackwell, Henry Browne, *186, 191*
Blackwell, Earl, Jr., *50*
Blaine, James G., *135, 138*
Blair, David, *74*
Blair, James, *99*
Blair, Linda, *227*
Blake, Amanda, *227*
Blake, Eugene Carson, *81*
Blake, Robert, *227*
Blake, William, *24*
Blakey, Art, *284*
Blalock, Jane, *210*
Blanc, Louis, *186*
Blanc, Mel, *289*
Blanda, George, *210*
Blankers-Koen, Fanny, *210*
Blass, Bill, *294*
Blavatsky, Helena Petrovna, *86*
Blériot, Louis, *121*
Bligh, William, *181*
Blish, James B., *48*
Bloch, Felix, *102*
Bloch, Konrad E., *102*
Bloch, Ray, *284*
Block, Herbert, *57*
Blok, Alexander, *37*
Blondell, Joan, *227, 245*
Blood, Sweat, and Tears, *268, 284, 286*
Bloom, Claire, *254*
Bloomer, Amelia, *186*
Bloomingdale, Joseph B., *194*
Blough, Roger M., *194*
Plücher von Wahlstaff, Gebhard, *181*
Blue, Ben, *275*
Blue, Vida, *210*
Blume, Judy, *10*
Blumenthal, W. Michael, *135*
Bly, Nellie, *294*
Bly, Robert, *10*
Blyth, Ann, *227*
Boas, Franz, *93*
Boccaccio, Giovanni, *37*
Bock, Jerry, *289*
Bocuse, Paul, *294*
Boehme, Jakob, *86*
Bogarde, Dirk, *255*
Bogart, Humphrey, *226, 227*
Bogdanovich, Peter, *278*
Boggs, Corinne ("Lindy"), *135*
Bohlen, Charles E., *135*
Böhm, Karl, *74*

Bohr, Aage, *108, 124, 127*
Bohr, Niels, *124, 125*
Boito, Arrigo, *74*
Bok, Derek Curtis, *99*
Bolden, Buddy, *284*
Bolger, Ray, *263, 290*
Boleyn, Anne, *155, 157*
Bolingbroke, Henry St. John, *155*
Bolivar, Simon, *161, 171, 172*
Boll, Heinrich, *37*
Bombeck, Erma, *50*
Bond, Julian, *135*
Bond, Ward, *227*
Bonnard, Pierre, *62*
Bono, Sonny, *265*
Boole, George, *112*
Boone, Pat, *265*
Boone, Richard, *227*
Boorstin, Daniel J., *93*
Booth, Ballington, *186, 187*
Booth, Edwin, *227*
Booth, Evangeline Cory, *186, 187*
Booth, John Wilkes, *145, 227, 294, 301*
Booth, Shirley, *227*
Booth, William, *186, 187*
Borah, William E., *135*
Borden, Gail, *102*
Borden, Lizzie, *294*
Bordet, Jules J. B. V., *124*
Borg, Bjorn, *210*
Borge, Victor, *275*
Borges, Jorge Luis, *37*
Borgia, Cesare, *161*
Borgia, Lucrezia, *161*
Borglum, Gutzon, *57*
Borgnine, Ernest, *227*
Borman, Frank, *129*
Borodin, Alexander, *74*
Boros, Julius, *210*
Borromini, Francesco, *62*
Borzage, Frank, *278*
Bosch, Hieronymus, *62*
Bosch, Juan, *161*
Bosley, Tom, *227*
Bossy, Mike, *210*
Bostock, Lyman, *210*
Boswell, James, *24*
Botha, Louis, *161*
Bothe, Walter W., *117*
Botticelli, Sandro, *62*
Bottoms, Timothy, *227*
Boucher, François, *62*
Boudreau, Lou, *210*
Bougainville, Louis Antoine de, *131*
Boulanger, Nadia, *74*
Boulez, Pierre, *74*
Boulle, Pierre, *32*
Boult, Sir Adrian, *74*
Bourke-White, Margaret, *50*
Boutelle, Richard S., *194*
Bouton, Jim, *210*
Bouts, Dierik, *62*
Bovet, Daniele, *124*
Bow, Clara, *227*
Bowa, Larry, *210*
Bowen, Elizabeth, *24*
Bowes, Major Edward, *289*
Bowie, David, *265*
Bowie, James, *174*
Bowles, Chester, *135*
Boycott, Charles Cunningham, *295*
Boyd, Malcolm, *81*
Boyd, Stephen, *255*
Boyd, William, *227*
Boyd Orr, John, First Baron Boyd Orr of Brechin Mearns, *93*
Boyer, Charles, *255*
Boyle, Peter, *227*
Boyle, Robert, *112*
Boyle, W. A., *194*
Brabham, Jack, *210*
Bracken, Eddie, *227*
Bradbury, Ray, *48*
Braddock, Edward, *130, 181*

328

NAME INDEX

Dostoyevsky, Fyodor, 38
Doubleday, Abner, 212
Doubleday, Nelson, 51
Douglas, Donald W., 196
Douglas, Helen, 139
Douglas, Kirk, 232
Douglas, Lloyd C., 12
Douglas, Melvyn, 139, 232
Douglas, Michael, 232
Douglas, Mike, 290
Douglas, Paul H., 139
Douglas, Paul, 232
Douglas, Stephen A., 139, 145
Douglas, William O., 139
Douglass, Frederick, 187
Douglass, Truman B., 81
Dow, Herbert H., 196
Dowding, Hugh C., 181
Downs, Hugh, 290
Dowson, Ernest C., 25
Doyle, Arthur Conan, 46
D'Oyly Carte, Richard, 26
Drabble, Margaret, 25
Dragon, Darryl, 273
Drake, Alfred, 266
Drake, Edwin L., 196
Drake, Sir Francis, 132
Dreiser, Theodore, 12
Dressler, Marie, 256
Drew, Charles R., 104
Drew, John, 212
Dreyfus, Alfred, 158, 181
Dreyfus, Pierre, 196
Dreyfuss, Richard, 232
Dru, Joanne, 232
Drury, Allen, 12
Dryden, John, 25
Drysdale, Don, 212
DuBarry, Comtesse, 296
Dubinsky, David, 187
Dubois, Marie Eugene F.T., 124
DuBois, W.E.B., 187
Duccio di Buoninsegna, 64
Duchamp, Marcel, 60, 64
Duchin, Eddy, 285
Duchin, Peter, 285
Duff, Howard, 232
Dufy, Raoul, 64
Dukas, Paul, 75
Duke, Benjamin N., 196
Duke, James B., 196
Duke, Patty, 232
Duke, Vernon, 70
Dulbecco, Renato, 102, 104, 110
Dullea, Keir, 232
Dulles, Allen, 139
Dulles, John Foster, 139
Dumas, Alexandre (père), 33
Dumas Alexandre (fils), 33
du Maurier, Daphne, 25
Dunant, Jean H., 97, 163
Dunaway, Faye, 232
Dunbar, Paul Lawrence, 12
Duncan, David Douglas, 58
Duncan, Isadora, 38, 70
Duncan, Sandy, 232
Dunham, Katherine, 70
Dunlop, John B., 113
Dunn, James, 232
Dunne, Irene, 232
Dunne, John Gregory, 12
Dunning, John Ray, 104
Dunnock, Mildred, 232
Dunster, Henry, 99
Du Pont, Eleuthère, Irénée, 94, 196
Du Pont, Francis Irénée, 104
Du Pont, Pierre S., 196
Du Pont de Nemours, Pierre
    Samuel, 94
Du Pont, Thomas Coleman, 196
Duran, Roberto, 212
Durand, Asher Brown, 58
Durant, Thomas C., 196
Durant, William J., 81
Durante, Jimmy, 276

Duras, Marguerite, 33
Durbin, Deanna, 232
Dürer, Albrecht, 64
Durkheim, Emile, 94
Durocher, Leo E., 212
Durrell, Lawrence, 25
Dürrenmatt, Friedrich, 38
Duryea, Dan, 232
Du Sable, Jean Baptiste Point, 129
Duse, Eleanora, 256
Duvalier, François, 163
Duvall, Robert, 232
Duvall, Shelly, 232
DuVigneud, Vincent, 104
Dvořák, Antonin, 75
Dylan, Bob, 266
Dystel, Oscar, 51

Eagels, Jeanne, 232
Eagleton, Thomas, 139
Eakins, Thomas, 58
Eames, Charles, 58
Earhart, Amelia, 129
Early, Jubal A., 175
Earp, Wyatt, 296
Eastland, James O., 139
Eastman, George, 104, 206
Eastwood, Clint, 232
Eaton, Cyrus S., 196
Eberhart, Mignon G., 46
Eberhart, Richard, 12
Eberle, Ray, 266
Ebsen, Buddy, 232
Eccles, Sir John C., 114, 124
Eccles, Marriner S., 196
Echegaray y Eizaguirre, José, 38
Echeverria Alvarez, Luis, 164
Eckhard, Johannes, 87
Eddy, Duane, 285
Eddy, Mary Baker, 81
Eddy, Nelson, 266
Edelman, Gerald M., 104, 115
Eden, Sir Anthony, 155
Eden, Barbara, 232
Ederle, Gertrude, 212
Edison, Thomas Alva, 103, 104, 116
Edmonds, Sarah, 175
Edward VII (Duke of Windsor), 155
Edwards, Blake, 279
Edwards, Cliff, 290
Edwards, Gus, 290
Edwards, Jonathan, 81
Edwards, Ralph L., 279
Edwards, Vincent, 232
Eggar, Samantha, 256
Eglevsky, André, 70
Ehrenburg, Ilya, 38
Ehrlich, Paul, 118, 127
Eichmann, Adolf, 164
Eiffel, Alexandre-Gustave, 64
Eigen, Manfred, 115, 118
Einstein, Albert, 104, 107, 110, 120,
    126, 128
Eisenhower, David II, 296
Eisenhower, Dwight D., 134, 139,
    156, 296
Eisenhower, Milton Stover, 100
Eisenstein, Sergei Mikhaylovich, 282
Eisley, Loren, 12
Eizenstat, Stuart E., 139
Ekland, Britt, 256
Eldridge, Florence, 232
Eldridge, Roy, 285
Eleanor of Aquitaine, 159
Elgar, Sir Edward, 75
Eliot, Charles William, 100
Eliot, George, 25, 26
Eliot, John, 82
Eliot, T. S., 25, 95
Elizabeth I, 113, 155, 156, 157, 300
Elizabeth II, 156
Ellington, Duke, 285
Elliot, Robert B., 276
Elliott, Cass, 266

Ellis, Havelock, 94
Ellison, Harlan, 49
Ellison, Ralph Waldo, 12
Ellsberg, Daniel, 139
Ellsworth, Lincoln, 129, 133
Elsheimer, Adam, 65
Eluard, Paul, 33
Emerson, Ralph Waldo, 12, 84
Emerson, Roy, 212
Emmett, Daniel D., 290
Empedocles, 87
Enders, John F., 104, 109, 110
Engels, Friedrich, 187, 189
Ensor, James Sydney, 65
Epictetus, 87
Epstein, Brian, 290
Erasmus, Desiderius, 87
Eratosthenes, 124
Erdman, Paul E., 12
Erhard, Ludwig, 164
Erickson, Leif, 232
Ericson, Leif, 132
Eric the Red, 132
Erlanger, Joseph, 104, 105
Erlichman, John D., 140
Ernst, Max, 65
Ervin, Samuel J., Jr., 139
Erving, Julius, 212
Erwin, Stuart, 232
Esaki, Leo, 105, 114, 125
Escoffier, Auguste, 296
Esenin, Sergei, 38
Esposito, Phil, 212
Esterhazy, Marie Charles, 182
Estrada, Erik, 232
Etting, Ruth, 266
Eucken, Rudolf, 87
Euclid, 125
Euler, Leonhard, 125, 126
Euler, Ulf S. von, 102, 114, 125
Euler-Chelpin, Hans von, 113, 125
Euripides, 38
Evans, Bergen, 94
Evans, Dale, 232, 247
Evans, Dame Edith, 256
Evans, Maurice, 256
Everett, Chad, 233
Everly, Don, 266
Everly, Phil, 266
Evers, James C., 188
Evert, Chris, 212
Ewbank, Weeb, 213
Ewell, Tom, 233
Ewing, William M., 104
Ewry, Ray, 213
Eyck, Jan Van, 65

Fabergé, Peter Carl, 65
Fabian, 267
Fabius Maximus Verrucosus,
    Quintus, 182
Fabray, Nanette, 267
Fadiman, Clifton, 52
Fahrenheit, Gabriel D., 118
Fain, Sammy, 290
Fairbanks, Chuck, 213
Fairbanks, Douglas, 233, 245
Fairbanks, Douglas, Jr., 233
Faisal, 164
Falk, Peter, 233
Falkenburg, Jinx, 290, 292
Fall, Albert B., 140, 195
Falla, Manuel de, 75
Fangio, Juan, 213
Fantin-Latour, Henri, 65
Faraday, Michael, 113
Fargo, William G., 196, 208
Farley, James A., 140
Farmer, Fannie Meritt, 296
Farmer, Frances, 233
Farmer, James L., 188
Farmer, Philip J., 49
Farquhar, George, 26
Farragut, David G., 175, 178

NAME INDEX

NAME INDEX

NAME INDEX

Hunt, E. Howard, *143*
Hunt, H. L., *199*
Hunt, Richard M., *59*
Hunt, Holman, *66*
Hunter, James ("Catfish"), *215*
Hunter, Evan, *15*
Hunter, Jeffrey, *237*
Hunter, Kim, *237*
Hunter, Ross, *279*
Hunter, Tab, *237*
Hunter, Thomas, *100*
Huntington, Henry E., *199*
Hurok, Sol, *279*
Hurst, Fannie, *15*
Huss, Jan, *88*
Husak, Gustav, *166*
Hussein, Abdul ibn, *166, 198*
Hussey, Ruth, *237*
Huston, John, 238, *258, 279*
Huston, Walter, *257*
Hutchinson, Anne, 81, *82,* 154
Hutchinson, Thomas, *143*
Hutson, Don, *215*
Hutton, Barbara, *257, 298*
Hutton, Betty, *237*
Hutton, James, *114*
Hutton, Lauren, *291*
Huxley, Aldous L., *27,* 88, *295*
Huxley, Andrew F., *114,* 125
Huxley, Thomas H., 88, *114*
Huygens, Christiaan, *126*
Huysmans, Joris Karl, *34*
Hyatt, John, *106*
Hyde, Edward, *156*
Hyde-White, Wilfrid, *258*

Ian, Janis, *268*
Ibarruri, Delores, 166
Iberville, Pierre LeMoyne, Sieur de, *132*
Ibn Saud, *166*
Ibsen, Henrik, *40,* 44
Ichazo, Oscar, *298*
Ieyasu, *166*
Ignatius of Loyola, Saint, *88*
Ikhnaton (Amenhotep IV), *166*
Iles, Francis (see Berkeley, Anthony)
Ingalls, John J., *143*
Inge, William, *15*
Inge, William R., 88
Ingenhousz, Jan, *126*
Ingersoll, Robert H., *199*
Ingersoll, Royal E., *176*
Ingram, Rex, *237*
Ingres, Jean-Auguste-Dominique, *66*
Innes, Michael, *46*
Inness, George, *59*
Inouye, Daniel K., *143*
Ionesco, Eugene, *34*
Ipatieff, Vladimir Nikolaevich, *106*
Ireland, John, *258*
Irving, Henry, *258*
Irving, John, *15*
Irving, Washington, *15*
Irwin, Hale, *215*
Isabella I, 92, 164, *166*
Isaiah, *88*
Isherwood, Christopher, 23, *27*
Issel, Dan, *215*
Ito, Prince Hirobumi, *166*
Iturbi, José, *76*
Ivan IV, *166*
Ives, Burl, *237*
Ives, Charles, 71
Ives, James M., *58, 59*

Jack, William S., *199*
Jackson, Andrew, *129, 143*
Jackson, Anne, *237, 252*
Jackson, Glenda, *258*
Jackson, Helen Hunt, *15*
Jackson, Henry M., *143*
Jackson, Jesse, *189*

Jackson, Kate, *237*
Jackson, Mahalia, *268,* 271
Jackson, Maynard, *143*
Jackson, Milt, *286*
Jackson, Reggie, *215*
Jackson, Robert H., *143*
Jackson, Shirley, *15*
Jackson, Thomas J. ("Stonewall"), *176*
Jackson 5, The, *268*
Jack the Ripper, *298*
Jacob, Francois, *122,* 123
Jacobs, Helen Hull, *215*
Jaffe, Sam, *237*
Jagger, Dean, *237*
Jagger, Mick, *268*
James, Harry, 235, *286*
James, Henry, *15,* 82
James, Henry, *82*
James, Jesse, *298,* 301
James, P.D., *46*
James, William, *82*
Janaček, Leos, *76*
Jan and Dean, *286*
Janeway, Eliot, *95*
Jannings, Emil, *258*
Jansky, Karl G., *106*
Janssen, David, *237*
Jarrell, Randall, *15*
Jarvis, Howard A., *143*
Jaspers, Karl, 88
Javits, Jacob K., *144*
Jaworski, Leon, *144*
Jay, John, *144*
Jeans, Sir James H., *114*
Jeffers, Robinson, *15*
Jefferson, Blind Lemon, *268*
Jefferson, Thomas, 52, 60, 66, 101, 130, 136, *144*
Jeffreys, Anne, *237*
Jenkins, Ferguson, *215*
Jenner, Bruce, *215*
Jenner, Edward, *114*
Jenney, William Le Baron, *59*
Jensen, J. Hans D., 105, 111, *119*
Jensen, Johannes V., *40*
Jeremiah, *88*
Jerome, Saint, 88
Jessel, George, 290, *291*
Jesus Christ, 88, 170
Jewett, Sarah Orne, *15*
Jimenez, Juan Ramon, *40*
Joan of Arc, *88,* 158
Jodl, Alfred, *182*
Joel, Billy, *268*
Joffre, Joseph J.C., *182*
Joffrey, Robert, *71*
John (Lackland), *156,* 159
John, Elton, *268*
John, Tommy, *215*
John of the Cross, Saint, *88*
John Paul I, *88*
John Paul II, *88*
Johns, Glynis, *258*
Johns, Jasper, *59*
John III Sobieski, *166*
Johnson, Andrew, 138, 140, *144,* 152
Johnson, Bunk, *286*
Johnson, Chic, *276,* 277
Johnson, Eyvind, *40*
Johnson, Hiram W., *144*
Johnson, Howard E., *291*
Johnson, J.J., *286*
Johnson, Jack, *216*
Johnson, Claudia Alta ("Ladybird"), *298*
Johnson, Lyndon Baines, 137, *144,* 298
Johnson, Philip C., *59*
Johnson, Rafer, *216*
Johnson, Samuel, 24, *27*
Johnson, Tom L., *199*
Johnson, Van, *237*
Johnson, Walter, *216*

Johnson, William E., *189*
Johnston, Joseph E., *176*
Joliot-Curie, Jean Frederic, *122*
Joliot-Curie, Irene, *122*
Jolliet, Louis, *132,* 133
Jolson, Al, *268*
Jones, Allan, *268*
Jones, Bert Hayes, *216*
Jones, Bobby, *216*
Jones, Buck, *237*
Jones, Carolyn, *237*
Jones, David ("Deacon"), *216*
Jones, Dean, *237*
Jones, Ed ("Too Tall"), *216*
Jones, Inigo, 66
Jones, Jack, *268*
Jones, James, *15*
Jones, James Earl, *237*
Jones, James Warren ("Jim"), *298*
Jones, Jennifer, *237, 258*
Jones, John Paul, 66, *176*
Jones, Mary ("Mother" Jones), *189*
Jones, Quincy, *286*
Jones, Shirley, 229, 265, *268*
Jones, Spike, *286*
Jones, Tom, *268*
Jong, Erica, *15*
Jonson, Ben, *27*
Jooss, Kurt, *76*
Joplin, Janis, *268*
Joplin, Scott, *71*
Jordan, Barbara, *144*
Jordan, Frank ("Fibber McGee"), *276*
Jordan, Hamilton, *144*
Jordan, Marian, ("Molly McGee"), *276*
Jordan, Vernon E., Jr., *189*
Jory, Victor, *258*
Joseph, Chief, *176,* 177
Josephson, Brian D., 105, *114,* 125
Jouffroy d'Abbans, Claude F., Marquis de, *122*
Jouhaux, Leon, *189*
Joule, James P., *114,* 119
Jourdan, Louis, *258*
Joyce, James, *27,* 51
Juan Carlos I, *166*
Juantorena, Alberto, *216*
Juarez, Benito, *166*
Judas Maccabaeus, *166*
Judd, Winnie Ruth, *298*
Jung, Carl, *95*
Jungreis, Esther, *82*
Jurgenson, Sonny, *216*
Justinian I, *166*
Juvenal, *40*

Kafka, Franz, *40*
Kahanamoku, Duke, *216*
Kahn, Albert, *59*
Kahn, Madeline, *237*
Kahn, Otto Hermann, *200*
Kaiser, Georg, *40*
Kaiser, Henry J., *200*
Kaline, Al, *216*
Kallen, Horace, *100*
Kalmus, Herbert T., *200*
Kamen, Martin D., *106*
Kamerlingh-Onnes, Heike, *126*
Kandinsky, Vassily, *66*
Kane, Helen, *268*
Kanin, Garson, 235, *279*
Kant, Immanuel, 87, *88*
Kantor, MacKinlay, *15*
Kapitsa, Pyotr, Leonidovich, 108, 111, *126*
Kaplan, Gabe, *276*
Karajan, Herbert von, *76*
Karamanlis, Constantine, *166*
Karlfeldt, Erik A., *40*
Karloff, Boris, *258*
Karras, Alex, *216*
Katz, Sir Bernard, 102, *114,* 125

NAME INDEX

NAME INDEX

Newman, Edwin, 54
Newman, John H., 90
Newman, John von, 108
Newman, Paul, 243, 253
Newman, Phyllis, 243
Newman, Randy, 270
Newton, Sir Isaac, 89, 104, 113, 115
Newton, Robert, 259
Newton, Wayne, 270
Newton-John, Olivia, 270
Ney, Michel, 184
Niarchos, Stavros S., 202
Nicholas of Cusa, 120
Nichols, Mike, 280
Nichols, Red, 287
Nichols, William H., 202
Nicholson, Jack, 243
Nicholson, William, 115
Nicklaus, Jack, 219
Nicolet, Jean, 133
Nicolson, Sir Harold G., 157
Niebuhr, Reinhold, 83
Nielsen, Arthur Charles, 54
Nielsen, Leslie, 243
Nietzsche, Friedrich, 37, 90
Nightingale, Florence, 115
Nijinsky, Vaslav, 78
Nilsson, Birgit, 69, 78
Nilsson, Harry, 270
Nilsson, Ulf, 219
Nimitz, Chester W., 178
Nimoy, Leonard, 243
Nin, Anaïs, 35
Nirenberg, Marshall W., 106, 108
Niven, David, 260
Niven, Laurence, 49
Nixon, Ransom M., 55, 56, 138, 139,
    140, 144, 148, 180, 296, 299,
    300
Nixon, Patricia, 299
Nizer, Louis, 300
Nkrumah, Kwame, 169
Nobel, Alfred B., 202
Nobile, Umberto, 129, 133
Noble, Edward J., 202
Noguchi, Isamu, 60
Nolan, Kathy, 243
Nolan, Lloyd, 243
Noll, Chuck, 219
Nolte, Nick, 243
Noone, Jimmie, 287
Nordhoff, Charles Bernard, 14, 18
Nordhoff, Heinz, 202
Norell, Norman, 300
Norris, Frank, 18
Norris, George W., 148
Norrish, Ronald G.W., 115, 118
North, Frederick, 157
Northrop, John Howard, 108, 109
Northrup, John Knudsen, 202
Norton, Eleanor Holmes, 148
Norton-Taylor, Judy, 243
Norton, Ken, 219
Norton, Oliver W., 202
Norvo, Red, 287
Novak, Kim, 243
Novarro, Ramon, 243
Novello, Ivor, 260
Nureyev, Rudolf, 78
Nurmi, Paavo, 219
Nyro, Laura, 270

Oakie, Jack, 243
Oakley, Annie, 129, 292
Oates, Joyce Carol, 18
Oberon, Merle, 260
Obici, Amedeo, 202
O'Brian, Hugh, 243
O'Brien, Edmond, 244
O'Brien, Edna, 29
O'Brien, Lawrence, 148
O'Brien, Margaret, 244
O'Brien, Pat, 244
O'Casey, Sean, 29

Ochoa, Severo, 108
Ockham, William of, 90
O'Connell, Arthur, 244
O'Connell, Daniel, 157
O'Connell, Helen, 270, 274
O'Connor, Carroll, 244
O'Connor, Donald, 244
O'Connor, Edwin Greene, 18
O'Connor, Flannery, 18
O'Connor, Una, 260
O'Day, Anita, 270
Odets, Clifford, 18
Odetta, 270
Oehlenschläger, Adam, 42
Oersted, Hans Christian, 127
Oerter, Al, 219
O'Faolain, Sean, 29
Offenbach, Jacques, 78
O'Flaherty, Liam, 29
Ogden, Robert Morris, 96
Ogilvy, David M., 202
Oglethorpe, James E., 148
Oh, Sadaharu, 219
O'Hair, Madalyn, 83
O'Hara, John, 18
O'Hara, Mary, 18
O'Hara, Maureen, 260
O'Hare, Edward H., 178
O'Herlihy, Dan, 260
Ohm, Georg S., 120
O'Keefe, Dennis, 244
O'Keeffe, Georgia, 60
Oland, Warner, 244
Olav V, 170
Olcott, Henry Steel, 83
Oldfield, Barney, 219
Olds, Ransom E., 202
Olin, John M., 203
Oliva, Tony, 219
Oliver, Al, 219
Oliver, Edna May, 244
Oliver, King, 286, 287
Olivier, Lord Laurence, 260
Olmsted, Frederick L., 60
Olsen, Merlin, 219
Olsen, Ole, 276, 277
Omar Khayyam, 42
Onassis, Aristotle Socrates, 202,
    203, 300
Onassis, Jacqueline Kennedy, 17,
    203, 300
O'Neal, Patrick, 244
O'Neal, Ryan, 244
O'Neal, Tatum, 244
O'Neill, Eugene, 18, 51, 99, 229,
    244
O'Neill, James, 244
O'Neill, Thomas P., Jr., 148
Ophüls, Marcel, 283
Oppenheimer, J. Robert, 108
Orbach, Jerry, 244
Orbison, Roy, 270
Orczy, Baroness, 42
Orlando, Tony, 271
Ormandy, Eugene, 71
Orr, Bobby, 219
Ortega y Gasset, José, 90
Orton, Joe, 29
Orwell, George, 29
Ory, Kid, 287
Osborne, John, 29
Osmond, Donald ("Donny"), 271
Osmond, Marie, 271
O'Sullivan, Maureen, 233, 244
Ostwald, Friedrich Wilhelm, 120
Oswald, Lee Harvey, 298, 300
Otis, Elisha Graves, 108
Otis, James, 148
O'Toole, Peter, 260
Ott, Mel, 219
Otto, Nikolaus A., 120
Oughtred, William, 115
Ouspenskaya, Maria, 244
Ovid, 42
Owen, Reginald, 244

Owen, Sir Robert, 115
Owen, Robert, 190
Owen, Robert Dale, 190
Owen, Wilfred, 29
Owens, Buck, 271
Owens, Jesse, 219
Ozaki, Kōyō, 42
Ozawa, Seiji, 78

Paar, Jack, 292
Pacino, Al, 244
Packard, James W., 203
Packard, Vance, 96
Paderewski, Ignace, 170
Padgett, Lewis, 49
Paganini, Niccolò, 78
Page, Alan, 219
Page, Geraldine, 244
Page, Patti, 271
Pahlavi, Mohammed Reza, 170
Paige, Leroy ("Satchel"), 219
Paine, Thomas, 83
Palade, George E., 108, 124
Palance, Jack, 244
Palestrina, Giovanni da, 78
Paley, William S., 54
Palillo, Ron, 244
Palladio, Andrea, 67
Palmer, Arnold, 220
Palmer, Jim, 220
Palmer, Lilli, 244
Palmer, Nathaniel B., 130
Palmer, Potter, 203
Palmerston, Viscount, 157
Pankhurst, Emmeline, 190
Papanicolaou, George N., 108
Papas, Irene, 260
Papp, Joseph, 280
Paracelsus, 127
Paré, Ambroise, 123
Pareto, Vilfredo, 96
Park, Brad, 220
Park Chung Hee, 170
Parker, Bonnie, 294, 300
Parker, Charlie, 287, 288
Parker, Dave, 220
Parker, Dorothy, 18
Parker, Eleanor, 244
Parker, Fess, 244
Parker, George S., 203
Parks, Bert, 292
Parks, Larry, 244
Parks, Rosa, 190
Parmenides, 90
Parnell, Charles Stewart, 157
Parnis, Mollie, 300
Parrish, Maxfield, 60
Parseghian, Ara R., 220
Parsons, Sir Charles A., 115
Parsons, Estelle, 244
Parsons, Louella, 54
Parsons, Talcott, 96
Parton, Dolly, 271
Partridge, Eric, 96
Pascal, Blaise, 90, 122
Passman, Otto E., 148
Passy, Frederic, 97, 163
Pasta, Guiditta, 78
Pasternak, Boris, 42
Pasternak, Joseph, 280
Pasteur, Louis, 123, 127
Paterno, Joe, 220
Patiño, Simón Iturri, 203
Patman, Wright, 148
Paton, Alan, 42
Patrick, Saint, 90
Patrick, John, 18
Patterson, Floyd, 220
Patterson, Frederick Douglas, 100
Patterson, John H., 203
Patton, George S., Jr., 178
Paul, Saint, 90
Paul, Alice, 190
Pauli, Wolfgang, 108

344

NAME INDEX

Pyle, Ernie, *54*
Pynchon, Thomas, *19*
Pythagoras, *90*

el-Quaddafi, Muammar, *170*
Quant, Mary, *204*
Quantrill, William C., *178*
Quasimodo, Salvatore, *43*
Quayle, Anthony, *260*
Queen, Ellery, *47*
Queeny, John F., *204*
Quevedo y Villegas, Francisco
   Gómez de, *43*
Quezon y Molina, Manuel Luis, *170*
Quidde, Ludwig, *170*
Quinn, Anthony, *245*
Quisling, Vidkun, *170*

Rabelais, Francois, *35*
Rabi, Isidor I., *108*
Rachmaninoff, Sergei, *78*
Racine, Jean, *35*
Rackmil, Milton R., *204*
Radcliffe, Ann, *47*
Radetzky, Joseph W., *184*
Radford, Arthur W., *178*
Radischev, Aleksandr, *43*
Radisson, Pierre, *133*
Raeder, Erich, *184*
Raft, George, *245*
Raglan, Fitzroy J. H. S., *184*
Ragland, John ("Rags"), *278*
Raikes, Robert, *101*
Rainer, Luise, *246*
Rainey, Joseph H., *149*
Rainey, "Ma", *271*
Rains, Claude, *246*
Rainwater, L. James, *108, 124, 127*
Raitt, John, *246*
Raleigh, Sir Walter, *300*
Raman, Sir Chandrasekhara V., *127*
Rambeau, Marjorie, *246*
Ramon y Cajal, Santiago, *125, 127*
Rampal, Jean-Pierre, *78*
Ramsay, Sir William, *116*
Ramsey, Sir Bertram Home, *184*
Rand, Ayn, *19*
Rand, James H., *204*
Rand, Sally, *264*
Randall, Tony, *246*
Randolph, A. Philip, *190*
Randolph, Edmund J., *149*
Randolph, John, *149*
Randolph, Peyton, *171*
Rankin, Jeanette, *149*
Rankin, Judy, *220*
Rankine, William John M., *116*
Ransom, John Crowe, *19*
Raphael, *68*
Rapp, George, *83*
Rasputin, Grigori Efimovich, *171*
Rathbone, Basil, *246*
Rathenau, Emil, *204*
Rather, Dan, *54*
Rattigan, Terence, *29*
Ravel, Maurice, *78, 79*
Rawlings, Margaret Kinnan, *19*
Rawls, Lou, *271*
Ray, Aldo, *246*
Ray, Dixy Lee, *246*
Ray, Johnnie, *271*
Ray, Man, *60*
Rayburn, Gene, *292*
Rayburn, Sam T., *144, 149*
Raye, Martha, *246*
Rayleigh, Baron John William Strutt,
   116
Raymond, Gene, *246*
Razin, Stenka, *171*
Reade, Charles, *29*
Reagan, Ronald, *145, 149, 254*
Reasoner, Harry, *54*
Réaumur, René A. F. de, *123*
Reber, Grote, *108*

Rebozo, Charles ('Bebe"), *300*
Redding, Otis, *271*
Reddy, Helen, *271*
Redford, Robert, *246*
Redgrave, Lynn, *260*
Redgrave, Michael, *260*
Redgrave, Vanessa, *260*
Reed, Sir Carol, *283*
Reed, Donna, *246*
Reed, Jerry, *271*
Reed, John, *54*
Reed, Lou, *271*
Reed, Oliver, *260*
Reed, Rex, *54*
Reed, Robert, *246*
Reed, Walter, *108*
Reed, Willis, *220*
Reese, Della, *271*
Regan, Phil, *246*
Regiomantanus, *120*
Rehnquist, William, *149*
Reichstein, Tadeusz, *106, 128*
Reid, Wallace, *246*
Reilly, Charles Nelson, *246*
Reiner, Carl, *246, 280*
Reiner, Fritz, *72*
Reiner, Rob, *246, 280*
Remarque, Erich Maria, *43, 235*
Rembrandt, *68*
Remick, Lee, *246*
Remington, Eliphalet, *204*
Remington, Frederic, *60*
Remsen, Ira, *109*
Renault, Mary, *29*
Rennie, Michael, *260*
Renoir, Jean, *283*
Renoir, Pierre-Auguste, *68, 283*
Renwick, James, *60*
Resnais, Alain, *283*
Restif de la Bretonne, Nicholas
   Edme, *35*
Reston, James, *54*
Reuben, David R., *97*
Reuss, Henry S., *149*
Reuter, Baron Paul Julius von, *204*
Reuther, Walter P., *190*
Revels, Hiram R., *149*
Revere, Paul, *178, 179*
Revson, Charles H., *204*
Reymont, Wladyslaw S., *43*
Reynaud, Paul, *160*
Reynolds, Burt, *246, 255*
Reynolds, Debbie, *246, 267*
Reynolds, Sir Joshua, *68*
Rhee, Syngman, *171*
Rhine, Joseph Banks, *97*
Rhodes, Cecil, *157*
Rhodes, John J., *149*
Rhys, Jean, *29*
Ribaut, Jean, *133*
Ribbentrop, Joachim von, *171*
Ribicoff, Abraham A., *149*
Ricardo, David, *97*
Rice, Elmer, *19*
Rice, Grantland, *220*
Rice, Jim, *220*
Rice, William M., *204*
Rich, Buddy, *287*
Rich, Charlie, *271*
Rich, Irene, *246*
Richard I, *157, 159*
Richard III, *157*
Richard, Maurice, *220*
Richards, Laura Elizabeth, *19*
Richards, Theodore W., *109*
Richardson, Elliot L., *149*
Richardson, Henry H., *60*
Richardson, Sir Owen W., *116*
Richardson, Sir Ralph, *260*
Richardson, Samuel, *29*
Richardson, Tony, *283*
Richelieu, Armand Jean du Plessis,
   160
Richler, Mordecai, *43*
Richman, Harry, *271*

Richter, Burton, *109, 110*
Richter, Charles F., *109*
Richter, Johann Paul Friedrich, *43*
Richtofen, Manfred F. von, *184*
Rickenbacker, Edward V., *178*
Rickey, Branch W., *220*
Rickles, Don, *278*
Rickover, Hyman G., *178*
Riddle, Nelson, *287*
Ridgway, Matthew B., *179*
Riefenstahl, Leni, *283*
Rigg, Diana, *260*
Riggs, Bobby, *216, 220*
Riis, Jacob A., *190*
Riley, James Whitcomb, *19*
Rilke, Rainer Maria, *43*
Rimbaud, Arthur, *35*
Rimsky-Korsakov, Nikolai, *43, 79*
Rinehart, Mary Roberts, *47*
Ringling, John N., *292*
Riperton, Minnie, *271*
Ripley, George, *190*
Ripley, Robert LeRoy, *60*
Ritchard, Cyril, *260*
Ritter, John, *246, 272*
Ritter, Tex, *246, 271*
Ritter, Thelma, *246*
Rivera, Chita, *264*
Rivera, Diego, *60, 68*
Rivers, Joan, *278*
Rivers, Johnny, *272*
Rivers, Larry, *60*
Rivers, L. Mendel, *149*
Roach, Max, *287*
Robards, Jason, Jr., *226, 246*
Robbe-Grillet, Alain, *35*
Robbins, Frederick C., *104, 109,*
   110
Robbins, Harold, *19*
Robbins, Jerome, *72*
Robbins, Marty, *272*
Robert I (Robert the Bruce), *157*
Roberts, Oral, *84*
Roberts, Kenneth, *19*
Robertson, Cliff, *241, 246*
Robertson, Dale, *247*
Robertson, Oscar, *220*
Robeson, Paul, *72*
Robespierre, Maximilien, *160, 296*
Robinson, Bill ("Bojangles"), *264*
Robinson, Brooks, *220*
Robinson, Edward Arlington, *19*
Robinson, Edward G., *247*
Robinson, Frank, *220*
Robinson, Jackie, *221*
Robinson, "Sugar" Ray, *221*
Robson, May, *247*
Rochambeau, Jean Baptiste
   Donatien de Vimeur, *184*
Rochester, *247*
Rockefeller, David, *204*
Rockefeller, John Davison, *149, 196,*
   204
Rockefeller, John Davison, Jr., *149,*
   204
Rockefeller, John D. IV ("Jay"), *149,*
   204
Rockefeller, Laurance Spelman, *149,*
   204
Rockefeller, Nelson A., *149, 204*
Rockne, Knute, *221*
Rockwell, Norman, *60*
Rodgers, Bill, *221*
Rodgers, Jimmie, *272*
Rodgers, Richard, *12, 17, 291, 292*
Rodin, Auguste, *68*
Rodino, Peter W., Jr., *149*
Rodney, Caesar, *149*
Roebling, John A., *109*
Roentgen, Wilhelm K., *120*
Roethke, Theodore, *19*
Rogers, Charles ("Buddy"), *247*
Rogers, Ginger, *263, 264*
Rogers, Henry H., *204*
Rogers, Kenny, *272*

NAME INDEX

Schweitzer, Albert, *191*, 296
Schwinger, Julian S., 104, *109*, 128
Scipio Africanus, Publius Cornelius, 182, *184*
Scofield, Paul, *261*
Scopes, John T., *101*
Scorsese, Martin, *281*
Scott, Dred, *191*
Scott, George C., 231, *248*, 251
Scott, Hugh D., Jr., *150*
Scott, Lizabeth, *248*
Scott, Martha, *248*
Scott, Randolph, *248*
Scott, Robert F., *133*
Scott, Sir Walter, *30*, 41
Scott, Winfield, *179*
Scott, Zachary, *248*
Scotto, Renata, 79
Scourby, Alexander, *248*
Scranton, George W., *205*
Scranton, William W., *150*
Scriabin, Aleksandr, 79
Scribner, Charles, 55
Scripps, E. W., 55
Scripps, Ellen Browning, 55
Scruggs, Earl, *285*
Scully, Vin, *221*
Seaborg, Glenn T., 107, *109*
Sears, Richard W., *205*
Seaver, Thomas, *221*
Sebastian, John B., *272*
Sedaka, Neil, *272*
Seeger, Pete, 270, *272*
Seferis, Giorgos, *43*
Segal, Erich, *20*
Segal, George, *248*
Segovia, Andrés, 79
Segre, Emilio G., *109*
Selassie, Haile (see Haile Selassie)
Selfridge, Harry G., *205*
Sellers, Peter, 256, *261*
Selznick, David O., 237, *281*
Semenov, Nikolai Nikolaevich, 114, *128*
Semmes, Raphael, *179*
Sendak, Maurice, *20*
Seneca the Younger, *91*
Senghor, Léopold Sédar, *43*
Sennett, Mack, 250, *281*
Sequoya, *191*
Serkin, Rudolf, 72
Serlin, Oscar, *281*
Serling, Rod, *20*
Serra, Junipero, *91*
Service, Robert William, *43*
Sessions, Roger, 70, *72*
Seton, Anya, *20*
Seton, Elizabeth, *101*
Seurat, Georges, 68
Sevareid, Eric, 55
Severinsen, Doc, *288*
Sévigné, Marie de Rabutin Chantal, *36*
Seville, David, *272*
Sewall, Samuel, *150*
Seward, William H., *150*
Sexton, Anne, *20*
Seyss-Inquart, Arthur, *171*
Shackleton, Sir Ernest H., *133*
Shaffer, Peter, *30*
Shaftesbury, Anthony Ashley Cooper, *158*
Shah Jehan, *171*
Shahn, Ben, *61*
Shakespeare, Frank, Jr., 55
Shakespeare, William, *30*, 43
Shankar, Ravi, *272*
Shannon, Claude E., *109*
Shannon, Del, *272*
Shapiro, Jacob, *301*
Shapiro, Karl, *20*
Sharif, Omar, *261*
Shatner, William, *248*
Shaw, Artie, 234, 238, *288*
Shaw, George Bernard, *30*, 261

Shaw, Irwin, *20*
Shaw, Robert, *261*
Shawn, Dick, *278*
Shays, Daniel, *179*
Shearer, Moira, 79
Shearer, Norma, *248*, 281
Shearing, George, *288*
Shedd, John G., *205*
Sheehy, Gail, 55
Sheen, Fulton John, *84*
Sheen, Martin, *248*
Sheldon, Sidney, *20*
Shelley, Mary Wollstonecraft, *30*, 48
Shelley, Percy Bysshe, *30*, 34, 48
Shepard, Alan B., Jr., *130*
Shepherd, Cybill, *248*
Sheraton, Thomas, *301*
Sheridan, Ann, *248*
Sheridan, Philip H., *179*
Sheridan, Richard B., *30*
Sherman, Allan, *278*
Sherman, John, *150*
Sherman, Roger, *150*
Sherman, William T., 150, 176, *179*
Shero, Fred, *221*
Sherrington, Sir Charles S., 111, *116*
Sherwood, Robert, *20*
Shield, Lansing P., *205*
Shields, Brooke, *248*
Shih Huang Ti, *171*
Shockley, William, 103, *109*
Shoemaker, Willie, *221*
Sholokhov, Mikhail, *43*
Shore, Dinah, 252, *272*
Shore, Eddie, *221*
Short, Bobby, *272*
Shorter, Frank, *221*
Shostakovich, Dimitri, 79
Shreve, Henry M., *205*
Shriner, Herb, *278*
Shriver, R. Sargent, Jr., *150*
Shubert, Lee, *281*
Shula, Don, *221*
Shulman, Max, *20*
Shute, Nevil, *30*
Sibelius, Jean, 79
Siddons, Sarah, *261*
Sidney, Sir Philip, *30*
Sidney, Sylvia, *248*
Siegbahn, Karl M. G., *128*
Siemens, Ernest Werner von, 204, *206*
Siemens, Sir William, *116*
Sienkiewicz, Henryk, *43*
Sieyes, Emmanuel Joseph, *191*
Signoret, Simone, 259, *261*
Sigsbee, Charles D., *179*
Sikorsky, Igor I., *109*
Silhouette, Étienne de, *160*
Sillanpaa, Frans E., *44*
Sillitoe, Alan, *30*
Sills, Beverly, 72
Silver, Horace, *288*
Silverberg, Robert, *49*
Silvers, Phil, *248*
Sim, Alistair, *261*
Simenon, Georges, *48*
Simmons, Al, *222*
Simmons, Jean, *261*
Simon, Carly, *272*
Simon, Neil, *20*
Simon, Paul, *272*
Simon, Richard Leo, 55
Simon, William E., *150*
Simone, Nina, *272*
Simpson, Adele, *301*
Simpson, Sir James Y., *116*
Simpson, Louis, *20*
Simpson, O.J., *222*
Sims, William S., *179*
Sinatra, Frank, 233, 234, *272*
Sinclair, Harry F., 195, *206*
Sinclair, Upton, *20*

Singer, Isaac Bashevis, *20*
Singleton, Zutty, *288*
Sinyavsky, Andrei, *44*
Sirhan, Sirhan Bishara, *301*
Sirica, John J., *151*
Sisler, George, *222*
Sisley, Alfred, 68
Sissle, Noble, *286*
Sitting Bull, 129, 177, *179*
Sitwell, Dame Edith, *30*
Sitwell, Sir Osbert, *30*
Sjöwall, Maj, *48*
Skelton, Red, *248*
Skidmore, Louis, *61*
Skinner, B. F., *97*
Skinner, Cornelia Otis, *248*
Skinner, Otis, *248*
Skoda, Emil von, *206*
Slater, Samuel, *206*
Slezak, Leo, 79, *248*
Slezak, Walter, 79, *248*
Slick, Grace, *273*
Slim, William J., *184*
Sloan, Alfred P., Jr., *206*
Sloan, John, *61*
Smeal, Eleanor C., *191*
Smetana, Bedrich, 79
Smith, Adam, *97*
Smith, Merriman, 55
Smith, Alexis, *248*
Smith, Alfred E., *151*
Smith, Bessie, 271, *273*, 288
Smith, Betty, *20*
Smith, Bob ("Buffalo Bob"), *293*
Smith, C. Aubrey, *261*
Smith, Cordwainer, *20*
Smith, Edward E., *49*
Smith, Hamilton O., 108, *109*, 123
Smith, Hedrick, 55
Smith, Holland M., *179*
Smith, Howard K., 55
Smith, Ian Douglas, *171*
Smith, Jaclyn, *249*
Smith, Jedediah S., *130*
Smith, Joe, *288*
Smith, John, *151*
Smith, Joseph, *84*
Smith, Kate, *273*
Smith, Keeley, *273*, 287
Smith, Maggie, *261*
Smith, Margaret Chase, *150*
Smith, Patti, *273*
Smith, Pinetop, *288*
Smith, Robert H., *191*, 192
Smith, Roger, 225, *249*
Smith, Walter W. ("Red"), *222*
Smith, Willie, *288*
Smithson, James, *116*
Smollett, Tobias, *31*
Smothers, Dick, *273*
Smothers, Tom, *273*
Smuts, Jan C., *171*
Snead, Sam, *222*
Snell, Peter, *222*
Snodgrass, W. D., *20*
Snodgress, Carrie, *249*
Snow, C. P., *31*
Snow, Hank, *273*
Snyder, Jimmy ("The Greek"), *222*
Soares, Mario, *172*
Sobell, Morton, *301*
Socrates, 90, *91*
Soddy, Frederick, 109, *116*
Solti, Sir Georg, 79
Solzhenitsyn, Alexander, *44*
Somers, Suzanne, *249*
Somes, Michael, 79
Sommer, Elke, *249*
Somoza, Anastasio, *172*
Somoza-Debayle, Anastasio, *172*
Sondheim, Stephen, *293*
Sontag, Susan, *97*
Soo, Jack, *249*
Sophocles, *43*
Sorvino, Paul, *249*

NAME INDEX

NAME INDEX

NAME INDEX

SUBJECT INDEX

SUBJECT INDEX

SUBJECT INDEX